Sports Medicine

Prevention, Assessment, Management, and Rehabilitation of Athletic Injuries

SECOND EDITION

Richard Irvin, A.T., C. (Retired), Ed.D.
Emeritus
Oregon State University

Duane Iversen, P.T., A.T., C.
University of Oregon

Steven Roy, M.D.
Past Director
Center for Sports Medicine and Running Injuries
Eugene, Oregon

Prentice Hall

Upper Saddle River, NJ 07458

Vice-President, Editor-in-Chief, Social Science: Sean W. Wakely

Publisher: Joseph E. Burns

Editorial Assistant: Sara Sherlock

Editorial-Production Administrator: Joe Sweeney

Editorial-Production Service: WordCrafters Editorial Services, Inc.

Composition Buyer: Linda Cox

Manufacturing Buyer: Megan Cochran

Cover Administrator: Linda Knowles

Compositor: Omegatype Typography, Inc.

Text Designer: The Davis Group, Inc.

Pearson Education
10 Bank St
White Plains, NY 10605

Internet: www.abacon.com
America Online: Keyword: College Online

Photos pages 1, 41 (top), 51, and 481 by Mike Shields

Library of Congress Cataloging-in-Publication Data
Irvin, Richard.
    Sports medicine : prevention, assessment, management, and
rehabilitation of athletic injuries.—2nd ed. / Richard Irvin,
Duane Iversen, Steven Roy.
      p.   cm.
    Roy's name appears first on the earlier edition.
    Includes bibliographical references and index.
    ISBN 0-13-037466-0
    1. Sports medicine.   2. Physical education and training.
  I. Iversen, Duane. II. Roy, Steven. III. Title.
    [DNLM: 1. Athletic Injuries. 2. Sports Medicine. QT 261 I72s
1998]
RC1210.R68 1998
617.1'027—dc21
DNLM/DLC
for Library of Congress

Printed in Canada

Sports Medicine

Brief Contents

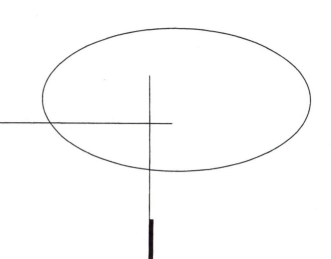

PART ONE

The Prevention of Athletic Injuries

PART TWO

The Management of Athletic Injuries

PART THREE

Specific Athletic Injuries and Related Problems

PART FOUR

Other Areas for Consideration

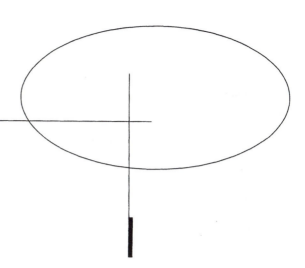

Contents

PART THREE

Specific Athletic Injuries and Related Problems

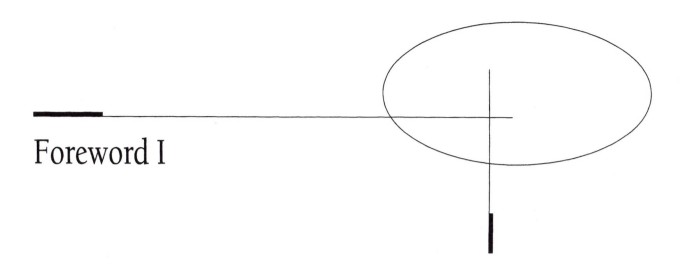

Foreword I

It is again my privilege to be asked to comment on the revised edition of *Sports Medicine*. In the decade since the first edition appeared, much in the field of athletic training has changed, and athletic trainers who have not improved themselves through continuing education have been left far behind. Educational curricula have matured and expanded, and the profession has started to utilize this wealth of knowledge to expand its outlook far beyond the traditional training room setting.

Technological advances in both assessment and treatment have changed markedly, as have knowledge of improved surgical techniques and post-surgical rehabilitation. This new edition reflects these changes. Rather than attempting to include information on all of the advances themselves, Dr. Roy and Dr. Irvin have wisely added Duane Iversen, with his considerable clinical expertise and practical experience, as a contributing author, and have included the contributions of numerous other experts in the sports medicine field.

Many principles in the practice of contemporary athletic training remain fundamentally unchanged since the publication of the first edition, and the authors have wisely chosen to avoid change simply for the sake of change. As in the first edition, however, this text continues to explore in depth areas of athletic training that other texts have only mentioned or even totally ignored. The expanded section on PNF exercise, for example, and the new chapter on athletes with disabilities provide good basic information that previously had to be sought out from a variety of sources. I am confident this book will remain one of the top classroom texts and desktop references in the field of athletic training.

Lindsy McLean
Head Athletic Trainer, San Francisco "Forty-Niners"
Former Chairman, Board of Certification,
National Athletic Trainers Association

Foreword II

When the first edition of *Sports Medicine: Prevention, Assessment, Management, and Rehabilitation of Athletic Injuries* was published in 1983, it was heralded as one of the most important texts in sports medicine to be produced in more than a decade. Since that time, the work has proven its early proponents to be correct: it has become one of the most utilized resources for students and professionals in sports injury management. Dr. Steven Roy and Dr. Richard Irvin incorporated contemporary exercise science and extensive clinical experience into a comprehensive volume that shed new light on managing the most perplexing medical problems facing the sports participant.

In the years since the publication of the first edition, participation in sport and exercise has continued to increase among all age groups. It is not unusual to see five- and six-year-old children on the soccer field and octogenarians in masters track and field competitions. The inevitable injuries that result from the stresses of repetitive and intensive physical activity require modern approaches to prevention and care. Our understanding of trauma in sport today is vastly improved over our knowledge a decade ago, and many new strategies for the diagnosis, treatment, and rehabilitation of injuries are available to sports medicine professionals.

In this new edition, the primary authors have employed experts from a variety of disciplines within the allied health sphere to update every chapter of the text and to add important new chapters consistent with the latest advances in the field. Discussions of new techniques in athletic conditioning, emergency care, equipment fitting, and taping have been added to the text to provide the reader with the mechanics and theory underlying contemporary methods of sports injury management.

The chapter on therapeutic modalities has been substantively updated and includes many changes in this rapidly progressing technological area. Similarly, the chapter on the female athlete has been completely rewritten to reflect the growth of knowledge in that area over the last ten years. In this new edition, the reader will find two chapters rather than one on illnesses, skin disorders, and medications—a change that permits a more detailed focus on medication in sport, a topic of increasing significance in recent years. The chapters on injuries to various body parts have all been updated to reflect current medical opinion on their management and significance.

The new chapter on athletes with disabilities addresses the concerns of special athletes who are competing with increasing frequency in organized sport. An additional new chapter on assessment of athletic injuries recognizes the criticality of precise identification of the impairment and provides the means to delineate its severity.

The entire work is skillfully and generously illustrated, and numerous tables complement the text. The revised volume is comprehensive in scope and is a most appropriate text for university courses in sports injury management, as well as a general reference for any allied medical professional interested in the health implications of physical activity.

Ralph Waldo Emerson wrote, "Knowledge exists to be imparted," and the authors of this text are to be congratulated for making a significant contribution of their knowledge toward a better understanding of the stress of sports participation and the most effective measures to minimize its adverse consequences.

Louis R. Osternig, PhD, ATC
University of Oregon

Preface

The primary goals of this edition are essentially the same as those of the first edition. The authors are dedicated to the task of providing applicable information for the health care provider of injured athletes. In addition, every effort has been made to contribute to the education of all individuals who desire to become involved with the field of sports medicine.

The authors believe in the values of athletic participation and recognize the dedication of athletes in their quest to achieve success. Since the quest involves physical as well as mental and emotional application of effort, there is always a risk of injury. The authors join with all individuals involved in the medical care of the injured athlete in attempting to minimize the effects of trauma and reduce the risks while maximizing the benefits.

The authors wish to thank many individuals who took the time and effort to submit their suggestions for improving this edition of *Sports Medicine*. Most of the recommendations concerned the content of the text. An effort has been made to increase the scope and depth as well as to update the content of the text. Since most readers were comfortable with the style of presentation, we have made an attempt to retain the original format.

As far as possible, an attempt has been made to avoid promoting any "pet" or biased techniques, protocols, or procedures. Acceptable alternatives are presented whenever possible, and the reader is encouraged to make choices based on good judgment, experience, and documentation.

The reader will recognize some familiar aspects of the original text that have been carried over to this edition. For example, the organizational structure has been retained, dividing the coverage into four parts:

Part 1   The Prevention of Athletic Injuries

Part 2   The Management of Athletic Injuries

Part 3   Specific Athletic Injuries and Related Problems

Part 4   Other Areas for Consideration

The reader will also find that the original internal format has been maintained in the chapters on anatomy: functional anatomy, evaluation (assessment), prevention, etiology, signs and symptoms, treatment, and rehabilitation.

Included among the additions and updating of materials in this edition are:

1.   Coverage of more pathologies and additional information on each of the original and added injuries

2.   An expanded glossary

3.   Two new chapters: Assessment of Athletic Injuries (Chapter 5) and Athletes with Disabilities (Chapter 24)

4.   Additional references

If this publication contributes in even a small measure to the care of the injured athlete, then the project was well worth the effort.

Acknowledgments

The authors would like to recognize the influence of their former teachers and mentors who provided the guidance and motivation for us to pursue a career in sports medicine. Our early experiences were valuable in providing us with the courage and confidence to even attempt to become involved in this project. Those role models and other colleagues and associates have, over the years, generously shared their expertise and ideas that gave us the foundation upon which to become involved in writing this text.

Completion of a project like this requires the efforts of many "behind-the-scenes" individuals. The typists, photographers, and illustrators, and the editorial and production staff of Prentice Hall and Allyn & Bacon, as well as Linda Zuk of WordCrafters, have provided the expert assistance that has transformed this project from a dream into a reality.

The second edition was possible only with the help of many sports medicine professionals who made themselves available to infuse new ideas and to expand the scope and depth of this publication. These contributions ranged from several specific items (figures, charts, tables) to revision of one or more chapters. The individuals who were involved in one or more chapter revisions expended an enormous amount of intellectual energy and utilized countless hours of their time; they are individually identified in the List of Contributors.

Finally, we wish to thank the reviewers of this edition: John Cottone, EdD, ATC, State University College at Cortland; David O. Draper, EdD, ATC, Brigham Young University; John P. Miller, School University of New Hampshire; Charles Redmond, Springfield College; and Christine Stopka, PhD, CSCS, University of Florida.

Introduction

Athletic health care is a broad and very inclusive profession that involves a variety of medical as well as paramedical personnel, including physicians, exercise physiologists, athletic trainers, physical therapists, coaches, and physical educators. This text is concerned with the various athletic health care professionals' responsibilities as related to the health care of the athlete.

Physicians concerned with sports medicine may be divided into a number of categories:

1. The physician who sees a sports medicine patient only occasionally, but who is interested in athletics and sports medicine.

2. The physician—especially the orthopedic surgeon, family practitioner or generalist, pediatrician, cardiologist, internist or podiatrist—who spends a substantial portion of the professional day treating sports medicine patients. Many team physicians fall into this group.[1,2]

3. The full-time sports medicine physician. This group has evolved from the local team physician whose sports medicine practice was limited to attending games in his or her spare time to the physician whose practice is devoted completely or primarily to the prevention, diagnosis, and rehabilitation of athletic injuries. This new breed is cutting through many of the traditional dividing lines that separated the specialties in the past. Sports medicine requires a special attitude, specific knowledge of many sports and their demands, and empathy with the athlete. The direction of growth of sports medicine as a profession, as well as the granting of specialty rank, is still under discussion.[3,4,5] A sports medicine physician is also knowledgeable about the skills and abilities of the athletic trainer and works closely with the trainer in a variety of settings, whether interscholastic, collegiate, professional, or clinical.

Athletic training was formally recognized as an allied health profession in 1990 by the American Medical Association.[6] This recognition gives athletic trainers official professional status in the health care field. Their new status will give athletic trainers greater potential for research funding and will provide additional avenues of practice for individual professionals and athletic trainers.

Athletic training is best defined by considering the major functions or responsibilities of the athletic trainer. These functions fall into three categories:

1. Prevention of athletic trauma from conditions that adversely affect the health or performance of an athlete. Some of these areas include conditioning, physical examinations, evaluation of playing fields and equipment, and preventive taping.

2. Management of athletic trauma or other medical problems that affect the athlete. Some of these areas include first aid, injury recognition, assessment, treatment, and rehabilitation.

3. Counseling of the athlete in various health-related areas such as nutrition (e.g., eating disorders), psychological and emotional fitness (e.g., relaxation and tension control), and personal health habits (e.g., alcohol, tobacco, and substance abuse). In addition, athletic trainers should be knowledgeable about the various performance-enhancing drugs to which athletes may be exposed.

In its state licensing bill (Texas Athletic Trainer Licensure Act), the state of Texas has defined the athletic trainer as: "A person with specific qualification . . . who, upon the advice and consent of his team physician, carries out the practice of prevention and/or physical rehabilitation of injuries incurred by athletes. To carry out these functions the athletic trainer is authorized to use physical modalities such as heat, sound, cold, electricity or mechanical devices related to rehabilitation and treatment."

The two major organizations most closely associated with athletic health care are: the National Athletic Trainers Association Inc. (NATA) and the American Physical Therapy Association (APTA), particularly its Sports Physical Therapy Section (see page xxx for a listing of other organizations).

The National Athletic Trainers Association was founded in 1949 primarily for the purpose of advancing, encouraging, and improving the athletic training profession in all its phases. NATA implements this goal by seeking to promote a better working relationship among those interested in the profession of athletic training, to further develop the abilities of each member, and to better serve the common interest of its members by providing a means for a full exchange of ideas within the profession.

The years since the formation of NATA have seen many advances. One area of achievement is the establishment of the certification of the athletic trainers. In August of 1970 the first NATA certification examination was administered, and by 1992 over 6,000 members had taken the examination. In 1990 athletic training was recognized by the American Medical Association as an allied health care profession. Total membership had grown from 5,000 members in 1982 to over 17,000 members in 1992. Certified male trainers comprise 58% of the membership, and females, 42%, a ratio that is considerably different from that in earlier years when training was a decidedly male-dominated profession.

Another committee of NATA, the Professional Education Committee, has worked hard to improve and upgrade education standards for athletic trainers. Currently approximately 79 colleges and universities offer approved NATA curricula in undergraduate athletic training. In addition, 13 universities offer graduate-level programs.[7] Currently an individual can qualify to apply to take the certification examination administered by the Board of Certification under two major sections: (1) students who have graduated from an undergraduate or graduate program; (2) internship program graduates. In the future, approved curricula will be the only avenue to certification. For complete details of specific certification requirements and procedures, write to:

NATA Board of Certification
3725 National Drive
Raleigh, NC 27612

The Sports Physical Therapy Section of the American Physical Therapy Association provides a common forum for the member therapist with an interest in sports medicine. Sports physical therapy is one of the areas of specialization identified by the American Physical Therapy Association. The sports physical therapist deals with the physiological, pathological, and performance problems of athletes and seeks means to overcome these problems. The sports physical therapist may practice in a variety of settings: private or hospital-based sports medicine centers or clinics, health and fitness facilities, or athletic organizations of all levels. Activities of the Sports Physical Therapy Section include:

1. Broaden the field of physical therapy in the areas of performance enhancement, conditioning, treatment, rehabilitation, and research of athletic injuries.

2. Disseminate information to its members on current physical physical therapy trends and practices to improve the care of sports injuries.

3. Improve the relationships with other organizations associated with the treatment of athletic injuries.

4. Promote the development of sports medicine within programs of the physical therapy curricula.

5. Sponsor continuing education programs and provide publications.

6. Provide a job placement service.

7. Sponsor a variety of projects to increase the awareness of the role of the sports physical therapist.

For complete information regarding the specialist certification examination and application to sit for the examination, write to:

Specialist Certification Department
APTA
1111 North Fairfax St.
Alexandria, VA 22314

Those involved in sports medicine should also be aware of the following organizations:

American Orthopaedic Society for Sports Medicine

American Academy of Family Physicians

American Academy of Pediatrics

American Alliance for Health & Physical Education, Recreation and Dance

American College of Sports Medicine

American Medical Society for Sports Medicine

American Trauma Society

Canadian Athletic Trainers' Association

Joint Commission on Sports Medicine

National Association of Collegiate Directors of Athletics

National Association of Intercollegiate Athletics

National High School Athletic Coaches Association

National Strength & Conditioning Association

National Collegiate Athletic Association (NCAA)

Ethics

The athletic health care specialist should be a very conscientious and caring individual. It is the responsibility of each specialist to put the medical needs of an athlete above all other considerations. Athletic trainers must be honest and loyal and possess high moral standards. Good athletic trainers are dedicated to the profession. An established professional code of ethics* expresses the ideals of the profession and a standard of conduct and integrity for individuals to follow in their day-to-day activities. High standards of conduct combined with clinical competency should result in quality care of the injured athlete. It has been noted that the obligation to act competently calls for a higher motivation than merely concerns for civil liability or disciplinary penalty.

The athletic trainer is frequently placed in situations that are less than enviable. Those who are or will be involved with the athlete should be aware of potential ethical problems so that they will be prepared to deal with them. The athletic trainer is usually employed by the team management, and this may lead to an implicit expectation on the part of management or coaching staff of loyalty to them. This arrangement may not always be in the best interests of the athlete, and in recent years movements have developed to organize athletes so they may have their own athletic trainer and/or physician. This would theoretically limit management's power in potentially controlling the actions of medical personnel.

The player's welfare should be placed above all other considerations, including pressure from the coaches and management, fears of job security, and ego. Although coaches and management do have valid concerns, the trainer must not allow a nonmedical consideration to influence his or her judgment. In order to serve both parties effectively, the athletic trainer needs to be accepted by the athlete as well as by the coaches and management, but there should be no doubt in anyone's mind that decisions regarding the health and welfare of the athlete will be made on a sound medical basis and will not be subject to manipulation or influence by others. All too frequently, subtle or blatant pressure is exerted on the athletic trainer "for the sake of team,"

with little or no regard for the potential health hazards to which the athlete might be exposed. The athlete's best interests should always be given first priority. If pressure is exerted and a question of judgment arises, the athletic trainer should call for a physician's opinion. The physician, not the trainer, should be the person who makes the unpopular decisions.

An athletic trainer is often asked to defy the natural process of healing and frequently does an amazing job of helping an athlete to return to participation. There is the risk, however, of cutting corners or proclaiming athletes ready to return when they are not. This situation arises if the athletic trainer feels that, in order to retain his or her status in the eyes of coach or management, the player should be ready by a particular deadline. Sometimes, however, controlled activity (rest) is the only answer, and the athletic trainer needs to be able to decide, in spite of external pressures, when rest is indicated and to explain the situation to the athlete as well as to the coach and management without creating hostility on either side.

Occasionally an athlete may be medically able to return to participation but may be a disadvantage to the team due to an inadequate level of fitness resulting from the enforced layoff. Premature return to competition should first be discussed with the athlete, but the coaching staff should know of the trainer's opinion regarding the level of fitness of an athlete who has been injured.

Another potential source of conflict is the issue of confidentiality of the athlete's background of injuries. Professional scouts or reporters may casually discuss a particular player. The athletic trainer should avoid being caught in a position of being asked informally (or formally) to disclose private medical information without a player's written release. All information that is given out verbally or in writing should be cleared by the player as well as by the management, and a notation should be made of the information, the date, and to whom it was released.

The athletic trainer may encounter unsafe coaching practices or facilities. If this occurs, the trainer should first advise the appropriate person. If the advice is ignored, a report of the findings and recommendations should be sent to the highest authority. If definite hazardous conditions exist, it is the athletic trainer's professional duty to ensure that corrective action is taken. The same situation applies to the use of inappropriate, illegal, or banned drugs in an athletic setting. An athletic trainer should never dispense prescription medication to an athlete, and every effort should be made to ensure a drug-free environment.

The athletic trainer may encounter conflicting demands and will often be confronted with extremely

---

*Because of limited space, the authors are not able to reproduce the code of ethics of the various organizations. The reader is encouraged to obtain copies of these documents from the appropriate organizations.

taxing situations. Mature judgment, a cool head, and frequent consultations with physicians, fellow trainers, and superiors can ensure that wise decisions are made.

Liability

The athletic trainer and all members of the athletic health care team need to consider the medical-legal aspects of their profession. Today it is as important to be well versed in the legal aspects of sports medicine as in the medical aspects. Those who deal with athletic injuries are in a potentially hazardous situation; two types of legal action may be brought against them:

1. *Civil action for tort.* The court may compensate the plaintiff for harm caused by the defendant's conduct involving an act of commission (performance of an unlawful act) or an act of omission (failure to perform a legal duty).

2. *Criminal action for tort.* The state may prosecute the defendant to protect the public from further wrongful acts.

A plaintiff may have a basis for tort action against another individual in one of these three categories:

1. *Intentional interferences.* An intentional act is performed with the knowledge or reasonable certainty that the act will cause or create a personal injury or property damage.

2. *Negligence.* Failure to act as a prudent person would under similar conditions. In determining whether the defendant acted as a reasonable prudent person, the court will determine whether the defendant took into account the surrounding circumstances and whether the defendant possessed such knowledge as is possessed by an ordinary reasonable person (considering the defendant's training and experience), and whether judgment and discretion were exercised as would have been done by persons of reasonable intelligence under similar circumstances.

Considerations for determining negligence include:

Defendant has a duty to protect others against unreasonable risks.

Defendant has a duty to exercise a standard of care commensurate with the risk involved.

The conduct of the defendant must have been the proximate cause or legal cause of the injury or harm. There must be a connection between the act or conduct and the resulting injury.

Actual injury or damage must have resulted from the action of the defendant.

3. *Strict liability.* Defendant's activity puts others in danger although there is no intentional interference or negligence.

The defendant may utilize the following defenses in a tort involving a charge of negligence:

- *Contributory negligence.* The plaintiff's own conduct may fall below the standard that he or she should conform to for his or her own protection, and this conduct legally contributes to the plaintiff's own harm.

- *Assumption of risk.* The plaintiff has knowledge of the danger of the situation and voluntarily enters into that situation (the plaintiff must have knowledge of the risks and understand the risks).

- *Unavoidable and nonforeseeable accident.* The harm or injury is not caused by negligence, but is the result of a true accident.

- *Intervening act or event.* The negligence is not the proximate cause of the injury, but was due to an intervening act or event (often resulting from the act of a third party).

The athletic trainer should not conduct a program out of "fear and intimidation," but should make every attempt to deliver a service that results from the best efforts of a complete, ethical, and caring philosophy. Nonetheless, in the real world of tort liability (allegations of malpractice, etc.) the athletic trainer needs to be aware of liability prevention (legal overexposure). The following topics should be considered in the development of a risk management plan:

1. Emergency medical plan

2. Liability insurance

3. A legal written contract

4. Good rapport with the athlete

5. Rapport, communication, and proper chain of command or supervision between the physician and the athletic trainer and the athletic trainer and the assistant trainer and/or student trainers

6. Professional credentials and continuing education

7. Records and documents of all types of medical information, and proper control and release of this information

8. Warning of injury risk and informed consent

I. EMERGENCY MEDICAL PLAN: Each athletic organization should develop a written document concerned with the management of a medical emergency. This document should contain all instructions, guidelines, and policies pertaining to the response of a staff member to an injured athlete. The plan should be updated constantly and made available to all staff members involved in the athletic program. This topic should be formally included on the agenda of at least one official staff meeting each year (preferably the first meeting of the year). (For additional information see Chapter 6.)

2. LIABILITY INSURANCE: The athletic trainer needs to be aware of the expense that may be involved to defend oneself in court. In addition to legal expense, there is always the possibility of a settlement being awarded to the plaintiff.

The athletic trainer should also be aware of the many exclusions that may be written into a liability insurance policy. Many state educational association policies contain exclusions, and the trainer should read the policy carefully. Following is an example of language in a university policy that offers the athletic trainer liability coverage:

> The state of _____ through the operation of the State liability fund shall defend, save harmless, and indemnify any of its officers, employees, and agents (including students in practicum and volunteers), whether elective or appointed, against any tort claim or demand, whether groundless or otherwise, arising out of an alleged act occurring while acting within the scope of their employment or duties, whether arising out of governmental or proprietary function including the operation of aircraft and motor vehicles within the state's control. This defense applies to any claim arising from Civil Rights action, malpractice, or general tort. No defense will be available in case of malfeasance of willful or wanton neglect of duty.

The athletic trainer should supplement this institutional coverage with a personal liability policy. Information on purchase of liability insurance may be obtained from athletic trainers professional organizations.

3. LEGAL WRITTEN CONTRACT: The written contract should describe as specifically as possible all of the duties and responsibilities of the athletic trainer. Following is an example of a job description that might appear in a contract for an assistant athletic trainer:

1. Assist the team physician and head athletic trainer in the prevention of athletic injuries in sports that fall under the Intercollegiate Athletic Program (baseball, basketball, crew, cross-country, football, golf, gymnastics, softball, swimming, tennis, track, volleyball, wrestling).
2. Assist the team physician and the head athletic trainer in first aid care of the injured athlete in all of the sports listed above.

3. Assist the team physician and the head athletic trainer in the treatment of the injured athlete in all of the above sports utilizing various medications and physical agents.
4. Assist the team physician and the head trainer utilizing rehabilitative modalities.
5. Assist the team physician and the head trainer in the supervision of the student trainers.

4. PATIENT RAPPORT: The athletic trainer needs to establish a close humanistic and therapeutic relationship with the athlete—the patient. The athletic trainer should have an understanding of the athlete as a person as well as being well versed in the medical aspects of the problem. A good relationship that includes an understanding and a feeling of empathy are important elements in promoting a desirable relationship with the athlete.

5. RAPPORT, COMMUNICATION, AND A CHAIN OF COMMAND OR SUPERVISION: The employing institution and the athletic trainer need to establish open communication and a "chain of command" among the physician, the athletic trainer, the assistant trainer, and so forth. Each member of the sports medicine team needs to be aware of their responsibility and the teamwork effort needed to provide optimum health care for the athlete. The team approach should result in the establishment of a common goal and all individual members should apply their expertise in the achievement of that goal. Verbal and written communication is an important aspect of keeping the program on track and working together for the welfare of the athlete.

Establishment of a chain of command ensures that all individuals are aware of events and that following actions and results are known by all team members. Each athletic organization needs to establish a flowchart that clearly indicates the level of responsibility of every staff member. From this organizational chart the various supervision assignments can also be declared. Supervision exists at many levels and everyone needs to know their supervision duties (for example, the athletic trainer supervises the assistant athletic trainer(s) and the student athletic trainer(s) in the injury care of an athlete).

6. PROFESSIONAL CREDENTIALS AND CONTINUING EDUCATION: Depending on the specific area of athletic health care involvement, the individual needs to obtain the current recognized certification and/or licensing credentials. The establishment of recognized competencies and the development of certification examinations to test these competencies has given the public a confidence in individuals working in the sports medicine field. Evidence of certification/licensing through the examination process leads to an assumption that the trainer has an acceptable level of competence and will provide a standard level of care. State licensing and/or registration denotes state approval and control of the athletic trainer.

The athletic trainer needs to update his or her database continually. Research in the sports medicine field has produced a large volume of related information that will continue to grow. The education of those who work in the healing arts is never complete. Continuing education requirements are a good extrinsic motivation for those employed in athletic health care. Many postgraduate opportunities are available, as are seminars, short courses, and workshops. A wide variety of professional journals are also available to members of the sportsmedicine team. Since the athletic trainer will be judged on whether he or she acted as a prudent professional in a situation, the athletic trainer needs to be aware of currently approved and accepted techniques.

7. RECORDS, DOCUMENTATION AND RELEASE OF INFORMATION:
Each athletic training program must have a comprehensive system for recording and filing appropriate medical records, as well as con-

trolling the release of medical information. The Buckley Amendment, part of the Educational Act of 1974, indicates that the opportunities for an individual to secure employment, insurance, and credit, and his right to due process and other legal protections are endangered by the misuse of certain informational systems; the right to privacy is a personal and fundamental right protected by the constitution of the United States. The athlete needs to be given an opportunity to agree to or restrict release of medical information. This authorization and the actual details of any release of medical information need to be documented.

Each institution or agency needs a variety of records that fit the needs of their own situation, including:

- Physical examination and medical history (see Chapter 1)
- Injury record
- Cumulative medical record
- Medical chart progress notes (see Figure 1)
- Emergency information
- Release of information (general)
- Release of medical information (see Figure 2)
- Rehabilitative records
- Training room record
- Daily injury report to the coach

Chart notes are written in either SOAP (**S**ubjective, **O**bjective, **A**ssessment and **P**lan) or narrative format. Subjective is what the patient or athlete tells you: where it hurts, what he/she did, any past medical history (PMH), etc. Objective is what you find upon examination: range of motion, inspection, palpation, strength, sensation, ambulation, etc. Assessment is your professional opinion of the injury. Plan is what you intend to do in the next treatment. Narrative is all of this information summarized in one paragraph. Many abbreviations are used in notes (see appendix A).

SOAP examples:
S: Pt is a 15 y.o. female with Ⓛ knee—med. meniscus from soccer on 10/9/92 when she was hit by another player. Pt. c/o pain Ⓛ knee—medial aspect. She iced it initially and saw Dr. on 10/10/92.
O: Inspection: Pt comes into clinic on crutches NWB w/knee immobilizer on L. ROM 10–80°, quad stren. 3/5, ham 4/5. Palpation—tender medial aspect. L knee. RX of US, SLR C O# X 20–4 planes, ice/ES.
A: Decreased motion and strength 2 to Ⓛ knee injury.
P: Progress exercises as tolerated. See 3 × wk—3 wk.

Narrative example:
Pt is a 15 y.o. female with Ⓛ knee—med meniscus from soccer on 10/9/92 when she was hit by another player. Comes into clinic on crutches NWB w/Knee immobilizer. Ⓛ knee—medical aspect. Eval shows ROM 10–80°, quad strength 3/5, ham 4/5. Was seen for Rx of US, SLR c o# × 20—4 planes, ice/ES. Will be seen 3 × wk for 3 wk.

Chart notes are important because they give you a running inventory of what you are doing and how the athlete is progressing; they are invaluable in insurance claims and litigation.

FIGURE I
Medical Chart Progress Notes

Release of Medical Information—NATA-suggested Form

RELEASE OF INFORMATION AUTHORIZATION

I, _____ , Do—Do Not, give my consent for the team physician, athletic trainers, or other medical personnel of _____ , to
(name of school)
release such information regarding my medical history, record of injury or surgery, record of serious illness, and
rehabilitation results as may be requested by the scout or representative of any professional or amateur athletic organization seeking such information.

I understand that such scout or representative of the team has made representations to the team physician,
athletic trainer or other medical personnel of _____ , that the
(name of school)
purpose of this request for my medical information is to assist the organization he or she represents in making
a determination as to offering me employment.

I understand that a record will be kept of all individuals requesting such information and the date of the request. This information is normally confidential and except as provided in this Release will not be otherwise released by the parties in charge of the information. This Release remains valid until revoked by me in writing.

Signed: _____ *Dated:* _____

Reprinted by permission of the National Athletic Trainers Association.

Release of Medical Information (*continued*)—NATA-suggested Log of Transaction

---

	Information Discussed
(Name)	
(Organization)	
(Date)	
(Interview or telephone)	

Reprinted by permission of the National Athletic Trainers Association.

FIGURE 2
Release of Medical Information—NATA-suggested form

Computer programs are available to maintain bio-
graphical information, medical histories, and track
injuries over a period of time on an individual, sport,
program, conference, league, or even national basis.[10]

**8. WARNING OF INJURY RISK AND INFORMED
CONSENT:** One of the most common allegations in
sports litigation has been the failure to properly warn
the athlete/parents of the injury risk and the failure to
obtain an informed consent to participation. Although
the athletic trainer should not be the only staff member
responsible for development of an injury risk and
informed consent program, he or she is logically the one
who plays a major role in such a program. Traditional
general release forms signed by athletes and parents do
not meet current requirements. Briefly, a release form
should include specific warning of injury risk, describ-
ing what harm may occur and how it can occur. The language used in the informed consent needs to be
understood by all of the parties. (See Figures 3 and 4.)

Frequency of Injury in Athletes

The number of individuals participating in all types
of athletic events is increasing annually. In a recent,
three-year (1986–1988) injury surveillance study con-

Participation in athletics requires an acceptance of the risk of injury.

Rules and guidelines for each sport are designed to help protect the athlete from injury, but enforcement of the rules by game officials is not a guarantee against injury, nor are printed warnings on equipment or instructions by coaches in proper techniques. These factors minimize the risk, but they can never completely eliminate the risk.

My trainer will acquaint me with the types of injury that I may incur in this sport and will instruct me in the techniques that will minimize the chance of injury in this sport.

I recognize that I have the responsibility to wear the required equipment, obey the rules of my sport, train my body to the best of my ability, utilize proper techniques, and avoid activities for which I have not been trained, or which I do not feel qualified to perform. I will report any injuries promptly to the athletic training staff and follow their recommendations for treatment and return to activities following injury.

I have read and understand the significance of this statement.

_____   _____   _____
Student-Athlete Signature   Date   Sport

_____
PRINTED NAME

_____   _____
Parent's Signature (if under 18)   Date

FIGURE 3
General Participation Informed Consent

---

ducted by the National Athletic Trainers' Association[8] involving 112 high schools across the United States, 36 percent of the 21,233 players monitored sustained a time-loss injury. Sixty percent of the injuries occurred in practice, and 40 percent occurred in games. While the overall injury toll fell to a projected 503,000 in 1988 from 636,000 two years earlier, major injuries (three or more weeks of time loss), rose to 65,634. (See Figure 5.) These statistics indicate that a significant number of injuries occur even though the sports medicine community is engaged in prevention of athletic injuries. The athletic trainer needs to be aware of the current incidence of injuries at various levels of competition. Up-to-date information and statistics may be obtained from the following organizations:[10]

Big Ten Injury Surveillance Survey
1110 Carver Pavilion
University of Iowa Hospitals
Iowa City, IA 52242

National Head and Neck Injury Registry
c/o University of Pennsylvania Sports
   Medicine Center
Wreightman Hall E-7
235 S. 33 St.
Philadelphia, PA 19104

National High School Athletic Injury Registry
National Athletic Trainer's Association, Inc.
2952 Stemmons Freeway
Dallas, TX 75247

National Injury Prevention Foundation
San Diego State University
San Diego, CA 92184

Regional Spinal Cord Injury Systems
University of Alabama at Birmingham
University Station
Birmingham, AL 35294

The Sports Medicine Center or Clinic

The various medical and paramedical specialties of the athletic health care team should be efficiently organized in order to make them available to all participants. A centralized sports medicine center or clinic seems to be a logical and appropriate way to utilize and mobilize available services, and in many instances the college or university community lends itself ideally to the development of such a clinic. The athlete and the medical and paramedical personal are in residence and centralization of the sports medicine services should be feasible. The college or university sports medicine center could provide the following services or functions:

1. Preventive program for various types of athletic endeavors

2. Athletic first aid and emergency care

3. Evaluation and diagnostic services

4. Nonsurgical treatment

5. Referral service, when appropriate

6. Rehabilitation

7. Research

Participation in athletics requires an acceptance of the risk of injury.

Rules and guidelines for each sport are designed to help protect the athlete from injury, but enforcement of the rules by game officials is not a guarantee against injury, nor are printed warnings on equipment or instructions by coaches in proper techniques. These factors minimize the risk, but they can never completely eliminate the risk.

My coach will acquaint me with the types of injury that I may incur in this sport and will instruct me in the techniques that will minimize the chance of injury in this sport.

I recognize that I have the responsibility to wear the required equipment, obey the rules of my sport, train my body to the best of my ability, utilize proper techniques and avoid activities for which I have not been trained, or which I do not feel qualified to perform. I will report any injuries promptly to the athletic training staff and follow their recommendations for treatment and return to activities following injury.

Serious head and neck injuries that may cause death, permanent brain damage, and/or paralysis occur each year in football due to the tremendous forces encountered in playing the game.

Compliance with rules, instruction in correct techniques, and use of proper equipment minimize these risks, but they cannot completely eliminate them.

Between 1976 and 1984 there were reported 123 brain hemorrhages resulting in 72 deaths and 134 permanent spinal cord paralyses in high school and college football players. The injury and death rates are low (1.3/100,000 deaths; 0.43/100,000 paralyses), but the athlete and his family must be made aware of the possibility that may occur in spite of all reasonable precautions.

The NOCSAE seal on a helmet indicates that a manufacturer has complied with the best available engineering standards for head protection. By keeping a proper fit, by not modifying its design, and by reporting to the coach or equipment manager need for its maintenance, the athlete is also complying with the purpose of the NOCSAE standard.

The rules against intentional head butting, ramming, or spearing of the opponent with the helmeted head are in place to protect the helmeted person much more than the opponent being hit. The athlete who does not comply with these rules is a candidate for catastrophic injury. For example, no helmet can offer protection to the neck, and quadriplegia now occurs more frequently than brain damage. The typical scenario of this catastrophic injury in football is the lowering of one's head while making a tackle. The momentum of the body bends the neck after the helmeted head is stopped by the impact, and the cervical spine cannot be "splinted" as well by the neck's muscles with the head lowered as in the preferred "face-up, eyes-forward, neck-bulled" position. When the force at impact is sufficient, the vertebrae in the neck can dislocate or break, cause damage to the spinal cord they had been protecting, and thereby produce permanent loss of motor and sensory function below the level of injury.

Because of the impact forces in football, even the "face-up" position is no guarantee against head or neck injury. Further, the *intent* to make contact "face up" is not a guarantee that the position can be maintained at the moment of impact. Consequently, the teaching of blocking/tackling techniques that keep the helmeted head from receiving the brunt of the impact are now required by rule and coaching ethics, and coaching techniques that help athletes maintain or regain the "face-up" position during the milieu of a play must be respected by the athletes.

I have read and understand the significance of these statements.

Student-Athlete   Date

Printed Name

Parent or Guardian Signature (if under 18)   Date

FIGURE 4
Football Participation Informed Consent

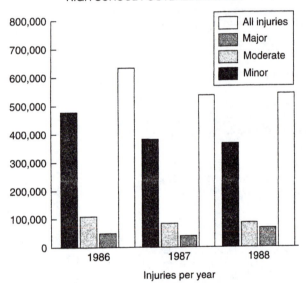

ANNUAL INJURY TOLL 1986-89

Legend:
- Football
- Girls' Basketball
- Boys' Basketball
- Wrestling

110,473   119,056   123,960   552,229

Total injuries

HIGH SCHOOL FOOTBALL INJURIES

Legend:
- All injuries
- Major
- Moderate
- Minor

1986   1987   1988

Injuries per year

Annual High School Football Injury Statistics			
	1986	1987	1988
All Injuries	636279	516716	503706
Major Injuries	54407	57241	65634
Moderate Injuries	104959	86028	86243
Minor injuries	476913	373447	351929

FIGURE 5
NATA Injury Surveillance Study 1986–1988

8. Teaching modules for utilization by various curricula in the sports medicine field.

The sports medicine center could provide services to the following programs:

1. Intercollegiate athletics
2. Intramural programs
3. Athletic clubs and recreational sports
4. Physical education departments
5. Community sports–fitness programs (recreation department, YMCA, etc.)

Other types of sports medicine centers[9] designed to serve specific athletic needs have been developed for the pre- and post-college athlete and for the general public. They are usually organized as either a regional sports medicine center (usually associated with a medical school) or a private sports medicine center. All-inclusive athletic health care facilities have evolved to include the services of various personnel to develop a complete approach to health and fitness.

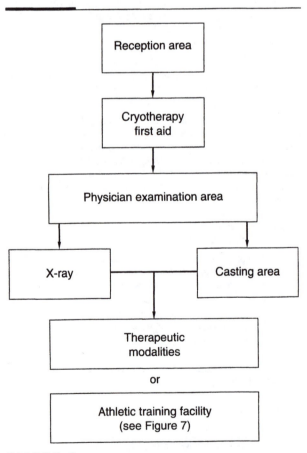

FIGURE 6
Example of a sports medicine clinic flow pattern

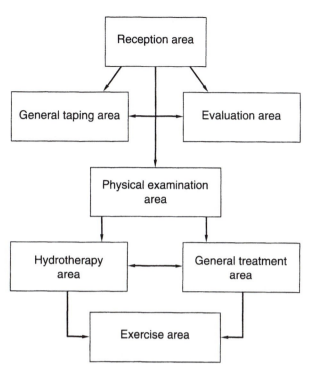

FIGURE 7
Example of an athletic training facility flow pattern

REFERENCES

1. Hirsch FJ: Generalist as team physician. *Phys Sportsmed* 7:88–90 and 92–95, August 1979.

2. Ryan AJ: Sports medicine history. *Phys Sportsmed* 6:77–82, October 1978.

3. Ryan AJ: Is sports medicine a "specialty"? *Phys Sportsmed* 6:3, January 1978.

4. Caldwell F: Physicians discuss sports medicine training. *Phys Sportsmed* 6:12, August 1978.

5. Prokop L: Sports medicine (Development and range of the field). *Olympian* 4:15–17, 1978.

6. National Athletic Trainers' Association, *NATA News*, Vol. 2, No. 4, September 1990.

7. Professional Education Committee, NATA, News Release, October 16, 1992.

8. National Athletic Trainers' Association, News Release, 1991.

9. Ferstle J: Olympic centers, money and muddle. *Phys Sportsmed* 6:22–23, June 1978.

10. Where to turn for sports injury statistics, *Phys SportsMed* 15:179–181, April 1987.

RECOMMENDED READINGS

Adkinson JW, Requa RK, Garrick JG: Injury rates in high school football. *Clin Orthop* 99:131–136, 1974.

Garrick JG, Requa R: Medical care and injury surveillance in the high school setting. *Phys Sportmed* 9:115–120, February 1981.

Goldberg B, Veres G, Nicholas JA: Sports medicine. *NY State J Med* 78:1406–1408, 1978.

National Athletic Trainers' Association, *NATA News*, October 1993.

Nicholas JA: What sports medicine is about. *Con Med* 42:4–8, 1979.

Ryan AJ: Do we need a federal institute? *Phys Sportmed* 6:45, April 1978.

Ryan AJ: Sports medicine today. *Science* 200:919–924, 1978.

Ryan AJ, Allman FL, editors: *Sports Medicine*. New York, Academic Press, 1974.

Shively RA, Grana WA, Ellis D: High school sports injuries. *Phys Sportmed* 9:46–50, August 1981.

Vinger PF, Hoerner EF, editors: *Sports Injuries: The Unthwarted Epidemic*. Littleton, MA, PSG Publishing Company Inc., 1981.

Williams JG: International Federation of Sports Medicine. American Medical Association: *Proceedings of the Medical Aspects of Sports*. Chicago, 1974, pp 48–51.

Contributors

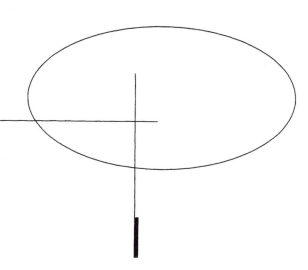

Russell J. Cagle, Ph.D., A.T., C.
    Head Athletic Trainer and Associate Professor
    Willamette University
    Salem, Oregon

Lori D. Carter, Ed.M., A.T., C.
    Assistant Professor of Sport and Exercise Science,
    Barry University
    Miami Shores, Florida

Kathleen A. Curtis, Ph.D., P.T.
    Associate Professor
    California State University at Fresno
    Department of Physical Therapy
    Fresno, California

David A. Draper, Ed.C., A.T., C.
    Assistant Professor,
    Sportsmedicine/Athletic Training
    Brigham Young University
    Provo, Utah

Karen Dyste, M.S., A.T., C.
    Head Athletic Trainer—North Eugene High School
    Eugene, Oregon

Robert E. Grams, M.S., A.T., C.
    Department of Physical Education
    Seattle Pacific University
    Seattle, Washington

Rod A. Harter, Ph.D., A.T., C.
    Associate Professor,
    Dept. of Exercise and Sport Science
    Oregon State University
    Corvallis, Oregon

Robert Johnson, P.T.
    Comprehensive Physical Therapy
    Eugene, Oregon

Kent Keyser, M.S., P.T., A.T., C., O.C.S., C.O.M.T.
    Comprehensive Physical Therapy
    Eugene, Oregon

Kenneth F. Kladnik, M.Ed., A.T., C.
    Head Athletic Trainer,
    Eastern Oregon State College
    La Grande, Oregon

Kenneth Kopke, M.Ed., A.T., C.
    President Athletic Training Services
    Formerly Head Athletic Trainer
    and Director of Sports Medicine
    Central Michigan University (1969–1986)
    Mt. Pleasant, Michigan

John Koth, M.P.T., M.S., A.T., C.
    Sun Valley Sports Medicine—Physical Therapy
    Ketchum, Idaho

Thomas E. Koto, Jr., A.T., C./R.
    Idaho Sports Medicine Institute
    Boise, Idaho

Richard J. Lindquist, M.D.
    Professor and University Physician
    University of Oregon Student Health Center
    Eugene, Oregon

Natalie Martin, M.A., A.T., C.
    Assistant Athletic Trainer,
    Barry University
    Miami Shores, Florida

Donald F. Mattern, M.Sc., A.T., C.
    Athletic Trainer, University of Lethbridge
    Lethbridge, Alberta, Canada

Jeff McCubbin, Ph.D.
    Associate Professor,
    College of Health and Human Performance
    Oregon State University
    Corvallis, Oregon

Kathryn E. Ralston, P.T., A.T., C.
    Rogue Valley Medical Center
    Medford, Oregon

O. Duane Royer, M.S., P.T., S.C.S., A.T., C
    Rebound (Physical Therapy
    and Sports Rehabilitation)
    Albany, Oregon

Michael "Sandy" Sandago, M.A., A.T., C.
    Heath Athletic Trainer,
    Oregon State University
    Corvallis, Oregon

Sayers John Miller, III, M.A., P.T., A.T., C.
    Cascade Orthopedic and Sports Therapy
    Seattle, Washington

Donna Scurlock, M.D., A.B.F.P., C.A.Q.
    Sports Medicine Professor
    and University Physician
    University of Oregon Student Health Center
    Eugene, Oregon

Kim S. Terrell, M.S., A.T., C.
    Director of Sports Medicine
    Northeastern University
    Boston, Mass.

Richard Troxell, M.S., A.T., C.
    Program Director, Athletic Training
    Department of Exercise and Movement Science
    University of Oregon

The Prevention of Athletic Injuries

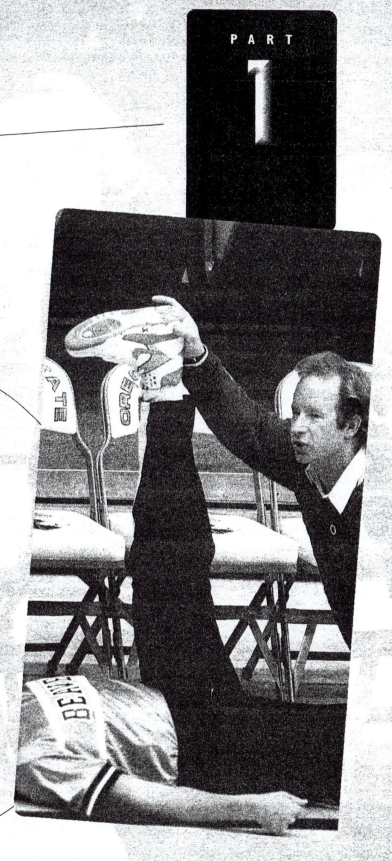

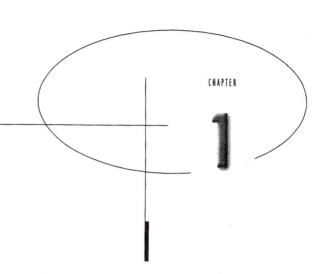

The Preparticipation Physical Examination

A preparticipation physical examination should have a definite purpose according to the type of athlete being examined.[1] For instance, the examination of a young teenager entails a different orientation from that of a professional football player. To quote from Garrick[2]:

important for young athletes

> A child athlete offers the most potential for accomplishing something meaningful in the preparticipation examination. As athletes become more experienced one is less likely to discover significant medical problems during the course of an examination, as the first few participation examinations uncover conditions that will preclude specific athletic activities. Later in the athlete's career one usually looks for (and finds) only the residuals of previous injuries. For the experienced athlete the examination serves primarily as a quality control of treatment and rehabilitation of previous injuries.

The primary objectives of the examination are to

1. Determine if any defects or conditions exist which might place that athlete at risk or increase the chances of injury in that particular sport

2. Bring to the athlete's attention any weakness or imbalance, so that correction of it may be undertaken before beginning a particular athletic activity

3. Determine whether an athlete may participate safely in spite of having a recognizable problem

4. Meet legal and insurance requirements. Each state, as well as many leagues and conferences, have their own regulations concerning the medical eligibility of student athletes. At least 35 states require a yearly evaluation, and 36 provide an official state form for this evaluation.

The secondary objectives of the examination include

1. Determining the general health of the athlete. (It has been shown that up to 78% of athletes view the PPE (preparticipation exam) as their annual health examination.)[3]

2. Counseling the athlete regarding findings—both normal and abnormal

3. Assessing maturity

4. Assessing fitness level and performance

TIMING: The physical examination should ideally be conducted 4–6 weeks before the beginning of the season in order to allow (1) further investigation of any questionable finding elicited during the examination, and (2) sufficient time to correct problems such as muscle weakness, infections, and other conditions. The American Academy of Pediatrics[4] recommends a full physical examination when the student enters a new school level (junior high, high school) and an annual interim history and limited exam. The examination should ideally take place in a health care facility. At least one of the rooms should be in an area of complete quiet and privacy so that a cardiac and a medical examination can be satisfactorily undertaken. The trainer can assist with or perform many parts of the examination, and may be asked to be responsible for the organization and record keeping.

Eight major areas are involved in the physical examination:

1. *History.* The inclusion of health questionnaires and interview has become a major element in the PPE. Indeed, the medical history may be the single most

important component of the PPE. A complete history can help identify up to 74 percent of all sports significant problems.[5] A thorough general history should address overall health, past hospitalizations and surgeries, chronic diseases, medication use, immunization status, allergies, missing organs, and family history of cardiovascular disease and Marfan Syndrome.[6] While the basic PPE should be similar for both male and female athletes, the history should address issues specific to the female athlete. Menstrual dysfunction and

TABLE 1.1 *Sports participation health record*

This evaluation is only to determine readiness for sports participation. It should not be used as a substitute for regular health maintenance examinations.

Name _____ Age (Yrs)_____ Grade _____ Date _____
Address _____ Phone _____
Sports _____

The Health History (Part A) and Physical Examination (Part C [table 3]) must be completed, at least every 24 months, before sports participation. The Interim Health History (Part B) must be completed at least annually.

Part A: Health History
To be completed by athlete and parent.

	YES	NO
1. Have you ever had an illness that:		
a. required you to stay in the hospital?	☐	☐
b. lasted longer than a week?	☐	☐
c. caused you to miss 3 days of practice or a competition?	☐	☐
d. is related to allergies (eg, hay fever, hives, asthma, insect sting reactions)?	☐	☐
e. required an operation	☐	☐
f. is chronic (eg, asthma, diabetes)?	☐	☐
2. Have you ever had an injury that:		
a. required you to go to an emergency room or see a doctor?	☐	☐
b. required you to stay in the hospital?	☐	☐
c. required x-rays?	☐	☐
d. caused you to miss 3 days of practice or a competition?	☐	☐
e. required an operation?	☐	☐
3. Do you take any medication or pills?	☐	☐
4. Have any members of your family under age 50 had a heart attack, had a heart problem, or died unexpectedly?	☐	☐
5. Have you ever:		
a. been dizzy or passed out during or after exercise?	☐	☐
b. been unconscious or had a concussion?	☐	☐
6. Are you unable to run 1/2 mile (2 times around the track) without stopping?	☐	☐
7. Do you:		
a. wear glasses or contacts?	☐	☐
b. wear dental bridges, plates, or braces?	☐	☐
8. Have you ever had a heart murmur, high blood pressure, or a heart abnormality?	☐	☐
9. Do you have any allergies to any medicine?	☐	☐
10. Are you missing a kidney?	☐	☐

11. When was your last tetanus booster? _____

12. For women.
    a. At what age did you experience your first menstrual period? _____
    b. In the last year, what is the longest time you have gone between periods? _____

Explain any "yes" answers.

_____

_____

disordered eating represent two problem areas specific to female athletes.

In the case of the precollege athlete, the best medical history is usually obtained from the family physician in conjunction with the parents. However, the history form should be reviewed in detail with the athlete, either on an individual basis or in a group. The athlete should not just be given a form and told to fill it in. The questions should be phrased so that any *yes* answer can be further evaluated (see Tables 1.1 and 1.2).

TABLE 1.1 *(Continued)*

I hereby state that, to the best of my knowledge, my answers to the above questions are correct.

Date _____
Signature of athlete _____
Signature of parent _____

Part B: Interim Health History
This form should be used during the interval between preparticipation evaluations. Positive responses should prompt a medical evaluation.

1. Over the next 12 months, I wish to participate in the following sports:
   a. _____
   b. _____
   c. _____
   d. _____

2. Have you missed more than 3 consecutive days of participation in usual activities because of any injury this past year? YES ☐ NO ☐
   If yes, please indicate:
   a. Site of injury _____
   b. Type of injury _____

3. Have you missed more than 5 consecutive days of participation in usual activities because of an illness, or have you had a medical illness diagnosed that has not been resolved in the past year? ☐ ☐
   If yes, please indicate:
   a. Type of illness _____

4. Have you had a seizure or a concussion or been unconscious for any reason in the last year? ☐ ☐

5. Have you had surgery or been hospitalized in this past year? ☐ ☐
   If yes, please indicate:
   a. Reason for hospitalization _____
   b. Type of surgery _____

6. List all medications you are currently taking and what condition the medication is for.
   a. _____
   b. _____
   c. _____

7. Are you worried about any problem or condition at this time? ☐ ☐
   If yes, please explain: _____
   _____

I hereby state that, to the best of my knowledge, my answers to the above questions are correct.

Date _____
Signature of athlete _____
Signature of parent _____

Reprinted with permission of the American Academy of Pediatrics, *Sports Medicine: Health Care for Young Athletes.* Elk Grove Village, IL, American Academy of Pediatrics, © 1991.

TABLE 1.2 *Supplemental health history questionnaire for the female athlete*

Name _____ Age _____

Directions: Please answer the following questions to the best of your ability.

1. How old were you when you had your first menstrual period? _____
2. How often do you have a period? _____
3. How long do your periods last? _____
4. How many periods have you had in the last 12 months? _____
5. When was your last period? _____
6. Do you ever have trouble with heavy bleeding? _____
7. Do you have questions about tampon use? _____
8. Do you ever experience cramps during your period? _____
   If so, how do you treat them? _____
9. Do you take birth control pills or hormones? _____
10. Do you have any unusual discharge from your vagina? _____
11. When was your last pelvic exam? _____
12. Have you ever had an abnormal PAP smear? _____
13. How many urinary tract infections (bladder or kidney) have you had? _____
14. Have you ever been treated for anemia? _____
15. How many meals do you eat each day? How many snacks? _____
16. What have you eaten in the last 24 hours? _____
17. Are there certain food groups you refuse to eat (eg, meats, breads)? _____
18. Have you ever been on a diet? _____
19. What is your present weight? _____
20. Are you happy with this weight? If not, what would you like to weigh? _____
21. Have you ever tried to control your weight by vomiting? _____
    Using laxatives? _____ Diuretics? _____ Diet pills? _____
22. Have you ever been diagnosed as having an eating disorder? _____
23. Do you have questions about healthy ways to control weight? _____

Source: M. Johnson, Tailoring the Preparticipation Exam for Female Athletes. *The Physician and Sportsmedicine,* 20 (7), pp. 61–72, July 1992. Reproduced with permission of McGraw-Hill, Inc.

2. *Measurement.* This should include height, weight, and blood pressure.

3. *Medical examination.* This examination should be conducted in a quiet, private room and should include cardiovascular, respiratory, abdominal, lymphatic, genital, dermatologic, and ear, nose, and throat systems. Males should be dressed in shorts, and females in shorts and bikini tops or tank tops. A thorough review of the athletes' medical history will help to identify predisposing conditions that may place them at risk for injury or death. Because over 95 percent of sudden deaths in athletes under 30 years of age involve the cardiovascular system, careful attention to cardiovascular history is vital.[3] A review of family medical history may also be relevant with regard to high blood pressure, diabetes, allergies, and sudden death in family members under 50. In addition, thoroughly review the athlete's history of neurologic conditions and injuries, such as seizures, severe or recurrent headaches, head injuries, burns/stingers, pinched nerves, or transient quadriplegia (Table 1.1).

4. *Orthopedic examination.* The purpose of the orthopedic examination is to identify congenital or acquired musculoskeletal problems that might be

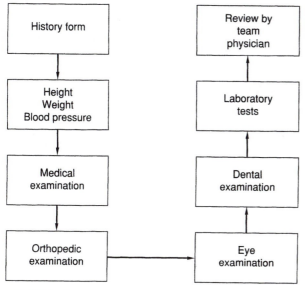

FIGURE I.I

The physical examination—flow pattern

(Adapted from Pediatric Clinics of North America, James G. Garrick, M.D., *Sports Medicine* 24:4, November 1977, p. 741.)

adversely affected by or interfere with athletic participation (see Table 1.3).

Complete examination of individual joints of the knee and shoulder may be performed if the history or screening examination indicates the need for such an evaluation.

5. *Eye examination.*

6. *Dental screening examination.*

7. *Laboratory tests.* These should consist of a minimum of a hemoglobin or hematocrit estimation and a urinalysis.

8. *Review of the physical examination by the physician in charge.* Undoubtedly one of the most important and difficult decisions in the PPE is clearance for an activity when an abnormality is found that may limit the athlete's participation or predispose him or her to further injury. The physician must determine which sports the athlete should be able to participate in. The American Academy of Pediatrics "Recommendations for Participation in Competitive Sports" (Table 1.4) should be

TABLE I.3   *The two-minute orthopedic exam*

Instructions	Points of Observation
Stand facing examiner	Acromioclavicular joints, general habitus
Look at ceiling, floor, over both shoulders; touch ears to shoulders	Cervical spine motion
Shrug shoulders (examiner resists)	Trapezius strength
Abduct arms 90° (examiner resists at 90°)	Deltoid strength
Fully rotate arms externally	Shoulder motion
Flex and extend elbows	Elbow motion
Pronate and supinate wrists with arms at sides, elbows flexed 90°	Elbow and wrist motion
Spread fingers; make fist	Hand or finger motion and deformities
Contract and relax quadriceps	Symmetry and knee effusion; ankle effusion
"Duck walk" four steps away from examiner with buttocks on heels	Hip, knee, and ankle motion
Stand with back to examiner	Shoulder symmetry, scoliosis
Straighten knees, touch toes	Scoliosis, hip motion, hamstring tightness
Raise up on toes	Calf symmetry, leg strength

Reprinted with permission of the American Academy of Pediatrics, *Sports Medicine: Health Care for Young Athletes.* Elk Grove Village, American Academy of Pediatrics, © 1991.

TABLE 1.4 *Recommendations for participation in competitive sports*

	Contact			Noncontact	
	Contact/ collision	Limited contact/collision	Strenuous	Moderately strenuous	Nonstrenuous
Atlantoaxial instability	No	No	Yes*	Yes	Yes
Swimming (no butterfly, breaststroke or diving starts)					
Acute illnesses	*	*	*	*	*
Needs individual assessment (e.g., contagiousness to others, risk of worsening illness)					
Cardiovascular					
Carditis	No	No	No	No	No
Hypertension					
Mild	Yes	Yes	Yes	Yes	Yes
Moderate	*	*	*	*	*
Severe	*	*	*	*	*
Congenital heart disease	†	†	†	†	†
Needs individual assessment					
†Patients with mild forms can be allowed a full range of physical activities; patients with mild or severe forms or who are postoperative should be evaluated by a physician					
Eyes					
Absence or loss of function of one eye	*	*	*	*	*
Detached retina	†	†	†	†	†
Availability of American Society for Testing Materials approved eye guards may allow competitor to participate in most sports, but this must be judged on an individual basis					
†Consult opthalmologist					
Inguinal hernia	Yes	Yes	Yes	Yes	Yes
Kidney (absence of one)	No	Yes	Yes	Yes	Yes
Liver (enlarged)	No	No	Yes	Yes	Yes
Musculosketetal disorders	*	*	*	*	*
Needs individual assessment					
Neurologic	*	*	Yes	Yes	Yes
History of serious head or spine trauma, repeated concussions or craniotomy					
Convulsive disorder					
Well controlled	Yes	Yes	Yes	Yes	Yes
Poorly controlled	No	No	Yes†	Yes	Yes‡
Needs individual assessment					
†No swimming or weight lifting					
‡No archery or riflery					
Ovary (absence of one)	Yes	Yes	Yes	Yes	Yes
Respiratory					
Pulmonary insufficiency	*	*	*	*	Yes
Asthma	Yes	Yes	Yes	Yes	Yes
May be allowed to compete if oxygenation remains satisfactory during a graded stress test					
Sickle cell trait	Yes	Yes	Yes	Yes	Yes
Skin (boils, herpes, impetigo, scabies)	*	*	Yes	Yes	Yes
No gymnastics with mats, martial arts, wrestling or contact sports until no longer contagious					
Spleen (enlarged)	No	No	No	Yes	Yes
Testicle (absent or undescended)	Yes*	Yes*	Yes	Yes	Yes
Certain sports may require protective cup					

Source: Preparticipation Physical Education (monograph). American Academy of Family Physicians, American Academy of Pediatrics, American Medical Society for Sports Medicine, American Orthopaedic Society for Sports Medicine, American Osteopathic Academy of Sports Medicine, Kansas City, 1992.

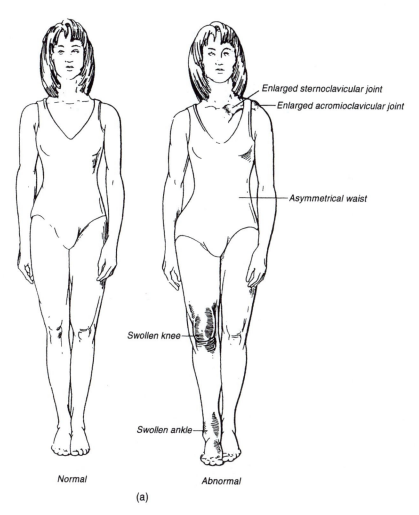

Enlarged sternoclavicular joint
Enlarged acromioclavicular joint

Asymmetrical waist

Swollen knee

Swollen ankle

Normal   Abnormal

(a)

Instructions: Stand straight with arms at sides.
Observations: Symmetry of upper and lower extremities and trunk.
Common abnormalities:
1. Enlarged acromioclavicular joint
2. Enlarged sternoclavicular joint
3. Asymmetrical waist (leg length difference or scoliosis)
4. Swollen knee
5. Swollen ankle

FIGURE 1.2a

Symmetry of upper and lower extremities and trunk (patient facing examiner)

used. The recommendations divide sports activities into several categories based on the amount of contact and the intensity of exercise. The physician must decide, based on the status of each athlete, the level of participation:

a. no athletic participation
b. limited participation with specific sports mentioned
c. clearance withheld until additional tests, examinations, or rehabilitation can be completed
d. no reason found to restrict participation

This physician may also review advice given to the athlete—for instance, "improve flexibility of the hamstrings, decrease body fat, increase strength of the quadriceps." For information specific to the female athlete see Chapter 24.

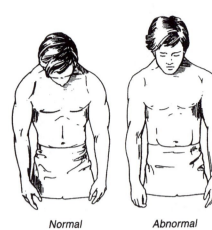

Normal   Abnormal

Neck range of motion–flexion.

Normal   Abnormal

Neck range of motion–extension.

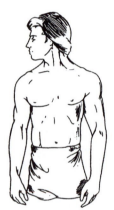

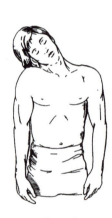
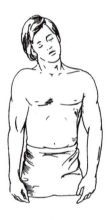

Normal   Abnormal

Neck range of motion–left and right lateral rotation.

Normal   Abnormal

Neck range of motion–left and right lateral flexion.

(b)

Instructions: Look at ceiling; look at floor; touch right (left) ear to shoulder; look over right (left) shoulder.

Observations: Should be able to touch chin to chest, ears to shoulders and look equally over shoulders.

Common abnormalities (may indicate previous neck injury):

1. Loss of flexion
2. Loss of lateral bending
3. Loss of rotation

FIGURE 1.2b

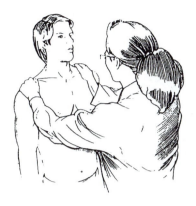

Normal   *Abnormal*

Resisted shoulder shrug–trapezius strength.

(c)

Instructions: Shrug shoulders while examiner holds them down.

Observations: Trapezius muscles appear equal; left and right sides equal strength.
Common abnormalities (may indicate neck or shoulder problem).
1. Loss of strength
2. Loss of muscle bulk

FIGURE 1.2c

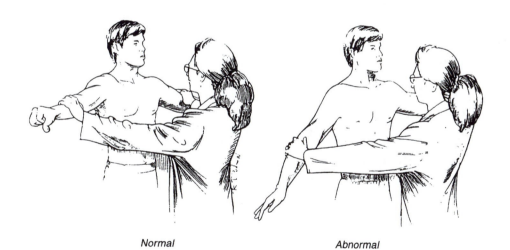

Normal   *Abnormal*

Resisted shoulder abduction–deltoid strength.

(d)

Instructions: Hold arms out from sides horizontally and lift while examiner holds them down.

Observations: Strength should be equal and deltoid muscles should be equal in size.
Common abnormalities:
1. Loss of strength
2. Wasting of deltoid muscle

FIGURE 1.2d

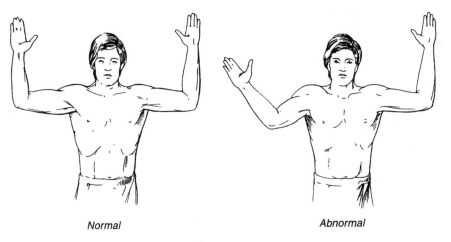

Normal   Abnormal

Shoulder range of motion–external rotation.

(e)

Instructions: Hold arms out from sides with elbows bent (90°); raise hands back vertically as far as they will go.

Observations: Hands go back equally and at least to upright vertical position.

Common abnormalities (may indicate shoulder problem or old dislocation):

1. Loss of external rotation

FIGURE 1.2e

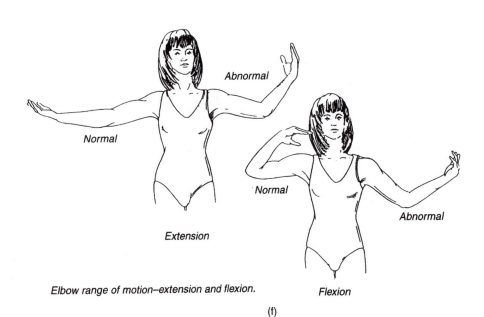

Normal

Abnormal

Normal

Abnormal

Extension

Flexion

Elbow range of motion–extension and flexion.

(f)

Instructions: Hold arms out from sides, palms up; straighten elbows completely; bend completely.

Observations: Motion equal left and right.

Common abnormalities (may indicate old elbow injury, old dislocation, fracture, etc.):

1. Loss of extension
2. Loss of flexion

FIGURE 1.2f

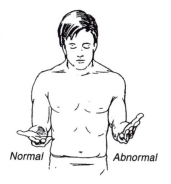
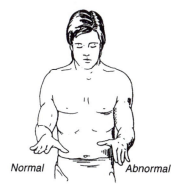

Pronation   Supination

Elbow range of motion–pronation and supination.

(g)

Instructions: Hold arms down at sides with elbows bent (90°); supinate palms;
pronate palms.
Observations: Palms should go from facing ceiling to facing floor.
Common abnormalities (may indicate old forearm, wrist, or elbow injury):
1. Lack of full supination
2. Lack of full pronation

FIGURE 1.2g

Normal

Abnormal

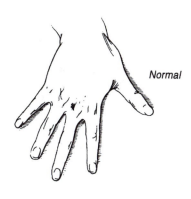
Normal

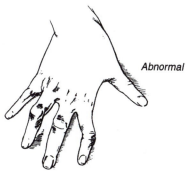
Abnormal

Instructions: Make a fist; open hand and
spread fingers.
Observations: Fist should be tight and fingers
straight when spread.
Common abnormalities (may
indicate old finger fractures or
sprains):
1. Protruding knuckle from fist
2. Swollen and/or crooked finger   (h)

*Hand and finger range of motion (patient
making a fist and spreading fingers).*

FIGURE 1.2h

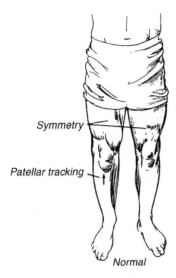

Symmetry

Patellar tracking

Normal

Contraction of quadriceps muscles

(i)

Instruction: Stand straight; contract quadriceps
Observation: Symmetry and knee effusion

FIGURE 1.2i

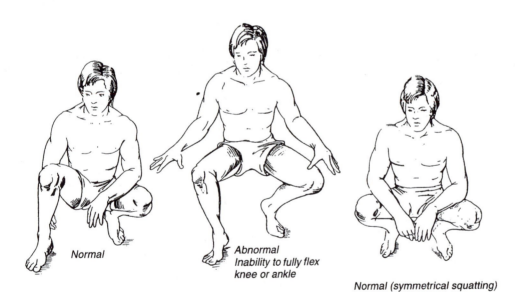

Normal

Abnormal
Inability to fully flex
knee or ankle

Normal (symmetrical squatting)

(j) Squat and "duck walk."

Instructions: Squat on heels; duck walk 4 steps and stand up.
Observations: Maneuver is painless; heel to buttock distance equal left and right; knee flexion equal
during walk; rises straight up.
Common abnormalities:
1. Inability to fully flex one knee
2. Inability to stand up without twisting or bending to one side

FIGURE 1.2j

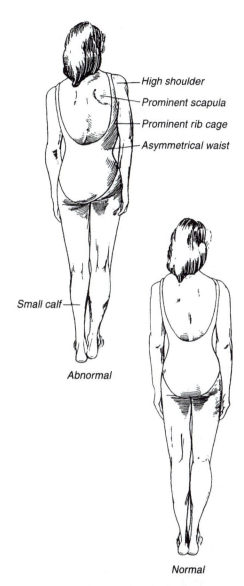

High shoulder
Prominent scapula
Prominent rib cage
Asymmetrical waist

Small calf

Abnormal

Normal

Symmetry of upper and lower extremities and trunk (patient facing away from examiner).

(k)

Instructions: With back to examiner stand up straight.
Observations: Symmetry of shoulders, waist, thighs, and calves.
Common abnormalities:
1. High shoulder (scoliosis) or low shoulder (muscle loss)
2. Prominent rib cage (scoliosis)
3. High hip or asymmetrical waist (leg length difference or scoliosis)
4. Small calf or thigh (weakness from old injury)

FIGURE 1.2k

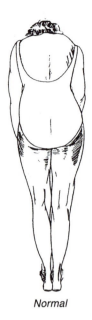
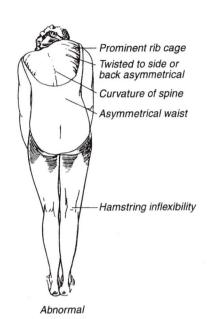

Prominent rib cage

Twisted to side or back asymmetrical

Curvature of spine

Asymmetrical waist

Hamstring inflexibility

Normal   Abnormal

Back flexion with knees straight (patient facing away from examiner).

(I)

Instructions: Bend forward slowly as to touch toes.
Observations: Bends forward straightly and smoothly.
              Common abnormalities:
                1. Twists to side (low back pain)
                2. Back asymmetrical (scoliosis)

FIGURE 1.21

Characteristics to Note during the Physical Examination

POSTURE: Posture is not only a reflection of the state of muscle tone, but often reflects on some aspects of the athlete's psychology as well. During a screening examination it is necessary to become aware of each athlete's posture and what can be done to correct any abnormality (Table 1.5).

FLEXIBILITY: The subject of flexibility has produced a great deal of controversy in recent years. There is no doubt, however, that some athletes are "tight" while others are "loose." Some authorities[7,8] feel that a tight-jointed individual is more prone to muscle strains, whereas a loose-jointed individual is more subject to ligament sprains. However, others[9] disagree with this assessment and feel that one cannot predict the occurrence of injuries based on these criteria alone.

Irrespective of these arguments is the athlete's subjective feeling of improved performance and comfort if a slow, passive stretching program is performed routinely. It appears that this type of stretching program is useful in injury prevention, particularly with certain muscle groups that tend to become too tight with repeated use, for example, the hamstrings, and the gastrocnemius-soleus-Achilles group. For these reasons it is considered desirable that athletes be encouraged to perform slow stretching exercises of specific muscle groups that might become tight in their particular sporting activity. On the other hand, however, certain high-performance athletes who are tight do not wish to stretch, yet do not appear to be prone to injury. Whether this is the exception that proves the rule is still a subject of debate.

SKINFOLD THICKNESS: There are almost no sports (except perhaps long-distance swimming and sumu wrestling) in which a large amount of subcutaneous fat is an advantage. If an athlete needs to put on weight, it should be as muscle mass only and not as fat.

An estimation of percentage of body fat can be made by a number of methods, one of the most accurate being total body immersion in an underwater weighing tank.

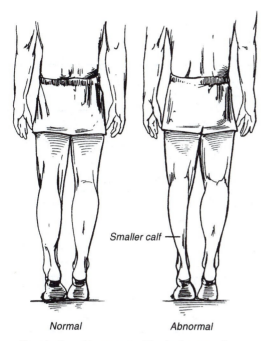

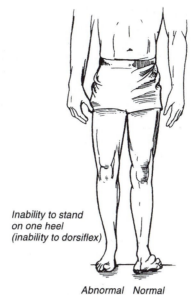

Smaller calf —

Inability to stand
on one heel
(inability to dorsiflex)

Normal   Abnormal   Abnormal   Normal

*Examination of lower extremities (patient standing
on toes, facing away from examiner).*

*Examination of lower extremities (patient
standing on heel, facing examiner).*

(m)

Instructions: Stand on heels; stand on toes.
Observations: Equal elevation right and left; symmetry of calf muscles.
Common abnormalities:
1. Wasting of calf muscles (Achilles injury or old ankle injury)

FIGURE 1.2m

Source: Preparticipation Physical Evaluation, a joint publication of the American Academy of Family Physicians, American Academy of Pediatrics, American Medical Society for Sports Medicine, and American Osteopathic Academy of Sports Medicine, 1992.

As this is not practical in many cases, skinfold thickness measurement by means of calipers is a useful technique, but one that needs to be continually practiced in order to achieve consistency and accuracy (Figure 1.3).

Women are normally considered to have a higher body fat content than men,[10] and most male athletes should fall below 12 percent to 15 percent body fat. Endurance athletes,[11] gymnasts of both sexes, and wrestlers are often below 7 percent but should not be below 5 percent. However, if an individual has a total body fat above the optimum for that sport, he or she is carrying excessive deadweight, which is detrimental to athletic performance as well as to health. Athletes should be educated in this area and advised accordingly.

A practical way to estimate the fluctuations in body fat is to measure a number of standard locations and add them together to obtain a total.[12,13,14] This procedure can be repeated on occasion throughout the season (Table 1.6).

STRENGTH: There are a number of different methods used to test muscle strength. One method is to place the extremity into the desired position and ask the athlete to maintain that position while a constant resistance is applied (Figure 1.4), Other methods include the use of a strain gauge for isometric contractions, a handgrip dynamometer (Figure 1.5), successive lifts on an isotonic machine (Universal Gym) until the maximum lift is achieved, or visual or printed readouts on one of the isokinetic machines (Cybex or Kincom, etc.).

MATURATION: The participation of a pre-adolescent or adolescent athlete should be determined not by age, but by size, weight, and degree of maturity. Two methods of evaluating physical maturity are:

1. *Skeletal development.* This is determined by comparing X-rays of the wrist with the norms found in a radiologic atlas[15,16] (Figure 1.6).

TABLE 1.5 *Physical examination record (Part C)*

Name _____ Date _____ Age _____ Birth date _____
Height _____ Vision: R _____/_____ corrected _____ uncorrected _____
Weight _____   L _____/_____ corrected _____ uncorrected _____
Pulse _____ Blood pressure _____ Percent body fat (optional) _____

	Normal	Abnormal Findings	Initials
1. Eyes			
2. Ears, nose, throat			
3. Mouth, teeth			
4. Neck			
5. Cardiovascular			
6. Chest, lungs			
7. Abdomen			
8. Skin			
9. Genitalia: hernia (male)			
10. Mulsculoskeletal: ROM, strength, etc.			
a. neck			
b. spine			
c. shoulders			
d. arms, hands			
e. hips			
f. thighs			
g. knees			
h. ankles			
i. feet			
11. Neuromuscular			

12. Physical maturity (Tanner stage)   1   2   3   4   5

Comments re abnormal findings: _____
_____
_____
_____
_____

Participation Recommendations

1. No participation in:_____
_____

2. Limited participation in:_____
_____

3. Requires: _____
_____

4. Full participation in: _____
_____

Physician Signature _____
Telephone number _____ Address _____

Reprinted with permission of the American Academy of Pediatrics, *Sports Medicine: Health Care for Young Athletes.* Elk Grove Village, American Academy of Pediatrics, © 1991.

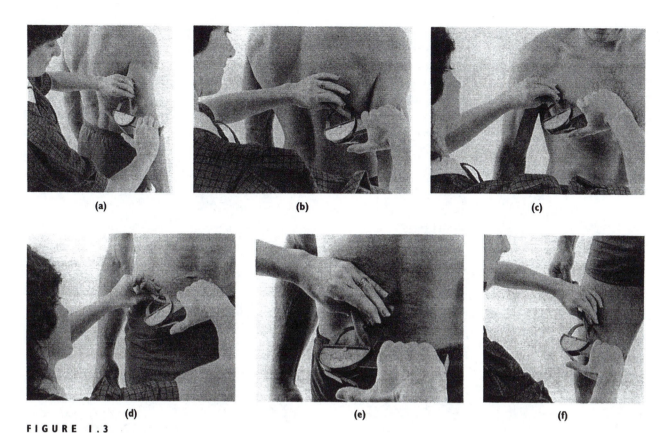

FIGURE 1.3

Estimation of body fat by the use of skinfold thickness calipers

The skin should be lifted away from the underlying muscle. The most commonly used sites are illustrated: (a) mid triceps; (b) scapula; (c) anterior chest; (d) iliac crest; (e) just below and lateral to the umbilicus; (f) the anterior thigh

---

TABLE 1.6 *Simple classification of skinfold measurements for athletes*

Classification	Triceps[a]	Scapula[b]	Abdomen[c]	Total
Lean (< 7% fat)	< 7 mm	< 8 mm	< 10 mm	< 25 mm
Acceptable (12–15% fat)	7–13 mm	8–15 mm	10–20 mm	25–48 mm
Over fat (> 15% fat)	> 13 mm	> 15 mm	> 20 mm	> 48 mm

[a]Back of upper arm, over triceps midway on upper arm—skinfold lifted to parallel to long axis of arm with the arm hanging.

[b]Below tip of right scapula, skinfold lifted along axis of body.

[c]Five centimeters lateral to umbilicus, avoid umbilical crease, skinfold lifted on axis with umbilicus.

Note: The scapular skinfold is the single best skinfold to measure; the triceps, the next best.

Source: E. S. Buskirk, *Sports Medicine* (A. J. Ryan, F. L. Allman, eds.). New York, Academic Press, 1974, p. 146.

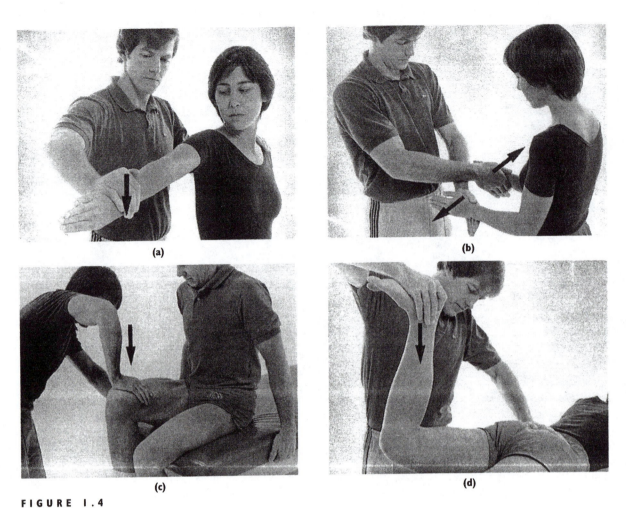

FIGURE I.4

Manual resistive muscle testing

Firm, constant pressure (not overpowering force) is applied by the examiner in order to detect muscle dysfunction or weakness. (a) deltoids; (b) internal rotators; (c) hip flexors; (d) gluteals

FIGURE I.5

A handgrip dynamometer

An accurate way to determine handgrip strength

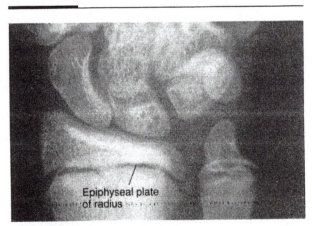

FIGURE I.6

Skeletal maturity

This wrist X-ray may be used to help determine the degree of bony maturity present. Note the epiphyseal plates which are still widely open. By using X-rays such as these, it may be possible to predict the potential height of the subject.

2. *Sexual development*. The presence and character of pubic or axillary hair, and breast development (in females) are satisfactory indications of the degree of maturity reached by that athlete (Figure 1.7). In adolescent females, the onset of menstruation may also be a suitable index of their degree of maturation and development (Figure 1.8).

According to Smith[17], collision contact sports such as football, wrestling, lacrosse, and ice hockey should not be recommended for boys until they have reached Stage V development. On the other hand, the highly skilled junior-high school athlete with Stage IV or V pubic hair development may be a suitable participant in many high school programs (Table 1.7).

Conditions that Might Disqualify an Athlete from Specific Athletic Participation

As mentioned in Table 1.4, some of the conditions listed as "disqualifying" apply only to particular sports. Other conditions are subject to the responsible physician's evaluating all the various factors involved.[18]

1. *Eye conditions*. An athlete with only one eye, severe myopia in one eye, or previous retinal detachment which has been repaired should be advised to refrain from contact sports.

The athlete should not wear hard contact lenses while boxing. Specially manufactured eyeglasses can be used for contact events if the athlete so chooses. However, soft contact lenses are usually readily accepted by most athletes and are probably superior and safer to use than glasses.

2. *Cardiac conditions*. Congenital cardiac disease now ranks as the major cause of death in high school and collegiate levels of participation. The incidence of indirect deaths (those attributed to systemic failure as a result of exertion while participating in sports), of which acute cardiovascular collapse is the most common cause, now outnumber direct deaths (those resulting from participating in the skills of the sport), by a ratio of nearly 2 to 1.[19] Heart murmurs are frequently heard in many athletes. In most cases these are functional in nature, but they usually need to be evaluated by a cardiologist in order to exclude more serious conditions which might result in sudden death during athletic participation (e.g., hypertrophic cardiomyopathy (HCM), congenital aortic stenosis (AS), and severe mitral valve prolapse).

Hypertrophic cardiomyopathy (HCM) is the most common cause of sudden death in young athletes.[3] In general, athletes with HCM accompanied by any of the following should not participate in competitive sports:

marked left ventricular hypertrophy, significant left ventricular outflow obstruction, significant arrhythmias, history of syncope, or family history of sudden death (HCM-related).

Athletes with HCM along with any of these five findings may participate in low-intensity activities if approved by a cardiologist.[3]

3. *Multiple concussions*. At present it is generally agreed than an athlete who has had three episodes of loss of consciousness with retrograde amnesia or other changes following the concussion should be disqualified from contact sports. This figure should be used as a guide only and should not be an inflexible number. Some athletes should be advised to refrain from contact activities after only one severe head injury. Other athletes who have had multiple episodes of minor concussions ("bell rung") may be candidates for disqualification even though they have not actually lost consciousness. These cases should be examined in conjunction with a neurologist or neurosurgeon in order to reach the most satisfactory conclusion with regard to the athlete's ability to continue with contact participation. Table 1.8 lists guidelines for grading concussions in sport and return to play.

4. *Burners/stingers*. Athletes with burners/stingers (nerve root or brachial plexus neuropraxia secondary to pinching or stretching of the cervical nerve roots or brachial plexus) may be cleared for all sports if they are asymptomatic and the physical examination is normal. Recurrent burners/stingers in one season may require further evaluation (cervical spine radiography) to rule out predisposing conditions such as c-spine instability or degenerative changes.

5. *Convulsive disorders*. Participation in athletics, and even in contact sports, can be undertaken by children and teenagers whose epilepsy is suitably controlled, if they are cooperative and emotionally stable. Those who suffer from epilepsy only while sleeping should be evaluated in the same manner as non-epileptics.[20,21,22]

There should, however, be restrictions on:

a. mountain climbing

b. working at heights

c. swimming alone

d. scuba diving

There should be restrictions on participation among:

a. those who experience daily or weekly seizures

b. those who display bizarre forms of psychomotor epilepsy

c. those whose post-convulsive state is prolonged or typically includes marked abnormal behavior.

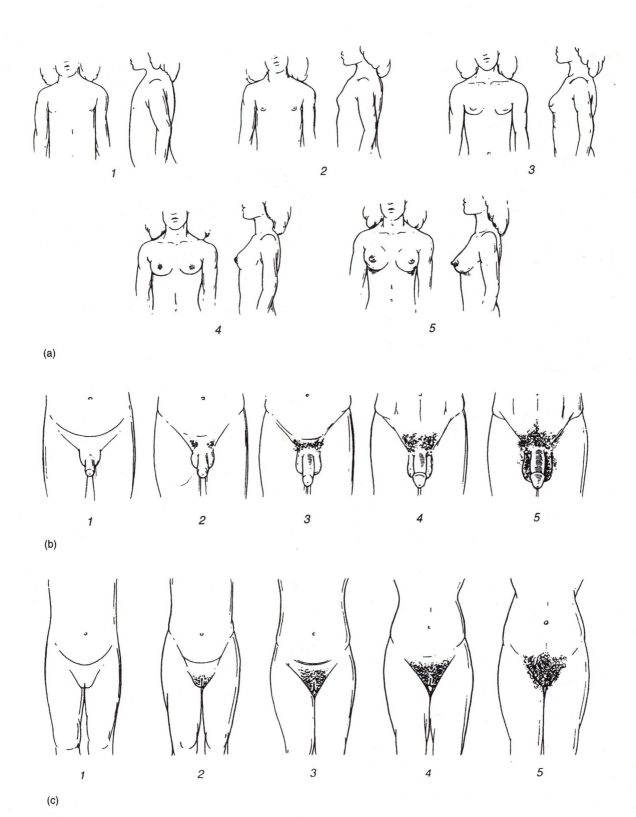

FIGURE 1.7

Tanner stage examination

Tanner stages: (a) breast; (b) pelvic (male); (c) pelvic (female)

Source: Preparticipation Physical Evaluation, a joint publicaton of the American Academy of Family Physicians, American Academy of Pediatrics, American Medical Society for Sports Medicine, and American Osteopathic Academy of Sports Medicine.

Mark a point on the line below to indicate months and years elapsed since her first menstruation. The point directly below on the second line shows the developmental age rating to use when considering programming this individual with girls of dissimilar chronological age.

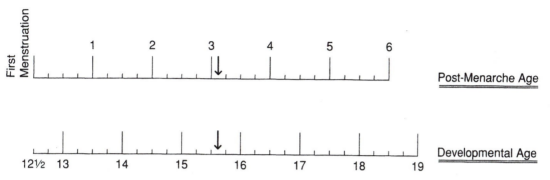

Example: Trudy J.

First menstruation: August 1976
Date of current evaluation: September 1979
Time elapsed since the onset of menstruation and evaluation dates: 3 years, 1 month. (Mark this on top line.)

The point directly below on the second line indicates a developmental level of 15 years, 7 months, although Trudy's chronological age is 14 years, 4 months. (Date of birth May 6, 1965.)

Thus, Trudy may be considered for programming with girls 15–16 years of age if other factors indicate superior levels of fitness and skills.

FIGURE 1.8
Scale to determine physical maturity of a girl
Source: Institute of Sports Medicine and Athletic Trauma, Lenox Hill Hospital, 130 East 77th Street, New York, New York 10021.

TABLE 1.7 *Tanner stages of pubertal development*

Stage	Pubic Hair	Breasts
1	None	Prepubertal, no glandular tissue
2	Sparse, long, straight, lightly pigmented	Breast bud, small amount of glandular tissue
3	Darker, beginning to curl and extend laterally	Breast mound and areola enlarged, no contour separation
4	Coarse, curly, abundant, less than adult	Breast enlarged, areola and papilla form mound projecting from breast contour
5	Adult type and quantity, extending to medial thigh	Mature, areola part of breast contour

Adapted from J.M. Tanner, Growth at Adolescence, 2d ed., Oxford, England, Blackwell Scientific Publications, 1962.

TABLE 1.8 *Grading concussions in sports and guidelines for return to play**

*—These guidelines are not absolute and therefore should not substitute for the clinical judgment of the examining physician.

| Grading | | Guidelines | | |
Severity	Signs/symptoms	First concussion	Second concussion	Third concussion
Grade I (mild)	Confusion without amnesia; no loss of consciousness	May return to play if asymptomatic‡ for at least 20 minutes	Terminate contest/practice; may return to play if asymptomatic†† for at least one week	Terminate season; may return to play in three months if asymptomatic††
Grade II (moderate)	Confusion with amnesia*; no loss of consciousness†	Terminate contest/practice; may return to play if asymptomatic for at least one week	Consider terminating season, but may return to play if asymptomatic†† for one month	Terminate season; may return to play next season if asymptomatic††
Grade III (severe)	Loss of consciousness†	Terminate contest/practice; transport to hospital; may return to play one month after two consecutive asymptomatic†† weeks; conditioning allowed after one asymptomatic†† week	Terminate season; may return to play next season if asymptomatic††	Terminate season; strongly discourage return to contact/collision sports

*—Posttraumatic amnesia (amnesia for events following the impact) or more severe retrograde amnesia (amnesia for events preceding the impact).
†—Some clinicians include "brief" loss of consciousness in Grade II and reserve "prolonged" loss of consciousness for Grade III. However, the definitions of "brief" and "prolonged" are not universally accepted.
††—No headache, confusion, dizziness, impaired orientation, impaired concentration or memory dysfunction during rest or exertion.
Source: Preparticipation Physical Evaluation (monograph), American Academy of Family Physicians, American Academy of Pediatrics, American Medical Society for Sports Medicine, American Orthopaedic Society for Sports Medicine, American Osteopathic Academy of Sports Medicine, Kansas City, 1992.

REFERENCES

1. Tennant FS, Sorenson K, Day CM: Benefits of preparticipation sports examinations. *J Fam Pract* 13:287–288, 1981.

2. Garrick JG: Pre-participation sports assessment. *Pediatrics* 66:803–806, 1980.

3. Preparticipation Physical Evaluation (PPE) a joint publication: American Academy of Family Physicians, American Academy of Pediatrics, American Medical Society for Sports Medicine, American Osteopathic Academy of Sports Med, 1992.

4. Committee on sports Medicine and Fitness, American Academy of Pediatrics: *Sports Medicine: Health Care for Young Adults.* Elk Grove Village, American Academy of Pediatrics, second edition, 1991).

5. Goldberg B, et al: Preparticipation sports assessment—an objective evaluation. *Pediatrics* 66(5): 736–745, 1980.

6. Johnson M: Tailoring the preparticipation exam to female athletes. *Phys Sports Med* 20 (7): 61–72, July 1992.

7. Nicholas JA: Risk factors: Sports medicine and the orthopedic system. An overview. *J Sports Med* 3:243–259, 1975.

8. Nicholas JA: Injuries to knee ligaments. Relationship to looseness and tightness in football players. *JAMA* 212:2236–2239, 1970.

9. Jackson DW, Jarrett H, Bailey D, et al: Injury prediction in the young athlete: A preliminary report. *Am J Sports Med* 6:6–14, 1978.

10. Durnin JV, Womersley J: Body fat assessed from total body density and its estimation from skinfold thickness:

measurements on 481 men and women aged 16 to 72 years. *Br J Nutr* 32:77–97, 1974.

11. Costill DL, Bowers R, Kammer WF: Skinfold estimates of body fat among marathon runners. *Med Sci Sports* 2:93–95, 1970.

12. Wilmore JH, Behnke AR: An anthropometric estimation of body density and lean body weight in young men. *J Appl Physiol* 27:25–31, 1969.

13. Jackson AS, Pollock MC, Ward A: Generalized equations for predicting body density in women. *Med Sci Sports Exerci* 12:175–182, 1980.

14. Jackson AS, Pollock MC: Generalized equations for predicting body density of men. *Br J Nutr* 40:497–504, 1978.

15. Greulich WW, Pyle SI: *Radiographic Atlas of Skeletal Development of the Hand and Wrist*. Palo Alto, Stanford University Press, second edition, 1959.

16. Tanner JM, Whitehouse RH, Marshall WA, et al: *Assessment of Skeletal Maturity and Prediction of Adult Height*. London, Academic Press, 1975.

17. Smith NJ: *Sports Medicine and Physiology,* edited by Strauss RH. Philadelphia, Saunders, 1979.

18. Shaffer TE: The health examination for participation in sports. *Pediatr Ann* 7:27–30, 1978.

19. Bonci C: Anatomy of a physical. *Training and Conditioning,* 3 (2): 40–46, June 1993.

20. Livingston S: *Comprehensive Management of Epilepsy in Infancy, Childhood and Adolescence*. Springfield, Ill., Charles C. Thomas, 1972.

21. Livingston S, Berman W: Participation of the epileptic child in contact sports. *J Sports Med* 2:170–174, 1974.

22. Livingston S: Should epileptics be athletes? *Phys Sportsmed* 3:67–72, April 1975.

RECOMMENDED READINGS

Allman Jr, FL: Moderator of Round Table on: The preparticipation physical examination. *Phys Sportsmed* 2:23–29, August 1974.

Blackburn Jr, TA, editor: *Guidelines for Pre-Season Athletic Participation Evaluation*. Columbus, Georgia, Sports Medicine Section of the American Physical Therapists Association, 1979.

Gomolack C: Problems in matching young athletes: Baby fat, peach fuzz, muscle, and mustache. In Lockerroom, *Phys Sportsmed* 3:96–98, May 1975.

Kendall HO, Kendall FP, Wadsworth GE: *Muscles: Testing and Function*. Baltimore, Williams and Wilkins, fourth edition, 1993.

Nicholas JA, Strizak AM, Veras G: A study of thigh muscle weakness in different pathological states of the lower extremity. *Am J Sports Med* 4:241–248, 1976.

Salem DN, Isner JM: Cardiac screening for athletes. Symposium on sports injuries. *Othop Clin North Am* 11:687–695, 1980.

Tanner JM: *The Physique of The Olympic Athlete*. London, George Allen and Unwin, 1964.

Johnson M: Tailoring the preparticipation exam to female athletes. *Phys Sportsmed* 20:61–72, July 1992.

Preparticipation Physical Evaluation (Monograph): American Academy of Family Physicians, American Academy of Pediatrics, American Medical Society for Sports Medicine, American Osteopathic Academy of Sports Medicine, Kansas City, 1992.

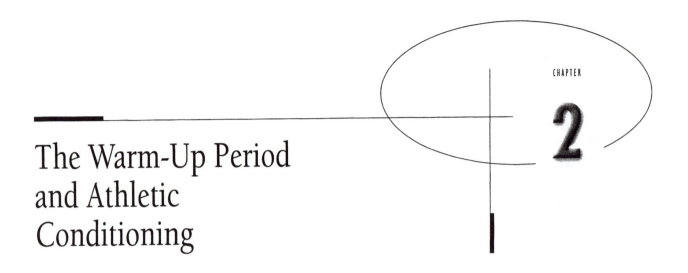

The Warm-Up Period and Athletic Conditioning

The Warm-Up Period

Is the Warm-Up Necessary?

Most athletes consider the warm-up an integral part of their event. It is something that helps get their bodies and minds ready for the workout or competition. They feel that it not only helps their performance, but it also helps prevent injuries.

Most research seems to agree with these subjective impressions. It appears that an increase in the temperature within the muscles is necessary for the attainment of optimal performance, though an elevation of the core temperature is also considered an important criterion. The athlete's body tends to work more efficiently, more safely, and at a higher level when "warmed up."

Some of the advantages of the warm-up include a raised maximal oxygen intake, a reduction in the oxygen needed for a specific activity, and a reduction in the resistance of pulmonary blood flow. In addition, there is an increased rate of neuromuscular transmission and recruitment of muscle fibers, as well as activation of "neuromuscular memory" for the specific movements that are necessary for the event. From the psychological standpoint the warm-up helps the athlete to focus on the forthcoming action.

Every athlete should be encouraged to find the type of warm-up that is best suited for his or her personality and sport. Much of this may be related to subjective impressions, superstitions, the influence of coaches, or what the athletes happened to do on a particular day when they performed well. It would seem, though, that a warm-up schedule that is related to the event would be preferable, particularly if certain aspects of the event could be practiced as part of the warm-up.

The intensity and duration of the warm-up should be governed by the event and the level of fitness of the athlete; for instance, a high-performance, well-conditioned athlete may require twenty to thirty minutes of fairly intense exercise in order to perform at his or her maximal potential. This type of warm-up would be totally inappropriate for a less conditioned athlete and would result in exhaustion. For the muscle temperature to be at a satisfactory level, the rectal temperature should have increased by two degrees. If an athlete is sweating freely in normal climatic conditions, it can be assumed this temperature has been reached.

In the final analysis, it appears that there is sufficient evidence to endorse the concept of a well-thought-out and organized warm-up program as long as it is adjusted to the level and the needs of the individual athlete.

An Outline of a Warm-Up Schedule

Here is an outline of a warm-up and warm-down schedule which combines general with specific warm-up activities:

1. *Stretching.* The initial stretching should be gentle, light, and limited to the muscles that will be stressed.

2. *Jogging.* The athlete should jog or run over a distance and at a pace related to his or her degree of fitness and type of sport. This should produce sweating and an increase in the core temperature.

3. *Stretching.* Following the jogging, the athlete should stretch slowly but thoroughly.

4. *Sport-specific warm-up activities.* These should be performed next and should consist of such exercises as skill-drills incorporating the actual activities of that sport.

5. *Rest period.* In order to regain body homeostasis the athlete should relax for a period of about ten minutes before participating. During this time he or she may wish to engage in visualization of the event and positive "psyching up" thoughts.

6. *The event.*

7. *Post-event warm-down.* Following the event, the athlete should be allowed a warm-down activity period of about three to five minutes. This has the effect of removing lactic acid and other products of metabolism from the muscles and tissues, thereby helping reduce some of the stiffness and tightness so often experienced the following day. This also allows the athlete time to settle down physically and psychologically after the outpouring of adrenalin and the excitement of the event.

8. *Stretching.* Following the warm-down period, stretching should be repeated. Many athletes find this to be mentally relaxing as well. The amount of stretching undertaken depends on the intensity and type of event.

Stretching

Various stretching techniques have been described in the literature.

1. *Ballistic* stretching utilizes repetitive bouncing motions (stretches) of the muscle in its lengthened position. It is considered less desirable and beneficial than other techniques since more tension is created in the muscle, and the risk of injury is increased.[1] The basic argument against ballistic stretching is that muscles will reflexively contract when suddenly stretched. Therefore the stretch will be against a contracted muscle which (a) can injure the muscle tissue, and (b) will not produce any actual stretching of the muscle. It also has undesirable psychological features compared with the slow, static stretch. It is not advised.

2. *Static* stretching is performed by placing the muscle in its lengthened position and maintaining a low-amplitude stretch for an extended period (15 to 60 seconds). With the slow build-up in tension, the inverse stretch reflex is invoked, which induces relaxation in the muscle and permits further stretching and increased flexibility.[2] This is the most widely used method of stretching, and has the least associated injury risk. The main advantages of this type of stretching are related to the athlete's increased body awareness and to learning how to relax. At the same time, it appears that the increased flexibility which is achieved also enhances performance and probably helps reduce injuries. This is particularly true for those who have tight muscles and those engaged in sporting activities that tend to produce muscle imbalances, such as long-distance running (tight hamstrings) and basketball (tight hamstrings and back muscles).

3. **Passive** stretching utilizes an external manual or mechanical force to stretch a muscle. The athlete is relaxed and makes no contribution towards increasing the range of motion. Passive stretching can allow the joint to be taken through a greater range than can be accomplished through active techniques. A major concern in passive stretching is the possibility of injury resulting from incorrectly applied external forces, either by a partner or mechanical device.

4. **Proprioceptive Neuromuscular Facilitation (PNF)** represents the most frequently used passive technique. The muscle is first taken to its lengthened position. The athlete is then asked to actively contract against an isometric resistance for five seconds. Following the isometric contraction, the muscle is passively stretched into its new available range. This process is repeated three to five times. Known as *contract-relax*, this technique applies the concepts of reflex activation and inhibition, i.e., a maximum contraction of the muscle leads to maximum relaxation of the same muscle.

An alternate PNF technique is known as *reciprocal inhibition*. The muscle is first taken to its lengthened position. At that point, contraction of the agonist muscle (for example the quadriceps group) at the antagonist's end of range (hamstrings group) leads to reciprocal inhibition and relaxation of the antagonist muscle, and the potential to stretch further.[1]

Some believe that PNF stretching is the most successful technique for developing increased flexibility. It is also believed that this technique may help reset the stretch reflex level and enhance relaxation of the muscles being stretched. A major disadvantage is that this technique requires a knowledgeable and well trained partner.

While he or she is stretching, the athlete's mind should be focused on the body as well as on slow, gentle, normal breathing. In this way the athlete begins to feel the subtleties of muscle tension, contraction, and relaxation, of which, in all likelihood, he or she was previously unaware. The athlete also learns that the body is never the same on two successive days—the degree of flexibility achieved on one day may not be repeatable on the next. This should be considered normal, and adjustments for these variabilities should be made on a day-to-day basis.

Coaches should be educated in the art of stretching, particularly with reference to encouraging the athlete's concentration on what he or she is doing at the time, and in the need to discourage competition between athletes in achieving increased flexibility. The athlete should, by concentration and experience, learn what is right for his or her particular body and thus achieve maximal results. The coach should discourage any bouncing or rapid movements and should point out muscle tensions unnoticed by the athlete. Such tensions are manifested by active muscle contractions, quivering of the muscles, a strained expression on the athlete's face, holding of the breath, or to-and-fro bouncing movements.

Stretching should be a pleasant, enjoyable experience. It should not be a painful, uncomfortable time spent wishing that one were doing something else. Each athlete needs to learn what stretches are most applicable to his or her particular athletic activity as well as what is necessary for his or her particular body type. Some basic stretches are shown in Figures 2.1 through 2.6.

FIGURE 2.3
Quadriceps stretch.
The hip should be extended in order to stretch the rectus femoris muscle.

FIGURE 2.1
Hamstring stretch—beginning position

FIGURE 2.2
Hamstring stretch.
By allowing the body and head to come forward towards the knee, the stretch includes not only the hamstrings, but also the back.

FIGURE 2.4
Groin stretch.
The elbows may be used to exert pressure and thus increase the stretch.

(a)   **(b)**

FIGURE 2.5

Achilles stretch.

This stretch needs to be done in two positions. (a) With the knee straight in order to stretch the gastrocnemius. (b) The knee is bent to concentrate the stretch on the soleus. *Note:* the foot should be pointing straight ahead, and the arch should be maintained and not allowed to flatten out.

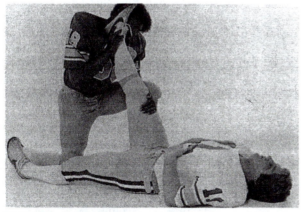

FIGURE 2.6

Passive stretching (using the contract/relax PNF technique).

The leg is held by the partner so the knee is straight and the hamstrings are comfortably stretched. The athlete then pushes the leg as firmly as possible against the partner's resistance, keeping the knee straight. This sequence is repeated several times.

Athletic Conditioning

The athlete who participates in a well-devised, scientifically based, and properly supervised athletic physical conditioning program should benefit in at least four areas:

a. Enhanced athletic performance
b. Decreased risk of injury
c. Decreased severity should an injury occur
d. Accelerated rehabilitation and return to activity after an injury

At the present time, it has not been definitely proven that improvement in the various components of conditioning or fitness offers the athlete a lessened risk of injury, though it has been suggested by many individuals that there are theoretical benefits for injury prevention from a preparticipation physical conditioning program. The following people have advanced a variety of thoughts on the effects of physical conditioning programs:

Reid and *Schiffbauer*—The importance of hypertrophy of muscle tissue as a protection against bodily injury should be stressed.[3]

Gallagher—To avoid injuries to the lower extremities and to the back area, athletes should supplement their normal activities with exercises to increase the size and the strength of the muscles, which will then protect the joints in these areas from injury.[4]

Rasch—The athlete who is in a fatigued state has less efficiency and slower reactions, and therefore may be unable to guard against situations that could result in an injury.[5]

Thorndike—Exercises to strengthen the ankle and the knee can reduce injuries to these areas.[6]

Adams—Habitual exercise can cause a significant increase in the strength of the ligaments surrounding the knee and therefore prevent injuries to the knee.[7]

Falls et al.—Improved movement skill is important in the avoidance of injury.[8]

Gallagher—Overdevelopment provides increased strength that helps to stabilize joints.[4]

Kraus—While general conditioning is an important factor in the prevention of athletic injury, it is also important in the prevention of re-injury.[9]

Cahill and *Griffith*—A pre-season general body conditioning program results in fewer and less severe knee injuries.[10]

Physical conditioning or athletic fitness can be classified in a variety of ways. Table 2.1 gives the specific physical conditioning components, a definition of each, and the application of the component to the prevention of injuries.

TABLE 2.1 *Athletic conditioning components*

Conditioning Component	Definition	Application to Injury Prevention
Strength	A maximal voluntary force exerted in a single muscular effort.	To stabilize an anatomical area against applied forces.
Power	Force × distance × time; or, strength × speed.	To shorten the time required to perform and/or increase the applied force (explosive type of movement), such as may be required to rapidly respond to a threat of injury.
Muscular endurance	The ability to repeat a series of muscular contractions.	A low muscular endurance capacity increases the potential for injury.
Flexibility	The range of movement of a joint that is permitted by the surrounding tissues.	To respond to forced extensibility without injury to the involved tissue.
Agility	The involvement of coordination and speed to permit rapid control in the movement or change of direction of the body.	To change the direction or position of the body rapidly, efficiently, and with precision in response to avoiding collision and the resulting injury.
Balance	Equilibrium of the body over its supporting base.	To control and maintain effective static and/or dynamic body position to prevent any awkward position that might contribute to injury.
Proprioception	The awareness of body position in space.	To perceive the position of the various body segments or be aware of the segment-space relationship to prevent injury (*example:* position of the foot as it comes in contact with the floor or the ground after being airborne).
Cardiovascular-respiratory endurance	The adequate function or response of those physiological systems that deliver fuel and oxygen to the active muscles.	To enable continuous muscular effort to be exerted in order to avoid the onset of fatigue which might then contribute to the occurrence of injury.

Injury, as well as injury prevention, is influenced by the position of the origin and insertion of a muscle, the relationship of this muscle to the joint, and the angle of pull of the muscles on the bone at a particular moment through the range of motion. For instance, if a muscle has its origin near the joint and its insertion at a distance from the joint, the major resultant action will be to keep the two articulating bones of the joint in close approximation. This type of muscle action contributes to the stability of the joint (a shunt muscle action).

An example of the stabilizing action of muscles on a joint is the glenohumeral joint, which consists of the head of the humerus articulating with the shallow glenoid fossa of the scapula. The joint capsule is loose and flexible, thus permitting a wide range of motion, and the supportive ligaments are relatively weak. The muscles around the shoulder need to be developed and conditioned in order to provide optimal stabilization of the shoulder.

Where a muscle primarily produces motion of the joint, proper conditioning can enable the muscle to prevent an unwanted or exaggerated movement. The knee joint is frequently at risk from a combination of internal forces (e.g., a pivoting or cutting action) and external forces (e.g., a tackle or block in football). Adequate conditioning of the muscles could contribute to the prevention of some of these knee injuries. All the muscles around the knee (the quadriceps in front, the hamstrings behind, the pes anserinus group medially, and the popliteus and biceps tendons and the iliotibial tract laterally) help maintain the stability of the knee. In particular, the quadriceps (especially the vastus medialis) provides resistance to lateral subluxation of the patella.

Cahill and Griffith conducted an eight-year study of groups of high-school football players.[10] Those involved in an active pre-season, general body-conditioning program (which included the thigh muscles) suffered fewer and less serious injuries than those who did not condition (see Table 2.2).

Well-conditioned and hypertrophied muscles or muscle groups can contribute to the protection of less stable underlying soft tissues. For example, adequate strength, hypertrophy, and reflexive action of the abdominal muscles can afford protection to the abdominal viscera.

These are just a few of the many possible examples where a degree of protection may be provided by adherence to a well-designed conditioning program. Other possible beneficial effects are discussed later in this chapter.

General Conditioning Principles

There are some common principles that apply to the development of the components of conditioning. These include:

1. *Overload.* To facilitate improvement, the system involved must be progressively and gradually challenged or placed under additional stress. Depending upon the component of conditioning being challenged, overload might be implemented by increasing the

   a. resistance
   b. repetitions or sets
   c. rate (intensity) of work or exercise
   d. duration of work or exercise

2. *Specificity.* The effects of the conditioning program are specific to the type of stress applied and to the particular system of the body that is exercised.

All of the above might be summarized in one principle, the SAID principle (Specific Adaptation to Imposed Demands). The SAID principle states that if the body is placed under stress of varying intensities and durations, it attempts to overcome the stress by adapting specifically to the imposed demands.[11] While it is

---

TABLE 2.2 *Knee injury summary*

	No Conditioning					Conditioning					Total
	1969	1970	1971	1972	Total	1973	1974	1975	1976	Total	Total
Number of players	318	312	307	317	1254	298	277	350	302	1227	2481
Number of injured	24	16	22	23	85	18	16	9	7	50	135
Number of operations	6	4	4	5	19	1	4	1	1	7	26

Source: B.R. Cahill and E.H. Griffith, "Effect of Preseason Conditioning on the Incidence and Severity of High School Football Knee Injuries," *American Journal of Sports Medicine* 6:180–183, 1978. Reprinted by permission of the American Orthopaedic Society for Sports Medicine.

important to overload or place demands on the body so that improvement may occur, the stress should not be so severe as to prevent the body from being able to cope or adapt.

Strength

One muscle fiber consists of many myofibrils, which in turn are made up of many thousands of sarcomeres. When the sarcomeres receive the appropriate stimulation from the nervous system, chemical reactions occur which provide energy from ATP breakdown. This results in contraction of the sarcomeres as the actin "slides" on the myocin.

For muscle growth or hypertrophy to occur, the muscle must be stressed. When repetitively subjected to high-intensity demands, the muscle will respond by increasing in size and strength.

The improvement that might occur as a result of a strength-developing program is influenced by the level of strength possessed by the individual at the onset of the program as well as by the method and intensity of the program. Strength programs can be classified according to the type of resistance that is applied to the limb (Table 2.3).

The first step in formulating an individual strength-training program is to determine the:

1. Type of resistance to be used
2. Amount of weight or resistance to be used
3. Number of repetitions per set
4. Number of sets per workout
5. Number of workout sessions per week

The level of strength may be determined by using devices such as a

1. Cable tensiometer
2. Dynamometer
3. Cybex isokinetic dynamometer

However, the most commonly used "in-the-field" determination of the starting level of strength is the one-repetition maximum, which seems to be adequate for that purpose.

When attempting to develop strength, it is necessary to work at maximum resistance in order to maximize gains. Berger's studies found that those individuals training with four, six, and eight repetitions per set showed significantly greater gains than those who trained with two, ten, and twelve repetitions per set.[12]

DeLorme[12,13] developed a system based upon a maximum of ten repetitions (10RM):

	Resistance	Repetitions
First set	50% of 10 RM	10 repetitions
Second set	75% of 10 RM	10 repetitions
Third set	100% of 10 RM	10 repetitions

The specific strength-development program should be individualized and determined according to the needs of the athlete. The athletic trainer should be familiar with the correct lifting techniques used in various types of strength-training programs.

Resistive Exercise

Traditional free weights and various guided weight apparatus are the most typical resistive devices used for strength development. Several other methods of strength training using nontraditional types of resistance have been developed. Many of these exercises offer opportunities to condition effectively with limited equipment and are adaptable to any level of fitness. The primary categories are:

1. Water resistance
2. Flexible tubing—tension bands
3. Body weight versus gravity
4. Friction
5. Sport-specific training

TABLE 2.3 *Commonly used types of resistance*

Type of Resistance	Type of Movement	Device Used
Isometric	Muscle contraction, no movement	Any immovable object or device
Isotonic	Fixed resistance, variable speed of movement	Free weights
concentric	Contraction with muscle shortening	Wall pulleys
eccentric	Contraction with muscle lengthening	Guided weight apparatus (Universal Gym, Nautilus, etc.)
Isokinetic	Fixed speed, resistance accommodates to force applied (accommodative resistance)	Cybex, Orthotron

Benefits of these exercises can range from specific isolated strength and power training with little or no aerobic component, to a general muscle toning activity with a high degree of aerobic conditioning. (Also see Chapter 8.)

WATER RESISTANCE STRENGTH TRAINING AND CONDITIONING: Aquatic exercise has long been considered an ideal activity for the development of both aerobic fitness and general body muscle strengthening.[14,15,16,17] Conditioning exercise using water as resistance can be classified into two primary categories. Running in water at a level in which the body is either partially or totally buoyant or performing specific joint motions against water resistance offer different yet extremely effective exercise options.

The three basic movement patterns (there are other movements) are as follows:

1. Running simulation

    Arms—Move your arms as if you were running on land. For more resistance keep your palm facing forward when moving your arm forward, and your palm facing back when your arm pulls back.

    Legs—Follow a running motion. Keep your strides short in order to create a smoother rhythm (Figure 2.7).

2. Cross-country skiing, simulation

    Arms—Move your arms forward and back, keeping your arms straight. For more resistance use the palm forward/palm back rotation as described above.

    Legs—Keep your legs almost straight and have your toes pointing downward for more resistance. Move your legs forward and backward in a scissor-type motion (Figure 2.7).

3. Cycling simulation

    Arms—Same as for running.

    Legs—Cycling motion.

The second category of water resistance exercises is concerned primarily with specific muscle strengthening exercises that are performed in an aquatic environment.

Paddle designs have been developed to add surface area resistance to motion performed in water. The amount of muscle stress can be adjusted by either changing paddle sizes, increasing or decreasing the speed of movement, or both (e.g., hydratone, aquaflex).

CROSS COUNTRY

Benefits

Improves aerobic fitness. Strengthens and tones THIGHS (quadriceps, hamstrings) BUTTOCKS (gluteals). TRUNK (abdominals, erector spinae) and HIP FLEXORS (iliopsoas). Maintains flexibility of HIPS.

Exercise

With legs straight and body erect, extend one leg forward and one leg back. Swing your legs through the water front-to-back and back-to-front. Stabilize yourself by keeping buoys at the surface with arms held out to your sides.

KNEE-HIGH JOG

Benefits

Improves aerobic fitness. Strengthens and tones THIGHS (quadriceps, hamstrings) and BUTTOCKS (gluteals). Maintains flexibility of LOW BACK and HIPS.

FIGURE 2.7

Example: Utilizing hand buoys and buoyancy cuffs (*Source:* Hydro Fit, Eugene, Oregon; reprinted with permission.)

In addition, traditional swimming pool activity (e.g., lap swimming, flutter kicking, treading water, and various games and activities) can be utilized to provide the conditioning effect. The imagination and creativity of the

Level one workout

Flutter kicking—front—1 min.
Flutter kicking—back—1 min.
Flutter kicking—right side—2 min.
Flutter kicking—left side—2 min.
Elementary treading—2 min.
Lap swimming—8 min.
Elementary treading—2 min.

Level two workout

Flutter kicking—front—2 min.
Flutter kicking—back—2 min.
Flutter kicking—right side—2 min.
Flutter kicking—left side—2 min.
Advanced treading—2 min.
Lap swimming—14 min.
One hand high treading—2 min.

Level three workout

Flutter kicking—front—3 min.
Flutter kicking—back—3 min.
Flutter kicking—right side—3 min.
Flutter kicking—left side—3 min.
Advanced treading—3 min.
Lap swimming—20 min.
Two hand high treading—3 min.

FIGURE 2.8
Example of swimming pool conditioning exercise program.

athletic trainer seems to be the only limiting factor in designing the scope and intensity of the aquatic program (see Figure 2.8).

Swimming Pool Conditioning Terminology:

Treading Water (water deep enough that toes will not touch bottom; swimmer in perpendicular position)

Elementary treading: Swimmer sculls or fins as he kicks—bicycle leg action, scissors, or frog style.

Advanced treading: Swimmer kicks bicycle, scissors, or frog style while hands are held shoulder high.

One-hand-high treading: Swimmer kicks bicycle, scissors, or frog style while holding one arm straight up and other hand shoulder high.

Two-hand-high treading: Swimmer kicks bicycle, scissors, or frog style holding both arms straight up out of the water.

Flutter Kicking

Front: In a prone position, hold onto side of pool with hand(s) and flutter kick.

Back: In a supine position, hold onto side of pool with hand(s) and flutter kick.

Left side: on a side position, hold onto side of pool with right hand and flutter kick.

Right side: Same as above, holding with left hand.

FLEXIBLE TUBING/TENSION BAND RESISTANCE: Exercise methods which utilize elastic or flexible tubing as the primary resistance to muscle contraction may offer the widest range of strength training alternatives. Tubing exercise can provide resistance to practically all joint motions with either a concentric or eccentric contraction. It can also be adjusted so that the speed of these contractions can range from isometric to very high speed. Combine these advantages with the relatively low cost and ease of use and the result is what many feel is an ideal means of providing strength training (see Figure 2.9).

(a) *Active knee extension against resistance* Sit with your thigh supported and your knee bent to 90 degrees. Tie the tubing off behind you. Raise your leg until your knee is almost, but not quite, straight. Return to the starting position.

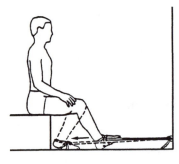

(b) *Active knee flexion against resistance* Sit on a chair with your leg comfortably extended and your heel resting on the floor. Place the tubing around your ankle and tie off the other end directly in front of you at the same height as your ankle. Begin with slight tension on the tubing, stabilize your thigh with your hands, and bend your knee as far as comfort will allow. Allow the leg to slowly return to the starting position under control.

FIGURE 2.9
Example of tubing exercises for knee extension and flexion

A wide range of commercially available products have been developed for use in rehabilitation, general conditioning, and many sport-specific training programs. With practically all of these products the resistance can be modified by simply increasing the stretch, using a band with a "stiffer" resistance, or adding additional bands (e.g., Fitter, Lifeline Gym, Theraband, Bow Flex, Total Gym, Sprint Resister).

BODYWEIGHT VS. GRAVITY: The basic concept of this category of resistance is simply to move the body against the constant force of gravity. The amount of resistance can be varied by adding weight to the body (e.g., weight vest), increasing the distance the body has to travel (e.g., increasing step height with step-up exercises), or altering the number and speed of the repetitions. These categories fall within the definition of closed-chain kinetic exercise and are widely used for rehabilitation. Advantages of this method include development of muscle and joint proprioception and synergistic muscle function.

Step-ups, stair climbing, mini-tramps, and jump ropes are all valuable tools for developing strength and endurance and increasing proprioception of the muscles of the low extremities. Equipment needs for this category of resistance can be very minimal and results can be excellent.

A variation of the step-up/down exercise, plyometrics, has gained wide acceptance as a valuable tool in the development of power (force × speed). Plyometric training involves the development of explosive power through hopping, bounding, and jumping exercises.[18,20] These activities (see Figure 2.10) combined with strength development programs should result in the enhancement or development of explosive power for the athlete. The main objective of plyometric training is to develop the stretch (eccentric phase)–shortening (concentric phase) cycle.

FRICTION RESISTANCE: Friction resistance has been incorporated into many types of specific muscle-strengthening exercise units. Most have been designed for a particular joint or muscle group and most have been for the upper extremities. Shoulder wheels, wrist rollers, rowing machines, and flywheel bicycle ergometers have been staples of gymnasiums for many years. Resistance is adjusted by the amount of tension applied to the friction pod. A relatively new and increasingly popular form of friction resistance exercise is the slide board. First developed for the conditioning of speed skaters, it has been adapted for both rehabilitation and general conditioning purposes. This exercise entails sliding laterally on a smooth flat surface in a skating-like position. As with many of the other alternative resistance exercises, the slide board can be adapted to a variety of conditioning goals. Another popular form of exercise using friction resistance has been cross-country ski simulators. These have proved to be excellent general body conditioners (e.g., Shoulder Wheel, Slide Board, Wrist Rollers, Nordic-Track).

Sport-Specific Training

In the world of sports conditioning, if the athlete is going to put all his effort into a sport or activity, the conditioning for that sport must be "sport specific." Sport specific training has been around for a long time, but since the early 1970s when our base of knowledge began to expand and we gained more understanding of muscle physiology, conditioning for athletes by training programs for the sport the athlete was engaged in became more popular. That is, a baseball player had to condition his arm to throw; therefore the conditioning program was designed to strengthen, become more flexible, and gain muscle endurance by training through exercise routines specifically for the arm. Pitchers had to have a great amount of leg strength to pitch so many innings; therefore a running program was initiated to gain endurance and leg power. These sport-specific programs are now an everyday occurrence in athletic life.

Every sport has some unique characteristics. Therefore certain performance parameters must be met in order for a person to compete or enjoy that particular activity. They may involve running, throwing, jumping, hitting an object, climbing, or any number of physical skills that require strength, endurance, and flexibility. Therefore, for the athlete to enjoy this activity to its fullest, those skills must become trained to their fullest. Introducing sport-specific training into an athlete's conditioning program combines conditioning as well as skill training. There is a "two-for-the-price-of-one" benefit, plus immediate feedback on skill level development. Skill levels increase, conditioning increases, enjoyment of the sport increases, and the level of competition increases—all the result of the use of sport-specific training habits instilled early in a sports conditioning program.

Power

An additional contribution to protection against injury is the ability of the muscle to contract or exert force at an accelerated speed (power may be defined as the product of force and speed). The isokinetic apparatus has been shown to be useful in the development of power.

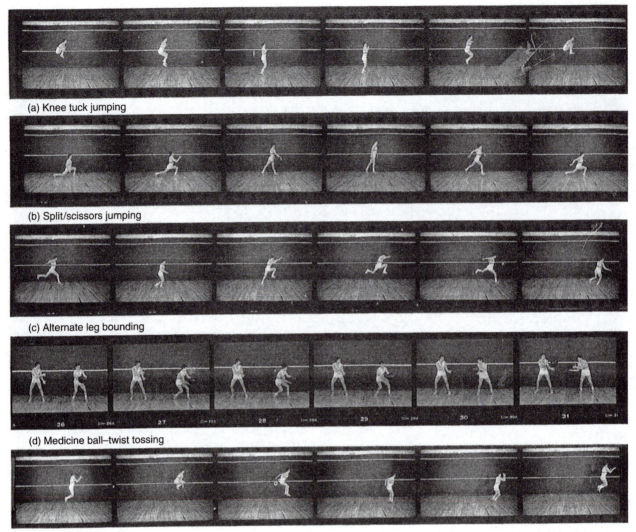

(a) Knee tuck jumping

(b) Split/scissors jumping

(c) Alternate leg bounding

(d) Medicine ball—twist tossing

(e) Double leg hopping

FIGURE 2.10
Basic plyometric sequences
(*Source:* James G. Radcliffe, Author/consultant/coach, University of Oregon, Eugene, Oregon, reprinted with permission.)

Muscular Endurance

In addition to muscular strength and power, muscular endurance plays a role in injury prevention. The athlete not only needs to attain the appropriate level of strength, but also needs to be able to maintain a high percentage of that strength over a period of time or through a series of repeated muscular efforts.

The general principles that apply to strength development also apply to the development of muscular endurance, so that strength-training methods can be adapted for use in muscular-endurance training with the following modifications:

1. Reduce the amount of resistance
2. Increase the rate of work
3. Increase the number of repetitions and, possibly, sets

Flexibility

Another quality of the muscular system that is important to the athlete is flexibility. It has been suggested that a lack of normal flexibility may lead to muscle strains.

Adequate flexibility is important to the athlete in at least two aspects:

1. Full range of motion is necessary for the successful execution of athletic skills.

2. Normal resting length and an adequate excursion of extensibility of the muscle-tendon unit might afford some protection against injury.

Cardiovascular-Respiratory (Aerobic) Endurance

The ability of the athlete to sustain repeated muscular effort requires adequately conditioned cardiovascular and respiratory systems. These systems need to be fully developed to extract, deliver, and utilize oxygen and so prolong the time before which fatigue will occur. Fatigue can leave the athlete vulnerable to injury through inability to effectively utilize the muscular system or respond to an injury-producing situation.

There are a number of laboratory tests available for assessing the level of cardiopulmonary fitness.

1. *Step-up tests.* These tests utilize the pulse-rate response to a standard work load as an indication of fitness. The recovery ability is also determined, by measuring the time required for the pulse rate to return to a predetermined percentage of the resting heart rate.

2. *Bicycle ergometer and treadmill testing.* This is used to measure the maximal oxygen uptake, the maximal rate at which oxygen can be utilized during exercise (VO_2Max).

"In-the-field testing" is more practical for the athletic trainer in assessing the cardiovascular-respiratory status of groups of athletes. Results from tests such as the Cooper twelve-minute run or the one-and-one-half-mile run can be compared to established norms; but it is probably of more value for the individual to establish his or her own base line of distance or time.

The development of cardiovascular-respiratory endurance should be specific to the needs of the athlete. The following variables should therefore be considered:

1. Intensity of training activity
2. Duration of workouts
3. Frequency of workouts

The *intensity* of activity can be simply determined by the response of the pulse, presuming the athlete has been adequately screened before participating in the endurance program. Utilizing the heart rate as an indicator of the effect of the activity on the athlete, the

appropriate level of intensity can then be prescribed. For instance, the age-related maximal heart rate for the twenty-to-thirty-year-old is usually listed at 190 beats per minute. If it is determined that the athlete should work at 80 percent of this maximal heart rate, then the appropriate "training heart rate" for the athlete would be 152 beats per minute for at least ten to fifteen minutes at a time. This is the training heart rate for the endurance portion of the program (Figure 2.11). However, the *duration* needs to be determined by the athlete's present level of conditioning. A session of at least 30 minutes, while maintaining the pulse at a target heart rate, should produce significant endurance conditioning. The minimal number of workouts (*frequency*) that will have an effect on the athlete's endurance is two sessions of aerobic activity per week; most athletes should have at least three or four sessions per week.

Anaerobic Conditioning

While aerobic fitness is important for the prevention of fatigue, there is a need for the development of the anaerobic systems of the body. The improvement of anaerobic conditioning will depend upon the type of athletic activity in which the athlete is engaged. For instance, rapid explosive movements of short duration demand this type of conditioning in order to build up a reserve of high energy compounds and to train the system to resynthesize these compounds at a faster rate. However, the anaerobic system also needs to be developed by athletes participating in longer-duration activities (e.g., by interval training).

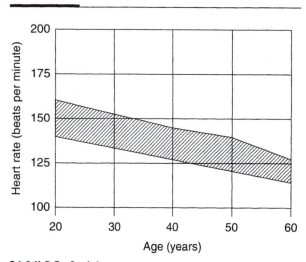

FIGURE 2.11

Training or target heart rate to develop endurance

Summary

This section has been concerned with the pre-season conditioning program. However, for complete injury prevention purposes there needs to be concern for:

1. *The in-season conditioning program.* Many athletes consider that mere participation in athletic activity can effectively produce a high state of physical conditioning, and they do not realize that without a specifically planned program the various components of physical fitness can deteriorate during the season.

2. *The post-season conditioning program.* This phase of the program should identify and emphasize the areas that need special rehabilitation, and should help to maintain at an adequate level each of the components that make up the term *physical fitness.*

3. *The year-round conditioning program.* Periodization (planned variation of intensity and volume) is a more sophisticated version of the year-round conditioning program. The cycling of physical training is based on research that has indicated gains in physical performance when there is a variation of volume (repetitions) and intensity (percent of maximum).

The Matveyev[19] model of periodization includes the following cycles (see Figure 2.12):

  a. preparation phase (intensity–low, volume–high)

  b. transition 1 (intensity increases and volume decreases)

  c. competition phase (further volume reduction with increased intensity during this in-season phase)

  d. transition 2 (active rest)

The Matveyev model of periodization incorporates the variation of training over the year (cycle training) rather than keeping the components static. The predicted advantages of this variable program are:

  a. *Physiological*—physical improvement that results from appropriate periods of effort and recovery.

  b. *Psychological*—an improved motivation, enthusiasm, and adherence to the task should prevent the chronic fatigue (staleness) effects that could result from a nonvariable conditioning program.

REFERENCES

1. Surburg PR: Neuromuscular facilitation techniques in sports medicine. *Phys Sportsmed* 9:114–127, September 1981.

2. Smith C: The warm-up procedure: To stretch or not to stretch. A brief review. *J Orthop Sports Phys Ther* 19 (1): 12–17, 1994.

3. Reid SE, Schiffbauer W: Role of athletic trainers in prevention, care and treatment of injuries. *Lancet* 77:83–84, 1957.

4. Gallagher JR: *Understanding Your Son's Adolescence.* Boston, Little, Brown and Company, 1951.

5. Rasch PJ: Endurance training for athletes. *J Assoc Phys Mental Rehabil* 13:182–185, 1959.

6. Thorndike A: *Athletic Injuries.* Philadelphia, Lea and Febiger, 1956.

7. Adams A: Effect of exercise on ligament strength. *Res Q* 37:163–167, 1966.

8. Falls HB, Wallis EL, Logan GA: *Foundations of Conditioning.* New York, Academic Press, 1970.

9. Kraus H: Physical conditioning and the prevention of athletic injury. American Medical Association, *Proceedings of the 7th National Conference on the Medical Aspects of Sports,* Chicago, November 30, 1966, pp. 98–103.

10. Cahill BR, Griffith EH: Effect of preseason conditioning on the incidence and severity of high school football knee injuries. *Am J Sports Med* 6:180–183, 1978.

11. Allman FL: *Sports Medicine.* Ryan AJ, Allman FL, editors. New York, Academic Press, 1974, p. 311.

12. DeLorme T: Heavy resistance exercises. *Arch Phys Med Rehabil* 27:607–630, 1946.

13. DeLorme T, Watkins A: Techniques of progressive resistance exercise. *Arch Phys Med Rehabil* 29:263–273, 1948.

14. Genuario S, Vegso J: The use of a swimming pool in the rehabilitation and reconditioning of athletic injuries. *Contemp Orthop* 20 (4): 381–87, 1990.

15. Avellini B, et al: The intensity of exercise in deep-water running. *Inter J Sports Med* 12: 27–9, 1991.

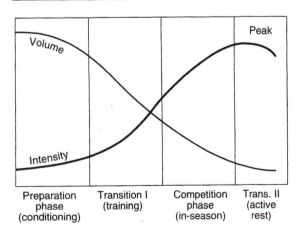

FIGURE 2.12
Matveyev's model of periodization

16. Koszuta L: Water exercise causes ripples. *Phys Sportsmed* 14 (10): 163–67, 1986.

17. Gleim G, Nicholas J: Metabolic costs and heart rate responses to treadmill walking in water at different depths and temperatures. *Am J Sports Med* 17 (2): 248–52, 1989.

18. Radcliffe JC, Farentinos RC: *Plyometrics—Explosive Power Training.* Human Kinetics 1985.

19. Matveyev LP: *Periodisienang dos Sportlichen Training* (Translated into German by P. Tschienne with a chapter by A. Kruger). Berlin, Beles and Wernitz, 1972.

20. Gambetta V: Leaps and bounds. *Train Cond* 3 (4): 4–14, December 1993.

RECOMMENDED READINGS

Alter MJ: *Sports Stretch.* Champaign, IL, Leisure Press, 1990.

Anderson B: *Stretching.* Bolinas CA, Shelter Publications, 1980.

Åstrand PO, Rodahl K: *Textbook of Work Physiology.* New York, McGraw-Hill, second edition, 1977.

Aten DW, Knight KL: Therapeutic exercise in athletic training—Principles and overview. *Athletic Training* 13:123–126, 1978.

Beaulieu JE: *Stretching for All Sports.* Pasadena, Athletic Press, 1980.

Bobbert MF: Drop jumping as a training method for jumping athletes. *Sports Med* 9(1): 7–22, 1990.

Caldwell F: The search for strength. *Phys Sportmed* 6:83–88, January 1978.

Case JG, DePalma BF, Zelko RR: Knee rehabilitation following anterior cruciate ligament repair/reconstruction: An update. *Athletic Training* 26:22–31, 1991.

Cook TM, et al: EMG comparison of lateral step-up and stepping machine exercise. *J Orthop Sports Phys Ther* 16(3): 108–13, 1992.

Cornelius WL: Two effective flexibility methods. *Athl Train* 16:23–25, 1981.

Cornelius WL, Hinson MM: The relationship between isometric contractions of hip extensors and subsequent flexibility in males. *J Sports Med Phys Fitness* 20:75–80, 1980.

Costill DL: Coyle WF, Fink GR, et al: Adaptations in skeletal muscle following strength training. *J Appl Physiol* 46:96–99, 1976.

deVries HA: *Physiology of Exercise for Physical Education and Athletics.* Dubuque, William C. Brown Company, third edition, 1980.

Franklin BA: Aerobic exercise training programs for the upper body. *Med Sci Sport Exerc* 21(5 suppl.) S149–157.

Gerberick SG, et al: Quadriceps strength training using two forms of bilateral exercise. *Arch Phys Med Rehabil* 74(3): 233–256, 1989.

Hamer P, Morton A: Water-running: Training effects and specificity of aerobic, anaerobic, and muscular parameters following an eight week interval training programme. *Austral J Sci Med Sport* 22(1): 13–22, 1990.

Knight KL: Cryostretch for muscle spasm. In Trainer's Corner, *Phys Sportsmed* 8:129, April 1980.

Lamb DA: A kinematic comparison of ergometer and on-water rowing. *Am J Sports Med.* 17:367–373, 1989.

Lundin P, Berg W: A review of plyometric training. *Nat Strength Cond J* 13(6): 22–30, 1991.

McCullough C: Stretching for Injury Prevention. *Patient Manage* (Aust.) 14:79–85, June 1990.

Miles S: Sports fitness and its relationship to sports injuries. *Br J Sports Med* 11:46–49, 1977.

Moore MA, Hutton RS: Electromyographic investigation of muscle stretching. *Med Sci Sports Exerci* 12:322–329, 1980.

Osternig LR: Optimal isokinetic loads and velocities producing muscular power in human subjects. *Arch Phys Med Rehabil* 56:152–155, 1975.

Panariello RA: The closed kinetic chain in strength training. *Nat Strength Cond J* 13(1): 29–33, 1991.

Peterson, et al: Influence of concentric strength training on concentric and eccentric strength. *Arch Phys Med Rehabil* 71(2): 101–105, 1990.

Pipes TV: Strength training modes: What's the difference? *Scholastic Coach* 46:96 and 120–124, 1977.

Rathnow KM, Mangum M: A comparison of single versus multi-modal exercise programs: Effects on aerobic power. *J Sports Med Phys Fitness* 30(4): 382–388, 1990.

Reese S, Lavery K: Slide boards: A conditioning and rehabilitation tool. *Nat Strength Cond J* 13(5): 22–24, 1991.

Rooks DL, et al: Musculoskeletal assessment and training: The young athlete. *Clin Sports Med* 7(3): 641–677, 1988.

Safran MR, Seaber AV, Garrett Jr, WE: Warm-up and muscular injury prevention. *Sports Med* 8:239–249, 1989.

Shellock FG, Prentice WE: Warming-up and stretching for improved physical performance and prevention of sports-related injuries. *Sports Med* 2:267–278, 1985.

Shephard RJ: Aerobic versus anaerobic training for success in various athletic events. *Can J Appl Sport Sci* 3:9–15, 1978.

Solveborn Sven–A: *The Book About Stretching.* New York, Japan Publications, 1985.

Stanton P, Purdam C: Hamstring injuries in sprinting—The role of eccentric exercise. *J Orthop Sports Phys Ther* 10(9): 343–349, 1989.

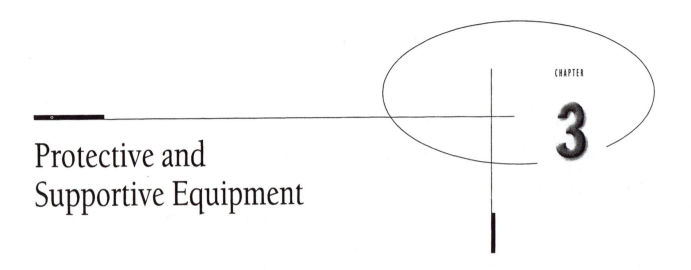

CHAPTER

3

Protective and Supportive Equipment

Protective Equipment

In some sports it may be necessary to utilize protective equipment to:

1. Protect the athlete from injury (acute injury)
2. Protect an injury from additional or accumulated trauma (chronic injury)

The athletic trainer needs to arrive at a philosophy that considers protection versus practicality (e.g., limitation of function). In addition, the rules of each athletic activity need to be reviewed.

A knowledge of high school, college, or youth organizations' current rules and regulations is in order when discussing protective and/or supportive equipment. Updates to rules will guide you with regard to materials allowed, padding required, and what devices may be used. Protective and supportive equipment is continually improved to provide athletes with a greater chance to compete safely. The athlete, as well as equipment personnel, athletic trainers, and coaches, have a responsibility to ensure that all equipment and supportive devices are kept in good condition. Athletes should be instructed in the purpose and function of such devices so that they may participate in the inspection of their equipment.[1,2]

Helmets

Some type of commercially produced protective and supportive equipment is available for virtually every body part. We have helmets for different sports for cranial protection, safety goggles for the eyes, mouthpieces for dental protection, shoulder devices, and so on for each body part. (Figure 3.1)

Two basic types of helmets are used in football: padded and air-filled (Figure 3.2). Other sports that require helmets include ice hockey, fencing, lacrosse, baseball, softball, and cycling.

The major difference in purpose between football helmets and others is the ability to protect over repeated collisions. The collisions that football helmets are designed to withstand are of a low-velocity nature for the most part, for example a collision with another player or contact with the ground. Other helmets are designed to withstand a high-velocity incident, such as being hit by a baseball or hockey puck.

Although the modern football helmet is not capable of eliminating head injuries completely, it does appear to significantly reduce their severity. Wearing an improperly fitted helmet increases the chances of head injuries. The following principles and testing procedures apply to the fitting of all types of football helmets (courtesy of the American Equipment Managers Association).

Fitting the Football Helmet

STEP #1: PREPARE HELMETS AND ORGANIZE FITTING AREA

Prepare helmets. Before beginning any helmet fitting session, all helmets should be properly prepared, as follows:

1. Clean and sanitize each helmet.

2. Inspect each helmet inside and out.

   a. Check the shell for cracks, especially around all holes drilled in the shell (such as facemask attachments, jaw pad snaps, etc.).

FIGURE 3.1
Example of protective equipment

b. Check the condition of the inside support system. Are there any cracks in the vinyl lining? If it is an air helmet, make sure that all liners are holding air (water test if there is any doubt). Is the sweat band in good condition?

FIGURE 3.2
Football helmets

c. Check the facemask. Is metal showing? Is the facemask the right size for the shell? Are attachments in new condition? Repair or replace as necessary.

d. Check the chin strap and corresponding attachments. Make sure they are in new condition.

3. Be sure that all required repair work has been completed.

4. Check each helmet to assure that it bears a *current* NOCSAE (National Operating Committee on Standards for Athletic Equipment) certification stamp (see manufacturer's recommendations for their definition of current).

5. Be certain that the helmet warning label is clearly legible on the outside of the helmet.

6. Be sure there is a full range of sizes ready to be issued.

Organize fitting area. Any helmets not ready to be issued should be removed from the fitting area and clearly marked so that they are not used accidentally. After assuring that all helmets are ready to be issued, organize your area to ensure a smooth flow.

STEP #2: OBTAIN INFORMATION FROM THE ATHLETE

Position. Athletes should be questioned informally during the beginning of the fitting process. Determine what position they will be playing; this helps you later decide the appropriate facemask and sometimes affects the style of helmet used.

Medical history. Check for any prior medical problems. If athletes have a history of concussions, you will want to keep a close eye on them. If they have had allergic reactions to some of the helmet materials that come in contact with the skin, you may need to change to another helmet with a different type of liner material. If they have had a broken nose on more than an isolated occasion, you will need to determine whether it was the result of a poor fit or whether the style of helmet used previously just did not grip the particular head shape well enough.

Past experiences. Ask athletes what type or types of helmets they have used in the past. Get their opinions on how the helmet performed. If they have had problems, simple questions such as, "Did it move on your head?" "Was it comfortable?" "Did it have pressure points and, if so, where?" provide little clues that can give you a good indication of their past experiences with helmets. This information will be valuable in determining what type of helmet to select and will allow athletes to provide input into the fitting process, helping them to be more comfortable with the fitting and giving them more confidence in the end result. Do not put a helmet on an athlete just because he wants to wear it, however; it must fit properly.

Physical abnormalities. Visually check the athlete's head for physical abnormalities. Use your hand to feel the areas of the head covered by hair. Examples of abnormalities might include a severely sloping forehead; lumps under the skin; an excessively extended brow; an extra-large occipital bone; protruding moles, warts, scars; or any other unusual occurrences that may cause problems with the helmet's fit or comfort.

STEP #3: OBTAIN MEASUREMENTS

Circumference. Two head measurements are commonly used when fitting helmets see (Table 3.1). The first is the head circumference measurement taken by a cloth tape measure. There are specially designed tapes for taking this measurement. They have a metal

TABLE 3.1 *Head measurement conversion chart*

Head Circumference Inches	Head Size
20 1/8	6 3/8
20 1/2	6 1/2
20 7/8	6 5/8
21 1/4	6 3/4
21 5/8	6 7/8
22	7
22 3/8	7 1/8
22 3/4	7 1/4
23 1/8	7 3/8
23 1/2	7 1/2
23 7/8	7 5/8
24 1/4	7 3/4
24 5/8	7 7/8
25	8
25 3/8	8 1/8
25 3/4	8 1/4
26 1/8	8 3/8
26 1/2	8 1/2

loop at one end and a full range of head sizes marked, so that the head can be measured by head size and not just inches. However, a common cloth tape will suffice. The measurement can be noted in either inches or by head size and should be recorded on the athlete's records.

Begin by placing the tape around the athlete's head at the widest point. The tape should be one inch above the eyebrow on the front and on the occipital lobe in the back. The tape should be over the hair, but check to make certain it is not over the ears. Pull the tape snug and take the measurement. To be certain of what snug is, first pull the tape verifiably tight, then back off just a little without letting it become loose.

Caliper. The second measurement is taken with a head caliper. Begin by having the athlete sit in a chair so that the caliper can be read more easily. Place the caliper one inch above the eyebrow in front and on the crest of the occipital lobe in the back. Carefully read the measurement before removing the caliper from the head. As before, record the measurement on a permanent record for the athlete.

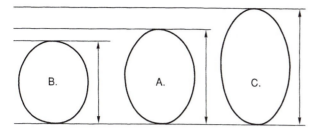

FIGURE 3.3
Determination of head size for helmet fit

It is highly recommended that both measurements be taken because they can be compared, providing information about the overall shape you are fitting. The "ideal" head shape should produce circumference and caliper measurements that are equal. The measurements may not equal each other, however. Then, depending on the difference, you will have either a "short squatty" head shape or a "long oval" head shape (Figure 3.3).

Assume that all three head shapes have an equal circumference. If you compress the normal head shape (A) into a more circular "short squatty" shape (B), the caliper measurement would be smaller. If you stretched head shape (A) into a "long oval" shape (C), the caliper measurement would be larger.

A variance of one or two head sizes is somewhat common; however, a variance of two to three head sizes or more usually means you have an unusually-shaped head that would require special attention.

Style. The first decision in selecting an appropriate helmet for the athlete is the style to be used. It is recommended that you not limit yourself to only one style of helmet, as the various styles tend to fit different types of head shapes differently—some better than others. Before choosing a style, consider the athlete's past experience, any abnormalities you have noted, and the level of play. At this point, you must combine product knowledge of the various helmet styles, your experience in fitting, and all the information on the athlete to choose the best helmet for the situation. Seldom are there clear-cut answers.

Size. Once the style has been selected, choose the appropriate size. First, check the athlete's measurements; second, refer to the appropriate sizing chart for the helmet style selected. These charts should be readily available for quick reference. The helmet size you choose should be considered as only a starting point; you may need to size up or down after completing the next step.

STEP #4: INITIAL POSITIONING AND SIZING CHECK

Preparation. Before the athlete tries the helmet on, it is recommended that you wet the hair down to approximate the sweaty conditions under which the helmet will be used. With younger players, a quick review of how to put the helmet on properly will be very helpful. The use of a face mask during the initial check is discretionary, as manufacturers show proper fitting procedures both with and without a facemask on the helmet.

> NOTE—The following procedures and the order in which they occur vary, depending on the helmet brand and style you are fitting. You *must* follow the manufacturer's guidelines and use the following only as supplemental information.

Prepare air-filled pads. If the helmet you are fitting uses air-filled pads for fitting purposes, you will need to follow the manufacturer's recommended procedures for either inflating or deflating the pads before placing the helmet on the athlete's head for fitting.

Height. Ask the athlete to put the helmet on. The first check will be for the correct height. The frontal rim of the helmet should be one inch (or one finger width) above the eyebrow. If the height is incorrect, follow the recommended procedure for adjusting the height. The correct height must be established before continuing the fitting, because many of the remaining fitting checks will vary depending on the height (see Figure 3.4).

Chin strap. Once the correct height has been established, the chin strap must be correctly fastened; this will keep the helmet in proper position while you check and adjust the remaining pads in the helmet. Hold the chin cup squarely on the athlete's chin, and then adjust and fasten the front straps and finally the back. Make certain that the tension is equal on all straps and that none is pulled out of alignment.

Neck. Use your fingers to feel just under the posterior rim of the helmet. The padding should be in firm but comfortable contact with the head. The neck padding is one of the major areas that grips the head to keep the helmet from sliding down onto the nose. If there are any gaps or if the helmet is too tight, follow the manufacturer's guidelines to make necessary adjustments.

Back to front. The fit of the front and the back pads should be checked at the same time, because they affect

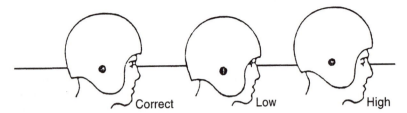

FIGURE 3.4
Helmet position

each other. The very center of the back pad cannot be reached, but the sides can be checked somewhat by placing a finger into the ear hole and feeling for firm contact with the head.

The front pad is visible, and several types of checks are recommended for this area. First, grip the helmet firmly on each side and rotate it gently from side to side, then up and down. The skin of the forehead should move with the helmet. If the helmet slips without moving the skin, an adjustment needs to be made.

Second, standing in front of the athlete, lock your fingers behind the athlete's head, and pull firmly toward you. If a gap appears between the front liner and the forehead, adjustments will have to be made to increase the thickness of the front and back pads. Care should be taken in this procedure; too much force can cause a gap, even in a good fit.

The last check requires that the helmet be on the athlete for at least one minute. After that time, remove the helmet and immediately check the color of the forehead. There should be no hint of whiteness, which indicates a loss of circulation (the helmet is too tight). Redness, however, is acceptable.

STEP #5: SELECT THE HELMET

Sides. The sides can be partially seen from the front and can be felt by slipping a finger through the ear hole. Check for firm but comfortable contact with the skin. If the sides are too tight or loose, follow the manufacturer's recommendations and make the needed adjustments.

Cheek pads. The cheek pads can be clearly seen from the front. As much of their surface area as possible should be in firm, but comfortable, contact with the skin without squeezing the cheeks into a puckered position.

Facemask. Use the manufacturer's guidelines to select the proper style and size of mask based on the athlete's position and helmet size. Follow the manufacturer's instructions to attach the mask, then check the fit. The clearance between the end of the nose and the inside of the mask should be two to three fingers' widths. Also, ensure that the athlete's vision has not been impaired by the placement of the horizontal bars.

Adjustments. Air-filled pads are the easiest to adjust by inflating or deflating the appropriate cells. Padded cells require a little more work. If any pad within the helmet does not fit properly, replace it with the appropriate-thickness pad. Each manufacturer supplies various thicknesses of pads that can be interchanged without voiding their warranty. This helps assure the athlete of a "custom" fit. If you are unsure of which pads to use, consult the helmet manufacturer, a reputable helmet dealer, a reconditioner, or an equipment manager.

STEP #6: THE FINAL "GRIP" CHECK: The final goal is to obtain a firm, yet comfortable, grip on the head. There are several quick methods to assure that this goal has been attained. With the helmet fully assembled, have the athlete put the helmet on and affix the chin strap.

Crown check. Lock your fingers on the very top of the helmet and firmly pull straight down on the athlete's head. Ask the athlete where the pressure is felt. Be cautious not to "lead" the athlete into giving you an answer. If the pressure is felt evenly distributed all over, then you have a good fit. If the athlete says that the pressure is felt on the top, the answer is still acceptable. However, if the athlete feels pressure mainly in front and back, then the helmet is too tight from front to back and you will need to make adjustments.

Lateral movement. Place your hands on each side of the helmet and ask the athlete to hold his head still. Gently force the helmet from side to side, watching the skin on the forehead. It should move with the helmet. There should be a firm resistance to the helmet. The cheek pad should bunch the cheeks, but not slide around toward the nose. If there is too much movement, check the cheek pads, side pads, and the chin strap.

Vertical movement.   Again, place your hands on each side of the helmet and ask the athlete to hold the head still. Gently force the helmet up and down. The skin on the forehead should move with the helmet, and with enough force it will eventually slip a little, but it should catch on the eyebrow without coming down on the nose. If it does come down on the nose, check the neck pad first, as it is designed to grab the base of the occipital lobe to keep the helmet from sliding forward. Also check the chin strap and the front and back pads. Be careful; with sufficient force, even a well-fitting helmet can be brought down onto the nose, especially if the force is exerted on the facemask and not the sides of the helmet.

Final check.   When you have completed the fitting, ask whether the athlete is comfortable with the helmet, and let him know that you are pleased with the fit. This will help build confidence in the equipment and the player's trust in you.

Comfort.   *Comfort* is a relative term at best. The phrase "firm but comfortable" has been used throughout the fitting process already described and therefore should be defined. The sensitivity of each individual will determine what is comfortable for that person. Some players, particularly those with little skin fat in the head area, will be more sensitive.

Recording.   Make certain that all pertinent information on the athlete's helmet has been permanently recorded in a file that will be easily accessible when needed. This information will be needed during future maintenance, inspections, and inventories. More important, it provides solid documentation if needed within the courtroom. Also, each helmet should be clearly marked with some type of serial number so that each may be clearly distinguished from others.

Customized padding.   Obtaining a good fit without customizing the helmet is desirable. However, if customizing is required, helmet manufacturers have provided various pad thicknesses, allowing for considerable customization when fitting the athlete. It is

imperative that you follow established guidelines when changing these pads. Following are some key points:

1.   Never interchange pads between different brands of helmets.

2.   Pads are often made to fit within a specified shell size, for example, M, L, or XL. Make certain that you are using the correct pad for the given shell size.

3.   Never alter a pad by "cutting it down."

4.   If you must add padding and already have the thickest pad the manufacturer provides, be careful not to inhibit the the function of the helmet as designed by the manufacturer.

5.   In the rare circumstance that you cannot get a helmet to fit "firmly but comfortably," and you are unsure how to customize the helmet, call the helmet manufacturer for advice. Never attempt customizing unless you know how to achieve your goal properly.

Specialized pads.   Many helmet manufacturers have specialized pads already designed for some of the more common problems. These pads include such items as the "Denver front" for severely sloping foreheads, side shims for the long narrow head, and special crown pads to lift up low-riding helmets. If you do not have any of these items, contact your helmet dealer for further information.

Fitting—A Continuing Process

The fitting process has only begun. The fitting of the football helmet will last as long as the athlete is with your team. The athlete will need to make daily checks, and there should be weekly checks by a staff member (equipment manager, athletic trainer, or coach). At the beginning of each season, each athlete's fit should be thoroughly checked, even if the athlete is wearing a helmet from the previous season. The goal is not only to *attain*, but also to *maintain a firm but comfortable* fit.

The protective value of a football helmet is indisputable, but research has not yet produced a helmet that can fully protect the brain in a vigorous contact sport such as football. The athletic trainer can help maximize the helmet's protective value by ensuring a perfect fit and by taking other precautions such as requiring the athlete to wear a mouth guard, develop strong neck muscles, and use proper blocking and tackling techniques (Figure 3.5).

Though the fitting of a protective helmet is illustrated by using the example of a football player, the same principles apply to other contact or collision sports such as ice hockey and lacrosse.

FIGURE 3.5
Football, a contact sport

FIGURE 3.6
Mouthpieces

Eyes are vulnerable to injury in all sports and care must be exercised to prevent injury. Various commercial protective lenses are available for use. These products are made from a polycarbonate material that is shatter-resistant and can provide either corrective or natural vision.

Use of commercial mouthpieces, either custom fit by a dental professional or by use of a moldable plastic (Figure 3.6) can greatly reduce the chance of dental and head injury. Mouthpieces aid in the reduction of forces transmitted to the head by preventing tooth-to-tooth contact. Through athlete education, use of these items is becoming more universal in all sports. It has become more common to see softball and basketball players with custom-fit mouthpieces. When fitting a mouthpiece one should be sure that:

1. The mouthpiece covers all upper teeth.

2. When the athlete opens the mouth the mouthpiece remains on the upper jaw.

3. If a strap type of mouthpiece is used, make sure that the strap is easily released with pressure to prevent dental injuries caused by pulling on the strap.

The American Equipment Managers Association's guidelines for the proper fit of shoulder pads are as follows, but include the essentials for fitting any athlete requiring the use of shoulder pad protection. Special devices are available for use with specific injuries and can aid in the diffusion of a direct blow or restrict range of motion to aid the athlete in the return to activity while minimizing the chance for recurrence or complications (Figure 3.7 and 3.8).

AEMA SHOULDER PAD FITTING GUIDELINES:
To fit the shoulder pad properly, keep these points in mind: personal history of injuries, birth defects, scars, and fit without shirt or T-shirt only.

Determine the athlete's shoulder width and/or chest size and, possibly, weight (use a tape measure to measure shoulder tip to shoulder tip). Next, determine the playing position(s) of this athlete. Match this player's position and shoulder width with a corresponding shoulder pad.

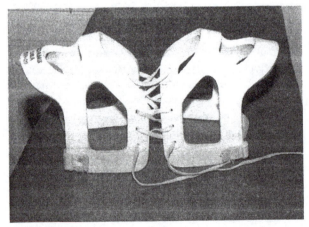

FIGURE 3.7
Shoulder protection

FIGURE 3.8
Shoulder protection

Try the pads on. *Secure the straps and laces.* Be sure that the sternum and spine are covered.

ANTERIOR VIEW

1. Check for proper AC joint coverage. The pad should extend $\frac{1}{2}$ inch over the deltoid.

2. Check for proper pectoralis muscle coverage.

3. The collar should provide comfortable range of motion to the neck ($\frac{1}{2}$ inch). Arms raised in an upward motion should not pinch the neck.

4. Check coverage of the deltoids (the cap should fit snugly).

5. Check trapezius coverage.

6. The arches should meet evenly, with no overlap.

LATERAL VIEW

1. Check for proper AC channel. Check to see whether it is off the AC joint.

2. Check for proper coverage of the caps over the deltoids.

3. Check the clavicle.

POSTERIOR VIEW

1. Check coverage of the rhomboids and the latissimus dorsi. The pad should fit neatly over this region, and the arches should not overlap.

2. Check the neck area again.

3. Check the staps

   - The shoulder pad should fit snugly over the entire shoulder region, yet still allow for range of motion
   - Player should raise the hands above the head

- Take a football stance
- Straps should be snug
- Pads should not choke or pinch the athlete
- No restriction of movement of the extended arm
- Pad should rest back into place after movement
- Medial portion of the neck should be snug to the neck; movement should not scissor the neck
- Properly worn jerseys and sleeves help keep the pad in place

Supportive Devices

The Knee

There are numerous supportive devices available for athletes with knee problems. These can be divided into three major areas:

1. "Sleeve" type braces that give compression and allow body heat to be retained (Figure 3.9). These devices commonly are made from neoprene rubber bonded with a nylon cover. These sleeves are used for a variety of conditions such as chrondomalacia and patella tendinitis.

2. Prophylactic knee braces that are used primarily in American football (Figure 3.10). These braces are adhered by either taping or a strap system to the lateral aspect of the knee. Their primary function is to protect from lateral blows to the knee. There are many different types and styles available, ranging from double-hinged double-axis braces to an interlocking gear type single

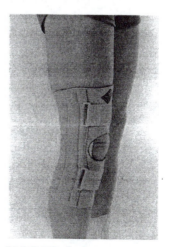

FIGURE 3.9
A neoprene sleeve, which may incorporate a patellar stabilizing pad, or medial and lateral metal stays.

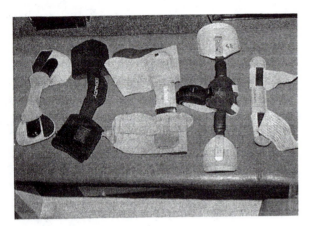

FIGURE 3.10
Prophylactic knee braces

hinge. They may or may not have stops to prevent hyperextension. Prophylactic braces are made from a variety of materials ranging from metal to polycarbonate plastic. These braces have gone through a period of widespread popularity and use, followed by increasing skepticism as to their effectiveness. Early use was unsupported by significant clinical or laboratory data. Multiple studies regarding prophylactic knee braces have since been presented in the orthopedic and sports medicine literature, often with conflicting findings and conclusions.[3]

3. Customized fitted knee braces that are used primarily after or in attempt to avoid surgery (Figure 3.11). These braces are available from a number of manufacturers and will reduce anterior tibial displacement at low loads depending upon the four-point nature of the design to protect the surgical repair or deficiency. These four points are located along the medial and lateral joint lines and across the quadriceps and the tibia. Use of a functional knee brace is standard care after injury or surgery, although some people believe the major benefit from this brace is proprioceptive.[4,5]

The Ankle

Ankle braces have seen a rapid rise in popularity as numerous studies have documented their effectiveness. Research with regard to prophylactic ankle taping has shown that it loses up to 50 percent of its initial support after 10 minutes.[7,8] There are many commercially designed ankle braces available specifically for athletes, including lace-up types with and without support straps such as the Swede-O by Swede-O-Universal, Ankle Guard by McDavid, The Arizona by Pro Orthopedic; and semi-rigid orthoses such as the Sports Stirrup by AirCast, Active Ankle by Active Innovation Inc., and the Ankle Ligament Protector by Don Joy Orthopedics (Figure 3.12).

Another factor in the rise in popularity of ankle braces is the cost involved. Quite simply, it is much more cost- and time-effective to use ankle braces over the course of an athletic season, leaving the athletic trainer time to spend with athletes in the areas of rehabilitation and prevention of athletic injuries.

Fabrication of Protective Devices

Imagination, necessity, and experience are the basis for most custom pads. There are three basic types of pads:

1. A direct cover that softens a direct blow
2. A "doughnut" type pad—one that allows the pad around an injured area to absorb a blow before it makes contact with the injured area.

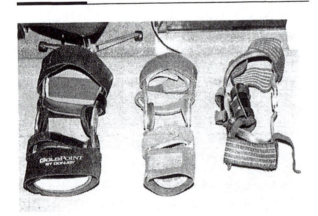

FIGURE 3.11
Customized prescription knee braces

FIGURE 3.12
Ankle braces

3. A "bubble" type pad that distributes a blow around an injured area while preventing the injured area from being touched (Figure 3.13).

The type of material used when constructing a custom-type pad needs to be carefully examined. What is its shock absorbability? Is it affected by temperature? Can it be reused or is it to be used on a one-time-only basis? Closed cell foam and felt (in an assortment of density and thicknesses), a variety of plastics (such as Orthoplast and Plastazote), and some forms of casting materials (fiberglass, silicone rubber) are commonly used to create special custom pads.

When preparing to create a custom pad, a construction plan should be in place. This plan should account for the following:

1. What area needs to be protected? Is it muscular? Is it a joint? How much movement is required of the area?

2. What will you protect the area from? A direct blow? On an isolated basis? Repeated basis? Will you need to restrict range of motion or movement, or protect in just one plane of motion?

3. What type of pad will you make? Bubble? Direct cover? Doughnut?

4. What material will be used for the pad? Moldable plastic? Fiberglass? Silicon rubber? Felt? Foam?

5. How thick will the pad be? This is determined by need and rules governing the sport involved and the consideration of required equipment and uniform constraints.

6. How will the pad be adhered to the body part after it's made? Elastic wrap? Adhesive Tape? Elastic tape? Velcro strap system?

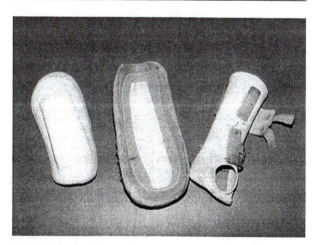

FIGURE 3.13
Protective fabricated pads

EXAMPLE: WHEN CREATING A "BUBBLE" PAD,

1. Mark the injured area to be protected.

2. Using a piece of foam or felt, at least a ½" thick, cover the identified injured area.

3. Prepare material to be used.

4. Stretch material over the pad covering the injured area.

5. Wrap the pad onto the area with either an elastic wrap or foam underwrap material.

6. After the material cools, unwrap and trim to shape, keeping enough area around the injured, now "bubbled," area to line the pad with an adhesive foam or felt.

7. Using a piece of adhesive foam, line the non-"bubbled" area of the pad.

8. Secure the pad in place by method of choice.

In conclusion, the authors recognize that not all athletic activities were adequately covered in this presentation and encourage the reader to utilize this football section as a guide to research other sports (e.g., ice hockey and lacrosse).

For each sport the athletic health care specialist should:

1. Be able to identify and describe the requirements and restrictions in the utilization of protective equipment for selected sports (as indicated by the rules, e.g., NCAA).

2. Be able to fit the major protective equipment for selected sports (e.g., football helmet).

3. Be able to identify and describe the various types of material utilized in the fabrication of selected protective equipment.

4. Be able to identify and describe the various supportive devices for the major anatomical areas of the body.

5. Be able to identify and describe the major fabrication designs for protective devices.

REFERENCES

1. American Academy of Orthopaedic Surgeons. *1991 Athletic Training and Sports Medicine,* American Academy of Orthopaedic Surgeons, 2nd Edition.

2. Arnheim D, et al: *Principles of Athletic Training.* Times Mirror/Moseby College, eighth edition, 1993.

3. Johnston J, Paulos L: Prophylactic lateral knee braces. *Med Sci Sports Exerc* 23 (7):783–787, 1991.

4. Branch T, Hunter R, Reynolds P: Controlling anterior tibial displacement under static load. *Orthop* 11:1249–1252, 1988.

5. Mishra DV, Daniel DM, Stone ML: The use of functional knee braces in the control of pathologic anterior knee laxity. *Clin Orthop* 241:213–220, 1989.

6. Rovere G, et al: Retrospective comparison of taping and ankle stabilizers in preventing ankle injuries. *Am J Sports Med* 16 (3):228–233, 1988.

7. Rarick L, et al: The measurable support of the ankle joint by conventional methods of taping. *J Bone Joint Surg* 44A:1183–1190, 1962.

8. Fumich R, et al: The measured effect of taping on combined foot and ankle motion before and after exercise. *Am J Sports Med* 9:165–170, 1981.

RECOMMENDED READINGS

Andrews and Harrelson: *Physical Rehabilitation of the Injured Athlete*. Philadelphia, W. B. Saunders, 1991.

Andrish JT, Bergfeld JA. Romo LR: Method for the management of cervical injuries in football. A preliminary report. *Am J Sports Med* 5:89–92, 1977.

Bassett III FH, Malone T, Gilchrist RA: A protective splint of silicone rubber. *Am J Sports Med* 7:358–360, 1979.

Bergfeld JA, Andrish JT, Weiker G, et al: *Soft Playing Splint*. In Cleveland Clinic Foundation, Section of Sports Medicine, Cleveland, Ohio.

Black RA: The football helmet crisis. *Interscholastic Athletics* 5:10–12, 1978.

Clarke KS, Powell JW: Football helmets and neurotrauma—an epidemiological overview of three seasons. *Med Sci Sports* 11:138–145, 1979.

Cushing D: Helmet reconditioning: Does NOCSAE ensure safety? *Phys Sportsmed* 8:101–104, October 1980.

Hughes JR, Wilms JH, Adams CL. et al: Football helmet evaluation based on players EEG's. *Phys Sportsmed* 5:73–77, May 1977.

Klein FC: Facts about the much abused football helmet. *Scholastic Coach* 48:4–6, 1978.

LaCava G: Environment. equipment and prevention of sports injuries. *J Sports Med Phys Fitness* 18:1–2, 1978.

Mac Collum MS: Protecting upper extremity injuries in sports. *Phys Sportsmed* 8:59–64, July 1980.

Michel LM: Special pads for special problems. *Athletic Training* 14:68–69, 1979.

Mueller FO: Moderator Round Table on Protective Equipment: problems and promise. *Phys Sportsmed* 4:66–73, February 1976.

Palumbo Jr PM: Dynamic patellar brace: A new orthosis in the management of patellofemoral disorders. A preliminary report. *Am J Sports Med* 9:45–49, 1981.

Ryan, AJ: Protective equipment—boon or bane? Editorial in *Phys Sportsmed* 4:80, February 1976.

Rylander RC: Custom-made protective pads and heel cup. *Athletic Training* 8:169–183, 1973.

Torg JS, Truex Jr R, Quedenfeld T. et al: National Football Head-Neck Registry—report and conclusions. *JAMA* 241:1477–1479, 1979.

Wershing CE: A specialized pad for the acromioclavicular joint. *Athletic Training* 15:103–108, 1980.

The Management of Athletic Injuries

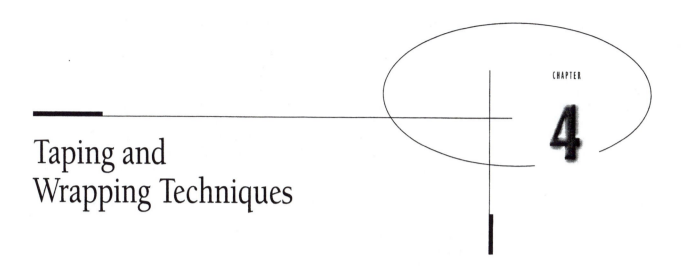

Taping and Wrapping Techniques

Adhesive Taping

The application of adhesive taping as an athletic training tool is both an art and a science and has been developed over the years by coaches, athletic trainers, and sports medicine physicians. However, questions regarding the effectiveness of adhesive taping have not as yet been adequately answered by scientific investigation. Therefore, at this time much of the information regarding adhesive taping is strictly empirical.

Before the athletic trainer becomes involved in the techniques and procedures of taping, there are a series of questions that need to be considered:

1. Does adhesive taping actually prevent ligament sprains? Garrick and Requa[1] conducted a study in which high-top shoes plus preventive ankle taping decreased the frequency of ankle sprains in intramural basketball.[2]

2. Does adhesive taping provide support for a joint and, if so, for what period of time? There have been several studies concerned with the length of time and the degree to which adhesive taping contributes to the support of a joint. Some have shown that correct ankle taping provides significant support for only a relatively short period of time, while others indicate that it is quite effective.[3, 4, 5, 6, 7, 8] McIntyre et al.,[9] studied the effectiveness of strapping techniques during prolonged dynamic exercises and found that all of the ankle strapping techniques examined were equally effective in maintaining consistent immobilization for 10 minutes of continuous uphill treadmill walking.

3. Does adhesive taping cause any adverse effects on the strength or the normal range of motion of the joint being taped? There has been some speculation that tap-

ing might result in the loss of muscular strength around the taped joint, but this idea has never been proven and does not appear to be clinically valid. Range of motion studies do not show significant impairment.[10, 11]

4. Does adhesive taping enhance or restrict normal motor athletic performance (speed, agility, jumping ability, etc.)? Most studies that have investigated the effects of taping on motor performance have not found any negative results.[11, 12]

5. Does adhesive taping cause an increased incidence of injury to an adjacent untaped joint? For instance, are there more knee injuries when the ankle is taped?[13, 14] Garrick and Requa report that there was no increase in knee sprains in athletes who taped their ankles.[1]

6. Does adhesive taping produce any other protective effects in addition to the physical reinforcement of the normal supportive structures? There has been a study suggesting that ankle taping stimulates the peroneal muscles, resulting in earlier firing of these muscles, thereby preventing inversion ankle sprains.[12]

7. Does adhesive taping produce a physiological dependence that causes the athlete to neglect the physical conditioning aspect of prevention? This is theoretically possible, but in practice does not appear to be significant. Psychological dependence on tape after an injury does occur, but does not appear to produce any harmful effects besides being costly.

8. How does taping compare to reusable "braces" in effectiveness for restricting unwanted motion (joint support)?[15, 16, 17] It appears that most of the research on the topic involves the ankle joint. Bunch and

colleagues[18] conducted a study that involved ankle taping, wrapping, and the use of five lace-on braces. Pre-exercise testing indicated that tape provided the best or highest level of support. After a simulated exercise condition (utilizing an instrument that created 350 inversions in a 20-minute period) there was a decrease of 21 percent in support of the taped ankle condition. The change for the lace-on braces ranged from 4.5 to 8.5 percent (decrease).

Gross and colleagues[19] studied the effectiveness of one particular method of taping and one semirigid orthosis in providing support for the ankle joint. The ankle support for both of these motion-limiting methods was measured before and after exercise (the exercise program consisted of running for 10 minutes on a figure-of-eight course and performing 20 toe raises). One of the results of this study indicated that the semirigid orthosis limited ankle motion (inversion) significantly more than the taping treatment following the bout of exercise.

Greene and Hillman[20] studied the relative effectiveness of athletic taping and a semirigid orthosis in providing inversion-eversion range restriction before, during, and after a three-hour volleyball practice. Statistical analysis showed maximal losses in taping restriction for both inversion and eversion at 20 minutes into exercise. Vertical jumping ability was not affected. Results suggested that a semirigid orthosis may be more effective than taping in providing initial ankle protection and in guarding against ligamentous reinjury.

Rovere and colleagues[21] investigated the effectiveness of taping and the effectiveness of wearing a laced stabilizer in preventing ankle injuries and reinjuries. Six seasons of collegiate football practices and games were assessed retrospectively. Tape had been worn when 159 of the injuries and 23 of the reinjuries occurred; a stabilizer had been worn when 37 of the injuries and one of the reinjuries occurred. The combination allowing the fewest injuries overall was low-top shoes and laced ankle stabilizers.

After studying the answers to the above questions, it becomes clear that more research is needed to define indications for, and effects of, taping. In particular, evidence needs to be accumulated regarding the advantage of one taping technique over another.

Each individual athletic trainer needs to develop a philosophy regarding the utilization of adhesive taping. In some cases it appears that taping is used more as a ritual than as a preventive and/or therapeutic tool. Evidence of this fact might be the taping of all athletes for a game or contest and not taping anyone for practice sessions. In addition, some coaches seem to be interested in the use of taping as a "quick fix" rather than as one part of a total program. These individuals need to be educated regarding the place of taping in the holistic, preventive, and/or treatment plan. There is no magic cure in covering of an injury with tape, but it does have a place with other treatment modalities and as part of a preventive or rehabilitation program.

Taping is one of the athletic trainer's most useful tools, and he or she should develop sufficient and effective techniques. Taping skills should be developed by first acquiring the necessary background on the general principles and then proceeding on to specific techniques and variations.

General Principles

The athletic trainer should:

1. Acquire a functional understanding of the normal joint and supportive structures (anatomy) and of joint movements (kinesiology)

2. Know the common mechanisms of injury as they might affect a particular joint

3. Visualize the purpose for which the adhesive taping is to be applied, that is, for full immobilization or for functional support of the joint through a particular range of motion

Guidelines for Adhesive Taping

The athletic trainer needs to learn to do the following:

1. Select the correct type and width of tape for the particular area in question.

2. Adequately prepare the area to be taped:

   a. Shave, clean, and dry the area to be taped if it is appropriate to do so.

   b. Utilize a suitable amount and type of tape adherent so the skin becomes "sticky." The trainer should be aware that skin sensitivity or allergic reactions to the adherent can develop, particularly to benzoin.[22, 23]

   c. Use protective material (e.g., underwrap, gauze pads) between the skin and the tape in selected areas. Applying tape directly to the skin does result in better tape adherence; however, it may also "break the skin down" and cause blisters or allergic reactions.

   d. Tape the affected part only when it is at normal body temperature—do not tape immediately after cold or hot treatments or after hydrotherapy.

  e. Be aware of skin sensitivity or an allergy to the tape itself. If this is found, apply the tape over a few layers of gauze pads or underwrap, or use nonallergenic tape.

3. Apply the tape in a smooth, firm manner, taking care not to crimp or wrinkle it, as this could interfere with the circulation, cause nerve, muscle, or tendon irritation, or result in blistering of the skin.

4. Position the joint correctly to achieve the objective or objectives of the taping procedure and at the same time permit free range of desirable and functional movements.

5. Properly tear the tape. The technique for this is to

  a. keep the tape in an extended or "stretched" position, not allowing the edge to fold over into the area of the tear

  b. use forearm movements and not finger movements when tearing the tape

  c. attempt to actually break the tape rather than tear it (Figure 4.1)

6. Approach each taping procedure as an individualized problem that needs a specific taping technique for the prevention of a particular injury or the protection of an injured part.

7. Use a minimum of tape without compromising the objectives of the taping procedure.

8. Properly remove, or instruct the athlete to remove, the tape after participation is completed:

  a. Do not use excessive force or violent movements to remove the tape.

  b. When cutting the tape off, use only bandage scissors or tape cutters designed for this specific purpose.

  c. Utilize the proper technique with bandage scissors or tape cutters to avoid damaging the skin, letting natural concave areas of the body serve as "paths" for the cutting instrument (Figure 4.2).

9. Take proper care of the skin once the tape has been removed:

  a. Clean the skin of all tape residue with soap and water, or use only those tape-removal liquids that are approved for this purpose.

  b. Apply a moisturizing cream if the skin is dry.

  c. Apply an antibiotic ointment if the tape has caused skin abrasions. If signs of infection or allergy develop, seek medical guidance.

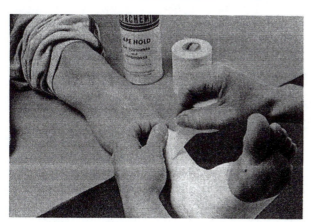

FIGURE 4.1
The technique of tearing tape

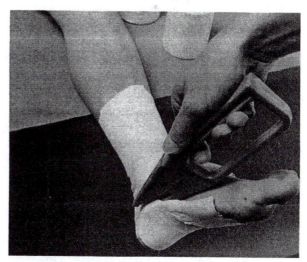

FIGURE 4.2
Using a tape cutter to remove tape

FIGURE 4.3

Big toe support

Indications: Pain, particularly a sprain of the first metatarsophalangeal (M/P) joint. **Objectives:** To limit dorsiflexion and/or abduction of the first M/P joint. **Tape:** 2.5 cm/1 inch tape. **Taping position:** Athlete supine on taping table with foot over edge of table. The toe is placed in a "corrected" position. **Taping technique:**

Option A:
1. Longitudinal strips are placed on the superior-medial aspect of the foot. These strips extend from the mid-portion of the distal phalanx to proximal to the first metatarsal head (**a**).
2. Overlap additional longitudinal strips around to the plantar aspect of the toe and foot (**b**).
3. Secure the longitudinal strips by encircling tie-down strips around the toe and arch. *Caution*—do not apply these strips too tightly. Leave a gap on top of the foot and then bridge this gap with additional strips (**c**) and (**d**).

Option B: Half-figure-eight procedure
1. Begin the first strip on superior-medial aspect of the foot and then go between the big toe and the second toe, encircle the big toe and end on the superior aspect of the foot. These strips may be applied in a reverse direction (depending on correction needed) (**e**).
2. Continue with overlapping strips (using the same procedure as used for strip number one).
3. Secure in place as in Option A (**f**).

Note: These two procedures may be combined:
1. Apply Option A longitudinal strips.
2. Apply Option B half-figure-eight strips.
3. Secure with tie-down strips.

Option C: Moleskin option
Tape: 2 inch elastic tape; 2.5 cm/1 inch tape; 3 inch moleskin (approximately 5 inches long).

Taping procedure:
1. Place one anchor around the great toe on the proximal phalanx with 1 inch adhesive tape. Place the second anchor around the midfoot beginning on the dorsal aspect, moving laterally, and ending on the dorsal aspect overlapping the ends (**g**).
2. Cut the moleskin in a "T" pattern (**h**).
3. Place the "T" portion of the moleskin around the anchor on the plantar aspect of the great toe (**i**).
4. Pull the moleskin firmly to place the great toe in slight flexion to limit hyperextension.
5. Place another anchor around the great toe on the proximal phalanx with 1 inch adhesive tape and a second anchor around the mid-foot (**j**).

Note: This technique can be used separately or in conjunction with other options.

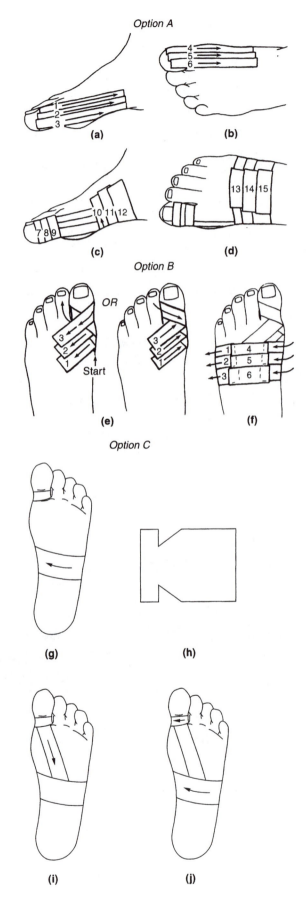

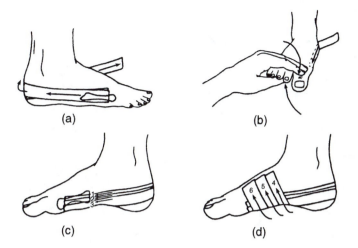

FIGURE 4.4

LowDye taping

Indications: Medial arch strain; plantar fasciitis; excessive pronation. **Objectives:** To reduce strain on the plantar fascia and medial
arch structures; to help control excessive pronation. **Tape:** 2.5
cm/1 inch tape. (Tape adhesive should also be used.) **Taping position:** Athlete sits on taping table with leg extended over the edge
of the table. The foot should be relaxed. **Taping Technique:** Tape
is applied to the lateral border of the foot, starting just proximal to
the head of the fifth metatarsal. This tape is brought around the
heel and lightly applied just proximal to the first metatarsal head
(**a**). The plantar aspect of metatarsal heads 2 to 5 are supported by
the thumb, and the first metatarsal head is depressed in a plantar
direction by the index and middle fingers. Do *not* pronate the foot
while doing this; keep the foot in a neutral position. Then secure
the tape just proximal to the medial aspect of the first metatarsal
head (**b**). Repeat this procedure 3 or 4 times (**c**). Then tie these
strips down with circumferential strips running from the dorso-
lateral aspect of the foot to the dorso-medial aspect (**d**).

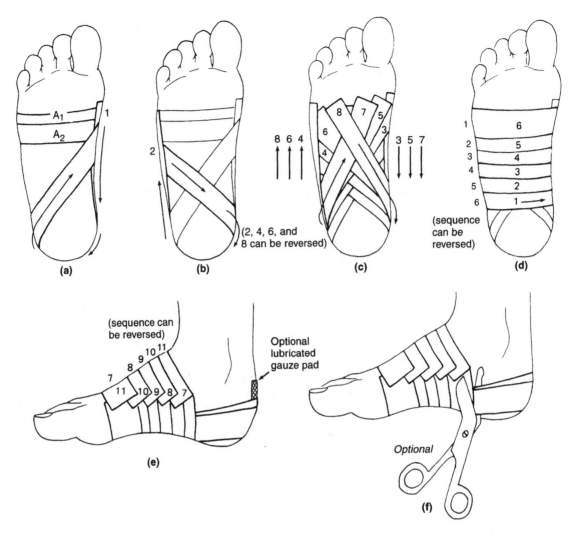

FIGURE 4.5

Longitudinal arch support

Indications: Plantar fasciitis; medial arch strain. **Objectives:** To reduce the tension on the plantar fascia and medial arch during the mid-support phase of gait. **Tape:** 2.5 cm/1 inch tape. **Taping position:** Athlete supine or prone on the taping table with foot over the edge. **Taping technique:** Place two anchor strips circumferentially just proximal to the metatarsal heads (apply lightly). Begin the first strip of tape on the medial side of the foot (just proximal to the head of the first metatarsal). Go behind the heel and angle the tape under the foot, crossing the longitudinal arch. Stop near the origin of this strip (**a**). Place the second strip of tape on the lateral side of the foot (just proximal to the head of the fifth metatarsal) and go under and around the heel, up the lateral side, and stop near the origin of this strip (**b**). Continue alternating strips in the same pattern until the "fan" is filled in (**c**). Tie down the entire procedure by placing circumferential strips over the previous strips by starting on the dorso-lateral aspect of the foot and then continue under the arch and finish on the dorso-medial aspect of the foot. Leave a gap on the top of the foot, bridging this by placing short strips of tape across the gap (**d**) and (**e**). *Option*—Once the "tie-down" strips are in place, the heel strips may be cut and removed (**f**). This may prevent excessive tightness and/or blisters, although some of the support will be lost.

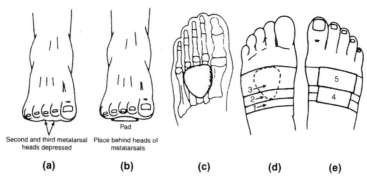

(a)   (b)   (c)   (d)   (e)

Second and third metatarsal heads depressed   Place behind heads of metatarsals   Pad

FIGURE 4.6

Metatarsal arch support

Indications: Metatarsal arch pain/strain; metatarsalgia. **Objectives:** To control the metatarsal arch and the stress on the intermetatarsal ligaments (a). **Tape:** 2.5 cm/1 inch tape; metatarsal arch pad. **Taping position:** Athlete lies prone on the taping table with the foot extended over the end. **Fabrication of the metatarsal pad:** Oval in shape, edges bevelled, thickest portion of pad should be placed where the most pressure is required. Place pad behind the metatarsal heads (b and c). **Taping technique:** Secure the pad in place: Begin the tape on the dorso-lateral aspect of the foot and then continue under the foot and up to the dorso-medial aspect of the foot (leave a gap by encircling only two thirds of the foot) (d). Fill in the gap by placing several short strips of tape on top of the foot. This permits expansion of the foot when weight-bearing (e).

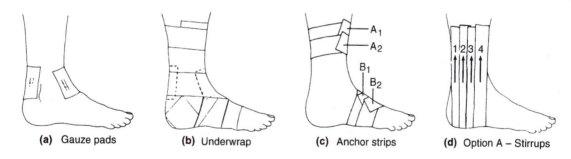

(a) Gauze pads   (b) Underwrap   (c) Anchor strips   (d) Option A – Stirrups

FIGURE 4.7

Ankle taping

Indications: Preventive ankle taping; following inversion sprains. **Objectives:** Support the lateral ligaments of the ankle without restricting functional motion. **Tape:** 3.75 cm/1½ inch tape. **Taping position:** Athlete sits on the taping table with the lower leg extended over the edge of the table. The ankle is held at right angles to the lower leg (neutral dorsi/plantar flexion), and slightly everted in a closed packed position. **Taping technique:**

1. Place lubricated gauze pads on the instep and behind the heel. Wrap the foot and lower leg with underwrap and secure the underwrap with two anchor strips at the top (A_1 and A_2) and the bottom (B_1 and B_2). The anchor strips should overlap the underwrap and adhere to the skin (a–c).
2. Apply vertical or stirrup strips:

Option A: Start the first stirrup on the medial aspect of the lower leg, go under the heel and up on the lateral aspect of the foot and lower leg. Continue overlapping these stirrup strips (three to five) until the last strip is well in front of the malleolus (d).

(Continued)

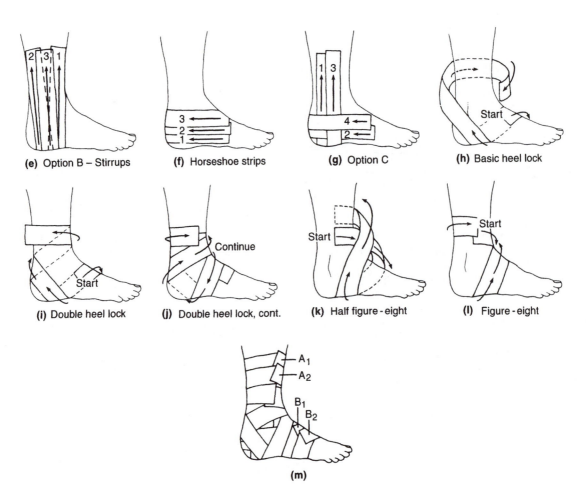

(e) Option B – Stirrups   **(f)** Horseshoe strips   **(g)** Option C   **(h)** Basic heel lock

(i) Double heel lock   **(j)** Double heel lock, cont.   **(k)** Half figure - eight   **(l)** Figure - eight

(m)

FIGURE 4.7 *(continued)*

Ankle taping

Option B: Start the vertical or stirrup on the medial side of the leg and behind the malleolus; go under the foot to the lateral aspect of the foot and lower leg (angle the tape so that it comes up in front of the malleolus). Start stirrup number two on the inside of the lower leg and in front of the malleolus and end with the tape angling upwards on the lateral aspect of the lower leg. The last stirrup strip covers both the medial and lateral malleolus (no angle) (**e**).

3. Following the application of the vertical stirrups, horizontal or "horseshoe" strips are then placed around the ankle. The first strip is started low on the outside of the foot and taken behind the heel and along the medial aspect of the foot (applying the "horseshoe" strips in this manner adds some support to the long arch). Continue applying these strips in an overlapping manner until the malleolus is covered (**f**).

Option C: In this procedure the stirrup and "horseshoe" strips are alternated, producing a basketweave effect (**g**).

4. A heel lock is applied by starting on the top of the instep and then taking the tape under the foot, behind the heel, and around the lower leg. Heel locks should be applied in both directions (**h–j**). The novice "taper" can begin applying heel locks by starting the procedure on the plantar surface of the foot.

5. Half figure-eights are applied by starting on the lateral aspect of the lower leg and crossing over the instep, then going under the foot and coming up on the lateral aspect of the lower leg before being attached medially (**k**). Several of these should be applied and they should overlap and progress down the foot. A full figure-eight is an option. This is accomplished by having the tape completely encircle the lower leg (**l** and **m**).

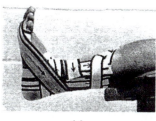
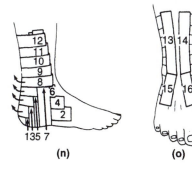

(n)

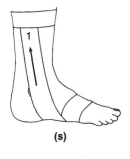

(o)

Ankle taping (for medial support)
Indications: Following eversion sprains. **Objectives:** Protect a mild sprain of the deltoid ligament or support medial laxity. **Taping technique:** Direction of pull on the stirrup should be reversed from that done for lateral support, i.e., apply from the lateral to the medial side with the foot in neutral position and slightly inverted. The half figure-eight should also be applied in the opposite direction.

Acute Ankle Injury—Open Basketweave
Swelling frequently occurs following an ankle sprain. In order to prevent constriction of the circulation, which may happen if tape encircles the ankle, open basketweave taping should be used in the acute ankle sprain until the swelling has stabilized (n and o).

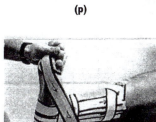

(p)

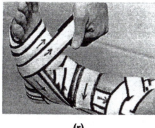

(q)

(r)

Option D: Wilkerson subtalar sling[24]
After the application of the stirrup and horseshoe:

1. The first strip of the semielastic tape is applied to the plantar surface of the forefoot over the head of the second metatarsal, wrapped around the base posterior aspect of the leg and terminated on the anterior aspect of the leg (p).
2. The second strip of the semielastic tape is applied along a slightly more posterior and inferior course, thereby overlapping the first strip approximately three-fourths of its width (q).
3. Short strips of nonelastic tape are applied to the dorsal forefoot in a lateral to medial direction to pull the subtalar sling down against the surface of the forefoot and ankle (r).

(*Source:* Gary B. Wilkerson, EdD, ATC, Sports Medicine Department, Trover Clinic, Madisonville, Kentucky. Printed with permission.)

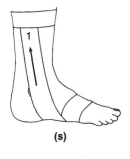

(s)

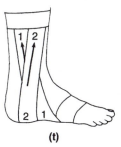

(t)

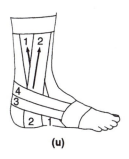

(u)

Option E: Moleskin stirrups
Tape: 3.5-cm/1½-inch adhesive tape; 2-inch moleskin.

Taping Procedure:
Option F: In this procedure 2-inch moleskin is used in place of or in addition to adhesive tape for the stirrups.

1. Cut two moleskin stirrups the length of the desired stirrup.
2. Start the first moleskin stirrup on the medial aspect of the lower leg, go under the heel and up on the lateral aspect of the foot and lower leg, covering both the medial and lateral malleoli. When applying stirrups, pull the foot into slight eversion to reduce available inversion (s).
3. Start the second moleskin stirrup slightly forward of the first stirrup on the medial aspect of the lower leg. Again pass under the heel and up on the lateral aspect of the foot and lower leg, covering both the medial and lateral malleoli. End this stirrup slightly forward of the first stirrup (t).
4. Following the application of the moleskin stirrups, place two horseshoe strips around the ankle (u).
5. Apply heel locks and figure-eights as previously described.
6. Apply final closure strips as previously described.

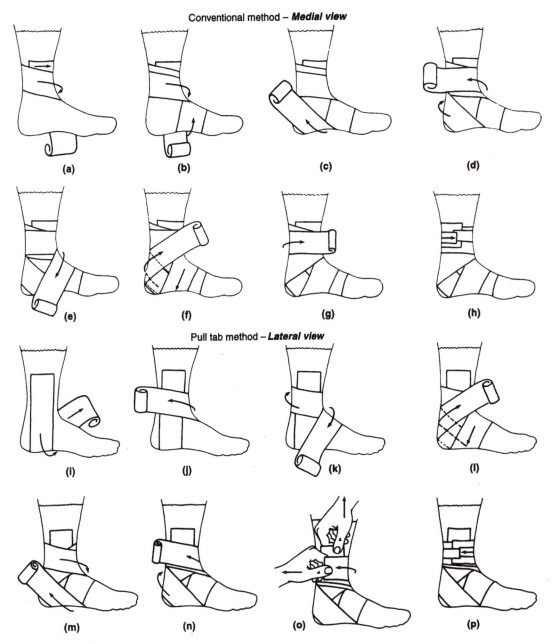

Conventional method – *Medial view*

(a) (b) (c) (d)

(e) (f) (g) (h)

Pull tab method – *Lateral view*

(i) (j) (k) (l)

(m) (n) (o) (p)

FIGURE 4.8

Ankle wrap: muslin wrap

Indications: Prevention of sprains; ankle support. **Objectives:** Generally support the structures around the ankle. **Wrap:** 5 cm/2 inch wide muslin wrap (approximately 270 cm/108 inches long). **Wrapping position:** Same as with ankle taping. **Wrapping technique:**

Option A: Conventional method (a–h).
1. Start the wrap on the lateral aspect of the lower leg, encircle the leg and go over the instep. Proceed under and around the foot.
2. Next, bring the muslin up at an angle and secure an ankle lock. Then proceed around the lower leg, over the instep, and under the foot to form a heel lock on the opposite side.
3. Depending on the length of wrap, additional heel locks may be applied. Finish with figure-eight or by encircling the lower leg.
4. Secure the procedure in place by duplicating the pattern with tape, or tie down with a short piece of tape.

Option B: Pull tab method (i–p).
1. Start on the lateral aspect of the lower leg and bring the wrap laterally under the heel. Swing over the lateral malleolus and add a heel lock. Repeat in the opposite direction.
2. After the completion of the procedure, the "tab" may be pulled up (this will place the ankle in more of an everted position) and then tied down.

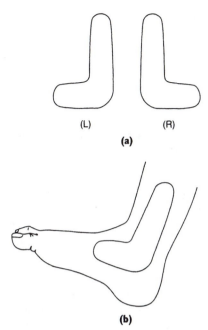

(L)   (R)
(a)

(b)

FIGURE 4.9

Tape and pad support for subluxing peroneal tendon

Indications: Subluxing peroneal tendon. **Objectives:** Secure peroneal tendons under lateral malleolus. **Tape:** 3.5-cm/1½ inch adhesive tape; J-shaped felt pad (approximately 2 inches long and ½ inch thick). **Taping position:** Same as ankle taping. **Taping procedure:**

1. Cut a J-shaped pad (approximately 2 inches long) out of adhesive foam.
2. Place the pad posterior to the lateral malleolus over the peroneal tendons with the long portion of the fibula.
3. Tape the ankle as you normally would.

FIGURE 4.10

Achilles tendon taping

Indications: Achilles tendinitis; gastrocnemius-soleus strain. **Objectives:** Prevent extreme dorsiflexion of the ankle. **Tape:** 3.75 cm/1½ inch tape. **Preparation:** Shave or clip body hair from midfoot to low-calf area if applicable; apply tape-holding spray to the skin. **Taping position:** Prone, foot over edge of the table. The foot should be placed midway between plantar and dorsiflexion, or slightly plantar flexed from that position (a). **Taping technique:**

1. Apply underwrap from midfoot to the low-calf area (b).
2. Place an anchor strip at midcalf and anchor at midfoot. The anchor strips should overlap the underwrap and attach to the skin (A and B in [b]).
3. Secure a restraining strap from the plantar surface of the foot, up the posterior aspect of the lower leg.

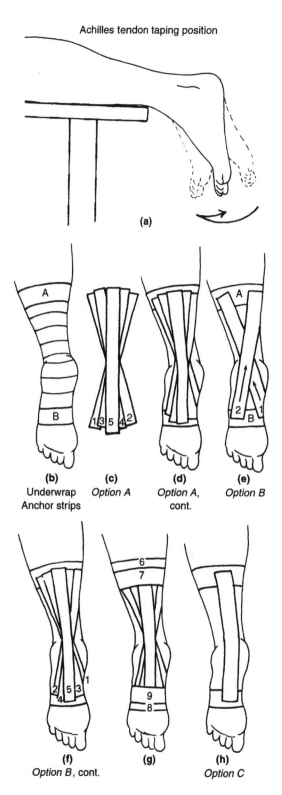

Achilles tendon taping position

(a)

(b) Underwrap Anchor strips   **(c)** Option A   **(d)** Option A, cont.   **(e)** Option B

(f) Option B, cont.   **(g)**   **(h)** Option C

Option A: Construct a "fan" on a table top or other smooth surface. Peel off and apply to the athlete. The individual strips of the fan should run from the foot to the calf in order to pull the foot into a plantar flexed position (c and d).

Option B: Construct the "fan" directly on the athlete (e–f) or utilize semi-elastic tape.

Option C: Split a bicycle inner tube and attach (h). Tie down as in (g).

4. Tie down the "fan" with circumferential strips (numbers 6–9 in [g]).

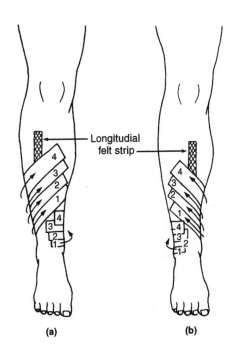

Longitudial felt strip

(a)   (b)

FIGURE 4.11

Taping for shin pain

Indications: Pain in the lower leg while running, not associated with a compartment syndrome or a stress fracture/reaction (see Chapters 9 and 21). **Objectives:** To support the lower leg musculature and reduce the symptoms. **Tape:** 3.75 cm/1 inch tape, 5 cm/2 inch elastic tape, and/or 7.5 cm/3 inch elastic wrap. **Preparation:** Shave or clip body hair from the lower leg. **Taping position:** Athlete may either stand or sit on taping table. **Taping technique:**

1. *Anterior leg symptoms.* Begin the first strip on the inside of the lower leg above the medial malleolus and apply the tape around and behind the leg, and then spiral upwards finishing on the anterior aspect of the leg. Overlap each strip of tape or wrap and apply as many strips as needed (a).

2. *Posteromedial leg symptoms.* Begin the first strip on the outside of the lower leg above the lateral malleolus. Apply the tape around and behind the leg, spiral upwards, and finish on the anterior aspect of the leg.

Options: Additional support may be obtained by securing the tape with elastic tape or wrap. If both anterior and posteromedial symptoms are present, a combination of the two techniques may be used. Apply alternating interlocking strips. In addition, medial arch taping or LowDye taping may be incorporated to help control excessive pronation (b). In addition, longitudinal felt strips may be placed over sensitive areas (to increase local or area pressure).

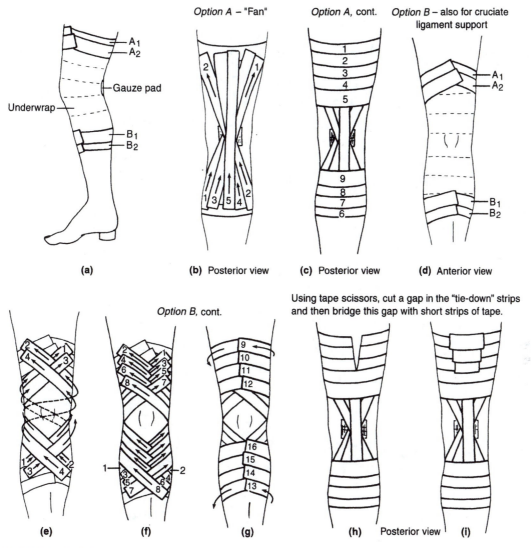

Option A – "Fan"
Option A, cont.
Option B – also for cruciate ligament support

(a)
(b) Posterior view
(c) Posterior view
(d) Anterior view

Option B, cont.

Using tape scissors, cut a gap in the "tie-down" strips and then bridge this gap with short strips of tape.

(e)
(f)
(g)
(h) Posterior view
(i)

FIGURE 4.12

Taping to prevent hyperextension of the knee

Indications: Sprained posterior capsule; strained lower hamstrings; anterior cruciate ligament laxity. **Objectives:** Prevent hyperextension of the knee. **Tape:** 3.75 cm/1½ inch tape; 5 cm/2 inch elastic tape optional. **Preparation:** Place adequate padding behind the knee (lubricated gauze pads) and then apply underwrap from the midcalf to midthigh. **Taping position:** Athlete stands on top of the taping table. Extend the knee until a strain is experienced. Allow the knee to bend slightly towards flexion. By placing a roll of tape under the heel, the knee can be kept in flexion (a). **Taping technique:**

Option A (**b** and **c**):
1. Secure the underwrap with anchor strips top (A₁ and A₂) and bottom (B₁ and B₂), which should adhere to the skin.
2. Construct a "fan" on the posterior aspect of the knee. Form the pattern by establishing the outer borders of the fan and then fill in the pattern.
3. The "fanned" strips of tape should run from distal to proximal.
4. Secure the fan by utilizing "tie-down" strips (either white tape or elastic tape).

Option B (**d–g**) This procedure is also utilized for cruciate ligament support:
1. Anchor strips (same as Option A).
2. Begin the first strip on the anteromedial aspect of the lower leg. Proceed below the patella, continue behind the knee, spiraling upwards to finish high on the thigh.
3. The second strip begins on the anterolateral aspect of the lower leg, runs below the patella, and spirals upwards to finish high on the opposite side of the thigh.
4. Continue with overlapping strips.
5. To finish, "tie down" the tape with white or elastic tape. Be careful not to over-tighten. If the tape is too tight around the thigh, release the tension by cutting the top posterior aspect, and then filling in the gap with short strips of tape (**h** and **i**).

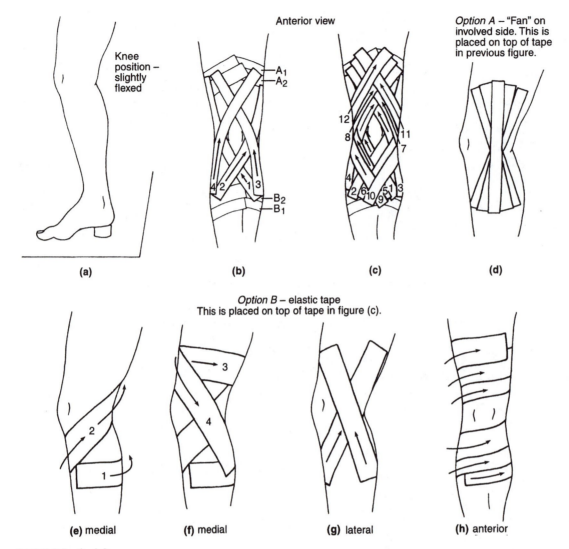

(a) Knee position – slightly flexed

Anterior view

(b)

(c)

Option A – "Fan" on involved side. This is placed on top of tape in previous figure.

(d)

Option B – elastic tape
This is placed on top of tape in figure (c).

(e) medial   **(f)** medial   **(g)** lateral   **(h)** anterior

FIGURE 4.13

Collateral ligament support

Indications: Mild sprain of the medial or lateral collateral ligaments; supporting established laxity of one of these ligaments.
Objectives: Support the knee against valgus or varus stress. **Tape:** 3.75 cm/1½ inch tape; 7.5 cm/3 inch elastic tape. **Taping position:** Athlete stands on top of the taping table with knee slightly flexed (a). **Taping technique:**

1. Wrap with underwrap from midcalf to above midthigh.
2. Secure the underwrap.
3. Begin the first strip on the anteromedial aspect of the lower leg and angle the tape up (near the inferolateral border of the patella) to high up the thigh.
4. Start the second strip on the anterolateral aspect of the lower leg and angle upwards (near inferomedial border of the patella) to high up the thigh.
5. Start the third strip near the first, and angle upwards (superomedial border of the patella) to high on the thigh.
6. Start the fourth strip near the second strip and angle upwards (near the superolateral border of the patella) to high on the thigh.
7. Continue alternating and overlapping strips of tape duplicating the pattern formed by the first four strips until the medial and lateral aspects of the knee are covered (**b** and **c**).
8. Proceed to either Option A or Option B:

Option A: Apply a "fan" on the involved side of the knee, and complete the taping (i.e., add a top layer to "tie down" the tape) (**d**).
Option B: Utilize 7.5 cm/3 inch elastic tape. Apply a modified figure-eight to reinforce the involved side of the knee. Apply an *X* procedure on the opposite side. Tie this tape down with elastic tape (**e–h**).

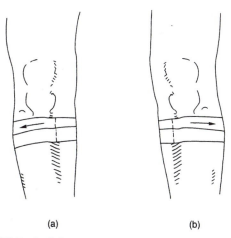

(a)   (b)

FIGURE 4.14

Patella tendon support strap

Indications: Patellar tendinitis. **Objectives:** Decrease stress on the patellar tendon. **Preparation:** Shave, clean, and dry area. **Tape:** 3.5-cm/1½-inch tape or 1-inch tape. **Taping position:** Knee joint slightly flexed. Place heel on 2-inch block. **Taping procedure:**

1. Tape should be applied directly to the skin when possible. Apply the first strip between the distal end of the patella and the tibial tuberosity. Begin on the lateral aspect of the lower leg, move anteriorly, then medially and encircle the lower leg and return to the lateral side* (**a**).

2. Apply the second strip one-half tape width inferior beginning on the medial aspect of the lower leg, move anteriorly, then laterally and encircle the lower leg and return to the medial side* (**b**).

*Most of the tape pressure should be directly over the patellar tendon.

OPTION: 1-inch elastic tape may be used in place of 3.5-cm/1½-inch or 1-inch adhesive tape.

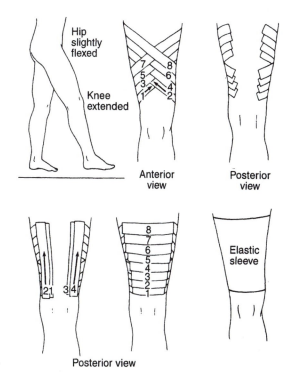

FIGURE 4.15

Taping for anterior thigh (quadriceps) strain

Indications: Strain of the quadriceps muscles; contusion of the quadriceps muscles. **Objectives:** Support the quadriceps muscle group and reduce the tensile stress on a minor strain. May also be used to support a pad to protect a quadriceps contusion. **Tape:** 7.5 cm/1½ inch tape. **Taping position:** Athlete stands with the hip slightly flexed and knee extended. **Taping technique:** Begin on the lateral side posteriorly and spiral up and around the leg to end on the posterior side medially. Repeat in the opposite direction. Alternate sides, producing an interweaving effect. Support the posterior edges of tape with vertical strips and fill in the gap. An elastic thigh sleeve may be worn over the tape or utilize elastic tape.

(a) Hip extended, knee flexed

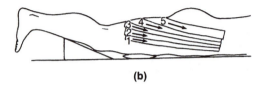

(b)

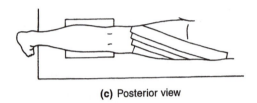

(c) Posterior view

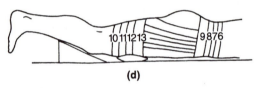

(d)

FIGURE 4.16

Taping for posterior thigh (hamstring) strain

Indications: Hamstring muscle group strain, particularly biceps femoris. **Objectives:** Reduce the tensile stress on the hamstring musculature. **Preparation:** Shave or clip body hair on the posterior thigh and buttock area—if applicable. **Tape:** 3.75 cm/1 inch tape. **Taping position:** Prone, with a bolster placed beneath the lower leg so as to flex the knee. **Taping technique:** Apply strips from low down on the thigh to the iliac crest area. "Tie down" with strips; these should not completely surround the limb. The gap should then be filled in. If the strain is mainly medial, e.g., the semitendinous muscle, the tape should be applied so as to cover the medial side as well as the posterolateral.

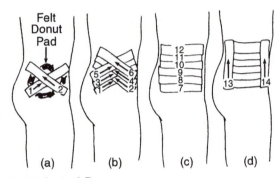

FIGURE 4.17

Taping for a "hip pointer"

Indications: Contusion to iliac crest area. **Objectives:** Protect the contused area; may be used in conjunction with a pad. **Preparation:** Shave or clip body hair over the involved area. **Tape:** 3.75 cm/1½ inch tape. **Taping position:** Standing erect. **Taping technique:** Interlocking strips over a felt "donut pad" (indicated in [a]), then cover with horizontal, overlapping layers. Secure with two vertical strips.

Internal rotation wrap

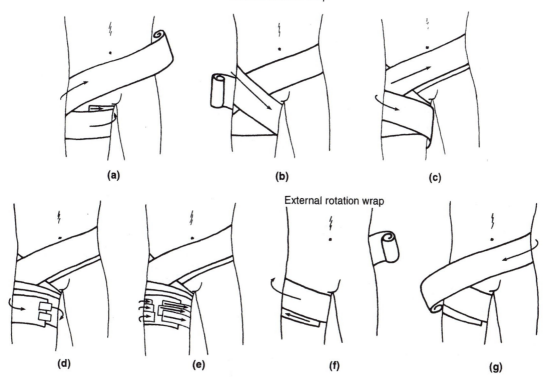

(a)   (b)   (c)

External rotation wrap

(d)   (e)   (f)   (g)

FIGURE 4.18

A hip spica for a groin strain

Indications: Groin and lateral hip strains. **Objectives:** Allow the hip to assume a relaxed position and to functionally limit motion. **Preparation:** Shave or clip body hair over the involved area if tape is used. **Tape:** 7.5 cm/3 inch elastic tape; 3.75 cm/1½ inch tape; or 7.5 cm/3 inch elastic wrap. **Taping position:** Standing erect. **Wrapping technique:** Surround the limb and body with either elastic tape or wrap. Secure with tape. The leg should be held in internal rotation when the adductors and/or anterior groin muscles are involved (a–e). The external rotation spica can be applied when the tensor fasciae latae, gluteals, and posterolateral buttock musculature are symptomatic (f and g).

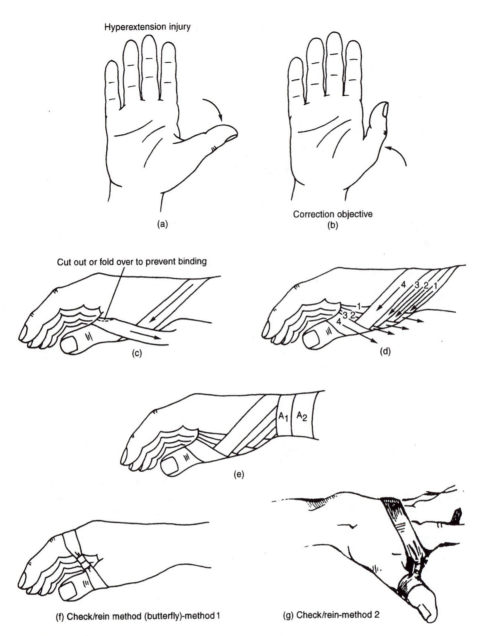

Hyperextension injury

(a)

Correction objective

(b)

Cut out or fold over to prevent binding

(c)

(d)

(e)

(f) Check/rein method (butterfly)-method 1

(g) Check/rein-method 2

FIGURE 4.19 *(this page and opposite)*

Taping for thumb injuries

Indications: Abduction and/or extension sprains of the thumb. **Objectives:** Protect the involved ligaments and prevent extension and abduction during healing. **Tape:** 2.5 cm/1 inch tape or 1-inch semi-elastic tape. **Taping position:** See diagram. **Taping technique:** See diagram. The option of additional support may be used under the basic figure-eight arrangement. The check rein method should be incorporated (**f, g**), and may be used by itself after healing has occurred. Additional support—*Option A—l–n. Option B—o.*

Abduction injury

(h)

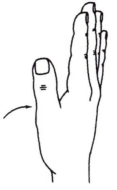

(i) Correction objective – adduction

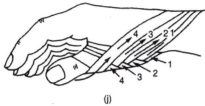

(j)

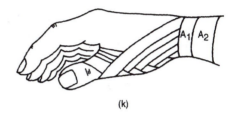

(k)

Additional support – *Option A* – utilize under basic figure eight (Figures [c] and [d])

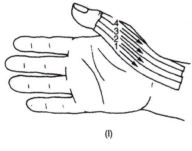

(l)

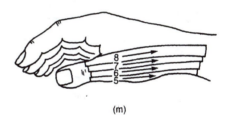

(m)

Additional support – *Option B* –
utilize under basic figure eight
(Figures [c] and [d])

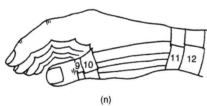

(n)

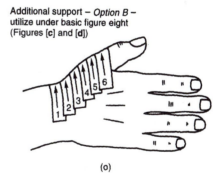

(o)

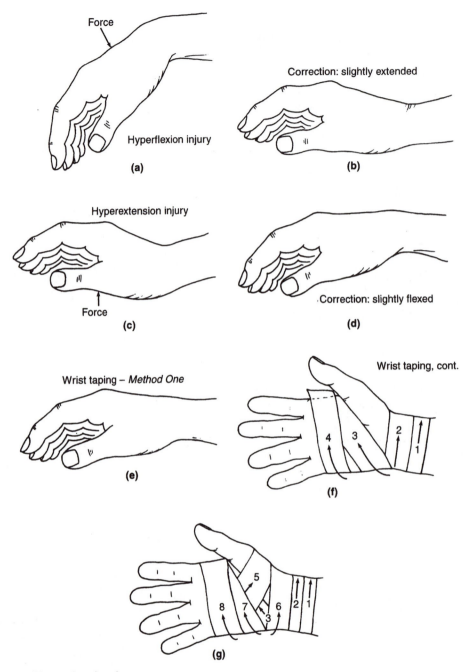

Force

Hyperflexion injury

(a)

Correction: slightly extended

(b)

Hyperextension injury

Force

(c)

Correction: slightly flexed

(d)

Wrist taping – *Method One*

(e)

Wrist taping, cont.

4 3 2 1

(f)

5

8 7 6 2 1
3

(g)

FIGURE 4.20 *(this page and opposite, top)*

Taping for wrist injuries

Indications: Mild sprains or contusions to the wrist. **Objectives:** Limit range of motion and support the wrist. **Preparation:** Shave or clip body hair from part to be taped. **Tape:** 2.5 or 3.75 cm/1 or 1½ inch tape. **Taping position:** See diagram. **Taping technique:** See diagram. Ensure that the tape over the palm of the hand is not too tight.

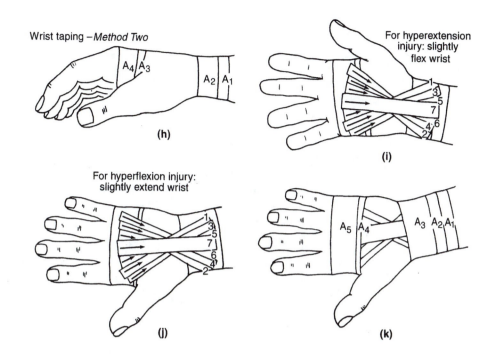

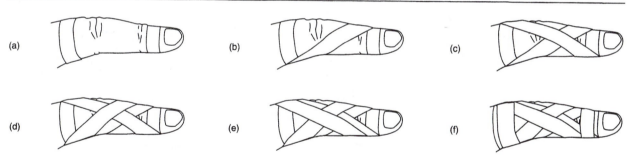

FIGURE 4.21

Collateral taping for intermediate phalangeal joint

Indications: Sprain of the interphalangeal collateral ligament(s). **Objective:** Provide support for collateral ligaments and prevent abduction/adduction during healing. **Tape:** ¼-inch to ½-inch adhesive tape. **Taping position:** Slight flexion of PIP joint. **Taping procedure:**

1. Place anchor strips around proximal and distal aspects of the affected phalanges (**a**).
2. Begin the first strip on the anteromedial aspect of the proximal anchor strip and angle the tape up across the medial joint line, ending on the distal anchor strip (**b**).
3. Start the second strip on the anterolateral aspect of the proximal anchor strip and angle the tape up across the lateral joint line, ending on the distal anchor strip (**c**).
4. Begin the third strip on the posteromedial aspect of the proximal anchor and angle up over the medial joint line and adhere to the anteromedial aspect of the distal anchor (**d**).
5. Begin the final strip on the posterolateral aspect of the proximal anchor and angle down over the lateral joint line, ending on the anterolateral aspect of the distal anchor (**e**).
6. Secure this technique by applying a second anchor over the proximal and distal tape ends (**f**).

Note: This technique can also be used for a lateral ligament sprain or a combination medial and lateral collateral ligament sprain.

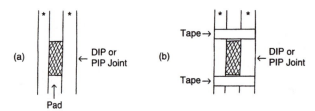

FIGURE 4.22

Adjacent finger(s) taping procedure

Indications: Support of the interphalangeal joint. **Objectives:** Protect the involved ligaments and prevent abduction/adduction of interphalangeal joint during healing. **Tape:** 2.5-cm/1-inch adhesive tape; ½-inch gauze, felt or foam rubber. **Taping position:** Extension of phalanges. **Taping procedure:**

1. Place gauze, felt or foam between affected and adjacent fingers in (**a**).
2. Apply a ½-inch or 1-inch (depending on size of finger) tape anchor proximal and distal to affected joint surrounding both the affected and adjacent finger (**b**).

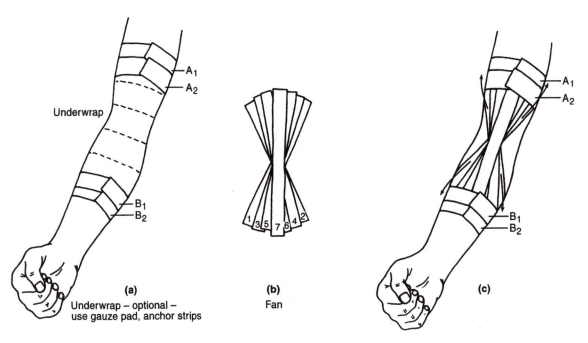

FIGURE 4.23

Taping for a hyperextension injury of the elbow

Indications: Hyperextension elbow injury; mild sprain to medial collateral ligament. **Objectives:** Prevent hyperextension of the elbow. **Tape:** 3.75 cm/1½ inch tape. **Taping position:** Elbow slightly flexed; forearm neutral to slightly supinated. **Taping technique:** Apply underwrap; secure with tape above and below (**a**). Construct a "fan" of tape (**b**) and apply to the front of the athlete's elbow. Secure with strips above and below (**c**). The athlete should not be able to fully extend the elbow.

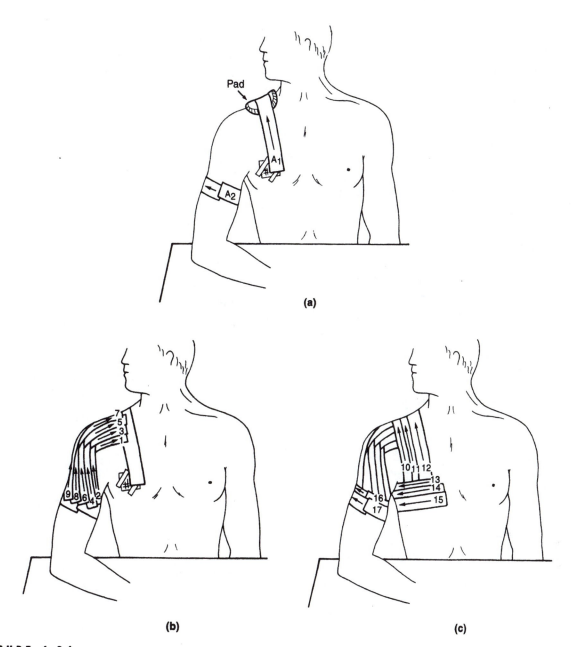

FIGURE 4.24

Taping for an acromioclavicular sprain

Indications: Mild strain of the shoulder musculature. Objectives: Support the shoulder in a nonspecific fashion. Preparation: Shave or clip body hair from area to be taped. Tape: 3.75 cm/1½ inch tape. Taping position: Sitting; shoulder relaxed and somewhat internally rotated. Taping technique: Apply a protective pad to the nipple area (a). An anchor strip should be applied from the scapula, over the clavicle, to (or just above) the nipple line. A second anchor is placed around the arm at the insertion of the deltoid. Interlocking strips are then applied, starting at the posterolateral aspect of the arm, crossing the shoulder to the anterior aspect of the chest. A felt donut or orthoplast/fiberglass shell can be incorporated under the tape, as indicated in illustration (a). (b) The second strip then runs from the anterior aspect of the arm to the scapular area. This alternating pattern is continued, and then tied down with strips applied over the anchors. The chest anchors are then secured (c).

Wrapping: Preparation and Guidelines

1. Shave, clean, and dry the area to be wrapped if appropriate to do so.

2. Utilize a suitable amount of tape adherent so the skin becomes "sticky." Folded adhesive tape can be used in conjunction with spray adhesive.

3. Use protective material between the skin and the tape and wrap as necessary.

4. Wrap the affected body part only when it is at normal body temperature—do *not* wrap immediately after cold or hot treatments or after hydrotherapy.

5. Begin distal to injury and wrap toward and beyond the injury, applying constant, even support.

6. Apply the wrap in a smooth, firm manner, but do not pull tight; skin should not "pucker." A too-tight wrap may compromise circulation or cause nerve, muscle, or tendon irritation. Wrapping should allow for contraction of major muscle groups.

7. Place wrap on a contracted muscle.

8. Position the joint correctly to achieve the objectives of the wrapping procedure and at the same time permit free range of desirable and functional movements.

9. Check circulation and function after wrap is in place.

Purposes of Elastic Bandage

1. First aid compression (reduce swelling and/or hemorrhaging)

2. Hold dressings, padding, splints, and ice bags in place

3. Joint support

4. Large muscle group support

5. Restrict movement

Securing Wraps

1. Angle the wrap distal to proximal and encircle the extremity.

2. Fold over the exposed one-inch "flap."

3. Continue to encircle the extremity with the wrap to cover the folded portion and proceed as directed.

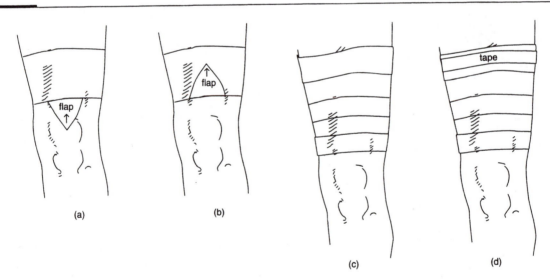

(a) (b) (c) (d)

FIGURE 4.25

Elastic wraps

Hamstring wrap

Indications: Hamstring strain. **Objectives:** Support hamstrings. **Tape:** 6-inch elastic wrap and 1½-inch adhesive tape or 2-inch elastic adhesive tape. **Wrapping position:** Standing, slight hip extension. Place heel on 2-inch block. **Prewrapping procedure:**

1. Shave the area to be wrapped.
2. Spray the area with tape adherent.

Wrapping procedure:

1. Secure the wrap on the distal thigh as described previously (**a** and **b**).
2. Proceed upward, overlapping the wrap one-half its width, pulling wrap more securely around the injured area. End wrap at the proximal thigh (**c**).
3. Anchor the wrap by using adhesive tape around the circumference of the proximal thigh (**d**).

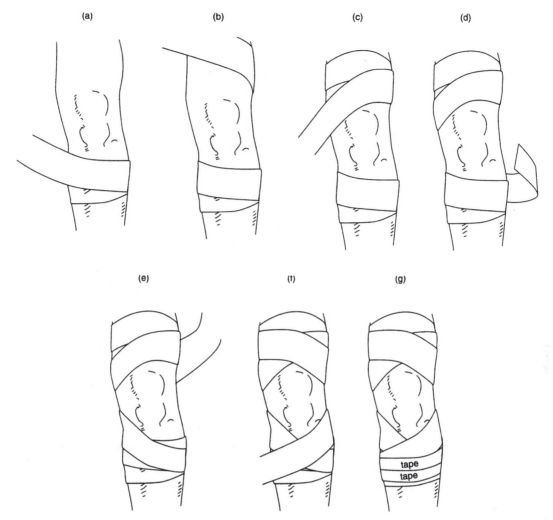

FIGURE 4.26

Knee wrap

Indications: Knee sprains and strains. **Objectives:** Support the knee joint. **Tape:** 4- or 6-inch elastic wrap (double-length wrap may be necessary for larger legs); 3.5-cm/1½ inch adhesive or 2-inch elastic tape. **Wrapping position:** Knee in slight flexion. Place heel on 2-inch block and place a pad over popliteal fossa. **Prewrapping procedure:**
1. Shave the area to be wrapped.
2. Spray the area with tape adherent.

Wrapping procedure:
1. Place pad over the popliteal fossa.
2. Begin on the posterolateral aspect of the lower leg. Begin wrapping, moving medially to laterally. Secure wrap end as previously described.
3. Angle the wrap to cross the medial joint line. Continue to the posterolateral aspect of the thigh.
4. Encircle the thigh and continue downward, back towards the medial joint line.
5. Cross the popliteal space; encircle the lower leg.
6. Continue the wrap to cross the lateral joint line and encircle the thigh and again cross the lateral joint line.
7. Secure the wrap with either 3.5-cm/1½-inch adhesive tape or 2-inch elastic tape.

Option: Use 3-inch elastic tape and follow the wrapping pattern.

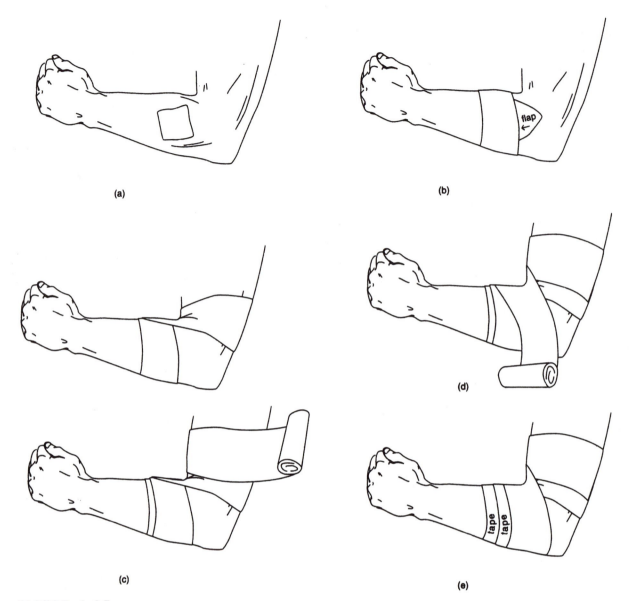

(a)

(b)

(c)

(d)

(e)

FIGURE 4.27

Elbow wrap

Indications: Elbow sprains and strains. **Objectives:** Support the elbow joint. **Tape:** 4-inch elastic wrap; 3.5-cm/1½-inch adhesive tape. **Wrapping position:** Elbow flexion (degree of flexion is dependent on amount of restriction required. Place pad over cubital fossa. **Prewrapping procedure:**

1. Shave the area to be wrapped.
2. Spray the area with tape adhesive.

Wrapping procedure:

1. Place pad over cubital fossa (a).
2. Encircle the forearm to anchor the wrap as described previously (b).
3. Bring the wrap upward, crossing the anterior cubital fossa; then encircle the upper arm and return to the beginning position by crossing the anterior cubital fossa (c).
4. Continue as described, but move toward the elbow one-half the width of the preceding layer (d).
5. Secure the wrap proximal (e).

Option: Use 3-inch elastic tape and follow the wrapping pattern.

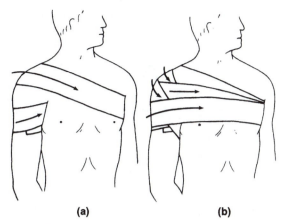

FIGURE 4.28

Shoulder spica

Indications: Occasionally used in the acute management of a shoulder injury in place of a sling; may be used in the later stages of rehabilitation as a functional support. **Objectives:** Support the shoulder joint; help relax the musculature; restrict motion to a limited extent. **Tape:** 7.5-cm/3-inch elastic wrap; 7.5-cm/3-inch elastic tape; or 3.75-cm/1½-inch tape. **Preparation:** Shave or clip hair from body area to be taped. **Wrapping technique:**

1. Apply the wrap or tape around the upper arm, then proceed across the chest, under the opposite axilla, across the back, and over the shoulder (**a**).
2. Repeat this a number of times overlapping by one-half of the wrap width, progressing down the arm and ending at the arm (**b**).
3. Secure with tape around the arm.

Bandaging

Although the use of a bandage may be appropriate for various anatomical areas of the body, this discussion of bandaging will be limited to the fingers. In addition, this section will be limited to gauze bandages of the "single-headed" roller type (a double-headed roller bandage consists of a bandage that is rolled from each end towards the center). Following are general principles to be followed in bandaging:

1. Utilize the correct width for the task (part to be bandaged). The roller bandage should be available in widths from 1 inch to 6 inches. If the exact width desired is not available, the athletic trainer should choose the next narrower width rather than one that is too wide.

2. Do not unroll more bandage than you can control easily. Always wrap from a tightly rolled bandage.

3. Bandage the body areas from a distal to proximal and from a medial to lateral direction.

4. Keep an even pressure throughout the procedure; utilize a slight decreasing tension from distal to proximal (avoid a tourniquet effect).

5. In the process of bandaging cover two-thirds of the previous layer.

The two types of bandaging that will be presented are:

1. Continuous (finger) bandage
2. Recurrent (finger) bandaging

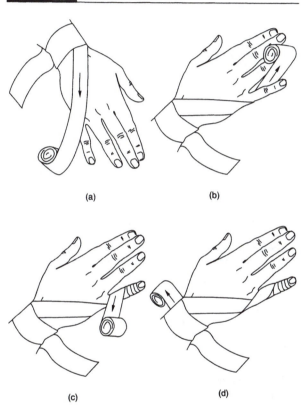

FIGURE 4.29

Continuous finger bandage (Example: little finger)

Indication: Wound injury. **Bandage:** 2.5 cm/1 inch. **Taping position:** Forearm supported, little finger abducted. **Bandaging technique:**

1. Leave about 6 inches of the end free, take a turn around the wrist, carry the bandage across the back of the hand to the little finger (**a**).
2. Take the bandage to the top of the little finger with a single turn (**b**).
3. Cover the finger to the base of the finger with spiral turns (**c**).
4. Take the bandage back across the hand to the wrist, and continue to the base of the next finger (**d**) and then tie down at wrist.

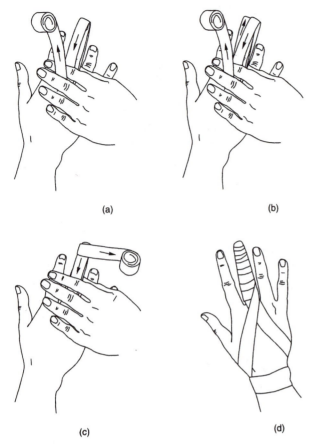

(a)

(b)

(c)

(d)

FIGURE 4.30

Recurrent finger bandage (Example: middle finger)

Indication: Wound injury. **Bandage:** 2.5-cm/1-inch. **Taping position:** Forearm supported, middle finger separated from the index and ring fingers. **Bandaging technique:**

1. Take the bandage once over center of the finger (hold bandage on each side) (**a**).
2. Make two more turns over the finger (one on each side of the first turn) (**b**).
3. Apply a spiral from the tip of the finger down the finger as far as necessary (**c**).
4. Finish off with a figure-of-eight around the wrist and tie down (**d**).

REFERENCES

1. Garrick JG, Requa RK: Role of external support in the prevention of ankle sprains. *Med Sci Sports* 5:200–203, 1973.

2. Garrick JG: The frequency of injury, mechanism of injury, and epidemiology of ankle sprains. *Am J Sports Med* 5:241–242, 1977.

3. Malina RM, Plagenz LB, Rarick LG: Effects of exercise upon the measurable supporting strength of cloth and tape ankle wraps. *Res Q* 34:158–165, 1963.

4. Sprigings EJ, Pelton JD: An EMG analysis of the effectiveness of external ankle support during sudden ankle inversion. *Can J Appl Sport Sci* 6:72–75, 1981.

5. Rarick GL, Bigley G, Karst R, et al: The measurable support of the ankle joint by conventional methods of taping. *J Bone Joint Surg* 44A: 1183–1190, 1962.

6. Laughman RK, Carr TA, Chao EY, et al: Three-dimensional kinematics of the taped ankle before and after exercise. *Am J Sports Med* 8:425–431, 1980.

7. McCluskey GM, Blackburn Jr TA, Lewis T: Prevention of ankle sprains. *Am J Sports Med* 4:151–157, 1976.

8. Seitz CJ, Goldfuss AJ: The effects of taping and exercise on passive foot inversion and ankle plantarflexion. *Athletic Training, JNATA* 19:178–182, 1984.

9. McIntyre DR, Smith MA, Denniston NL: The effectiveness of strapping technique during prolonged dynamic exercises. *Athletic Training, JNATA* 18:52–55, 1983.

10. Fumich RM, Ellison AE, Guerin GJ, et al: The measured effect of taping on combined foot and ankle motion before and after exercise. *Am J Sports Med* 9:165–170, 1981.

11. Abdenour TE, Saville WA, White RC, et al: The effect of ankle taping upon torque and range of motion. *Athletic Training* 14:227–228, 1979.

12. Glick JM, Gordon RB, Nishimoto D: The prevention and treatment of ankle injuries. *Am J Sports Med* 4:136–141, 1976.

13. Ferguson AB: A case against ankle taping. *J Sports Med* 1:46–47, 1973.

14. Wells J: The incidence of knee injuries in relation to ankle taping. *Athletic Training* 4:10–13, 1969.

15. Burks RT, Bean BG, Marcus R and Barker HB: Analysis of athletic performance with prophylactic ankle devices. *Am J Sports Med* 19:104–106, 1991.

16. Firer P: Effectiveness of taping for the prevention of ankle ligament sprains. *Br J Sports Med* 24(1):47–50, 1990.

17. Martin N, Harter R: Comparison of inversion restraint provided by ankle prophylactic devices before and after exercise. Unpublished Master's Thesis. San Jose State University, 1990.

18. Bunch RP, Bednarski I, Holland D, et al: Ankle joint support: A comparison of reusable lace-on braces with taping and wrapping. *Phys Sports Med* 13(5):59–62, 1985.

19. Gross MT, Bradshaw MK, Ventry LC, Weller KH: Comparison of support provided by ankle taping and semirigid orthosis. *J Orthop Sports Phys Ther* 9:33–39, 1987.

20. Greene TA, Hillman SK: Comparison of support provided by a semirigid orthosis and adhesive ankle taping before, during, and after exercise. *Am J Sports Med* 18:498–506, 1990.

21. Rovere GD, Clarke TJ, Yates CS, Burley K: Retrospective comparison of taping and ankle stabilizers in preventing ankle injuries. *Am J Sports Med* 16:228–233, 1988.

22. Ryan AJ: Taping prevents acute and repeated ankle sprains. *Phys Sportsmed* 1:40–47, November 1973.

23. Cooper DL, Fair J: Contact dermatitis, benzoin, and athletic tape. In Trainer's Corner, *Phys Sportsmed* 6:119, December 1978.

24. Wilkerson GB: Comparative biomechanical effects of the standard method of ankle taping and a method designed to enhance subtalar stability. *Am J Sports Med* 19:588–595, 1991.

RECOMMENDED READINGS

Davies GJ: The ankle wrap—variation from the traditional. *Athletic Training* 12:194–197, 1977.

DeLacerda FG: Ankle strapping with tape. *J Sports Med Phys Fitness* 18:18, 1978.

DeLacerda FG: Effects of underwrap conditions on the supportive effectiveness of ankle strapping with tape. *J Sports Med Phys Fitness* 18:77–81, 1978.

Drake EC: The case for ankle taping. Letter to the editor. *J Sports Med* 1:45, 1973.

Emerick CE: Ankle taping: Prevention of injury or waste of time? *Athletic Training* 14:149–150 and 188, 1979.

Felder CR, McNeeley J: Ankle taping: An alternative to the basketweave. *Athletic Training* 13:152–156, 1978.

Libera D: Ankle taping, wrapping and injury prevention. *Athletic Training* 7:73–75, 1972.

McConnell J: The management of chondromalacia patella: a long-term solution. *Aust J Physiother* 32:215–223, 1986.

Myburgh KH, Vaughn CL, Issacs SK: The effects of ankle guards and taping on joint motion before and after a squash match. *Am J Sports Med* 12:441–446, 1984.

Ross SE: The supportive effects of Modified Duke Simpson strapping. *Athletic Training* 13:206–210, 1978.

Simon JE: Study of comparative effectiveness of ankle taping and ankle wrapping on the prevention of ankle injuries. *Athletic Training* 4:6–7, 1969.

Stover CN: Functional semirigid support system for ankle injuries. *Phys Sportsmed* 7:71–75, May 1979.

Whitesel J, Newell SG: Modified Low-dye strapping. *Phys Sportsmed* 8:129, September 1980.

Wright KE, Whitehill WR: *The Comprehensive Manual of Taping and Wrapping Techniques.* Gardner, Kansas, Cramer Products, 1991.

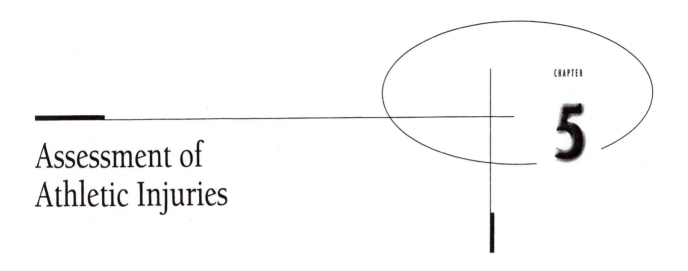

Assessment of Athletic Injuries

Chapter 6 (Emergency Care and Athletic First Aid) covers the immediate need(s) of the acutely injured athlete,[1] while this chapter concerns the assessment phase of responding to an injured athlete. The various injury exposures may range from life-threatening situations to very minor conditions.[2] The immediate post-injury assessment should consist of a protocol with systematic comprehensive observation and tests that will clarify details of the injury. The recognition of these injury details will facilitate accurate management of the injury, development of a clinical impression of the problem, and then a diagnosis. The assessment enables the athletic trainer to determine appropriate immediate responses that could range from initiation of CPR to the application of other first aid, or perhaps even permitting the athlete to return to athletic activity (with proper medical approval).

This chapter attempts to present the reader with an introduction to the rationale and principles of acute injury assessment procedures, providing a foundation for the specific injury assessment protocols that will follow in chapters concerned with ankle, knee injuries, and so forth. Other values of acute injury assessment are:

1. To provide necessary information to formulate a formal diagnosis

2. To obtain information needed for the required documentation

3. To establish a database of information pertaining to the mechanism of injury, specific athletic activity engaged in at the time of injury, the time of injury, and the severity and location of the injury. All of this information can be valuable for the continuing care of the injured athlete as well as providing data for those involved in research.

It is recognized that the first responder might be an athletic trainer, coach, EMT, M.D., or any one of a number of other individuals.

For organizational purposes, acute injuries that might occur can be classified as:

1. Life-threatening injuries

2. Injuries that are not currently life-threatening but require monitoring because of potential of becoming life-threatening

3. Low-priority injuries or non-urgent injuries requiring proper first-aid procedures.

The athletic trainer who responds quickly and documents an injury finds himself or herself with the unique opportunity to take advantage of the "golden period" of the injury (within the first 10 to 20 minutes post-injury). If this window of opportunity is missed, a great deal of valuable information related to the injury may be masked by protective muscle spasm, swelling, increased pain, or other physiological events. However, the motivation and desire for only a quick post-injury assessment should not supersede the goal of a complete, accurate and logically sequenced assessment.

The acute injury assessment is only one of the many evaluations that the involved injured athlete should be subjected to over the course of an injury episode. To meet the possibility of dynamic medical changes that occur, the athlete should periodically be reevaluated until rehabilitation has been achieved. The athletic trainer should follow an established plan for injury assessment. This procedure provides confidence and results in an accurate assessment.

It is gratifying to see that the athletic training educational programs place a high priority on developing competent assessment skills and techniques. The student athletic trainer needs an opportunity to learn and perfect the assessment skills to the highest degree possible. In addition, it is prudent that athletic organizations employ personnel who demonstrate the highest order of expertise in the area of acute injury assessment as well as emergency medical skills.

The Primary Assessment

The primary assessment survey is concerned with identifying the function or lack of function of the life-support systems (usually referred to as the ABCs—airway, breathing and circulation). In addition, severe bleeding (although not as prevalent in athletic injuries as in motor vehicles or industrial injuries) is a major concern. An in-depth discussion of ABCs assessment as well as the management of other medical emergencies will be provided in Chapter 6.

In athletes, life-threatening injuries are possible and a fatality might result from missed findings in the assessment process. The recognition of a serious life-threatening situation should result in an expedient application of the appropriate emergency care. It is fortunate that only a small percentage of all athletic injuries are of life-threatening priority. However, the athletic trainer needs to be well prepared and on the alert for a life-threatening situation.[3,4,5]

The Secondary Assessment

Beyond the recognition and assessment of life-threatening injuries, all levels of injuries need to be properly evaluated. The athletic trainer will find that the secondary survey can be achieved with a well designed and logically sequenced plan. While the primary survey may have ruled out any obvious life-threatening injuries, it must be remembered that under certain circumstances some lower-level injuries may develop into a serious or even life-threatening situation.

The athletic trainer must keep in mind an awareness of the *vital signs*: pulse, respiration, and the skin condition. These vital signs need to be continuously monitored throughout the acute assessment process.

1. *Pulse:* The pulse can be determined by placing two fingertips (not the thumb) over the radial pulse point, or if circumstances prevent this, by placing them over the carotid pulse point (avoid pressure on the carotid sinus). Characteristics such as the speed (fast or slow) and strength (strong or weak) of the pulse should be noted.

2. *Respiration:* Beyond the primary survey that determines if respiration is present (which may be accomplished by placing a metal object near the mouth of the victim and noting any condensation), the rate of respiration should be monitored. Additionally, abnormal sounds such as wheezing, constricted airway, or gurgling sounds (fluid in the airway), should be noted.

3. *Skin condition:* Ascertain the condition of the skin by observing the temperature, color, and the presence of excessive moisture or extreme dryness. Identify any changes during the assessment process.

Another portion of the secondary assessment is the recognition of signs and symptoms. The signs and symptoms that result from an injury are valuable clues readily identified by the athletic trainer. A *sign* is an objective finding that indicates the body's reaction to an injury. It is something that the athletic trainer can see, hear, or feel (such as dilated pupils, cold clammy skin, swelling). A *symptom* is a subjective finding relayed to the athletic trainer by the injured athlete (for example, sensory disturbances such as nerve "tingling" and pain).

The progressive steps of a secondary assessment are:

1. History   H
2. Observation   O
3. Palpation   P
4. Special tests   S
5. Resulting decision(s)[7]

The History

The athletic trainer must establish a history of the injury incident while building a rapport with the injured athlete and acquiring his/her confidence. The athletic trainer needs to project a caring attitude along with a purposeful sequence of questing. By asking clear questions, the trainer can learn the essential details of the involvement as well as subtle factors that may emerge from the athlete's expressions and movements as the conversation progresses.

The athletic trainer carefully avoids making an early assumption and directing questions leading to a conformation of the assumptions. It is critical to maintain a proper demeanor to avoid making value judgments and yet reassure the injured athlete. Questions asked in order to compile a history of the incident must be clear, objective, and relevant.[6,8]

EXAMPLE QUESTIONS FOR AN ACUTE KNEE INJURY:

1. Was it a contact or a non-contact injury? If contact, from what direction was the force applied?

2. Was the foot planted?

3. In which direction did the knee go?

4. Was there a pop?

5. Did you feel anything slip out?

6. Where was the pain?

7. Did the knee feel unstable or give way?

8. Did the knee swell immediately?

9. Have you had previous knee injuries?

Refer to Chapter 19 for further information related to the history of knee injury assessment, and to other chapters on obtaining a history of other specific injuries. While there is a recommended standard method of obtaining the history, some individuality is permitted. This allows for differences in personality, education, and abilities of each athletic trainer. An athletic trainer will have his or her own style (in medicine it is sometimes referred to as bedside manner) of assessing the injury situation. The combination of a natural ability to relate to injured athletes and the use of an established protocol is essential in obtaining an accurate history.

Observation

This phase of the secondary assessment can be in operation from the moment the athletic trainer becomes involved with the injured athlete. There is really no formal beginning or end to the process of being aware of the injured athlete and his or her physical and mental responses to that injury. During the first exposure to the victim and during the period of obtaining verbal information, the athletic trainer can obtain additional assessment data by being alert and observant.

The athletic trainer needs to resist the urge to touch the athlete at this stage of the assessment. This time is for using the eyes, realizing it is very easy to miss important observations and associated information. An example of an omission would be an athletic trainer picking up and moving a limb, which might reduce a dislocation. In this case, the fact there had been a dislocation would not be recognized. The athletic trainer needs to

be observant for signs such as immediate swelling, which could indicate the presence of a serious injury.

Palpation

Up to this point the athletic trainer has gathered a great deal of information but has not physically touched the athlete. The following information regarding the injury should have been obtained:

1. The mechanism of injury

2. What the athlete experienced and what seems to be the major complaint

3. A variety of signs and symptoms related to the injury

The athletic trainer builds on this foundation and continues to progress through the evaluation, sorting out the information, aware of not zooming in on any one preconceived conclusion, as this may result in skewing data. Avoid shortcuts and stay with the step-by-step plan to ensure an accurate assessment.

Some valuable principles of conducting the palpation phase of the assessment are:

1. Palpate in a set sequence. The palpation should start away from the injury and work toward the apparent injured site. As a result of this format, the most tender area(s) should be palpated last. Example—suggested order of palpating a suspected lateral ankle injury.[8,10]

   a. Neck of the fibula

   b. Squeeze the midshaft of the fibula (pain felt at the ankle during this maneuver may well indicate a fracture)

   c. Interosseous membrane and anterior compartment

   d. Deltoid ligament

   e. Anterior tibiofibular ligament

   f. Navicular

   g. Achilles tendon

   h. Bifurcated ligament

   i. Base of the fifth metatarsal

   j. Posterior talofibular ligament and peroneal tendon

   k. Calcaneofibular ligament

   l. Anterior talofibular ligament

Refer to Chapter 20 for further information related to ankle assessment.

2. The athletic trainer's touch should radiate confidence, competence, and compassion. Be confident and precise with your contact and pressure as you proceed during the palpation. The athlete receives non-verbal messages through touch and may need assurance that care is being taken not to cause any more pain. Your hands should indicate that you are confident, competent, and caring.

3. Begin palpation gently with pressure increasing to a firm level. Experience is the best teacher to acquire the proper feel for the amount of force to be applied to obtain the appropriate response. In the case of an acute injury, there is usually no need to press as hard as for a chronic injury.

4. Palpation should be specific, ensuring that each distinct anatomical structure is palpated in a set pattern to prevent any areas from being excluded. The athletic trainer needs to make a mental note of the palpation findings which then can be added to the results of the history and observation phases of the evaluation.

5. If relevant, always compare the apparent abnormal findings with the bilateral corresponding area (being aware that the comparison area is normal). Remember that many areas of the body are normally tender to deep palpation. The athletic trainer should be able to localize pain or discover abnormal sensations through an accurate palpation process.

Tests

Tests are injury-specific. For instance, in a head injury evaluation, tests will be administered which will determine the extent of the head injury.

EXAMPLES:

1. The 100–7 test—This test can reveal the capacity for concentrated (cognitive) thought.

2. Romberg test—This test can determine the ability to control balance.

Tests that evaluate nerve function may also be appropriate for certain types of suspected injuries.

EXAMPLES:

1. Sensory assessment–axillary nerve—This can be achieved by checking the sensation over the lateral aspect of the upper arm (see Chapter 12).

2. Motor assessment–long thoracic nerve—This can be achieved by testing for "winging" of the scapula (paralysis of the serratus anterior muscle).

3. Tendon reflexes assessment–biceps (C5 & C6) and triceps (C7 & C8).

Vascular tests are important in the evaluation of local circulation. Peripheral pulses, if absent, can indicate impairment of the circulation. If vascular impairment is not discovered and followed up with the appropriate medical response, severe complications can result.

Range of motion tests (ROM), when properly applied, can determine the functional ability of specific anatomical areas, the loss of range of motion, or deficient strength. There are three range of motion tests: evaluating active, passive, and resistive range.

1. Active range of motion—These tests are performed by the athlete to demonstrate a range of motion with no added resistance or assistance by the athletic trainer. The amount of movement, smoothness of movement and the ability of the athlete to demonstrate voluntary muscle control should be observed.

Example: The expected active normal range of motion for the shoulder joint (see Chapter 12).

2. Passive range of motion—The athletic trainer moves the limb through the ROM and attempts to feel for the quality of movement, establish the end point of the ROM, and note any abnormalities (such as clicks and pops).

3. Resistive range of motion—The athletic trainer should request that the athlete perform the same movements (as the active ROM) against resistance.[11,12] The athletic trainer needs to be familiar with normal muscle testing guidelines.

   a. The athlete should be properly positioned to provide stabilization of proximal joints and prevent muscle substitution. The athletic trainer should be careful to not grasp or exert pressure on an antagonist muscle, which results in an improper sensory input.

   b. The examiner should properly apply the manual resistance to overload the targeted muscle or muscle groups.

   c. The athletic trainer should be aware of any loss of strength (weakness) by comparing the results obtained with the corresponding bilateral uninjured area. The results obtained by this grading system should suffice for an on-the-field/floor acute injury assessment. However, a more detailed result can be obtained by grading the results using one of the established manual muscle testing grading systems (Figure 5.1).

LIGAMENT STABILITY STRESS TESTING:

These tests provide clinical information on the ligament stability of the joint. A rule of thumb is to first test the uninjured extremity. The athletic trainer needs to learn and practice the recognized tests designed to test the supportive ligament structures surrounding the involved joint. It is important to examine the various ligaments in a set sequence with the correct technique and then again compare the results with the corresponding uninjured extremity.

EXAMPLE: ANKLE LIGAMENT STABILITY STRESS TESTS (SEE CHAPTER 20).

1. Eversion stress test (stresses the deltoid ligament)

2. Side-to-side movement test (stresses the tibiofibular ligament)

3. Anterior drawer test (stresses the anterior talofibular ligament)

4. Inversion stress test (stresses the calcaneofibular ligament)

Important ligament stress assessment guidelines:

1. Apply adequate support (stabilize) to the proximal structures.

2. The assessment is concerned with locating the instability or laxity and the absence of the firm end point or feel.

3. Always apply the least amount of force that will adequately test the targeted ligament(s). The stress does need to be forceful enough and with enough speed to distinguish the presence or absence of a firm end point.

4. The ligament stress assessments should start away from what appears to be the injured area.

5. If it is obvious that there is extreme laxity or "looseness" (sometimes described as a soft or "mushy" feel), the athletic trainer should terminate stress tests.

6. Do not force stress tests if there are muscle spasms or continue tests if pain is not tolerated by the athlete.

Many other special injury tests need to be utilized to assess acute injuries:

1. The Apprehension Sign Test—This test is used to check for the stability of the glenohumeral joint (see Chapter 12).

2. The Thompson (Simmonds) Test—This test is used to check for a ruptured achilles tendon (see Chapter 20).

3. The McMurray Test—This test is used to check the knee for suspected meniscal injury (see Chapter 19).

Functional tests require the athlete to perform exercises or movements relevant to the activity that caused the injury. If the injury assessment indicates the possibility of permitting the athlete to return to the activity, then functional testing should be undertaken. This testing should be comprehensive and progressional (see Chapter 8 for clarification). Note: For additional adjuncts to the assessment process, utilize established assessment protocols or injury assessment flow charts (Figures 5.2 and 5.3).

Decision(s)

The athletic trainer determines management of the injury based on the clinical findings obtained from the complete assessment. The resultant decisions could include the following:

1. Obtain the services of an advanced life support system.

2. Refer to a variety of other medical specialists, a hospital, or other allied health professionals.

3. Continue the assessment process, which might include a variety of more complex and technical examination procedures. (Examples are tomography, magnetic resonance imagery, and so on) (Figures 5.4 and 5.5).[13]

4. Permit the athlete to return to athletic activity (with appropriate medical approval).

It needs to be recognized that the athletic trainer does not produce a diagnosis, but rather develops a clinical evaluation that can be invaluable and can contribute to the development of a diagnosis. Up to this point, the athletic trainer should have been utilizing preapproved procedures (standing orders) by the team physician and will need additional support and direction in order to proceed to the next phase of injury management.

The attending athletic trainer needs to keep an ongoing record throughout the assessment process and then transfer this information to a formal system (for example the SOAP system), which can easily and systematically be kept on file and referred to by the athletic trainer and other medical personnel (see Introduction).

Completes range of motion against gravity	*Completes range of motion*	*No range of motion*
N Normal—with full resistance at end of range	F Fair—against gravity	T Trace—slight contraction
G Good—with some resistance at end of range	P Poor—with gravity decreased	0 Zero—no contraction

Knee Extension—Testing

NORMAL AND GOOD

Sitting with legs over edge of table. Patient grasps edge of table to stabilize trunk.

Patient should be allowed to lean back until tension in the hamstrings is relieved. Pain or discomfort in this muscle group will inhibit knee extension.

Stabilize thigh without pressure over Quadriceps.

Patient extends knee through range of motion without terminal locking.

Resistance is given above ankle joint. (Pad should be used under knee.)

Note: Resistance to a locked knee can be injurious to the joint and is not a valid indicator of the strength of the extensors because a co-contraction of other muscles around the knee is required for the locking action.

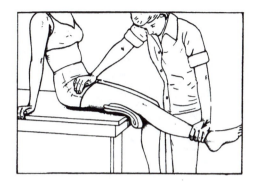

FAIR

Sitting with legs over edge of table.

Stabilize thigh.

Patient extends knee through range of motion without medial or lateral rotation at the hip (rotation allows extension at an angle, not in a vertical line against gravity).

POOR

Sidelying with upper limb supported. Limb to be tested is flexed at the knee joint.

Stabilize thigh above knee joint. (Avoid pressure over Quadriceps.)

Patient extends knee through range of motion.

Note: Do not allow the hip to be in flexion as extending the hip from the flexed position can cause passive knee extension.

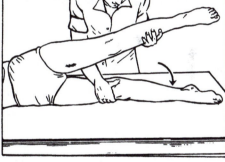

TRACE AND ZERO

Supine with knee flexed and supported.

Patient attempts to extend knee.

Contraction of Quadriceps is determined by palpation of tendon between patella and tuberosity of tibia, fibers of muscle on the anterior surface of the thigh, and the tendon of Rectus femoris near its origin between the Sartorius and the Tensor fascia lata.

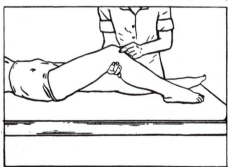

FIGURE 5.1

Example grading system and manual testing techniques

Source: Daniels, Lucille, M.A., and Catherine Worthingham, Ph.D., D.SC. *Muscle Testing: Techniques of Manual Examination,* 5th edition. Philadelphia: W. B. Saunders Company, 1986, Reprinted with permission.

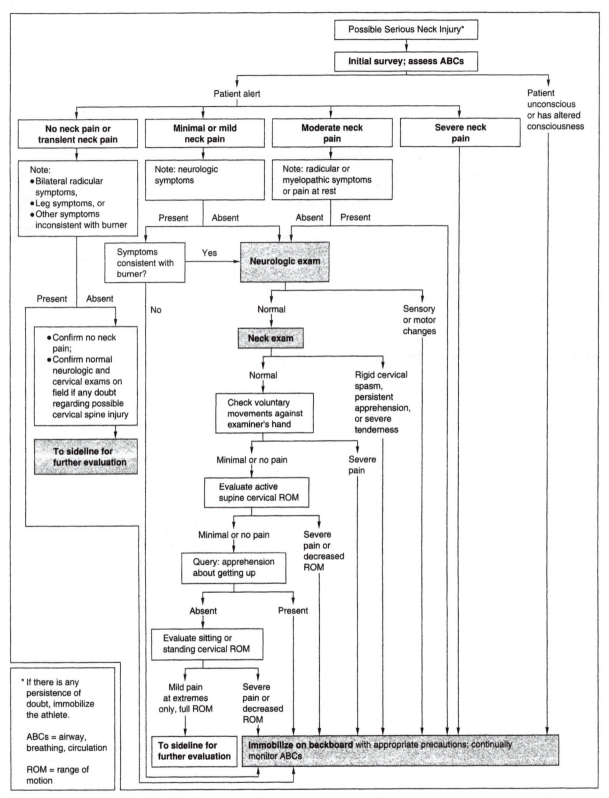

FIGURE 5.2

Neck injuries flowchart

Source: Anderson, C: Neck Injuries, Figure 3. *The Physician and Sportsmedicine*, McGraw-Hill, August 1993. Reprinted with permission of McGraw-Hill, Inc.

SIDELINE EVALUATION (Revised May, 1991)	SIDELINE EVALUATION (Revised May, 1991)
Grading Scale for Concussion in Sports	**Mental Status Testing**
Grade 1 Confusion without amnesia No loss of consciousness Grade 2 Confusion with amnesia No loss of consciousness Grade 3 Loss of consciousness	Orientation: Time, place, person and situation (Circumstances of injury) Concentration: Digits backward 3 – 1 – 7 4 – 6 – 8 – 2 5 – 9 – 3 – 7 – 4 Months of year in reverse order Memory: Names of teams in prior contest, President, Governor, Mayor, Recent newsworthy events, 3 words and 3 objects at 0 and 5 minutes, Details of contest (plays, moves, strategies, etc.)
Guidelines for Return to Competition	
Grade 1—Remove from contest. Examine immediately and every five minutes for the development of amnesia or post-concussive symptoms at rest and with exertion. May return to contest if amnesia does not appear and no symptoms appear for at least twenty minutes. Grade 2—Remove from contest and disallow return. Examine frequently for signs of evolving intracranial pathology. Re-examine the next day. May return to practice only after one full week without symptoms. Grade 3—Transport from field by ambulance (with cervical spine immobilization if indicated) to nearest hospital. Thorough neurological evaluation emergently. Hospital confinement if signs of pathology are detected. If findings are normal, instructions to family for overnight observation. May return to practice only after two full weeks without symptoms. Prolonged unconsciousness, persistent mental status alterations, worsening post-concussion symptoms or abnormalities on neurological exam require urgent neurosurgical consultation or transfer to a trauma center.	**Exertional Provocative Tests** 40 yard sprint 5 push-ups 5 sit-ups 5 knee bends (Any appearance of associated symptoms is abnormal, e.g., headache, dizziness, nausea, unsteadiness, photophobia, blurred or double vision, emotional lability, or mental status changes.) **Neurological Tests** Pupils: Symmetry and reaction Coordination: Finger-nose-finger and tandem Sensation: Finger-nose (eyes closed) and Romberg

FIGURE 5.3

Head injury

Source: Sports Medicine Committee of the Colorado Medical Society: *Management of Concussions in Sports,* Reprinted with permission.

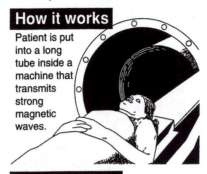

MRI benefits athletes

Magnetic Resonance Imaging has become sports medicine's newest diagnostic tool. How the procedure works:

How it is used

▶ The 20-40 minute procedure is especially effective in diagnosing knee and shoulder injuries and bone bruises, which do not show up on the traditional X-ray.

▶ Can provide information about injuries to the ligaments, cartilage, bones and soft tissue surrounding the joints.

▶ It's not used for broken bones.

Cost

Approximately $400-$800 for each procedure.

How it works

Patient is put into a long tube inside a machine that transmits strong magnetic waves.

A computer reads the magnetic waves as they bounce back from the area being scanned and relays them to a computer screen, where the signals are transformed into masses—top, side and frontal views.

MRI vs. X-rays

PROS

▶ Allows doctor to view area in question from multiple planes.

▶ One hundred times more sensitive to differences in a joint than a CAT scan.

▶ Eliminates need to use arthroscope for diagnostic purposes.

CONS

▶ "You feel like you're in a tube in a submarine," which can be a problem if you're like Rob Dibble and suffer from claustrophobia.

▶ Patient hears loud clicking or tapping sound, which can be overcome by using headphones and taped-in music.

Source: Dr. Anton Hasson, a neuroradiologist at Loma Linda (Calif.) University Medical Center, USA TODAY research.

By Rod Coddington, USA TODAY

FIGURE 5.4

Source: USA Today. Copyright 1992, Reprinted with permission.

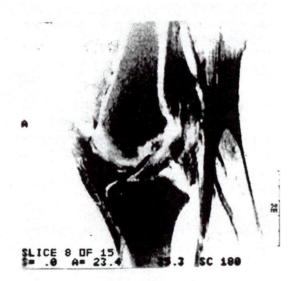

FIGURE 5.5

Example MRI (knee-anterior cruciate)
Source: John Erkkila, M.D. Corvallis Clinic P.C. Corvallis, OR. Printed with permission.

REFERENCES

1. National Safety Council: *First Aid and CPR,* Boston: Jones and Bartlett, 1991.

2. Vinger PF , Hoerner EF: *Sports Injuries: the Unthwarted Epidemic,* Boston: Wright-PSG, Inc., 1982.

3. Booher JA, Thibodeau GA: *Athletic Injury Assessment,* St. Louis: Times Mirror/Mosby College Publishing, second edition, 1989.

4. Arnheim D, Prentice W: *Principles of Athletic Training,* St. Louis: Times Mirror/Mosby College Publishing, eighth edition, 1993.

5. American Academy of Orthopaedic Surgeons: *Athletic Training and Sports Medicine,* Park Ridge, IL: American Academy of Orthopedic Surgeons, second edition, 1991.

6. O'Donohue DH: *Treatment of Injuries to Athletes,* Philadelphia: W.B. Saunders Co., fourth edition, 1984.

7. Hoppenfeld S: *Physical Examination of the Spine and Extremities,* New York: Appleton-Century-Crofts, 1976.

8. Cyriax J: *Textbook of Orthopedic Medicine, Vol 1: Diagnosis of Soft Tissue Lesions,* London: Bailliere Tindall, 1982.

9. Magee DJ: *Orthopedic Physical Assessment,* Philadelphia: W.B. Saunders Co., 1987.

10. Kannus VP: Evaluation of abnormal biomechanics of the foot and ankle in athletes. *Br J Sports Med* 26(2): 83–9, June 1992.

11. Daniels L, Worthingham C: *Muscle Testing,* Philadelphia: W.B. Saunders Co., fifth edition, 1986.

12. Kendall EP, McCreary EK: *Muscles: Testing and Function,* Baltimore: Williams and Wilkins Co., 1985.

13. Galloway HR, Suh JS, Everson Ll, Griffiths HJ: Radiologic case study: MRI and sports injuries. *Orthopedics,* 15(2): 249, 252–6, February 1992.

RECOMMENDED READINGS

Mirabello SC, Loeb PE, Andrews JR: The wrist: field evaluation and treatment. *Clin Sports Med* 11(1): 1–25, 1992.

Mirabello SC, Loeb PE, Andrews JR: The hand: field evaluation and treatment. *Clin Sports Med* 11(1): 27–37, 1992.

Kannus VP: Evaluation of abnormal biomechanics of the foot and ankle in athletes. *Br J Sports Med* 26(2): 83–89, June 1992.

Sterling JC, Edelstein DW, Calvo DR, Webb R: Stress fractures in the athlete. Diagnosis and management. *Sports Med (Auckland)* 14(5): 336–346, November 1992.

Howard CB, Bonneh DY, Nyska M: Diagnosis of popliteus tenosynovitis by ultrasound. *J Orthop Sports Phys Ther* 16(2): 58–59, August 1992.

Sallis RE, Jones K: Stress fractures in athletes. How to spot this underdiagnosed injury. *Postgrad Med* 89(6): 185–189, May 1991.

Abrams JS: Special shoulder problems in the throwing athlete: pathology, diagnosis and nonoperative management. *Clin Sports Med* 10(4): 839–846, 1991.

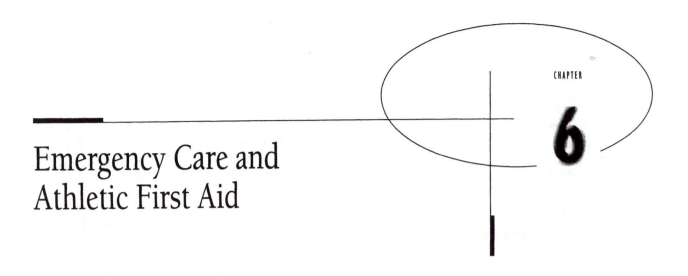

Emergency Care and Athletic First Aid

Because an athletic trainer is often at the site of an athletic accident, he or she should therefore have the appropriate educational background, experience, certification, and/or licensing to handle the situation. Included should be certification in standard first aid, advanced first aid, and cardiopulmonary resuscitation. The trainer should know how to deal with the following situations in a sports environment:

1. Cardiopulmonary emergencies
2. Head and neck injuries
3. Shock—anaphylactic shock
4. Internal injuries
5. Medical emergencies
6. Superficial bleeding
7. Fractures
8. Dislocations
9. Soft-tissue injuries

Cardiopulmonary Emergencies

The area of primary respiratory and/or cardiac arrest is such an extreme emergency situation that any attempt to adequately and accurately cover the topic in this publication would be an impossible task. The reader needs to obtain this information by completing an official CPR course.[1,2,3]

Obstruction by a Foreign Object

In athletics there is always the possibility of inhaling a foreign object. The trainer should make every effort to discourage the use of chewing gum and to educate the athlete in removing dentures or dental appliances before athletic participation. If any obstruction to the upper airway should occur, the athlete will suddenly be unable to speak or cough and will make exaggerated attempts to breathe. However, no air movement will be present. If a foreign object is suspected as being the cause of the obstruction, the trainer should deliver a series of four or five sharp blows to the spine between the scapulae. If this fails to remove the obstruction, the Heimlich maneuver should be performed. This maneuver has proven effective in removing a variety of foreign objects from the upper airway.

The Heimlich Maneuver

The Heimlich maneuver consists of a series of rapid thrusts to the upper abdomen. It is performed with the athlete in either a vertical or horizontal position.

1. With the athlete vertical—the trainer

   a. stands behind the athlete and wraps his or her arms around the athlete's waist.

   b. grasps one fist with the other hand, placing the thumb side of the fist against the athlete's abdomen between the xiphoid and the umbilicus.

   c. presses the fist into the athlete's abdomen with a quick upward thrust.

2. With the athlete horizontal (the horizontal technique is more applicable to the situation in which a cervical spine injury may exist):

    a. Put the athlete in a supine position, kneel close to the athlete's hips, or straddle the hips or one leg.

    b. Place the heel of one hand against the athlete's abdomen, between the xiphoid and the umbilicus; place the second hand on top of the first.

    c. Press the hands into the athlete's abdomen with a quick upward thrust.

In cases where the foreign object cannot be dislodged, mouth-to-mouth resuscitation may provide an adequate amount of air to maintain the victim until the obstruction is removed or a tracheotomy is performed. (Figure 6.1).

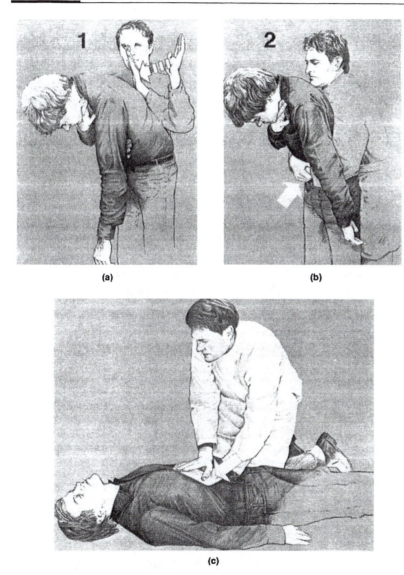

(a)   (b)

(c)

FIGURE 6.1

*Parts (a), (b) and (c) show the **Heimlich maneuver**.*
(Reproduced with the permission of Laerdal Medical Corp.)

Head and Neck Injuries

In many situations a head and a neck injury may occur simultaneously.

A head injury may result in intracranial bleeding, either venous or arterial. Immediate management consists of

1. Assessment of the state of consciousness

2. Assessment and observation of the athlete's airway, breathing, and circulation

3. A decision as to the appropriate form of management

The trainer needs to be aware that an athlete may relapse after apparently recovering and may suddenly lose consciousness. (For a complete discussion of head injuries, see Chapter 11).

A neck injury is often associated with a head injury. When dealing with a head injury, *the trainer should assume that a neck injury is present until it is proven otherwise.* In a sport where a helmet is worn (such as football), the helmet should *not* be removed until a neck injury has been ruled out.

Since the football helmet is individually fitted for optimum protection of the head, the helmet fits very snugly and is not easily removed by another individual. Athletic trainers have accepted the fact that attempting to remove the helmet can be dangerous because removal can cause excessive movement to the cervical spine area. For athletes suffering respiratory and cardiac arrest and an airway management problem, the athletic trainer needs to be prepared to quickly and effectively remove the face mask.[4,5,6,7,8]

Recently it has been reported that in some instances there is a conflict between the attending athletic trainer and the emergency medical technician (EMT) on the decision to remove or not to remove the helmet. Many EMTs are taught to always remove the helmet when there is a need for airway access although reports from the field indicate there is no universal conformity in this EMT protocol.

Athletic trainers need to develop a rapport with the EMTs with whom they will be working (ambulance personnel, etc.) to develop a rationale for not removing the helmet. These discussions should resolve any conflict that might arise in a time of crisis. Perhaps one area of discussion should be concerned with the differences between the football helmet and other types of helmets (e.g., motorcycle helmet). The motorcycle helmet, which is more familiar to EMTs, has a full solid face mask and the emergency removal of that face mask is not required. The football helmet presents the opportunity for face mask removal, if the attending personnel are properly trained and prepared.

Being adequately trained and prepared for removing the face mask is the key to a successful resolution to an airway access emergency situation. Removal of the face mask is a skill that should have a high priority for every athletic trainer. The athletic trainer needs to know how the face mask is attached to the helmet (there are a variety of methods of attachment) and the procedure for its safe and efficient removal. This acquisition of the skill of face mask removal should result in a recognized standard of care for the profession.

At the time of the emergency, the athletic trainer must be well versed in the proper procedures and equipped with the devices needed to solve the problem.

EXAMPLE:

1. Older type helmets with a double-bar face mask may still require bolt cutters.

2. Plastic clip attachments may be:

   - cut with a sharp instrument (e.g., scalpel, "anvil pruner")

   - unscrewed from the helmet

   - in need of a specialized tool to completely remove the face mask (e.g., trainer's angel).

The National Athletic Trainers' Association has adopted the following guidelines with regard to the on-site removal of the athletic helmet.

Removing helmets from athletes with potential cervical spine injuries may worsen existing injuries or cause new ones. Removal of athletic helmets should, therefore, be avoided unless individual circumstances dictate otherwise.

Before removing the helmet from an injured athlete, appropriate alternatives such as the following should be considered:

- Most injuries can be visualized with the helmet in place.
- Neurological tests can be performed with the helmet in place. The eyes may be examined for reactivity, the nose and ears checked for fluid and the level of consciousness determined.
- The athlete can be immobilized on a spine board with the helmet in place.
- The helmet and shoulder pads elevate the supine athlete. Removal of helmet and shoulder pads, if required, should be coordinated to avoid cervical hyperextension.
- Removal of the face mask allows full airway access to be achieved. Plastic clips securing the face mask can be cut using special tools, permitting rapid removal.

In all cases, individual circumstances must dictate appropriate actions.

Source: National Athletic Trainers' Association. Reprinted with permission.

FIGURE 6.2
Laerdal™ Pocket Mask.™
(*Source:* Laerdal Medical Corporation. Reprinted with permission.)

In situations where the face mask cannot be removed, a barrier device may be utilized in the delivery of artificial respiration or cardiopulmonary resuscitation (e.g., Laerdal™ Pocket Mask;™ see Figure 6.2).

The athletic trainer needs to palpate for possible deformities of the spine and test the power and sensation in the extremities. If a neck or spinal cord injury is suspected, the head and neck should be adequately immobilized and the athlete moved only with supervision by a physician or trained personnel (see Chapters 11 and 16).

Shock

The term *shock* implies a state of collapse of the cardiovascular system and constitutes a medical emergency. Every significant injury has the potential to lead to a state of shock. If this should occur, the trainer needs to realize that treating shock is the immediate priority and that the original injury can be treated once this problem is under control.

Shock can occur from

1. hemorrhage (internal or external)
2. pooling or stagnation of the blood flow

If the shock cycle is allowed to progress, serious and even irreversible changes may occur. The athletic trainer should attempt to prevent shock from occurring and, if it does develop, should treat it as follows (Figure 6.3):

1. If the injured athlete is conscious, respond in a confident, reassuring, and controlled manner.

2. Position the athlete correctly in view of other injuries that might be present. In general, the optimal position is *reclining with the feet higher than the head.* This position will allow available blood to perfuse the brain.

3. If bleeding is present, use the proper procedures to bring it under control.

4. Relieve or minimize the pain. For instance, if a fracture or fractures are present, adequate immobilization of the injured area will reduce the amount of pain.

5. Control heat loss, but do not actively warm the athlete, as the cutaneous blood vessels will dilate and remove much-needed blood from the vital organs.

SUMMARY—SHOCK TREATMENT

W–armth
A–irway
R–est
R–eassurance
M–echanical Aid

Anaphylactic Shock

Anaphylactic shock is triggered by contact with a substance that the individual has previously been exposed to and has developed antibodies against. With the antibodies present, contact with the offending agent will cause chemicals to be released within the body, resulting in a severe allergic response.

In athletics, the offending agent is usually an insect sting. However, the reaction might be due to sensitivity to certain foods or medications (oral or injected). The allergic reaction may be an inability to breathe because of a severely swollen air passage.

The attending athletic trainer needs to be especially aware of any athletes with known allergies. Signs and symptoms (see Chapter 5) that may be present are: difficult breathing, tightness and swelling of the throat, hives, nausea, abdominal cramps, and even unconsciousness.

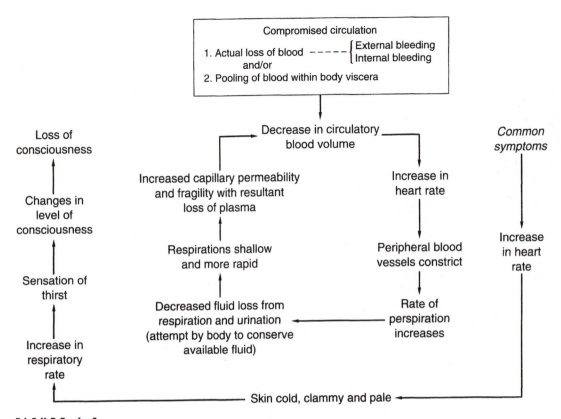

FIGURE 6.3
The shock cycle.
(Adapted from *Emergency Care and Transportation of the Sick and Injured,* American Academy of Orthopaedic Surgeons, 2nd ed. [Chicago, 1977]. Reprinted by permission of the publisher.)

Treatment of the involved athlete must be prompt, as severe complications may develop within minutes or even seconds. For a victim of anaphylactic shock there needs to be an emergency kit (syringe) of epinephrine (0.3 ml. epinephrine) available. In addition, CPR might be necessary. The victim needs to be closely monitored until transportation to a medical facility is completed.

The occurrence of anaphylactic shock is a life-threatening event. Death can occur by inability to breathe or insufficient circulation through the body.

Internal Injuries

THE THORACIC AREA: An injury to the thorax may result in damage to the lungs, possibly causing a *pneumothorax* (tearing of part of the lung, leading to the accumulation of air between the lung and the chest wall), a *hemothorax* (blood between the lung and the chest wall), or both.

The athlete will be short of breath and may cough up blood. The trainer should supply oxygen, place the athlete in a comfortable position (usually a semi-reclining, 45 degree position) and transport him or her to a medical facility. In addition, there is a possibility of a lung contusion if the athlete is coughing up pink, frothy blood.

Occasionally, contusions of the heart result in swelling of the pericardial sac, which will impair heart function. This is a dire emergency in which the athlete needs urgent medical attention.[9]

THE ABDOMINAL AREA: The most common serious abdominal injuries are to the spleen and kidneys. Rupture of the spleen[10] which could include symptoms of referred pain* may be indicated by Kehr's sign—pain of the left shoulder and upper arm. Suspicion might be registered if the athlete has had a recent

---

*Referred pain—pain in a part other than that in which the cause is produced or situated. Boyd[11] reports that pain relative to visceral injury has a tendency to irradiate and result in referred pain.

bout with mononucleosis, which leads to splenic enlargement and an increased chance of splenic rupture. The management of an injury to the abdominal area should include the possibility of (a) delayed splenic rupture and (b) contusion or rupture of the kidney, which might be expressed in the evidence of hematuria. Other organs, such as the liver, may also be involved.

For these types of injuries the initial signs and symptoms, besides abdominal pain, are those of early shock, especially a rapid pulse and decreased blood pressure. The athlete should be placed in a supine position, with padding beneath the knees to relax the abdominal musculature, and rapidly transported to a medical facility.

Medical Emergencies

Management of the Diabetic Emergency

Diabetes is a disease that affects the way in which the individual metabolizes carbohydrates. One of the hormones secreted from the pancreas, which regulates the rate and amount of glucose in the blood, is insulin. If insulin is not available in sufficient amounts and at the proper rate, an emergency situation may arise that can lead to coma and possibly death. There are basically two situations that can precipitate a diabetic emergency. The diabetic may have too much sugar in the blood (hyperglycemia), which can lead to diabetic coma, or the diabetic may have too little sugar in the blood (hypoglycemia), which can lead to insulin shock. Therefore, it

is important to know that the following events may precipitate a diabetic emergency:

1. The athlete has undiagnosed diabetes.
2. The athlete with diabetes has not taken required insulin injection.
3. The athlete with diabetes has overeaten.
4. The athlete with diabetes has an injury, illness, or stress that affects insulin levels.
5. The athlete with diabetes has taken too much insulin.

Management of the diabetic emergency is similar whether the problem is diabetic coma resulting from hyperglycemia or insulin shock resulting from hypoglycemia. The initial step is to provide sugar-containing food or drink. The athlete suffering from diabetic coma needs to be in a hospital for definitive care; the athlete suffering from insulin shock, on the other hand, should respond to the administration of sugar-containing food or drink within 10 to 15 minutes. If this does not occur, he or she needs to be taken to a hospital.

Some precautions must be taken before participation by the athlete with diabetes is allowed. It is imperative that, before the diabetic is allowed to be involved in physical activity, the diabetes must be under control. This means that the athlete must be cleared for activity by a physician. Also, the importance of hydration before activity begins needs to be constantly reinforced. This is especially true in cases where they may be participating in activities in conditions of high heat and humidity; the

TABLE 6.1   *Indicators of a diabetic emergency*

	Diabetic Coma	Insulin Shock
History	gradual onset	sudden onset
	extreme thirst	weakness
	frequent urination	sudden hunger
	abdominal pain	diplopia (double vision)
	vomiting	headache
	eventual stupor/unconsciousness	eventual stupor/unconsciousness
Sensory Observation	drowsiness	staggering, poor coordination
	flushed skin	anger, bad temper
	deep rapid breathing	pale color
	fruity or wine-like breath odor	sweating
		drooling
Palpation	rapid, weak pulse	normal pulse
Tests	decreased blood pressure	normal blood pressure

diabetic athlete is more prone to suffer from dehydration and subsequent heat illnesses.

Management of the Athlete with Epilepsy (Seizures)

Seizure disorder is a neurological disorder often referred to as epilepsy. It is characterized by occasional, temporary changes in the way electrical signals are conducted through the brain. Epileptic episodes are the result of a surge of electrical signals passing between brain cells which can affect a small area of the brain or involve the entire structure. The outward manifestation of these disruptive signals is evidenced by loss of body control, loss of consciousness, and possibly behavioral changes as well. These physical changes are referred to as an epileptic seizure.

Epileptic seizures are divided into two categories: convulsive (also known as tonic-clonic or grand mal seizures) and non-convulsive. The category of seizure taking place is determined by which area and how much of the brain is involved in the particular episode. Convulsive seizures usually last from two to five minutes and are characterized by complete loss of consciousness and uncontrolled muscle spasms. Non-convulsive seizures can be a blank stare lasting a few seconds, an uncontrolled twitching movement of an arm or leg, or even a period of unawareness of one's surroundings.

Several factors need to be considered prior to participation in athletic activity. Consider the nature of the activity and the environment in which it takes place. For instance, study the risks involved in contact versus non-contact sports, activities performed at great heights, and activities in a deep aquatic environment. The athlete must be honest about the rate of occurrence and severity of seizures, whether the seizures are adequately controlled by medication, and how motivated he or she is to participate in a particular activity.

The management of the epileptic emergency can be quite simple if the athletic trainer is prepared ahead of time to handle it. Quite often the epileptic seizure is preceded by an aura, which means the athlete has a sensation of a halo-like glow and possible hallucinations or a dream-like state. When this sensation begins, the athlete should inform the athletic trainer. The athletic trainer should be alert in observing this particular athlete during activity and should be aware of unusual behavior that may be signaling the start of an epileptic seizure (see Chapter 27).

Once the seizure begins it is important for the athletic trainer to remain calm and take the athlete to a safe area where the seizure can run its course without risk of further injury. The basic role for the trainer at this time is to monitor the athlete. Make sure that the airway remains open and the athlete's breathing is not being compromised in any way. This is best accomplished by having the athlete lie on his or her side and loosen any restrictive clothing. If possible, protect the athlete by putting a pillow under his or her head. Don't unnecessarily restrict the athlete's movement unless there is a chance of further injury. Make a note (mental or otherwise) of the time at which the seizure started, so that the duration of the seizure can be reported to the athlete's physician. Be available to reassure the athlete as he or she begins to regain consciousness. Hospitalization is required only if there are multiple seizures, if one seizure lasts longer than ten minutes, or if there has been injury to the athlete during the seizure. Regardless of the type or length of seizure, the athlete should always be given the option of going to the hospital.

Superficial Bleeding

In athletics, serious bleeding from superficial wounds is an uncommon, but potentially significant injury.[12] Various types of superficial wounds include:

1.   L–Lacerations. The skin and deeper tissues are cut, torn, or both.

2.   I–Incised wounds. The edges of the skin or mucous membranes are smooth and bleed freely as determined by the number and size.

3.   P–Puncture wounds. Sharp and deeply penetrating the skin.

4.   S–Special wounds—Example abrasions. The outer layer of the skin is scraped or abraded away.

The athletic trainer can usually control bleeding by means of a dressing and direct pressure over the wound. In addition, cold can be applied (but not to the unconscious athlete) and the body part elevated if possible. If there are serious bleeding problems not controlled by the simple measures mentioned here, the trainer should consider pressure to the supplying artery.

HIV infection and transmission as it relates to the athlete and the attending athletic trainer need to be reviewed and discussed.[13,14,15,16,17] Although bleeding from an open wound carries a risk of transmission, this it is regarded as a minimal risk. Other methods of transmission are:

1.   Sexual activity with exchange of semen and/or vaginal and cervical secretions.

2.   Blood transfusions (blood not sufficiently screened).

3. Puncture wounds by contaminated needles and other sharp objects.

Since participants in sports are subject to the same rules of HIV infection as an individual in the general population, there needs to be an awareness of transmission to the health provider. Therefore the athletic trainer should:

1. Wear waterproof gloves for direct contact with another individual's blood or body fluids. Change gloves after treating each individual.

2. Wash hands with soap and water after removing gloves.

3. Wash off any blood or body fluid that contacts the skin of the care provider with an antiseptic or soapy water.

4. If an athlete or care provider is at risk of an HIV viral infection, contact a physician as soon as possible to assess the situation and initiate appropriate action.

The athletic trainer needs to be aware of:

1. Federal and state OSHA standards pertaining to the exposure to blood and other potentially infectious materials and the disposal of these materials.

2. NCAA (or other appropriate governing agencies or conferences) rules and regulations dealing with removing athletes from contests with open wounds and/or blood-stained uniforms.

3. Individual institutional guidelines.

Fractures

Fractures (Figure 6.4) can be:

1. *Closed*—The bone is broken, but the skin is not damaged.

2. *Open (compound)*—There is an associated open wound in the area of the fracture. The fractured bone may or may not be visible.

A fracture can be caused by a number of different forces.

1. *Direct force*—The bone is broken at the site of the force.

2. *Indirect force*—Trauma is inflicted at a distance from the resulting fracture. An example of this is falling on the outstretched hand and sustaining a fracture of the clavicle.

3. *Avulsion force*—A portion of the bone is pulled off by the attached muscle, tendon, or ligament.

If a fracture is present, the main features are

1. Unnatural mobility of the part
2. Deformity
3. Local tenderness over the bone
4. Crepitation

The early management of a closed fracture consists of applying a splint or some form of immobilization.

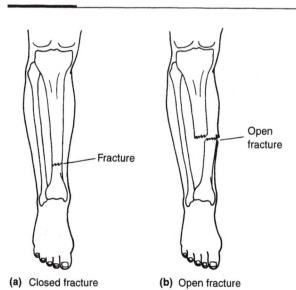

(a) Closed fracture   (b) Open fracture

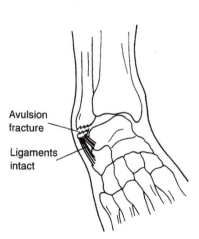

(c) Avulsion fracture

FIGURE 6.4
Types of fractures

Immobilization will reduce the pain, protect the underlying blood vessels and nerves from further damage, and reduce the likelihood of shock.

When dealing with an open fracture, the trainer needs to cover the wound with a sterile dressing and control the bleeding. The fracture should then be immobilized and elevated if possible.

Prompt medical attention should always be obtained when a fracture is suspected.

Splinting Techniques

There are a variety of splints that can be utilized:

1. Ordinary wooden splints, preferably padded

2. Improvised materials substituting for wooden splints (e.g.. cardboard or rolled-up papers or magazines)

3. Commercially available disposable and reuseable splints (e.g., SAM splint).

4. Pneumatic or air splints (*Caution:* This type of split should not be overinflated, as this may impair the circulation and the nerve supply to the toes or the fingers). When utilizing this method, care should be taken to leave toes and fingers exposed so that circulation can be more easily monitored

5. Vacuum splints

Vacuum Splint

A vacuum splint (see Figure 6.5) is a nylon sleeve that is shaped to fit one of the limbs or the cervical spine area. A vacuum splint differs from an air splint in one important way: whereas an air splint has air blown into it to stiffen it and splint the body part, a vacuum splint uses a hand pump to draw air out of the splint and create a vacuum within the splint. As the vacuum is created, small styrofoam beads inside the splint are pulled tightly together to form a solid, rigid structure that conforms precisely to the covered body part. The major advantage of using a vacuum splint as opposed to an air splint is that the vacuum splint does not exert circumferential pressure on the body part, thereby reducing the risk of occluding blood flow to the area (Figure 6.5).

SPLINTING TERMINOLOGY:

1. Traction—the act of exerting a pulling force

2. Immobilize—to restrict, stop, or control the normal motion of a joint

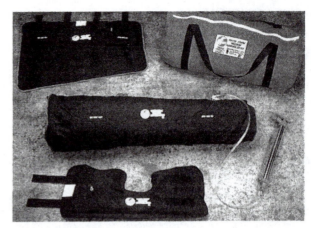

FIGURE 6.5
Vacuum splint
(*Source:* Cramer Products, Inc. Gardner, Kansas. Printed with permission.)

3. Stabilize—to hold in place (usually a temporary procedure) until immobilizing and splinting are feasible

4. Alignment—return of a bone or joint that has been deformed to its normal anatomical position in relationship to other structures.

FRACTURE OF THE HUMERUS:

Splints. Two padded wooden or improvised-material splints (Figure 6.6).

Technique. Holding the elbow at 90°, place the shorter padded splint on inner surface of upper arm; the longer padded splint, on outer surface.

Position. Arm against chest, hold in position with two cravats. The forearm is supported in a narrow sling suspended from the neck.

Alternative. Air splint; vacuum splint.

FRACTURE OF THE FOREARM:

Splints. Two padded wooden splints or improvised-material splints (Figure 6.7).

Technique. With splints in palm-down position, apply inside splint from elbow to palm; outside splint, from elbow to backs of fingers. Utilize two cravats to fix splints in place (one above and one below the fracture). Hold arm across chest with cravat sling.

Alternative. Air splint; vacuum splint.

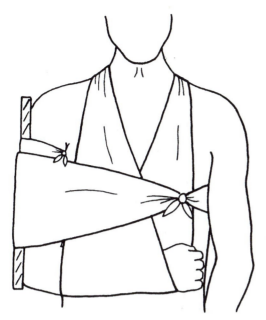

FIGURE 6.6
Emergency splinting for a fractured humerus

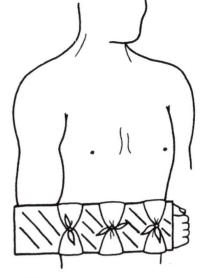

FIGURE 6.7
Emergency splinting for a fractured forearm

FRACTURE OF THE WRIST:

Splint. Padded wooden or folded-newspaper or magazine splint.

Technique. Place wrist onto splint and wrap in place with bandage or elastic wrap.

Special Consideration. The trainer needs to be aware of the differential diagnosis of a suspected wrist fracture (see Chapter 15).

FIGURE 6.8
Emergency splinting for a fracture of the metacarpals

FRACTURE OF THE HAND (METACARPALS):

Splint. Rolled bandage (Figure 6.8).

Technique. Place rolled bandage in palm of hand and wrap in place with another rolled bandage or elastic wrap. Secure the fingers of the affected metacarpals to the adjacent fingers.

FRACTURE OF THE FINGERS:

Splint. Padded tongue depressor or padded aluminum splint (Figure 6.9).

Technique. Place splint from palm to past the end of the finger, and wrap loosely in place (Figure 6.9). Secure the adjacent finger or fingers to the affected finger for added support.

FIGURE 6.9
Emergency splinting for a fractured finger

FRACTURE OF THE FEMUR:

Splints. Two padded wooden splints four to six inches wide, one long and one short.

Technique. Place the longer splint on the outside (lateral) surface of the leg, extending from the axilla to the heel. The shorter splint should extend from the groin to the heel on the inside (medial) surface of the leg. Use seven to eight cravats to secure the splints in place (Figure 6.10).

FRACTURE OF THE PATELLA:

Splint. Four-to-six inch well-padded wooden splint.

Technique. The splint should reach from the buttock to below the heel. Place it under the leg and secure it by four to six cravats. The patella should be left exposed. The knee should be kept straight (extended).

FRACTURE OF THE LOWER LEG:

Splints. Two padded wooden splints four to six inches wide, one long and one short (Figure 6.11).

Technique. Place the longer splint on the lateral surface of the leg, extending from the upper thigh to the heel. The shorter splint should extend from the groin to the heel on the medial surface of the leg. Use four to five cravats to secure the splints in place.

Alternative. Air splint, extending from the upper thigh to the foot; vacuum splint.

FRACTURE NEAR THE ANKLE (TIBIA, FIBULA, OR BOTH):

Splints. Two padded wooden splints four to six inches wide.

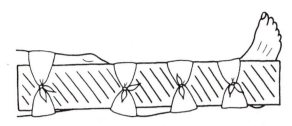

FIGURE 6.11
Emergency splinting for a fractured lower leg or ankle

Technique. Place the longer splint on the lateral surface of the leg from the upper thigh to the heel. The shorter splint extends from the groin to the heel on the inner surface of the leg. Use four to five cravats to secure the splints in place and be sure the foot is secured.

Alternative. Air splint extending from below the knee to the foot.

FRACTURE OF THE FOOT (TARSALS AND METATARSALS):

Splint. Padded, right-angled splint.

Technique. Place the splint onto the posterior aspect of the lower leg and foot, extending to the ball of the foot, and secure it in place with four to five cravats.

Alternative.

1. Ankle air splint
2. Four well-padded splints, secured so little or no movement can take place at the ankle joint

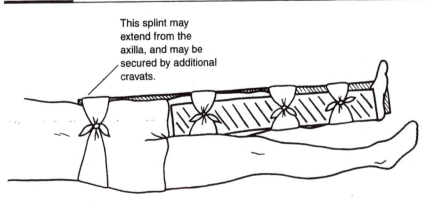

This splint may extend from the axilla, and may be secured by additional cravats.

FIGURE 6.10
Emergency splinting for a fractured femur

FRACTURE OF THE CERVICAL SPINE:

Splint. Cervical spine board.

Technique. The handling of an injury to the cervical spine is discussed in the section on neck injuries, and in the section on stretchers at the end of this chapter.

   Note: An athlete with an injury to the cervical spine or evidence of cord compression should be moved only by personnel adequately trained to handle this type of injury, preferably under the supervision of a physician.

FRACTURE OF THE THORACIC OR THE LUMBAR SPINE

Splint. Long spine board.

Technique. The handling of the thoracic or the lumbar spinal injury is discussed in the section on stretchers at the end of this chapter.

   Note: An athlete with a thoracic or a lumbar fracture should be moved only by personnel adequately trained to handle this type of injury, preferably under the supervision of a physician.

SUMMARY—GENERAL GUIDELINES FOR SPLINTING

1. Manage the fracture very carefully to prevent a simple fracture from becoming a compound fracture. Consider the victim's comfort in order to avoid shock.

2. Immobilize joints proximal and distal to the fracture site.

3. Tie the splint, if appropriate, above and below the fracture site.

Dislocations

A dislocation is a displacement of a bone from its joint and usually involves an injury to the capsule and the ligaments. Sometimes the dislocation may involve the articular surface and the tearing of muscles and tendons.

   The following general symptoms and signs are associated with a dislocation:

1. Deformity of the joint (sometimes fixed or "locked" in the deformed position)

2. Pain, especially with movement

3. Inability to use the joint

   The initial management of the dislocation consists of immobilizing or splinting the involved joint and extremity. Attempts to reduce the dislocation should be performed by a physician. It is important to realize that an improper or ill-advised attempt to reduce a dislocation may cause additional tearing of ligaments, muscles, or tendons, or injury to blood vessels and nerves.

Soft-Tissue Injuries

Soft-tissue injuries include:

1. Contusion—injury to tissues without breakage of skin; a bruise
2. Strain—injury to a musculotendinous tissue
3. Sprain—injury to a ligament

Although most soft-tissue injuries do not fall into the life-threatening category, there is still a need to apply the correct athletic first-aid procedure to minimize the extent of the injury and effect a quick and complete recovery. Most soft-tissue injuries are treated by the standard formula of I.C.E plus S^2 (Figure 6.12).

ICE OR COLD APPLICATION: The application of cold[19] is a very important first-aid procedure. Cold is used in the acute soft-tissue injury because it decreases the metabolism of the injured tissues, thereby reducing the need for oxygen at a time when there may be a limited amount available at the cellular level (secondary hypoxic syndrome). A possible increase in the viscosity of the blood may reduce the blood flow into the injured area, thus reducing the extent of the internal bleeding. The analgesic effect reduces the pain, and the stretching in combination with ice may reduce the pain–spasm–pain vicious cycle (see Fig. 6.13). Various types of cold application include:

1. *Ice*—Place crushed ice in a double plastic bag, a wet towel, or a conventional ice bag. Use an elastic wrap that

---

I.C.E. *plus* S^2

I = *ice* (cold) application
C = *compression*
E = *elevation* of the affected limb if applicable
S^2 = *stabilization* or protection of the original injury from additional trauma
gentle *stretching* of the injured area over ice if applicable

FIGURE 6.12

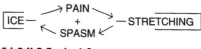

FIGURE 6.13

has been presoaked in cold water to hold the ice in position. The time schedule for the ice application depends on the type and severity of the injury, but twenty to thirty minutes every hour for the first twentyfour hours is a good rule of thumb.

2. *Chemical cold pack*—Although many varieties of cold packs are available, their ability to lower the temperature of the deeper soft tissues is limited[9], and their use should be restricted to emergency situations where there are no other options.

3. *Inflatable (pressure) cold devices*—Combination units may be very useful in initial and subsequent management of soft-tissue injury of the extremities.

4. *Ethyl chloride and related chemical sprays*—Sprays are used in soft-tissue injury, particularly when it is accompanied by muscle spasm. These sprays must be applied cautiously because skin damage from freezing may occur.

COMPRESSION: Compression is usually accompanied by application of an elastic wrap, which can first be soaked in cold water to aid the cooling process. A dry elastic wrap has insulation properties and may counteract the effect of cold. There are a variety of commercial devices that can achieve a combination of compression and cold and may be very useful in treating the acute injury.

Since an injury disrupts the fluid balance within the body, the application of compression and elevation can be utilized to reestablish homeostasis in the body fluid balance system.

ELEVATION: Elevation is most applicable to an extremity. Where practical, the involved part should be elevated higher than the heart for much of the first twenty-four hours following injury. Elevation works mainly by limiting the amount of dependent edema and swelling that can occur after an injury.

STABILIZATION: Placing the injured tissue in a protective situation will encourage healing by first "intention," which then will minimize the amount of scar tissue formation. In addition, the effect of the reflex inhibition may also be reduced. Stabilization could also include placing the tissue in a gentle stretch position over ice, if applicable.

Other Emergency Care Information

Crutch Fitting

While there are a variety of crutches available, the axillary adjustable (wooden or aluminum) crutch is most commonly used. The method of adjusting or fitting the crutch to the individual includes these steps:

1.   Have the athlete stand erect, place the crutch tips about six inches away from the sides of the feet and slightly in front of the toes (Figure 6.14).

2.   Adjust the length of the crutches so that two or three fingers can fit between the top of the crutch and the axilla.

3.   Adjust the handgrip so as to permit the elbow to bend 25° to 30° (Figure 6.15).

GAIT INSTRUCTION: While there are a number of gaits, the *three-point* or *featherweight-bearing* gait is the one most applicable to the athlete and most commonly used. It is important for the athlete to attempt to

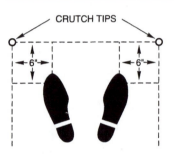

FIGURE 6.14
Fitting Position

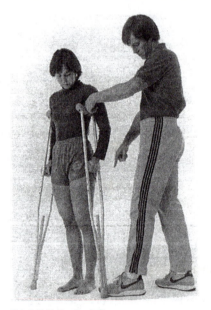

FIGURE 6.15
Fitting crutches

go through the action of a normal gait motion without actually putting weight on the affected limb. Not only does this maintain relative flexibility of the ankle joint and Achilles tendon, but more importantly, it allows proprioceptive contact to be maintained so that the sensory system does not "switch off" the affected limb.

The three-point gait permits controlled weight bearing. The athlete should

1. Place both crutches and the involved limb forward at the same time

2. Push down against the handles of the crutches as his or her weight shifts forward (bringing the body forward as the hands push down). Do not allow the top of the crutches to press into the axillae. Most of the weight is taken on the crutches, but a controlled amount is taken on the affected limb. The athlete should attempt a normal heel-to-toe movement, not allowing the affected foot to be maintained in a position of plantar flexion

3. Move the uninvolved foot through, and step ahead of, the crutches

If the affected limb is immobilized in a cast and no weight bearing is prescribed, the athlete should

1. Move the crutches forward together, one to a position about twelve inches in front, and the other six inches to the side, of the toes

2. Push down against the handles of the crutches

3. Permit the body to swing through between the crutches

4. Land in front of the crutches and on the heel of the uninvolved foot

5. If the involved leg is not in a cast and weight bearing is not allowed, the athlete should not plantar flex the ankle but dorsiflex the foot as the leg is brought forward, without taking any weight on that foot.

Ascending stairs: First lift the healthy leg up a step, then follow with the injured leg *and* the crutches.

Descending stairs: Lower the crutches *and* the injured leg first, then follow by lowering the healthy leg (Figure 6.16).

Stretcher Use

Stretchers[10] and spine boards should be readily available during any athletic activity, but particularly during contact and high-risk sports such as football, wrestling, rugby, lacrosse, and gymnastics.

The scoop stretcher has become popular, because the athlete does not have to be moved and is easily secured to the stretcher. When using this type, one must be careful not to pinch the patient or catch clothing

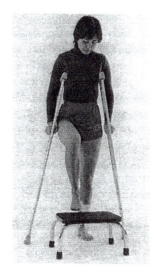

(a)	**(b)**

FIGURE 6.16
Crutch walking:
(a) Ascending stairs (b) Descending stairs

between the halves of the stretcher as it is closed together (Figure 6.17).

Any sports-medicine team needs to prepare for the emergency transportation of an athlete from the scene of play. Practice drills should be set up and a team leader appointed to be in charge of deciding the timing of the lift, the placement of the personnel, and the control of the injured part.

The stretcher is most commonly used in athletics to remove a player with an ankle or knee injury from the scene of participation to the sidelines. Placing the

FIGURE 6.17
The Army-type stretcher (above) and the scoop stretcher (below)

athlete on a stretcher is usually easily accomplished with this type of injury. The injured joint or limb should be adequately supported by the leader as the athlete is placed onto the stretcher. The athlete can either roll onto the unaffected side with the stretcher placed underneath, and then roll back onto the stretcher, the injured limb supported by the team leader; or, other players, trainers, or bystanders can help lift the player as the stretcher is placed underneath. The player is then gently lowered onto the stretcher while the injured extremity is carefully supported. If a fracture is suspected, the limb should be splinted before the player is moved. If circumstances permit, an injured knee should be placed into a postoperative knee immobilizer before the athlete is placed upon the stretcher.

When moving an unconscious player, or one who is suspected of having a cervical, thoracic, or lumbar spine injury, special care needs to be taken. A short or, preferably, a long spine board is used. The player is placed onto the spine board as one solid unit while the head, shoulders, pelvis, and legs are controlled under the direction of the leader (see Chapter 16). The spine board is then placed in position and the athlete rolled back onto it and secured to it (Figure 6.18).

THE INTEGRITY OF THE SPINE MUST BE PROTECTED—USE THE BACKBOARD.

As mentioned, if an athlete has a cervical, thoracic, or lumbar spine injury, he or she should only be moved by personnel adequately trained to handle this type of injury, preferably under the supervision of a physician. This may mean a delay in the athletic event, but the player's health and well-being must be the prime consideration.

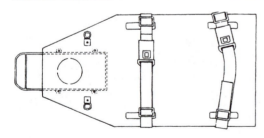

FIGURE 6.18

Cervical spine board.

(Modified from Joseph S. Torg, Theodore C. Quedenfeld and William Newell, "When the athlete's life is threatened," *The Physician and Sports Medicine* 3:54–67, March 1975. Reproduced by permission of the publisher, McGraw-Hill Book Company, and courtesy of William Newell, Purdue University.)

Medical Emergency Plan

Every sponsoring athletic organization needs to develop a medical emergency plan.[20] This document should provide direction for each staff member in determining the appropriate course of action when responding to an injured athlete. In addition, this evidence of advanced planning could prove valuable in any legal action(s) that might ensue. Developing a plan concerned with medical emergencies requires consideration of four broad areas. These include: prevention, training and education, communication, and on-site injury management.

Prevention

The area of prevention seems self-evident. It is much better to prevent an emergency situation than to have to deal with it after the fact. With some thought, planning, and careful implementation, much can be accomplished that is very worthwhile in the area of prevention.

Some areas to be considered in preventing emergency situations include: the players, the sport, the external environment, and the health support system.

Assessment of the players involves factors such as the size of the players in terms of height, weight, relative body composition, and the range of these factors among the players.

- Are bigger people competing against smaller people?
- What is the skill level of these players, considered both as a group and as individuals?
- What is the level of conditioning (in terms of strength, endurance, power, flexibility, aerobic/anerobic conditioning) of the group and the individual?
- What level of conditioning is required to compete safely in this sport and at this level of competition?
- What is the physical and emotional maturity level of the group and the individual?

Consideration of these factors can help in creating policies that determine safe participation levels in various athletic activities. Additionally, questions need to be asked about the specific nature of each sport:

- Is body contact involved in this sport?
- Is the body contact incidental to the play or is it an inherent part of the play action?
- Does the body contact occur at the head, neck, or trunk?

- What are the chances the body contact would cause the player to be knocked down with the risk of landing on his/her head, neck, or trunk?

- Other than body contact, is there any action or situation that might arise during play that could cause a player to lose balance with a risk of landing on his/her head, neck, or trunk?

- At what speed is this sport played? Are impact forces great or minimal?

- Can the magnitude of impact forces be compensated for by use of protective equipment or by controlling the environment around the playing area?

- Are the use of implements and projectiles an integral part of this sport?

The greater the number of affirmative answers to the above questions, the more planning must go into controlling and eliminating hazards wherever feasible, and preparing to manage an emergency situation.

Evaluation of the external environment includes factors such as playing surface, designated structures, non-playing areas, lighting, air quality, and extremes of climate (e.g., heat, cold, humidity, smog, rain, snow, sleet, wind, lightning). All of these factors need to be accounted for and a plan developed to modify or postpone the athletic activity as necessary.

The health (medical) support system is an integral part of the emergency prevention program. It is extremely important to be aware of medical conditions among the athletes under supervision. A thorough preseason medical exam is crucial to being prepared to cope with potential emergencies. This information, although confidential in nature, should be disseminated to personnel working with the athlete. Also, some type of medical information card or sheet for each athlete must be available at the competition site, whether at home or away.

The medical examination is also used as a screening device to protect athletes at risk for serious injuries from participating in potentially dangerous activities. This is a legitimate and necessary use of the information gathered and should not be viewed as an infringement of the individual athlete's rights.

Training/Education

Generally in the athletic situation, the resident expert and manager of medical emergencies is the certified athletic trainer. It is the athletic trainer's responsibility to have sufficient and appropriate education in emergency medical protocol, and to have designated, trained personnel to assist with a medical emergency.

Any and all athletic staff (e.g., coaches, managers, student trainers) who have direct contact with and responsibility for athletes need to have at least rudimentary knowledge of first aid and cardiopulmonary resuscitation techniques. These people, minimally, need to be able to differentiate between a life-threatening and non-life-threatening emergency. It is very prudent for athletic staff members to be certified at the basic level in first aid and CPR, and to maintain that level of certification.

Communication

The most critical factor in managing emergency medical situations is communication. The hub of the communication wheel quite often is the athletic trainer, who is usually the first person on the scene in an emergency. Figure 6.19 provides a summary of communication management in an athletic emergency.

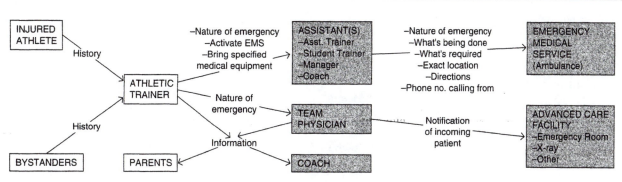

FIGURE 6.19

Managing communication in a medical emergency in the athletic situation
(*Source*: Donald F. Mattern, A.T.C., Athletic Trainer, University of Lethbridge.)

Other considerations for expediting and facilitating communications in an emergency situation might include:

- The use of walkie-talkies among the athletic trainer, the assistants on the bench, the team physician, and the visiting trainer.
- The use of a cellular phone, which is kept on the bench with whoever is in charge of emergency equipment. The phone could be preprogrammed with the numbers for EMS, hospital emergency room, X-ray, and so on. The cellular phone could also be equipped with a speed dialer.
- The use of an emergency checklist, completed before each athletic event and signed by both host and visiting athletic trainers to ensure complete understanding of procedures by both parties in case of emergency.

On-Site Injury Management

Competent management of injury situations begins with effective supervision of the activity. Being a good athletic trainer comes with experience. It involves knowing the sport, the demands it makes on the players, the skills necessary to play, the potential areas for injury, and types and severities of injuries to be expected. Good management also involves knowing the athletes, their level of conditioning at the particular point of the season, how they react to injuries within the game–both their own and those of their teammates, and what each athlete is like as a person.

In order to develop this kind of knowledge, it is important to initiate injury profiles for each sport. This will help identify the who, what, where, and when of injuries occuring in that sport. It follows that keeping an injury profile for each sport requires an accurate, consistent injury reporting system.

The knowledge gained by keeping accurate injury profiles facilitates improved injury management. Also, an injury profile aids in choosing the type and amount of emergency medical equipment required for each sport and determining whether that equipment needs to be on-site or merely available.

In conclusion, it is always possible for injuries to occur in athletic events.[21] Those in a position of responsibility need to anticipate injuries and be prepared to provide appropriate care for the athletes. An emergency care plan needs to take into consideration the level of training and the competence of the designated injury care provider. A thorough understanding of the emergency care plan needs to be demonstrated by those attending to the needs of the injured athlete. To what-

ever degree is feasible, for each situation and/or level of competition, an appropriate emergency care/accident procedure plan needs to be formulated. (See the following example of a medical emergency plan, courtesy of Charles Fisher, Intramural Director, Oregon State University.)

EXAMPLE: ON-SITE MEDICAL EMERGENCY PLAN—INTRAMURAL SITUATION

1. Emergency/first aid—The minimum of first aid equipment is available to each sport supervisor.

   a. Bags of ice
   b. First-aid kit (containing band-aids, gauze pads, tape, rubber gloves, and a clean towel)
   c. When the supervisor notices the supplies are getting low, he or she should inform the equipment supervisor to replace them.

2. General plan of action when a participant is injured and either campus police or an ambulance is needed.
   NOTE: Campus police will transport students only—and *not* faculty/staff members or non-students—to the health center.

   a. Quickly assess the situation and provide treatment within your first-aid training capabilities.
   b. If a radio is available, call the intramural office. If no answer, call for base station. If only a telephone is available, call campus police directly.
   c. Explain the nature and extent of the injury. If an ambulance is needed clearly state, "We need an ambulance."
   d. Relay the specific location of the injured person(s).
   e. Briefly describe the nature of the injury and the number of injured people needing assistance.
   f. State the name of the injured person *or* the name of the person in charge at the injury site.
   g. After the injured person has been attended to, collect information to complete the "game site" portion (front side) of the accident report form.
   h. Return the accident form to the office with the scorecards and supervisor's report.
   i. An accident follow up will be conducted by the office personnel.

3. If the radio communication system is unavailable:

   a. The supervisor should stay with the injured participant at all times and provide treatment within their first-aid capabilities.

b. Direct a game official or bystander to telephone campus police.

c. Before that person leaves, provide as much information as is available for the action plan listed above. If possible, send two individuals to make the telephone call.

d. After the injured person has been attended to, complete the accident form.

Those involved in athletic health care need to be aware that when medical emergencies and/or life threatening injuries are mismanaged, serious negative consequences are possible.

Be prepared for any possible medical emergency and provide the highest level of care for each athlete.

REFERENCES

1. American Heart Association : Guidelines for cardiopulmonary resuscitation and emergency cardiac care (Recommendations of the 1992 National Conference). *JAMA:* 268:16, 2171–2302, October 28, 1992.

2. Thygerson A: *First Aid and Emergency Care Workbook,* Boston: Jones and Bartlett Publishers, pp. 193–215, 217–235, 1982.

3. Torg JS, Quedenfeld TC, Newell W: When the athletes life is threatened. *Phys Sports med* 3:54–60, March 1975.

4. Putman LA: Alternative methods for football helmet facemask removal (Tip from the field). *Athletic Training* 27:2, 170–172, 1992.

5. Partin N: New emergency care guidelines. *NATA News* 24–25, January 1993.

6. Clover J, Baker D: Removing football face masks (Letters to the editor). *Athletic Training* 27:3,198, 1992.

7. Stephenson MD, Ray R, Ortolani A: Helmets and face masks (Letters to the editor). *Athletic Training* 27:4, 294–295.

8. Rehlerg RS: Football helmets: to remove or not to remove . . . should there be a question. *NATA News* 4–6, 1993.

9. Wilder PE: Thoracic injuries: mechanics, characteristics, management. *Athletic Training* 26:230–234, 1988.

10. Loomis JL, Johnson A, Hochberg WJ, et al.: Equipment update: Penn State's foldable rigid stretcher. *Phys Sportsmed* 7:135–136, October 1979.

11. Boyd CE: Refocused visceral pain in athletics. *Athletic Training* 20–25, Spring 1980.

12. Webster DJ, Kaiser DA: An infection control policy for the athletic setting. *Athletic Training* 26:12, 70–74, Spring 1991.

13. Position Statement: HIV as it relates to sport: *Canadian Academy of Sport Medicine,* April 1992.

14. World Health Organization Consensus Statement: Consultation on AIDS and sports. *Journal of American Medical Association* 267(10):1312,1992.

15. When sports and HIV share the bill, smart money goes on common sense. *JAMA* 267(10):1311–1314, 1992.

16. Aids and intercollegiate athletics. *NCAA Sports Medicine Handbook.* (NCAA, 6201 College Boulevard, Overland Park, Kansas 66211-2422).

17. American Academy of Pediatrics: Human immunodeficiency virus [acquired immunodeficiency syndrome (AIDS) virus] in the athletic setting. *Pediatrics* 88(3): 640–641,1991.

18. Heckman JD: Fractures-emergency care and complications. *Clin Symposium* 43:3, 2–32, 1991.

19. Wilkenson GB: Treatment of the inversion ankle sprain through synchronous application of focal compression and cold. *Athletic Training* 26:220–234, Fall 1991.

20. Harris AJ: Disaster plan—a part of the game plan. *Athletic Training* 232:1, 59, 1988.

21. Booher JA, Thibodeau, GA: *Athletic Injury Assessment.* St. Louis: Times Mirror/Mosby College Publishing, 2nd edition, 1989.

RECOMMENDED READINGS

Compton R: The four "S" shoulder wrap. *Athletic Training* 12:94–96, 1977.

Elam JO, Greene DG: Mission accomplished: successful mouth-to-mouth resuscitation. *Anesth Analg.* 40:578–580, 1961.

Elam JO, Greene DG, Schneider MA, et al: Head-tilt method of oral resuscitation. *JAMA* 172:812–815, 1960.

Guildner CW: Resuscitation—opening the airway: a comparative study of techniques for opening an airway obstructed by the tongue. *JACEP* 5:588–590, 1976.

Moore R: Emergency medical care of athletic injuries. *Emergency* 3:184–186, 1975.

Ruben H: The immediate treatment of respiratory failure. *Br J Anaesth* 36:542–549, 1964.

Ruben HM, Elam JO, Ruben AM, Greene DG: Investigation of upper airway problems in resuscitation: studies of pharyngeal x-rays and performance by laymen. *Anesthesiology* 22:271–279, 1961.

Safar P: Ventilatory efficacy of mouth-to-mouth artificial respiration: airway obstruction during manual and mouth-to-mouth artificial respiration. *JAMA* 167:335–341, 1958.

Safar P, Escarraga LA, Chang F: Upper airway obstruction in the unconscious patient. *J Appl Physiol* 14:760–764, 1959.

Smith WS: Esophogeal airway—an alternative to mouth-to-mouth. *Athletic Training* 14:38–39, 1979.

Therapeutic Modalities and Procedures

Hippocrates, recognized as the founder of medicine, who lived from 460 to 370 B.C., wrote, "Healing is a matter of time, but it is also a matter of opportunity." Over the centuries, medical practitioners have used numerous techniques and devices in their efforts to enhance the opportunities for healing of musculoskeletal injuries. These techniques and procedures ranged from the practical to the bizarre, including medicinal uses of massage with specially-formulated herbs and oils, hot water mineral baths, blood-letting with leeches, and the topical application of a variety of poultices (e.g., mud, rhinoceros dung, epsom salts).

Since the discovery of electricity, a wide variety of modalities have been developed which use different forms of electromagnetic and acoustic energy. These therapeutic devices have been used by physical medicine practitioners to treat the five principal physical signs and symptoms associated with a significant musculoskeletal injury or inflammatory condition: pain (*dolor*), edema (*tumor*), increased local tissue temperature (*calor*), skin redness (*rubor*), and loss of function (*functio laesa*).

Currently, many different therapeutic modalities are available to facilitate removal of these physical barriers to healing. When deciding which modality is appropriate for use in the treatment of a given musculoskeletal ailment, the clinician must consider the known physiologic effects produced by that modality. Each therapeutic modality is thought to produce a particular set of physiologic effects, and the sports medicine clinician must have the desired outcome in mind when selecting among the various devices and treatment protocols. Unfortunately, the means by which

some modalities achieve a therapeutic benefit is not completely understood and in some cases is theoretical. Thus, the appropriateness of such treatments remains controversial. These issues will be addressed in discussions of individual modalities within this chapter.

After obtaining all necessary subjective and objective information from the athlete and making an assessment regarding the nature and severity of a particular musculoskeletal problem, either by oneself or through physician referral, a treatment plan must be formulated. The treatment plan includes short-term, intermediate, and long-term goals, with the ultimate goal being pain-free movement and the complete restoration of functional ability.[1]

Exercise is perhaps the optimal therapeutic modality, given its portability and low cost. Therapeutic exercise of appropriate duration, frequency, and intensity facilitates healing through increases in blood flow, metabolic rate, and nutrients delivered to the site of injury. Often the severity of the injury prevents the athlete from performing voluntary activity. In these cases, therapeutic modalities such as electrical muscle stimulation or continuous passive motion are used to produce physiological and biomechanical responses similar to those which would occur with exercise.

Every treatment plan involving therapeutic modalities must also include phase-of-injury-appropriate therapeutic exercises. The healing process associated with a musculoskeletal injury or inflammatory condition has three distinct phases or stages: an acute phase, a subacute phase, and a chronic phase (Table 7.1). While the ultimate goal of treatment with therapeutic modalities is the complete restoration of function, there are numerous short-term and intermediate goals which should be identified. For each particular phase of healing there are specific goals to be achieved. For example, in the *acute phase*

TABLE 7.1 *Three phases of healing: acute, subacute, and chronic*

	Acute Stage *Inflammatory-Reaction*	Subacute Stage *Repair and Healing*	Chronic Stage *Maturation and Remodeling*
Characteristics	Vascular changes Exudation of cells and chemicals Clot formation Phagocytosis, neutralization of irritants Early fibroblastic activity	Removal of noxious stimuli Growth of capillary beds into area Collagen formation Granulation tissue Very fragile, easily injured tissue	Maturation of connective tissue Contracture of scar tissue Remodeling of scar Collagen aligns to stress
Clinical Signs	Inflammation Pain before tissue resistance	Decreasing inflammation Pain synchronous with tissue resistance	Absence of inflammation Pain after tissue resistance

Treatment Approach	Control effects of inflammation:
	  Modalities
	  Immobilization
	Cautious gentle movement
		Prevent or minimize contracture and adhesion formation:
		  Gentle active movement, gradually increasing in intensity and range
			Restore function:
			  Progressive stretching, strengthening, and functional exercises

Source: C Kisner, LA Colby, *Therapeutic Exercise: Foundations and Techniques,* 2d ed., Philadelphia, F. A. Davis, 1990, p. 215.

(the first 24 to 72 hours after a traumatic injury), the main objectives are to control pain and internal hemorrhaging, and to limit the extent of the inflammatory response. Later, in the *subacute phase* (approximately 3 to 7 days post-injury), appropriate treatment goals include edema reduction and the prevention of muscle atrophy. For more severe injuries (e.g., fractures requiring lengthy periods of immobilization), prevention of contractures and muscle re-education are important clinical goals. Since healing collagenous tissues continue to mature and remodel for 6 to 12 months following injury, appropriate levels of mechanical stress upon these tissues during the *chronic phase* of healing is vital.[2]

The Applied Physics of Therapeutic Modalities

Two basic types of energy used to create the healing effects associated with therapeutic modalities: electromagnetic and acoustic. *Electromagnetic* energy is a constant in our daily lives and is produced by a variety of sources, the most common source emanating from our solar system. All forms of electromagnetic energy travel through space at the same velocity, but differ in their effects and appearance due to an inverse relationship between their frequencies and wavelengths (Figure 7.1). The electromagnetic energy spectrum, first defined in 1934, encompasses the entire range of wavelengths and frequencies of electromagnetic energy, ranging from radio waves (longest) to gamma rays (shortest), and includes visible light.[3] Specific to non-ionizing radiation and therapeutic modalities, the longer the wavelength emitted by a device, the greater the depth of penetration of its energy into human tissues.[4]

Electromagnetic energy requires no medium for transmission, and therefore may be transmitted through the earth's atmosphere, human tissues, or in a vacuum. The transmission of energy in the form of heat involves the exchange of kinetic energy, or the energy that an object possesses due to its motion. Heat is transferred from the source to the recipient by one or more of the following methods:

1. *Conduction.* The transference of heat by conduction involves the diffusion of energy through the collision of molecules. In order to transfer heat by conduction, the recipient needs to be in direct physical contact with the source [e.g., a hydrocollator (moist heat) pack, paraffin bath].

2. *Convection.* Convection requires movement of a medium, usually water or air, which transfers heat by a flow from the source to the recipient. With therapeutic modalities, the actual transfer of heat still occurs by conduction, but the process is made more efficient due to

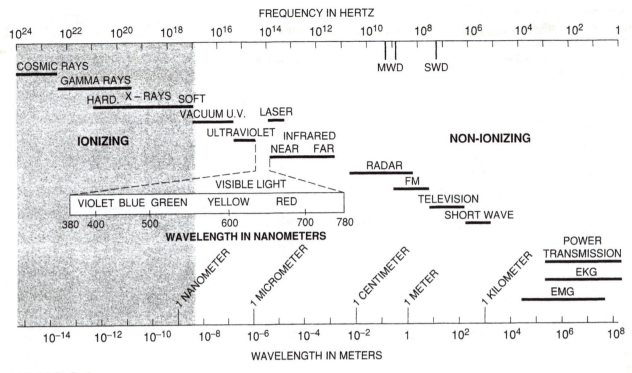

FIGURE 7.1

A graphical representation of the electromagnetic spectrum
(*Source:* SL Michlovitz, *Thermal Agents in Rehabilitation,* 2d ed., Philadelphia, FA Davis, 1990, p. 46.)

circulation of the medium (e.g., the movement of the water across a body segment during a whirlpool treatment).

3. *Radiation.* The transfer of electromagnetic energy via radiation occurs in the absence of any medium, that is, through space. Radiant energy is defined as the heat gained or lost through radiation, and is emitted from any object having a temperature greater than absolute zero, the theoretical temperature characterized by the complete absence of heat (−273.2°C). Therapeutic modalities which transfer heat by radiation include infrared lamps and moist heat packs.

4. *Conversion.* In some cases, the electromagnetic energy released from a modality, particularly microwave and shortwave diathermy devices, creates a magnetic field that is changed into heat. This phenomenon is known as conversion.

Unlike electromagnetic energy, *acoustic energy* requires a medium for transmission. The only therapeutic modality which uses acoustic energy, *ultrasound,* emits high-frequency mechanical waveforms, inaudible to the human ear, that produce both thermal and nonthermal physiological effects. Acoustic energy travels much faster through denser mediums; in human tissues,

ultrasound travels an average of 1,540 meters per second.[5] Acoustic energy does not travel in a vacuum.

Electromagnetic energy travels in a straight line when in a vacuum. When traveling through a medium such as human tissue, its pathway is affected by changes in the density of tissue. Electromagnetic as well as acoustic energy may be either completely or partially *reflected* upon striking the surface, have its direction of travel through the medium changed (*refracted*), *absorbed* by the medium, or *transmitted* unaffected to the next density level.

Several fundamental principles govern the therapeutic application of electromagnetic and acoustic energy to the human body. The amount of energy applied by the modality selected by the clinician must be of sufficient magnitude to elicit a physiologic response, while simultaneously not causing any damage to the treated tissues. This phenomenon is known as the *Arndt-Schultz principle.*

The *Law of Grotthus-Draper* states that energy that is not absorbed by the tissues is transmitted to the deeper layers of tissue. For example, the greater the amount of ultrasound energy absorbed in superficial tissues, the less energy available to be transmitted to deeper layers; consequently the maximum depth of penetration of the ultrasound energy is decreased.[6]

Two key laws of physics apply to radiation: the inverse square law and the cosine law. The *inverse square law* states that the intensity of the radiation varies inversely with the square of the distance from the source of the radiation. For example, when the distance from the therapeutic modality to the treatment area is decreased by 50 percent, the intensity of the radiation delivery is increased by 200 percent. The *cosine law* holds that optimal radiation is received when the source of the radiation is perpendicular ($\perp$) to the area being treated. For example, when the angle of radiation is focused at 30 degrees relative to the treatment surface, twice the exposure is required to produce the same intensity as when the angle of radiation is set at 90 degrees.

Fundamental Concepts of Electricity

Electricity is the force created by an imbalance in the distribution of electrons at two points. An electrical current can be defined as a stream of free electrons passing along a conductor from a higher concentration to a lower concentration. To understand the key principles of electricity that apply to electrotherapy, five terms need to be defined.

Coulomb: the charge produced by 6.25×10^{18} electrons (negatively-charged particles) or protons (positively-charged particles).

Ampere: the rate of flow of an electrical charge; 1 ampere equals the flow of 1 coulomb per second past any point or through a conducting wire.

Volt: a measure of the tendency for current flow to occur; that is, the electrical potential difference between two poles. As a unit of measure, 1 volt represents the amount of work required to move 1 coulomb of charge.

Ohm: the degree of resistance to electrical current flow by a given material. Precious metals such as copper and silver are good *conductors* and offer relatively little resistance to electrical current.

Watt: a unit of electrical power; also, the rate at which electricity is being used.

Over the years therapeutic electrical currents have been known by many different, often confusing terms, but the recent establishment of a standard nomenclature for electrotherapeutic terminology by the American Physical Therapy Association has greatly improved the understanding of electrical currents and their related descriptive terms. These terms for the three basic forms of electrical current utilized in physical medicine are direct current, alternating current, and pulsed current.[7]

Direct current (DC) is defined as the continuous, unidirectional flow of either positively- or negatively-charged particles, whereas *alternating current* (AC) is the continuous, bidirectional flow of charged particles. *Pulsed current* is a term specific to electrotherapeutic modalities, and is defined as a direct or alternating current which is periodically interrupted for a finite period of time. A single *pulse* is defined as an isolated electrical event separated from the next electrical event by a finite period of time. Each pulse can be described as a *waveform*, possessing magnitude, polarity (positive, negative, or both), and duration. The more vertical the slope of the electrical waveform, the more rapid the increase in amplitude, the greater its potential to excite human tissue.[8]

General Principles of Therapeutic Modalities and Procedures

During the formulation of a treatment plan involving therapeutic modalities, the clinician should consider: (a) the type and severity of the injury or condition, (b) the specialized anatomy of the region, (c) the indications and contraindications governing the use of the available modalities, (d) the efficacy of selected treatment protocols, and (e) the need for continual monitoring of the athlete's progress in the rehabilitation process.

The discussion of individual therapeutic modalities within this chapter will, in most instances, be presented in outline format. The reader is encouraged to consult the list of recommended modalities texts at the conclusion of this chapter for additional information. The three major subcategories of modalities to be presented in this chapter are superficial thermal agents, deep thermal agents, and electrical agents. In addition, massage and manipulation therapy are presented as possible treatment modalities.

Superficial Thermal Agents

Superficial thermal agents are therapeutic modalities that lie within the infrared band of the electromagnetic energy spectrum and transfer energy either to (heating modalities) or from (cold modalities) the tissues (see Figure 7.1). The majority of thermal agents penetrate human tissue superficially, either heating or cooling tissues to depths approximating 1 cm in clinical doses.

Extensive research with various thermal agents has resulted in the identification of numerous physiological effects associated with therapeutic applications of heat and cold within the infrared portion of the electromagnetic spectrum and the acoustic spectrum (ultrasound). The known physiological effects of heat and cold are summarized in Tables 7.2 and Table 7.3, respectively.

TABLE 7.2 *Known physiological effects of superficial heat application*

Vasodilation of arterioles and capillaries
Analgesia
Increased local tissue temperature
Increased local metabolic rate
Increased capillary permeability
Increased nerve conduction velocity
Increased lymphatic and venous drainage
Increased removal of metabolic wastes
Increased elasticity of soft tissues
Increased edema formation
Decreased muscle spasm
Decreased muscle tone

Adapted from C Starkey, *Therapeutic Modalities for Athletic Trainers*. Philadelphia, F. A. Davis, 1993, pp. 62–63; and GW Bell, WE Prentice, Infrared modalities. In *Therapeutic Modalities in Sports Medicine*, 3rd ed., ed. WE Prentice, St. Louis: Mosby, 1994, p. 178.

TABLE 7.3 *Known physiological effects of superficial cold application*

Vasoconstriction of arterioles and capillaries
Analgesic and anesthetic effects
Decreased local tissue temperature
Decreased local metabolic rate
Decreased formation and accumulation of edema
Decreased delivery of phagocytes and leukocytes
Decreased nerve conduction velocity
Decreased muscle spasm

Adapted from C Starkey, *Therapeutic Modalities for Athletic Trainers*. Philadelphia, F. A. Davis, 1993, p. 54; and GW Bell, WE Prentice, Infrared modalities. In *Therapeutic Modalities in Sports Medicine*, 3rd ed., ed. WE Prentice, St. Louis: Mosby, 1994, p. 178.

Hydrocollator (Moist Heat Packs)

As one of the most affordable and widely used modalities, moist heat packs transfer their heat energy to the body by means of conduction. When the hot pack is applied, it is at a much higher temperature than the skin surface being treated and the clinician must take precautions to avoid overheating and burning of the athlete's skin.

INDICATIONS: Hydrocollator packs are appropriate for use in the subacute and chronic phases of healing of soft-tissue injuries, such as contusions, muscle strains, and localized muscle spasms. Due to a depth of penetration of approximately 1 cm, moist heat packs should be used primarily for superficial musculoskeletal problems.

CONTRAINDICATIONS: Moist heat packs are not appropriate for use during the acute phase of healing. The use of hot packs is also contraindicated in cases of open skin infection. Other general contraindications include individuals with impairment or deficiency in thermal sensation and thermoregulatory control.

PRECAUTIONS: A minimum of six layers of toweling (approximately 1 inch thickness of toweling) or a commercially available hydrocollator pack holder should be used to protect the athlete's skin from overheating. Approximately 5 minutes into the treatment, the clinician should lift the hot pack to check the athlete's skin for signs of *mottling* (blotchy areas of red and white skin areas in whites, uneven lighter and darker areas in blacks) as a warning sign of burning. Extra layers of toweling should be used when treating fair-skinned and/or red-headed individuals, or when the patient complains that the heat is too intense.

THERAPEUTIC AND PHYSIOLOGIC EFFECTS: Analgesia; reduction in muscle spasm; increase in cutaneous and subcutaneous (superficial) circulation.

TREATMENT TECHNIQUES: The thermostat of a hydrocollator unit is typically preset by the manufacturer to maintain a constant water temperature of approximately 71°C (160°F).[9] Depending on the treatment area, three different sizes of heat packs are available: (a) standard size (12" × 12") for most body segments, (b) double size (24" × 24") for the thoracic and lumbar spinal areas, and (c) cervical packs (6" × 18") for treating the cervical region.

To use, remove the hot pack from the hydrocollator unit using forceps and permit the excess water to drain back into the unit. The hot pack is hottest initially and cools as the treatment progresses. Place at least six layers of towels between the athlete and the moist heat pack, using more layers as needed to prevent burns. The duration of treatment is usually 15 to 20 minutes.

Hydrotherapy (Whirlpool)

Hydrotherapy is one of the oldest therapeutic methods employed in physical medicine, and is done in water tanks of varying shapes and sizes. Facilitating the patient's movement through buoyancy, hydrotherapy employs Archimedes' principle, which states that a body immersed in a liquid experiences an upward force equal to the weight of the displaced liquid. Therefore, the patient senses that the body or the extremity being immersed "weighs less" in the liquid (water) than in air, and that therapeutic exercises can be performed with less effort.

INDICATIONS: Hydrotherapy is appropriate for the acute phase of injury care, in which case a low water temperature is utilized (12.8°C or 55°F). Hydrotherapy is commonly used during the subacute and chronic phases of healing of sprains, strains, contusions, bursitis, and tenosynovitis. Whirlpool treatments are also used in the care of open wounds, typically to aid in the removal of necrotic tissue, or with the addition of a bactericidal agent such as betadine, povidone-iodine, or sodium hypochlorite to the water, cleansing the open wound. When using warmer water, wound healing can be facilitated through increased cutaneous circulation, with concomitant increases in oxygenation, nutrition, and metabolism of the treated tissues.[10]

CONTRAINDICATIONS: Warm or hot whirlpools should not be used with acute injuries, nor in the presence of active hemorrhaging or swelling.

PRECAUTIONS: A ground fault circuit interrupter (GFCI) that stops the flow of electricity to the whirlpool when a ground fault is sensed is a necessary part of the electrical system. In this application, a ground fault is defined as a difference of 5 milliamperes or more between the electrical currents in the hot and neutral wires that supply the outlet used to power a whirlpool, suggesting a leakage of current into the ground wire. In general, GFCIs are required for all electrical outlets within 1.5 meters of therapeutic hydrotherapy units.[11] A monthly test of the GFCIs should be conducted to

determine if they are functioning properly, with an electrical safety inspection performed annually by a qualified technician to ensure that the GFCIs are properly calibrated. Even with a GFCI, the athlete should never be allowed to turn the whirlpool on or off, due to the potential for electrical shock.

The concept of universal precautions, the assumption that all blood and certain body fluids are to be treated as if contaminated with human immunodeficiency virus (HIV), hepatitis B virus (HBV), or other bloodborne pathogens, must be observed when utilizing the whirlpool for open wound care. The current list of potentially infectious materials for which universal precautions must be observed, according to Occupational Safety and Health Administration regulations, includes blood, any body fluid with visible blood (e.g., exudate from a healing abrasion), and any unidentifiable body fluid (e.g., pus from an infected wound).[12] The clinician must be aware of the potential role of the whirlpool as a vector for disease transmission and utilize various virucidal and bactericidal chemical products available to disinfect the water and the whirlpool itself following treatment of individuals with open wounds. It is suggested that personal protective equipment such as latex gloves be used when scrubbing the whirlpool after such a treatment.

THERAPEUTIC AND PHYSIOLOGIC EFFECTS: The physiological effects of hydrotherapy are temperature dependent (Table 7.4). For warm to hot whirlpools (temperatures ranging from 36°C to 43°C), decreased

---

TABLE 7.4   *Suggested water temperatures for hydrotherapy treatments*

Description:	Celsius°:	Fahrenheit°:
Very cold	1–13	35–55
Cold	13–18	55–65
Cool	18–27	65–80
Tepid	17.5–33.5	80–92
Neutral	33.5–35.5	92–96
Warm	35.5–36.5	96–98
Hot	36.5–40	98–104
Very Hot	40–46	104–115

Adapted from MT Walsh, Hydrotherapy: the use of water as a therapeutic agent. In *Thermal Agents in Rehabilitation*, 2d ed., ed. SL Michlovitz, Philadelphia: F. A. Davis, 1990, p. 117.

pain (analgesia), sedation, decreased stiffness, increased tissue extensibility, and increased blood flow (vasodilation) are among the primary physiological effects. For cold to very cold whirlpools (temperatures ranging from 10°C to 15°C), decreased edema, decreased sensation (anesthesia), decreased metabolism, and decreased blood flow (vasoconstriction) are the key physiological effects.

TREATMENT TECHNIQUES: There are numerous scenarios in the treatment of sports-related injuries when hydrotherapy may involve use of either hot or cold water in order to achieve the treatment goals, and cases when the physiological effects of one temperature are more appropriate than another. Prior to making a choice between hot or cold whirlpool treatment, several factors must be considered: (a) the stage of the injury, (b) the region or body part to be treated, (c) the presence of a hypersensitivity or allergy to cold or heat, and (d) the athlete's preference, a particularly important consideration to ensure his/her compliance with a home treatment program.[13]

The whirlpool's intake valve should be submerged at least 3 cm below the water line to avoid drawing air through the turbine. The clinician must position the whirlpool's jet properly so that the flow of water does not directly contact a painful, acute lesion. Treatment time varies individually with the condition, but usually ranges from 20 to 30 minutes.

Cryotherapy

The therapeutic application of cold to the body is referred to as *cryotherapy*. When applied to the injured part, cold produces a series of local and systemic responses. The major physiologic responses include: (a) decreased blood flow through vasoconstriction of local blood vessels, (b) reduction of the inflammatory process via reduction in metabolic rate, (c) reduced muscle spasm through decreased motor nerve conduction velocity, and (d) reduction of pain through cold-induced anesthesia.

INDICATIONS: It is commonly accepted that the application of cold is an appropriate treatment for virtually all injuries, whether as a first aid procedure or for chronic inflammatory condition, with the possible exception of frostbite. However, recent changes in the initial management of cases of backcountry frostbite have made the use of cold on frozen tissues appropriate until care can be initiated and all danger of refreezing of the tissues has been eliminated.[14]

Any of the soft tissue injuries associated with sports participation such as sprains, strains, and contusions can be treated with cryotherapy. It is important to note that both acute and chronic injuries may be treated. Cryotherapy can also be used for relieving muscle spasms and myofascial (trigger point) pain.[15,16] Cold therapy has also been used successfully in the postoperative management of pain in patients following anterior cruciate ligament reconstruction.[17]

CONTRAINDICATIONS: The presence of known circulatory disturbances such as Raynaud's disease or hypersensitivity to cold preclude the use of cryotherapy. Individuals with cardiac or respiratory conditions should not receive cryotherapy treatments. Athletes who have an area of anesthetic skin, perhaps from severance of cutaneous nerves as a result of surgical incisions, should not have that area treated with cryotherapy.

PRECAUTIONS: The clinician must also be cautious about placing cold near or onto a superficial nerve, as this can lead to temporary or permanent nerve damage. There have been several published reports of superficial peroneal nerve damage producing foot drop from cryotherapy treatments at the level of the fibular head.[18,19] When using gel or chemical cold packs always use a layer of insulation (e.g., wet elastic bandage or towel) between the pack and the skin; otherwise, the temperature at the skin interface may be less than 32°F and damage to the skin may result, producing blisters, or with prolonged exposure, damage to deeper tissues in the form of frostbite may result.

THERAPEUTIC AND PHYSIOLOGIC EFFECTS: The ability of cryotherapy to reduce pain and edema is widely accepted.[20,21] Although the exact mechanisms are not yet completely understood, cryotherapy following musculoskeletal trauma also appears to reduce the inflammatory reaction, decrease hematoma formation, and reduce the metabolic and oxygen needs of injured tissues.[22,23,24] Cryotherapy also decreases muscle spasm by reducing nerve conduction velocity and muscle spindle excitability.

Easily the most controversial issue surrounding the use of cryotherapy relates to its effects upon arterial circulation. Starting with research by Lewis in 1929,[25] claims of increased blood flow as the result cold-induced vasodilation have been investigated for decades. Lewis' study involved immersion of the fingers in cold water and he observed alternating periods of warming and cooling of the skin, a phenomenon he termed the *hunting response*. This term was used to describe the series of fluctuations in the local blood vessels between vasodilation and vasoconstriction in an effort to adapt to the change in temperature.

Knight[26] investigated this phenomenon extensively in a series of studies whose collective results have not substantiated the existence of a therapeutic cold-induced vasodilation. He suggests that in response to cold application, an initial vasoconstriction is followed by a mild posttreatment dilation of blood vessels; however, the diameter of these dilated blood vessels never reaches the diameter which existed prior to treatment. Several recent studies using impedance plethysmography, a noninvasive technique which measures arterial and venous blood flow based upon the amount of electrical resistance in a given region, failed to observe physiologically significant cold-induced vasodilation following 20-minute cryotherapy treatments.[27,28,29]

TREATMENT TECHNIQUES: When using water ice packs, crushed or shaved ice is preferred because it molds easily to the shape of the body part being treated. The ice should be placed in a sturdy plastic bag that does not leak. This treatment should be applied for approximately 20 minutes of every hour during the acute phase of an injury, and repeated throughout the day. If using refreezable commercial cold packs, be sure to place a layer of wet toweling or elastic bandage between the pack and the skin to prevent cold injury. Follow the specific instructions for use provided by the manufacturer.

For ice massage treatments, freeze water in 6- to 8-ounce paper cups. Peel away the paper cup to expose the ice and instruct the athlete to rub the ice over the injured area in a circular or similar patterned movement. Ice massages should be applied for 5 to 15 minutes, depending upon the superficial or deep nature of the injury, until anesthesia occurs. This protocol can be repeated several times per day.

Cryokinetics

The combination of therapeutic application of cold and exercise, more commonly referred to as *cryokinetics,* has been widely adopted for the treatment of musculoskeletal injuries. In this case, cold is applied to produce a level of analgesia necessary for the athlete to perform the desired exercises without pain.

INDICATIONS: The use of cryokinetics is appropriate for all conditions that cryotherapy alone would be employed.

CONTRAINDICATIONS AND PRECAUTIONS: Athletes with circulatory problems associated with Ray-

naud's disease or a hypersensitivity to cold should not be treated with cryokinetics. The clinician must closely monitor the duration of treatment to produce analgesia, but not anesthesia. The temporary absence of (or decrease in) sensation caused by cold application prior to rehabilitative exercises can be dangerous, particularly during closed kinetic chain activities. Proprioception is typically decreased following musculotendinous or ligamentous injury, and numbing the injury with cold will further diminish peripheral feedback, placing the athlete at increased risk of aggravating the injury.

An additional concern is the effect of cold on the viscoelastic properties of soft tissue. Cryotherapy reduces the temperature in the treated tissues, thereby decreasing the extensibility and increasing the viscosity of collagenous tissues. If used improperly the athlete may be more susceptible to microscopic and macroscopic lesions during the first few minutes of the exercise phase of cryokinetics, since soft tissues are less elastic at lower temperatures. The injury risk is analogous to beginning a vigorous exercise session without performing a proper warm-up beforehand.

THERAPEUTIC AND PHYSIOLOGIC EFFECTS: The goal of cryokinetics is to use the physiologic effects of cold to diminish the level of pain in the injured body segment, and then subject that segment to stage-appropriate range of motion and resistance exercises. Cryokinetics enhances the healing process by stimulating circulation through exercise while simultaneously preventing inhibitory neural responses from pain and allowing the surrounding tissues to engage in early activity.[30]

TREATMENT TECHNIQUES: The duration of the cold treatment is affected by: (a) the cooling agent chosen, (b) the size of the area being treated, (c) the location of the injury (deep or superficial), and (d) the amount of insulating subcutaneous fat present. Generally 10 to 12 minutes of cold application is sufficient to create the desired analgesic effect.[31] After applying cold to the injured part, an exercise program specific to the particular injury is begun. If the athlete experiences pain in the injured part while exercising, the intensity of the exercise should be decreased or stopped altogether. The cycle of cold treatment and exercise may be repeated several times during one clinical session.

EXAMPLE: An athlete sustains a moderate (grade 2) inversion sprain involving the lateral ligaments of the ankle and requires crutches for ambulation. During the acute phase of the injury the treatment program should include cold, coupled with compression and elevation. Gentle passive- or active-assisted range of motion exercises or joint mobilization techniques should also be employed. As the inflammatory response diminishes and the injury progresses to the subacute phase a program of cryokinetics is begun. Cold should be applied to the athlete's ankle for 10 to 15 minutes, followed by attempts at a normal heel-to-toe walking gait. If this can be achieved without a limp, the athlete should continue until pain is felt. The cold should be applied again and the process repeated three to five times. As the condition continues to improve, range of motion, manual resistance, and partial to full weight-bearing exercises (e.g., stationary cycling, slide board) are added to restore functional abilities, combat atrophy, build strength, and maintain cardiovascular fitness. Each treatment session should always conclude with application of cold, compression, and elevation.

Vapocoolant (Cold) Spray

While watching a major league baseball game, who has not seen a batter hit by a pitch? As the player writhes in pain the team's athletic trainer rushes out of the dugout with a container to spray the contusion. Almost instantly the player is up off the ground and heading off to first base, staying in the game. What was the magical potion the athletic trainer used to help the athlete? Most likely it was a topical freeze spray such as FluoriMethane to instantly relieve the pain. Vapocoolants such as FluoriMethane and ethyl chloride are liquids bottled under pressure that are emitted as a fine spray onto the skin to produce an instantaneous, significant cooling effect.

The most common therapeutic uses of vapocoolant sprays are in the treatment of myofascial pain or *trigger point therapy*. Trigger points are small areas of intense localized pain and/or increased sensitivity in muscles or connective tissues. The technique of "spray and stretch" has been used for many years with ethyl chloride and, more recently, FluoriMethane spray. Ethyl chloride was originally used for trigger point therapy but is no longer recommended because it is flammable, volatile, and can freeze the skin.[32] (Figure 7.2)

INDICATIONS: The spray and stretch technique is used to relieve pain arising from muscle spasm or an irritable myofascial trigger point.

CONTRAINDICATIONS: Hypersensitivity of the skin to cold.

PRECAUTIONS: The clinician must be very careful not to cause skin damage or frostbite when using spray coolants. Both FluoriMethane and ethyl chloride are

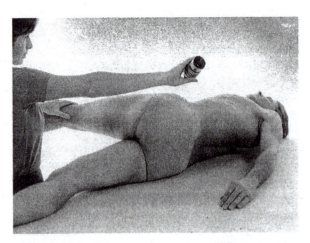

FIGURE 7.2
Spray and stretch technique as used for piriformis muscle spasm

prescription medications which athletic trainers should use under the supervision of a physician.

THERAPEUTIC AND PHYSIOLOGIC EFFECTS: The concept that underlies the spray and stretch technique is that a muscle that is in spasm produces pain, regardless of the cause. In order to relieve the spasm and achieve normal resting length in the affected muscle, the cycle producing the muscle spasm must be interrupted. The effectiveness of cold spray in relieving muscle spasm is attributed to the cold receptors conducting the sensation more rapidly than pain impulses. This results in the muscle pain impulses being blocked and normal reflex patterns being restored. While not well understood, the counterirritation of cold, together with stretching the muscle, interrupts the cycle of muscle spasm in many cases, particularly when treating trigger points.[15,33]

TREATMENT TECHNIQUES: The muscle to be sprayed should first be stretched to the point of discomfort. The vapocoolant container should be held between 18 to 24 inches (45 to 60 cm) away from the skin in such a way that the stream of spray will strike the skin surface at an angle.[34] Move the stream of spray from the trigger point or origin of the muscle to the reference area or insertion of the muscle. In order not to frost the skin, the speed of movement should be approximately four inches (10 cm) per second.[34] Typically, three or four parallel lines are sprayed in the one direction along the length of the muscle, not across the muscle. Have the athlete move the treated body segment through the available active range of motion immediately after treatment or assist the athlete in moving the limb.

Contrast Bath

In the past, clinicians have used contrast bath hydrotherapy to reduce edema or joint effusion through the alternate use of cold and heat treatments. Hayes[35] suggested that contrast baths be used as a type of "vascular exercise" to induce alternate vasoconstriction and vasodilation of the blood vessels. This alternation stimulates peripheral blood flow and helps to stimulate healing.

However, Myrer[36] and associates are of the opinion that the effects of contrast baths are purely psychological. They base this on the results of their research that showed no significant increases or decreases in muscle temperature during contrast whirlpool therapy. They are quick to point out that they didn't measure blood flow, only temperature change, and that it might be possible to get vasodilation and vasoconstriction without a resultant change in tissue temperature.

INDICATIONS: Contrast baths are appropriate for the reduction of edema during the subacute and chronic stages of traumatic and inflammatory conditions.

CONTRAINDICATIONS: Since contrast baths employ both heat and cold, the risks associated with both modalities must be considered. Refer to the contraindications for thermotherapy and cryotherapy listed previously. Of particular concern is peripheral vascular disease and lesions in which an active hemorrhage is occurring.

PRECAUTIONS: Athletes who have anesthetic areas of skin cannot judge temperatures very well; be sure water temperatures and durations of immersion are set according to accepted protocols.

THERAPEUTIC AND PHYSIOLOGIC EFFECTS: While both heat and cold applications have been shown to produce beneficial therapeutic effects, each has some undesired physiologic effects which could interfere with the healing process. The alternate use of cold and heat is thought to offset the negative physiologic effects of each form of treatment, resulting in increased circulation to the injured area, in turn reducing edema and improving range of motion.

TREATMENT TECHNIQUES: Fill two whirlpools or similar containers, one with cold water (10°C to 15°C) and one with warm or hot water (36°C to 43°C). The actual treatment protocol and duration are left to the discretion of the clinician as the most effective ratio of hot-to-cold immersion has not been scientifically determined. Among the most commonly used ratios of hot-to-cold are 3:1 and 4:1, with the total duration of treatment ranging from 15 to 20 minutes, depending upon the stage of injury and the condition being treated. If a subacute stage injury such as a grade 2+ ankle sprain is being treated, the treatment session should finish with cold water immersion to facilitate vasoconstriction. Conversely, if vasodilation is desired, as is the case with many chronic stage injuries, then the treatment session should finish with warm or hot water immersion, followed by several minutes of elevation of the treated area above the level of the heart in order to reduce edema formation.

Intermittent Compression Units

Intermittent pneumatic compression (IPC) units employ mechanical pressure to reduce edema by facilitating increased lymphatic and venous flow in the affected extremity. The systematic external pneumatic compression of an extremity reduces venous stasis by intermittently squeezing the limb and accelerating deep venous blood flow. Intermittent pneumatic compression has been shown to be effective in a wide range of clinical applications and conditions, from the prevention of deep vein thromboses following surgery to the reduction of both acute and chronic edema in the lower and upper extremities.[37–39]

The components of IPC devices include a pump unit and several different-shaped fabric sleeves designed to fit over a particular body segment (e.g., half arm, full arm, half leg, full leg), connected by inflow and outflow hoses. Intermittent compression units have evolved since their introduction several decades ago as single-cell inflatable devices that inflate and deflate with uniform (circumferential) pressure applied to the extremity being treated. A second type of IPC device is a single-cell inflatable appliance with cooling capabilities. A third and most recent version of these units has the capability to apply sequential compression to an injured extremity through the distal-to-proximal filling of a series of chambers within the appliance. In a sequential IPC device, the most distal compartment inflates first, followed by the next most distal, and so on until pressure has been increased and is maintained in all compartments of the device until released.[40]

When the combination of IPC and cryotherapy is used, water or some similar fluid is typically cooled to 10° to 13°C (50° to 55°F) and pumped through the device.[41]

INDICATIONS: In sports medicine applications IPC units are appropriate for use on acute posttraumatic and postinflammatory edemas, particularly soft tissue injuries with significant swelling. Intermittent compression is an effective treatment against venous thrombosis in patients undergoing general surgery, major knee surgery, and neurosurgery.[39]

CONTRAINDICATIONS: In the early management of athletic injury cases where tibial compartment compression syndrome is a possibility in the differential diagnosis, the use of IPC devices is not appropriate. Additionally, IPC units should not be used until a physician has ruled out the existence of a fracture in the affected extremity.

PRECAUTIONS: With regard to the treatment pressure applied by the device, the amount of compression must not exceed the athlete's diastolic blood pressure. When using the cryotherapy aspect of this modality, the clinician must always be alert for individuals with circulatory disturbances and/or hypersensitivity to cold.

THERAPEUTIC AND PHYSIOLOGIC EFFECTS: The intermittent pneumatic compression device acts as an artificial muscle pump, replicating the natural pumping action of the muscles lost during immobilization due to a variety of causes (e.g., pain, extensive tissue damage, edema). Venous stasis is reduced while lymphatic movement and blood fibrinolytic activity are enhanced by intermittent pneumatic compression treatment.[39]

TREATMENT TECHNIQUES: With IPC devices, three parameters can be adjusted: (a) the duty cycle (ratio of time-on to time-off), (b) the total treatment time, and (c) the treatment pressure. There is little scientific evidence to support a particular treatment time protocol. The time on-time off pressure sequences have been developed through clinical trials and are based on athlete comfort levels. Some of the treatment duty cycles used by clinicians include 1:2 (one minute on, two minutes off), 2:1 (two minutes on, one minute off), and 4:1 (four minutes on, one minute off).[42]

One recommendation for total treatment time is based upon a 1955 clinical finding that significant reductions in limb volume occurred following 30 minutes of intermittent pneumatic compression.[43] Currently, suggested total IPC treatment time protocols range from 20 minutes to several hours per day.[40,41]

With regard to treatment pressure, recommendations are influenced by the blood pressure and comfort level of the athlete. For treatment of upper extremity edema, one major manufacturer recommends that treatment pressure be within a range of 30 to 50 mm Hg, and

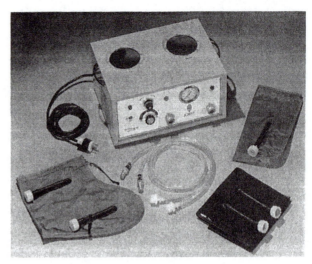

FIGURE 7.3
Intermittent cold and pressure unit
(Photo courtesy of Jobst Institute, Inc.)

within a range of 30 to 60 mm Hg when treating lower extremity conditions.[40] These pressure range recommendations are based on average arterial capillary pressures (approximately 30 mm Hg), and any pressure that exceeds this value should facilitate lymph movement and edema reabsorption.[42] (Figure 7.3)

Paraffin Bath

The paraffin bath is an inexpensive, infrared modality that provides superficial heating of tissues. The use of paraffin baths is common in the treatment of patients with rheumatoid arthritis and osteoarthritis, or newly healed burns to the smaller joints of hands and feet. When mixed with mineral oil, the melting point of paraffin wax drops from 54°C to 48°C and remains as a liquid at temperatures above 47.8°C. The mixture of paraffin and mineral oil has a low specific heat and is well tolerated by athletes at temperatures ranging from 47°C to 54°C (118°F to 130°F). In contrast, a hot whirlpool at or above 49°C (120°F) is perceived as scalding and typically will burn the skin.[13]

INDICATIONS: Paraffin bath treatments are appropriate for any subacute or chronic joint injury or condition, but are typically limited to the smaller joints of the hands and feet, which must fit inside the walls of the paraffin bath. One common use in sports medicine is for the subacute stage treatment of sprained or dislocated joints of the hand.

CONTRAINDICATIONS AND PRECAUTIONS:
Paraffin baths are contraindicated in acute injury cases, in the presence of an active hemorrhage of inflammatory response, and in cases of impairment of local circulation. Paraffin baths should not be used with open wounds, nor in the treatment of athletes with skin infections.

THERAPEUTIC AND PHYSIOLOGIC EFFECTS:
The paraffin bath is particularly useful in enhancing cutaneous circulation and providing temporary relief from pain. The cutaneous receptors are shut off from all stimuli except the warmth of the paraffin, and the insulation provided by the layers of hardened paraffin prevents rapid heat loss following treatment.

TREATMENT TECHNIQUES: The thermostat of the paraffin heating unit should be set to maintain the temperature between 47°C to 54°C (118°F to 130°F). Several different methods of treatment are available. In the paraffin "dip and wrap" method, the affected extremity should be dipped into the melted paraffin for 2 to 3 seconds, then removed to permit air drying. This procedure is repeated six to twelve times, then the treated extremity is covered with a plastic bag and then a cotton towel. The paraffin is left on for 20 to 30 minutes. In the "dip and soak" treatment method, the same procedure as in the dip and wrap technique is performed except that once the paraffin "glove" is formed, the treated part is not wrapped. Instead the affected extremity is immersed and soaked in the liquid paraffin for 15 to 20 minutes. For clinicians who want to treat larger body parts, paraffin "painting" of the injured part with a paint brush is appropriate. The paint brush is dipped in the melted paraffin and the paraffin applied to the body part. This procedure is repeated six to twelve times and then the paraffin is allowed to air dry. Total treatment time is from 20 to 30 minutes.

Infrared Light

Infrared lamps are electromagnetic energy devices that produce radiant energy which can be used for superficial heating of tissues. Infrared light is classified as a radiant modality since no medium (water or air) is required for the transmission of energy. There are two types of infrared light modalities, luminous (near infrared) and nonluminous (far infrared). Luminous infrared lamps output some visible light, while the output from nonluminous infrared lamps cannot be seen. Luminous infrared light penetrates to a depth of 0.5 to 1.0 cm, while nonluminous infrared light penetrates to only 0.2 cm.

INDICATIONS: Superficial soft tissue injuries and skin conditions in the subacute to chronic stages. Infrared light is also useful in the treatment of conditions in which the athlete cannot tolerate the pressure or weight of a moist heat pack or other conductive heating modality. Given the vast array of thermal agents available for use by the clinician, infrared light is not frequently employed in the treatment of sports-related injuries.

CONTRAINDICATIONS: Infrared light treatments are contraindicated for acute conditions and for individuals who have a deficiency in heat perception. Once thought to be effective in the treatment of superficial skin wounds such as abrasions (turf burns), infrared light treatment has been found to be detrimental to the healing process because it dehydrates the tissues.[44]

PRECAUTIONS: The clinician must employ the cosine law and position the lamp so that the infrared energy will be delivered at a right angle to the targeted tissues. The inverse square law must also be considered with the therapeutic use of infrared light; the lamp should be located approximately 50 to 75 cm (20 to 30 inches) away from the athlete.

THERAPEUTIC AND PHYSIOLOGIC EFFECTS:
Produces superficial vasodilation, increased capillary blood flow, and analgesia.

TREATMENT TECHNIQUES: The clinician controls the intensity of infrared light by manipulating the distance from the lamp to the patient, and by adjusting the electrical current flow through the tungsten or carbon filament generator. Treatment times typically range from 20 to 30 minutes, and may be repeated as necessary.

Deep Thermal Agents

Thermotherapeutic agents are divided into two major categories, superficial and deep. We have previously discussed the superficial thermal agents, those which produce thermal effects to tissue depths of approximately 1 cm. In contrast, deep thermal agents can increase tissue temperatures to depths of 3 cm or more. There are two different deep thermal agents, diathermy and ultrasound, with ultrasound by far the more commonly used.

Diathermy

Two general types of diathermy units are used clinically: shortwave and microwave, with shortwave diathermy used more commonly than microwave.[45] Their effects on human tissues are produced mainly as a result of increases in local tissue temperature to depths of 3 to 5 cm, and through reflexes associated with temperature receptors.

Shortwave diathermy is a form of electromagnetic radiation that uses a high-frequency electrical current to heat the deeper tissues. Most shortwave diathermy machines operate at a frequency of 27.12 MHz, although other frequencies are available.

Microwave diathermy also uses electromagnetic radiation to heat deeper tissues by means of conversion. Tissues with a higher water content, such as muscle and fat, are more likely to absorb microwave energy than is bone, and heat is likely to be produced at the muscle-fat interface.

A third method of diathermy treatment involves the delivery of *pulsed* shortwave electromagnetic waves, and depending upon the total amount of energy applied, local tissue temperature may or may not increase. Pulsed shortwave diathermy has been in use for many years with mixed results; however, a recent double-blind, prospective study substantiated the efficacy of a single treatment in reducing edema in grade I and II acute ankle sprains.[46]

INDICATIONS: Shortwave and microwave diathermy treatments are appropriate for subacute and chronic soft tissue injuries to muscle, tendon, ligament, and other connective tissues which require deeper heating than provided by superficial penetrating modalities such as hot packs, whirlpools, paraffin baths, and infrared lamps. Pulsed shortwave diathermy has been suggested in the treatment of acute as well as chronic conditions in which nonthermal physiological effects such as increased collagen formation, phagocytosis, and hematoma reduction are desired.[46]

CONTRAINDICATIONS: Shortwave and microwave diathermy is generally contraindicated in the treatment of acute injuries, specifically areas of acute inflammation, active hemorrhage, nondraining infections, limited circulation, and peripheral vascular disease. Shortwave and microwave diathermy should not be administered over clothing, wound dressings, casts, or metal implants.

PRECAUTIONS: The clinician must not use a metal table when treating an athlete with shortwave and microwave diathermy, as serious burns may result. Diathermy should not be used during pregnancy or over the joints of skeletally immature patients.

THERAPEUTIC AND PHYSIOLOGIC EFFECTS: Generally, the same physiological effects as other heating modalities; specifically, vasodilation, increased blood flow, and increased metabolic rate. Both shortwave or microwave diathermy can be used to effect an increase in tissue temperature to the therapeutically desirable range of 40°C to 44°C.[45]

Draper[47] and colleagues recently measured the rate of temperature increase in human muscle via pulsed shortwave diathermy. At an intramuscular depth of three centimeters, the temperature increased 4°C with a 15 minute treatment. Since the size of their diathermy drum was 15 cm^2, they are of the opinion that pulsed shortwave diathermy can cause vigorous heating over a larger area than ultrasound.

TREATMENT TECHNIQUES: Shortwave diathermy is administered either through the application of one condenser plate on each side of the area to be treated or by means of an induction coil which uses a magnetic field to induce increased temperature within the tissues. The condenser method of treatment produces more current density superficially than in the deeper tissues. One layer of absorbent cotton toweling is required to prevent the concentration of the electric field on the perspiration that may accumulate on the skin area being treated. Treatment time is usually 20 to 30 minutes.

In the majority of pulsed shortwave diathermy applications, the treatment goal is to select the highest possible pulse power while generating the least amount of heat.[45] Numerous protocols for pulse duration and repetition rates and peak power exist, with little scientific evidence regarding the most effective protocol. One manufacturer suggests treatment durations of 15 to 45 minutes, depending upon patient comfort and tolerance, repeated up to four times per day.

Ultrasound

To this point in the chapter we have discussed modalities that utilize some aspect of the electromagnetic energy spectrum in order to create their therapeutic effects. In this section we will discuss *ultrasound*, a deep heating modality which utilizes the acoustic energy spectrum to produce its therapeutic result (Figure 7.4). *Phonophoresis*, the use of ultrasound to drive medications through the skin into underlying tissues, will also be discussed.

FIGURE 7.4
Recent ultrasound research on humans has led to new understanding and improved use of this modality.
(*Source:* Sports Injury Research Lab of Brigham Young University, Provo, UT 84057.)

Ultrasound therapy involves the creation and transfer of high-frequency sound waves into the body for therapeutic purposes. Present-day therapeutic ultrasound equipment is designed to emit waves well beyond the human audible acoustic range of approximately 16 cycles per second (Hz) to 20,000 Hz. Acoustic waveforms with frequencies greater than 20,000 are termed ultrasound. Therapeutic ultrasound follows the Law of Grotthus-Draper, discussed earlier in this chapter, in that ultrasound penetrates through tissues high in water content, is absorbed by tissues high in protein, reflects off bony surfaces, and refracts through joints.[6]

The most commonly used ultrasound frequencies in sports medicine today are 1 MHz (1 million cycles per second) and 3 MHz (3 million cycles per second). Unlike audible sound, which travels well through the air, these much higher ultrasound frequencies require a more dense medium for efficient transmission.

A well documented inverse relationship exists between the frequency of the ultrasound and the depth of penetration of the acoustic energy. That is, the greater the frequency of the ultrasound, the less depth of penetration in human tissues (e.g., the output from a 1 MHz ultrasound transducer will penetrate to greater depths than the output from a 3 MHz transducer).[46] For the sports medicine clinician different therapeutic indications exist for these two most common ultrasound frequencies. When treating superficial conditions such as olecranon bursitis or Achilles tendinitis, a 3 MHz ultrasound transducer should suffice. For treatment of a deeper injury such as a gluteal muscle strain or ischial bursitis, use of a 1 MHz transducer would be more appropriate (Figure 7.5).

Several key terms associated with ultrasound devices must be defined. The strength of an ultrasound beam is determined by its *intensity,* the rate at which energy is delivered per unit area. Using SI units, ultrasound intensity is expressed in watts per square centimeter (W/cm^2), and is calculated by measuring the total

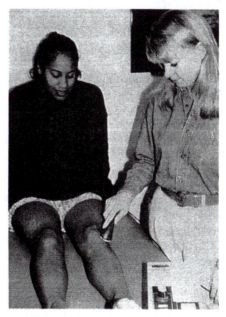

FIGURES 7.5
Ultrasound application

power output of the ultrasound generator (in watts) and dividing by the area of the transducer face (in cm^2). Therapeutic ultrasound intensities employed to treat sports-related injuries range from about 0.25 W/cm^2 to 3.0 W/cm^2.

The *effective radiating area* (ERA) of a particular transducer represents the portion of the transducer that emits ultrasound waves, and is always smaller than the transducer surface. The ERA of a given ultrasound transducer is measured at a distance of 5 mm from the transducer by recording all the areas that emit more than 5% of the maximum power output found at any location on the transducer's surface. When the ERA of an ultrasound transducer is unknown, this value can be estimated as 70% of the transducer's surface area.[48]

The variability within an ultrasound beam is referred to as its *beam nonuniformity ratio* (BNR). This parameter is defined as the ratio of the highest intensity within the ultrasound beam (known as the *spatial peak intensity*) to the average intensity indicated on the device's output meter. In accordance with a recent federal law, the BNR value must be indicated on the ultrasound unit. The significance of knowing the BNR value becomes apparent in the following example: If the ultrasound unit you are using has a BNR of 5:1, and you are treating a subacute case of Achilles tendinitis using an intensity of 1.5 W/cm^2, some portion of the ultrasound beam will have an intensity of 7.5 W/cm^2, a level that may cause periosteal burning in your patient. Thus, the higher the BNR, the more important that the clinician move the transducer constantly throughout the treatment in order to avoid creating hot spots and tissue damage. The lower the BNR, the more uniform the ultrasonic output; when contemplating purchase of a new ultrasound generator, consider any device with a BNR greater than 8:1 unacceptable.[49]

Dependent upon the nature of the injury, the ultrasound treatment may be delivered in a *continuous* or *pulsed* (interrupted) mode. The clinician can specify the length of time that the ultrasound wave is present during one pulse period. This ratio value is called the *duty cycle* and can be calculated using the following formula:[50]

$$duty\ cycle = \frac{duration\ of\ pulse\ (time\ on)}{pulse\ period\ (time\ on + time\ off)}$$

The maximum duty cycle (ratio) value is 1.0; the nearer the duty cycle value is to 1.0, the greater the thermal effects of the ultrasound treatment. The duty cycle most commonly used in pulsed ultrasound is 0.20 (i.e., ultrasound waves flowing 20 percent of the time), with other protocols employing duty cycles ranging from 0.05 (5%) to 0.50 (50%). If pulsed ultrasound is used to treat an acute injury, typically only the nonthermal effects of ultrasound are desired; the clinician might select a 1 MHz frequency transducer, pulsed-wave ultrasound set at a low intensity (e.g., 0.5 or 1.0 watts/cm^2) using a duty cycle of 20% (2 msec "ON", 8 msec "OFF") for 10 minutes so as not to increase blood flow and promote edema formation.

According to Lehmann,[51] a continuous ultrasound treatment must increase tissue temperature by 2°C in order for pain reduction, increased blood flow, and reduction in muscle spasm to occur. To produce increased tendon extensibility and affect collagen viscoelastic properties, the ultrasound treatment must increase treated tissue temperature by 4°C. Draper and associates[52] recently studied the thermal effects of continuous ultrasound treatments of 10-minute duration using 1 MHz frequency at 1.5 W/cm^2 and 2.0 W/cm^2, and observed local temperature increases of 3°C and 4°C, respectively, at tissue depths of 3 cm. These authors suggested that the area being treated be no larger than twice the ERA of the ultrasound transducer used in order to ensure a therapeutic rise in tissue temperature. They also discovered that 3 MHz ultrasound heats three times faster than the more common 1 MHz frequency.[53] They were able to increase muscle temperature 4°C in three to four minutes with 3 MHz ultrasound at 1.5–2 W/cm^2.

Average ultrasound treatment times range from five to eight minutes, but should depend on the ERA of the transducer and the size of the area treated. The actual net dosage of ultrasound delivered is difficult to determine. Assuming the surface to be treated is planar, Grey[54] suggested that the total treatment time can be estimated with the formula:

$$total\ treatment\ time = \frac{time\ per\ cm^2\ surface\ area \times treated\ surface\ area}{effective\ radiating\ area}$$

INDICATIONS: Therapeutic ultrasound has been used for more than four decades in the treatment of a variety of soft-tissue conditions including sprains, strains, tendinitis, and bursitis. Ultrasound is also used in pain management and wound healing, elimination of calcific deposits, joint contractures and scar tissue formation, and the treatment of plantar warts. Recent studies have found ultrasound to be an effective deep heating agent, thus preparing tissues for stretching, joint mobilization, and cross-friction massage.[55,56]

The results of a double-blind, multi-institutional prospective study of noninvasive, low-intensity (30 mW/cm^2) pulsed ultrasound recently confirmed the findings of previous animal and human studies that low-intensity ultrasound accelerates the tibial fracture healing rate in humans. Heckman et al.[57] treated 67 tibial fractures with either ultrasound or a placebo device (sham ultrasound), and found that one 20-minute low-intensity ultrasound treatment per day for a period of 20 weeks or until the fracture was sufficiently healed increased fracture healing rate by nearly 38 percent with no serious complications related to its use.

CONTRAINDICATIONS: Ultrasound should not be applied to the eyes, heart, testes, or pregnant uterus. The clinician should minimize the exposure of active growth plates of adolescents to ultrasound.

PRECAUTIONS: The sports medicine clinician must be wary of treating individuals who have a diminished ability to perceive changes in tissue temperature and pain level. For example, an athlete who has just undergone surgery to an extremity or spine may temporarily have reduced sensory input from nerves cut during the operation and might not be able to sense when tissue damage from an ultrasound treatment is occurring. An additional concern involves the use of ultrasound over areas with reduced circulation, as the heat produced by the treatment may not dissipate rapidly enough.[50]

Reflection of ultrasound energy at the muscle-bone interface may cause burning of the periosteum and must be avoided. The most common instances of periosteal burning occur when delivering ultrasound over bony prominences of the body with little fat or muscle covering. When treating a superficial condition such as an acromioclavicular joint sprain or olecranon bursitis, the intensity of the ultrasound treatment should be reduced if periosteal pain is perceived.

THERAPEUTIC AND PHYSIOLOGIC EFFECTS: Ultrasound treatment protocols may be manipulated to create both thermal and nonthermal effects. Thermal effects of ultrasound are those effects that accompany the elevation in tissue temperature to depths of 5 cm produced by ultrasound, and are similar to those produced by deep thermal agents discussed previously. These include increased blood flow, increased nerve conduction velocity, increased collagenous tissue extensibility, and decreased pain.[50]

Tissues that contain a high percentage of collagen are particularly affected by ultrasound energy; thus bone, tendons, ligaments, and joint capsular structures are common targets for ultrasound treatments. The amount of heat created by ultrasound is dependent upon the intensity of the signal and the size of the area being treated.

The nonthermal effects produced by ultrasound are defined as effects attributed to some mechanism other than an increase in tissue temperature. Nonthermal effects are not as well understood as are thermal effects, but they include *cavitation,* the vibrational effect on gas bubbles by the ultrasound beam. *Stable cavitation* refers to the creation of stable cavities between the gas bubbles which can produce positive changes in cell membrane diffusion and alter cell function. Sufficiently intense pulsation of these gas bubbles in the treated area, known as *unstable cavitation,* can cause changes in cellular activity, as well as tissue and blood vessel damage. At present, however, there is insufficient research to know if any beneficial nonthermal effects of ultrasound occur, or if they can be attributed to stable cavitation.[50]

TREATMENT TECHNIQUES: In general, a 3.0 MHz frequency ultrasound transducer should be used for treating lesions from 1 to 2 cm in depth, while a 1 MHz frequency ultrasound transducer is recommended for treating injuries at depths of 2 cm or more from the skin surface.[50]

Since ultrasound waves cannot pass through the air, a coupling agent must be employed so that as much of the ultrasound energy as possible passes from the transducer head into the tissues being treated. Treatment techniques can employ either a direct contact or an indirect contact method, and are selected based upon the contour of the body segment being treated. The mode of delivery can be either pulsed ultrasound, designed to produce only nonthermal effects, or continuous ultrasound, which heats the tissues.

Direct contact technique. This method is useful when treating flat contoured body segments such as the low back or anterior thigh regions. A thin layer of water-soluble coupling medium (gel) is applied to the skin so as to transmit the sound waves from the transducer into the area in need of treatment. Many clinicians heat the coupling medium to body temperature (37°C) for improved patient comfort; however, the viscosity of the medium should remain high enough so that it stays in a gel form.

The transducer must be kept at right angles to the treatment surface or else the ultrasound waves will be reflected off the skin due to poor coupling (refer to the cosine law previously discussed in this chapter). The transducer head must be kept moving constantly with small circular or longitudinal strokes at a rate of about four centimeters per second.[58] Overlap each previous stroke by approximately one half.

The clinician must consider the major goal of the ultrasound treatment and the quantity of tissue to be treated when selecting the intensity of ultrasound. This dosage intensity should be set and subsequently adjusted as necessary while the transducer is in contact with the patient. When the primary objective is vigorous heating of the tissues, the ultrasound output should be increased to a level that produces a dull ache and then reduced slightly to just below the athlete's pain threshold.[9] It is permissible for the patient to have a mild sensation of warmth beneath the transducer during the treatment, but otherwise the ultrasound treatment should remain at a subsensory level.

There are three general categories of therapeutic ultrasound dosage: (a) low intensity, ranging from 0.1 to 0.8 W/cm^2, (b) medium intensity, from 0.8 to 1.5 W/cm^2, and (c) high intensity, ranging from 1.5 to 3.0 W/cm^2. Lower intensity ultrasound can be utilized when the primary objective of the treatment is the relief of muscle spasms or pain management, conditions that respond to smaller increases (2°C) in tissue temperature.

Indirect contact technique. This ultrasound technique is used on unevenly contoured body surfaces and/or segments that are highly sensitive to pressure. The most common indirect method is the underwater technique, in which the body part to be treated is immersed in water. The injured area should be submerged underwater and the ultrasound transducer should be held approximately 1 to 2 centimeters from the skin surface, but should not make contact. As with the direct contact technique, the clinician must keep the transducer moving. The clinician should not immerse his/her hand holding the transducer in the water as demineralization of the bones of the hand has been reported among those who have performed repeated underwater ultrasound treatments.

Williams[59] recommended use of a ceramic tub for underwater ultrasound treatments due to the excellent reflective qualities of the ceramic material, in effect creating an "echo chamber" which causes the ultrasound output to contact the immersed body part from all angles. It should be noted that the presence of air bubbles in the water or on the face of the ultrasound transducer tends to reduce the transmission of ultrasound.[50]

A second indirect technique utilizes a water-filled balloon or gel pack positioned between the transducer head and the area to be treated. In this technique, the gel pack or balloon helps the clinician maintain transducer contact with the irregularly shaped injured areas that do not fit easily into a ceramic tub (e.g., an acromioclavicular joint injury). A coupling gel is also used between the balloon or gel pack and the skin.

A minimum of three ultrasound treatments per week are needed to achieve a therapeutic benefit, but the recommended frequency of ultrasound is daily administration. An upper limit of 12 to 14 consecutive ultrasound treatments has been recommended in several published reports; however, other sources contend that properly applied ultrasound has no negative long-term side effects and that a maximum number of treatments has yet to be determined scientifically.[60]

Phonophoresis

Phonophoresis is a technique whereby whole molecules of medication are driven through the skin by means of ultrasound. The most common medications used in phonophoresis are anti-inflammatories (e.g., 10% hydrocortisone), salicylates (e.g., Myoflex, Theragesic), and local anesthetics (e.g., Xylocaine, lidocaine).

INDICATIONS: Phonophoresis has been used for superficial, acute, and subacute soft-tissue conditions, such as tendinitis, strains, and contusions. Among the specific conditions commonly treated with phonophoresis are iliotibial band friction syndrome, Achilles tendinitis, medial and lateral humeral epicondylitis, plantar fasciitis, and supraspinatus tendinitis.

CONTRAINDICATIONS: The contraindications for phonophoresis are similar to those listed previously for ultrasound, with the addition of any potential adverse reaction to the specific medication being driven transdermally.

PRECAUTIONS: The skin overlying the area to be treated should be washed thoroughly to remove any bacteria and skin oils. The most frequent medication used for phonophoresis is a 10 percent hydrocortisone ointment, sometimes in conjunction with a local anesthetic agent such as lidocaine. The clinician must be aware of the possibility of suppression of adrenal gland function and the tendon-weakening effect of corticosteroids. Sensitivity to local anesthetic agents should also be noted if these medications are to be used. These medications are prescription drugs whose use requires the supervision of a physician.

THERAPEUTIC AND PHYSIOLOGIC EFFECTS: The therapeutic effects are the same as those associated with ultrasound, with the additional biochemical and/or physiological effects of the substances driven through the skin.

TREATMENT TECHNIQUES: When administering phonophoresis, the coupling method may be either direct or indirect. The medication to be used is applied directly to the skin surface to be treated, a coupling gel is then spread over the medication, and then a continuous ultrasound treatment is performed. An optional technique involves massaging the medication into the muscle, followed by application of the coupling gel, followed by ultrasound. If an indirect technique is utilized, the medication is applied to the skin first, and the body segment is immersed in water and then treated with continuous-mode ultrasound.

Recent research has revealed that many of the most popular coupling mediums used with phonophoresis cause reflection, rather than transmission, of ultrasound energy at the skin-transducer interface. Generally, thick, white corticosteroid creams were found to be poor conductors of ultrasound, with some causing 100 percent reflection of the ultrasound output. If the coupling agent used in phonophoresis does not allow ultrasound transmission, then no penetration of the medication, nor ultrasound energy, will occur. A recent study reported that a 10 percent trolamine salicylate cream (Myoflex) did not transmit ultrasound, while other salicylate products (e.g., Theragesic) permitted ultrasound transmission.[61]

Another study[62] compared the heating effects of Flex-all and Biofreeze at muscle depths of 3 centimeters during a 10-minute, 1-MHz ultrasound treatment. Concentrations of 50% ultrasound gel mixed with 50% Flex-all or Biofreeze were used as coupling media. Pure 100% ultrasound gel was used as the control, and caused an increase of 3.4°C; the Flex-all mixture resulted in a 2.8°C increase; and the Biofreeze raised muscle temperature only 1.8°C. Thus, the contents of Flex-all impedes ultrasound transmission by 20 percent, while Biofreeze impedes ultrasound transmission by 47 percent.

Additional research studies are required on this subject before any conclusions regarding the clinical efficacy of phonophoresis may be drawn.

Electrical Agents

The first documented use of an electrical modality in medicine was described by Hippocrates in the 5th century B.C. in his recommendation to include boiled torpedo fish as part of the diet of individuals with asthma.[63] He believed that eating the flesh of the torpedo fish, a species which can generate an electrical charge to shock its prey, would in some way be beneficial to asthmatic patients. Clearly, the use of electricity in physical medicine has been refined in the nearly 2500 years since the days of Hippocrates. Most notably, the last two decades have brought unparalleled advances in the scientific understanding of how electricity affects human neuromuscular function, and in the technology of the devices used to deliver therapeutic doses of electricity to human tissues.

Recall our discussion earlier in this chapter of the terms used to describe the electrical currents used in physical medicine. To review, direct current (DC) is the continuous, unidirectional flow of either negatively- or positively-charged particles. Alternating current (AC) involves the continuous, bidirectional flow of charged particles, while pulsed current is either alternating or direct current which is periodically interrupted for a finite period of time. To achieve desired therapeutic effects, the sports medicine clinician manipulates the type of electrical current used, along with other device-specific parameters such as waveform, magnitude, voltage, frequency, pulse rate, and treatment duration.

When electrodes from an electrotherapeutic device are applied to the skin and the amplitude of the electrical stimulation is gradually increased, three progressive responses are typically observed in normal individuals: *sensory level stimulation, motor level stimulation,* and *noxious level stimulation.* When the amplitude of the electrical stimulation is at a relatively low level, the initial response perceived by the patient is sensory in nature, and depending upon the frequency, may be described as a "pins and needles" or "tapping" sensation. These sensations result from the stimulation of sensory nerve fibers which lie in close proximity to the surface electrodes, under which the electrical current density is the greatest. If the clinician continues to increase the amplitude of the current, the patient's sensory perception becomes stronger and commonly more diffuse, particularly within the soft tissues located between the electrodes.[64]

A physiologic phenomenon called *adaptation* occurs if a static level of sensory stimulation is maintained for a prolonged period of time, and the athlete being treated will sense a gradual decrease in the amount of sensation perceived. Adaptation can be reduced by modulating the frequency or amplitude of electrical stimulation, or by simply increasing the amplitude of stimulation at a midpoint (e.g., 5 to 7 minutes) of the treatment period.

Continued gradual increases in the amplitude of electrical stimulation will next produce motor level stimulation. Specifically, alpha motoneuron axons in the peripheral nerves innervating the muscle being treated are excited to create either isometric or concentric isotonic muscle actions, as predetermined by the clinician.

If joint movement is mechanically or manually restrained, or if both agonist and antagonist muscle groups are stimulated simultaneously, then an isometric muscle action will result. If movement at the joint at which the muscle being stimulated acts is not constrained, then a concentric isotonic muscle action will be produced.

Continued increases in electrical amplitude will next produce a noxious level response in the patient. While this form of electrical stimulation is painful and cannot be tolerated for extended periods of time, it produces very forceful muscular actions and may be beneficial in the relief of pain and muscle spasms. Given the individual differences in pain tolerance among athletes, the exact stimulation parameters (e.g., amplitude, waveform, electrode location) which evoke a painful response vary considerably.[64]

In this section, three specific clinical uses of electrical agents will be discussed: neuromuscular electrical stimulation, transcutaneous electrical nerve stimulation, and transdermal delivery of medication via iontophoresis.

Neuromuscular Electrical Stimulation

Neuromuscular electrical stimulation (NMES) is defined as the application of electrical current to stimulate a response from a muscle. The electrical current introduced to biologic tissues must be of sufficient amplitude and duration to cause excitable cells to reach the threshold required for them to release an *action potential* (see Arndt-Schultz principle). An action potential is a large, transient depolarization event that is conducted along the membrane of a muscle cell or nerve fiber, and necessary (either singly or in succession) for muscle stimulation to occur.

INDICATIONS: The U.S. Food and Drug Administration has approved NMES devices as safe and effective for (a) the treatment of disuse atrophy, (b) the increase and maintenance of range of motion, and (c) muscle reeducation and facilitation.[65] Additional indications for NMES use include the supplementation of motor recruitment in healthy muscle, the management of spastic disorders, and the enhancement of function of weak or paralyzed muscles as a substitute for braces or orthoses.[66]

CONTRAINDICATIONS: Electrotherapy is generally contraindicated in individuals with known or suspected cardiac arrhythmias or conditions managed by demand-type pacemakers because of the potential for grim consequences, the severely obese, and persons whose fracture is immobilized with a metal external fixation device. The clinician must also avoid use of electrical stimulation over the carotid sinus.[67]

PRECAUTIONS: The skin of some individuals may have an allergic response to, or be irritated by, coupling gels, the electrode materials, or adhesives used to hold electrodes in place. This problem can typically be avoided by using hypoallergenic electrodes and by not placing the electrodes in the same exact location from one treatment to the next.

THERAPEUTIC AND PHYSIOLOGIC EFFECTS: Research on the effects of NMES on human skeletal muscle has revealed significant changes in muscle fiber characteristics (e.g., hypertrophy of both Type I and Type II muscle fibers) and metabolism (e.g., increased mitochondrial oxidative capacity and higher levels of adenosine triphosphatase) following repetitive electrical stimulation.[66]

Delitto and Robinson[68] reviewed existing research studies that compared the abilities of NMES and voluntary exercise to alter muscle performance in healthy subjects with no apparent muscle weakness. The collective results of NMES research suggests that: (a) usually an increase in strength is found in the NMES treatment group when compared with an unexercised control group; (b) no difference typically exists between strength levels in the NMES group and the voluntary exercise group; (c) no additional strength gains are observed when voluntary exercise and NMES were performed simultaneously, when compared to the results of voluntary exercise alone or NMES alone; and (d) it is possible with NMES to create (electrically) isometric muscle tension to as much as 80 to 90 percent of maximum *voluntary* isometric torque values.

In studies of patient populations (i.e., persons with muscle weakness), the collective summary of the literature suggests that certain NMES treatment regimens produce strength gains which exceed those found with voluntary exercise. Not surprisingly, a positive relationship has been found between the intensity of NMES stimulation and the amount of strength gained.[68] Refer to Table 7.5 for specific characteristics of a typical NMES strengthening protocol.

TREATMENT TECHNIQUES: Although a number of waveforms are available in electrotherapeutic devices, the symmetrical biphasic rectangular (preferred for stimulation of large muscle groups) and the asymmetrical biphasic rectangular waveforms (preferred for selective recruitment of smaller muscles) are the two most

TABLE 7.5 *Characteristics of neuromuscular electrical stimulation (NMES) strengthening programs*

Type of current	Pulsatile or burst-modulated AC
Amplitude of stimulation	Maximum tolerable
Phase duration	20 to 1000 μsec
Waveform	Subject preference
Duty cycle	10 to 15 sec ON / 50 to 120 sec OFF
Frequency of stimulation	30 to 50 pulses/sec or bursts/sec
Type of muscle action	Isometric
Number of stimulations per session	10 to 20 at maximum tolerable intensity
Frequency of sessions	3 to 5 times per week minimum

Adapted from A Delitto, AJ Robinson, Electrical stimulation of muscle: techniques and applications. In *Clinical Electrophysiology: Electrotherapy and Electrophysiologic Testing*, ed. L Snyder-Mackler, AJ Robinson, Baltimore: Williams and Wilkins, 1989, p. 112.

commonly used in NMES. These waveforms provide an equal amount of current flow in each of the phases (negative charge and positive charge), thus eliminating the possibility of undesired electrochemical effects.[66]

Carbon-impregnated silicon rubber electrodes are commonly used in the sports medicine setting, as they are flexible and available in a variety of shapes and sizes. More recent technology has provided the clinician with new electrode options from which to choose: self-adhesive synthetic copolymer gel pads, conductive gel pads, and karaya pads (made of a natural conductive gum). These types of electrodes, although disposable, can be reused several times if the skin surface is cleansed prior to application. DeVahl[66] suggests that an effective electrode must (a) promote low skin-electrode resistance to current flow (*impedance*), (b) uniformly conduct electrical current, (c) be sufficiently flexible to maintain uniform contact with the skin throughout the treatment, (d) avoid skin irritation, and (e) be cost effective.

The size of the electrode is inversely proportional to the current density; the larger the electrode, the less its current density for a given amplitude. Larger electrodes have a lower resistance to current flow than smaller electrodes.[67] Additionally, larger electrodes have been found to be significantly more comfortable to the patient (less pain due to a lower current density) and are able to induce greater magnitude muscle actions than are smaller electrodes.[69]

Three different treatment techniques are associated with NMES, based upon electrode size and placement: *monopolar* technique, *bipolar* technique, and *quadripolar* technique. With the monopolar technique, the surface areas of the electrodes are of unequal size; this technique is commonly used when treating small muscles or trigger points. The *active electrode* (where the treatment effect occurs) is placed over the motor point of the muscle to be treated, while the *dispersive electrode* (where the electrical current is transmitted into the body) is placed at a point distant to the area being stimulated. In this protocol, the surface area of the dispersive electrode is substantially larger than that of the active electrode(s) in order to achieve a higher electrical current density at the active electrode(s).

With the bipolar technique, the electrodes are of equal size and are used to stimulate large muscles or a group of muscles. The clinician positions both electrodes on the same muscle or muscle group. Since the electrodes are of equal size, their current densities are equal, and therefore an equivalent amount of stimulation occurs under each electrode. For instance, when treating the quadriceps muscles, one electrode (active) is positioned over the motor point on the lower one-third of the thigh while another electrode (dispersive) is placed over the proximal portion of the femoral nerve. Typical duty cycles used with NMES protocols range from 1:5 (10 seconds on, 50 seconds off) to 1:6 (10 seconds on, 60 seconds off) in order to avoid muscle fatigue.[68]

The quadripolar stimulation technique requires the use of an NMES device with two channels with a set of electrodes emanating from each channel. Perhaps the clearest explanation of quadripolar technique is to envision two concurrent bipolar treatment techniques. Based upon the goal(s) of the treatment and the clinician's preference, the four equal-sized electrodes may be arranged so that the currents from the two channels either: (a) run parallel to each other (e.g., when attempting to strengthen the lumbar erector spinae musculature bilaterally), (b) intersect in an interferential mode (e.g., when trying to resolve a chronic rotator cuff muscle weakness), or (c) work in opposition (e.g., when stimulating agonist and antagonist muscle groups).[67]

Transcutaneous Electrical Nerve Stimulation (TENS)

For the purposes of our discussion, the term *transcutaneous electrical nerve stimulation* (TENS) refers to all therapeutic devices that transmit electrical waveforms across the skin (transcutaneously) for the primary purpose of pain management. When discussing TENS and pain management, most sports medicine clinicians envision a small, portable, battery-powered one- or two-channel stimulator unit with self-adhesive electrodes worn by the athlete for extended periods of time. However, low voltage *interferential current* (IFC) units as well as *microcurrent electrical nerve stimulation* (MENS) devices also have their place in the clinician's armamentarium against acute and chronic pain.

INDICATIONS: While the majority of TENS units have the capacity to stimulate muscular contractions (with the lone exception being MENS devices), the primary use of TENS is to control acute and chronic pain. Transcutaneous electrical nerve stimulation has been used successfully in the treatment of postsurgical pain and following musculoskeletal injury.[70–72]

CONTRAINDICATIONS: TENS is a very safe, non-invasive therapeutic procedure with few contraindications. These include the same general contraindications discussed previously with NMES (e.g., patients with pacemakers, use over the carotid sinus, pregnancy).

PRECAUTIONS: The skin of some individuals may have an allergic response to or be irritated by coupling gels, the electrode materials, or adhesives used to hold electrodes in place. This problem is of greater concern when the electrodes are worn for extended periods of time, but the incidence can be diminished by use of non-irritating coupling gels and/or hypoallergenic electrodes.

THERAPEUTIC AND PHYSIOLOGIC EFFECTS: Electrical stimulation for the relief of pain has been performed for more than a century by physical medicine practitioners, yet this practice was not accepted by the scientific community until Melzack and Wall introduced their gate control theory of pain transmission in 1965.[73]

The exact mechanism by which TENS works remains subject to speculation, as its clinical efficacy has not been well established through controlled scientific studies. Perhaps most controversial are the conclusions of a well controlled clinical study by Deyo and colleagues that, in the treatment of chronic low back pain, TENS was no more effective than treatment with a placebo (sham TENS), and that TENS added no apparent benefits to those achieved with a program of stretching exercises alone.[74]

Establishing the clinical efficacy of TENS is no easy task because one unavoidable problem exists in all research designs. TENS is a modality that produces a sensory stimulation so that those treated with TENS are quite aware of the treatment. Sham TENS, as was used in the Deyo et al. study to provide the requisite control group, does not result in sensory level stimulation and may be perceived by patients as a less-than-credible treatment, perhaps one not capable of producing a legitimate placebo effect.[75]

TREATMENT TECHNIQUES: Snyder-Mackler[76] observed that electroanalgesia is accomplished by one of three methods, and virtually all commercially available TENS stimulators are able to produce each of these responses. Using terms previously discussed in this chapter, pain can be modulated through sensory level stimulation, motor level stimulation, and noxious level stimulation. The clinical treatment protocols for each of these methods is presented in Table 7.6.

Sensory level stimulation for pain control, also known as "conventional TENS" or "high frequency TENS," employs the original gate control theory of Melzack and Wall. According to this pain control theory, the nonpain sensory information traveling at a faster rate through larger-diameter nerves (A-fibers) activates T-cells in the dorsal horn of the spinal cord and "closes the gate" to painful impulses traveling toward the spinal cord at a slower rate on smaller-diameter sensory nerves (C-fibers).[67] When this protocol is administered correctly, the clinician should neither be able to observe nor palpate muscle contraction. Sensory level stimulation is very comfortable because of its low-intensity current level, is beneficial for relief of both acute and chronic pain, and is the technique of choice for many clinicians seeking electroanalgesia.[76]

Motor level stimulation for pain control is used primarily for the cases of nonacute pain, and has been most effective when applied to a site either anatomically or physiologically related to the locus of pain.[76] This mode of TENS application is also known as "acupuncture-like TENS" or "low frequency TENS." Research indicates that greater-intensity muscle contractions evoke increased levels of analgesia, perhaps through the gate control theory or through activation of the endogenous opiate mechanisms of pain relief. The clinical response of patients to motor level stimulation for pain reduction is not usually immediate but tends to be long lasting, which supports the endogenous opiate mechanism.[76]

Noxious level stimulation for pain modulation, also known as "brief-intense TENS," produces a painful stimulus at or away from the injury site. Pain relief is thought to be achieved by activation of mechanisms in the brain stem that attentuate or amplify pain signals.[67] Unlike motor level stimulation, the analgesic effects of

TABLE 7.6 *Electroanalgesia produced with TENS protocols: (a) conventional, (b) acupuncture-like, and (c) brief-intense*

Parameter	Conventional TENS	Acupuncture-like TENS	Brief-Intense TENS
Mode of stimulation	Sensory level	Motor level	Noxious level
Amplitude	Perceptible tingling	Strong, visible contractions	Noxious, below motor threshold
Pulse frequency	50 to 100 pps	1 to 5 pps	1 to 5 or 100 pps
Pulse duration	30 to 300 μsec	200 to 500 μsec	250 to 500 μsec
Mode	Modulated rate	Burst	Modulated amplitude
Duration of treatment	As needed	30 to 45 minutes	Seconds to minutes
Onset of relief	< 10 minutes	20 to 40 minutes	< 15 minutes
Duration of analgesia	Few residual post-treatment effects	Hours to days	30 to 60 minutes

Adapted from L Snyder-Mackler, Electrical stimulation for pain modulation. In *Clinical Electrophysiology: Electrotherapy and Electrophysiologic Testing*, ed. L Snyder-Mackler, AJ Robinson, Baltimore: Williams and Wilkins, 1989, p. 209; and C. Starkey, *Therapeutic Modalities for Athletic Trainers*, Philadelphia: F. A. Davis, 1993, p. 147.

noxious level stimulation are short-lived, and thus, this technique is recommended for pain reduction prior to therapeutic exercise sessions.[77] (Figure 7.6)

Iontophoresis

Iontophoresis is a process whereby ions in solution (medication) are driven through the intact skin by means of low-voltage bipolar electrodes. Prescription anesthetics, analgesics, and anti-inflammatory agents are the most commonly used medications for iontophoresis.[78,79] One popular combination is an ionized solution of dexamethasone (an anti-inflammatory agent) with lidocaine (an anesthetic).

Because of an ionic reaction that occurs between the negative and positive poles of the iontophoresis generator, the medication molecules are driven through the skin and into the superficial tissues along the lines of

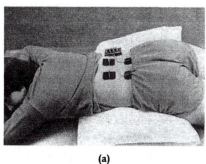
(a)

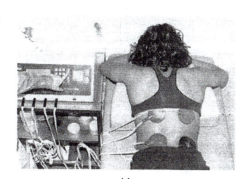
(b)   (c)

FIGURE 7.6
Transcutaneous electrical nerve stimulation for pain relief

force created by the electrical current. At the negative electrode, negative ions are driven through the skin while positive ions are electrically forced through the skin at the positive pole. A direct current generator is required for iontophoresis in order to ensure the unidirectional flow of ions during the treatment, with the extent of ion transfer proportional to the duration and intensity of the current.[80] Hasson and associates reported penetration of dexamethasone to depths of 2 cm below the skin.[81]

INDICATIONS: Due to its relatively superficial depth of penetration, iontophoresis is indicated for the treatment of inflammatory conditions such as tendinitis, bursitis, and epicondylitis. This modality has also been used in the treatment of adhesions, bone spurs, scar tissue formation, myositis ossificans, adhesive capsulitis (frozen shoulder), and delayed-onset muscle soreness.[79,82,83]

CONTRAINDICATIONS: The particular contraindications of iontophoresis are specific to the medication being used. Toxic and allergic reactions to the medications employed have been reported.

PRECAUTIONS: Skin irritation and chemical burning are the most frequent side effects associated with iontophoresis.

THERAPEUTIC AND PHYSIOLOGIC EFFECTS: The therapeutic and physiologic effects of iontophoresis are specific to the medications used. Anti-inflammatory medications such as hydrocortisone and dexamethasone have been shown to reduce inflammation. Similarly, use of an anesthetic such as lidocaine is intended for pain reduction through anesthesia.

TREATMENT TECHNIQUES: Prior to administration of iontophoresis, the clinician should brief the patient on the typical sensations experienced during the treatment (i.e., a tingling sensation usually followed by warmth). The area to be treated should be cleansed thoroughly to remove any potential insulators against the electrical current, such as dirt, skin oils, and lotions. Treatment durations range from 20 to 60 minutes.

The efficacy of transdermal delivery of a desired medication (iontophoresis) has been compared against oral and injection delivery methods. Each method has its advantages and disadvantages, but perhaps the primary criticism of iontophoresis is the inability to drive adequate concentrations of a given medication through the skin into a treatment area and contain it there. To address this issue, Riviere and associates[84,85] coupled lidocaine with vasoactive medications (vasoconstrictors or vasodilators) in a process they termed *co-iontophoresis*. These researchers observed that when lidocaine and epinephrine (a vasoconstrictor) were phoresed in combination, a higher concentration of lidocaine was transferred into the tissues and a longer period of time was required to dissipate the medication from the treatment area. Thus, the lidocaine had longer lasting effects and greater concentration when phoresed in combination with the vasoconstrictor than when administered alone. Conversely, when lidocaine was combined with a vasodilator (tolazoline), opposite effects were demonstrated, as the lidocaine concentration at the treatment site decreased more rapidly and distributed throughout the circulatory system. While these research findings are preliminary, it appears the use of vasoactive medications can improve the effectiveness of medications delivered via iontophoresis.

Massage

INDICATIONS: Postacute soft-tissue trauma, particularly strains.

CONTRAINDICATIONS AND PRECAUTIONS: Acute injuries with ongoing hemorrhaging, infections, thromboses, and situations where calcification might occur with massage, for example, thigh contusion with the possibility of myositis ossificans and conditions in which the nervous system has suffered some damage.

THERAPEUTIC AND PHYSIOLOGICAL EFFECTS: The effects vary according to the specific type of massage applied. However, these effects are usually classified as either mechanical or reflexive.

TREATMENT TECHNIQUES: Determine the specific type of massage to be utilized for the particular situation and injury. Types of massage are:

1. *Effleurage*—Superficial or deep stroking movements administered with the flat of the hand and fingers:

   a. *Deep massage*—Mechanical forces are applied to the deeper structures such as the muscles.

   b. *Superficial massage*—No pressure is applied, so that the main effect is that of sensation rather than of mechanical force.

2. *Petrissage*—Kneading of the muscles. All movement is executed by grasping or picking up the muscle tissue, then compressing, rolling, or squeezing it. The pressure is usually applied into the muscle rather than along the body surface.

3. *Tapotement*—This technique involves mechanical percussion with the fingers, the fingertips, the palms, or the sides of the hands to create tapping, cupping, slapping, or hacking movements.

4. *Vibration*—The hand is kept in contact with the athlete to produce a trembling, vibratory forward-and-backward movement. The direction of massage is usually distal-to-proximal—for example, in the upper extremity, from the fingers to the wrist or from the elbow to the shoulder; in the lower extremity, from the ankle to the knee or from the knee to the hip; on the back, from the buttocks to mid-scapula along the spine.

5. *Friction*—In frictional and, especially, cross-frictional massage, firm fingertip pressure is applied to or across the muscles, tendons, or both. This is a particularly useful technique for breaking down scar tissue, for example, lateral epicondylitis or rotator-cuff tendinitis.[86]

Manipulative Therapy

The use of manipulative therapy (also called mobilization therapy) is undoubtedly controversial.[87] However, this does not mean that the subject should not be explored. Exponents of manipulative therapy find athletes to be particularly good subjects, as they are prone to problems that tend to be amenable to manipulation and are less likely to have the contraindications nonathletes might have.

For those wishing to use manipulative techniques, it is important to understand the indications, limitations, and possible dangers. Manipulation should not be undertaken without a thorough understanding of the subject and should be guided by an experienced therapist. Manipulation should not be used as a cure-all, for it can certainly be dangerous if used in the wrong circumstances.[88]

What Does Manipulation Do?
Why Does It Work?

There are many theories as to why manipulation works. One of the most acceptable and easily understood is that presented by John Mennell, M.D., as the concept of joint play and joint dysfunction.[89,90]

Joint play refers to the normal range of involuntary movement of which a joint is capable. An example that

Dr. Mennell often refers to is the metacarpophalangeal joint, which has joint play in several directions. For instance, the joint can be opened by pulling the finger in a long-axis direction (long-axis extension). The phalanx can be moved anteriorly and posteriorly (anteroposterior glide). Also, it can be tilted either to the medial or the lateral side, as well as rotated medially or laterally. These are all normal movements of that particular joint and constitute joint play.

The theory states that if normal joint play is not present, pain will be experienced either in that joint or as referred pain. Pain will be felt both when the joint is moved voluntarily and when it is moved in testing for joint play. This pain is referred to as *joint dysfunction*. Stated another way, the normal range of voluntary movement depends upon the normal range of involuntary movement, i.e., joint play.

Manipulation restores normal joint play by taking the movement of that joint to its limits. If this is done in a correct manner, the pain in that joint will disappear, if due to joint dysfunction as defined above.

Athletes involved in running activities are particularly prone to joint dysfunction of the lower back and feet. Gymnasts and rowers are subject to lower-back joint dysfunction, and wrestlers to neck joint dysfunction. Those involved in weight training often develop joint dysfunction of the wrists. Immobilization of a joint for a period of time to allow healing may result in dysfunction of that joint. All these problems may, after careful evaluation, be suitable for manipulative therapy.

Muscle spasm can follow or be associated with joint dysfunction and can make it very difficult for manipulative techniques to be employed. Muscle spasm can indeed persist after normal joint play has been restored and should be specifically treated by massage, cold spray, cryotherapy, or other suitable techniques.

BEFORE MANIPULATION IS CONSIDERED:

1. A positive diagnosis of joint dysfunction should be made. In order to make this diagnosis, the trainer must appreciate the extent of normal joint play for each individual and should compare the affected joint with the normal opposite joint in making this determination.

2. The contraindications for manipulative therapy should be thoroughly understood. For instance, if joint or bone inflammation or disease exists, then no manipulation should take place. It is not indicated during the healing phase of ligament sprains or muscle strains, nor if there are any signs of a disc protrusion or rupture in the cervical or lumbar areas. It is therefore important to make a distinction between radiating pain, indicating a probable disc protrusion, and referred pain, which might be associated with joint dysfunction.

RULES FOR EMPLOYING MANIPULATIVE THERAPY:

1. Both patient and therapist must be completely relaxed. A patient cannot relax if there is a feeling of tension in the grip or the movements of the therapist.

2. Only one joint should be moved during each manipulation (though there are occasional exceptions to this rule).

3. Only one movement should be performed at each joint at a time.

4. One bone of the joint should be stabilized while the other is moved.

5. There should be very little force and no abnormal movements. Manipulation is achieved by velocity of acceleration, without any real force being applied to the movement. The joint itself should be moved through its full range of normal joint play (which is thought to be nearly always less than three millimeters).

REFERENCES

1. Kisner C, Colby LA: *Therapeutic Exercise.* Philadelphia: F. A. Davis, second edition, p. 3, 1990.

2. Houglum PA: Soft tissue healing and its impact on rehabilitation. *J Sport Rehab* 1:19–39, 1992.

3. *Webster's 9th New Collegiate Dictionary.* Springfield, MA: Merriam-Webster, p. 401, 1991.

4. Prentice WE: Therapeutic modalities in relation to the electromagnetic and acoustic spectra. In *Therapeutic Modalities in Sports Medicine,* edited by Prentice WE. St. Louis: Times Mirror/Mosby College Publishing, second edition, p. 24, 1990.

5. Spiker JC: Ultrasound. In *Therapeutic Modalities in Sports Medicine,* edited by Prentice WE. St. Louis: Times Mirror/Mosby College Publishing, second edition, p. 131, 1990.

6. Draper DO, Sunderlund S: Examination of the Law of Grotthus-Draper: does ultrasound penetrate subcutaneous fat in humans? *J Athletic Training* 28:246–250, 1993.

7. Kloth LC, Cummings JP: *Electrotherapeutic Terminology in Physical Therapy.* Alexandria, VA: Section on Clinical Electrophysiology and the American Physical Therapy Association, 1990.

8. Prentice WE: Basic principles of electricity. In *Therapeutic Modalities in Sports Medicine,* edited by Prentice WE. St. Louis: Times Mirror/Mosby College Publishing, second edition, p. 36, 1990.

9. Lehmann JF, deLateur BJ: Therapeutic heat. In *Therapeutic Heat and Cold,* edited by Lehmann JF. Baltimore: Williams and Wilkins, fourth edition, 1990.

10. Walsh MT: Hydrotherapy: The use of water as a therapeutic agent. In *Thermal Agents in Rehabilitation,* edited by Michlovitz SL. Philadelphia: F. A. Davis, second edition, p. 123, 1990.

11. *National Electrical Code.* Therapeutic pools and tubs in health care facilities. National Fire Protection Association 70, Quincy, MA, 1990.

12. National Safety Council. *Bloodborne Pathogens.* Boston: Jones and Bartlett, 1993.

13. Michlovitz SL: Biophysical principles of heating and superficial heat agents. In *Thermal Agents in Rehabilitation,* edited by Michlovitz SL. Philadelphia: F. A. Davis, second edition, pp. 104–105, 1990.

14. Hafen BQ, Karren KJ: *Prehospital Emergency Care and Crisis Intervention.* Upper Saddle River, NJ: Prentice-Hall, fourth edition, pp. 565–567, 1992.

15. Mennell J McM: The therapeutic use of cold. *J Am Osteopath Assoc* 74:1146–1152, 1975.

16. Grant AE: Massage with ice (cryokinetics) in the treatment of painful conditions of the musculoskeletal system. *Arch Phys Med Rehabil* 45:233–238, 1964.

17. Cohn BT, Draeger RI, Jackson DW: The effects of cold therapy in the postoperative management of pain in patients undergoing anterior cruciate ligament reconstruction. *Am J Sports Med* 17:334–349, 1989.

18. Collins K, Storey M, Peterson K: Peroneal nerve palsy after cryotherapy. *Phys Sportsmed* 14:105–108, May 1986.

19. Green GA, Zachezewski JE, Jordan SE: Case report: cold-induced nerve palsy. *Phys Sportsmed* 17:63–72, 1989.

20. Bierman W: The therapeutic uses of cold. *JAMA* 157:585–592, 1955.

21. Abramson D: The physiologic basis for the use of physical agents in peripheral vascular disorders. *Arch Phys Med Rehabil* 46:216–244, 1965.

22. McMaster WC, Liddle S: Cryotherapy influence on posttraumatic limb edema. *Clin Orthop* 150:283–287, 1980.

23. Janssen CW, Waaler E: Body temperature, antibody formation, and inflammatory response. *Acta Pathol Microbiol Scand* 69:557–566, 1967.

24. Knight KL: Effects of hypothermia on inflammation and swelling. *Athletic Training* 11:7–10, 1976.

25. Lewis T: Observations upon the reactions of the vessels of the human skin to cold. *Heart* 15:177–208, 1929.

26. Knight KL: *Cryotherapy: Theory, Technique and Physiology.* Chattanooga: Chattanooga Corporation, 1985.

27. Baker RJ, Bell GW: The effect of therapeutic modalities on blood flow in the human calf. *J Orthop Sports Phys Ther* 13:23–27, January 1991.

28. Taber C, Countryman K, Fahrenbruch J, LaCount K, Cornwall M: Measurement of reactive vasodilation during cold gel pack application to nontraumatized ankles. *Phys Ther* 294–299, 1992.

29. Weston M, Taber C, Casagranda L, Cornwall M: Changes in local blood volume during cold gel pack application to traumatized ankles. *J Orthop Sports Phys Ther* 19:197–199, April 1994.

30. Michlovitz SL: Biophysical principles of heating and superficial heat agents. pp. 96–97, 1990.

31. Smith W: The application of cold and heat in the treatment of athletic injuries. In *Thermal Agents in Rehabilitation,* edited by Michlovitz SL. Philadelphia: F. A. Davis, second edition, pp. 246–247, 1990.

32. Michlovitz SL: Cryotherapy: the use of cold as a therapeutic agent. In *Thermal Agents in Rehabilitation,* edited by Michlovitz SL. Philadelphia: F. A. Davis, second edition, p. 82. 1990.

33. Travell J, Rinzler SH: The myofascial genesis of pain. *Postgrad Med* 11:425–431, 1952.

34. Travell J: Ethyl chloride for painful muscle spasm. *Arch Phys Med* 33:291–298, 1952.

35. Hayes KW: *Manual for Physical Agents.* Norwalk: Appleton-Lange, fourth edition, pp. 55–56, 1993.

36. Myrer JW, Draper DO, Durrant E: Contrast therapy and intramuscular temperature in the human leg. *J Athletic Training* 29:318–322, 1994.

37. Airaksinen O: Changes in posttraumatic ankle joint mobility, pain, and edema following intermittent pneumatic compression therapy. *Arch Phys Med Rehab* 70:341–344, 1989.

38. Griffin JW, Newsome LS, Stralka SW, Wright PE: Reduction of chronic posttraumatic hand edema: a comparison of high voltage pulsed current, intermittent pneumatic compression, and placebo treatments. *Phys Ther* 70:279–286, 1990.

39. Hull RD, Raskob GE, Gent M, McLoughlin D, Julian D, Smith FC, Dale I, Reed-Davis R, Lofthouse RN, Anderson A: Effectiveness of intermittent pneumatic leg compression for preventing deep vein thrombosis after total hip replacement. *JAMA* 263:2313–2317, 1990.

40. Hooker DN: Intermittent compression devices. In *Therapeutic Modalities in Sports Medicine,* edited by Prentice WE. St. Louis: Times Mirror/Mosby College Publishing, second edition, pp. 245–255, 1990.

41. Starkey C: *Therapeutic Modalities for Athletic Trainers.* Philadelphia, F. A. Davis, pp. 215–219, 1993.

42. Rucinski TJ, Hooker DN, Prentice WE, Shields EW, Coté-Murray DJ: The effects of intermittent compression on edema in postacute ankle sprains. *J Orthop Sports Phys Ther* 14:65–69, August 1991.

43. Watkim KG, Martin GM, Krusen FH: Influence of centripedal rhythmic compression on localized edema and early mobilization. *Arch Phys Med Rehab* 36:98–103, 1955.

44. Cummings J: Role of light in wound healing. In *Wound Healing: Alternatives in Management,* edited by Kloth LC, McCulloch JM, Feedar JA. Philadelphia: F. A. Davis, pp. 287–301, 1990.

45. Kloth LC, Ziskin MC: Diathermy and pulsed electromagnetic fields. In *Thermal Agents in Rehabilitation,* edited by Michlovitz SL. Philadelphia: F. A. Davis, second edition, pp. 170–199, 1990.

46. Pennington GM, Danley DL, Sumko MH: Pulsed, nonthermal, high-frequency electromagnetic energy (Diapulse) in the treatment of Grade I and Grade II ankle sprains. *Military Med* 158:101–104, 1993.

47. Draper DO: When you're hot, you're hot: Thermal modalities from research to practice. Presented at the 47th Annual Meeting and Clinical Symposium of the National Athletic Trainer's Association, Orlando, FL, June 14, 1996.

48. Dyson M: Mechanisms involved in therapeutic ultrasound. *Physiother* 73:116–120, 1987.

49. Starkey C: pp. 178–181.

50. Ziskin MC, McDiarmid T, Michlovitz SL: Therapeutic ultrasound. In *Thermal Agents in Rehabilitation,* edited by Michlovitz SL. Philadelphia: F. A. Davis, second edition, p. 134–169, 1990.

51. Lehmann JF: *Therapeutic Heat and Cold.*

52. Castel C, Draper DO, Castel D: Rate of temperature increase during ultrasound treatments: are traditional treatment times long enough? (Abstract) *J Athletic Training* 29:156, 1994.

53. Draper DO, Castel JC, Castel D: Rate of temperature increase in human muscle during 1 MHz and 3 MHz continuous ultrasound. *J Orthop & Sports Phys Therapy* 22:142–150, 1995.

54. Grey K: Surface areas in ultrasound therapy: evaluation of seven methods for measuring the treated skin area in physiotherapeutic application of ultrasound. *Scand J Rehab Med* 25:11–15, 1993.

55. Draper DO, Ricard, MD: Rate of temperature decay in human muscle following 3 MHz ultrasound: the stretching window revealed. *J Athletic Training* 30:304–307, 1995.

56. Rose S, Draper DO, Schulthies SS, Durrant E: The stretching window part two: Rate of thermal decay in deep muscle following 1 MHz ultrasound. *J Athletic Training* 31:139–143, 1996.

57. Heckman JD, Ryaby JP, McCabe J, Frey JJ, Kilcoyne RF: Acceleration of tibial fracture-healing rate by non-invasive, low-intensity pulsed ultrasound. *J Bone Joint Surg* 76-A: 26–34, 1994.

58. Kramer JF: Ultrasound: evaluation of its mechanical and thermal effects. *Arch Phys Med Rehab* 65:223–228, 1984.

59. Williams R: Production and transmission of ultrasound. *Physiother* 73:113–120, 1987.

60. Gann N: Ultrasound: current concepts. *Clin Management* 11:64–69, 1991.

61. Cameron MH, Monroe LG: Relative transmission of ultrasound by media customarily used for phonophoresis. *Phys Ther* 72:142–150, 1992.

62. Draper DO: Ten mistakes commonly made with ultrasound use: Current research sheds light on myths. *Athletic Training: Sports Health Care Perspectives* 2:95–107, 1996.

63. Kellaway P: The William Osler Medal essay: Part played by electric fish in early history of bioelectricity and electrical therapy. *Bull Hist Med* 20:112, 1946.

64. Robinson AJ: Physiology of muscle and nerve. In *Clinical Electrophysiology: Electrotherapy and Electrophysiologic Testing*, edited by Snyder-Mackler L, Robinson AJ. Baltimore: Williams and Wilkins, pp. 90–93, 1987.

65. Food and Drug Administration Compliance Policy Guidelines. Guide Number 7124.26, Chapter 24. Devices, July 1, 1982.

66. DeVahl J: Neuromuscular electrical stimulation (NMES) in rehabilitation. In *Electrotherapy in Rehabilitation*, edited by Gersh MR. Philadelphia: F. A. Davis, pp. 218–268, 1992.

67. Starkey C: pp. 97–172.

68. Delitto A, Robinson AJ: Electrical stimulation of muscle: techniques and applications. In *Clinical Electrophysiology: Electrotherapy and Electrophysiologic Testing*, edited by Snyder-Mackler L, Robinson AJ. Baltimore: Williams and Wilkins, pp. 110–111, 1987.

69. Alon G, Kantor G, Ho HS: Effects of electrode size on basic excitatory responses and on selected stimulus parameters. *J Orthop Sports Phys Ther* 20:29–35, 1994.

70. Paris DL, Baynes F, Gucker B: Effects of the Neuroprobe in the treatment of second degree ankle inversion sprains. *Phys Ther* 63:35–40, 1983.

71. Smith MJ, Hutchins RC, Hehenberger D: Transcutaneous neural stimulation use in postoperative knee rehabilitation. *Am J Sports Med* 11:75–81, 1983.

72. Rosenberg M, Curtis L, Bourke DL: Transcutaneous electrical nerve stimulation for the relief of postoperative pain. *Pain* 5:129–134, 1978.

73. Melzack R, Wall PD: Pain mechanisms: a new theory. *Science* 150:971–979, 1965.

74. Deyo RA, Walsh NE, Martin DC, Schoenfeld LS, Ramamurthy S: A controlled trial of transcutaneous electrical nerve stimulation (TENS) and exercise for chronic low back pain. *New Engl J Med* 322:1627–1634,1990.

75. Mendel FC, Fish DR: The TENS issue: what can we learn? (letter). *Phys Ther* 71:623–624, 1991.

76. Snyder-Mackler L: Electrical stimulation for pain modulation. In *Clinical Electrophysiology: Electrotherapy and Electrophysiologic Testing*, edited by Snyder-Mackler L, Robinson AJ. Baltimore: Williams and Wilkins, pp. 205–227, 1987.

77. Kloth LC: Electrotherapeutic alternatives for the treatment of pain. In *Electrotherapy in Rehabilitation*, edited by Gersh MR. Philadelphia: F. A. Davis, pp. 197–217, 1992.

78. Bertolucci LE: Introduction of anti-inflammatory drugs by iontophoresis: double blind study. *J Orthop Sports Phys Ther* 4:103–108, 1982.

79. Harris PR: Iontophoresis: clinical research in musculoskeletal inflammatory conditions. *J Orthop Sports Phys Ther* 4:109–112, 1982.

80. Glick E, Snyder-Mackler L: Iontophoresis. In *Clinical Electrophysiology: Electrotherapy and Electrophysiologic Testing*, edited by Snyder-Mackler L, Robinson AJ. Baltimore: Williams and Wilkins, pp. 247–260,1987.

81. Hasson SM, Wible CL, Reich M, Barnes WS, Williams JH: Dexamethasone iontophoresis: effect on delayed onset muscle soreness and muscle function. *Can J Sport Sci* 17:8–13, 1992.

82. Weider DL: Treatment of traumatic myositis ossificans with acetic acid iontophoresis. *Phys Ther* 72:133–137, 1992.

83. Hasson SH: Exercise training and dexamethasone iontophoresis in rheumatoid arthritis: a case study. *Physiother Can* 43:11–18, 1991.

84. Riviere JE, Monteiro-Riviere NA, Inman AO: Determination of lidocaine concentrations in skin after transdermal iontophoresis. *Pharmaceutical Res* 9:211–214, 1992.

85. Riviere JE, Sage B, Williams PL: Effects of vasoactive drugs on transdermal lidocaine iontophoresis. *J Pharmaceutical Sci* 80:615–620, 1991.

86. Cyriax J, Russell G: *Textbook of Orthopaedic Medicine: Treatment by Manipulation, Massage, and Injection*, Vol II, New York, Macmillan, tenth edition, 1980.

87. Schiötz EH, Cyriax J: *Manipulation, Past and Present.* London, William Heinman Medical Books Ltd, 1975.

88. Schellhas KP, Latchaw RE, Wendling LR, et al: Vertebrobasilar injuries following cervical manipulation. *JAMA* 244:1450–1453, 1980.

89. Mennell J McM: *Joint Pain.* Boston, Little Brown and Company, 1964.

90. Mennell J McM: *Back Pain.* Boston, Little Brown and Company, 1960.

RECOMMENDED READINGS

Draper DO: Ten mistakes commonly made with ultrasound use: current research sheds light on myths. *Athletic Training: Sports Health Care Perspectives* 2:95–107, 1996.

Gersh MR editor: *Electrotherapy in Rehabilitation.* Philadelphia: F. A. Davis, 1992.

Hayes KW: *Manual for Physical Agents.* Norwalk: Appleton-Lange, fourth edition, 1993.

Michlovitz SL editor: *Thermal Agents in Rehabilitation.* Philadelphia: F. A. Davis, second edition, 1990.

Prentice WE editor: *Therapeutic Modalities in Sports Medicine.* St. Louis: Times Mirror/Mosby College Publishing, third edition, 1994.

Snyder-Mackler L, Robinson AJ editors: *Clinical Electrophysiology: Electrotherapy and Electrophysiologic Testing.* Baltimore: Williams and Wilkins, second edition, 1995.

Starkey C: *Therapeutic Modalities for Athletic Trainers.* Philadelphia: F. A. Davis, 1993.

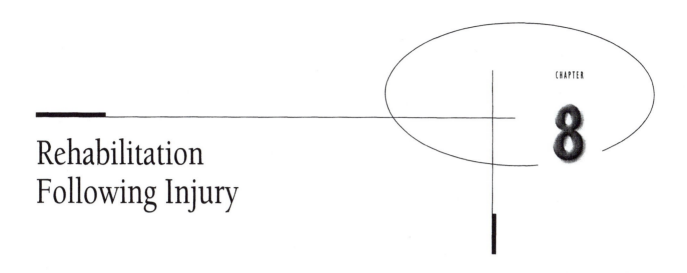

Rehabilitation Following Injury

One of the major contributions the athletic trainer can make to the welfare of the athlete is in the area of rehabilitation and/or reconditioning. The prescribed rehabilitation program frequently determines what level of athletic participation will be possible in the future.

The quality of rehabilitation also influences the frequency of injury. An example comes from a study by the New York Public High School Athletic Association (report of 1971) that included over 61,000 high school football players. This study showed that the rate of knee injury was 15 to 17 times greater for those with previously injured knees than for players who had not sustained knee injuries. Most of those reinjured *had not* had adequate rehabilitation. The study recommended that any athlete with a knee injury be placed in a planned rehabilitation program under the direction of a physician, and that no athlete be allowed to return to varsity football without completing the program.

The West Point Military Academy study of 1969[1] pointed out that 80 percent of knee injuries at the academy were incurred by athletes previously injured in high school. As a result of these findings, cadets with weak thigh muscles were prohibited from participating in contact sports and were prescribed a remedial program. The rehabilitation program resulted in a significant decrease in the total number of knee injuries.

A longitudinal study, the North Carolina Study (over six years) cited by Gieck, Lowe, and Kenna,[2] indicated a reinjury rate that either dropped or remained static, from 71 percent to 11 percent, depending on whether the rehabilitation program was managed by a coach or a teacher/trainer.

Goals of Rehabilitation

The goals of rehabilitating an injured athlete are usually considered different from those for the injured general population. Vigorous, intense, *but load-controlled* exercise enhances early return to participation and ensures that the injured part is as optimally conditioned as possible. As Dr. Fred Allman[3] has said many times, "The goal of treatment must be restoration of function to the greatest possible degree in the shortest possible time." That means that rehabilitation should begin at the same time as initial treatment of the injured part. Treatment and rehabilitation should blend imperceptibly into one, as acute care and early rehabilitation can minimize the effects of the injury. However, the tissue-healing process must be understood. Strain to the injured tissue in its attempts to repair must not be greater than the tissue's ability to accommodate stress, or the intensification of tissue breakdown will occur. Yet significant stress reduction, rest, or immobilization will result in disuse atrophy and assure reinjury and improper rehabilitation. Thus a fine balance must be established in the use of stress to enhance proper tissue repair, yet not cause tissue breakdown.[4]

No longer is rehabilitation put off until the injured part is "healed"; rather, rehabilitation is started while healing is taking place, resulting in an earlier return to activity and perhaps an improvement in the quality of the tissue that forms during the healing process. The aim is not necessarily to speed up healing (which cannot as yet be accomplished), but rather to do all that is possible to avoid slowing it down.[5, 6, 7, 8, 9]

For example, the past several years has seen an increase in the accelerated ACL reconstructed (knee) rehabilitation protocol which incorporates earlier weight-bearing, immediate full range of motion, early closed chain activities, and earlier return to sport. There is much enthusiasm for this and other accelerated protocols because there appear to be no detrimental effects of a faster rehabilitation process when specific guidelines are adhered to.[10] Thus, acquiring an appreciation of the healing process permits the development of an efficient rehabilitation program that is based upon rational principles and appropriate guidelines. The following statement is extremely important:

> Guidelines can be established for a rehabilitation program, but it is important that the sports medicine specialist avoid a cookbook approach when designing an athlete's rehabilitation program. There are too many factors that enter into each athlete's situation to be able to apply a standard treatment regimen for all. Rather the specialist must develop an individual program based on general guidelines and his or her own knowledge and make adjustments for each athlete as the situation dictates. (Houglum, pp. 28–29).[7]

A rehabilitation program for an athlete permits few exceptions that justify rest. If an injury prevents normal use, the athlete should find alternate activities that do not impede or aggravate the injury. These activities should maintain components of fitness for the athlete, for example cardiovascular endurance and strength maintenance of noninvolved structures. The rehabilitation program should not merely treat the symptoms of an injury. For example, many bursitis and tendonitis conditions are secondary problems. The primary pathology should be resolved. If the primary cause of the symptoms is not corrected, then the secondary factors (itis) will return when the athlete resumes normal levels of activity.[4] Thus, an athlete cannot be generically rehabilitated. It must be remembered that normal for the athlete is not the same as for the nonathlete; nor is it the same for all sports and levels of competition. The biomechanical and future stresses that the athlete will strive toward must be anticipated, and an understanding of the involved stresses specific to the athlete's sport is required of the manager of the rehabilitation program.

An area of the rehabilitation process that is often neglected but that should be given as much regard as the obvious injury is the psychological aspect. The separation of the physiological and psychological aspects of injury impedes the rehabilitation of the athlete.[11, 12] It is especially important to understand the motivational factors that an athlete will bring to the rehabilitation process. Noncompliance to rehabilitation programs will interfere with the rehabilitation process and increase the reinjury factor.[13] Studies on rehabilitation adherence indicate that the most important factors in producing a high degree of adherence are: (1) good rapport between

athletic trainer and athlete; (2) explanation of the rehabilitation process; (3) convenience with regard to the athlete's schedule; and (4) support from peers and coaches.[14, 15] Each athlete will approach their individual program with a different vigor and rationale. Thus the program must account for these factors and categorically design each aspect to accommodate those differences.[16]

In summary, the rehabilitation program is influenced by, yet not limited to, a number of factors:[4, 7, 17, 18, 19]

1. Severity of the injury

2. Stage of tissue healing

3. Type of treatment, including surgery and all precautions and restrictions of the particular injury or surgical procedure affecting the rehabilitation program

4. Muscular strength of the involved limb

5. Pain during joint motion

6. Range of joint motion limitations

7. Joint swelling

8. Functional anatomy of the involved structure and segment

9. Neuromuscular pattern of the moving parts

10. Tissue sites capable of elicting pain

11. Responsible faulty neuromuscular mechanism

12. Other conditions within the joint, for example, chondromalacia of the patella

13. Knowledge of the controllable and uncontrollable stresses that will be made by the injured athlete's sport upon the damaged tissues and its associated segments

14. Limiting factors of surrounding joints or muscles; for example, most of the lower-extremity muscles have actions on two joints

15. Motivational rationale of the athlete as well as psychological aspects (fear of reinjury). Thus the athlete favors the noninvolved limb, predisposing it to overuse syndromes.

Rehabilitation Program

An individualized program drawn up for each athlete is a necessity. This rehabilitation prescription should include duration of each session, frequency per week or day, intensity, and the progression of these three factors. A long-term yet adjustable and individual plan should also include estimates of when each exercise type and stress load should be applied. The incorporation of periodization programs, eccentric loading, kinematic chain (closed versus open chain),[20, 21] and criteria that determines progression are only a few of the complexities of a rehabilitation program.

While there are many pieces of specialized equipment on the market—and they are very useful—one can also use little or no equipment and still obtain adequate results—often better than obtained by incorporating special or expensive equipment. Thus, having the most expensive machinery will not guarantee results if there is an inadequate program, little motivation, or poor supervision. The latter is especially true during the re-entry phase. Supervision of this phase requires progressive simulations of the sport's particular stresses on the athlete. Even the most sophisticated rehabilitation program cannot mimic the true stress and load accommodations that controlled participation in the athlete's sport will ensure. Thus, if the program is carefully, knowledgeably, and innovatively designed for a particular athlete's needs, and if the athlete is adequately motivated and supervised for the duration of the program, the program is usually successful.

The program should be progressive, so that an increasing amount of work is performed at each session, as long as predetermined limits and the limits of discomfort are not exceeded. Athletes with minor injuries may be started on high-intensity, short-duration exercises initially, while those with more serious injuries may need to begin at a low to moderate intensity and then progress into the high-intensity program. Correct form with each exercise should be stressed constantly in order to maximize the results and prevent reinjury. There should be a definite rhythm and timing to the exercises.

Stages of Rehabilitation Program

The rehabilitation program should proceed in an orderly fashion through a number of planned stages. In judging an athlete's rate of recovery and attempting to determine the timing of return to participation, factors such as functional tests and pain are considered. Guidelines of arbitrary time periods have limited, if any, value in modern athletic treatment as long as healing time is within physiological limits. These stages need to be individualized, but they generally include:

1. *Immediate or acute rehabilitation phase.* Initially, emphasis should be on cardiovascular fitness and isometric contractions if a joint is immobilized.[22] Exercising the opposite limb may evoke a crossover reaction and maintain the muscles of the injured limb.[7, 23, 24] If permitted, an attempt at limited motion within the confines of the immobilizer may speed healing.[6, 25]

Muscle stimulation and continuous passive motion (CPM) are also frequently used at this stage.[26] CPM is a machine-dependent device that moves a joint though its functional ROM at a constant rate of motion (Figure 8.1). The various machines use a limb carriage to support the proximal and distal segments of a joint. The control system of the device can change (a) the range of the motion, (b) the position of the motion arc, and (c) the rate at which the motion occurs.[27, 28, 29]

2. *Protective phase.* When the immobilization is lifted, a pain-free range of motion is regained through graded exercises, proprioceptive neuromuscular facilitation patterns (PNF),[30, 31] adjuncts of transcutaneous electrical nerve stimulation (TENS), and cryotherapy (See Chapter 7). All of these techniques are used to overcome the neural inhibitions that frequently limit progress at this stage.[32]

3. *Restoration of motion, strength, and proprioception.* As joint motion and flexibility return, resistance exercises can be increased. Some programs start with limited-range isotonic exercises, but others are achieving excellent and rapid results with low-resistance, moderately high-speed exercise on isokinetic machines, using submaximal intensity through a limited range of motion.

4. *Restoration of power and endurance.* As strength is developed, more emphasis is placed on speed, power and endurance. These qualities can be achieved through the utilization of circuit training, plyometrics, flexibility exercises, and following the periodization principle.

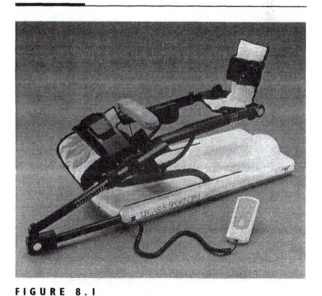

FIGURE 8.1

An example of a continuous passive motion (CPM) machine (*Source:* Sutter Corporation, Biomotion Specialists®. Printed with permission.)

5. *Progressive control of Re-entry phase.* As the last step, specific skill patterns and sport-related skills are prescribed, with progressively complex drills.[33] This re-entry phase is paramount, and a progressively controlled stress and/or load implementation must be monitored. The athlete must be effectively observed by the trainer and strict limitations on intensity, frequency, and duration of sport specific skills (drills) must be implemented. Particular attention must be given proprioceptive enhancement to ensure that the athlete has developed sufficient neural protective mechanisms to avoid reinjury. For the athlete, this phase is the most critical, most carefully monitored, and most individualized portion of the rehabilitation phases.

The criteria listed below should be measured during and at the end of the rehabilitation program. Before releasing the athlete for full activity, these criteria should be met and equal measurements of opposite uninjured (contralateral) side should be achieved. These criteria include:

1. Strength of each muscle group
2. Power of each muscle group
3. Endurance of each muscle group
4. Balance between antagonistic muscle groups
5. Flexibility of the muscles of the involved joint along with flexibility of the adjacent joints.
6. Proprioception of the injured joint and affected limb
7. Functional use of that limb in the athlete's sport[34]

Common Mistakes

The most common mistakes in rehabilitation are:

1. Rehabilitation is focused on a single muscle group. After evaluation of the athlete to find out which muscles are particularly weak, all muscles of the limb need to be exercised, concentrating on the weaker ones. As Norkin and Levangie[20] so adequately state:

> Some of the joints of the human body are linked together into a series of joints in such a way that motion at one of the joints in the series is accompanied by motion at an adjacent joint. For instance, when a person in the erect standing position bends both knees, simultaneous motion must occur at the ankle and hip joints. However, when the leg is lifted from the ground, the knee is free to bend without causing motion at either the ankle or hip.

The limitations imposed by the injury or surgery should be understood and observed.

2. Rehabilitation is discontinued before the injured limb is found to be equal or superior to the uninjured side. The 15 parameters previously mentioned need to

be continuously reassessed and the results documented before a return to *uncontrolled* participation. The athlete must progress through the re-entry phase before full and unlimited participation is permitted.

3. Exercises for developing proprioception and functional exercises are forgotten and do not correspond to neuromuscular patterns.[35]

4. Postural defects, anatomical malalignment, and muscular or anatomical asymmetry, as well as biomechanical imbalances, are neglected when the rehabilitation program is developed.

5. Eccentric exercises are neglected, especially in the management of tendonitis.[36, 37]

6. Specific sport skills and the SAID principle (specific adaptation to imposed demands) are not incorporated into the program, nor are periods of active rest. Exercises should be adapted to the specific needs of the athlete's *particular position* in a sport.

Types of Exercises

Isometric Contractions

Isometric exercise occurs when pressure or force is applied to muscle fibers that prevent external movement and offer resistance inherently proportional to the muscles' static tension-developing capacity at one shortening length. No dynamic work is accomplished in isometric exercise. In other words, the muscular tension is and will continue to remain proportional to the applied external force whether the outside force is gravity and the weight of the limb or a fifty-pound weight attached to the limb. Thus, there is no limb movement. The contraction is often performed against a fixed resistance and frequently is the only type of exercise that can be used—for instance, if a limb is immobilized in a cast. Isometrics are often used to help maintain strength and enhance vascularization during the immediate and protective phases.

Isometrics, while useful, do not increase muscle bulk significantly, and they strengthen the muscle mainly at the joint angle at which the contraction is performed. With prolonged isometric exercise, the speed of a joint may actually be decreased, while endurance is not improved to any extent. Isometrics will not directly improve a joint's range of motion. To achieve the greatest benefit from isometric exercises, the joint should be at an angle that permits the muscle to contract maximally within the parameters of the rehabilitation protocol. For example, the quadriceps will contract maximally (maximal voluntary contraction, MVC) with the knee joint fully extended, and contraction will be further enhanced if the foot is dorsiflexed. This is a proprioceptive neuromuscular principle.[38] The frequency and duration of isometric exercises depend on the state of the athlete's musculature as well as on the underlying reason for performing the exercises. For example, an athlete who has excellent quadriceps musculature, but whose limb is immobilized for a sprain of the medial collateral ligament, should be able to perform twenty quadriceps sets at maximal intensity every hour during the waking day, as well as one session each day of three quadriceps sets held for one minute. Isometric contraction force can be measured with a strain-gauge device or on isokinetic machines. Contrast this with a case of chondromalacia patellae with poor quadriceps strength. Performing intensive quadriceps sets may actually cause a flareup of the condition. The trainer needs to work closely with the athlete in this situation; he may find that contracting the quadriceps with the knee fully extended causes pain. Therefore these contractions may need to be performed initially with the knee slightly flexed. If genu recurvatum is present, the athlete needs to learn where the zero position of extension is and to perform the contractions in this position. In the beginning, an athlete may be allowed to perform only two or three quadriceps sets at 50 to 70 percent of MVC, each lasting five seconds, three times a day. If this does not cause pain, the intensity and number of contractions can be increased. This example again emphasizes the need for an individualized program for each athlete.

Isotonic (Eccentric/Concentric) Contractions

Isotonic exercise occurs when pressure is applied against a force that allows movement but offers a constant resistance through a range of movement. In actual practice, the term isotonic is usually construed as applying to any form of dynamic exercise where the resistance is not proportionate to the muscle's actual dynamic force curve.

Normally the magnitude of an isotonic resistance must be limited to the greatest load that can be moved at the weakest point in some range of movement. This resistance will be less than maximal during the remainder of the range; thus it will not load the muscle to its full tension-developing capacity in much of its shortening range. The exercise is also subject to various changes in acceleration and output.

ECCENTRIC CONTRACTION. If the external resistance exceeds the muscle power generated, a forcible lengthening of the active muscle occurs.

CONCENTRIC CONTRACTION. If the force generated by the muscle is greater than the external resistance, a shortening of the muscle will occur.

The weight (force) may be a sandbag, a weighted boot, an N-K table, a Universal Gym, or some other similar machine. Thus, concentric (or positive) work occurs when the muscle shortens as the weight is lifted; eccentric (or negative) work occurs when the muscle lengthens while the weight is being slowly lowered.[39, 40] Or, in the words of Staub, "Simply stated, the tension developed by an active muscle decreases as the shortening velocity increases (concentric). If the external force overcomes the ability of the muscle to actively resist, the muscle lengthens (eccentric), but only after producing additional tension."

Eccentric work appears to effect a greater gain in strength, but is also more stressful, resulting in muscle soreness and, in the case of the knee, an overload on the patella. Contemporary rehabilitation programs typically incorporate eccentric load principles. It is often possible to lower a much heavier weight than can be lifted. This knowledge can be utilized in a variation of the standard exercise whereby the athlete lifts the weight with two legs and then lowers the weight with the affected leg only (Figure 8.2).

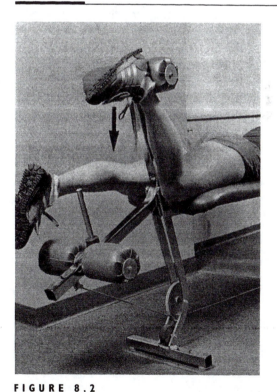

FIGURE 8.2
Isotonic exercise
To maximize isotonic resistance, the weight is lifted with two legs and then lowered with only one leg.

Isotonic exercise produces improvement by developing tension within the muscle. More tension is developed at a slow, controlled rate of movement (for example, lifting to a count of three, holding for two counts, lowering for four counts). Much of the effect may be lost due to the ballistic movement of the weight if the procedure is done too rapidly.

There are disadvantages to isotonic exercise:

1. When using isotonic exercise in knee rehabilitation, the patellofemoral joint is subjected to reactive forces that may cause pain and even articular cartilage injury or degeneration.

2. The amount of weight is fixed and usually determined by the "sticking point" or weakest part of the range of motion of the lift. This means that, except for this point, the muscles moving the weight are working at below-maximum intensity. For this reason in particular, weight-machine manufacturers have produced an isotonic machine (variable-resistance isotonic exercise machine) that varies the resistance to correspond to the changes in muscle strength throughout the range of motion. Such machines include the Nautilus and DVR Universal. Whether these actually result in greater gains in strength is subject to much controversy, with each manufacturer claiming spectacular results. There is also the question of the ability of the muscles developed by these machines to transfer the strength gains into a sport-specific activity. In summary, these machines appear to be an advance over the standard isotonic machines, but how much better they may be awaits further investigation. These machines are classified as variable resistance and not as isokinetic. (Figures 8.3 and 8.4)

The use of free weights, while a very controversial area, probably has greater benefit and is more sport-specific because free-weight techniques incorporate more functionality and usually do not violate kinematic chain principles.[35] (Refer to further comments after the section on isokinetics in this chapter.)

Isokinetic Contractions

If the movement involved is of a constant speed and, therefore, the rate of change of the muscle length is relatively constant, the movement and the contraction are identified as *isokinetic*. This definition can be expanded by considering the movement as exercise against a load that allows movement at a mechanically fixed rate of speed, offering resistance inherently proportional to the muscle's dynamic tension-developing capacity.

When an individual applies maximum effort on an isokinetic exerciser, the machine will instantly accelerate to its set speed. Then, by preventing any further acceleration, it will load the dynamically harnessed

FIGURE 8.3
An example of a Universal DVR (variable resistance) isotonic machine

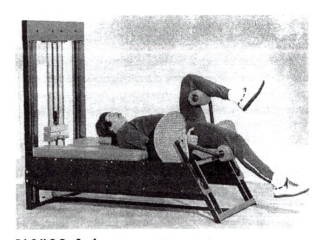

FIGURE 8.4
Nautilus hip and back machine
Variable resistance isotonics

muscle exactly proportionate to its maximum dynamic tension capacity through a full range of motion. As the muscle's tension capacity and skeletal advantage vary through the range of motion, the resistance caused by the speed-governing action of the exerciser will fluctuate accordingly and naturally accommodate the muscle's force-transmitting capacity at every point in the range. As the muscle's tension capacity improves, the loading automatically keeps perfect pace with improvement.

In isokinetic loading, the desired exercise speed always occurs immediately, with resistance then developing as a function of the amount of tension. The muscle can develop at that speed, and the reverse will not occur—resistance initially and speed secondarily—as occurs in isotonic exercise.

By determining an appropriate exercise speed and presetting it on the isokinetic exerciser, it is possible to allow a muscle to contract at the specific shortening speeds on the tension-velocity curve so that the muscle can develop either (a) maximum peak tension, (b) most work per repetition, (c) highest power output, or (d) some submaximal average power output per repetition for a maximum time duration. The exerciser can also be loaded at a specific joint speed corresponding to some special physical activity.

In performing isokinetic exercise, an individual simply concentrates on generating greater and greater contractile force through a range of motion at a fixed speed. He or she can rely on the fact that the exercising device will safely and accurately control the resultant motion at the preset speed and along the desired exercise pattern.

Isokinetic exercise is dependent upon velocity accommodated by resistance and may be applied to a force–velocity curve. These mechanically controlled dynamometers were made available with the introduction of Cybex I in the late 1960s.[41] The development of these devices provides tools by which the contractile properties of muscles under conditions of constant velocity *in vivo* (dynamic) can be measured.[42] Isokinetic dynamometers contain either an electronic servomotor or hydraulic valves as speed-control mechanisms, which theoretically prevent acceleration of the limb regardless of increases in applied force once a preset speed is attained.

The possible speed settings range from 0° per second to 450° per second. Strength is usually developed between 60° per second and 120° per second and power, at 180° per second. However, clinical evidence is being accumulated to show that strength and power gains are also excellent at faster speeds, possibly due to an increase in muscle recruitment.

Endurance may also be developed at faster speeds. One technique is to attempt to perform as many flexion/extension movements as possible (or whatever movement is appropriate) in a set time (e.g., one minute). (See section on knee rehabilitation.)

One advantage of using isokinetic exercise is the visual readout possible with these machines and the mechanical reliability of isokinetic dynamometer systems, which has been found to be as high as 0.99.[42] Thus the isokinetic devices, with their integrated software and computer interfacing, help the trainer evaluate progress, but also provide a powerful psychological stimulus for the athlete. Also, as an appropriate resistance is applied throughout the range of motion, the athlete can reduce the force at the point of pain. In addition, a condition such as chondromalacia patellae or lateral epicondylitis of the elbow which, when painful, is often difficult to treat by means of isotonic exercise, frequently responds to high-speed isokinetic exercise.

A definite disadvantage of the isokinetic machines is their cost, which limits their availability to a fraction of those who could benefit from the advantages of isokinetics. Isokinetic machines are also potentially dangerous when used in an uncontrolled manner on joints that are not stable. For instance, anterolateral rotatory instability of the knee can be produced if too vigorous a contraction is attempted through the last 30° of extension in a knee lacking an intact anterior cruciate ligament, and chondromalacia patellae can be aggravated by high torque at slow speed. However, there are devices and dynamometer configurations that control for such potential problems. Contemporary therapeutic protocols might use isoacceleration, isodeceleration, as well as eccentric and the traditional concentric contractile procedures on the isokinetic dynamometer.[43]

A major disadvantage of any resistive machine-dependent exercise is that motion is limited in a linear plane; rarely does a machine effectively incorporate multiplanar, multiaxialar, or multijoint applications to the body. Simply stated, many believe that machines are only an adjunct to the therapy and that functional and closed kinetic chain activities are not effectively accomplished by machine-resistive devices.

Therapeutic Exercise Classifications

Therapeutic exercises are classified into the following categories: passive exercises, relaxed movements, and active exercises (static, assistive, free or unassistive, resistive, and progressive-resistive exercises).

Passive Exercises

Passive exercises are movements of the muscles and associated tissues (bones, joints, connective tissues) by application of an external force by either a therapist or by a mechanical device. The chief purposes of passive movement are to promote circulation to maintain or increase range of motion, and reduce or inhibit adhesions, fibroses, and contractures. Passive exercises should not be confused with joint mobilization and manipulation techniques. Passive exercise is frequently used in athletics to achieve contracture reduction. Such attempts may produce pain or elicit the muscle spindle response. (It may be helpful to heat the structures prior to passive exercise.) [44] Other classifications of exercise and relaxation techniques generally provide better results; passive exercise has no real value in athletics.

Relaxed Movement

This classification differs from passive exercises in two principal ways: (1) passive exercise demands maximal relaxation of the involved structures; (2) neither active resistance nor resistance by the patient is permitted. Relaxed movement can be described by using the example of Codman shoulder exercises. These exercises are performed by holding a weight using wrist strength while the shoulder muscles are supported and completely relaxed. In this position the patient initiates a pendulum motion, intended to increase range of motion. PNF techniques can be substituted to also achieve the same results: an increase in range of motion and in strength.

JOINT MOBILIZATION: Joint mobilization is certainly not new, however it is becoming more widely accepted. Expanded knowledge of joint kinematics has provided more rationale for its usage.[4] Excellent auto-mobilization techniques are also available.[45] The mechanics and principles of this valuable technique can be investigated by reading the works of Cyriax[46] and Maitland.[47]

Active Exercises

STATIC EXERCISES: Muscle setting is synonymous with static exercises. Isometric contraction lasting approximately six seconds alternated with an equal period of relaxation are performed repeatedly by the patient for a prescribed length of time. This technique is employed extensively in the treatment of fractures and in cases in which soft tissue is immobilized. These exercises may also be used for treatment of various inflammatory conditions when movement of the involved structure produces pain. Static exercises are often difficult to initiate when the patient has a reflex inhibition. As the muscles become stronger, easier to contract, and less painful, more active types of exercises are included in the rehabilitation program. Static exercise hastens the repair and recovery of damaged tissue. In addition, muscle tonus and muscle strength are maintained, and muscle atrophy may be retarded or prevented.

ASSISTIVE EXERCISES: In assistive exercises the patient is aided in the performance of some type of active movement. The assistance may be either manual (provided by the therapist) or mechanical (supplied by slings, pulleys, weights, springs, elastic bands, or rubber tubes). The assistance procedure is usually arranged to counterbalance the forces of gravity usually acting on a part of or on the entire involved extremity. The assistance is applied only in the direction in which the patient requires aid to perform an active motion of the involved structure. For example, the patient may not be able to perform a concentric contraction of the upper extremity but retains enough strength to perform an eccentric contraction. In this case minimal assistance would be provided to allow the patient to perform the concentric motion. Thus the patient will now be able to properly control an eccentric motion. This technique should be used to assist the patient only minimally; therefore, the patient must always exert a maximal effort upon the structures that are assisted. Rarely does this procedure become necessary in the athletic treatment clinic.

HYDROTHERAPY: Certain underwater exercises are regarded as assistive exercises. In such cases the buoyancy of the water provides the assistance needed for the patient to complete the desired movement. The buoyancy of the water reduces the stress loads and the viscosity of the water adds resistance to many land therapy protocols. With the use of a flotation vest (Figure 8.5) many standard rehabilitation procedures can be performed without stress; thus aquatic therapy may be used to strengthen without creating loads that would be detrimental with land exercises.

The decreased joint and bone compression forces water exercise offers have proven to be valuable in rehabilitating athletes. Running in water has gained broad acceptance as an effective method of conditioning and reconditioning, particularly for the athletes who are experiencing overuse injuries to the spine or lower extremities. Various flotation devices have been designed to maintain the body in an upright position in deep water. Near-normal running form can be achieved in a neutrally buoyant position with the aid of these devices. Self-contained deep-water running tanks (e.g., Aqua-ark) have been developed to provide this type of alternative exercise in situations where physical space is limited or access to a deep-water pool is not available. These units also provide adjustable water jet resistance and can serve as a water treadmill by altering the speed of water flow.

A second category of water resistance exercises, buoyancy cuffs and hand buoys (Figure 8.6), are used

FIGURE 8.5
An example of a flotation device
(*Source:* Bioenergetics, Inc., Dallas, Texas. Printed with permission.)

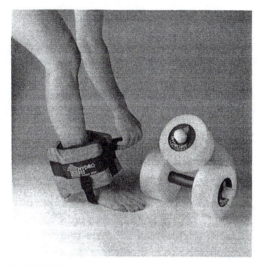

FIGURE 8.6
An example of buoyancy cuffs and hand buoys
(*Source:* Hydro-Fit® Eugene, Oregon. Printed with permission.)

for muscle strengthening exercises that are performed in an aquatic environment.

There are few references for use of aquatic therapy, but most typical land exercises can easily be transferred to water once the basic principles of aquatic therapy are understood. An excellent reference is *Aquatic Rehabilitation* by Glenn McWaters.[48]

UNASSISTIVE EXERCISES: Unassistive exercises or free exercises are active movement executed solely by the patient's efforts, without any resistive mechanism or motion.

Resistive Exercises

Resistive exercises are active exercises performed by the patient while the muscular contractions are resisted by an external force. Resistive exercises exist in two forms: manual resistive exercises and mechanical resistive exercises. The latter make use of some type of variable resistance equipment or apparatus such as pulley weights, dumbbells, or a stationary bicycle.

MANUAL RESISTIVE: Manual resistive exercise is one of the most useful exercise therapies and is frequently the method of choice in rehabilitation. The amount of resistance can be accurately regulated by the athletic trainer or sports therapist throughout the range of active movements; the direction of the movement can be accurately guided, and muscle substitution can be virtually eliminated. In addition, manual resistive exercises can accommodate maximal resistance to the muscles throughout the entire range of motion.

Theoretically, manual resistive exercise could be categorized within the isokinetic group. As in the case of isokinetic exercises, there is accommodation maximally throughout the range of motion, but no eccentric contraction occurs.

Usually manual resistive exercises are prescribed in accordance with the tolerance or fatigue factors of the patient. Therefore no set number of resistive movements are performed; the movements are continued until the therapist elicits a desired result from the patient. The onset of fatigue should occur gradually; the therapist must not attempt to fatigue the patient immediately. Naturally the desired results include the achievement of both endurance and strength improvement.

The advantage of manual resistance is the application of a variable resistance that accommodates specific objectives. The athletic trainer can apply resistance at specific ranges of motion and thus avoid painful ranges of motion. Or the trainer may permit the athlete to tolerate an accommodating resistance that does not have the disadvantage of isotonic exercise, in which the subject able to achieve full range of motion with the resistance only if the load is accommodating the weakest portion of the range. A specific advantage of manual resistance is the elimination of linear constraints that are present with most machine resistive devices. The primary disadvantage is the skill acquisition, adherence to structural-functional criteria (if using multiplanar and multiaxial exercises) in order not to enhance biomechanical incongruities. Another primary complaint of using manual resistance is the labor intensity required to provide adequate benefit.

Regardless of these disadvantages, manual resistance is a form of exercise in which the trainer should develop a special skill. When properly done, it falls under the category of accommodative variable resistance, with the trainer adjusting the speed of movement and resistance to the best suited of the athlete's needs at the particular moment, which varies according to the stage of rehabilitation and the state of fatigue. Almost any movement can be performed, and manual resistance can accomodate patterns of movement that cannot be duplicated on machines (Figure 8.7).

PROGRESSIVE-RESISTIVE EXERCISES: The utilization of weights and pulleys to provide a resistance load against which muscle force is applied has been developed into numerous well-organized systems. The principle of maximal resistance and *slow repetition* of the exercise is recommended as the basic procedure. Two methods of loading the muscles are employed. In one method, resistive weight is added to the natural weight of the body part to be moved, and in the other method a load is arranged to counterbalance a desired amount of gravitational force. The purpose is to make the weakened muscle relatively stronger and, at the same time, maintain the maximal amount of resistance that can be lifted commensurate with the weakened tension capacity. The former of these two methods is referred to as load-resisting exercise, and the latter is known as load-assisting exercise. Load assisting is rarely required with injured athletes, and manual resistive exercise can be incorporated into the rehabilitation program if the athlete should require assistance. Generally manual resistive exercises will promote better results than will load-assisting exercises.

Muscle power is evaluated by measuring one resistive movement (1 RM). After muscle power has been established, the resistance is reduced in order for the athlete to perform 10 RMs in succession. Progressive-resistance exercises are performed by the patient upon completion of a brief warm-up period consisting of lighter resistance. The patient will then perform a prescribed number of sets. A set is comprised of either eight or ten repetitions of one RM.

The more frequently used method for progressive-resistance exercises was originally developed by DeLorme, whose procedure uses the following formula: ½ max 10 RM, ¾ max 10 RM, Full max 10 RM. An illustration of this method would have the maximal weight established at 40 pounds; one-half of that weight would be 20 pounds, and three-fourths would be 30 pounds. A successful modification of the DeLorme method could be performance of three to five sets at the maximal resis-

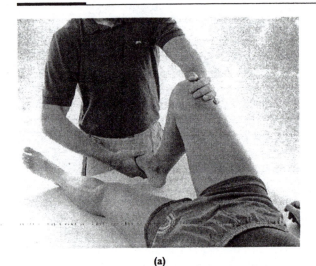

(a)

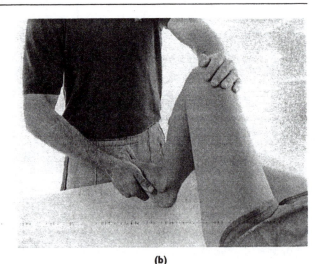

(b)

FIGURE 8.7
Manual resistance exercises
The trainer should learn to apply the correct resistance for each individual athlete and injury. These illustrations demonstrate resistance to (a) inversion and (b) eversion of the ankle.

tance. Isotonic is a simple and easily accessible form of exercise developed by DeLorme as progressive-resistance exercise (PRE).[49,50] His formula is to first determine the maximum weight that can be lifted more than eight but less than twelve times (this equals ten repetitions maximum). Three sets of ten repetitions are then performed at 50, 75, and 100 percent of the ten-repetition maximum and the load is progressively adjusted accordingly.

A variation on DeLorme's technique is the Oxford technique, in which the weight is taken off rather than added on (e.g., sets of 100, 75, and 50%). This method is probably less effective and is seldom used in sports medicine. (An injury may occur due to a strenuous first set.)

To achieve a rapid increase in strength, the muscle group needs to be subjected to loads that will cause momentary failure. This high-intensity work is mandatory to rehabilitation techniques in sports medicine in order to develop the muscles as fully as possible over the shortest time. For this reason, DeLorme's PRE program has been modified to include daily adjustments (the DAPRE technique[51]; see action on knee rehabilitation). Another modified program uses one set at 50 and 75 percent, but three sets at 100 percent.

The performance of the full maximal resistance, not a warm-up phase, will achieve results; therefore, most therapists prescribe either a modified method or use no warm-up phase. The author prefers the warm-up phase because the patient is usually more responsive during the maximal resistance period following a warm-up; the patient is usually less apprehensive and more confident; muscle substitution is usually reduced; and the patient's range of motion and muscle capacity are more fully prepared.

The one-half and three-fourths as expressed in the formula above usually do not have to be exact. Many athletic trainers or sports therapists, for lack of weights required for a precise use of the DeLorme method, use increments of five-, two-, and one-half-pound weights to achieve a close approximation of the one-half and three-fourths increments as specified in the formula.

Frequently the athletic trainer or sports therapist chooses not to attempt the establishment of maximal muscle capacity with 1 RM. Instead a more conservative method is used which applies resistance that is not a true maximum. This procedure is becoming the method of choice because the athlete patient is usually reluctant to apply maximal muscle capacity and because pain is often involved with such an attempt.

ELASTICIZED RUBBER BANDS OR TUBING: Rubber tubing and bands are available in various thicknesses and can therefore provide a variety of resistances,

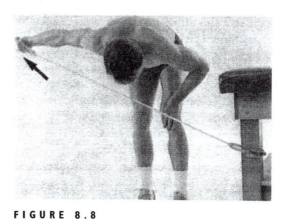

FIGURE 8.8
Elasticized rubber tubing (surgical tubing)
This simple exercise technique is one of the most useful and practical ways to exercise individual muscles as well as groups of muscles. This illustration demonstrates the exercise for the posterior deltoid muscle.

which permits a type of resistive exercise to be done in almost any setting. Almost any muscle of the extremities or the back can be exercised by adjusting the direction of the pull (Figure 8.8).

An interesting technique uses high-speed motion through particular planes to place localized stress on muscle. When performed in this manner until the onset of fatigue, a recruitment of muscle fibers appears to occur, resulting in immediate improvement in the function of the muscle. There may also be some gains in strength. Tubing can also be used to produce eccentric movements and to incorporate most functional and both kinematic chains, closed or open.

CIRCUIT TRAINING: When the athlete is nearing full recovery, all muscle systems can be placed under maximal stress by incorporating a circuit into the rehabilitation program. Such a circuit may incorporate thirty repetitions on the isotonic knee flexion/extension machine, followed immediately by high-speed knee flexion/extension on an isokinetic machine performed submaximally until the thigh muscles burn from fatigue (elasticized rubber tubing may be substituted). Following is a one-minute isometric contraction of the quadriceps. The circuit is repeated as many times as possible without a break.[52] This type of training can be adapted to almost any major joint of the extremities.

SPORT-SPECIFIC SKILLS: No rehabilitation program is complete until the athlete is graduated back into a specific sport and has developed the ability to perform the required movements efficiently and is able to tolerate the specific stresses required by his or her sport. The athlete can be helped with exercises and skills that are an integral part of the sport. These exercises should become increasingly complex as the rehabilitation program progresses. There must be someone who can effectively evaluate and determine whether the athlete can return to *unrestricted* participation. This aspect of the rehabilitation process, if not handled correctly, will frequently result in reinjury to the athlete.

Progressive-resistance exercises must be performed daily, and the patient must be encouraged to increase the number of sets or the amount of resistance daily. But instructing the athlete to apply a fixed amount of weight daily should be avoided. The resistance increase is dependent upon the patient's previous response to the maximal resistance and any post-exercise soreness, swelling, or pain. Unfortunately the increase is dependent upon numerous variables; thus, general guidelines cannot be easily established. The patient's responses and the therapist's knowledge and prior experience must be considered in each individual case.

In summary, the following criteria must be kept in mind. All resistive exercises must be performed with slow repetitions to allow control of concentric and eccentric contractions. Muscle substitution by stronger muscles to assist the weaker group must also be prevented. No patient should be allowed to throw the weight through a specified range of movement, nor should gravitational assistance be permitted. In other words, athlete patients will cheat and must be closely supervised by the therapist if the exercise program is to be successful.

Open versus Closed Kinetic Chain Exercises

Choosing exercises for a rehabilitation program involves decisions about multiple variables. One of the most important variables is how to appropriately influence the kinetic chain of the injured body part to promote optimal healing and function. Exercises can be performed utilizing either open or closed kinetic chain biomechanics. Open-chain exercises involve movement along a series of connected joints where the distal segment is free. The swing phase of gait is an example in the lower extremity. Closed-chain exercises involve movement along a series of joints where the distal segment is fixed. The support phase of gait is an example in the lower extremity.

Osteokinematics and neuromuscular function are different in open versus closed kinetic chain movements. Dorsiflexion of the ankle joint provides a perfect

example. Open-chain dorsiflexion occurs when a concentric contraction of the ankle dorsiflexors brings the dorsum of the foot up towards the lower leg. Closed-chain dorsiflexion occurs when the ankle plantarflexors contract eccentrically to control forward movement of the lower leg over the stationary foot.[53]

Closed-chain exercises have several advantages over open-chain exercises in the lower extremities for athletes using closed-chain biomechanics in their sport:

1. They promote integrated movement of the entire kinetic chain instead of isolated joint movement.

2. They utilize concentric and eccentric muscle contractions specific to functional activities instead of primarily concentric contractions in nonfunctional patterns.

3. They produce normal physiological loads instead of artificial loads.

4. They produce normal physiological stress and strain in tissues instead of abnormal and inconsistent stress and strain, which can be harmful to tissues.

5. They allow for functional and variable velocities instead of nonfunctional velocities, accelerations, and decelerations.

6. They produce triplanar instead of uniplanar motion.

7. They promote stabilization through normal intrinsic postural mechanisms instead of artificial external means.

8. They force the athlete to react to the environment instead of acting on it.

9. They facilitate normal proprioceptive feedback mechanisms instead of abnormal or foreign mechanisms.[37, 54, 55, 56, 57, 58]

Due to the specificity principle of training, closed-chain exercises are more likely to facilitate optimal tissue healing and normal function in the athlete participating in sports requiring the lower extremities to function in a closed kinetic chain manner. There should be a greater carryover to functional progressions and the athlete will regain the "feel" of functional activities more rapidly. Some sports requiring open-kinetic chain lower-extremity movements, such as swimming and gymnastics, would have more functional carryover from open-chain exercises, as demonstrated in PNF techniques. Open chain exercises may also be preferable when trying to isolate a specific muscle for strengthening.

Closed-chain exercises have become the staple of ACL reconstruction rehabilitation programs in recent years due to the simultaneous contraction of the quadriceps and hamstring muscles around the knee joint, minimal anterior shear forces on the graft, and the facilitation of normal proprioceptive feedback mechanisms.[37, 55, 56, 57] These factors make closed-chain exercises safe as early-stage ACL rehabilitation tools.[55, 59] Squats, leg presses, step-ups/downs, skips, jumps, bounds, balance boards, slideboards, ski machines, and stair machines can be utilized to stress the lower extremities in a closed-chain manner.

Open-chain exercises are more functionally appropriate in rehabilitating athletes using the upper extremities in an open kinetic chain fashion. They facilitate normal movement patterns with appropriate muscle contractions and synergy along the kinetic chain, produce normal physiological loads, produce normal stress and strain in tissues, facilitate normal proprioceptive feedback mechanisms, and allow for the use of functional and variable velocities. In addition, they are better able to isolate and work a weak muscle since substitution of other muscles is less likely to occur. Free weights, plyoballs, surgical tubing, manual resistance, and isokinetics are valuable for stressing the upper extremities in an open-chain manner.

Closed-chain exercises can be valuable in simulating normal forces and neuromuscular reactions in sports requiring closed-chain use of the upper extremities, such as gymnastics and wrestling. They are also useful for strengthening scapular stabilizer muscles, facilitating cocontraction of muscles around the glenohumeral joint, and enhancing dynamic joint stability.[60, 61] To balance compression and shear forces, 90 degrees of shoulder elevation is the optimal position for joint stability and closed-chain exercises.[62] Pushups, pushups with a plus, dips, quadruped positioning, and physioball exercises are valuable for stressing the upper extremities in a closed-chain manner.

The appropriate choice of open versus closed kinetic chain exercises according to the specificity principle of training is essential to promote optimal tissue healing and the quickest functional return to activity.

Proprioceptive Neuromuscular Facilitation (PNF)

This category of exercise rehabilitation is challenging. Other rehabilitation methods may achieve equal results, yet proprioceptive neuromuscular facilitation (PNF) incorporates many techniques to accomplish a variety of rehabilitation objectives (Figure 8.9).

Proprioceptive neuromuscular facilitation[31, 63] consists of techniques based upon specific procedures that incorporate neuromuscular and neurophysiological principles and developmental constraints. When admin-

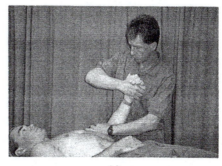

(a)

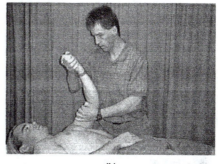

(b)

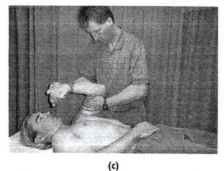

(c)

FIGURE 8.9
Proprioceptive neuromuscular facilitation
This sequence demonstrates a pattern that is used in shoulder rehabilitation.

istered properly, PNF can be very effective in sports medicine. Each word of the acronym, PNF, can lend itself equally to a complete definition of the term. Proprioceptive means receiving stimulation within the tissues of the body. Neuromuscular pertains to nerves and muscles. Facilitation is the reverse of inhibition, and is defined as the promotion or hastening of a natural process. Therefore, PNF may be defined as methods of promoting or hastening the response of the neuromuscular mechanisms through stimulation of the proprioceptors and other sensory potentials of the sport participant. The patterns that dictate PNF movements are based on well-established developmental patterns acquired from birth, and they integrate the most efficient neuromuscular patterns given the limitations of anatomical structure. Growth of sensory activity moves in a cephalic-caudal and proximal-distal direction, with a final and normal coordinated and/or sequenced movement developing to a distal-proximal priority.[38] Thus the components of motion are an orderly sequence of developed movement patterns. According to Beevor's axiom,[38] the brain knows nothing of individual muscle action, only of functional movement. This axiom is relevant to most sports activities, which are dependent on functional movement patterns during coordinated movement rather than on isolated muscles.

Although opponents of PNF used in the athletic setting claim that the techniques are relevant only for the neurologically impaired, one has only to analyze the biomechanics of sports to realize that the PNF patterns apply to athletic motion and can be specifically related to the most efficient sports movements. However the application of PNF techniques to sport participants focuses primarily on a few selected stretching and strengthening techniques.

Patterns and Principles

The basic extremity patterns and principles for PNF are as follows:

PNF patterns adhere to specific movement combinations and consistencies within the three linear planes and axes. However, PNF patterns are spiral-diagonally directed actions that cross linear planes and axes. Thus the patterns are functional patterns of movement. All the muscles of the extremities create the four patterns (or 2 complete diagonals), with each having three movement components: (a) flexion and extension are combined with the other two components, (b) adduction and abduction, as well as (c) internal and external rotation.[62]

Referring to Figures 8.10 and 8.11, the three components of motion are considered in order of importance: (a) flexion/extension, (b) adduction/abduction, and (c) internal/external rotation. The diagram indicates that the opposite end of one diagonal will be the antagonist component. The intermediate pivot may remain straight or may flex and extend. The adduction or abduction and rotations will remain congruent with the proximal joint. The distal pivot will remain consistent with the proximal joint regardless of the intermediate joint. Further study of the diagram indicates that certain combinations of a component are consistent: (a) the upper extremity is coupled with flexion and external rotation, and extension is combined with internal rotation; and (b) the lower extremity is coupled with adduction and external rotation and therefore the antagonist of these components must be coupled with abduction and internal rotation. The agonist are the muscles within the pattern that are in their shortening position, whereas the antagonist are those muscles within the pattern that are nearer their lengthened state.

These diagonal patterns must be adhered to because each set of patterns is congruent with motor patterns and consistent with functional-structural constraints which include both the joint structures as well as the musculature.

The line of movement for the components is usually in the lengthened state to facilitate maximal stretch. Thus the muscles within a pattern are allowed to be in their lengthened state initially and then to progress to their shortened state. Therefore the extension and flexion component accomplishes the greatest degree of stretch, the abduction and adduction component, an intermediate amount; and finally the internal and external component accomplishes the least.

PNF should place a demand within the movement pattern where a response is desired. The resistance is graded according to patient need and response. Stimulation of weaker components can be achieved by demand on stronger components within the pattern, and with additional emphasis on the stronger pivots of motion. Specific techniques use isometric and isotonic contractions. A "hold" refers to *maintaining* a muscular contraction within the diagonal and spiral pattern, whereas a "push" or "pull" requires movement within the pattern.

Attention to sensory cues will direct the patient in components of motion, and movement will stimulate further sensory cues. This produces coordinated and purposeful movement.

Manual contact (hand placement) should be with appropriate pressure and should be applied to facilitate muscular contraction within the pattern and attain maximal response. Hand positioning and pressure change during pattern movement should provide appropriate sensory cues and assure coordinated movement. Manual contact should not be applied simultaneously to the agonist and antagonistic patterns because this produces improper muscular response and voids the facilitating effect.

To demonstrate the influence of hand placement and other neural influences, perform the technique following a muscle testing procedure on the biceps brachii (give no verbal cues to the athlete). Encircle the subject's distal forearm with your hand (pressure on both anterior and posterior surfaces). Next, try muscle test-

FIGURE 8.10

Upper extremity diagonals
(Modified from: Alder, S., Beckers, D., and Buck, M. *PNF in Practice: An Illustrated Guide.* New York: Springer–Verlag, p. 68, 1993.)

SHOULDER: Flexion, adduction, external rotation

SCAPULA: Anterior elevation
FOREARM: Supination
WRIST: Radial flexion
FINGERS: Radial flexion
THUMB: Flexion, adduction

SHOULDER: Flexion, abduction, external rotation

SCAPULA: Posterior elevation
FOREARM: Supination
WRIST: Radial extension
FINGERS: Radial extension
THUMB: Extension, abduction

FLEXION AND EXTERNAL ROTATION ARE CONSISTENT*

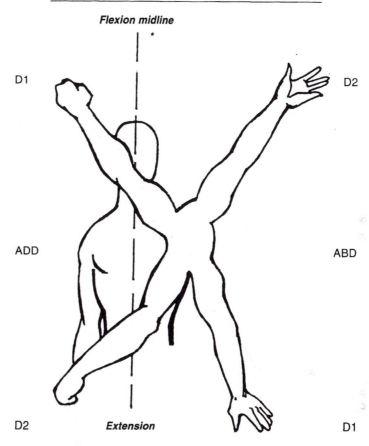

Flexion midline

D1

D2

ADD

ABD

D2

Extension

D1

SHOULDER: Extension adduction internal rotation

SCAPULA: Anterior depression
FOREARM: Pronation
WRIST: Ulnar flexion
FINGERS: Ulnar flexion
THUMB: Flexion, opposition

SHOULDER: Extension abduction internal rotation

SCAPULA: Posterior depression
FOREARM: Pronation
WRIST: Ulnar extension
FINGERS: Ulnar extension
THUMB: Extension, palmar abduction

ing the biceps brachii with contact on only anterior surface of the forearm. If you do not inform the athlete which direction to move in the initial test, he or she probably will not contract any particular muscle group or will alternate contraction between the biceps brachii and the triceps. Without any verbal command the athlete "knew," in the second procedure, which direction to resist when only the anterior forearm received tactile sensation. Such examples demonstrate the propriocep-

tive influences upon movement and how improper hand pressure contributes to ineffective PNF procedures if the sensor mechanisms, via hand placement, are not properly used; or, if properly used, that movement is influenced and/or enhanced by correct hand placement.

Other proprioceptive influences can be applied to other areas of rehabilitation. For example, the distal component of a limb is frequently permitted to be in the wrong position in therapeutic procedures. A trainer may

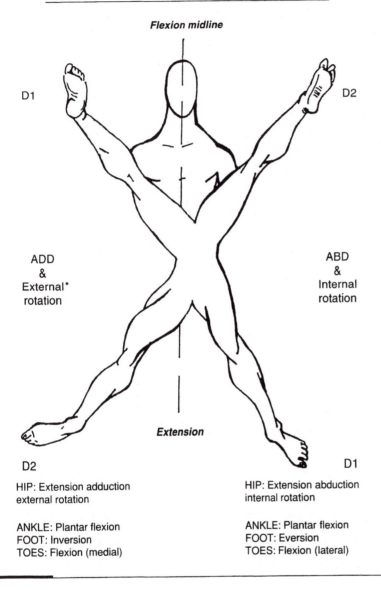

HIP: Flexion adduction
external rotation

ANKLE: Dorsi flexion
FOOT: Inversion
TOES: Extension (medial)

HIP: Flexion abduction
internal rotation

ANKLE: Dorsiflexion
FOOT: Eversion
TOES: Extension (lateral)

FIGURE 8.11
Lower extremity diagonals
(Modified from: Alder, S., Beckers, D., and Buck, M. *PNF in Practice: An Illustrated Guide*. New York: Springer–Verlag, p. 104, 1993.)

ABDUCTION AND INTERNAL ROTATION ARE CONSISTENT*

Flexion midline

D1

D2

ADD
&
External*
rotation

ABD
&
Internal
rotation

Extension

D2

D1

HIP: Extension adduction
external rotation

ANKLE: Plantar flexion
FOOT: Inversion
TOES: Flexion (medial)

HIP: Extension abduction
internal rotation

ANKLE: Plantar flexion
FOOT: Eversion
TOES: Flexion (lateral)

request the athlete to contract the leg extensors while the foot is plantar flexed rather than dorsiflexed, influencing the contraction of the leg extensors.

Proper body mechanics of the applicator (the person providing manual contacts) to the athlete is paramount to avoid injury to the applicator and to assure proper contraction throughout the determined pattern by the patient. An applicator should position his or her body along the diagonal plane of the pattern and in such

a position as to ensure complete control of the athlete in accordance with the pattern's components.

The amount of resistance should facilitate a maximal response from the participant. Resistance should be applied progressively and should be accommodating.

Timing is relative to the sequence of muscular contraction during the pattern. Movements should occur distally first and then progress proximally.

Verbal cues are used to encourage proper response. The commands must be short and concise (e.g., "push," "pull," "hold," and "relax"). Verbal cues should be coordinated with the movement pattern and sensory cues. A common problem in the athletic treatment setting is conversation that arises during the exercise. Casual conversation could obscure the verbal commands and inhibit maximal effort by the patient.

Demonstrate a movement pattern by passively moving the athlete through the desired pattern to assist the patient's understanding of the pattern movement.

Note: PNF patterns are not limited to extremities; they are also applicable for trunk and neck techniques.

The techniques can be performed with the patient in any one of many positions (e.g., supine, sitting, side-lying, kneeling, prone, or on all-fours). Techniques of facilitation are superimposed on the basic patterns.[62] Application to athletes are usually dominated by use of two different stretching and strengthening techniques, which can be applied throughout a movement pattern or restricted to the available range of motion, depending on the rehabilitation objective. There are many other techniques and combination of techniques, including:

1. Rhythmic initiation
2. Hold-relax active movement
3. Repeated contractions
4. Rhythmic rotation
5. Timing for emphasis
6. Normal timing
7. Resisted progression agonist reversals.[64]

These techniques require further reading and necessitate competent instruction, so they are not discussed in this text. Finally, the following brief explanation of the most commonly used techniques in the athletic setting does not assure skill acquisition, only basic understanding.

Techniques to Increase Range of Motion

HOLD-RELAX (HR): Hold-relax is a relaxation technique based upon maximal resistance of an isometric contraction. Since an isometric contraction is involved, the command must be "hold" *instead of "push."* Remember that "hold" should be progressive resistance and not application that creates sudden maximal contraction. The isometric contraction must not be broken or defeated. If the hamstrings are tight, for example, the isometric resistance would be applied to the D1 and D2 (Figure 8.10) extensor patterns with the patient supine and the knee extended. The isometric contraction is gradually maximized over a period of seconds, then it is followed by a command to relax. Once relaxation has been achieved, the limb actively moves against minimal resistance through the newly gained range to the new point of limitation and the procedure is repeated. The limb position is supported by the applicator throughout the repeated sequences. The athletes themselves can be taught to become the applicator and apply this technique.

The applicator will frequently apply minimal resistance with hand placement on the agonist to assist the concentric contraction. In the hamstring example, the hand would be placed upon the thigh as the athlete contracts the hip flexors and moves further into hip flexion. This combination of active movement following HR may be referred to as slow reversal hold-relax.[38, 63] If the agonistic muscles are too weak to move the part into the gained range, passive movement is an alternative. Frequently the applicator will first move the limb to the limited range prior to applying resistance to the antagonist. In the hamstring example, the lower extremity is moved into hip flexion until limitation is felt and "hold" is then applied. Simultaneous hand placements should not be on the antagonist and agonist. As in the hamstring example, hand placement should not be posterior thigh or leg and also the anterior thigh, nor should manual contact be in the popliteal region as this will encourage leg flexion.

The distal component position must also be considered. Thus in the hamstring example, manual contact upon the plantar surface of the foot will encourage leg flexion and hip extension, whereas hand placement upon the dorsum of the foot will encourage hip flexion.

CONTRACT-RELAX (CR): Contract-relax, is a combination of *isotonic* and *isometric* contractions, and is applicable when decreased range of motion is on one side of a joint. The difference between CR and HR is in the verbal commands and the type of muscle contraction. With the joint at the point of limitation, the subject is asked not to hold, but to turn and push as hard as possible. The result is an isotonic contraction of the *rotatory* component and an isometric contraction of the *other two components* (flexion-extension and adduction-abduction) of the antagonistic pattern. Thus, as with HR, a change in joint angle of flexion-extension, abduction-adduction is not allowed to occur; but unlike HR, rotation is allowed. The buildup in tension is immediate, not gradual, and the release is abrupt. The applicator then passively moves the joint to another limitation in the range and repeats the entire procedure, or the athlete may actively move into the agonist pattern after relaxation. This repetition is performed several times. Contract-relax is not an appropriate choice in cases of pain. It has been shown, however, to yield greater increases in motion than HR on two joint muscles in normal subjects.[63]

Strengthening

SLOW REVERSAL (SR): This technique consists of a reversal of the direction of the pattern, beginning with concentric contractions of the agonist followed by concentric contractions of the antagonist. The second step of the pattern involves again reversing from agonist to antagonist and applying maximal resistance, but resistance is graded to allow the patient to move through the components of the pattern. Therefore, the components of motion must be completed in the maximum (allowable) range of motion of the first part of the pattern and immediately reversed into the antagonist pattern and subsequent repeats of this procedure. The effects of slow reversal are best explained by Sherrington's law of successive induction,[65] which maintains that a pattern of movement is facilitated by the immediate preceding contraction of its antagonist.[63]

RHYTHMIC-STABILIZATION (RS): This procedure consists of alternate isometric contraction of the agonist and antagonist. The applicator applies maximal resistance to the agonist and the antagonist alternately without the involved body part moving in either direction of the pattern. The applicator must be careful not to force the patient's involved structures into an increase in range of motion. This technique can be incorporated at any position within the pattern and may begin and end with slow reversals. Rhythmic stabilization is beneficial in the *strengthening* and *relaxation* of weak component motions.

SUMMARY OF PNF: PNF is the application of specific principles and techniques that depend on the proficiency of the applicator. Although the patterns and the principles of application may appear simple, they are by no means easily acquired or implemented. The trainer should not attempt these procedures on the basis of mere observation. Effective use of PNF patterns is dependent on comprehension of the principles, techniques, and appropriate integration within the therapeutic objective. Recommended readings on PNF include: Sullivan, P. E., Markos, P. D., and Minor, M. A.;[63] Voss, D., Ionta, M., and Myers, B.;[62] and Alder, S., Beckers, D. and Buck, M.[66] These texts will expedite comprehension of PNF. To gain proficiency, however, practice and proper instruction of the various techniques and the integration of procedures and principles is required.

Prescription of Rehabilitation Programs

For those who are unfamiliar with the prescription of rehabilitation programs, a short summary of some common conditions follows. This outline shows the progression of an exercise prescription program. Many details obviously need to be included. Remember: Each athlete is different, and each program needs to be individualized.

1. A mild second-degree sprain of the lateral ligaments of the ankle

   Following the initial treatment of ice, compression, and elevation; start a cardiovascular fitness program that does not aggravate the ankle (i.e., swimming). The ankle exercise program may consist of:

   a. initially, isometric eversion, followed by isotonic and isokinetic. OR manual resistive exercises (i.e., PNF). Include exercises that stretch the Achilles tendon

   b. proprioception exercises, such as Bab's board, Stork Stand, and tubing exercises that are applied to the uninvolved limb while standing; Fitter exerciser

   c. additional work on the entire extremity

   d. specific return-to-sport exercises and activities

2. A mild second-degree medial collateral ligament sprain of the knee

   a. initially, quadriceps and hamstring isometric exercises, followed by isotonic and isokinetic exercises and stationary cycling

   b. hamstring stretching exercises and strengthening of the other muscle groups

   c. internal tibial rotation, abduction, toe raises, and work on the hip stabilizers

   d. Hopping and stationary running, followed by stair running

   e. eventually, figure eights, cariocas, and other functional exercises

3. Following a surgical repair of an anterior shoulder dislocation

   a. initially, isometric internal rotation, followed by isotonic and isokinetic exercises

b. later, exercises for the deltoid, the rotator cuff, and the trapezius muscles

c. eventually, arm hanging, pull-ups, and peg-board climbs

4. Rotator-cuff impingement under the coracoacromial arch, for instance in an athlete who does much throwing

   a. initially, gentle exercise, with gradual increasing intensity. At first, pendulum circles and isometric exercises for the trapezius, the latissimus dorsi, the deltoid, and the rotator-cuff muscle groups

   b. progression into isokinetic followed by isotonic exercises and elasticized tubing exercises

   c. eventually, throwing exercises following the FUNGO routine

REFERENCES

1. Abbott HG, Kress JB: Preconditioning in the prevention of knee injuries. *Arch Phys Med Rehabil* 50:326–333, 1969.

2. Gieck J, Lowe J, Keena K: Trainer malpractice: A sleeping giant. *Athletic Training* 1: 41–46, 1984.

3. Allman FL: *Sports Medicine*, edited by Ryan AJ, Allman FL. New York, Academic Press, 1974.

4. Kessler RM, Hertling D: Peripheral joint mobilization techniques. In *Management of Musculoskeletal Disorders: Physical Therapy Principles and Methods*, edited by Kessler R and Hertling D. Philadelphia: J.B. Lippincott, second edition, pp. 87–125, 1990.

5. Leach RE: The prevention and rehabilitation of soft tissue injuries. *Int J Sports Med* 3:18–20, 1982.

6. Dehne E, Torp RP: Treatment of joint injuries by immediate mobilation: Based upon the spinal adaptation concept. *Clin Orthop* 77:218–232, 1971.

7. Houglum, P.A. Soft tissue healing and its impact on rehabilitation. *Journal of Sports Rehabilitation* 1: 19–39, 1992.

8. Kisner C, Colby LA: *Therapeutic Exercise: Foundations and Techniques*. Philadelphia: F.A. Davis, second edition, 1990.

9. Moyer JA: Rehabilitation goals in sports medicine. In *Rehabilitation Techniques in Sports Medicine*, edited by Prentice WE. St. Louis: Mosby, pp. 24–33, 1990.

10. Draper V, Ladd C: Subjective evaluation of function following moderately accelerated rehabilitation of anterior cruciate ligament reconstructed knees. *J Athletic Training* (28) 1: 38–41, 1993.

11. Pease DG: Psychologic factors of rehabilitation. In *Physical Rehabilitation of the Injured Athlete*, edited by Andrews JR and Harrelson GL. Philadelphia: W. B. Saunders, pp. 1–12, 1991.

12. Tuffey S: The role of athletic trainers in facilitating psychological recovery from athletic injury. *J Athletic Training* 26: 346–351, 1991.

13. Worrel TW: The use of behavioral and cognitive techniques to facilitate achievement of rehabilitation goals. *J Sports Rehabil* 1: 69–75, 1992.

14. Fisher CA, Mullins SA, Frye PA: Athletic trainers' attitudes and judgements of injured athlete's rehabilitation adherence. *J Athletic Training* (28) 1: 43–47, 1993.

15. Fisher CA, Hoisington LL: Injured athlete's attitudes and judgments toward rehabilitation adherence. *J Athletic Training* (28) 1: 48–54, 1993.

16. Wiese DM, Wiese MR: Psychological rehabilitation and physical injury; implications for the sportsmedicine team. *Sport Psych* 1: 318–330, 1987.

17. Paulos L, Noyes FR, Grood E, et al: Knee rehabilitation after anterior cruciate ligament reconstruction and repair. *Am J Sports Med* 9:140–149, 1981.

18. Kellett J: Acute soft tissue injuries. *Med Sci Sports Exerci* 18(5): 489–498, 1986.

19. Caillet R: *Soft Tissue Pain and Disability*. Philadelphia: F. A. Davis, second edition, 1988.

20. Norkin CC, Levangie PK: *Joint Structure and Function: A Comprehensive Analysis*. Philadelphia: F.A. Davis, second edition, 1992.

21. Bunton EE, Pitney WA, Kane AW, Cappaert TA: The role of limb torque, muscle action and proprioception during closed kinetic chain rehabilitation of the lower extremity. *J Athletic Training* (28) 1: 10–22, 1993.

22. Hettinger ERT, Muller EA: Influence of training and of inactivity on muscle strength. *Arch Phys Med* 51:449–462, 1970.

23. Hellebrandt FA: Cross education: Ipsilateral and contralateral effects of unimanual training. *J Appl Physiol* 4:136–144, 1951.

24. Hellebrandt FA, Waterland JC: Indirect learning. The influence of unimanual exercise on related muscle groups of the same and the opposite side. *Am J Phys Med* 41:45–55, 1962.

25. Tipton CM, Matthes RO, Maynard JA, et al: The influence of physical activity on ligaments and tendons. *Med Sci Sports* 7:165–175, 1975.

26. Eriksson E, Haggmark T: Comparison of isometric muscle training and electrical stimulation supplementing isometric muscle training in the recovery after major knee ligament surgery. *Am J Sports Med* 7:169–171, 1979.

27. Howard M: *Continuous passive motion*. Paper presented at the meeting of the National Athletic Trainers Association, Las Vegas, NV, June 1986.

28. Rosen M, Jackson D, Atwell A: The efficacy of continuous passive motion in the rehabilitation of anterior cruciate ligament reconstructions. *Am J Sports Med* 20(2): 122–127, 1992.

29. Bohannon, R: Clinical applications of continuous passive motion. *Postgraduate advances in physical therapy,* 1987.

30. Houglum P: Techniques of PNF in athletic training. *Athletic Training* 10:44–45, 1975.

31. Prentice WE, Kooima EF: The use of proprioceptive neuromuscular facilitation of sport-related injury. *Athletic Training* 26–31, Spring 1986.

32. Aten DW, Knight KL: Therapeutic exercise in athletic training—principles and overview. *Athletic Training* 13:123–126, 1978.

33. Yamamoto SK, Hartman CW, Feagin Jr JA, et al: Functional rehabilitation of the knee. A preliminary study. *J Sports Med* 3:288–291, 1975.

34. Allman, FL: *Sports Medicine,* edited by Ryan AJ, Allman FL. New York, Academic Press, p. 311, 1974.

35. Jesse JP: Misuse of strength development programs in athletic training. *Phys Sports Med* 10(7): 46–52, 1979.

36. Curwin S, Standish WD: *Tendonitis: Its Etiology and Treatment.* Lexinton: Collamore Press, 1984.

37. Gray GW: Rehabilitation of running injuries; biomechanical and proprioceptive considerations. In *Top Acute and Trauma Rehabilitation.* Gaithersburg, MD: Aspen Publishers, 1986.

38. Knot M, Voss D: *Proprioceptive Neuromuscular Facilitation: Patterns and Techniques.* New York, Harper and Row, 1968.

39. Komi PV, Buskirk ER: Effect of eccentric and concentric muscle conditioning of tension and electrical activity of human muscle. Ergonomics 15:417–434, 1972.

40. Stuab WT: Eccentric action of muscles: Physiology, injury, and adaptation. In *Exercise and Sport Science Reviews,* 17: 157–185, Baltimore: Williams & Wilkins, 1989.

41. Malone TR: Introduction. In Evaluation of isokinetic equipment, edited by Malone TR. *March Sports Injury Management* 1:1, pp. 1–5, Baltimore: Williams & Wilkins, 1988.

42. Osternig LR: Isokinetic dynamometer. Implications for muscle testing and rehabilitation. In *Exercise and Sport Science Reviews,* American college of sports medicine series. Baltimore: Williams & Wilkins, pp. 45–80, 1986.

43. Weating SH, Seger JY, Thorstensson A: Isoacceleration: A new concept of resistive exercise. *Med Sci Sports Exerci* (23) 5: 631–635, 1991.

44. Draper DO, Ricard MD: Rate of temperature decay in human muscle following 3 Mhz ultrasound: The stretching window revealed. *J Athletic Training* 30: 304–307, 1995.

45. Hertling D: Automobilization techniques for the extremities. In *Management of Musculoskeletal Disorders: Physical Therapy Principles and Methods,* edited by Kessler R and Hertling D. Philadelphia: J. B. Lippincott, second edition, pp. 125–136, 1990.

46. Cyriax J, Coldham M: Treatment by manipulation, massage, and injection. In *Textbook of Orthopedic Medicine Vol 2.* Baltimore: Williams & Wilkins, eleventh edition, 1984.

47. Maitland GD: *Peripherial Manipulation.* Stoneham, MA: Butterworth, second edition, 1977.

48. McWaters G: Aquatic therapy. In *Physical Rehabilitation of the Injured Athlete,* edited by Andrews J and Harrelson G. Philadelphia: W.B. Saunders, pp. 473–503, 1991.

49. DeLorme TL: Restoration of muscle power by heavy resistance exercises. *J Bone Joint Surg* 27:645–667, 1945.

50. DeLorme TL, Watkins AL: Techniques of progressive resistance exercise. *Arch Phys Med* 29:263–273, 1948.

51. Knight KL: Knee rehabilitation by the daily adjustable progressive resistive exercise technique. *Am J Sports Med* 7:336–337, 1979.

52. Steadman JR: Rehabilitation after knee ligament surgery. *Am J Sports Med* 8:294–296, 1980.

53. Tibero D, Gray GW: Kinematics and kinetics during gait. In *Orthopaedic Physical Therapy,* edited by Donatelli R and Wooden MJ. New York: Churchill Livingstone, pp. 305–320, 1989.

54. Chandler TJ, Stone MH: The squat exercise in athletic conditioning: A review of the literature. *Nat Strength Cond Assoc J* 13(5): 52–57, 1991.

55. Gray GW: *Chain Reaction: Successful Strategies for Closed Chain and Open Chain Testing and Rehabilitation* (course manual). Adrian, MI: Wynn Marketing, 1993.

56. Ohkoshi Y, Yasuda K, Kaneeda K, Wada T, Yamanaka M: Biomechanical analysis of rehabilitation in the standing position. *Am J Sports Med* 19(6): 605–611, 1991.

57. Palmitier RA, Kai-nan A, Scott SG, Chao EYS: Kinetic chain exercise in knee rehabilitation. *Sports Med* 11(6): 402–413, 1991.

58. Pope MH, Stankewich CJ, Beynnon BD, Fleming BD: Effect of knee musculature on anterior cruciate ligament strain in vivo. *J Electromyography Kinesiology* 1(3): 191–198, 1991.

59. Shelbourne KD, Wilckens JH: Current concepts in anterior cruciate ligament rehabilitation. *Orthop Rev* 19(11): 957–964, 1990.

60. Davies GJ, Dickoff-Hoffman S: Neuromuscular testing and rehabilitation of the shoulder complex. *J Orthop Sports Ther* 18(2): 449–458, 1993.

61. Wilk KE, Arrigo C: Current concepts in the rehabilitation of the athletic shoulder. *J Orthop Sports Ther* 18(1): 365–378, 1993.

62. Rowe C: *The Shoulder.* New York: Churchill Livingstone, 1987.

63. Voss D, Ionta M, Myers B: *Proprioceptive Neuromuscular Facilitation: Patterns and Techniques.* Philadelphia: Harper & Row, 1985.

64. Sullivan PE, Markos PD, Minor MA: *An Integrated Approach to Therapeutic Exercise: Theory and Clinical Application.* Reston, VA: Reston, 1982.

65. Sherrington C: *The Intergrative Action of the Nervous System.* New Haven, Conn: Yale Press, reprinted edition (1961), 1906.

66. Alder S, Beckers D, Buck M: *PNF In Practice: An Illustrated Guide.* New York: Springer-Verlag, 1993.

RECOMMENDED READINGS

Blair DE, Willis RP: Rapid rehabilitation following anterior cruciate ligament reconstruction. *J Athletic Training* 26: 32–43, 1991.

Clarke DH: Adaptation in strength and muscular endurance resulting from exercise. *Exerc Sport Sci Rev* 1:73–102, 1973.

Eriksson E: Sports injuries of the knee ligaments: Their diagnosis, treatment rehabilitation and prevention. *Med Sci Sports* 8:133–144, 1976.

Fry A, Powell D, Kraemer W: Validity of isokinetic and isometric testing for assessing short-term resistance exercise strength gains. *J Sports Rehabil*, 1(4): 275–283, 1992.

Gieck J: Psychological considerations of rehabilitation. In *Rehabilitation techniques in Sports Medicine*, edited by Prentice WE. St. Louis: Times Mirror/Mosby, pp. 107–121, 1991.

Hinson MN: Isokinetics: A clarification. *Res Q* 5:30–35, 1979.

Kessler RM: Arthology. In *Management of Musculoskeletal Disorders: Physical Therapy Principles and Methods*, edited by Hertling D and Kessler RM. Philadelphia: J.B. Lippincott, second edition, pp. 9–39, 1990.

Knight K, Ingersoll C: Isokinetic contractions may be more effective than isometric contractions in developing muscle strength. *J Athletic Training*, 1993.

Kraus H: Evaluation and treatment of muscle function in athletic injury. *Am J Surg* 98: 353–362, 1959.

Krejci V, Koch P: *Muscle and Tendon Injuries in Athletes*. New York, Stuttgart, Thieme, 1979.

Olson K, Knight K, Ingersoll C, Ozmum: Strength, speed, and power gains with isokinetic training versus isotonic training with the DAPRE technique. *J Athletic Training*, 1993.

Pipes TV, Wilmore JH: Isokinetic versus isotonic strength training in adult men. *Med Sci Sports* 7:262–274, 1975.

Rogers JL: PNF: A new way to improve flexibility (Proprioceptive Neuromuscular Facilitation). *Track Technique* 74:2345–2347, 1978.

Sargeant A, Davies CTM, Edwards RJHT, et al: Functional and structural changes after disuse of human muscle. *Clin Sci Mol Med* 52:337–342, 1977.

Smith M, Melton P: Isokinetic versus isotonic variable resistance training. *Am J Sports Med* 9:275–279, 1981.

Standish WD, Rubinovih RM, Curwin S: Eccentric exercise in chronic tendonitis. *Clinical Orthop* 208: 65–68, 1986.

Steadman JR: Rehabilitation of athletic injuries. *Am J Sports Med* 7:147–149, 1979.

Tanigwa MC: Comparison of the hold-relax procedure and passive mobilization on increasing muscle length. *Phys Ther* 52:725–735, 1972.

Voss D, Knott M: Patterns of motion for proprioceptive neuromuscular facilitation. *Br J Phys Med* 17(9): 191–198, 1954.

Specific Athletic Injuries and Related Problems

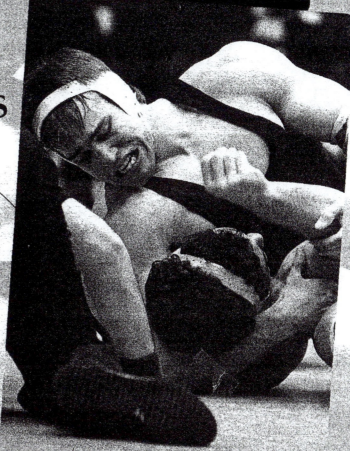

Inflammation, Microtrauma, and Stress-Related Injuries

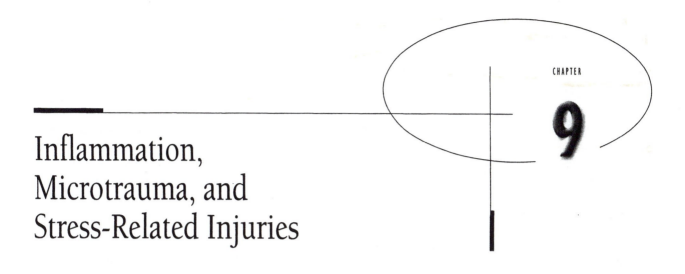

Modern sports place intense demands on the recovery and restorative powers of the body. The present-day athlete is asked to do far more training and to subject his or her body to more stress than ever before. Very often, however, we find that the adaptive and healing processes have not kept pace with the imposed demands, resulting in overuse injuries that are frequently difficult and frustrating to treat.

In this chapter we discuss the process of inflammation as it applies to acute and chronic overuse injuries, the concept of microtrauma, and, finally, the stress-related injuries of bone.

The Inflammatory and Healing Process

It is important to realize that the body's initial reaction to an injury is similar to its reaction to an infection. This reaction is termed *inflammation* and may manifest macroscopically (such as after an acute injury) or at a microscopic level, the latter occurring particularly in chronic overuse conditions.

The trauma, or initial lesion, leads to an increase in the friction that occurs between moving tissues as well as to a release of chemical mediators, both of which may start the inflammatory process.[1] This process may present macroscopically with a number of signs, particularly (a) pain and loss of normal function, (b) swelling, and (c) redness and warmth. These signs are often referred to as the "cardinal signs" of inflammation. However, microtrauma may not present with any of these signs, particularly during the early stages, even though the inflammation is proceeding at the microscopic level.

1. *Pain.* Pain is thought to be due to a combination of factors acting in a vicious circle. For instance, the trauma itself may stimulate the pain receptors. Pain may also result from cell anoxia, because of interference with the blood supply, due to damage suffered by the capillaries at the time of the injury. Oxygen and nutrients are essential for cellular survival, and their lack releases chemical substances such as bradykinin and prostaglandin, further aggravating the pain.

2. *Swelling.* Swelling results from a number of causes. There is bleeding from the torn arteries, veins, and capillaries. Damaged cells fail to retain intracellular fluid, losing it to the extracellular compartment. Cell damage also stimulates activity in the mast cells, which are present throughout the body in loose connective tissue. The mast cells release histamine, which in turn increases vascular and cell membrane permeability, resulting in additional loss of intracellular fluid and plasma. As more cells succumb to anoxia, more fluid leaks out. The increased protein in the extracellular fluid raises the osmotic pressure of the extracellular compartment surrounding the site of the injury. Fluid is therefore drawn out of the cells, which are alive but functioning suboptimally. If the limb is held in a dependent position, gravity adds yet another factor that may increase the swelling.

3. *Redness and warmth.* Redness and warmth are indications of an increase in the blood supply to an injured area, which occurs once the healing process is initiated. Redness and warmth may also result from the release of histamine, serotonin, bradykinin, and the production of eicosanoids—prostaglandins, thromboxanes, and leukotrienes—by the injured tissues.

The purpose of the inflammatory process is to heal the injured tissues. In order to clarify the process of inflammation and healing, we divide it in three stages: (1) cellular response, (2) regeneration, and (3) remodeling.

Cellular Response

The cellular response in acute inflammation results in leukocytes (white blood cells) invading the traumatized area. Neutrophils comprise the largest group of the leukocytes, followed by the lymphocytes, monocytes, and macrophages. Neutrophils and macrophages are phagocytic and have the ability to engulf and digest invading organisms and/or debris from cellular damage. Lymphocytes play a primary role in the immune response of the body. The monocyte and macrophage also participate in the debridement of damaged tissue and in stimulation of tissue healing. All of the leulocytes produce substances that further stimulate and/or regulate the inflammatory response. This stimulation, in turn, may result in an increased vasodilatory effect on the surrounding blood vessels and lead to the stimulation of several humoral factors or systems, including the fibrolytic system, the clotting system, the complement system, and the kinin system (Figure 9.1).

Regeneration

After the cellular response, the body initiates mechanisms with which it attempts to regenerate the damaged tissue. The body's potential for regeneration is somewhat limited, however, and usually a less specialized tissue or form of *collagen* is produced. The first step in the regenerative phase is to remove the debris that results from the trauma, as well as the cells that have succumbed to anoxia. The granulocytes and macrophages accomplish this, for they can survive under relatively anaerobic conditions. The next stage is the forming of capillaries in order to bring oxygen and nutrients (amino acids, sugars, vitamins, and enzymes) into the damaged area. Thus, endothelial cells regenerate, leading to the proliferation of capillary buds, which connect to form a new capillary system.

Fibroblasts then become active. This leads to collagen production, which can begin once there is sufficient oxygen at the cellular level; the manufacture of collagen takes place in the ribosomes of the reticulum, which requires oxygen. Three polypeptide chains are formed when proline is hydroxylated by the enzyme prolinehydroxylase, together with vitamin C, into hydroxyproline. Glycine is also added. These chains, which consist of about a thousand amino acids each, are coiled into a spiral. Three of these chains then join, forming a triple helix. The triple-helix configuration adds strength to the collagen, as does cross-linkage, which occurs by the joining of aldehydes produced from lysine (Figures 9.2 and 9.3).

At the same time as the collagen is being produced, it is being broken down by the lytic process of the

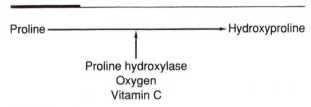

FIGURE 9.2

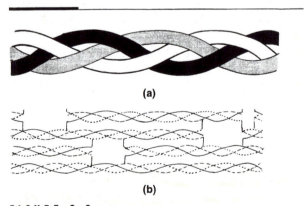

FIGURE 9.3
(a) The triple helix (b) The structure of collagen
Triple helix plus cross linkages

Trauma (either macroscopic or microscopic)
→ Release of chemicals such as serotin, histamine, bradykinin, and prostaglandin

Cellular response — Leukocytes invade the traumatized area

Stage of regeneration — Fibroblasts lead to the production of collagen

Stage of remodeling — Ground substance added and the collagen assumes its final form

FIGURE 9.1
Stages of inflammation and subsequent healing

enzyme collagenase, which is produced by macrophages and granulocytes. This occurs particularly during the first two weeks following the injury. For adequate healing to occur, there should be a balance between the synthesis and breakdown of collagen, but as less energy is needed for the lytic process, more breakdown than synthesis may occur initially. The result is that, during the first two weeks after an injury, the tissues may have a decreased tensile strength. The healing tissues are then reinforced by ground substance which adds strength and defines the type of collagen that will eventually develop.

Remodeling

The injured tissues next undergo remodeling, which can take up to one year to complete in the case of major tissue disruption.[2] The remodeling stage blends in with the latter part of the regeneration stage, which means that motion of the injured tissues will influence their structure when they are healed. This is one reason why it is necessary to consider controlled motion during the recovery stage. If a limb is completely immobilized during the recovery process, the tissues may emerge fully healed but poorly adapted functionally, with little chance for change, particularly if the immobilization has been prolonged. Another reason for encouraging controlled motion is that any adhesions that develop will be flexible and will thus allow the tissues to move easily on each other. Caution should be observed during the first two weeks, as mentioned previously, as the tensile strength of the tissues may be markedly reduced.

Tissue Constriction

One of the problems related particularly to inflammation from chronic overuse stress is the constriction of the tissues by the healing process. Myofibroblasts, which contain relatively large amounts of actin, migrate into the damaged tissue and induce a contraction of the wound margins. This serves to decrease the overall area of the injured tissue and thus facilitate faster healing and a reduction in scar formation. As this process occurs, it affects not only the movement of tissues on each other, but also controls the amount of blood (and therefore oxygen) that is available to the tissues, especially during high-demand situations.[3] This hypoxia may explain the occurrence of pain after an injury has apparently healed. Tissue constriction can result from repetitive stress, which leads to microtrauma and an inflammatory reaction, or it can be due to adhesion formation following a period of immobilization.

Microtrauma

Constant repetitive maximal stressing of the body day after day leads not only to adaptive changes which enhance performance, but also to changes in some athletes which result in pathological microscopic lesions involving the tendon, or the junction of muscle and tendon or tendon and bone. These pathological changes result from an inflammatory response to the microtrauma of repeated stress and lead to edema and hemorrhage, followed by the invasion of inflammatory cells. If this reaction is not reversed at an early stage, the permanent organization of fibrin and the formation of adhesions and scar tissue may follow. This in turn may lead to constant pain both during and after activity. An example of this is patellar tendinitis, which results from the repetitive stress of jumping and landing, and leads to an inflammatory response to microtrauma at the attachment of the patellar tendon to the patella.[4,5]

The microtraumatic lesion appears to be an individual reaction in particular athletes, with some being more disposed to develop the problem than others, even though they may all be engaged in the same activity.

SYMPTOMS: The inflammatory response to microtrauma can be divided into phases according to the severity of the symptoms.

Phase I. Pain *after* activity only

Phase II. Pain *during and after* activity, with no significant functional disability

Phase III. Pain during and after activity *with* significant functional disability

Phase IV. Pain *all the time,* with significant functional disability

TREATMENT: Discussing the concept of microtrauma with the athlete is important so that he or she has a clear understanding of the condition and the prognosis, and is thereby more inclined to cooperate in the treatment program.

PHASES I AND II:

1. Modification of the athlete's activity, if possible
2. Removal of any aggravating exercises
3. Ice massage or heat before activity, depending on which modality is more comfortable for the athlete
4. Ice and ice massage after activity
5. Accessory supports according to the area involved (e.g., patellar neoprene support and/or in-shoe orthotic devices)

6. Strengthening exercises of the muscles involved, so long as these exercises do not aggravate the condition

7. Anti-inflammatory medication (e.g., aspirin, Naprosyn, or Motrin)

8. Physical therapy modalities (e.g., high-voltage galvanic stimulation and transcutaneous electrical nerve stimulation)

PHASE III:

1. Modification of activity, ice massage both before and after activity, and the treatment modalities mentioned for Phases I and II

2. Intralesional cortisone injections in the more refractory cases once or twice only, if at all

PHASE IV: Surgery in selected cases

Stress Reactions and Stress Fractures

If an overuse condition affects the bones rather than the soft tissues, a stress fracture or a pre-stress fracture (a stress reaction) can result. Stress fractures are among the most common athletic injuries and should always be considered when an athlete complains of pain related to bone, particularly if the pain is aggravated by activity and relieved by rest. The trainer needs to maintain a high index of suspicion for this condition in order to make an early diagnosis and apply the correct treatment, thereby decreasing the morbidity and complication rate.

The term *stress reaction* is used to describe a condition in which microfractures of the bone are present.[6] Some of these microfractures will heal if the athlete decreases the intensity of the causative activities. However, if the force on the bone is increased, an actual stress fracture may result (see the discussion of tibial stress reaction).

It is becoming apparent that the diagnosis of a stress fracture is increasing in frequency. Part of this is due to earlier detection both clinically and by utilization of procedures such as the bone scan, but part may also be due to an actual increase in fractures because of greater athletic participation by the general public (Figure 9.4).

↓ definition

ETIOLOGY: A stress fracture occurs when the forces applied repetitively to a bone exceed the structural strength of the bone. Though most stress fractures are related to impact forces associated with weight bearing, others are not (such as the fractured humerus of the ball thrower or javelin thrower). The factors that seem to be most clearly associated with the development of stress fractures are:

Increased Muscular Forces
+
Increased Rate of Remodeling
↓
Resorption and Rarefaction
↓
Focal Microfractures
↓
Periosteal and/or Endosteal Response
("Stress Reaction")
↓
Linear Fracture
("Stress Fracture")
↓
Displaced Fracture

FIGURE 9.4
The development of stress fractures
(Adapted from C. L. Stanitski et al. On the nature of stress fractures, *American Journal of Sports Medicine* 6:391–396, 1978. Reprinted by permission.)

1. Muscle forces acting across the bone

2. Repetitiveness of the activity

The muscle forces, or torque, across the bone may stress that bone if an imbalance between antagonistic muscles exists.[7] In addition, though muscles may be rapidly strengthened by a particular activity, bone is thought to adapt and strengthen at a much slower rate and is thus subjected to forces for which it is not ready. Initially, as mentioned, microfractures may occur and in some cases may progress to become complete fractures.

Types of Stress Fractures

There are four basic types of stress fractures (see Figure 9.5):

1. Oblique fracture—the most common variety

2. Compression fracture

3. Transverse fracture—the most dangerous because it can displace

4. Longitudinal fracture—very rare

Bones Most Frequently Affected

Almost any bone in the body can be affected by a stress fracture. In athletes, the ones most commonly affected (Figure 9.6) are the following:

1. Tibia—either the upper third or the junction of the mid-third and lower thirds. Occurs particularly in running activities.

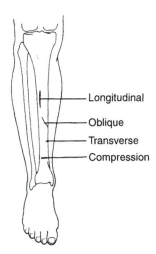

FIGURE 9.5
Types of stress fractures

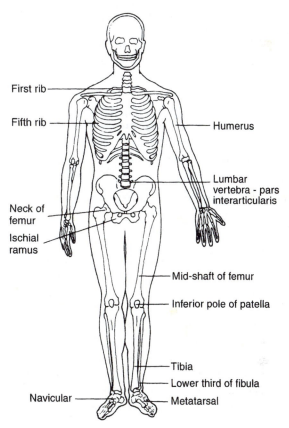

FIGURE 9.6
Sites of stress fractures

2. Fibula—usually the lower third. Occurs mostly in running athletes.

3. Metatarsal shaft—especially the second through fourth. Can result from marching, walking, running, or jumping.

4. Calcaneus.

5. Femur—either the lower third or the femoral neck. These are serious fractures which can displace if not adequately treated.

6. Pars interarticularis of the lumbar vertebrae—stress fractures in this area can result in spondylolysis. These fractures are particularly common in gymnasts and football linemen.

7. Rib fractures—especially the first rib in weight lifters and the eighth rib in tennis players.

8. Humerus—oblique-spiral fractures of the midshaft of the humerus have been recorded in throwing sports.

SYMPTOMS AND SIGNS: The athlete complains of pain which initially occurs during the activity and is relieved by rest, though occasionally a stress fracture will present with sudden acute pain. In the next stage the pain continues for hours, perhaps through the night, or it might become worse during the night (pain that becomes worse at night is highly suggestive of bone pain). Swelling may occur, particularly after activity.

Localized tenderness with or without swelling is almost always present over the fracture (Figure 9.7). Percussion is often very painful and should be performed gently. One may also percuss away from the affected area. For example, with a suspected stress

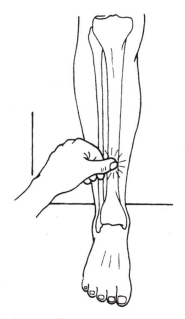

FIGURE 9.7
Localized tenderness is highly suggestive of a stress fracture

fracture of the tibia, percussing the heel may produce pain in the area of the fracture.

The tuning-fork test may help to add weight to the presumptive diagnosis of a stress fracture. With this test a vibrating tuning fork with a flat base is placed onto the tender area. If discomfort or pain is felt (which is not present when the unaffected limb is tested), it is suggestive of a stress fracture. While this test is not always positive, it is seldom positive if a stress fracture is not present (Figures 9.8 and 9.9).

X-RAYS: It is important to realize that a stress fracture may not be visible on ordinary X-rays for two to eight weeks after symptoms commence. It is therefore important to X-ray the painful area again if symptoms persist, or to obtain a bone scan.

The first signs on ordinary X-rays are rarefaction of bone, a hairline fracture, a thin layer of callus along the periosteum, or all three. In the compression-stress fracture, a dense sclerotic line appears in the substance of the bone. The dangerous transverse variety has a clear fracture line running at right angles to the bone shaft which may appear to involve only part of one cortex, but the weakness usually extends right across the shaft (Figures 9.10 and 9.11).

BONE SCAN: A radioactive-labeled substance (technetium-99m) is taken up by metabolically active bone. This produces the increased uptake or "hot spot"

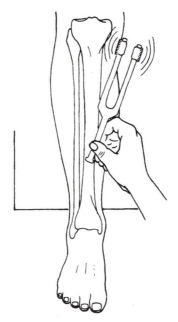

FIGURE 9.9
The tuning-fork test to diagnose a stress fracture

of a positive bone scan and can be seen within the first few days of the symptoms presenting.[8,9,10,11] The *stress reaction state* may produce a "hazy" bone scan (see tibial stress reaction, Figure 9.12).

COMPLICATIONS: The most serious complication involves displacement of a complete stress fracture. This is particularly dangerous when it occurs through the neck of the femur, as avascular necrosis may follow.

Occasionally, nonunion of a stress fracture occurs, necessitating surgery and possibly bone grafting. Some stress fractures require a long period of relative inactivity to heal completely and may recur after apparent healing.

TREATMENT: Rest is the basic treatment for stress fractures, but each case has to be evaluated on its own merits. For instance, it is frequently permissible for the athlete to continue participation while suffering from a stress fracture of the third or fourth metatarsal shaft as long as a special in-shoe modification is used. However, the individual with a stress fracture at a site such as the femur should not be permitted to continue with athletic activity until the fracture has healed.[12,13]

Resumption of training should be graduated so that enough time is allowed for adequate bone adaptation to take place. If training is resumed too rapidly, the symptoms will frequently recur.

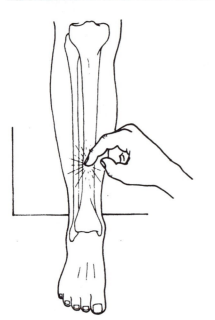

FIGURE 9.8
Percussion used to diagnose a stress fracture

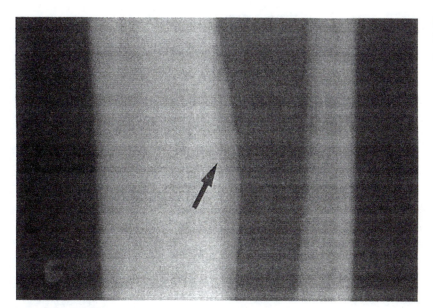

FIGURE 9.10
Transverse fracture of the anterior crest of the tibia

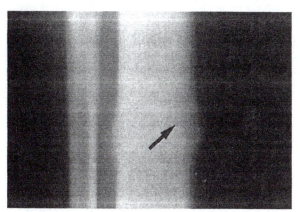

FIGURE 9.11
A stress fracture at six weeks
Note the callus indicating that healing is taking place.

REFERENCES

1.   van der Meulen JCH: Present state of knowledge on processes of healing in collagen structures. *Int J Sports Med* 3:4–8, 1982.

2.   Paulos L, Noyes FR, Grood E, et al: Knee rehabilitation after anterior cruciate ligament reconstruction and repair. *Am J Sports Med* 9:140–149, 1981.

3.   Kvist M, Järvinen M: Clinical, histochemical and biochemical features in repair of muscle and tendon injuries. *Int J Sports Med* 3:12–14, 1982.

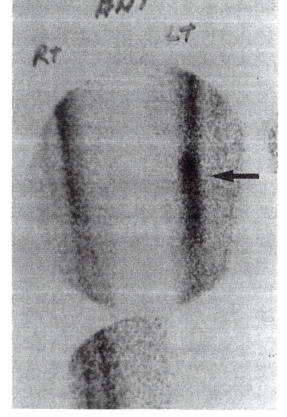

FIGURE 9.12
Bone scan of the tibiae
A "hot spot," signifying a stress fracture, can be seen.

4. Williams JGP: Wear and tear injuries in athletes—an overview. *Br J Sports Med* 12:211–214, 1979.

5. Blazina ME, Kerlan RK, Jobe FW, et al: Jumper's knee. *Orthop Clin North Am* 4:665–678, 1973.

6. Jackson DW: Shin splints: common, painful, and confusing. *Consultant* 16:75, 1976.

7. Devas M: *Stress Fractures.* London, Churchill Livingstone, 1975, pp. 224–227.

8. Geslien GE, Thrall JH, Espinosa JL: Early detection of stress fractures using 99m Tc-polyphosphate. *Radiology* 121:683–687, 1976.

9. Prather JL, Nusynowitz ML, Snowdy HA, et al: Scintigraphic findings in stress fractures. *J Bone Joint Surg* 59A:869–874, 1977.

10. Daffner RH: Stress fractures: Current concepts. *Skeletal Radiol* 2:221–229, 1978.

11. Garrick JG: Presentation, 43rd American Academy of Orthopedic Surgeons, New Orleans, Louisiana, February 1976.

12. Kaltsas D-S: Stress fractures of the femoral neck in young adults. *J Bone Joint Surg* 63B:33–37, 1981.

13. Todd RC, Freeman MAR, Pirie CJ: Isolated trabecular fatigue fractures in the femoral head. *J Bone Joint Surg* 54B:723–728, 1972.

RECOMMENDED READINGS

Belkin SC: Stress fractures in athletes. Symposium on sports injuries. *Orthop Clin North Am* 11:735–741, 1980.

Cohen K, Diegelmann R, Linblad W: *Wound Healing: Biomechanical and Clinical Aspect.* Philadelphia, WB. Saunders Co, 1992.

DeLee J, Drez D: *Orthopaedic Sports Medicine: Principles and Practices.* Philadelphia, WB. Saunders Co. 1994.

Latshaw RF, Kantner TR, Kalenak A, et al: A pelvic stress fracture in a female jogger. A case report. *Am J Sports Med* 9:54–56, 1981.

Morris JM, Blickenstaff LD: *Fatigue Fractures: A Clinical Study.* Springfield Ill., Charles C Thomas Company, 1967.

Orava S, Puranen J, Ala-Ketola L: Stress fractures caused by physical exercise. *Acta Orthop Scand* 49:19–27, 1978.

Stanitski CL, McMaster JH. Scranton PE: On the nature of stress fractures. *Am J Sports Med* 6:391–396, 1978.

Taunton JE, Clement DB, Webber D: Lower extremity stress fractures in athletes. *Phys Sportsmed* 9:77–86, January 1981.

Woo SLY, Kuei SC, Amiel D, et al: The effects of prolonged physical training on the properties of long bone: A study of Wolff's law. *J Bone Joint Surg* 63A:780–787, 1981.

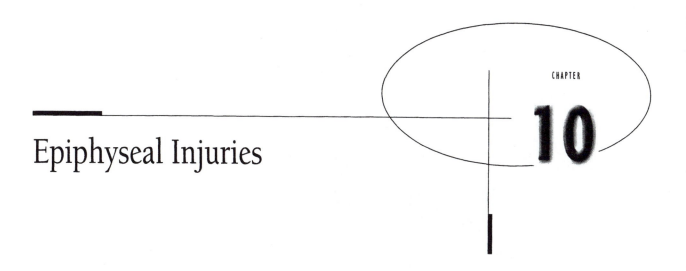

Epiphyseal Injuries

Bone Growth in Adolescents

Adolescents and pre-adolescents are subject to a special group of injuries because their bones have not yet matured. These injuries, which affect the growth centers, should be known to those involved in the health care of the young athlete.

Pre-adolescence is defined as the time from childhood until the onset of secondary sex characteristics, whereas adolescence is considered to begin after secondary sex characteristics appear and to continue to the point of skeletal maturity.

The highest incidence of epiphyseal injuries occurs in twelve- to fourteen-year-olds, with boys being injured more frequently than girls.

Physiology of Bone Growth

The growth center (Figure 10.1) consists of three main parts:

1. Epiphysis, in which a secondary center of ossification may form

2. Growth plate (or physis)

3. Metaphysis

Epiphyses may be divided into pressure and traction epiphyses. Pressure epiphyses relate to the longitudinal growth of long bones and are found at the ends of the bones. Traction epiphyses, or *apophyses,* are located at the attachment of certain tendons to the bones, for example, the patellar tendon's attachment to the tibia, and the medial epicondylar epiphysis from which originate the forearm flexor muscles of the humerus.

The growth plate consists of four layers of cartilaginous cells. The first lies adjacent to the epiphysis and is called the reserve zone. The cells of the reserve zone increase in number (proliferate) and form the second layer, the zone of proliferating cells. These cells then mature and increase in size (hypertrophy). This zone of hypertrophied cells in turn becomes calcified (zone of provisional calcification) and, finally, ossified (Figure 10.2). The zone of hypertrophying cells is the weakest part of the growth plate and is the area through which separation usually occurs in the event of an injury. Mild injuries do not usually interfere with the blood supply or the zone of resting cartilage cells, so that growth is not disturbed.

Prevention of Epiphyseal Injuries

Though epiphyseal injuries occur in organized sports, they are more likely to happen during unorganized play

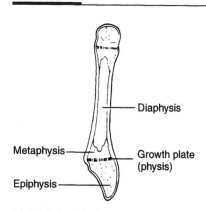

FIGURE 10.1
The growing bone

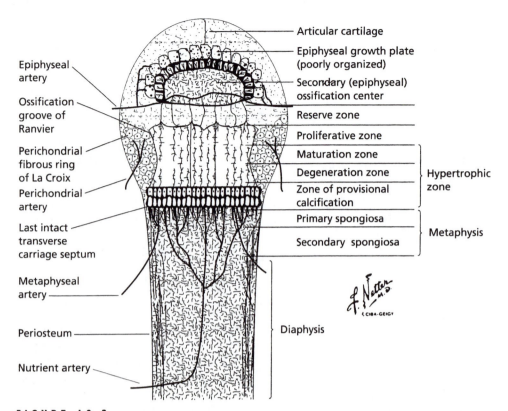

FIGURE 10.2

Structure and blood supply of a typical growth plate.

Source: Netter FH, *The CIBA Collection of Medical Illustrations,* Vol 8, p. 166, 1987. Reprinted with permission of Curtis Management Group, Indianapolis, IN.

activity.[1] For instance, only 15 percent of fractures of the distal femoral epiphyseal plate were found to result from organized athletic participation.

In order to reduce to a minimum the number of epiphyseal and other injuries that do occur in organized athletics, certain points should be remembered.

1. An athlete who suffers an injury or illness that results in muscular atrophy or loss of tone should be placed on a program of rehabilitation exercises before being allowed to return to a competitive environment.

2. The adolescent may be more likely to suffer epiphyseal injuries during certain developmental stages (e.g., "growth spurts") particularly if involved in contact sports.

3. There are adolescents who should be encouraged to take up activities other than contact sports, for example, an extremely obese adolescent or the tall, thin, rapidly growing youth who is uncoordinated and has poor muscle development. These youths should be re-examined when their bodies have matured and at that time it should be determined whether they are better able to withstand the forces of contact-sport participation.

4. Heavily muscled or more mature adolescents should not be allowed to compete in contact sports with those who are smaller and relatively immature in their development, because this exposes the smaller athletes to a higher rate of injury. Contact sports should be organized so that weight, size, and strength are taken into consideration. In an attempt to reduce the injury rate, the New York Public High School Association devised a program that grouped adolescents on the basis of physical fitness, skills, and physical maturity. This program has apparently resulted in a 50 percent reduction in the injury rate.

Classification of Epiphyseal Injuries

The most frequently used classification is that developed by Salter and Harris,[2] which divides the injuries into five types—type I producing the least damage to the epiphysis and type V being the most serious (Figure 10.3).

The most common types of epiphyseal fractures seen in athletes are type I and type II. It has often been stated that the epiphyseal plate is the weakest link in the tendon-

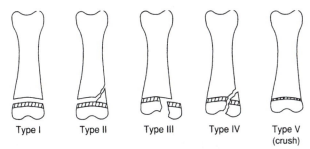

FIGURE 10.3

The Salter-Harris classification of epiphyseal fractures
Source: BA Torre, Epiphyseal Injuries in the Small Joints of the Hand, *Hand Clinics,* 4 (1), pp. 113–121, 1988.

Type I   Type II   Type III   Type IV   Type V (crush)

TABLE 10.1 *Adolescent and pre-adolescent injuries*

1. An adolescent or pre-adolescent is much more likely to sustain an injury to the growth plate than to suffer a ligamentous injury.

2. The growth plate is the weakest link in the chain involving the muscles, tendons, ligaments, and bone.

3. Any injury or "sprain" around a joint in a growing child should be considered an epiphyseal injury until proven otherwise.

bone chain. Some studies have shown that the capsule and ligaments around joints are between two to five times stronger than the growth plate. This means that an injury that would result in ligament damage in an adult leads to an epiphyseal injury in a child (Table 10.1).

Treatment of Epiphyseal Injuries

1. Type I or type II epiphyseal injuries, in which minimal separation is present and no remodeling is necessary, need be immobilized only for about three weeks, followed by a period of rehabilitation.

2. Type I or II where there is slightly more separation or where remodeling is necessary should be immoblized for about six weeks, followed by a gradual rehabilitation program before return to participation.

3. Type III, IV, or V injuries include an osseous component in the injury and thus are slower to heal than when the growth plate alone is injured. Adolescents with these injuries should be off contact and collision sports for at least one year. If the involved epiphysis is related to a weight-bearing joint, the athlete should not participate in running or jogging activities for at least one year, but he or she can swim. At the end of the year, the athlete should be reassessed with regard to further participation.

Complications and Prognoses of Epiphyseal Injuries

Injuries to the growth plate may have a number of possible effects, though the majority do not result in interference with bony growth. Significant growth disturbance occurs in approximately 10 percent of epiphyseal injuries. This relatively low figure is due to the fact that most fractures occur through the zone of hypertrophying cells or of provisional calcification, neither of which interferes with blood vessels supplying the epiphyseal cells.

The complication rate depends on the bone involved, the extent of the damage to the epiphyseal plate, and the degree of maturity reached by that epiphysis. In some cases, a temporary increase in the growth of the bone is produced, but this does not usually result in any deformity.

Most type I, II, and III injuries have a good prognosis as long as the epiphyseal blood supply remains intact. Type IV has a relatively poor prognosis, particularly if the epiphyseal plate is not perfectly realigned.

Type V injuries are associated with crushing of the epiphysis and therefore have the poorest prognosis, but fortunately this injury accounts for only about 2 percent of all epiphyseal fractures.

In the small number of cases in which the growth plate closes, bony growth is disturbed. If the whole epiphysis is affected, one limb will be shorter than the other, though this deformity does not produce any angulation. If the bone involved is one of a pair (e.g., the ulna and the radius or the tibia and the fibula), shortening of one bone will result in the development of a deformity of the related joint. On the other hand, if only part of the epiphyseal plate closes while the other part continues to grow, an angulation of the limb will result.

Overuse Injuries of the Growth Plate

The growth plate may also be injured by an overuse type of stress.[3] Though this is not a common injury, it is nevertheless an area of concern as more and more adolescents and pre-adolescents subject themselves to intense training techniques.[4,5]

X-ray changes are seen in stress fractures of the proximal humeral epiphyses in baseball players[6]; distal humeral epiphyses in baseball pitchers and gymnasts[7,8]; ischial crest epiphyses[9] and proximal tibial epiphyses stress fractures in runners[10]; and stress changes to the distal radial epiphyses in gymnasts[11,12] (Figure 10.4).

X-RAY EXAMINATION: It should be remembered that usually very little change shows on the X-rays, even though the epiphysis has been injured. The epiphysis can be displaced at the moment of injury and then return to the normal anatomical position. Comparison X-rays of the opposite extremity should be taken. Slight widening or irregularity of the growth plate may be noted, but often the only way to prove that an epiphyseal fracture has occurred is to perform stress X-rays (usually under anesthesia) and note if this results in any opening of the growth plate. Stress X-rays should be performed in certain areas, such as around the knee joint, especially with injuries to the distal femoral epiphysis (Figure 10.5). Laxity on physical examination in

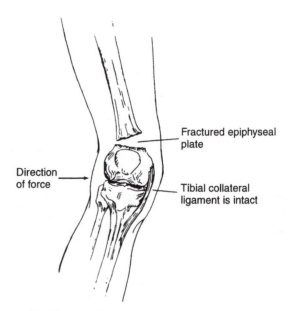

FIGURE 10.5
Epiphyseal fracture—distal femoral epiphysis
This injury may result from a valgus force (as illustrated).

this setting is presumptively epiphyseal injury, rather than ligamentous sprain, until proven otherwise.

OTHER IMAGING STUDIES: Tomograms may be helpful if limited additional information is necessary, but often fail to provide sufficient detail.[13]

Computed tomography (CT) scanning with coronal and sagittal reconstruction can be useful in imaging complex fractures such as a severely comminuted epiphyseal and metaphyseal ankle fracture not adequately visualized on plain films.[13]

Magnetic resonance imaging (MRI) is commonly used in assessing soft tissue injury, but may also be useful for detecting subtle growth plate injuries before radioscopic changes are evident.[13,14]

Ultrasound can be more sensitive than plain films in detecting and grading slipped capital femoral epiphyses and in following remodeling after surgical fixation.[15]

Multiphase bone scintigraphy (bone scanning) may occasionally be useful for detecting physiologic bone growth cessation before they are visible using other techniques.[16]

WHICH EPIPHYSES ARE MOST COMMONLY INJURED? The epiphyses most likely to be injured in athletic participation are the:

1. Distal radius (wrist injuries)
2. Phalanges (finger injuries)
3. Distal tibia (ankle injuries)

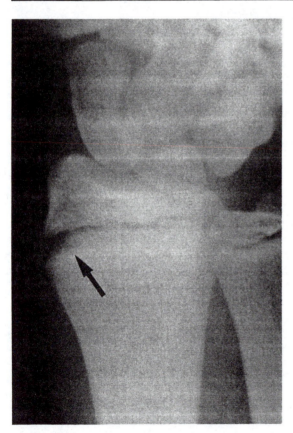

FIGURE 10.4
Stress changes of the distal radial epiphysis
as seen in gymnasts (compare with Figure 10.6). Some of the changes include widening and irregularity of the epiphyseal plate.

4. Distal humerus (elbow injuries)
5. Phalanges (toe injuries)
6. Proximal humerus (shoulder injuries)
7. Distal fibula (ankle injuries)
8. Distal ulna (wrist injuries)
9. Distal femur (knee injuries)
10. Metacarpals (hand injuries)

These 10 locations account for approximately 90 percent of epiphyseal injuries. Distal epiphyses are more commonly injured than proximal; notable exceptions are the proximal phalanges and proximal humerus.[17]

Specific Areas

The Wrist

The *distal radial and ulnar epiphyseal plates* may be injured by a fall on the hand of an outstretched arm. All "sprains" of the wrist in the adolescent and the pre-adolescent should therefore be examined with this possibility in mind and referred for X-ray examination. Chronic injuries may be more common in adolescent gymnasts and weightlifters.[11,18] The distal radius is responsible for approximately 30 percent of epiphyseal injuries and the distal ulna for about 3 percent.[17]

The Hand and Fingers

The proximal phalangeal and thumb metacarpal epiphyseal plates are the most commonly injured, and represent approximately 15 percent of epiphyseal injuries.[17,18,19]

The Ankle Joint

The *distal fibular and tibial epiphyseal plates* are commonly injured, usually due to an inversion plantar flexion injury to the ankle (though sometimes they are injured by an eversion force). A high index of suspicion is necessary to avoid missing the diagnosis and calling the injury a sprain. It is therefore important that all ankle sprains be evaluated not only clinically but also by X-rays.[20] These epiphyseal injuries account for about 18 percent of the total, with the distal tibia alone responsible for about 14 percent.[17]

The Knee Joint

A valgus force applied to the lateral side of the knee is likely to result in a sprain of the medial collateral ligament in an adult, whereas in the growing athlete the growth plate is more commonly injured. It is not unusual for a sixteen-year-old to have open epiphyses which will take the force of the injury rather than tear the ligaments.[21] This is because the capsule and the ligaments surrounding the joint are two to five times stronger than the growth plate. Also, the anatomy of the ligamentous attachment is important. At the knee, the collateral ligaments are attached below the distal femoral epiphysis, while the proximal tibial epiphysis is above the ligament, thus making the distal femoral epiphysis more susceptible to injury. In a pre-adolescent, ligamentous and meniscal injuries are relatively rare.

The symptoms and signs of an epiphyseal knee injury may be very similar or even identical to a knee ligament injury. Obtaining a complete series of X-rays (including valgus-stress views) before making a definitive diagnosis is often important (see Figure 10.5). As with any knee ligament injury, examine for damage to the popliteal artery or nerve (particularly with proximal tibial epiphyseal injuries).

If the adolescent presents with pain around the knee but no specific knee injury is found, remember that a hip or back problem may be the cause of the pain. For instance, a slipped capital femoral epiphysis or Perthes disease of the hip may present with knee pain without hip pain.

The Elbow Joint

The distal humeral epiphysis has four separate ossification centers. Epiphyseal injuries here represent approximately 10 percent of the total, while the proximal radius and proximal ulna combine for approximately 2 percent.[17]

1. *The medial epicondylar epiphysis* of the elbow may be avulsed in a Little League baseball pitcher.[22,23,24] There may be a history of pain with a particular pitch, or the symptoms may come on gradually. Tenderness is localized to the medial epicondylar epiphysis, and swelling may be present. Extension of the elbow may be limited and valgus stress may produce pain, as may forced resistance to wrist flexion. The epiphysis is usually minimally avulsed, but occasionally may slip into the elbow joint (special X-ray views of both elbows may be necessary).

2. *The proximal radial epiphysis.* The head of the radius may be injured by a fall on the outstretched hand, and a type II injury to the radial head may be produced by compression against the capitulum of the humerus.[8,25] The head of the radius may also be injured in a posterior dislocation of the elbow.

Chronic stress such as occurs in baseball pitching or in gymnastics can produce traumatic osteochondrosis of the capitulum and the articular surface of the radial head[7] as well as injury to the olecranon[7,8] (see section on throwing injuries of the shoulder and elbow).

The Hip Joint

A slipped capital femoral epiphysis occurs in young teen-agers, most frequently in extremely obese or thin, rapidly growing males. This condition may present with pain either in the hip or in the knee; *there may be no pain in the hip at all—the only complaint being vague knee pain.*

Diagnosis is made from X-rays, where the displacement of the capital femoral epiphysis can be seen (Figure 10.6).

Treatment is usually by surgical correction.

Other Epiphyseal Problems

The preceding discussion has dealt primarily with acute or chronic injuries in the adolescent athlete. There are a number of other problems the trainer or care provider may encounter in the same or younger age group. It is beyond the scope of this chapter to list definitive methods of diagnosis or treatment, but the care provider should have some familiarity with the major entities.

Dorsal Epiphysitis (Scheurermann's Disease)

Dorsal epiphysitis is a disturbance of the dorsal thoracic epiphyses. The cause is unknown. It occurs in early adolescence and may result in permanent kyphosis if untreated. It presents with thoracic back pain and is diagnosed by X-ray evaluation, which may show vertebral wedging, irregularity of epiphyseal rings, and concave osteolytic defects in the disc surfaces of the vertebral bodies (Schmorl's nodes). Treatment includes exercises and possibly Milwaukee type bracing.[26]

Aseptic Necrosis of the Capital Femoral Epiphysis (Legg-Perthes' Disease)

Aseptic necrosis is most common in children from 5 to 10 years of age. While the exact cause is unknown, it is thought that loss of blood supply leads to avascular necrosis of the femoral head. With appropriate treatment and sufficient time (two to two-and-a-half years) the necrotic bone may be absorbed and replaced with new viable bone. Ultimate outcome is variable[27,28] with younger children, and those with a smaller area of involvement of the femoral head have a better prognosis.[29]

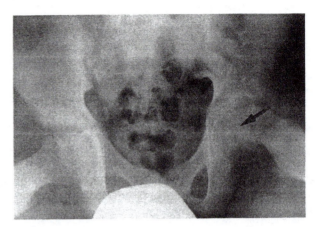

FIGURE 10.6
Slipped capital femoral epiphysis

Pain at the Tibial Tubercle (Osgood-Schlatter Disease)

Osgood-Schlatter is not a disease but rather a group of conditions involving the tibial tubercle epiphysis. The patient presenting with an Osgood-Schlatter lesion is usually between 11 and 15 years of age. Boys are more frequently involved than girls.[30]

TRACTION EPIPHYSITIS: Traction epiphysitis implies separation of a portion of the cartilaginous apophysis from the proximal tibial epiphysis, due to stress at the insertion of the patellar tendon (an apophysis is a non–weight-bearing epiphysis). The onset of this condition is often related to a particular episode, but it may develop spontaneously over a period of time. Some clinicians feel it may be related to a growth spurt.

Symptoms and Signs. Athletic participation is usually impaired by pain, which may occur both during and after activity. There may be swelling over the tibial tubercle, and a lump is often visible, palpable, or both. Tenderness is localized to the tibial tubercle area and the distal patellar tendon.

Bilateral X-rays of the tibial tubercles may show some sclerosis or a moth-eaten appearance of the proximal tibial epiphysis, which is considered by some to be indicative of a stress fracture.

Treatment. Traction epiphysitis is usually treated by decreasing the activity level to one of comfort and by commencing rehabilitation exercises, particularly quadriceps-strengthening exercises with the leg fully extended, hamstring-stretching exercises, and ice massage to the tibial tubercle. A gradual increase in activity is then permitted. Some physicians may elect to inject corticosteroids to dampen down the inflammatory response, though this form of treatment is not generally recommended.

TENDINITIS AT THE INSERTION OF THE PATELLAR TENDON: Tenderness is localized to the distal patellar tendon, and it may be difficult to differentiate tendinitis of the patellar tendon from traction epiphysitis. The bursa between the patellar tendon and the tibia may be inflamed; other symptoms and signs may be very similar. However, there are usually no abnormal findings on X-ray examination.

Treatment. Activity, particularly jumping, may need to be decreased for a period of time, during which the quadriceps muscle should be strengthened with isometric exercises and the hamstrings stretched. Ice massage should be applied frequently to the tender area. Mild oral anti-inflammatory medication can be used, and though corticosteroid injections are used on occasion, this should be done with discretion and the utmost caution.

FORMATION OF PATELLAR TENDON OSSICLE(S): Ossicles usually occur in the older adolescent. The symptoms are often magnified by an activity such as excessive jumping or squatting (e.g., in a baseball catcher). The diagnosis is based on X-ray examination (Figure 10.7).

Treatment. If the ossicles are considered the cause of the presenting symptoms, surgical removal is necessary, often with excellent results.[31]

Complete Avulsion of the Epiphysis of the Tibial Tubercle

Complete avulsion is a dramatic injury and occurs as a result of a sudden deceleration, such as when a basketball player comes to a rapid stop or a long jumper lands. The epiphysis is pulled upward by the contracting quadriceps; the fracture may extend right through into the knee joint.[32]

This injury may occur with the same mechanism as that which would cause an anterior cruciate ligament tear in an adult and should be considered in the differential diagnosis of a large knee hemarthrosis in an adolescent.

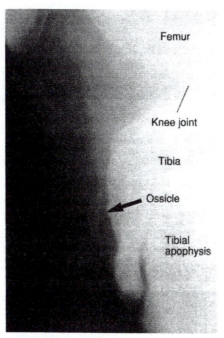

FIGURE 10.7
Ossicle within the patellar tendon

Other Avulsion Injuries Involving Apophyses

Avulsion fractures may occur at the:

1. anterior superior iliac spine at the origin of the sartorius muscle

2. anterior inferior iliac spine at the origin of the rectus femoris

3. ischial tuberosity at the origin of the hamstring group (Figure 10.8)

4. lesser trochanter at the insertion of the iliopsoas.

Other Adolescent Injuries

Calcaneal apophysitis (Sever's Disease) may be considered the young adolescent equivalent of Achilles tendinitis. X-rays may or may not be abnormal. Treatment is conservative, with heel lifts, relative rest, and gentle stretching followed by strengthening of regional musculature. The outcome is usually good.[33,34,35]

Aseptic necrosis of the tarsal navicular (Kohler's Disease) can occur in the prepubertal child. The cause is unknown and males are affected more often than females. There is tenderness at the medial midfoot and supination is painful. X-rays are normal early in the course, but eventually show necrosis. Treatment is

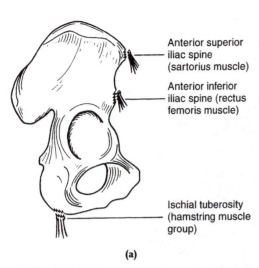

Anterior superior
iliac spine
(sartorius muscle)

Anterior inferior
iliac spine (rectus
femoris muscle)

Ischial tuberosity
(hamstring muscle
group)

(a)

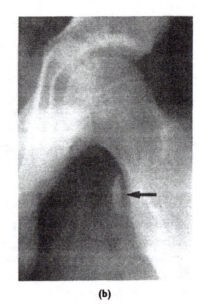

(b)

FIGURE 10.8
(a) Avulsion injuries involving the pelvic apophyses
(lateral view of right pelvis)
(b) Avulsion fracture of the lesser trochanter from excessive traction of the iliopsoas muscle

typically conservative and successful with four to six months of immobilization in a walking cast.[27,33]

Aseptic necrosis of the second metatarsal head (Freiberg's Disease) can occur in adolescence either secondary to trauma or for unknown reasons. It presents as pain and local tenderness of the second metatarsal head and X-rays will show necrosis within two to three weeks. Treatment ranges from four to six months of immobilization in a walking cast to metatarsal head bone grafting or excision. The outcome is variable.[27,33]

Drugs and environmental factors may affect the growing bones of young athletes. Chemotherapeutic agents may affect the growth plate, and antibiotics such as the tetracyclines and quinolones (ciprofloxin, norfloxacin, etc.) can affect growth at various stages of development. Infections such as osteomyelitis may localize at growth plates, and both benign and malignant tumors may have effects on growing bone. Nutritional disorders such as vitamin C or D deficiencies can also affect bone growth.[13,36]

REFERENCES

1. Larson RL: Epiphyseal injuries in the adolescent athlete. *Orthop Clin North Am* 4:839–851, 1973.

2. Salter RB, Harris WR: Injuries involved in the epiphyseal plate. *J Bone Joint Surg* 45A:587–622, 1963.

3. Orava S, Saarela J: Exertion injuries to young athletes. *Am J Sports Med* 6:68–74, 1980.

4. Godshall RW, Hansen CA, Rising DC: Stress fractures through the distal femoral epiphysis in athletes. A previously unreported entity. *Am J Sports Med* 9:114–116, 1981.

5. Hunter LY, O'Connor GA: Traction apophysitis of the olecranon. A case report. *Am J Sports Med* 8:51–52, 1980.

6. Cahill BR, Tullos HS, Fair RH: Little league shoulder. *J Sports Med* 11:150–153, 1974.

7. Brown R, Blazina ME, Kerlan RK, et al: Osteochondritis of the capitellum. *J Sports Med* 2:27–46, 1974.

8. Chan D, Aldridge MJ, Maffuli N, Davies AM: Chronic stress injuries of the elbow in young gymnasts. *Br J Radiol* 64: 1113–1118, 1991.

9. Clancy WG, Foltz AS: Iliac apophysitis and stress fractures in adolescent runners. *Am J Sports Med* 4:214–218, 1976.

10. Cahill BR: Stress fracture of the proximal tibial epiphysis: A case report. *Am J Sports Med* 5:186–187, 1977.

11. Caine D, Roy S, Singer KM, Broekhoff J: Stress changes of the distal radial growth plate. A radiographic survey and review of the literature. *Am J Sports Med* 20 (3): 290–8, 1992.

12. Roy S, Caine D, Singer KM: Stress changes of the distal radial epiphysis in young gymnasts. *Am J Sports Med* 13: 301–308, 1985.

13. Bright RW: Physeal injuries. In *Fractures in Children*, Vol. 3, edited by Rockwood CA. Philadelphia: J. B. Lippincott, third edition, 2: 87–186, 1991.

14. Jaramillo ED, Hoffer EA, Shapiro F, et al: M. R. imaging of fracture of growth plate. *AJR* 155: 1261–1265, 1990.

15. Kallio PE, Patterson DC, Foster BK, et al: Classification in slipped capital femoral epiphysis; sonographic assessment of stability and remodeling. *Clin Orthop* 294: 196–203, 1993.

16. Harckeht HT, Mandell GA: Scintigraphic evaluation of the growth plate. *Sem Nuc Med XXIII* (4):266–273, 1993.

17. Peterson HA: Physeal Injuries of the Distal Humerus. *Orthop* 15 (7): 799–808, 1992.

18. Markiewitz AD, Andrish JT: Hand and wrist injuries in the preadolescent and adolescent athlete. *Clinics in Sports Medicine* 11 (1): 203–25, 1992.

19. Torre BA: Epiphyseal injuries in the small joints of the hand. *Hand Clinics* 4 (1): 113–21, 1988.

20. Goldberg VM, Aadalen R: Distal tibial epiphyseal injuries: The role of athletics in 53 cases. *Am J Sports Med* 6:263–268, 1978.

21. Salter RB: Epiphyseal plate injuries in the adolescent knee. In *The Injured Adolescent Knee*, edited by Kennedy JC. Baltimore, Williams and Wilkins, 1979, pp. 77–102.

22. Tullos HS, King JW: Lesions of the pitching arm in adolescents. *JAMA* 22:264–271, 1972.

23. Lipscomb AB: Baseball pitching injuries in growing athletes. *J Sports Med* 3:25–34, 1975.

24. Francis R, Bunch T, Chandler B: Little league elbow: A decade later. *Phys Sportsmed* 6:88–89, April 1978.

25. Micheli LJ, Santore R, Stanitski CL: Epiphyseal fractures of the elbow in children. *Am Family Physician* 22:107–116, 1980.

26. Hensinger RN: Fractures of the thoracic and lumbar spine. In *Fractures in Children*, Vol 3, edited by Rockwood CA. Philadelphia: J. B. Lippincott, third edition, 958–989, 1991.

27. Steinberg GG: Hip, pelvis and proximal thigh. In *Ramamurti's Orthopedics in Primary Care*, edited by Steinberg GG. Baltimore: Williams and Wilkins, second edition, pp. 159–193, 1992.

28. Weinstein SL: Segg-Calve'-Perthes Disease. In *Pediatric Orthopedics,* Vol 2, edited by Morrisy RT. Philadelphia: J.B. Lippincott, third edition, 23:851–883, 1990.

29. Rarquinio TA: Foot. In *Ramamurti's Orthopedics in Primary Care,* edited by Steinberg GG. Baltimore: Williams and Wilkins, second edition, 9:258–289, 1992.

30. Roberts JM: Fractures and dislocations of the knee. In *Fractures in Children,* Vol 3, edited by Rockwood CA.

Philadelphia: J. B. Lippincott, third edition, 1165–1233, 1991.

31. Mital MA, Matza RA, Cohen J: The so-called unresolved Osgood-Schlatter lesion. A concept based on fifteen surgically treated lesions. *J Bone Joint Surg* 62A:732–739, 1980.

32. Ogden JA, Tross RB, Murphy MJ: Fractures of the tibial tuberosity in adolescents. *J Bone Joint Surg* 62A:205–215, 1980.

33. Gross RH: Fractures and dislocations of the foot. In *Fractures in Children*, Vol 3, edited by Rockwood CA. Philadelphia: J. B. Lippincott, third edition, 1383–1453, 1991.

34. Garrick JG, Webb DR: *Sports Injuries: Diagnosis and Management.* Philadelphia: WB Saunders, first edition, 11:257–277, 1990.

35. Teebagy AK: Leg and Ankle. In *Ramamurti's Orthopedics in Primary Care*, edited by Steinburg, GG. Baltimore: Williams and Wilkins, second edition, 8:231–257, 1992.

36. Iannotti JP: Growth plate physiology and pathology. *Orthop Clin N A* 21 (1): 1–17, 1990.

RECOMMENDED READINGS

Butler JE, Eggert AW: Fracture of the iliac crest apophysis. An unusual hip pointer. Brief communications. *J Sports Med* 3:192–193, 1975.

DeHaven KE: Athletic injuries in adolescents. *Pediatr Ann* 7:96–119, 1976.

Ogden JA: The development and growth of the musculoskeletal system. In *The Scientific Basis of Orthopaedics.* Albright JA, Brand RA, editors. New York, Appleton-Century-Crofts, 1979, pp. 41–103.

Pappas A: The osteochondroses. *Pediatr Clin North Am* 14:549–570, 1967.

Rockwood, CA, Wilkin KE, King RE: *Fractures in Children.* Philadelphia, third edition, J. B. Lippencott, 1991.

Stanitski CL, DeLee JC, Drez DD: *Pediatric and Adolescent Sports Medicine,* Vol 3. Philadelphia, W. B. Saunders, 1994.

Wilkins KE: The uniqueness of the young athlete: Musculoskeletal injuries. *Am J Sports Med* 8:377–382, 1980.

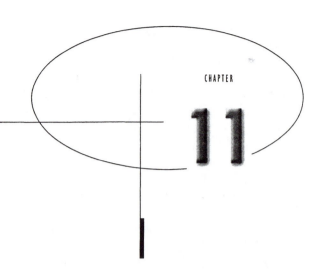

CHAPTER

11

Head and Face Injuries

 Both head and face injuries are of great concern to the athletic health care specialist. Brain injuries have the highest priority and can result in catastrophic situations. But this concern does not lessen the importance of injury to such structures as the eye.

A variety of forces can be identified as contributors to brain injury in sports. The Sports Medicine Committee, Colorado Medical Society,[1] in their *Guidelines for the Management of Concussion in Sports,* indicate the following:

1. Rotational (angular) forces more commonly cause loss of consciousness associated with deep shearing injuries of nerve fibers (diffuse axonal injury).

2. Translational (linear) forces are less likely to cause unconsciousness but more commonly lead to skull fractures, intracranial hematomas, and cerebral contusions.

Anatomy

The skull is covered by the scalp on the outside, and it protects the brain on the inside. Between the skull and brain are three layers of tissue: the dura mater, the arachnoid, and the pia mater. In order to understand the various bleeding problems that can occur after a head injury, it is necessary to have a basic knowledge of the anatomy of these three layers.

1. *The dura mater.* The dura mater lies under the skull and is a thick fibrous membrane that encloses the various venous sinuses, for instance, the superior sagittal sinus.

2. *The arachnoid.* Under the dura mater lies the arachnoid. This layer is crossed by bridging cerebral veins. Between the dura mater and the arachnoid is a potential space called the *subdural space.*

3. *The pia mater.* The pia mater is a thin tissue enclosing the brain. Between the pia mater and the arachnoid is the *subarachnoid space,* in which flows the cerebral spinal fluid. Here are found the major arterial blood vessels and bridging cerebral veins.

The brain is supplied by two arterial systems:

1. Internal carotid arteries anteriorly

2. Vertebral arteries posteriorly

These arteries link up on the under surface of the brain to form the circle of Willis.

An important artery that may be injured in head trauma is the *middle meningeal artery,* which crosses through the skull above the ear (Figures 11.1 and 11.2).

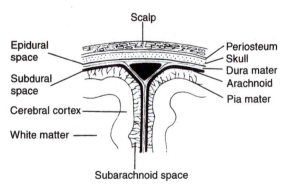

FIGURE 11.1

Cross-sectional anatomy of the skull and meninges

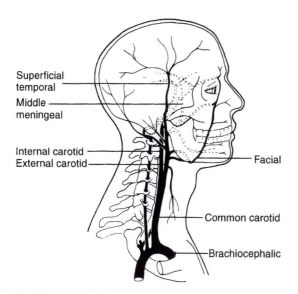

FIGURE 11.2

Blood supply of the head and neck.

(Modified from Jacob and Francone, *Structure and Function in Man,* published by W. B. Saunders Co., Philadelphia.)

Injuries to the Head

The effects of a head injury depend on the amount of damage to the brain and its surrounding structures. A blow to the head, as occurs when a basketball player falls and strikes his or her head against the floor, may lead to a superficial *contusion* of the scalp in one athlete, while in another it may lead to a rapidly fatal intracranial hemorrhage. The possibility of developing a serious condition after a simple contusion should, therefore, not be forgotten. A blow to the head can lead to:

1. Scalp hematoma
2. Fracture of the skull
3. Concussion
4. Cerebral edema
5. Intracranial bleeding

Scalp Hematoma

A scalp hematoma is a collection of blood within the layers of the scalp superficial to the skull. Treatment with ice is usually sufficient unless there is also a laceration of the scalp. If there is any suggestion of a skull fracture or concussion, the athlete should be referred to a physician for a full evaluation and X-rays.

Skull Fracture

The presence of a fracture indicates that a very forceful injury has occurred, and brain damage or injury to the surrounding structures must be carefully excluded. It should be realized, however, that serious or fatal intracranial injuries can occur in the absence of a fracture.

A fracture in the area of the middle meningeal artery has the potential to damage that artery and may result in the development of an extradural hematoma. Any fracture that occurs within the anatomical area of the middle meningeal artery should be very closely observed for the development of symptoms or signs suggestive of intracranial bleeding.

An additional danger from a skull fracture is the introduction of bacteria through the laceration and fracture site into the intracranial cavity, which can result in septic meningitis. Also, a depressed fracture can injure the brain substance, leading to future scarring and possible epilepsy.

Concussion

Concussion is defined as "a clinical syndrome characterized by immediate and transient impairment of neural function, such as alteration of consciousness, disturbance of vision, equilibrium, etc., due to mechanical forces."[2] The term "concussion" therefore, *does not* require the patient to have had a complete loss of consciousness, and is a diagnosis made only in retrospect—after there has been a return to the normal level of consciousness. It is possible for an athlete to appear normal following a blow to the head, but later lapse into unconsciousness. This period of normalcy is referred to as a "lucid interval." The lucid interval often occurs with an epidural hematoma, but generally does not occur with an acute subdural hematoma.[3] For this reason, it is important that an athlete not be left alone after suffering what appears to be a concussion, as a relapse into unconsciousness may occur.

Concussion is classified according to the length of time of unconsciousness and the symptoms and signs (see Table 11.1). Although various classification schemes have been developed, the following guidelines are generally accepted.

1. *First-degree concussion.* No actual loss of consciousness occurs, only a blurring of consciousness lasting less than ten to twenty seconds. Minimal or no symptoms or signs are present.

2. *Second-degree concussion.* A blurring or loss of consciousness occurs, lasting from twenty seconds to

TABLE 11.1 *Classification and management of the unconscious athlete*

	First-Degree Concussion	Second-Degree Concussion	Third-Degree Concussion
Period of Unconsciousness	No actual loss of consciousness ("dinged" or "bell-rung") but blurring of consciousness lasting less than 10–20 seconds	Blurring or loss of consciousness lasting from 20 seconds to 1–2 minutes	Loss of consciousness lasting 2 or more minutes
On-Field Management	Check for neck injury. The athlete, when recovered, can walk off the field if no neck injury is present.	Check for neck injury. The athlete, when recovered, can walk off the field if no injury is present.	
Off-Field Examination			
Symptoms	No amnesia No headache No nausea	Headache and amnesia often present.	
Signs	No positive signs on neurologic testing and examination. Athlete should be fully oriented and emotionally in control.	Confusion and disorientation. May have some neurologic signs (e.g., nystagmus).	
Return to Participation	If all the above criteria are present, and if the diagnosis is a first-degree concussion, athlete may return to game.	No return to game	No return to game
Management	Observe frequently during the game and reexamine afterward.	Observe frequently during game while athlete sits on the sideline. Hospitalize for observation for 24 hours.	Hospitalize immediately for observation and treatment.
Time Off from Practice and Competition	If headache, nausea, amnesia or other signs develop later, athlete should be off contact for 2 days after this clears.	Usually three to five days, longer if necessary; each case should be evaluated individually.	One season[a]
Disqualifying Factors	If repeatedly suffers "dings," particularly with minor trauma, carefully evaluate status with regard to contact participation.	More than two episodes in a season disqualifies athlete for the rest of that season. Each athlete should be individually evaluated with regard to further participation in contact sports.	Two or three third-degree concussions in a career should preclude athlete from further participation in contact sports.

[a]The New York State Athletic Commission has stated that every boxer knocked unconscious must be kept out for 90 days. In addition, full neurological examinations must be performed, including EEGs and CAT scans.

one or two minutes. Minimal to moderate symptoms and signs are found.

3. *Third-degree concussion.* There is loss of consciousness lasting two or more minutes.

Cerebral Edema

A fairly frequent and sometimes alarming complication of a blow to the head is the development of cerebral edema. In this condition there is an increase in pressure

TABLE 11.2 *Symptoms and signs of increasing intacerebral pressure*

1. Persistent and/or increasing headache
2. Nausea and/or vomiting
3. Slowing of the pulse below the athlete's norm
4. Increase in systolic blood pressure while diastolic pressure decreases
5. Pupil irregularity

inside the skull, probably due to an increase in the amount of cerebrospinal fluid and, possibly, the occurrence of a self-limited intracranial bleed. The symptoms and signs of a rise in intracranial pressure may be present (Table 11.2).

Intracranial Bleeding

Intracranial bleeding is a life-threatening situation that needs to be evaluated and diagnosed rapidly. Depending on the anatomical layer affected, bleeding may occur in the

1. extradural (epidural) space
2. subdural space
3. subarachnoid space

EXTRADURAL (EPIDURAL) HEMORRHAGE:

If the middle meningeal artery is damaged, bleeding occurs between the skull and the dura. This represents arterial bleeding, which leads to rapid compression of the brainstem and will be fatal unless the pressure is relieved and the bleeding stopped (Figure 11.3).

The classic history is that of a blow to the head followed by a temporary loss of consciousness. The athlete then recovers and appears to be normal. As mentioned earlier, this is sometimes referred to as the "lucid interval." This lucid interval may last for a few minutes or up to an hour or two, following which the athlete may lapse into lethargy, become unconscious, or suffer a seizure and then rapidly deteriorate unless treated. In some cases, the lucid interval may not occur. The athlete may never recover from the initial loss of consciousness. Or there might not be an initial loss of consciousness at all, only a momentary stunning as a result of a blow to the head.

An extradural hemorrhage is one of the true emergencies in which seconds or minutes are vital in determining whether the athlete will succumb or survive.

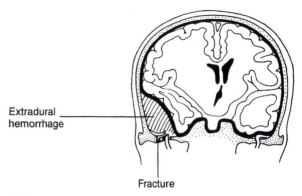

FIGURE 11.3
An extradural hemorrhage
due to a skull fracture and damage to the middle meningeal artery

SUBDURAL HEMORRHAGE: Bleeding occurs in the subdural space as a result of tearing of the bridging cerebral veins, which run from the cerebral cortex to the dural sinuses (Figure 11.4).

In an *acute* subdural hemorrhage, the athlete is knocked out and seldom regains consciousness. In a *subacute* subdural hemorrhage, there may or may not be loss of consciousness, and the indications that this injury has occurred may not be present for a number of hours or even days.

A *chronic* subdural hematoma is a rare condition that follows trauma to the head. A relatively small amount of bleeding becomes surrounded by a semipermeable membrane that attracts tissue fluid by osmotic pressure. The fluid passes through the membrane, increasing the size of the hematoma. This process may continue for a number of months as the brain adapts to the gradually increasing pressure.

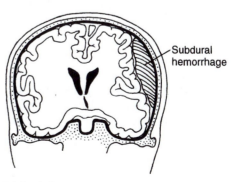

FIGURE 11.4
A subdural hemorrhage

SUBARACHNOID HEMORRHAGE: A subarachnoid hemorrhage in an athlete is usually due to a rupture of a congenital aneurysm (an aneurysm is an abnormal dilation of one of the arteries). This is a not-infrequent cause of sudden death in young people, and while it may occur in athletic activities, it is probably unrelated.

A subarachnoid hemorrhage may also occur in conjunction with diffuse cerebral damage resulting from a serious head injury. This type of injury implies severe impairment in cerebral function.

Evaluation

Evaluation Following a Head Injury

A number of different symptoms, signs, and tests should be used to evaluate the seriousness of a particular head injury:

1. *Headache.* This is a fairly constant finding following a blow to the head and indicates all is not as it should be. The athlete should not be allowed to return to participation until the headache has completely cleared.

2. *Nausea and vomiting.* An increase in intracerebral pressure stimulates the reflex onset of nausea and vomiting. This sign indicates that a fairly significant increase in cerebrospinal fluid pressure has occurred.

3. *Amnesia.* A loss of memory frequently occurs following a blow to the head. Start by asking the athlete simple questions (e.g., score, date, what he or she ate earlier that day). If these are easily answered, ask more complicated questions related to the athletic event. For instance, in football the reserve quarterback can be asked to question the injured athlete about plays.

Amnesia may vary with time. An athlete who has received a blow to the head may have full recollection of the blow and other events immediately afterwards, and may be able to answer questions clearly, and yet fifteen minutes later, the same questions may produce a totally different response, with amnesia for recent events being the most obvious. *Post-traumatic (anterograde) amnesia* is a fairly common symptom following a second degree concussion.

A good test for anterograde amnesia is to ask the athlete to remember three items, for example: blue shirt, red tie, and yellow pencil. Five or ten minutes later, ask the injured athlete to repeat the three items. An individual with post-traumatic amnesia will typically not be able to recall the original items.

Retrograde amnesia (loss of memory of events that occurred prior to the injury) is associated with more severe head injury.

4. *The 100-minus-7 test.* This is a useful procedure to determine ability for concentrated thought. The athlete is asked to subtract seven from one hundred, then seven from the answer, and to continue in that manner as rapidly as possible.

5. *Tinnitus (ringing in the ears).* Mild tinnitus may be reported by an athlete with a first-degree concussion. A more severe concussion may be accompanied by more intense tinnitus.

6. *The pupils.* The pupils should be carefully evaluated and compared. Note their size, equality, and reaction to light. A normally responsive pupil will visibly constrict when light is directed into it. The opposite pupil should also constrict simultaneously. This response is termed the *consensual eye reflex* and may be impaired following serious head injury. The failure of either pupil to constrict when light is directed into it is a sign of potentially significant injury. An extradural hematoma may compress one side of the brain, resulting in an enlarged pupil on the side of the hematoma. (Note, however, that in some people one pupil is normally larger than the other [Horner's syndrome].)

7. *Eye movements (nystagmus).* Nystagmus is the occurrence of rapidly oscillating movements of the eyes. It is most easily observed when the athlete is asked to look to the side while keeping the head still. This test is a sensitive indicator that all is not right with cerebral function. If nystagmus is present, it is advisable to keep the athlete out of participation.

8. *Finger/nose coordination test.* The athlete is asked to place his or her finger alternatively on the examiner's finger and then on his or her own nose. The examiner's finger is moved to a different position each time. Again, if not performed satisfactorily, it is an indication that the athlete should not be allowed to resume playing.

9. *Romberg's test.* The athlete is asked to stand with the feet together with the arms held out at 90° of forward flexion. Closing the eyes should not result in any loss of posture, and the athlete should not sway excessively. The test can be made more sensitive by asking the athlete to perform the same maneuver standing on the heads of the metatarsals.

10. *Heel/toe walking.* The athlete should be able to accomplish this test easily.

11. *The pulse.* A slowing of the pulse below that which is normal for the athlete may be an indication of an increase in intracerebral pressure.

12. *Blood pressure.* Another indication of possible increasing cerebrospinal-fluid pressure is an increase in systolic blood pressure with a decrease in diastolic pressure. Blood pressure should therefore be monitored over a period of time.

13. *Respiratory difficulty.* Complete cessation or difficulty with respiration may occur following a head or neck injury (Table 11.3). This is one reason why a trainer should always carry an oral airway during an athletic practice or event.

14. *Leakage of cerebrospinal fluid.* If a fracture of the cribriform plate occurs, cerebrospinal fluid may leak from the nose. This may be diagnosed by testing the fluid with a urine Multistix (or similar "stix" with a glucose indicator). If glucose is present in the discharge, it strongly suggests the fluid is cerebrospinal.

A fracture of the base of the skull may result in bleeding or leakage of cerebrospinal fluid from the ear. If the eardrum is not perforated, the buildup of blood behind the eardrum can be observed.

15. *Loss of emotional control.* Loss of emotional control or irrational behavior may indicate a disturbance of normal cerebral function and should preclude the athlete's returning to play.

16. *Papilledema.* Examination of the fundus with an ophthalmoscope may reveal blurring of the medial margins of the optic disk. This can indicate early papilledema—an important sign of an increase in intracerebral pressure.

On-Field Evaluation and Management of the Unconscious Athlete

An unconscious athlete should be assumed to have a *neck injury* in addition to any head injury.

The following steps should be taken in the immediate management of an unconscious athlete:

1. Check the airway and if impaired make preparation to begin resuscitation. If managing an injured football player one must remove the face mask to gain access to the mouth and nose. (See Chapter 6 for a discussion of facemask removal.)

2. Do not remove helmet (if applicable).

3. Stabilize head and neck.

4. Do not hyperextend neck, but bring jaw forward. If the airway has been opened and self-breathing has not started, begin resuscitation while maintaining a stabilized head and neck and an open airway with a chin lift method.

5. Check the pulse. If not present, commence CPR with the head and neck stabilized.

6. Check the blood pressure.

7. Check the pupils.

8. Remove athlete from the field on a spine board. The head and neck *must be stabilized.* At no time should an attempt be made to revive an unconscious athlete with

TABLE 11.3 *Cessation of breathing resulting from injury to the head or neck*

Cessation of breathing may occur with or without cardiac arrest. Noncardiac causes include:

1. *A direct head-on contact injury* which results in (a) impingement of the vascular supply to the brain stem and (b) brain stem contusion, or (c) both.

2. *Impingement of the cord above C4–5* (a C4–5 lesion will result in the ability to breathe abdominally only; a lesion above this will lead to complete cessation of respiration).

3. *Ruptured intervertebral disc* (C3–4).

ammonia capsules or smelling salts; this could cause the athlete to jerk and exacerbate a neck injury. If in any doubt, obtain help from specially trained EMTs before removing the athlete from the field.

If there are signs of an *extradural (epidural) hemorrhage,* for instance unconsciousness with a dilated pupil on one side and paralysis of the opposite side of the body, transport the athlete to a hospital as rapidly as possible. If it is just as quick for the ambulance to be summoned to remove and transport the athlete from the field to the hospital, then this should be done. If you have to remove and transport the athlete yourself, ensure that he or she is removed from the field on a spine board with the neck stabilized and, if possible, supply oxygen. While the athlete is being transported, a responsible person should be sent to telephone the emergency room at the hospital, informing them an athlete with a potentially serious head injury is en route.

Sideline Examination of a Possible Concussion

An athlete who has had a less severe episode of possible concussion, or who has been dazed, needs a neurological evaluation. Start the examination by asking the athlete simple questions to check for amnesia. Proceed onto the 100-minus-7 test, look for nystagmus, test finger-to-nose coordination, and perform Romberg's test. Check the pupils, monitor the pulse and, if possible, the blood pressure. Always examine the neck to ensure no injury has occurred.

A number of classification systems can be useful in determining the appropriate course of action to take when caring for an athlete who has sustained a possible concussion. To make an accurate assessment of severity, the

Glasgow Coma Scale for Assessing Level of Consciousness can be used (Table 11.4). It uses eye opening, motor, and verbal response to assess level of consciousness.[4]

Another grading scale for concussion in sports is presented in Table 11.5.

If there was only a momentary blurring of consciousness, no amnesia, and all the sideline tests are normal, the athlete may return to participation, but should be observed while in action and then be reexamined at the end of the event. If there is any question as to the athlete's coordination, ability to concentrate, or emotional stability, he or she should be removed from the event immediately.

If the athlete has blurring or loss of consciousness lasting from twenty seconds to one or two minutes, return to participation should not be allowed that day. He or she should be under constant surveillance during the initial postconcussion period (see the "lucid interval" of the extradural hemorrhage).

TABLE 11.4 *Glasgow coma scale for assessing level of consciousness*

Response	Points	
Eye-Opening		
Spontaneous	4	____
To speech	3	____
To pain	2	____
None	1	____
Motor		
Obeys on command	6	____
Localizes pain	5	____
Withdraws from pain	4	____
Decorticate flexor response	3	____
Decerebrate extensor response	2	____
No movement	1	____
Verbal		
Oriented	5	____
Confused conversation	4	____
Inappropriate words	3	____
Incomprehensible sounds	2	____
None	1	____

Total Points: 14–15 = 5; 11–13 = 4; 8–10 = 3; 5–7 = 2; 3–4 = 1. The lower the score, the more severe is the extent of brain injury.

The athlete should be carefully examined and observed on the sideline and then placed under medial care for the following 18 to 24 hours. Thereafter, the athlete should be examined on a daily basis and evidence of *postconcussion syndrome* should be noted. Postconcussion syndrome is manifested by residual headache, inability to concentrate, and irritability. It may last for weeks or even months in individuals who have experienced a significant head injury. An athlete with postconcussion syndrome should be under a physician's care, and any athlete with persistent headache or neurological signs and symptoms should not be allowed to return to participation until a full examination is normal. Of particular concern is the *second impact syndrome,* which can occur when an athlete returns to activity before the symptoms of a previous concussion have completely resolved. Following a second concussion, the brain may lose its ability to regulate cerebral blood flow. This results in a massive increase in intracranial pressure, which is extremely dangerous and can lead to death.[3] The final decision concerning when the athlete may return to activity should be made by the attending physician.

Because the pathology of multiple concussions has been shown to be cumulative, consideration must be given to this factor when determining the point at which the athlete may return to activity. The guidelines in Table 11.5 are for return to collision sports.

Lacerations of the Face and Scalp

Lacerations of the Scalp

Scalp lacerations frequently bleed copiously. The initial bleeding can usually be controlled by pressure from a sterile dressing. As with any bleeding wound, care should be taken to follow standard blood-borne pathogen safety procedures for the treatment of open wounds (See Chapter 6). The wound should be kept covered and clean until it can be sutured.

Laceration of the Eyebrow

Lacerations of the eyebrow may bleed freely but are relatively easy to temporarily tape with Steri-Strips or similar skin closures. Ice and compression can be applied over the strips. If the athlete wishes to resume participation, he or she may be permitted to do so providing the laceration does not affect the eye itself and bleeding has stopped. If bleeding recurs, the athlete should be withdrawn from participation until the wound is sutured, but can frequently return soon after suturing, depending on the circumstances.

TABLE 11.5 *Grading scale for concussion in sports*

The history of recent head trauma outside the sports setting (e.g., motor vehicle accident) should be considered in the "Return to Play" section for each grade of concussion.

Grade 1	Confusion without amnesia **No loss of consciousness** **Remove from event pending on-site evaluation prior to return**

This is the most common yet the most difficult form of concussion to recognize. The athlete is not rendered unconscious and suffers only momentary confusion. The majority of concussions in sports are of this type, and players commonly refer to it as having been "dinged" or having their "bell rung." All athletes with Grade 1 concussions should be removed from the game and evaluated before reentering the contest.

Return to Play Following Grade 1 Concussion

Following a first Grade 1 concussion, if the athlete has no symptoms at rest or exertion, return to the game may be permissible after at least 20 minutes observation. In every instance when the athlete is symptomatic, removal from the game is mandatory. All symptoms (headache, dizziness, impaired orientation, impaired concentration, memory dysfunction) must have disappeared, first at rest and then with exertional provocative testing before return to competition (see "Sideline Evaluation" below). Return is allowed only if the athlete is asymptomatic during rest and exertion for at least 20 minutes. A second Grade 1 concussion in the same contest eliminates the player from competition that day. CT scanning or MRI scanning is recommended in all instances in which headache or other associated symptoms either worsen or persist longer than one week. It is recommended that three Grade 1 concussions terminate a player's season. No further contact sports are permitted for at least 3 months, and then only if asymptomatic at rest and exertion.

Grade 2	Confusion with amnesia **No loss of consciousness** **Remove from event and disallow return**

With a Grade 2 concussion, the athlete is not rendered unconscious but exhibits confusion and has amnesia for the events following the impact (post-traumatic amnesia). After a Grade 2 concussion the athlete should be removed from the game and given a thorough neurological evaluation. The athlete should be evaluated frequently over the next 24 hours for signs of evolving intracranial pathology by direct medical observation or with explicit, written instructions given to the family.

Return to Play Following Grade 2 Concussion

Return to competition after a first concussion may be as soon as one week after the athlete is asymptomatic at rest and exertion. A neurological exam should be performed by a physician prior to return to practice. CT scanning or MRI scanning is recommended in all instances in which headache or other associated symptoms either worsen or persist longer than one week. Return to contact play should be deferred for at least one month after a second Grade 2 concussion, and termination of the season should be considered. Terminating the season for that player is mandated by three Grade 2 concussions, as it would be by any abnormality on CT or MRI scan consistent with brain contusion or other intracranial pathology.

Grade 3	**Loss of consciousness** **Remove from event and transport to appropriate medical facility**

It is usually quite easy to recognize a Grade 3 concussion. This level of head injury applies to any athlete who is rendered unconscious for any period of time. Initial treatment includes transport to the nearest hospital by ambulance (with cervical spine immobilization if indicated). A thorough neurologic evaluation should be performed emergently, including CT scan or MRI scan when appropriate. Hospital confinement is indicated if any signs of pathology are detected or if the mental status of the athlete remains abnormal. If findings are normal, explicit written instructions may be given to the family for overnight observation. Neurological status should be assessed daily thereafter until all symptoms have resolved.

(Continued)

TABLE 11.5   *(Continued)*

Prolonged unconsciousness, persistent mental status alterations, worsening post-concussion symptoms, or abnormalities on neurological exam require urgent neurosurgical consultation or transfer to a trauma center.

Return to Play Following Grade 3 Concussion

One month is the typical period the athlete should be held from contact sports after a Grade 3 concussion. Return to play after one month is allowed only if the athlete has been asymptomatic at rest and exertion for at least 2 weeks. CT scanning or MRI scanning is recommended in all instances in which headache or other associated symptoms either worsen or persist longer than one week. If asymptomatic, conditioning drills may be resumed prior to one month. A season is terminated by two Grade 3 concussions or by any abnormality on CT or MRI consistent with brain contusion or other intracranial pathology. Return to any contact sport should be seriously discouraged in discussions with the athlete.

In most instances when an athlete has suffered a head injury which requires intracranial surgery, return to contact sports is contraindicated. However, the final determination as to whether an athlete may return to competition is the team physician's clinical decision.

Reprinted with permission from *Management of Concussions in Sports,* published by the Sports Medicine Committee of the Colorado Medical Society.

Lacerations of the Central Portion of the Face

Almost any laceration on the central portion of the face should be carefully sutured for an acceptable cosmetic result. This should be done within a few hours of the injury, not the next day.

Immediate treatment consists of either Steri-Strips or similar skin closure and bandage or pad. Ice should be used to reduce the swelling. How soon an athlete with a facial laceration may return to activity varies with the severity of the laceration and the type of anticipated activity. Generally an athlete can return to activity without delay after a laceration has been sutured. More severe laceration may require two or three weeks without stress before return is safe.[5] Adhesive skin closures should be applied over the sutures as reinforcement when the athlete is active.

Some lacerations do not need to be sutured, and can be treated satisfactorily with Steri-Strips or similar closures. A decision as to the necessity for suturing should preferably be made by a physician, but if the wound is linear and is superficial, so that it does not gape, and satisfactory approximation of the wound can be made with the application of adhesive skin closures, then this may be an alternative to suturing. Continue use of the skin closures until the wound is completely healed, which is usually five to seven days for a face laceration.

Until a facial wound has completely healed, it is necessary to continue protecting it with adhesive skin closures if there is continued participation in contact sports. Protection should be continued for at least another seven days.

Facial Fractures

Fracture of the Jaw

Fractures to the mandible are the most common facial fractures resulting from athletic competition.[5]

Following a blow to the jaw, there is frequently intense pain, making it difficult to determine if a fracture is present. The following points may help in deciding:

1. Ask the athlete to open and close his or her mouth. Note any asymmetry in movement.

2. Ask the athlete to bite, and note any malocclusion.

3. Feel for any irregularity along the jaw, both when it is at rest and when it is being opened and closed.

4. Note any crepitis to palpation or movement of the jaw.

5. Note any slurred speech.

If a fracture is suspected, the athlete should be referred for X-rays and specialized treatment. Follow-up treatment of a mandibular fracture may include observation and closed or open reduction, including rigid or non-rigid fixation.[6]

Weight loss is common among athletes who require stabilizing fixation following a fractured jaw because of the inability to chew normally. The athletic trainer and/or nutritional consultant should work with the athlete to help ensure that proper nutrition is compromised as little as possible. Both commercial and homemade high-calorie liquid supplements should be used along with normal foods that can be blended for consumption.

Fracture of the Maxilla or Sinuses

A fracture of the maxilla, the sinuses, or both usually occurs from a direct blow. Tenderness is present over the injured area, and diffuse swelling may occur. The examiner should palpate for a "step-off" fracture and should test for hypesthesia in the distribution of the infraorbital nerve beneath the eye and along the side of the nose. On occasion, nose blowing will cause a swelling to appear around the eye. This is suggestive of a fracture of the maxilla or ethmoid sinus. The athlete should be sent for X-rays and a specialist's evaluation.

Dental Injuries

Prevention

Dental injuries can occur in almost any contact activity, and often result in permanent damage. They can be somewhat more complicated to manage than many sports injuries because the healing processes for teeth differ from the other repair processes in the body. The full extent of injury and the actual status of the tooth may not be known for up to five years after injury.[7]

Mouth guards and preventive dental appliances have become increasingly accepted as important pieces of equipment, and they should be worn by athletes in both practice and game situations for sports such as football, ice hockey, rugby, boxing, and wrestling.[8] Additionally, there is little doubt that the number and severity of oral injuries in the sports of basketball, soccer, lacrosse, baseball, and volleyball would be reduced with more frequent use of mouth guards. For example, one study has reported that while football players had an oral injury rate of only 2.8 percent with 98 percent using mouth guards, basketball players had an oral injury rate of 10% with only 10% of the participants using mouth guards.[9]

Another study that compared the oral injury rates of college women's basketball players who used mouth guards to those who did not found that the injury rate was 2.8 percent for those who used mouth guards compared to 30.3 percent for those who did not.[10]

It is recommended that the use of mouth guards (see Chapter 3) be vigorously encouraged in at least bas-ketball and soccer and that continued vigilance be practiced to ensure that mouth guards are indeed worn when mandated in collision sports.

Mouth guards vary from inexpensive plastics that are heat-molded to conform to the athlete's dental pattern to those that are custom-made. The latter are particularly useful for athletes who have to be able to communicate clearly during the game (e.g., quarterbacks in football and basketball and soccer players).

Custom-made mouth protectors are generally agreed to be the most effective; however, since they are fabricated by a dentist from a model of the athlete's maxillary teeth, they are relatively expensive and usually require two visits to the dentist's office.[11] Mouth-formed (boil and bite) protectors may be more practical for many athletes, but it is important that the manufacturer's directions for fitting be carefully followed for maximum protection.

The use of mouth guards has not only dramatically reduced the incidence of dental injuries, but has been shown to reduce the incidence of concussion. The mechanism of this effect is thought to relate to the shock absorbency characteristics of the mouth guard, which decreases the force with which the jaw snaps shut on head impact.[12,13]

Dislocated Tooth

The loss of a tooth is a painful injury that can cause great expense and lead to lost time on the playing field. Virtually all avulsed teeth that are improperly treated will be lost, leading to extensive and long-term dental work. On the other hand, proper treatment as recommended by the American Dental Association and the American Association of Endodontists can save over 90 percent of all avulsed teeth for the life of the athlete.[14,15,16]

When a tooth is knocked out, the periodontal ligament that joins the tooth to the bony socket is ruptured. The portion that remains attached to the socket stays viable with no additional treatment because it remains bathed in blood and saliva. If the portion of the ligament attached to the tooth root can also remain viable, chances are quite good that the tooth can be saved. To keep the tooth portion of the periodontal ligament viable, it must be transported to the dentist's office in an environment that closely matches that found in the empty socket. The best way to achieve this is simply to replace the tooth in the empty socket. If possible, the tooth should be rinsed off with a pH-balanced preserving solution or sterile saline and held in place by having the athlete bite on gauze.[16]

If for some reason (e.g., unconsciousness, debris, or uncooperativeness) the tooth cannot be replaced in the socket, it should be placed in an emergency tooth-preserving system that simulates the environment of the mouth and keeps the damaged ligament moist. This system can keep the tooth cells viable for up to 4 to 12 hours.[16]

In either case, the athlete should be *immediately* transported to dentist.

Fractured Tooth

Injured teeth that are not obviously fractured should be X-rayed within a day or two to rule out possible unseen fractures to the root. Fractures may occur through the enamel, or through the dentine and the enamel, or they may include the pulp.

Small fractures through the enamel produce minimal symptoms. The player should be able to breathe vigorously through the mouth without pain or sensitivity. First aid consists of using pain-relieving tooth drops and a temporary filling material to cover any exposed portion of the tooth. Dental emergency kits containing these and other first aid supplies are available. Fluids should be kept off the tooth if this causes sensitivity. The tooth can later be smoothed down with satisfactory results.

If the fracture extends through the dentine as well, there is increased sensitivity to heat, cold, and fluids. If the symptoms are severe, an injection of a local anesthetic near the root of the tooth can be performed by a dentist or physician to decrease the symptoms. The tooth can then be covered with temporary or permanent filling material.

Severe pain and marked increase in sensitivity occur with exposure of the pulp. This can be noted by carefully looking to see if the pink pulp is visible through a thin layer of dentine. Again, a local anesthetic may relieve symptoms temporarily, but this type of injury will usually require a root-canal filling (Figure 11.5).

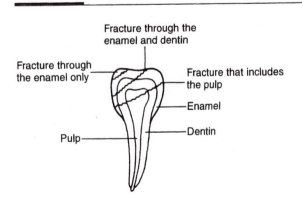

FIGURE 11.5
Dental fractures

Fracture through the enamel and dentin

Fracture through the enamel only

Fracture that includes the pulp

Enamel

Dentin

Pulp

TABLE 11.6 *Dental injuries that need immediate referral*

1. The tooth is avulsed or dislodged
2. The tooth is displaced by 2 mm or more
3. A fractured crown where the tooth is still alive

Loose Tooth

If there is any suspicion that the tooth's position has shifted, the athlete should be immediately referred to a dentist, since the blood supply may have been disrupted. In cases where there is no actual displacement, but only minimal loosening of the tooth, a precautionary X-ray should be taken at a convenient time. The athlete should be warned not to bite with the tooth for at least one to two weeks.

If the tooth is displaced two millimeters or more, it should be pushed back with the finger into its anatomical position. The athlete should then be referred immediately to a dentist so the loose tooth can be stabilized.

Fractured Crown

This is not always an emergency, as very often the crown will be situated over a dead tooth and, therefore, sensitivity will not be increased. If the tooth *is* sensitive, a temporary cap can be molded from the fill material found in emergency dental kits until the athlete can get to a dentist. If the tooth is not dead, the crown should be replaced as soon as possible.

Artificial Plates

Removable artificial plates should *not* be kept in the mouth during either practice or competition, as they are liable to be broken, resulting in some pieces being accidentally swallowed, inhaled, or lodged in the gum or palate (Table 11.6).

Eye Injuries and Conditions

Our eyes are among our most precious organs, but they are taken quite casually by many athletes even though they are exposed to potential trauma (Figure 11.6). The potential for long-term consequences is great. The American Academy of Opthamology estimates that 25 percent of all those with eye injuries develop serious complications or even loss of vision.[17]

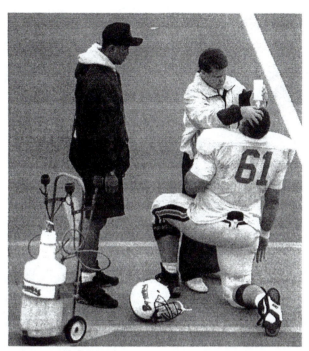

FIGURE 11.6
On-field eye injury
(Photo by Ben Danley)

FIGURE 11.7
An eye protector should be used for racquetball and squash

In sports such as racquetball and squash, serious injuries and permanent damage can easily be prevented by the use of eye protectors.[18,19,20] It is strongly recommended that no athlete be allowed to participate in racquetball or squash without wearing eye protectors, and that in sports such as tennis, badminton, baseball, and basketball the use of eye protectors be encouraged.[20,21,22] Eye protectors should be of the "closed" variety, with polycarbonate lenses that meet American Society for Testing and Material (ASTM) standards (Figure 11.7).

The U.S. Consumer Product Safety Commission estimates that baseball and basketball are the leaders in sports-related eye injuries in the United States.[23]

Approximately 30 percent of sports-related ocular injuries occur to children 16 and under; 90 percent of these are considered preventable.[24]

Fractures

The "blow-out fracture" of the orbit is an injury that needs to be recognized and managed, and then the involved athlete should be referred to an ophthalmologist for further evaluation and treatment.

The mechanism of injury is usually by blunt trauma to the area. The traumatic force is usually transmitted by an athletic implement (e.g., hockey stick) or by another athlete (e.g., elbow). Any athlete who sustains orbital trauma should be assessed for visual acuity, diplopia (two images), periorbital edema, anesthesia or hypoaesthesia over the infraorbital nerve distribution (lateral nose and/or upper lip), and pain (aching discomfort).

Contusions to the Lids

Because the tissues surrounding the lids are very loose, they permit a large amount of swelling to occur. The eye can rapidly become closed by swollen lids. The possibility of an underlying orbital fracture should be considered.

EXAMINATION: When initially examining an athlete with a swollen lid, it is important to try to assess the function and condition of the underlying eye. Visual acuity should be tested with the unaffected eye covered, and the results should be recorded. Then, with the athlete lying supine, the lids should be very gently retracted. The eyes should then be inspected for obvious abnormalities. The pupils should be equal, regular, and reactive to light; eye movements should be full, unrestricted, and symmetrical. Fluorescin dye can be instilled in order to exclude or identify corneal abrasions. The athlete should then sit up, and the anterior chamber should be inspected for evidence of bleeding. This will appear as a layer of blood with a meniscus (Figure 11.8).

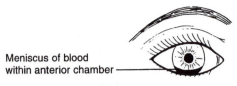

Meniscus of blood within anterior chamber

FIGURE 11.8
Anterior chamber hemorrhage

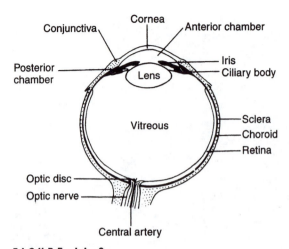

FIGURE 11.9
The anatomy of the eye

TREATMENT: Ice should not be applied in the form of a heavy ice pack. Rather, the use of specially made cold packs for eyes is recommended, or else crushed ice or cold water in a latex surgical glove that is placed on the affected eye. With contusions around the orbit of the eye, the early and intermittent application of cold can significantly reduce the swelling and ecchymosis that results in a "black eye." It is especially important to perform a thorough evaluation of any facial injury to rule out fractures or injury to other structures such as the eye itself. If there is any doubt about the condition of the eye, the athlete should be referred immediately for ophthalmologic consultation. The athletic trainer should never instill medication into the eye. At times it may be acceptable to gently irrigate (with water) the superficial area around the eye to remove debris that could cause an irritation to the eye (Figure 11.6).

Levator Injury

The levator palpebrae superioris muscle elevates the upper lid. If a finger is jammed into the eye, the muscle can be damaged. If there is difficulty in opening the eye after a few days of ice treatment, patching, and rest, a specialist's opinion should be sought.

Corneal Abrasions

The athlete will complain of pain, a gritty feeling, or the sensation of a foreign body being present. A drop or two of local anesthetic solution will make the athlete feel more comfortable and permit an adequate examination. A foreign body should be sought on the cornea and, if not present, the upper lid should then be everted (if there is not too much swelling) so the conjunctiva can be adequately inspected (Figure 11.9). A corneal abrasion can best be seen by applying a strip impregnated with fluorescin dye, which will outline the area of abrasion by staining it a deep yellow. Corneal abrasions usually heal rapidly when adequately treated. The eye should be placed at rest so that a patch may be applied, and mydriatric and antibiotic drops should be used as indicated. The patch must be tight enough to prevent opening of the lid under it, and the tape should be applied in a manner that will not permit it to become loose when the athlete chews food. Analgesics may be required (Figure 11.10).

Occasionally a complication such a iritis will develop; it should be referred immediately to an ophthalmologist. The first symptom of iritis is often photophobia (avoidance of bright light) and an increase in pain and redness of the eye.

Subconjunctival Hematoma

A condition causing the athlete a considerable amount of anxiety is subconjunctival hematoma. It is a harmless condition occurring as a result of the spontaneous rupture of a small blood vessel, but it may appear rather alarming due to the red color against the white sclera.

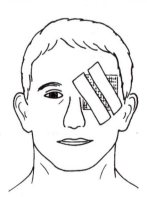

FIGURE 11.10
An eye patch

One can usually detect the posterior margin of the hematoma, which helps confirm the diagnosis. No treatment besides reassurance is necessary.

Conjunctivitis (Pink Eye)

Inflammation of the conjunctiva may be the result of a bacterial infection. Signs and symptoms may include pain, itching, burning, sensitivity to light, redness, and discharge. The condition is contagious and care should be taken to avoid spreading the infection to the other eye or to other people. The athlete should be referred to a physician for diagnosis and treatment with antibiotic ointment.

Injury to the Lens or Iris

Lens or iris injuries can be seen by inspecting the pupil, which may be irregular, dilated, or constricted. Expert consultation should be sought immediately.

Hemorrhage into the Anterior Chamber (Hyphema)

An anterior chamber hemorrhage is a potentially very serious injury usually resulting from blunt trauma. Observe if a meniscus of blood is present (Figure 11.8). Visual acuity may be reduced. A hyphema requires prompt medical attention. The initial treatment is to loosely patch the eye with a sterile or clean dressing, elevate the head to prevent venous ingestion and reduce intraocular pressure, and transport to a medical facility. The mainstay of treatment is rest. Patches may be needed on both eyes. The ophthalmologist should determine the length of time such immobilization is necessary. Secondary hemorrhage may occur if the athlete returns to participation too soon, the danger period being three to seven days after the injury. If this occurs, it could lead to permanent impairment of vision. Complications of hyphema include glaucoma later in life; periodic follow-up by an ophthalmologist is therefore recommended.

Hemorrhage into the Posterior Chamber

Posterior-chamber bleeding may present with a visual defect. It may be painful but is often painless. If there is considerable bleeding within the globe, the "red reflex" will be lost (normally, when a light is shown into the eye the retina is seen through the pupil as red.).

Bleeding into the posterior chamber is a serious injury. It should immediately be referred for specific diagnosis and treatment.

Detached Retina

Patients frequently describe the occurrence of a detached retina using phrases like "a curtain fell in front of my eye" or "multiple lights flashed on and off," or mention the appearance of "floaters" (caused by the retina tearing across a blood vessel). Such a history should make the athletic trainer aware of the possibility of a detached retina, which might occur days or weeks after the traumatic event. The athlete should immediately be referred to an ophthalmologist.

Nasal Injuries

Bleeding (Epistaxis)

Because of the copious blood supply of the nasal mucosa, bleeding is often a problem, particularly in sports such as wrestling. In most cases the bleeding is easily controlled by manually pinching the nostrils and applying ice. However, in situations where the athlete must return to participation, a plug of cotton or gauze will temporarily alleviate the bleeding (it is important to remember to remove the cotton once the bleeding has stopped). If this does not suffice, adrenalin in the concentration of 1:1,000 solution or an OTC nasal spray can be applied to the cotton before inserting. This encourages vasoconstriction. Should the bleeding persist in spite of manual pressure and the application of ice, the athlete should be referred to a medical facility for examination and possible cauterization and packing.

Septal Hematoma

A hematoma of the septum can develop quite insidiously following a blow to the nose. The first indication may be difficulty in breathing through one of the nostrils. This condition can lead to infection, tissue necrosis, scarring, and the eventual destruction of the nasal cartilage, especially if left undrained. These complications can cause functional as well as cosmetic problems; the internal thickening and fibrosis can result in a partially obstructed airway or, in the case of necrosis of the septum, a perforation may occur. A large perforation will result in a "saddle nose" deformity. Spreading of the infection to the brain, with the development of a brain abscess, is a rare but serious complication.

Once a septal hematoma is diagnosed, it should be drained and antibiotics prescribed if necessary. It is important for the athlete to avoid contact activities for a few days after the injury to minimize the risks of infection and the recurrence of the hematoma. If the athlete is participating in contact sport, a face mask should be worn for seven to ten days to prevent further nasal trauma.

Nasal Fractures

Due to their prominence and relative thinness, the bones of the nose are the most frequently fractured face bones.[25] If a nasal fracture is suspected, one should look for bony deviation, which can be done visually if the athlete is seen before swelling has developed. Simple observation by the examiner as well as the athlete can often accurately assess the need for treatment. The examiner should also inspect the nose with the athlete supine, observing the athlete from behind, along the bridge of the nose. Excessive swelling of the nasal dorsum, ecchymosis around the eyes, and nasal bone crepitus should also raise one's suspicion of a nasal fracture. If there is any question as to whether a fracture exists, the athlete should be referred for a specialist's opinion. There is some controversy over the timing for the reduction of nasal fractures. Recommendations vary from a maximum of 10 or 12 days post-injury to several months.[26] Certainly if significant swelling and ecchymosis is present it can be difficult to visualize the nasal dorsum and septum, making precise reduction difficult. Thus, unless the reduction can be made immediately after injury, time to permit swelling to sufficiently resolve should be allowed before reduction is attempted.[27] The immediate application of ice may help to reduce swelling.

Of particular concern is the fact that repeated nasal fractures can cause both long-term functional and cosmetic damage. As many as 15 percent of nasal fractures are repetitive.[28] When returning to activity following a nasal fracture, the use of a protective nose guard to distribute the forces of a blow to the forehead and cheekbones is highly recommended.

A nose that is deformed as a result of repeated injuries is probably best repaired by plastic surgery after the athlete has ended his or her competitive athletic career.

Ear Injuries

Hematoma of the Pinna ("Cauliflower Ear")

Injuries to the pinna resulting in a cauliflower ear were notorious in past years. They are the result of contact sports and are still found in professional boxers, rugby players, and wrestlers who do not wear ear protectors.

A cauliflower ear is the result of one or more episodes of trauma to the pinna, which results in sub-

perichondral hemorrhage with pressure or infection destroying the underlying cartilage. This results in a progressively increasing distortion of the pinnal shape.[29]

PREVENTION: Any athlete at risk should wear an adequate protective device designed for the sport. In rugby the positions most frequently associated with cauliflower ears are the front-row forwards, the locks, and the eighth man. Wrestling without an ear protector should not be permitted. It is important for the athlete to be sure the protector fits adequately, as friction between the protector and the ear can itself cause a hematoma. Should the hematoma occur, complications can be prevented by adequate treatment performed under aseptic conditions.

TREATMENT: Once the earlobe becomes traumatized, it should be packed with ice and a moderate amount of compression should be applied. If a hematoma develops, it should be drained under aseptic conditions at the earliest convenient time. A compressive dressing of a material such as cotton soaked in flexible collodion can be used[30] (Figure 11.11). Compression should be continued for a few hours after drainage. The dressing should be kept in place for at least five days to allow adequate healing to occur. If swelling recurs, this same procedure should be repeated. Restricting the athlete's activity is not considered necessary unless a complication ensues.

Rupture of the Eardrum

Rupture of the eardrum (tympanic membrane) results from a direct blow to the ear, which causes a sudden violent increase in the pressure within the external auditory canal. Such a blow may occur from a soccer ball hitting the side of the head, from a slap of the hand against the pinna, or from a fall while water skiing. It may also occur as a result of barotrauma from diving.

SYMPTOMS AND SIGNS: The athlete presents with a history of the incident and describes an intense pain followed by hearing loss and, in some cases, severe dizziness and nausea. A small amount of bleeding from the external auditory meatus may be present. On inspection of the drum with an otoscope the diagnosis is readily apparent.

TREATMENT: Most small ruptures will heal spontaneously, but it is important that the athlete understand

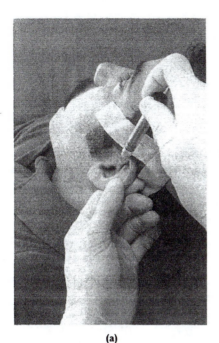
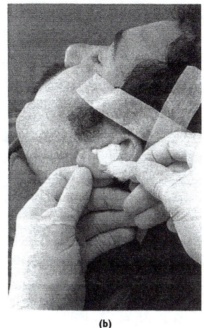
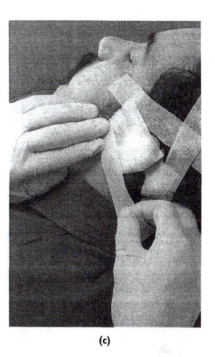

(a)   **(b)**   **(c)**

FIGURE 11.11

Draining an ear hematoma.

(a) After thoroughly cleaning the pinna with an alcohol or Betadine solution, drain the hematoma with a narrow-bore needle. This should be done using strict aseptic technique. (b) The external auditory meatus is plugged with a dry piece of cotton. Strips of cotton are then soaked in collodion and applied in layers to the pinna. (c) Paper tape is used to maintain pressure on the cotton strips. These are left in place for 3 to 5 days, after which the cotton, collodion, and tape are reapplied if necessary.

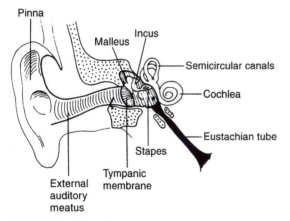

FIGURE 11.12

The anatomy of the ear
(frontal cross-section)

that water should not be allowed to enter the external auditory meatus until the drum has completely healed. If the rupture is large or persists, it may have to be repaired surgically or a graft may have to be inserted. Auditory testing should be repeated.

Ear and Sinus Barotrauma in Diving

One of the reasons the ear is often affected by diving is that there is an increase in pressure of 14.7 pounds (one atmosphere) for every 33 feet of descent. This increase in pressure may damage the middle ear and sinus cavities unless there is continuous equalizaion of the pressure between the cavities and the exterior.

PREVENTION:

1. *Adequate diving instruction.* This is a must. Prior to any diving attempt, the student diver should develop the ability to perform the Valsalva maneuver (the nose and mouth are held closed while an attempt is made to explosively blow out air). This will open the eustachian tubes so the pressure within the pharynx, the middle ear, and the sinuses is equalized. With experience, divers may be able to equalize pressure simply by yawning or swallowing. In addition, the novice diver must learn how to ascend and how to deal with panic situations.

2. *Physical examination of a diving candidate.* This exam should include the cardiovascular and respiratory systems but, most importantly, it should include a

thorough evaluation of the otolaryngological structures, including:

a. inspection of the tympanic membranes

b. having the diving candidate attempt to perform the Valsalva maneuver while the examiner observes movement of the tympanic membrane

c. inspection of the external canal with particular reference to otitis externa, osteomas, and cerumen

d. inspection of the position of the nasal septum, particularly with regard to hypertrophy of the turbinates

e. inspection of the nasopharynx, especially the area of the eustachian tube orifices.

Chronic sinusitis should be controlled. Any hearing loss should be appropriately recorded and individually assessed. A profound unilateral hearing loss probably contraindicates diving, in order to prevent damage to the good ear. Any tendency to vertigo (e.g., active Meniere's disease) or a perforated eardrum is a contraindication to diving.

SYMPTOMS AND SIGNS: An inexperienced diver, or one who has a nasopharyngeal problem such as an infection or allergy, might find it impossible to equalize the pressure, resulting in damage to the tympanic membrane or sinuses. A reverse external ear barotrauma sometimes occurs when a plug of wax or an earplug blocks the external auditory canal and results in the tympanic membrane extending outward. A rebound phenomenon after use of a vasoconstrictor may cause the eustachian tube to become blocked, thereby preventing equalizaton of pressure while ascending.

If the pressure is sufficient to cause rupture of the tympanic membrane, the effects of cold water on the labyrinth may lead to dizziness, disorientation, nausea, and vomiting, which in a diving situation can be life threatening.[31] Rupture of the round window can lead to permanent loss of hearing and to vertigo.

TREATMENT: *Mild* cases, which show a reddening of the tympanic membranes with or without slight hemorrhage within the drum, should be treated with vasoconstrictors, decongestants, or both. Diving should be prohibited until the symptoms have disappeared and the eardrum appears normal. This usually takes five to seven days.[32,33]

In *severe* cases, the drum may or may not be ruptured, but there is free blood in the middle ear. This condition requires the use of systemic antibiotics, oral vasoconstrictors, decongestants, and a topical nasal decongestant (avoid antihistamines). Traumatic perfo-

ration of the tympanic membrane should be referred to an otolaryngologist.

Damage to the sinuses may cause hemorrhage, marked edema of the mucosa, or extravasation of fluid. Secondary infection may occur unless adequate drainage is established. Occasionally surgical drainage is required.

External Auditory Canal—"Swimmer's Ear" (Otitis Externa)

Swimmer's ear (see Chapter 22) is a bacterial or fungal infection involving the lining of the external auditory canal. It occurs frequently in those who neglect to adequately dry the canal.

PREVENTION: The best protection is to ensure that the swimmer dries the external auditory canal after each workout. This may be achieved by shaking the head to the side or by using a hair dryer. The use of a cotton-tipped applicator is not recommended. The instillation of a few drops of VoSol or 1% boric-acid solution (5.0 grams boric acid and 70% ethyl alcohol made up to 500 milliliters) three or four times a week may help retain the normal acid conditions of the external auditory canal and thereby prevent infection.

SYMPTOMS AND SIGNS: The athlete presents with an itching or intensely painful ear that may or may not be discharging. Pus and debris are easily seen through the otoscope. Local pressure around the external auditory meatus or pulling on the pinna will cause pain. If left untreated, the infection may spread to the middle ear and cause disturbances of balance as well as hearing.

TREATMENT: A special wick can be inserted for 24 to 48 hours and antibiotic or steroid drops can be used. Alternatively, Burrow's Solution (aluminum acetate) can be used initially to decrease swelling. When the swelling and pain have subsided, the ear canal should be cleared of debris. Eardrops containing alcohol or boric acid and an antibiotic should be used as necessary.

REFERENCES

1. The Sports Medicine Committee, The Colorado Medical Society, *Guidelines for the Management of Concussion in Sports,* May 1990 (Revised May 1991).

2. Committee on Head Injury Nomenclature of the Congress of Neurological Surgeons: Glossary of head injury including some definitions of injury of the cervical spine. *Clin Neurosurg* 12:388, 1966.

3. Roberts WO: Who Plays? Who Sits? Managing concussions on the sidelines. *Phys Sportsmed* 20:66–72, June 1992.

4. Cantu RC: Guidelines for return to contact sports after a cerebral concussion. *Phys Sportsmed* 14:75–83, 1986.

5. Matthews B: Maxillofacial trauma from athletic endeavors. *Athletic Training* 25:132–137, Summer 1990.

6. Koloskie J, Orr DL: Management and treatment of a mandible fracture in an athlete. *JNATA* 27:177–179, 1992.

7. Castaldi CR: First aid for sports-related dental injuries. *Phys Sportsmed* 15:81–89, September 1987.

8. Schwartz R, Novich MM: The athlete's mouth-piece. *Am J Sports Med* 8:357–359,1980.

9. Morrow RM, Seals RR, Barnwell GM, Day EA, Moore RN, Stephens MK: Report of a survey of oral injuries in male college and university athletes. *Athletic Training, JNATA* 26:338–242, Winter 1991.

10. Morrow RM, Bonci T, Seals RR, Barnwell GM: Oral injuries in Southwest Conference Women Basketball Players. *Athletic Training, JNATA,* 26:344–345, Winter 1991.

11. Doberstein ST: A procedure for fitting mouth-formed mouthguards. *Athletic Training, JNATA* Fall 1990.

12. Hickey JC, Morris AL, Carlson LD, et al: The relation of mouth protectors to cranial pressure and deformation. *JADA* 74:735, 1967.

13. Stenger JM, Lawson EA, Wright JM, et al: Mouthguards: Protection against shock to head, neck, and teeth. *JADA* 69:273, 1964.

14. Accepted Dental Therapeutics. *American Dental Association* 72, 1984.

15. Ad hoc committee on treatment of the avulsed tooth. American Association of Endodontists. Recommended guidelines for the treament of the avulsed tooth. *J Endod* 9:571, 1983.

16. Krasner P: The athletic trainer's role in saving avulsed teeth. *Athletic Training; JNATA* 24:139–142, Summer 1989.

17. Whyte JD: Eye Injuries. *Athletic Training, JNATA* 22:207–210, Fall 1987.

18. Bishop PJ, Kozey J, Caldwell G: Performance of eye protectors for squash and racquetball. *Phys Sportsmed* 10:62–69, March 1982.

19. Easterbrook M: Eye protection for squash and racquetball players. *Phys Sportsmed* 9:79–82, February 1981.

20. Labell P, Mercier M, Podtetenev M, Trudeau F: Eye injuries in sports: Results of a five-year study. *Phys Sportsmed* 16:126–138, May 1988.

21. Easterbrook M: Eye injuries in racket sports: A continuing problem. *Phys Sportsmed* 9:91–101, January 1981.

22. Easterbrook M: Eye Injuries in squash and racquetball players: An update. *Phys Sportsmed* 10:47–56, March 1982.

23. US consumer product safety commission: Eye injuries only, all products. Washington, DC, 1989.

24. Strahlman E, Elman M, Daub E. et al: Causes of pediatric eye injuries: A population-based study. *Arch Ophthalmol* 108(4):603–606, 1990.

25. Sane J: Comparison of maxillofacial and dental injuries in four contact team sports: American football, bandy, basketball, and handball. *Am J Sports Med* 161196):647–651, 1988.

26. Martinez SA: Nasal fractures: what to do for a successful outcome. *Postgrad Med* 82(8):71–74,77, 1987.

27. Schendel SA, Sports-related nasal injuries. *Phys Sportsmed* 18:59–74, October 1990.

28. Illum P: Long-term results after treatment of nasal fractures. *J Laryngol Otol* 100(3):273–277, 1986.

29. Eichel BS, Bray DA: Management of hematoma of the wrestler's ear. *Phys Sportsmed* 6:87–90, November 1978.

30. Stuteville OH, Janda C, Pandya NJ: Treating the injured ear to prevent a "cauliflower ear." *Plastic and Reconstructive Surgery* 44:310–312, 1969.

31. Pipkin G: Caloric labyrinthitis: A cause of drowning. A case report of a swimmer who survived through self-rescue. *Am J Sports Med* 7:260–261, 1979.

32. Strauss MB, Cantrell RW: Ear and sinus barotrauma in diving. *Phys Sportsmed* 8:38–43, August 1974.

33. MacFie DD: ENT problems in diving. *Med Serv J Can* 20:845–861, 1964.

RECOMMENDED READINGS

Behnke AR, Austin LF: Introduction to scuba diving. *J Sports Med* 2:276–290, 1974.

Blyth CS, Schindler RD: *Forty-eighth Annual Survey of Football Fatalities 1931–1979.* National Collegiate Athletic Association and American Football Coaches Association 1980.

Cantu RC: Guidelines for return to contact sports after a cerebral concussion. *Phys Sportsmed* 14:75–83, 1986.

Downs JR: Facial trauma in intercollegiate and junior hockey. *Phys Sportsmed* 7:88–92, February 1979.

Mueller FO, Blyth CS: Catastrophic head and neck injuries. *Phys Sportmed* 7:71–74, October 1979.

Putnam LA: Alternative methods for football helmet face mask removal. *J Athletic Training* 27: 170–172, 1992.

Reid SE, Epstein HM, Louis MW: Brain trauma inside a football helmet. *Phys Sportsmed* 2:32–35, August 1974.

Schneider RC: *Head and Neck Injuries in Football.* Baltimore, Williams and Wilkins Company, 1973.

Torg JS editor: *Athletic Injuries to the Head, Neck, and Face.* Philadelphia, Lea and Febiger, 1982.

Torg JS, Truex Jr R, Quedenfeld T, et al: National Football Head-Neck Registry—report and conclusions. *JAMA* 241:1477–1479, 1979.

Travell J: Temporomandibular joint dysfunction—Temporomandibular joint pain referred from muscles of the head and neck. *J Prosthet Dent* 10:745, 1960.

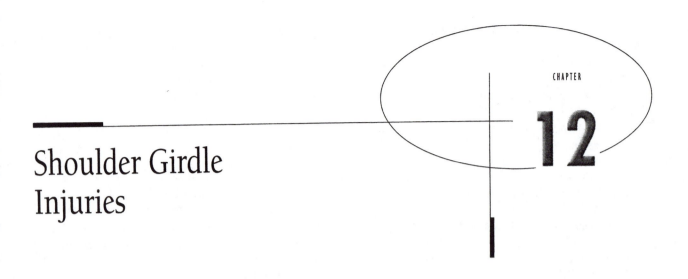

Shoulder Girdle Injuries

Functional Anatomy

Because the shoulder girdle is designed to permit maximum mobility, there is a compromise in the degree of structural stability. In addition, there is only one point at which the shoulder girdle is attached to the skeletal system—at the sternoclavicular joint (Figure 12.1).

Bones and Joints

The bones of the shoulder girdle include the clavicle, scapula, and humerus.

THE CLAVICLE: The clavicle prevents the shoulder from dropping across the chest and thus helps maintain the distance between the upper arm and the sternum. It is concave posteriorly in its proximal two-thirds and concave anteriorly in its distal third. The weakest point of the clavicle is at the junction of the middle and outer thirds, and it is in this area where fractures frequently occur.

The clavicle is attached to the the sternum through the sternoclavicular joint. This joint represents the only true articulation between the upper extremity and the trunk. Its stability is maintained by a fibrous capsule reinforced by the sternoclavicular and costoclavicular ligaments.

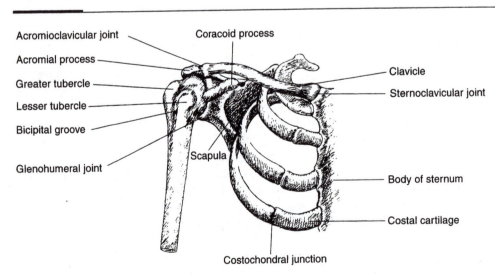

FIGURE 12.1
The shoulder girdle

FIGURE 12.2

The sternoclavicular joints (anterior view). The right joint is shown without ligaments to reveal the articular structures.

(*Source:* Frankel, Nordin, *Basic Biomechanics of the Musculoskeletal System,* 2nd ed., Lea & Febiger, Malvern, PA, 1989, p. 233.)

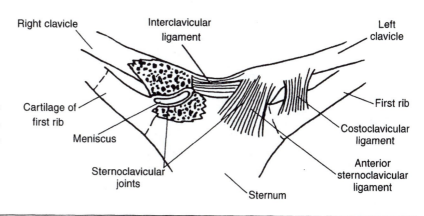

These run between the medial aspect of the clavicle, first rib, and sternum (Figure 12.2). Interposed between clavicle and sternum is also a meniscus. The sternoclavicular joint permits some motion in all planes. Calliet[1] describes elevation of the distal clavicle through the first 30 degrees of scapular rotation. The remaining 30 degrees of scapular rotation occurs as the "crankshaped" clavicle rotates about its long axis (Figure 12.3).

At the outer end of the clavicle lies the acromioclavicular joint (Figure 12.3). Linking the distal end of the clavicle to the acromion process, the AC joint is surrounded by a dense, fibrous capsule (the capsular, or AC

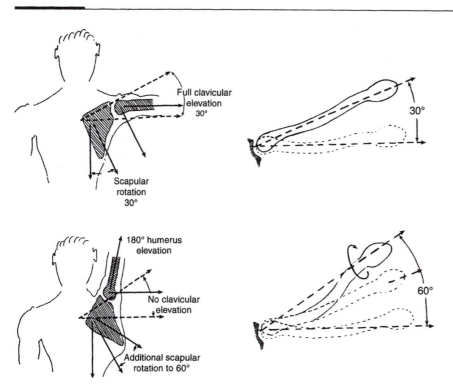

FIGURE 12.3

Scapular elevation resulting from clavicular rotation

The upper drawing shows the elevation of the clavicle without rotation to 30°. The remaining 30° of scapular rotation, which is imperative in full scapulohumeral range, occurs by rotation of the "crankshaped" clavicle about its long axis.

(*Source:* R. Calliet, *Shoulder Pain,* Philadelphia, FA Davis, 1966, p. 26.)

ligament). A meniscus, when present, may be complete or incomplete. AC joint stability is provided by two sets of ligaments and two muscles:

1. Acromioclavicular ligament
2. Coracoclavicular ligaments: trapezoid and conoid

The acromioclavicular ligament that envelops the structure is thick superiorly and thin inferiorly. The deltoid muscle fibers and the trapezius muscle that surround the joint merge with the superior AC ligament and attach to the superior clavicle and the acromion process. The coracoclavicular ligaments (the conoid and trapezoid), extend from the coracoid process to the outer undersurface of the clavicle (Figure 12.4). The coracoclavicular ligaments suspend the scapula from the clavicle and allow the scapula to move on the clavicle. Inman and coworkers[2] found that during shoulder abduction and forward flexion, the range of acromioclavicular joint motion is 20 degrees. If the ligaments holding the distal end of the clavicle are damaged, the clavicle will be displaced in a cephalad direction.

THE SCAPULA AND SCAPULOTHORACIC AR-TICULATION: The scapula (or shoulder blade) lies flat against the posterior chest wall, and its movements are closely integrated with those of the shoulder (Figure 12.5). To it are attached numerous important muscles. Some of the more important structures include:

1. Acromion process
2. Coracoid process
3. Glenoid fossa
4. Spine of the scapula

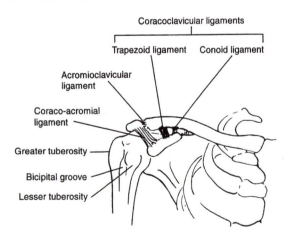

FIGURE 12.4
Ligaments at the lateral end of the clavicle

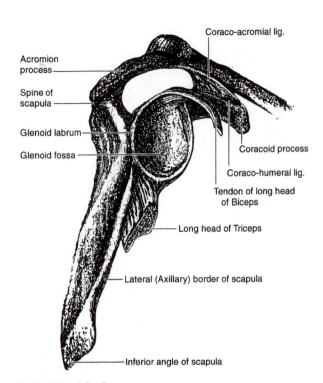

FIGURE 12.5
Glenoid fossa, lined along the periphery by the glenoid labrum
(Modified from JCB Grant, *Grant's Atlas of Anatomy,* 6th ed., Williams & Wilkins, Baltimore, 1972, p. 38.)

Between the acromion process and the coracoid process is a thick band of ligament-like tissue called the coraco-acromial ligament. The coraco-acromial ligament and the acromion make up the coraco-acromial arch. The coraco-acromial ligament may cause impingement of the structures running beneath it, particularly in an athlete who uses the shoulder frequently (such as a baseball player or swimmer). The structure most frequently pinched under the arch is the supraspinatus tendon.

The glenoid fossa is lined by the labrum, a fibrocartilaginous rim that serves to deepen the glenoid fossa and thereby increase the stability of the glenohumeral joint. Except for its attachment through the acromioclavicular and sternoclavicular joints, the scapula is without bony or ligamentous connection to the thorax. While this seemingly unstable situation literally has the shoulder "hanging by the clavicle," it does allow for a wide range of scapular motion. These motions include protraction, retraction, elevation, depression, and rotation.[3]

THE HUMERUS: The head of the humerus fits into the glenoid fossa. Other landmarks on the proximal humerus include the greater tuberosity (to which the supraspinatus tendon is attached) and the lesser tuberosity (to which the subscapularis muscle is attached). The tendon of the long head of the biceps runs in a special groove (the bicepital) that lies between the lesser and greater tuberosities. The transverse humeral ligament helps to prevent the biceps tendon from slipping out of the groove.

THE GLENOHUMERAL JOINT: The convex articulating surface of the head of the humerus is two to three times as large as the shallow, concave socket of the glenoid (Figure 12.6). Although the glenoid fossa is deepened to a certain extent by the fibrocartilaginous labrum (Figure 12.5), its shallowness allows significant freedom of movement of the humeral head on the glenoid surface. Motion at the glenohumeral joint is typical of ball-and-socket joints. Three types of surface motion may take place in any given plane: rotation (spin), rolling, and translation (gliding). Surface motion at the glenohumeral joint is primarily rotational, but some combination of gliding and rolling also takes place.[3] The glenohumeral joint is secured largely by a thick capsule composed of a number of ligaments (Figure 12.7), and allows the upper limb to move through an extensive range of movement. These ligaments, particularly the inferior glenohumeral ligament, can be torn with an antero-inferior dislocation of the shoulder. Incompetency of the capsule can result in recurrent subluxation or dislocation of the shoulder joint.[4] Static stability of the glenohumeral joint is assisted by the peripheral thickness of the glenoid labrum. The rotator cuff muscles act to dynamically stabilize the humeral head within the glenoid fossa during all activities. The internal rotator muscles, including the subscapularis, help protect the anterior and inferior glenohumeral complex from injury by preventing unchecked external rotation.[5]

SCAPULOHUMERAL RHYTHM: Inman[2] examined arm elevation in the frontal and sagittal planes and found that about two-thirds of the motion (approximately 120 degrees) took place at the glenohumeral joint and one-third (approximately 60 degrees) at the scapulothoracic articulation. A range of sixty degrees of scapular motion at the scapulothoracic articulation is possible only because of an equal amount of elevation and rotation occurring at the AC and SC joints. Without rotation of the clavicle, arm elevation would be limited to about 120 degrees.[1] (Figure 12.3.)

Muscles

The main muscles associated with the shoulder girdle include the following (Figure 12.8):

THE TRAPEZIUS: This is a triangular muscle which covers the neck and shoulder. It arises from the occiput and the spines of the cervical and thoracic vertebrae and inserts into the posterior border of the outer third of the clavicle as well as into part of the acromion process and spine of the scapula. The insertion of this

---

FIGURE 12.6
Physiologic motions occurring at the glenohumeral joint
(*Source:* Frankel, Nordin: *Basic Biomechanics of the Musculoskeletal System,* 2nd ed., Lea & Febiger, Malvern, PA, 1989, p. 231.)

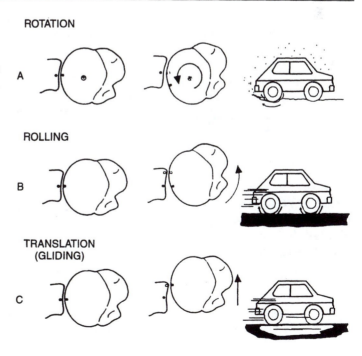

ROTATION

A

ROLLING

B

TRANSLATION
(GLIDING)

C

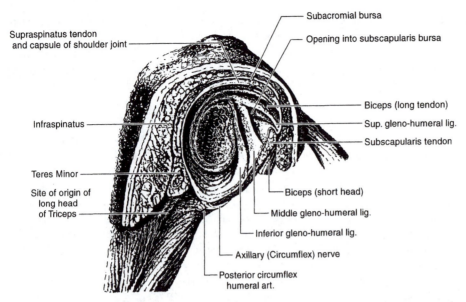

FIGURE 12.7

Illustration depicts both static (ligamentous) and dynamic (muscular) support of the glenohumeral joint (*Source:* JCB Grant, *Grant's Atlas of Anatomy,* 6th ed., Williams & Wilkins, Baltimore, 1972, p. 39.)

muscle into the clavicle varies in extent—in some individuals it may reach as far as the middle of the clavicle and on occasion may even blend with the posterior edge of the sternocleidomastoideus muscle. The trapezius helps to stabilize the scapula during movements of the upper limb.

THE LATISSIMUS DORSI: This is a large triangular muscle which covers the lumbar region and the lower half of the thoracic area. It inserts into the upper third of the humerus. Before its insertion it wraps around the lower border of the teres major muscle, and as a result the lowest fibers are inserted highest into the humerus while the highest fibers pass into the lowest end of the tendon. The latissimus dorsi helps form the posterior fold of the axilla. Its actions are mainly those of adduction, extension, and internal rotation of the humerus, but it also acts with the pectoralis major and teres major to help depress the raised arm against resistance.

THE PECTORALIS MAJOR: The pectoralis major is a thick muscle covering the upper and front part of the chest. It arises from the medial half of the clavicle, from the sternum, from the cartilages of the ribs, and from the aponeurosis of the external oblique muscle. It inserts into the upper third of the humerus and gives off an expansion which covers the bicipital groove. Its main actions are those of adduction and internal rotation of the humerus. When the arm is extended, the pectoralis

major draws it forward and medially. When the arm is flexed, the clavicular portion of the pectoralis major acts with the anterior fibers of the deltoid. When the arms are used for movement, such as climbing, the muscle helps draw the trunk forward and upward.

THE SERRATUS ANTERIOR: This muscle lies between the ribs and the scapula and inserts into the costal surface of the medial border of the scapula. When the serratus anterior acts with the pectoralis minor muscle, it helps draw the scapula forward, and is the main muscle concerned with pushing and punching movements. It assists the trapezius in rotating the scapula forward around the chest wall and is therefore important in raising the arm above the head. During the action of abduction, the serratus anterior works together with other muscles that are inserted into the scapula to help steady the scapula and allows the deltoid to abduct the humerus. If the serratus anterior is paralyzed from damage to the long thoracic nerve, it will be unable to hold the scapula against the chest wall. If the athlete is asked to push the arm forward into protrusion, the inner border of the scapula will "wing," especially in its lower two-thirds.

THE DELTOID: This muscle covers the shoulder joint and gives it its smooth, rounded contour. The deltoid arises from the lateral third of the clavicle as well as from the acromion process and the spine of the scapula.

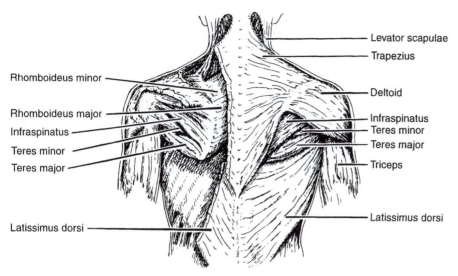

FIGURE 12.8
Muscles of the upper back and shoulder girdle

It inserts by means of a thick tendon into the lateral side of the shaft of the humerus. It has three portions: anterior, middle, and posterior.

The actions of the deltoid muscle are numerous. It may act with the pectoralis major to bring the arm forward and to internally rotate the humerus. In combination with the latissimus dorsi and the teres major, it extends the arm backward. Together with the supraspinatus, it raises the arm from the side. While the deltoid is abducting the arm, the scapula is being rotated by the serratus anterior and the trapezius muscles. As this is happening, the head of the humerous is prevented from moving upward by the downward pull of the subscapularis, the infraspinatus, and the teres minor.

The axillary nerve supplies the deltoid muscle. If this nerve is damaged, the deltoid will atrophy. This can be seen when the rounded contour of the normal side is compared with the flattening of the shoulder and the prominence of the acromion process on the affected side.

THE ROTATOR CUFF: The rotator cuff consists of the following muscles:

1. The *supraspinatus* arises from the supraspinous fossa and passes under the acromion to form a tendon which inserts into the most superior portion of the greater tubercle of the humerus. It is separated from the acromion process, the coraco-acromial ligament, and the deltoid muscle by the subacromial bursa.

2. The *infraspinatus* arises from the infraspinous fossa on the scapula and inserts as a tendon into the middle portion of the greater tubercle of the humerus.

3. The *teres minor* arises from the upper two-thirds of the lateral border of the scapula on its dorsal surface. It inserts into the lowermost portion of the greater tubercle of the humerus, below the insertion of the infraspinatus.

4. The *subscapularis* is a large triangular muscle which arises from the subscapular fossa and is inserted into the lesser tubercle of the humerus.

The most important action of the rotator cuff muscles is to stabilize the head of the humerus in the glenoid (Figure 12.9). For instance, during abduction the subscapularis, the infraspinatus, and the teres minor counteract the strong pull of the deltoid and the supraspinatus, to enable the arm to be abducted away from

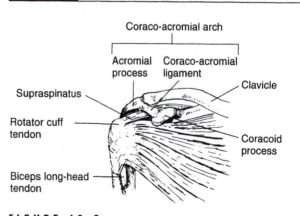

FIGURE 12.9
The relationship of the supraspinatus (and rotator cuff) to the coraco-acromial ligament

the body. Otherwise the deltoid and the supraspinatus would tend to elevate the head of the humerus instead of abducting the arm. (The initiation of abduction is one of the main functions of the supraspinatus.) The supraspinatus also acts as an internal rotator of the humerus when the arm is hanging next to the side, while the infraspinatus and the teres minor, together with the posterior fibers of the deltoid muscle, externally rotate the humerus. (These are the only external rotators of the humerus.)

THE BICEPS: The biceps has two heads:

1. The *short head* arises from the coracoid process.

2. The *long head* originates from the glenoid labrum at the superior aspect of the glenoid cavity within the shoulder joint. It then arches over the head of the humerus and descends into the bicipital groove. The groove is covered by the transverse humeral ligament and by the tendon of the pectoralis major muscle.

Insertion is by means of a single tendon into the tuberosity of the radius. The main action of the biceps is to supinate the forearm. It also flexes the elbow and has a weak effect on forward flexion of the shoulder joint. The long head can exert some downward pressure on the upper end of the humerus and in this way may prevent the head of the humerus from moving upward as the deltoid muscle contracts.

THE TRICEPS: The triceps muscle is situated on the back of the upper arm and has three heads.

1. The *long head* arises from the glenoid on the scapula.

2. The *lateral head* arises from the posterior surface and the lateral border of the humerus.

3. The *medial head* arises from the posterior surface of the humerus below the radial groove.

The three heads blend together to form a tendon, which inserts into the olecranon on the ulna. The long head of the triceps helps form two spaces as it travels between the teres minor and the teres major muscles. One of these spaces is the "quadrangular space," bounded by the subscapularis and the teres minor above, the teres major below, the long head of the triceps medially, and the humerus laterally. This space contains the posterior circumflexed humeral vessels and the axillary nerve. Both of these are important, for if they are damaged or compressed in this space, they cause pain and incapacity of the shoulder joint.

The main function of the triceps is that of extension of the forearm and the arm. When the arm is extended,

the long head also assists in extending the shoulder and adducting it (Table 12.1).

Nerves and Arteries

The brachial plexus and the brachial artery run in close proximity to the shoulder joint and can be damaged in an injury of the shoulder girdle, such as an anterior dislocation of the humerus or a posteriorly displaced fracture of the clavicle. When an injury involves the shoulder girdle, it is therefore important to check the blood and nerve supply to the upper limb. The dermatome areas (that is, the areas of skin supplied by a particular nerve root) should be noted (Figure 12.10).

Evaluation Procedures

1. *Observe* the athlete.

    a. From the *front* (Figure 12.11), note

        (1) general posture

        (2) prominence of the sternoclavicular joint (subluxation)

        (3) deformity of the shaft of the clavicle (fracture)

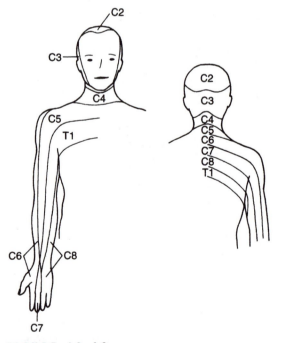

FIGURE 12.10
Dermatomes of the upper extremity

TABLE 12.1 *Main action of muscles around the shoulder girdle*

Movement	Main Muscles Involved
Flexion	Deltoid (anterior portion) Coracobrachialis Pectoralis major (clavicular portion)
Extension	Latissimus dorsi Teres major Deltoid (posterior portion)
Abduction	Deltoid (middle portion) Supraspinatus Serratus anterior (helps steady scapula; allows deltoid to function)
Adduction	Pectoralis major Latissimus dorsi
External rotators	Infraspinatus Teres minor (Deltoid—posterior portion)
Internal rotators	Subscapularis Pectoralis major Latissimus dorsi Teres major (Deltoid—anterior portion)
Depresses raised arm against resistance	Pectoralis major Latissimus dorsi Teres major
Arm abducted with the head of the humerus prevented from moving upwards by:	Subscapularis Infraspinatus Teres minor Biceps—long head
Scapula stabilization	Trapezius Serratus anterior Rhomboids
Scapula protraction (reaching and punching)	Trapezius Serratus anterior Rhomboids
Scapula retraction (pulling scapulae toward each other)	Rhomboid major Rhomboid minor
Elevation of scapulae (shoulder shrugs)	Trapezius Levator scapulae

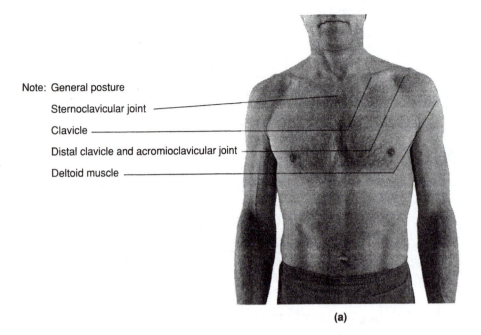

Note: General posture

Sternoclavicular joint

Clavicle

Distal clavicle and acromioclavicular joint

Deltoid muscle

(a)

Observing the athlete from behind

Note: Alignment of the head and neck

Any muscle atrophy, especially
the deltoid
and supraspinatus

The position and movement
of the scapula

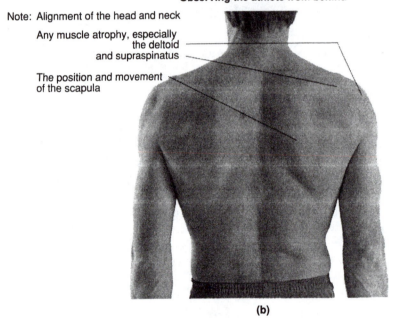

(b)

FIGURE 12.11
(a) Observing the athlete from the front (b) Observing the athlete from behind

(4) prominence of the distal clavicle and the acromioclavicular joint (shoulder separation or a shoulder pointer)

(5) wasting of the deltoid muscle (axillary nerve lesion)

b. From the *side*, note

(1) alignment of the cervical and thoracic spines

(2) swelling over the front of the shoulder joint

(3) position of the acromioclavicular joint

c. From *behind*, note

    (1) posture of the head and neck

    (2) muscle atrophy—particularly the deltoid and supraspinatus

    (3) position of movement of the scapula

2. Ask athlete to *point* with one finger to the area of pain.

3. *Palpate* for

    a. skin temperature (warmth suggests inflammation)

    b. tenderness (avoiding painful area until last)

      (1) sternoclavicular joint

      (2) clavicle

      (3) acromioclavicular joint

      (4) biceps tendon, long head

      (5) under acromion process

      (6) greater tuberosity of humerus

      (7) anterior capsule

      (8) posterior capsule

      (9) posterior glenoid

      (10) scapula

      (11) trapezius and rhomboid muscles, and trigger points in the area of these muscles

4. Examine the following areas first, as they may refer pain to the shoulder.

    a. cervical spine (see p. 300)

    b. thoracic outlet (see section on thoracic outlet syndrome p. 231)

    c. temporomandibular joint

      (1) observe range of motion

      (2) observe symmetry of mouth opening and closing

      (3) palpate for tenderness, swelling, and clicking of the joint

5. *Check skin sensation* of the shoulder and arm and feel the distal pulses.

6. *Check active range of motion* of the shoulder—performed by the athlete (Table 12.2 and Figure 12.12).

7. *Check active range of motion*—performed against resistance. The same movements are performed, this time against isometric manual resistance provided by the examiner. Note if any weakness is present, and observe the position of the arm and the location of the pain.

TABLE 12.2   *Movement of the arm at the shoulder*

> *Following are the main movements of the shoulder girdle that need to be tested (Figure 12.13). Note range as well as smoothness of motion at the glenohumeral, acromioclavicular, and sternoclavicular joints, as well as scapulothoracic action.*

1. Forward flexion
2. Backward extension
3. Abduction—observe the scapulohumeral rhythm from behind
4. Adduction
5. Internal rotation with arm at side
6. External rotation with arm at side
7. External rotation with arm in abduction
8. Internal rotation with arm in abduction
9. Horizontal extension with arm in abduction
10. Horizontal flexion with arm in abduction—try to place the hand on the opposite shoulder
11. Internal rotation posteriorly—attempt to touch the opposite scapula
12. Protraction and retraction
13. Shoulder shrugs
14. Perform the particular movement that causes pain, or is thought to be associated with the condition, e.g., a tennis serve or a baseball pitch

8. *Check passive range of motion*—feel for the quality of the end point in the range of motion and for any clicks or pops.

9. *Test for stability*

    a. Glenohumeral joint (apprehension tests or signs)—Apprehension tests are designed to induce anxiety and protective muscular response as the shoulder is brought into a position associated with instability. In the anterior apprehension test, the arm is placed at 90 degrees of abduction in an externally rotated position (Figure 12.13a). Anterior pressure is then applied to the back of the shoulder while the shoulder is rotated externally. Immediate discomfort and apprehension may be experienced by the athlete if the glenohumeral joint is unstable in an anterior and inferior direction. The deltoid muscle will also contract

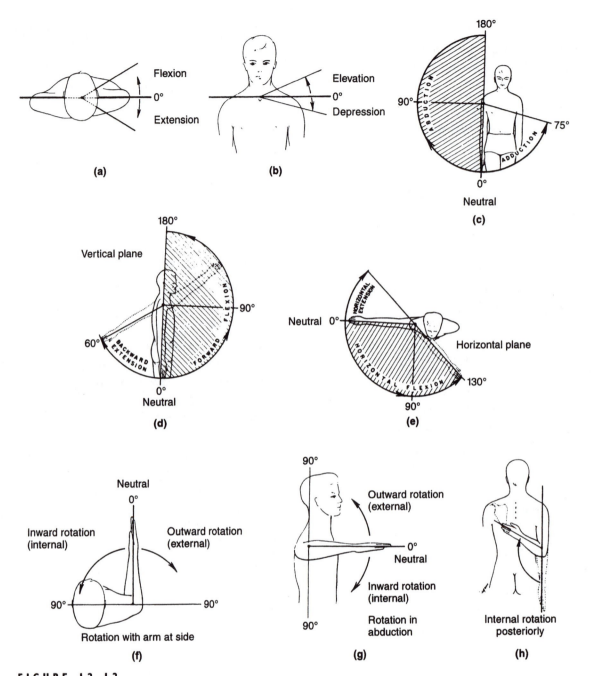

FIGURE 12.12
Shoulder joint—range of motion
(Reproduced with permission of the American Academy of Orthopaedic Surgeons)

reflexively. Pain may be experienced along the inferior rim.

A variation of this test is to place the athlete's arm at 90 degrees of abduction (Figure 12.13b). The elbow is supported on the examiner's shoulder and the examiner's cupped hands are placed over the proximal humerus. The muscles surrounding the shoulder should be relaxed while the examiner directs a downward force on the proximal humerus. The humerus will displace in an inferior direction if laxity is present.

An additional variation of the apprehension test is performed with the athletic supine and the shoulder abducted and rotated externally. The examiner progressively increases the degree

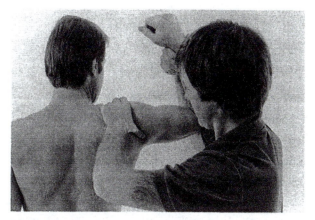

FIGURE 12.13a
Examining for anterior stability of the glenohumeral joint
The arm is externally rotated while an anteriorly directed force is applied to the posterior aspect of the humeral head.

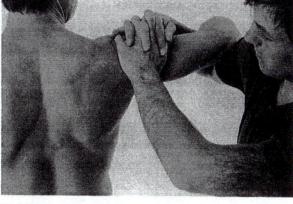

FIGURE 12.13b
Testing for antero-inferior glenohumeral instability
The deltoid muscles should be completely relaxed as a downward force is applied to the proximal humerus.

of external rotation and notes the development of pain or apprehension (Figure 12.13c).

The *relocation test* (or Fowler's test)[6] is also helpful in evaluating anterior instability. After having performed and noted the response to the supine apprehension test described above, the examiner places his or her hand over the anterior shoulder of the athlete. A posterior-directed force is applied with the hand to prevent anterior translation of the humeral head. The arm is then again abducted and rotated externally to end range. A positive result is obtained when this posteriorly-directed force

allows increased external rotation and diminishes associated pain and apprehension (see Figure 12.13d).

To detect apprehension when the humerus is forced posteriorly, the athlete should stand with arms at the side. The shoulder girdle is stabilized by the examiner and pressure is exerted in a posterior director against the humeral head.

Another method to detect posterior instability is to have the athlete lying supine with

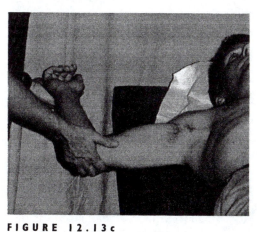

FIGURE 12.13c
Apprehension test in supine
The arm is abductal and rotated externally. The examiner progressively increases the degree of external rotation and notes the development of athlete's apprehension.

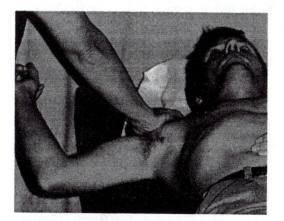

FIGURE 12.13d
Relocation test or Fowler's sign
The arm is placed in the abducted, externally rotated position until pain or apprehension is elicited. The maneuver is then repeated with a posterior-directed force applied to the humeral head. Relief of pain or apprehension with improved external rotation is indicative of anterior subluxation.

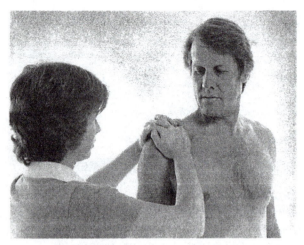

FIGURE 12.14
Testing for acromioclavicular joint stability
A squeezing action may demonstrate abnormal motion or produce pain.

the shoulder at 90 degrees of forward flexion and rotated internally. Posteriorly-directed pressure is then applied against the elbow in an attempt to sublux the humerus posteriorly.

b. Acromioclavicular joint—Stability may be tested by placing cupped hands over the acromioclavicular joint.[7] One palm is placed on the anterior aspect of the clavicle, while the other is placed over the spine of the scapula. The hands are then squeezed together, which causes a "glide" motion through the acromio-clavicular joint and may demonstrate abnormal laxity or produce pain (Figure 12.14).

c. Sternoclavicular joint—Stability of the stern-oclavicular joint should be tested mainly in the anteroposterior direction. Care should be exercised in grasping the proximal clavicle, as this

may be uncomfortable for the athlete. Abnormal motion or pain should be noted.

10. *Demonstrate impingement signs.* There are two methods of demonstrating impingement of the humerus, supraspinatus, and biceps tendons against the inferior surface of the acromion and coraco-acromial ligament:

a. Bring the arm into the extreme of forward flexion, with the forearm held in supination. If pain is experienced when the arm is brought to maximum forward flexion against resistance, a positive impingement sign is present.[8]

b. An alternative method is to have the athlete hold the arm at 90° of flexion in internal rotation and pronation. The elbow is stabilized and the forearm brought rapidly downward, which attempts to force the forearm into maximal internal rotation and brings the head of the humerus sharply up against the inferior aspect of the acromion. Pain that is localized to the area of the coraco-acromial arch is indicative of impingement (Figure 12.15).[9]

11. *Muscle testing.* Test individual muscle groups to locate any weakness (Table 12.3).

12. *Test nerve functions:*

a. Axillary nerve—Loss of sensation over the lateral aspect of the upper arm (Figure 12.16), as well as weakness and lack of tone of the anterior and middle deltoids during abduction, indicates an axillary nerve lesion.

b. Long thoracic nerve—Test for "winging" of the scapula (paralysis of the serratus anterior muscle) by having the athlete resist downward pressure against the arm when held at 90° of flexion (Figure 12.17).[10] An alternative is the "climb-the-wall" test.

c. Dorsal scapular nerve (to the rhomboids)—Test for partial winging of the scapula when

(a)

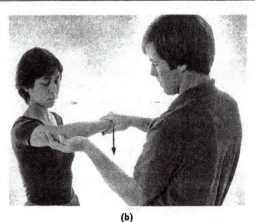

(b)

FIGURE 12.15
Impingement signs
(a) Bring the arm into extreme forward elevation (flexion) with the humerus in external rotation (the forearm in supination). (b) The elbow is stabilized as the forearm is forced downward, bring the shoulder into internal rotation. The head of the humerus is thus forced against the acromion and the coraco-acromial arch.

TABLE 12.3 *Manual muscle testing*

The following tests localize the strain to the particular muscle group tested, and comparison of the two extremities helps detect weaknesses.[9]

1. Arm at 90° of abduction, full external rotation and supination, force directed downward (*anterior deltoid*)

2. As above, but with some internal rotation and palm facing downward (*middle deltoid*)

3. As above, with full internal rotation and palm facing backward (*posterior deltoid*)

4. Arm at the side, elbow at 90°, force directed toward midline (*teres minor*)

5. Arm at 90° of abduction, elbow bent, force directed downward (*infraspinatus*)

6. Arm at 90° of abduction, force directed upward (*subscapularis*)

7. Resistance to initiation of abduction (*supraspinatus*)

8. Arm at 90° of abduction, 60° of horizontal flexion, full internal rotation, force directed downward (*supraspinatus*)

9. Resistance to shoulder shrugs (*trapezius*)

10. Arm at 90° of flexion, palm facing downward force directed downward (*serratus anterior*)

11. Hand on hip, elbow at 90°, force directed forward on the elbow (*rhomboids*)

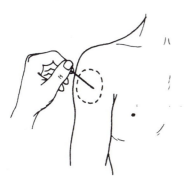

FIGURE 12.16
Sensation loss over lateral side of upper from an axillary nerve lesion

the shoulder is extended in a slightly abducted position against resistance; or, with the hand on the waist, the elbow is forced forwards (Figure 12.18).

   d. Suprascapular nerve (to the supraspinatus and infraspinatus)—Test by initiating abduction

FIGURE 12.17
Testing the long thoracic nerve
If the long thoracic nerve is damaged, the serratus anterior muscle will cease to function, resulting in winging of the scapula.

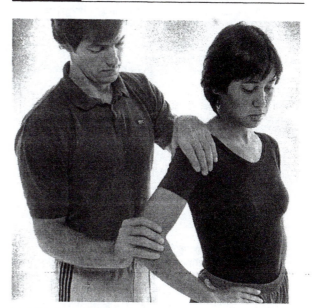

FIGURE 12.18
Testing the dorsal scapular nerve, which supplies the rhomboid muscles
The athlete resists the forward force on the elbow, while the trainer observes contraction of the rhomboids and partial winging of the scapula.

against resistance (supraspinatus) and by resisting external rotation (infraspinatus).

The trainer should be aware that pain may be referred to the shoulder from irritation of the diaphragm due to free gas or blood, from infection, and from cardiac ischemia or gallstones.

Table 12.4 is designed to help differentiate the common shoulder conditions that may present during an athletic event.

TABLE 12.4 *On-field examination of acute shoulder injuries*

Examination Procedure	Possibilities Examiner Should Consider
I. Symptoms 1. Pain and/or burning around shoulder area, initially diffuse. 2. Weakness of arm and shoulder girdle. 3. Arm just hangs down, or is supported with opposite arm.	Acromioclavicular joint separation. Shoulder dislocation. Fractured clavicle. Brachial plexus lesion. Rotator-cuff tear. Biceps subluxation. Fractured humerus.
II. Ask athlete to point out tender area (this is often very difficult for the athlete to do initially).	
III. *Observe* and then *palpate* gently: 1. Sternoclavicular joint 2. Clavicle, midshaft 3. Clavicle, outer end 4. Acromioclavicular joint 5. Contour of shoulder 6. Rest of shoulder and upper arm	Sprain/dislocation. Fracture. Pointer or acromioclavicular separation. Acromioclavicular separation Shoulder subluxiation or dislocation. Fractured humerus.
IV. If all above are negative, *palpate more firmly* over: 1. Anterior capsule 2. Biceps 3. Lateral to and under acromion process 4. Posterior capsule 5. Greater and lesser tuberosities of humerus	Shoulder subluxation. Subluxation of long head of biceps. Supraspinatus (rotator-cuff) tear. Posterior dislocation or anterior subluxation. Avulsion fracture; greater tuberosity (supraspinatus insertion) or lesser tuberosity (subscapularis insertion).
V. *Range of motion* Check shoulder through full range of active motion. Then test range of motion against resistance.	If athlete can't bring arm across chest (adduction and internal rotation) an anterior dislocation is probably present. If athlete can't abduct and externally rotate, a rotator-cuff (and deltoid) injury or posterior dislocation is probably present. Weakness of flexion and abduction may mean: 1. Muscle strain, e.g., supraspinatus strain 2. Brachial plexus lesion 3. Localized nerve lesion, e.g., axillary nerve 4. Inhibition due to pain
VI. Check sensation over neck, shoulder, and arm.	Possible neck injury.
VII. If all above are negative, examine for tenderness over brachial plexus, neck musculature, and posterior spinous process of cervical vertebrae.	
VIII. If all the above are negative: 1. Test for subluxation of shoulder— apprehension sign. 2. Put neck through full range of motion, then full range of motion against resistance; also, compression test. 3. Test power of each muscle group of the arm.	

Prevention of Shoulder Injuries

1. *Falling technique.* Perhaps the most important preventive measure is for the athlete to learn how to fall correctly. This technique should be developed until it becomes a habit. The athlete should learn not to fall on the outstretched arm or the point of the shoulder, but rather to roll over so as to absorb the shock of impact. Falling down flat and hard is bound to cause an injury. Most people, however, fall incorrectly, and the correct techniques have to be developed by practicing falling drills. Coaches and trainers should be educated in the importance of this type of drill, particularly for athletes engaged in contact sports.

2. *Shoulder pad placement.* In football, incorrect fitting of the shoulder pads may be responsible for the occasional acromioclavicular dislocation seen in this sport. Not tying the jersey down, or cutting the sleeves, are other predisposing factors because they allow the shoulder pads to slip out of position and expose the acromioclavicular joint to possible injury.

3. *Tackling technique.* Shoulder dislocations are most frequently encountered through poor tackling technique, particularly when the arm is abducted and externally rotated while trying to stop the ballcarrier. The danger of this form of tackling should be constantly stressed so that it will not be attempted.

4. *Muscle development.* It is imperative, particularly in contact sports, that the musculature around the shoulders be strengthened to protect the shoulder girdle. This applies especially to the larger muscle groups such as the trapezius, the deltoid, the subscapularis, and the latissimus dorsi.

5. *Warm-up techniques.* In throwing activities (as well as in sports such as gymnastics, tennis, and swimming) it is important to perform a gradual warm-up program before undertaking vigorous activity. Minor injuries which occur before adequate warm-up has taken place tend to plague participants of these sports because of the repetitive nature of the shoulder-girdle motion. Included in warm-up is an adequate stretching program. This should be a slow, relaxed type of stretching that keeps the stretch well within the limits of discomfort.

6. *Throwing technique.* A large percentage of injuries in the throwing sports occur because of incorrect technique. This predisposing factor needs to be corrected as early as possible in an athlete's career so as to prevent permanent injury.

Types of Injuries

Injuries to the Sternoclavicular Joint

SPRAINS AND DISLOCATIONS: The most common injury to the sternoclavicular joint is a *sprain*, which occurs particularly in such activities as football and wrestling, when the athlete falls on his or her side with the opposition on top. This drives the shoulder forward and inward, applying a force to the clavicle which can disrupt the costoclavicular and the sternoclavicular ligaments (Figure 12.19). If the force is severe enough, a third-degree tearing of the ligaments can occur, resulting in a *dislocation* of the sternoclavicular joint. The proximal end of the clavicle may be forced medially, upward and forward, commonly resulting in swelling and deformity over the sternoclavicular joint on the side involved.

On occasion, however, the force may drive the clavicle backward (a posterior dislocation). This will produce little in the way of deformity, but may cause a great deal of distress if the clavicle impinges on the trachea and interferes with breathing. If this happens, the athlete may find that it is more comfortable to sit forward than to lie down. A posterior dislocation is also dangerous because it can rupture the underlying blood vessels.

Treatment consists of ice application, an arm sling, and anti-inflammatory medication if necessary. If the instability is severe, a plaster-of-Paris, figure-eight bandage should be used. In some cases, if reduction cannot be maintained, open reduction with fixation may be necessary.

Fracture of the Shaft of the Clavicle

A fracture of the clavicular shaft is a common injury, particularly in the child or adolescent. It usually occurs

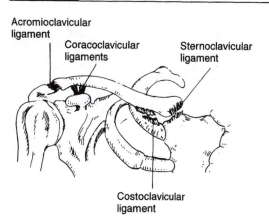

FIGURE 12.19
The sternoclavicular and costoclavicular ligaments showing a complete sprain of these ligaments

from a fall on the outstretched arm or on the point of the shoulder, less commonly from a direct blow. Most fractures occur in the middle third. Displacement is due to the muscle pull—the proximal portion is pulled superiorly in relation to the distal fragment (Figure 12.20).

In most cases the diagnosis is obvious, with a visible and palpable deformity that is accompanied by marked ecchymosis and pain. In some cases, such as the pre-adolescent with a greenstick fracture, a deformity may not occur and pain and swelling may be the only signs. If the initial X-rays are negative but pain and tenderness persist, X-rays should be repeated, because a fracture may not show up for a week or two after the initial injury.

Treatment consists of ice and a figure-eight bandage to support the shoulders and pull them backward (Figure 12.21).

Contusion to the Outer End of the Clavicle ("Shoulder Pointer")

Contusions to the outer end of the clavicle are frequent and painful injuries. It is most important to be sure that one is not dealing with an acromioclavicular joint injury.

SYMPTOMS AND SIGNS: The symptoms are usually localized to the distal end of the clavicle, but may radiate into the trapezius muscle on that side. Swelling and tenderness are localized to the area of the distal clavicle and do not involve the acromioclavicular joint. There may be some tenderness and spasm of the trapezius muscle. Careful palpation should be made, to ensure that neither the acromioclavicular joint nor the coracoclavicular ligament is involved. There should be

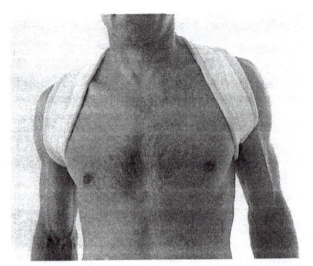

FIGURE 12.21
Figure-eight support used for treating a fractured clavicle

no instability of the clavicle either on clinical examination or on X-rays (Figure 12.22).

X-RAYS: These should be taken in order to exclude a fracture of the distal clavicle or a separation of the acromioclavicular joint.

TREATMENT: Ice immediately. Early use of anti-inflammatory medication is beneficial. An injection of local anesthetic containing a cortisone preparation and hyaluronidase is particularly useful to reduce pain and

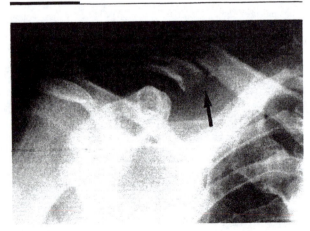

FIGURE 12.20
X-ray—fracture of the clavicle

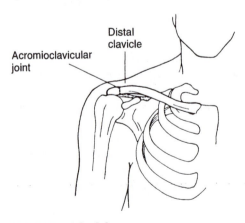

FIGURE 12.22
A contusion to the distal end of the clavicle will produce localized tenderness
If there is tenderness over the acromioclavicular joint, a sprain of this joint should should be suspected.

tenderness. A pad can be used to protect the area (a donut pad should be fashioned and placed over the tender area). Progressive exercises of the shoulder, particularly of the trapezius muscle, should be instituted to prevent any atrophy from occurring.

COMPLICATIONS: Long-term complications may occur, particularly when the athlete is inadequately treated. Progressive calcification around the distal end of the clavicle can cause a painful deformity. Osteophyte formation and degeneration of the acromioclavicular joint can also occur, necessitating excision of the distal clavicle. Osteolysis of the distal clavicle is an uncommon condition but one which can occur as a result of a contusion to the distal clavicle.

Osteolysis of the Distal Clavicle

Osteolysis of the distal clavicle is a relatively rare condition in which a portion of the distal clavicle may resorb. The diagnosis is made by X-ray visualization of the distal clavicle (Figure 12.23).

ETIOLOGY: The exact etiological mechanism is poorly understood. It may be related to a type of vascular necrosis, although this is not clearly understood. Osteolysis of the distal clavicle usually develops following:

1. A relatively minor injury to the distal clavicle such as a first-degree or a mild second-degree acromioclavicular joint sprain or contusion to the distal clavicle.

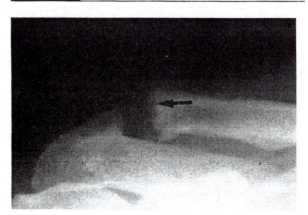

FIGURE 12.23
X-ray showing osteolysis of the distal clavicle
Note the "moth-eaten" clavicle, as well as the widening of the acromioclavicular joint.

2. Repeated minor traumata such as happens to weight lifters, gymnasts, ice-hockey players, and judo exponents.

3. A severe injury to the acromioclavicular joint or distal clavicle—much less common than the preceding two causes.

SYMPTOMS AND SIGNS: Pain in the region of the acromioclavicular joint and limitation of extreme shoulder motion appear to be the predominant symptoms. Enlargement of the soft tissue around the distal clavicle can be observed. This lump is often very tender to the touch.

X-RAYS: It usually takes a minimum of two to three weeks for the X-ray changes to appear after the initial acute injury. However, in cases of repetitive minor trauma, symptoms may be present for some weeks or months before the changes appear on the X-ray. The earliest changes are sclerosis or cystic degeneration in the distal clavicle, followed by frank osteolysis.

COURSE: Some cases resolve spontaneously, though this is uncommon if the athlete continues to participate.

TREATMENT: Athletes such as weight lifters and gymnasts find their effectiveness limited. It appears at this time that rest for a period of six months or more is required to allow the lesion to heal so that return to participation may be pain-free.

Corticosteroid injections have not been reported to be beneficial and may, in fact, be harmful. They should be used judicially. Surgical removal of the distal clavicle (distal to the coracoclavicular ligament) may be necessary in cases that are resistant to conservative treatment. This surgery has been successful in selected cases, but should not be considered until at least 6 to 12 months of activity limitation has failed to result in improvement.

Acromioclavicular Joint Sprain (Shoulder Separation)

The acromioclavicular joint is a relatively unstable joint that is easily disrupted. A separation implies a sprain of the ligaments supporting the acromioclavicular joint (Figure 12.24). Mild sprains may involve only the acromioclavicular capsule, while severe sprains may totally disrupt not only the acromioclavicular capsule, but also the costoclavicular ligaments (the conoid and trapezoid). These ligaments are discussed in the section

(a)   **(b)**

FIGURE 12.24

Acromioclavicular joint separation mechanisms of injury (a) Falling on the point of the shoulder
(b) Falling on the hand of an outstretched arm
This mechanism is nonspecific, and may result in an injury to one or more structures from the wrist
to the clavicle.

on functional anatomy at the beginning of the chapter, and illustrated in Figure 12.4.

Allman[11] has classified acromioclavicular sprains as Grades I, II, or III representing, respectively, no involvement, partial tearing, and complete disruption of the acromioclavicular and coracoclavicular ligaments (Figure 12.25 and Table 12.5).

Grade I (mild) injuries are characterized by sprained but intact acromioclavicular ligaments and an intact coracoclavicular ligament.

In Grade II (moderate) injuries, the acromioclavicular ligament is completely torn and the coracoclavicular ligament is sprained but intact. There may be a slight relative upward displacement of the distal end of the clavicle secondary to a minor stretching of the coracoclavicular ligament.

In Grade III (severe) injuries, complete acromioclavicular dislocation occurs, as both the acromioclavicular and coracoclavicular ligaments are completely disrupted. Separation in the coracoclavicular interspace is 25 to 100 percent greater than the normal shoulder.

Rockwood[12] has further classified the more severe injuries as grades IV to VI, depending upon the direction and amount of acromioclavicular displacement and the extent of associated injury to the deltoid and trapezius muscles.

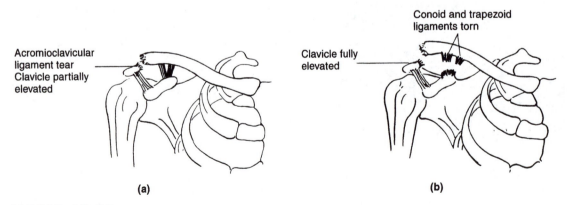

(a)   **(b)**

FIGURE 12.25

(a) Second-degree acromioclavicular joint sprain (b) Third-degree acromioclavicular joint sprain

TABLE 12.5 *Findings in an acromioclavicular-joint sprain*

Degree of Sprain	Pathology	Clinical Findings
First-Degree	Sprain of the acromioclavicular ligament or capsule. Coracoclavicular ligament intact.	Tenderness and swelling over the acromioclavicular joint only. Minimal limitation of shoulder's range of motion. Clavicle stable when moved. No elevation of the clavicle.
Second-Degree	Severe sprain of the acromioclavicular ligament. Partial sprain or stretching of the coracoclavicular ligament.	Tenderness over the acromioclavicular joint (2+). Swelling over the acromioclavicular joint (2+). Some tenderness over the coracolavicular ligaments. Shoulder motion considerably limited due to pain. Slight elevation of the clavicle relative to the acromion process.
Third-Degree	Complete tearing of the acromioclavicular and coracoclavicular ligaments. There is often damage to the deltoid and trapezius muscles.	The athlete supports the arm, as the symptoms are markedly increased when the arm hangs. Tenderness 3+. Swelling 3+. Obvious elevation of the clavicle relative to the acromion process.

MECHANISM OF INJURY

1. The typical mechanism of injury is a direct blow to the superior aspect of the acromion, as may occur in a fall onto the tip of the shoulder. The force drives the acromion process of the scapula downward. The clavicle, which initially moves with the acromion, may become blocked by the first rib, driving it in an upward direction.[13] This is the commonest mechanism of injury.

2. The athlete falls on the outstretched hand, transmitting the force up the arm and through the acromioclavicular joint.

3. The athlete falls on the outstretched hand which is at right angles to the body. Contact is then made by the opposition against the shoulder, forcing the shoulder forward on the fixed arm.

4. In some sports, such as ice hockey, the acromioclavicular joint frequently gives rise to chronic symptoms.[14] The injury seems to be due to the indirect forces on the shoulder that are inherent in that sport.

SYMPTOMS AND SIGNS:

The arm and the shoulder on the side of the injury usually droop. Severe pain accompanies most acromioclavicular sprains, but localization by the athlete is often vague. Tenderness to palpation is more specific, located directly over the acromioclavicular joint. There may also be tenderness along the clavicle and the attachments of the trapezius and the deltoid muscle. In very severe sprains there may be tenderness over the coracoclavicular ligaments as well.

The athlete should be observed from the front, from the side, and from behind. The clavicle may ride above the level of the acromion process. This can be accentuated by gentle downward traction on the arm. The clavicle should also be gently mobilized while palpating over the acromioclavicular joint in order to observe if any excessive motion is present.

X-RAYS:

Anteroposterior X-rays of the acromioclavicular joint should be taken to exclude fractures of the clavicle, acromion, coracoid, or humerus. Stress views of both shoulders should then be taken with the athlete standing. Weights are suspended from the wrists in order to apply traction through the arms to the acromioclavicular joint. A second-degree separation may show a slight elevation of the clavicle relative to the acromion process, and a slight increase in the distance between the coracoid process and the clavicle. In the severe third-degree separation, the clavicle rides high above the acromion process and there is a wide gap between the coracoid process and the clavicle, compared with the opposite side (Figure 12.26 a and b).[15]

If the trainer suspects a rare posterior dislocation of the clavicle (i.e., the clavicle moves in a posterior

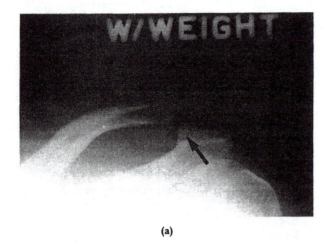

(a)

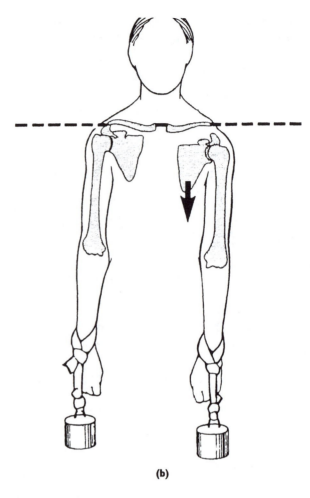

(b)

FIGURE 12.26

(a) X-ray of a third-degree acromioclavicular sprain
Note the clavicle riding above the level of the acromion process, and the widening of the space between the coracoid process and the clavicle, as well as between the acomion and the clavicle.

(b) Schematic drawing of a patient with a complete grade III acromioclavicular dislocation
The major deformity seen in this injury is a downward displacement of the scapula and upper extremity—*not* an upward elevation of the clavicle.

(Modified from Rockwood, C, and Green, D, *Fractures in Adults,* 3rd ed., Philadelphia, J. B. Lipincott, Philadelphia, 1991.)

direction and not upward), then the Alexander view[16] should be taken (this is a shoulder-forward position with the shoulder against the X-ray plate).[17]

DIFFERENTIAL DIAGNOSIS: It is important to differentiate acromioclavicular joint lesions from contusions to the distal end of the clavicle (shoulder pointer). A shoulder pointer implies a contusion only—there is no ligamentous involvement. The primary differentiating feature is the area of tenderness. In the shoulder pointer there is no tenderness over the acromioclavicular joint. However it is not uncommon to have a combination of the two injuries (i.e., an acromioclavicular

joint sprain plus a contusion to the distal end of the clavicle).

TREATMENT: With the exception of certain type III injuries, most authors agree on treatment for all types of AC separations.

1. *First-degree separation:* First-degree acromioclavicular sprains usually respond well to ice and immobilization in a sling, with analgesics and/or anti-inflammatories until discomfort dissipates (usually seven to ten days). Gentle range-of-motion exercises can be initiated to preserve joint arthrokinematics as discomfort allows. Ranges of motion to be avoided are

horizontal adduction past neutral, and the extremes of forward flexion and abduction. A donut pad may be placed over the acromioclavicular joint when the athlete participates in contact sports.

2. *Second-degree separations.* Second-degree separations generally also respond well to symptomatic treatment followed by early pain-free motion. Because by definition a second-degree acromioclavicular sprain involves the coracoclavicular ligaments with possible elevation of the clavicle, some practitioners advocate the use of immobilizing devices such as the Kenny Howard sling (Figure 12.27), taping, or casting. These bracing techniques attempt to place a downward force on the distal clavicle, while simultaneously lifting at the elbow to approximate torn ligament ends. Such immobilizing forces must be maintained twenty-four hours a day for up to four to six weeks. Patient compliance is a problem, as is skin breakdown beneath straps and padding.

In a retrospective study of 62 partial, and 54 complete acromioclavicular separations by Jacobs et al.,[18] no difference in the satisfactory results were noted between no treatment and those treated with prolonged immobilization. "In our opinion, poor results are dependent not so much on the type of treatment as on such factors as damage to the meniscus, inverted intra-articular ligaments, post-operative attritional changes in the AC joint, biceps tendinitis, and associated muscle tears." Their recommendation was that immobilization as the primary method for treatment need only restrict acromioclavicular joint motion during the usually short period after injury when the patient has pain. A sling and swathe for approximately two weeks was deemed adequate.

3. *Third-degree separation.* Third degree (Type 3) injury treatment remains controversial.

   a. conservative treatment: If the clavicle can be reduced and is easily held in place, use of a Kenny Howard sling, taping, or casting may be attempted. It is applied for a period of six to eight weeks.

   b. skillful neglect: Many sports medicine physicians feel it is unnecessary to immobilize or repair third-degree acromioclavicular separations.[19] Failure to reconstruct the acromioclavicular joint has not been found to result in impaired strength or functional use of the arm.[20] Many athletes can and do function well with complete dislocations of the AC joint. Symptomatic treatment followed by early pain-free motion to maintain joint arthrokinematics is stressed. When this motion can be accomplished comfortably, further rehabilitation exercises are progressively instituted. The athlete is then permitted to return to activities with padding placed over the joint. Modifications of the shoulder pads are made on football players so that the forces are borne on the chest rather than on the point of the shoulder. Muscle strengthening exercises (with particular emphasis on the trapezius, deltoid, and biceps) are continued until the two arms have equal power through a full range of motion. Physicians using this method claim equally good long-term results as compared to other methods of treatment, and they point out that athletes treated this way are usually able to return to participation much earlier than those who have had long-term immobilization or surgical treatment. Even if the functional results are good, there is a definite cosmetic deformity as a result of the clavicle protruding above the acromion process.

   c. surgical treatment: Some surgeons feel that functional relationships should be maintained in the shoulder and that a high-riding clavicle will disrupt normal upper extremity arthrokinematics. In their opinion, restoration of normal anatomy gives the patient the best chance to attain normal function. Numerous surgical procedures are available; they generally either fix the reduced clavicle to the coracoid or stabilize across the acromioclavicular joint.

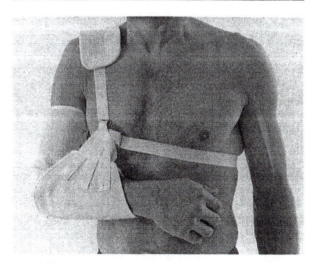

FIGURE 12.27
The Kenny Howard sling

COMPLICATIONS:

1. Pain, disability, and decrease in the range of shoulder motion may occasionally be troublesome complications. They are particularly common following first- and second-degree separations.[21,22,23]

2. Acromioclavicular joint injuries of all grades are associated with some risk of subsequent degenerative joint disease and chronic pain. This may result in spur formation, which leads not only to pain in the acromioclavicular joint but to an impingement syndrome involving the rotator cuff.

3. Soft-tissue calcification can also develop over the distal clavicle and render this area painful for a period of time.

4. Osteolysis (resorption) of the distal clavicle can occur.

5. Cosmetic deformity from an unreduced separation consists of an unsightly bulge over the clavicle.

REHABILITATION: Once swelling and pain are controlled, full range-of-motion activities can be initiated. Ranges of motion to avoid initially include horizontal adduction past neutral and extremes of forward flexion and abduction. Isometric shoulder strengthening (flexion, extension, abduction, adduction, and rotation) can usually be introduced relatively early into rehabilitation to maintain and increase static muscle strength without causing increased joint irritation. Isotonic activities (low weight/high reps) can be introduced as pain-free range improves, but weight should be limited initially to avoid overloading the involved joint. The range of strengthening exercises should be limited initially to no more than 90 degrees of flexion and abduction. Beyond about 90 degrees of shoulder elevation, the clavicle begins to rotate like a crank, increasing the rotational and shear forces at the AC joint. Rehabilitation exercises for the entire shoulder-girdle muscle complex should be continued until pre-injury power, strength, endurance, and flexibility are attained. Once the athlete has returned to competition, a strength maintenance program should be continued to ensure muscular support of the joint. Bench press, military press, and dips should be avoided, or at least limited in range until they can be performed pain-free.

Anterior Dislocation of the Glenohumeral Joint (Shoulder Dislocation)

The glenohumeral joint allows for great mobility of the shoulder. In comparison with the hip joint (another ball-and-socket type joint), there is minimal bony articulation between the head of the humerus and the glenoid fossa. In addition, the capsular ligaments are lax in all but the extremes of motion. Control of the joint is provided primarily by the dynamic action of the rotator cuff. When the forces driving the glenohumeral joint toward the limits of its normal ROM exceed the restraining strength of the shoulder muscles and capsular ligaments, the humeral head may tear out of the glenoid fossa and lodge outside. The majority of dislocations cause the humeral head to lie anterior and inferior to the glenoid rim, with only about 2 percent posterior (Table 12.6 and 12.7).

MECHANISM OF INJURY: The arm is forced into external rotation, usually while abducted and elevated. The greater tuberosity of the humeral head is levered against the acromion process, which forces it anterior and inferior. This tears the inferior glenohumeral ligament, the anterior capsule, and perhaps the labrum. The humeral head slips out, commonly in an antero-inferior direction; when the arm is dropped to the side, the head usually comes to rest under the coracoid process (Figure 12.28).[24]

SYMPTOMS: The athlete usually knows that the shoulder has dislocated and is very alarmed and apprehensive. Intense pain accompanies the initial dislocation (though recurrent dislocations may be much less painful). There may be tingling and numbness down the arm to the hand.

TABLE 12.6 *Dislocation of the glenohumeral joint (shoulder dislocation)*

1. *Anterior dislocation (98%)*

   (1) antero-inferior
   (2) inferior

   May end up in a subcoracoid (most common) or subglenoid position.

2. *Posterior dislocation (2%)*

   (1) subcramial (other positions have rarely been reported).

TABLE 12.7 *Anterior dislocation—antero-inferior type (most common)*

Severity	Sprain of Anterior Capsule and Ligaments	Subluxation of the Humerus	Dislocation
Glenohumeral movement	Arm abducted and externally rotated. Greater tuberosity forced against acromion.	Head of humerus levered partially out of glenoid.	Humerus slips out of glenoid and in an anterior and inferior direction. Usually located under the coracoid process (sub-coracoid) or under the anterior aspect of the glenoid (subglenoid).
Tissue damage	Partial tearing of the anterior and inferior capsule and ligaments with a variable decrease in tensile strength.	More complete tearing. Serious decrease in tensile strength. Rotator-cuff may be damaged.	Severe stretching and tearing. Limited or no tensile strength. Rotator-cuff may be damaged or torn.
Common complications	If laxity is present after healing, subluxation may occur.	Repeated subluxations with limitation of function. Compression and/or avulsion of greater tuberosity.	Repeated dislocations from progressively less force. Fracture of the greater tuberosity. Rotator-cuff injury or tear. Nerve damage. Axillary artery damage.
	$\longrightarrow$ $\longrightarrow$	increasing severity	$\longrightarrow$ $\longrightarrow$

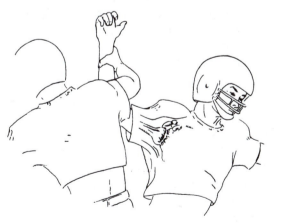

FIGURE 12.28

Mechanism of an anterior dislocation

The arm is forced into extension, abduction and external rotation.

SIGNS: Immediate recognition of anterior dislocation is often possible due to the characteristic position of the athlete's arm. Once the clothes are removed, note the:

1. Sharp contour of the affected limb in comparison with the smooth deltoid outline on the opposite side

2. Prominent acromion process

3. Humeral head beneath the coracoid process

4. Resistance by the athlete to any attempt to adduct or rotate the arm internally (i.e., the arm cannot be brought across the chest)

Always examine:

1. Sensation of the:

  a. lateral arm (Figure 12.16) The axillary nerve can be damaged as it circles around the surgical neck of the humerus. It may be bruised or torn during anterior dislocation and can lead to localized paresis or paralysis of the deltoid

b. radial aspect of the forearm (musculocutaneous nerve)

c. remainder of the arm, forearm, and hand
(other brachial plexus nerves)

2. Strength (this may be difficult to examine due to
pain) of the:

a. deltoid, as well as tone (C5)

b. forearm pronation and supination (C6)

c. wrist flexion and extension (C6 and C7)

d. finger flexion and extension (C7 and C8)

e. finger abduction and adduction (T1)

3. Radial pulse

4. Peripheral circulation to the fingernails. To check
this, the nails should be lightly squeezed, which produces a whiteness of the nail bed. When the pressure is
released, an almost immediate return to normal nail
color takes place if the circulation is normal; however, if
the microcirculation is impaired, there will be a lag
before this occurs.

X-RAYS: An anterior dislocation is usually easy to
see on the anteroposterior view. In addition, a West
Point or axillary view should be obtained to help evaluate the status of the glenoid.

Use of an arthrogram has been advocated by some
authorities. They point out that there is an ever-constant
threat of a rotator cuff tear occurring in conjunction
with an initial dislocation.[25]

COMPLICATIONS:

1. Two gross pathological lesions are frequently found
following anterior dislocations. Both predispose to
recurrent dislocations (Figure 12.29).

a. A Bankart lesion represents a group of anatomical lesions involving the anterior capsule,
labrum, and glenoid rim. As the humeral head
is wedged forward at the extreme of abduction
and external rotation, further motion is
restricted by the ligamentous capsule. If the
capsule and its anchors into the labrum and
glenoid rim are not of sufficient strength to
limit further translation, tearing can occur.
Laxity in the capsule, as well as a defect in the
labrum, can predispose the shoulder to recurrent dislocations when it is placed near the
extremes of abduction and external rotation.

b. A Hill-Sachs lesion represents an indentation
or eroded area on the articular surface of the
posterior humeral head. This occurs when the

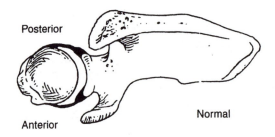
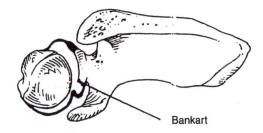
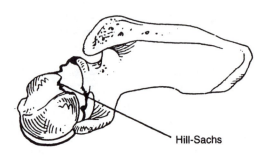

FIGURE 12.29
Gross pathological lesions in anterior shoulder dislocation.
(*Source: Athletic Training and Sports Medicine*, American
Academy of Orthopaedic Surgeons, Chicago, 1984.)

humeral head is wedged anterior and inferior
to the glenoid rim during a dislocation. The
posterior humeral head is compressed by the
bony edge of the anterior glenoid. The position
of this bony defect can predispose the shoulder
to repeated subluxations or dislocations.

2. In addition to injuries to the anterior capsule and
labrum, anterior dislocations can cause damage to the
nerves around the glenohumeral joint, in particular the
axillary nerve (which supplies the deltoid muscle) and
the musculocutaneous or ulnar nerve.

3. The primary artery traversing the shoulder region is
the axillary artery. Damage from a dislocating humeral
head can impair blood flow to the hand. Early recognition is essential.

4. Rotator cuff tears may occur especially in conjunction with an inferior type of anterior dislocation, even in
a young athlete.

5. Fractures of the humeral head and glenoid are relatively frequent in the older athlete. The greater tuberosity is the area most commonly fractured due to its shearing against the acromion process and the coracoacromial ligament.

REDUCTION OF A SHOULDER DISLOCATION:

The ideal time to reduce a shoulder dislocation is immediately after it has occurred. If there is a delay, pain and involuntary muscle spasm can make reduction difficult and necessitate a general anesthetic. *Reduction should be done by a physician.* An evaluation of the neurological and vascular structures should be performed and recorded before the reduction. If possible, X-rays should be taken before reduction is attempted; post-reduction X-rays should always be taken (Table 12.8).

Techniques of Reduction.

1. *Traction method.* This is the preferred and least traumatic method of reducing the dislocation (Figure 12.30). The athlete lies supine. The arm is held at between 30 and 45 degrees of abduction. Countertraction is applied by means of a swathe around the upper thorax, the pull being in the opposite direction to the traction on the affected arm. The affected arm is very gently pulled in its longitudinal axis while the patient is reassured and encouraged to relax. The traction should be very gentle, with a slow increase in the amount of force exerted. It often takes two to five minutes of gentle traction to reduce the shoulder. In most cases the arm will be felt to slip back into the glenoid fossa as the athlete relaxes. The arm should then be turned into internal rotation and held in place across the chest.

2. *Hippocratic method.* If countertraction is not possible, then place an unshod foot against the chest wall (not in the axilla). Apply the same technique of gentle traction while encouraging the patient to relax.

3. *Kocher's maneuver.* If the aforementioned methods do not work, a modified Kocher's maneuver can be performed by a physician who is skilled and experienced in using this technique. Complications can occur if the Kocher's maneuver is used in a forceful manner by an unskilled person.

The arm is gently rotated externally while traction is applied in the long axis of the humerus. This usually results in the humeral head slipping back into the glenoid. As this is felt to occur, the arm is then brought into a slightly adducted and internally rotated position, which should complete the reduction.

4. *Self-reduction technique.*[11] The patient is instructed to clasp his hands about his (ipsilateral) knee and then relax his shoulder muscles, allowing the weight of the lower limb to provide gentle in-line traction on the upper limb as the hip is extended. Countertraction is provided by the patient's own muscles (back extensors) (Figure 12.31).

5. *Stimson technique.* The patient lies prone on a flat surface with the injured limb dangling over the side. A weight is suspended from the wrist. Countertraction is provided by the flat surface.

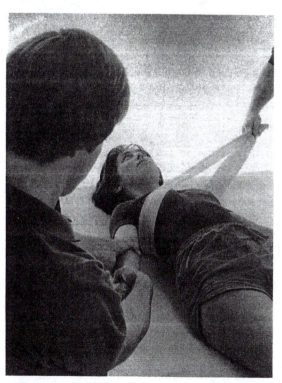

FIGURE 12.30

Traction method of reducing an anterior dislocation of the shoulder

Gentle traction is applied along the long axis of the arm, while counter-traction is applied in the opposite direction by means of a swathe. The main emphasis during this maneuver is on helping the athlete to relax, and on the gentleness of the traction.

TABLE 12.8 *Complications that can occur from reducing a dislocated shoulder*

1. Damage to one or more of the underlying nerves
2. Axillary artery damage
3. Fractures of the humerus and/or glenoid or epiphyseal damage

FIGURE 12.31
Self-reduction technique for anterior dislocation of the shoulder

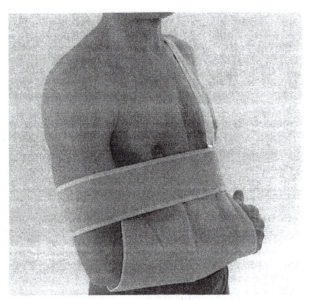

FIGURE 12.32
The arm is immobilized across the chest in a sling and swathe

Note: The techniques of Aronen and Stimson are useful to athletes who have experienced multiple recurrent dislocations and are capable of self-reducing.

POST-REDUCTION IMMOBILIZATION: A post-reduction check of the neurological and vascular structures should be routinely performed. The arm should be held against the side, internally rotated, and maintained in this position by means of a sling and swathe. No abduction or external rotation should be allowed (Figure 12.32). Analgesics and anti-inflammatory medication can be used as indicated. Ice should be used immediately afterward and continued for the first few days.

TREATMENT: The standard treatment for an anterior dislocation of the shoulder in an athlete may be summarized as:

1. Three to four weeks of immobilization, followed by rehabilitation

2. Return to participation when the shoulder is rehabilitated

It has been said that if the shoulder is immobilized for three to four weeks following the initial dislocation, the chances of a repeat dislocation are very small.[26] Not all agree on this point, as some sports medicine physicians do not consider that this form of treatment necessarily influences later shoulder stability. For this reason, the following alternative programs of treatment have been suggested and are under investigation:

1. Reduction of the dislocation, followed by early surgery.[27] An arthroscopic examination and repair of an acute Bankart lesion, if present, is sometimes recommended in young athletes, as the recurrent dislocation rate is so high. However, most orthopedists still advocate conservative treatment after the initial dislocation.

2. Immobilization until the shoulder is asymptomatic (usually ten days to three weeks), and then initiation of a vigorous but controlled rehabilitation program. The role of an extensive rehabilitation program should not be underestimated. Return to participation is permitted only when the shoulder is fully rehabilitated.

While the injured shoulder is immobilized, the athlete can still perform the following exercises under supervision:

1. Handgrip and forearm exercises (pronation and supination, flexion and extension of the elbow)

2. Isometric abduction and adduction with the arm at the side

3. Isometric internal and external rotation with the arm held in internal rotation

4. Isotonic internal rotation from 45° to 90° of internal rotation

When movement of the shoulder is permitted, the initial exercises are pendulum and internal-rotation exercises. Abduction and external rotation are attempted only when sufficient healing has taken place to allow these movements (see rehabilitation of the shoulder).

Recurrent Anterior Dislocation of the Shoulder

If the anterior capsule and inferior glenohumeral ligaments have been badly stretched after an anterior dislocation, the stability of the shoulder may be compromised. A torn labrum is unlikely to heal. In addition, inadequate rehabilitation increases the chances of recurrent problems.

TREATMENT: Because recurrent dislocations signify that the anterior supporting structures (the anterior, capsule, the inferior glenohumeral ligaments, and the subscapularis muscle) are not functioning adequately, there does not seem much point in suggesting that the athlete with an acute but recurrent dislocation be immobilized for a period of three to six weeks. A more practical approach is to

1. Immobilize while symptoms are present

2. Rehabilitate vigorously soon after the injury

3. Assess the athlete for possible surgery only after complete rehabilitation has been attempted

SURGICAL PROCEDURES: Commonly used surgical procedures include the *Bankart* repair, which is designed to reattach the capsulolabral lesion to the anterior glenoid; the *inferior capsule shift* procedure,[28] designed for patients with capsular laxity; and the *Bristow* operation,[29,30] in which a portion of the coracoid process is removed and placed at the anterior glenoid.

Recurrent Anterior Subluxation of the Shoulder

Subluxation of the shoulder implies a partial dislocation of the humeral head. It occurs when the humeral head slips up over the glenoid rim and then relocates spontaneously. Subluxation occurs most commonly in an anterior direction when the athlete's arm is forced into a position of abduction and external rotation. Subluxations may also occur without contact, particularly in the throwing athlete. (See section on injuries to throwing athletes.)

PATHOLOGY: Frequently a rent in the labrum and/or stretched anterior capsule is present. Without the static support of these structures, the humeral head is somewhat free to glide in and out of the glenoid fossa. Generally the humeral head will slip out forward with abduction and external rotation, and spontaneously reduce when the deforming stress is removed. Subluxation injuries from throwing and other overhead activities are thought to result from excessive strain on both passive (ligamentous) and dynamic stabilizers of the shoulder during the the overhead motion.[31,32]

SYMPTOMS: A good history is vital in making the diagnosis of a subluxing shoulder. For instance, a back-stroke swimmer doing a turn or a wrestler having his arm forced into an abducted, externally rotated position may relate a feeling of apprehension at the particular moment he felt the shoulder slip out of place. Often, however, the chief symptoms are limited to poorly defined pain and a vague feeling of instability with certain actions.

SIGNS: There is a full range of movement without pain when the arm is moved both actively and passively. Tenderness may be found at the:

1. Insertion of the inferior glenohumeral ligament anteriorly

2. Origin of the ligament posteriorly (Figure 12.33)

3. The most important test is the apprehension sign (Figure 12.14 a and b). This tests for laxity of the anterior capsule, the inferior glenohumeral ligament, or both. A positive apprehension sign, together with tenderness anteriorly, posteriorly, or both, is highly suggestive of a shoulder subluxation.[33,34,35]

X-RAYS: The routine radiographs of the shoulder (anteroposterior, internal, and external rotation views) are usually normal in the subluxing shoulder. The technique that demonstrates the lesions associated with a shoulder subluxation is the West Point view, a modified axillary view.[36] This X-ray shows the antero-inferior lip of the glenoid, the area commonly traumatized, which may show:

1. A chip fracture off the antero-inferior rim of the glenoid. This is a most significant X-ray finding (Figure 12.34)

2. Calcification within the anterior capsule

3. Hill-Sach's lesion (Figure 12.29). This is a defect of the humeral head caused by compression of the head against the glenoid as the humerus subluxes. (The Hill-Sach's defect can also be seen occasionally on an antero-posterior view with the arm in internal rotation.)[37]

TREATMENT:
CONSERVATIVE. Conservative treatment in the form of vigorous, controlled rehabilitation should be attempted before surgery is suggested (see section on

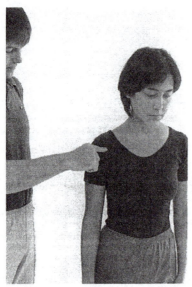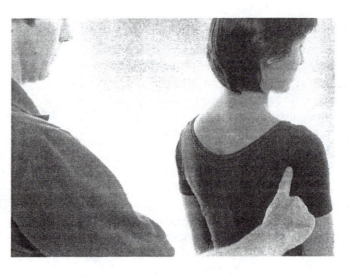

FIGURE 12.33
Recurrent anterior subluxation of the shoulder
Areas where tenderness is frequently elicited anteriorly and posteriorly.

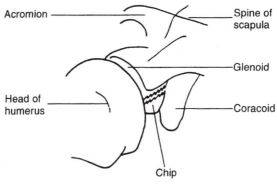

Acromion — Spine of scapula

— Glenoid

Head of humerus

— Coracoid

Chip

FIGURE 12.34
West Point view of the shoulder
This view demonstrates a large chip off the glenoid, strongly suggesting that an anterior subluxation has occurred.

shoulder rehabilitation). If the athlete desires to continue activity in spite of the disability, a self-adjusting elastic support (e.g., the West Point harness) may be used.[38] This harness allows a fairly wide range of movement but prevents full external rotation and abduction.

Surgical. Surgical repair is similar to that used in recurrent anterior dislocations. Certain surgical procedures may not be appropriate for all athletes with shoulder instability. Some procedures build in so much stability that the shoulder can no longer attain the range of motion needed for certain high-level athletic activities.[39] In throwing athletes, in particular, these procedures tend to severely limit end-range external rotation, and may prevent a return to pre-injury levels of performance.[40] The "capsulolabral" reconstruction technique and the anterior capsule "shift" techniques[41] have been promoted for use with the overhand athlete. These procedures attempt to restore normal bony and soft tissue anatomy while attempting to limit restrictions to ROM. The capsulolabral reconstruction technique is designed to reattach the cartilaginous lesion (Bankart) to the anterior glenoid. The anterior capsule shift procedure is designed for patients with capsular laxity. The anterior/inferior capsular "pouch" is incised, and the inferior portion is advanced superiorly.

Posterior Dislocation of the Glenohumeral Joint

A posterior dislocation is a rare lesion in the athlete, accounting for less than 2 percent of shoulder dislocations. However the diagnosis of a posterior dislocation is often missed on the initial examination. When examining an injured shoulder, always consider the possibility of a posterior dislocation.

MECHANISM OF INJURY: The force drives the humeral head backward while the arm is in flexion (usually below 90 degrees) and internal rotation. The head slips out posteriorly and comes to rest under the acromion process. The posterior capsule is stretched, torn, or disrupted from the posterior glenoid. A reverse Hill-Sach's lesion may be created on the anterior articular surface by the posterior lip of the glenoid.

SYMPTOMS: Symptoms consist of generalized shoulder pain and inability to rotate externally or abduct the arm. In contrast to anterior shoulder dislocation, where the deformity is easily visible and the position of the arm is extreme, posterior dislocations present with a normal contour. The athlete with a posterior dislocation might not realize that a dislocation has occurred.

SIGNS:

1. The arm is held across the front of the chest.

2. There is flattening of the anterior shoulder when viewed from the side.

3. There is a bulge posteriorly when viewed from above.

4. The coracoid process is prominent.

5. The athlete cannot externally rotate or abduct the arm.

6. The athlete finds that, as the arm is held in internal rotation, on elevating it he or she cannot supinate the hand.

X-RAYS:

1. Anteroposterior views may look normal.

2. Axillary and tangential views will reveal the diagnosis.

3. If a fracture of the lesser tuberosity is present, a diagnosis of a posterior dislocation should be considered until disproven.

COMPLICATIONS:

1. Fracture of the lesser tuberosity of the humerus
2. Comminuted intra-articular fracture of the proximal humerus

REDUCTION:

1. Longitudinal forward traction with the elbow bent

2. Downward pressure on the humeral head

3. Adduction of the arm, then external rotation, followed by internal rotation[48]

IMMOBILIZATION: Immobilization is from four to six weeks in slight abduction and external rotation.

Recurrent Posterior Dislocation and Subluxation

This is an unusual condition which may not occur as infrequently as was previously thought. It is more commonly seen in those with loose ligaments, and on occasion may be combined with anterior instability (the so-called "global instability").[49] If recurrent subluxation occurs posteriorly, the posterior glenoid lip may indent the humeral head.

TREATMENT: Initially, treatment is by attempted rehabilitation of the posterior shoulder musculature. Surgery is occasionally necessary.[50]

Voluntary or Habitual Dislocators

There are some individuals who are able to voluntarily dislocate their shoulders either anteriorly or posteriorly.

Others find that their shoulders slip out of joint with very little provocation and without an initial injury. These conditions may be due to

1. Congenital malformations of the glenoid fossa, the labrum, or the humeral head

2. Excessive laxity of the structures around the glenohumeral joint

3. Ability of the individual to dissociate some of the muscles of the rotator cuff from the others, so that voluntary contraction of part of the rotator cuff moves the humeral head into a subluxed or dislocated position, while the counteracting forces of the other muscles of the rotator cuff are not called into play.

Voluntary subluxation or dislocation in either direction (i.e., anteriorly or posteriorly) is a difficult condition to treat. It may be associated with psychiatric problems in some cases.

Impingement of the Rotator Cuff

Rotator cuff impingement is an important and common lesion in the athletic population. Repetitive overhead activities such as throwing and serving vigorously accelerate the shoulder through extremely large ranges of motion. The speed of a professionally thrown baseball ranges from 85 to 105 mph. The hand at release must go from 85 mph or more to 0 mph at the end of the follow-through, all within a distance of little more than four feet.[51] In essence, throwing a baseball or serving a tennis ball is an attempt to throw the upper limb away from the body. This type of activity places a tremendous strain on those structures responsible for maintaining the humeral head within a central location on the glenoid fossa. Inability to control the upper limb adequately may result

in abnormal excursion of the humeral head within the glenoid. Excessive use, leading to fatigue of the dynamic stabilizers of the humeral head (rotator cuff) and scapula, is felt by many to be a primary cause of shoulder impingement.[39] As the cuff muscles fatigue, fine motor control degrades, and the ability to control humeral head motion diminishes. The rotator cuff tendons (especially the supraspinatus tendon) and the tendon of the long head of the biceps are squeezed up against the underside of the acromion and the coraco-acromial ligament. A vicious cycle is set up in which fatigue of cuff muscles leads to impingement and swelling, which, in turn, leads to further muscle inhibition and dysfunction.

While overuse is the most common cause of shoulder impingement, trauma to subacromial structures from a fall or blow can also contribute to the injury.

ANATOMY: Traversing the gap between the coracoid and the acromial process is the coraco-acromial ligament, which forms an arch over the humeral head. Beneath this arch runs the supraspinatus tendon and the intra-articular portion of the tendon of the long head of the biceps. Between the acromion process and the supraspinatus tendon lies the sub-acromial bursa (Figure 12.35).

ETIOLOGY:

1. *Chronic microtrauma.* The glenohumeral joint is inherently unstable, with stability provided predominantly by the capsular, ligamentous, and muscular structures. Repetitive high-velocity overhead activities push the shoulder to its physiological limits, which may result in microscopic damage to the tissues under the coraco-acromial arch.[52]

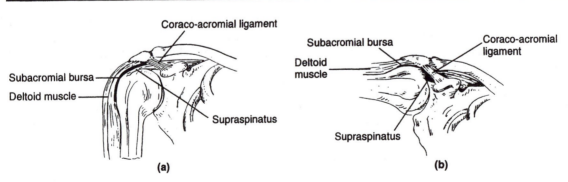

FIGURE 12.35

Impingement of the rotator cuff

(a) With the arm at the side there is no impingement under the coraco-acromial arch. (b) With the arm in abduction, the space beneath the coraco-acromial arch is reduced.

2. *Vascular impairment.* In sports such as swimming, particularly the butterfly, where the swimmer is required to rotate the arm on the shoulder many hundreds if not thousands of times a day, there may be interference with the blood supply to the supraspinatus tendon. This can result in a localized area of necrosis of the supraspinatus tendon, which can lead, in turn, to edema and an inflammatory reaction.[53]

3. *Partial tear of the rotator cuff, particularly the supraspinatus tendon.* This has the same results as vascular impairment.

4. *Previous trauma.* Previous trauma to the acromion process or acromioclavicular joint (e.g., a previous AC separation) can cause distortion of the acromion process and reduce the space available under the arch.

5. *Strength and Flexibility imbalances.* Numerous studies have documented asymmetry patterns in the shoulders of overhead athletes. Athletes involved in unilateral sports classically demonstrate increased external rotation on the dominant side as compared with the nondominant extremity.[54] Beach et al.,[55] demonstrated that swimmers in their study were hypomobile in internal rotation compared with published standards, and that external rotation ROM was 10 to 11 degrees greater than normal. Inability to adequately stabilize the humeral head during the extremes of both the cocking and follow-through phases of the throwing motion may lead to overuse of the posterior rotator cuff muscle-tendon unit. Both cuff and capsule may become fibrotic and shortened as a result of repeated trauma. Increased posterior capsular tightness may lead to increased anterior translation of the humeral head during the extremes of overhead activities.

Falkel and Murphy[56] reported that swimmers with shoulder pain have significantly lower absolute external rotation endurance than swimmers without shoulder pain. This relative weakness of external rotators has also been demonstrated in a number of other studies.[5,57]

SYMPTOMS:

1. The principal symptom is pain, which is often elicited by activities such as bringing the arm through the acceleration phase of the throwing motion, when the arm is whipped rapidly from external to internal rotation, such as occurs when hitting an overhead smash or serve in tennis, or in swimming the butterfly stroke. The pain is usually localized to the superolateral aspect of the shoulder, in the area just lateral or anterior to the acromion process. However the pain may be more diffuse, particularly in cases involving the tendon of the long head of the biceps or a more generalized inflammatory response to microtrauma.

2. A snapping feeling or sensation may occur when the arm is brought from an externally to an internally rotated position or when the arm is abducted between 70 and 120 degrees.

SIGNS: The inflammatory response to microtrauma can be divided into phases or stages according to the severity of the symptoms. Based on Neer's[58] mechanical model of impingement, the typical Stage I patient is 25 years of age or younger, although the lesion may appear at any age. Repetitive overhead use in athletics or activities of daily living result in edema and hemorrhage in the supraspinatus tendon. The tendonitis is usually localized.

STAGE I

1. The chief complaint is a dull ache following activity. This may eventually progress to pain during activity, and eventually alteration of that activity if there is no intervention.

2. Tenderness is usually vague except when the arm is passively abducted to 45 degrees and pressure is exerted under the acromion process. When this is done, localized tenderness is often apparent. Pain may also be elicited when the arm is passively extended and the supraspinatus tendon is palpated anteriorly.[59]

3. Pain is experienced when the arm is actively abducted between 70 and 120 degrees. Shoulder impingement is sometimes referred to as the *painful arc syndrome.*

4. The impingement test may be positive. The arm is brought to 90 degrees of forward flexion. The elbow is flexed and the arm is simultaneously adducted and internally rotated in an effort to reproduce the athlete's pain (Figure 12.15 b.).[60]

5. There may or may not be atrophy of the muscles around the shoulder.

6. Evidence of biceps tendinitis may also be present (see section on biceps tendon). Edema and hemorrhage in the subacromial space are the basis of the toothache-like pain noted with Stage I impingement. The hallmark of Stage I is that the lesion is reversible with activity modification.

STAGE II

Stage II symptoms are an extension of Stage I complaints. With continued irritation, the bursa may become involved, adding to the mechanical impingement. The bursa as well as the supraspinatus and biceps tendons become fibrotic and thickened. Night pain may be a problem. The pain begins to limit activities, whether overhead tennis serves or reaching for objects in a cabinet. The distinguishing feature of Stage II is that the impingement process is no longer reversible with only time and activity modification. In Neer's scheme, Stage II lesions are typically found in athletes ranging from 25 to 40 years of age. However, Hawkins and Kennedy[43] note that Stage II can occur at any age.

STAGE III

Pathological changes in Stage III result from the continued mechanical impingement of subacromial soft tissue. A prolonged history of chronic tendinitis with tendon degeneration is the hallmark of Stage III impingement. Athletic endeavors are frequently impossible due to pain and weakness. Partial or complete rotator cuff tears, capsule/labral lesions, biceps tendon lesions, or bony changes to the anterior acromion, acromioclavicular joint, or greater tuberosity are frequently seen. Stage III lesions typically occur in athletes and in those whose occupations demand excessive overhead work, with onset usually at 40 years or older.

FURTHER INVESTIGATIONS:

1. Injection of a local anesthetic under the coracoacromial arch abolishes the impingement sign if the pain is due to rotator cuff impingement.

2. X-rays of the shoulder are usually normal.

3. An arthrogram may be performed to exclude a complete tear of the rotator cuff.

4. Ultrasound examination, in some peoples' hands, is a good technique for demonstrating rotator cuff tears.

5. It is seldom necessary to obtain an MRI, as impingement syndrome is a clinical diagnosis and not a radiographic diagnosis. The MRI is a valuable tool if a tumor is suspected.

TREATMENT OF SHOULDER IMPINGEMENT: Early intervention should be stressed in the treatment of Stage I shoulder impingement.

1. Activity modification, or possibly even complete rest, may be indicated to limit the degree of injury to the rotator cuff, capsule, and other soft tissue structures of the subacromial space

2. Ice therapy, including ice massage

3. Gentle stretching exercises if muscular or capsular limitations exist. Stretching should be selective, and any that put undue stress on already compromised soft tissue structures should be avoided

4. Anti-inflammatory medications, if indicated. Occasionally a local steroid injection beneath the cora-

coacromial arch is attempted. Care must be taken to avoid injecting into the tendon

5. Consultation with the coach about altering the technique of the athlete's arm motion

6. Other conservative forms of treatment such as ultrasound, TENS, friction massage, and iontophoresis

7. Vigorous and complete rehabilitation of all the muscles around the shoulder once signs of inflammation have settled down. It is especially important that the dynamic stabilizers of the humeral head and scapula be fully rehabilitated. The strengthening and functional activities listed in the section on rehabilitation of the dislocating shoulder are appropriate for this condition

8. Return to play, when strength, range of motion, and function of the affected arm begin to approach preinjury levels, the athlete may start a functional activities progression (see functional activities progression in rehabilitation of dislocating shoulder).

TREATMENT OF STAGES II AND III: Conservative management of Stage II impingement is essentially the same as for Stage I. Modalities such as ice, ultrasound, phonophoresis and iontophoresis, and electrical stimulation continue to be of benefit in Stage II. Exercises for Stage II are unchanged from those in Stage I. Pain-free range of motion activities to maintain full mobility are important. Strengthening exercises probably need to be of lower intensity in the initial stages. Stage II impingement is no longer a completely reversible event. Some type of activity modification may be necessary to prevent further damage to soft tissue structures. Technique and training schedules may need to be carefully scrutinized. Occasionally Stage II impingement requires surgical intervention. Neer[57] states that shoulder surgery should be considered only when symptoms have persisted in spite of conservative treatment for 18 months.

Patients with Stage III degeneration are typically treated surgically. Surgery may involve decompression of the subacromial space, usually through an anterior acromioplasty. If a full-thickness rotator cuff tear exists, repair is required. Postsurgical rehabilitation protocols vary from surgeon to surgeon. Goals of rehabilitation include:

1. Restoration of normal joint mechanics through active and passive range of motion exercises.

2. Improving the strength and endurance of the muscles surrounding the shoulder girdle to prevent the upward migration of the humeral head.

3. Assessing the manner in which functional activities are carried out and making necessary modifications.[61]

Tear of the Rotator Cuff

A tear of the rotator cuff may be partial or complete. The partial tear may have very similar clinical features to the impingement syndrome and may, indeed, be a cause of that syndrome. Complete tears are rare under 30 years of age, but they do occur. A rotator cuff tear results from an acute shoulder injury. Common mechanism of acute injury to the rotator cuff includes:

1. A fall on the outstretched arm, with the force transmitted through the humeral head to the rotator cuff

2. Impingement of the tuberosity against the acromion when the arm is rapidly and forcibly abducted. It most frequently involves the supraspinatus tendon, but it may also include the infraspinatus tendon and the tendon of the long head of the biceps.

SIGNS: The signs may be very similar to the impingement syndrome. In addition:

1. Tenderness may be present at the insertion of the supraspinatus tendon into the greater tuberosity of the humerus. More commonly, localized tenderness is found in the coraco-acromial arch when the arm is passively abducted at 45 degrees and pressure is applied under the arch, or when the arm is extended and pressure is applied anteriorly over the supraspinatus insertion. On occasion tenderness is also present over the biceps long head or around the acromioclavicular joint.

2. Pain is experienced on abducting the arm between 70 and 120 degrees. (This may be one of the causes of the painful arc syndrome.)

3. Supraspinatus crepitus may be felt as the arm is actively abducted.

4. Impingement signs may or may not be present (Figure 12.15). Their absence may be evidence differentiating rotator cuff tear from the impingement syndrome.

5. Wasting or poor contraction of the supraspinatus may be observed when the athlete is viewed from above and from behind.

6. An athlete who has a complete tear may not be able to abduct the arm against even minimal resistance.

Note: It is possible for a muscular athlete to have a partial tear of the rotator cuff and yet be able to actively initiate abduction, even against resistance, without too much pain or difficulty. In addition, no muscle weakness may be elicited unless specific muscle tests are performed and the shoulder muscles are fatigued by repetitive testing.

FURTHER INVESTIGATIONS:

1. If the impingement sign is present, it may be relieved by a local anesthetic injected under the coraco-acromial arch.

2. X-rays of the shoulder are usually normal.

3. An arthrogram or MRI (magnetic resonance imaging) may be useful in making the diagnosis.

TREATMENT:
CONSERVATIVE. The initial treatment can be conservative if the exact severity of a partial tear is in question.

1. Place the affected arm in a sling.
2. Use ice therapy and anti-inflammatory medication.
3. Limit external rotation and abduction for a period of time, depending upon the severity of the condition.

This treatment should be followed by:

1. Rehabilitation exercises
2. Gentle stretching
3. Cortisone injections, a single steroid injection in a partial rotator cuff tear may be acceptable in some instances.

Surgical. If an arthrogram shows leakage of dye, surgical repair is indicated.[62] If the arthrogram is negative and the symptoms do not clear up within a reasonable period of time (varying from athlete to athlete and from sport to sport), surgical exploration should be performed to release the impingement and repair any tear.

Impingement Syndrome and the Biceps Tendon

The origin of the long head of the biceps tendon is closely associated with the rotator cuff tendons and the glenoid labrum. Anatomically, the tendon arises from the supraglenoid tubercle and superior margin of the labrum. It rides over the top of the humerus encased in a synovial sheath, coursing intracapsularly before exiting through the bicepital groove[63] (Figure 12.36). Acting with the rotator cuff, the long head of the biceps imparts a downward force during overhead activities to help contain the humeral head within the glenoid.

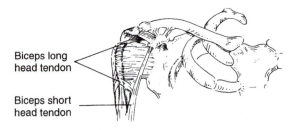

FIGURE 12.36
The biceps—long and short heads

Biceps long head tendon

Biceps short head tendon

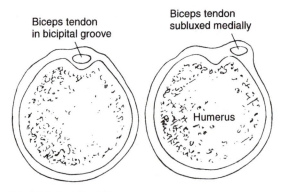

Biceps tendon in bicipital groove

Biceps tendon subluxed medially

Humerus

FIGURE 12.37
Cross-section through proximal humerus

Weakness in the dynamic stabilizers of the shoulder (rotator cuff) as well as capsular insufficiency can cause the humeral head to translate excessively, subjecting the biceps tendon to increasing microtrauma. Tenderness is usually present over the bicepital groove, and a snap may be felt when the arm is rotated externally or brought from an externally rotated to an internally rotated position. This snap is due to the impingement of the biceps tendon under the coraco-acromial arch. Impingement signs should be positive.

If bicepital tendinitis is associated with the shoulder-impingement syndrome, therapy directed to the impingement syndrome can result in spontaneous resolution of the bicepital tendinitis.

Subluxation of the Tendon of the Long Head of the Biceps

Subluxation of the tendon of the long head of the biceps is another cause of shoulder pain, although a relatively infrequent one.

ANATOMY: The bicipital groove is formed by the lesser tuberosity medially and the greater tuberosity laterally. The roof is formed by the transverse humeral ligament. The tendon does not actually slide in the groove; rather, the groove slides over the tendon. This occurs particularly when the arm is moved from internal to external rotation and back again from external to internal rotation (Figure 12.37).

PATHOLOGY: There are usually a number of factors which together allow the biceps tendon to sublux. There may be an initial forceful injury (usually with the arm resisting abduction and external rotation), which may cause the transverse humeral ligament to become stretched, permitting subluxation of the tendon. Repetitive movement, such as throwing, may further aggravate the ligament laxity.

The shape of the groove is considered by some to predispose to the development of the condition in a particular athlete.[64] If the medial aspect of the groove (the lesser tuberosity) is flat, the groove will be shallow and the tendon may easily sublux toward the medial side.

In its course over the humeral head, the biceps tendon is angulated approximately 30° medially, so that tightening of the biceps, together with external rotation of the arm, tends to cause the tendon to bowstring toward the medial side. Most subluxations are thought to occur in the medial direction, but some cases of lateral subluxation have been noted.

SYMPTOMS: Most symptoms are associated with pain and a snapping sensation, particularly when the arm is rapidly moved from internal to external rotation. This pain is followed by a dull ache, which persists for the next few hours or days. Crepitus may be noted on moving the arm.

SIGNS: Tenderness is located over the bicipital groove. This area of tenderness will be observed to move laterally as the arm is externally rotated. Other areas around the anterosuperior aspect of the shoulder may also be tender, due to inflammation spreading out to include the rotator cuff and the proximal portion of the biceps muscle.

There are various clinical tests which may induce subluxation and may help with the diagnosis. Some of these are designed to bowstring the biceps tendon over the medial wall of the bicipital groove.

1. Yergason's test—The affected arm is held with the elbow at 90° and against the chest wall. Against resistance, the shoulder is externally rotated, the elbow flexed, and the forearm supinated, while downward traction is applied to the elbow.[65] The examiner palpates

the tendon in the bicipital groove in order to detect subluxation of the tendon. Pain is produced by either subluxation or biceps tendinitis.

2. With the elbow at the side, and flexed to 90°, supinating from a pronated position against resistance may cause pain over the biceps tendon. This may also be due to biceps tendinitis.

3. Gilcrest's sign—The athlete raises the weight of a light dumbbell with elbow extended to above the head, then lowers the arm to a position of 90° of abduction while supinating the forearm and externally rotating the shoulder.[7] This may elicit subluxation of the tendon from the bicipital groove and cause discomfort.

4. With the shoulder at 90° of abduction and the elbow extended, the forearm is pronated and supinated against resistance. The tendon may be felt to snap out of the groove.

5. The affected arm is passively abducted and externally rotated. The arm is turned into internal rotation and then back to external rotation while the bicipital groove is palpated for instability of the tendon.

TREATMENT:

Conservative. Conservative treatment should initially be tried in order to decrease inflammation and allow the tissues to heal in a functional position. If significant functional incapacity, swelling, and tenderness are present, the arm should be splinted for a week or two in order to allow healing to occur. Ice should be applied, and anti-inflammatory medication used as indicated. A progressive rehabilitation program should then be prescribed, including strengthening of the dynamic stabilizers of the rotator cuff and scapula.

Surgical. In the chronic case where conservative therapy has been tried but throwing has become nearly impossible, surgical intervention should be considered.[64] The operation consists of removal of the long head from the glenoid and suturing of the tendon into the bicipital groove. Good results from this procedure have been reported.

Thoracic Outlet Syndrome

The name *thoracic outlet syndrome* implies compression of the neurovascular components that travel from the neck through the thoracic outlet area and supply the upper extremity.

ETIOLOGY: Many etiologies have been associated with this syndrome. The commonest include:

1. Compression of the neurovascular bundle between the anterior and middle scalene muscles

2. Compression between the first rib and the clavicle (costoclavicular syndrome)

3. Abnormalities of the first rib

4. Compression under the pectoralis minor muscle

5. Compression under a cervical rib

6. Poor posture with sagging shoulders. However, it is rare to find a thoracic outlet syndrome in tennis players and pitchers, many of whom have a dominant shoulder that sags but also have excellent muscle tone

7. Other etiologies such as fascial fusion of muscles

8. A combination of two or more of the above

PATHOMECHANICS: There is compression of the neurovascular bundle, affecting particularly the inferior portion of the brachial plexus, most commonly in the distribution of the ulnar nerve, and occasionally, the median nerve.

SYMPTOMS: The symptoms may include burning and numbness of the shoulder, the inner side of the arm, the forearm, and the hand. This usually follows a pattern corresponding to a dermatome. However, on occasion, pain may be localized to the shoulder, elbow, or forearm region alone.[66]

SIGNS: There may be some decrease in sensation as well as atrophy and weakness of the muscles supplied by the involved nerves. A number of tests aimed at decreasing the pulse and reproducing the symptoms are used (Figure 12.38).

1. *Adson's maneuver*—Tests for compression of the neurovascular bundle between the anterior and middle scalene muscles. The arm is held at the side and slightly abducted and extended. The athlete looks to the side being tested, slightly extends the neck, and takes a deep breath and holds it for ten seconds. There is some downward traction of the arm while the pulse is being observed.

2. *Hyperflexion-abduction test*—The arm is held in full flexion and abduction, and the neck is somewhat extended. The arm is supinated. Obliteration of the pulse and reproduction of pain suggest tightness of the pectoralis minor muscle.

3. *Test for the costoclavicular syndrome*—Done with the athlete sitting with shoulders pulled backward and downward. The arm is in 30° of abduction and extended.

(a)   (b)

FIGURE 12.38
(a) Adson's maneuver (b) Hyperflexion-abduction test with the neck in extension

INVESTIGATIONS: Tests include: (a) an X-ray of the neck to detect the presence of a cervical rib, (b) nerve conduction studies, and, in particular, (c) a Doppler blood-flow sensor with the head and the arms in different positions.

TREATMENT: Most cases respond to a program of exercise therapy designed to relieve tension on the structures involved.[66,67,68] This program should be individualized according to the etiology. Following are some exercises that may be generally useful (Figure 12.39):

1.   Athlete supine, hands behind head, elbows in front of face. As the athlete inhales, elbows are drawn slowly apart and lateral to the head. As the athlete exhales, elbows are brought back together. This can be performed against manual resistance.

2.   Serratus anterior exercise—shoulder protraction using dumbbells, barbells, or the universal gym.

3.   Mid-trapezius exercise—athlete prone, arm abducted 90° at the shoulders, elbows bent 90° over the edge of a table. Athlete holds a dumbbell in each hand and lifts the weights and the elbows straight upward, keeping the elbows bent so the scapulae approximate each other.

4.   Erector spinae strengthening—athlete prone, back extended, and shoulders pulled backward.

5.   Lower trapezius exercise—athlete prone, forearm and elbow lifted upward to hyperflexed position of the shoulder.

6.   Pectoralis stretching—athlete standing in a corner, leaning forward with feet firmly planted, stabilizing body with elbows against the wall and bringing chest forward toward the corner.

7.   Upper trapezius exercises or shoulder elevation—can be done using a barbell for resistance.

8.   In addition, passive or active stretching of the pectoralis minor and the scalene muscles, as well as cross-frictional massage, may be useful.

Shoulder Rehabilitation Following Reconstruction/Repair of Anterior Shoulder

This program, while designed as a post-operative shoulder instability protocol, can also be used in a modified, speeded-up form in cases of anterior subluxation or a conservatively treated anterior dislocation. Many of these exercises and activities may also be appropriate for conditions associated with shoulder impingement and overuse. Prior to implementation of this program, the patient's activity level, age, sex, goals, tissue status, and muscular status should all be carefully considered.

The program allows early, protected motion, and incorporates activities designed to dynamically strengthen the muscles surrounding the glenohumeral joint, as well as to develop neuromuscular control. The various phases, in addition to representing a timeline for rehabilitation, also represent a progression of ever-challenging activities.

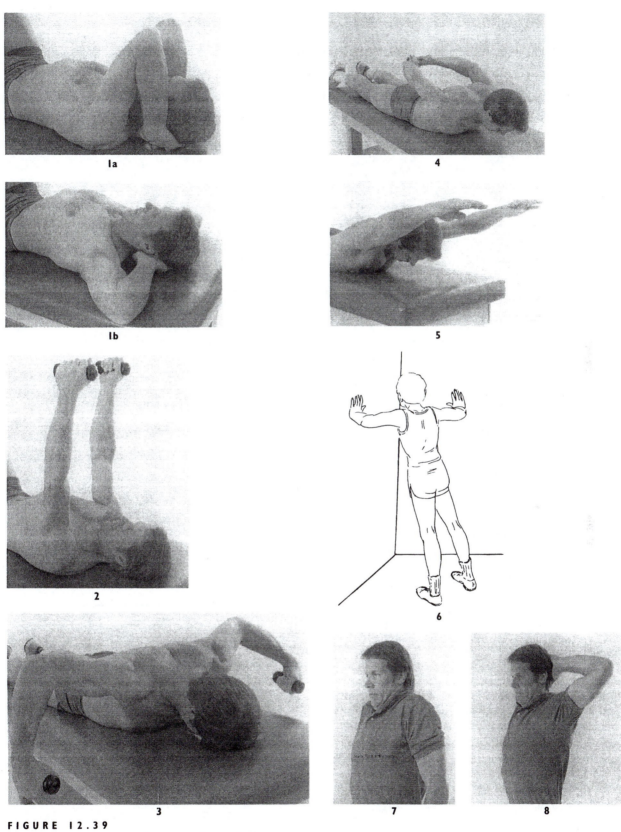

FIGURE 12.39
Exercises for treatment of thoracic outlet syndrome

la

lb

2

3

4

5

6

7

8

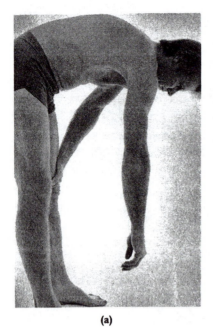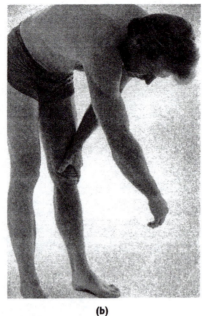

(a)	(b)

FIGURE 12.40
Codman's pendulum exercise
(a) The arm should be allowed to relax and hang freely. The motion, small circles that slowly increase in size, should be gravity-assisted. (b) Abduction and adduction motions should also be performed.

PHASE I: "Protection" phase (weeks 0–4). Goals:

1. Decrease pain and inflammation
2. Protect the surgery/healing tissue
3. Retard muscle atrophy
4. Maintain mobility

Weeks 0–2. Period of protected immobilization:

1. Immobilizing device removed twice daily for modified Codman's pendulum exercise.
2. Use of TNS and muscle stimulation as indicated
3. Isometric exercises for wrist and elbow flexion and extension, forearm supination and pronation, to minimize stiffness

Weeks 2–4. Initiate range of motion activities. Flexion and scapular plane abduction should be limited to 90 degrees, external rotation to neutral only first 3 to 4 weeks. Active external rotation should only be allowed first 8 weeks.

1. Codman's pendulum exercise (Figure 12.40)
2. Wand-assisted ROM
3. Finger climbing on the wall (Figure 12.41)
4. Use of overhead pulleys

Initiate Isometric activities

1. Punch and retract (Figure 12.42)
2. Shoulder abduction and adduction
3. Shoulder internal and external rotation

EMS, TNS, cold, other modalities may be used as indicated. Stress functional use of the shoulder during ADLs. The athlete needs to be aware of and avoid flexion/internal rotation synergy pattern.

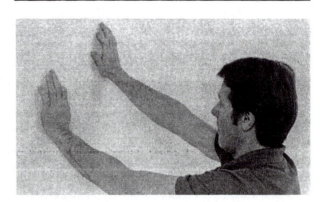

FIGURE 12.41
Finger-climbing-up-wall
to increase the shoulder range of motion

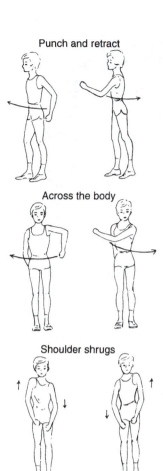

Punch and retract

Across the body

Shoulder shrugs

FIGURE 12.42

Initially performed in an isometric position, these exercises may be progressed by adding resistance such as elastic tubing.

(Modified from: R. K. Kerlan, F. W. Jobe, M.E. Blazina, et al., "Throwing injuries of the shoulder and elbow in adults." *Current Practice in Orthopaedic Surgery* 6:41–58. 1975.)

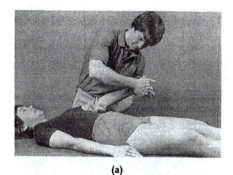
(a)

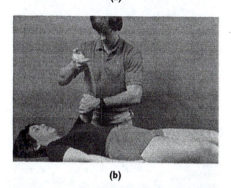
(b)

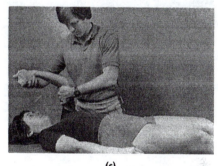
(c)

FIGURE 12.43

PNF D2 Flexion/Abduction/external rotation, modified.
In stages (a), the therapist emphasizes greater resistance to the Flexion/Abduction component with hand placement at the distal humerus. Lesser resistance is placed at the wrist. In stage (b) to (c), the emphasis shifts to the wrist for resistance of the external rotation component.

PHASE 2: (weeks 4–10). Goals:

1. Protect the repair

2. Increase shoulder mobility

3. Increase functional strength

Continue to work on shoulder mobility (120 degrees of active flexion and scapular plane abduction, 15 degrees of active external rotation by 4 to 6 weeks). Introduce PNF to help establish and strengthen functional movement patterns (Figure 12.43).

Isotonic activities may be used to improve shoulder strength and endurance (upper body ergometry, rotator cuff, and scapular stabilization exercises). ROM should be limited initially to avoid excessive stress to capsule and/or repair (Figures 12.44, 12.45, 12.46).

Closed chain activities will enhance strength and shoulder stability (balance board, slide board, wall/kneeling push-ups, press-ups, etc.) (Figure 12.47).

Proprioceptive activities may be introduced to help develop kinesthesia and awareness of joint position (Figure 12.48).

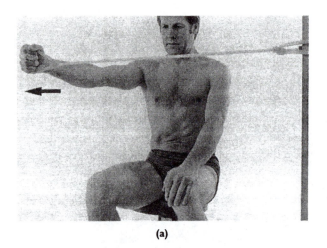

(a)

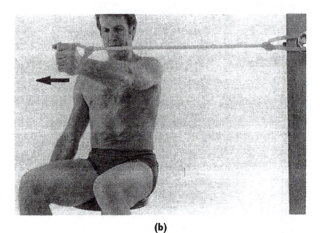

(b)

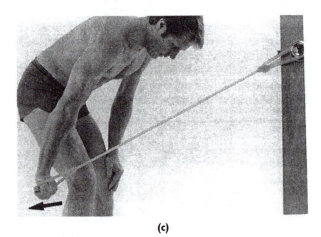

(c)

FIGURE 12.44
Elasticized tubing exercises
A few examples of the many possible exercises are shown.

FIGURE 12.45
Use of an upper body ergometer to improve shoulder strength and endurance

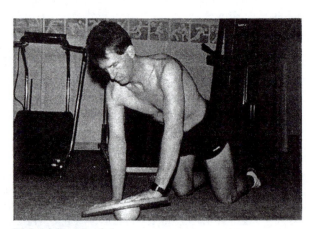

FIGURE 12.46
Use of a balance board to challenge shoulder stabilization and balance

FIGURE 12.47
Limited-range bench press
Note the pin which controls the range of descent of the weight stack. The position of the pin can be altered as a greater range of motion against resistance is allowed.

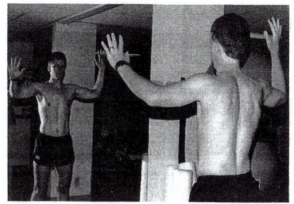

FIGURE 12.48
Positioning exercises (both with eyes open and closed) in front of a mirror

PHASE 3: (weeks 11–16) Period of dynamic strengthening. Goals:

1. Full range of motion

2. Improve functional strength

3. Improve functional stability

4. Continue proprioception activities

5. Initate low-impact plyometrics

Initiate high-speed, low-load isokinetic strengthening. Employ faster-paced PNF activities.

Continue weight training for shoulder strength and endurance (bench press, push-ups, press-ups, rowing, "lat" pull-downs, scapular plane abduction, prone horizontal abduction, etc.) (Figures 12.49a–d).

Use closed chain activities for enhanced proprioception and shoulder stability (single-and double-arm balancing on unstable surfaces such as gymnastic ball, foam rollers, balance board, fitter, etc.). Also, low-impact plyometrics activities can be introduced (press, release, and catch on shuttle; medicine ball sequential activities, trunk rotation; chest pass; 2-hand-overhead pass; single catch and throw, etc.)[40,42] (Figure 12.50).

PHASE 4: (weeks 17–23). Goal:
Introduce demands of athlete's specific sport to exercise program.

Once the athlete has demonstrate good strength and flexibility and synchronous control of the shoulder during exercise, he or she may begin to simulate activities through progressive functional drills. Athletes who will be returning to "collision" sports (football, hockey, gymnastics, wrestling, etc.) need to start with a very structured environment and specific drills. An example for football might include such drills as arm and shoulder pops on a blocking bag, controlled falls, rolls, form tackling, etc.

Rehabilitating overhead athletes also benefit from a structured rehabilitative environment. Several excellent references regarding return-to-throw protocols exist.[31,43,44,45,46] (see Table 12.9.)

It should be remembered that the legs and trunk are responsible for over 50 percent of the kinetic energy developed during the throwing motion. Rehabilitation should also stress activities for the legs, hip, trunk, and back.[47]

PHASE 5: (weeks 24–36). Goals:

1. Strength of affected shoulder at least 90 percent that of unaffected shoulder

2. Full pain-free shoulder ROM with normal scapulo-humeral rhythm

3. Good proprioceptive function

Return to full unrestricted activity.

(a)

(b)

(c)

(d)

FIGURE 12.49

(a) Lateral Step-up; (b) Double arm support on unstable base; (c) Prone horizontal abduction; (d) Functional tubing patterns (external rotation)

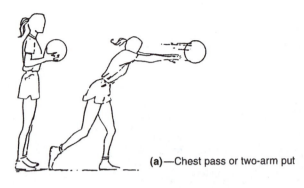

(a)—Chest pass or two-arm put

(b)—Two-handed overhead step and throw

(c)—Single-arm overhead throw

FIGURE 12.50

Medicine ball sequential throwing activities.

(Source: C.M. Bonci, B. Sloane, and K. Middleton, "Non-surgical/surgical rehabilitation of the unstable shoulder," *Journal of Sports Rehabilitation* 1(2), 146–171. Copyright 1992 by Human Kinetics Publishers. Reprinted by permission.)

TABLE 12.9 *Progression of throwing activities*

Mirror Throwing—With a light (1#) weight in the throwing hand, the athlete is instructed to use his or her normal throwing motion in front of a mirror. He or she must execute slowly, exaggerating each phase of the throwing act.

Short-Distance Throwing—Begin to play catch with a ball for short distances of 20 to 30 feet for periods of 5 minutes to 15–20 minutes daily. The purpose of this drill is to regain the throwing motion in a coordinated fashion. Proper throwing mechanics are stressed, as are fluidity of motion and accuracy. Velocity is not a concern at this point.

Long-Distance Throwing—Once short-distance throwing for 20 minutes daily is tolerated, long distance throwing can be initiated. Distances gradually increase to 150 feet, but velocity remains limited. Emphasis should be on proper throwing mechanics.

Form Throwing—Once the athlete can throw comfortably for short and long distances, begin to throw from a mound. This period usually starts 6 to 8 weeks into a conditioning program. Initially the pitcher should throw only fast balls. After reaching near-maximum velocity, breaking balls can be introduced gradually.

Modified from A. Pappas, R. Zawacki, and C. McCarthy, "Rehabilitation of the pitching shoulder," *American Journal Sports Medicine* 13: 223–235, 1985.

REFERENCES

1. Calliet R: *Shoulder Pain*, F A Davis, Philadelphia, 1996.

2. Inman VT, Saunders JB, Abbot LC: Observations on the function of the shoulder joint. *J Bone Joint Surg* 26A:1–30, 1944.

3. Nordin M, Frankel V: *Basic Biomechanics of the Musculoskeletal System*. Lea and Febiger, second edition, Malvern, PA, 1989.

4. Turkel SP, Panio MW, Marshall JL, et al: Stabilizing mechanisms preventing anterior dislocation of the glenohumeral joint. *J Bone Joint Surg* 63A:1208–1217, 1981.

5. Warner J, Micheli L, Arslanian L, Kennedy J, Kennedy R: Patterns of flexibility, laxity, and strength in normal shoulders and shoulders with instability and impingement. *Am J Sports Med* 18:366–375, 1990.

6. Davies GJ, Gould JA, Larson RL: Functional examination of the shoulder girdle. *Phys Sportsmed* 9:82–102, June 1981.

7. DeLee J, Drez D: *Orthopaedic Sports Medicine: Principles and Practice*. WB Saunders, Philadelphia, 1994.

8. Neer CS, Welsh RP: The shoulder in sport. *Orthop Clin North Am* 8:583–591, 1977.

9. Hawkins RJ, Kennedy JC: Impingement syndrome in athletics. *Am J Sports Med* 8:151–158, 1980.

10. Gregg JR, Labosky D, Harty M, et al: Serratus anterior paralysis in the young athlete. *J Bone Joint Surg* 61A:825–832, 1979.

11. Garrick J, Webb D: *Sports Injuries—Diagnosis and Management*. WB Saunders, Philadelphia, 1990.

12. Rockwood C, Green D, Bucholz: *Rockwood and Green's Fractures in Adults*. Philadelphia, J.P. Lippincott, third edition, 1991.

13. Pettrone F, Nirschl R: Acromioclavicular dislocation. *Am J Sports Med* 6:160–164, 1978.

14. Norfray JF, Tremaine MJ, Groves HC, et al: The clavicle in hockey. *Am J Sports Med* 5:275–280, 1977.

15. Allman FL: Fractures and ligamentous injuries of the clavicle and its articulation. *J Bone Joint Surg* 49A:774–784, 1967.

16. Alexander OM: Radiography of the acromioclavicular articulation. *Med Radiogr Photogr* 30:34–39, 1954.

17. Waldrop JI, Norwood LA, Alvarez RG: Lateral roentgenographic projections of the acromioclavicular joint. *Am J Sports Med* 9:337–341, 1981.

18. Jacobs B, Wade P: Acromioclavicular joint injury—An end result study. *J Bone Joint Surg* 48A: p 475–486, 1966.

19. Glick JM, Milburn LJ, Haggerty JF, et al: Dislocated acromioclavicular joint. Follow-up study of 35 unreduced acromioclavicular dislocations. *Am J Sports Med* 5:264–270, 1977.

20. Tibone J, Sellers R, Tonino P: Strength testing after 3rd degree acromioclavicular dislocations. *Am J Sports Med* 20:328–331, 1992

21. Bergfeld JA, Andrish JT, Clancy WG: Evaluation of the acromioclavicular joint following first- and second-degree sprains. *Am J Sports Med* 6:153–159, 1978.

22. Cox JS: The fate of the acromioclavicular joint in athletic injuries. *Am J Sports Med* 9:50–53, 1981.

23. Park JP, Arnold JA, Coker TP, et al: Treatment of acromioclavicular separations. A retrospective study. *Am J Sports Med* 8:251–256, 1980.

24. De Palma AF, Flannery GF: Acute anterior dislocation of the shoulder. *J Sports Med* 1:6–15, 1973.

25. Bateman JE: Cuff tears in athletes. *Orthop Clin North Am* 4:721–745, 1973.

26. Rowe CR: Prognosis in dislocations of the shoulder. *J Bone Joint Surg* 38A:957–977, 1956.

27. Rockwood Jr, CA: Dislocations about the shoulder. In *Fractures,* edited by Rockwood Jr, CA, Green DP. Philadelphia, Lippincott, 1975, p 656.

28. Rowe CR, Patel D, Southmayd WW: The Bankart procedure: A long term end result study. *J Bone Joint Surg* 60A: 1–16, 1978.

29. Lombardo SJ, Kerlan RK, Jobe FW, et al: The modified Bristow procedure for recurrent dislocation of the shoulder. *J Bone Joint Surg* 58A:256–261, 1976.

30. Hill JA, Lombardo SJ, Kerlan RK: The modified Bristow-Helfet procedure for recurrent anterior shoulder subluxations and dislocations. *Am J Sports Med* 9:283–287, 1981.

31. Pappas A, Zawacki R, McCarthy C: Rehabilitation of the pitching shoulder. *Am J Sports Med* 13:223–235, 1985.

32. Irrgang J, Whitney S, Harner, C: Nonoperative treatment of rotator cuff injuries in throwing athletes. *J Sport Rehab* 1:197–222, 1992.

33. Rowe CR, Zarins B: Recurrent transient subluxation of the shoulder. *J Bone Joint Surg* 63A:863–872, 1981.

34. Blazina ME, Satzman JS: Recurrent anterior subluxation of the shoulder in athletics—A distinct entity. In Proceedings of the American Academy of Orthopaedic Surgeons. *J Bone Joint Surg* 51A:1037–1038, 1969.

35. Hastings DE, Coughlin LP: Recurrent subluxation of the glenohumeral joint. *Am J Sports Med* 9:352–355, 1981.

36. Rokous JR, Feagin JA. Abbott HG: Modified axillary roentgenogram. *Clin Orthop* 82:84–86, 1972.

37. Hill HA, Sachs MD: The grooved defect of the humeral head. A frequently recognized complication of dislocations of the shoulder. *Radiology* 35:690, 1940.

38. Feagin JA: Elastic arm-torso harness. *J Sports Med* 2:99–101, 1974.

39. Jobe F, Pink M: Classification and treatment of shoulder dysfunction in the overhead athlete. *J Orthop Sports Phys Ther* 18:427–432, 1993.

40. Bonci C, Sloane B, Middleton K: Nonsurgical/surgical rehabilitation of the unstable shoulder. *J Sport Rehab* 1:146–171, 1992.

41. Jobe B, Giangurra C, Kvitne R, Glousman R: Anterior capsulolabral reconstruction of the shoulder in athletes in overhand sports. *Am J Sports Med* 19: 428–434, 1991.

42. Gambetta V: The complete guide to medicine ball training. *Opt Sports Training* Sarasota, FL, 1991.

43. Hawkins R, Kennedy J: Impingement syndrome in athletes. *Am J Sports Med* 8:151–158, 1980.

44. Kerlan R, Jobe F, Blazina M, et al: Throwing injuries of the shoulder and elbow in adults. *Curr Pract Orthop Surg* 6:41, 1974.

45. Jobe F, Bradley J: Rotator cuff injuries in baseball: prevention and rehabilitation. *Sports Med* 6:378–387, 1988.

46. Brewster C, Moynes-Schwab D: Rehabilitation of the shoulder following rotator cuff injury or surgery. *J Orthop Sports Phys Ther* 18:422–426, 1993.

47. Wilk K, Arrigo C: Current concepts in the rehabilitation of the athletic shoulder. *J Orthop Sports Phys Ther* 18 (1): 365–378, 1993.

48. Connolly JF, editor: De Palma's *The Management of Fractures and Dislocations.* Philadelphia. WB Saunders, Vol I, third edition, 1981, p 634.

49. Neer CS, Foster CR: Inferior capsular shift for involuntary inferior and multidirectional instability of the shoulder. A preliminary report. *J Bone Joint Surg* 62A:897–908, 1980.

50. Tibone JE, Prietto C, Jobe FW, et al: Staple capsulorrhaphy for recurrent posterior shoulder dislocation. *Am J Sports Med* 9:135–139, 1981.

51. Horigan J, Robinson J: The seven minute rotator cuff solution. *Health for Life.* Los Angeles, 1990.

52. Jackson DW: Chronic rotator cuff impingement in the throwing athlete. *Am J Sports Med* 4:231–240, 1976.

53. Rathbun JB, Macnab I: The microvascular pattern of the rotator cuff. *J Bone Joint Surg* 52B:540–553, 1970.

54. Lichfield R, Hawkins R, Dillman C, Atkins J, Hagerman G: Rehabilitation of the overhead athlete. *J Orthop Sports Phys Ther* 18(2):433–441, 1993.

55. Beach M, Whitney S, Dickhoff-Hoffman: Relationship of shoulder flexibility, strength, and endurance to shoulder pain in competitive swimmers. *J Orthop Sports Phys Ther* 16:262–268, 1992.

56. Falkel J, Murphy T: Case principles—Swimmer's shoulder. In *Shoulder Injuries, Sports Injury Management,* edited by Malone TE. Vol 1, Williams and Wilkins, Baltimore, 109–125, 1988.

57. Jobe F, Pink M: Shoulder injuries in athletes. *Clin Manag* 11:39–47, 1991.

58. Neer C: Impingement lesions. *Clin Orthop* 173:70–77, 1983.

59. Hoppenfeld S: *Physical Examination of the Spine and Extremities.* New York, Appleton-Century-Crofts, 1976, p 12.

60. Jobe FW, Moynes DR: Delineation of diagnostic criteria and rehabilitative program for rotator cuff injuries. *Am J Sports Med* 10:336–339, 1982.

61. Simon E, Hill J: Rotator cuff injuries: an update. *J Orthop Sports Phys Ther* 10(10), 394–397, April 1989.

62. Nixon JE, DiStefano V: Rupture of the rotator cuff. *Orthop Clin North Am* 6:423–447, 1975.

63. Simon W: Soft tissue disorders of the shoulder. *Orthop Clin North Am* 6:521, 1975.

64. O'Donoghue DH: Subluxing biceps tendon in the athlete. *J Sports Med* 1:20–29, 1973.

65. Hoppenfeld S: *Physical Examination of the Spine and Extremities.* New York, Appleton-Century-Crofts, 1976, p 32.

66. Strukel RJ, Garrick JG: Thoracic outlet compression in athletes. A report of four cases. *Am J Sports Med* 6:35–39, 1978.

67. Britt LP: Nonoperative treatment of the thoracic outlet syndrome symptoms. *Clin Orthop Rel Res* 51:45–48, 1967.

68. Smith KF: The thoracic outlet syndrome: A protocol of treatment. *J Orthop Sports Phys Ther* 1:89–99, 1979.

RECOMMENDED READINGS

Bateman JE: *The Shoulder and Neck*. Philadelphia, WB Saunders, 1972.

Booth Jr, RE, Marvel Jr, JP: Differential diagnosis of shoulder pain. *Orthop Clin North Am* 6:353–379, 1975.

Bonci C, Sloane B, Middleton K: Nonsurgical/surgical rehabilitation of the unstable shoulder. *J Sports Rehab* 1:146–171, 1992.

Clancy WG, editor: Symposium on shoulder problems in overhead-overuse sports. *Am J Sports Med* 7:138, 1979.

Current shoulder issues—Part 1. *J Orthop Sports Phys Ther* 18(1): 1993.

Current shoulder issues—Part 2. *J Orthop Sports Phys Ther* 18(2): 1993.

DeLee J, Drez D: *Orthopaedic Sports Medicine: Principles and Practice*. Philadelphia, WB Saunders, 1994.

Garrick J, Webb D: *Sports Injuries—Diagnosis and Management*. Philadelphia, WB Saunders, 1990.

Irrgang JJ, Whitney S, Harner C: Nonoperative treatment of rotator cuff injuiries in throwing athletes. *J Sports Rehab* 1:197–222, 1992.

Voss D, Knot M, Kobat H: The application of neuromuscular facilitation in the treatment of shoulder disabilities. *Phys Ther Rev* 33:536–541, 1953.

13

Arm and Elbow Joint Injuries

Functional Anatomy

The elbow is the anatomic area that joins the arm with the forearm. The elbow-forearm complex represents the second link in a mechanical chain of levers that begins at the shoulder and ends at the fingertips. The shoulder, as the first link, functions to permit the hand to be positioned anywhere within an imaginary sphere that represents the full excursion of shoulder motion. Elbow motion allows the height and length of the upper extremity to be adjusted, whereas forearm rotation allows the hand to be placed in the most effective position for function.[1]

ARTHROLOGY: The elbow joint complex is composed of the humeroulnar, radioulnar, and the superior and inferior radioulnar articulations. The humeroulnar joint, commonly referred to as the elbow joint, is a modified hinge joint. The elbow proper and the superior radioulnar articulation are enclosed in a single joint capsule.[2] Motion at the elbow is of two types: flexion-extension and pronation-supination (forearm rotation).

CARRYING ANGLE: When standing in the anatomic position (palms facing anteriorly), the upper arm and the forearm form a valgus (lateral) angle. This is known as the *carrying angle*. In adults this angle is usually 10 to 15 degrees, and normally it is greater, on average, in women. In the mature pitcher's arm, this angle may be 10 to 15 degrees greater than that of the non-dominant arm; this change is a secondary result of adaptive remodeling to repetitive bony stress.[3]

BONES: At the elbow, the *humerus* has two articulating areas: the convex *capitellum* laterally and the

trochlea medially. The trochlea has a spool-shaped depression where it articulates with the proximal ulna. Extending proximally from the humeral condyles are the *medial* and *lateral epicondyles*. The forearm flexor-pronator muscles attach at the medially epicondylar ridge, while the extensor-supinator muscles attach along the lateral epicondylar ridge. The medial epicondyle is more prominent than the lateral, and its cartilaginous apophyseal growth plate does not close until 16 or 17 years of age.[4] (Figures 13.1–13.3)

The *ulna* is a large bone proximally, but becomes more narrow as it extends distally toward the wrist. The central ridge of the proximal ulna runs between two bony projections, the olecranon posteriorly and the coronoid process anteriorly. This central bony projection is called the trochlear ridge. On either side of the ridge is a concave region known as the trochlear notch, which corresponds to the convex surface of the humeral trochlea.[5] The olecranon process of the ulna extends posteriorly and provides a bony block to hyperextension, while the coranoid process of the ulna extends anteriorly and aids in limiting hyperflexion (Figure 13.2).

The radius is larger distally at the wrist, and narrow proximally. The proximal radial head is a cup-shaped disk that articulates with a convex capitellum of the humerus to form the humeroradial joint.

The proximal radioulnar joint (superior radioulnar joint) is formed by the convex medial rim of the head of the radius and the concave radial notch of the proximal ulna. The annular ligament completely surrounds the radial head with a firm ring, thus holding the radial head against the ulna. Motion at the superior radioulnar joint is in the form of pronation and supination.

An *interosseous membrane* connects the radial and ulnar shafts through the forearm. The fibers run

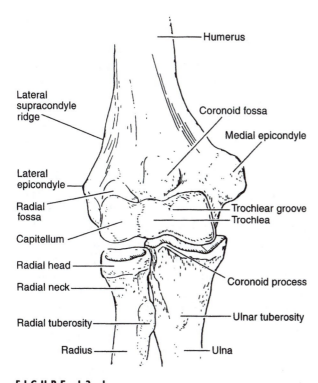

FIGURE 13.1

Anterior view of the elbow

(From JR Andrews, K Wilk, Y Satterwhite, and J Tedder, "Physical examination of the thrower's elbow," *Journal of Orthopaedic Sports Physical Therapists* 17(6): 297, 1993.)

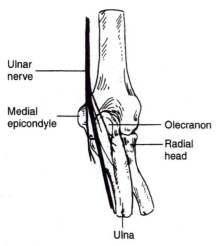

FIGURE 13.2

Posterior view of the elbow

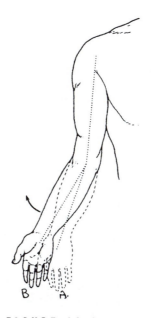

FIGURE 13.3

Carrying angle of the elbow

(From American Orthopaedic Association: *Manual of Orthopaedic Surgery.* Chicago, 1972, p. 138. Reprinted by permission.)

obliquely downward and medially (from radius to ulna), and limits separation and migration of the radius and ulna. The interosseous membrane separates the anterior flexor compartment from the posterior extensor compartment.

Elbow Joint Stability

Theoretically, elbow stability can be considered to be 50 percent a function of collateral ligaments and anterior capsule and 50 percent a function of the bony articulation, primarily from the ulno-humeral joint.[6]

BONY ARTICULATION: Unlike the shoulder, the elbow joint complex possesses significant inherent stability because of the interlocking configuration of the articulating surfaces. The main contributor to bony stability is the articulation between the trochlea of the humerus and the trochlear fossa of the ulna. The coronoid process provides an important block to posterior displacement as the elbow flexes. The humeroradial articulation provides some resistance to valgus stress across the elbow and inhibits posterior dislocation at 90 degrees of flexion or more. The proximal radioulnar articulation does not provide significant elbow stability, but simply allows forearm pronation and supination to take place.[1]

LIGAMENTS:

MEDIAL COLLATERAL LIGAMENT.
The medial (or ulnar) collateral ligament is the major stabilizer against valgus stress at the elbow. It originates from the inferior surface of the medial epicondyle of the distal humerus and fan outs to insert along the medial edge of the olecranon from the coronoid process anteriorly to the midportion of the olecranon. It is composed of three portions (Figure 13.4):

1. Biomechanically and anatomically, the *anterior oblique* component of the medial collateral ligament is the major ligamentous support of the medial aspect of the elbow. It originates on the inferior surface of the medial epicondyle of the humerus and inserts at the medial aspect of the coranoid process.

2. The *posterior oblique* portion of the medial (ulnar) collateral ligament is fan shaped. It originates inferior to the origin of the anterior oblique portion and inserts into the posteriomedial aspect of the olecranon.

3. The *transverse bundle* portion of the medial ligament complex originates from the medial olecranon and inserts into the coronoid process of the ulna. It is difficult to differentiate it from the medial joint capsule. The majority of investigators believe that this portion of the ligament complex contributes little, if any, elbow stability.[5]

In athletics the elbow is often forced into a valgus position, placing a strain on the medial collateral liga-

ment. The medial ligaments are tight when the elbow is in full extension and the olecranon is "locked" into the olecranon fossa. As the elbow moves from full extension to varying degrees of flexion, the anterior oblique portion of the medial collateral ligament becomes relatively lax and can be more easily stressed. Most ligamentous injuries take place when the arm is in this vulnerable position.[1]

THE LIGAMENTS ON THE LATERAL ASPECT.

1. The elbow does not possess a true *lateral collateral ligament*. The anatomic structure designated as such originates on the lateral epicondyle of the distal humerus and attaches to the annular ligament, but does not attach directly to bone (Figure 13.5). Therefore this lateral stabilizing structure is able to resist only minimal tensile forces.[1] The anconeus, a muscle located on the lateral aspect of the elbow, provides additional stability against varus stress. The lack of strong lateral stabilizing structures does not pose a significant problem, because valgus stability is much more important functionally than is varus stability. From a consideration of typical elbow motions involving high forces (throwing, falling on an outstretched arm), it is clear that the primary tensile stresses are sustained on the medial side.[1]

2. The *annular ligament* completely surrounds the radial head with a firm ring, thus holding the radial head against the radial notch of the ulna (Figure 13.5).

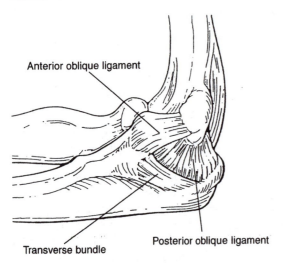

FIGURE 13.4

Normal anatomy of ulnar (medial) collateral ligament complex (From J Whiteside and J Andrews, "Common elbow problems in the recreational athlete," *Journal of Musculoskeletal Medicine* 6(2): 24, 1989.)

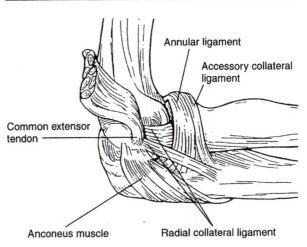

FIGURE 13.5

Normal anatomy of radial (lateral) collateral ligament complex (From J Whiteside and J Andrews, "Common elbow problems in the recreational athlete," *Journal of Musculoskeletal Medicine* 6(2): 24, 1989.)

Muscles

MUSCLES ORIGINATING ABOVE THE ELBOW:

1. *Biceps brachii: Long head*—From the upper margin of the glenoid rim to the tuberosity of the radius. *Short head*—From the coracoid process to the tuberosity of the radius. *Function:* Flexes the elbow joint, supinates the forearm.

2. *Brachialis:* From the lower half of the anterior of the humerus to the tuberosity of the ulna and the coronoid process. *Function:* Flexes the elbow joint.

3. *Triceps: Long head*—From the axillary border of the scapula. *Lateral head*—From the lateral and posterior surfaces of the shaft of the humerus. *Medial head*—From the posterior surface of the shaft of the humerus below the lateral head. The three heads insert into the olecranon of the ulna. *Function:* Extends the elbow joint.

4. *Anconeus:* From the posterior aspect of the lateral epicondyle of the humerus to the olecranon and the dorsal surface of the ulna. *Function:* Extends the elbow.

5. *Brachioradialis:* From the supracondylar ridge of the humerus to the coronoid process of the ulna. *Function:* Flexes the elbow.

MUSCLES ON THE MEDIAL ASPECT OF THE ELBOW (FIGURE 13.6):

1. *Flexor carpi radialis:* From the medial epicondyle of the humerus to the base of the second and third metacarpals. *Function:* Flexes and abducts the wrist.

2. *Flexor carpi ulnaris:* From the medial epicondyle of the humerus and the upper two-thirds of the ulna into the pisiform bone. *Function:* Flexes and abducts the wrist.

3. *Palmaris longus:* From the medial epicondyle of the humerus to the transverse carpal ligament and the palmar aponeurosis. *Function:* Flexes the wrist.

4. *Pronator teres:* From the medial epicondyle of the humerus and the coronoid process of the ulna to the middle of the radial shaft. *Function:* Pronates the forearm.

MUSCLES ON THE LATERAL SIDE OF THE ELBOW (FIGURE 13.7):

1. *Extensor carpi radialis longus and brevis:* From the lateral epicondyle and the supracondylar ridge of the humerus to the base of the second and third metacarpals. *Function:* Extends and abducts the wrist.

2. *Extensor carpi ulnaris:* From the lateral epicondyle of the humerus to the common extensor tendon sheath. *Function:* Extends the wrist and fingers.

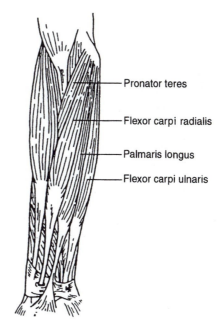

FIGURE 13.6

The flexor-pronator muscle group of the elbow
(From J Andrews, K Wilk, Y Satterwhite, and J Tedder, "Physical examination of the thrower's elbow," *Journal of Orthopaedic Sports Physical Therapists* 17(6): 298, 1993.)

3. *Supinator:* From the lateral epicondyle of the humerus and the radial ligament of the elbow to the proximal shaft of the radius. *Function:* Supinates the forearm.

Movements

1. *The radio-ulnar-humeral joint.* The movement of this joint is limited solely to extension and flexion. In full extension the joint is stable, but with flexion the joint is dependent upon the ligaments for stability.

2. *The radio-ulnar joint* The proximal radio-ulnar joint allows for pronation and supination of the forearm and hand. This movement takes place between the radial head and the radial notch of the ulna, and allows for about 140° of movement. If rotation of the humerus is also included, movements up to 360° can be achieved (Figure 13.8).

Injuries above the Elbow Joint

Exostoses of the Mid-Humerus

The lateral aspect of the mid-humerus is very vulnerable to direct blows because the bone is close to the surface and receives little protection from muscle. There

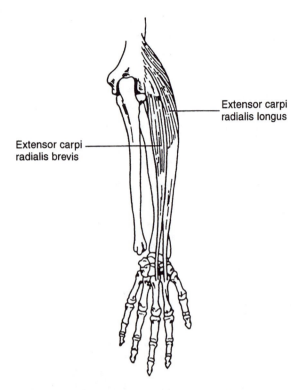

Dorsal view of forearm and hand

FIGURE 13.7
The extensor carpi muscles of the wrist 1) extensor carpi radialis longus. 2) extensor carpi radialis brevis.
(From J Andrews, K Wilk, Y Satterwhite, and J Tedder, "Physical examination of the thrower's elbow," *Journal of Orthopaedic Sports Physical Therapists* 17(6): 298, 1993.)

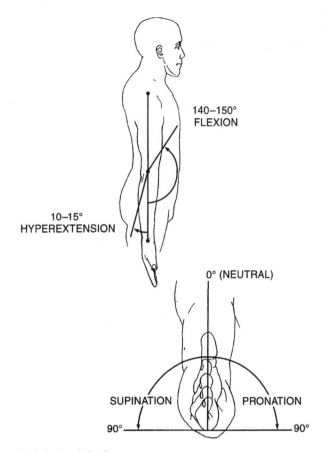

FIGURE 13.8
Range of motion at the elbow
(From D Magee, *Orthopedic Physical Assessment*, Philadelphia, WB Saunders, 1987, p. 5. Reprinted by permission.)

are two conditions that arise from contusions to this area. They have, however, totally different prognoses (Figure 13.9).

EXOSTOSIS INVOLVING THE LATERAL ASPECT OF THE HUMERUS ("LINEBACKER'S ARM" OR "TACKLER'S EXOSTOSIS"): The exostosis results from repeated contusions to the outer aspect of the mid-humerus, with development of a hematoma and subsequent calcification. This calcification is usually in the form of a spur, which can be palpated on the lateral aspect of the humerus but seldom interferes with arm function even though it may be very tender when repeatedly contused.

Treatment.
PREVENTIVE. Wearing a pad or protector over the vulnerable area when playing a sport such as football can help prevent the hematoma. Once the contusion has

occurred, it should be iced and compressed and an anti-inflammatory medication commenced. Repeated contusions to the area should be avoided by making sure adequate protection is worn.

DEFINITIVE. Treatment is aimed at preventing further contusions to the area, because once calcification has formed, symptoms are rare unless there is repeated trauma. Surgical excision of the calcification is seldom necessary, but when it is, it should not be performed until the calcification is mature, usually in twelve to eighteen months.[7,8]

MYOSITIS OSSIFICANS INVOLVING THE ANTEROLATERAL ASPECT OF THE ARM AND THE BRACHIALIS MUSCLE: Myositis ossificans refers to the heterotrophic formation of bone in traumatized soft tissue, especially muscle. The initial injury may be a contusion, strain, sprain, fracture, or disloca-

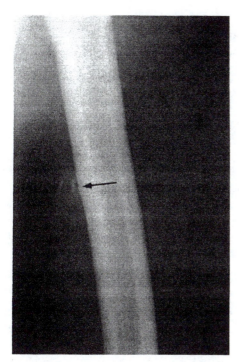

FIGURE 13.9
X-ray of an exostosis, lateral aspect, humerus
This calcific spur can often be palpated, and should be protected in contact activities.

tion. Evidence of heterotrophic bone formation may be found as early as three weeks post-injury. Complaint of excessive pain and swelling following the initial injury should alert the practitioner to the suspicion of myositis ossificans. This calcification is particularly apt to occur if:

1. the athlete returns to participation too soon

2. the area is reinjured before healing occurs

3. massage, heat, ultrasound, or other modalities have been aggressively applied to the hematoma

4. vigorous strengthening and stretching is initiated before the area is healed

5. the bleeding is associated with hemophilia (a rare bleeding disorder)

Symptoms. Unusually prolonged pain and swelling following the initial injury; undue difficulty regaining lost motion, particularly elbow extension; or excessive pain on motion should alert the practitioner. The usual presenting symptom is a painful "lump" in front of the arm.

Treatment. Treatment with ice and anti-inflammatory medication may be supplemented by splinting the elbow. The athlete should avoid all painful activities and no forced movement of the elbow should occur until symptoms have subsided. As symptoms subside and if no evidence of ongoing myositis ossificans exists, gentle active range of motion can begin. There should be no forced or passive motion. Resistance exercises should not be introduced until radiographic and bone scan evidence shows that the lesion has finally matured.

Return to participation should be allowed only after symptoms have completely subsided. The arm should be protected from further contusions. Again, if surgical intervention is necessary (which it seldom is), it should not be contemplated until the calcification has matured.

Supracondylar Fracture

A child under twelve years of age who falls and complains of pain around the elbow should be suspected of having a supracondylar fracture (Figure 13.10). In many cases the deformity and diagnosis are obvious, but it may sometimes appear to be a dislocated elbow because the olecranon and distal humerus are displaced backward. It is therefore important to make no attempt at reduction of an apparently dislocated elbow until the diagnosis is confirmed. The forward displacement of the proximal humeral shaft, which occurs with most supracondylar fractures, endangers the blood vessels and nerves—this is the most serious immediate complication (Figure 13.11).

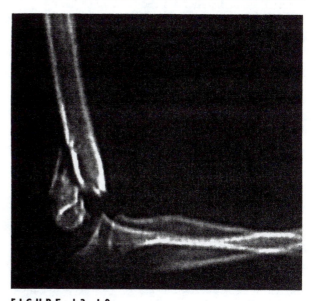

FIGURE 13.10
Supracondylar fracture on x-ray film
(From *Athletic Training and Sports Medicine,* American Academy of Orthopaedic Surgeons, Chicago, 1984, p. 217.)

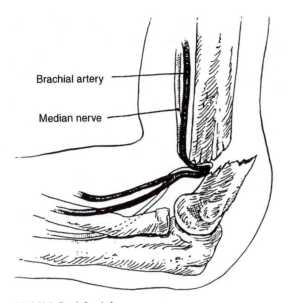

FIGURE 13.11
Complications of supracondylar fracture
(From *Athletic Training and Sports Medicine*, American Academy of Orthopaedic Surgeons, Chicago, 1984, p. 217.)

TREATMENT: The arm is splinted in a comfortable position and ice applied. The nerve supply to the hand must be examined, particularly the median nerve, and the radial pulse and peripheral circulation to the nail beds must be closely monitored. This fracture should be referred immediately for orthopedic consultation.

A supracondylar fracture results in very rapid swelling, which may compress the blood vessels around the elbow. If there is interference with the circulation, necrosis of the forearm muscles can result, which in turn can lead to Volkmann's ischemic contracture. This contracture is a permanent deformity that leaves the child with a useless limb. The supracondylar fracture must therefore be treated with the utmost care and urgency.

Injuries around the Elbow Joint

Strain of the Medial Flexor-Pronator Muscles

A strain of the flexor-pronator muscle group commonly results from a valgus force (i.e., during a wrestling match or football scrimmage) or a noncontact injury (i.e., as in javelin, baseball or softball throwing). Frequently this injury occurs together with a medial collateral ligament sprain.

SYMPTOMS: Pain is present on the medial side of the elbow, particularly when the wrist is flexed and the forearm pronated.

SIGNS: Some swelling may be noted in the flexor muscles or over the medial epicondyle. Tenderness is present on the medial epicondyle or along the course of the muscles. The main finding is pain when resisting forced flexion of the wrist and pronation of the forearm. The pain is localized to the involved muscle, usually at the medial epicondyle or the musculotendinous junction just distal to the elbow (Figure 13.12) The ulnar nerve may also be injured, therefore it is necessary to check for sensation or power changes in the little and ring fingers.

SEVERITY:
FIRST-DEGREE STRAIN. Only a few muscle fibers have been microscopically torn and rapid healing is to be expected.

SECOND-DEGREE STRAIN. More muscle fibers are involved, or the attachment of the tendon to the medial epicondyle may be partially avulsed. This can prolong recovery, with possible recurrence of the condition if it does not heal adequately.

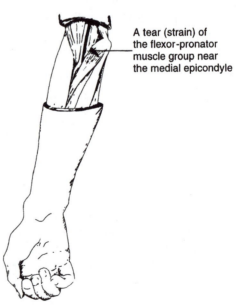

A tear (strain) of the flexor-pronator muscle group near the medial epicondyle

FIGURE 13.12
Strain of the flexor-pronator muscle group

THIRD-DEGREE STRAIN. A third-degree strain implies a complete tearing of the muscle or a complete avulsion of the tendon from the medial epicondyle. An additional variation is an avulsion fracture of the medial epicondyle with the tendon remaining intact.

TREATMENT:

INITIAL. Ice, splinting of the elbow and possibly the wrist, and early prescription of analgesics and anti-inflammatory medication.

DEFINITIVE.

First-degree strain—Icing and gentle stretching of the involved muscle group. Strengthening exercises should follow as soon as symptoms permit. Physical modalities such as ultrasound and muscle stimulation may be useful.

Second-degree strain—The elbow should be splinted until symptoms subside. Anti-inflammatory medications and physical modalities can be used. The musculature should be rehabilitated before allowing return to participation.

Third-degree strain—A decision should be made as to the advisability of surgical intervention. If the medial epicondyle is avulsed, it should be replaced to ensure pain-free function of the elbow (particularly in throwing sports). If surgery is not performed, the elbow and wrist should be immobilized for at least four to six weeks. The muscles should then be thoroughly rehabilitated.

A progressive return to throwing activities can help limit reinjury to this area. Several return-to-throw protocols are illustrated and discussed in Chapter 12's section on rehabilitation.

Golfer's elbow, Little League elbow, medial epicondylitis, and flexor/pronator tendonitis are all terms that describe conditions closely associated to strains of the flexor-pronator muscle group. The mechanism of injury is the same in many cases.

Sprain of the Medial Collateral Ligament

The medial collateral ligament of the elbow can be injured by valgus force, hyperextension force, or overuse, such as excessive throwing.

VALGUS FORCE: A valgus force can occur in a contact sport such as wrestling or in a non-contact activity such as javelin throwing, if either is done incorrectly. In addition to the injured ligament, the flexor-pronator muscles of the forearm as well as the ulnar nerve may also be involved. Most of these injuries occur

when a force is applied to the elbow flexed at approximately 30 to 60 degrees.

Signs: Tenderness and swelling are usually present over the medial side of the elbow joint, and posteromedially if the posterior band is involved. Stability of the elbow joint should be tested by placing a valgus force on the elbow when it is bent to between 15 and 30 degrees (Figure 13.13).[9] The elbow is normally lax in this position. The amount of laxity should be compared with that of the normal side. If the athlete cannot relax the musculature due to pain, the injured area can be anesthetized and retested.

Stress X-rays are taken with the athlete supine and the shoulder abducted and externally rotated to 90 degrees. The humerus is supported by the table, but the forearm is allowed to hang in a valgus position at about 45 degrees of flexion.[10] No stress besides gravity is necessary to demonstrate an opening of the joint if a third-degree sprain is present. Comparison views should always be taken.

HYPEREXTENSION INJURIES: A partial or complete dislocation of the elbow can result from a hyperextension injury. The complete dislocation may reduce spontaneously. Frequently the athlete will give a history of having felt the elbow slip out of place and then pop back. This type of injury can damage the capsule, the ligaments, and the muscle attachments around the elbow and the arm.

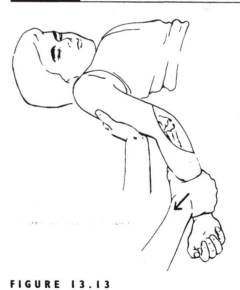

FIGURE 13.13
Valgus stress test for the medial collateral ligament of the elbow

SYMPTOMS AND SIGNS. There is considerable pain around the elbow both medially and laterally, and the athlete is usually very apprehensive. Swelling occurs soon after the injury and tenderness may be diffuse. Applying valgus stress is frequently very painful and is resisted by the athlete. Nerve function and the integrity of the vascular system should be checked. X-rays need to be taken to exclude the possibility of fractures or dislocations, and valgus stress used to detect any opening of the medial side of the joint, as previously described.

Treatment.

Immediate: The elbow should be inspected for bony deformity or dislocation. Ice should be applied around the elbow and the arm splinted, to relieve the muscle spasm that invariably accompanies such an injury. Analgesics and anti-inflammatory medication can be commenced.

Definitive: Most sprains of the medial collateral ligament are treated conservatively.

First-degree sprain—Following the initial treatment, the elbow should be iced and moved through a full range by active muscle contraction in a cold whirlpool. Isometric, followed by isotonic and isokinetic, exercises can be commenced immediately. Rehabilitation to strengthen all the musculature of the shoulder, elbow, and forearm should be continued for two to four weeks.

Second-degree sprain—A posterior splint should be used until the symptoms have subsided, followed by range of motion utilizing a cold whirlpool. Isometric exercises can be started immediately, and isotonic and isokinetic resistance can be used when symptoms permit. The length of time of immobilization depends on the severity of the sprain and the type of sport in which the athlete is participating. For instance. it is possible for a wrestler to wrestle fairly soon after a moderately severe hyperextension injury if the elbow is adequately taped to prevent extension through the final 20°. On the other hand, the javelin thrower may take many weeks to recover sufficiently and rehabilitate enough to be able to return to throwing activities.

Third-degree sprain—A complete tear of the medial collateral ligament often occurs in conjunction with dislocation of the elbow. The elbow should be splinted with posterior and anterior splints initially (to allow for swelling), followed by a cast with the elbow at 90° of flexion. This cast is retained for three to six weeks. Surgery is occasionally required.

During this time, isometric contractions are performed every hour. When the cast is removed, active range-of-motion and strengthening exercises should commence. The athlete should not return to participation until normal strength has been regained throughout the affected arm.

Limitation of motion is not an uncommon occurrence following severe sprains, particularly limitation of extension. One should never try to achieve full range of motion by forced passive movements. All this will do is encourage the formation of more scar tissue and possibly calcification. The only movements permitted are active ones (i.e., movements performed by the athlete using the muscles of the affected arm only).

REHABILITATION FOLLOWING A SPRAIN OF THE MEDIAL COLLATERAL LIGAMENT:

1. *While immobilized:* Isometric as well as limited isokinetic and isotonic exercises can be started. The isometric contraction should include setting the biceps, triceps, pronators and supinators, lateral and medial wrist flexors, and wrist and finger extensors. Squeezing a tennis ball is a useful exercise. Shoulder exercises, particularly range-of-motion and isometric, should not be forgotten. Muscle stimulation and transcutaneous electrical nerve stimulation (TENS) can begin soon after the injury.

2. *While partially immobilized:* Partial immobilization means that the athlete can remove the immobilizing device under the direction and control of the trainer, but he or she should wear it at all other times.

Active range-of-motion exercises in a cold whirlpool can begin early in the rehabilitation process, as can isokinetic exercises (limited-arc elbow flexion and extension, pronation and supination, and wrist flexion and extension). Manual-resistance exercises may also be useful.

Strength may be increased before a full range of motion has been achieved. Isokinetic exercise should be combined with isotonic strengthening using dumbbells for curls, triceps extensions, and abduction of the arm with the elbow in different degrees of flexion.

3. *When immobilization is discontinued:* Adduction of the arm and the use of elastic tubing should be undertaken only when there has been sufficient healing of the medial collateral ligament to permit such movement. Wrist and shoulder strengthening should be continued and increased. Finally, curls, upright rowing, military and bench presses, pull-ups, and dips should be performed with progressively increased resistance.

OVERUSE: Sixty-five percent of the load to valgus strain is taken up by the medial collateral ligament. Repetitive valgus stress, which is associated with the act of throwing, may result in microtrauma to the anterior oblique portion of the medial collateral ligament. Repetitive insult can result in attenuation and stretching of this area, as well as subsequent compression of the radiocapitellar articulation.[6]

Signs and Symptoms. This condition occurs predominately in pitchers, but may also be observed in other athletes engaged in an overhead throwing motion (volleyball, javelin). There may be pain with palpation over either the humeral or ulnar attachments of the medial collateral ligament. The pain is usually intensified by forced extension and valgus stress, as occurs during the acceleration phase of the overhand throwing act. Due to painful inhibition, the pitcher is usually effective for two or three innings and then suffers a gradual loss of control, especially with early release, which causes him to throw high.[6]

Treatment. In most cases abstinence from the aggravating activity results in cessation of symptoms. Ice and anti-inflammatory may be used initially to help alleviate symptoms. After symptoms resolve, a gradual return to throwing is permitted. Modification of throwing mechanics may be indicated.

Dislocation of the Elbow

Dislocation of the elbow is not a common occurrence, in either the general population or the athlete (.1% to 1%).[6] Activity associated with contact, such as football or soccer, or a fall onto an outstretched arm (wrestling, gymnastics, rollerblading, skateboarding, cheerleading, etc.) can result in a dislocation.

Anterior/posterior stability of the elbow joint is the function primarily of an intact coranoid process and its abutment into the coranoid fossa of the distal humerus, and the integrity of the medial and lateral collateral ligaments. An elbow dislocation is generally an injury of hyperextension, in which the olecranon process is forced into the olecranon fossa and the trochlea is then levered over the coranoid process (Figure 13.14). In a complete dislocation the ulna comes to lie behind the humerus, while in a "perched" dislocation the elbow is subluxed, with the coronoid process impinged upon the trochlea. In a complete dislocation, the medial collateral ligament, the anterior capsule, and, less frequently, the lateral collateral ligament may be disrupted (Figure 13.15). The dislocation may be simple without associated fractures, or it may involve radial head or capitellar fractures as well. Although elbow dislocations may occur in any direction, in most instances the dislocation is posterior.[11] Severely displaced fractures or dislocations at the elbow place the brachial artery as well as the median, ulnar, and radial nerve at risk.

Three bony landmarks—the olecranon, the medial epicondyle, and the lateral epicondyle—form a straight

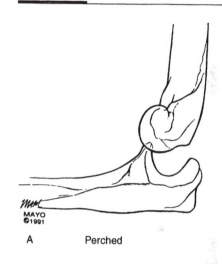

A   Perched

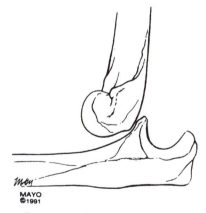

B   Posterior–Complete

FIGURE 13.15
Illustration of perched and complete posterior elbow dislocations
(From J DeLee and D Drez, *Orthopaedic Sports Medicine: Principle and Practice,* Philadelphia, WB Saunders, 1994, p. 837. Reprinted by permission of Mayo Foundation.)

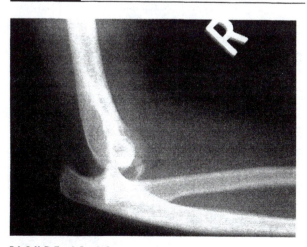

FIGURE 13.14
Elbow dislocation on x-ray film

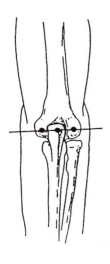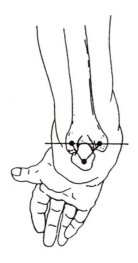

FIGURE 13.16
Relation of the medial and lateral epicondyles and the ole-cranon at the elbow in extension and flexion
(From D Magee, *Orthopaedic Physical Assessment*, Philadelphia, WB Saunders, 1987, p. 95. Reprinted by permission.)

line when the elbow is extended, and an equilateral triangle when flexed (Figure 13.16). This relationship is lost with dislocation but is usually maintained with a supracondylar fracture.[4]

SYMPTOMS AND SIGNS: The athlete usually has intense pain and is often aware that the elbow has dislocated. Swelling is frequently rapid. The elbow cannot be extended and the olecranon is prominent posteriorly, with the forearm appearing to be shortened. Palpation of the elbow usually confirms the diagnosis clinically.

IMMEDIATE COMPLICATIONS: The following complications should be looked for:

1. Vascular impairment—check the

    a. radial pulse

    b. peripheral circulation, by compressing the nail beds and noting the return of normal color

2. Nerve damage—in particular, examine for signs of median nerve impairment. Examine sensation over the palm, the thumb, the index finger, and the middle fingers, and note the ability to contract the abductor pollicis brevis by resisting forced abduction.

TREATMENT AT THE SCENE OF THE INJURY:
POST-REDUCTION TREATMENT. In cases of simple dislocations, the elbow is immobilized for one to two weeks, depending on the severity of the bony and

soft-tissue injuries. It is important to avoid prolonged immobilization. Isometric setting of the forearm muscles, the biceps, and the triceps can begin soon after reduction is complete.

Once mobilization of the arm is permitted, those in charge should instruct the athlete not to allow any passive stretching of the elbow. All movements should be done *actively by the athlete,* using the affected arm only. If at the end of three weeks a significant flexion contracture remains, use of a hinged turnbuckle splint may be employed to regain extension range.[12] Loss of terminal extension range (up to 10 percent) is not unusual, even at two to three years post-injury.[13]

Gentle strengthening exercises are allowed at three weeks, and may be performed without restriction at eight to ten weeks. However, all movements and exercises should be done within the limits of comfort; the elbow should never be forced beyond the pain-free range.

COMPLICATIONS:

1. The most serious long-term complication of a dislocated elbow is *myositis ossificans* and calcification of the soft tissues around the elbow, which limits normal elbow movement. This can be prevented to some extent by early and gentle reduction and avoidance of any passive motion of the elbow joint during rehabilitation.

2. Limitation of full elbow motion can result from the formation of scar tissue.

3. Ulnar nerve injury or entrapment is caused by scar tissue or irritation by bony spurs.

Injuries to the Ulnar Nerve

The ulnar nerve runs a course that exposes it to a variety of injuries. Arising from the C5 through C8 levels of the medial cord of the brachial plexus, it is both a motor and sensory nerve. In the middle of the arm the ulnar nerve pierces the medial intramuscular septum and then passes deep to the medial head of the triceps, passing between the olecranon and the medial epicondyle in the ulnar groove[11] (Figure 13.17). It can be:

1. contused by a direct blow

2. stretched by a valgus force to the elbow

3. entrapped in scar tissue following trauma to the elbow

4. irritated by bony spurs

5. injured from recurrent subluxation out of the ulnar groove

6. compressed by hypertrophy of the flexor-pronator musculature

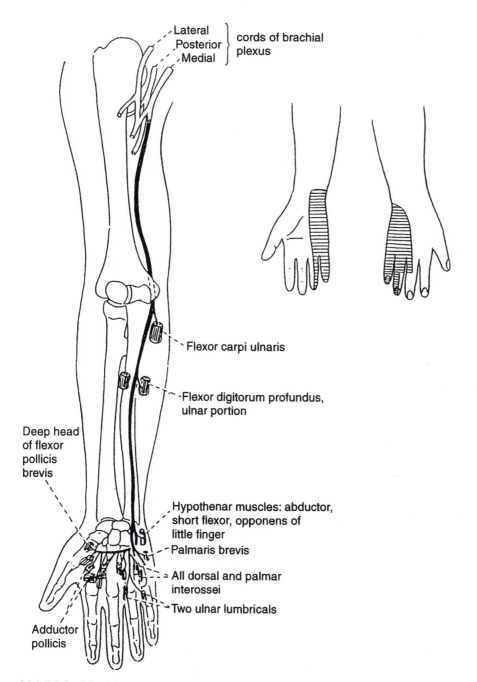

FIGURE 13.17
Distribution of the ulnar nerve
(From W Hollingshead and C Rosse, *Textbook of Anatomy*, 4th ed., New York, Harper & Row, p. 157.)

SYMPTOMS AND SIGNS: Pain in the elbow may or may not be present. The cardinal symptoms of an ulnar nerve injury are tingling and burning of the little finger and the ulnar half of the ring finger. In chronic cases, the muscles of the hand will atrophy as many are supplied by the ulnar nerve.

To test for motor function of the ulnar nerve, place a thin sheet of cardboard between the ring finger and the little finger. This is easily removed if an ulnar nerve lesion is present. Sensation impairment can be determined by a pinprick test over the little finger and the ulnar half of the ring finger (Figure 13.17).

TREATMENT: If ulnar nerve symptoms or signs persist after an injury or recur with repetitive use of the arm, the athlete should be referred for nerve conduction studies and an opinion on removing the ulnar nerve from its bony canal and transposing it to the anterior aspect of the medial side of the elbow.[14] This procedure is usually successful, provided permanent changes have not occurred within the ulnar nerve.

Olecranon Bursitis

The olecranon bursa lies between the skin and the posterior aspect of the proximal ulna. Acute swelling may follow a contusion. The swelling may be either from bleeding or from the outpouring of fluid into the bursal sac. Repetitive pressure and friction, as is common in wrestling, can also injure the bursa. Olecranon bursitis may present in a number of ways:

1. No symptoms may be present other than swelling, which may not interfere with the athlete's activities.

2. The bursa may become inflamed and extremely tender to the touch, particularly after an acute contusion.

3. The bursa may become infected. Abrasions such as turf burns, road rash, lacerations, and puncture wounds can result in infection.[15]

PREVENTION: Athletes who frequently fall on their elbows (e.g., football wide receivers) should wear elbow pads to protect themselves from contusions to the olecranon bursa. This applies particularly to those who play on an artificial surface. A neoprene (wetsuit material) elbow sleeve has been developed for this purpose[16] (Figure 13.18).

TREATMENT: An ice pack should be applied to the tender area and held in place firmly with an elastic wrap. The ice should be applied for twenty to thirty minutes every hour for the first twenty-four hours. Anti-inflammatory medication should be administered immediately.

In cases of considerable swelling and tenderness, the olecranon should be drained under sterile conditions, the fluid should be cultured, and a long-acting local anesthetic should be injected. Ice, compression, and anti-inflammatory medication should be continued. Compression must be continuous during the first forty-eight hours following aspiration. Cold should be applied over the compression wrap. Antibiotics should be used if an infection is suspected. The athlete may be allowed to return to participation as long as the elbow is adequately protected from further contusions. In most

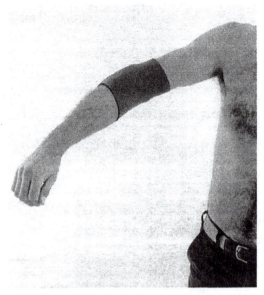

FIGURE 13.18
Neoprene elbow sleeve
The pad helps protect the olecranon.

cases this protection should be continued for the remainder of the season.

In chronic olecranon bursitis, a long-acting corticosteroid preparation can be injected into the bursa after it is drained, provided there is no infection. It may be necessary to surgically remove the bursa if it becomes chronically inflamed or is painful constantly.

Fracture of the Head of the Radius

A fracture of the head of the radius commonly occurs as the result of a fall on the hand of an outstretched arm. Occasionally, however, the radial head is fractured as the result of a severe valgus force that tears the medial collateral ligament and places compression and shearing stress on the radial head (Figure 13.19).

SYMPTOMS AND SIGNS: Pain is the main symptom, and it is frequently poorly localized. There may be some swelling lateral to the olecranon. Flexion and extension may or may not be limited, but pronation and supination are usually very painful and cannot be adequately performed. Tenderness is experienced directly over the head of the radius (only gentle palpation is required). In the absence of other injuries, complications of the nerves or blood vessels seldom occur.

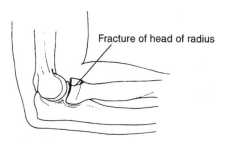

FIGURE 13.19
Fracture of head of radius

TREATMENT:

Initial: Ice and splinting of the arm to prevent muscle spasm; analgesics and anti-inflammatory medication can be started immediately. The athlete should be referred for X-rays. Frequently, multiple views need to be taken to demonstrate the fracture. With nondisplaced fractures, the fracture line may not be evident on X-ray, but a positive fat pad sign (Figure 13.20) is suggestive of the diagnosis.

Definitive: Most cases of fracture of the radial head are minimally displaced and can be treated with a sling or posterior splint for a few days until symptoms abate. Treatment usually consists of early mobilization and rehabilitation of the muscles of the arm and forearm as symptoms allow. If the radial head is more severely displaced, an opinion on surgery should be obtained.

Prognosis: If normal anatomic alignment of the radial head is not achieved, limitation to pronation, supination, or both may result. Otherwise the prognosis should be excellent.

Common Extensor Tendinitis (Tennis Elbow, Lateral Epicondylitis)

Common extensor tendonitis or tennis elbow is clearly the most common cause of chronic lateral elbow pain in athletes. Overuse tends to be the cause. The onset is usually gradual, and pain is most severe after activity. The inflammatory response that characterizes the disorder represents the body's attempt to deal with the microtrauma to the structures involved. (Refer to chapter 14 for additional information on diagnosis and treatment of this condition.)

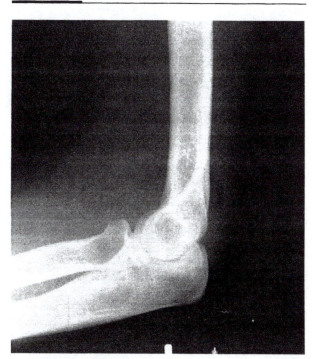

FIGURE 13.20
Lateral x-ray of elbow illustrating "fat pad" sign

REFERENCES

1. Nordin M, Frankel V: *Basic Biomechanics of the Musculoskeletal System.* Lea and Febiger, second edition, 1989.

2. Magee D: *Orthopedic Physical Assessment.* Philadelphia, W. B. Saunders, 1987.

3. Andrews J, Wilk K, Satterwhite Y, Tedder J: Physical examination of the throwers elbow. *J Orthop Sports Phys Ther* 17 (6): 246–304, 1993.

4. *Athletic Training and Sports Medicine.* American Academy of Orthopaedic Surgeons, Chicago 1984.

5. Stroyan M, Wilk K: The functional anatomy of the elbow complex. *J Orthop Sports Phys Ther* 17 (6): 279–295, 1993.

6. DeLee J, Drez D: *Orthopaedic Sports Medicine: Principle and Practice.* Philadelphia WB Saunders, 1994.

7. Diamond P, McMaster J: Tackler's exostosis. *J Sports Med* 3:238–242, 1975.

8. Huss C, Puhl J: Myositis ossificans of the upper-arm. *Am J Sports Med* 8: 419–424, 1980.

9. Norwood L, Shook J, Andrews J: Acute medial elbow ruptures. *Am J Sports Med* 9:16–19, 1981.

10. Woods G, Tullos H: Elbow instability and medial epicondyle fractures. *Am J Sports Med* 5:23–30, 1977.

11. Andrews J, Whiteside J: Common elbow problems in the athlete. *J Orthop Sports Phys Ther* 17 (6): 289–295, 1993.

12. Protzman R: Dislocation of the elbow joint. *J. Bone Joint Surg* 60A:539–541, 1978.

13. Josefsson P, Johnell O, and Gentz C: Long-term sequelae of simple dislocation of the elbow. *J Bone Joint Surg* 66A:927–930, 1984.

14. Kerlan R, Jobe F, Blazina M, et al: Throwing injuries of the shoulder and elbow in adults. *Curr Pract Orthop Surg* 6:41–58, 1975.

15. Garrick J, Webb D: *Sports Injuries: Diagnosis and Management.* W. B. Saunders Philadelphia, 1990.

16. Larson R., Osternig L: Traumatic bursitis and artificial turf. *J Sports Med* 2: 183–188, 1974.

RECOMMENDED READINGS

DeLee J, Drez D: *Orthopaedic Sports Medicine: Principles and Practice.* Philadelphia, 1994. W. B. Saunders.

Halpern AA, Nagel DA: Compartment syndrome of the forearm: Early recognition using tissue pressure measurements. *J Hand Surg* 4:258–263, 1979.

Hartz CR, Linscheid RL, Gramse RR, et al: The pronator teres syndrome: Compressive neuropathy of the median nerve. *J Bone Joint Surg* 63A:885–890, 1981.

Priest JD, Weise DJ: Elbow injury in women's gymnastics. *Am J Sports Med* 9:288–295, 1981.

Rockwood C, Green D, Bucholz: *Rockwood and Green's Fractures in Adults,* 3rd ed. Philadelphia, J. P. Lippincott Co., 1991.

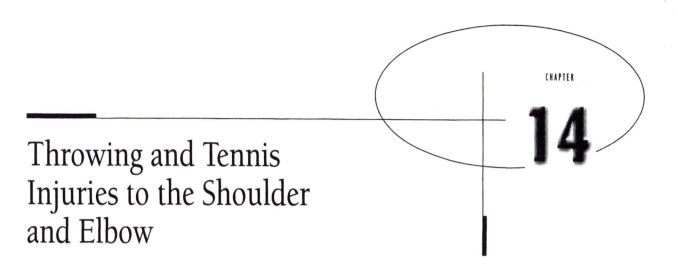

Throwing and Tennis Injuries to the Shoulder and Elbow

Acute and chronic overuse injuries to the throwing arm occur frequently in athletes of all age groups. Professional baseball pitchers are perhaps the group most studied, but injuries are also found in the pre-adolescent and adolescent Little League competitor.[1,2,3,4] In the shoulder, the acceleration and deceleration forces generated during the act of throwing are quite great and produce a tendency for the humeral head to be forced out of the glenoid cavity.[5] This tendency for excessive motion must be controlled by both active (muscular) and passive (capsule/ligament/labral) restraints. While the elbow joint is inherently more stable than the shoulder, it too is quite vulnerable to the high forces generated during the throwing act.

In order to understand the various injuries that may occur during the throwing act, it is necessary to be familiar with the throwing action as well as with the changes that occur in the throwing arm. The throwing action is divided into four phases[5] (Figure 14.1):

1. Windup
2. Cocking (includes early and late)
3. Acceleration
4. Deceleration/follow-through

Changes that Can Occur in the Arm of a Pitcher

With constant, repetitive throwing, the dominant arm undergoes hypertrophy not only of the muscles, but of the bones as well. This hypertrophy is selective in that not all components are equally involved (Table 14.1).

MUSCULAR HYPERTROPHY: The main muscles of the throwing arm that undergo hypertrophy are the pectoralis major and the latissimus dorsi. These act as powerful internal rotators of the throwing arm. The flexor muscles of the wrist and fingers also hypertrophy considerably, as can easily be seen by comparing the upper forearms.

BONY HYPERTROPHY: There is hypertrophy of all the bones of the upper limb on the dominant side, particularly the humerus.[6] A stress reaction can occur in the mid-humerus. With hypertrophy of the humerus, there is a relative decrease in the size of the olecranon. This results in an inability of the professional pitcher to fully extend the dominant arm, because the olecranon jams into the olecranon fossa. There is also an increase in the carrying angle in longtime pitchers.[7]

RANGE OF MOVEMENT: As mentioned, extension of the elbow may be limited. Shoulder range of movement increases, in that the pitching arm may be able to rotate externally more than it can rotate internally. This results in the internal rotation becoming increasingly more effective, and it allows a greater acceleration in arm motion and an increase in the velocity of ball release.

Shoulder Problems Resulting from Overhead Sports

Tennis, swimming, baseball, volleyball, football, javelin throwing, and so on subject the shoulder to extremely large ranges of motion, acceleration forces, and

FIGURE 14.1

Four phases (stages) of overhead throw:
(a) wind-up; (b) cocking (both early and late); (c) acceleration; (d) deceleration/follow-through
(*Source:* Modified from C. Dillman, G. Fleisig, & J. Andrews: "Biomechanics of Pitching with Emphasis upon Shoulder Kinematics," *Journal of Orthopedic Sports Physical Therapy* 18(2), p. 297, © 1993 by Williams & Wilkins.)

repetitions. The throwing act itself is in essence an attempt to throw the arm away from the body.[8] The forces generated are great enough to force the humeral head out of the glenoid (Figures 14.2 and 14.3). The shoulder joint's stability is attained through a complex interrelationship of static stabilizers (glenohumeral ligaments and labrum) and the dynamic action of the rotator cuff. In evaluating an athlete with potential rotator cuff pathology, it is essential that both active and passive restraints to shoulder motion be considered.

The various conditions affecting the shoulder are discussed under the following headings:

1. Anterior symptoms and signs
2. Posterior symptoms and signs
3. Superior symptoms and signs
4. Proximal humerus

Anterior Symptoms and Signs

Some of the conditions that should be considered when a pitcher presents with symptoms related to the anterior aspect of the shoulder include the following:

1. *Biceps tenosynovitis/tendinitis* The tenderness is localized over the long head of the biceps. It moves from the anterior part of the shoulder medially when the arm is internally rotated and laterally when the arm is externally rotated. The biceps (long head) has its origin along the superior margin of the glenoid labrum; it has been found to be very active both in the late stages of the cocking phase (exerts a downward force on the head of the humerus) and the deceleration/follow-through phase (helps to decelerate the humerus).[9] Due to their ability to assist in dynamically stabilizing the humeral head within the glenoid, the biceps is frequently referred to as a fifth rotator cuff muscle.

2. *Tendinitis of the pectoralis major, latissimus dorsi, or subscapularis muscles* Symptoms of involvement of these structures are usually present late in the cocking phase (they decelerate external rotation) and at the beginning of the acceleration phase, since they are the main internal rotators of the shoulder.[10]

3. *Subluxation of the tendon of the long head of the biceps* usually presents when the arm is drawn back into external rotation at the end of cocking, and beginning of acceleration phase.

TABLE 14.1 *The mechanism of throwing*

Shoulder and Arm Movements	Primary Muscles Involved	Stress Involved
Phase I. Wind-up		
Begins with both feet on the ground, throwing shoulder shifted away from direction of throw. Opposite leg is raised, ends when ball is removed from glove	Muscle activity in the shoulder is minimal and quite erratic	Little
Phase II. Cocking (includes both early and late)		
Trunk and lower body move forward while arm and ball lag behind. Shoulder abducts to 90 degrees, horizontally extends to 30 degrees, and by the end of this phase externally rotates 160 to 180 degrees. Early cocking occurs from when ball leaves player's glove until opposite foot makes contact with ground Late cocking occurs from when foot makes contact with ground until point of maximum external rotation.	During early cocking the anterior, mid, and posterior deltoid fire to allow the arm to abduct to 90 degrees. The supraspinatus, infraspinatus, and teres minor begin to fire to stabilize the humeral head During late cocking, the posterior rotator cuff firing increases to produce more external rotation while at the same time controlling anterior translation of the humeral head. Toward end of cocking phase the subscapularis becomes active to decelerate external rotation of the humeral head and prepare for rapid acceleration of the arm and ball. Strong activity also of serratus anterior and pectoralis major.	At the end of the cocking phase the anterior capsule and internal rotators are maximally stretched Arthrokinematically the head of the humerus tends to sublux anteriorly during the extremes of abduction and external rotation. Resisted primarily by the inferior G.H. ligament, assisted by the dynamic action of the rotator cuff and posterior deltoid Overuse injuries to secondary stabilizers (rotator cuff, biceps tendon) may occur with excess humeral head motion Altered biomechanics at G.H. joint may cause "kissing lesions" to occur when the posterior aspect of the humeral head impinges against the posterior glenoid rim and labrum. Tightness in the posterior capsule may cause abnormal anterior and superior translation of the humeral head during this phase.

(Continued)

TABLE 14.1 *(Continued)*

Shoulder and Arm Movements	Primary Muscles Involved	Stress Involved
Phase III Acceleration		
Begins with forward movement of the shoulder and arm, ends with release of the ball Very short (less than 1/10 sec.) in which arm and ball accelerate to more than 80 MPH, angular velocity in excess of 7000 degrees/sec During acceleration the scapula protracts and G.H. joint internally rotates and humerus adducts. At release, pitcher's trunk should be tilted forward and the lead knee extended.	The muscles responsible for internal rotation and horizontal adduction of the shoulder show strong activity during acceleration phase (subscapularis, pectoralis major, latissimus dorsi) The scapula must be stabilized so that glenohumeral internal rotation can occur about a fixed point. The mid traps and rhomboids eccentrically contract, while the lower and upper traps and serratus anterior concentrically contract to hold the scapula rotated up.	Compressive and shear forces in the anterior shoulder drop, as posterior and inferior forces grow Valgus stress to the medial elbow (the medial epicondyle) may be avulsed or the medial ligament may be torn.
Phase IV Deceleration/ Follow-through		
After the ball is released from the hand, the shoulder continues to internally rotate and horizontally adduct across the body. During deceleration and follow-through, arm motion must be decelerated to maintain the humeral head within the glenoid. The body continues to move forward with the arm, reducing distraction forces at the G.H. joint. The planted contralateral leg is critical at this time, as it allows for balance and a smooth transition during deceleration. Arm maintains abducted position of approximately 100 degrees.	Strong muscle activity during deceleration and follow-through (posterior deltoid, supraspinatus, infraspinatus, teres minor, latissimus dorsi, subscapularis) Strong activity occurs in the upper traps, mid traps, and rhomboids in an attempt to decelerate the scapula.	Deceleration forces 2× as great as acceleration forces, great eccentric stress on dynamic stabilizers of G.H. joint. Eccentric injury to rotator cuff, with intra and undersubstance tears. Compressive traction forces may lead to degeneration of labral and biceps complex. Eccentric load to posterior capsule leads to inflammation and fibrosis; cuff and capsule may tighten, leading to altered dynamics of humeral head. Scapular stabilizers (traps, serratus, rhomboids, levator scap) subjected to eccentric load as they attempt to decelerate the scapula.

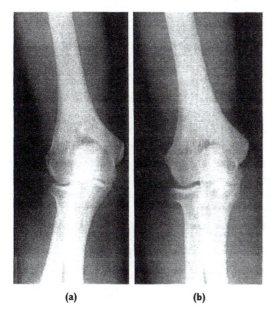

(a)   **(b)**

FIGURE 14.2

Humeral hypertrophy in response to exercise
X-rays of the elbows of a 23-year-old right-handed tennis player who started playing at the age of nine: (a) AP view of the left arm; (b) AP view of the right arm

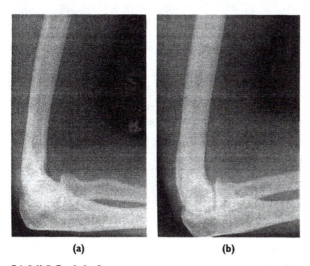

(a)   **(b)**

FIGURE 14.3

(a) Lateral view of the left arm (b) Lateral view of the right arm
The changes are typical of those that occur in the baseball pitcher, as well as the tennis player.
(*Source:* H. H. Jones, J. D. Priest, W. C. Hayes et al., Humeral hypertrophy in response to exercise. *The Journal of Bone and Joint Surgery* 59-A:2:204–208, 1977. Illustrations reproduced with the kind permission of the authors and the publisher.)

4. *Anterior subluxation of the glenohumeral joint, resulting in shoulder instability.* During the terminal cocking phase of a throw, the shoulder of a professional pitcher may be externally rotated in excess of 180 degrees.[11] At this point in the range, the anterior capsule and internal rotators are maximally stretched. If the dynamic stabilizers of the humeral head (cuff muscles) do not function well to centralize and hold the humeral head within the glenoid during this period, the capsule may be subjected to stretching forces. The end result may be a "subluxation" or increased "play" of the humeral head anteriorly on the glenoid. Increased joint play in the subluxing shoulder places even greater demands on the dynamic stabilizers, and can lead to further capsule and labral injuries. In addition, the mechanics of motion may change, as subluxations deny maximal congruency of the glenoid and the humeral head. This excess motion increases the chances of impingement of the soft tissue structures of the sub-acromial space (bursa, rotator cuff tendons, labrum) into the underside of the acromion and coraco-acromial ligament. Anterior instability during the cocking stage of throwing may cause a sudden sharp or paralyzing pain, which is characteristic of the so-called "dead arm" syndrome.

Pain during the deceleration phase and follow-through typically implicates injury to posterior structures, but may also indicate compressive forces to the anterior capsule or labrum.

5. *Impingement of the rotator cuff.* If the rotator cuff muscles are weak, fatigued, or overused during overhead activities, their ability to help centralize the humeral head within the glenoid may be compromised. Excessive translation of the humeral head can cause impingement lesions of the rotator cuff against the acromion and coraco-acromial ligament.[12] Impingement and instability are usually part of a continuum (Figure 14.4).

6. *Subdeltoid Bursitis* is an inflammatory reaction to microtrauma occurring over a long period of time. It

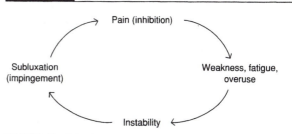

FIGURE 14.4
Overuse/injury continuum

occurs particularly in pitchers who have poor mechanics, tend to be overachievers, and go on pitching in spite of pain. Adhesions develop within the subdeltoid and sub-acromial bursa that keep the rotator cuff from gliding smoothly under the acromion process and coracoacromial ligament. The pain occurs mainly during the acceleration and early follow-through phases.

The tenderness is felt over the long head of the biceps, but it remains persistently anterior despite internal and external rotation of the humerus. Symptoms are reproduced when manual resistance is applied to the arm during the acceleration and early follow-through phases.

7. *Miscellaneous conditions* include such conditions as fracture of the coracoid process, stress fracture of the first rib, fracture of the anterior lip of the glenoid, and fracture of the acromion process. They may all present with anterior shoulder symptoms and signs.

Posterior Symptoms and Signs

1. *Posterior cuff strain* is a vague diagnosis. However, the pain may be noted during the windup phase, during the follow-through phase, or both. Tenderness is usually present over the posterior glenoid. During the acceleration phase of throwing, the arm internally rotates at an extremely high rate of speed. The study by Dillman et al.[11] of angular motion at the shoulder during the throwing act noted speeds in excess of 7,000 degrees/second during the acceleration phase of a throw. From the end range of external rotation (end of the cocking phase) to ball release requires but .03 second. The posterior cuff muscles, along the posterior deltoid and scapular stabilizers, act to eccentrically control the horizontal adduction and internal rotation of the humeral head that occurs during the deceleration/follow-through phase of throwing. An inability to control this motion may cause the passive restraints (capsule, labrum) to be overloaded as the head of the humerus rolls forward out of the glenoid fossa. In addition, fatigue and overload can cause intrasubstance tears within the rotator cuff. Pain during the deceleration and follow-through phase of throwing usually implicates overload injury to posterior stabilizing structures. Some of these cases show changes of the posterior glenoid on X-rays (the so-called Bennett lesion) that may be associated with tears of the glenoid labrum.[13]

2. *Tight posterior cuff/capsule.* The posterior cuff muscles are active during both the cocking and follow-through phases of throwing. Overuse can lead to localized inflammation and scarring. The end result may be a tight posterior capsule, with limited internal rotation

and horizontal adduction. Tightness in the posterior capsule has been proposed as contributing to impingement syndrome by causing abnormal anterior and superior translation of the humeral head during shoulder elevation.[9]

3. *Chondromalacia of the posterior humeral head.* Abnormal translation of the humeral head is thought to be responsible for the "kissing lesion," an area of chondromalacia on the posterior aspect of the humeral head where it impinges against the posterior glenoid rim during abduction and external rotation.[9] Instability of glenohumeral mechanics, or in the case of tight posterior structures, "limited" glenohumeral mechanics is thought to contribute to this abrasion-type injury.

An indentation fracture of the posterior humeral head (Hill-Sachs lesion) may also be present in athletes with severe instability.[14]

Superior Symptoms and Signs

1. *"SLAP" lesion.* Superior labral pathology is a common arthroscopic finding in throwing athletes.[15] Most common is a superior labral avulsion at the insertion of the long head of the biceps tendon, the "SLAP" lesion. The biceps insertion at the superior margin of the glenoid labrum helps to dissipate the forces placed on the inferior glenohumeral ligament during the cocking phase of the throwing motion. In addition it appears the biceps may play a significant role in the deceleration of the pitching arm.[9]

2. *Supraspinatus tendinitis.* Injury to the undersurface of the supraspinatus is thought to occur secondary to repetitive overload of the tendon during the eccentric phase of throwing. With increasing instability in the shoulder, the supraspinatus tendon may also be impaled against the underside of the acromion and coraco-acromial ligament as the humeral head moves excessively upward. In the middle-aged individual, this may eventually lead to degenerative spurring along the underside of the acromion or acromioclavicular joint.

Proximal Humerus

Conditions involving the proximal humerus are rare, but they do occur. Stress fractures of the humeral shaft have been reported,[3,16] as well as stress fractures in the proximal humeral epiphysis in pre-adolescent and adolescent athletes. In these cases, tenderness is present over the affected area. X-rays should always be taken; they may show a stress fracture or widening of the epiphysis.

Influence of Scapular Stabilization on Injuries to the Shoulder

Shoulder instability and impingement among throwers may also occur as a result of weakness/fatigue of the scapular stabilizers. A stable scapula provides a solid base from which the scapulo-humeral muscles (primarily rotator cuff) can act. With weak scapulothoracic muscles the efficiency of the rotator cuff is decreased. Kibler[17] has suggested that with weakness of the posterior scapular stabilizers (trapezius, serratus anterior, rhomboids, levator scapula), the scapula may glide laterally, leading to an increase in the distance from the posterior midline of the body to the inferior angle of the affected scapula. Kibler found that, in comparing a group of symptomatic throwers with an activity-matched control, a significant (greater than one centimeter side to side) increase in scapular glide was noted. This lateral orientation of the scapula in symptomatic throwers might represent a functional scapulothoracic instability pattern. Inability to position the glenoid as a stable base for its articulation with the humeral head may further contribute to glenohumeral instability and overuse of cuff stabilizers. This lateralized position may also contribute to the development of a tight posterior capsule on the involved side.

Treatment of Overuse Problems around the Shoulder

The primary problem for many young overhead athletes with shoulder injuries seems to be glenohumeral instability associated with overuse. Initial treatment is designed to control inflammation and decrease stress to anterior capsular structures, and may include activity modification, active rest, anti-inflammatories, and therapeutic modalities. The long-term goal should be to provide increased strength to the dynamic stabilizers of the shoulder complex (a treatment protocol is illustrated in Chapter 12).

Once pain has been controlled and weaknesses resolved, a progressive return-to-activity protocol must be employed. This stage should allow the overhead athlete to gradually reproduce forces and loading rates that approach the athlete's functional demands. The fungo routine represents a graduated, progressive throwing protocol (Table 14.2). Other examples of rehabilitation throwing protocols for baseball are included in the chapter on shoulder injuries. Similar activities in modified form could be crafted for tennis, volleyball, javelin, and other overhead sports.

TABLE 14.2 *Fungo routine*

1. Make long, easy throws from the deepest portion of the outfield with the ball just getting back to the FUNGO hitter. Perform for thirty minutes on two consecutive days, then rest the arm for a day.

2. Make stronger throws from the middle of the outfield, getting the ball back on five or six bounces. Perform for thirty minutes on two consecutive days, then rest for a day.

3. Make strong, crisp throws from the short outfield with relatively straight trajectory so that the ball bounces once on the way back to the FUNGO hitter. Perform for thirty minutes on two consecutive days, then rest for a day.

4. Return to the mound or other normal position for usual activities.

Source: "Throwing Injuries of the Shoulder and Elbow in Adults," R. K. Kerlan and others, *Current Practice in Orthopedic Surgery* 6:41–58, 1975. Reprinted by permission.

Strength and Flexibility

Muscle imbalances are frequently found in the throwing athlete.[5] Generally the anterior muscles are short and strong, and the posterior muscles are elongated and weak. This results from the specific pattern of use that throwing requires. These muscle imbalances will force the shoulder girdle to adopt an abnormal position (shoulders rounded and arm internally rotated), and will place additional stress on shoulder stabilizers (see section on problems related to throwing). Flexibility exercises should address possible tightness in pectoralis major and minor, subscapularis, latissimus dorsi, teres major, and internal and external rotators. Slow static stretching exercises should be performed on a year-round basis. Any muscle weakness in overhand athletes should be identified and corrected in the preseason. The treatment of shoulder instability in young athletes is focused at building up stability. Dynamic stabilization of both glenohumeral and scapulothoracic joints should be emphasized (see specific examples in Chapter 12).

Technique

The correct throwing technique can dramatically alter the stress applied to the shoulder and the medial aspect of the elbow. When major-league pitchers are studied in high-speed movies, a surprisingly similar series of pitching mechanics is seen. Athletes should be taught the overhead or three-quarter arm action rather than the sidearm action, which often produces elbow symptoms.[18] With a vertical position of the arm, the elbow is almost fully extended at the time of ball release, which decreases stress on the elbow and shoulder. Whipping and/or snapping of the pitching elbow and forearm, particularly with the sidearm action, increases speed but also increases stress on the elbow and forearm. If the body opens up too soon (i.e., the body gets too far ahead of the arm), there is increased stress on the arm. A good pitching coach should observe and correct this before symptoms appear.

Extension of the nonpitching arm and a too-early lifting of the back foot off the ground results in an imbalance in body mechanics. It may also indicate a technique problem elsewhere that requires correction.

Prevention

Prevention is the key to handling shoulder problems. The first sign of shoulder discomfort should alert the athlete and his or her coach and medical advisors to the possibility of a developing problem. At that stage the player should be treated vigorously, and on no account should he or she throw while there is pain. If the player does continue throwing, a reversible condition may progress into one that is not necessarily reversible.

Routine Care of the Throwing Arm

The following program was developed by Frank Jobe, M.D., and William Buhler, trainer of the Los Angeles Dodgers.[19] Such a program helps prevent many of the injuries that occur from incorrect and inadequate arm care.

1. Gently stretch and massage the elbow and shoulder before throwing.

2. Perform the throwing action without the ball.

3. Start with gently throwing, wearing a warm-up jacket.

4. Gradually increase the velocity of the throw.

5. After throwing, replace the warm-up jacket, perform gentle stretching, and allow a period of time to cool down.

6. Apply ice to the arm and shoulder or place in an ice whirlpool for thirty minutes.

Elbow Problems Resulting from Throwing

Most throwing-related injuries to the elbow result from a valgus overload that occurs during the late cocking and acceleration phases of the throwing act (Figure 14.5). The injuries that occur from throwing may be divided into:

1. Medial tension injuries

2. Lateral compression injuries

3. Posterior injuries

Medial Lesions

During late cocking and early acceleration, the shoulder begins to propel the arm forward. Because of the inertia of the aftercoming arm, the elbow is thrust forward ahead of the wrist, forcing it into valgus.[20] This valgus

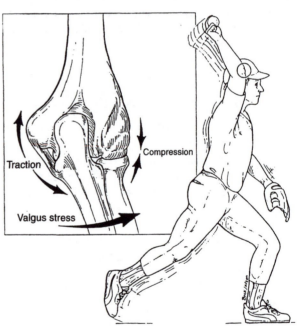

FIGURE 14.5
In the acceleration phase of pitching, the humerus is whipped forward with the elbow bent, placing great valgus stress on the trailing elbow. This produces strong medial traction and concurrent lateral compression as shown in this posterior view of the right elbow (inset).
(Source: J. Whiteside, J. Andrews, Common elbow problems in the recreational athlete, *Journal Musculoskeletal Medicine* 6(2). Beck Visual Communications, Inc. Minneapolis, 1989.)

load to the medial elbow, combined with the strong contraction of the flexor-pronator muscles as the arm is started on its forward journey, puts the medial ligaments, the flexor tendon attachment, and the medial epicondyle at risk for injury.[21]

The Little League player's problems are related to unfused epiphysis and immature bones. Injury to the epiphysis of the medial epicondyle of the humerus is the most common problem of the Little Leaguer. This epiphysis is usually the last epiphyseal center around the elbow to close. It is also one of the weakest and is, therefore, susceptible to injury. Pain and tenderness over the medial epicondylar epiphysis are the presenting symptoms.

During adolescence, muscle mass, strength, and throwing force are all increasing. Valgus stresses to the elbow are increased, and a traumatic avulsion of the medial epicondyle through the epiphyseal plate can occur with a single throw, or damage can be more gradually caused by repetitive throwing maneuvers. X-rays should always be taken of both elbows to determine if an avulsion of the epiphysis has occurred. The results are graded as follows:

Grade I: No X-ray changes, minimal symptoms

Grade II: No X-ray changes or less than 5 mm displacement of the epiphysis on the X-ray, more severe symptoms.

Grade III: Displacement on the X-ray greater than 5 mm; should be treated surgically.

By young adulthood, the medial epicondyle is fused, and injuries of the muscular attachments and ligaments of the epicondyle become more prevalent. During this time the flexor muscles and ulnar collateral ligament are at increased risk of injury.[22]

1. *Acute lesions.*

   a. Epicondylitis: Tenderness over the medial epicondyle resulting from a strain of the origin of the medial flexor/pronator muscle group.

   b. Medial epicondyle avulsion fracture: Results from an excessive force of contraction of the medial flexor/pronator muscles.

   c. Medial ligament sprain: Palpating along the medial ligament produces pain, particularly over the medial joint line. The ligaments should be stressed at 30 degrees to 45 degrees of flexion. No instability will be found unless the ligaments have been completely torn. If

there is a partial tear, pain will be produced with valgus stress.

   d. Flexor/pronator muscle strain: Produces pain near the elbow when active wrist flexion, or forearm pronation, is resisted. Local tenderness is usually present at the musculotendinous junction just distal to the elbow.

   e. Ulnar nerve subluxation: Produces a sudden electric shock-like pain, shooting down the forearm to the ring finger and the little finger. Tingling and numbness may also be present.

2. *Chronic conditions.*

   a. Ulnar neuritis: The pain is localized in the elbow area, and there is tenderness over the ulnar nerve. This condition may be provoked by a fracture of a traction spur.

   b. Ulnar nerve entrapment: Scar tissue formation around the ulnar nerve can cause this condition, which produces pain, numbness, tingling, and muscle weakness of the ring finger and the little finger, as well as wasting of the small muscles of the hand.[23]

   c. Soft-tissue calcification: This is an X-ray diagnosis. A number of different types of soft-tissue calcifications have been noted, as follows:

      (1) Traction spur from the ulna results from a constant repetitive valgus stress pulling on the capsule attached to the ulna at the joint line. This traction spur can be symptomless in many pitchers and may not cause discomfort unless it fractures.

      (2) "Stalagmite" is a buildup of calcium along the medial capsular attachment to the proximal ulna. It is probably secondary to an inflammatory response to microtrauma from valgus overload.

      (3) Calcification of the flexor muscle mass may occur adjacent to the medial epicondyle of the humerus. It is thought to be caused by microtearing of the muscle fibers, particularly when associated with fast- or curveball throwing.

   d. Miscellaneous conditions: These include inflammation of the medial capsule, the pronator teres muscle, the interosseous membrane, and a medial forearm compartment compression syndrome. The formation of an ossicle or an incomplete fusion of the medial epiphysis may also give rise to the problems (Figure 14.6).

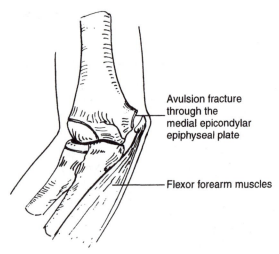

FIGURE 14.6
Avulsion of the medial epicondylar epiphysis, as may occur from pitching

---

Lateral Lesions

As the arm is forced into valgus at the elbow, high compressive forces, as well as shear stresses, are created laterally, particularly between the radial head and the capetellum.

1. *The adult pitcher.*

   a. Lateral epicondylitis: Results from excessive or incorrect use of the wrist extensor muscles, usually in those who throw a "screw ball" or a fast ball with marked pronation of the forearm.

   b. Avascular necrosis: An area of dead or necrotic bone of the capitulum, with adjacent calcification.

   c. Loose bodies within the joint on the lateral side: Probably the result of avascular necrosis of the capitulum or radial head.

2. *The Little League player.* Though injury to the lateral compartment rarely occurs in the younger athlete, when it does, it results in the tragedy of a permanently damaged elbow joint.[24] The following lesions have been described:

   a. Osteochondritis dissecans of the capitulum: This area of dead bone may be displaced, forming a loose body within the joint. This condition results in an incongruous joint surface and the possible onset of osteoarthritis.

   b. Osteochondrosis of the radial head: This is the same lesion, occurring in the proximal radial epiphysis.

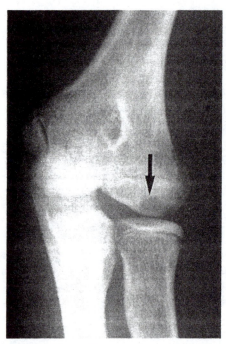

FIGURE 14.7
X-ray—osteochondritis dissecans of the capitulum
Note the cystic changes within the bone, and the irregular joint margin.

---

   c. Proximal radial epiphyseal compression and angulation: This epiphysis usually fuses at about age fourteen or later. If damaged, limitation of elbow extension, pronation, and supination can result. It is one of the most serious elbow injuries.

As mentioned previously, the professional pitcher can develop a limitation to full extension because of the relative increase in size of the olecranon as compared to the olecranon fossa. *An adolescent does not have the limitation of extension that is found in the professional pitcher.* If limitation to extension is found, pathology around the elbow joint must be excluded by a thorough clinical and X-ray evaluation.

Posterior Lesions

Posterior articular surface damage develops during two phases of the throwing act: during late cocking/early acceleration, excessive valgus stress at the elbow can cause a wedging effect of the olecranon into the medial wall of the olecranon fossa; and throughout follow-through, hyperextension of the elbow is prominent, placing stress on the olecranon and anterior capsule.

Injuries include:

1. *Loose bodies.* These are probably formed by the jamming of the olecranon into the olecranon fossa (see Figure 14.8).

2. *Osteochondral fracture of the middle of the trochlear notch.* This usually occurs on one particular pitch, when the elbow is rapidly extended while the valgus stress is continued. Severe pain and a "crunch" are usually felt.

3. *Hyperextension sprain.* This may include the medial ligament as well as the biceps tendon.

4. *Triceps strain.*

5. *Stress fracture of the olecranon (rare).*

Javelin Throwing

Throwing a javelin places considerably more stress on the elbow than does pitching a baseball. Some of the factors involved are the heavier javelin and the greater forces produced by a running javelin thrower compared with the stationary pitcher. The shoulder is also stressed, though to a lesser extent. If the technique is not quite right, an immediate elbow injury will occur, in contrast to the pitcher, who usually develops an injury over a

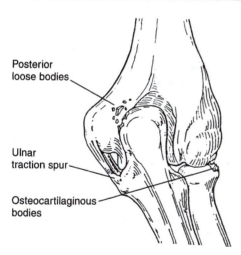

FIGURE 14.8

Compression forces on the lateral side of the elbow during pitching may produce osteocartilaginous lesions in the distal humerus and the radial head. Other bony changes that may develop in the chronically stressed elbow may include ulnar traction spur and posterior loose bodies.

(*Source:* J. Whiteside, J. Andrews, Common elbow problems in the recreational athlete, *Journal Musculoskeletal Medicine* 6(2). Beck Visual Communications, Inc. Minneapolis, 1989.)

period of time. The technique in javelin throwing is vital to the prevention of injury. The forearm should be kept vertical during the acceleration phase, and the elbow should not move into a valgus position.

Football

The football quarterback has a limited windup and a short acceleration phase. Most of the action involves the wrist flexion or snap, which is probably the most important part of the quarterback's throw. However, injuries involving the medial elbow and triceps muscle do occasionally occur.

TREATMENT OF ELBOW INJURIES RESULTING FROM THROWING: The concepts of microtrauma and muscle imbalance should again be stressed, along with the importance of preventing an injury or treating it early and vigorously should it occur. The standard treatment of ice and immobilization applies to most injuries. This treatment is continued for a period of time as dictated by the severity of the injury. A sling should be used whenever necessary. Anti-inflammatory medication, as well as physical therapy modalities, may be helpful.

Following the athlete's recovery from the initial symptoms, elbow mobility exercises should be initiated (within the limits of pain) to nourish articular cartilage and to limit the formation of elbow-flexion contractures. The anterior capsule of the elbow is relatively thin and is very sensitive to injury.[25] Excessive scar tissue formation within the anterior capsule and its attachments to the brachialis muscle can lead to loss of motion at the elbow. Active motion, joint mobilization, and long duration/low amplitude passive stretches can be initiated relatively early on.

STRENGTH TRAINING: The biceps muscle is an important stabilizer of the elbow during the follow-through phase of throwing. It functions eccentrically to decelerate the elbow and prevent hyperextension. The flexor/pronator group also functions dynamically to control medial stress (valgus stress) during the acceleration and follow-through phase of throwing. If these muscle groups are not functioning optimally prior to the resumption of throwing activities, potential for reinjury exists. In addition to muscle groups functioning at the elbow, the rotator cuff and shoulder musculature must be strengthened to ensure dynamic stability of both shoulder and elbow during the throwing act. Dynamic stabilizers and "steerers" of the shoulder and elbow need a great level of endurance. Begin with controlled sub-maximal efforts. Progress to faster speeds of movement with quick changes of direction. Plyometric activities can be added in "functional" positions in the latter stages of rehabilitation (see section on shoulder rehabilitation Chapter 12).

In chronic conditions involving the ulnar nerve, it is possible to surgically release or relocate the nerve.[23,26] This is a relatively minor procedure producing good results, providing the ulnar nerve is undamaged. Surgery for soft-tissue calcification or a loose body is also a relatively successful procedure in selected cases. Most other surgical procedures around the elbow of the professional pitcher produce unpredictable results and are avoided whenever possible. In chronic conditions resistant to other forms of therapy, a limited number of local corticosteroid injections can be used with care.

The Little League Pitcher

The importance of limiting the number of throws to prevent excessive elbow stress to the ununited epiphysis and growing bones has been a frequently discussed subject over the past decade, and rules and regulations are now in force in the various Little Leagues. The Little League coach should stress to the players not only the importance of limiting the number of pitches during organized practice, but also the danger of excessive throwing in unorganized and sandlot situations. The number of curve balls pitched should also be limited.

The technique of the Little League pitcher should not differ from that of the professional pitcher, and correct throwing mechanics should be stressed. The coach should use discretion as to the frequency and length of time each player is allowed to pitch. It is important that both younger and older pitchers be brought along slowly. In treating medial epicondylar conditions of the

Little League thrower, the importance of an adequate period of rest cannot be overemphasized. Not only should this athlete be off throwing for quite a few weeks, but a gradual buildup in the number and speed of the throws should be carefully supervised before return to full activity.

Elbow and Shoulder Injuries from Tennis

The elbow, and to a lesser extent the shoulder, are notoriously susceptible to injury in tennis players (Table 14.3).

INCIDENCE:

1. *Lateral epicondyle.* Involvement of the lateral epicondyle occurs commonly in the "club player," especially the one who plays frequently and for long periods of time, who is competitive, and who has a poor technique, particularly on the backhand. In addition, these players are usually over thirty-five years of age.[27,28] The condition also affects the adult beginner, who invariably has a poor technique and an insufficient musculature.[29]

The expert tennis player is not excluded from lateral epicondylitis, but suffers from it far less frequently than the less proficient club player. In the expert, however, symptoms are related to both the backhand and the forehand and are probably associated with overuse and muscle imbalances rather than faulty technique.[30]

2. *Medial side of the elbow.* The medial side of the elbow is the site of injuries commonly found in the expert player who hits a hard American twist serve.

TABLE 14.3 *Elbow injuries in tennis players*

Medial Side of Elbow	Stroke Involved	Presumed Predisposing Factors	Lateral Side of Elbow	Stroke Involved	Presumed Predisposing Factors
70% of expert males with elbow problems	Serve	American twist serve	30% of expert males with elbow problems	Forehand and/or backhand	Overuse
50% of expert females with elbow problems	Serve	Force of serve relative to musculature	50% of females with elbow problems	Forehand and/or backhand	Overuse
25% of club players with elbow problems	? Serve		75% of club players with elbow problems	Backhand	Technique, muscle weakness

PATHOLOGY:

1. *Lateral side.* The symptoms on the lateral side of the elbow are invariably localized to the lateral epicondyle at the extensor aponeurosis (which consists of the extensor communis and extensor carpi radialis muscles). Changes found at surgery in those who have suffered from this condition for a long time include fissuring and tears of the underside of the musculotendinous junction of the wrist extensor muscles.[31,32] Occasionally calcific deposits are found in the tendon. Very seldom does a complete rupture occur.

2. *Medial side.* Medial symptoms are related to one of two areas:

A. Medial epicondyle—to which are attached the wrist and the finger flexor muscles, the pronator teres, and the medial ligament. Repetitive forces in this area lead to changes of the medial epicondyle and the coranoid process and calcification in the medial soft tissues.

B. Cubital tunnel—the flexor carpi ulnaris arises from this area, and it is thought that constant repetitive straining of the muscle attachment gives rise to symptoms here. In experienced players, bony changes such as spurring of the coranoid process have been found. In contrast with baseball players, the ulnar nerve itself is rarely involved.

MECHANISM OF INJURY:

1. *Lateral side.* The lateral epicondyle appears particularly prone to injury in activities that overuse the forearm muscles. These muscles frequently have relatively inadequate strength, power, endurance, and flexibility. Add to this the poor technique of the average club player, particularly with regard to the backhand (Figure 14.9). A number of factors relating to technique have been implicated, including the "leading-elbow-backhand syndrome," off-center ball contact, poor timing, poor body-weight transfer, and poor use of the forearm muscles.

2. *Medial side.* As mentioned, medial symptoms occur mainly in the expert player and seem to be related to the action of the serve. Surveys show that males are predominantly affected, the implication being that the injury is stress related, since males tend to serve harder than females. This stress may be magnified by a defect in technique, such as spinning the ball excessively during the American twist serve, where maximum pronation, ulnar deviation, and wrist flexion put a considerable strain on the medial epicondylar structures.

FIGURE 14.9
The "leading-elbow" backhand
A mistimed shot with the arm in this position may produce microtrauma to the muscles and tendons attached to the lateral epicondyle.

SYMPTOMS AND SIGNS: Symptoms usually develop insidiously and tend to become progressively worse. Occasionally they originate from one single stroke, particularly a mistimed shot.

Tenderness is localized precisely to the attachment of the extensor aponeurosis to the lateral epicondyle (Figure 14.10). On the medial side, the exact site depends on the area involved. There is very seldom swelling or ecchymosis. Weakness of the extensor muscles on the lateral side, and one of the flexor and pronator muscles on the medial side, may be found. This is due either to actual muscle weakness or to weakness related to the discomfort of the condition. Frequently weakness of one of the shoulder muscle groups is found. A decrease in wrist flexibility, particularly flexion, is often present (Figure 14.11). Spasm of the extensor carpi radialis muscles is frequently related to lateral epicondylar symptoms.

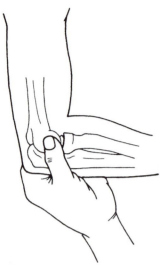

FIGURE 14.10
Lateral epicondylitis
Tenderness is localized to one specific area of the lateral epicondyle.

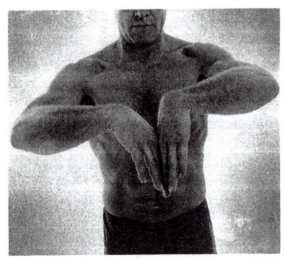

FIGURE 14.11
Limitation of passive wrist flexion due to tightness and spasm of the extensor carpi radialis muscles

TREATMENT:

1. *The acute case.* Initial treatment consists of ice packs, resting the arm in a sling, avoidance of tennis activity for a number of days (depending on the severity of the condition), and anti-inflammatory medication.

2. *The chronic case.*

   A. *Before playing:* One hour before playing, apply ice or heat, depending on which modal-ity gives the best results. Massage the tender area and the surrounding muscles. Half an hour before playing, take two aspirin. Before going onto the court, do calisthenic exercises to raise the body temperature; stretching exercises (which will be outlined) for the extensor muscle groups; and shadow-playing, hitting forehands, backhands, and serves without the ball. On the court, hit forehands only for five minutes before attempting backhands.

   B. *On-court modifications:*

      a. Average club players need, in most cases, to improve their *technique of hitting a back-hand*; in particular, the "leading elbow" should be eliminated. A good coach can do more than medical personnel to help prevent lateral epicondylitis in a tennis player. Some players benefit from a change from the standard one-handed to a two-handed backhand, which takes the strain off the muscles and therefore off the lateral epicondyle.

      b. The *racquet* can be changed to one that produces little vibration up the forearm, particularly when the ball is hit off center. A racquet with a large "sweet spot" may also be advantageous. A lighter rather than a heavier racquet is usually better.

      c. A smaller *grip size* is usually recommended, but it is more important to get the right size for the particular player.

      d. The *strings of the racquet* should be 16-gauge gut, strung at the correct tension for that particular racquet, in most cases in the area of 50–52 pounds. Very tightly strung racquets are usually dangerous for the less accomplished player, as the forces of vibration are conducted up the arm when the ball is hit off center.

      e. A *slower ball and slower court* have the advantage of producing fewer mistimed shots and less force in racquet-ball contact.

   C. *Muscle strength:* Together with the change of backhand technique, improvement of muscular strength is probably the most important change that the average tennis player can make. Muscle-strengthening exercises should affect the shoulder girdle, the wrist extensor muscles, and the finger extensor muscles (Figure 14.12).

   D. *Flexibility:* Improving the flexibility of the wrist and elbow may improve the symptoms of lateral epicondylitis. Ice massage applied

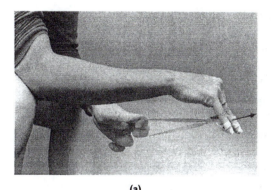 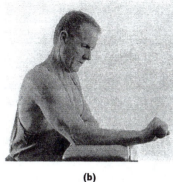 

(a)   (b)   (c)

FIGURE 14.12

(a) Finger extension exercise, using rubber bands as resistance
The wrist should be kept stationary during this exercise.
(b) Wrist extension exercise using a dumbell.
(c) Combination exercise for strengthening of both forearm and shoulder girdle.

to the stretched muscle may help to relieve symptoms and muscle spasm (Figure 14.13).

E. *Elbow band:*   The elbow band is a 2½" (6 cm) nonelastic band worn just below the elbow. The counterforce of the band is thought to disseminate the forces of muscle contraction over a wider area and help decrease the strain on the lateral epicondyle (Figure 14.14).

    Numerous other devices and braces (including a neoprene elbow sleeve) are on the market and seem to succeed in reducing symptoms in some players.

F. *Physical therapy:*   Physical therapy procedures such as ultrasound with hydrocortisone

(phonophoresis) may be useful, as may high-voltage galvanic stimulation over the tender area and muscle stimulation to enhance the contractile properties of the extensor carpi radialis muscles.[33]

G. *Medical treatment:*   Anti-inflammatory medication can be used in the form of oral aspirin, an ibuprofen-type drug (Motrin), or a short course of phenylbutazone. If necessary, intralesional cortisone injections can be given. The need for these injections is reduced, however, if the previously mentioned suggestions are faithfully followed. Sling immobilization can be used during flare-ups. Cast immobilization

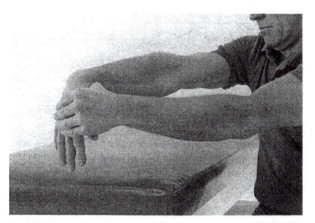 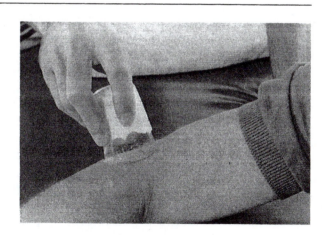

FIGURE 14.13

Gentle passive stretching of the extensor carpi radialis muscles, together with ice-massage, is often useful in treating "tennis elbow."

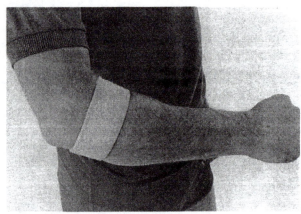

FIGURE 14.14
An elbow band for lateral epicondylitis
Elbow band is worn just below the elbow and appears to reduce the tension of the extensor aponeurosis at its attachment to the lateral epicondyle.

is not advised, but is occasionally used. As a last resort, surgery can be undertaken.

As medial epicondylar symptoms are mainly related to the serving action and occur in advanced and expert players, an expert coach should be employed to help modify the serving technique. Players should also be sure to warm up slowly and to avoid practicing the serve for too long. They should be aware of the dangers of repetitive all-out serving and should adjust their strategies to include a large number of three-quarter pace serves, using only a moderate amount of spin. Icing and anti-inflammatory medication are very beneficial. Cortisone injections may be used as indicated.

REFERENCES

1.   Tullos HS, King JW: Lesions of the pitching arm in adolescents. *JAMA* 22:264–271, 1972.

2.   Larson RL: Epiphyseal injuries in the adolescent athlete. *Orthop Clin North Am* 4:839–851, 1973.

3.   Cahill BR, Tullos HS, Fair RH: Little league shoulder. *J Sports Med* 11: 150–153, 1974

4.   Lipscomb AB: Baseball pitching injuries in growing athletes. *J Sports Med* 3:25–34, 1975.

5.   Irrgang JJ, Whitney S, Harner C: Nonoperative treatment of rotator cuff injuries in throwing athletes. *J of Sport Rehab* 1:197–222, 1992.

6.   Jones HH, Priest JD, Hayes WC, et al: Humeral hypertrophy in response to exercise. *J Bone Joint Surg* 59A:204–208, 1977.

7.   Woods GW, Tullos HS, King JW: The throwing arm: Elbow joint injuries. *J Sports Med* 1:43–47, 1973.

8.   Horrigan J, Robinson J: *The Seven Minute Rotator Cuff Solution*. Health for Life, Los Angeles, 1990.

9.   Litchfield R, Hawkins R, Dillman C, Atkins J, Hagerman G: Rehabilitation for the overhead athlete. *J Orthop Sports Phys Ther* 18(2):433–441, 1993.

10.   Norwood LA, Del Pizzo W, Jobe FW, et al: Anterior shoulder pain in baseball pitchers. *Am J Sports Med* 6: 103–105, 1978.

11.   Dillman C, Fleisig G, Andrews J: Biomechanics of pitching with emphasis upon shoulder kinematics. *J Orthop Sports Phys Ther* 18(2):402–408, 1993.

12.   Jobe F, Pink M: Classification and treatment of shoulder dysfunction in the overhand athlete. *J Orthop Sports Phys Ther* 18(2): 427–432, 1993.

13.   Lombardo SJ, Jobe FW, Kerlan RK, et al: Posterior shoulder lesions in throwing athletes. *Am J Sports Med* 5:106–110, 1977.

14.   Savoie JH: Arthroscopic examination of the throwing shoulder. *J Orthop Sports Phys Ther* 18(2):409–412, 1993.

15.   Andrews JR, Carson WG, McLeod WD: Glenoid labrum tears related to the long head of the biceps. *Am J Sports Med* 13:337–341, 1985.

16.   Devas M: *Stress Fractures*. London, Churchill Livingstone, 1975.

17.   Kibler BW: Role of the scapula in the overhead throwing motion. *Contemp Orthop* 22:525–532, 1991.

18.   Albright JA, Jokl P, Shaw R, et al: Clinical study of baseball pitchers: Correlation of injury to the throwing arm with method of delivery. *Am J Sports Med* 6:15–21, 1978.

19.   Kerlan RK, Jobe FW, Blazina ME, et al: Throwing injuries of the shoulder and elbow in adults. *Curr Pract Orthop Surg* 6:41–58, 1975.

20.   Whiteside J, Andrews J: Common elbow problems in the recreation athlete. *J Musculoskeletal Med* (6)2, 17–34, Feb. 1989.

21.   DeLee J, Drez D: *Orthopaedic Sports Medicine: Principle and Practice*. Philadelphia, W. B. Saunders, 1994.

22.   Pappas AM: Elbow problems associated with baseball during childhood and adolescence. *Clin Orthop* 164:30–41, 1982.

23.   Del Pizzo W, Jobe FW, Norwood L: Ulnar nerve entrapment syndrome in baseball players. *Am J Sports Med* 5: 182–185, 1977.

24. Brown R, Blazina ME, Kerlan RK, et al: Osteochondritis capitellum. *J Sports Med* 2:27–46, 1974.

25. Wilk K, Arrigo C, Andrews J: Rehabilitation of the elbow in the throwing athlete. *J Orthop Sports Phys Ther* 17(6): 305–317, 1993.

26. Brondy A, Leffert R, Smith R: Technical problems with ulnar nerve transposition at the elbow: Findings and results of reoperation. *J Hand Surg* 3:85–89, 1978.

27. Priest JD, Braden V, Gerberich SG: The elbow and tennis. Part 1. An analysis of players with and without pain. *Phys Sportsmed* 8:81–91, April 1980.

28. Priest JD, Braden V, Gerberich SG: The elbow and tennis. Part 2. A study of players with pain. *Phys Sportsmed* 8:77–85, May 1980.

29. Priest JD: Tennis elbow. The syndrome and a study of average players. *Minn Med* 59: 367–371, 1976.

30. Priest JD, Jones HH, Nagel DA: Elbow injuries in highly skilled tennis players. *J Sports Med* 2:137–149, 1974.

31. Nirschl RP: Etiology and treatment of tennis elbow. *J Sports Med* 2:308–323, 1974.

32. Nirschl RP, Pettrone FA: Tennis elbow: The surgical treatment of lateral epicondylitis. *J Bone Joint Surg* 61A: 832–839, 1979.

33. Nirschl RP, Sobel J: Conservative treatment of tennis elbow. *Phys Sportsmed* 9:42–54, June 1981.

RECOMMENDED READINGS

Barnes DA, Tullos HS: An analysis of a hundred symptomatic baseball players. *Am J Sports Med* 6:62–67, 1978.

Berhang AM, Dehner W, Fogarty C: Tennis elbow: A biomechanical approach. *J Sports Med* 2:235–259, 1974.

DeHaven KE, Evarts EM: Throwing injuries of the elbow in athletics. *Orthop Clin North Am* 3:801–808, 1973.

DeLee J, Drez D: *Orthopaedic Sports Medicine: Principle and Practice.* Philadelphia, W. B. Saunders, 1994.

Gruchow HW, Pelletier D: An epidemiologic study of tennis elbow. *Am J Sports Med* 7:234–238, 1979.

Gunn CC, Milbrandt WE: Tennis elbow and the cervical spine. *Can Med Assoc J* 114:803–809, 1976.

Indelicato PA, Jobe FW, Kerlan RK: Correctable elbow lesions in professional baseball players: A review of 25 cases. *Am J Sports Med* 7:72–75, 1979.

Ingham B: Transverse friction massage for relief of tennis elbow. *Phys Sportsmed* 9:116, October 1981.

Kulund DN, McCue FC, Rockwell DA: Tennis injuries: Prevention and treatment. A review. *Am J Sports Med* 7:249–253, 1979.

Priest JD, Nagel DA: Tennis shoulder. *Am J Sports Med* 4:28–42, 1976.

Slocum DB: Classification of elbow injuries from baseball pitching. *Tex Med* 64:48–53, 1968.

Wrist and Hand Injuries

Functional Anatomy

The hand is a very versatile organ, largely due to the wide range of movement possible at the shoulder, the hinge action of the elbow, and the rotation of the forearm. The area between the scapulae is the only region of the body the hand cannot reach. It can open and become completely flat or it can clench into a fist. The fingers can spread wide apart or converge to pick up tiny objects. The thumb has a wide range of movement and works with the fingers to pinch and grasp (Figures 15.1 and 15.2).

Muscles

The muscles supplying the hand are divided into two groups:

1. Those arising from the forearm—the *extrinsic* muscles (these have their muscle bellies in the forearm, but their tendons are in the hand)

2. Those arising from the hand—*intrinsic* muscles

EXTRINSIC MUSCLES: The extrinsic muscles play an important part in the following hand movements:

1. Supination of the forearm—mainly controlled by the biceps muscle, assisted by the supinator

2. Pronation of the forearm—pronator teres and pronator quadratus

3. Adduction of the hand at the wrist—produced by the combined action of the flexor carpi ulnaris and extensor carpi ulnaris muscles

4. Abduction of the hand at the wrist—flexor carpi radialis with extensor carpi radialis longus and brevis

5. Flexion of the wrist—effected by the flexor carpi radialis and the flexor carpi ulnaris

6. Extension of the wrist—extensor carpi radialis longus and brevis and extensor carpi ulnaris

7. Flexion of the fingers—due to the action of flexor digitorum sublimis (or superficialis) and the flexor digitorum profundus (assisted by the lumbricals and interosseous muscles)

8. Extension of the fingers—combined action of the extrinsic and intrinsic muscles:

   a. The extensor digitorum communis extends the proximal phalanges and stabilizes the metacarpophalangeal joints so that the interossei can extend the middle and distal phalanges and move the fingers laterally. This is the reason why, with a "mallet finger," it is possible to extend the metacarpophalangeal (MP) and proximal interphalangeal (PIP) joints even though the tendon is avulsed from the distal phalanx.

   b. The interosseous and lumbrical muscles are intrinsic muscles and will be discussed under the section on intrinsic muscles.

9. Movements of the thumb—the most important digit of the hand, capable of many types of movement.

   a. Abduction—produced by the abductor pollicis longus and brevis.

   b. Adduction—produced by the adductor pollicis (supplied by the ulnar nerve).

   c. Opposition—flexor pollicis brevis and opponens pollicis (supplied by the median nerve). In opposition, the opponens pollicis arches the thumb toward the tips of the fingers, while the

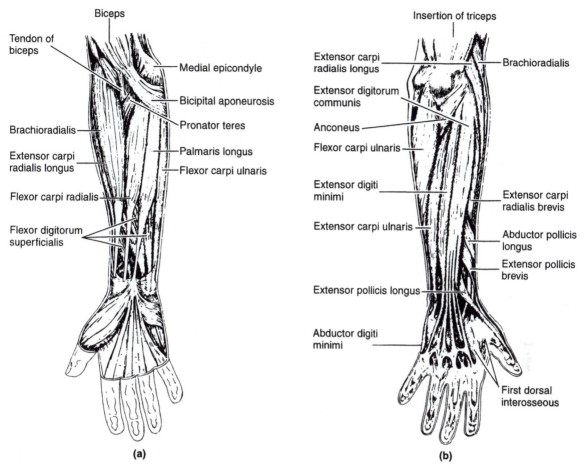

FIGURE 15.1
Muscles of the forearm:
(a) anterior view; (b) posterior view

adductor pollicis slides the thumb across the palm toward the ulnar side of the hand. However, when pinching the tips of the fingers, pressure is exerted by the action of the flexor pollicis longus and adductor pollicis. If the ulnar nerve is damaged and the adductor pollicis inactive, it is difficult to make an *O* with the thumb and index finger (Figure 15.3).

   d. Circumduction—of the muscle groups supplying the thumb.

   e. Flexion—by the flexor pollicis longus and opponens pollicis, assisted by the flexor pollicis longus.

   f. Extension—by the extensor pollicis longus and brevis and the abductor pollicis longus. This muscle not only extends and abducts the first metacarpal, but also stabilizes the first metacarpophalangeal (MP) joint.

INTRINSIC MUSCLES: The intrinsic muscles of the hands consist of:

1.   Muscles of the hypothenar eminence
2.   Muscles of the thenar eminence
3.   Interosseous muscles
4.   Lumbrical muscles

   The seven *interosseous* muscles have three main functions:

1.   Abduct and adduct the proximal phalanges, that is, spread and approximate the fingers.

2.   Help flex the proximal phalanges (when the extensor tendons are relaxed).

3.   Extend the middle and distal phalanges. These latter two movements occur as a result of the attachment of the interosseous and lumbrical muscles into the dorsal expansion or "hood" (Figure 15.4).

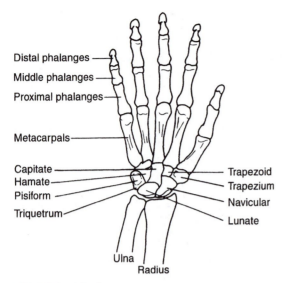

FIGURE 15.2
Bones of the hand and wrist

Distal phalanges
Middle phalanges
Proximal phalanges
Metacarpals
Capitate
Hamate
Pisiform
Triquetrum
Trapezoid
Trapezium
Navicular
Lunate
Ulna
Radius

FIGURE 15.3
Test for ulnar nerve lesion
When the adductor pollicis muscle is inactive, the pinch action of the thumb lacks strength.

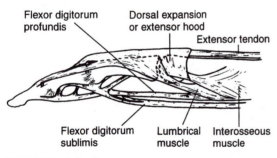

Flexor digitorum profundis
Dorsal expansion or extensor hood
Extensor tendon
Flexor digitorum sublimis
Lumbrical muscle
Interosseous muscle

FIGURE 15.4
Muscles and tendons of the finger

In a boutonnière deformity, the central slip to the dorsum of the middle phalanx is damaged, resulting in overactivity of the lateral bands (interosseous and lumbricals). This results in flexion of the PIP joint and extension of the distal interphalangeal (DIP) joint.

The four *lumbrical* muscles arise from the flexor digitorum profundus tendons in the palm of the hand. They are attached to the dorsal expansion (hood) like the interosseous muscles, and they form the lateral bands that insert into the middle and distal phalanges. This enables these muscles to flex the proximal phalanges when the extensor digitorum longus is relaxed and to extend the middle and distal phalanges when the extensor digitorum longus is extending the proximal phalanx. The ulnar nerve supplies the medial lumbricals and the median nerve supplies the lateral two (Figure 15.5).

Ligaments

Of the many ligaments in the hand, the important ones in athletic injury are:

1. *The ulnar collateral ligament of the thumb.* The collateral ligaments reinforce the capsule on each side of the MP joint of the thumb. They run from the sides of the metacarpal head to the base of the proximal phalanx. There is also an accessory ulnar collateral ligament which links up with the volar plate.

When the thumb is in extension, the accessory ulnar collateral ligament and the volar plate are tight, whereas the ulnar collateral ligament proper becomes tight only when the thumb is flexed (Figure 15.6). Therefore, when one is testing the ulnar collateral ligament for laxity, it is necessary to test with the MP joint in flexion as well as in full extension.

2. *The collateral ligaments and the volar plate of the PIP and the DIP joints of the fingers.* The volar plate and expansion of the joint capsule may be injured if the finger is forced into hyperextension. The collateral ligaments stabilize the interphalangeal joints laterally. If severe lat-

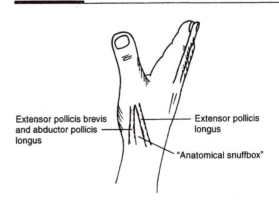

Extensor pollicis brevis and abductor pollicis longus
Extensor pollicis longus
"Anatomical snuffbox"

FIGURE 15.5
Tendons of the thumb—dorsal surface

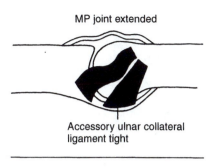

MP joint extended

Accessory ulnar collateral
ligament tight

MP joint flexed

Ulnar collateral
ligament tight

FIGURE 15.6
Ulnar collateral ligaments of the thumb

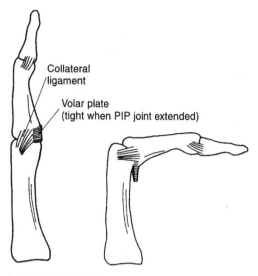

Collateral
ligament

Volar plate
(tight when PIP joint extended)

FIGURE 15.7
The collateral ligaments and volar plate of the fingers

eral stress is placed on the finger, the collateral ligaments
tear first, followed by the volar plate (Figure 15.7).

Blood Supply

Blood is supplied to the hand by the radial and ulnar
arteries. These join to form two arches in the palm: the
superficial palmar arterial arch, which is the larger, and
the deep palmar arterial arch. The blood supply to the
fingers arises from these arches.

Nerve Supply

DERMATOMES OF THE HAND: The hand is
supplied by three neurological levels: C6, C7, and C8
(see Figure 12.10).

PERIPHERAL NERVE SUPPLY: The hand is
supplied by three nerves: the radial, the median, and the
ulnar.

1. *The radial nerve.* The radial nerve supplies sensation to the radial side of the dorsum of the hand. Sensation is best tested between the thumb and the index
finger (Figure 15.8). Motor function is tested by extension of the fingers at the MP joints against resistance
(Figure 15.9), and by flexion of the elbow against resistance with the forearm in a neutral position (brachioradialis muscle).

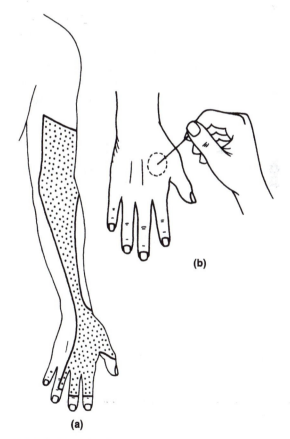

(b)

(a)

FIGURE 15.8
The radial nerve
(a) **sensory distribution** (lower forearm dorsally and dorsum of the hand) (b) **sensation test** (dorsum of the hand)

FIGURE 15.9

The radial nerve—motor function test

The fingers are extended at the metacarpophalangeal joints against resistance.

(Modified from R. McRae, *Clinical Orthopaedic Examination*, 1976. Printed with permission of Churchill Livingstone, Edinburgh.)

2. *The median nerve.* The median nerve supplies sensation mainly to the radial side of the palm and the fingers, and usually the dorsum of the terminal phalanges of the thumb, the index finger, and the middle finger. Sensation is best tested on the palmar aspect of the index finger (Figure 15.10). To test the motor function of the median nerve, have the athlete resist abduction of the thumb and note the tone of the thenar eminence. This tests the abductor pollicis brevis muscle (Figure 15.11).

3. *The ulnar nerve.* The ulnar nerve supplies sensation to the palmar and dorsal surfaces of the little finger and of the ulnar half of the ring finger. Sensation is best

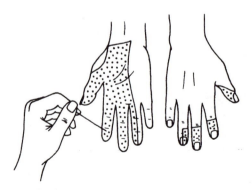

FIGURE 15.10

The median nerve—sensation test

(Modified from R. McRae, *Clinical Orthopaedic Examination*, 1976. Printed with permission of Churchill Livingstone, Edinburgh.)

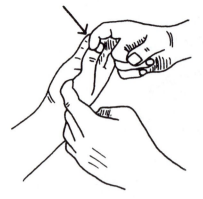

FIGURE 15.11

The median nerve—motor function test

Test the abductor pollicis brevis by resisting abduction.

(Modified from R. McRae, *Clinical Orthopaedic Examination*, 1976. Printed with permission of Churchill Livingstone, Edinburgh.)

FIGURE 15.12

The ulnar nerve—sensation test

(Modified from R. McRae, *Clinical Orthopaedic Examination*, 1976. Printed with permission of Churchill Livingstone, Edinburgh.)

tested toward the tip of the little finger (Figure 15.12). Muscle tests include adduction (interosseous muscles) and abduction (abductor digiti minimi) of the little finger, adduction of the thumb (adductor pollicis), and abduction of the index finger (first dorsal interosseous) against resistance (Figure 15.13).

Wrist Injuries

A diagnosis of a sprained wrist should never be made unless the following conditions have been excluded:

1. Fracture of the distal radius (Colles' fracture)

2. Displaced distal radial epiphysis (in an adolescent or pre-adolescent)

3. Fractured navicular (scaphoid)

4. Injury to the distal radio-ulnar joint

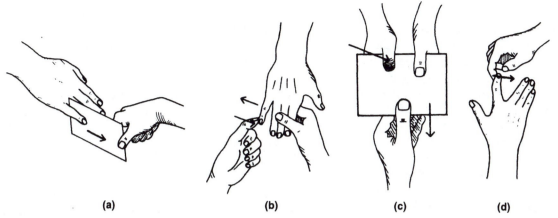

(a) **(b)** **(c)** **(d)**

FIGURE 15.13

The ulnar nerve—motor function tests

(Modified from R. McRae, *Clinical Orthopaedic Examination,* 1976. Printed with permission of Churchill Livingstone, Edinburgh.)

Fracture of the Distal Radius (Colles' Fracture)

A Colles' fracture is very common in the general population, but does not occur frequently in athletes. It usually results from a fall on the dorsally flexed hand of an outstretched arm.

SYMPTOMS AND SIGNS: There is usually severe pain, swelling, and deformity in which there is a depression or hollow in the lower third of the forearm, followed by a prominence at the wrist due to the displaced fracture.

TREATMENT:
 Initial: Ice, splint, and analgesia.
 Definitive: Reduction under anesthesia, followed by immobilization.

Displaced Distal Radial Epiphysis

In the pre-adolescent and the adolescent, the most common epiphyseal injury involves displacement of the distal radial epiphysis. If this occurs in a child with a fair amount of subcutaneous tissue, the displacement may not be readily visible. For this reason, if a child has tenderness around the wrist after falling, the wrist should be X-rayed.

TREATMENT:
 Immediate: Ice, splint, elevation, and analgesia.
 Definitive: Reduction if necessary, immobilization for a period of time, depending on the severity of the injury (see Chapter 10).

Fractured Navicular (Scaphoid)

The navicular fracture is notorious for

1. not being readily visible on initial X-rays

2. requiring prolonged immobilization before healing occurs

3. having a high rate of complications, such as nonunion or avascular necrosis

MECHANISM OF INJURY: The fracture is usually due to a fall on the dorsally flexed hand of an outstretched arm.

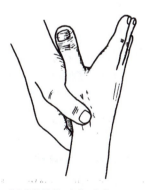

FIGURE 15.14

The "anatomical snuffbox"

Tenderness on palpation is highly suggestive of a fractured navicular.

(Modified from R. McRae, *Clinical Orthopaedic Examination,* 1976. Printed with permission of Churchill Livingstone, Edinburgh.)

SYMPTOMS AND SIGNS: Symptoms may be minimal, with little or no swelling. Tenderness is the most important physical finding, located directly over the navicular ("anatomical snuffbox," Figure 15.14). A valuable sign is pain in the area of the navicular when the forearm is rotated.

Any athlete who has had a wrist injury and has tenderness in the area of the navicular should be considered to have a fractured navicular until proven otherwise. Do not treat this athlete for a sprained wrist. X-rays are mandatory.

As mentioned, the initial X-rays are frequently negative. In some cases it may be desirable to obtain a tomogram or a bone scan in order to help establish the presence of a fracture. In most cases, tenderness over the navicular dictates that injury be treated as a fractured navicular and the wrist be immobilized. After two weeks the cast is removed and the wrist re-X-rayed.[1]

TREATMENT:

Immediate: Ice, elevation, analgesics, and splinting.

Definitive: A navicular cast is applied, extending from below the elbow to the interphalangeal joint of the thumb, with the wrist in slight radial deviation and dorsiflexion. It is necessary to keep the wrist immobilized until X-rays show the fracture to be healed.

COMPLICATIONS:

1. If the fracture does not mend and the wrist is symptomatic, a bone graft is often necessary.

2. The blood supply to the proximal fragment may be impaired and can result in avascular necrosis (death of the bone due to a lack of blood), which could cause a permanently painful wrist.

Injury to the Distal Radio-Ulnar Joint

MECHANISM OF INJURY: The injury is usually caused by a fall with the wrist hyperextended and the forearm hyperpronated. This results in an injury to the

1. inferior dorsal radio-ulnar ligament

2. ulnar collateral ligament

3. fibrous cartilaginous disc between the ulna and the carpals

4. interosseous membrane

In a mild injury, only the inferior dorsal radio-ulnar ligament is involved, whereas in a severe injury all the structures are damaged.

SYMPTOMS AND SIGNS: Swelling and tenderness are present over the distal radio-ulnar joint, particularly on the dorsal aspect of the wrist. Pain is increased by active and passive pronation. The ulna might be slightly more prominent in some cases, and compressing the distal ulna toward the volar aspect will increase the pain.

X-RAYS: X-rays are frequently interpreted as being normal. However, close inspection may reveal a spread of the distal radio-ulnar joint and possibly some dorsal displacement of the ulna, which can be seen on the lateral view.

TREATMENT: The ulna is reduced by dorsal compression and by supinating the wrist and the forearm. The wrist is held in an above-elbow cast for four weeks or longer.

Rotatory Instability of the Navicular (Scaphoid)

MECHANISM OF INJURY: A fall on the hand of the outstretched arm is the usual cause. The wrist goes into dorsiflexion, and there is damage to the naviculolunate articulation and to the ligaments of the wrist.

SYMPTOMS AND SIGNS: There is pain on dorsiflexion of the wrist, and often a limited range of motion. Tenderness is usually present over the lunate and the naviculolunate joint dorsally. There is frequently a painful click, and occasionally the navicular can be felt to slip as the wrist is moved.

X-RAYS: Special views are usually necessary to confirm the diagnosis. A widening of the space between the lunate and the navicular can be seen on the anteroposterior view.[2]

TREATMENT: Treatment depends on the extent of the instability and on when the diagnosis is made.

Fracture of the Hamate

MECHANISM OF INJURY: Fracture of the hamate is a fairly rare injury that occurs in baseball catchers or tennis players. The fracture is due to repeated trauma to the area, usually of a fairly minor nature (such as holding a tennis racquet or suffering a blow on the hamate from a baseball).[3]

SYMPTOMS AND SIGNS: There is tenderness over the base of the hypothenar eminence, some pain on flexing the fourth and fifth fingers, and possibly a mild ulnar nerve lesion (Figure 15.15).

X-RAYS: Special X-ray views are often necessary to detect the fracture.

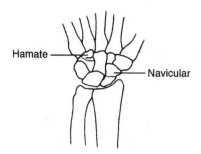

FIGURE 15.15
A diagrammatic representation of fractures of the navicular and hamate

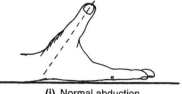
(i) Normal abduction

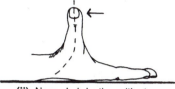
(ii) Normal abduction with stress

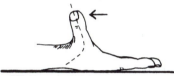
(iii) Abnormal abduction with stress

FIGURE 15.16
Abduction stress test indicating laxity of the ulnar collateral ligament

TREATMENT: Surgical treatment is frequently required.

Hand and Finger Injuries

Sprain of the Ulnar Collateral Ligament of the Thumb ("Gamekeeper's Thumb")

An ulnar collateral ligament sprain of the thumb is both a common and an important injury that is often overlooked initially or dismissed as a minor sprain.[4] The ulnar collateral ligament is necessary for the stability of the thumb-index finger pinch. If a tear of the ligament is not diagnosed and adequately treated, the thumb-index finger-pinch ability will be lost and chronic pain will probably develop at the metacarpophalangeal (MP) joint of the thumb. Instability will be greatest if both the accessory and the ulnar collateral ligament itself are torn. The ligament is most frequently torn at its distal attachment (Figure 15.16).

MECHANISM OF INJURY: Abduction or hyperextension forces are the usual mechanisms of injury, but damage to the ligament can also occur with a torsion force.

SYMPTOMS AND SIGNS: Pain and swelling are present in the web space at the base of the thumb. There is tenderness over the ulnar collateral ligament and sometimes hemorrhage in the MP joint. Swelling may also be present along the ulnar side of the metacarpal head.

Severe pain is experienced if the examiner attempts to abduct the thumb. Instability will be present if the tear is complete (i.e., a third-degree sprain). It should be remembered that it is necessary to test for instability with the thumb both in extension and in slight flexion, and always to compare the amount of laxity present with that on the opposite side. Very often it will be difficult to assess the degree of laxity because of the pain produced by the stress test, and local anesthesia may have to be administered. The amount of laxity present may be documented by means of X-rays. Arthrography may be useful in confirming the diagnosis in difficult cases.[5,6]

TREATMENT:
Immediate: Ice with compression, elevation, and splinting of the thumb, usually with tape. Anti-inflammatory medication can be given if necessary.

Definitive: First-degree and mild second-degree sprains are adequately treated with proper taping;[7] the taping can be modified for everyday activity and reinforced for athletic participation (see section on taping). More severe second-degree sprains should be immobilized in a cast for four to six weeks. Third-degree sprains should be treated by early surgery, followed by adequate immobilization.[8] When the athlete returns to participation, the thumb should be taped for the first month.

The importance of early detection and management of this condition cannot be overemphasized. Loss of proper MP joint function may produce significant functional disability. Third-degree sprains, in which recognition and surgical repair is delayed, often require reconstruction rather than simple repair and thus have the potential for a much less favorable outcome than an injury managed in an early stage.[9]

Collateral Ligament Sprain Involving the Proximal Interphalangeal Joint

A proximal interphalangeal joint (PIP) sprain of the collateral ligament is probably the most common athletic injury. It is often mistreated, mainly because of inadequate diagnosis, which may lead to permanent disability with swelling, stiffness, loss of finger movement, and pain.[10]

MECHANISM OF INJURY: The finger is pulled to the side, usually toward ulnar deviation, and any subluxation either reduces spontaneously or is immediately reduced by the athlete.

SYMPTOMS AND SIGNS: Tenderness is present over the collateral ligament involved and over the volar plate. Swelling occurs rapidly.

Stress testing of the PIP joint is usually possible soon after the injury. If the athlete is seen later, however, a local anesthetic should be administered proximal to the PIP joint, in order to adequately examine and stress test the ligaments. For complete instability to occur, both the collateral ligament and the volar plate must be torn.[11,12]

DIAGNOSIS:

First-degree sprains show no laxity of the collateral ligament, and the X-rays are normal.

Second-degree sprains may have some laxity of the collateral ligament and X-rays are normal.

Third-degree sprains show considerable instability of the joint when stress tested. X-rays reveal an avulsion fracture involving the volar plate.

TREATMENT: *Immediate:* Ice and compression should be applied to the involved ligament, and the finger should be splinted. Anti-inflammatory medication should be commenced if necessary (Figure 15.17).

Definitive: X-rays need to be taken to exclude fracture or avulsion fracture. The PIP joint is usually immobilized by means of a dorsal splint in 20° to 30° of flexion for three weeks, followed by gentle, active range-of-motion exercises. The finger is then taped to the adjacent finger for the following two to three weeks, and thereafter during all athletic participation for as long as symptoms persist. Surgery is indicated if there is functional instability of the PIP joint or if an avulsion fracture involving 20 percent or more of the articular surface has occurred.

Boutonnière Deformity

The classic boutonnière deformity consists of hyperextension of the metacarpophalangeal (MP) joint, flexion of the proximal interphalangeal (PIP) joint, and hyperextension of the distal interphalangeal (DIP) joint. It results from an injury to the central slip (Figure 15.18).

MECHANISM OF INJURY: A severe flexion force often causes the injury, though occasionally a direct blow to the PIP joint crushes the central slip.

The PIP joint goes into flexion when the central slip tears, and the lateral bands (hood) then drop anteriorly. This maintains the PIP joint in flexion as the DIP joint is extended (Figure 15.19).

SYMPTOMS AND SIGNS: Pain and swelling of the PIP joint. General joint tenderness is present, but specific point tenderness should be looked for over the dorsum of the middle phalanx.

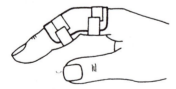

FIGURE 15.17
PIP sprain of the collateral ligaments
This may be treated with a dorsal splint. The finger is flexed 20°–30° at the PIP joint, and may be taped to the adjacent finger.

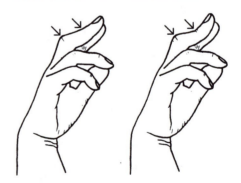

FIGURE 15.18
The Boutonnière deformity
The metacarpophalangeal joint is extended, the proximal interphalangeal joint is flexed, and the distal interphalangeal joint is extended.

(i) Tearing of the central slip

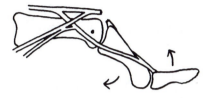

(ii) The extensor hood drops anteriorly, resulting in the PIP joint being held in flexion while the DIP joint is extended.

FIGURE 15.19

The Boutonnière deformity

(Modified from R. I. Burton and R. G. Eaton, "Common hand injuries in the athlete," *Orthopedic Clinics of North America* 4:3:812, July, 1973.)

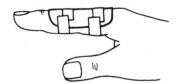

FIGURE 15.20

The Boutonnière deformity

The proximal interphalangeal joint is splinted in extension.

Pseudo-Boutonnière Deformity

This deformity appears similar to the boutonnière deformity. It is due to a hyperextension injury (not a flexion injury) to the PIP joint (e.g., a ball striking the end of the finger or a fall on the outstretched finger). The mechanism of injury does not therefore involve the central slip; rather, there is damage to the volar plate. This results in progressive contraction and calcification of the scar tissue that subsequently forms. Radiological evidence of calcification appears three to six months after the injury, usually in the area of the proximal attachment of the volar plate.

TREATMENT: Surgical intervention is often required.

Dislocation of the Metacarpophalangeal Joint

The index finger is most frequently affected. The proximal phalanx is dislocated dorsally on the metacarpal. This is called an irreducible dislocation because it often requires open reduction. Immobilization is for three weeks, after which active range of motion is started.

Dislocation of the Metacarpophalangeal Joint of the Thumb

The diagnosis is usually obvious.

TREATMENT:

Immediate: A gentle attempt to reduce the dislocation can be made by a trained physician. If this fails, it should not be repeated. The thumb should be iced, the limb elevated, the athlete transferred for X-rays, and the reduction attempted in a more appropriate setting.

Definitive: After X-raying of the dislocation, a local anesthetic is usually given. Direct traction should not be applied; the thumb should first be adducted and flexed

A diagnostic point is that the PIP joint cannot be fully extended. This is often assumed to be due to pain and swelling, so that the diagnosis is missed. A local anesthetic nerve block should be given and the athlete should be asked to actively extend the PIP joint. If the athlete is unable to fully extend the finger (e.g., there is an extension lag), the diagnosis of a ruptured central slip and a potential boutonnière deformity should be suspected.

Note: Extension of the PIP joint does not usually occur soon after the injury.

TREATMENT:

Immediate: Ice and anti-inflammatory medication should be commenced immediately and the finger should be splinted (Figure 15.20).

Definitive: The PIP joint alone is immobilized in full extension for at least eight weeks (Figure 15.20), followed by eight weeks of splinting at night and for athletic participation. The splint should be continued during athletic participation until there is at least 45° of flexion and full extension.

If the diagnosis is missed and the finger is splinted in flexion, the disrupted ends of the central slip will be held apart. This will only aggravate the condition and establish a deformity. Splinting in as much extension as possible can be tried for awhile to assess the response, but if the extension lag remains, surgical correction should be undertaken.

across the palm, after which traction usually reduces the dislocation. The X-rays should also be taken following the reduction. If attempts at reduction prove unsuccessful, surgery may be necessary. Immobilization is for three to four weeks, followed by four weeks of protective taping during athletic participation.

Dislocation of the Proximal Interphalangeal Joint

Dislocation of the PIP joint is usually in a dorsal direction, that is, the middle phalanx dislocates dorsally on the proximal phalanx (rarely in a volar direction). The nature of this dislocation means there must be either a tear or an avulsion of the volar plate of the middle phalanx.

TREATMENT:

Immediate: Reduction is usually relatively easy. Long-axis traction is applied, together with gentle hyperextension of the PIP joint. Following reduction, the joint should be tested for stability. Ice and a splint should be applied. The athlete should be sent for X-rays, to establish whether an avulsion fracture of the volar plate or an articular fracture (which involves the joint) has occurred.

Definitive: Anti-inflammatory medication should be commenced, and the finger should be immobilized with the PIP joint in a position of 20° to 30° of flexion for about three weeks. This is followed by gentle, active range-of-motion for about three weeks. The affected finger should be taped to the adjacent finger for an additional two weeks to keep it immobile. Thereafter, taping should be continued for athletic participation as long as there are symptoms.

With a straight dorsal dislocation, the collateral ligaments are usually intact and so no collateral instability is present. However, if a large fracture has occurred which includes the insertion of the collateral ligament, reduction is often unstable and if functionally unstable, requires surgery.

Dislocation of the Distal Interphalangeal Joint

DIP joint dislocation can be in either a dorsal or a lateral direction or in a combination of the two. The flexor and the extensor mechanisms are usually not disrupted.

TREATMENT:

Immediate: Reduction is fairly easily accomplished by gently increasing the deformity while applying trac-

tion. Once reduction is achieved, the joint is usually stable, but it should be examined both for stability and for range of motion. Incomplete range of motion may indicate that the volar plate has been entrapped within the joint. Ice and a splint should be applied and the athlete should be referred for X-rays to exclude any accompanying fractures.

Definitive: The DIP joint should be immobilized in a position of function (30° of flexion) for three weeks, then taped during athletic participation for at least another three weeks.

Fractures of the Metacarpals

Fractures of the metacarpals can occur at the

1. base
2. shaft
3. neck

These fractures can be transverse, oblique, or spiral. In addition, certain types (e.g., "boxer's fracture") can be impacted.

SYMPTOMS AND SIGNS: The athlete complains of pain and swelling of the hand following the injury. There is tenderness over the affected metacarpal and crepitation is elicited in an unstable fracture.

One of the most useful signs for differentiating between a contusion and a fracture is the percussion test. In this test the athlete holds the fingers in full extension. The ends of the fingers are firmly percussed, transmitting force down the shaft of the metacarpal and producing pain if a fracture is present (Figure 15.21). The same test can be applied with the fingers flexed while the MP joint is percussed.

Finger alignment should be checked. Most important is nail alignment on flexion of the MP and finger joints. If there is a disturbance in the normal fingernail

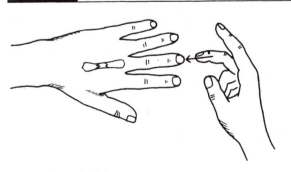

FIGURE 15.21
The percussion test for a suspected fracture of the metacarpal

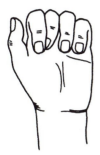

FIGURE 15.22
Rotation of a fractured metacarpal will cause a disturbance in the normal fingernail alignment

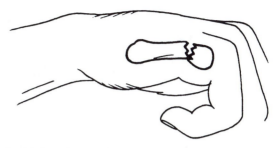

FIGURE 15.23
Fracture of the neck of the fifth metacarpal—the "boxer's fracture"

alignment, a fracture with rotational deformity should be suspected (Figure 15.22). The diagnosis is confirmed by X-ray examination.

TREATMENT:

Immediate: Ice, compression, and elevation of the limb are combined with anti-inflammatory medication if necessary.

Definitive: This varies with the metacarpal involved, the type of fracture, and the amount of displacement or angulation. Generally speaking, the third and fourth metacarpals are usually more stable than the index-finger and the little-finger metacarpals. Immobilization is achieved with the MP joint held in flexion (this allows muscle relaxation because the MP joint is in the position of function). Four or five weeks of immobilization are usually sufficient for healing. Open reduction may be necessary if rotation, shortening, or angulation are detected.

Boxer's fracture is a fracture of the neck of the fifth metacarpal and usually produces a flexion deformity. It usually results from a mistimed punch. Many physicians consider that up to 40° of volar angulation is acceptable for normal functioning, as long as no rotation is present. Some physicians, however, reduce the fracture if less angulation is present. The fracture should be immobilized for four to six weeks (Figure 15.23).

Fracture-Dislocation of the Base of the First Metacarpal (Bennett's Fracture)

A fracture-dislocation of the first metacarpal base is really a dislocation in which the small medial fragment of the proximal metacarpal is left in the joint, where it is held by the attachment of the volar ligament. The fracture is very unstable and can usually be diagnosed clinically; because of this metacarpal instability, maintenance of the reduction may be troublesome. Thus,

operative reduction with internal fixation is not uncommon.

Fractures of the Proximal Phalanges

The proximal phalanx is fractured more commonly than the other phalanges, usually by a hyperextension force. This fracture is often disabling because of complications.

SYMPTOMS AND SIGNS: The diagnosis may be suspected clinically by the presence of swelling, tenderness, and percussion tenderness. Fingernail alignment should be checked to determine if rotation or angulation has occurred.

TREATMENT:

Immediate: Ice, elevation of the limb, and splinting of the finger are combined with anti-inflammatory medication as required.

Definitive: Since this fracture is frequently unstable, it may have to be surgically immobilized with Kirschner wires (fine wires placed through the bone across the fracture to hold the fragments in place).

COMPLICATIONS: Complications include rotation, nonunion (if immobilized inadequately), or adherence of adjacent tendons to the healing fracture site. This last complication can limit motion of the finger joints.

Fractures of the Middle Phalanges

Middle phalangeal fractures usually occur in the narrow midshaft and are either transverse or oblique. Diagnosis is based on swelling, local tenderness, possibly crepitus, and percussion tenderness at the end of the extended finger. Rotation should be checked by examining nail alignment. These fractures heal slowly and may require six to eight weeks of immobilization. If unstable, Kirschner wires should be used.

Articular Fractures Involving the Phalangeal Joints

Fractures extending into the joint may require surgery if they involve more than a quarter of the articular surface, if there is displacement of a condylar fracture, or if a volar lip fracture is present.

Fracture-Dislocation of the Volar Lip

A fracture-dislocation usually involves the volar lip of the base of the middle phalanx. There is frequently a history of longitudinal compression force, for example, a ball hitting the fingertip. Some dorsal subluxation of the joint may also occur. If this condition is not adequately diagnosed and treated, permanent stiffness and pain result. Examination usually requires local anesthesia and stress X-rays. If the fracture involves more than approximately 20 percent of the articular surface, it should be replaced surgically, for it is often found during operation to be considerably larger than expected from the X-rays.[11,12]

Rupture of the Flexor Tendon (Flexor Digitorum Profundus) of the Distal Phalanx

MECHANISM OF INJURY: In a contact sport such as football or rugby, the athlete may grab the opponent's jersey by bringing the fingers into flexion. If the force extending one of the fingers is too great, the attachment of the flexor digitorum profundus may be avulsed from its insertion into the distal phalanx.[13]

SYMPTOMS AND SIGNS: Pain, swelling, and tenderness of the finger, particularly at the tendon attachment just distal to the DIP joint on the volar surface. Pain and tenderness are felt in the palm if the tendon has retracted, and a small mass can be felt in that area. Ecchymosis can be seen under the skin along the course of the tendon if the athlete is examined a day or two after the injury. The diagnostic feature is an inability to fully flex the DIP joint, particularly when the PIP joint is held in extension (Figure 15.24). An X-ray should be taken to rule out an avulsion fracture.

TREATMENT:
Immediate: Ice, anti-inflammatory medication, and elevation.
Definitive: Surgery as soon after the injury as feasible.

Acute Mallet Finger

Acute mallet finger (rupture of the extensor tendon of the distal phalanx) can occur in any sport involving

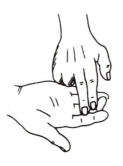 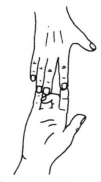

(i) Test for flexor digitorum profundus   **(ii)** Test for flexor digitorum sublimis

FIGURE 15.24
Tests for the function of the flexor tendons of the hand (Modified from R. McRae, *Clinical Orthopaedic Examination,* 1976. Printed with permission of Churchill Livingstone, Edinburgh.)

catching a ball. The injury is caused by a longitudinal force to the fingertip which occurs when the hand is slightly closed before the ball is caught. The ball therefore strikes the extended finger, forcing it into flexion and avulsing the tendon (extensor digitorum) from the distal phalanx, with or without a piece of bone. The DIP joint thus cannot be fully extended (Figure 15.25).

SYMPTOMS AND SIGNS: The diagnosis is usually obvious. There is a "dropped finger" and tenderness over the distal phalanx at the attachment of the tendon to the dorsal surface. A secondary reaction can result if the condition is not corrected—the PIP joint may be forced into hyperextension (especially if there are lax ligaments at the PIP joint) as the force of the extensor mechanism is increased due to lack of pull on the distal phalanx. This results in a "swan neck" deformity (Figure 15.26).

TREATMENT:
Immediate: Treatment is with ice, some compression, splinting of the finger in extension, and anti-inflammatory medication if indicated. An X-ray should be taken to exclude an avulsion fracture.
Definitive: Consists of splinting the DIP joint at 0° of extension. It is not considered necessary to hyperextend the DIP joint, nor to include the PIP joint. In the case of an avulsion fracture, X-rays should be obtained to ensure proper positioning of the bone fragments so that optimal healing may occur. Splinting of the DIP joint at 0° should be continued for approximately eight weeks. The splint should not be removed if the joint and

TABLE 15.1 *Common finger injuries*

Mechanism	Injured Structures	Treatment
Injuries to the metacarpophalangeal joint of the thumb		
Abduction or torsional stress	Ulnar collateral ligaments	First-Degree: Tape Second-Degree: Cast Third-Degree: Surgery
Adduction	Radial collateral ligaments	First- and Second-Degree:
Direct blow or longitudinal force	Fracture, proximal phalanx	Tape Cast
Injuries to the proximal interphalangeal joint		
Hyperextension	Volar plate Fracture, proximal or middle phalanx	Splint PIP joint in 30° of flexion for 6 weeks
Valgus or varus stress	Collateral ligament with or without the volar plate	Splint PIP joint in 30° flexion, with adjacent fingers as stabilizers, for 6 weeks
Forced flexion or dorsal contusion	Central slip rupture (point tenderness on dorsal surface of middle phalanx—boutonniere deformity)	Splint PIP joint in full extension for 8–16 weeks
Injuries to the distal interphalangeal joint		
Forced flexion—unable to extend distal phalanx	Attachment of extensor tendon (extensor digitorum—"mallet finger")	Splint DIP joint in extension for 8–16 weeks, occasionally surgery
Forced extension—unable to flex distal phalanx (particularly when PIP joint is held in extension)	Attachment of flexor tendon (flexor digitorum profundus)	Surgery

FIGURE 15.25
Mallet finger
(Modified from R. McRae, *Clinical Orthopaedic Examination*, 1976. Printed with permission of Churchill Livingstone, Edinburgh.)

FIGURE 15.26
Mallet finger
The extensor tendon itself or the tendon plus a piece of bone may be avulsed.

distal phalanx are not fully supported, even for a moment. After eight weeks, the splint should be worn only at night and when participating in athletics. This should be continued for at least another six weeks. Surgery should be considered if a large piece of bone is avulsed, particularly if it involves the surface of the joint (Figure 15.27).

Note: An injury to the PIP joint often coexists with a mallet finger but is frequently overlooked. When examining a mallet finger, always remember to exclude an injury to the PIP joint.

Tenosynovitis of the Tendons of the Thumb

Inflammation of the tendon sheaths of the extensor pollicis longus, the extensor pollicis brevis, and the abductor pollicis longus (occasionally the extensor digitorum) are particularly common in sports requiring a great deal of wrist action such as in crew or basketball. It occurs especially when the athlete has a deficient technique.

SYMPTOMS AND SIGNS: Pain, swelling, and crepitus along the tendons at the wrist and up the arm are the presenting symptoms. Performance is impaired and there is local tenderness along the tendons. Resistance to abduction and extension of the thumb is frequently painful and weak.

TREATMENT: Ice, immobilization of the wrist and the thumb, and anti-inflammatory medication should be used initially, followed by ultrasound and ice massage. Injection of corticosteriods under the tendon sheath (but not into the tendon) may prove beneficial if a more conservative regime does not work. When the athlete returns to participation, the coach should attempt to correct the faulty technique.

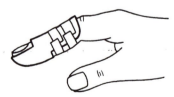

FIGURE 15.27
Mallet finger
The distal interphalangeal joint is splinted in extension (0°).

Lacerations

A laceration that involves the hand should not be passed off as a minor injury. It should be taken seriously, and the nerve and tendon function should be carefully checked (see tendon and nerve tests of the hand). If there is any doubt as to the integrity of either of these structures, an orthopedic or hand surgeon should be consulted immediately. Standard antiseptic management should be applied before referral.

"Bowler's Thumb"

Bowler's thumb (perineural fibrosis of the ulnar digital nerve) is found in tenpin bowlers, who constantly irritate the ulnar digital nerve of the thumb when placing it within the thumbhole of the ball. Some of these athletes have transient symptoms that subside when bowling is curtailed, but others have permanent damage to the nerve.[14,15] Enlarging the thumbhole and/or padding the thumb are useful for preventing or decreasing symptoms. However, if symptoms do not subside, surgical exploration of the nerve may be indicated.

"Handlebar Palsy"

Handlebar palsy occurs in cyclists, who present with motor weakness involving the ulnar innervated muscles of the hand. There are minimal sensory findings. It results from repeated irritation of the deep branch of the ulnar nerve just distal to the canal of Guyon. Prevention of this condition consists of applying sufficient padding to the handlebars and changing the position of the hand at frequent intervals while cycling.[16,17]

Carpal Tunnel Syndrome

Another injury of the wrist worthy of attention is carpal tunnel syndrome (CTS), which is the most common focal nerve entrapment syndrome.[18] This injury is more often found in the work setting and has long been associated with repetitive motion activities such as typing or frequent and sustained use of the wrist flexors. It also may occasionally occur in the athletic population in both the acute and chronic forms. Careful history and evaluation is the key to early recognition and may help the athlete avoid prolonged disability or surgery.

ETIOLOGY: The carpal tunnel is formed anteriorly by the volar (or transverse) carpal ligament and posteriorly by the carpal bones (Figure 15.28). CTS involves the compression of the median nerve, most commonly as it passes through the carpal tunnel in conjunction

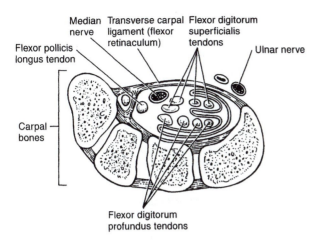

FIGURE 15.28

A cross-sectional view of the wrist and proximal palm
shows that the carpal tunnel, bounded above by the transverse carpal ligament (flexor retinaculum) and below by the carpal bones, contains the median nerve and nine tendons. Mechanical compression of the median nerve causes carpal tunnel syndrome.

(From Steyers C, and Schelkun P., Practical management of carpal tunnel syndrome, *The Physician and Sportsmedicine* 23(1), 1995. Reproduced with permission of McGraw-Hill, Inc.)

with the nine flexor tendons of the wrist and fingers. Chronic CTS is most often associated with inflammation and subsequent swelling of the synovial sheaths that surround the flexor tendons, while acute forms of the disease may involve compression by an invasive structure, such as an intrusion of a fractured or dislocated carpal bone or compression from a ganglion cyst.

Chronic diseases such as rheumatoid arthritis or diabetes increases the incidence of CTS. The onset of the condition is frequently insidious in nature.

SYMPTOMS AND SIGNS: CTS presents with paresthesia and discomfort of the wrist and of the distal median nerve sensory distribution—primarily the radial digits 1 through 3, although the discomfort may extend proximally into the forearm and shoulder. The athlete may complain of symptoms during activity or encounter discomfort at night after a period of vigorous use of the hands in practice or competition.

Athletes involved in sports that require sustained gripping are at greater risk of developing CTS. Atrophy of the thenar muscles and autonomic nerve dysfunction may be observed in the patient with an advanced case of CTS, but such manifestations are unusual in the athlete (Figure 15.29).

Clinical examination of the wrist should include a complete history and a careful examination to rule out

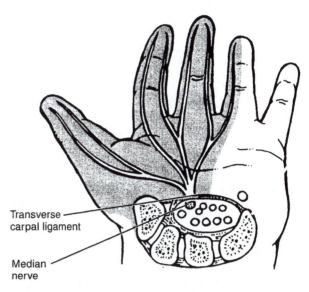

FIGURE 15.29

Sensory symptoms of carpal tunnel syndrome
localize to the sensory distribution of the median nerve. They most commonly consist of pain, numbness, and burning or tingling of the palmar surfaces of the thumb, index finger, middle finger, and the radial half of the ring finger (shaded area).

(From Steyers C, and Schelkun P., Practical management of carpal tunnel syndrome, *The Physician and Sportsmedicine* 23(1), 1995. Reproduced with permission of McGraw-Hill, Inc.)

acute etiologies. Special tests to evaluate nerve lesions are indicated. Phalen's Test (up to several minutes of sustained wrist flexion) and Tinel's Sign (local percussion of the carpal tunnel region) may be helpful in reaching a diagnosis by reproducing symptoms, although the reliability of the latter test has recently been questioned.[19] Nerve conduction studies can assist in making a final diagnosis when combined with other more conventional diagnostic measures.

TREATMENT: Initial treatment of CTS is most often conservative, with rest, ice, splinting, and anti-inflammatory medication. If conservative measures fail, or if the condition returns with further activity, a surgical decompression of the carpal tunnel contents may be indicated.[20]

Subungual Hematoma (Bleeding Under the Nail)

A hematoma can develop under the nail of a finger or toe following localized trauma to that area. This is an exceptionally painful condition, due to the sensitivity of the subungual nerve endings to any increased pressure.

As the pressure increases, the pain is accentuated by throbbing that interferes with the athlete's rest.

TREATMENT: Following trauma to a nail, the area should be iced continuously for a number of hours in the hope of preventing the development of a hematoma under the nail.

Once blood is present it should be released. The old technique is to use the straightened end of a paper clip, which is heated until red hot and then immediately placed end-on against the nail. The heat rapidly and painlessly produces a hole in the nail and so releases the entrapped blood (Figure 15.30).

If a hot paper clip seems objectionable, a wide-bore needle (No. 18) can be used. The needle is rotated like a drill bit, and if done gently, may be an adequate, though time consuming, technique. A number of holes should be made to ensure complete release of all the entrapped blood and serous fluid. The nail should be cleaned with an antiseptic solution, and antibiotic ointment applied for the following few days.

Regardless of the technique utilized, proper precautions for protection against contaminated blood and waste materials should be observed.

FIGURE 15.30
Releasing a subungual hematoma with a heated paper clip

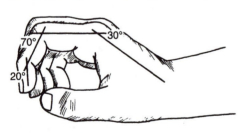

FIGURE 15.31
The so-called "position of function" of the hand

REFERENCES

1. Leslie IJ, Dickson RA: The fractured carpal scaphoid. *J Bone Joint Surg* 63B:225–230, 1981.

2. Mayfield JK, Johnson RP, Kilkoyne RK: Carpal dislocations: Pathomechanics and progressive perilunar instability. *J Hand Surg* 5:226–241, 1980.

3. Stark HH, Jobe FW, Boyes JH, et al: Fracture of the hook of the hamate in athletes. *J Bone Joint Surg* 59A:575–582, 1977.

4. McCue FC, Hakala MW, Andrews JR, et al: Ulnar collateral ligament injuries of the thumb in athletes. *Am J Sports Med* 2:70–80, 1974.

5. Engel J, Ganel A, Ditzian R, et al: Arthrography as a method of diagnosing tear of the ulnar collateral ligament of the metacarpophalangeal joint of the thumb ("Gamekeeper's thumb"). *J Trauma* 19:106–109, 1979.

6. Bowers WH, Hurst LC: Gamekeeper's thumb. Evaluation by arthography and stress roentgenography. *J Bone Joint Surg* 59A:519–524, 1977.

7. Rovere GD, Gristina AG, Stolzer WA, et al: Treatment of gamekeeper's thumb in hockey players. *J Sports Med* 3:147–151, 1975.

8. Sakellarides HT: Treatment of recent and old injuries of the ulnar collateral ligament of the MP joint of the thumb. *Am J Sports Med* 6:255–262, 1978.

9. O'Donoghue DH: *Treatment of Injuries to Athletes.* Philadelphia, W. B. Saunders, 1984.

10. McCue FC, Andrews JR, Hakala M: The coach's finger. *J Sports Med* 2:270–275, 1974.

11. Melchionda AM, Linburg RM: Volar plate injuries. *Phys Sportsmed* 10:77–84, January 1982.

12. Bowers WH, Fajgenbaum DM: Closed rupture of the volar plate of the distal interphalangeal joint. *J Bone Joint Surg* 61A:146, 1979.

13. Reef TC: Avulsion of the flexor digitorium profundus. An athletic injury. *Am J Sports Med* 5:281–285, 1977.

14. Howell AE, Leach RE: Bowler's thumb: Perineural fibrosis of the digital nerve. *J Bone Joint Surg* 52A:379–381, 1970.

15. Dobyns JH, O'Brien ET, Linscheid RL, et al: Bowler's thumb: Diagnosis and treatment. Review of seventeen cases. *J Bone Joint Surg* 54A:751–755, 1972.

16. Burke ER: Ulnar neuropathy in bicyclists. *Phys Sportsmed* 9:52–56, April 1981.

17. Smail DF: Handlebar palsy. Letter to editor in *New Eng J Med* 292:322, 1975.

18. Katz RT: Carpal Tunnel syndrome: a practical review. *Amer Fam Phys* 49(6): 1371–9, 1385–6, May 1994.

19. Kuschner SH, Ebramzadeh E, Johnson D, Brien WW, Sherman R: Tinel's Sign and Phalen's Test in Carpal Tunnel Syndrome. *Ortho* 15(11): 1297–1302, November 1992.

20.   Weiss AP, Akelman E: Carpal Tunnel Syndrome: A Review. *Rhode Island Medicine* 75(6): 303–306, June 1992.

RECOMMENDED READINGS

Burton RI, Eaton RG: Common hand injuries in the athlete. *Orthop Clin North Am* 4:809–839, 1973.

Dobyns JH, Simm FH, Linscheid RL: Sports stress syndromes of the hand and wrist. *Am J Sports Med* 6:236–254, 1978.

MacCollum MS: Protecting upper extremity injuries in sport. *Phys Sportsmed* 8:59–64, July 1980.

McCue FC, Bangher WH, Kulund DN, et al: Hand and wrist injuries in the athlete. *Am J Sports Med* 7:275–286, 1979.

Ruby LK: Common hand injuries in the athlete. Symposium on sports injuries. *Orthop Clin North Am* 11:819–839, 1980.

DeLee J, Drez D: *Orthopaedic Sports Medicine: Principles and Practice* Vol I–III. W. B. Saunders, Philadelphia, 1994.

Cervical and Thoracic Spine Injuries

Anatomy

The *vertebral column* consists of 24 movable vertebrae (7 cervical, 12 thoracic, and 5 lumbar) and numerous fixed vertebrae (5 sacral and a number of coccygeal bones) (Figure 16.1). It is rigid enough to support the body and protect the spinal cord, yet flexible enough to permit a wide variety of movements. This flexibility is due largely to the *intervertebral discs* between all the movable vertebrae (except the first two cervical vertebrae) (Figure 16.2), and to the angle of articulation of the facet joints in the various areas of the vertebral column. (See section on functional anatomy of the lumbar spine, chapter 17.) Each region of the spine (i.e., the cervical, thoracic and lumbar regions) has its own characteristics. There are also minor differences within each region.

The *spinal cord* is enclosed within the bony spinal canal. Nerve roots emerge from the spinal cord through the superior portions of the intervertebral foramina, which are formed by the pedicles of two adjacent vertebrae (Figure 16.3).

Cervical Vertebrae

Cervical vertebrae are the smallest in the spinal column. They are oblong and are broader from side to side than from front to back. The transverse foramen contains the vertebral artery (Figure 16.4).

The first cervical vertebra is the *atlas,* which articulates with the skull. The atlas has no body, but is pierced by the odontoid process of the second cervical vertebra, the *axis.* The odontoid process allows the head and the atlas to rotate by pivoting on the articular facets of the axis (Figure 16.5).

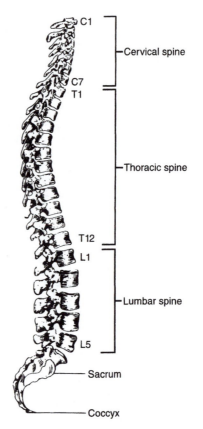

FIGURE 16.1
The spinal column (from the side)

The seven cervical vertebrae normally form a gentle curve which is convex anteriorly. When injured, the paravertebral muscles go into spasm and eliminate the curve. An excessive curve can indicate poor posture of the entire vertebral column and pelvis.

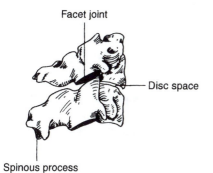

FIGURE 16.2
Lateral view of two cervical vertebrae—note angle of facet joints

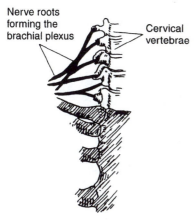

FIGURE 16.3
Nerve roots emerging through the intervertebral foramina of the cervical spine

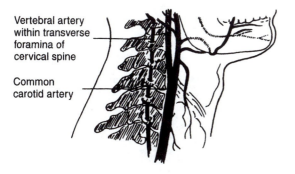

FIGURE 16.4
Anatomy of the vertebral artery in the neck

Ligaments

The primary ligaments are:

1. *Ligamentum flavum:* Contains much elastin, which gives it a yellowish color. This ligament is able to stretch and contract, unlike most other ligaments. It secures the lamina of the adjacent vertebrae and prevents excessive motion of one vertebra upon another. Another of its important functions is to maintain the tension on the capsule of the facet joint, thus keeping the capsule from becoming trapped within the joint.

2. *Ligamentum nuchae:* Runs from the external occipital protuberance to the posterior spinous processes of the seven cervical vertebrae, below which it becomes the supraspinous and interspinous ligaments. It separates the muscles of the posterior portion of the neck at the midline.

3. *Alar ligaments:* Strong ligaments that link the skull with the axis. They help to control lateral flexion and rotation, but do not restrain flexion or extension in normal circumstances.

4. *Transverse ligament of the atlas:* Runs horizontally from one side of the atlas to the other. It holds the odontoid process against the anterior arch of the atlas.

5. *Anterior longitudinal ligament:* Attaches to the anterior surface of the intervertebral discs and vertebral bodies. It is a strong band that has a firm attachment cranially to the basilar part of the occipital bone.

6. *Posterior longitudinal ligament:* Attaches to the posterior surface of all the cervical vertebral bodies and intervertebral discs. It forms the tectorial membrane, which helps hold the skull on the atlas and axis (Figure 16.6).

Cervical Muscles

Because the neck combines extreme mobility with protection of the spinal cord, there is an intricate interdigitation of the muscles that help to support and protect the neck. The muscles work synergistically to permit movement and support at the same time. Some of the important muscles associated with movement of the cervical spine include:

1. *Longissimus cervicis:* From the transverse processes of the fourth and fifth thoracic vertebrae. Inserts at the transverse process of the second through sixth cervical vertebrae. *Function:* Extends the neck.

2. *Longissimus capitis:* From the transverse processes of the fourth and fifth thoracic vertebrae. Inserts at the mastoid process of the temporal bone. *Function:* Extends the neck and rotates the head.

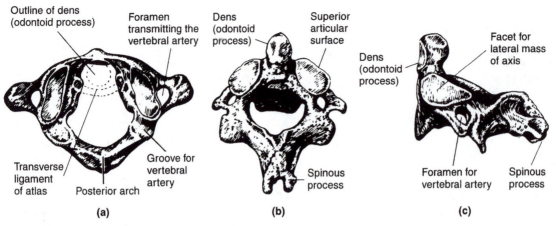

FIGURE 16.5

(a) Looking down on the superior aspect of the atlas (first cervical vertebra); (b) looking down (and slightly obliquely) on the superior aspect of the axis (second cervical vertebra); (c) lateral view of the axis

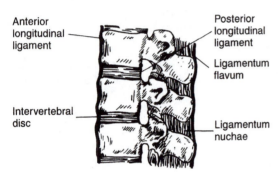

FIGURE 16.6

Schematic representation of the ligaments of the cervical spine

3. *Splenius capitis:* From the lower half of the ligamentum nuchae and the spines of C7 through T8. Inserts into the mastoid process.

4. *Splenius cervicis:* From the spines of T3 to T6. Inserts into the transverse processes of C1 through C3. *Function:* Extension of the neck when the two sides work together. When one side acts separately, the head is drawn to one side and the face is rotated to the same side.

5. *Iliocostalis cervicis:* From the angles of the first six ribs. Inserts into the transverse processes of the fourth through sixth cervical vertebrae. *Function:* Extends the neck (Figure 16.7).

6. *Other muscles involved in neck movements are:*

    INTRINSIC:

    a. rectus capitus anterior major and minor

    b. longus colli

    c. rectus capitus posterior major and minor

    d. superior and inferior obliques

    EXTRINSIC:

    a. trapezius

    b. levator scapulae

    c. sternocleidomastoideus

NERVE PLEXUSES OF THE CERVICAL SPINE: Two plexuses arise from the cervical spine. The *cervical plexus* is formed from the anterior rami of C1, C2, C3, and C4, and has three major branches; the *cutaneous,* the *motor,* and the *phrenic.* The *brachial plexus* arises from the anterior rami of C5, C6, C7, C8, and T1, and provides the nerve supply to the upper extremities (Figure 16.8). The brachial plexus consists of roots that join together to form trunks and then divide to form the cords of the brachial plexus. From these cords arise the *ulnar,* the *radial,* the *median,* and the *musculocutaneous* nerves.

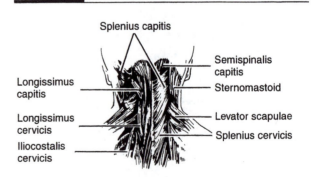

FIGURE 16.7

Muscles of the cervical spine (viewed from the posterior aspect)

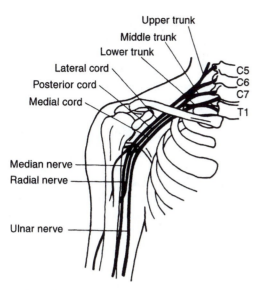

FIGURE 16.8
The brachial plexus

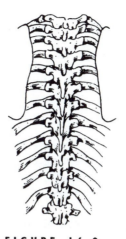

FIGURE 16.9
Thoracic spine—from the back—showing the costovertebral articulations

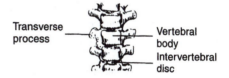

FIGURE 16.10
Thoracic vertebrae—from the front

CIRCULATION: The neck contains the vital arteries that supply the brain. Anterior are the external and internal carotid arteries, which are divisions off the common carotid arteries at the upper border of the thyroid cartilage. The vertebral arteries run posteriorly within the vertebrae. The artery typically enters at the C6 level and runs vertically through a canal formed by the transverse foramina and overlying muscles. The most tortuous part of the artery is through the suboccipital region as it changes direction on exit from C2.

Thoracic Vertebrae

The thoracic spine is part of the bony cage that encloses the heart, the aorta, the lungs, and other vital structures. Thoracic vertebrae are larger than cervical vertebrae and have a long spinous process that points downward. Each thoracic vertebra (except the eleventh and twelfth) articulates with a rib on each side by means of three articular facets, one located on the transverse process and two on the vertebral body itself. Each thoracic vertebra, that articulates with a rib, therefore, has six articular facets (Figures 16.9 and 16.10).

Thoracic Muscles

Some of the muscles surrounding the thoracic spine are:

1. *Spinalis thoracis:* Originates from the spinous processes of the upper lumbar and lower thoracic vertebrae and runs to the spines of the upper thoracic vertebrae. *Function:* Extends the thoracic spine.

2. *Longissimus thoracis:* Originates from the transverse processes of the lumbar vertebrae and lumbosacral fascia and inserts into the transverse processes of all the thoracic and upper lumbar vertebrae and the ninth and tenth ribs. *Function:* Extends the thoracic vertebrae.

3. *Iliocostalis thoracis:* Runs from the upper border of the angle of the lower six ribs to the angles of the upper six ribs. *Function:* Helps keep the thoracic spine erect.

4. *Other muscles:* Also involved with the movement of the thoracic spine are the *rhomboid major* and *minor,* the *trapezius,* the *serratus anterior,* and the *latissimus dorsi.*

5. *Other muscles:* Muscles that effect the thoracic spine through their respiratory functions are the internal and external intercostals, levator costae, serratus posterior superior, and, most importantly, the diaphragm.

Injuries to the Neck

Mechanism of Cervical Injuries

Cervical spine injuries usually result from the neck being forced into hyperflexion or, less commonly, hyperextension, often with rotation.[1] Axial loading is also considered to be a cause in some cases.[2] In football, where the mechanics have been well documented, injuries occur by one of the following mechanisms: the head or face mask is struck by the knee; the face mask is grabbed by an opponent; the athlete receives a karate-type blow; or, most frequently, the athlete lowers his or her head when making contact with an opponent. A number of serious injuries, including quadriplegia and paraplegia, have occurred in recent years from the athlete using the head as a battering ram, forcing the crown of the head to make contact with the top of the helmet. This action transmits forces axially through the spine.

Most severe injuries from hyperflexion and hyperextension (with or without rotation) result in cord damage from a fracture, a dislocation, or both. Injuries from axial loading usually occur at the level of the third and fourth cervical vertebrae. They include acute rupture of the disc between C3 and C4, anterior subluxation of C3 and C4, or unilateral or bilateral dislocation of the joints between the articular processes.[2]

Occasionally a cervical spinal cord injury occurs without a fracture or a dislocation and is thought to be the result of a vascular injury. In the less severe cases, the lesion consists of sprained cervical ligaments with secondary muscle spasm.

Prevention of Neck Injuries

The main *functions* of the cervical portion of the spine are:

1. Protection of the spinal cord
2. Mobility
3. Stability

Since mobility is one of the main requirements of the cervical spine, stability suffers. When stability suffers, the spinal cord is placed at increased risk. It is therefore imperative that an athlete engaging in a contact sport use all available methods to strengthen the muscles and ligaments supporting the cervical vertebrae. At the same time, appropriate measures must be taken to decrease the possibility of injury to this area.

NECK MUSCULATURE: Strength, power, and endurance of the neck musculature should be maintained year around, particularly for athletes in contact sports. Too often football linemen work on improving their neck musculature while defensive backs do not consider such conditioning necessary. Statistics have shown that the thinner, lighter, and speedier defensive back and wide receiver suffer the greatest incidence of quadriplegia and paraplegia following neck injuries in football.[3]

Athletes with long necks are theoretically at greater risk than those with short, thick necks. However, it is not only the length of the neck that is important, but also the ability to fully contract the muscles at the appropriate time (proprioceptive awareness). Some exercises that should be performed throughout the year by all athletes in contact activities (see section on neck rehabilitation) include:

1. Isometric resistance—resistance to flexion, extension, lateral flexion, rotation, and diagonals at various angles throughout the range of movement.

2. Manual resistance using a partner—a full range of flexion, extension, lateral flexion, rotation, and diagonals while the partner applies resistance (Figure 16.11).

3. Isokinetic-type resistance (e.g., Mini-Gym)—flexion, extension, and lateral flexion exercises.

4. Weighted football helmet, neck harness, or spring resistance flexion, extension, lateral flexion, and circular motions (Figure 16.12).

5. Bridging—using the *back of the head*—is useful for athletes in wrestling and other contact sports and should be part of the prevention exercise program (Figure 16.13).

6. Shoulder shrugs—important primarily for the trapezius muscles. They can be done either with free weights or, more easily, using the bench-press bars on the Universal gym (Figure 16.14).

7. Scapular exercises—emphasis on the dynamic placement of the scapulae on the thorax to provide stabilizing forces for the neck. In particular the middle and lower trapezius, rhomboids, and serratus anterior muscles.

8. Variable resistance equipment—a series of machines using variable isotonic resistance for flexion, extension, lateral flexion, rotation, and shoulder shrugs. These machines provide an excellent neck-muscle workout (Figure 16.15). It is recommended that exercises on these machines be performed slowly, with no more than three workouts per week.

TECHNIQUE:

1. *Football.* The protection afforded by the helmet has unfortunately allowed the head to be used as a weapon, exposing the neck to nonphysiological forces.

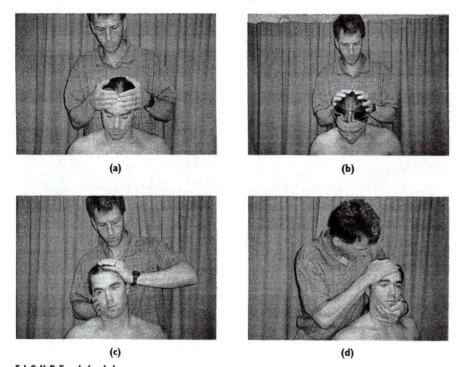

(a)   (b)

(c)   (d)

FIGURE 16.11

Isometric neck-strengthening exercises
(a) Resisting neck flexion; (b) resisting neck extension; (c) resisting lateral flexion;
(d) resisting rotation.

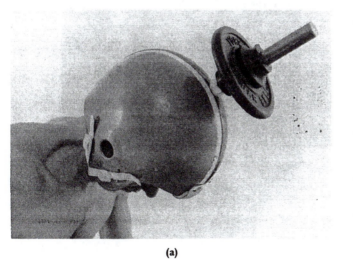

(a)   (b)

FIGURE 16.12

Devices used to strengthen the neck musculature
(a) An adapted football helmet; (b) head attachment, with chain and weights

 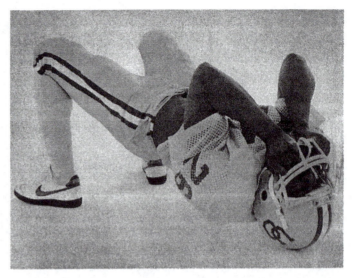

FIGURE 16.13
Bridging exercises
The top of the head or helmet should not be used; this avoids hyperflexion or hyperextension of the neck.

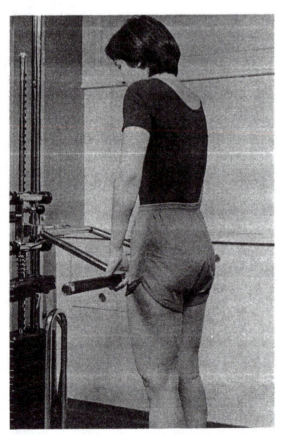

FIGURE 16.14
Shoulder shrugs to build up the trapezius muscles

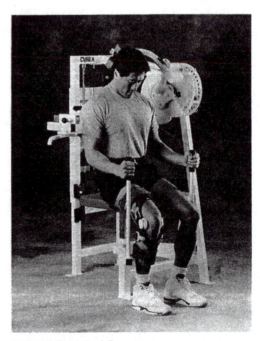

FIGURE 16.15
Variable resistance neck exercise equipment.
(Photo furnished by Cybex.)

This danger should be emphasized to the athlete and the correct techniques of blocking and tackling should be pointed out. Spearing in any form should not be tolerated.[4] Coaches should emphasize the importance of keeping the paracervical musculature "on guard" (shoulder-shrug position) so an unexpected blow will not catch the neck unprotected.

2. *Rugby.* Neck injuries in rugby are related primarily to the collapse of the scrum, placing the hooker at risk.[5,6,7] If a team purposely collapses the scrum, they should be heavily penalized. The high tackle may also injure the neck.[8]

3. *Wrestling.* Neck injuries in wrestling occur most frequently as a result of slamming the opponent onto the mat. The official should disqualify any wrestler who performs this maneuver.[9]

4. *Falling techniques.* Correct falling techniques should be taught so they become automatic and routine for all participants in any sport where a fall from a height might occur.

EQUIPMENT:

1. *Football.*

   a. *Helmet:* Experiments are being undertaken to change the helmet to afford adequate head protection yet discourage its use as a weapon. This should eliminate injuries to opponents and possible cervical damage to offenders.

   b. *Face mask:* "Face-masking" is illegal but occurs with some frequency. Fortunately, very few injuries occur from such a maneuver. Many observers see the face mask as being responsible for the development of an attitude of invulnerability because of the protection it affords. Some authorities feel that removing the face mask would discourage overaggressive use of the head in blocking and tackling, and would thereby decrease the chances of serious cervical injury (though the incidence of less serious but potentially disfiguring facial injuries could well increase).

   c. *Neck collar:* An appropriately designed and well-fitted neck collar prevents lateral flexion and hyperextension injuries. This is probably due as much to proprioceptive feedback and muscular contraction as to the actual physical limitation of movement by the collar (Figure 16.16).

   d. *Restrictive straps:* Some college teams strap the helmet to the shoulder pads in front, behind,

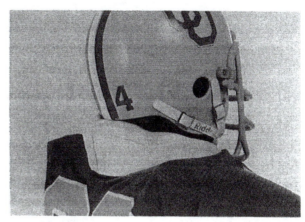

FIGURE 16.16
Football neck-collar

and at the sides to limit extremes of neck movement.[10] This may help decrease the incidence of recurrent brachial plexus lesions and the chance of serious spinal cord injury (Figure 16.17).

2. *Gymnastics and wrestling mats.* It is the coach's responsibility to ensure that mats used in gymnastics and wrestling provide adequate protection for the particular maneuver the athlete is undertaking. For example, with certain new or difficult maneuvers on the

FIGURE 16.17
Helmet-to-shoulder pad strap

to restrict excessive neck flexion and extension. These have been used experimentally by some college teams in an attempt to decrease the incidence of neck injuries.

balance beam, the mats may need to be piled to a height almost parallel to the beam. A foam-filled "pit" should be used for learning new tricks, so confidence can be developed and mistakes can be made without injury.

Tragedies from improper use of the trampoline have resulted in the American Academy of Pediatrics issuing a statement urging that the trampoline be banned.[11,12] Suggestions have been made regarding safe use of the trampoline,[13] including:

a. The potential for severe injuries on the trampoline should be recognized, and all participants should be well coached before they use the apparatus.

b. All trampolines should be locked when they are not in use.

c. Proper specifications for trampoline equipment, including frame, pads, and safety spotting decks, should be created.

d. The six basic learning positions should be mastered early.

e. The gymnast should proceed in a systematic progression of twist routines as his or her ability improves.

f. There should be no somersaults or tricks requiring inversion of the head in any basic physical education class. The use of the trampoline should always be elective.

Office or Training-Room Examination of the Cervical Spine

With the athlete sitting on the examination table:

1. Palpate tenderness of the

a. spinous processes

b. transverse processes

c. muscles

d. brachial plexus-roots and trunks

2. Check active voluntary range of motion (Figure 16.18):

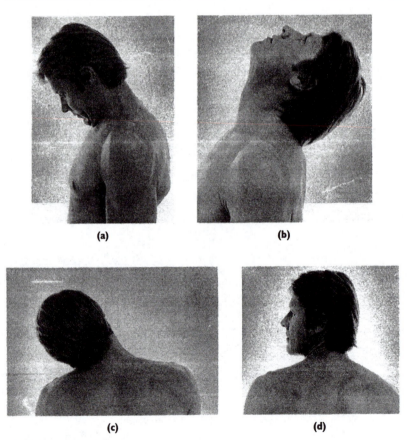

(a)   (b)

(c)   (d)

FIGURE 16.18
Neck range-of-motion
(a) flexion; (b) extension; (c) lateral flexion; (d) rotation.

a. flexion

b. extension

c. lateral flexion to both sides

d. rotation to both sides

e. circle left and right

3. Check cranio-vertebral stability (Figure 16.19a,b).[14,15] Cranio-vertebral instability manifests itself by:

   a. signs and/or symptoms of transient spinal cord compression (i.e., paraesthesia, hyper-reflexia, etc.)

   b. signs and symptoms of vertebral and/or basilar artery compromise:

      (1) history of "drop attacks"

      (2) cerebellar ataxia (loss of muscular coordination)

      (3) nystagmus (rhythmical oscillation of the eyeballs)

      (4) facial paraesthesia

4. Check sensation:

   a. occipital area and angle of the jaw (C2, C3)

   b. supraclavicular area (C4)

   c. lateral aspect of the shoulder (axillary nerve patch)

d. lateral upper arm (C5)

e. lateral forearm, thumb, and index finger (C6)

f. middle finger palmar aspect (C7)

g. little finger and ring finger palmar aspects (C8)

h. medial side of forearm and elbow (T1)

5. Check reflexes:

   a. biceps (C5, C6)

   b. supinator (C5, C6)

   c. triceps (C7, C8)

6. Check strength-tested against isometric resistance:

   a. neck flexion chin tuck (C1, C2)

   b. extension (C1–C2)

   c. lateral flexion (C3)

   d. shoulder shrugs (C4)

   e. resistance to elbow flexion, elbow at 90° (C5)

   f. resistance to elbow extension, elbow at 90° (C6)

   g. resistance to wrist extension (C7)

   h. resistance to thumb extension (C8)

   i. resistance to finger opening and closing (T1)

If there is no evidence of neurological deficit and X-rays are normal, test strength of full range of neck movement against resistance.

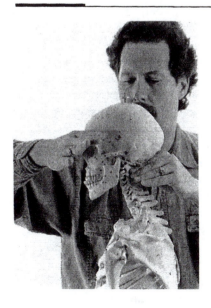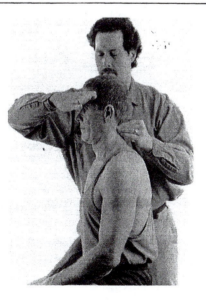

FIGURE 16.19
Sharp-purser test for cranial vertebral stability

On-Field Management of a Neck Injury

When dealing with a potential neck injury, the trainer must be aware that the spinal cord may be involved. It is essential that a pre-established plan be developed so the injury can be dealt with in the most satisfactory manner. The following points should be considered by anyone likely to be faced with this situation:

1. Keep an airway and resuscitative equipment on hand during practice and participation in a contact sport.

2. If there is any question as to the seriousness of a cervical injury, always assume that the *most serious* injury has occurred. This approach may result in some relatively minor injuries being dramatized. On the other hand, if a serious injury is neglected, it could cost a life or cause permanent paralysis (Table 16.1).

3. Designate a leader to be in charge of evaluation, decision making, and removal of the athlete from the field. Evaluation and removal from the field of play may hold up the event for a period of time. This should not influence the attitude of the examiner, who must be unhurried in the evaluation and beyond reproach in the removal of the athlete from the field (Figure 16.20).

4. A neck injury that at first seemed to be minor may become complicated later by some inadvertent movement. It is therefore imperative that any neck injury be thoroughly evaluated and followed. This will help eliminate the tragedies that do occur after the athlete has left the field.

TABLE 16.1 *On-field evaluation of a potentially serious neck injury (with particular reference to football)*

Athlete Unconscious	Athlete Conscious

1. Assume athlete has *neck injury* in addition to head injury.	1. Ask athlete
	  a. Where is the injury?
	  b. Is there any neck pain?
	  c. Is there any tingling, burning, or numbness down the limbs?
	  d. Is there any difficulty with breathing?
	  e. Any problem in moving the limbs?

2. Check airway. If impaired, cut face mask with bolt cutters or similar tool. Do not remove helmet. Stabilize head and neck. Do not hyperextend neck but bring jaw forward. Insert airway or supply oxygen.	2. *If any of above are present* treat as potentially serious neck injury (i.e., take off field on spine board with head and neck stabliized). Do not allow athlete to sit up, stand up, or walk off until thoroughly evaluated.
3. Check pulse. If not present, commence CPR with head and neck stabilized.	3. *If neck pain only* (i.e., no limb tingling, burning, numbness, weakness, or difficulty with breathing), check for posterior neck tenderness and deformity (do not remove helmet or move neck). Check for deficiency in grip strength and leg power.
4. Check blood pressure.	4. *If above are negative* ask athlete to put neck through voluntary range of movement (flexion, extension, lateral flexion, and rotation). Ask if there is any tingling, burning, or numbness in limbs with any neck movement.
5. Check pupils.	5. *If any are positive* suspect a neck injury. Remove from field on spine board with head and neck stabilized.

6. Remove from field
  • on spine board
  • head and neck stabilized
If any doubt, obtain help from trained EMTs in removing athlete from field.
	6. *If above are satisfactory* athlete can walk off the field. Evaluate fully at sideline.

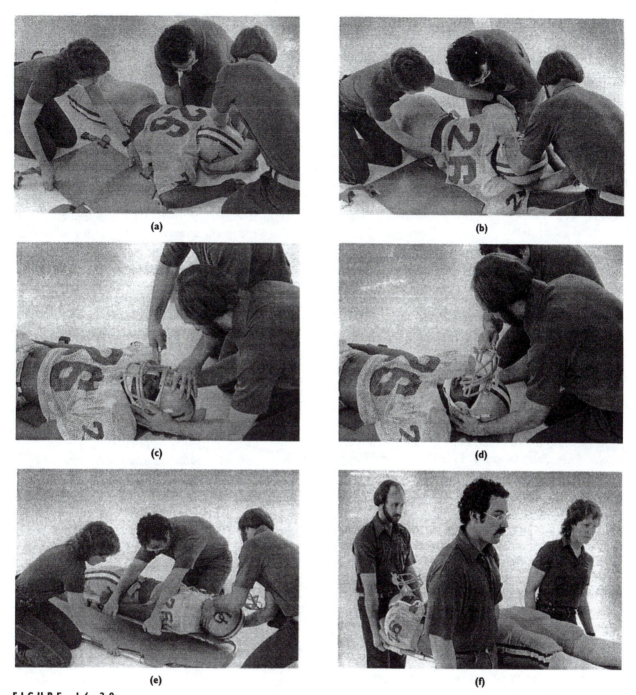

FIGURE 16.20

Removal of a player with a suspected neck injury from the field

(a) A leader should be designated. He or she should control the position of the head and neck, and apply traction.

(b) The leader directs the other member of the team. The injured player in carefully rolled onto the spine board. The leader continues to apply traction to the neck.

(c) The face mask may need to be removed. This is accomplished either by using a bolt-cutter, or, if the face mask is fastened to the helmet by rubber ties, these may be cut by using a sharp penknife.

(d) The face mask is then removed and an airway inserted if necessary.

(e) Secure the player to the spine board, and place on a stretcher. The neck should be controlled, or secured by means of straps.

(f) Place sand-bags on each side of the head to control its position, or secure the head with straps. Under the direction of the leader, the player is lifted and carried off the field for further evaluation or transportation by ambulance.

Sideline Evaluation of a "Minor" Neck Injury

Following are procedures involving minor injuries to the neck, after which the athlete is allowed to walk off the field:

1. Repeat questions about tingling, burning,[16] numbness, or weakness.

2. Ask the athlete to localize the area of discomfort.

3. Check grip strength and leg power.

4. Check sensation along dermatome areas of neck, shoulder, upper arm, forearm, hand, trunk, and legs.

5. Check reflexes of biceps, triceps, supinators, finger flexion, and the patella.

6. If all the above are normal and symmetrical, remove the helmet (if one is worn).[17]

7. Check for tenderness and deformity in the neck area.

8. Ask the athlete to move the neck through a voluntary (active) range of movement (flexion and extension, lateral flexion, and rotation).

9. If the active motion is normal and relatively painless, test these movements against resistance; also test power of shoulder shrugs.

10. Perform the compression test. With the chin directed toward the supraclavicular fossa, apply a compressive force downward on the head. If the athlete experiences any pain in the neck or any radiation of pain down the arm, a cervical disc protrusion or rupture may have occured.

11. If the athlete has normal neck muscle power, a full range of motion, no pain with any maneuver, and no tingling, burning, numbness, or weakness of any limb, a minor neck injury can be assumed. Return to participation can be permitted (Tables 16.2 and 16.3).

TABLE 16.2 *Criteria for return to activity after a neck injury*

1. Minimal or no neck tenderness

2. Full, voluntary active range of motion

3. Normal and symmetrical neck muscle power when neck movements are tested against resistance—with no pain

4. Normal and symmetrical limb power, sensation, and reflexes

5. No tingling, burning, or numbness in any limb

TABLE 16.3 *NATA guidelines regarding helmet removal*

The National Athletic Trainers' Association has adopted the following guidelines with regard to the on-site removal of the athletic helmet.

Removing helmets from athletes with potential cervical spine injuries may worsen existing injuries or cause new ones. Removal of athletic helmets should, therefore, be avoided unless individual circumstances dictate otherwise.

Before removing the helmet from an injured athlete, appropriate alternatives such as the following should be considered:

- Most injuries can be visualized with the helmet in place.
- Neurological tests can be performed with the helmet in place. The eyes may be examined for reactivity, the nose and ears checked for fluid and the level of consciousness determined.
- The athlete can be immobilized on a spine board with the helmet in place.
- The helmet and shoulder pads elevate the supine athlete. Removal of helmet and shoulder pads, if required, should be coordinated to avoid cervical hyperextension.
- Removal of the facemask allows full airway access to be achieved. Plastic clips securing the facemask can be cut using special tools, permitting rapid removal.

In all cases, individual circumstances must dictate appropriate actions.

From NATA, 1995.

Spinal Cord "Concussion"

A "concussion" of the spinal cord implies a temporary paraplegia or quadriplegia with complete recovery. The mechanisms that can cause spinal cord concussion are the same as those that result in more serious injury with permanent spinal cord damage. Possible causes include:

1. Vertebral impingement of the spinal cord, with or without sprain of the ligaments (see cervical stenosis)

2. Anterior spinal artery compression or impingement

3. Protruded or ruptured intervertebral disc

Cervical Stenosis

The term *cervical stenosis* implies a narrowing of the spinal canal, usually the mid-cervical area. This narrowing is due to a developmental abnormality and probably predisposes an athlete to a spinal cord injury.[18]

Hyperextension force is the usual mechanism of injury when cervical stenosis is present, though some cases may be due to hyperflexion. The athlete presents with paraplegia or quadriplegia, which may be temporary or permanent.

The diagnosis is made on examination of the lateral X-ray or by means of computerized axial tomograms (CAT) scan. The width of the spinal canal should not be less than 14.5 mm for vertebrae C3, C4, C5, and C6; if it is less, the diagnosis of cervical stenosis should be considered. An athlete who is discovered to have cervical stenosis after recovering from an episode of paraplegia or quadriplegia should be advised to refrain from contact sports, as continued activity may result in permanent quadriplegia or even death.[19]

Contusions to the Posterior Cervical Spine

INVOLVING MUSCLE: A contusion to the posterior muscle group is usually painful and causes varying degrees of muscle spasm. Treatment should be with ice, anti-inflammatory medication if indicated, and active range-of-motion exercises when the initial spasm has subsided. Inappropriately or inadequately treated contusions to this area can result in the formation of calcification within the hematoma in the muscle. A blow to this area may also be associated with a sprain or strain, which can further complicate the contusion.

INVOLVING BONE: The posterior spinous process of one or more cervical vertebrae may be fractured from a direct blow to that area or from an avulsion fracture caused by sudden contraction of the neck muscles when, for instance, the head or neck is forcibly struck.

Contusions to the Anterior Neck and Throat

A contusion anteriorly to the larynx and/or trachea usually results in severe distress, apprehension, aphonia (inability to talk), and some dyspnea (shortness of breath) lasting for a few seconds. These symptoms should pass rapidly, and relatively normal phonation and breathing should return within a minute or two. If they do not, then a severe injury to the larynx and trachea should be suspected, and the athlete should be immediately referred to a laryngologist.

Pinched-Nerve Syndrome

SYNONYMS: Nerve pinch, burner, stinger, nerve stretch.

ETIOLOGY: A pinched-nerve syndrome can result from one or more of the following causes:

1. Brachial plexus lesions—Thought to be the most frequent cause. Commonly, the head is forced to one side while the opposite shoulder is depressed. This usually affects the upper trunk of the brachial plexus.[20] However there are many variations, such as stretching, contusing, or, rarely, tearing of the brachial plexus. Occasionally the plexus is compressed between the clavicle and the first rib, particularly when the shoulder is abducted and the neck extended (Tables 16.4 and 16.5).

2. Entrapment of the nerve root or roots in the spinal column—A hyperextension or hyperflexion injury can cause subluxation of the facets, resulting in entrapment of a nerve root.

3. Protruded or ruptured intervertebral disc—Can result in a combined spinal cord and nerve root lesion, though it is an uncommon mechanism of injury.

4. Combination of nerve root and brachial plexus lesion—The cervical nerves pass almost horizontally through the nerve root canals and are therefore subject to traction injuries (Figure 16.21).

SYMPTOMS AND SIGNS: The athlete experiences a sudden, severe burning pain that radiates along the shoulder and down the arm, sometimes to the hand, and is usually associated with varying degrees of numbness, weakness, and neck pain. There may be sensation changes and the reflexes may be depressed. The most frequently affected area is the upper trunk of the brachial plexus, involving C5 and C6, leading to weakness of the deltoid, biceps, infraspinatus, and supraspinatus. X-rays of the cervical spine should be taken to exclude any bone injury or displacement.

The symptoms and signs are usually transient, but occasionally permanent damage results. Any athlete with a pinched nerve should be watched and checked for at least two weeks so that objective muscle weakness can be excluded.

GRADING THE SEVERITY OF A PINCHED-NERVE LESION.

Grade I	Full recovery within a few minutes (to a few days)
Grade II	a. Recovery within a few days to two months
	b. Recovery within two to six months
Grade III	Recovery not complete within six months (catastrophic injury)

TABLE 16.4 *Differentiation between brachial plexus and nerve root lesions*

Brachial Plexus Lesions	Nerve Root Lesions
1. Numbness and burning of entire arm, hand, and fingers.	1. Numbness and burning confined to one or more definable dermatomes.
2. Sensation loss over two to four dermatomes.	2. Sensation loss confined to a definable dermatome.
3. Complete transient paralysis of arm.	3. Partial transient paralysis of arm.
4. Tenderness over brachial plexus.	4. No tenderness over brachial plexus.
5. No tenderness over neck posteriorly.	5. Tenderness over neck posteriorly.
6. Increase in symptoms with passive movement of head and neck to *opposite side*.	6. Hyperflexion, extension, or lateral flexion of neck to *same side* as the symptoms may aggravate symptoms.
7. Symptoms do no occur with downward pressure on head with chin in supraclavicular fossa on same side as lesion.	7. Symptoms occur with downward pressure on head with chin in supraclavicular fossa on same side as lesion.

Note: It may not be possible to differentiate these two because the symptoms and signs may be mixed.

TABLE 16.5 *Effects of a brachial plexus lesion*

Nerve Root	Symptoms: Pain, Numbness, Tingling	Signs: Sensation Impairment	Weakness	Reflexes Absent
C4	Supraclavicular and shoulder area	Supraclavicular and shoulder area	On attempting to resist forced lateral flexion of the neck to the opposite side	
C5	Outer border of upper arm	Outer border of upper arm	Shoulder abduction Elbow flexion	Biceps Supinator
C6	Down radial side of arm to include radial side of hand	Radial side of forearm, thumb, and index fingers	Shoulder abduction Elbow flexion Pronation and supination Wrist flexion and extension	Biceps Supinator
C7	Down arm to hand including middle finger	Middle finger and corresponding area on palmar aspect of hand	Shoulder adduction Elbow extension Wrist flexion and extension Finger flexion and extension	Triceps Flexor finger jerk
C8	Down ulnar side of forearm to include ulnar side of hand	Ulnar side of forearm, ring, and little finger	Elbow extension Finger flexion and extension	Flexor finger jerk
T1	Inner border of mid and upper arm	Inner border upper arm	Finger abduction and adduction	

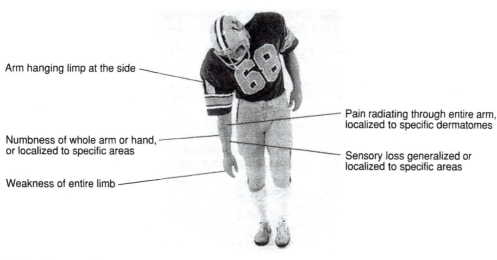

Arm hanging limp at the side

Numbness of whole arm or hand, or localized to specific areas

Weakness of entire limb

Pain radiating through entire arm, localized to specific dermatomes

Sensory loss generalized or localized to specific areas

FIGURE 16.21
Football player with a "pinched-nerve" lesion

TREATMENT: No specific form of treatment will "cure" a pinched-nerve lesion. A number of modalities help reduce some of the inflammation around the damaged nerves. Perhaps the most important aspect of treatment is to ensure that the athlete does not return to participation too soon. (See criteria for return to play, Table 16.6.) The treatment of a pinched nerve includes:

1. Cervical collar

2. Ice

3. Anti-inflammatory medication, muscle relaxants, and analgesics if necessary

4. Cervical traction and electrical muscle stimulation if necessary

5. Active range-of-motion exercises that are steadily increased within the limitations of discomfort

6. Strength exercises as described under the section on neck rehabilitation when symptoms subside

7. Direct mobilization and self-mobilization (when appropriate) to the nervous system[21]

8. Electromyography studies if sensation is not recovered completely within three to six weeks[22]

9. Investigation for a cervical disc lesion if and when the clinical situation warrants

---

TABLE 16.6 *Criteria for return to play following a pinched-nerve lesion*

1. *Full range of active neck movement* with minimal pain

2. *Full strength of neck movements* as tested against resistance—without pain

3. *Full strength, power, and endurance* of shoulder shrugs, abduction, elbow flexion and extension, and grip as compared with the opposite side

4. *Normal sensation* over all dermatomes

When a footballer returns to play following a pinched-nerve lesion, use of a cervical collar or straps on the football helmet should be encouraged. (See section on prevention.)

Other Nerve Lesions

AXILLARY NERVE: An axillary nerve injury may present as an isolated lesion. It is caused by an injury to the anterior aspect of the axilla, either from an anterior shoulder dislocation or from a direct blow. The nerve can also be involved as part of a brachial plexus or cervical nerve root lesion. Loss of sensation is localized to a small patch on the lateral aspect of the shoulder, and often weakness and wasting of the deltoid muscle occurs.

SUPRASCAPULAR NERVE: Injury to the upper root of the brachial plexus may damage the suprascapular nerve, resulting in weakness of the supraspinatus and infraspinatus. No sensation defect is found, as this nerve is purely a motor nerve.

An isolated lesion of the infraspinatus may occur if the nerve is entrapped or damaged in the suprascapular notch. This lesion will present with weakness and atrophy localized to the infraspinatus. Occasionally pain is a prominent symptom.

LONG THORACIC NERVE: The long thoracic nerve arises from C5, C6, and C7, and can be damaged either at the root level or along its course. It supplies the serratus anterior muscle and, if damaged, results in "winging" of the scapula (Figure 16.22).

Neck Rehabilitation Exercises

The exercises outlined in Table 16.7[23] can be performed as part of a prevention and conditioning program by athletes who have poor neck musculature but who wish to engage in contact sports such as football, wrestling, and rugby. These sports are the most frequent sources of neck injuries.

The outline presented here is meant to serve only as a guide. Many variations have been and can be developed on this theme. This program is divided into three stages and each stage should be completed before progressing on to the next, though it is not necessary to perform all the exercises mentioned in each stage. The program should always be individualized.

The Roman numerals refer to the stage, and the + indicates in which stage a particular exercise should be performed.

In the neck rehabilitation program, hyperextension exercises should not be attempted until neck motion is

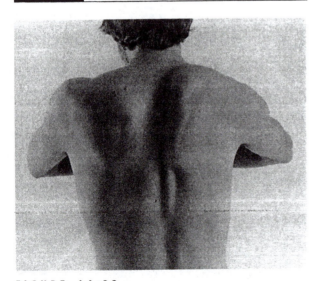

FIGURE 16.22
Winging of the scapula, due to a lesion of the long thoracic nerve

painless. Neck muscle spasm may be improved by using one of the many neck traction devices available.

BRIDGING: This is a controversial exercise; some writers have stated that it may be associated with vertebral artery impingement and potential brain damage. It is the authors' contention, however, that if a wrestler does not strengthen his or her neck and does not practice bridging limited to the back and foreparts of the head, he or she is in all likelihood at greater risk of a neck injury. Wrestling requires the ability to perform a vigorous bridging maneuver, and if the athlete is going to be engaged in such an activity, then the neck must be strengthened and the correct bridging exercise mastered (Figure 16.13).

Injuries to the Thoracic Spine

Examination of the Thoracic Spine

1. *Athlete standing with back to examiner.* Athlete outlines area of pain.

   a. Palpate area of tenderness over:
      (1) spinous processes
      (2) costovertebral joints
      (3) muscles
      (4) trigger areas (See section on stretch and spray)

   b. Note pain and limitation of active, voluntary range of motion with:
      (1) flexion—note manner of bend; percuss spinous processes, note manner of return
      (2) extension
      (3) lateral flexion
      (4) rotation

2. *Athlete sitting on examination table.*

   a. Note rotation to each side

   b. Test sensation. Useful landmarks are:
      (1) medial forearm (T1)
      (2) medial side of upper arm (T2)
      (3) medial side of upper arm and axilla to the nipple line (T3)
      (4) umbilicus area (T10)

   c. Test reflexes:
      (1) triceps (C7 and C8)
      (2) abdominal (upper—T8 to T10; lower—T11 and T12)
      (3) knee patella (L4)

TABLE 16.7 *Neck rehabilitation exercises*

Stage I: There is neck pain and stiffness		Stages I II III		Stage III: No pain, full range of movement		Stage III
No.	Exercise	I II III		No.	Exercises	III
1.	Traction	+		1.	Isometric exercises utilizing athlete's own resistance—flexion, extension, lateral flexion left and right, and diagonal flexion/rotation from neutral position to end range positions progression	+
2.	Range of movement to point of pain, but no hyperextension	+		2.	Full isometric resistance using a partner (Figure 16.11)—flexion, extension, lateral flexion left and right, rotation left and right, and diagonal flexion/rotation from neutral position to end range positions progression	+
3.	Ice massage and/or heat	+ +		3.	Shoulder shrugs and scapular mm. retraining using free weights (Figure 16.14).	+
4.	TENS	+		4.	Neck strengthening utilizing light resistance devices (Figures 16.23 and 16.24).	+

Stage II: Almost no pain, though still some limitation of range of movement

No.	Exercise	Stages II III
1.	Range of movement with hold-relax[23] (isometric) contraction at end of movement—flexion, lateral flexion (no hyperextension yet)	+
2.	Gentle isometric partner resistance exercises—flexion, lateral flexion to left and right, rotation to left and right	+

(Stage III, continued)

5. Helmet with weights, or weight loaded head strap (Figure 16.12)—flexion extension, lateral flexion left and right.[22] +

6. Bridging—the back of the head or helmet should contact the ground, not the top of the head (variation: athlete face down using forehead or front of helmet as contact point (Figure 16.13). +

If machines are available:

1. Universal bench press apparatus for shoulder shrugs and other scapular mm. strengthening (Figures 16.14, 16.25, and 16.26).

2. Isokinetic special neck machines, eg. Nautilus, Cybex Eagle, etc. (see Figure 16.15)
   (a) Shoulder shrug machine
   (b) Four-way neck machine
   (c) Rotation neck machine

Injuries to the Thoracic Facet Joint and Costovertebral Articulation

The numerous thoracic facet and costovertebral articulations are subject to frequent trauma. Joint dysfunction (called subluxation by some) often results. Frequently a joint dysfunction is overlooked because the pain is referred along the rib, and intercostal muscle spasm is considered the etiology.

The mode of injury is usually from compression of the chest, as occurs when a football player falls onto a football with another player on top of him. Also, side-to-side compression can occur, as in wrestling. A flexion injury to the thoracic spine, as well as landing rigidly on the feet, can also cause joint dysfunction involving the thoracic area.

Examination of the thoracic spine and costovertebral articulation should always be performed in cases of chest and rib compression injuries, as well as in cases of injuries involving rotation, flexion, and extension. Once rib and thoracic spine fractures have been excluded by X-rays, joint dysfunction can usually be

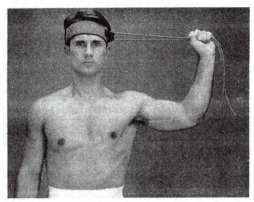

FIGURE 16.23
Elastic resistance with head strap
(Photo furnished by the Saunders Group Inc.)

FIGURE 16.24
Pressurized ball isometrics

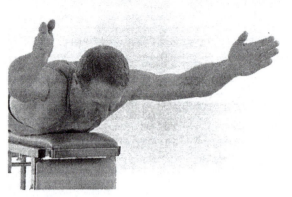

FIGURE 16.25
Prone horizontal abduction for scapular stabilization

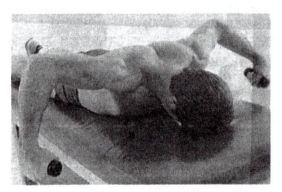

FIGURE 16.26
Horizontal rowing

accurately diagnosed by a combination of localized tenderness, palpation of the position of the posterior spinous processes, skinfold rolling, and sometimes sensory changes. If these are present in the absence of X-ray bone changes, mobilization/muscle energy techniques or manipulation of the facet joints and costovertebral articulations can safely be undertaken, usually with dramatic improvement of symptoms.[24] Trauma to the ribs can also cause restrictions in the overlying muscles or the intercostals. These restrictions can lead to torsional dysfunctions of the vertebrae and sternum, as well as affecting the vital capacity of the athlete's lungs.

Compression Fracture of the Vertebral Body

A compression fracture of the vertebral body often results from a hyperflexion injury. The anterior aspect of the vertebra is compressed; usually the amount of compression is minimal, but the symptoms may be severe. An extension brace may need to be worn for a few weeks until the symptoms improve.

Occasionally the force on the spine is directed axially up the spinal column, resulting in a fracture of the hyaline cartilaginous end plate of the intervertebral disc. Nuclear material may be extruded into the body of the vertebra, resulting in a Schmorl's nodule (Figure 16.27).

Dislocation of the Thoracic Spine

A dislocation involving the thoracic vertebrae is a very unusual injury in athletics. When it does occur, the

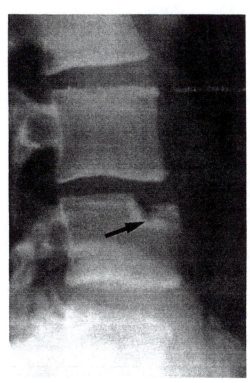

FIGURE 16.27
X-ray—Schmorl's nodule
This endplate fracture may be seen in the lower thoracic and lumbar vertebrae

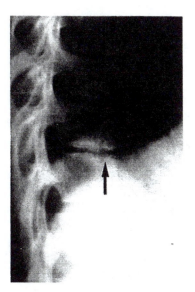

FIGURE 16.28
X-ray—juvenile epiphysitis (Scheuermann's disease)
Note the irregularity of the thoracic vertabrae. The amount of wedging present is minimal.

spinal cord is almost always involved. Always test for tingling, numbness, loss of power, reflexes, and sensation of the lower legs in an injury involving the spine. If there is any suggestion of spinal cord damage, the athlete should not be moved except by a highly trained team of emergency medical technicians.

Juvenile Epiphysitis (Spinal Osteochondrosis or Scheuermann's Disease)

The exact etiology of juvenile epiphysitis is unknown. A disturbance of the growth plate results in a patchy and irregular transition of cartilage to bone. This affects mainly the thoracic vertebrae in the teenager and results in wedging of a variable number of dorsal vertebrae (Figure 16.28). The symptom is usually diffuse thoracic discomfort. If the discomfort is severe, the athlete might need to be placed in a Milwaukee brace. It is possible for this condition to result in kyphosis (forward angulation of the spine) if left untreated.

REFERENCES

1. Schneider RC: *Head and Neck Injuries in Football*. Baltimore, Williams and Wilkins, p. 110, 1973.

2. Torg JS, Truex Jr, RC, Marshall J, et al: Spinal injury at the level of the third and fourth cervical vertebrae from football. *J Bone Joint Surg* 59A:1015–1019, 1977.

3. Torg JS, Truex Jr. RC, Quedenfeld TC, et al: The national football head and neck registry, report and conclusions. *JAMA* 241:1477–1479, 1979.

4. Duff JF: Spearing: Clinical consequences in the adolescent. Sports safety supplement. *J Sports Med* 2:175–177, 1974.

5. Williams JPR, McKibbin B: Cervical spine injuries in rugby union football. *Brit Med J* 2:1747, 1978.

6. Scher AT: Vertex impact and cervical dislocation in rugby players. *S Afr Med J* 59:227–228, 1981.

7. Scher AT: Rugby injuries to the cervical spinal cord. *S Afr Med J* 51:473–475, 1977.

8. Scher AT: The high rugby tackle—an avoidable cause of cervical spinal injury? *S Afr Med J* 53:1015–1018, 1978.

9. Roy SP: Intercollegiate wrestling injuries. *Phys Sportsmed* 7:83–94, November 1979.

10. Andrish J, Bergfeld J, Romo L: A method for the management of cervical injuries in football. A preliminary report. *Am J Sports Med* 5:89–92, 1977.

11. Committee on accident and poison prevention: *Trampoline*. Evanston, Ill., American Academy of Pediatrics, September 1977.

12. Hammer A, Schwartsbach AL, Paulev PE: Trampoline training injuries—one hundred and ninety-five cases. *Br J Sports Med* 15:151–158, 1981.

13. Rapp GF, Nicely PG: Trampoline injuries. *Am J Sports Med* 6:269–271, 1978.

14. Sharp J, Purser DW: Spontaneous atlanto-axial dislocation in ankylosing spondylitis and rheumatoid arthritis. *Ann Rheum Dis* 20:47–72, 1961.

15. Derrick LJ, Chesworth BM: Post-motor vehicle accident alar ligament laxity. *JOSPT* 16(1): 6–11, 1992.

16. Maroon JC: "Burning hands" in football spinal cord injuries. *JAMA* 238: 2049–2051, 1977.

17. Long SE, Reid SE, Sweeney HJ, et al: Removing football helmets safely. In Trainer's Corner, *Phys Sportsmed* 8:119, October 1980.

18. Grant T, Puffer J: Cervical stenosis: A developmental anomaly with quadriparesis during football. *Am J Sports Med* 4:219–221, 1976.

19. Cantu, RC: Functional cervical spinal stenosis: a contraindication to participation in contact sports. *Med Sci Sports Exerci* 25(3) 316–320, 1993.

20. Robertson WC, Eichman PL, Clancy WG: Upper trunk brachial plexopathy in football players. *JAMA* 241:1480–1482, 1979.

21. Butler, DS: *Mobilisation of the Nervous System.* Melbourne, Churchill Livingstone, 1991.

22. Clancy WG, Brank RL, Bergfeld JA: Upper trunk brachial plexus injuries in contact sports. *Am J Sports Med* 5:209–216, 1977.

23. Saliba V, Johnson G, Wardlaw C: Proprioceptive neuromuscular facilitation, In *Rational Manual Therapies,* edited by Basmajian J, Nyberg R. Baltimore, Williams and Wilkins, p. 243–284, 1993.

24. Greenman, PE: *Principles of Manual Medicine,* Baltimore, Williams and Wilkins, 1989.

RECOMMENDED READINGS

Albright JP, Moses JM, Feldick HG, et al: Nonfatal cervical spine injuries in interscholastic football. *JAMA* 236:1243–1245, 1976.

American Academy of Pediatrics, Trampolines 11. *Pediatrics* 67:438, 1981.

Anderson C: Neck injuries—backboard, bench, or return to play, Primary Care Series, *Phys Sportsmed,* 21(8): 23–24, 1993.

Bogduk N, & Marsland A, The cervical zygoapophyseal joints as a source of neck pain. *Spine* 13(6), 610–617, 1988.

Bourdillion JF, Day EA, & Bookhout MR, *Spinal Manipulation.* New York, Butterworth Heinemann Ltd., fifth edition, 1992.

Croft A: Soft Tissue Injury: Long and Short Term Effects. In *Whiplash Injuries: The Cervical Acceleration and Deceleration Syndrome,* edited by Foreman S, Croft A. Baltimore, Williams and Wilkins, p. 172–327, 1988.

Hammer A, Schwartzbach A, Pauley PE: Some risk factors in trampolining illustrated by six serious injuries. *Brit J Sports Med* 16:27–32, 1982.

Maroon JC: Catastrophic neck injuries from football in western Pennsylvania. *Phys Sportsmed* 9:83–86, November 1981.

Maroon JC, Kerin T, Rehkopf P, et al: A system for preventing athletic neck injuries. *Phys Sportsmed* 5:77–79, October 1977.

Mueller FO, Blyth CS: Catastrophic head and neck injuries. *Phys Sportsmed* 7:71–74, October 1979.

Pecina, MM: *Tunnel Syndromes.* Boca Raton, CRC Press, 1991.

Riley D: Strength training for the neck. In Trainer's Corner, *Phys Sportsmed* 9:165, May 1981.

Roback DL: Neck pain, headache, and loss of equilibrium after athletic injury in a 15-year-old boy. *JAMA* 245:963–964, 1981.

Torg JS, editor: *Athletic Injuries to the Head, Neck, and Face.* Philadelphia, Lea and Febiger, 1982.

Torg JS, Quedenfeld TC, Moyer RA, et al: Severe and catastrophic neck injuries resulting from tackle football. *J Am Coll Health Assoc* 25:224–226, 1977.

Travell, J, Simmons, D: *Myofascial Pain and Dysfunction: The Trigger Point Manual.* Baltimore, Williams and Wilkins, 1983.

Wyke, M: Neurology of the cervical spinal joints, *Physiotherapy* 65(3), 72–76, 1979.

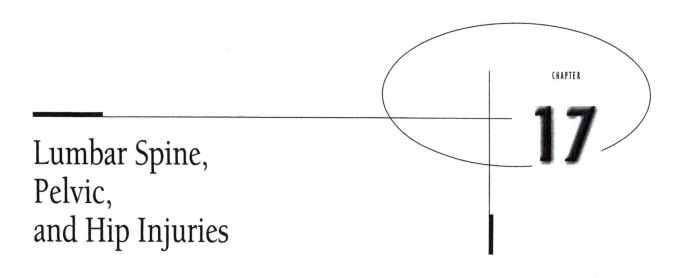

Lumbar Spine, Pelvic, and Hip Injuries

Functional Anatomy

Bones

The *lumbar vertebrae* attach the powerful lumbar muscles and support the body's weight. They are therefore much stronger and larger than the other vertebrae and have short, thick processes (Figure 17.1).

The *pars interarticularis* is subject to severe angular forces from certain athletic activities such as football and gymnastics. This results in a high incidence of spondylolysis and stress fractures of the pars interarticularis (Figure 17.2).[1,2]

The *sacrum* articulates with the fifth lumbar vertebra above, the coccyx below, and the two iliac bones on either side. The intervertebral disc between the fifth lumbar vertebra and the sacrum is subjected to severe shear and torsional forces, so that this articulation is subjected to the highest incidence of disc protrusion and degeneration.

The *coccyx* articulates with the distal end of the sacrum. It is occasionally contused, leading to annoying discomfort when sitting.

The *pelvis* consists of a ring of bone that articulates with the sacrum posteriorly and with itself at the pubic symphysis anteriorly. The bones of the pelvis consist of the ilium superiorly, the ischium inferiorly, and the pubic bone anteriorly. Landmarks that can be palpated easily are the anterior superior iliac spines, the iliac crests, and the posterior superior iliac spines. All three portions of the pelvic bone meet laterally at the *acetabulum*, a deep socket which, together with the head of the femur, forms the hip joint. Below the head of the femur is the neck, which projects at an angle from the main

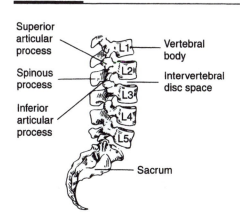

FIGURE 17.1
The lumbar spine—from the lateral aspect

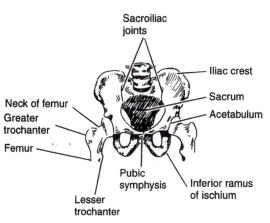

FIGURE 17.2
The pelvis

shaft of the femur. At this junction are the *greater* and *lesser trochanters,* to which are attached a number of important muscles (Figure 17.2).

INTERVERTEBRAL DISCS: The intervertebral discs are important structures that are frequently subjected to injury, particularly in the lower lumbar and lumbosacral areas. The disc consists of the *annulus fibrosus,* composed mainly of dense fibrous rings surrounding the soft gel-like interior—the *nucleus pulposus.* Connection to the vertebrae above and below is through a hyaline cartilage layer. Most of the resistance to rotational or torsional stress appears to be taken by the annulus, the hyaline cartilage, and the posterior articulating processes/facet joints.

The articular facet joints are synovial joints with articular cartilage. The capsule surrounding these joints is very sensitive to pressure and motion and is thought to have the same nerve supply as the dura. The synovial lining contains meniscoid-like bodies that can become entrapped within the joint, causing it to lock and producing pain.

Ligaments

The *anterior longitudinal ligament* is very powerful and serves to limit hyperextension of the spine as well as forward motion of one vertebra upon another, especially of the fifth lumbar onto the sacrum. It is attached to the annulus and the intervertebral discs and prevents forward bulging of the annulus.

The *posterior longitudinal ligament* lies anterior to the spinal cord and has strong attachments to the rim of the vertebral body posteriorly and to the central portion of the annulus. The posterolateral corner of the annulus is poorly covered, producing a weak area where disc protrusion frequently occurs.

The *posterior ligamentous system* is well developed in the lumbosacral area. It consists of the lumbar dorsal fascia and the interspinous and supraspinous ligaments. It helps resist shear stress as well as forward bending. However the interspinous and supraspinous ligaments are frequently weak or ruptured at L4–5, L5–51 or both in people over thirty years of age.

The most important ligament at the hip joint is the *iliofemoral ligament,* which is usually torn in dislocations of the hip because it is intimately blended with the hip capsule. Two other ligaments support the hip while allowing wide ranges of motion: the *pubofemoral ligament* and the *ischiofemoral ligament* (Figure 17.3).

Muscles

Numerous muscles support the lower back and aid in stabilization of the pelvis and motion of the leg during walking and running. These include:

1. *Longissimus thoracis:* Runs from the transverse processes of the lumbar vertebrae and the lumbosacral fascia to the transverse processes of all the thoracic and upper lumbar vertebrae and the ninth and tenth ribs. *Function:* Extends the vertebral column and maintains erect posture.

2. *Iliocostalis lumborum:* Runs from the iliac crests to the angles of the sixth and seventh ribs. *Function:* Extends the lumbar spine and maintains erect posture.

3. *Quadratus lumborum:* Originates at the iliac crests and iliolumbar ligament and inserts into the last rib and the upper four lumbar vertebrae. *Function:* Flexes the trunk laterally when the pelvis is fixed. Hikes the pelvis superiorly when the trunk is fixed. Functions prominently in the gait cycle.

4. *Transversospinalis:* A variety of deep, short back muscles (i.e., multifidus) that run obliquely upwards

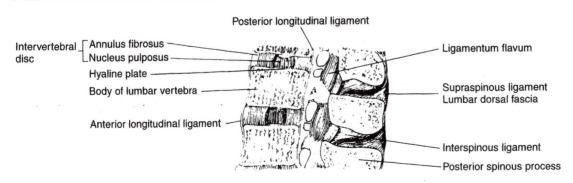

FIGURE 17.3
Lumbar intervertebral disc and ligaments

and medially from the transverse processes to the vertebrae. *Functions:* Primarily as postural and proprioceptive stabilizers of the trunk.

5. *Psoas major:* Originates from the transverse processes, bodies, and discs of the lumbar vertebrae and inserts into the lesser trochanter of the femur. *Functions:* Flexes the hip and medially rotates the thigh when the trunk is fixed. If it is tight and/or restricted, it may cause increased sway (lordosis) in the lumbar spine with decreased symmetrical flexion at the lumbar spine. This restriction may lead to a mistaken assessment of tight hamstrings.

6. *Iliacus:* Runs from the margin of the iliac fossa to the lateral side of the tendon of psoas major. *Function:* Flexes the hip and medially rotates the thigh when the the trunk is fixed.

7. *Psoas minor:* Runs from the last thoracic and the first lumbar vertebrae to the iliopectineal eminence. *Function:* Flexes the trunk with the iliacus and psoas major muscles when the lower extremity is fixed.

8. *Gluteus maximus:* Runs from the posterior gluteal line of the ilium and the posterior surface of the sacrum and the coccyx to the fasciae latae and gluteal ridge. *Function:* Extends the thigh when the pelvis is fixed.

9. *Gluteus medius:* Runs from the lateral surface of the ilium into the lateral surface of the greater trochanter. *Function:* Abducts the hip and medially rotates the thigh when the pelvis is fixed. Stabilizes the pelvis in gait when the femur is fixed in the stance phase.

10. *Gluteus minimus:* Runs from the outer surface of the ilium to the anterior border of the greater trochanter. *Function:* Abducts the hip and medially rotates the thigh when the pelvis is fixed.

11. *Piriformis gemelli, quadratus femoris,* and *obturator* muscles: Run from the sacrum, the posterior portion of the ischium, and the obturator foramen to the greater trochanter of the femur. *Function:* Primarily, rotate the thigh laterally when the lower extremity is moving freely. Rotate the pelvis contralaterally when the ipsilateral lower extremity is fixed.

12. *Abdominal muscles:*

    a. *Rectus abdominis:* Runs from the pubic crest to the xiphoid process, costal cartilages of the fifth, sixth, and seventh ribs. *Function:* Helps flex the lumbar vertebrae, support the abdomen, and control the position of the pelvis (Figure 17.4).

    b. *Transversus abdominis:* Runs from the costal cartilages of the lower six ribs, the thoracolumbar fascia, the iliac crest, and the inguinal ligament to the linea alba through the rectus

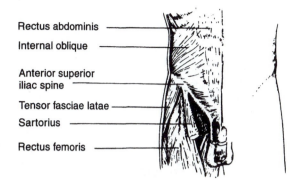

FIGURE 17.4
Superficial abdominal and groin muscles

sheath and the conjoined tendon to the pubis. *Function:* Helps support and control the abdominal viscera.

c. *Obliquus externus abdominis* (external oblique): Runs from the lower eight costal cartilages to the iliac crest and the linea alba through the rectus sheath. *Function:* Flexes and rotates the vertebral column. Acts as a stabilizer of the trunk and spine through its bony and fascial attachments.

d. *Obliquus internus abdominis* (internal oblique): Runs from the lumbar aponeurosis, the iliac crest, and the inguinal ligament to the lower three or four costal cartilages, the linea alba, and the conjoined tendon to the pubis. *Function:* Flexes and rotates the vertebral column on the pelvis. Acts as a very important stabilizer of the lumbar spine through its attachment to the lateral raphe of the lumbodorsal fascia.[3]

Nerves

The *sciatic nerve* is the longest nerve in the body. It is formed by the sacral plexus of nerves and consists of rami L4 and L5 and S1, S2, and S3. It runs deep to the gluteus maximus after passing under the piriformis muscle. Thereafter, it travels down the posterior aspect of the thigh to supply the lower leg and foot via its main branches, the tibial nerve and the common peroneal nerve.

Nerves forming the sciatic nerve can be compressed by a protruding or herniated lumbar disc, particularly at the L4–L5 and the L5–S1 interspaces. Pain is also produced by irritation or locking of the facet joints. The sciatic nerve can, in addition, be compressed by a spasm of the piriformis muscle, producing radiating pain down

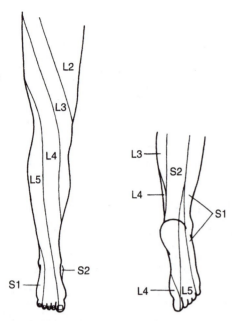

FIGURE 17.5
Dermatomes of the lower extremity

the leg. The *femoral nerve* originates from L2, L3, and L4 and supplies mainly the anterior aspect of the thigh. The *femoral artery* and *vein* lie alongside the femoral nerve in the groin (Figure 17.5).

Lower-Back Pain

Lumbar Backache

Lumbar backache is one of the most common afflictions of the human race, and unfortunately athletes are not exempt from this most annoying and at times incapacitating malady. There are many hypotheses as to the causes of and cures for backache, and, while no unanimous opinion can be reached, two broad schools of thought seem to have the largest following.

The standard view of lumbar backache suggests that, while backache has many causes, the pain is commonly due to disc degeneration involving the hyaline cartilage, the annulus fibrosus, or both.[4] This degeneration results in subluxation of the posterior articular facet joints.[5] However disc protrusion or herniation is thought by some to be the main cause, accompanied by symptoms and signs of nerve compression or irritation such as radiating pain.[6]

While not disputing that disc degeneration and disc protrusion are important causes of lower backache, another school of thought contends that most cases of backache without radiating pain are due to joint dys-

function of the facet and sacroiliac joints. This view postulates that normal movement takes place at each sacroiliac joint independently of each other joint, and if normal movement cannot take place, this joint dysfunction will cause backache[7,8,9]

This view is not accepted by many orthopedic surgeons, who generally state that the sacroiliac joint is of little importance in backache. Some state that pain and tenderness at the sacroiliac joint area are due to referred pain of disc degeneration (especially from T12–L1 and L5–S1 discs) or from stretching of the supraspinous ligaments.[6]

This division of opinion awaits resolution based on further research, but the athletic trainer should be aware of these views, as the controversy surrounding lower back pain is commonly discussed in athletic circles and is a familiar topic to many coaches and athletes.

PREVENTION OF LUMBAR BACKACHE: Many lower backaches that affect the athlete could be prevented by attention to some predisposing factors (Table 17.1).

TABLE 17.1 *Lower backache in athletes*

> ### Common Causes
> 1. Mechanical backache (i.e., pain arising from a disorder of one of the structures of the spinal column)
>   a. joint
>   b. bone
>   c. soft tissue (e.g., capsule, ligament, or muscle)
> 2. Discogenic backache
>   a. disc protrusion or rupture which may involve the nerve root
>   b. disc regeneration
>
> ### Rare Causes
> 1. Neurogenic backache—arising from pathology of the nerve root or of the spinal cord.
> 2. Vascular backache—arising from changes in blood vessels (e.g., an athlete with Marfan's syndrome suffering from a dissecting aneurysm of the aorta may present with back pain).
> 3. Viscerogenic backache—arising from visceral disorders (e.g., gallbladder or kidney stones may present with backache).
> 4. Inflammatory disorder—such as ankylosing spondylitis, Reiter's syndrome, etc.

1. *Standing posture:* Observe from the side and ask the athlete to hyperextend the knees. Note how this may cause hyperlordosis of the back. Standing in this position for a period of time can aggravate lower backache. A kyphotic position of the thoracic spine can induce both thoracic and lowerback pain, as can hyperlordosis of the cervical spine with the head held forward.

2. *Sitting posture:* Sitting with the legs extended together and the hips flexed puts a severe strain on the lumbosacral joint. This can produce symptoms in a susceptible athlete. Some feel that sitting for a period of time with the back flattened (e.g., with the knees higher than the hips) can induce backache. They contend that a certain amount of lordosis is necessary for normal back functioning.[10,11]

3. *Lifting posture:* Weightlifting has become an increasingly important part of almost all sports and is commonly performed on a year-round basis by both males and females. The coach and trainer should be aware of the correct technique for each particular type of lift, and should constantly observe athletes while they are lifting in order to correct deficiencies in their technique.[11] The athlete should keep the back erect and the knees bent, with the weight close to the body at all times. A lumbosacral belt should be used for heavy weight lifting, as this is thought to help stabilize the lumbosacral and sacroiliac joints. Rotational movements put a severe strain on the facet joints and can induce acute joint dysfunction or subluxation (Figure 17.6).

4. *Sit-ups:* Many athletes have surprisingly weak abdominal muscles (in particular the obliquus and tranversus muscles), which predisposes to hyperlordosis and poor control of the pelvis. This, in turn, puts a strain on the posterior articular facets, the discs, and the lumbosacral and sacroiliac joints. An abdominal strengthening program of sit-ups should be employed to counteract this strain.

There are many variations in technique for performing a sit-up. Some of these may actually be harmful to people with potential back problems. The correct forms should be stressed. Incorrectly performed sit-ups tend to cause an imbalance in the strength and tone of the iliopsoas muscle in relationship to the abdominal muscles, causing it to be functionally shorter (Figure 17.20). This, in turn, can increase hyperlordosis. Another reason for weak abdominal muscles is that a functionally short and tight iliopsoas muscle remains facilitated constantly, causing the abdominals to be reciprocally inhibited.[12]

5. *Muscle tightness:* Inflexibility of the hamstrings, iliotibial tracts, and iliopsoai tends to aggravate lower backache. Stretching exercises for the hamstrings, the iliotibial tracts, the iliopsoai, and the back muscles help

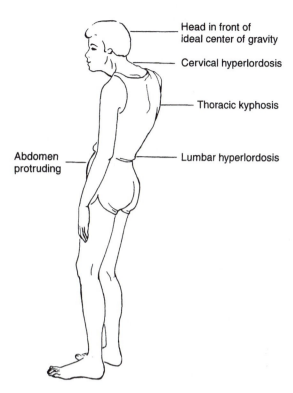

FIGURE 17.6
Postural defects

prevent back problems. Tightness of the Achilles tendon can cause a weight distribution problem that affects the articular facets. If inflexibility of the Achilles tendon is noted, heel lifts can be used temporarily while the athlete works on improving the flexibility of both the gastrocnemius and soleus muscles and tendons.

6. *Back exercises:* Employing the correct form for back exercises is important in preventing lower-back pain. (See section on back rehabilitation.)

Examination of the Lumbar Spine

1. *Athlete standing with back to examiner.* The athlete outlines area of pain.

   a. Note alignment of iliac crests, posterior superior iliac spines, and other obvious landmark comparisons.

   b. Visually note local signs of the *skin* (color, texture, scars, etc.) and *soft tissue contours* (wasting, swelling, etc.).

   c. Note range, rhythm, and deviation during voluntary range of motion of:

      (1) flexion

      (2) extension

(3) lateral flexion to both sides

(4) rotation to both sides

   d. Note movement and symmetry of posterior superior iliac spines on forward flexion and on return to erect position.

   e. Test strength of calf muscles by repeated unilateral heel-raises (this tests for an S1 lesion).

   f. Test strength of anterior tibial muscles by heel-walking (L5).

2. *Athlete leaning forward over examining table.* Test tenderness of spinous processes (anterior and lateral pressure) including lower thoracic spines.

3. *Athlete sitting on examining table.*

   a. Compare standing and sitting alignments of iliac crests and posterior superior iliac spines.

   b. Note position and alignment of sacrum.

   c. Compare voluntary range of motion as performed in standing position.

   d. *Perform dural mobility test*—Slump test[13] (Figure 17.11) *and* Passive neck bend (PNB) test[13] (Figure 17.12).

4. *Athlete lying supine.*

   a. Note level of anterior superior iliac spines and symmetry of the pubes.

   b. Test power of:

     (1) abdominals (Figure 17.7)

     (2) hip flexors (L2)

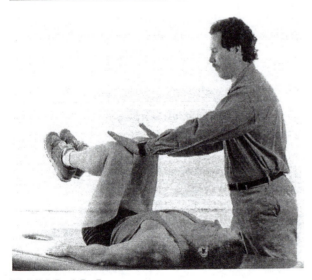

FIGURE 17.7
Testing abdominal muscles

(3) quadriceps (L3)

(4) anterior tibial (L4)

(5) extensor hallucis longus (L5)

(6) flexor hallucis longus (S1)

(7) hamstrings (S2)

   c. Test sensation by dermatome areas:

     (1) groin area/iliac crest (L1)

     (2) medial mid-thigh (L2)

     (3) superior aspect of medial knee (L3)

     (4) anterior lateral knee spiraling on anterior leg across the medial arch (L4)

     (5) lateral knee down anterior lateral leg across the dorsum of the foot (L5)

     (6) posterior lateral leg and along the lateral border and lateral plantar aspect of the foot (S1)

     (7) posterior calf, posterior thigh into gluteal cleft area with particular note of the popliteal fossa (S2)

   d. Test muscle tenderness:

     (1) quadriceps (L4)

     (2) anterior tibial (L5)

     (3) calf (S1)

   e. Test reflexes:

     (1) patella (L4)

     (2) Achilles tendon (SI)

     (3) plantar (Babinski's sign)—pyramidal tract (tensor fasciae latae component of this reflex is lost with S1 lesion)

   f. Test sciatic nerve irritation:

     (1) straight-leg raise using the unaffected leg with foot dorsiflexed (contralateral straight-leg raising test) (Figure 17.8)

     (2) straight-leg raise using the affected leg with dorsiflexion of foot and neck flexion—Lasègue's sign (Figure 17.9)

     (3) "bowstring" test (Figure 17.10)

     (4) Note that the slump test[13] (Figure 17.11) and passive neck bend test[13] (Figure 17.12) were done earlier in the exam while the athlete was sitting. However, if sitting causes too much discomfort, these tests can be done sidelying or supine.

   g. Measure:

     (1) leg length

     (2) muscle bulk of thigh and calf

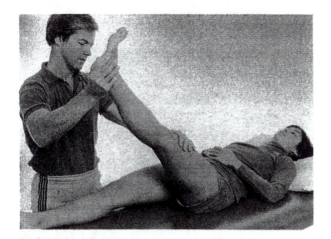

FIGURE 17.8

Contralateral straight-leg-raising test

When testing for sciatic nerve irritation, begin by slowly raising the opposite (non-affected) leg with the knee held straight. If pain radiates down the affected leg, this test is strongly suggestive of a disc protrusion or herniation.

---

   h. Examine abdomen

   i. Examine chest

5. *Athlete lying on side.*　Test Gaenslen's sign

6. *Athlete lying prone.*

   a. Test tenderness in lower back and buttocks

   b. Test stretching of femoral nerve (L4), also known as prone knee bend (PKB)[13]

   c. Test flexibility of Achilles tendon

   d. Examine feet (See Chapter 21)

Tests for Examination of the Lumbar Spine

1. *Straight-leg-raising test (Lasègue's sign):*　In this test (SLR), the leg is raised with the knee straight until pain is felt. The leg is then lowered by approximately 1 inch (2.5 cm) until there is no longer any pain. The foot is then dorsiflexed; if the pain returns, the test is considered positive for sciatic nerve stretch. This test can be made more definitive by flexing the neck while dorsiflexing the foot (Figure 17.9).

2. *Bowstring test:*　This test is performed by raising the affected leg until radiating pain is felt. The knee is then bent to relieve the discomfort (Figure 17.10). The lower leg is placed on the examiner's shoulder and firm pressure is applied to and just above the popliteal fossa in the area of the sciatic nerve. If this maneuver produces pain that travels up into the back or down the leg, it suggests the sciatic nerve is under tension—that is, there is likely to be a disc protrusion or rupture.[5]

3. *Babinski's sign:*　In the neurologically intact person over two years of age, stimulation of the plantar aspect of the foot should cause the toes to curl downward; upward fanning of the toes (especially the big toe) is a pathological response. In the context of lower backache, the plantar aspect of the foot is stimulated to elicit a reflex contraction of the tensor fasciae latae. This pertinent feature is lost with an S1 lesion.

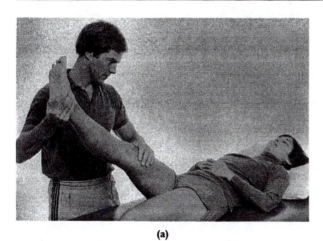
(a)

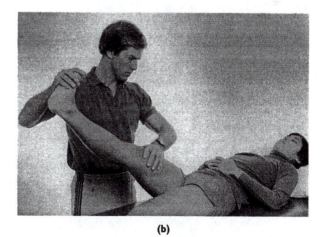
(b)

FIGURE 17.9

Lasègue's sign

This test is performed by (a) raising the straight leg to the point where pain radiating down the leg is experienced. The leg is then lowered slightly so no pain is felt. Then, (b) dorsiflex the foot; if this reproduces radiating pain down the leg, the test is positive for sciatic nerve stretch or irritation.

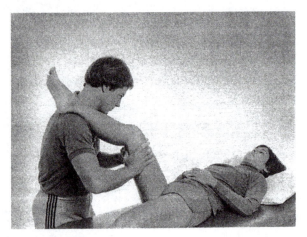

FIGURE 17.10
Bowstring sign
Pressure is applied to the sciatic nerve in the popliteal area. If positive, pain is felt locally and frequently radiates up the leg to the back.

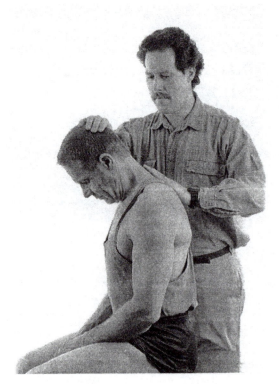

FIGURE 17.12
Passive neck bend test

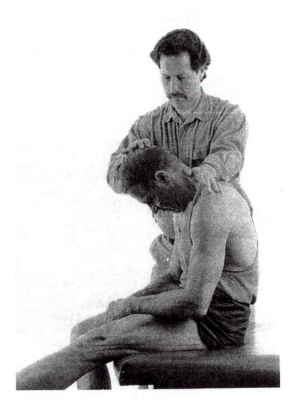

FIGURE 17.11
Dural mobility—slump test

4. *Gaenslen's sign:* This test determines the presence of pain related to the sacroiliac joint. It is performed with the patient lying on the unaffected side. The upper leg is retracted by the examiner until the hip is fully extended. At the same time the athlete flexes the opposite hip and knee up against his or her chest. If he or she feels pain in the sacroiliac region when the hip is extended, a lesion of the sacroiliac joint may be present.

Presenting History of Lower-Back Discomfort

MECHANICAL BACKACHE:

Etiology.

1. *Sudden onset:* May be due to an unguarded twisting motion such as stepping into a pothole while running or mistiming a particular movement. The athlete will frequently give a history of being "unable to move," or feeling that the "back was locked." He or she may or may not have pain in the buttock, groin, hip, or thigh. Occasionally the pain may go down the leg to the knee, or even as far as the ankle.

2. *Slow onset:* The athlete may complain of a dull ache, usually localized to one or the other sacroiliac

TABLE 17.2 Definitions of radiating pain and referred pain

1. *Radiating pain.* Results from irritation and/or compression of a nerve root. It is localized to the distribution of that particular nerve root, and may travel the entire length of the leg along that particular dermatome. It my present with or without backache.

2. *Referred pain.* Experienced in a site removed from that of the origin—in the back, buttock, groin, or thigh, but usually not beyond the knee. Occasionally a referred pain may mimic nerve root irritation (radiating pain) and present around the ankle and foot.

---

joint areas. It is usually relieved by rest but aggravated by activity. Secondary muscle spasm may follow, further decreasing the range of motion and the effectiveness of running. The legs often feel weak and not fully under the athlete's control. Referred pain may or may not be present (Table 17.2).

Signs. Tenderness is commonly elicited over the lumbosacral or sacroiliac joint on one side. The height of the posterior superior iliac spines or the iliac crests may be uneven, indicating either a difference in leg length or pelvic asymmetry. In the case of such a finding, the athlete should sit on the table and the heights should again be compared. If the crests and spines are not level when standing but are level when sitting, a discrepancy in length should be suspected of either (a) functional or (b) anatomical origin. (See section on backache in the runner, Chapter 21.) An asymmetry of movement when the athlete is asked to bend forward while the posterior superior iliac spines are palpated, particularly on arising from a flexed position, may be another indication of pelvic asymmetry.

When the athlete lies supine, the reflexes are symmetrical and sensation is unimpaired, but power may be altered. Ipsilateral straight-leg raising should not cause pain. Contralateral straight-leg raising and the bowstring signs are usually negative.

Treatment. Initially ice in the form of cold towels or ice packs (heat may be used for relaxation if the athlete feels this modality is more helpful than ice). Pain medication when indicated and muscle relaxants may be used, but their effects are variable. Anti-inflammatory medications are often useful. Pelvic traction may provide short-term relief of muscle spasm and pain. A lumbosacral corset is often used if muscle spasm persists.

The athlete should start rehabilitation exercises to ensure improved strength and flexibility, with gentle, active stretching within the limits of discomfort (see section on back rehabilitation), as well as gentle active pelvic range of motion exercises. Transcutaneous electrical nerve stimulation (TENS) is also useful.

Mobilization and manipulation of the lower back is an everyday form of therapy in training rooms throughout the country, even though these procedures are controversial in some medical circles.[14] Side effects are infrequent or nonexistent, provided the guidelines and requirements mentioned next are adhered to. (See section on manipulation.)

1. The diagnosis should be that of joint dysfunction (e.g., mechanical backache).

2. There should be no sign of disc prolapse or rupture or nerve root compression.

3. The therapist should have adequate training and experience in manipulative techniques.

4. The manipulation should always be gentle and nonforceful.

Relapses are often an indicator that muscle imbalances are still present and need to be addressed first. In these cases repeated manipulation is a disadvantage, but can be minimized by utilizing a full stretching and strengthening program. (See section on back rehabilitation.)

DISCOGENIC BACKACHE:

Etiology.

1. *Sudden onset:* Results from a very sudden movement, for example, while performing a dead lift using incorrect technique the athlete suffers a severe, sharp pain localized to the back and radiating down the leg to the ankle or the foot. Coughing or sneezing aggravates this radiating pain.

2. *Second injury:* Following a fairly severe back injury, a fairly minor incident can initiate back pain with radiating symptoms.

3. *Radiating pain only:* This is the presenting symptom and localizes either in the affected nerve root distribution or in a particular area of the leg (e.g., the lower hamstring area).

The most common areas for discogenic prolapse or rupture are the L4–L5 disc (L5 nerve root compression) and the L5–S1 disc (S1 nerve root compression) (Table 17.3).

TABLE 17.3 *Symptoms and signs suggesting nerve root compression and/or irritation (radiating pain)*

Decreased sensation	
Decreased reflexes	
Decreased power	
Muscle tenderness (and later wasting)	These should all correspond to the same dermatome or nerve root distribution.
Positive straight-leg raising increased by dorsiflexion (Lasègue's sign)	
Positive contralateral straight-leg raising	
Positive bowstring sign	

Pathomechanics Of Disc Rupture.

1. The initial injury leads to separation of the hyaline cartilage plate from the adjacent vertebral bodies.

2. Further stress leads to fissuring and weakness of the annulus.

3. Subsequent injury leads to the nucleus pulposus protruding or extruding through the torn fibers of the annulus, usually at the posterolateral corner (Figure 17.13).

Signs. Tenderness in the back may or may not be present. The posterior superior iliac spines are usually level. Scoliosis, or listing *away* from the site of pain, may be present if the herniation is lateral to the nerve, but listing to the side of the pain will occur if the herniation is medial to the nerve (the latter is less common). Forward flexion may produce sciatic nerve radiation down the leg.

Power, sensation, and reflexes may decrease over the affected nerve root distribution, and muscle tenderness may be present in the corresponding muscle group. A sagging of the gluteal fold may be present in an S1 lesion (gluteus maximus weakness). There may be a loss of the iliotibial tract reflex on testing Babinski's sign (S1 lesion). Straight-leg raising tests should then be performed, starting with the contralateral leg (Figures 17.8 and 17.9). This will indicate tightness of the hamstrings, but, more importantly, if it produces radiating pain down the affected leg, it is very suggestive of a disc protrusion or rupture. (This is the contralateral straight-leg raising test mentioned earlier). Lasègue's sign using the affected leg should then be performed, followed by the bowstring test. The contralateral straight-leg raising test, Lasègue's sign, and the bowstring test are reliable indicators of tension on the sciatic nerve, which in most instances results from a disc protrusion or rupture (Table 17.4).

Investigations.

1. *X-rays* include the anteroposterior, lateral, and perhaps oblique views of the lumbosacral spine.

The following investigations are most useful when surgery is contemplated, but are not performed routinely.

2. *Epidural phlebography* investigation is particularly useful in the young athlete.[15] Contrast material is injected into the epidural veins; if a disc protrusion is present, an interruption of the dye flow in the veins is usually observed.

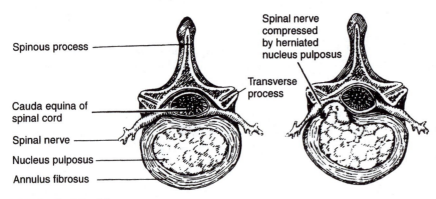

Spinous process

Spinal nerve compressed by herniated nucleus pulposus

Transverse process

Cauda equina of spinal cord

Spinal nerve

Nucleus pulposus

Annulus fibrosus

FIGURE 17.13
A normal and herniated intervertebral disc
(Modified from Netter.)

TABLE 17.4 *Differentiating signs of L4–L5 and L5–S1 disc lesions*

Signs	L4–L5 Lesion (L5 signs)	L5–S1 Lesion (S1 signs)
Power decrease	Extensor hallucis longus (dorsiflexors)	Flexor hallucis longus (plantar flexors)
Sensation decrease	Dorsum of foot and anterior aspect of lower leg	Sole and outer border of leg and foot
Reflexes		Decreased ankle jerk
Plantar stimulation with iliotibial tract response	Iliotibial tract response	No iliotibial tract response
Muscle tenderness	Anterior tibial	Calf muscle
Sciatic nerve stretch tests	Positive	Positive

3. *Myelography* is used to rule out the possibility of nerve root tumor and to localize the level of a disc herniation.

4. *Nerve root infiltration* A local anesthetic is injected into the root sleeve as the nerve root emerges through the root canal. Disappearance of the radiating pain following the injection of anesthetic into a specific sleeve confirms the particular lesion site.

5. *Electromyography* demonstrates the inability to fully contract a particular group of muscles and thus confirms the diagnosis of nerve compression at a particular level.[16]

6. *Discography,* injection of a disc with dye, is used in some centers.

7. *Computerized axial tomography* (CAT) scan may be very useful.

8. *Magnetic resonance imaging* (MRI) is becoming a very popular scanning tool.

Treatment.

1. Symptomatic therapy (e.g., ice, heat, or both)

2. Pain medication if necessary

3. Anti-inflammatory medication

4. Muscle relaxants

5. Pelvic traction for up to two weeks

6. Lumbosacral corset in conjunction with rehabilitation exercises, continued for at least as long as corset is worn

7. Transcutaneous electrical nerve stimulation (TENS)

8. No manipulation and mobilization if there are signs of nerve irritation, compression, or both

9. Bed rest with or without traction up to two or three weeks (controversial). Early mobility and walking is more typically the norm currently.

10. Epidural cortisone[17]

11. Surgery is indicated when one or more of the following are present:

   a. bowel and bladder paralysis

   b. marked muscle weakness, especially if increasing in severity

   c. deterioration of neurological signs in spite of complete bed rest

   d. unrelieved pain

12. Surgical intervention may be contemplated if an athlete is unable to perform and the diagnosis of a ruptured disc is certain.

Other Specific Problems

Cauda Equina Syndrome

The cauda equina syndrome results from compression of the cauda equina below L1 (Figure 17.14). It occurs, for instance, with disc protrusion or rupture or from spondylolisthesis. Athletes who develop the cauda equina syndrome usually have lower back pain, sciatica, decreased sensation in the saddle area (most importantly, a lack of the anal wink sign—no external anal sphincter muscle contraction with sensory or light touch testing), bilateral weakness of the lower extremities (even frank paraplegia), loss of ankle or knee reflexes, and bowel and bladder incontinence.[18,19] In the early stages, the symptoms and signs may be unilateral and rapidly progressive. The first signs of impending

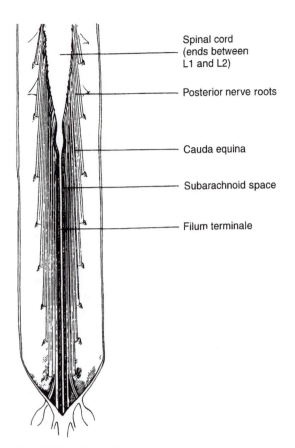

FIGURE 17.14
The cauda equina
(exposed from behind)

Spinal cord
(ends between
L1 and L2)

Posterior nerve roots

Cauda equina

Subarachnoid space

Filum terminale

cauda equina compression may be difficulty in voiding and the development of constipation. Signs of loss of sensation, reflexes, and motor function may then become bilateral.

Piriformis Syndrome

Spasm of the piriformis muscle can compress the sciatic nerve, producing sciatica-like symptoms of radiating pain down the leg.[20] Sometimes there is pain in the buttock as well. Localized tenderness may be present in the area of the piriformis muscle. The condition is treated either by applying ice or by ice massaging the piriformis muscle while it is being stretched. FluoriMethane™ spray and stretch and other forms of trigger point treatments will usually produce dramatic results.[21,22]

Contusion to the Lumbar Spine

Contusions to the lumbar spine are common. This area is covered by large muscle groups, so a contusion here should be treated in the same manner as soft-tissue

trauma occurring anywhere else (i.e., with ice, anti-inflammatory medication, gentle stretching, and protection from further contusions).

Occasionally the tips of the spinous processes are involved, causing a periosteal hematoma and marked muscle spasm. This may be treated with an injection of cortisone and hyaluronidase into the site of the hematoma, in addition to ice and anti-inflammatory medication. TENS can also be used, and a lumbosacral corset may be useful until adequate muscle relaxation and rehabilitation are achieved.

Ankylosing Spondylitis

The trainer should be aware of the possibility of this medical inflammatory condition being a cause of backache. Ankylosing spondylitis is a relatively rare condition occurring mostly in males in their late teens or early twenties. It starts as an inflammation of the sacroiliac joints.

Initially there is vague lower backache with pain around the sacroiliac joints; some morning stiffness may also be present. Tests such as Gaenslen's sign and pelvic compression may cause pain in the sacroiliac region. As the disease advances, decreased chest expansion may be noted (careful examination of this area is vital) together with limitation of back extension. There may also be symptoms related to the iris, the cardiovascular and pulmonary systems, and the pubic area. The course of this disease is usually slow and variable.

X-RAY: Changes of the sacroiliac joints include fuzziness, with sclerosis of the iliac and sacral bones developing later. Eventually there is ossification of the vertebral ligaments.

TREATMENT: Consists mainly of anti-inflammatory medication and extension exercises of the spine. Posture reeducation and back care in daily living is also very important.

Instabilities of the Lumbar Spine

Fracture of the Transverse Spinous Process of the Lumbar Vertebra

The transverse processes can be fractured by (a) direct blow, or (b) an avulsion due to violent muscular contraction (Figure 17.15). Many cases produce relatively little discomfort besides localized tenderness, and the athlete is able to return to activities soon afterward. In severe cases, there is marked iliopsoai spasm, and the athlete is unable

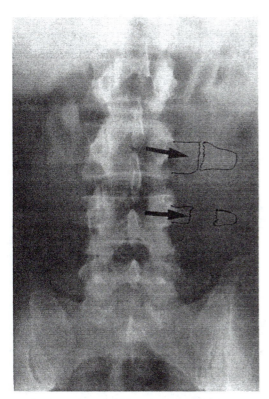

FIGURE 17.15
X-ray—fracture, transverse process lumbar spine

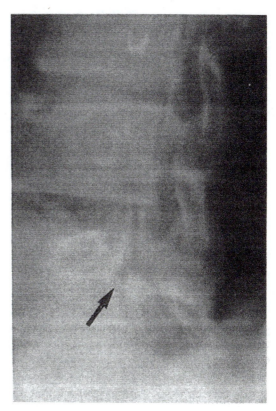

FIGURE 17.16
X-ray—spondylolysis of the fifth lumbar vertebra
Note the crack through the neck of the "Scotty dog."

to straighten the legs and back simultaneously. Treatment includes ice, muscle relaxants, anti-inflammatory medication, analgesics, traction, TENS, and often a lumbosacral corset. After the fracture(s) heals, examine closely for secondary facet joint dysfunctions.

Spondylolysis

Spondylolysis in an athlete is often a stress fracture through the pars interarticularis of one or more of the lumbar vertebrae[23] (Figure 17.16). Presence of a definite spondylolysis on X-rays, indicates that the condition has been present for weeks or months. Early diagnosis is possible with radioactive isotope scans using technium, which shows areas of bone stress as "hot spots." If an athlete presents with a backache localized to one of the lumbar vertebrae and ordinary X-rays do not show any lesion but the scan shows a hot spot, "prespondylolysis" is probably present. If this area continues to be stressed, actual spondylolysis can ultimately develop.[24,25]

Spondylolysis is thought to be a cause of backache, particularly in gymnasts[2] and offensive linemen in football.[1,26] If an athlete has pain at a level other than that of the spondylolysis, it may mean that (a) a prestress fracture is developing at another level, or (b) there is

another cause of the pain (e.g., mechanical dysfunction). The X-ray visualization of spondylolysis does not necessarily mean the backache is due to the spondylolysis per se. Spondylolysis may, however, predispose the athlete to backache from joint dysfunction due to the instability it produces.

Spondylolisthesis

Spondylolysis may be the precursor of spondylolisthesis, a group of conditions in which the proximal spinal column moves forward on a distal vertebra (Figure 17.17). But spondylolisthesis is often due to hereditary factors. The condition usually occurs in the lower lumbar region. The two most common types of spondylolisthesis are spondylitic spondylolisthesis and isthmic spondylolisthesis.

1. *Spondylitic spondylolisthesis.* The spondylitic spondylolisthesis defect is found in the neural arch in the region of the pars interarticularis, and probably represents a stress fracture. Pain from the spondylolisthesis can develop if the defect is held together by a loose fibrous syndesmosis that separates on flexion or straining,

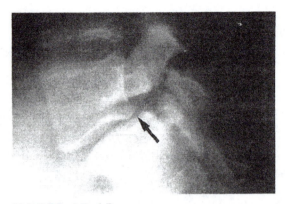

FIGURE 17.17
X-ray—spondylolisthesis—Grade 1 (out of IV)
Note disc-space narrowing between L5 and S1, as well as the spondylolysis of L5.

putting additional stress on the supraspinous ligament. However a forward slip is often associated with degenerative changes of the underlying disc, so the symptoms may be more from the secondary disc changes than the slippage per se. Presenting symptoms are:

a. localized back pain

b. referred pain

c. nerve root irritation or compression or both (including the cauda equina syndrome)

A clinical sign suggesting spondylitic spondylolisthesis is a step, which can be palpated and often actually seen, usually at the L5 level. There may also be dimples above the posterior superior iliac spines, and the normal lumbar lordosis may be replaced by a very flat lumbar spine.

The diagnosis is made after examining the X-rays. However, the amount of slippage seen on X-rays can be totally out of proportion to the symptoms: there may be a marked slip on X-rays with no backache or nerve root compression. Again, X-ray visualization of spondylolisthesis does not necessarily mean the backache is due to that condition. It may be the result of some other cause, most commonly joint dysfunction. Surgery is indicated only if pain becomes progressive or if nerve root compression or cauda equina symptoms are present. Symptomatic spondylolisthesis in an athlete such as a gymnast will probably preclude him or her from further participation.

2. *Isthmic spondylolisthesis.* Isthmic spondylolisthesis usually presents in a young teenager. On X-rays the pars interarticularis appears thinned and elongated, but no actual defect is visible. This probably represents a number of previous stress fractures, resulting in an elongation of the pars.

This condition behaves differently from the spondylitic spondylolisthesis. The onset can be sudden and dramatic. The athlete presents with a rigid lumbar spine; a functional scoliosis; a pelvis that rotates forward, resulting in a flat sacrum; and hamstring spasm. Walking is possible only with bent knees. In contrast to the spondylitic spondylolisthesis, surgery is often required to prevent further slippage, as cauda equina symptoms may occur. However, in the majority of cases there is no nerve compression.

Transitional Vertebrae

In some cases the S1 segment is a mobile segment resulting in a relative sixth lumbar vertebra. This condition is known as *lumbarization*. In contrast, are cases in which fusion of the fifth lumbar vertebra to the sacrum/ilium complex occurs, known as *sacralization*.

In rare cases a pseudoarthrosis appears as a defect of the fifth lumbar transverse process and ilium, resembling an ununited fracture. Surgical management of this condition is seldom successful.[27] The trainer should be aware that lumbarization and sacralization occur in only 2 to 8 percent[28] of the population; however, they are readily diagnosed with anteroposterior radiological views.

Treatment. Consists of strict discipline to neutral stabilization]concepts.[29] (See section on rehabilitation of the back.) The neutral lumbar spine range allowed for the athlete is minimized. This controlled range *must* be maintained over time.

Rehabilitation of the Back

The outline presented in Table 17.5 is meant to serve purely as a guide. Many variations have been developed on this theme. The program is divided into four stages,

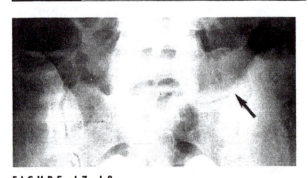

FIGURE 17.18
Example of sacralization of the 5th lumbar vertebra, forming a pseudoarthrosis with the first sacral segment. Note the sclerosis on either side of the pseudoarthrosis.

and each stage should be completed before progressing to the next, although it is not necessary to perform all the exercises mentioned in each stage. The program should always be individualized. The Roman numerals refer to the stage, and the + indicates in which stage a particular exercise should be performed. The basic concepts in back rehabilitation are to improve the:

1. Abdominal muscle strength and control of the pelvis and trunk

2. Flexibility of the lower back, the iliopsoai muscles, the hamstring muscles, the iliotibial tract, and the Achilles tendons. In addition, the fascial investments in these areas, in particular the lumbodorsal fascia and the fascia latae, need to be free of restrictions and have adequate mobility to allow for muscle flexibility and broadening[30]

3. Proprioception of the trunk in relation to the upper and lower extremities[31]

Once these areas have been strengthened mobility has improved, the athlete can undertake additional exercise to strengthen the back musculature. The first thing the athlete needs to learn is how to control the position of the pelvis and the amount of lordosis of the lower back. Numerous theories exist as to the best position (bias) of the pelvis during exercise. The posterior pelvic tilt is useful when the posterior ligamentous system (PLS) is desired to produce stabilization of the spine or if a flexion bias is desired, as in cases of severe spondylolisthesis or stenosis (foraminal narrowing). Anterior pelvic tilt bias may be desired in advanced-level control of the trunk with heavy lifts, or if an extension bias is desired as in cases such as disc prolapse or herniation. The most popular current idea is to train athletes to stabilize their trunk and pelvis in *neutral*. The neutral position of the lumbar spine is a mid-range controlled position. It is in this position that the body should align so that vertical compressive forces can be dissipated throughout the axial skeleton. This position provides the trunk with options for unlimited movement responses to outside forces. It is vitally important that an athlete be able to brace, initiate, and resist in a controlled manner to avoid high shear and compressive forces on the back in the rehabilitation process[32] (Figure 17.19).

The sit-up (or curl-up) is useful for improving the strength of the abdominal musculature. The athlete bends his or her knees to approximately 90° with the hips at 45°. The legs or feet are not held down. The athlete then positions the pelvis to the appropriate bias (Figure 17.19a-b) and curls the chin up to the chest. The shoulders and upper back are then slowly curled to approximately 30° off the ground; this position is held for two seconds. The back is then uncurled, one verte-

TABLE 17.5 *Rehabilitation of the back*

Stage I: Minimal or No Muscle Spasm Present and No Flexion Sensitivity					
No.	Exercise	I	II	III	IV
1.	Lying on back—bend knee to chest—one leg at a time	+			
2.	Lying on back, both legs together—bend knees to chest	+			
3.	Lying on back—isometric neutral and/or pelvic tilt (Figure 17.19)	+			
4.	Rock backward and forward smoothly (Figure 17.21)	+	+		
5.	Beginning sit-ups—lift to 60° position using elbows and arms, return to table with pelvic tilt action, arms across chest	+			
6.	Curl-ups and returns down, arms outstretched in front of body (Figure 17.20a)	+			

The above exercises assume that the athlete is not flexion sensitive. If the diagnosis needs ruling out of a discogenic condition, then caution with the above exercises is needed.

No.	Exercise	I	II	III	IV
7.	Hip-lift—push down with feet and shoulders, raise hips in neutral generally but use pelvic tilt in diagnosis of spondylolisthesis and stenosis (Figure 17.22)	+	+		
8.	Prone pressups—keep hips on mat and buttock relaxed (Figure 17.23)	+	+		
9.	Hanging from overhead bar—in neutral generally but use pelvic tilt in diagnosis of spondylolisthesis and stenosis.	+	+		
10.	Stretching exercises				
	a. iliopsoas stretch—beginning (Figure 17.24)	+	+		
	b. lying on back—rotate legs and lower back slowly to each side, shoulders flat on floor.	+	+	+	+
	c. iliotibial tract stretch	+	+	+	+
	d. hamstring stretch (see chapter 2).	+	+	+	+
	e. Achilles tendon stretch (see chapter 2)	+	+	+	+

(Continued)

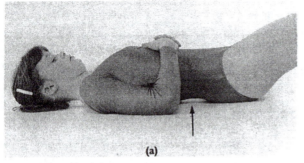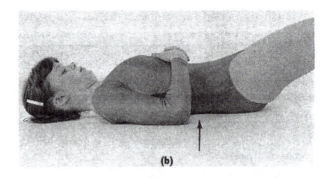

FIGURE 17.19

Pelvic positions of bias for stabilization of the lumbar spine.

(a) Pelvic neutral is a relative midrange position between the extremes of flexion and extension. In this position any long-axis forces are dissipated through the entire spine.

(b) Posterior pelvic tilt flattens the arch and holds the lumbar spine against the ground. These positions are maintained isometrically for 5 to 10 seconds, and repeated 5 to 10 times each. They form the basis for many lower back exercises.

bra at a time, while maintaining the pelvic position. The lowering process should take at least two to three seconds. The chin-tuck position is maintained throughout the series of curl-ups. Proper pelvic positioning is performed before each curl-up. The number of curl-ups is limited by an inability to hold a proper pelvic position/tilt or by loss of form (Figure 17.20a).

The reverse sit-up (or reverse curl-up) is an excellent strengthening exercise for the athlete who is flexion sensitive and/or desires emphasis of the obliques and transversus abominus musculature. The athlete holds onto a secured object overhead (the arms can be supporting the trunk at the sides if desired) with the hips at

90° and the knees fully bent. The athlete tightens the lower abdominal muscles by concentrating effort on pulling the muscles flat and in an upward motion (hollow/flat abdomen). Care is taken not to allow the rectus abdominus muscles to dominate, which occurs when the abdomen area is in a bunched contraction versus a flat, broadened contraction and the athlete is unable to breathe freely due to restriction of the diaphragm. The athlete then curls the knees toward the chin as far as possible without losing proper form. Variations of leg position and angles of movement can be made to create progressions in difficulty and intensity (Figure 17.20b).

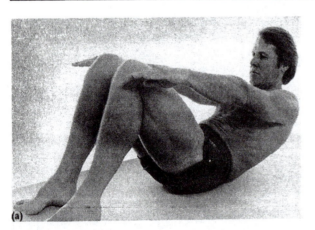

FIGURE 17.20

(a) The sit-up

The knees are bent to 90° and the feet are free. A pelvic tilt is performed and held, and the shoulders are curled forward with the chin tucked in. The movement is slow and held at 30°, and then the trunk is slowly lowered. The chin should be kept tucked in.

(b) Reverse curl exercise

Many back injuries are aggravated by improper exercise, such as lowering and raising the legs when held straight out and sit-ups with the legs secured and the back arched into hyperlordosis. These exercises should not be performed, particularly by an athlete prone to back problems.

As is true of any area that is injured, the pelvis and trunk can experience diminished or lost sensory input of its orientation in space (proprioception). Stabilization exercises are used to synthesize the strength and control concepts of care with progressively challenging balance improvements of the the trunk and extremities (Figures 17.26a–e). The level of difficulty is determined by the stage of healing of the injury in question, the athlete's current abilities, and the sports-specific requirements that the athlete will need to return to play. The use of equipment such as therapeutic gym balls and cylinders[33] has become a staple of back rehabilitation programs. Low-level clinical plyometric training with medicine balls is an inexpensive way to finalize the rehabilitative training process prior to release to full participation.

Table 17.5 covers guidelines for rehabilitation of the back without significant complications. A few comments should be made regarding modifications for specific cases. Athletes with spondylolisthesis should avoid hyperlordosis in any exercise or activity. Extension of the spine to 0° under supervision is permitted, but the pelvis must be in neutral (or possibly in a posterior pelvic tilt) at all times. Increasing flexion range is important to athletes with spondylolisthesis. The same is true in athletes with transitional vertebrae, except that both hyperflexion and hyperlordosis need to be avoided. Rehabilitation of the athlete with this condition should be aimed at stabilization and control in the midspine range/neutral.

TABLE 17.5 *(Continued)*

	Stage II: No Muscle Spasm Present				
No.	*Exercise*	*I*	*II*	*III*	*IV*
1.	Beginning to moderate proprioceptive training on ethafoam cylinder[33] (Figure 17.26a)		+	+	+
2.	Beginning to moderate stabilization exercises (Figure 17.26b,c,d)		+	+	+
3.	Isometric, concentric, eccentric bracing (Figure 17.26e)		+	+	+
4.	Isometric pelvic neutral/tilt against a wall		+	+	+
5.	Reverse curl-ups (Variations for increasing difficulty can be performed) (Figure 17.20b)		+	+	+
6.	Curl-ups and return, arms across chest		+		
7.	Leg extensions—prone, with legs and pelvis over end of table,				
	(a) single leg lift to 0° only with progression from knees bent to knees straight,		+		
	(b) double leg lift to 0° only with progression from knees bent to knees straight.		+	+	
8.	Slump stretch[13] (Figure 17.11)		+	+	+

(Continued)

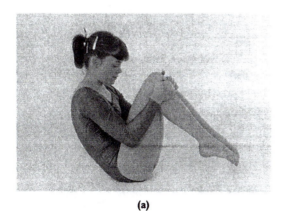

(a)   (b)

FIGURE 17.21
The rock-up and roll—a useful flexibility exercise
The pelvic tilt should be maintained throughout the roll, ensuring a smooth action.

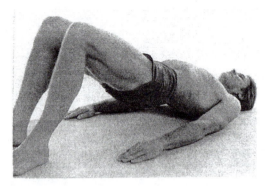

FIGURE 17.22
The hip-lift

FIGURE 17.23
Prone press-up

FIGURE 17.24
Iliopsoai stretch—beginning

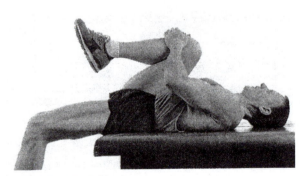

FIGURE 17.25
Psoai stretch

TABLE 17.5 *(Continued)*

		Stage			
	Stage III: More Advanced				
No.	Exercise	I	II	III	IV
1.	Curl-up and return, arms behind head		+		
2.	Reverse curl-up with hip extension, press knees (Figure 17.27)		+		
3.	Lying prone, legs supported, torso over end of table—back extensions from 90° to 0° only (Figure 17.28)			+	+
4.	Hyperextension—in bridging position.			+	+
5.	Pull-ups from bar.			+	+
6.	Hanging from bar—bring knees to chest			+	+
7.	Advanced ethafoam cylinder[33] and gym ball proprioceptive exercises			+	+
8.	Advanced psoai stretch (Figure 17.25)		+	+	+

(Continued)

FIGURE 17.26
(a–d) Proprioception exercises utilizing a foam roller;
(e) bracing

FIGURE 17.27
Reverse curl-up

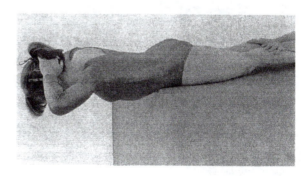

FIGURE 17.28
Back strengthening
With the legs held, the athlete should extend to the horizontal only.

A flexion-sensitive athlete with discogenic backache should avoid flexion until the disc is stable. Emphasis is initially on stabilization in neutral and low-level extension activities.[34] As symptoms subside, low-level rotational exercises are introduced to help in the fibrogensis at the injured vertebral segment. As continued improvement occurs, initiation of the four stages presented can be started.

FIGURE 17.29
Reverse curl-up in a pike position

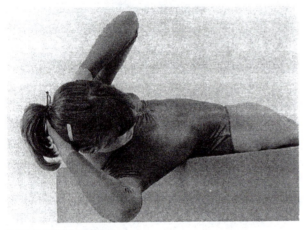

FIGURE 17.30
Trunk strengthening
The feet and legs are supported and the buttocks are in contact with the edge of the table. The trunk is held horizontal and slowly rotated. If the athlete is sufficiently strong and well-conditioned, a weight may be grasped while the arms are outstretched.

TABLE 17.5 *(Continued)*

	Stage IV: For Suitably Conditioned Strong and Advanced Competitive Athletes Only with Individual Prescription and Supervision				
No.	*Exercise*	*I*	*II*	*III*	*IV*
1.	Reverse curl-up with knee toward ceiling press and progressions into a pike position (Figure 17.29)				+
2.	Curl-up and touch elbows to opposite knee				+
3.	Curl-up and return, hold weight behind neck				+
4.	Lying prone, legs supported, torso over end of a table— a. back extensions from 90° to 0° with weights b. hyperextensions without weights, i.e. come up above 0° c. hyperextensions without weights, i.e. come up above 0° (as long as there is no discomfort and only done at final rehabilitation)				+
5.	Supine, arms outstretched, holding weight, rotate torso with feet held; or no weight, hands behind head (Figure 17.30)				+
6.	Prone, feet held, torso off end of table—back extensions with rotation.				+
7.	High advanced proprioceptive training with cylinders, gym ball, balance boards, and etc.[11,31,33]				+
8.	Dead lifts, cleans, and squats.				+

Injuries to the Groin and the Hip

Groin Muscle Strain

A strain of one of the groin muscles—the sartorius, part of the rectus femoris, one of the adductors, or the iliopsoai[35]—tends to be a slow-healing condition. The athlete complains of discomfort localized in the groin area, particularly when greater speed and a higher knee lift are attempted. Tenderness is usually localized to the muscle involved. For instance, placing the muscle under stress, isometric resistance, or forced hip flexion reproduces the pain.

TREATMENT: After the initial icing, gentle prolonged stretching of the involved muscle should be instituted (Figure 17.31a,b,c), together with a strengthening program for all the groin muscles (Figure 17.32a,b,c). These exercises are isometric at first. Once performed painlessly, the athlete progresses to high-speed isokinetic workouts.

Taping/wrapping the upper thigh to hold the hip in slight flexion, which prevents extension, often provides symptomatic relief and may help the athlete to continue participating (Figure 17.33). Compression shorts are readily available and are popular with many athletes (Figure 17.34). Ultrasound and, in particular, TENS are accessory means that may help the athlete return to participation. Corticosteroid injections are sometimes used in resistant cases.

Lateral Hip Pain

Lateral hip pain may be due to:

1. Strain or weakness of the quadratus lumborum, the abdominal muscles, or the iliotibial tract, presenting with pain along the iliac crest

2. Friction of the iliotibial tract over the greater trochanter, often associated with trochanteric bursitis

3. Strain of the gluteus medius, the piriformis, or both, at the attachment to the greater trochanter

4. Lower back dysfunction or discogenic disease, with radiation or referred pain in the hip area

5. Stress fracture of the femur

TREATMENT: Appropriate strengthening and stretching exercises and therapeutic modalities usually relieve the symptoms. A discrepancy in leg length should be diagnosed and corrected. In cases of trochanteric bursitis or iliotibial friction, a cortisone injection may be indicated.

"Hip Pointer"

Hip pointer indicates a *contusion to the iliac crest*, the anterior superior iliac spine, or both. This contusion results in bleeding, swelling, and pain. Sometimes avulsion of a portion of the muscles attached to the crest

(a)

(b)

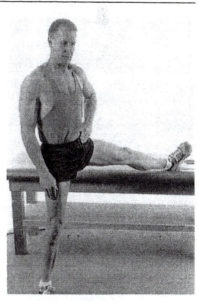
(c)

FIGURE 17.31
Groin stretches

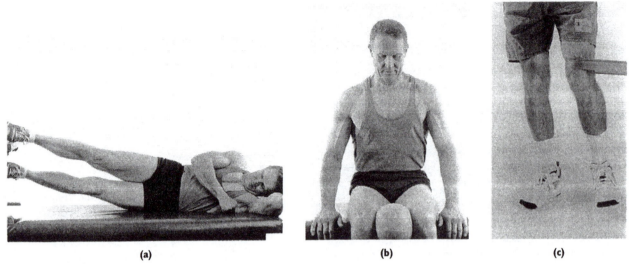

FIGURE 17.32
(a) Isometric/active side lift; (b) seated leg squeeze; (c) hip adduction against resistance of elastic band

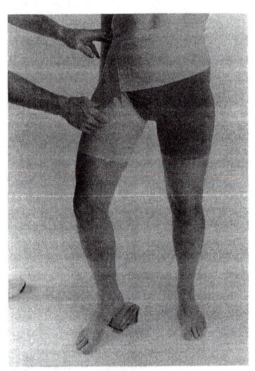

FIGURE 17.33
Taping/wrapping of the groin

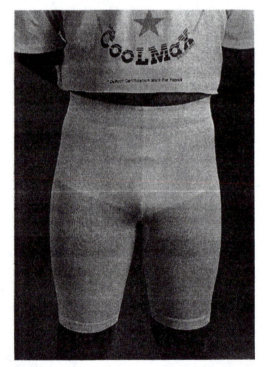

FIGURE 17.34
Compression shorts
(Photo furnished by Lontex Corp., Perkasie, PA)

occurs. Rarely is a fracture of the crest found. The athlete has difficulty walking normally and standing upright due to the pain and muscle spasm. The area is very tender to the touch. It is important for the trainer to exclude an intra-abdominal injury.

TREATMENT: Ice should be placed on the painful area immediately. Injection of a corticosteroid preparation in conjunction with a long-acting anesthetic agent is often indicated soon after the injury. Following such treatment, symptoms rapidly decrease, though it may take a few days of icing and gentle stretching to enable the athlete to run normally. Oral anti-inflammatory medication can be used if necessary, and TENS is a useful adjunct. The athlete should wear adequate protective padding upon return to participation.

Injury to the Lateral Cutaneous Nerve of the Thigh

The lateral cutaneous nerve of the thigh supplies the proximal two-thirds of the lateral thigh. It is purely sensory in function. Contusions to this nerve can result in impaired sensation laterally over the thigh. Muscle power is not affected. Recovery depends on the degree of damage the nerve has sustained. Usually no active treatment is necessary.

Occasionally the nerve becomes entrapped in scar tissue, producing constant pain in the lateral groin area or along the lateral border of the thigh. Manual connective tissue mobilization is often an effective conservative treatment. The condition can also be treated with a local anesthetic and a cortisone preparation. If these measures fail to relieve the symptoms, exploratory surgery aimed at releasing the entrapped nerve should be considered.

Dislocation of the Hip

A hip dislocation is a severe injury resulting from a considerable force which usually drives the hip backwards. A fracture may be associated with this posterior dislocation. An anterior dislocation rarely occurs.

The athlete cannot walk after the injury. A large prominence may be felt over the greater trochanteric area with pain localized in the hip. The affected foot tends to rest on top of the opposite foot. Though the diagnosis may be immediately apparent clinically, no attempt should be made to reduce the dislocation on the field. The athlete should be removed by stretcher and taken to an emergency room for further examination and X-rays.

TREATMENT: Reduction under general anesthesia will most frequently be necessary. It may then take many months before full athletic activity can be resumed.

COMPLICATIONS:

1. Compression of the sciatic nerve can result in an impairment of foot function.
2. Avascular necrosis of the femoral head can occur up to six months after injury. This complication seems to be more common when the femur remains unreduced for a number of hours. It is therefore important to act immediately after the dislocation.
3. Osteoarthritis can occur later in life.

When a dislocation occurs in the adolescent with an unfused capital femoral epiphysis, *a fracture through the epiphysis* can result. This usually presents in a very similar way to dislocation of the hip, and careful X-ray studies may be necessary before deciding on the diagnosis. The condition may require reduction and internal fixation.

Pain around the Pubic Symphysis from Overuse

Pubic symphysis pain can be due to:

1. Adductor strain
2. Stress fracture of the inferior ramus
3. Osteitis pubis

Osteitis pubis is an unusual condition that can affect a running athlete, especially a long-distance runner, though it may result from direct local trauma.[36,37,38] Presenting symptoms are pain and tenderness over the symphysis pubis, resulting in spasm of the adductor muscles. In severe cases the athlete may develop a waddling gait. There may be radiation of pain down the inner aspect of the thigh and up into the lower abdomen.

TREATMENT: Anti-inflammatory medication to help alleviate the symptoms is combined with ice, ultrasound, and TENS. If a localized tender spot exists, a local injection of corticosteroid may prove beneficial. In the severely acute case with a markedly inflamed symphysis pubis and high fever, four to six weeks of oral cortisone may be indicated.[39] After the acute symptoms have subsided, treatment consists of slowly and progressively strengthening abdomen, groin, adductor, or lower back muscle.

REFERENCES

1. Ferguson KJ, McMaster JH, Stanitski CL: Low back pain in college football lineman. *J Sports Med* 2:63–69, 1974.

2. Jackson DW, Wise LI, Cirincione RJ: Spondyloysis in the female gymnast. *Clin Orthop* 117:68–73, 1976.

3. Bogduk N, Twomey L: *Clinical Anatomy of the Lumbar Spine*. Melbourne, Churchill Livingstone, 1987.

4. Levine DB: The painful low back. In *Arthritis and Allied Conditions: A Textbook of Rheumatology,* edited by McCarty DJ. Philadelphia, Lea and Febiger, ninth edition, 1979.

5. Macnab I: *Backache.* Baltimore, Williams and Wilkins, 1977.

6. Cyriax J: *Textbook of Orthopaedic Medicine: Diagnosis of Soft Tissue Lesions,* Vol. 1. New York, Macmillian, seventh edition, 1978.

7. Mennell J McM: *Back Pain.* Boston, Little Brown and Company, 1960.

8. Kirkaldy-Willis WH, Hill NJ: A more precise diagnosis for low-back pain. *Spine* 4:516–523, 1979.

9. Greenman P: *Principles of Manual Medicine.* Baltimore, Williams and Wilkins, 1989

10. McKenzie RA: Prophylaxis in recurrent low back pain. *NZ Med J* 89:22–23, 1979.

11. Johnson GS, Saliba VL: *Back Education and Training: CME course.* San Anselmo, Institute of Physical Art, 1988.

12. Janda V: Muscle weakness and inhibition (pseudoparesis) in back pain syndromes. In *Modern Manual Therapy of the Vertebral Column,* edited by Grieves G. London, Churchill Livingstone, 1986.

13. Butler DS: *Mobilisation of the Nervous System.* New York, Churchill Livingstone, 1991.

14. Schiotz E, Cyriax J: *Manipulation, Past and Present.* London, Heinemann and Son, 1975.

15. Rettig A, Jackson DW, Wiltse LI., et al: The epidural venogram as a diagnostic procedure in the young athlete with symptoms of lumbar disc disease. *Am J Sports Med* 5:158–164, 1977.

16. Leyshon A, Kirwin EOG, Wynn Parry CB: Electrical studies in the diagnosis of compression of the lumbar root. *J Bone Joint Surg* 63B:71–75, 1981.

17. Jackson DW, Rettig A, Wiltse LL: Epidural cortisone injections in the young athletic adult. *Am J Sports Med* 8:239–243, 1980.

18. Gindin RA, Volcan IJ: Rupture of the intervertebral disc producing cauda equina syndrome. *Am Surgeon* 44:585–593, 1978.

19. Floman Y, Wiesel SW, Rothman NH: Cauda equina syndrome presenting as a herniated lumbar disk. *Clin Orthop* 147:234–237, 1980.

20. Pace JP, Nague D: Piriformis syndrome. *West J Med* 124:435, 1976.

21. Travell JG, Simons DG: *Myofascial Pain and Dysfunction: The Trigger Point Manual,* Vol. 2. Baltimore, Williams and Wilkins, 1992.

22. Jones LH: *Strain and Counterstrain.* Colorado Springs, The American Academy of Osteopathy, 1981.

23. Wiltse LL, Widell EH, Jackson DW: Fatigue fracture: The basic lesion in isthmic spondylolisthesis. *J Bone Joint Surg* 57A:17–22, 1975.

24. Jackson DW, Wiltse LL, Dingeman RD, et al: Stress reactions involving pars interarticularis in young athletes. *Am J Sports Med* 9:304–312, 1981.

25. Jackson DW: Low back pain in young athletes. Evaluations of stress reaction and discogenic problems. *Am J Sports Med* 7: 364–366, 1979.

26. Kotani PT, Ichikawa N, Wakabayashi W, et al: Studies of spondylosis found among weight lifters. *Br J Sports Med* 6:4–8, 1970.

27. Macnab I, McCulloch J: *Backache.* Baltimore, Williams and Wilkins, second edition, 1990.

28. Magee DJ: *Orthopedic Physical Assessment.* Philadelphia, WB Saunders, 1987.

29. Basmajian JV, Nyberg R: *Rational Manual Therapies,* Chapter 15. Baltimore, Williams and Wilkins, 1993.

30. Johnson GS, Saliba VL: Soft tissue mobilization, chapter 18. In *Conservative Care of Low Back Pain,* edited by White A and Anderson R. Baltimore, Williams and Wilkins, 1991.

31. Keyser KV, Hauswirth B: *Integrating Function: The Foam Roller Approach: CME course.* San Anselmo, Institute of Physical Art, 1993.

32. Johnson GS, Saliba VL: Lumbar protective mechanism, Chapter 13. In *Conservative Care of Low Back Pain,* edited by White A and Anderson R. Baltimore, Williams and Wilkins, 1991.

33. Hauswirth B, Keyser KV: Ideas at work: Ethafoam™ roller. *PT—Magazine of Phys. Ther* 1(2): 93–94, 1993.

34. McKenzie RA: *The Lumbar Spine—Mechanical Diagnosis and Therapy.* New Zealand, Spinal Publications, 1981.

35. Birnbaum DA: Missed avulsion fracture of the lesser trochanter in a tennis professional. *Med Trial Tech Q* 27:121–125, 1980.

36. Koch RA, Jackson DW: Pubic symphysitis in runners. A report of two cases. *Am J Sports Med* 9:62–63, 1981.

37. Cochrane GM: Osteitis pubis in athletes. *Br J Sports Med* 5:233–235, 1971.

38. Williams JGP: Limitations of hip joint movement as a factor in traumatic osteitis pubis. *Br J Sports Med* 12:129–133, 1978.

39. Pyle LA: Osteitis pubis in athletes. *J Am Coll Health Assoc* 23:238–239, 1975.

RECOMMENDED READINGS

Bogduk N, Twomey L: *Clinical Anatomy of the Lumbar Spine.* Melbourne, Churchill Livingstone, 1987.

Bourdillon JF: *Spinal Manipulation.* London, William Heinemann Medical Books, fourth edition, 1987.

Breig A: *Adverse Mechanical Tension in the Central Nervous System.* New York, John Wiley & Sons, 1978.

Chrisman OD, Mittnacht A, Snook GA: A study of the results following rotatory manipulation in the lumbar interverterbral-disc syndrome. *J Bone Joint Surg* 46A:517–524, 1964.

Cibulka MT, Delitto A, Koldehoff RM: Changes in innominate tilt after manipulation of the sacroiliac joint in patients with low back pain. *Phys Ther* 68:9, 1988.

Cyriax J, Russell G: Treatment by manipulation, massage, and injection. In *Textbook of Orthopaedic Medicine.* Vol. II. London, Baillière Tindall, eleventh edition, 1984.

Evjenth O, Hamburg J: *Muscle Stretching in Manual Therapy, A Clinical Manual,* Vol. 1 and 2. Sweden: ALFTA Rehab., 1984.

Fahrni WH: Conservative treatment of lumbar disc degeneration: Our primary responsibility. *Orthop Clin North Am* 6:93–103, 1975.

Gracovetsky S, Farfan H: The optimum spine. *Spine* 11: 543–572, 1986.

Greenman P: *Principles of Manual Medicine.* Baltimore, Williams and Wilkins, 1989.

Grieve G: *Modern Manual Therapy of the Vertebral Column.* London, Churchill Livingstone, 1986.

Grieve G: *Common Vertebral Joint Problems.* London, Churchill Livingstone, second edition, 1988.

Handal J, Selby D: Spinal Instability, Chapter 13. In *Rehabilitation of the Spine, Science and Practice,* edited by Hochschuler SH, Cotler HB, and Guyer RD. St. Louis, Mosby, 1993.

McKenzie RA: Manual correction of sciatic scoliosis. *NZ Med J* 76:194–199, 1972.

Merrifield HH, Cowan RF: Groin strain injuries in ice hockey. Research summaries. *J Sports Med* 1:41–42, 1973.

Micheli L: Low back pain in the adolescent. Differential diagnosis. *Am J Sports Med* 7:362–364, 1979.

Nachemson AL: The load on lumbar discs in different positions of the body. *Clin Orthop* 45:107–122, 1966.

Nachemson AL: The influence of spinal movements on the lumbar intradiscal pressure and on the tensile stresses in the annulus fibrosus. *Acta Orthop Scand* 33:183–207, 1963.

Stanish W: Low back pain in middle-age athletes. *Am J Sports Med* 7:367–369, 1979.

Sturesson B, Selvik G, Uden A: Movements of the sacroiliac joints: A roentgen stereophototgrammetric analysis. *Spine* 14(2): 162–165, 1989.

Travell JG, Simons DG: *Myofascial Pain and Dysfunction: The Trigger Point Manual,* Vol. 2. Baltimore, Williams and Wilkins, 1992.

White AA, Panjabi MM: *Clinical Biomechanics of the Spine.* Philadelphia, JB Lippincott, 1978.

Wyke B: The neurology of joints: A review of general principles. *Clin Rheum Diseases* 7:223–239, 1981.

Chest, Abdominal, and Genital Injuries

Chest Injuries

Direct blows to the chest can result in one or more of the following injuries:

1. Contusions
2. Rib fractures, which can result in a pneumothorax
3. Costochondral separations
4. Cardiac contusions, which can result in a pericardial effusion with cardiac tamponade (constriction of the heart)

Contusions

A severe contusion to the ribs is often very difficult to distinguish from a fracture. Because of bruising of the intercostal muscles, there may be both pain on inspiration and localized tenderness. These cases should be X-rayed to exclude a fractured rib or other intrathoracic problems such as a pneumothorax.

Having excluded the more serious conditions, the involved area should be iced and anti-inflammatory medication administered if necessary. A rib belt can be used for comfort. If the athlete is participating in a contact sport, sufficient padding should be applied over the contusion for adequate protection.

Rib Fractures

A fractured rib may present with localized tenderness and pain on inspiration, resulting in shallow, rapid breathing. It is sometimes possible to feel crepitus over a fractured rib, but often the symptoms are indistinguishable from those of a contusion. The athlete should

always be X-rayed to establish the diagnosis and exclude any complication. Complications include a pneumothorax, which is clinically confirmed by the presence of hyper-resonance to percussion and the absence of breath sounds when listening with a stethoscope to the affected site.

Treatment of the uncomplicated case is symptomatic, using a rib belt or tape on the involved side of the chest wall. Healing should be complete before the athlete is allowed to return to participation, mainly because of the danger of a pneumothorax, caused by a fractured rib penetrating the pleura. The healing process in the average case is usually sufficiently completed within three to four weeks, but the athlete should use protective padding over the fracture if participating in a contact sport.

Emergency care of a pneumothorax includes administration of oxygen and rapid removal of the player by stretcher from the area of participation to the nearest emergency room.

Spontaneous Pneumothorax

A spontaneous pneumothorax can occur in a previously healthy athlete. There is sudden shortness of breath and a sharp chest pain, which may be referred to the tip of the shoulder. If a large pneumothorax is present, cyanosis can be seen (blueness of the tongue, mucous membranes, and nails).

Signs include shallow, rapid respiration with poor air entry into the affected lung and hyperresonance to percussion over the affected area. Treatment consists of administration of oxygen and rapid transportation of the athlete to an emergency facility capable of handling this type of problem.

Costochondral Separations

Costochondral separations frequently occur in a sport such as wrestling, when the rib cage is squeezed or when one arm is pulled over to the side, stretching the attachment of the rib at the costochondral junction. Frequently the injured athlete feels a pop.

Symptoms and Signs. Tenderness is localized specifically to the costochondral junction, and often swelling and/or displacement of the rib can be seen and felt. The displaced rib can sometimes be manipulated back into place and held there by means of semi-circumferential taping. These cases should be X-rayed to exclude fractured ribs.

Treatment. Treatment consists of ice, tape, and analgesics. The judicious use of a corticosteroid injection around the painful area often helps reduce the symptoms and may allow the athlete to return to participation, though many athletes have prolonged discomfort.

Cardiac Contusions

A cardiac contusion can result in a pericardial effusion, which may lead to cardiac tamponade. This is clinically confirmed by muffled heart sounds, engorgement of the neck veins, small pulse pressure when taking the blood pressure, and a pulse that tends to disappear on inspiration.

As cardiac tamponade is a life-threatening condition that needs to be treated immediately, the athlete needs to be taken by ambulance to an emergency room without delay.

Abdominal Injuries

Injuries to the abdominal viscera are not common in most athletic activities, but they do occur in contact events. Such accidents most frequently cause

1. Rupture of the spleen[1]
2. Rupture of the liver
3. Contusion or rupture of the kidney
4. Such uncommon conditions as retroperitoneal hemorrhage and rupture of the bowel

Splenic Rupture

The spleen can rupture at any time but is more likely to do so when it is enlarged and fragile, as it becomes with infectious mononucleosis. Many times the athlete has splenomegaly without being aware of it and can rupture the spleen during a relatively innocent movement or blow. At other times rupture results from a severe impact injury to the left upper quadrant of the abdomen or to the lower left rib cage.

Symptoms and Signs. In most cases the diagnosis is not made initially, though it should be suspected. The athlete may have severe pain immediately after the injury and then recover and be thought to have had either "the wind knocked out" or a contusion to the lower ribs. With continued bleeding into the peritoneal cavity, the athlete will begin to suffer increasing abdominal pain and may have referred shoulder pain from the blood irritating the diaphragm. Because of the blood loss, dizziness or fainting may be the first clue to the diagnosis.[1]

The earliest signs are a pale athlete (from constriction of the blood vessels) and a rapid pulse—this is an important sign. The blood pressure may remain normal for a considerable period of time after the injury. If there is a suspicion of a ruptured spleen, the athlete should be immediately transported to an emergency facility for further investigation and observation. If there is some distance to be traveled to the emergency facility, an intravenous infusion of normal saline or Ringer's lactate solution should be given as a precautionary measure before clinical shock sets in.

Treatment. A ruptured spleen almost always needs to be removed surgically, and a blood transfusion is frequently necessary.

Hepatic Rupture

Because the liver is encased in a capsule, it is possible to have a controlled amount of bleeding from a blow to the upper right quadrant. If the liver is severely lacerated and bleeding into the intraperitoneal cavity, symptoms and signs similar to a ruptured spleen rapidly develop.

As with a ruptured spleen, the suspicion of a contused or lacerated liver should be followed by emergency treatment and rapid transfer of the athlete to a facility for further investigation. An athlete with a contused liver is usually kept under observation, as the condition often resolves spontaneously. Lacerations of the liver frequently need to be surgically repaired.

Renal Contusion or Rupture

A renal injury is usually caused by a blow to the flank and presents with a backache, blood in the urine, or both. Any athlete who has a contusion to the flank should be asked to produce a urine specimen which, even though clear, should be tested for microscopic bleeding. If blood is present the athlete should be referred for urological investigation, which frequently includes an intravenous pyelogram (IVP). An athlete with a contusion to or partial rupture of the kidney can be merely placed under observation, as this condition frequently resolves spontaneously. A large laceration of the kidney may need to be surgically repaired.

Contusion to the Solar Plexus ("Having the Wind Knocked Out")

Solar plexus contusion is a frequent injury resulting from irritation of the solar plexus by a blow to the epigastric area. Spasm of the diaphragm reflexly causes temporary paralysis of respiration. Occasionally, the feeling of having the wind knocked out is due to a forceful expiration of the residual volume of air normally present in the lungs and leads to an inhibition of inspiration for the following few seconds.

The athlete suffering from such a contusion should lie still and wait for spontaneous recovery, then be escorted from the area of participation. The abdomen should be examined to ensure no damage to the spleen, liver, or other abdominal structures and to ensure full recovery, after which return to participation may be permitted.

Genital Injuries

Contusion to the Testes

The intense pain and discomfort associated with contusion to the testes is relieved by a simple procedure. The athlete is given a brief explanation of what is to follow, and is then lifted approximately six inches above the ground. This is accomplished by the trainer placing his or her hands beneath the athlete's axilla. The athlete is then dropped to the ground. The impact appears to break the spasm of the cremasteric muscles, often producing dramatic disappearance of the pain.

If swelling of the scrotum occurs, the area involved should be iced and the scrotum elevated by placing towels between the legs. If a large hematoma develops, the athlete should be examined by a urologist and assessed for possible aspiration.

Contusion to the Vulva

A vulval contusion results from a fall, such as falling astride a balance beam, and a large hematoma rapidly develops. In severe cases, lacerations occur and need to be sutured.

Vaginal Injuries

High-speed water-skiing injuries can result in rupture of the wall of the vagina. Or water may be forced through the fallopian tubes, resulting in localized pelvic peritonitis. If such an injury occurs, the athlete should be referred immediately to a gynecologist. These injuries can be prevented by the athlete's wearing a neoprene wet suit while water-skiing.

REFERENCE

1. Hahn DB: The ruptured spleen: Implications for the athletic trainer. *Athletic Training* 13:190–191, 1978.

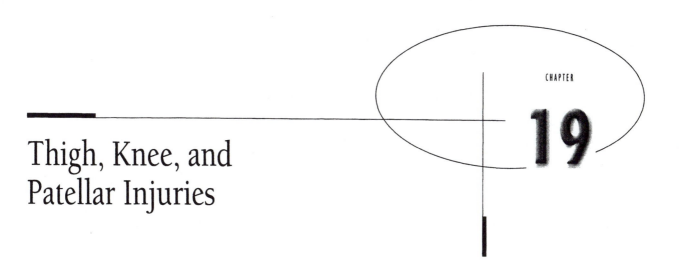

CHAPTER

19

Thigh, Knee, and Patellar Injuries

Functional Anatomy

Knee Movements

The knee consists of the *tibiofemoral joint* and the *patellofemoral joint*. The tibiofemoral joint appears to move as a hinge, but actually other movements occur as the knee flexes from the extended position. These movements include[1]

1. A rocking action
2. A gliding action
3. Rotational movements

1. In full extension (0°) there is no rotational movement. The tibia is externally rotated on the femur and "locked" in this position.

2. From 0° to 20° of flexion, a rocking action takes place. The tibia begins to internally rotate on the femur (depending on how one looks at it, it is also correct to say that the femur externally rotates relative to the tibia).

3. From 20° on, the tibia starts to glide on the femur. An increasing amount of tibial rotation is now possible—up to 40° when the knee is bent to 90°. More external rotation is usually present than internal rotation (Figure 19.1).

4. The knee can normally bend until the calf comes into contact with the thigh at approximately 135°.

5. On extension of the knee from the flexed position, the tibia externally rotates relative to the femur during the last 20°.[2] This is the so-called "screw-home" mechanism, which helps to stabilize the knee in full extension.[3]

The *patellofemoral articulation* is a gliding joint. The patella slides along the intercondylar groove between the lateral and medial femoral condyles.

Ligaments

The knee has a complex system of ligaments which enclose it from all directions except over the anterior portion.

MEDIAL STABILIZING COMPLEX: The medial ligament is divided into two portions:

1. *Medial capsular ligament:* Consists of the meniscofemoral and the meniscotibial bands lying on either

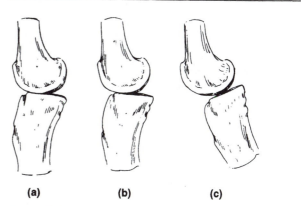

| (a) | (b) | (c) |

FIGURE 19.1
Initial movements of the tibiofemoral joint
(a) At 0° the joint is locked; (b) With the initiation of flexion, a rocking action occurs; (c) From 20° onwards, the tibia glides on the femur. Rotation is now possible.

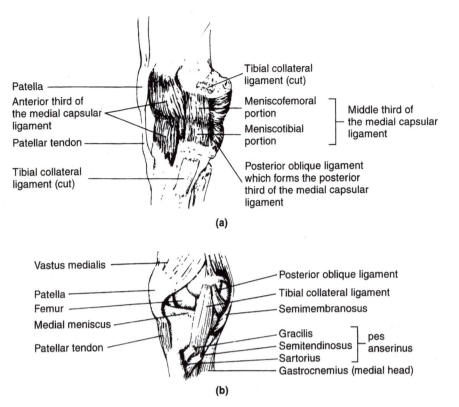

Patella

Anterior third of the medial capsular ligament

Patellar tendon

Tibial collateral ligament (cut)

Tibial collateral ligament (cut)

Meniscofemoral portion

Meniscotibial portion

} **Middle third of the medial capsular ligament**

Posterior oblique ligament which forms the posterior third of the medial capsular ligament

(a)

Vastus medialis

Patella

Femur

Medial meniscus

Patellar tendon

Posterior oblique ligament

Tibial collateral ligament

Semimembranosus

Gracilis
Semitendinosus
Sartorius
} **pes anserinus**

Gastrocnemius (medial head)

(b)

FIGURE 19.2

(a) The medial capsular ligament; (b) Medial stabilizing structures (the capsular ligament is partially removed)

side of the joint line and is attached to the periphery of the medial meniscus. It is divided into anterior, middle, and posterior thirds (Figure 19.2).

The *posterior oblique ligament* is really the posterior third of the medial capsular ligament, but is named as a separate ligament because it is thought to help prevent valgus laxity and medial rotatory instability.

2. *Tibial collateral ligament:* Runs from the medial epicondyle of the femur to the medial side of the tibia and inserts into the tibia underneath the pes anserine group of muscles, about 7 cm below the joint line. It is one of the main stabilizers against valgus stress and medial rotation. The anterior portion of this ligament is taut throughout the range of motion, from full extension to 90° of flexion, which helps prevent valgus opening[4] (Table 19.1).

LATERAL STABILIZING COMPLEX:

1. *Lateral capsular ligament:* Similar to the medial capsular ligament in that it consists of both meniscotibial and meniscofemoral bands, and is divided into anterior, middle, and posterior thirds (Figure 19.3).

2. *Fibular collateral ligament:* Runs from the lateral femur to the head of the fibula and consists of a band of firm tissue that is easily palpated when the knee is held at 90° of flexion and forced into a varus position (such as when the lateral malleolus is placed on the opposite

TABLE 19.1 *Medial stabilizing complex of the knee*

Consists of two parts:

1. *Medial capsular ligament* (deep capsular ligament) This is divided into thirds:
   Anterior third
   Middle third
   Posterior third (this is the same as the
                    posterior oblique ligament)

   Each division has a meniscofemoral part and a meniscotibial part

2. *Tibial collateral ligament* (superficial)

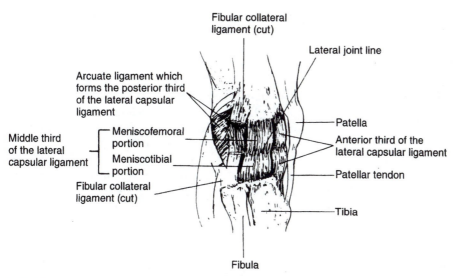

FIGURE 19.3
The lateral capsular ligament

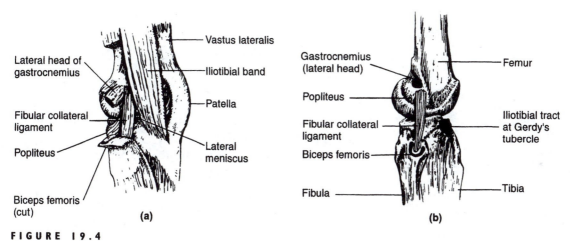

FIGURE 19.4
(a) Some of the structures comprising the lateral stabilizing complex (the capsular ligament is not included); (b) Attachment of the structures comprising the lateral stabilizing complex

knee while the athlete is sitting). Lateral stability is achieved (Figure 19.4) in conjunction with the

a. iliotibial band

b. biceps tendon

c. popliteus tendon and arcuate ligament complex (Table 19.2)

CRUCIATE LIGAMENTS:

1. *Anterior cruciate ligament:* Runs from the anterior part of the tibial plateau just medial and posterior to the anterior tibial spine, and goes posteriorly and laterally to attach to the posterior-most portion of the medial aspect of the lateral femoral condyle. This ligament is of vital importance in preventing hyperextension and excessive rotation of the tibia on the femur during running and cutting.[5]

2. *Posterior cruciate ligament:* Lies in the long axis of the leg. It runs from the posterior part of the tibial plateau to the lateral part of the medial femoral condyle. Its main function is to prevent posterior displacement of the tibia on the femur, particularly during the gliding phase of flexion (Figure 19.5).

TABLE 19.2 *Lateral stabilizing complex of the knee*

The following structures support the lateral side of the knee joint:

1. *Lateral capsular ligament*—as on the medial side, this part is divided into thirds:
   Anterior third
   Middle third
   Posterior third

Each of these divisions has a meniscofemoral and a meniscotibial part.

2. *Fibular collateral ligament*—runs between the femur and the fibular head

3. *Biceps tendon*—attaches to the fibular head

4. *Iliotibial band*—attaches to Gerdy's tubercle

5. *Popliteus tendon* and *arcuate ligament complex*—cover the posterolateral corner of the knee

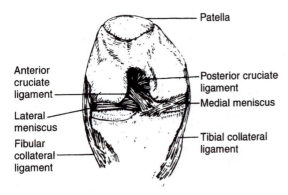

FIGURE 19.5
The ligaments of the knee from the front with the knee bent

Anterior cruciate ligament

Lateral meniscus

Fibular collateral ligament

Patella

Posterior cruciate ligament

Medial meniscus

Tibial collateral ligament

OTHER LIGAMENTS:

1. *Popliteal oblique ligament:* On the posterior aspect of the knee, it blends in with the posterior capsule and the fibers from the semimembranosus muscle.

2. *Posterior capsule:* A thick band of tissue situated posteriorly, it appears to be one of the structures preventing hyperextension of the knee. It is taut in extension, but lax in flexion.

The Menisci

There are two menisci in the knee joint: the *medial meniscus* and the *lateral meniscus*. These fibrocartilaginous disks deepen the joint, thereby permitting a more stable articulation between the femur and the tibia. They also act as shock absorbers (weight transmitters) and help smooth the gliding action of the tibia on the femur (Table 19.3).

The medial meniscus lies on the medial tibial plateau, which is concave; the lateral meniscus lies on the lateral tibial plateau, which is convex. The menisci move with the tibia during flexion and extension and with the femur during rotation.

The blood supply to the menisci is via peripheral vessels from the synovial and capsular tissues, and is relatively poor, especially that to the central section of the meniscus. Most of the nutritional needs are therefore met by the diffusion of synovial fluid.

The menisci are thicker at their peripheries than at their centers (Figure 19.6) and are circular in shape. Smillie has stated that, "The contour of the lateral meniscus is most accurately described as a large segment . . . of a small circle. Whereas, by comparison, the medial is a small segment of a large circle."[6]

TABLE 19.3 *Functions of the menisci*

1. Share the load in weight-bearing and increase the joint contact area

2. Absorb shock, thereby protecting the articular cartilage

3. Help stabilize the joint by deepening the articular surfaces of the tibial plateau

4. Help facilitate control of some rotational movements (such as the "screw-home" movement)

5. Aid in joint nutrition and lubrication

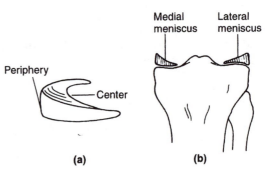

Medial meniscus

Lateral meniscus

Periphery

Center

(a)

(b)

FIGURE 19.6
(a) The meniscus
The menisci are thicker at the periphery than at the center;
(b) Silhouette of the menisci

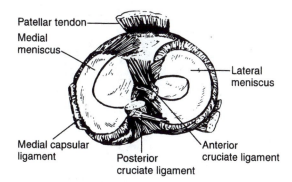

Patellar tendon
Medial meniscus
Lateral meniscus
Medial capsular ligament
Posterior cruciate ligament
Anterior cruciate ligament

FIGURE 19.7
The menisci (from above)

The *medial meniscus* is C shaped and consists of an anterior portion, or body, and a posterior segment, or horn. There is an important attachment to the deep capsular portion of the medial capsular ligament. A peripheral detachment of the meniscus can result if this medial capsular ligament is torn (Figure 19.7).

The semimembranosus muscle is attached to the posterior aspect of the medial meniscus (via the posteromedial capsule) and tends to pull the meniscus back out of the way during flexion. However, mobility of the medial meniscus is limited, which leaves the posterior horn vulnerable to tearing.

The *lateral meniscus* is more O shaped and is more mobile than the medial meniscus because it does not have any attachment to the deep posterolateral capsule, from which it is separated by the popliteal tendon sheath. The arcuate ligament is firmly attached to the lateral meniscus, and, as the popliteus muscle is attached to both the arcuate ligament and the lateral meniscus, the posterior segment of the meniscus can be pulled backward during medial rotation of the tibia in flexion.

Muscles

The muscles surrounding the knee joint are of extreme importance in preserving the stability of a basically unstable joint. It has been shown that athletes who condition all the muscles around the knee have a far lower incidence of injury than those who do not. The muscles surrounding the knee are:

QUADRICEPS MUSCLE GROUP: The quadriceps are the main stabilizers of the knee joint. They lie on the front of the thigh and form the quadriceps tendon, which inserts into the patella. The patellar tendon originates from the inferior pole of the patella and inserts into the tibial tubercle. The main function of the quadriceps muscle group is to extend the flexed knee.

The quadriceps consist of four muscles:

1. *Vastus medialis*—makes up most of the medial bulk of the muscle. It has a separate part, the vastus medialis obliquus (VMO). The vastus medialis is important in stabilizing the patella. It is a very sensitive index of knee derangement, as it is the first muscle to atrophy.

2. *Vastus intermedius*—forms the bulk of the muscle.

3. *Vastus lateralis*—runs on the lateral side. These three vastus muscles originate from the femur and, with the rectus femoris, insert into the quadriceps tendon.

4. *Rectus femoris*—runs from the anterior inferior iliac spine to join the quadriceps tendon above the patella. The rectus femoris is the most superficial of the four muscles. It flexes the hip and extends the knee.

PES ANSERINE MUSCLE GROUP: This group is composed of the sartorius, the gracilis, and the semitendinosus muscles, of which the semitendinosus is the strongest. The sartorius runs from the anterior superior iliac spine; the gracilis, from the pubis; the semitendinosus, from the ischial tuberosity. These muscles insert into the tibial crest (as the pes anserine tendon) anteriorly and superficial to the tibial attachment of the tibial collateral ligament, about 7 cm below the medial joint line. They act mainly to flex the knee but can, under certain conditions, internally rotate the tibia (Figure 19.8).

HAMSTRINGS: The hamstrings are situated on the posterior aspect of the thigh and are nearly as important as the quadriceps in preserving the stability of the knee. The main functions of the hamstrings are to

1. Flex the extended knee.

2. Work in conjunction with the quadriceps muscle group during knee extension. As the quadriceps extend the knee, the hamstrings act as a brake to slow down the tibia. If the quadriceps are too powerful relative to the hamstrings, a strained (or "pulled") hamstring can result from their being unable to adequately counteract the force of the quadriceps during extension.

3. Extend the hip.

The hamstrings consist of three muscle masses which originate from the ischial tuberosity (Figure 19.9).

1. *Semitendinosus*—runs down the medial aspect of the thigh posteriorly and inserts into the tibia with the gracilis and the sartorius as the pes anserine muscle group.

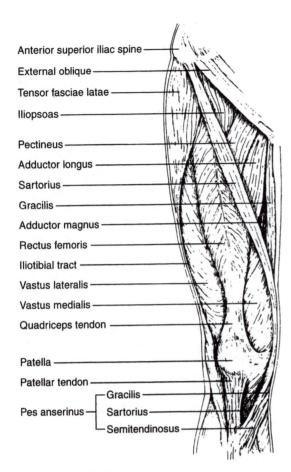

Anterior superior iliac spine
External oblique
Tensor fasciae latae
Iliopsoas

Pectineus
Adductor longus
Sartorius
Gracilis
Adductor magnus
Rectus femoris
Iliotibial tract
Vastus lateralis
Vastus medialis
Quadriceps tendon

Patella
Patellar tendon
Pes anserinus — Gracilis
Sartorius
Semitendinosus

FIGURE 19.8
Muscles of the thigh—anterior view

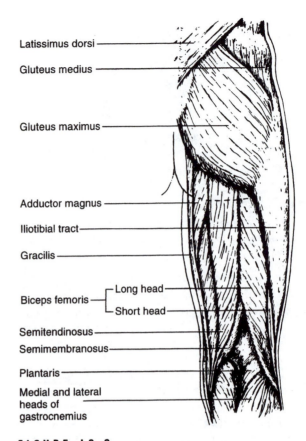

Latissimus dorsi
Gluteus medius

Gluteus maximus

Adductor magnus
Iliotibial tract
Gracilis

Biceps femoris — Long head
Short head
Semitendinosus
Semimembranosus
Plantaris
Medial and lateral heads of gastrocnemius

FIGURE 19.9
Muscles of the thigh—posterior view

2. *Semimembranosus*—forms the bulk of the hamstring muscle group. It dynamically tightens the posteromedial corner, helping to prevent excessive rotation of the tibia from medial to lateral. The semimembranosus, on reaching the knee, branches into five divisions which fan out and attach to

a. the oblique popliteal ligament

b. the posterior capsule and the medial meniscus, where there is dynamic action retracting the meniscus from the joint

c. the tibia medially, which helps to increase its internal rotatory action

d. the posterior tibial tuberosity

e. the popliteal fascia

3. *The biceps femoris.* This muscle has two heads—the *long head* originating from the ischial tuberosity and the *short head* originating from the lateral femur. The biceps runs down the lateral aspect posteriorly and inserts into the head of the fibula. This helps dynamically stabilize

the lateral aspect of the knee, particularly in flexion, as contraction of the biceps tightens the fibular collateral ligament and the posterior capsule.

ILIOTIBIAL TRACT: This muscle originates from the anterior superior iliac spine and the iliac crest as the tensor fasciae latae. It becomes the iliotibial tract at the lower third of the thigh and then sweeps across the lateral side of the knee to insert into the tibia at Gerdy's tubercle.

POPLITEUS: This muscle originates from the femur just above the lateral joint line, where it is covered by the fibular collateral ligament and the biceps femoris tendon. It is intimately connected with the posterior horn of the lateral meniscus, helping to retract it back out of the way. It inserts into the posterior aspect of the upper medial tibia above the soleal line. The popliteus has a number of functions which include:

1. Internal rotation of the tibia relative to the femur or, alternatively, external rotation of the femur if the tibia is fixed

2. Prevention of forward movement of the tibia on the femur when the foot is fixed

3. Tightening of the posterior capsule and the arcuate ligament

4. Retraction of the lateral meniscus

GASTROCNEMIUS: As the gastrocnemius crosses the knee joint, it splits into two heads which insert posteriorly into the medial and lateral aspects of the femur respectively and play a part in stabilizing the knee joint.

Thigh Injuries

Contusion to the Quadriceps

A contusion to the lateral and, more importantly, the anterior aspect of the thigh is often undertreated. It should be realized that this can be one of the most disabling injuries to afflict an athlete. Following a severe blow to the thigh, two things occur: (1) Blood vessels are broken and a lesser or greater degree of bleeding occurs and (2) a variable amount of muscle is crushed. The bleeding can be considerable and can increase the damage to the muscle.

SYMPTOMS AND SIGNS: The athlete may attempt to continue participating after the injury. The thigh becomes progressively more stiff while at the same time the quadriceps muscles become more and more unresponsive. If the injury is severe, swelling and tightness of the thigh musculature are observed soon afterwards, together with loss of knee flexion.[7] If the athlete does not receive adequate treatment immediately, there may be increased swelling of the leg, stiffness of the muscles, inability to flex the knee and contract the quadriceps muscles, and severe pain.

TREATMENT: The sooner treatment is commenced the better the prognosis for the athlete.[8] Immediately after the injury, it is usually not possible for either the athlete or the examiner to determine if the injury will result in a major or minor hematoma. It is best to err on the conservative side and treat all contusions to the thigh as potentially serious. The following procedure is recommended:

1. Firmly apply a cold, wet elastic wrap to the thigh at the level of the contusion. After one or two turns of the wrap, apply ice. Further layers of wrap add compression to the contused area; the cold, wet bandage conducts the cold onto the thigh area.

2. While the athlete lies prone, an elastic bandage (or similar device) is tied around the ankle, and the knee

flexed until minimal discomfort is felt. The athlete holds the elastic bandage over the shoulder to maintain the desired amount of knee flexion (Figure 19.10). *On no account should any force be applied in flexing the knee.* The idea behind this maneuver is to maintain the flexibility of the knee and the quadriceps muscles; it is *not* designed to increase flexibility. If the leg is kept straight, marked stiffness will be present the next day; with this method, flexibility is usually maintained at or near normal. It should again be emphasized that this procedure does not actually stretch the muscles, rather it holds the leg in a comfortable position.

3. Give analgesics if necessary.

4. Have the athlete use crutches for ambulation.

5. Begin anti-inflammatory medication if necessary.

After a few hours of icing the thigh with the knee held in flexion (the ice should be applied for 45 to 60 minutes at a time, and then taken off for 20 minutes), reassess the injury (Table 19.4). If there appears to be significant damage, continue the ice and the knee-flexed position for at least another twelve to twenty-four hours. If damage is mild, tell the athlete to repeat the icing with the leg in a flexed position two or three times during the night and the following day, each time keeping the ice in place for about an hour. If the leg continues to swell in spite of these measures, consideration should be given to exploring the hematoma and aspirating the blood.

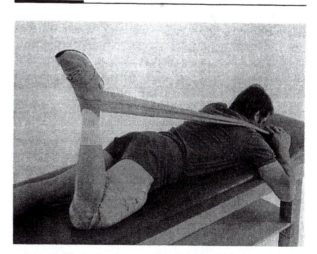

FIGURE 19.10
Early treatment of a quadriceps contusion
Ice, together with a cold, wet elastic compression wrap, is applied to the anterior aspect of the thigh. A gentle stretch is then applied to the quadriceps muscle. This stretch should not be forceful, nor should it cause any pain. The stretch should be released and the ice removed for 20 minutes every hour.

TABLE 19.4 *Assessing the severity of a thigh injury*

	Mild	Potentially Severe
1. The ability to actively bend the knee through a normal range of motion	Yes	No
2. The ability to actively set the quadriceps and to raise the leg without any discomfort	Yes	No
3. Localized swelling	No	Yes
4. Localized tenderness	+	+ + +

+ = minimal tenderness

+ + + = marked tenderness

CONTINUING TREATMENT: Icing in a prone position with the knee flexed for 30 to 60 minutes at a time is continued on a daily or bi-daily basis until full flexibility is achieved, and thereafter, following each workout, until the leg becomes completely asymptomatic.

Quadriceps sets should be started when they can be performed painlessly. Until that time, electrical stimulation of the quadriceps and hamstrings can be used if it causes no pain. When doing isometric setting exercises, the athlete should hold each set for about five to eight seconds, doing ten of these each hour. When full contraction of the quadriceps is achieved, straight-leg raising (as described in the section on knee rehabilitation) should begin. The full knee rehabilitation program should then be instituted (Table 19.5).

COMPLICATIONS:

EARLY. As mentioned, a *poorly treated* contusion of the anterior thigh can result in a prolonged recovery, with stiffness, poor quadriceps action, and muscle wasting. A period of four to eight weeks is necessary before the athlete can start to rehabilitate the injured leg. The most important time to start treating this injury is immediately after it happens!

LATE. Myositis ossificans (calcification within the muscles at the site of the injury) can develop. Calcification is a feared complication and is particularly apt to occur if (a) the athlete returns to participation too soon, (b) the thigh is re-injured before healing occurs, (c) massage or heat has been applied to the hematoma, (d) the

TABLE 19.5 *Contusion to the quadriceps*

During the recovery phase there should be

NO MASSAGE to the thigh

NO HEAT to the thigh

NO ULTRASOUND

NO CORTISONE INJECTIONS

NO ACTIVE STRETCHING of the quadriceps musculature

hematoma has been poorly treated, or (e) the bleeding is associated with hemophilia (a rare bleeding disorder).[9]

Myositis ossificans can permanently limit the amount of knee flexion and can also produce a hard, painful lump in the thigh. If this occurs, the athlete should be withdrawn from athletic participation until the calcification has matured (this can be observed on serial X-rays), at which time a decision as to the advisability of surgical removal of the calcified mass can be made. Removal of the mass before it is mature frequently causes a recurrence of the calcification (Figures 19.11 and 19.12).

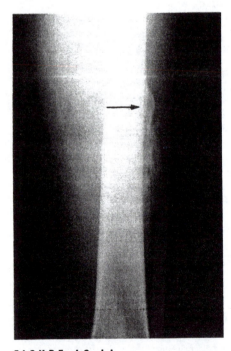

FIGURE 19.11

X-ray—myositis ossificans of the thigh

This basketball player suffered a contusion to the thigh six weeks before this X-ray was taken. Note the marked calcification arising from the femur.

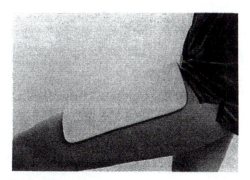

FIGURE 19.12

Anterior thigh pad

A heat-molded pad is made from Orthoplast or Plastazote (white material) and a foam inner lining. The pad should be worn to protect the thigh following a contusion. Myositis ossificans is more likely to form if a second contusion occurs to the same area shortly after recovery from the first.

PROGNOSIS: If the athlete is adequately treated immediately after the injury, the chance of complications is small. However, if the initial bleeding is severe and the treatment is not started for a few hours, it may be four or five weeks or longer before the athlete can return to participation (Table 19.6).

Strain of the Quadriceps Musculature

This usually implies a strain of the rectus femoris muscle, but occasionally one or more components of the vastus, the sartorius, or both are involved. A strain may vary from a mild "pull" of the rectus femoris to a complete rupture of the muscle. When the latter occurs, a large bulge is seen in the upper thigh.

TABLE 19.6 *Criteria for return to participation after a contusion to the quadriceps*

1. There should be full flexibility of the thigh musculature when compared with the opposite unaffected leg (Figure 19.13)

2. There should be equal power, strength, and endurance of the quadriceps mechanism compared with the opposite leg

3. There should be minimal or no tenderness present in the thigh

4. The athlete should return to play with substantial protective padding over the affected area (Figure 19.12)

MECHANISM OF INJURY: Most pulls occur in an athlete who is not sufficiently warmed up or stretched out before beginning rapid acceleration during a sprint. Other predisposing factors include (1) tight quadriceps muscles, (2) an imbalance between the quadriceps power of the two legs, and (3) a short leg. The rectus femoris can also be strained when a kick is mistimed in rugby, soccer, or football.

SYMPTOMS AND SIGNS: The athlete is immediately aware that the muscle has been strained. There is pain down the entire length of the rectus femoris, with tenderness localized to the area of the strain. There is inability to contract the rest of the quadriceps mechanism, and knee flexion is usually limited. Swelling, should it occur, may mask a complete rupture of the rectus femoris initially. A complete rupture leaves a permanent bulge high up in the thigh but, surprisingly, often produces little functional disability.

TREATMENT: *Initial:* Ice on a firmly applied, cold, wet elastic wrap is the treatment of choice. This should be followed by anti-inflammatory medication, analgesics, and crutch ambulation.

Later: Once the initial bleeding has settled down, ice therapy should be combined with TENS, ultrasound, gentle frictional massage, and *gentle, controlled* stretching exercises. At no time should these stretching exercises be painful. As soon as the quadriceps can adequately contract, the athlete may be progressed through an effort-limited exercise program for maintenance of quadriceps function. As healing continues and strength returns, a full quadriceps rehabilitation program should be commenced (see section on knee rehabilitation). Avoid excessive and ballistic stretches during these activities (Figure 19.13 and Table 19.7).

Acute Strain of the Hamstring Group

An acute hamstring "pull" is a common and frustrating injury occurring particularly in sprinters. It can be related to some of the following factors:

1. Lack of flexibility of the hamstring group.

2. Imbalance in the ratio of strength and power between the hamstrings and the quadriceps. In sprinters the quadriceps are usually stronger than the hamstrings, while in long-distance runners the ratio of quadriceps to hamstring strength may be closer to 1:1.

3. Inequality of strength of the left versus the right hamstring group.

4. The fact that the biceps muscle receives two nerve supplies, one to the short head and one to the long head.

FIGURE 19.13
Quadriceps strain
This test should demonstrate equal flexibility of both left and right quadriceps before return to participation is permitted.

TABLE 19.7 *Criteria for return to participation after a strain of the quadriceps musculature*

The athlete should not be allowed to sprint until there is:

1. Equal power, strength, and endurance of both quadriceps muscle groups
2. Equal flexibility of both quadriceps (Figure 19.13)
3. No pain with any of these tests

This theoretically results in an inappropriate contraction of the one head while the other is relaxing.

5. A poor running style, particularly leaning backward when decelerating at the end of a sprint or when attempting to lengthen the stride.

SYMPTOMS AND SIGNS: With an acute strain the athlete is immediately aware of the condition. Occasionally it feels as if something has "popped" in the back of the thigh. In severe cases the athlete will describe an intense tearing sensation, with pain from the ischial tuberosity down to the back of the knee. There is usually generalized pain, but tenderness is localized to the area of the actual disruption. Swelling can occur fairly rapidly and obscure the defect of a severe tear. Passive straight-leg raising is limited, and there is inability to fully contract the hamstrings against resistance. After a few days, considerable ecchymosis might be noted in the back of the thigh, which will gradually descend to behind the knee.

TREATMENT: Immediate treatment is with ice and compression, using a cold, wet elastic wrap. The athlete should gently stretch the hamstrings while icing, to help prevent the loss of flexibility that would otherwise occur (Figure 19.14). Should spasm of the hamstrings prevent stretching, spraying with Fluori-Methane and TENS may be useful. An anti-inflammatory drug and analgesics are given as necessary. If the athlete cannot walk normally, crutches should be used.

A few days after the initial bleeding has subsided, ice therapy can be augmented with isometric contractions of the hamstrings, TENS, ultrasound, gentle frictional massage, and gentle, controlled hamstring stretching.

Once hamstring setting exercises are painless, the athlete may be progressed onto an isokinetic apparatus.

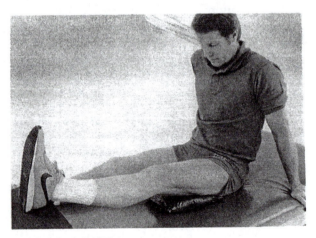

FIGURE 19.14
Acute hamstring strain
While icing the injured area, place a gentle stretch on the hamstrings. This may help prevent spasm and loss of flexibility that might otherwise occur. The foot is placed on a stool, the quadriceps are relaxed, and the hamstrings gently stretched. Compression may be added.

TABLE 19.8 *Criteria for return to participation after an acute strain of the hamstring group*

1. There should be at least equal flexibility of the hamstrings bilaterally (preferably more than was present before the injury)
2. There should be equal bilateral strength, power, and endurance of the hamstring group
3. There should be a satisfactory ratio of quadriceps-to-hamstrings strength, power, and endurance

Hamstring rehabilitation should continue for some time after the athlete has returned to participation.

Then, both the hamstring and the quadriceps groups should be progressively developed. Stretching should be emphasized. When satisfactory strength, power, and flexibility have been achieved, the athlete may begin to jog. A useful exercise is running backwards. Straight ahead running should be gradually increased, but no sprinting should be allowed until the criteria for return to full participation have been fulfilled (Table 19.8).

Slow-Onset Hamstring Strain

With this type of strain, which occurs particularly in the long-distance runner, progressive tightness and discomfort are noted in the uppermost third of the posterior aspect of the leg. Localized tenderness may or may not be present. Hamstring flexibility is limited, weakness is usually apparent, and asymmetry in the heights of the posterior superior iliac spines is sometimes present, suggesting the association of lower-back joint dysfunction or other lumbar spine pathology.[10] Tenderness is sometimes localized to the ischial tuberosity, suggesting either microtrauma of the hamstring attachment or ischial bursitis.

TREATMENT: Progressive stretching of the hamstrings, together with various therapy modalities such as ultrasound, muscle stimulation, TENS, ice massage, cross-frictional massage, and stretching with ice massage, may all effect an improvement. Mobilization of the lower back may be indicated. An intensive muscle-balancing and muscle-strengthening program for the hamstring, gluteal, adductor, and quadriceps muscle groups should then be undertaken. A cortisone injection may be indicated in cases of ischial bursitis.

Complete Rupture of the Quadriceps or Patellar Tendon

A tendon rupture is a major injury which occurs when the athlete lands in an off-balance position from a long jump or from a basketball rebound. There is a sudden giving-in of the knee with severe pain.

SYMPTOMS AND SIGNS: The exact diagnosis might not be immediately apparent and, in fact, it might be possible for the athlete to extend the knee even though the quadriceps mechanism has been completely torn. There is tenderness either at the attachment of the quadriceps tendon into the superior pole of the patella or below the patella in the area of the patellar tendon. In the latter case, the patella is also pulled upward to some extent. A defect in the muscle-tendon at the area of tenderness can be felt.[11]

If the athlete is not seen until some time after the actual injury, a large hemarthrosis of the knee may mislead the examiner into thinking that an intra-articular knee injury has occurred. It is therefore important to consider this condition in the differential diagnosis of a hemarthrosis of the knee.

TREATMENT:

Immediate: Ice, a knee splint (preferably a postoperative knee splint), and crutches or a stretcher should be used. Analgesics will probably be necessary.

Definitive: Surgical repair of the injured tissues frequently needs to be undertaken.

The Knee

Prevention of Knee Injuries

RULE CHANGES: Rule changes in contact sports, particularly football, have had a marked effect in reducing certain types of knee injuries. As long as these rules are enforced, many knee injuries will be prevented.

LEG MUSCULATURE: The development of strength, power, endurance, and proprioception of the muscles surrounding the knee has been shown to be closely related to a decrease in the incidence of knee injuries, particularly in contact sports. However, if the thigh muscles are not in a state of contraction at the time of impact, they cannot contract rapidly enough to effectively protect the ligaments.[12]

The quadriceps are often thought of as the main group of muscles supporting the knee joint; however, it is vital that the other muscles around the knee be given equal attention. These include the hamstrings, the gastrocnemius, the abductors and adductors, the popliteus, and the pes anserine muscles. Not only will development of these muscle groups reduce the rate of acute injuries, but it will also decrease the recurrence of injuries in unstable knees. Surveys have shown that there is up to seventeen times greater chance of suffering a knee ligament injury when the athlete participates with incompletely rehabilitated or atrophied leg muscles.[13] Exercise for developing the muscles around the knee joint are discussed in the section on rehabilitation.

SHOE-SURFACE INTERFACE: In contact sports such as football, most knee injuries occur when the foot is planted and fixed. A force is applied against the knee, and if the foot cannot move away from its fixed position as contact occurs, knee ligaments are the first to be injured. However, if the athlete is wearing a shoe with a low coefficient of friction, there is a definite chance the foot will move with the blow, thereby eliminating the force on the ligaments. In this way the knee is protected from a potentially serious ligament injury.

Studies have shown that a soccer-style shoe with a relatively large number of cleats (e.g., fourteen) that are low and wide (e.g., 3/8" [9 mm] high and 1/2" [12 mm] in diameter) is probably the safest type of shoe available. This shoe tends to slip under impact, reducing the incidence of knee injuries, but it holds sufficiently well to enable normal cuts and turns to be performed.[14]

The type of shoe sole in contact with the playing surface is particularly important on artificial turf, where rubber soles have been shown to adhere too firmly, increasing the incidence of knee injuries. For artificial turf, the soccer-style shoe with low, wide cleats and a polyurethane sole is recommended.[15]

Wearing long cleats on grass might be useful for increasing traction, but unfortunately, long cleats have the potential to lock the foot into the surface, increasing the chance of a knee injury. It is suggested that the same soccer-style shoe that is recommended for artificial surfaces also be worn on grass.

THE SURFACE: A well-maintained field is always far safer for the athlete than a surface full of potholes and irregularities. This type of surface not only produces a large number of ankle injuries, but is also responsible for many knee injures.[14]

Controversy exists over whether the artificial surface (AstroTurf) is more dangerous than grass, and over which produces a greater incidence of knee injuries.[16,17] Certain types of injuries tend to predominate on the harder surface of the artificial turf (such as posterior cruciate ligament injuries, which occur when the tibial tubercle comes into contact with the unrelenting surface, forcing the tibia backward).

The History and Evaluation

It has been said that the history in a knee injury is worth 80 percent of the diagnosis. The following questions should be routinely asked in an *acute injury:*

1. Was it a contact or a noncontact injury? If contact, from what direction was the force applied?
2. Was the foot planted?
3. In which direction did the knee go?
4. Was there a "pop"?
5. Did you feel anything slip out?
6. Where was the pain?
7. Did the knee feel unstable or give way?
8. Did the knee swell immediately?
9. Have you had any previous knee injuries?

The *nonacute* or the *chronic* injury needs to have a number of additional points clarified:

1. Length of time the symptoms have been present
2. Mechanism of injury
3. Primary symptoms
4. Other symptoms
5. Site of the pain
6. Any swelling, locking, or giving in?
7. Is there any pain on going up or down stairs?
8. Are any symptoms related to jumping, running, cutting, or squatting?
9. Are there any abnormal voluntary movements of the knee joint?
10. Has there been any previous knee injury?
11. Has there been any injury to the opposite knee?

SALIENT POINTS IN THE HISTORY: The examiner should be aware of what the following symptoms might indicate.

1. *Rapid swelling of the knee* within twelve hours of the injury indicates bleeding into the joint and is usually associated with a significant injury.[18,19] In many instances a torn anterior cruciate ligament injury, or possibly a subluxed patella or osteochondral fracture, gives this history.

2. *Swelling of the joint* with relatively gradual onset, occurring more than twelve hours after an injury, is

indicative of synovial irritation and a joint effusion. A meniscal tear might be the causative factor.

3. *Giving-in* should be carefully interpreted:

   a. Did the knee give-in while walking straight ahead, which might indicate a meniscal lesion?

   b. Did the knee give-in while rotating, which might indicate a rotatory instability problem?

4. *Locking* is suggestive of a meniscal tear. Locking means that the knee actually locks in one position and is then released by some movement which allows it to become "unlocked." The term "locking" is also used when full extension is blocked, which may be due to a torn meniscus, but may also be caused by spasm of the hamstrings.

5. *The history of a "pop"* in an acute injury is very significant. In most cases it is due to an anterior cruciate ligament tear; in some, it is due to a subluxing patella; and in a few, to a torn meniscus or an osteochondral fracture.

6. *Pain on going up or down stairs,* particularly on walking down, is indicative of retropatellar irritation.

7. *Pain under the patella and along the patellar tendon,* after such jumping activities as basketball, is indicative of patellar tendinitis.

8. *Pain behind the patella,* after sitting with the knee flexed at approximately 90° for a period of time, is indicative of retropatellar irritation.

9. *A subluxing patella* can produce vague symptoms, or even symptoms attributable to injuries of other structures; for instance, it can produce a history of giving way, locking, and swelling.

OBSERVATION:

1. Note the *bulk and tone* of the quadriceps, the hamstrings, and the calf muscles.

2. Note any *limitation of full flexion or extension or any limp.* Have the athlete stand eight to ten feet away and observe the alignment of the lower limb, the position of the patellae, the amount of genu varum or genu valgum, the amount of tibia varum, and the position of the feet while standing (particularly with regard to excessive pronation or a high-arched cavus foot). These features can cause knee pain in those undertaking running activities.

3. Apply *functional tests.*

   a. Ask the athlete to hop on the affected leg, first pointing the foot into internal rotation while hopping and then pointing it into external rotation.

   b. Have the athlete hop in a 360° circle while leaning over to the side, first clockwise and then counterclockwise.

   c. Ask the athlete to run in place, first slowly and then with maximum effort, raising the knees as high as possible. Look for any abnormality in the running pattern.

   d. Have the athlete attempt to squat down as far as possible. Note any limitation, crepitus, or pain.

   e. Ask the athlete, while in the squatting position, to walk in a full-squat, duck-waddle fashion. Note any pain or inability to do this maneuver.

   f. Have the athlete lightly hold the examining table with one hand while attempting to squat all the way down on the affected leg. This is a useful test of quadriceps strength. Observe his or her ability to return to the standing position using the affected leg alone. This test often shows up a latent weakness of the quadriceps (Table 19.9).

MEASUREMENTS: Measurements are sometimes useful, but they are often misleading. Probably a better way to pick out subtle differences in the bulk of the quadriceps musculature is by careful observation. When measurements are taken, a reference point such as the medial joint line or the medial malleolus should be used. Measurements taken from the patella tend to be inaccurate, as the position of the patella varies and the patellae may be asymmetrical.

A useful series of measurements involves the

1. Mid-calf area
2. Midpatellar area
3. Ten centimeters above the medial joint line
4. Twenty centimeters above the medial joint line

PALPATION: Any swelling in the joint should be noted. One method of determining if the swelling is intra-articular or extra-articular is to perform ballottement on the patella. If the patella is ballotable, then the swelling is intra-articular. Another test for intra-articular swelling involves compressing any fluid to the medial side of the knee. The swelling is then tapped and a fluid wave is felt for on the lateral side (Figure 19.15).

Then palpate for any tender area. Starting on the medial side, palpate along the tibial collateral ligament from the femoral condyle down to the tibia, proceeding down about 7 cm. Tenderness along this area suggests injury to the tibial collateral ligament. Tenderness over

TABLE 19.9 *Outline of a knee examination*

1. *Observe with athlete standing*
   (1) Stance, leg alignment, attitude of feet
   (2) Swelling, muscle bulk, muscle definition
2. *Functional tests (if appropriate)*
   (1) Hopping (foot externally rotated, then internally rotated)
   (2) Rotational lean-hop (clockwise, then counter-clockwise)
   (3) Running-in-place
   (4) Squat
   (5) Duck-waddle
   (6) One-legged squat
3. *Athlete sitting at end of examining table*
   (1) Position of patallae
   (2) Vastus medialis obliquus with legs held at 45° against resistance
   (3) Retropatellar crepitus
4. *Athlete supine on examining table*
   (1) Measure circumference of thighs at 10 cm and at 20 cm above medial joint line
   (2) Check range of motion (note retropatellar crepitus)
   (3) Palpate for swelling
   (4) Palpate for tenderness
   (5) Test muscle strength (quadriceps and hamstrings)
   (6) Lift leg into hyperextension (observe for postero-lateral rotatory instability)
5. *Ligament stress tests*
   (1) Valgus and varus stress at 0° and at 30° of flexion
   (2) Lachman test at 10° of flexion
   (3) With the knee at 90° and the hip at 45°, sit on foot and test for anterior and posterior drawer with the foot
      (a) in neutral position
      (b) externally rotated
      (c) internally rotated
   (4) Pivot-shift tests
      (a) MacIntosh test
      (b) Jerk test of Hughston
      (c) Lateral position of Slocum
6. *Meniscus Test*
   (1) McMurray's meniscal test
7. *Patella tests*
   (1) Moving the patella laterally with the knee at 0° and at 30° of flexion, test for
      (a) lateral laxity
      (b) pain with movement
      (c) apprehension
   (2) Retropatellar pain on compression
8. *Hip movement tests*
   (1) Measure internal and external rotation
9. *Athlete prone*
   (1) ·Examine the popliteal fossa for tenderness and swelling
   (2) Use Apley's meniscal test
10. *Peripheral circulation tests*
   (1) Always palpate the posterior tibial and the dorsalis pedis pulses after an acute knee injury
   (2) Check peripheral circulation to the toes

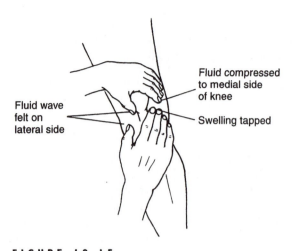

FIGURE 19.15
Palpating swelling within the knee

the medial joint line is due to injury either to the medial meniscus or to the medial capsular ligament. Continue the palpation posteriorly on the medial side, to include the posteromedial corner. Then palpate the anteromedial joint line. Tenderness here suggests a medial meniscal injury or possibly osteochondral pathology.

Palpate the quadriceps insertion into the patella, the medial facet of the patella, and the patellar tendon. An important area is the origin of the patellar tendon at the lower pole of the patella. To adequately palpate this area, the patella needs to be stabilized superiorly while the lower pole is palpated firmly with the thumb (Figure 19.55).

Palpation continues onto the lateral facet of the patella and the anterolateral joint line. Tenderness here can indicate an osteochondral, fat-pad, or lateral meniscal injury. The length of the fibular collateral ligament from the lateral femoral condyle to the fibula should be palpated. Tenderness over the lateral joint line may be associated with a lateral meniscal injury. While palpating the fibular head, do not forget to palpate over the biceps insertion. Palpate the iliotibial tract as it inserts into Gerdy's tubercle. Tenderness over the posterolateral corner suggests an injury to the posterior horn of the lateral meniscus or an involvement of the popliteal tendon and the arcuate ligament complex. Examine the popliteal area for any swelling or tenderness.

RANGE OF MOVEMENT: Any limitation of flexion or extension should be measured. Compare the two sides. To test for hyperextension, lift both feet off the table simultaneously and note how far the knee drops back (Figure 19.16). Ensure that the thigh muscles are completely relaxed.

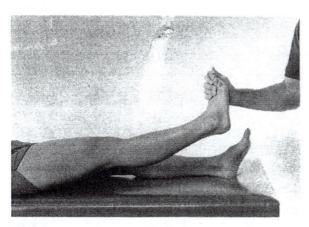

FIGURE 19.16
Test for hyperextension

LIGAMENT STABILITY TESTS: There is still controversy as to the exact meaning and interpretation of many of the ligament stress tests. A workable guideline to the interpretation of these tests is presented, but the reader should bear in mind that there may be disagreement on the subject (Table 19.10).

1. *Hyperextension test:* The foot is raised so as to let the knee drop back into hyperextension; this is compared with the opposite side (Figure 19.16). If hyperextension is excessive on the affected side, it may indicate rupture or incompetency of the anterior cruciate ligament, with or without a tear of the posterior cruciate ligament. Posterolateral rotatory instability is said to be present if the tibia rotates to the lateral side and drops posteriorly during the hyperextension test.

2. *Valgus and varus stress tests:* The stress tests are designed to demonstrate laxity of the collateral ligaments, but they may also give information on the status of other structures.

    a. Valgus and varus stress at 0°: If there is valgus or varus opening beyond the normal limb, it indicates involvement not only of the stabilizing complex involved, but also of the anterior or posterior cruciate ligaments, and perhaps of other structures as well (Figure 19.17).

    b. Valgus or varus stress at 30°: This localizes the stress to the medial or the lateral stabilizing complex, and any excessive opening indicates laxity of that complex of ligaments.

3. *Drawer tests at 90° of knee flexion:* The athlete lies supine, hip flexed to 45° with knee bent to 90°. The examiner sits on the foot to stabilize it and makes sure that the hamstrings are completely relaxed (Figure 19.18).

TABLE 19.10 *Knee ligament instabilities*

Instabilities	Tests
One-plane instabilities[a]	
Medial	Valgus stress at 0° and 30° of flexion
Lateral	Varus stress at 0° and 30° of flexion
Anterior	Anterior drawer at 90° of flexion
	Lachman test
Posterior	Posterior drawer at 90° of flexion
Rotatory instabilities[b]	
Anteromedial	Valgus stress at 30° of flexion
	Anterior drawer with foot in external rotation at 90° of flexion
Anterolateral	Anterior drawer with foot in internal rotation at 90° of flexion
	Pivot shift tests
Posterolateral	Hyperextension of leg
	Posterior drawer with foot in internal rotation at 90° of flexion
Posteromedial	Posterior drawer with foot in external rotation at 90° of flexion (rare)
Combined instabilities	
Anteromedial *plus* anterolateral (most common)	
Anterolateral *plus* posterolateral	
Anteromedial *plus* anterolateral and posterolateral	

Note: This classification of instabilities was devised by the Research and Education Committee of the American Orthopaedic Society for Sports Medicine.

[a]*Movement of the tibia in relation to the femur,* that is, medial means the tibia is moving away from the femur on the medial side.

[b]*Movement of the tibia in relation to the femur,* that is, anteromedial rotatory instability means the tibia is rotating anteriorly and moving away from the femur on the medial side.

    a. Anterior drawer sign with foot in *neutral* position (Figure 19.19a): Forward movement of the tibia on the femur in this position indicates incompetence of the anterior cruciate ligament. However, it is important to realize that

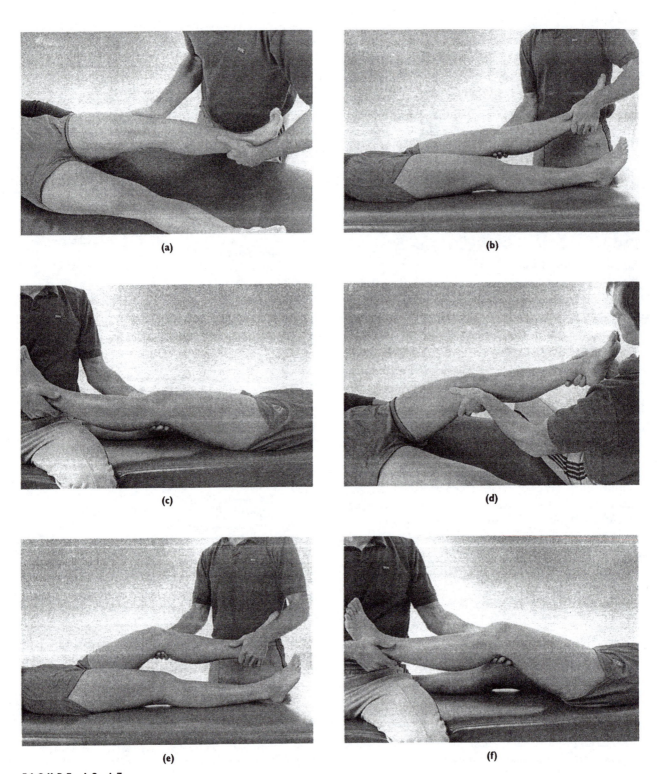

FIGURE 19.17

Valgus and varus stress tests

(a) Valgus stress test performed at 0°—viewed from above; (b) Valgus stress test performed at 0°—viewed from the side; (c) Varus stress performed at 0°—viewed from the lateral side; (d) Varus stress test performed at 0°—viewed from above and medially; (e) Valgus stress test performed at 30°—viewed from the medial side; and (f) Varus stress test performed at 30°—viewed from the lateral side.

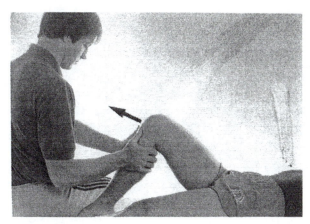

FIGURE 19.18
The drawer tests
The examiner should sit on the foot to help stabilize the leg and ensure that the hamstrings are relaxed.

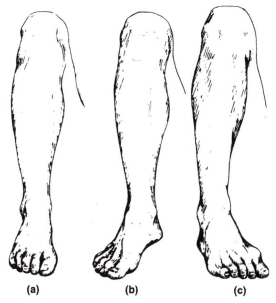

(a)   (b)   (c)

FIGURE 19.19
Anterior drawer test—foot positions
(a) The foot is first placed in a neutral position and an anteriorly directed force is applied to the tibia. If anterior motion in excess of the normal opposite limb is produced, an anterior cruciate ligament tear should be strongly suspected. (b) If this motion is also present when the test is performed with the foot in external rotation, and the medial tibial plateau is noted to rotate laterally, anteromedial rotatory instability may be diagnosed. (c) The foot is internally rotated 10° to 15° and the test repeated. If it is noted that the lateral tibial plateau comes forward and medially, then the rotatory instability is anterolateral.

this test may not be positive in a significant percentage of anterior cruciate ligament tears, especially acute injuries.

b. Anterior drawer sign with foot in *external rotation* (15°) (Figure 19.19b): This is the Slocum test for anteromedial rotatory instability.[20] It is positive if the medial tibial plateau advances anteriorly and rotates from the medial to the lateral side. A positive test indicates damage to the anterior cruciate ligament, the postero-medial corner, or both.

c. Anterior drawer sign with foot in *internal rotation* (Figure 19.19c): With anterior stress, the lateral tibial plateau moves anteriorly and rotates medially from the lateral side when there is incompetency of either or both the anterior cruciate ligaments or the lateral collateral ligament and the posterolateral corner.

This test should be repeated with progressive internal rotation of the foot and the tibia. When the tibia is rotated to approximately 20° the test should become negative, as the posterior cruciate ligament holds the tibia from moving forward in this position. If there is forward motion with the foot in maximal internal rotation, suspect the possibility of a posterior cruciate ligament injury.

d. *Posterior drawer sign* with foot in neutral position (Figure 19.20): If laxity in a posterior direction is present, it indicates damage to the posterior cruciate ligament.

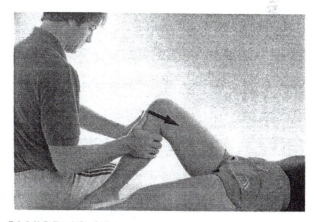

FIGURE 19.20
Posterior drawer test
The foot is placed in the neutral position and a posteriorly directed force is applied to the tibia. If the tibia is noted to move posteriorly, then a posterior cruciate ligament injury is probably present.

Sometimes it is difficult to decide if there is an anterior drawer or a posterior drawer sign present, as the neutral position of the knee becomes obscured. A useful way of deciding is to place both knees in the same position of 45° of hip flexion and 90° of knee flexion and note the relative position of the tibial tubercles from the side. If the posterior cruciate ligament is completely torn, the tibial tubercle on the affected side will sag backward in relation to the unaffected leg (Figure 19.21).

4. *Lachman test:* The Lachman test is one of the most important and sensitive tests for detecting a tear or incompetency of the anterior cruciate ligament.[21] The test will often be positive when all other tests, including the anterior drawer tests, are negative, particularly when performed soon after an injury. It is performed with the knee flexed approximately 5° to 10°. With the thigh supported, the tibia is brought forward on the femur (Figures 19.22 and 19.23). Excessive forward movement of the tibia on the femur suggests a torn

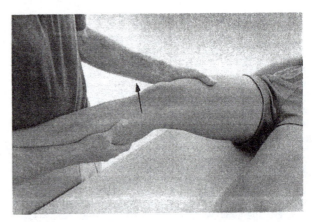

FIGURE 19.23
The Lachman test
To detect abnormal motion, observe the tibial tubercle as it moves anteriorly in relation to the inferior pole of the patella.

anterior cruciate ligament. One can usually observe, as well as feel, any excessive movement but this may be quite subtle.

5. *Pivot-shift tests:* Pivot-shift tests are designed to demonstrate anterolateral rotatory instability and can be used in both acute and chronic situations. Together with the Lachman test, they constitute the most sensitive index for detecting an anterior cruciate ligament injury. In order to appreciate the biomechanics of anterolateral rotatory instability, it is necessary to assume that the tibia is in a subluxed position when the knee is hyperextended. As the knee reaches 20° to 30° of flexion, the tibia relocates on the femur with a sudden shift which is both seen and felt. As the knee returns to extension, the reverse procedure takes place. This is the basis for these tests.

The three tests described all appear to test the same pathological entity. However, in many instances only one or two of the tests will be positive.

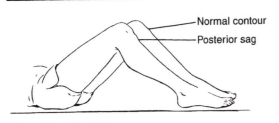

FIGURE 19.21
Posterior sag
When a posterior cruciate ligament tear is present, the tibia may sag posteriorly. The thigh musculature must be relaxed. Line up the legs at 90° of knee flexion and observe the outlines (silhouettes) of the tibiae from the side.

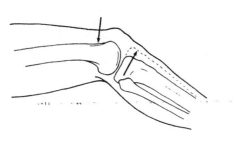

FIGURE 19.22
The Lachman test
This test is designed to detect injury to the anterior cruciate ligament. With the knee in 10° to 15° of flexion, the tibia is brought forward on the femur.

a. *Pivot-shift test of MacIntosh:*[22] The athlete lies supine and the leg is lifted approximately 30° to 45° at the hip, with the knee fully extended so that it falls backward into hyperextension. The foot and the tibia are internally rotated (sometimes a positive response is elicited when the foot is externally rotated). A valgus force is applied to the knee at the same time as it is flexed. While the valgus force is being applied, pressure is directed against the head of the fibula in an attempt to rotate it forward and around from the lateral to the medial side (Figure 19.24).

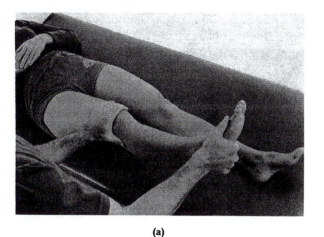

(a)

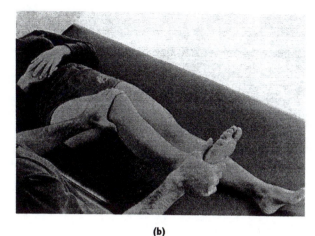

(b)

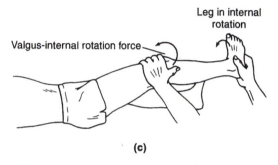

(c)

FIGURE 19.24
The pivot-shift test of MacIntosh
A pivot-shift is produced if anterolateral rotatory instability is present, most commonly as a result of an anterior cruciate ligament injury.

b. *Jerk test of Hughston:* This is really the same as the MacIntosh test but is performed in the opposite direction. Start with the knee flexed at about 45° and the foot internally rotated. Apply a valgus force while attempting to rotate the fibula medially as the knee is being straightened. The jerk takes place at approximately 20° of flexion.

c. *Pivot-shift test in the lateral position as described by Slocum:*[23,24] The athlete lies on the unaffected side, the unaffected leg drawn up into flexion and out of the way. The pelvis is positioned so that the affected leg is internally rotated and the knee fully extended. The thumb of one hand is placed on the fibular head. A valgus force is applied as the knee is flexed. The pivot shift (i.e., reduction of the tibia from its subluxed position) occurs at between 20° and 30° of flexion. As the knee is brought back into full extension, the reverse procedure occurs (Figure 19.25 and Table 19.11).

MENISCAL TESTS: *McMurray's meniscal test:* The athlete lies supine with the knee fully flexed. The foot is held in one hand while the other hand palpates the joint line on both sides of the knee. Keeping the knee fully flexed, rotate the tibia from external to internal rotation and back again. A click or a grinding probably indicates a tear of the posterior segment of the meniscus (Figure 19.26).

Another method involves extending the leg with the foot internally rotated, at the same time applying a varus force, which will compress the medial compartment. A tear is revealed by a click and by the pain felt in the vicinity of the joint line (Figure 19.27).

The knee is again flexed, the foot externally rotated, and the leg extended while a valgus force is applied to the knee. This compresses the lateral compartment and may reveal a lateral meniscal injury.

Apley's meniscal test: The athlete lies prone and the knee is flexed to 90°. Pressure is then applied to the heel while the foot is rotated. If this produces pain in the knee, it suggests a posterior horn injury. The foot is then pulled upward to distract the joint and remove the pressure from the meniscus. If no pain is felt on rotation of the foot, this adds further weight to the diagnosis (Figure 19.28).

EXAMINATION OF THE PATELLA:

1. With the athlete standing, note the alignment, height, and shape of the patella.

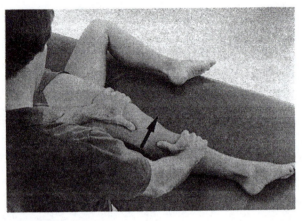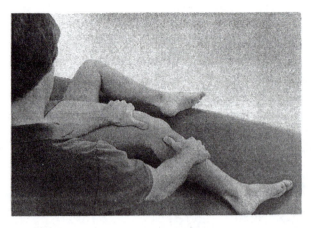

FIGURE 19.25
The pivot-shift test in the lateral position (Slocum test)
A valgus force is applied as the knee is flexed. The pivot shift will usually occur at 20° to 30° of flexion.

TABLE 19.11   *Clinical tests for ligament instability*

Tests	Position of the Knee	Ligaments Involved
Valgus stress	0°	Medial stabilizing complex, ACL,[a] posteromedial corner, and sometimes PCL.[b]
	30°	If stable at 0°, and other tests are negative, then more or less of the medial stabilizing complex is involved, depending on severity.
Varus stress	0°	Lateral stabilizing complex, biceps tendon, posterolateral corner,[c] ACL, and often PCL.
	30°	Same as valgus stress at 30° except the lateral stabilizing complex is involved.
Lachman	5–10°	ACL (with or without other structures).
Anterior drawer	90°	
	1. neutral position of foot	ACL (with or without medial or lateral collateral ligament).
	2. foot externally rotated	ACL and/or medial stabilizing complex and posteromedial corner.[d]
	3. foot internally rotated	ACL (with or without lateral complex and posterolateral corner).
		If positive at 20° of internal rotation, probably PCL.
Posterior drawer	90°	PCL (with or without structures in the posteromedial and posterolateral corners).
Pivot-shift	Various	ACL (with or without posterolateral corner, and/or lateral stabilizing complex).

[a]anterior cruciate ligament
[b]posterior cruciate ligament
[c]popliteus muscle and arcuate ligament complex
[d]posterior oblique ligament and some attachments of the semimembranosus muscle

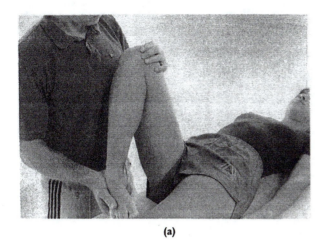
(a)

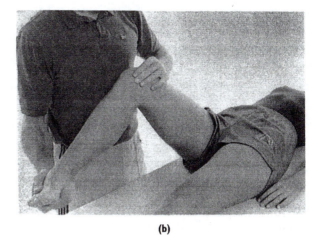
(b)

FIGURE 19.26

The McMurray test

(a) To test for a torn meniscus, the knee is fully flexed, rotated, and extended. The fingers are placed on the joint line and a click or a grinding sensation are palpated for within the joint. (b) By extending the knee while applying a varus force and internal rotation of the tibia, a torn medial meniscus may be compressed and produce a click or pain.

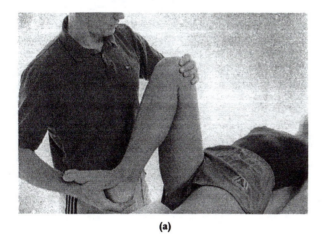
(a)

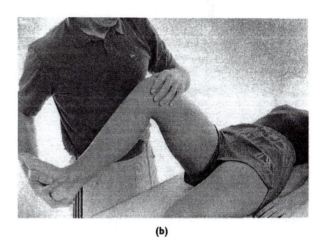
(b)

FIGURE 19.27

The McMurray test

(a) The same procedure is then performed with the foot in external rotation. The knee is hyperflexed and the fibia rotated. (b) The knee is then extended, maintaining the position of external rotation of the foot, and a valgus force is applied to the knee.

2. With the athlete standing, measure the Q angle by taking a line from the anterior superior iliac spine down the thigh to the midpoint of the patella, and from there to the tibial tubercle (Figure 19.29). To be considered normal, it should be under 16° in females and 10° in males; over 20° is probably abnormal.

3. With the athlete sitting at the end of the examining table, legs hanging at 90°, note the position of the patellae, particularly lateral squinting of the patellae or high-riding patellae (Figure 19.30).

Note the tracking of the patella as the knee is extended and flexed. The VMO can be well seen when the knees are held at 45° against resistance (Figure 19.31). Also, note if retropatellar crepitus is present.

4. With the athlete supine and the legs extended, note tenderness of any of the facets of the patella.

5. Then attempt to sublux the patella by moving it laterally. If the patella moves more than half of its width across the lateral femoral condyle, it suggests subluxation, particularly if the so-called "apprehension test" is

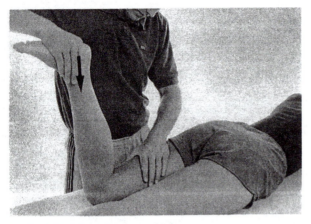

FIGURE 19.28
The Apley test
By applying downward pressure and rotating the tibia, a posterior horn tear of the medial meniscus may produce pain. This pain should not be present if the tibia is distracted from the femur and rotated.

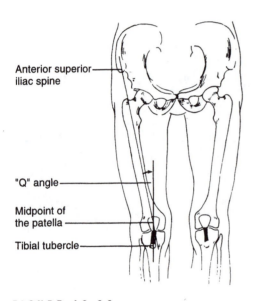

FIGURE 19.29
Measuring the "Q" angle
A wide "Q" angle may predispose the athlete to patella problems.

Labels on figure:
- Anterior superior iliac spine
- "Q" angle
- Midpoint of the patella
- Tibial tubercle

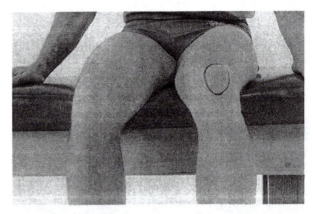

FIGURE 19.30
Patellar position when sitting
Note if the patellae are located in the midline or if they squint medially or laterally. Also, note if they point towards the ceiling (patella alta) or are near the tibial tubercle (patella infera).

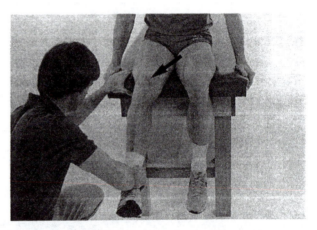

FIGURE 19.31
The vastus medialis obliquus (VMO)
Note the development and insertion of the VMO into the patella when the knee is held at 45° against resistance.

ing femur with the leg extended and the quadriceps relaxed. Feel for crepitus and inquire if pain is felt.

Note: The most striking demonstration of retropatellar crepitus is usually felt when the athlete squats from a standing position.

Mechanisms of Knee Ligament Injuries

When a knee injury occurs, one or more ligaments may be involved. In addition, the patella, the menisci, or both may be affected. Most knee ligament injuries result from an *external force*. However, some knee ligament injuries occur *without* an external force being applied to

positive, that is, if the athlete becomes alarmed or grabs the examiner's hand (Figure 19.32). Repeat this maneuver with the knee at 30° of flexion and the quadriceps relaxed and then tightened.

6. To detect the presence of retropatellar crepitus, move the knee through a full range of motion while at the same time palpating the patella. Another test is to move the patella firmly but gently against the underly-

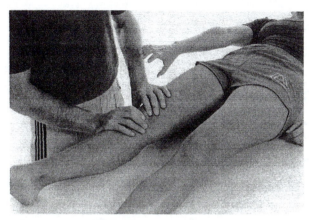

FIGURE 19.32
The "apprehension test" for patellar instability
If the athlete becomes alarmed when the patella is moved laterally, it is suggestive of patellar instability.

FIGURE 19.33
Valgus knee injury
If a valgus force is applied to the knee while the foot is fixed, a tear of the medial ligamentous structures will occur. If the force is sufficiently great, the anterior cruciate ligament may also be torn as well as the medial meniscus.

the knee. For instance, a basketball player may stop suddenly, hear or feel a "pop," and find that the knee gives in (an anterior cruciate ligament tear). Each major ligament will now be discussed in turn (Table 19.12).

MEDIAL LIGAMENT INJURIES: Medial ligament injuries are caused by a valgus force, for example:

1. If the foot is planted and fixed, a tackle or block against the lateral aspect of the knee will drive the knee medially (Figure 19.33).

2. If one ski becomes entrapped in snow while momentum carries the skier onward, a valgus, external rotational movement at the knee results. In this example the foot is unweighted (Figure 19.34).

If the force is not severe, only the medial capsular ligament will be involved. This may also lead to a peripheral detachment of the medial meniscus. If the force is more severe, there is involvement of the medial capsular ligament, the tibial collateral ligament, and the posteromedial corner (posterior oblique ligament). Finally, the cruciate ligaments will tear (the anterior cruciate is more often involved). A tear through the body of one of the menisci (usually the medial meniscus) can also occur.

LATERAL LIGAMENT INJURIES: The lateral ligament is injured less than the medial ligament as it is not as vulnerable to injury. This is because the force, or blow, necessary to damage the ligament must be applied to the medial aspect of the knee in order to force it into a varus position.

TABLE 19.12   *A "pop" associated with an acute knee injury*

> The examiner should always ask if the athlete heard or felt a "pop" (particularly following a hyperextension or internal rotation injury).
>
> In most cases, this will indicate an *anterior cruciate ligament injury*.
>
> In a few cases, it will be due to a *subluxed patella*, though a tearing sound or sensation is more common with this injury.
>
> In a small number of cases, the "pop" will be due to a *torn meniscus*.
>
> An *osteochondral fracture* may give more of a "snap" than a "pop."

FIGURE 19.34
A valgus, external rotation injury to the right knee, which will result in a medial ligament sprain
The anterior cruciate ligament may also be injured.

Usually the lateral capsular ligament and the fibular collateral ligament are the first structures to be torn on the lateral side. With more severe injuries, the biceps tendon and the iliotibial band may come loose from their attachment to the head of the fibula and Gerdy's tubercle respectively, and the peroneal nerve may be injured. The popliteal tendon and the posterolateral corner of the knee may also be damaged. As with valgus injuries, the cruciate ligaments (particularly the anterior cruciate ligament) may be involved, and one or both of the menisci may be damaged.

ANTERIOR CRUCIATE LIGAMENT INJURIES:
The anterior cruciate ligament alone can be torn. This is called an "isolated tear," but it is probably a misnomer because there is usually microscopic damage to other structures around the knee. The anterior cruciate ligament is also injured as part of a more complex injury, which occurs through one of the following mechanisms:

1. Hyperextension
2. Internal rotation of the leg with external rotation of the body. The leg usually hyperextends as well (Figure 19.35).

FIGURE 19.36
External rotation injury
The tibia is externally rotated, the foot is fixed, the femur rotates internally, and the athlete pushes off and cuts to the left. This mechanism may result in a patellar dislocation, with or without a medial collateral ligament tear. An anterior cruciate ligament tear may also occasionally result from this cutting maneuver.

3. External rotation–valgus cutting action (Figure 19.36)
4. Deceleration, as in basketball
5. A force which drives the tibia in an anterior direction when the knee is flexed at 90° (Figure 19.37)
6. In conjunction with medial or lateral collateral ligament injuries, as previously described

POSTERIOR CRUCIATE LIGAMENT INJURIES:
The posterior cruciate ligament is also injured in a number of ways:

1. A force applied to the anterior aspect of the tibia while the knee is at 90° will drive the tibia backward and tear the posterior cruciate ligament. Such a force can occur when a football player lands on the tibial tubercle with his knee flexed, particularly on artificial turf (Figure 19.38).
2. In conjunction with either a lateral or a medial ligament injury, as described.
3. A severe hyperextension injury.
4. Hyperflexion injury (Table 19.13).

FIGURE 19.35
Anterior cruciate ligament injury
The right tibia is internally rotated, the foot is fixed, the femur and body rotate externally as the athlete cuts to the right.

FIGURE 19.37

Anterior cruciate ligament injury

If an anteriorly directed force is applied to the tibia when the foot is fixed, the anterior cruciate ligament may be injured.

FIGURE 19.38

Posterior cruciate ligament injury

A forceful landing on the tibial tubercle may drive the tibia backwards on the femur, rupturing the posterior cruciate ligament.

Classification, Diagnosis, and Treatment of Ligament Injuries

MEDIAL STABILIZING COMPLEX: A medial stabilizing complex injury may best be described with the example of a football injury. If an athlete's right foot is planted, and the athlete is then blocked or tackled on the lateral side of the right knee, the knee is forced into a valgus position. Because of a number of factors (the force involved in the block, the strength of the athlete's leg muscles, and whether the foot remains fixed to the ground, etc.), the injury may vary from a mild, first-degree sprain to a complete rupture of the different structures, perhaps ending as the "unhappy triad" (medial ligament plus anterior cruciate tear plus medial meniscal tear).

FIRST-DEGREE SPRAIN:

Symptoms and Signs. In a first-degree sprain, assume that the integrity of the ligament is undisturbed and that there is almost normal tensile strength (Table 19.14). Visualize the disruption of a few collagen fibers, perhaps in the capsule, sometimes in the superficial portion of the ligament.

The athlete usually complains of some pain on twisting the leg or forcing it into a valgus position. He or she might be aware of the injury, but often continues to play without complaining, only seeking advice afterwards when the leg becomes increasingly stiff.

There is usually minimal or no swelling over the medial side of the knee, and the tenderness is localized to one area, usually close to the joint line. There is a full range of movement, with perhaps a minor decrease in flexion due to stiffness. Ligament testing shows normal strength with no abnormal laxity. Functionally, the athlete might run with little impairment soon after the injury, or with a slight limp if the leg has become stiff, but is able to perform straight-ahead and backward running. There may be some difficulty in cutting and in running figure-eight patterns (Figure 19.39).

Treatment. Treatment is with ice, compression, perhaps anti-inflammatory medication, and isometric quadriceps and hamstring contractions. This is soon followed by a progressive functional rehabilitation program. (See section on knee rehabilitation.) Icing

TABLE 19.13 *Forces that injure ligaments of the knee*

---

1. *Valgus force*

For example, a block or tackle to the outside of the knee (the foot is fixed) may result in a tear of the:
   a. medial stabilizing complex
   b. anterior cruciate ligament
   c. medial meniscus

   } this is the "unhappy triad" or "O'Donaghue's Triad"

2. *Varus force*

For example, a force applied to the medial side of the knee, forcing the knee to bend into a varus direction (less common than a valgus force), may tear the:
   a. lateral stabilizing complex
   b. anterior cruciate ligament
   c. lateral meniscus

(It should be realized that there are many variations of the above.)

3. *Anteriorly directed force with the knee bent*

Results in an "isolated" anterior cruciate tear

4. *Posteriorly directed force with the knee bent*

Results in an "isolated" posterior cruciate tear

5. *Hyperextension force*

For example, jumping and landing with a straight leg may tear the:
   a. anterior cruciate ligament
   b. then the posterior cruciate ligament if the knee is forced posteriorly far enough

6. *Internal rotation force*

For example, one ski crossing while the body externally rotates and the leg hyperextends may tear the:
   a. anterior cruciate ligament
   b. other structures according to the forces applied

TABLE 19.14 *Criteria for rapid rehabilitation of second-degree grade II medial collateral ligament sprain*

---

1. No (or minimal) swelling
2. Tenderness localized to one area of the tibial collateral ligament, not diffuse
3. Knee stable when tested at 0° (in full extension)
4. Less than 10° of valgus opening at 30° of flexion
5. A definite end point when valgus stress is applied at 30° (the hamstring muscles should be completely relaxed)
6. No anteromedial rotary instability with the knee at 90° and the foot externally rotated
7. No other injured ligaments, in particular, no evidence of an anterior cruciate ligament tear

If the injury meets all of these criteria, the athlete may be placed onto a rehabilitation program aimed at returning him or her to participation in the shortest possible time without jeopardizing the knee (see section on knee rehabilitation).

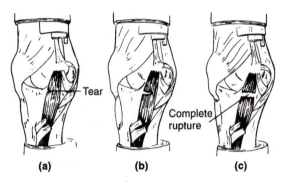

FIGURE 19.39

Degrees of a medial ligamentous injury
(a) First degree: only a few collagen fibers are disrupted. There is almost normal tensile strength. Minimal, if any, valgus laxity is present. (b) Second degree: partial tearing of the ligamentous structures occurs. There is a significant decrease in tensile strength. Valgus laxity is present, but an end point can be felt. (c) Third degree: The ligamentous structures are completely torn. No tensile strength remains. There is marked instability on valgus stress.

---

and perhaps protective taping are used until the symptoms subside, probably a few days. The athlete is allowed to return to participation when functionally capable of performing. With this routine, no strength, power, or endurance should be lost. If there is any weakening of the musculature, the athlete should be kept out of contact participation until the leg has developed strength, power, and endurance equal to or greater than the opposite side. Stretching exercises may be undertaken, but they should be performed cautiously immediately after the injury. Rather, the athlete should work gradually toward normal flexibility over a period of days.

SECOND-DEGREE SPRAIN: A second-degree sprain covers the whole range between a minor ligament injury (first-degree sprain) and a complete rupture of the ligament (third-degree sprain). To make this category meaningful, it is divided into two types:

1. *Second-degree (grade I)*—Sprains that more closely approximate first-degree injuries

2. *Second-degree (grade II)*—Sprains that more closely approximate third-degree sprains

SECOND-DEGREE SPRAIN (GRADE I):

Symptoms and Signs. There is some tearing of the medial capsule and the tibial collateral ligament may also be affected. There is usually some decrease in tensile strength of the collagen fibers, but integrity is present. As with first-degree sprains, the athlete might be able to continue playing for a period of time and then afterwards complain of pain and stiffness, but will be more aware that a definite injury has occurred.

Slight swelling may be apparent, though there is no gross hemarthrosis or effusion. Tenderness is more marked but is limited to a small localized area, usually close to the joint line. Full flexion is often difficult to obtain for a while after the injury because of the discomfort, and full extension may be limited by hamstring spasm.

Ligament testing should reveal no laxity on valgus stress at 0° of flexion. There is no, or very minimal (less than 5°), laxity when testing at 30° of flexion. Stressing causes definite pain in the injured area as may testing for anteromedial rotatory instability by means of Slocum's test with the knee at 90° and the foot externally rotated.

Treatment. This injury is treated in the same way as the first-degree sprain, except that it is probably wise to keep the athlete in a postoperative knee splint for a few days until pain and swelling diminish. As with grade I injury, rehabilitation can begin as symptoms allow.[25,26]

SECOND DEGREE SPRAIN (GRADE II):
Grade II implies a more complete tearing of the ligaments, though there is still some tensile strength.

Symptoms and Signs. The athlete usually complains of the knee buckling when attempting to cut, and may feel unhappy or apprehensive about continuing to play (however, some highly motivated athletes will ignore the instability and continue to participate unless restrained by those in charge).

On examination, swelling is usually slight unless there is an additional injury to one of the other ligaments. Tenderness may be localized to one area or may extend along the entire length of the tibial collateral ligament and along the joint line. There is usually a fairly substantial decrease in the range of motion, with flexion being more limited than extension. Ligament stability testing may show the following:

1. At 0° there may be slight laxity, indicating a severe injury.

2. At 30° there may be some laxity (up to approximately 10° of joint opening) but a definite end point can be felt.

The Lachman test should be negative (assuming there is no involvement of the anterior cruciate ligament).

With the knee at 90° and the tibia in the neutral position of rotation, there should be no laxity on testing anterior or posterior drawer signs. Externally rotating the foot with the knee at 90° usually causes severe pain along the posteromedial joint line and the medial ligaments. Testing for anteromedial rotatory instability (Slocum's test) is usually negative or only minimally positive. Rotating the foot into internal rotation at 90° should not cause pain, and the anterior and posterior drawer tests should be stable. Pivot-shift tests should be negative unless there is involvement of the anterior cruciate ligament, but they are often painful and probably should not be performed when there is a damaged tibial collateral ligament.

McMurray's test may be positive for pain if there is peripheral tearing of the meniscus. The test may be negative initially even when there is a meniscal tear, particularly if the knee cannot be fully flexed.

Treatment. A grade II medial collateral ligament (MCL) injury usually does not require surgical repair, and after an initial period of acute care it may be rehabilitated aggressively. Initial care consists of ice (30 minutes every 3 to 4 hours through the first 24 hours), a compression wrap, a hinged brace to limit valgus stress, and crutches (weight-bearing as tolerated). If the athlete can tolerate them, isometric quad exercises and gentle range-of-motion activities may be initiated on day one. Strength maintenance activities (stationary cycling, isotonic PREs for quads and hamstrings) can be started once sufficient pain-free range of motion is restored. Crutches are discarded when the athlete is able to walk with minimal or no limp.

Upon restoration of full range of motion, minimal pain, and leg control, the athlete may progress through a functional exercise program. (See section on knee rehabilitation.) A return-to-sport progression might start with straight-ahead, controlled-speed jogging. The athlete gradually increases effort from half to three-quarters, and finally to 100 percent effort. When the athlete can successfully tolerate high-speed straight-ahead sprints, cutting drills are introduced (starting at half speed). If there is more than minimal pain or if a limp develops, the athlete should stop, progressing to the next phase of intensity only when pain free.[27] The athlete must demonstrate ligamentous stability, full range of motion, good strength (90 percent of contralateral leg), and functional stability before returning to practice sessions.[28]

THIRD-DEGREE SPRAIN (GRADE III):

Symptoms and Signs. In a third-degree sprain, there is complete disruption of the ligaments (*no* tensile strength is present). The athlete is fully aware that a serious injury has occurred and usually does not attempt to walk on the leg. There may be severe pain at the time of the injury, which then decreases in intensity and leads into a relatively pain-free period of two or three hours. The athlete should not be allowed to walk on the leg during this time, because of the danger of damaging one of the uninjured ligaments, which are now unsupported and unprotected by the medial stabilizing complex.

On examination, there is usually some swelling (though in some cases there is none). Tenderness is often localized to one end of the tibial collateral ligament and over the joint line. A full range of motion is usually present if the athlete is examined soon after the injury, though this is often followed by severe hamstring spasm which permits only limited movement.

Stress testing of the ligaments demonstrates the following: At 0° there is usually some valgus opening, particularly if the anterior or posterior cruciate ligaments have been torn as well. If complete hamstring relaxation is achieved, testing at 30° will produce marked opening of the joint (greater than 10°) with no definite end point.

The Lachman test is negative unless the anterior cruciate is involved. With the knee bent at 90° and the foot in neutral position, there are negative anterior and posterior drawer signs unless the cruciates are torn. Slocum's test may reveal some anteromedial rotatory instability, especially with a tear of the anterior cruciate ligament. Anterior stress at 90° with the foot internally rotated does not reveal any instability. Pivot-shift tests are usually negative (when there is only a medial ligament injury), but they are very painful and are not advised when a third-degree ligament injury has been demonstrated, as damage to other structures can occur. McMurray's test may or may not be positive (it may not even be possible to perform this test).

Treatment. There has been some controversy regarding the treatment of complete (grade III) sprains. O'Donoghue popularized the early (first three to five days) surgical repair of grade III sprains. However, the results of successful nonoperative treatment of incomplete grade II sprains, as well as mounting evidence that ligaments heal more quickly and become stronger when not rigidly immobilized, has led to the practice of allowing early motion following surgical repairs. Currently a nonsurgical, aggressive rehabilitative approach is taken for even grade III sprains.[27] The key to successful treatment of MCL injuries is to establish the existence of an isolated MCL lesion with no associated damage to other vital medial stabilizing structures, particularly the anterior cruciate ligament.[29] (Tables 19.15 and 19.16).

Lateral Stabilizing Complex

The same findings, classification, and treatment are used for lateral stabilizing complex injuries as for the medial side. There are some differences, however:

1. There is normally some physiological laxity of the lateral stabilizing complex when tested at 30°.
2. Slight instability may be tolerated on the medial side; the lateral side cannot compensate for instability and will collapse into a varus position if stressed.

Anterior and Posterior Cruciate Ligament Tears

Though there may be partial tears of the cruciate ligaments, it is difficult or even impossible to make this diagnosis clinically. If instability of one of the cruciates can be demonstrated, a third-degree sprain should be suspected.

Anterior cruciate ligament tears. The clinical diagnosis of an acute anterior cruciate ligament tear depends on the mechanism of the injury, the history of a pop and the rapid swelling of the knee, together with the findings of a positive Lachman test, possibly a positive MacIntosh test, and occasionally some laxity on the anterior drawer test.[30] An arthroscopic examination of the joint is usually necessary to confirm the diagnosis.[18,19]

On many occasions the cruciates have been found intact at surgery, but instability develops over a period of time. One must envision that a microscopic lesion has occurred with loss of collagen integrity. With continued use, the ligament can stretch and this can lead to functional incompetence even though it is macroscopically intact.

SURGICAL TREATMENT: The treatment of anterior cruciate ligament (ACL) injuries has changed over the years. The first reconstructive procedure was described by Campbell[31] in 1939, using a patellar tendon as a graft. Next, primary ACL repairs were

TABLE 19.15 *Rehabilitation and return to sport progression, grade III medial collateral ligament sprain*

Phase 1 0–10 days post injury	Weight bearing as tolerated 0°–90° in hinged brace (post-op or functional) PROM out of brace (pain-free) Quad isometrics Hamstring PREs
Phase 2 10–20 days post injury	Continue brace (crutches as needed) Begin stationary bike for strength and endurance Closed-chain exercise progression
Phase 3 three weeks to four months post injury	Continue strength program Begin functional exercise program (see rehabilitation section) Isokinetic test at 6–8 weeks
Return to sports/activity criteria	Six to eight weeks Full ROM Quads at 80–90% of opposite Good functional test Good valgus stability

TABLE 19.16 *Medial and lateral knee ligament injuries*

	First-degree Sprain	Second-degree Sprain		Third-degree Sprain
		Grade I	Grade II	Grade III
Tissue Damage	Minimal tissue damage	Partial tearing Some decrease in tensile strength	More complete tearing Serious decrease in tensile strength	Complete disruption Zero tensile strength
Clinical Laxity	Stable	Slight laxity	Moderate laxity	Complete instability
Treatment	Standard immediate care Muscle strengthening exercises Minimal protection	Standard immediate care Muscle strengthening exercises Postoperative splint	Standard immediate care Muscle strengthening exercises Good splinting Cast or cast-brace	Standard immediate care Post-op hinged knee brace Progressive weight bearing Nonoperative care if isolated MCL with no associated ACL involvement
Prognosis	Normal function No laxity	Good function Minimal or no laxity	Good function if adequate healing occurs	Good function if adequate healing occurs

attempted. Unfortunately, the success rate of repair was low unless a piece of bone had been avulsed with the ligament (an uncommon occurrence). This led to a trend in conservative, nonoperative treatment. Consequences noted with an ACL-deficient knee include osseous degenerative changes, increases in meniscal tears, arthritis, and/or chronic knee instability.[32] Noting these poor outcomes, the move was back to reconstructive procedures, including extraarticular reinforcements such as the pes anserine or iliotibial band transfers.[33,34] In addition, synthetic and cadaver grafts continue to be experimented with today.

Today's "gold standard" in reconstructing ACL tears is an arthroscopically assisted bone-tendon-bone graft using primarily the central one-third of the patellar tendon.[32,35,36] The success of this surgery is enhanced by precise graft placement, tensioning, and fixation, complemented by rapid rehabilitation protocols emphasizing early full range of motion and weight bearing.[37,38,39,40]

Posterior cruciate ligament partial tears are also difficult or impossible to diagnose. If the history is suggestive of a posteriorly-directed force, and if posterior drawer laxity is present, then the diagnosis of a complete tear of the posterior cruciate ligament should be made.[41,42] However, there are some instances in which the clinical tests are negative, and then an arthroscopic examination is needed to make the diagnosis.[43] The hyperextension test may indicate postero-lateral rotatory instability.[44]

Posterior cruciate ligament tears are usually repaired acutely. The success rate is variable.

Rotatory Instabilities

The term *rotatory instability* refers to a *subluxation* of the tibial plateau on the femoral condyles. A number of these rotatory instabilities have been described (see Table 19.10), the commonest ones being:

1. Anteromedial rotatory instability
2. Anterolateral rotatory instability
3. Combined anteromedial and anterolateral rotatory instability

ANTEROMEDIAL ROTATORY INSTABILITY:

Symptoms. The athlete may first become aware of this instability when planting the affected foot in external rotation while attempting to cut to the opposite direction. The tibia rotates and subluxes from the medial side anteriorly, and the knee tends to buckle into a valgus position. Instability varies from mild apprehension to complete giving way of the knee.

Pathology. The pathology is usually associated with an injury to the posteromedial corner (posterior oblique ligament), the anterior cruciate ligament, or both. However, the symptoms may only begin after an associated tear of the medial meniscus has occurred. These tears are frequently associated with anteromedial rotatory instability.

Examination. There may or may not be valgus laxity at 30° of flexion. However, when the anterior drawer test is performed with the knee at 90° and the foot externally rotated 15°, the tibia is seen and felt to move forward and to rotate from the medial side laterally. This condition is also diagnosed with the anterior drawer test with the foot in the neutral position. If the medial tibial plateau comes forward, but the lateral plateau does not, anteromedial rotatory instability is present.

ANTEROLATERAL ROTATORY INSTABILITY:

Symptoms. Anterolateral rotatory instability seems to incapacitate the athlete more frequently than does the anteromedial variety. The athlete will state that when cutting to the same side as the planted leg, there is a feeling of instability. This is often described as the tibia subluxing forward and medially while the femur is felt to rotate laterally. After an episode of this subluxation, pain and swelling are present for a few days. Any sport that uses a pivot-type activity tends to accentuate this instability, particularly basketball and football.

Pathology. In most cases the basic fault is a rupture or incompetency of the anterior cruciate ligament, together with damage to the posterolateral corner, the lateral stabilizing complex, or both. This injury frequently leads to tears of the medial, and often the lateral, meniscus.

Examination: The clinical findings associated with this instability usually consist of a positive anterior drawer sign when the foot is in the neutral position and when it is internally rotated to 10°. However, it is possible for these signs to be absent. The main diagnostic criterion is a positive pivot-shift test, obtained by using one or all of the mechanisms presently available:

1. MacIntosh test
2. Jerk test of Hughston
3. Lateral position of Slocum

For the jerk or sudden pivot-shift to occur, the iliotibial band must be intact. If the band has been incised during surgery, the pivot-shift test may be negative, even though anterolateral rotatory instability is present.

PROGRESSION OF EVENTS FOLLOWING AN ANTERIOR CRUCIATE LIGAMENT TEAR: Many former athletes give a history of hearing or feeling a "pop" in their knee, which resulted from a cutting action or hyperextension. Swelling may have developed rapidly or it may have been completely absent; the initial examination may have been negative for gross ligament instability. A year or two after the injury, the knee may buckle and give way during a cutting maneuver. A torn medial meniscus may be diagnosed and removed.[45]

The athlete may find that increasing instability develops over time, and that the knee gives way both when cutting with the foot externally rotated and when pivoting to the same side as the planted foot. At this stage there may also be pain at the posterolateral corner of the knee. The athlete has now developed anteromedial and anterolateral rotary instability.[46,47]

Wasilewski et al.,[48] in their study on the effects of surgical timing on recovery and associated injuries after anterior cruciate ligament disruption, noted that chondral lesions were found in 44 percent of chronic knees (surgery at least six months post injury) compared to 17 percent of those who had surgery within one month of initial injury. In addition, only 6 percent of the chronic group had two normal menisci at surgery, compared to 29 percent of the acute group. The time interval between the initial injury and the subsequent development of instability varies from athlete to athlete and appears to depend on many individual factors. However, the scenario described above is a fairly typical sequence of events.

Before the advent of modern surgical techniques, the loss of an ACL was probably the most serious injury that could affect a high-performance athlete. It signaled the end of many promising careers. [49, 50, 51, 52]

Meniscal Lesions

INCIDENCE: The medial meniscus appears to be injured more frequently than the lateral meniscus. This may be due to the relative lack of freedom of movement of the medial meniscus, since the lateral meniscus can move out of the way of the lateral femoral condyle as it rotates.[52] Also, the medial meniscus is often injured in conjunction with medial ligament injuries. However, in certain sports, for instance, wrestling, there is an increased incidence of lateral meniscal tears. This may be because of the frequently flexed attitude of the knee with the foot in external rotation, and also because lateral ligament injuries occur relatively more often in wrestling.

There appears to be a high percentage of meniscal injuries in such sports as soccer, particularly when compared with football, where ligament injuries predomi-

nate. Meniscal tears are rare in pre-adolescents and uncommon in adolescents.

TYPES OF TEARS: Tears of the menisci are divided into

1. Peripheral tears or detachments
2. Tears of the body or substance of the meniscus, which are either longitudinal (vertical) or horizontal cleavage tears

The well-known "bucket-handle" tear is a longitudinal tear through the body of the meniscus (Figure 19.40). In some instances there may in fact be a double bucket-handle tear, in which two separate longitudinal tears are present. This occurs particularly in the midportion and the posterior horn of the medial meniscus.

The type of lesion that occurs differs at different ages, as it appears to be related to the status of the articular cartilage overlying the femur (or tibia), which interacts with the meniscus. A movement in a young athlete can produce the classical longitudinal tear, whereas the same mechanism in an older knee causes a horizontal cleavage tear.

ETIOLOGY: The meniscus is injured in the following ways:

1. In an isolated episode, when the knee is twisted while weight bearing, resulting in a combination of compression and rotational forces being exerted on the meniscus.

The medial meniscus can be injured by a rotational force, in which the tibia rotates externally with respect to the femur. Another possible mechanism exists when the foot is fixed to the ground by cleats. This prevents the tibia from externally rotating on forced extension of the knee.

The lateral meniscus is protected largely by its mobility. If this mobility is lost due to some aging process, rotational movements may take place within the substance of the meniscus (instead of between the

FIGURE 19.40
The "bucket-handle" tear of the medial meniscus

FIGURE 19.41
A "parrot-beak" tear of the lateral meniscus

condyle and the meniscus). This results in a horizontal cleavage tear which later causes a "parrot-beak" tear of the meniscus (Figure 19.41).[54] In these cases the ligaments are usually not affected.

2.   As part of a ligamentous injury. This is usually, but not always, associated with an external force.

3.   When abnormal movements take place in a chronically unstable knee, which occurs particularly with anterolateral rotatory instability. The femur tends to ride over the posterolateral corner of the lateral meniscus, causing a tear to develop with time. Or the abnormal movement can produce an acute medial meniscal tear.

4.   When the meniscus is abnormal (e.g., a discoid lateral meniscus).[55]

SYMPTOMS: In the acute injury, there may be a sudden locking of the knee, with inability to move the leg. Occasionally there may also be a "pop" heard as well.

The more common symptoms are joint-line or intra-articular pain localized to one side of the knee. The pain is elicited by squatting or twisting. A feeling of uncertainty may be experienced when the athlete walks on uneven ground, or an actual giving way of the knee may occur. The athlete may feel that there is a block when attempting to fully extend the knee. Sometimes swelling is the only symptom. If the athlete gives a history of the knee locking near full extension and then suddenly "unlocking" ("snapping back into place"), the diagnosis is fairly certain.

SIGNS: A mild to moderate effusion may be present. There may be some wasting of the quadriceps (particularly the vastus medialis obliquus) if the injury has been present for some time.

Hopping tests may produce a feeling of insecurity, and squatting may cause pain. Duck-waddling is almost always painful. Joint-line tenderness is usually present.

If tenderness is experienced over the anterior joint line when the athlete extends the knee from a flexed position, a longitudinal tear of the body of the meniscus should be suspected. Another suspicious finding is tenderness that moves anteriorly with extension and posteriorly with flexion.

There may be limitation to full extension or flexion, and forced flexion may be painful, particularly with posterior horn lesions. Pain on forced extension can indicate an anterior horn tear. Occasionally there will be pain through the midrange of knee movement, with the extremes of flexion and extension being pain-free. This indicates a tear of the midportion of the meniscus and is called the "painful arc sign."

If the knee can be fully flexed, McMurray's test is usually positive if there is a posterior horn tear. This tear causes a palpable or audible click over the torn meniscus (in longitudinal tears) or a grating associated with pain (in horizontal tears). Apley's test is sometimes positive for pain when there is a posterior horn tear (Table 19.17).

X-RAYS: X-ray findings are usually normal except in the case of a meniscal tear that has been present for some time and that has produced changes of degeneration within the joint space. This is best appreciated on the standing A.P. view. Arthrography, magnetic resonance imaging (MRI), and arthroscopy are useful procedures for confirming the diagnosis and localizing the tear.

TREATMENT: As early as the 1970s some surgeons were removing the entire meniscus if any doubt existed regarding its integrity.[56] The menisci were considered vestigial structures that had little effect on joint func-

TABLE 19.17   *Symptoms and signs of a mensical injury*

Symptoms:	Pain
	Pain + swelling
	Pain + giving way
	Locking and unlocking
Signs:	Vastus medialis atrophy
	Effusion
	Joint-line tenderness (important)
	Pain on forced flexion or extension
	Block to complete flexion or extension
	Positive McMurray's test

tion. Today we know that the menisci are not expendable structures but, in fact, play an integral role in normal knee joint mechanics. The menisci transmit load and reduce stress and compression to the articular cartilage and subchondral bone of the knee during weight bearing. Removal of even small portions of the meniscus may increase joint contact forces dramatically and lead to early degenerative changes in the knee.[57] The goal of meniscus surgery (both partial removal as well as repair) is to preserve as much functional meniscus tissue as possible.

REPAIR VS. REMOVAL: Once the diagnosis of a meniscal tear has been made, the tear can be left to heal, can be repaired, or the torn fragment can be resected.[56] This decision is typically based on a number of variables, including age, location of tear, and integrity of the meniscus. The presence of an adequate blood supply to the torn portion of the meniscus is an essential component in its potential for repair. The blood supply to the menisci is limited to perhaps 10 to 25 percent of the peripheral widths of the medial and lateral meniscal rims.[58,59] Peripheral tears, if small and minimally displaced, may be left alone, while larger, vertical longitudinal tears in the vascular zone may be repaired with great potential for healing. The prognosis for healing of complex tears and tears occurring in the avascular central portion of the meniscus is poor. These tears may be treated with a partial meniscectomy, attempting to remove only the torn portion of the meniscus while leaving as much of the fibrocartilagenous rim as possible.

REHABILITATION FOLLOWING MENISCUS SURGERY: At the present time quite a wide variation exists in post-meniscal repair rehabilitation protocols. Some authors[56] advocate restricted mobility and limited weight bearing during the first four to six weeks post repair, while others[60] permit immediate motion and early weight bearing. Long-term studies that would substantiate one program over another are currently lacking.

In developing a protocol, care should be taken not to place the meniscus in a biomechanical position that may cause excessive stress to the suture line. Excessive loading with deep squats, twisting or pivoting activities, and early plyometric activities can all adversely affect the healing meniscus. Table 19.18 outlines a rehabilitation and return-to-sport progression following meniscal repair. Table 19.19 outlines a similar rehabilitation protocol following partial menisectomy.

The failure rate of meniscus repair in ACL-deficient knees is higher than that of knees in which the ACL has been reconstructed.[61] In patients with concomitant ACL reconstruction and meniscus repair, ACL rehabilitation protocol is followed for the advancement of weight bearing and muscle training, while for the advancement of range of motion, the meniscus repair protocol takes precedence.

Differential Diagnoses of Meniscal Tears

OSTEOCHONDRAL FRACTURES: An osteochondral fracture (a fracture through the articular cartilage and a portion of the bone) may be associated with a twisting, weight-bearing type of injury, as is a meniscal tear. A dislocating patella can also cause an osteochondral fracture. There may be limitation of extension (as with the meniscal injury) and joint-line tenderness.

SUBLUXING PATELLA: The athlete with a subluxing patella may also give a history of giving-way and even of "locking." There may be an effusion, vastus medialis wasting, and joint-line tenderness from medial retinacular irritation. There is often pain on forced flexion, though the pain is more anterior than posterior. Tenderness is usually present along the medial facet of the patella, and moving the patella laterally causes pain and sometimes apprehension.

LIGAMENT INJURY: This injury produces localized joint-line tenderness and pain if the capsular ligament alone is involved. In fact, a capsular ligament tear is often associated with a peripheral tear of the medial meniscus.

TENDINITIS—OVERUSE INJURIES: Pes anserine tendinitis may present with pain and tenderness over and just below the medial joint line. On the lateral side of the knee, symptoms of popliteal and iliotibial tract inflammation, particularly in long-distance runners, can be confused with those of a lateral meniscal injury. Usually the tenderness is just above the joint line, though occasionally it may be over the joint line itself.

OSTEOCHONDRITIS DISSECANS: Osteochondritis can produce joint-line tenderness, but it is usually anterior and is best felt with the knee at 90° of flexion. It can cause locking if the fragment is detached. Wilson's test may be positive (with the foot internally rotated, the knee is extended from 30° of flexion while a valgus force is applied).[62] Osteochondritis dissecans tends to occur in adolescents (an unusual age for meniscal injuries).

TABLE 19.18 *Meniscal repair*

Phase 1	Immediate post-op	Straight-leg knee brace Weight bearing at tolerance (weight bearing status limited for unstable tears—perhaps as long as 6–8 weeks) Modalities (TNS, EMS, etc.) to decrease pain and swelling, maintain quad function Gentle ROM (0°–90°) Initiate quad isometrics
Phase 2	4–14 days post surgery	Full weight bearing Straight-leg knee brace PROM out of brace (0°–125° by three weeks) Quadriceps isometrics Proprioception activities
Phase 3	3–4 weeks post surgery	D.C. brace for walking when patient has full active ROM, good quad control, functional gait Stress endurance work (pool, cycling, upper body ergometer, treadmill walking, cross-country ski machine), limiting time and intensity initially Strength training for lower extremities (limit ROM to 30°–90°). Low weight/high rep initially
Phase 4	4–8 weeks post surgery	Continue strength work Continue endurance work Introduce closed kinetic chain activities (mini-squats, stepping, stairclimbing)
Return-to-sports/activity criteria		Usually 12–24 weeks Quad strength at 80–90% of opposite leg Power training (bounding, jumps, hops) and sport-specific activities can be initiated at 10–12 weeks (limit deep squats, pivoting activities for 3 months)

In patients with concomitant anterior cruciate ligament reconstruction and meniscus repair:

*For the advancement of weight bearing and muscle training, the ACL takes priority.

*For the advancement of range of motion, meniscus repair protocol takes precedence.

The Patella

Functional Anatomy

The patella is a sesamoid bone situated in the tendon of the quadriceps muscle. The quadriceps muscle group is attached to the superior pole of the patella, while the patella tendon originates from the inferior pole. The main functions of the patella are:

1. To increase the effective power of the quadriceps muscle by

   a. increasing the extensor lever arm of the quadriceps mechanism

   b. increasing the area of the action-force of the quadriceps muscles

   c. decreasing friction associated with quadriceps contraction

2. To protect the femoral condyles from direct blows

The patella glides in the intercondylar groove between the medial and the lateral femoral condyles. This movement is influenced and controlled by a number of factors (Figure 19.42).

1. Quadriceps muscle group, in particular the vastus medialis obliquus (VMO).

2. Medial retinaculum.

TABLE 19.19 *Rehabilitation and return to sport progression*

Partial Menisectomy (No Arthritic Changes)		
Phase 1	Immediate post-op	Weight bearing at tolerance Modalities to decrease pain and swelling Gentle ROM activities Quad isometrics, adductor squeezes
Phase 2	4–14 days post-surgery	Full weight bearing Aggressive ROM Proprioception activities Stationary bike Intro to open- and closed-chain activities
Phase 3	2 weeks to 2 months post-surgery	Continue strength work Introduction to functional exercise progression Isokinetic strength test at 6–8 weeks
Return-to-Sports/Activity Criteria		Six to eight weeks Quad strength at 80–90% of opposite leg Good functional strength

3. Medial patellofemoral ligaments (thickening of the deep capsule).

4. Shape of the patella (a patella with a flat undersurface is more likely to move laterally than one with a deep central ridge).

5. Height of the patella. With a patella alta, or high patella, the VMO loses some of its effect in stabilizing the patella.[63]

6. Shape and height of the femoral condyles. A low lateral femoral condyle allows the patella to shift laterally more easily than a high lateral condyle.[64]

7. Vastus lateralis. If there is an imbalance, with the vastus lateralis being more powerful than its medial counterpart, there is a tendency for the patella to be pulled laterally.

8. Lateral retinaculum. If excessively tight, this, too, tends to pull the patella laterally and cause excessive pressure between the patella and the femoral condyles.[65,66]

9. Lateral patellofemoral ligaments (thickening of the deep capsule).

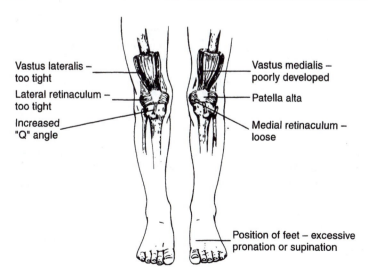

Vastus lateralis – too tight
Lateral retinaculum – too tight
Increased "Q" angle

Vastus medialis – poorly developed
Patella alta
Medial retinaculum – loose
Position of feet – excessive pronation or supination

FIGURE 19.42
Factors influencing the movement of the patella towards subluxation (schematic)

10. Location of the tibial tubercle. A laterally positioned tibial tubercle increases the Q angle.

11. External tibial torsion. This has the same effect as a laterally located tibial tubercle.

12. Q angle (this is the angle formed by a line drawn from the anterior superior iliac spine through the midportion of the patella to the tibial tubercle. This angle is increased by a wide pelvis or external tibial torsion). The normal Q angle is thought to be up to 10° in males and 16° in females.

13. A angle (a measure of the relationship of patellar orientation to the tibial tubercle—Figure 19.43). This measurement may be useful in designing a patellofemoral treatment plan. Recent literature, however,[67] suggests that this measurement may be difficult to reproduce.

14. Factors around the hip joint (e.g., anteversion of the femoral neck results in inward squinting of the patella).

15. The position of the foot (e.g., excessive pronation).

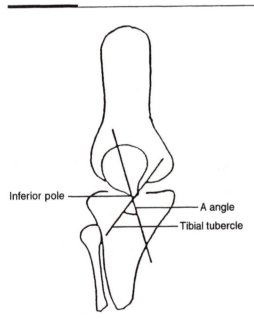

FIGURE 19.43
The A angle.
To calculate the A angle, the body of the patella is palpated both superiorly and inferiorly, and a line is drawn which bisects that patella longitudinally. The intersection of this line, with a line drawn from the tibial tubercle to the apex of the inferior pole forms an angle the compliment of which is the A angle.
(*Source*: Arno S: "The 'A' angle: A quantitative measurement of patella alignment and realignment," *Journal of Orthopaedic Sports Physical Therapists* 12(6): 237–242, © 1990 by Williams & Wilkins.)

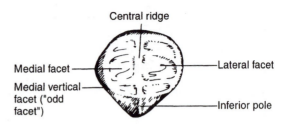

FIGURE 19.44
The articular surface of the patella

The articular surface of the patella is divided into large areas called facets (Figure 19.44). The lateral facet, which is broader and deeper than the medial facet, is divided from the medial facet by the central ridge. This ridge runs vertically and corresponds to the intercondylar groove on the femur. The medial facet has a small area on the most medial aspect termed the "odd facet," which is only in contact with the femur during extremes of knee flexion.

The entire articular surface of the patella is not in contact with the femur at any one time. Various areas of the patella articulate at different angles of the flexing knee. For instance, with the knee in extension, the distal portion of the patella has the highest contact force and the contact area moves proximally as the knee flexes. Between 90° and 135° most of the contact is on the medial facet, and this moves to the odd facet with complete flexion. Any abnormal movement of the patella along its course in the groove results in excessive patellofemoral pressure, pain, and eventually may result in articular cartilage degeneration on the undersurface of the patella or on the femoral condyles.

PATELLAR SHAPE: The patella has a very individual shape which differs from person to person. This variability may influence congruency and stability of the patella in the patellofemoral joint. A classification by Wiberg[68] and Baumgartl[69] is used to describe the patellar shape (Figure 19.45).

Type I Medial and lateral facets are equal and slightly concave.

Type II Medial facet is smaller; both facets are concave.

Type III Medial facet is smaller and convex; the larger, lateral facet is concave.

Type II–III Medial facet is small and flat.

Type IV Medial facet is very small and almost vertical.

Type V Jagerhut ("hunter's cap") patella is almost flat.

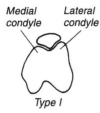

Medial condyle   Lateral condyle

Type I
Facets symmetrical
Both facets concave

Type II
Lateral facet longer

Type II /III
Medial facet convex

Type III
Medial facet convex
Lateral facet concave
Lateral facet longer

Type IV
Medial facet small
and steeply sloped

Type V Jagerhut
No central ridge
No medial facet

FIGURE 19.45

Classification of patellar shapes
(by Wiberg and Baumgartl). (Modified from R. L. Larson, "Fractures and dislocations of the knee. Part II, Dislocations and Ligamentous injuries to the knee," in *Fractures*, C. A. Rockwood and D. P. Green [eds.], Vol. 2, p. 1183, published by J. B. Lippincott Co., Philadelphia, 1975.).

Injuries to the Patella

The main injuries affecting the patellofemoral joint are:

1. Patellar fracture
2. Acute dislocation
3. Subluxation and spontaneous reduction of a dislocated patella

PATELLAR FRACTURE: This is an uncommon injury usually caused by a direct blow. The fracture can be horizontally across the patella, or it can shatter the patella into numerous pieces.

Treatment.

Initial: Immobilization with the leg in full extension, plus icing.

Definitive: Surgery is necessary if the fracture is displaced.

ACUTE DISLOCATION:

1. Commonly, patellar dislocations occur as noncontact injuries and result from the force of contraction of the quadriceps combined with the angle of the leg. For instance, during a cutting maneuver the foot is planted in external rotation and the knee is flexed to about 45° and forced into a valgus position (Figure 19.36). The quadriceps then forcefully contracts and, because of the angle of pull with the leg in this position, it actively dislocates the patella (Figure 19.46). This type of dislocation occurs in an athlete with a relatively normal lower extremity alignment and without gross abnormality of the quadriceps mechanism, *if* the forces pulling the patella laterally are powerful enough.

2. Dislocation can occur in those with genetic or developmental factors that predispose to lateral displacement of the patella. In these, a very small force may be all that is required to cause a dislocation.

Pathology. There is usually tearing of the attachments of the following structures from the patella:

1. Medial retinaculum
2. Medial patellofemoral ligaments
3. Vastus medialis obliquus (and perhaps other parts of the quadriceps muscle group)

If these heal in a lengthened position, chronic subluxation or recurrent dislocations can occur. In addition, there is frequently damage to the underlying cartilage or bone, which can result in one of the following (Figure 19.47):

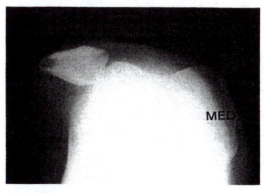

FIGURE 19.46

Patellar dislocation (laterally)
With this injury, there is damage to the medial retinaculum, the patellofemoral and patellotibial ligaments, and sometimes the vastus medialis. In addition, articular cartilage fractures frequently occur, particularly of the lateral femoral condyle.

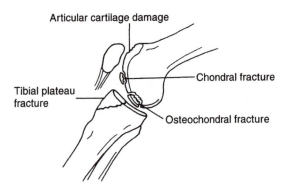

Articular cartilage damage

Chondral fracture

Tibial plateau
fracture

Osteochondral fracture

F I G U R E   1 9 . 4 7
Varieties of articular cartilage injury

1. Articular cartilage damage—partial thickness: Minimal symptoms.

2. Articular cartilage damage—full thickness: An articular cartilage fracture that can develop significant symptoms.

3. Avulsion fracture—on the medial side of the patella at the attachment of the medial retinaculum and patellofemoral ligaments.

4. Osteochondral fracture—involves the articular cartilage and the underlying bone of either the patella or the lateral femoral condyle. It often occurs during relocation of the patella, as it strikes the lateral femoral condyle.

5. Fracture of the patella—occurs through the entire thickness of bone.

Articular cartilage damage can occur on the patella, the femoral surface, or both, and can lead to permanent patellofemoral joint problems.

Symptoms. The athlete usually describes feeling the "knee going out of joint." There is intense pain and inability to move the knee.

Signs. On observation of the injured knee, the laterally dislocated patella is usually obvious. However, if the athlete is first seen some hours after the dislocation has occurred, gross intra-articular swelling can obscure the position of the patella. There should still be little difficulty in making the diagnosis after palpating the anterior aspect of the knee. While palpating this area, be sure that the quadriceps muscle group and the patellar tendon are intact, because it is possible for one of these structures to rupture, the presenting feature being a large hemarthrosis. In addition, a tibial collateral ligament injury frequently

occurs in conjunction with a patellar dislocation, producing medial tenderness and valgus instability.

Treatment.
Initial: If the athlete is seen at the site of the injury, the affected leg should be gently straightened. This is sometimes sufficient to produce reduction. If it does not, *gentle* medial pressure should then be applied. When a reduction is achieved, the knee should be packed with ice and splinted with whatever means are available, with the leg fully extended. The athlete is then transported for X-rays and definitive treatment.

If the patella cannot easily be reduced by the simple procedures outlined, no further attempts at reduction should be made. The knee should be iced and splinted with the leg in the position of greatest comfort while the athlete is being transported for X-rays and reduction.

Definitive: Most dislocations reduce easily. A nonsurgical approach to treatment is currently advised, unless the patella cannot be reduced or another indication for surgery exists such as an osteochondral fracture. This is diagnosed by finding fat globules in the hemarthrosis when it is aspirated.

Rehabilitation. Initial care must be designed to control pain, limit the size of the hemarthrosis, and maintain quadriceps function. Acute care should consist of ice, compression, knee immobilization in a posterior splint, and elevation. Crutches should be used until weight bearing is relatively pain-free.

If a first-time dislocator does not show excessive laxity of medial patellar restraints (significant lateral tilt on Merchant's view, palpable defect medially), a rehabilitation program may be started once symptoms subside. Quad-setting activities should begin as soon as the athlete can tolerate them. Biofeedback and electrical stimulation can be utilized to help gain and maintain control over the vastus medialis obliquus (the most important dynamic stabilizer of the patella). Active range-of-motion exercises are usually started within one week. The athlete can remove the splint and attempt to actively flex the heel to the buttocks while sitting on the floor or a table. Knee flexion can be assisted passively by looping a towel around the foot or ankle and gently pulling the heel to the buttocks. The athlete should continue to wear the knee immobilizer until 100 degrees of painless flexion is present.[27]

Early gait training out of the immobilizer should be done with the aid of crutches. Athletes should gradually increase the amount of time they can walk without the immobilizer. Starting in the morning and progressing throughout the day, the immobilizer should be replaced when fatigue or a limp becomes apparent. Initial knee

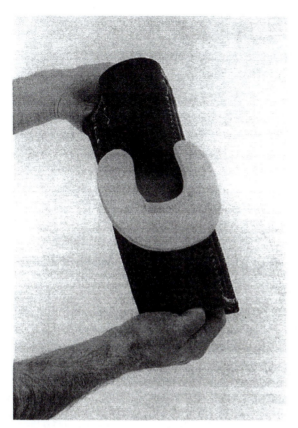

FIGURE 19.48
Neoprene sleeve with a felt patella stabilizing pad

strengthening activities should be performed submaximally with an emphasis on functional activities. (See rehabilitation section.) The athlete should use a knee brace such as a neoprene sleeve with a lateral pad when returning to activity, to protect the patella and prevent lateral displacement (Figure 19.48). An in-shoe orthotic device may be helpful in certain cases.

If it appears that the medial stabilizing structures of the patella have been compromised (significant lateral tilt or lateral glide of the patella, a palpable rent in the medial retinaculum) the physician may elect to:

1. Surgically repair the laxity in the medial restraints

2. Immobilize the knee in extension for 6 to 8 weeks to allow for healing of soft tissue restraints. Allowing the soft tissues to heal in a relatively shortened position is thought to help avoid future chronic medial patellofemoral laxity and instability.

RECURRENT DISLOCATIONS: If an athlete has had previous patellar dislocations, a knee immobilizer is used only until acute symptoms subside. Although subsequent dislocations may result in less pain and swelling, each redislocation can potentially cause more damage to patellar and femoral articular cartilage and soft-tissue structures. Traumatic arthritis is a distinct possibility with multiple patellar dislocations.[70] An assessment should be made as to whether surgical repair is warranted.

SUBLUXATION AND SPONTANEOUS REDUCTION OF A DISLOCATED PATELLA: The difference between spontaneous reduction of a dislocated patella and subluxation of a patella may be very subtle and difficult to distinguish clinically, though the two are really separate entities. Spontaneous reduction of a dislocated patella is usually a clearly defined event in which the patella is seen or felt to slip over the lateral femoral condyle and then return to the intercondylar groove. With a subluxation, a significant number of athletes are totally unaware that the patella has partially or completely dislocated, only knowing that something serious has occurred in the knee. However, as the two conditions overlap, they will be discussed together.

A subluxation or a dislocation occurs relatively often in athletes.[71,72] The etiology and pathological findings are those described under the section on acute dislocations. Many of the symptoms and signs of patellar subluxation are compatible with a meniscal tear, and for this reason the examiner's index of suspicion must be high; otherwise the diagnosis can be missed.

The athlete may state that the knee suddenly buckled and gave way, usually with a tearing sensation and much pain, sometimes with a "pop." Or the history may be much more vague and may include statements to the effect that the knee "went out of joint" or that there was locking, catching, or giving way. It may be stated that when the leg was straightened, something shifted back into place. Occasionally swelling is the only complaint.

If the athlete gives a history of the knee giving way, or of a pop, it is important to try to obtain a description of the mechanism of the injury and the exact position of the affected foot and leg at the time of these symptoms.

Signs. In the case of spontaneous reduction of a dislocated patella, there is usually a large hemarthrosis of rapid onset. Any flexion, passive or active, causes intense pain. In less severe or recurrent cases, there may be joint effusion, but this may be absent and the range of movement may be normal.

The athlete should sit at the end of the examining table, legs hanging down at 90° and should be observed for the following:

1. Lateral squinting of the patella. This is a sign which should immediately make the examiner suspect subluxation.

2. Patella alta, or high-riding patella. The patella tends to "look up" at the ceiling (Figure 19.30).

3. Tracking of the patella in the intercondylar notch when the knee is moved through the range of flexion to extension.

The athlete then holds the leg at 45° against resistance, at which time the vastus medialis is inspected and palpated. Then the knee is palpated. Tenderness is often elicited along the medial joint line and over the femoral attachments of the patellofemoral ligaments. The medial retinaculum and the vastus medialis obliquus may also be extremely tender, and the medial facet of the patella is almost always so.

The examiner should then test for lateral hypermobility of the patella, first with the leg fully extended, then at 30° of flexion. The quadriceps muscles should be relaxed. This maneuver can be exceedingly painful to perform in the acute case; if so, further testing for lateral mobility should not he undertaken at this time.

If the medial retinaculum and the patellofemoral ligaments are loose, it may be possible to displace the patella completely without discomfort or apprehension. In most instances, however, as the articular surface of the patella begins to slip over the lateral femoral condyle, the athlete becomes apprehensive and tightens the quadriceps in an attempt to straighten the leg, or grabs the examiner's hand to prevent further lateral displacement. This is termed a "positive apprehension test" and is highly suggestive of patellar instability (Figure 19.32). Compressing the patella against the underlying bone should be performed gently, as it may cause exquisite pain.

Testing the medial ligaments produces no laxity, though with valgus stress there is often some discomfort along the medial joint line and the tibial collateral ligament. This might lead the examiner into thinking that a sprain of the tibial collateral ligament has occurred, which indeed may have happened.

Examination of the menisci is usually best deferred in the acute case, as attempts to completely flex the knee will cause severe pain. However, in the chronic case, McMurray's test may also produce tenderness over the medial joint line, again possibly misleading the examiner into thinking that a meniscal injury is present.

X-rays of both knees are most useful in confirming the diagnosis. Sometimes a subluxed patella shows up on an anteroposterior (AP) view. Some osteochondral fractures of the patella or the femur can also be seen on this view (osteochondral fractures of the femur are usually best seen on the tunnel view). Look carefully for osteochondral avulsion fractures off the medial facet of the patella, as they may be difficult to see at first glance. The lateral view will demonstrate a patella alta or an

FIGURE 19.49
X-ray—avulsion fracture, medial facet of the patella
The attachment of the medial retinaculum and patellotibial ligaments may result in an avulsion fracture if the patella subluxes laterally.

osteochondral defect in one of the femoral condyles. However, it is the tangential view which gives the most information. A number of different techniques should be used to substantiate the diagnosis and to avoid missing any osteochondral fragments[72,73] (see section on knee X-rays) (Figure 19.49).

Treatment.

INITIAL. Ice, compression, elevation, and a posterior splint or postoperative immobilizer holding the knee in full extension constitute the initial treatment in the acute case. Anti-inflammatory medication, if used, should be started immediately.

DEFINITIVE.
Conservative: First-time subluxation or dislocation: If no indication for surgery exists, it is best to place the severe case in a postoperative knee immobilizer. The main point is to keep the knee straight, in order to avoid any pressure on the articular surfaces of the patellofemoral joint and to allow the soft tissues on the medial side of the patella to heal in the optimal position.

Recurrent subluxation or dislocation: In this case the medial retinaculum and the patellofemoral ligaments have probably elongated, due to previous episodes. There is no value in prolonged immobilization; they are therefore splinted only until asymptomatic, which usually takes from a few days to two weeks. However, they should be assessed for elective surgical repair.

Rehabilitation of both the first-time subluxation or dislocation and the recurrent case should be performed routinely. (See section on knee rehabilitation.)

Surgical: Surgical treatment may be indicated in certain cases.

Patellofemoral Joint Pain

Patellofemoral pain is a common condition, affecting up to one in four of the general population.[74] It can be a difficult condition to treat. The term *patellofemoral syndrome* covers a number of common conditions associated with articulation of the patella on the femur. One of these conditions is chondromalacia. The term *chondromalacia* should be reserved for situations in which pathologic changes of the articular cartilage of the patella (cartilage softening and disruption) has been documented, and should not be used to describe the whole spectrum of patellofemoral joint pain.[75, 76, 77, 78] Often no pathological findings are present in patients (especially young patients) who otherwise complain of severe pain and functional disability. Patellofemoral pain usually develops gradually and is characterized by a diffuse ache in the anterior knee. Pain is a significant factor because it may alter function and inhibit muscular activity.[79]

Extensor mechanism malalignment is by far the most common cause of patellofemoral pain in athletes. Extensor malalignment is influenced by a variety of factors, including:

1. Weakness and/or laxity of the medial stabilizers of the patella (VMO, patellofemoral ligaments, retinaculum)

2. Tightness of the lateral stabilizing structures (retinaculum, Iliotibial band)

3. Unbalanced lower limb mechanics—the "miserable malalignment syndrome" (genu varum/valgum, tibial torsion, abnormal foot mechanics, soft tissue tightness, etc) (Figure 19.50)

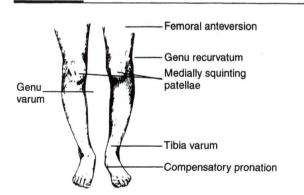

FIGURE 19.50
The miserable malalignment syndrome

The end result is a patella that does not track properly, resulting in excess pressure between particular areas of the under surface of the patella and the corresponding articular surface of the femur.

PATHOMECHANICS: Frequently referred to as *"excessive lateral pressure syndrome" (ELPS)*,[80] the pain is thought to be due either to compression of the lateral retinaculum (which is highly innervated) or to irritation of the nerve endings in the subchondral bone (articular cartilage has no nerve supply); this irritation occurs because of the loss of the normal energy-absorbing function of the intermediate and deep zones of the articular cartilage.[81,82] Other theories contend that the pain is secondary to an alteration of the blood supply in the chondral bone, or that it is caused by venous stasis and congestion within the patella.[83] Also, transverse plane rotation malalignments may account for abnormal forces on the articular cartilage and subchondral bone in many cases. (This topic is discussed further under the section on the runner's knee.)

Other causes of pain (many of which are interrelated) include:

1. Direct trauma
2. Bursitis
3. Recurrent subluxation or dislocation of the patella
4. Fat pad syndrome
5. Plica syndrome
6. Knee ligament or meniscal injury
7. Patellar tendinitis
8. Post-surgical or immobilization state
9. Systemic synovitis
10. Patellofemoral joint incongruencies
11. Reflex sympathetic dystrophy

NATURAL HISTORY AND SYMPTOMS: The typical sufferer of malalignment is in his or her teens or early twenties and is usually active and athletically involved at the onset of symptoms. It has been stated that the majority of symptoms resolve spontaneously over a period of time. While some do resolve spontaneously, it is unusual for the person who continues athletic activities to experience a spontaneous remission of symptoms without changing the type and/or amount of activity. Many athletes have pain in only one knee at a time, though some cases are bilateral. The primary complaints are:

1. Pain when going up and, particularly, down stairs or hills

2. Aching when sitting with the knees at 90° for a period of time. This ache is usually accompanied by stiffness that disappears rapidly after walking a short distance.

3. Pain during activity, after activity, or both, particularly after squatting and cycling

4. Catching, grating, transient locking, and a feeling of giving way at times

Swelling is an uncommon presenting symptom with patellofemoral syndrome, but even mild swelling can have a significant inhibitory effect on muscle function.

SIGNS: The following sequence should be followed in an examination of an athlete with patellofemoral pain. The athlete should:

1. Stand facing the examiner. The examiner should observe for signs of malalignment.

2. Stand sideways. The observer should examine for genu recurvatum, patella alta, and tight Achilles tendons.

3. Sit with the legs hanging down at 90°. Examiner should note "squinting" of the patellae and patella alta.

4. Sit with the legs at 45° against resistance. Examiner should inspect and palpate the vastus medialis obliquus muscles.

5. Lie supine. Observer should examine the patellae.

6. Finally, the examiner should observe functional activities such as walking, squatting, stepping up and down from stairs, and balancing:

   a. assess for normal sequencing of pronation and supination during gait

   b. assess knee and patellar position relative to the supporting foot during squatting and eccentric stepping activities

   c. assess ability of stance leg to stabilize pelvis during single-leg balancing activities

Pertinent physical findings that should be noted are:

1. Tenderness along the medial facet of the patella

2. Pain on compression of the patella against the underlying femur, particularly the lateral facet of the patella (this is the lateral patellar sign and suggests the possibility of the *patellar compression syndrome*, that is, higher-than-normal forces between patella and the femur[66,84]

3. Lateral laxity of the patella when tested with the leg in full extension and in 30° flexion

4. Positive apprehension sign

5. Malalignment of lower extremities and the patella

6. Weak, poorly functioning VMO and/or tight lateral structures

Crepitus may or may not be demonstrable, but it is not considered an important sign *by itself* in most cases, because there is little association between crepitus and symptoms in the athlete. Crepitus is often present in joints that have no patellofemoral pain, and vice versa. However crepitus that becomes more apparent as the severity of the symptoms increases is likely to be related to articular cartilage wear and deterioration.

An examination of hip rotation and feet should be included.

TREATMENT: The mainstay of treatment of patellofemoral joint pain is conservative management, including the following. The most important early measure in the treatment of patellofemoral joint pain is the *decrease in activities* involving great or prolonged patellofemoral compressive loads. Activities such as stair climbing, jumping, squatting, and weight training should be decreased until the condition has become asymptomatic. Once asymptomatic, the athlete should begin a program designed to increase the strength and power of the quadriceps muscle group. The athlete may be allowed to gradually return to former activities. Should the symptoms recur, the activity level must be reduced immediately.

An attempt must be made to *normalize patellar tracking* through stretching of tight lateral structures, stimulation and strengthening of medial stabilizers (VMO), and improvement in lower limb mechanics. Stretching of tight lateral structures may include:

1. Passive stretch of ITB/hip external rotators (Figure 19.51a)

2. Mobilizing techniques to enhance medial tilt and glide of the patella (Figure 19.51b)

3. Passive taping of the patella to enhance patellar position and stretch lateral structures (Figure 19.52). Repositioning of the patella through passive taping is designed to redistribute forces between the patella and femoral groove. A reduction of compressive forces (and pain) may also allow for more effective VMO activation

The vastus medialis obliquus represents the primary dynamic medial stabilizer of the patella. Because of the orientation of its fibers (and the resultant angle of pull), it has the ability to influence patellar tracking and decrease patellofemoral joint compressive forces. TNS, cold, and anti-inflammatories can all be used early on to decrease pain. Electrical stimulation, biofeedback, and muscle-setting exercises can all help the athlete gain

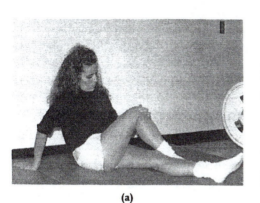

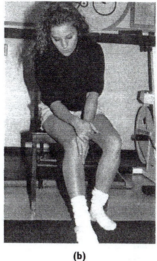

FIGURE 19.51
(a) Stretch to iliotibial tract/hip external rotators; (b) Seated passive mobilization of the patella (medial tilt)

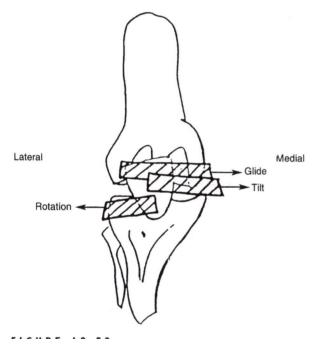

Lateral

Medial

Glide

Tilt

Rotation

FIGURE 19.52
An illustration of the taping technique to control patella lateral glide, medial tilt, and internal rotation.
(*Source:* Asno S: "The 'A' angle: A quantitative measurement of patella alignment and realignment," *Journal of Orthopaedic Sports Physical Therapists* 12(6):237–242, © 1990 by Williams & Wilkins.)

voluntary control over the muscle. Pain-free activities must be chosen whenever possible. Active exercise on a painful, swollen knee is counterproductive.

Functional strengthening activities should be chosen whenever possible. A functional strengthening pro-

gram might start with seated or standing quadriceps, adductor, and gluteus setting; it would progress to partial squats with emphasis on VMO activation and optimal lower limb mechanics (patella centered over feet, arches actively supported to limit excessive lower limb pronation). A progression from controlled, limited-range activities to more aggressive rehabilitation should take place only if and when the movements are pain free. Progressing from two-legged controlled squats to single-leg squats and/or lunging activities will further stress the athlete's ability to dynamically control patellofemoral forces. (See section on knee rehabilitation.) Use of stair-climbing and stationary cycling represent an excellent means of maintaining and building muscular strength and endurance. Cadence, knee flexion angles, resistance, duration, and frequency are all variables that can be controlled. Be aware that the biomechanics of the knee are different when loading the joint from above (closed chain) than when loading from below (open chain). When loading from above (i.e., kneebends) there is overall a pattern of increased patellofemoral joint reaction forces (PFJRF) with increased flexion of the knee. An increase in joint contact area with increasing flexion serves to distribute the forces over a broad area to normalize stress per unit load. When loading from below (open-chain knee extension) the PFJRF are increasing (due to increased demand on the quadriceps) while the contact area is decreasing.[85]

Increases in flexibility by means of slow, static stretching should be instituted for the quadriceps, hamstrings, iliotibial band, and gastrocnemius. Tightness of the hamstrings and heel cords may cause an increase in the amount of ankle dorsiflexion required during gait. If maximum dorsiflexion has already occurred at the talocrural (ankle) joint, then additional motion is possible only through compensation at the subtalar joint. Such compensation occurs in conjuction with pronation, causing additional internal rotation of both the tibia and femur, increasing the functional Q angle.

In-shoe orthotic devices may be helpful. Prolonged pronation of the subtalar joint may occur as compensation for forefoot abnormalities (forefoot varus), rearfoot abnormalities, or lower limb irregularities. The end result may be malalignment of the patella as the femur rotates medially while the quadriceps pull laterally. In McConnel's study of adolescent boys[86] subtalar pronation, not Q angle, was found to be the most significant predictor of patellofemoral pain.

The patella should be mobilized to enhance normal medial tilt and glide. The patella may also be taped to enhance patellar position and VMO contraction. The theory behind this taping technique is that the corrected position allows for a more even distribution of forces along the undersurface of the patella during activities (Figure 19.52). Finally, movement of the patella may be reduced by a neoprene patellar sleeve with a supportive ring. The sleeve also helps to keep the knee warm during activities and may give symptomatic relief. Other braces have also been used.[87]

Aspirin or Ibuprofen should be administered.

SURGICAL TREATMENT. Surgery is reserved for the exceptionally unresponsive and difficult cases and should not be undertaken until all conservative measures have been tried. Various surgical procedures have been devised, from a simple lateral retinacular release for patellar compression[88,89] to an operation in which the vastus medialis muscle is advanced, the lateral retinaculum released, and the tibial tubercle moved medially to decrease the Q angle.[90,91] A localized area of unhealthy articular cartilage is sometimes also removed. The surgical procedure needs to be individualized for each athlete.

Differential Diagnoses

Other causes of anterior knee pain need to be considered.

1. *Recurrent subluxation or dislocation of the patella.* This must be suspected in every case as it is associated with many cases of patellofemoral joint pain due to malalignment.

2. *Patellofemoral compression syndrome.* This may be part of, or independent of, the malalignment syndrome. If the reaction forces between the patella and the femur increase, anterior knee pain may result. The diagnosis is made by finding a tight lateral retinaculum and pain on compression of the lateral facet of the patella (lateral

patellar sign), and the pain may be relieved by surgical release of the lateral retinaculum.

3. *Meniscal lesion(s).* See section on the menisci.

4. *Bipartite patella.* The unfused portion of the patella is usually found at the superior lateral pole, and when symptomatic, pain and tenderness are localized to that site. Occurrence is mainly in males and may give rise to symptoms in athletes participating in sports that require much jumping and squatting.[92] The diagnosis is confirmed by X-rays (best seen on anteroposterior and tangential views of the patella) and often occurs bilaterally.

5. *Infrapatellar fat-pad lesions.* An uncommon finding, these are usually due to direct trauma of the fat pad, which results in swelling and hemorrhage, though the fat pads may become inflamed from general overuse. A differentiating feature is that the pain is often relieved by keeping the knee in slight flexion.

6. *Synovial plica.* The athlete usually complains of pain and swelling, accompanied by a catching or snapping sensation. The articular cartilage can degenerate from recurrent impingement of the plica on the patella and the femoral condyles. This is a relatively rare condition which is becoming more frequently diagnosed with increasing use of the arthroscope.[93]

7. *Quadriceps contracture.* This can occur after a fractured femur or a quadriceps injury, creating pain by increasing the patellofemoral joint reaction forces.

Other Conditions in or around the Knee

Osteochondral Fractures

The term "osteochondral" implies that the fracture is through the articular cartilage as well as a portion of the bone, and that it usually results in a fragment being detached from the underlying bone. While these fractures need to be diagnosed by means of X-rays, they can be suspected clinically.

MECHANISM OF INJURY: There are two basic mechanisms:

1. A direct blow to the knee, for instance, contacting a sharp object like the corner of a table with the knee flexed while moving at speed. The medial femoral condyle is more exposed and therefore more often involved.

2. A noncontact injury. The shearing force of twisting and weight bearing may be enough to cause a fracture through one or the other femoral condyle, for instance, when cutting sharply to the opposite side.

TYPES OF FRACTURES:

Femur: Osteochondral fractures of the medial femoral condyle tend to be smaller than those of the lateral femoral condyle.

Patella: Small or large osteochondral fractures may be produced during a patellar dislocation, when both the lateral femoral condyle and the patella can sustain fractures.

SYMPTOMS: The history is of an acute injury, either contact of the knee against an object or sudden twisting with the knee flexed. This is followed by a "snapping" sensation or sound and the rapid onset of swelling. There is severe pain, particularly if the athlete attempts to walk.

SIGNS: Signs include a large hemarthrosis, joint line tenderness which is usually localized to one specific area, and inability to fully extend the knee.

X-RAYS: X-rays may only show the osteochondral fragment when the special tunnel or tangential views are taken. Arthroscopy is helpful in difficult cases.

TREATMENT: Treatment is by surgery, preferably immediately following the diagnosis. The osteochondral fragment is replaced and pinned into position if this is possible, or else removed. If there is any delay before the diagnosis is made and surgery is undertaken, replacing the fragments may not be possible. Joint degeneration can result.

Osteochondritis Dissecans

Osteochondritis dissecans is a condition in which an area of bone undergoes changes which result in a loose piece of bone (also called a loose body) within the joint. In the knee the area of osteochondritis dissecans is mainly found on the posterolateral aspect of the medial femoral condyle (Figure 19.53).

ETIOLOGY: This is still a matter of debate although a number of factors have been associated with it, such as:

1. Trauma (some think it is a compression fracture)

2. Impairment of the blood supply to the affected area of the femur

3. Heredity in some cases

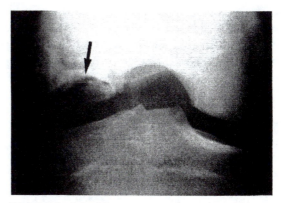

FIGURE 19.53
X-ray—osteochondritis dissecans of the knee

TYPES: As a generalization, osteochondritis dissecans is divided into two groups. These are distinguished from each other by an age difference.

UNDER 15 YEARS: In this group, osteochondritis dissecans is generally unrelated to trauma. It presents with nonspecific knee pain that may continue for a period of time (possibly months), and it is often bilateral.

Signs. Pre-adolescents and adolescents appear to have external tibial rotation when walking. A slight effusion may be present, and perhaps some quadriceps atrophy. Tenderness to palpation is present over the affected condyle when the knee is flexed beyond 90°.

Wilson's sign for osteochondritis dissecans may be positive.[62] This test is performed by placing the affected knee at 90° of flexion, then internally rotating the tibia and extending the knee. As the knee is extended, a valgus force is applied. Pain at 30° of flexion indicates a positive sign for osteochondritis dissecans, usually of the lateral portion of the medial femoral condyle. However, this test can be negative although osteochondritis dissecans is present.

Diagnosis. The diagnosis is made by means of X-rays, with the lesion commonly seen on the tunnel view.

There is also a growth variant or developmental abnormality affecting the secondary center of ossification, which is seen only on X-rays and does not produce any clinical symptoms and signs. This variant will go on to normal ossification without treatment being necessary.

Treatment. Usually the treatment is simple rest from activities that produce pain; sometimes enforced rest in a cast is necessary. The prognosis for this age group is usually excellent.

OVER 15 YEARS: These are usually males, and the symptoms are often related to a specific traumatic event. They may present with locking and giving way if the osteochondral fragment becomes detached and slips into the joint, or they may present with the same symptoms and signs as those under 15.

Diagnosis. Diagnosis is made by means of X-rays.

Treatment. The over-15 age group, or those with a loose fragment in the under-15 age group, may need surgical pinning or excision of the fragment.

Prognosis. The prognosis for this age group is much poorer than for the under-15 age group, and seems to worsen with increasing age.

Baker's Cyst

Actually a herniation of the synovium, this swelling is usually found on the posteromedial aspect of the knee. The herniation forms a sac and fills with synovial fluid. It is often associated with a tear or a degenerative condition of the medial meniscus.

By itself, the cyst is of little significance, though it can cause discomfort when the athlete is running at full speed. If it causes considerable impairment of athletic performance, or if it is associated with some intra-articular condition, an arthrogram should be ordered to rule out the presence of a meniscal tear. Should a tear be present, it may be an indication for a meniscectomy with or without removal of the cyst. On occasion, the cyst spontaneously ruptures followed by cessation of all symptoms.

Synovial Plica

A normal anatomical variation of the synovium, the plica is a band of tissue that runs from the lateral femoral condyle around the superior and medial aspects of the patella downward to the fat pad anteriorly. It usually does not cause any particular problem, but if it becomes inflexible and taut, it may give rise to symptoms of irritation, usually of the medial facet of the patella, though sometimes the superior or lateral aspects of the knee are involved[93,94,95] (Figure 19.54).

SYMPTOMS AND SIGNS: In some cases, direct trauma to the knee (and to the plica) initiates symptoms similar to those of a meniscal injury—pain, pseudolocking, and swelling. Pain referable to the patella, such as retropatellar pain when sitting, with relief on extension of the leg, may also be noticed. A snapping and popping

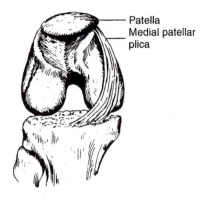

Patella
Medial patellar plica

FIGURE 19.54
Medial patellar plica

may occur, particularly over the medial femoral condyle, when the knee is moved through about 60° of flexion. Even though a plica may be causing some of the symptoms, there may be other pathology such as a medial meniscal injury or an extensor mechanism malalignment.

TREATMENT: Hamstring and quadriceps stretching exercises relieve symptoms in some cases, though most require surgical removal if symptomatic.

Patellar and Quadriceps Tendinitis ("Jumper's Knee")

Jumper's knee refers to tendinitis involving either the patellar tendon, the quadriceps tendon, or both. This condition is peculiar to athletic activities, particularly those involving constant repetitive jumping and landing such as basketball, the long and high jump, and the triple jump.

Patellar tendinitis is the more common of the two and may present with localized pain and tenderness in one of three areas:

1. Attachment of the patellar tendon to the inferior pole of the patella (the most common)
2. Midportion of the patellar tendon
3. Insertion of the patellar tendon into the tibial tubercle

Quadriceps tendinitis usually manifests with pain and tenderness localized to the insertion of the quadriceps group of muscles into the superior pole of the patella.

ETIOLOGY: This appears to be related to microtrauma to the tendon and to the attachment of the tendon to the patella. (See section on microtrauma.) Repetitive jumping with acceleration or deceleration is the primary causative mechanism. It seems that this condition is becoming more common, due to a longer playing season and increasing daily participation. Other factors which may aggravate the condition include squatting with heavy weights and malalignment of the patella.

Patellar tendinitis seldom disappears on its own if the athlete continues to play at the same level and for the same amount of time. A decrease in one of these factors (plus treatment) helps modify the progress of the condition to some extent.

SYMPTOMS: Symptoms are mainly confined to pain in the involved area. Occasionally there may be some catching, giving way, and weakness, which is often due to quadriceps wasting.

SIGNS: Tenderness localized to the involved area is the most prominent sign. In the common variety (i.e., patellar tendinitis localized to the inferior pole of the patella), tenderness is best elicited by stabilizing the patella superiorly with one hand while directing localized pressure against the distal pole of the patella and the most proximal portion of the patellar tendon (Figure 19.55). Occasionally there is swelling localized to the involved area. There is almost never any generalized swelling of the knee. As mentioned, various abnormalities of the extensor mechanism with malalignment of the lower extremity are often present.

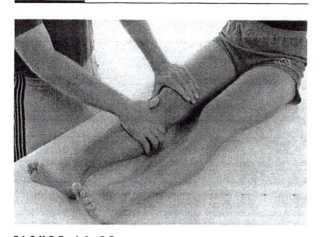

FIGURE 19.55
Patellar tendinitis
Stabilize the patella in order to elicit tenderness of the inferior pole of the patella and the proximal portion of the patellar tendon.

X-RAYS: Generally there is little to see on the AP and lateral X-ray views besides radiolucency and sometimes elongation and spurring of the distal pole. Evidence of old Osgood-Schlatter disease may be present. On the tangential view, there may be evidence of patellar instability, that is, lateral patellar tilting. A soft-tissue lateral X-ray may help to identify abnormalities of the tendon.

DIAGNOSIS: The diagnosis is purely clinical. One can grade the severity of the condition according to the symptoms (as outlined under the section on microtrauma).[96]

Phase I: Symptoms only after activity

Phase II: Symptoms during and after activity

Phase III: Symptoms present all the time

TREATMENT: The concept of microtrauma and the progressive nature of patellar tendinitis should be discussed with the athlete. An understanding of this concept by the athlete will facilitate a more successful therapeutic program.

CONSERVATIVE TREATMENT OF PHASES I AND II.

1.   Modification of activity if possible.

2.   Removal of any aggravating exercises such as heavy squatting.

3.   Icing and ice massage after activity, as well as at various intervals throughout the day.

4.   Ice massage or moist heat before activity, depending on which modality is more comfortable to the athlete.

5.   Use of a neoprene knee support with a ring to stabilize the patella if patellar instability is present.

6.   Once inflammation and pain are controlled, begin a progressive eccentric training program.

7.   Additional exercises listed under knee rehabilitation can be introduced with care not to aggravate the condition. The hamstrings should also be evaluated, with particular attention paid to flexibility and strength deficits (quadriceps to hamstring ratio).

8.   Use of in-shoe orthotic devices if indicated.

9.   Anti-inflammatory medication (for example, aspirin or ibuprofen taken an hour before practice).

CONSERVATIVE TREATMENT OF PHASE III.
When in Phase III, the athlete will have considerable difficulty maintaining an optimum level of athletic

performance. In addition to the treatment program outlined for Phases I and II, the following are suggested:

1. The advantages of modifying activity for a period of time should be discussed with the athlete.

2. It is advised that the athlete *not* receive an injection of a corticosteroid because of the potentially dangerous weakening of an already damaged tendon, and also because of the chronic nature of the condition, which tends to make the athlete desirous of repeated injections in spite of awareness of potential dangers. If a corticosteroid injection is given, it should be placed *around* the tendon and *not into it*. The athlete should understand that this injection is not to be repeated.

3. Iontophoresis, or ultrasound with hydrocortisone cream is sometimes useful.

4. Occasionally it is necessary to have the athlete walk in a postoperative knee splint, to rest the inflamed area.

5. TENS is sometimes useful in alleviating symptoms but does not appear to halt progression of the condition.

SURGICAL TREATMENT. Various surgical procedures, from localized excision of the necrotic area in the tendon to major patellar realignment with removal of necrotic material from the inferior pole of the patella, are currently used with relatively good results in selected cases.

On-Field Management of Knee Injuries

Those who are called upon to examine an athlete's knee at the site of injury should be familiar with a definite plan of action so that a quick, yet thorough, evaluation may be made. The on-field examination consists of the initial examination and the sideline examination.

Initial On-Field Examination

This examination is applicable when a decision must be made as to how the athlete will be removed from the field. In essence, the on-field examination is a *screening for ligament stability.* True, a dislocated patella or other serious injury may have occurred, but these are fairly obvious and there is no doubt that the athlete must be removed by means of a stretcher.

A brief history should be obtained as to the mechanism of injury and what the athlete experienced—whether there was a pop, snap, or tearing sensation and where the pain was initially felt. The player should then be asked to lie back and attempt to relax while the knee is being evaluated.

ON-FIELD TESTS FOR LIGAMENT STABILITY:

1. Outline the area of tenderness,

2. Apply valgus stress to the knee at both 0° and 30° of flexion.

3. Apply varus stress at both 0° and 30° of flexion.

4. Perform the Lachman test.

5. Apply anterior and posterior drawer tests with the knee at 90° and the foot fixed.

These tests should enable the examiner to make an accurate assessment as to the stability of the knee. From these findings, a decision should be made as to whether the player can be allowed to walk off the field or whether a stretcher should be used. If there is any doubt, get the stretcher! Do not allow the athlete to be carried off in a sitting position, as this can further disrupt an already damaged knee. The athlete should walk off only if the knee joint is completely stable and no other serious injury is found.

The Sideline Examination

When the athlete is at the sideline, both knees should be exposed. The shoe, sock, and tape of the affected limb should also be removed, so that circulation can be monitored. An ice bag should be applied to the knee while the history is reviewed.

The examiner should take great care to record the findings accurately. This is the ideal time to examine the knee, the so-called "golden period," as there is usually very little muscle spasm, swelling, or pain. These will undoubtedly develop later and will then preclude an exact and thorough examination.

Comparison between the healthy and the injured knee should be made at each stage of the examination.

1. Clearly define areas of tenderness.

2. Note any sign of hemarthrosis.

3. Check the range of movement, particularly with regard to hyperextension.

4. Test varus and valgus laxity at 0° and 30° of flexion.

5. Perform the Lachman test.

6. Place the knee at 90° and test the anterior drawer sign:

   a. in the neutral position

   b. with the foot externally rotated 15°

   c. with the foot internally rotated 10°

7. Test the posterior drawer sign at 90° of knee flexion (if positive, carefully monitor the peripheral circulation).

8. Perform pivot-shift tests:

   a. MacIntosh test

   b. jerk test of Hughston

   c. pivot-shift test in the lateral position (Slocum). These pivot-shift tests, if positive, suggest anterolateral rotatory instability. This might be found after an isolated anterior cruciate ligament rupture. Thus, these tests can be very useful in making this diagnosis when other tests are ambiguous

9. Carefully evaluate the patella for evidence of subluxation. Make sure of the integrity of the quadriceps and the patellar tendons.

10. Attempt McMurray's test of the menisci (not always possible because of pain and limitation of movement; Apley's test is sometimes used).

11. Check the peroneal nerve (sensation on the dorsal aspect of the foot; dorsiflexion of the foot).

12. Check the peripheral pulses.

MANAGEMENT: Apply ice and a postoperative knee splint if there is any evidence of ligament or patellar damage, and start the athlete on pain medication if this is necessary. If there is any suggestion of an unstable knee, the athlete should use crutches when walking and should not bear weight even though in a postoperative splint. The peripheral circulation should also be frequently monitored.

Order of Exclusion of Common Acute Knee Injuries

Table 19.20 presents a line of thinking that a trainer can follow when dealing with an acutely injured knee. Initially, it is important to observe any obvious abnormality, such as a fracture or a dislocated patella. With these conditions excluded, a history of sudden knee pain and disability means that a ligamentous tear is present, until proven otherwise. Once a ligament injury has been

---

TABLE 19.20 *Order of exclusion in an acute knee injury*

1. **LIGAMENT TEAR**
2. **PATELLAR SUBLUXATION**
3. Meniscal Tear
4. Osteochondral Fracture

---

excluded (within the limits of clinical evaluation), think of the possibility of patellar subluxation. Then examine for a meniscal tear. Finally, consider the possibility of an osteochondral fracture.

Criteria for Return to Play

The athletic trainer or sideline physician has to decide whether the athlete with a knee injury should return to play. Definite guidelines must be used to avoid further aggravation of an already injured structure (Table 19.21).

Rehabilitation of Injuries Involving the Knee

While designed primarily as a postoperative protocol following isolated anterior cruciate ligament (ACL) injury and reconstruction, the following exercises and timelines may be modified to accommodate a variety of both operative and nonoperative knee conditions.

   Over the past ten years a significant change has occurred with regard to the type and timeline of

---

TABLE 19.21 *Guidelines for return to play for an athlete with a knee injury*

1. If there is any instability during the examination, no return to play should be allowed.

2. If there is no evidence of any ligament instability or laxity, and the patella and the menisci appear normal, then the athlete should be put through a series of functional tests:

   a. Lean-hopping: the athlete hops on one leg while leaning, rotates 360° clockwise and then counterclockwise

   b. Duck-waddle

   c. Running-and-cutting: the athlete runs fairly rapidly over a 10-yard distance and then cuts to the right and then to the left

   d. Running backwards

   e. Running in figure eights: the athlete starts with fairly large figure eights, then rapidly does progressively smaller ones

If the athlete has no problem with these functional tests, return to play is permitted.

At no time should a local anesthetic or cortisone preparation be injected for the purpose of allowing the athlete to return to competition.

---

postoperative rehabilitation protocols. Shelbourne et al.,[39] observed during the mid 1980s that patients who failed to comply with the restrictions dictated by traditional rehabilitation protocols seemed to do better than those who were totally compliant. The noncompliant patients did not develop instability and, in fact, seemed to have a lower incidence of postoperative complications. Full range of motion was obtained more quickly and more completely, severe muscle atrophy was prevented or reversed sooner, and patellofemoral joint symptoms occurred less frequently. ACL protocols in effect at that time focused on protection of the new ligament through blocking of full extension and avoidance of active quadriceps function when the knee was in terminal extension.[97] In addition many of the protocols called for rigid immobilization with relatively long (6- to 8-week) periods of limited to non-weight bearing. Postoperative complications including joint stiffness and contractures, weakness, and patellofemoral problems were not uncommon. In addition, many patients had difficulty returning to pre-injury activity levels even after 9 to 12 months of rehabilitation. Given the results that they had observed among their noncompliant patients, Shelbourne et al.[39] devised a study to compare the subjective and objective results of the traditional program with a more aggressive rehabilitation protocol, incorporating: (1) early restoration of knee extension, (2) early weight bearing, and (3) use of closed-chain exercises to strengthen and improve lower extremity function. Their findings indicate that after ACL reconstruction, full knee motion and leg strength can be regained more quickly than previously thought, and without adverse effects on ligament stability. Additional advantages of the accelerated approach were:

1. Increased patient cooperation and compliance

2. Earlier return to normal function and athletic activities

3. Decrease in the incidence of patellofemoral joint symptoms

4. A marked decrease in the number of procedures required to attain full knee extension

The following protocol, in a somewhat modified form, was adapted from Shelbourne's findings.[98] The rehabilitation protocol can be broken down into three phases.

Acute/Preoperative Period

Emphasis should be placed on reducing swelling and inflammation and regaining full range of motion, strength, and normal gait. Traditional ICE or cryocuff, CPM, TENS, or EMS are helpful modalities. All muscles around the knee, hip, and ankle should be treated to develop strength and endurance insofar as the injury permits. Preoperative therapy familiarizes the athlete with exercises that will be performed during the immediate postoperative period. If the athlete's injury will necessitate future protective bracing, measuring and/or casting for a functional brace may also be done during the acute period. If swelling allows for preoperative brace fitting, it will permit the athlete to be in a functional brace as soon as possible, rather than waiting for return of normal bulk and girth of the surrounding musculature. Finally, contralateral limb rehabilitation may be started for possible crossover benefits.

Phase I

Includes the initial two weeks following surgery. The athlete is given five specific goals to work on during this period of time:

1. Full extension (passive only)

2. Wound healing

3. Quadriceps leg control (good quad set, no lag with straight leg raise)

4. Minimal swelling

5. Flexion to 90°

While protocols differ, many immediate postoperative programs incorporate use of CPM (continuous passive motion) devices to gently flex and extend the knee and a cryocuff to provide compression and cold and help control postoperative pain and swelling. Athletes with access to a CPM at home should be encouraged to use it as much as possible the first week postoperative.

The patient can begin work on extension on the evening of the operative day. Ten minutes of every hour should be spent attempting to allow the knee to relax into full extension. Full extension allows the correctly placed reconstructed ligament to fit into the intercondylar notch. Failure to achieve full extension within the first few weeks after surgery may allow the notch to fill with scar tissue, possibly leading to an extension block.[99]

Leg control is emphasized early after ACL reconstruction. Active quadriceps contraction with quad sets and straight leg raises mobilize the patella and lengthen the patellar tendon in order to avoid infrapatellar contracture.

In addition to full extension and leg control, active assisted motion to facilitate flexion is begun. Upon discharge from the hospital (usually day two) the athlete should be able to actively flex the knee to 90°. Active and assisted flexion off the side of the bed, as well as passive heel slides using a towel or sheet, will help to maintain and regain motion (Figure 19.56).

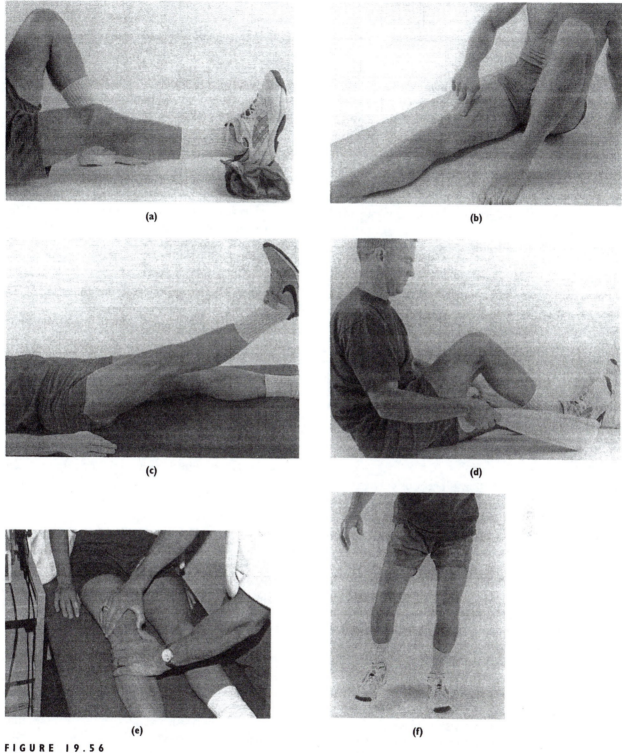

FIGURE 19.56

Phase I rehabilitation activities

(a) Passive knee extension—Athlete attempts to relax the leg, allowing the knee to drop into full extension. (b) Quadriceps sets—tighten and hold isometrically for 5–10 seconds. (c) Straight-leg raise—maintaining a good "quad set," the athlete attempts to raise the leg off the supporting surface without a lag. (d) Passive heel slide (with towel) to regain knee flexion ROM. (e) Patellar mobilization to minimize contractures and scarring. (f) Weight-shifting activities can be helpful in developing confidence during single-leg stance.

The patient is permitted to bear weight as tolerated with the aid of crutches, but is encouraged to be up and about only for bathroom privileges and meals. During the remainder of the time the patient is to rest, limit walking, and elevate the affected extremity.

During the second week of this two-week phase, patients are allowed some increase in activity, depending upon the amount of swelling in the knee. Regaining full-extension range of motion is the most critical factor in this phase. Prone knee-hangs may be added to help push the extension range. Wall slides, heel slides, and active assisted flexion over the edge of a table will help to restore flexion.

The patient is encouraged to progress from partial to full weight-bearing without crutches. Normal gait pattern should be encouraged as much as possible. Crutches are discontinued when the patient achieves full extension, has no quad lag, and can demonstrate a normal gait pattern. The patient should attempt to decrease use of the immobilizer at home and continue using it outside the house only as necessary until sufficient leg control has returned and gait is normalized. It is important to emphasize leg control early in the rehabilitation program. Through early extension, decreased use of the straight leg immobilizer, and normal gait, the patient should be able to regain good quadriceps tone and leg control.

Phase II

Phase II of the rehabilitation process usually encompasses weeks three to five postoperatively. During this phase patients are encouraged to develop a normal gait pattern and gradually resume normal activities. Walking without aids and without a limp probably does more to encourage early return of quadriceps strength than any specific exercise.[97] It is imperative that the patient maintain full extension with minimal swelling. While 90° of flexion is the goal of the initial postoperative phase, phase II is a time to work on improving flexion. Most patients achieve full ROM (full extension to 135° flexion) five weeks after reconstruction.

Closed kinetic chain exercises are advocated as soon as weight bearing of the involved extremity is possible. Closed-chain activities place functional stresses on the joint and extremity in ways similar to normal weight-bearing activities. In addition, closed-chain exercises minimize patellofemoral stress and do not produce significant stress to the reconstructed ACL ligament.[100] Knee bends, leg presses, step-ups, and calf raises all begin at about two weeks post-operatively. Bicycling and swimming workouts may also be initiated during this phase. Initially the bike is used as a mechanical means of attaining flexion, but once the patient has gained approximately 120° of flexion the bike may be used for endurance and strengthening workouts. Stairclimbing workouts can also usually begin at two to three weeks postoperatively (Figure 19.57).

Phase III

Phase III of the rehabilitation process starts at about five to eight weeks postoperatively. Emphasis during this phase is on functional return to activity. At this point the athlete should have attained full range of motion. Quad function and tone should be well established by this time (70 percent of contralateral side). Low impact, functional activities such as speed walking, lateral shifts (running from side to side while not allowing legs to cross midline), slide board activities, and rope jumping can be started. These activities should be performed initially while wearing an activity brace. Return to a running program is allowed only when the athlete is without inflammation; has full range of motion; and has sufficient leg strength, endurance, and proprioception to successfully complete the functional activities described above.

As the athlete's strength and function continue to improve, more vigorous agility drills are added. Carriocas, figure-of-eights, backward running, position changes while running in place, bounding, and jumping activities can all be introduced. Half-speed progressing to full-speed sprints can be added as the athlete proves ready. Numerous functional progressions exist.[97,101] It may take two to three months of sport-specific training before the athlete is capable of performing at a normal level.[102] Return to sport is allowed based upon the level of twisting activity required of the particular sport, as well as upon full completion of a functional rehabilitation program. Range of motion must be full, no effusion may be present, strength tests (both isokinetic and functional) must demonstrate greater than 90 percent of the uninvolved leg, and stability should be good.[103]

Performance testing should assess leg strength, power, endurance, balance, and impact conditioning (plyometrics). Activities such as single-leg hopping, vertical jumping for height, speed running, and sport-specific drills are frequently utilized to assess functional capacity. Table 19.22 lists return-to-sport timelines for various levels of activities (Figure 19.58).

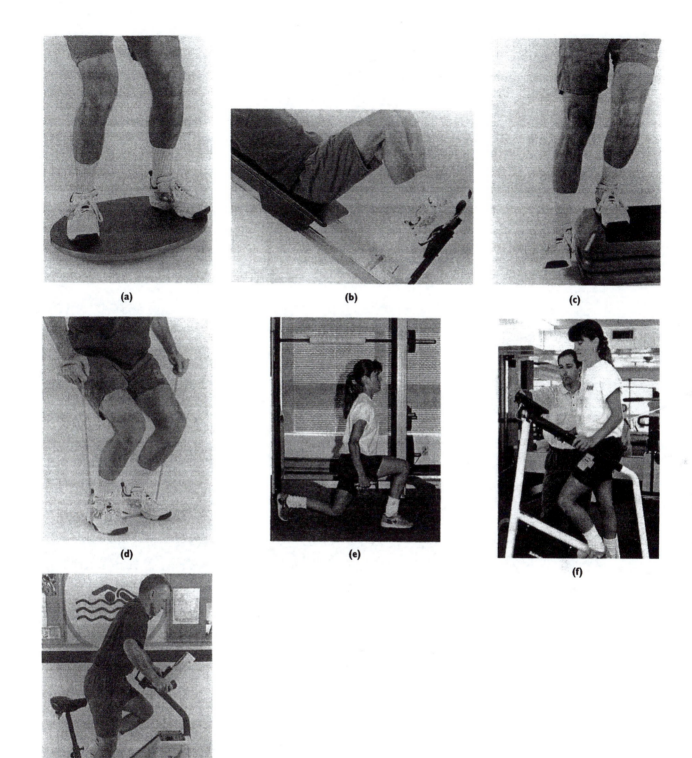

(a)

(b)

(c)

(d)

(e)

(f)

(g)

FIGURE 19.57

Phase II rehabilitation activities

Phase II activities include continued work on balance and stabilization. In addition, closed-chain activities for lower extremity strength and endurance are introduced. (a) Balance board; (b) Leg press; (c) Eccentric stepping; (d) Shallow squats against elastic resistance; (e) Lunges; (f) Stairclimbers; (g) Stationary cycling.

FIGURE 19.58

Phase III rehabilitation activities
Progressively demanding activities for balance, strength, and endurance are introduced; some of the many possible activities are illustrated. (a) Slide board; (b) Forward running against elastic resistance; (c) Side slide (defensive position) against an elastic resistance; (d) "Quick foot" drill; (e) Side step-up for strength and balance; (f) Modified lunge.

X-ray Views of the Knee

Following is a brief review of some of the views commonly used in a knee examination.

1. *Anteroposterior view.* The anteroposterior (AP) view is best taken with the athlete standing with both knees on the same plate, so that a comparison of the joint spaces (particularly the medial joint space) can be made.

In acute knee injuries, there should be a careful examination of the lateral aspect of the knee, particularly of the lateral tibial plateau where a lateral capsular sign may be found (Figure 19.59).[104] This sign is an indication that serious ligamentous damage has ccurred, and it usually denotes a rupture of the anterior cruciate ligament.

2. *Lateral view.* The lateral view should be taken with the knee bent approximately 30°, in order to standardize measurements of the patellar tendon and the patella. A rule of thumb: If the patellar tendon length exceeds the patellar length by 1 cm or more it is consid-

TABLE 19.22   *Return to sports following anterior cruciate ligament reconstruction*

Time Frame	Criteria	Sport Level
1 to 2 Months	80% PROM No effusion	**Class I** (Cycling, swimming, walking)
3 Months	90% PROM Good stability No effusion 70–80% of isokinetic quad strength	**Class II** (Running, mountain biking, intermediate roller blading, hiking)
4 to 5 Months	Full PROM No effusion Good stability 80% of isokinetic quad strength Good sport specific functional strength	**Class III** (Recreational tennis, recreational skiing, snow boarding, hockey)
5 to 8 Months	Full AROM No effusion and good stability 90–100% of isokinetic quad and hamstring strength Normal functional strength compared to opposite side	**Class IV** (Contact/cleated/racquet sports, competitive skiing, competition sports)

(Source: Wasilewski, Koth: Effect of surgical timing on return to athletic activity after significant knee injury. *Sports Medicine (Adis International)*, Auckland, New Zealand. 18(3):156–161, 1994.)

ered a patella alta (Figure 19.60).[63] Patella infera is indicated by a reverse ratio. The femoral condyles should be observed for any osteochondral defect.

3. *Tunnel view.* The tunnel view is a postero-anterior view taken with the knee bent a varying number of degrees. It is used to visualize the femoral condyles, particularly when looking for osteochondral fractures or osteochondritis dissecans.

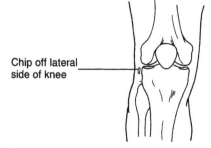

FIGURE 19.59
Lateral capsular sign
A chip off the lateral side of the knee following an acute knee injury is suggestive of a major internal derangement, especially an anterior cruciate ligament tear. When seen on X-ray it is called the "lateral capsular sign."

Chip off lateral side of knee

4. *Tangential views.* Tangential views are used to obtain information about the patella and the patellofemoral articulation. There are a number of views presently in common use and each has certain limitations. It may therefore be useful to take more than one tangential view when a patellar lesion is suspected (Figure 19.61).

   a. *Sunrise view:* The knee is bent nearly into full flexion, so that views of the inferior surface of the patella can be obtained in cases of a suspected osteochondral fracture.

   b. *Hughston view:* The knee is bent approximately 45°, with the tube angle at 30°. This gives a useful view of the intercondylar notch as well as the articulation of the patella in the groove. However, the X-ray beam contacts the plate at an angle and thereby distorts the appearance of the joint.

   c. *Merchant view:* The knees are bent approximately 30° with the plate placed on the tibia and held in place by a special piece of equipment. The Merchant view gives an accurate estimation of the intercondylar notch, the congruency angle, and the situation of the patellae.

   d. *Laurin view:* The Laurin view is the same as the Merchant view except that the plate is placed on the thigh and the X-ray tube is held near

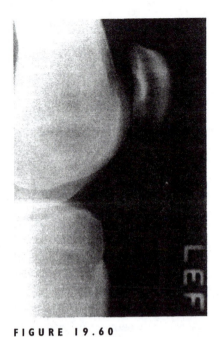

FIGURE 19.60
Patella alta
If the distance from the tibial tubercle to the inferior pole of the patella is 1.2 cm greater than the distance from the inferior to the superior pole of the patella, a patella alta should be suspected.

the feet. Advantages of this technique are: (1) no special piece of apparatus is needed, as the athlete can hold the plate, and (2) the X-ray beam contacts the plate at 90°, giving an undistorted picture. It also gives an accurate assessment of the location and articulation of the patella, particularly with regard to subluxation or tilting. The disadvantage is the dose of radiation the patient receives.

5. *Stress views:*

  a. *AP stress view:* Used to demonstrate medial or lateral joint opening in collateral ligament rupture or an epiphyseal opening when a fracture through the epiphysis has occurred in the pre-adolescent and the adolescent. Stress is applied in either the valgus or varus direction with the knee at 0° or 30° of flexion.

  b. *Lateral stress views:* The knee is flexed to 90°. The anterior and the posterior drawer tests are attempted, in order to demonstrate incompetency of the anterior or posterior cruciate ligaments. Comparison X-rays of the opposite limb are always taken (Figure 19.62).

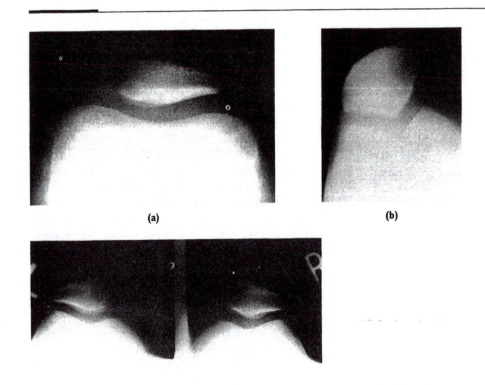

(a)

(b)

(c)

FIGURE 19.61
Tangential views of the patella
(a) Sunrise view; (b) Hughston view; (c) Merchant view.

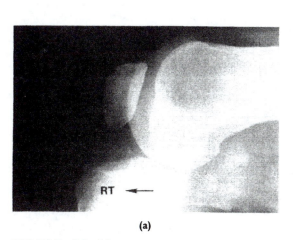
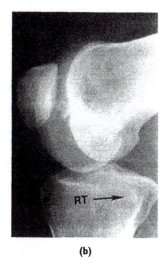

(a)   **(b)**

FIGURE 19.62
X-ray—knee, (lateral view)
(a) anteriorly directed stress; (b) posteriorly directed stress. Note the anterior laxity of the tibia on the femur in (a) as compared with the normal position (b).

REFERENCES

1. Kapandji IA: *The Physiology of the Joints.* London, E & S Livingston, 1970.

2. Lindahl O, Movin A: The mechanics of extension of the knee-joint. *Acta Orthop Scand* 38:226–234, 1967.

3. Hallen LG, Lindahl O: The "screw-home" movement in the knee joint. *Acta Orthop Scand* 37:97–106, 1966.

4. Warren LF, Marshall JL, Girgis F: The prime static stabilizer of the medial side of the knee. *J Bone Joint Surg* 56A:665–674, 1974.

5. Kennedy JC, Weinberg HW, Wilson AS: The anatomy and function of the anterior cruciate ligament. *J Bone Joint Surg* 56A:223–235, 1974.

6. Smillie IS: *Injuries of the Knee Joint.* Edinburgh, Churchill Livingstone, fifth edition, 1978, p. 71.

7. Jackson DW, Feagin JA: Quadriceps contusion in the young athlete: Relation of severity of injury to treatment and prognosis. *J Bone Joint Surg* 55A:95–105, 1973.

8. Kalenak A, Medlan CE, Fleagle SB, et al: Treating thigh contusions with ice. *Phys Sportsmed* 3:65–67, March 1975.

9. Jokl P, Federico J: Myositis ossificans traumatica. Association with hemophilia (factor X1 deficiency) in a football player. *JAMA* 237:2215–2216, 1977.

10. Muckle DS: Associated factors in recurrent groin and hamstring injuries. *Brit J Sports Med* 16:37–39, 1982.

11. Zernicke R, Garhammer J, Jobe F: Human patellar tendon rupture. *J Bone Joint Surg* 59A:179–183, 1977.

12. Pope MH, Johnson RJ, Brown DW, et al: The role of the musculature in injuries to the medial collateral ligament. *J Bone Joint Surg* 61A:398–402, 1979.

13. Callahan WT, Crowley FJ, Hafner JK: A statewide study designed to determine methods of reducing injury in interscholastic football competition by equipment modification. New York State Public High School Athletic Association, Albany, 1971.

14. Mueller FO, Blyth CS: North Carolina High School Football Injury Study: Equipment and prevention. *J Sports Med* 2:1–10, 1974.

15. Torg JS, Quedenfeld TC, Landau S: The shoe-surface interface and its relationship to football knee injuries. *Am J Sports Med* 2:261–269, 1974.

16. Stanitski CL, McMaster JH, Ferguson RJ: Synthetic turf and grass: A comparison study. *J Sports Med* 2:22–26, 1974.

17. Ryan AJ: Moderator of Round Table on: Artificial Turf: Pros and Cons. *Phys Sportsmed* 3:41–50, February 1975.

18. De Haven KE: Diagnosis of acute knee injuries with hemarthrosis. *Am J Sports Med* 8:9–14, 1980.

19. Noyes FR, Bassett RW, Grood ES, et al: Arthroscopy in acute traumatic hemarthrosis of the knee. Incidence of anterior cruciate tears and other injuries. *J Bone Joint Surg* 62A:687–695, 1980.

20. Slocum DB, Larson RL: Rotatory instability of the knee and its pathogenesis and clinical test to demonstrate its presence. *J Bone Joint Surg* 50A:211–225, 1968.

21. Torg JS, Conrad W, Kalen V: Clinical diagnosis of anterior cruciate ligament instability in the athlete. *Am J Sports Med* 4:84–93, 1976.

22. Galway RD, Beaupré A, MacIntosh DL: Pivot shift: a clinical sign of symptomatic anterior cruciate insufficiency. *J Bone Joint Surg* 54B:763–764, 1972.

23. Cabaud HE, Slocum DB: The diagnosis of chronic anterolateral rotatory instability of the knee. *Am J Sports Med* 5:99–105, 1977.

24. Slocum DB, James SL, Larson RL, et al: Clinical test for anterolateral rotatory instability of the knee. *Clin Orthop* 118:63–69, 1976.

25. Derscheid GL, Garrick JG: Medial collateral ligament injuries in football. Nonoperative management of grade I and grade II sprains. *Am J Sports Med* 9:365–368, 1981.

26. Steadman JR: Rehabilitation of 1st- and 2nd-degree sprains of the medial collateral ligament. *Am J Sports Med* 7:300–302, 1979.

27. Reider B, Sathy MR, Talkington J, Blyznak N, Kollias S: Treatment of isolated medial collateral ligament injuries in athletes with early functional rehabilitation—A five year follow-up study. *Am J Sports Med* 22:470–477, 1994.

28. Garrick J, Webb D: *Sports Injuries: Diagnosis and Management*. Philadelphia, WB Saunders, 1990.

29. Inoue M, McGurk-Burleson E, Hollis JM, Woo S: Treatment of the medial collateral ligament injury, I: The importance of anterior cruciate ligament on the varus-valgus knee laxity. *Am J Sports Med*, 15 (1): 15–21, 1987.

30. Marshall JL, Rubin RM, Wang JB, et al: The anterior cruciate ligament: The diagnosis and treatment of its injuries and their serious prognostic implications. *Orthop Rev* 7:35–46, 1978.

31. Campbell WC: Reconstruction of the ligaments of the knee. *Am J Surg* 43:47–480, 1939.

32. Chick RR, Jackson DW: Tears of the anterior cruciate ligament in young athletes. *J Bone Joint Surg* 60A:970–973, 1978.

33. Ellasaser JC, Reynolds FC, Omohyndro JR: The non-operative treatment of collateral ligament injuries of the knee in professional football players. An analysis of seventy-four injuries treated non-operatively and twenty-four injuries treated surgically. *J Bone Joint Surg* 56A:1185–1190, 1974.

34. Slocum DB, Larson RL, James SL: Late reconstruction of ligamentous injuries of the medial compartment of the knee. *Clin Orthop* 100:23–55, 1974.

35. Alm A, Gillquist J: Reconstruction of the anterior cruciate ligament by using the medial third of the patellar ligament. Treatment and results. *Acta Chir Scand* 140:289–296, 1974.

36. Jones KG: Reconstruction of the anterior cruciate ligament using the central one-third of the patellar ligaments. A follow-up report. *J Bone Joint Surg* 52A:1302–1308, 1970.

37. Blair D, Wills R: Rapid rehabilitation following anterior cruciate ligament reconstruction. *JNATA* 26:32–40, Spring 1991.

38. Wilk K, Andrews J: Current concepts in the treatment of anterior cruciate ligament disruption. *J Orthop Sports Phys Ther* 15:279–293, 1992.

39. Shelbourne DK, Nitz PA: Accelerated rehabilitation after anterior cruciate ligament reconstruction. *Am J Sports Med* 18:292–299, 1990.

40. Rosenberg TD, Paulos LE, Parker RD, Abbott PJ: Arthroscopic surgery of the knee: In *Operative Orthopaedics*, Vol 3, edited by Chapman MW. Philadelphia, JB Lippincott, pp. 1585–1604, 1988.

41. Kennedy JC: Posterior cruciate ligament injuries. *Orthop Digest* 7:19–31, 1979.

42. Loos WC, Fox JM, Blazina ME, et al: Acute posterior cruciate ligament injuries. *Am J Sports Med* 9:86–92, 1981.

43. Lysholm J, Gillquist J, Liljedahl SO: Arthroscopy in the early diagnosis of injuries to the knee joint. *Acta Orthop Scand* 52:111–118, 1981.

44. Flemming Jr, RE, Blatz DJ, McCarroll JR: Posterior problems in the knee. Posterior cruciate insufficiency and postero-lateral rotatory insufficiency. *Am J Sports Med* 9:107–113, 1981.

45. Hughston JC: A simple meniscectomy. *J Sports Med* 3:179–187, 1975.

46. Feagin JA: The syndrome of the torn anterior cruciate ligament. *Orthop Clin North Am* 10:81–90, 1979.

47. Arnold JA, Coker TP, Heaton LM: Natural history of anterior cruciate tears. *Am J Sports Med* 7:305–313, 1979.

48. Wasilewski S, Covall D, Cohen S: Effect of surgical timing on recovery and associated injuries after anterior cruciate ligament reconstruction. *Am J Sports Med* 21 (3):338–342, 1993.

49. Feagin JA, Walton CW: Isolated tear of the anterior cruciate ligament. Five year follow-up. *Am J Sports Med* 4:95–100, 1976.

50. Feagin JA, Abbott HG, Rokous JR: The isolated tear of the anterior cruciate ligament. *J Bone Joint Surg* 54A:1340–1341, 1972.

51. Youmans WT: The so-called "isolated" anterior cruciate ligament syndrome: A report of 32 cases with some observations on treatment and its effect on results. *Am J Sports Med* 6:26–30, 1978.

52. Jacobsen K: Osteoarthrosis following insufficiency of the cruciate ligaments in man. *Acta Orthop Scand* 48:520–526, 1977.

53. Yocum LA, Kerlan RK, Jobe FW, et al: Isolated lateral meniscectomy: a study of 26 patients with isolated tears. *J Bone Joint Surg* 61A:338–342, 1979.

54. Smillie IS: *Injuries of the Knee Joint*. Edinburgh, Churchill Livingstone, fifth edition, 1978, p. 92.

55. Kaplan EB: Discoid lateral meniscus of the knee joint. *J Bone Joint Surg* 39A:77–87, 1957.

56. DeLee J, Drez D: *Orthopaedic Sports Medicine: Principles and Practice*, Vol I, II. Philadelphia: WB Saunders, 1994.

57. O'Meara P: The basic science of meniscus repair. *Orthop Rev* 22 (6):681–686, 1993.

58. Arnoczky S, Warren R: Microvasculature of the human meniscus. *Am J Sports Med* 10:90 1982.

59. Arnoczky SP: Arthroscopic surgery: Meniscal healing. *Contemp Orthop* 10:31, 1985.

60. Barber F: Accelerated rehabilitation for meniscus repairs. *Arthroscopy* 10 (2):206–210, 1994.

61. Mc Laughlin J, Demaio R, Noyes F, Mangine R: Rehabilitation after meniscus repair. *Orthop* 17 (5):463–471, 1994.

62. Wilson JN: A diagnostic sign in osteochondritis dissecans of the knee. *J Bone Joint Surg* 49A:477–480, 1967.

63. Lancourt JE, Cristini JA: Patella alta and patella infera. Their etiological role in patellar dislocation, chondromalacia and apophysitis of the tibial tubercle. *J Bone Joint Surg* 57A:1112–1115, 1975.

64. Brattstrom H: Shape of the intercondylar groove normally and in recurrent dislocation of the patella. *Acta Orthop Scand Suppl* 68:1–148, 1964.

65. Larson RL: Subluxation-dislocation of the patella. In *The Injured Adolescent Knee*, edited by Kennedy JC. Baltimore, Williams and Wilkins, 1979, pp. 161–204.

66. Larson RL, Cabaud HE, Slocum DB, et al: The patellar compression syndrome. *Clin Orthop Rel Res* 134:158–167, 1978.

67. Ehrat M, Edwards J, Hastings D, Worrell T: Reliability of assessing patellar alignment: The A angle. *J Orthop Sports Phys Ther* 19:22–27, 1994.

68. Wiberg G: Roentgenographic and anatomic studies on the femopatellar joint. *Acta Orthop Scand* 12:319–410, 1941.

69. Baumgartl F: *Das Kniegelenk, Berlin,* Springer-Verlag, 1944.

70. *Athletic Training and Sports Medicine.* American Academy of Orthopaedic Surgeons, Chicago 1984.

71. Zimbler S, Smith J, Scheller A, et al: Recurrent subluxation and dislocation of the patella in association with athletic injuries. Symposium on sports injuries. *Orthop Clin North Am* 11:755–770, 1980.

72. Hughston JC: Subluxation of the patella. *J Bone Joint Surg* 50A:1003–1026, 1968.

73. Merchant AC, Mercer RL, Jacobsen RH, et al: Roentgenographic analysis of patellofemoral congruence. *J Bone Joint Surg* 56A:1391–1396, 1974.

74. McConnell J: McConnell patellofemoral course notes. Seattle, Washington, 1990.

75. Leach RE: Malalignment syndrome of the patella. *Instructional course lectures.* St Louis, CV Mosby Company, Vol 25, 1976, pp. 49–54.

76. Insall J, Faivo KA, Wise DW: Chondromalacia patellae. A prospective study. *J Bone Joint Surg* 58A:1–8, 1976.

77. Goodfellow JW, Hungerford DS, Woods C: Patellofemoral mechanics and pathology. II. Chondromalacia patellae. *J Bone Joint Surg* 58B:291–299, 1976.

78. Insall JN: Current concepts review. Patellar pain. *J Bone Joint Surg* 64A: 147–152, 1982.

79. Felder CR, Leeson MA: Patellofemoral pain syndrome—The use of EMG biofeedback for training the vastus medialis obliquus in patients with patellofemoral pain. Protocol from Thought Technology, 1990.

80. Ficat R, Hungerford: *Disorders of the Patellofemoral Joint.* Baltimore: Williams and Wilkins, 1977.

81. James SL: Chondromalacia of the patella in the adolescent. In *The Injured Adolescent Knee,* edited by Kennedy JC. Baltimore, Williams and Wilkins, 1979, pp. 205–251.

82. Goodfellow JW, Hungerford DS, Zindel M: Patellofemoral mechanics and pathology. I. Functional anatomy of the patello-femoral joint. *J Bone Joint Surg* 52B:287–290, 1976.

83. Brookes M, Helal B: Primary osteoarthritis, venous engorgement and asteogenesis. *J Bone Joint Surg* 50 B:493–504, 1968.

84. Insall J: Chondromalacia patellae: Patellar malalignment syndrome. *Orthop Clin North Am* 10:117–127, 1979.

85. Hungerford D, Lennox D: Rehabilitation of the knee in disorders of the patellofemoral joint: Relevant biomechanics: *Orthop Clinics of North America* 14:397–402, April 1983.

86. McConnell J: The management of chondromalacia patellae: A long term solution. *Aus J Physiother* 32:215–223, 1986.

87. Levine J: A new brace for chondromalacia patellae and kindred conditions. *Am J Sports Med* 6:137–140, 1978.

88. Merchant AC, Mercer RL: Lateral release of the patella. A preliminary report. *Clin Orthop* 103:40–45, 1974.

89. Micheli LJ, Stanitski CL: Lateral patellar retinacular release. *Am J Sports Med* 9:330–336, 1981.

90. Hughston JC: Reconstruction of the extensor mechanism for subluxating patella. *Am J Sports Med* 1:6–13, 1972.

91. Maquet PGJ: *Biomechanics of the Knee.* New York: Springer-Verlag, 1976, pp. 134–143.

92. Weaver JK: Bipartite patellae as a cause of disability in the athlete. *Am J Sports Med* 5:137–143, 1977.

93. Patel D: Arthroscopy of the plicae-synovial folds and their significance. *Am J Sports Med* 6:217–225, 1978.

94. Hughston JC, Andrews JR: The suprapatellar plica and internal derangement. Proceedings of the American Academy of Orthopaedic Surgeons. *J Bone Joint Surg* 55A:1318, 1973.

95. Hardacker Jr WT, Whipple TL, Bassett FH: Diagnosis and treatment of the plica syndrome of the knee. *J Bone Joint Surg* 62A:221–225, 1980.

96. Blazina ME, Kerlan RK, Jobe FW, et al: Jumper's knee. *Orthop Clin North Am* 4:665–678, 1973.

97. Shelbourne K, Klootwyk T, DeCarlo M: Update on accelerated rehabilitation after anterior cruciate ligament reconstruction. *J Orthop Sports Phys Ther* 15:303–316, 1992.

98. DeCarlo M, Shelbourne D, McCarrol J, Rettig A: Traditional versus accelerated rehabilitation following ACL reconstruction: A one-year follow-up. *J Orthop Sports Phys Ther* 15:309–316, 1992.

99. DeCarlo M: Notes on ACL Reconstruction Rehabilitation Program. Presented March 10–12 at 1994 Sports Rehabilitation Conference, San Diego, CA, 1994.

100. Fu F, Woo S, Irrgang J: Current concepts for rehabilitation following anterior cruciate ligament reconstruction. *J Orthop Sports Phys Ther* 15:270–278, 1992.

101. Mangine R, Noyes F: Rehabilitation of the allograft reconstruction. *J Ortho Sport Phys Ther* 15:295–302, 1992.

102. Malone T, Garrett W: Commentary and historical perspective of anterior cruciate ligament reconstruction. *J Ortho Sports Phys Ther* 15:265–269, 1992.

103. Wasilewski S, Koth J: Effect of surgical timing on return to athletic activity after significant knee injury. *Sports Medicine (Adis International),* Auckland: New Zealand. 18:156–161, 1994.

104. Woods GW, Stanley RF, Tullos HS: Lateral capsular sign: X-ray clue to a significant knee instability. *Am J Sports Med* 7:27–33, 1979.

RECOMMENDED READINGS

Butler DL, Noyes FR, Grood ES: Ligamentous restraints to anterior-posterior drawer in the human knee. *J Bone Joint Surg* 62A:259–270, 1980.

DeLee J, Drez D: *Orthopaedic Sports Medicine: Principles and Practice,* Vol I, II. Philadelphia: WB Saunders, 1994.

Detnbeck LC: Function of the cruciate ligaments in knee stability. *J Sports Med* 2:217–221, 1974.

Ellison AE: Skiing injuries. *CIBA Clinical Symposia* 29:3–40, 1977.

Ficat PR, Hungerford DS: *Disorders of the Patellofemoral Joint.* Baltimore, Williams and Wilkins, 1978.

Goldfuss AJ, Morehouse CA, LeVeau BF: Effects of muscular tension on knee stability. *Med Sci Sports* 4:267–271, 1973.

Greenfield B: *Rehabilitation of the Knee: A Problem-Solving Approach.* Philadelphia: FA Davis, 1993.

Hughston JC, Andrews JR, Cross MJ, et al: Classification of knee ligament instabilities. Part I. The medial compartment and cruciate ligaments. *J Bone Joint Surg* 58A:159–172, 1976.

Hughston JC, Andrews JR, Cross MJ, et al: Classification of knee ligament instabilities. Part II. The lateral compartment. *J Bone Joint Surg* 58A: 173–179, 1976.

Kennedy JC editor: *The Injured Adolescent Knee.* Baltimore: Williams and Wilkins, 1979.

Larson RL: Dislocations and ligamentous injuries of the knee. In *Fractures,* edited by Rockwood Jr, CA, Green DP. Philadelphia: JB Lippincott, Vol 2, 1975, pp. 1182–1260.

McLaughlin, Demaio, Noyes, Mangine: Rehabilitation after meniscus repair. *Orthop* 17 (5):463–471, 1994.

Outerbridge RE: The etiology of chondromalacia patellae. *J Bone Joint Surg* 43B:752–757, 1961.

Ritter MA, Gosling C: *The Knee: A Guide to the Examination and Diagnosis of Ligament Injuries.* Springfield Ill.: Charles C Thomas, 1981.

Staudte HW, Brussatis F: Selective changes in size and distribution of fibre types in vastus muscle from cases of different knee joint affections. *Z Rheumatol* 36:143–160, 1977.

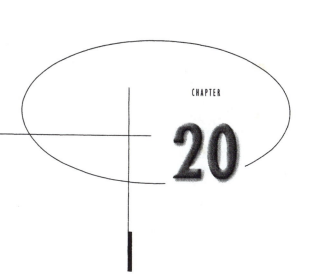

Lower Leg, Ankle, and Foot Injuries

CHAPTER

20

Ankle injuries are very common in many sports and in some athletic activities. These injuries (i.e., basketball) may rank first in the incidence of injuries. Because only a few sports don't require running and jumping, particpants in almost all athletic events (with only a few exceptions such as swimming) can expect lower leg, ankle, or foot injuries.

Functional Anatomy of the Lower Leg, Ankle, and Foot

The Lower Leg

The bones of the lower leg are the tibia and the fibula. The tibia is the larger of the two, articulating with the knee superiorly and with the ankle inferiorly. It has an anterior crest and a posteromedial crest, both of which can be palpated subcutaneously. The medial malleolus forms the inner ankle bone.

The fibula articulates with the tibia both superiorly and inferiorly, and bears very little of the body's weight. It does not articulate with the knee; but inferiorly it forms the lateral malleolus, to which are attached the lateral ankle ligaments. At the ankle the fibula articulates with the tibia and the talus.

The muscles of the lower leg are divided by thick fascial sheaths into four distinct compartments (Figure

20.1). These compartments can give rise to symptoms when the pressure within them becomes excessive. The *anterior compartment*, the one that most frequently develops symptoms, consists of the anterior tibial, extensor hallucis longus, and extensor digitorum muscles. Within these muscles are the deep peroneal nerve and the anterior tibial artery. *The lateral compartment*, composed of the peroneal muscles, contains the superficial peroneal nerve. The *deep posterior compartment* is made up of the posterior tibial, flexor digitorum longus, and flexor hallucis longus muscles; and the *superficial posterior compartment* is made up of the gastrocnemius, soleus, and plantaris muscles.

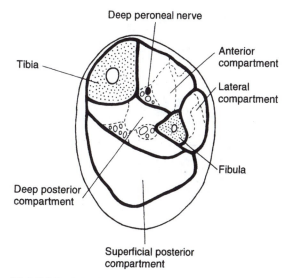

FIGURE 20.1
A cross-sectional view of the compartments of the lower leg

The reader is reminded to refer to other chapters (i.e., Chapter 21, Injuries to the Running Athlete, Particularly The Long Distance Runner) for additional information on injuries to the lower extremity.

FUNCTIONAL ANATOMY OF THE LOWER LEG, ANKLE, AND FOOT | 401

MUSCLE ORIGIN, INSERTION, AND FUNCTION:

1. *Tibialis anterior:* From the lateral condyle and upper portion of the lateral surface of the tibia to the medial cuneiform and base of the first metatarsal. *Function:* Dorsiflexes and supinates the foot and gently lowers the foot to the ground during the initial contact phase of standing (Figure 20.2).

2. *Extensor hallucis longus:* From the fibula and interosseous membrane to the dorsal surface of the base of the distal phalanx of the first toe. *Function:* Dorsiflexes the ankle and extends the first toe.

3. *Extensor digitorum longus:* From the anterior surface of the fibula, the lateral condyle of the tibia, and the interosseous membrane to the common extensor tendon of the lateral four toes. *Function:* Dorsiflexes the foot and extends the toes.

4. *Tibialis posterior:* From the interosseous membrane between the tibia and fibula to the navicular and cuneiforms. *Function:* Plantar flexes and supinates the foot.

5. *Flexor hallucis longus:* From the posterior surface of the fibula to the base of the distal phalanx of the great toe. *Function:* Plantar flexes the ankle and flexes the great toe.

6. *Flexor digitorum longus:* From the posterior surface of the shaft of the tibia to the distal phalanges of the lateral toes. *Function:* Plantar flexes the ankle and flexes the toes.

7. *Peroneus longus:* From the lateral surface of the fibula to the lateral side of the first metatarsal base and medial cuneiform. *Function:* Everts the foot and plantar flexes the ankle.

8. *Peroneus brevis:* From the lower two-thirds of the lateral surface of the fibula to the base of the fifth metatarsal. *Function:* Everts the foot and plantar flexes the ankle.

9. *Peroneus tertius:* From the lower third of the anterior surface of the fibula to the dorsal surface of the base of the fifth metatarsal. *Function:* Dorsiflexes the ankle and everts the foot.

10. *Gastrocnemius:* Has two heads, one from the lateral and one from the medial condyle of the femur posteriorly to the Achilles tendon. *Function:* Flexes the knee, plantar flexes the ankle, and supinates the foot.

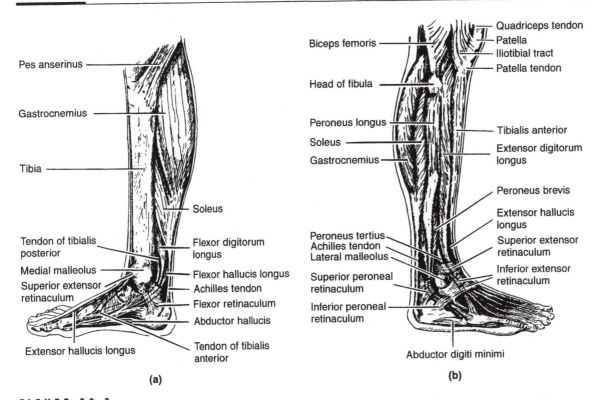

(a)

Pes anserinus
Gastrocnemius
Tibia
Soleus
Tendon of tibialis posterior
Flexor digitorum longus
Medial malleolus
Flexor hallucis longus
Superior extensor retinaculum
Achilles tendon
Flexor retinaculum
Abductor hallucis
Extensor hallucis longus
Tendon of tibialis anterior

(b)

Biceps femoris
Quadriceps tendon
Patella
Iliotibial tract
Patella tendon
Head of fibula
Peroneus longus
Tibialis anterior
Soleus
Extensor digitorum longus
Gastrocnemius
Peroneus brevis
Extensor hallucis longus
Peroneus tertius
Superior extensor retinaculum
Achilles tendon
Lateral malleolus
Inferior extensor retinaculum
Superior peroneal retinaculum
Inferior peroneal retinaculum
Abductor digiti minimi

FIGURE 20.2

(a) Muscles on the medial aspect of the lower leg; (b) Muscles on the lateral aspect of the lower leg

11. *Soleus:* From the posterior aspect of the head of the fibula and the medial border of the tibia to the Achilles tendon. *Function:* Plantar flexes the ankle and supinates the foot.

12. *Plantaris:* From the lateral condyle of the femur posteriorly to the Achilles or directly into the calcaneus. *Function:* Plantar flexes the foot and slightly flexes the knee.

ACHILLES TENDON: This is the common tendon of the gastrocnemius and soleus muscles, which unite distally to form it in conjunction with the plantaris muscle that lies between the gastrocnemius and the soleus. The Achilles inserts into the calcaneus.

Two bursae surround the Achilles, one between the skin and the Achilles (subcutaneous bursa) and the other between the Achilles and the calcaneus (retrocalcaneal bursa). The Achilles is surrounded by a peritendon, or, as it is sometimes called, a *paratenon* (there is no true synovial sheath), which allows it free movement against the surrounding tissue (Figure 20.3).

AREA POSTERIOR TO THE MALLEOLI: Running posteriorly to the medial malleolus are the posterior tibial, flexor digitorum longus, and flexor hallucis longus tendons; the posterior tibial artery; and the posterior tibial nerve (which divides and gives off the medial calcaneal nerve). Behind the lateral malleolus run the tendons of the peroneus longus and brevis. Covering these structures is a thick retinaculum.

The Ankle

Because the bony ankle is shaped like a mortise and tenon, it functions as a hinged joint and allows movement in one plane only—flexion and extension. The mortise is formed by the lateral malleolus of the fibula and by the undersurface and medial malleolus of the tibia. The tenon is the talus, which fits into the mortise. The talus is wider anteriorly, allowing it to fit more snugly into the mortise when the ankle is in dorsiflexion. Conversely, when the ankle moves into plantar flexion, the narrower part of the talus moves into the mortise, resulting in instability and predisposing the ankle to injury.[1]

The ligaments around the ankle are frequently injured and should be well known to the athletic trainer. On the medial side of the joint is the powerful deltoid ligament, which consists of two parts. The superficial part runs from the medial malleolus to the calcaneus and distally to support the arch of the foot; the deep part runs from the medial malleolus to the talus (Figure 20.4).

The tibiofibular syndesmosis consists of the anterior and posterior tibiofibular ligaments and the interosseous membrane, allowing very little movement between the tibia and fibula at the ankle joint. The tibiofibular syndesmosis is frequently damaged in rotational-type sprains of the ankle.

The lateral ligaments are much weaker than their medial counterparts and are frequently injured. These ligaments consist of three main parts: (a) the anterior talofibular ligament, (b) the calcaneofibular ligament, and (c) the posterior talofibular ligament. The arrangement of the lateral ligaments is such that at least one of them is tense throughout the range of ankle

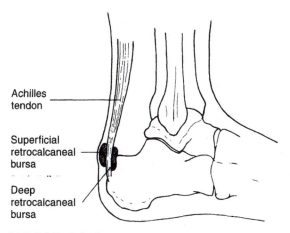

FIGURE 20.3
The Achilles tendon and the retrocalcaneal bursae (lateral view)

Achilles tendon
Superficial retrocalcaneal bursa
Deep retrocalcaneal bursa

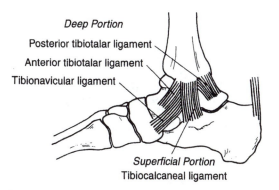

FIGURE 20.4
The deep and superficial portions of the deltoid ligament (viewed from the medial side)

Deep Portion
Posterior tibiotalar ligament
Anterior tibiotalar ligament
Tibionavicular ligament
Superficial Portion
Tibiocalcaneal ligament

movement—the calcaneofibular ligament in dorsiflexion, the anterior talofibular ligament in plantar flexion (Figure 20.5–20.7).

The retinaculum securing the peroneus longus and the peroneus brevis behind the lateral malleolus is in close continuity with the calcaneofibular ligament and can be damaged when this ligament is injured.

The Foot

The foot is truly a remarkable organ. It must absorb shock, adapt to the underlying surface, keep the body balanced, propel the body forward, and change from one of these functions to another—all within a minute period of time. It may be possible to continue to participate with a sore knee or a painful shoulder, but if one or both feet are hurt, the athlete is often incapacitated.

The foot is divided into three areas: (a) rearfoot, consisting of the calcaneous and the talus; (b) midfoot,

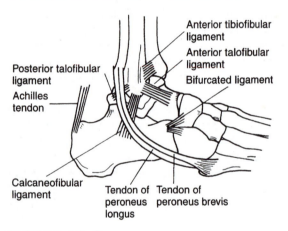

FIGURE 20.5
The lateral ligaments (viewed from the lateral side)

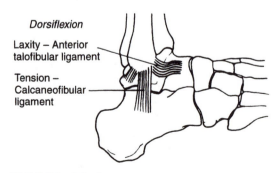

FIGURE 20.6
The position of the foot and ankle, and its influence on the lateral ligaments—dorsiflexion

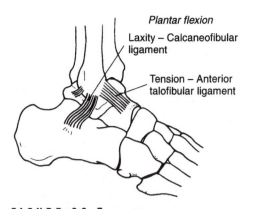

FIGURE 20.7
The position of the foot and ankle, and its influence on the lateral ligaments—plantar flexion

consisting of the navicular, the cuboid, and the cuneiforms; and (c) forefoot, consisting of the metatarsals and the phalanges.

Two joints often referred to are the *subtalar* and the *midtarsal*. The subtalar joint lies between the calcaneus and the talus. The midtarsal joint is actually two joints: (a) the talonavicular joint and (b) the calcaneocuboid joint (Figure 20.8).

MOVEMENTS: The subtalar joint imparts a triplane movement to the bones that allow motion in a side-to-side direction so pronation and supination can occur. *Pronation* consists of dorsiflexion, abduction, and eversion; *supination* is the opposite, namely, plantar flexion, adduction, and inversion. These movements take place at the subtalar joint.[2] The range of motion of the foot depends on the bony configuration as well as the ligaments and muscles acting on the bones.

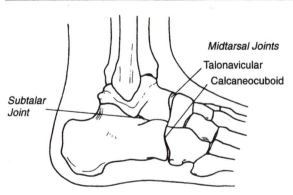

FIGURE 20.8
The subtalar and midtarsal joints

When the foot is pronated, it becomes loose and "unlocked," allowing for shock absorbency and adaptation to the underlying surface. Supination of the subtalar joint mechanically aligns the bones of the foot to "lock" the foot. This decreases the range of motion of the midtarsal joint and allows the foot to act as a rigid lever during the take-off and propulsive phase of gait. (See the biomechanics of running in the section on running injuries.)

LIGAMENTS AND FASCIA: There are a number of ligaments in the foot. Only a few will be discussed.

"SPRING" LIGAMENT. The calcaneonavicular or "spring" ligament helps to maintain the medial longitudinal arch. If forces are excessive, injury to this ligament causes discomfort and tenderness localized to the medial arch of the foot in the region of the calcaneonavicular joint.

BIFURCATED LIGAMENT. A ligament running between the calcaneus, the navicular, and the cuboid, this ligament can be injured in inversion sprains of the foot.

PLANTAR FASCIA. A white band of tissue running from the calcaneus to the heads of the metatarsals, the fascia supports the plantar aspect of the foot. It is often subjected to microtrauma, can become inflamed, and can tear under severe stress (Figure 20.9).

FIGURE 20.9
The plantar fascia

MUSCLES: Like the hand, the foot is supplied with extrinsic and intrinsic muscles. The extrinsic muscles are discussed later in this chapter.

The muscles on the posteromedial aspect of the leg (posterior tibial, flexor digitorum longus, and flexor hallucis longus) help to support the arch and promote the rigid lever action of the foot during the propulsive phase of gait.

The anterior muscles (tibialis anterior, extensor digitorum longus, and extensor hallucis longus) prepare the foot for contact with the ground. They also help absorb shock by dorsiflexing the foot before impact and then gently lowering it to the ground.

The lateral muscles (peroneals) act mainly as everters of the foot, helping to stabilize the ankle. They also help plantar flex the foot.

Intrinsic muscles: There are numerous intrinsic muscles in the foot, the primary ones being:

1. *Abductor hallucis:* Originates from the medial aspect of the calcaneus and runs to the medial side of the base of the proximal phalanx of the great toe. *Function:* Abducts and flexes the great toe. This muscle is thought to be important in some of the painful conditions around the medial arch.

2. *Abductor digiti minimi pedis:* Arises from the medial and lateral tubercles of the calcaneus in the plantar fascia and inserts into the lateral surface of the base of the proximal phalanx of the fifth toe. *Function:* Abducts the fifth toe.

3. *Flexor hallucis brevis:* Arises from the cuboid and the third cuneiform and inserts into the base of the proximal phalanx of the first toe. *Function:* Flexes the first toe.

4. *Flexor digitorum brevis:* Runs from the medial tuberosity of the calcaneus and the plantar fascia to the middle phalanges of the four lateral toes. *Function:* Flexes the toes.

NERVE SUPPLY: The *sciatic nerve* supplies the branches that innervate the lower leg and foot. Thus a lower-back disc herniation or protrusion may present with sensory or motor changes that manifest in the lower leg. The dermatome supplied by L4, L5, and S1 should be noted. (See the section on the lumbar spine, in Chapter 17.)

The sciatic nerve gives off a number of branches just proximal to the popliteal fossa: the *sural nerve* (supplies the lateral aspect of the foot); the *tibial nerve* (innervates the muscles on the posterior aspect of the leg); and the *common peroneal nerve*, which gives off the *deep peroneal nerve*. The deep peroneal nerve then runs within the anterior compartment, where it can become compressed in the anterior compartment compression syndrome. Because it innervates the skin of the first web space of the toes on the dorsal aspect of the foot, this area can lose sensation if the pressure increases sufficiently within the anterior compartment. This nerve also supplies the dorsiflexor muscles. The *superficial peroneal nerve* innervates the evertor muscles that lie within the lateral compartment and the skin of the dorsum of the lateral side of the foot (second, third, and fourth toes).

The *femoral nerve* supplies the saphenous nerve that innervates the medial aspect of the ankle.

ARTERIAL BLOOD SUPPLY: Just distal to the popliteal space, the popliteal artery divides into the anterior and posterior tibial arteries. The anterior tibial runs through the anterior compartment and supplies the dorsalis pedis pulse over the dorsum of the foot between the first and second metatarsals (though this pulse may be congenitally absent in some people).

The posterior tibial artery runs down the posterior aspect of the calf, giving off the peroneal artery to the lateral compartment. The posterior tibial also provides a pulse behind the medial malleolus, where one also finds the flexor tendons and the posterior tibial nerve (Figure 20.10).

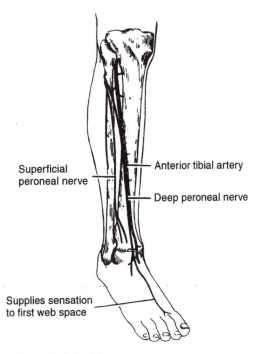

FIGURE 20.10
The nerve and blood supply that passes through the anterior compartment of the lower leg

Labels in figure:
Superficial peroneal nerve
Anterior tibial artery
Deep peroneal nerve
Supplies sensation to first web space

LYMPHATIC DRAINAGE: There is extensive lymphatic drainage from the foot to the lymph nodes in the popliteal area and the groin. Infection of the foot spreads rapidly through the lymphatic drainage system and often presents with a painful swollen lymph node in the groin.

Injuries to the Lower Leg

Contusions to the Anterior Lower Leg

The results of a contusion to the lower leg may vary from a mild bruise to a serious injury. The sport of soccer will undoubtedly produce injuries to this area, particularly if the athlete neglects to wear shin guards.

A kick directly on the tibia can cause a *tibial fracture*. When examining an athlete with this injury, gently palpate the tibia. If no fracture is obvious, percuss the tibial shaft and then the heel. If this produces pain over the tender area, a fracture should be suspected. Ice should be applied and the leg splinted. The athlete should not be allowed to bear weight on the leg until X-rays have been taken. Another method of incurring a fracture of the tibia in soccer or football is shown in Figure 20.11.[3]

A blow over the anterior compartment can cause bleeding within the compartment, resulting in increased pressure and development of the anterior compartment compression syndrome. (See compartment compression syndrome in the section on running injuries.) This condition may not develop immediately, and an attempt to prevent it should be made by placing ice over the anterior compartment. Icing and elevation should continue for a number of hours. Anti-inflammatory medication can be given if necessary. Any athlete who has an injury which could develop an anterior compartment compression syndrome should be informed of its symptoms and signs and should be instructed, if they arise, to seek immediate emergency care.

A *hematoma* over the tibia, or elsewhere in the lower leg, can, in rare instances, become infected. Infection should be suspected if, after a few days, the hematoma becomes red, increasingly painful, or swollen. The athlete should be referred to a physician for appropriate treatment.

An athlete returning to play after suffering a contusion to the lower leg should ensure that the injured area is adequately protected.

Rupture of the Gastrocnemius Muscle ("Tennis Leg")

"Tennis leg" is a condition formerly attributed to rupture of the tiny plantaris muscle, but it has now been

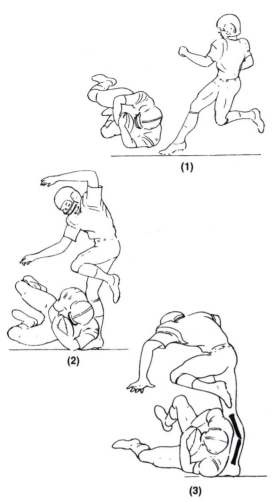

FIGURE 20.11

A mechanism for fracturing the tibia
(Modified from S. F. Gunther, "An avoidable soccer injury,"
Journal of Sports Medicine 2:167, 1974.)

demonstrated by surgical exploration to be due to a tear of the musculotendinous junction of one of the heads of the gastrocnemius muscle (usually the medial) (Figure 20.12).[4, 5]

MECHANISM OF INJURY: The injury occurs when the knee is suddenly extended while the foot is dorsiflexed, or when the foot is suddenly dorsiflexed while the knee is in extension.

PREDISPOSING FACTORS: Tennis leg occurs most frequently in the middle-aged athlete, after some degeneration of the muscle or musculotendinous junction of the gastrocnemius has occurred.

FIGURE 20.12
Tear of the medial head of the gastrocnemius ("tennis leg")

SYMPTOMS AND SIGNS: A sudden sharp pain is felt in the medial (sometimes the lateral) upper calf. It is often described as feeling like a "shot in the leg." The athlete is unable to bear full weight on the affected leg; swelling is fairly rapid, particularly if a substantial amount of the muscle is torn; and ecchymosis is frequently present.

It is usually very difficult to palpate a defect in the muscle. The affected area can be localized by tenderness to direct pressure. The athlete is often unable to stand on the metatarsal heads of the affected leg, but it is difficult to be certain whether this is due to weakness or pain.

Prodromal symptoms (e.g., symptoms appearing before the actual rupture has occurred) have been noticed by some athletes and consist mainly of aching and pain in the musculotendinous junction of the gastrocnemius after activities such as tennis.

TREATMENT:

Immediate: Apply a cold, wet elastic bandage for compression. Apply ice on top of one or two layers of this bandage and hold it firmly in place with additional wraps. Elevate the leg and the foot held in gentle plantar flexion. Instruct the athlete to use crutches and put no weight on the leg. Commence analgesics and anti-inflammatory medication if necessary.

Definitive:

1. Mild cases—weight-bearing as tolerated, using a felt heel lift for comfort. Strengthening exercises for the gastrocnemius muscle should be initiated, together with Achilles stretching and muscle stimulation.

2. Moderate to severe cases—should be treated with ice, heel lift for comfort, and use of a cane or crutch until weight-bearing can be tolerated. Strengthening exercises and gradual calf stretching should be performed daily within limits of pain.

3. Severe cases—When there is a substantial tearing of the gastrocnemius muscle together with separation of the affected ends, surgical exploration and repair is considered the best form of treatment by some authorities, but there is controversy on this issue.

PROGNOSIS: If this injury is adequately treated, the prognosis for returning to sports activities is excellent. However, an athlete who has had this condition is likely to suffer the same problem in the opposite leg. For those who have not been treated adequately, or who have not sought attention, return to full sports activity may be delayed for a considerable period of time, and normal function may be impaired.

Plantaris (Muscle-Tendon) Rupture

This injury appears to be rather rare in athletics, but it may occur and not be identified. The gastrocnemius and soleus muscle has a functional dominance over the plantaris, which may mask involvement of the plantaris.

MECHANISM OF INJURY: See rupture of the gastrocnemius muscle.

SYMPTOMS AND SIGNS: Pain deep in the upper calf area and a deep soreness may develop. Bleeding and swelling are not usually present.

TREATMENT: See rupture of the gastrocnemius muscle.

Total Rupture of the Achilles Tendon

This well-known but relatively uncommon athletic injury occurs particularly in middle age, but can occur in the prime of a young athlete's career.

MECHANISM OF INJURY: The rupture is usually the result of a sudden contraction of the gastrocnemius and soleus complex, as occurs when pushing off with the knee in extension (as in running) or when the foot is forced into a dorsiflexed position (as in landing from a jump). A direct blow to the Achilles can cause it to rupture, though this is rare. The tendon usually ruptures at its mid-portion, about 3 cm to 6 cm above the calcaneus, but it may be avulsed from the calcaneus or torn at the musculotendinous junction.

Predisposing factors include nonspecific degeneration of the tendon (possibly due to vascular impairment in the middle third of the tendon) and repeated subclinical tears leading to areas of necrosis. The use of corticosteriods, particularly administered by local injection (but also orally), has been implicated in weakening of the tendon.[6, 7]

SYMPTOMS AND SIGNS: The classic case of acute rupture presents with the history of a sudden snap which is clearly audible but often painless. In fact, the athlete may describe looking around for the source of the noise. In other cases, the rupture may be associated with the sensation of having been shot or kicked in the leg.

There is subsequent weakness of the foot, particularly when an attempt is made to stand on the metatarsal heads, followed by pain and swelling. However, the swelling may be a very minor symptom, particularly if a rupture of an avascular portion of the tendon has occurred.

When the athlete stands and is viewed from behind, the affected Achilles tendon appears thicker than the one on the opposite side. Localized swelling may be present over the tendon with possible ecchymosis. There may be tenderness directly over the rupture site, and sometimes a palpable gap can be felt. Weakness of ankle plantar flexion is demonstrated by inability to stand on the metatarsal heads of the affected limb. There may be some increase of dorsiflexion compared with the other limb, but this is often difficult to determine because of pain.

One of the most important tests is manual compression of the calf (also called the Thompson[8] or Simmonds test[9]). With the athlete prone, the knee bent, and the foot hanging, squeeze the calf. This maneuver normally produces plantar flexion of the foot. If plantar flexion does not occur, a ruptured Achilles tendon should be suspected (Figure 20.13).

X-RAYS: X-rays are sometimes useful because changes anterior to the Achilles tendon can be seen on the lateral view. Kager's triangle should be carefully examined for abnormalities (Figure 20.14).

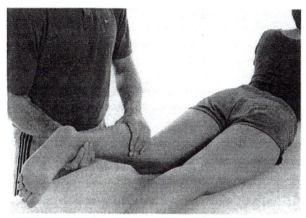

FIGURE 20.13

The Thompson (or Simmonds) test
The foot should plantar flex when the calf muscle is squeezed. If it does not, a rupture of the Achilles tendon should be suspected.

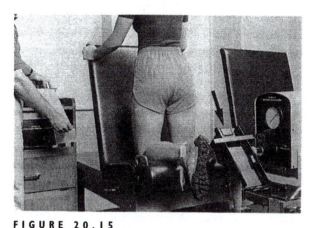

FIGURE 20.15

Rehabilitation of an injured Achilles tendon
Isokinetic training has been found to be of value in returning athletes with Achilles injuries to full function. This position exercises the soleus muscle when the foot is plantar flexed. The arrow points to the side being rehabilitated.

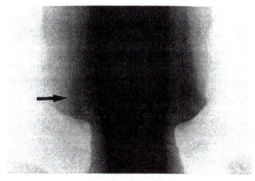

FIGURE 20.14

Soft-tissue lateral X-ray of the Achilles tendons
The arrow points to Kager's triangle, which has lost its radiolucency. The Achilles tendon is also noted to be indistinct on that side (compare with opposite Achilles).

TREATMENT: *Immediate* treatment consists of applying ice to the affected area, immobilizing the ankle in slight plantar flexion, and having the athlete use crutches. Analgesics and anti-inflammatory medication may be used if desired.[10] Surgical repair is the *definitive* treatment for the athlete. There is some controversy as to whether surgery is indicated in a non-athlete.[11] Cast immobilization, cast bracing or post-op walker brace, plantarflexed, is usually incorporated from four to eight weeks.[12]

REHABILITATION: Manual resistance, followed by progressive resistive exercises, closed kinetic chain

exercises, then isokinetic equipment. Carefully controlled dorsiflexion stretches should also be started. All progression throughout the rehabilitation should be done under consultation with the referring physician (Figure 20.15).

PROGNOSIS: Following a complete rupture of the Achilles tendon, the prognosis for returning to top-class athletic competion is guarded.[24] It should, however, be possible for the athlete to return to a high-level of activity in the majority of cases.

Partial Rupture of the Achilles Tendon

Partial rupture of the Achilles tendon, or tendinosis, is fairly common but infrequently diagnosed due to lack of awareness of the condition, together with the difficulty of making a confident diagnosis.[13] The onset may be dramatic—sudden pain, limited motion, and weakness localized to the Achilles—following an acute dorsiflexion of the ankle, a hard push-off, or even an innocent movement. Or the onset may be more vague, with the athlete presenting with "tendinitis"-type symptoms that do not clear with the standard treatment. (See section on injuries to the Achilles tendon.)

SYMPTOMS AND SIGNS: At one extreme is a situation similar to that of a complete rupture, only the Thompson test is negative. At the other extreme is the athlete with the usual symptoms of Achilles tendinitis—swelling, pain with motion, crepitus at times, and inability to perform. Signs include localized tenderness on squeezing the Achilles tendon and pain on either forced passive dorsiflexion or resistance to active plantar flexion. Crepitus may be present. Manual squeezing of the calf muscles does not produce a positive Thompson test, in other words, the foot *will* plantar flex. It is often possible for the athlete to stand on the metatarsal heads without weakness but with much discomfort.

TREATMENT: Initially treatment is with ice, immobilization, and anti-inflammatory medication. If the examiner feels strongly about the diagnosis and suspects that a substantial portion of the Achilles tendon has been torn, the Achilles should be immobilized in a cast with the foot in slight plantar flexion for four to six weeks. Casting is followed by a gradual return to normal activities together with a carefully controlled rehabilitation program.

If symptoms do not disappear after an adequate trial of conservative therapy, the question of surgical exploration of the Achilles tendon should be discussed with the athlete.[14] If it is felt on initial examination that a significant portion of the Achilles tendon has been torn, early operative treatment may be considered desirable. It should be remembered that many cases of Achilles "tendinitis" are actually partial tears of the Achilles tendon. This is probably the main reason why injection of a corticosteroid preparation should not be used in or around the Achilles tendon in these cases.

Injuries to the Ankle

Prevention of Ankle Injuries

STRETCHING: Recurrent ankle sprains are often associated with a tight Achilles tendon placing the ankle in a plantar-flexed position. Daily, slow, static stretching of the Achilles tendon can reduce the incidence of recurrent ankle sprains.[15] (See the technique for Achilles stretching.)

EXERCISES: A well-functioning peroneus muscle group helps prevent ankle sprains. The peroneus muscles must contract early enough in the foot's contact cycle to slow down or prevent excessive movement if the foot is forced into inversion.[16] Eversion exercises, as well as other exercises, should be used to train the peroneal muscles to contract maximally when needed. (See the ankle rehabilitation exercises.)[17]

Proprioception is also of great importance in preventing ankle sprains, particularly for the athlete who has had previous sprains and who might have injured the proprioception receptor-conduction mechanism. Ankle proprioception is easily tested by having the athlete stand on one foot with eyes closed to see if balance can be maintained (Figure 20.26).[18] Athletes with poor proprioception are able to balance on one foot for only a very short time. Proprioception can be improved by various exercises, as outlined in the ankle rehabilitation section.

Some athletes are obviously better coordinated than others and have a more highly refined proprioceptive system. This does not mean that the poorly endowed athlete (from the neuromuscular point of view) cannot do anything about his or her genetic plight. By embarking on simple eversion and proprioceptive exercises, the athlete can definitely improve his or her awareness of the body's position in space and the ability to control previously uncontrolled sudden inversion movements of the foot and ankle.

SHOES:

1. Soccer-style shoes for football: When a field is well maintained, so that ankle sprains from twists in potholes or poorly kept surfaces are eliminated, the type of shoe worn for football can influence the rate of ankle sprains.[18] It appears that the shoe with the lowest incidence of ankle sprains is the same shoe that should be worn to decrease the incidence of knee injuries—a soccer-style shoe with a polyurethane sole and about fourteen relatively flat, wide cleats.[18]

2. Shoe width: Many athletes, particularly football players, wear shoes which are much too narrow for their feet, allowing the foot to bulge over the edges of the soles in a very unstable manner and predisposing them to ankle sprains. It is therefore important that each athlete be individually fitted with a shoe that is not only adequate for the foot's length, but also of the correct width.

3. High-top shoes: In the past it was thought that high-top shoes would stimulate the proprioceptive receptors, leading to early firing of the peroneal muscles and thereby improving ankle stability. Recent studies indicate little difference in high- versus low-top shoes.[19] However, the main factor may not lie in the type of shoe, but rather in the type of ankle stabilization used.

TAPING VS. BRACING: Hundreds of thousands of rolls of tape are used each year in an attempt to reduce the incidence of ankle sprains. Whether tape actually achieves this goal has never been adequately proven. Many athletic trainers feel that taping a previously sprained ankle or an ankle that is prone to sprains is helpful. A growing number of athletic trainers are using ankle stabilizers in lieu of ankle taping, citing decreased number of ankle sprains or re-injuries, decreased time for application, and decreased annual cost per athlete.[19,20] (See Chapter 4.)

In a study comparing high- versus low-top shoes and taping versus bracing, the authors found, as did others, that the support provided by tape decreases with repeated mechanical stress.[20, 21] The support provided by braces did not appear to decrease as much during the same stresses as did the tape. It was possible, however, to retighten the braces to maximal support at intervals during the activity. The authors hypothesized that athletes wearing low-top shoes with braces had more incentive to retighten the braces during activities than did their counterparts who were taped and wearing high-top shoes, thereby reducing the incidence of injury or re-injury to the ankle.[22]

Taping or bracing is logical and necessary for those who have recently suffered an ankle sprain and who are still undergoing rehabilitation, as well as for those who are subject to frequent ankle sprains. These individuals should, however, also maintain a vigorous rehabilitation program to strengthen the muscles around the ankle, improve flexibility, and sharpen their proprioception.

PLAYING SURFACE: An irregular playing surface with potholes is an invitation to ankle sprain and negates the positive aspects of the ankle injury prevention program.[23]

Mechanism of Ankle Sprains

INVERSION SPRAINS: Over 80 percent of all ankle sprains are inversion injuries, occurring while the athlete is running straight ahead or cutting. The foot or ankle suddenly turns into plantar flexion and inversion, and the athlete feels a sharp pain on the anterolateral aspect of the ankle. The anterior talofibular ligament is the first ligament to be affected, and thus it is the most commonly injured structure around the ankle. If the sprain is more severe, the calcaneofibular ligament is also involved[22] (Figure 20.16).

With the rotational sprain (cutting across the plantar flexed, inverted foot), the tibiofibular ligament and the interosseous membrane may be involved in addition to the lateral ligaments.[24] With this inversion-rotational sprain, it is possible to fracture the neck of the fibula (maisonneuve fracture).[25]

Occasionally the athlete suffers a pure inversion sprain, for instance when coming down from a rebound in basketball and landing entirely on the side of the foot with no plantar flexion occurring.

EVERSION SPRAINS: Eversion sprains occur less frequently than inversion sprains, due to the anatomy of the ankle joint and the strength of the deltoid ligament. An eversion sprain may tear the deltoid ligament; or the ligament may be stronger than the bone, in which case the medial malleolus will be avulsed. The pure eversion sprain tears the deltoid ligament only. The milder sprain

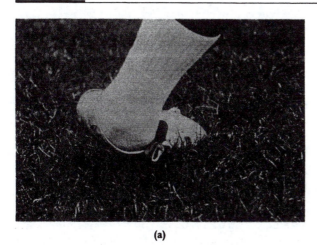

(a)

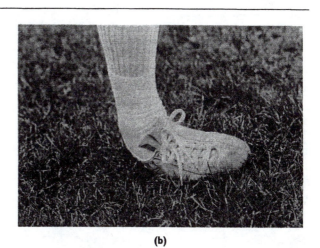

(b)

FIGURE 20.16

Mechanism of an ankle sprain

(a) An inversion-plantar flexion sprain. This motion usually sprains the anterior talofibular ligament, and if severe, the calcaneofibular ligament is also involved. A fracture of the fibula occasionally occurs. (b) An inversion sprain. This injury may affect only the calcaneofibular ligament, though the anterior talofibular ligament is also frequently sprained.

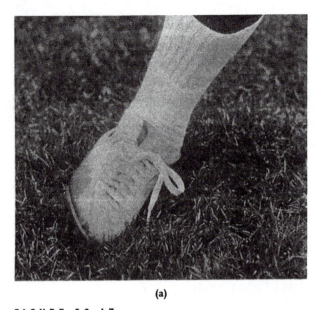

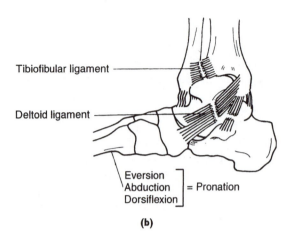

Tibiofibular ligament

Deltoid ligament

Eversion
Abduction = Pronation
Dorsiflexion

(a)   (b)

FIGURE 20.17

Mechanism of an ankle sprain

(a) An eversion sprain. This motion may tear the deltoid ligament, or may produce an avulsion fracture off the tip of the medial malleolus. (b) An eversion sprain may tear the deltoid ligament and the tibiofibular ligament (viewed from the medial side)

tears the deeper part of the ligament, whereas more severe forces tear both the deep and the superficial portions (Figures 20.17 and 20.18).

DORSIFLEXION SPRAINS: An excessive dorsiflexion force jams the talus into the mortise, since the anterior portion of the talus is wider than the posterior part. This may separate the syndesmosis and, in addition, cause an osteochondral fracture of the talus. The Achilles may be injured by the stretching forces of dorsiflexion, and the tibia may jam against the talar neck. Repeated forced dorsiflexion such as that seen in gym-

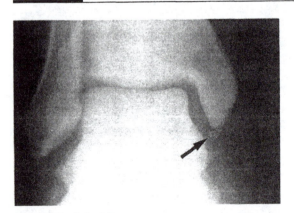

FIGURE 20.18

X-ray—avulsion fracture from the tip of the medial malleolus

nastics and basketball may cause anterior ankle impingement, resulting in anterior ankle pain due to inflammation and/or osteophyte formation.[26] Tibiotalar impingement due to a talar spur can be diagnosed by history and confirmed with an X-ray. Surgical removal of the spurs may be necessary (Figure 20.39).

PLANTAR FLEXION SPRAINS: Pure plantar flexion sprains are rare, although they may be sustained by soccer players, ballet dancers, and javelin throwers. There is usually some degree of inversion as well. The lateral ligaments, tibiofibular ligaments, and the anterior retinaculum are usually involved. In addition the ostrigonum may be damaged, resulting in pain and tenderness over the posterior aspect of the ankle (Table 20.1–20.5).[26]

More often the foot goes into excessive pronation (this implies abduction, eversion, and dorsiflexion), particularly when cutting to the opposite side. The resultant forces may tear the deltoid ligament.

ANKLE SYNDESMOSIS SPRAIN: Ankle syndesmosis sprain is an external force applied to the ankle, either in a downed athlete whose foot is stepped on, or in a weight-bearing player whose foot is in external rotation and at the same time receives a blow to the lateral aspect of the knee. The anterior tibiofibular ligament, interosseous membrane, posterior tibiofibular ligament,

TABLE 20.1 *Mechanism of common ankle sprains—ligaments involved*

Mechanism	Stage I	Stage II (More Severe)	Stage III (Most Severe)
Inversion + plantar flexion	Anterior talofibular ligament sprain	Stage I + calcaneofibular ligament sprain	Stage II + posterior talofibular ligament sprain
Inversion + plantar flexion + rotation (most common)	Anterior talofibular ligament sprain + Tibiofibular ligament sprain	Stage I + calcaneofibular ligament sprain	Stage II + posterior talofibular ligament sprain
Pure inversion (rare)	Calcaneofibular ligament sprain	Stage I + anterior talofibular ligament sprain	Stage II + posterior talofibular ligament sprain
Pronation (abduction + eversion + dorsiflexion)	Deltoid ligament sprain or avulsion fracture of medial malleolus	Stage I + tibiofibular ligament and interosseous membrane	Stage II + fibular fracture above mortice line

TABLE 20.2 *Anterior talofibular ligament sprain—symptoms and signs*

Degree	History	Tenderness	Swelling	Pain with Stress	Ligament Laxity	Other Structures
Stable						
Mild	Plantar flexion-inversion	Anterolateral	Anterolateral	Slight	0	0
Moderate	Plantar flexion-inversion	Anterolateral	Anterolateral	More pain	0	0
Severe	Plantar flexion-inversion + pop	Anterolateral	Anterolateral, more diffuse	Usually very painful; occasionally no pain, especially soon after injury	Slight anterior drawer sign	Calcaneofibular and/or tibiofibular ligaments
Unstable						
	Plantar flexion-inversion + pop	All over the lateral and anterolateral sides	Anterolateral, more diffuse	Usually very painful; occasionally no pain, especially soon after injury	More definite anterior drawer sign	Calcaneofibular (inversion stress) and/or tibiofibular (side-to-side) stress laxity

TABLE 20.3 *Tibiofibular ligament sprain—symptoms and signs*

Degree	History	Tenderness	Swelling	Pain with Stress	Ligament Laxity	Other Structures That May Be Involved
Stable						
Mild	Inversion or eversion rotation	Over tibiofibular ligament	Over anterior aspect in region of syndesmosis	Slight	0	0
Moderate	Inversion or eversion rotation	Over the tibiofibular ligament and often the medial or lateral ligaments	Over anterior aspect in region of syndesmosis	More pain	0	Lateral or medial ligaments and/or interosseous membrane
Severe	Inversion or eversion rotation	Over the tibiofibular ligament and often the medial or lateral ligaments	Over anterior aspect in region of syndesmosis	Usually very painful; occasionally no pain, especially soon after injury	Slight laxity on side-to-side test	Lateral or medial ligaments and/or interosseous membrane
Unstable						
	Inversion or eversion rotation	Over the tibiofibular ligament and often the medial or lateral ligaments	Over anterior aspect in region of syndesmosis	Usually very painful; occasionally no pain, especially soon after injury	Laxity on side-to-side test	Lateral or medial ligaments and/or interosseous membrane

and even a fracture of the distal or proximal fibula (maisonneuve fracture) may result from the external rotational forces applied to the ankle joint. This can lead to a widening of the ankle mortise[27] (Figure 20.19).

Evaluation of the Injured Ankle:

The purpose of evaluating an injured ankle is to

1. Attempt to exclude the presence of a fracture (relatively uncommon)

2. Make an anatomical diagnosis of the structures involved

3. Decide on the severity of the injury

4. Differentiate the unstable from the stable ankle sprain (probably the most important function of the clinical evaluation)

HISTORY: The following questions should be asked:

1. What was the mechanism of the injury (e.g., inversion with plantar flexion, eversion, rotation, etc.)?

2. Where was the pain initially?

3. Did you hear a pop, snap, or crack?

4. Were you able to bear weight immediately after the injury?

5. Did you continue to play?

6. Did the ankle feel unstable?

7. Did the ankle swell up immediately? Later?

8. What treatment was applied immediately? later?

9. Do you have any previous history of injuries to your ankles?

TABLE 20.4 *Calcaneofibular ligament sprain—symptoms and signs*

Degree	History	Tenderness	Swelling	Pain with Stress	Ligament Laxity	Other Structures
Stable						
Mild	Inversion	Over ligament	Over lateral side	Slight	0	0
Moderate	Inversion	Over ligament ± anterior talofibular and/or tibiofibular ligaments	Over lateral side	More pain	0	0
Severe	Inversion + pop	Over ligament ± anterior talofibular and/or tibiofibular	Over lateral side with or without anterior swelling	Usually very painful; occasionally no pain, especially soon after injury	Slight inversion laxity	Anterior talofibular and/or tibiofibular ligaments
Unstable						
	Inversion + pop	Over ligament ± anterior talofibular and/or tibiofibular	Over lateral side with or without anterior swelling	Usually very painful; occasionally no pain, especially soon after injury	Inversion laxity	Anterior talofibular (anterior drawer sign) and/or tibiofibular (side-to-side) laxity

OBSERVATIONS: Note areas of ecchymosis and of localized swelling. Immediate and diffuse swelling is usually, but not always, associated with a severe sprain. If there is bleeding within the joint, suspect a severe sprain. The athlete should then sit with legs hanging over the end of the examining table and the effect of gravity on the position of the ankle should be observed (the leg musculature must be completely relaxed). An obviously noticeable difference in the amount of inversion on the injured side when compared with the unaffected side indicates there is probably a severe unstable sprain of the lateral ligaments. The same test can be applied to injuries of the medial side involving the deltoid ligament, where a third-degree sprain would result in a position of excessive eversion.

PALPATION: The structures involved can usually be well localized by careful palpation. Start away from the suspected area of injury (leaving the most painful part of palpation to the end) and systematically palpate each important structure in turn. This way, no area will be overlooked. A suggested order for palpating a suspected lateral ligament injury follows (Figure 20.20):

1. Neck of the fibula
2. Squeeze the midshaft of the fibula (pain felt at the ankle during this maneuver may well indicate a fracture)
3. Interosseous membrane and anterior compartment
4. Deltoid ligament
5. Anterior tibiofibular ligament
6. Navicular
7. Achilles tendon
8. Bifurcated ligament
9. Base of the fifth metatarsal
10. Posterior talofibular ligament and peroneal tendons
11. Calcaneofibular ligament
12. Anterior talofibular ligament
13. Any other area indicated

TABLE 20.5 *Deltoid ligament sprain—symptoms and signs*

Degree	History	Tenderness	Swelling	Pain with Stress	Ligament Laxity	Other Structures
Stable						
Mild	Pronation (eversion + abduction + dorsiflexion)	Over deltoid ligament	Over deltoid ligament	Slight	0	0
Moderate	Pronation	Over deltoid ligament + tibiofibular ligament and interosseous membrane	Over deltoid ligament	More pain	0	Anterior tibiofibular sprain
Severe	Pronation	Over deltoid ligament + tibiofibular ligament and interosseous membrane	Over deltoid ligament + anterior ankle	Usually very painful; occasionally no pain, especially soon after injury	Eversion laxity	Anterior tibiofibular sprain ± interosseous membrane
Unstable						
	Pronation	Over deltoid ligament + tibiofibular ligament and interosseous membrane	Over deltoid ligament + anterior ankle	Usually very painful; occasionally no pain, especially soon after injury	Eversion laxity ± side-to-side laxity	Tibiofibular ligament ± interosseous membrane ± fibular fracture

LIGAMENT STABILITY TESTS: After obtaining the history, observing, and palpating, it should be possible to make an anatomical diagnosis as to the structures involved. The ligaments should then be stressed to determine if the ankle is stable or unstable.

Five tests are used to evaluate stability. Again, start on the unaffected side and move toward the affected side. For example, with a lateral ligament injury, start on the medial side and work across the ankle; with a deltoid ligament injury, start on the lateral side and move medially. Be aware of movement occurring at the subtalar joint when examining the ankle, and differentiate this movement from that of the ankle joint proper. In many athletes with so-called loose ankles, the excessive motion takes place at the subtalar joint and does not necessarily indicate abnormal laxity of the ankle ligaments.[17]

Before testing the affected ankle, remember to check the unaffected ankle and compare the two. Be sure that the athlete is completely relaxed and that no muscles around the ankle are held in involuntary contraction. The five tests (Figure 20.21) are:

1. *Eversion stress.* Stress the deltoid ligament by moving the calcaneus and talus into eversion.

2. *Side-to-side movement of the talus.* The side-to-side motion tests for widening of the mortise, which can occur if the tibiofibular ligament has been stretched.[28] Move the calcaneus and talus to each side as a unit. Do not tilt the ankle into either eversion or inversion. If the mortise (syndesmosis) is widened, the talus will be able to move sideways, producing a definite thud ("clonk") as it hits the fibula, and when moved in the opposite direction, it butts against the tibia.

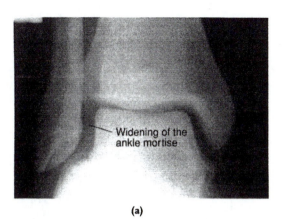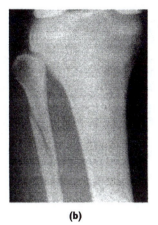

(a)   (b)

FIGURE 20.19

X-ray—a tear of the deltoid and tibiofibular ligament,
resulting in widening of the mortise (a). Part (b) shows a fracture of the upper fibula (Masionneuve fracture) which occurred from the ankle injury shown in part (a).

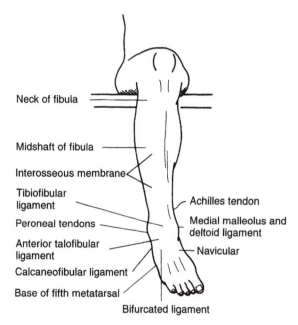

FIGURE 20.20

Ankle sprain—areas that should be specifically palpated for tenderness

3. *Anterior drawer test.* The ankle should be held in slight plantar flexion. One hand holds the lower tibia and exerts a slight posterior force while the other grasps the posterior aspect of the calcaneus and attempts to bring the calcaneus and talus forward on the tibia. Excessive forward movement indicates that at least the anterior talofibular ligament has been completely rup-

tured.[29] Also test for instability in a posterior direction by moving the tibia forward on a fixed heel.

4. *External rotation stress test.* This test is performed with the knee flexed at 90° and an external force applied to a neutral foot and ankle. A positive test will elicit pain over the anterior tibiofibular ligament, interosseous membrane, and even the posterior tibiofibular ligament.[30, 31]

5. *Inversion stress.* On attempting to tilt the talus into inversion when a severe lateral ligament injury exists, a spongy, indefinite end point will be felt. This test is often very painful and may be difficult to accomplish.

If pain and muscle spasm preclude an adequate evaluation of ligament stability, a local anesthetic can be injected (under the direction of a physician) into the joint and around the injured area or around the sural or peroneal nerves. Occasionally it may be necessary to examine the ankle under general anesthesia.

Having completed these tests. you should now be able to:

   a. Make an anatomical diagnosis
   b. Determine the severity of the injury
   c. Decide whether the ankle is stable or unstable

X-RAYS: Most ankle sprains should be referred for routine X-ray examination, to exclude any co-existing fractures. Routine X-rays include AP, lateral, and oblique views. If there is any question about the degree of stability, stress X-rays will further aid the diagnosis.[32] However, it should be emphasized that the clinical evaluation is usually sufficient to make the diagnosis; it is

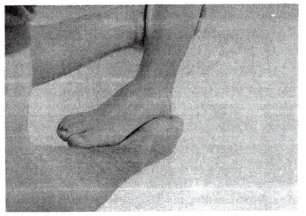

(a) Eversion test. The heel is grasped in one hand, the lower tibia in the other, and the ankle moved into eversion.

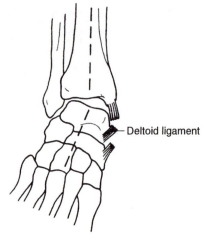

(b) Eversion test. A torn deltoid ligament will permit the ankle to open into eversion.

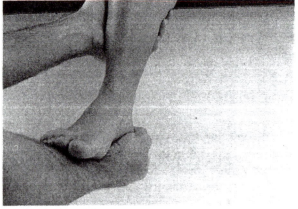

(c) Side-to-side test. The heel is moved from side to side, *not* into eversion or inversion. If the tibiofibular ligament is stable, no movement will occur. Attempt to move the calcaneus and talus as one unit.

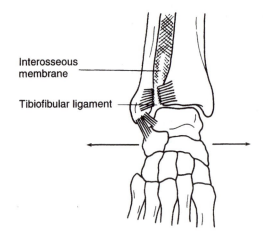

(d) Side-to-side test. If the mortise is widened, the talus will move from side to side.

FIGURE 20.21
Ankle ligament stability tests

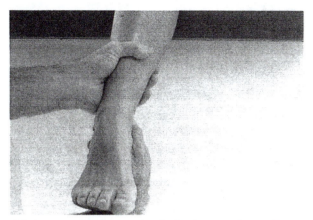

(e) Anterior drawer test. With the foot in plantar flexion and the tibia stabilized, the heel is brought forward on the tibia. The reverse procedure should also be performed, i.e., moving the heel backwards on the tibia.

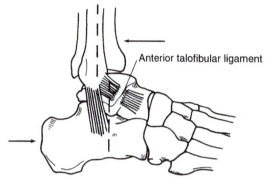

(f) Anterior drawer test. A torn anterior talofibular ligament will permit a positive drawer sign.

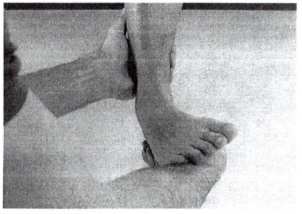

(g) Inversion test. The heel is brought into inversion while the tibia is stabilized.

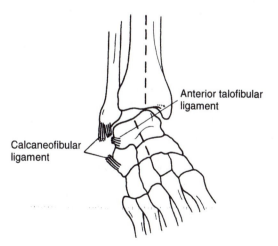

(h) Inversion test. A torn calcaneofibular ligament, usually with a torn anterior talofibular ligament, will permit the ankle to open into inversion.

FIGURE 20.21 *(continued)*

not necessary to take stress X-rays routinely. If stress X-rays are considered necessary to define the severity of the injury, they should include both AP and lateral views.[33]

1. *Anteroposterior view (talar tilt):* The stress should be directed either toward inversion or eversion (depending on whether the injury has involved the lateral or deltoid ligament), to demonstrate excessive talar tilt. Always compare with the unaffected side.

2. *Lateral view (anterior drawer test):* Anterior stress is applied to the calcaneus while holding the tibia stable. Again, this is compared with the opposite side.

On-Field Management of the Injured Ankle

Having sustained an ankle injury on the field of play, the athlete should be helped off the field bearing no weight, and should remain non-weight-bearing until the ankle has been evaluated. Immediately on reaching the sideline, the shoe, sock, and tape/brace of the affected leg should be removed. If the athlete is relatively uncooperative because of the discomfort being experienced at that moment, a cold, wet elastic wrap (4 inches [10cm] wide) should be applied to support the ankle (eversion support should be given with an inversion sprain). After one or two wrappings have been applied, place an ice bag on the bandage and continue the wrapping. This provides compression and support to the ankle and holds the ice bag in place.

When the athlete has regained composure, usually within three or four minutes, take a history and examine the ankle. The shoe, sock, and tape/brace of the opposite ankle should also be removed so the two ankles can be compared. The examination should be as complete as possible for an accurate assessment, because examining the ankle soon after the injury is easier than on any subsequent occasion.

If the ankle is completely stable and a fairly minor injury is diagnosed, and if the athlete wishes to return to participation, a series of functional tests should be undertaken before allowing the athlete to return to action (Table 20.6). The ankle should be retaped or braced before these tests are performed.

For the more severe injury, replace the elastic wrap and ice bag and elevate the leg for at least half an hour. If a fracture is suspected, splint the ankle. Do not allow weight bearing until after the X-ray examination.

Continuing Treatment of the Stable Ankle Sprain

Ice should be applied for at least twenty minutes every hour (longer in more severe cases) during the first

TABLE 20.6 *Criteria for return to play following an ankle injury*

1. No suggestion from the examination that a fracture might be present.
2. No evidence of ligament instability.
3. The athlete should be able to
   a. run forward
   b. run backward
   c. hop
   d. run-and-cut
   e. run in figure eights at normal speed without limp
4. Range of motion should be pain free.
5. Various muscle groups of the ankle and foot should have their full strength.
6. A positive attitude and confidence regarding further athletic performance.

If all the above criteria are met, the athlete is permitted to return to participation. However protective taping should be applied to support the injured structures. Immediately after the game, the ankle should be re-evaluated and treated as indicated.

twelve to twenty-four hours, while compression and elevation continue. X-rays should have been taken to exclude any fracture. The sprain is diagnosed as a first-, second-, or third-degree sprain.

The stable ankle sprain (first- or moderate second-degree sprain) is treated with tape (Gibney's open basketweave) or an elastic bandage utilizing a felt pad for compression over the affected malleolus. This pad is cut into the shape of a horseshoe for compression and can be removed for periodic icing (Figure 20.22). The best way to achieve elevation is to raise the leg against the wall at 90° to the body while lying down. The elastic bandage holding the pad in place is used mainly for compression and not for stability.

The athlete should be instructed to elevate the leg and ankle for the rest of that day and night.

Over the next 24 hours, the athlete should start stretching and exercising as tolerated. Stretching is performed by placing a band or towel around the plantar surface of the foot. The ankle is then passively dorsiflexed, stretching the gastroc-soleus complex within limits of pain, and then actively plantarflexed to strengthen the complex.

Exercises may begin with isometric or manual therapy. Inversion, eversion, plantar, and dorsiflexion

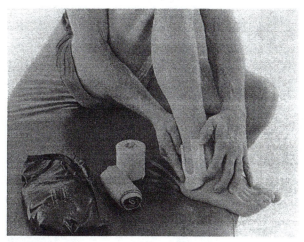
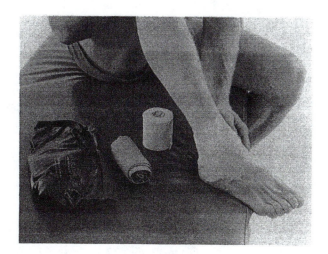

FIGURE 20.22
Ankle sprain
A felt horseshoe pad may be used for compression.

should all be performed within limits of pain. Elastic resistance can be added later. "Writing the alphabet" with the toes in a slush bucket (ice and water) is also a useful exercise.

The next stage is cryokinetics, in which the ankle is iced for twenty minutes, after which the athlete attempts to walk as normally as possible until the numbing effect of the ice wears off and the ankle again becomes painful. This procedure is repeated a number of times.

Crutches should be used if the athlete is unable to walk normally without pain, and even with crutches the athlete should use partial or touch-weight bearing. (See section on crutch usage.) Use of crutches should continue until the athlete can walk normally without any limp. Touch-weight bearing is used in order to

1.   Encourage a normal sequence of muscle response to proprioceptive stimuli, which occurs when the foot touches the ground. These responses will be lost if the foot is kept immobilized and away from the ground for a period of time.

2.   Prevent stiffness of the posterior tissues. Rehabilitation is started immediately in all cases of mild-to-moderate ankle sprains and in some cases of severe, stable sprains. (See section on ankle rehabilitation.)

SEVERE SECOND-DEGREE OR THIRD-DEGREE SPRAINS: The severe second-degree or third-degree sprain may be treated for six weeks in a cast, but usually requires a U-type splint, ankle-foot orthoses (AFO), or a reinforced lace-up ankle brace for a dura-

tion of four to six weeks postinjury (Figure 20.23).[31, 34, 35] A brace should then be worn for activities during the remainder of the season. The ankle will be rehabilitated in a protected manner without the negative effects of cast immobilization. With this form of protection, the athlete is able to apply ice, compression, and elevation, and to perform range-of-motion exercises.

In very severe cases of ligamentous rupture, surgical repair may be required.[26]

Ankle and Foot Rehabilitation

The rehabilitation program is divided into five stages (Table 20.7 and 20.8). Each stage is a relative period of time, varying from perhaps fifteen minutes for a mild ankle sprain to perhaps five to seven days for a more severe injury. The goal of the program is to literally prevent the athlete from running before he or she can walk. Each stage should be completed before progressing to the next. This means that the athlete should be able to do heel-raises before hopping and should jog before running and cutting.

The purpose of ankle rehabilitation is to

1.   Increase the strength of the muscles around the ankle joint

2.   Educate the athlete about where the ankle and foot actually are in space, as proprioceptive feedback is frequently impaired following an ankle injury

3.   Prevent the stiffness that often accompanies a poorly treated ankle sprain

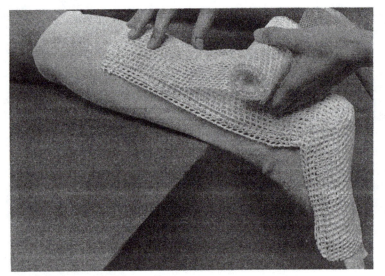
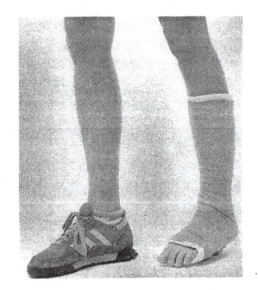

FIGURE 20.23
A posterior splint made from Hexcelite casting material

TABLE 20.7 *Outline of an ankle rehabilitation program*

	Stage I	
No.	Exercise	Stage I II III IV V
1.	Ice, compression and elevation	+
2.	Taping—Gibney's open bas-ket-weave or elastic wrap with horseshoe pad or pos-terior splint (severe) or air-stirrup/lace-up ankle brace	+
3.	Gentle dorsiflexion and plantar flexion	+
4.	Crutches with partial weight-bearing	+

4. Return to functional mobility while protecting the injured ligament(s)

STAGE I: (See sections on on-field management of the injured ankle, and continuing treatment.)

STAGE II:

1. It is often helpful to use a cold whirlpool (4°C to 16°C [39.2°F to 60.8°F]) on the day after an ankle

TABLE 20.8 *Outline of an ankle rehabilitation program*

	Stage II				
No.	Exercise	Stage I	II	III	IV V
1.	ROM in cold whirlpool	+			
2.	Achilles stretching with towel (can be done in a cold whirlpool	+			
3.	Alternate icing and walking	+			
4.	Contrast bath	+	+		
5.	Isometric ankle exercises	+	+		
6.	Manual therapy, eversion, inversion, dorsiflexion, and plantarflexion	+	+		
7.	Proprioceptive training	+	+	+	+
8.	Toe curls, marble pick-ups	+	+	+	+
9.	Cardiovascular training, upper body conditioning, contralateral training	+	+	+	+
10.	Swimming and running in pool	+	+	+	+
11.	Ice after rehabilitation ses-sion	+	+	+	+
12.	Supportive bracing	+	+	+	+

injury. The ankle and foot should be gently but actively moved in the whirlpool.

2. Achilles stretching in the whirlpool is performed with a wrap or towel around the end of the foot (Figure 20.24).

3. The cycle of pain-immobility-stiffness-pain often hinders rapid return to participation. One way to break this cycle is by means of ice therapy (cryokinetics).[34] Ice or ice massage is applied to the injured area for about ten to fifteen minutes (it is often useful to use ice for about five minutes, followed by ice massage for about five to seven minutes). When the ankle is well numbed, the athlete walks as normally as possible until discomfort is felt. The leg should again be elevated and iced and the walking repeated. It must be stressed that a normal walking motion should be achieved and that there should be no limp. If there is a significant limp, it indicates that the athlete is not yet ready for this exercise.

4. Some athletic trainers prefer to use "contrast baths," as they claim that this helps decrease swelling around the ankle (although there is no compelling research to support this finding). Many variations of the baths are used. Table 20.9 shows an example of one variation. Note that the athlete starts in the warm water and finishes in cold water. During treatment in warm water, the athlete is instructed to work on range of motion, primarily plantar/dorsiflexion.

5. Isometric peroneal exercises are performed by the athlete's keeping the heel fixed against the ground or floor while sitting with the knee bent at 90°. A weighted object, such as a 10 lb (4.5 Kg) sandbag, is placed against the outside of the foot near the toes. The per-

TABLE 20.9 *Contrast bath*

Warm water	104°–108° (or as tolerated)
Cold water	40°–50°

Start with the warm water for three minutes.

Move immediately to the cold water for two minutes.

Complete this cycle of hot and cold six times.

After completing the final cycle, stay in the cold water for 10 to 15 minutes.

Repeat the contrast bath two to three times per day, or until the swelling decreases.

Note: Not all athletic trainers agree on one specific contrast bath formula. (See Chapter 7 on therapeutic modalities.)

oneal muscles are isometrically contracted in an attempt to move the foot toward eversion. This contraction is maintained for five seconds or longer (Figure 20.25).

6. Manual therapy may also be applied to ankle ligament and foot injuries. The athlete moves the foot and ankle into eversion against the light resistance provided

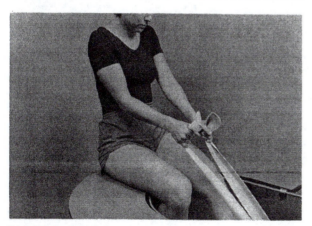

FIGURE 20.24
Ankle sprain
Active motion as well as passive Achilles stretching can be performed in a cold whirlpool bath.

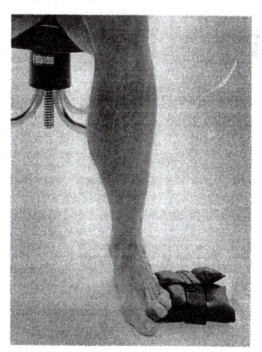

FIGURE 20.25
Isometric eversion exercise

by the athletic trainer, and then brings it back to neutral. This exercise is repeated for inversion, plantar, and dorsiflexion.

7.   This is a simple way to exercise proprioceptive feedback. The athlete stands on the injured foot, closes his or her eyes, attempts to maintain balance without wobbling or falling over.* This exercise should be performed for one or two minutes at a time (Figure 20.26).[19]

8.   Toe-curling exercises can be done with a towel on the floor. The athlete curls up the towel with his or her toes. Other exercises include picking up marbles with the toes or writing the alphabet in a bucket of ice slush (Figure 20.27).

9.   There is no reason for any athlete suffering from an ankle injury to lose cardiovascular fitness. A bicycle ergometer should be used from the first day onward. The ankle can be stabilized by taping the foot or by using a posterior splint. A combination high-resistance, low-speed and low-resistance, high-speed cycling should be used for a minimum of twenty to forty minutes each day. Most fit athletes in their late teens or early twenties should maintain a heart rate of at least 150 beats per minute while working out on the ergometer. Conditioning exercises for the upper body, the unaffected leg, and the upper part of the affected leg should be performed.

10.   Swimming and running in the swimming pool also maintains cardiovascular fitness.

11.   The ankle should be iced for 15 to 20 minutes at the end of the rehabilitation session. This should continue as long as there is swelling, pain, or tenderness.

12.   Grade II and III ankle sprains should be protected at all times with some form of bracing or support. Grade I sprains may require only ankle taping or bracing during rehabilitation or weight-bearing.

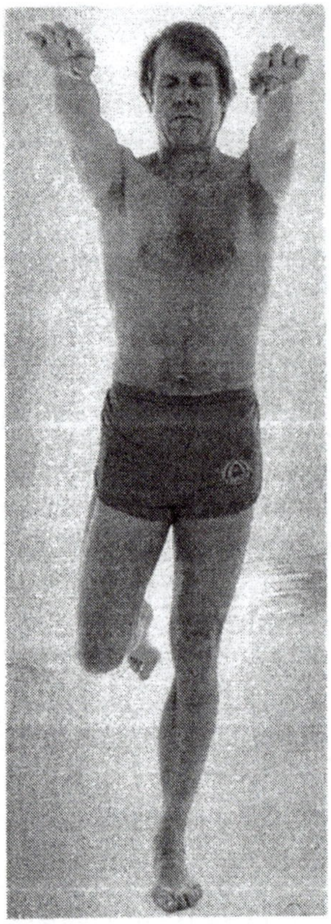

STAGE III:

1.   In this stage the athlete advances from the initial treatment phase and walking to heel raises and other progressive resistive exercises. Heel raises are first performed with the athlete's own body weight. Weight is supported mainly on the unaffected side and is gradually shifted to the injured ankle/foot. Sets of 12 to 15 repetitions should be completed through the pain-free range of motion (Figure 20.28).

2.   When the athlete is able to complete the single leg heel raises, without pain or difficulty, then heel raises

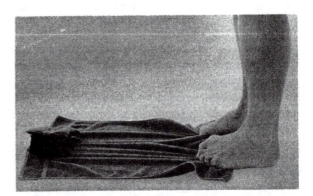

FIGURE 20.26
Ankle proprioception exercise
The athlete balances on one leg with eyes closed.

FIGURE 20.27
Toe-curling exercise
Using a towel to help develop the intrinsic muscles of the foot

with weight should begin. Again, start weight bearing on both feet and progress to single leg raises with weight, alternating from the injured to the uninjured limb. Several sets of 12 to 15 repetitions should be completed.

---

*With caution—balance board(s) might be utilized.

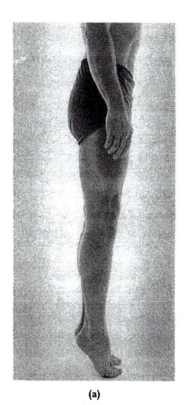

(a)

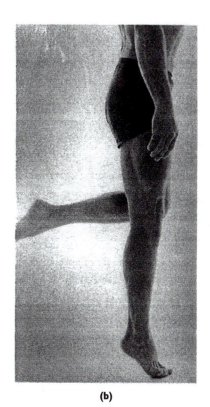

(b)

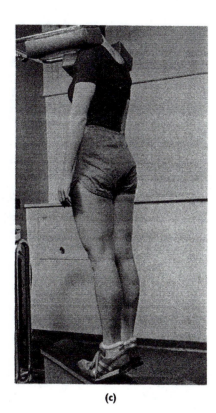

(c)

FIGURE 20.28

(a & b) Heel-raising exercise

To progress rapidly, this exercise should initially be performed using both legs and the support of a table. As confidence and strength are gained, the affected leg may be worked independently of support. (c) Advanced heel-raising exercise—weighted resistance plus the use of a slant board.

3.   Various types of isotonic machines are available for strengthening the muscles around the ankle (Figure 20.32). However, the use of an elastic band (sections of innertube, surgical tubing, Thera-band™) is effective. Eversion exercises strengthen the peroneal muscles, which dynamically stabilize and help protect the ankle from inversion sprains. The athlete sits with the knee flexed 45° to 90°, the heel resting firmly on the floor. The affected foot is positioned in line with the knee, and the band is attached around the forefoot so that resistance will increase with eversion of the foot. The other end of the band should be firmly attached to a stable object (e.g., leg of a table). The athlete moves the ankle/foot away from the stabilizing object while maintaining heel and knee position throughout the motion. Once the athlete has reached terminal motion, the ankle/foot is then returned to the starting position. The athlete must control the band eccentrically as well. Inversion with resistance should be performed in much the same manner, with the elastic band placed on the opposite side of the foot. Dorsiflexion can be achieved by placing the band across the dorsum of the foot with

the Achilles resting on a 5- to 6-inch roll. This allows the ankle to move freely throughout the range of motion. Three to five sets of 12 to 15 repetitions should be completed for each exercise. Both the injured and uninjured ankle/foot should be exercised. As the athlete's strength increases, he/she should increase the resistance by moving further from the point of attachment of the band (Figure 20.29).

4.   Refer to Chapter 2 for Achilles stretching. One leg is stretched at a time. The athlete leans forward against the wall. The leg is fully extended at the knee and the heel is on the ground. He or she holds for twenty seconds. The knee is then bent and the stretch repeated for twenty seconds. This should be a very gentle stretch without any force or bounce, and though there may be a slight burning, no pain should be felt. It is important that the athlete keep the foot pointed forward and not abducted, with the weight on the lateral side of the foot, so that the foot does not pronate. A slant board (Figure 20.30) can also be used. Achilles stretching should be done on the affected as well as the unaffected side, and

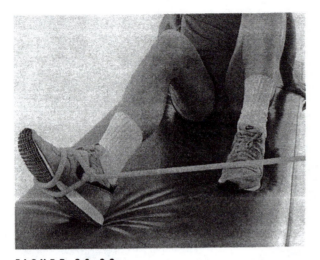

FIGURE 20.29
Peroneal strengthening exercise
Elasticized tubing or a rubber band is used as resistance. The heel is kept firmly on the ground as the forefoot is brought into abduction.

TABLE 20.10 *Outline of an ankle rehabilitation program*

		Stage				
No.	Exercise	I	II	III	IV	V
1.	Heel raises with body weight using both legs, progressing to single leg/heel raises				+	
2.	Heel raises with resistance starting with double-leg and progressing to single-leg raises			+	+	+
3.	Isotonic ankle exercises, including inversion, eversion, and dorsiflexion			+	+	+
4.	Achilles stretching—standing with knee bent and with leg straight			+	+	+
5.	Heel- and toe-walking			+	+	

it should become a standard exercise in the athlete's workout schedule.

5. Heel- and toe-walking are useful, simple methods of strengthening the lower leg muscles (Tables 20.10).

STAGE IV:

1. Isotonic exercises should continue, incorporating an explosive eversion motion and a controlled eccentric motion. This exercise will educate the lateral ankle stabilizers to contract in a powerful manner, thus stabilizing the ankle before the lateral ligaments are stressed or torn.

2. If isokinetic resistance is available, it should be employed on a daily basis for strength, power, and endurance. Inversion-eversion and plantar-dorsiflexion movements should be performed.

3. Useful proprioceptive exercises are hopping on one foot, hopping in pre-set patterns, hopping while bouncing a ball, and balancing on a balance board. Commercial balance boards are available. However a simple but effective board can be constructed by cutting a 2 × 4 into two semicircles. Cut one in half and secure it to one side of a 20-inch round plywood. The athlete should be careful when using this board, and should probably be assisted initially; otherwise re-injury might occur (Figure 20.33).

FIGURE 20.30
A slant board
This is useful for stretching the gastrocnemius-soleus muscle group and the Achilles tendon.

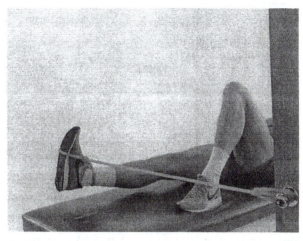

FIGURE 20.31
Strengthening hip abduction (gluteus medius) using elastic tubing
The gluteus medius muscle is often found to be weak following an ankle sprain.

FIGURE 20.32
Ankle-strengthening device

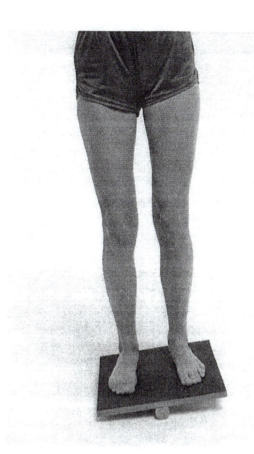

FIGURE 20.33
Balancing on a tilt board
This exercise helps improve balance and proprioception. It may be done as a training exercise, but is particularly useful in the later stages of ankle rehabilitation.

4.   Running can now be incorporated into the program—straight-ahead jogging only at first. The speed can gradually be increased until a full sprint is achieved. This can be augmented by running rapidly in place with the feet toeing slightly inward and arms pumping vigorously. (See section on knee rehabilitation.)

5.   Rope jumping should begin with low jumps on both feet. One-legged jumping on the affected leg can be started when there is no discomfort or apprehension of instability.

6.   Hopping onto a raised platform and in figure eights develops strength and proprioceptive feedback. Initially, hopping from side to side should be attempted, moving to a slightly raised platform and gradually increasing the height and number of repetitions (Table 20.11).

STAGE V: The final functional exercises are designed to put the ankle through its fullest range of movement and to make certain it can withstand the stress of active competition.

TABLE 20.11 *Outline of an ankle rehabilitation program*

No.	Exercise	Stage I	II	III	IV	V
	Stage IV					
1.	Isotonic ankle exercises				+	+
2.	Isokinetic exercises				+	+
3.	Hopping and bouncing a ball simultaneously				+	+
4.	Proprioceptive exercises, balance boards				+	+
5.	Running in place rapidly				+	+
6.	Straight-ahead jogging, gradually increasing to a run				+	+
7.	Jumping rope				+	+
8.	Hopping onto raised platforms and in figure-eight patterns				+	+

TABLE 20.12 *Outline of an ankle rehabilitation program*

No.	Exercise	Stage I	II	III	IV	V
	Stage V					
1.	Running sprints					+
2.	Weave patterns					+
3.	Cutting patterns					+
4.	Running—figure eights, crossovers sideways, and sport-specific patterns					+

1. Sprints alternating with jogging are started. The athlete marks off a running path approximately the length of a football field, making sure the running surface is smooth and without holes or bumps. The athlete accelerates over the first ten yards to full speed, then decelerates the last ten yards, avoiding abrupt stops.

2. Once the athlete is able to complete 8 to 10 100-yard lengths without pain or limp, decrease the speed to a jog and begin a gradual weave pattern, turning from left to right every ten yards. As the athlete is able to complete this stage of the running program, increase the speed to a sprint.

3. Begin with a jog again and begin a cutting pattern from left to right every five yards. Increase the speed as tolerated until a full-speed cut is achieved.

4. At this point begin with figure eights, crossovers, sideways running, and sport-specific patterns. Figure eights should be large at first and performed at a slow pace. As confidence increases, smaller and smaller figure eights are run with increasing speed. Crossovers are used in two different forms: the same leg can cross over in front each time, or alternate legs can cross over in front. Crossovers should be done in both directions (to the right and to the left). Sideways running consists of vigorous sprints over a distance of approximately fifteen yards. The athlete runs sideways and touches the ground at the farthest mark, then returns to the starting

place. This is repeated nonstop about twenty times. Sport-specific patterns should also be run as applicable.

When the athlete is able to complete the agility drill in its entirety without complaint of demonstration of a limp, swelling, or pain, and the ankle strength is within 80 to 90 percent of the uninjured ankle, then he or she should be able to return to activities. If the athlete has a grade II or III sprain, a brace should be worn at all times for at least six weeks postinjury, and only during activities after that time. The athlete should continue the ankle progressive exercises throughout the rest of the season. All resistive exercises should be performed after activities, followed with ice to reduce the possibility of reinjury and inflammation (Table 20.12).

Conditions Associated with Ankle Sprains

The following conditions may be associated with an ankle sprain, or they may occur independently but with mechanisms similar to those causing ankle sprains.

Syndemosis Sprains of the Ankle

Less frequent than inversion ankle sprains, tibiofibular syndesmosis sprains characteristically require prolonged recovery. The mechanism of injury may result in an external rotational force to the ankle and foot. This injury sometimes involves some or all of the following structures:

1. Anterior tibiofibular ligament
2. Posterior tibiofibular ligament

3. Transverse tibiofibular ligament
4. Interosseous membrane[20, 27]

Evaluation consists of performing an external rotational force to the ankle in a neutral position. In addition, a "squeeze test" should be performed. Ossification of the interosseous membrane may occur in the syndesmotic ankle sprain[20, 27] (Figure 20.40). Individuals with this type of injury usually recover with conservative measures, including bracing; however sprains associated with unstable ankle fractures and a widening of the joint mortise may require surgery.

Osteochondral Fracture of the Dome of the Talus

This fracture is often missed or may not be detected at all on the initial X-rays. The injury can follow any type of ankle sprain. The lesions are more widely spread across the talus than previously reported, with a high incidence in the anterolateral and posteromedial quadrant, respectively.[36] Tenderness over these areas, ankle

effusion, and lingering disability should lead one to suspect this type of injury (Figure 20.34). Bone scan and CT scan will aid in the detection of these lesions. Talar dome osteochondral fractures are usually treated conservatively and watched closely; they may need to be treated surgically if they do not heal.[36]

Subluxing Peroneal Tendon

A peroneal tendon subluxation can be confused with and ankle sprain, because is may give the athlete a feeling of instability as well as producing tenderness and swelling over the lateral malleolus. The initial injury may follow sudden dorsiflexion and eversion of the ankle, as when correcting an inversion twist.[37] However, it can occur from plantar flexion and eversion. The retinaculum gives way and the tendon slips out over the lateral malleolus and usually spontaneously returns.

The subluxing tendon is best diagnosed with the foot in dorsiflexion and everted against resistance. The tendons may be felt to slip over the lateral malleolus. Treatment, after the inflammation has resolved, is to place a horseshoe-shaped pad around the lateral malleolus, attempting to compress the tendons and keep them in place. If this is unsuccessful, surgery may be necessary if the condition is symptomatic.

Injury to the Os Trigonum

The os trigonum can be fractured or contused during plantar flexion injuries to the ankle. This condition presents with severe discomfort on the posterior aspect of the ankle, particularly with plantar flexion. In certain individuals, like ballet dancers, removal of the os trignonum may be required (Figure 20.35).

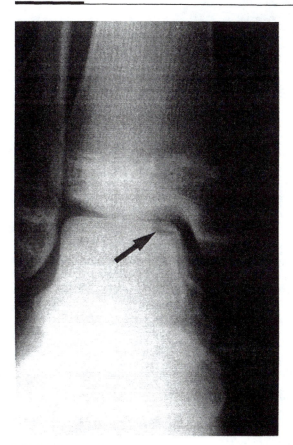

FIGURE 20.34
X-ray—osteochondral fracture of the dome of the talus

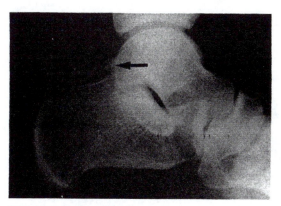

FIGURE 20.35
X-ray—os trigonum

Achilles Tendon Strain

The Achilles tendon and its surrounding soft tissues are sometimes injured during an ankle sprain and, in fact, may require a longer healing period than the ankle itself. Care should be taken when taping the ankle to avoid increasing pressure across the achilles when using heel locks.

Diagnosis is made by noting tenderness and swelling directly over the bifurcated ligament. X-rays are normal unless an avulsion fracture of the distal end of the calcaneus is present (Figure 20.36).[33] A bifurcated ligament sprain should be treated like an ankle sprain. Figure-eight taping or bracing should be used (see Chapter 4). If an avulsion fracture is present, the fragment may need to be excised (Figure 20.37).[37]

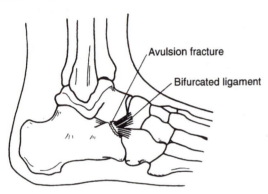

FIGURE 20.36
Avulsion fracture, distal calcaneus

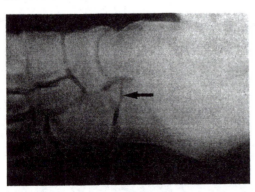

FIGURE 20.37
X-ray—an avulsion fracture off the distal calcaneus at the site of attachment of the bifurcated ligament

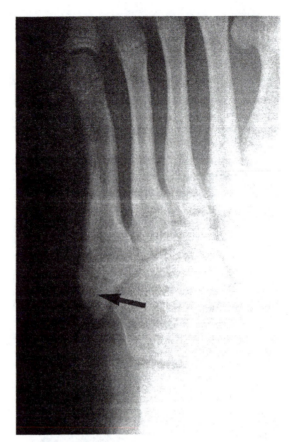

FIGURE 20.38
Avulsion fracture of the base of the fifth metatarsal, due to an inversion injury

Avulsion Fracture of the Base of the Fifth Metatarsal

An avulsion fracture of the fifth metatarsal base often occurs in conjunction with an inversion sprain. The peroneus brevis muscle contracts during an inversion, straining the tendon or avulsing a fragment of bone from the base of the fifth metatarsal (Figure 20.38). This condition usually heals if protected either by casting or use of a foot orthotic, as long as the fragment is not avulsed too far off the fifth metatarsal base, in which case surgical correction may be necessary.[26]

Other Conditions of the Ankle and Foot

Talar Spur (Tibiotalar Impingement)

Repetitive-force dorsiflexion can cause a building of spurs over the contact points of the tibia and talas. This can produce pain on dorsiflexion and inability to push off rapidly from a dorsiflexed position. Sometimes the talar spur is palpable. Diagnosis is best made with weight-bearing X-rays with the foot in a maximally dorsiflexed position (Figure 20.39). This syndrome can be differentiated from anterolateral soft tissue impingement of the lateral gutter with the use of magnetic resonance imaging (MRI) and mechanism. In the case of anterolateral soft tissue impingement, MRI indicates a thickening of the synovium about the anterolateral gutter. A typical mechanism is inversion stress versus forced dorsiflexion in tibiotalar impingement. Both injuries may develop osteophytes that may, in turn, require surgical removal.[26, 30]

Tibiofibular Synostosis

Calcification of the interosseous membrane between tibia and fibula at the inferior tibiofibular syndesmosis can occur after an ankle sprain, particularly after an inversion–internal-rotation sprain, but occasionally after an eversion sprain (Figure 20.40). Some athletes

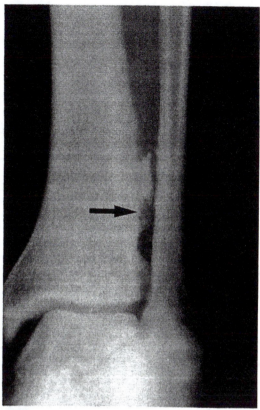

FIGURE 20.40
X-ray—tibiofibular synostosis
Calcification of the interosseous membrane between the tibia and fibula.

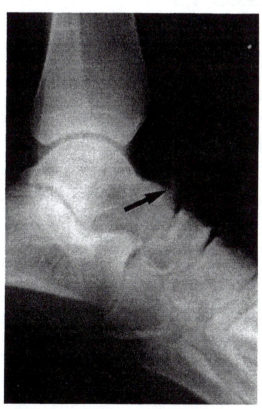

FIGURE 20.39
Tibiotalar impingement—due to a talar spur

suffer prolonged symptoms, with pain and impaired performance, presumably because of interference with the normal to-and-fro bowing action of the fibula which occurs while running.

Initially, rest followed by rehabilitation exercises may improve the problem in a percentage of these athletes. Some will require surgical treatment, however, which consists of removal of the calcification after it has matured. If surgery is performed too soon, the calcification will recur. Calcification may occur between the tibia and fibula without producing any significant symptoms and does not require any treatment.

Tarsal Tunnel Syndrome

Tarsal tunnel syndrome (entrapment neuropathy of the posterior tibial nerve) generally occurs where the nerve passes through the osseofibrous tunnel between the flexor retinaculum (lacinate ligament) and the medial malleolus. The entrapment is usually the result of abnormal foot function, especially of excessive pronation, which causes tightening of the flexor retinaculum. But it may be caused by a direct injury to the area (i.e., fracture of the medial malleolus or the talus).

SYMPTOMS AND SIGNS: Compression of the medial plantar branch of the posterior tibial nerve results in a burning or tingling sensation or pain in the medial arch region and the ball of the foot. A decrease in sensation may also be present over this area. If the medial calcaneal branch is entrapped, pain may be felt in the heel.

Tenderness is usually elicited over the nerve and just below and above it. Compressing the nerve against the underlying bone may cause pain in the arch or heel area. Tinel's sign (percussion over the nerve) is usually positive for tingling and pain along the course of the nerve.

TREATMENT: The tarsal tunnel syndrome may respond to a neutral-position, orthotic device designed to control excessive pronation. Local cortisone injections may be given in an attempt to free the entrapped nerve, but surgical release of the soft tissue causing the entrapment may be necessary.

Fracture of the Diaphysis of the Base of the Fifth Metatarsal

A transverse fracture of the diaphysis of the base of the fifth metatarsal (Jones fracture, Figure 20.41) should be differentiated from the more common avulsion fracture. The Jones fracture may begin as a stress fracture, becoming a complete fracture with an inversion injury, or may be an acute injury resulting from abnormal loading of the lateral part of the foot as the heel is elevated and the metatarsophalangeal joints are hyperextended.[38]

TREATMENT: Treatment for Jones fracture remains controversial, with conservative treatment utilizing a non-weight-bearing and, eventually, a weight-bearing cast. Surgical intervention includes bone grafting and the use of an intramedullary screw.[38] Nonunions and refractures are common with this type of injury.

The form of treatment that is most appropriate varies from case to case and is influenced by many factors, including the type of athlete (whether professional or recreational) and the type of sport in which the athlete participates. When healed, an in-shoe orthotic device may help redistribute the forces and prevent recurrence.

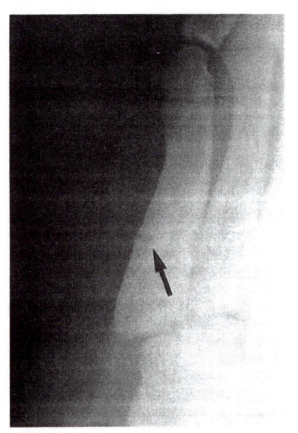

FIGURE 20.41
Stress fracture of the proximal diaphysis of the fifth metatarsal

Stress Fracture of the Metatarsal

ETIOLOGY: Metatarsal stress fractures appear to be related to either excessive hyper- or hypomobility of the foot. Prolonged pronation during the propulsive phase of gait may add considerable stress to the metatarsals. A cavus (high-arched) foot may not be able to pronate enough to absorb the forces generated by the ground on the foot and lower leg, thus increasing stress across the metatarsal arch, affecting primarily the second, third, and to a lesser extent the fourth and fifth metatarsals.

TREATMENT: Supportive (i.e., Lowdye; Figure 20.42) taping and off-the-shelf or custom foot orthotic devices with a metatarsal support may allow the athlete to continue activities. However, the intensity and duration of workouts should be decreased for a time. Metatarsal pads should be placed so that the bulk of the pad is just proximal and not distal to the head of the metatarsal (Figure 20.42). Distal placement will increase pressure on the metatarsal head and at the fracture site. Ice, elevation, and anti-inflammatory medica-

FIGURE 20.42
(a) Lowdye taping technique.
(b) Metatarsal pad placement

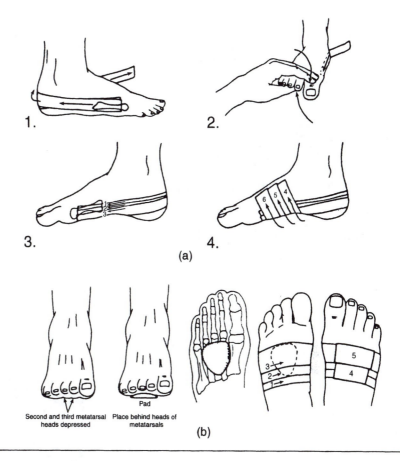

1.
2.
3.
4.

(a)

Second and third metatarsal
heads depressed

Pad
Place behind heads of
metatarsals

(b)

tion may be necessary if swelling is present. If ambulation is painful, crutches along with stiff-soled shoes and foot orthoses may be used until the athlete is able to ambulate with minimal pain (Figure 20.43).

Morton's Neuroma (Interdigital Neuroma)

ETIOLOGY: Compression of the bifurcation of the neurovascular bundle between the metatarsal heads can result in the formation of a neuroma (Figure 20.44).[39] This compression is usually due to a shearing force caused by a hypermobile foot with excessive pronation during heel-off in the stance phase, just as the toes are maximally dorsiflexed prior to toe-off. Tight-fitting shoes with a narrow toe box may also be blamed for this phenomenon.[39]

SYMPTOMS: There are two varieties of presenting symptoms.

Acute—Usually occurring in a sprinter and presenting with an acute electric-shock-like pain radiating from the forefoot down to the toes (usually the third and fourth toes, but it can occur between any two). The athlete rapidly removes the shoe from the foot to obtain relief.

Chronic—Presents with dull discomfort under the foot which, on palpation, is localized to the metatarsal interspace involved. If the condition has been present for some time, changes in sensation along the inside of the toes supplied by that particular nerve can be observed.

TREATMENT: Initially a metatarsal pad is used to relieve pressure on the nerve by uplifting the metatarsal arch at the heads and distal shafts. An in-shoe orthotic device may be used to prevent excessive pronation and also to hold the metatarsal pad in place, eliminating the need to tape the pad to the foot. Footwear must have adequate room in the toe box to accommodate the appliance and metatarsal pad. If these treatments do not produce satisfactory results, a local anesthetic and corticosteroid injection should be administered around

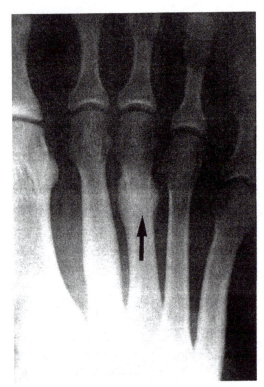

FIGURE 20.43
X-ray—stress fracture of the shaft of the third metatarsal, showing profuse callus formation

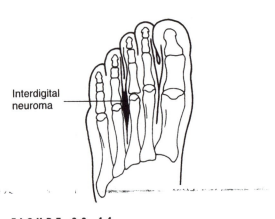

FIGURE 20.44
Morton's neuroma
Interdigital neuroma between the third and fourth metatarsal heads.

the neuroma. Surgical excision may be necessary in resistant cases.

Sesamoiditis

A sesamoid bone is one that is found within the substance of a tendon, for example, the patella. In the foot, sesamoids are found within the tendons of the flexor hallucis brevis. These sesamoids distribute and disperse the weight of the take-off phase of gait and increase the mechanical advantage of the flexor tendons.[40] It is surprising that so few athletes develop problems related to the sesamoids, as these bones are subjected to considerable force with each strike of the foot.

Usually two sesamoids are present—a medial, or tibial, sesamoid and a lateral, or fibular, sesamoid. The medial sesamoid is not infrequently *bipartite*, that is, the bone shows as two separate pieces on X-rays and this can be confused with a fracture (Figure 20.45).

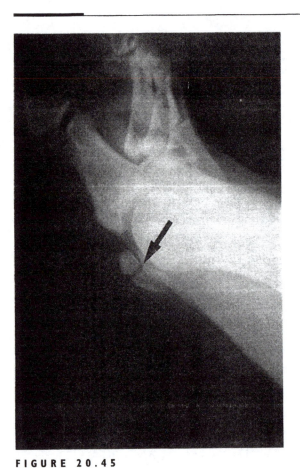

FIGURE 20.45
X-ray—sesamoids
A bipartile sesamoid usually has smooth edges, whereas an irregular crack may indicate a fracture or stress fracture.

Sesamoiditis is an inflammation of the tissues surrounding the sesamoids, which usually affects the medial more than the lateral sesamoid. It occurs most frequently in the cavus type of foot with a rigid, plantar flexed first ray, a high arch, and a tight Achilles tendon, but it can occur in any type of foot.

Tenderness, and sometimes swelling, is localized to the head of the first metatarsal on its plantar aspect. On passive dorsiflexion of the foot and palpation over the head of the first metatarsal, significant discomfort may be felt.

This condition is best treated with a foot orthotic that places the foot near its neutral position and balances the forefoot so as to reduce the stress at the first metatarsal head and distribute the forces across the lesser metatarsal heads. Ice massage, ultrasound, and other modalities, including anti-inflammatory medication and, occasionally, a corticosteroid injection may also be used.

The metatarsal sesamoids can also develop stress fractures or, rarely, acute fractures. Conservative treatment, which may include non-weight-bearing on the appropriate part followed by a foot orthoses, usually provides adequate results, though surgical excision of the affected sesamoid after failure of conservative treatment may be necessary.[40]

Acute Hyperdorsiflexion Injuries to the Metatarsophalangeal Joint of the Big Toe

This type of injury has become more prominent with the use of synthetic surfaces in conjunction with more flexible shoes. Another factor predisposing an athlete to "turf toe" may be decreased range of motion, both in plantar and dorsiflexion of the metatarsophalangeal joint, compared to the uninjured side.[41]

Most injuries occur when there is excessive dorsiflexion at the MP joint—the heel is often in the air. If the athlete is then forced toward the ground, the MP joint of the first toe is stressed. Occasionally the second, third, and fourth MP joints are involved, which can cause fractures of the metatarsal shafts, dislocations of the MP joints, or both.

Hyperdorsiflexion of the MP joint results in capsular tears, articular cartilage damage, and possibly a fracture of the medial sesamoid. These injuries may produce major incapacity in terms of discomfort and return to participation[42] (Figure 20.46).

TREATMENT: Initially treatment should be ice, anti-inflammatory medication, and protective taping. Walking should be allowed only when performed in a normal fashion without a limp.

In the meantime, the athlete should be cycling, swimming, and doing foot and toe exercises that do not cause discomfort. (See section on ankle rehabilitation.) As the athlete improves, graduated running activities can be started, but these should be undertaken only when the athlete is pain free, which might take a considerable amount of time. The toe should be taped (see Chapter 4) in neutral or slight plantarflexion, and the shoe should be firm enough to prevent excessive dorsiflexion of the MP joint. A steel spring plate or thermoplastic insert with a great toe extension can be incorporated into the

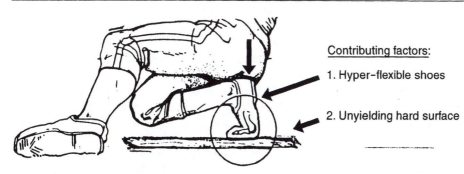

Contributing factors:

1. Hyper-flexible shoes

2. Unyielding hard surface

FIGURE 20.46
Mechanism for hyperextension injury to the first metatarsophalangeal joint
(Modified from SA Rodeo, S O'Brien, RF Warren, R Barnes, TL Wickiewicz, and MF Dillingham. "Turf-toe: An analysis of metatarsophalangeal joint sprains in professional football players," *The American Journal of Sports Medicine* 18(3):280–285, 1990.)

shoe. Surgery is usually undertaken only in resistant cases where healing does not occur.

Plantar Fasciitis (Also see Chapter 21)

ETIOLOGY: Plantar fasciitis is an injury to the plantar fascia on the bottom of the foot caused by stepping on a rock in the heel region or by the repetitive stress of running or other weight-bearing activities when good arch support is lacking in the shoes.

SYMPTOMS AND SIGNS: Pressure over the plantar fascia on its origin on the calcaneal or when the toes are extended may cause pain. The first step on getting out of bed in the morning may generate a great deal of pain—as would occur if a piece of glass was embedded in the heel. The pain may decrease but, as the day progresses, it may intensify.

TREATMENT: Plantar fascia responds well to phonophoresis or iontophoresis followed by ultrasound, stretching of the plantar fascia and Achilles tendon, followed by ice or ice with electrical stimulation. Low-dye taping may help to support the arch and take the pressure off the plantar fascia as it heals. If low-dye taping helps, an orthotic may be beneficial as a long-term solution. The orthotic needs to be of medium density. Hard plastic orthotics tend to irritate the plantar fascia, and soft orthotics do not provide the support needed.

Corns and Calluses

Both corns and calluses are composed of the same type of tissue and are a thickening of the skin in response to friction or trauma. Corns are typically found on the toes around the non-weight-bearing areas, whereas calluses are lesions on the plantar aspect of the foot.[43]

Corns may be either hard or soft. Hard corns (heloma durum or clavus durus) usually occur on top of the toes; soft corns (heloma molle or clavus mollis) are found between the toes and are kept soft by perspiration. Soft corns result from pressure of one toe against another and are often caused by shoes that are too narrow.[44]

Calluses (tyloma) are generally found on the weight-bearing plantar surface of the foot around the metatarsal heads and the heel. Callus formation, especially in athletes, is normal; however, when allowed to form in excess, the callus may become painful. A well defined and symptomatic callus, called an *intractable plantar keratosis*, is formed by a combination of internal pressure from bone to the skin and external forces of footwear against the foot.[43, 44] Like a corn, this callus

can be painful and is best treated by correcting the mechanical problem causing the shearing action of the foot. Customized orthotic devices may provide relief, but caution should be used, as ill-fitting orthoses may also cause abnormal callous formation.

Because shoes are the most important causative factor of both corns or calluses, the athletic trainer should examine and evaluate them. In addition to proper length and width, depth of the toe box is of primary consideration in shoe selection. If there is a great deal of deformity in the toes, or if there is a plantar displacement of the metatarsal heads, foot orthoses or protective padding may be necessary. If these measures fail to alleviate the problem, surgical correction provides good results in most cases.

Blisters

Blisters are best left alone if possible, and the layers should be allowed to heal together. It may be necessary to drain the fluid to allow for tissue adhesion. The clinician should cleanse the skin with alcohol or Betadine and a sterile needle or blade should be used to lance the blister. If a blister has already ruptured and the tissue flap is loose, the peripheral tissue should be trimmed. In both cases, the area should be cleansed and a topical antibiotic applied. Donut padding or hydrogel dressings such as Spenco SecondSkin may also reduce pressure and shearing across the blister site. Care should be taken not to apply tape or other adhesives across the blister, as it may adhere to or increase damage to the blister site. Risk of complications such as infection increase when raw skin is exposed or nonsterile techniques are performed. Medical referral may be required if infection is suspected (Figure 20.47 and 20.48).[45]

Ingrown Toenails

Ingrown toenails result from the nail plate becoming imbedded in the surrounding tissue. This occurs for a variety of reasons, including direct trauma to the toenail, improperly fitted shoes, and incorrect trimming of the toenails.

The ingrown toenail may require local antibiotic ointment if the area becomes infected, and the offending nail border may need to be surgically removed. If the nail is then kept properly trimmed, and shoes which provide adequate depth, width, and length are worn, permanent relief can result. However, if these measures fail, it may be necessary to remove the offending nail completely. This will usually provide permanent relief from the problem.

Note: Additional injuries of the lower leg and foot are discussed in Chapter 22.

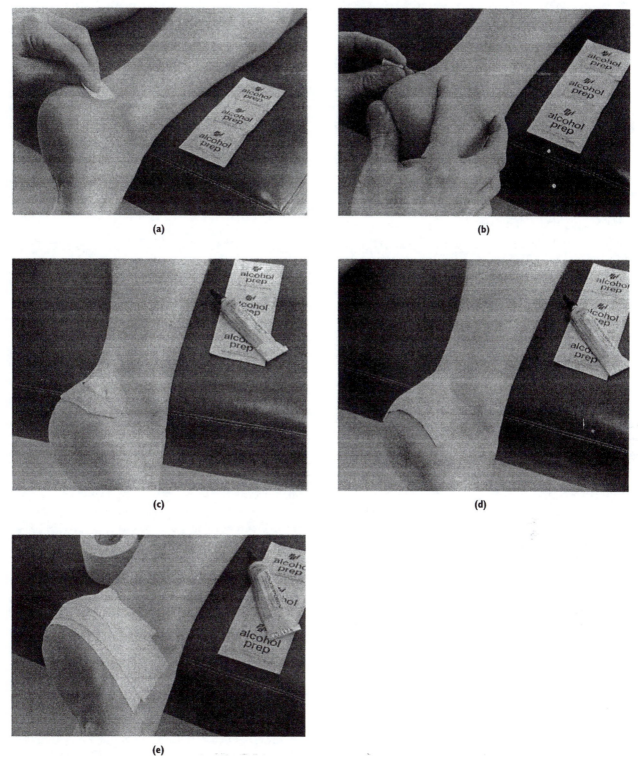

FIGURE 20.47

Draining a blister

(a) The area around the blister is thoroughly cleaned with alcohol or Betadine. (b) The trainers's hands should be surgically clean or sterile gloves should be worn. A sterile needle is used to pierce the blister. (c) The roof of the blister is left on. Antibiotic ointment (such as Polysporin) is applied over the blister. A moleskin "donut" is applied around the blister. (d) A moleskin cover is then applied. (e) If desired, a final layer of tape may be useful in securing the moleskin.

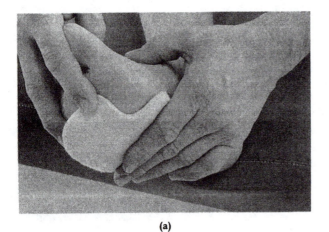
(a)

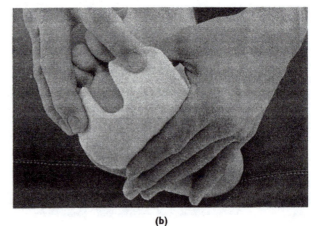
(b)

FIGURE 20.48

Felt pad accommodations

(a) Pain under the first metatarsal head may result from a callus, blister, or sesamoiditis. The felt is cut out to accomodate the painful area, and tapered off towards the second through fifth toes. (b) Pain under the head of one of the other metatarsals, from a callus, metatarsalgia, or a neuroma.

REFERENCES

1. Laurin C. Mathieu J: Sagittal mobility of the normal ankle. *Clin Orthop* 108:99–104, 1975.

2. Root ML, Orien WP, Weed JH: *Normal and Abnormal Function of the Foot.* Los Angeles, Clinical Biomechanics Corporation, 1977.

3. Gunther SF: An avoidable soccer injury. *Am J Sports Med* 2:167–169, 1974.

4. Arner O, Lindholm Å: What is tennis leg? *Acta Chir Scand* 116:73–77, 1958.

5. Miller WA: Rupture of musculotendinous juncture of the medial head of gastrocnemius muscle. *Am J Sports Med* 5:191–193, 1977.

6. Lee HB: Avulsion and rupture of the tendo calcaneus after injection of hydrocortisone. *Brit Med J* 2:395, 1957.

7. Melmed EP: Spontaneous bilateral rupture of the calcaneal tendon during steroid therapy. *J Bone Joint Surg* 47B:104–105, 1965.

8. Thompson TC, Dougherty JH: Spontaneous rupture of tendo achilles. A new clinical diagnostic test. *J Trauma* 2:126–129, 1962.

9. Ranney DA: A good test by any other name. Letter to the editor. *Phys Sportsmed* 8:10, December 1980.

10. Rubin BD, Wilson HJ: Surgical repair of the interrupted achilles tendon. *J Trauma* 20:248–249, 1980.

11. DiSteffano VJ, Nixon JE: Ruptures of the achilles tendon. *J Sports Med* 1:34–37, 1975.

12. Cetti R, Christensen S, Ejsted R, Jensen NM, Jorgensen U: Operative versus nonoperative treatment of Achilles tendon rupture. *Am J Sports Med* 21(6):791–799, 1993.

13. Skeoch DU: Spontaneous partial subcutaneous ruptures of the tendo achilles. Review of the literature and evaluation of 16 involved tendons. *Am J Sports Med* 9:20–22, 1981.

14. Denstad TF, Roaas A: Surgical treatment of partial achilles tendon rupture. *Am J Sports Med* 7:15–17, 1979.

15. McCluskey GM, Blackburn A, Lewis T: Prevention of ankle sprains. *Am J Sports Med* 4:151–157, 1976.

16. Freeman MAR, Dean MR, Hanham IW: Etiology and prevention of functional instability of the foot. *J Bone Joint Surg* 47B:678–685, 1965.

17. Laurin CA, Quellet R, St Jacques R: Talar and subtalar tilt: An experimental investigation *Can J Surg* 11:270–279, 1968.

18. Roy SP: Evaluation and treatment of the stable ankle sprain. *Phys Sportsmed* 5:60–63, August 1977.

19. Barrett JR, Tansi JL, Drake C, Fuller D, Kawasaki RI, Fenton RM: High versus low top shoes for prevention of ankle sprains in basketball players. *Am J Sports Med* 21(4):582–585, 1993.

20. Taylor DC, Englehardt DL, Bassett FH: Syndesmosis sprains of the ankle: The influence of heterotropic ossification. *Am J Sports Med* 20(2):146–150, 1992.

21. Henry JH, et al: Tibiofibular synostosis in professional basketball players. *Am J Sports Med* 21(4):619–622, 1993.

22. Rovere GD, Clarke TJ, Yates CS, Burley K: Retrospective comparison of taping and ankle stabilizers in preventing ankle injuries. *Am J Sports Med* 16(3):228–233, 1988.

23. Blyth CS, Mueller FO: *Football Injuries.* Minneapolis, McGraw-Hill Inc., 1974, p. 19.

24. Broström L: Sprained ankles. V. Treatment and prognosis in recent ligament ruptures. *Acta Chir Scand* 132:537–550, 1966.

25. Garrick JG: When can I . . . ? A practical approach to rehabilitation illustrated by treatment of an ankle injury. *Am J Sports Med* 9:67–68, 1981.

26. McDermott EP: Basketball injuries of the foot and ankle. *Clin Sports Med* 12:373–393, April 1993.

27. Boytim MF, Fischer DA, Neumann L: Syndesmotic ankle sprains. *Am J Sports Med* 19(3):294–298, 1991.

28. Smith GR, Winquist RA, Allan NK, et al: Subtle transchondral fractures of the talar dome: a radiological perspective. *Radiology* 124:667–673, 1977.

29. Canale ST, Belding RH: Osteochondral lesions of the talus. *J Bone Joint Surg* 62A:97–102, 1980.

30. Ferkel RD, Karzel RP, Pizzo WD, Friedman MJ, Fischer SP: Arthroscopic treatment of anterolateral impingement of the ankle. *Am J Sports Med* 7(5):440–446, 1991.

31. Laurin CA, Fleming LL, Hamilton WG, Hanson ST, Johnson KA: Symposium: Ligamentous injuries about the ankle. *Contemp Orthop* 25(1):81–100, July 1992.

32. Marti R: Dislocations of the peroneal tendons. *Am J Sports Med* 5:19–22, 1977.

33. Arner O, Lindholm Å: Avulsion fracture of the os calcaneus. *Acta Chir Scand* 117:258–260, 1959.

34. Ryan JB, Hopkinson WJ, Wheeler JH, Arciero RA, Swain JH: Office management of the acute ankle sprain. *Clin Sports Med* 7(3):477–495, July 1989.

35. Johnson KA, Teasdall RD: Sprained ankles as they relate to the basketball player. *Clin Sports Med* 12(2):363–367, April 1993.

36. Loomer R, Fisher C, Lloyd-Smith R, Sisler J, Cooney T: Osteochondral lesions of the talus. *Am J Sports Med* 21(1):13–19, 1993.

37. Degan TJ, Morrey BF, Braun DP: Surgical excision for anterior-process fractures of the calcaneus. *J Bone Joint Surg* 64A:519–524, 1982.

38. Meyer SA, Salzman CL, Albright JP: Stress Fractures of the foot and leg. *Clin Sports Med* 12(2):395–413, April 1993.

39. Mann RA: Diseases of the nerves of the foot. In *Surgery of the Foot*. St. Louis: C.V. Mosby, pp. 199–208, 1986.

40. McBryde AM, Anderson RB: Sesamoid foot problems in the athlete. *Clin Sports Med* 7(1):51–61, January 1988.

41. Rodeo SA, O'Brien S, Warren RF, Barnes R, Wickiewicz TL, Dillingham MF: Turf-toe: An analysis of metatarsophalangeal joint sprains in professional football players. *Am J Sports Med* 18(3):280–285, 1990.

42. Coker TP, Arnold J, Weber D: Traumatic lesions of the metatarsophalangeal joint of the great toe in athletes. *Am J Sports Med* 6:326–334, 1978.

43. Brainard BJ: Managing corns and plantar calluses. *Phys Sports Med* 19(12):61–67, December 1991.

44. Katchis SD, Hershman EB: Broken nails to blistered heels. Managing foot lesions in the office. *Phys Sports Med* 21(5):95–104, May 1993.

45. Ramsey ML: Managing friction blisters of the feet. *Phys Sports Med* 20(1):117–124, January 1992.

RECOMMENDED READINGS

Arrowsmith SR, Fleming LL, Allman FL: Traumatic dislocation of peroneal tendons. *Am J Sports Med* 11(3):142–146, 1983.

Black KP, Schultz TK, Cheung NL: Compartment syndromes in athletes. *Clin Sports Med* 9(2):471–486, 1990.

Brostrôm L: Sprained ankles. III. Clinical observations in recent ligament ruptures. *Acta Chir Scand* 130:560–569, 1965.

Brostrôm L: Sprained ankles. IV. Histologic changes in recent and "chronic" ligament ruptures. *Acta Chir Scand* 132:248–253, 1966.

Bunch RP, Bednarski K, Holland D, Macinanti R: Ankle joint support: A comparison of reusable lace-on braces with taping and wrapping. *Phys Sports Med* 13(5): 51–62:May 1985.

Burks RT, Bean BG, Marcus R, Barker HB: Analysis of athletic performance with prophylactic ankle devices. *Am J Sports Med* 19(2):104–106, 1991.

Case WS: Recovering from ankle sprains. *Phys Sports Med* 21(11):43–44, November 1993.

Cetti R: Conservative treatment of injury to the fibular ligaments of the ankle. *Brit J Sports Med* 16:47–52, 1982.

Cleaves G: Orthoplast Splint: Support method for a sprained ankle. *Athletic Training* 15:94–95, 1980.

Cox JS, Hewes TF: "Normal" talar tilt angle. *Clin Orthop* 140:37–41, 1979.

Evans GA, Frenyo SD: The stress-tenogram in the diagnosis of ruptures of the lateral ligament of the ankle. *J Bone Joint Surg* 61B:347–351, 1979.

Freeman MAR: Treatment of ruptures of the lateral ligament of the ankle. *J Bone Joint Surg* 47B:661–668, 1965.

Frost HM, Hanson CA: Technique for testing the drawer sign in the ankle. *Clin Orthop* 123:49–51, 1977.

Glasgow M, Jackson A, Jamieson AM: Instability of the ankle after injury to the lateral ligament. *J Bone Joint Surg* 62B: 196–200, 1980.

Glick JM, Gordon RB, Nishimoto D: The prevention and treatment of ankle injuries. *Am J Sports Med* 4:136–141, 1976.

Greene TA, Wight CR: A comparative support evaluation of three ankle orthoses before, during and after exercise. *J Orthop Sports Phys Ther* 11(10):453–466, April 1990.

Inman V: *The Joints of the Ankle*. Baltimore, Williams and Wilkins, 1976.

Jackson DL, Haglund B: Tarsal tunnel syndrome in athletes—case reports and literature review. *Am J Sports Med* 19(1):61–65, 1991.

Johannsen A: Radiological diagnosis of lateral ligament lesion of the ankle. A comparison between talar tilt and anterior drawer sign. *Acta Chir Scand* 49:295–301, 1978.

Knight KL: Ankle rehabilitation with cryotherapy. *Phys Sportsmed* 7:133, November, 1979.

Lindstrand A: Clinical diagnosis of lateral ankle sprains. In *Injuries of the Ligaments and their Repair: Hand—Knee — Foot,* edited by Chapchal G. Littleton MA, PSG Publisher, 1977, pp. 178–180.

McCluskey GM, Blackburn A, Lewis T: A treatment for ankle sprains. *Am J Sports Med* 4:158–161, 1976.

Rodeo SA, O' Brien S, Warren RF, Barnes R, Wickiewicz TL: Turf-toe: Diagnosis and treatment. *Phys Sports Med* 17:132–147, April 1989.

Shields CL, Kerlan RK, Jobe FW, et al: The Cybex II evaluation of surgically repaired achilles tendon ruptures. *Am J Sports Med* 6:369–372, 1978.

Stein SR, Luekens CA: Methods and rationale for closed treatment of achilles tendon ruptures. *Am J Sports Med* 4:162–169, 1976.

Symposium: Soft tissue injuries about the ankle. Is there a rational approach to the diagnosis and treatment? *Am J Sports Med* 5:225–257, 1977.

Walsch WM, Blackburn TA: Prevention of ankle sprains. *Am J Sports Med* 5:243–245, 1977.

Zinman H, Keret D, Reis ND: Fracture of the medial sesamoid bone of the hallux. *J Trauma* 21:581–582, 1981.

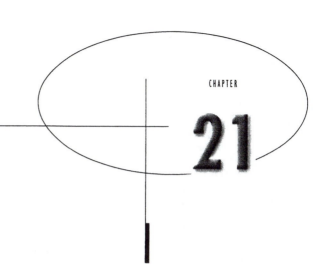

Injuries to the Running Athlete, Particularly the Long-Distance Runner

As the keynote speaker at the 47th Annual Meeting and Clinical Symposium of the National Athletic Trainers Association in Orlando, Florida, in 1996, two-time Olympic marathon medalist Frank Shorter praised athletic trainers. When he was 15 years old, he had a metatarsal condition that was correctly evaluated and treated by an athletic trainer. He stated that if his foot pain had continued much longer, he might have given up running. Thus, we have, in part, an athletic trainer to thank for the United States Olympic marathon gold medal in 1972 and the silver medal in 1976. Athletic trainers do have an impact in keeping runners healthy.

Biomechanics of a Normal Running Gait

One of the major differences between walking and running is that during running the body is totally airborne for a period of time. When observing a runner from the side, notice that the stride is divided into two distinct phases:

1. Phase I: The *contact* phase—one foot is in contact with the ground

2. Phase II: The *swing* phase—the leg and foot are swinging through the air[1,2]

Each of these phases may be further broken down as follows:

1. Contact phase (Figure 21.1)

    a. foot strike

    b. mid-support

    c. take-off

2. Swing phase (Figure 21.2)

    a. follow-through

    b. forward swing

    c. foot descent

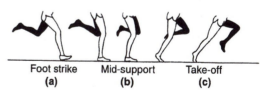

FIGURE 21.1
The running gait—the contact phase (note the movement of the unshaded leg)

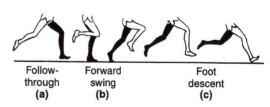

FIGURE 21.2
The running gait—the swing phase

Contact Phase

Runners contact the ground in one of three ways[3] (Figure 21.3):

1. With the heel
2. Flat-footed or with the ball of the foot, followed by rocking back onto the heel
3. On the ball of the foot

For purposes of description, this discussion assumes that the contact phase is initiated by heel contact. This phase consists of three parts.

1. *Foot strike:* Initial heel contact is normally on the lateral aspect. This is due to the varus angle formed by the lower leg in relation to the ground during running, as well as by the supinated position of the foot at the moment of impact. The entire foot then sequentially makes contact with the ground, as the heel moves toward eversion and the midtarsal joint moves toward pronation.

2. *Mid-support:* During foot strike and mid-support, the foot is loose and is easily able to adapt to the uneven surface and act as a shock absorber. This is because of the pronatory action of the subtalar and midtarsal joints, which allows the foot to be a *loose adaptor.* During mid-support, the tarsal joint reaches the limit of pronation. At the same time, the lower leg passes over the foot and the heel starts to rise from the ground. This is a critical time for the foot to change its function—from being a loose "bag of bones" adapting to the surface and absorbing shock to being a powerful and firm lever propelling the body forward.

3. *Take-off:* During this phase the foot is moving toward a supinated position. The muscle action and the angular relationships of the tarsals result in the foot being *locked.* In most athletes the big toe is passively dorsiflexed, and it very seldom actively plantar flexes. In these athletes it does not "flip" the foot off the ground. The value of the big toe being able to actively plantar flex is still unknown.

Effects of Foot Movements on the Lower Extremities

The lower leg is forced to follow the action of the foot, as evidenced by looking at someone who is standing. When the arch of the foot is lowered, the tibia rotates inwardly; when the arch is raised, the tibia rotates externally. This also has an effect on the patella and the femur and gives rise to overuse injuries at the knee. (Figure 21.4)

While watching an athlete run (particularly with the aid of a high-speed movie), notice how the tibia is slightly externally rotated at the beginning of foot strike. As pronation occurs during the mid-support phase, the tibia is forced to follow the subtalar joint movement, and it rotates internally. The tibia again rotates exter-

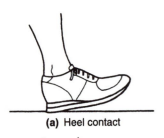

(a) Heel contact

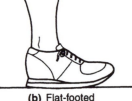

(b) Flat-footed

(c) On the ball of the foot

FIGURE 21.3
Variations in foot contact in runners

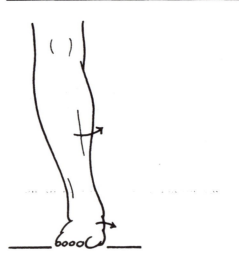

FIGURE 21.4
Foot pronation results in internal rotation of the tibia

nally when supination occurs during the latter part of the take-off phase.

The angle of the femoral neck influences the angle of the knee and the position of the foot. The femur rotates in the same direction as the tibia (internal rotation during midsupport; external rotation during takeoff), but it is not quite so obliged to follow the foot. The patella tends to follow the movement of the femur by virtue of its position in the intercondylar groove of that bone.

The posture of the athlete, particularly the lower back, greatly influences the way the legs and feet are able to function. An erect posture allows the legs to work in the most efficient manner and the feet to strike the ground in the optimum position (Figure 21.5). Conversely, foot function affects the posture of the lumbar spine.

Anatomical Variations

The description provided above is of the ideal. There are many variations on this theme, some of which may result in the development of injuries associated with running.

1. Tibia varum and calcaneus varus may require a considerable amount of pronation through the midtarsal joint so that the first metatarsal head is brought down to the ground (Figure 21.6).

2. A tight Achilles tendon can cause either early heel lift-off or excessive pronation in order to enable the leg to pass over the foot (Figure 21.7).

3. A tight Achilles tendon can be associated with a high-arched (cavus) foot, a rigid first ray which is plan-

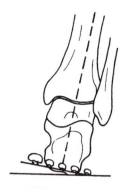

FIGURE 21.6
Tibia varum requiring compensatory pronation

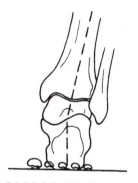

FIGURE 21.7
Compensatory pronation

tar flexed, and a supinated subtalar joint. The cavus foot causes poor shock absorbency and an unstable ankle (Figures 21.8 and 21.9).

4. Forefoot varus may require excessive pronation to bring the first metatarsal head to the ground (Figure 21.10).

5. The low-arched (pes planus) foot may have lax ligaments and poor muscle support, resulting in excessive medial movement of the talonavicular joint. This causes many problems arising from the excessively prolonged pronation and a loose foot (instead of a rigid foot) during the take-off phase.

From this list it is evident that there are two main areas where problems can arise. First, if insufficient pronation occurs (such as with the high-arched, cavus foot), too much shock is transmitted by the foot to the leg. Second, if excess pronation continues for too long during the mid-support and take-off phases, one of the many overuse syndromes can develop.

FIGURE 21.5
An erect posture can help the legs drive the body forward.

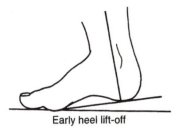

Early heel lift-off

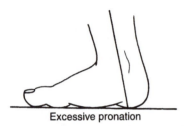

Excessive pronation

FIGURE 21.8

Tight Achilles—mechanisms of compensation

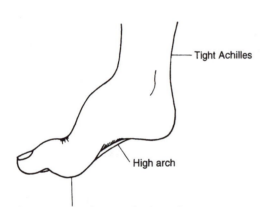

(a) Plantar flexed first ray – forefoot valgus

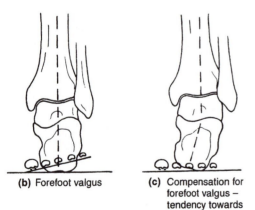

(b) Forefoot valgus   (c) Compensation for forefoot valgus – tendency towards supination

FIGURE 21.9

A cavus foot

(a) and (b) show the forefoot valgus. (c) shows the compensatory supination.

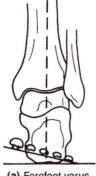
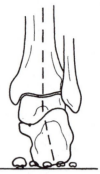

(a) Forefoot varus   (b) Compensation for forefoot varus – tendency towards pronation

FIGURE 21.10

Forefoot varus and its compensation

Causes of Overuse Injuries

It is important for the trainer to understand the mechanism that leads to overuse injuries. With this background he or she can guide runners in their training routines.

IMPACT SHOCK: Studies have shown that a runner strikes the ground with a force between three and five times that of walking. The ankle and the lower leg receive the most force, at 10 to 13 times body weight. The achilles tendon and knee are reported to receive forces 7 to 11 times body weight; and the plantar fascia, 1 to 3 times body weight.

Imagine what considerable repetitive forces are transmitted to bones, joints, and muscles of the lower extremities of the long-distance runner. This is especially true when an athlete starts distance running for the first time or when he or she starts to move up from, say, three miles a day to seven to ten miles a day. The muscles and bones have to strengthen in order to accept this new challenge. (Wolfe's Law).* Sometimes the athlete is unable to handle the force, and is compelled to temporarily back down. Muscle strength usually increases more rapidly than bone strength (in fact, some think the bone actually gets weaker before it gets stronger). This in-between phase, during which the bone is not yet fully ready to accept the force imposed on it, is the time when stress fractures and other overuse syndromes are apt to occur.

---

*Every change in the form and function of bones, or in their function alone, is followed by certain definite changes in their external configuration in accordance with mathematical laws.

A very carefully worked out training schedule, avoiding hard surfaces and excessive mileage, is needed to prevent impact-related injuries during this critical time.

VARUS ANGLE OF THE LEG AT FOOT STRIKE: Most people have a small amount of tibia varum, but this angle is increased during running, particularly in female athletes, who tend to "cross over" during their running gait. An increased varus angle means the foot must compensate in order to bring the first metatarsal head into contact with the ground. This compensation takes the form of an increase in pronation and, if excessive, can result in the foot being unstable rather than rigid during the take-off phase of gait (Figure 21.11).

FOOT FUNCTION: Poor foot function results from a poor angular relationship between the bones of the foot or from weak lower extremity muscles and loose foot ligaments. Again, this can result in the development of excessive pronation as well as inability of the foot to move toward a supinated position during the take-off phase. Poor foot function can therefore be the end result of a combination of genetic endowment (a poor bony angular relationship) together with inadequacy of muscles and ligaments to compensate for this defect. How often has one seen a runner with "terrible

feet" run long distances with no lower extremity problem at all? If for some reason a weakness in one of the key muscles supporting this foot develops, one or another overuse injury occurs and the "terrible foot" takes all the blame.

MUSCLE TIGHTNESS: The more an athlete runs, the greater the likelihood of developing tightness of the gastrocnemius-soleus and hamstring muscle groups. The tighter the gastrocnemius-soleus group becomes, the more it may interfere with optimum foot function. A tight hamstring muscle can alter the movement of the leg, particularly during the swing phase. It can also affect the posture of the lower spine and pelvis and, through this mechanism, influence the biomechanics of foot and leg function.

MUSCLE WEAKNESS: While the gastrocnemius-soleus and hamstring muscle groups are becoming tighter and stronger with long-distance running, the anterior tibial and quadriceps muscle groups may be getting weaker. A weak quadriceps muscle can cause patellar and peripatellar pain, while a weak anterior tibial muscle is frequently associated with an increase in impact shock and the development of lower leg pain and fatigue (Figure 12.12).

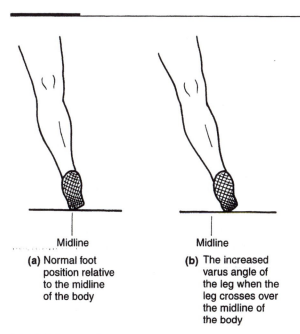

FIGURE 21.11
Increased varus angle of the leg due to "cross-over"

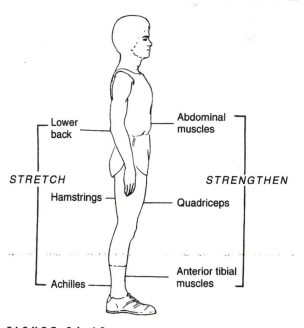

FIGURE 21.12
Common muscle imbalances that may develop in the long-distance runner

OVERAMBITIOUS TRAINING PROGRAM: This is one of the most important, and yet one of the most neglected, reasons why runners develop injuries. Doing too much too soon or trying to put in extra miles when the body is not ready to take them is an almost sure way of developing overuse injuries. Athletes must learn to "listen" to their own bodies. Those who do will avoid injuries; those who do not may suffer one injury after another (Table 21.1).

Prevention of Overuse Injuries

FLEXIBILITY: Flexibility should be maintained or improved by the use of slow, static stretches. The main muscle groups to be stretched are the Achilles tendon (gastrocnemius-soleus group), the hamstring muscles, the lower-back muscles, the groin muscles, and the quadriceps.

Stretching exercises should be done *both* before and after a run or workout. The after-workout stretching routine should be emphasized because this is the optimum time to increase flexibility, particularly of those muscle groups that tend to become tighter with long-distance running.

STRENGTH, POWER, AND ENDURANCE: Developing adequate strength, power, and endurance in all muscle groups, but particularly in the groups that tend to become weak or develop imbalances, should be stressed in a prevention program. In a long-distance runner the muscles to concentrate on are the lower-back and abdominal muscles, the quadriceps, the anterior and posterior tibial muscles, and the intrinsic foot muscles. Simple exercises include:

1. *Sit-ups:* These are best done with knees bent, arms folded over the chest, and pelvis tilted to flatten out any lumbar lordosis. (See section on back rehabilitation.)

2. *Quadriceps exercises:* The quadriceps are strengthened with isometric quadriceps sets and SLRs, the muscles being contracted for at least five seconds at a time. (See section on knee rehabilitation.)

Another technique for strengthening the quadriceps group consists of the athlete's sitting on the end of a table with a weight on the foot or ankle and then straightening out the knee. Patellae that are sensitive to this type of isotonic movement can become irritated, so this exercise should be avoided in runners who have peripatellar or retropatellar pain.

TABLE 21.1 *Factors associated with overuse injuries in runners*

Impact force	The impact force of running is three to five times that of walking. This can lead to stress fractures or "stress reactions" of bone.
Hard surface	Increases the impact force.
Change of surface	Particularly from soft to hard, but can also occur from hard to soft.
Downhill running	Especially associated with iliotibial tract irritation, popliteus tendinitis, and patellar tendinitis.
Lack of flexibility	Especially the Achilles tendon and the hamstrings.
Muscle weakness	Especially the intrinsic muscles of the foot, the anterior and posterior tibial muscles, and the quadriceps.
Overstriding	Results in the hamstring pulls and knee pain.
Poor posture	Especially leaning too far forward and hyperlordosis of the lumbar spine.
Overdistance	A relatively high incidence of injuries occurs in runners running over forty miles a week.
Overtraining	Being at the peak of training means being a hair's breadth from an injury.
Anatomical factors	Malalignment of the lower extremity, foot, or the relationship between them. Symptoms are usually associated with muscle weakness.
Shoes	Should provide control and shock absorbency.
Side of road	Running on the same side of a sloped road for a long time can produce knee pain.
Too much too soon!	

To strengthen the anterior tibial muscle group, the athlete sits on the end of a table with legs hanging down and sandbags or similar weights suspended from the feet. He or she then actively dorsiflexes the feet, using the anterior tibial muscles. Variations of this exercise include rotating both feet internally and in circles, to exercise the anterior *and* posterior tibial muscles. The feet can also be rotated externally in a circular motion, which helps strengthen the peroneal muscles (Figure 21.13).

The intrinsic foot musculature is exercised by the athlete's using his or her toes to curl up a towel placed on a smooth floor. A weight on the towel increases resistance. Picking up marbles with the toes and trying to actively spread the toes apart are other simple forms of exercise designed to strengthen the intrinsic foot musculature (Figure 21.14). Research has shown significant increase in toe flexon strength after six weeks of intrinsic muscle exercise.

SHOES: Shoes are the runner's only real piece of equipment and should be carefully chosen. They are important in protecting the runner's bones and joints from the hard pavement.[4] During the past few years there has been a revolution in the design and number of

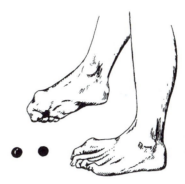

FIGURE 21.14
Picking up marbles with the toes

brands of shoes for running, but as yet there is no ideal running shoe, nor is there one shoe that is better than all others for every runner. New models have tended to come on the market before they have been adequately tested, and whole new injury syndromes have been produced by new shoe models. The subject is fraught with numerous difficulties and much confusion.

It is important to realize, that though a shoe may attain a high rating in shoe surveys, these surveys may not relate to a particular athlete's needs. Each shoe has certain qualities of shock absorbency, foot control, and flexibility. Every athlete needs a proportion of each of these qualities, but one athlete's needs may be totally different from any other athlete's needs. In the future it may be possible to quantify these unknowns, match them against each other, and choose the ideal shoe for a given foot from the data.

Consideration of the following biomechanical factors is appropriate in the selection of the correct shoe for an individual runner:

1. Amount each foot crosses the midline during running

2. Angle of the foot at footstrike (i.e., inverted, neutral, everted)

3. Footstrike—at heel, midfoot, or forefoot

4. Tibial varum or genu valgum

5. Hip width, hip excursion (vertical)

6. Foot shape (e.g., metatarsus adducts)

7. Assymetries (e.g., foot length, ROMs)

8. Ligamentous laxity

Although the best policy is to evaluate each runner's shoe individually for various factors, there are certain general features to note when examining a running shoe. (Figure 21.15). The heel counter should support the heel and Achilles tendon adequately. The sole at

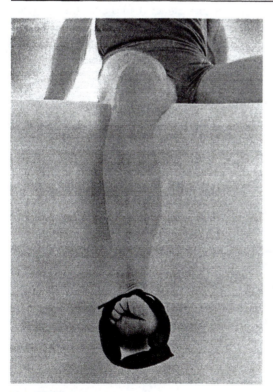

FIGURE 21.13
Anterior tibial muscle strengthening

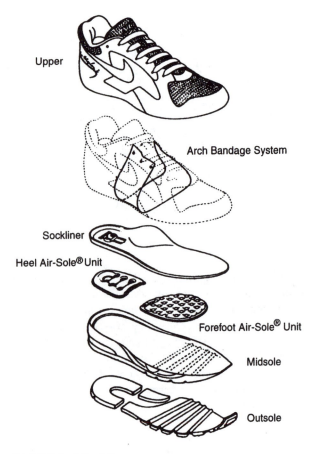

Upper

Arch Bandage System

Sockliner

Heel Air-Sole® Unit

Forefoot Air-Sole® Unit

Midsole

Outsole

FIGURE 21.15
One brand/model running shoe construction (Nike-Air, Skylon-2)
(*Source:* NIKE Inc., Beaverton, Oregon. Reprinted with permission.)

tend to stretch sideways slightly, but there should be no compromise in length. The amount of space available in the toe box is also important. A good rule of thumb is that the length of the shoe from the tip of the big toe to the tip of the shoe should be a thumb's width.

Next the athlete should try on both shoes at the same time and walk around again, making sure they feel just right. Having done this and having decided which brand and model to buy, he or she should place these shoes on the counter and view them from the back to see if there is any asymmetry in the way the uppers are placed on the sole. Lack of quality control in the manufacture of athletic shoes is possible and has led to injuries in a number of runners (Figure 21.16).

An athlete should not run in shoes immediately after purchasing them, but should walk in them for a day or two to allow them to adapt to the feet. After a few days of walking around, he or she can go on a short run of about 30 percent of normal distance, gradually increasing the length of time the shoes are worn so that after about five days the new shoes "fit like a glove."

Most shoes tend to wear down on the outside of the heel, but this should not be allowed to progress too far. The sole in this area should be filled in with either a glue gun made for this purpose or a preparation which is spread on the outside of the sole (e.g., Shoe Goo) to build it up to normal height. When using this type of substance, the athlete should be very careful not to build the area up any higher than the height of the rest of the sole. A very thin layer is all that is usually required. If the outside of the sole is built up too high, the foot tends to tilt inward, resulting in increased

the heel should be built up about ¾" (1.8 cm). The material used for the heel should not be so soft that it is easily compressed, but it should not be rock-hard either. There should be adequate cushioning for the ball of the foot because much force is directed through that area. There should be some flexibility of the front sole—otherwise the foot and the lower leg are strained during the push-off phase of gait—but it should not be so flexible that the shoe can easily be bent into a *U* shape.

When trying shoes on, the athlete should wear the socks that will be used for running. He or she should try on one shoe at a time, keeping the old running shoe on the opposite foot, lacing the new shoe up the same way as the old shoe, and walking around the store wearing the new shoe. Then the athlete should try on the other shoe, wearing the old shoe on the opposite foot. They should both be adequate in length and width. An athlete can certainly accept a bit of snugness in width, as shoes

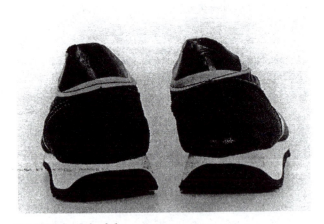

FIGURE 21.16
New shoes—lack of quality control
Note the valgus (or pronated) position of the right heel counter.

pronation, which could easily lead to new injuries. Before the shoes wear down completely, it is prudent for the athlete to obtain a new pair so they can be slowly broken in before the old ones are discarded.

With the recent flood of "airshoes" or gel-filled shoes into the market, there is an increasing need for consumer awareness regarding these shoes. Although air-soled shoes may decrease impact forces, they are not for everyone. Those who overpronate, especially, need a firm shoe that prevents excessive movement.

SURFACE: As previously mentioned, many injuries are due to impact shock. Though concrete might be the only surface available, it should be avoided whenever possible and a more forgiving surface chosen. Conversely, the athlete should be careful not to run on too soft a surface, which can cause excessive pronation or stretching of the Achilles tendon. Uneven ground often causes ankle sprains.

It is not only the surface hardness that is important, but also a change from one type of surface to another. This change, even though to a softer surface, can result in overuse injuries in certain susceptible individuals.

TRAINING SCHEDULE: The sensitivity of some athletes to the body's response to overtraining divides those who suffer from those who continue unscathed. As a rule, it is useful to think of the training schedule as being designed to enable the athlete to reach his or her maximal performance (or peak) when necessary. Once over the peak, one has to start at a lower level and build up to the peak once again (Figure 21.17).

General principles of training should include a hard-day, easy-day routine, with enough periods of rest to recover from really hard workouts. Early warning signs of overfatigue include:

1. Faster-than-normal pulse on awakening
2. Loss of body weight or body fat when in optimum condition
3. Scratchy sore throat
4. Easy fatigability
5. Insomnia

If these signs develop, the athlete should lower the mileage being run and put in a few easy days before returning to the normal schedule of vigorous workouts. He or she should also be aware of undue or unusual stress, such as the changing of time zones.

Probably more athletes have been ruined by overtraining than by any single biomechanical or muscular impairment. Figure 21.18 shows a form used to gather information from a runner who has been injured. The

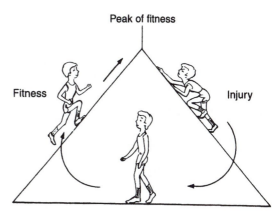

FIGURE 21.17
The pyramid of fitness and injury
As the runner reaches a high level of fitness and nears the peak, the chance of an injury increases. Once over the peak and in the area of injury, the runner cannot immediately return to that same level (as depicted by crawling up the other side of the slope), but must first back down to a lower level and then gradually work up again.

most important injury-prevention advice to give a runner is:

Listen to your body and work with it, not against it.

Sallade and Koch[5] have published what they believe to be the top ten training errors for distance runners:

1. Running on crowned roads
2. Excessive hill running
3. Track work in predominately one direction
4. Running on extremely hard surfaces
5. Running on unstable terrain
6. Changing shoes (types)
7. Increasing mileage too quickly
8. Increasing training speed too quickly
9. Not responding to body strain
10. Lack of variety in training

Returning to Running Following Injury

As stated earlier, overtraining is a major cause of running injuries. Once the athlete has nearly recovered from injury, he or she may be tempted to return to pre-injury mileage too soon. The athletic trainer should question the runner to ascertain at what part of their typical run they started to experience pain. Once this

center for sports medicine & running injuries of eugene

RUNNER'S HISTORY FORM   DATE:_____

Name _____   Age ____ Sex: M F   Wt: ____ Ht: _____

1. When did you first notice symptoms? _____
   Reinjury: ☐ Yes   ☐ No

2. Describe symptoms: (Right, Left, Both) _____
   _____

3. Type of pain: ☐ Dull   ☐ Throbbing   ☐ Intermittant
                  ☐ Sharp   ☐ Constant   ☐ Burning
                  ☐ Sore   ☐ Bruised

4. Onset: ☐ Gradual   ☐ Sudden

5. What was the onset of your symptoms related to?

   ☐ Change in surface   ☐ Running hills: up / down
   ☐ Increase in mileage   ☐ Change in speed: faster / slower / sprints
   ☐ Don't know   ☐ Change in shoes: from_____ to_____
   ☐ Other_____

6. When do your symptoms occur?

   ☐ As soon as you start to run   ☐ After you finish the run
   ☐ During the run   ☐ During normal activity (like walking)
   ☐ Always   ☐ _____

7. How long do your symptoms last? _____

8. What helps relieve your symptoms? _____

9. What increases your symptoms? _____

10. Have you been treated for this condition previously? ☐ Yes   ☐ No

    When? _____ By whom? _____

    What treatment? _____

11. Have you had any other running-related problems? ☐ Yes   ☐ No

    What? _____

    When? _____ Treatment _____ By whom? _____

12. What effect do your symptoms have on your workout?

    ☐ Pain during workout but able to run   ☐ Unable to workout
    ☐ Workout compromised by pain   ☐ Self-imposed rest
    ☐ Other _____

FIGURE 21.18
Runner's history form

distance or duration is known, the runner should start running at no greater than one-third the distance or time that caused the initial pain that led to the injury. For example, an athlete who started to experience ITB band pain at three miles into a run, but who was able to block out the pain and finish a six-mile run, would start on return from injury at a distance of one mile (one-third the distance of the original onset of pain). The athlete can gradually increase to pre-injury levels once he or she is able to tolerate this initial distance.

13. Type of runner:

- [ ] Fitness
- [ ] Recreation
- [ ] Club
- [ ] Serious

- [ ] High School
- [ ] College
- [ ] Professional
- [ ] World Class

14. Distance: Daily _____   Speed per mile: Training _____

     Weekly _____   Competition _____

15. How long have you been running? _____

16. How long have you been running at this distance and speed? _____

17. What types of surfaces do you run on ? Check all that apply.

- [ ] Composition track
- [ ] Cinder track
- [ ] Chips

- [ ] Asphalt
- [ ] Cross Country
- [ ] Grass

- [ ] Beach
- [ ] Dirt or Gravel
- [ ] Other _____

18. Where do you do most of your running? Check all that apply.

- [ ] Hills
- [ ] Flat

- [ ] Crowned roads
- [ ] Trails

19. Brand and model of shoes you wear now? _____

    How long have you been running in these? _____

    Any comments? _____

20. Brands and models of shoes previously worn, plus comments. _____

    _____

21. Do you wear orthotics or other corrective devices now? If yes,...

    What type? _____ How long have you worn them? _____

    Who prescribed them?_____What effect do they have?_____

22. Have you worn orthotic devices in the past? If yes,...

    What type? _____ How long did you wear them? _____

    Why did you stop wearing them? _____

23. Do you stretch regularly? If yes,...   Before Running   After Running

                        How Long?

- [ ] 5 minutes
- [ ] 10 minutes
- [ ] 15 minutes
- [ ] 20 minutes
- [ ] More

- [ ] 5 minutes
- [ ] 10 minutes
- [ ] 15 minutes
- [ ] 20 minutes
- [ ] More

24. What other sports do you participate in on a fairly regular basis? _____

    _____

FIGURE 21.18

Runner's history form (continued)

Biomechanical Examination of the Running Athlete's Alignment

Notice the general alignment of the athlete when he or she is standing. Specifically, notice the heights of the iliac crests, the posterior superior iliac spines, and the greater trochanters; the position of the patellae; the amount of genu varum or valgum, tibia varum; and the angle of the calcaneus. Then observe the type of arch configuration, the shape and angle of the metatarsals, the shape of the toes in relation to the metatarsals, and the length and general configuration of the toes. Ask the athlete to flex the knees as far forward as possible while

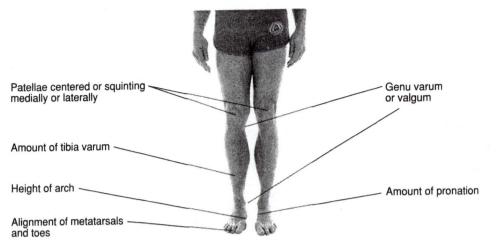

Patellae centered or squinting
medially or laterally

Amount of tibia varum

Height of arch

Alignment of metatarsals
and toes

Genu varum
or valgum

Amount of pronation

FIGURE 21.19

Examination of lower extremity alignment
Note the configuration of the feet when observed from the front and from the back.

keeping the heels firmly fixed to the ground. This indicates the amount of functional Achilles flexibility (Figure 21.19).

If the iliac crests and posterior superior iliac spines are not level, they should be observed while the athlete is sitting on the examining table. If they then become level, a discrepancy in leg length should be suspected. If they remain unchanged, lower-back joint dysfunction should be suspected.

The amount of tibia varum is determined by having the athlete stand on a firm platform with the foot in the neutral position. The lowest third of the leg is bisected, and the angle between this line and a line perpendicular to the ground is measured. This should also be measured with the foot in its compensated standing position (Figure 21.20).

The athlete should then lie prone with feet and ankles hanging over the end of the examining table. Observe the type of calluses present and their positions on the feet. This indicates not only the weight-bearing pressure areas but also what shearing forces are acting on the feet during running.

Grasp the heads of the fourth and fifth metatarsals just proximal to the metatarsophalangeal joint and gently move the relaxed foot through the full range of movement—from full pronation to full supination. This demonstrates whether or not there is limited or excessive range of movement at the subtalar joint, and whether the foot is rigid or flexible (Figure 21.21).

THE NEUTRAL POSITION: To determine the neutral position of the subtalar joint, have the athlete lie prone as previously described. When examining the left

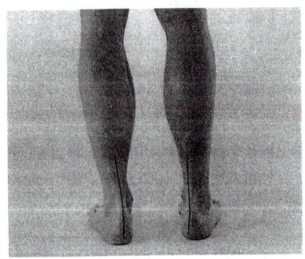

FIGURE 21.20
Bisection of the lower third of the leg (as well as bisection of the heel) assessed while standing

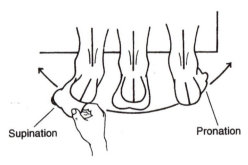

Supination

Pronation

FIGURE 21.21
Testing range of motion of the subtalar joint

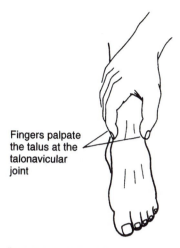

FIGURE 21.22

Fingers palpate the talus at the talonavicular joint

Determining the neutral position—the position of congruency of the talonavicular joint

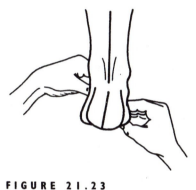

FIGURE 21.23

Determining the neutral position with the athlete lying prone
In this example, the rearfoot is in approximately 2° of varus

foot, use the left hand to move it through the range of movement by grasping the distal heads of the fourth and fifth metatarsals, while the middle finger and thumb of the right hand palpate the talus. The talus is the key to the neutral position and is best felt by placing the thumb just distal to the medial malleolus at the talonavicular joint, with the middle finger distal to the tibiofibular syndesmosis. As the foot is brought into pronation, the talus will be felt by the thumb to bulge on the medial side. As it is brought into full supination, it will be felt by the middle finger to bulge on the lateral side. A point will be reached between full supination and full pronation where the talus will either be felt equally on both sides, or will not be felt at all (Figure 21.22). This has to do with the talus being congruently positioned, so that the subtalar joint is assumed to be in the neutral position. The neutral position can also be felt as a "peak" of movement as the foot is passively moved from pronation to supination and back again.

Having determined the neutral position of the subtalar joint, it is now possible to estimate the relationship of the calcaneus to the lower leg. To do this, bisect the calcaneus and the lowest third of the leg (Figure 21.23) while the subtalar joint is held in the neutral position. In most cases, the calcaneus will be in a slightly varus position (2° to 4°) in relation to the lower leg.

Now determine the angular relationship of the rearfoot to the forefoot, making sure the subtalar joint is in the neutral position and the midtarsal joint is maximally pronated (Figure 21.24). Load the fourth and fifth metatarsal heads in a dorsal direction until resistance is felt. The relationship of the metatarsal heads (the forefoot) to the rearfoot is now estimated by again bisecting the calcaneus and then taking a line from the head of the fifth metatarsal to the first head of the metatarsal. This

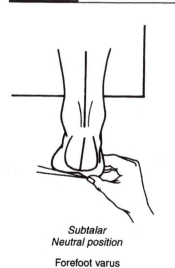

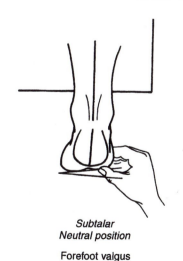

Subtalar
Neutral position

Forefoot varus

Subtalar
Neutral position

Forefoot valgus

FIGURE 21.24

Determining the position of the forefoot when the subtalar joint is in the neutral position

line is then related to the bisection of the calcaneus. If it is perpendicular (90°), then the forefoot is in a neutral position in relation to the rearfoot. If, however, the first metatarsal head lies on a higher plane than the fifth metatarsal head, the foot is in a forefoot supination or a forefoot varus position. Conversely, if the first metatarsal head is on a lower plane in relation to the fifth metatarsal head, then there is a forefoot valgus (as is commonly found with a cavus, or high-arched, foot) (Table 21.2).

Estimate the range of movement of the first ray by grasping the heads of the first and second metatarsals and moving the first metatarsal up and down in relation to the second. From this observation, judge whether the first ray is rigid, has some movement, has normal move-

ment, or is hypermobile. A hypermobile first ray allows the foot to pronate more than it may appear to do on the initial examination[6] (Figure 21.25).

Finally, perform gait analysis to closely study the foot and lower extremity in motion. Ask the athlete to walk back and forth over a distance of about thirty feet, and then to run in the shoes normally worn.

Lower Backache Caused by Faulty Mechanics of Foot and Leg

Backache is a common complaint in a running athlete. Often the problem arises from faulty mechanics of the foot or leg, the effects being felt in the back. For example, asymmetry of leg length of ⅛" to ¼" (3 to 6 mm) is sufficient to produce symptoms in a runner. Symptoms may be localized to the back, or may be felt in the back buttock or the leg.

EXAMINATION: A full examination of the back and a biomechanical examination of the feet should be undertaken. (See section on examination of the back.) The following points in particular should be noted:

1. Alignment of the lower leg, emphasizing symmetry and amount of pronation or supination of the foot.

2. Heights of the iliac crests and posterior superior iliac spines, with the athlete both standing and sitting.

3. Heights of the greater trochanters.

4. Heights of the anterior superior iliac spines, with the athlete both standing and lying supine.

5. Range of back movement and symmetry of posterior superior iliac spine movement on forward flexion and on return to erect position.

6. Apparent leg lengths, as evidenced by the levels of the medial malleoli observed with the athlete lying. Leg lengths are usually measured from the anterior superior iliac spine to the medial malleolus, but this measurement fails to take into account variables of the foot and pelvis.

Having excluded the major causes of backache discussed in Chapter 17, consider the possibility that back pain in the runner could be due to one of the following causes:

1. *Functionally short leg.* The actual leg lengths are equal, but that the legs are functionally unequal because of a difference of pronation or supination of one foot relative to the other, or because of some other functional asymmetry. For instance, the right foot may be in its

---

TABLE 21.2 *Summary of the examination of a running athlete*

1. Athlete standing:
   a. Facing examiner
   b. Facing sideways
   c. Back to examiner

   View from the hips to the feet (include entire back and shoulders if athlete has back problem)

2. Athlete sitting on examining table:
   a. Level of posterior superior iliac spines and iliac crests
   b. Position of patellae
   c. Lower legs

3. Athlete lying supine on back:
   a. Back
   b. Hip
   c. Knee

4. Athlete lying prone on abdomen:
   a. Hips
   b. Biomechanical examination of feet
      1) Amount of tibia varum of lower third of tibia
      2) Range of motion of subtalar joint and first ray
      3) Heel or subtalar varus with foot in neutral position
      4) Forefoot varus or valgus with foot in neutral position
      5) Position of first ray relative to rest of forefoot

5. Examine area of complaint in detail

6. Observe while walking

7. Observe while running

8. Examine walking and running shoes

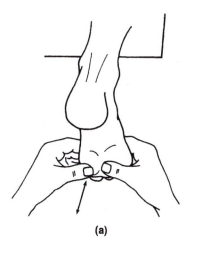 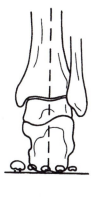 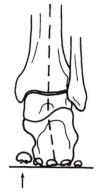

(a)

(b) The foot non-weight-bearing

(c) With weight-bearing, pronation occurs due to instability of the first ray

FIGURE 21.25

The influence of first ray motion on pronation
(a) Determining the amount of motion of the first ray. (b) and (c) Pronation due to a mobile first ray.

---

normal position while the left foot is excessively pronated. This causes the left leg to be "shorter" than the right, causing the left posterior superior iliac spine to be lower than the right when the athlete is standing. However, when the back is examined with the athlete sitting on the examining table, the posterior superior iliac spines are horizontally level in height. If the excessively pronated foot is placed in the neutral position, the height of the posterior superior iliac spines should once more be horizontally level when the athlete stands (Figures 21.26 and 21.27).

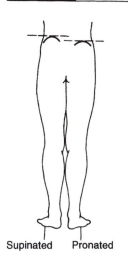

Supinated   Pronated

FIGURE 21.26
Functional short leg

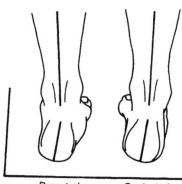

Pronated   Supinated

FIGURE 21.27
If one foot is pronated while the other is supinated, it may lead to a functional leg-length difference. However, if one leg is structurally longer it may result in the foot pronating on that side in order to equalize the leg-lengths and thus balance the pelvis.

---

2. *Anatomically short leg.* One leg is actually physically shorter than the other. The posterior superior iliac spine on the shorter side is lower than the opposite side when the athlete is standing, but the spines are level when the athlete is sitting. The body may try to compensate for this leg length difference by, for instance, pronating the foot on the longer side while supinating the foot on the shorter side. This compensation tends to level the pelvis when the athlete is standing (Figure 21.28).

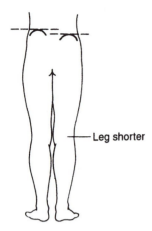

FIGURE 21.28
Anatomical short leg

Both the functionally and the anatomically short leg can cause complications of joint dysfunction in the lower back. Such dysfunction is detected in an asymmetry of movement of the posterior superior iliac spines on forward flexion and on return from a flexed position, and also by the spines' remaining unequal in height when the athlete is sitting on the examining table.

3. *Bilateral excessive pronation of the feet.* Results in a forward tilt of the pelvis with excessive lordosis of the back.

4. *Muscle imbalances.* Weakness of the abdominal, buttock, and lower-back muscles, with or without excessive tightness of the hamstrings, back, and iliotibial tract can cause or predispose to lower backache.

5. *Muscle spasm.* Spasm of the piriformis or quadratus lumborum muscles occasionally gives rise to lower backache and even to referred pain down the leg to the foot (Table 21.3).

TREATMENT:

1. Excessive pronation should be corrected by an orthotic device and the use of foot and lower leg exercises.

2. Anatomical discrepancy in leg length should be compensated for by building up the height of the heel and the sole of the shoe. For instance, a discrepancy of leg length of ¼" (6 mm) may require ¼" (6 mm) heel lift plus ⅛" (3 mm) continuation of the lift under the forefoot.

3. Any tightness of the Achilles, the hamstrings, or the iliotibial tract should be reduced by repetitive, slow, stretching exercises.

4. Weakness of the abdominal, back extensor, and buttock muscles should be corrected. (See section on rehabilitation.)

5. If dysfunction of the posterior facets or sacro-iliac joints is a problem even after implementation of the first four steps listed, manipulative therapy may be performed. Manipulation should be used only if the diagnosis is one of joint dysfunction or posterior facet joint subluxation. If there is evidence of nerve root irritation or compression, manipulation is not advised (see Chapters 7 and 17).

Common Running-Induced Injuries to the Hip

There are a number of causes of hip pain in a runner, some of which are outlined in Table 21.4. However overuse injuries to the hip constitute only 5 to 7 percent of total running injuries.

Running-Related Injuries to the Knee

Problems related to the knee comprise at least 25 percent of the injuries incurred by the runner. Many of these conditions have not been clearly defined and are listed according to anatomical area rather than etiology.

Medial Patellar Pain

Studies have shown that the prevalence of meniscal tears in marathon runners is no higher than the prevalence reported for sedentary persons, and that runners have the same amount of meniscal degeneration as do nonrunning athletes.

With a meniscal tear or an internal derangement excluded as the cause of medial patellar pain, pain related to the medial aspect of the patella, the medial joint line, or the medial tibial plateau is usually associated with excessive pronation during the mid-support and take-off phases. One theory about the occurrence of this pain relates to the excessive internal rotation of the tibia that accompanies a prolonged pronatory phase. As the knee starts to extend after reaching its maximal point of flexion, the tibia and femur usually start to rotate externally. As a result of excessively prolonged pronation, the tibia stays in internal rotation. Stress is thus placed on the medial patellar structures because the patella tends to follow the external rotational movement of the femur (Figure 21.29).

TABLE 21.3 *Causes and treatment of backache in the running athlete*

Causes	Complications	Treatment[a]
Functionally short leg (one foot pronates more than the other)	No lumbar complications	In-shoe orthotic device
	Lumbar joint dysfunction or subluxation	In-shoe orthotic device, manipulation if necessary
Anatomically short leg (one leg actually shorter than the other)	Uncompensated for by changes in the feet	Heel-and-sole lift
	Compensated for by pronation of longer leg and/or supination of shorter leg	In-shoe orthotic device and a heel-and-sole lift
	Lumbar joint dysfunction or subluxation	Manipulation and a heel-and-sole lift and/or in-shoe orthotic device
Excessive pronation of both feet	No lumbar complications	In-shoe orthotic device
	Lumbar joint dysfunction or subluxation	In-shoe orthotic device, manipulation if necessary
Dysfunction or subluxation of one of the joints of the lower back—foot alignment or leg length unrelated		Manipulation, stretching, and strengthening exercises
Back pathology—other than joint dysfunction (e.g., disc protrusion or rupture)		Orthopedic examination and treatment

[a]*Always stretch*: hamstrings, iliotibial tracts, Achilles tendons, back, and iliopsoas muscles
Always strengthen: abdominals and back extensors

An occasional cause of medial patellar pain is the synovial plica.

TREATMENT: Initially, treatment with ice and aspirin four times a day helps. However, it is usually necessary to improve the musculature, particularly of the vastus medialis, the posterior tibial, and the flexor hallucis longus muscles. Orthotic devices are often used as well, and they effect improvement in a high percentage of cases. Again, in this case, an "air shoe" may add to the trauma. This individual needs a firm, anti-pronation shoe. While the athlete is recovering, it may be necessary to decrease the mileage and perhaps change the running shoe and/or the surface.

Pes Anserine Bursitis

The cause of pes anserine bursitis in a runner is uncertain. Possibly it is related to an attempt by the pes to compensate for excessive tibia varum at heel strike. Fre-quently a weak vastus medialis muscle is found in association with the condition.

SYMPTOMS AND SIGNS: There is pain and swelling of the pes anserine bursa, which lies in close proximity to the insertion of the pes anserine tendon. This condition needs to be differentiated from a stress fracture of the upper tibia, which can present with the same findings.

TREATMENT: Initially, treat with ice and aspirin or other anti-inflammatory medication, along with exercises to improve the vastus medialis and the pes anserine muscle groups. Orthotic devices are often useful. On occasion, a local injection of corticosteroids helps.

Patellar Tendinitis

Patellar tendinitis can occur particularly in a runner, who runs hard down hills. (See section on jumper's knee in Chapter 19.)

TABLE 21.4 *Common running-induced injuries to the hip*

Condition	Symptoms and Signs	Causes	Treatment
Vague hip pain (in one or both hips)	Pain and aching within the hip No positive findings suggestive of intra-articular hip pathology Normal X-rays Normal bone scan	Malfunction or malalignment of foot and lower leg Leg length inequality—anatomical or functional Lower-back abnormality with referred pain Muscle imbalance	Localize and correct cause
Iliotibial tract irritation	Pain down lateral aspect of thigh, possibly localized to hip Symptoms worse on downhill running, relieved by uphill running Click or snapping as I-T band rubs over the greater trochanter	Excessive downhill running Tight iliotibial tract Shock absorbency problem Malalignment problem Leg length discrepancy	Apply ice Stretch iliotibial tract Anti-inflammatory medication and/or ultrasound Avoid downhill running Use orthotic devices if indicated Strengthen muscle weaknesses Cortiocosteroid injection
Strain of one of the muscles around the hip (iliopsoas, rectus femoris, sartorius, gluteus medius, or piriformis)	Pain localized to one muscle group	Often due to weakness of other muscles overloading the affected muscle	Isolate specific muscle weakness and correct Use physical modalities as indicated
Trochanteric bursitis	Pain around hip, localized tenderness over trochanteric bursa	May be associated with irritation of the iliotibial tract and tensor fascia lata May be associated with leg length difference, malalignment problem, or muscle weakness	Correct cause Apply ice Anti-inflammatory medication and/or ultrasound Occasionally, inject corticosteroid into the bursa Rarely, surgery
Stress fracture of femoral neck	Pain deep within hip. If condition suspected, obtain bone scan (the stress fracture may not show on an X-ray for weeks or even months. This fracture may displace.	Uncertain. May be related to excessive crossover, hard downhill or mountain running.	Insist on complete rest from all activity, preferably non-weight-bearing using crutches
Slipped capital femoral epiphysis	Hip pain or only knee pain X-ray diagnosis	Often occurs in overweight teenager, usually male	Usually surgical
Congenital dysplasia or other abnormality	Vague, constant hip pain after running X-ray diagnosis		Requires orthopedic consultation

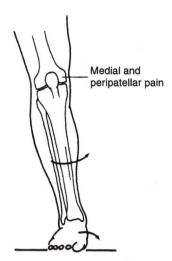

FIGURE 21.29
Excessive pronation may lead to patellar pain in a runner

Medial and peripatellar pain

SYMPTOMS AND SIGNS: Pain and tenderness are localized to the inferior pole of the patella at the origin of the patellar tendon, and sometimes farther down the tendon. An excessive Q angle may be found in association with bowing of the top third of the tibia (not necessarily related to genu varum).

TREATMENT: Of particular relevance to the runner is the use of orthotic devices, ice, and aspirin. Neoprene with a patellar support can be used on those with an excessive Q angle. On occasion, velcro straps such as the CHOPAT, designed to limit movement of the patella, have been found to help reduce the pain associated with this condition. The quadriceps muscles should be strengthened. Anti-inflammatory medication may also help.

Retropatellar Pain

See section on patellofemoral joint pain.

SYMPTOMS AND SIGNS: Pain occurs behind the patella when the athlete runs. It may also occur when he or she walks up or down stairs, cycles (or after cycling), or sits for some time with the knee bent at 90°. Frequently there is an extensor mechanism malalignment related to the hips, tibiae, feet, or all three.

TREATMENT: Carefully managed vastus medialis and quadriceps exercises are the mainstays of treatment, along with in-shoe orthotic devices. Gentle quadriceps stretching should be performed as long as it is not painful. High doses of aspirin (perhaps with vitamin C added) may prove helpful. Ice should be used for symptomatic relief of discomfort.

The runner should avoid hills, and he or she may actually have to discontinue running for a period of time to allow the retropatellar irritation to subside. During this time, treading water or running in place in a swimming pool while wearing a life jacket may prove very beneficial from the cardiovascular and muscular standpoint. Occasionally surgical realignment of the extensor mechanism and/or release of patellar compression must be performed.

Lateral Patellar Pain

Lateral patellar pain is thought to be due to an alignment defect involving the patella, but it is sometimes related to the feet as well. There may be a muscle imbalance of the vastus, with the vastus lateralis being more powerful or tighter than the medialis. Rarely is a fat-pad impingement the cause of symptoms.

SYMPTOMS AND SIGNS: There is pain as well as tenderness on the anterolateral aspect of the patella. The lateral patellar structures may be tight, allowing little medial movement of the patella when pressure is applied to the lateral facet.

TREATMENT: Ice and aspirin may be used initially. Quadriceps exercises need to be carefully controlled, emphasizing the vastus medialis. It is important to attempt to gently stretch the quadriceps over a period of time. In-shoe orthotic devices and an occasional cortisone injection may be helpful. A lateral retinacular release procedure is sometimes used.

Lateral Knee Pain

Frequently, lateral knee pain is due to a soft-tissue problem, which is due to tendinitis or friction of the iliotibial tract as it runs over the lateral femoral condyle.[7, 8, 9, 10] Occasionally the popliteal tendon or the lateral ligament become inflamed.[11] Irritation of these tissues appears to be related to mileage beyond normal and to poor shock absorbency, either through the shoes or through the body alignment; it therefore shows up quite frequently in runners with rigid feet (Figure 21.30).

SYMPTOMS AND SIGNS: Pain occurs during running and may be localized to the lateral epicondyle or may run diffusely along the iliotibial tract. It is usually initiated by hard downhill running and may

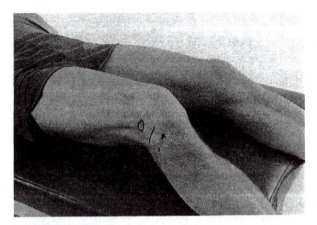

FIGURE 21.30
Lateral knee pain in a runner
Most commonly this is due to iliotibial tract friction over the lateral femoral epicondyle. The illustration shows the area of frequent tenderness (0) as well as other areas that might be tender (X). The line marks the lateral joint line.

disappear when the athlete runs uphill. Often pain is felt as the leg is brought forward through the swing phase.[12]

There is tenderness over the lateral epicondyle (occasionally over the lateral joint line), at the origin of the popliteal tendon, or at Gerdy's tubercle. There is inflammation where the iliotibial tract crosses the lateral epicondyle, and occasionally crepitus can be palpated. The iliotibial tract is frequently noted to be tight in these runners. Pain is usually elicited by full weight-bearing with the knee at 30° of flexion. Compressing the iliotibial tract against the lateral epicondyle while moving the knee through 30° of flexion may reproduce the symptoms.

TREATMENT: Athletes with this problem need to wear shoes with good shock absorbency and should attempt to run on a softer surface. They should also avoid hills. Carefully designed orthotic devices may help. Ice, aspirin, or other anti-inflammatory medication may be necessary. Iliotibial tract stretching has been found useful.[12] Strengthening of specific muscle weaknesses should be undertaken. Corticosteroid injections around the iliotibial tract and/or popliteal tendon are beneficial. In very resistant cases, surgical exploration and partial release of the iliotibial tract may be necessary[13, 14] (Figure 21.31).

Biceps Femoris Tendinitis

SYMPTOMS AND SIGNS: Biceps femoris tendinitis may present with pain and tenderness at, or just

FIGURE 21.31
Iliotibial tract stretch
To stretch the left side, place the left leg slightly forward with the body's weight on that leg. Drop the pelvis down on the right side. This will result in a stretching of the tensor fasciae latae and iliotibial tract on the left. Placing the hands on the iliac crests may help reinforce the sensation of when the correct position is obtained.

proximal to, the insertion of the tendon into the head of the fibula. Swelling occasionally localizes at the tendon insertion.

TREATMENT: Ice, decreased running activities, anti-inflammatory medication; occasionally a corticosteroid injection.

It should be clearly understood that many conditions within the knee joint may be unrelated to running (such as a torn medial meniscus), but may be brought out by running. These conditions are not discussed here, but should *always* be included in the differential diagnosis and excluded by means of a thorough knee examination.

Common Running-Induced Injuries to the Lower Leg

The term *shin splints* is a lay term that refers to any lower leg pain in a runner or in any athlete engaged in a running activity.[15] It is a nonspecific term, avoid using it; make a specific diagnosis. This is the only way that appropriate treatment can be instituted. The anatomical classification of lower leg pain in the runner is based on knowledge of the anatomical compartments. (See Chapter 20 and Table 21.5.)

Tibial Stress Reaction and Stress Fracture

The term *tibial stress reaction* applies to a condition in which the tibia attempts to adapt to the stress placed on it. The main components of a stress fracture are microfractures, which will heal if circumstances permit. This condition could be called a *prestress fracture* or *microfracture*. However, if the stress continues or increases, a proper stress fracture can occur.[16]

The tibial stress reaction therefore encompasses a spectrum of conditions. At one end is the athlete with slight tibial pain, no X-ray changes, and no increase in uptake on bone scan (there may be X-ray evidence of bone adaptation over a period of time if the stress continues). With a slight decrease in intensity of training, or perhaps a change in footwear, the pain may subside and not return when the previous level of activity is again reached.

At the other end of the spectrum is the athlete who suddenly develops severe pain, usually at the junction of the mid- and lower-third of the tibia. The symptoms are severe enough to prevent the athlete from continuing training. A bone scan at this time demonstrates a dense localized area of uptake. After two weeks ordinary X-rays reveal a definite fracture line extending at least part of the way, if not completely, through the cortex of the tibia. Callus is minimal or nonexistent. This condition represents a definite stress fracture.

Between these two extremes are many variations. One common variation is chronic recurrence of pain whenever an athlete exercises beyond a certain point. X-rays will be normal initially, but may change if the athlete is followed over a period of many months or years, provided that activity is continued at the same level. The cortex becomes thick and the actual width of the bone increases. Bone scans demonstrate a diffusely increased uptake, which is usually vertical, localized to the posterior aspect of the tibia, and less intense than the acute stress fracture. This area of increased uptake indicates the area of bony change that will be visualized much later on regular X-rays.

TABLE 21.5 *Anatomical classification of lower leg pain in the running athlete ("shin splints")*

1. *Posteromedial pain* (pain and tenderness along the posteromedial aspect of the tibia—the commonest area)
   a. Tibial stress reaction, which can develop into a stress fracture
   b. Muscle strains, inflammation, tendinitis, and periosteal irritation of the posterior tibial muscle and tendon and other soft tissues attached to the posteromedial border of the tibia ("medial tibial stress syndrome")
   c. Combination of the above
   d. Deep posterior compartment compression syndrome

2. *Tibial pain* (pain and tenderness directly on the tibia)
   a. Tibial stress reaction, which may develop into a stress fracture
   b. Pes anserine tendinitis and/or bursitis

3. *Anterior tibial compartment pain* (pain and tenderness within the anterior compartment)
   a. Muscle strains, inflammation, and tendinitis
   b. Anterior compartment compression syndrome

4. *Lateral compartment pain* (pain in the lateral compartment of the leg)
   a. Muscle strains, inflammation, and tendinitis
   b. Lateral compartment compression syndrome

5. *Fibular pain* (pain and tenderness directly on the fibula)
   a. Fibular stress reaction, which may develop into a stress fracture
   b. Biceps tendinitis at the head of the fibula

6. *Posterior pain* (pain on the posterior aspect of the lower leg)
   a. Muscle strains, inflammation, and tendinitis
   b. Posterior compartment compression syndrome of either the superficial or deep posterior compartment
   c. Thrombophlebitis

7. *Miscellaneous*
   a. Fascial herniae
   b. Popliteal artery entrapment syndrome
   c. Interosseous membrane calcification
   d. Varicose veins
   e. Pain referred from the lower back

Another frequent occurrence is pain in the tibia—not severe enough to prevent the athlete from performing, but constantly present with activity. Bony adaptation is much more rapid and is visualized on X-rays within a month or two as new periosteal bone and tibial molding. An actual stress fracture line is not visualized. Bone scans usually show a more diffuse uptake than that seen in the acute stress fracture, but of a similar horizontal pattern.

It should be understood that bone is an ever-adapting structure, but it adapts less rapidly than muscles and soft tissues. During running activities, certain muscles may increase in strength, adding to the forces generated across the bone, particularly if one set of muscles is considerably stronger than another. This muscle imbalance is thought to be the main etiologic mechanism of both stress reactions and stress fractures.[14,17] Impact is undoubtedly important in the case of the tibia, as are biomechanical factors, foot and leg alignment, flexibility, and other variables; but the one constant feature of stress reactions and stress fractures is related to muscle action. (See section on stress fractures.)

It is important to try to differentiate the tibial stress reaction from inflammation of the soft tissues of the lower leg (posterior tibial, flexor digitorum, and hallucis muscles and tendons). Differential points are shown in Table 21.6.

Medial Tibial Stress Syndrome

This stress syndrome includes tendinitis and periosteal irritation involving the posterior tibial muscle and tendon, the flexor muscles and tendons, and other soft tissues attached to the posteromedial border of the tibia. It is a very common condition and is frequently confused with the tibial stress reaction.

ETIOLOGY: The usual cause is abnormal foot pronation, with the posterior tibial, flexor hallucis, and digitorum longus muscles attempting to stabilize the foot. If the forces are severe, microtearing of the soft-tissue attachment to the periosteum can cause inflammation of the musculotendinous attachment to the bone.

An excessive number of foot strikes or the impact force of each foot strike, combined with an attempt at stabilization by the muscles mentioned, can cause the same result. ("Excessive" is relative and depends on the level of training of a particular athlete and the degree of adaptation of the tibia and the tissues connected to it. Excessive may be 150 miles [240 Km] per week for one athlete, but only 5 miles [8 Km] per week for another.)

TABLE 21.6 *Differentiation between tibial stress fractures and lower leg soft-tissue inflammatory conditions*

Tibial stress	Posterior Tibial Muscle-Tendon Inflammation
Tenderness may be at an area devoid of muscles (lowest third of the tibia) or it my be on the tibial shaft itself.	Tenderness mainly over the soft tissues.
Percussion of the tibia increases intensity of the pain.	Percussion on the tibia does not increase intensity of the pain.
Tuning fork vibration test may or may not be positive.	Tuning fork vibration test is negative.
Swelling is present over the bone and possibly in the soft tissues.	Swelling is usually present over the soft tissues.
Stressing the muscles does not increase pain.	Stressing involved muscles may cause increased pain.

SYMPTOMS AND SIGNS: There is pain and some swelling over the muscles on the posteromedial crest of the tibia, particularly in the middle third. The pain may be localized, or it may extend down the leg along the course of the posterior tibial muscle and tendon and around the medial malleolus to the attachment of the tendon to the navicular and first cuneiform.

In the early stages of the condition, the symptoms can occur after running only, but as it becomes more severe the pain also occurs at other times. Tenderness is present over the muscles and over the muscular attachment to the tibia (Table 21.6). Small lumps of hematoma are often felt on the posteromedial aspect of the lower leg, usually in the middle third.

There is seldom tenderness over the tibia itself, and percussion and vibration tests are negative.[18] Testing the posterior tibial and the flexor hallucis longus muscles often produces pain and weakness of the muscle being tested.

TREATMENT: The painful area should be iced and ice-massaged. Anti-inflammatory medication may be given if necessary. In-shoe orthotic devices are usually successful in controlling the pronation and relieving the excessive forces on the muscles. The posterior tibial, the flexor digitorum longus, and the flexor hallucis longus muscles should be strengthened, as should the intrinsic muscles of the foot.[17, 19]

Good shock-absorbent shoes that do not allow excessive pronation should be worn, and a softer training surface should be used for a time. Occasionally, taping the arch and lower leg helps. If necessary, decreased frequency and duration of weight-bearing workouts, with swimming as a substitute, should be suggested.

Compartment Compression Syndromes of the Lower Leg

There are four osseofascial compartments in the lower leg: (See Chapter 20.)

1. Anterior
2. Lateral
3. Superficial posterior
4. Deep posterior

Any of these compartments can develop a compression syndrome. This syndrome is defined as a condition in which the circulation and function of the tissues within the compartment become compromised by an increase in pressure within that compartment.

ETIOLOGY: The anterior compartment will be used as an example to explain the development of the syndrome; it is an almost-closed compartment and is the most commonly affected. In the case of the anterior compartment, the interosseous membrane lies posteriorly, the tibia on one side and the fibula on the other. Anteriorly a relatively nonexpansile fascia covers the compartment. If pressure within the compartment increases, there is no space for the compartment to expand to accommodate it. Therefore symptoms and possibly changes in the muscles develop.[20, 21, 22]

The exact initiating mechanism of compartment compression in a runner is unknown in most cases. Sometimes mild trauma with bleeding into the compartment is the cause. (Severe bleeding into the compartment, for instance after a fracture, is probably the most common etiologic mechanism of the syndrome, but this does not apply to the runner.) In the case of runners, it is thought that muscle swelling produces the initial increase in pressure. This increased pressure leads, in turn, to impairment of venous outflow, resulting in a further rise in intracompartmental pressure. If the pressure becomes great enough, arterial circulation is impeded. leading to ischemia (lack of blood supply) of the muscles and then necrosis[19] (Figure 21.32).

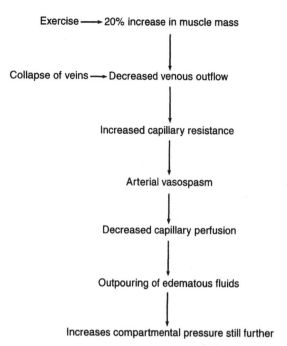

FIGURE 21.32
The development of a compartment compression syndrome

VARIETIES: The compartment compression syndrome manifests in one of three ways:

1. Acute
2. Recurrent (less severe than the acute)
3. Acute-on-recurrent

1. *Acute.* An acute compartment compression syndrome is a surgical emergency. Those involved with athletes should always be aware of the possibility of this condition suddenly presenting in the guise of shin splints. The commonly affected compartment is the anterior. The lateral is less often affected, and acute compression of the posterior is rare.

Symptoms and Signs.
The symptom is intense pain developing during a run and not subsiding afterward. Palpation reveals a "woody-hard" tender muscle mass. Passive plantar flexion stretching of the foot may evoke pain. The dorsalis pedis and the anterior tibial pulses are usually present. However decreased sensation may be noted in an area localized to the web of the first and second toes. If found, decreased sensation suggests that the condition is quite advanced, with a definite indication for emergency surgical evaluation. Other signs of advanced tissue change include spreading numbness over the dorsum of the foot and weakness of the anterior tibial muscle, the

extensor hallucis longus muscle, the extensor digitorum longus muscle, and the ankle evertors (Figure 21.33). When other compartments are involved, signs relative to their anatomy are found.[23, 24, 25, 26]

Diagnosis and Treatment. The diagnosis should be made on clinical grounds. It may be confirmed by using a wick catheter or similar device to measure the intra-compartmental pressure.[27, 28, 29] If the pressure is only slightly increased, the athlete may be treated conservatively with ice and observed carefully. If, however, the pressure reaches dangerous levels for more than a short while, surgical incision of the entire length of the fascia covering the affected compartment (fasciotomy) is indicated.[30]

2. *Recurrent.* This variety is more common in athletes than is the acute variety. The etiology is unclear. It is also unclear what regulates the pressure so that dangerous levels are not reached.

Symptoms and Signs. The athlete complains of pain localized to the affected compartment whenever a particular level of activity is reached. Symptoms are much less severe than in the acute variety, but performance can be affected by pain and weakness of the muscles in the affected compartment. There is pain during or after a workout, but there is never "woody hardness" or

extreme pain. The symptoms disappear fairly rapidly after activity ceases, especially if ice is applied. There is usually no evidence of any change in sensation over the dorsum of the foot.

Treatment. The most valuable form of therapy is ice applied after activity. Some athletes find it useful to apply ice before exercising as well. Other suggestions for decreasing symptoms include: stretching the anterior tibial muscles, balancing the strength of the muscles of the lower leg, changing the surface, wearing shoes with beveled heels, and using in-shoe orthotic devices.[31]

If the condition persists, the diagnosis should be confirmed by obtaining intracompartmental pressure readings before and after exercise, to help decide whether a fascial release should be performed.[32]

A recurrent compartment syndrome involving the deep posterior compartment has been described. Athletes with this condition have medial tibial pain with tenderness over the middle or lower portion of the posteromedial crest.[33, 34, 35]

Tightness of the deep posterior compartment is difficult to evaluate clinically, but is sometimes mentioned by the athlete. There may be a feeling of numbness deep within the plantar aspect of the foot, as well as weakness of toe-off that coincides with the onset of pain. Usually no pain or weakness is apparent on testing the posterior tibial, the flexor hallucis longus, or the flexor digitorum longus muscles when in a resting state, though these muscles may demonstrate weakness once symptoms are present.

This condition is usually treated with ice, exercises, anti-inflammatory medication, and stretches. But if the symptoms do not improve rapidly, surgical release of the fascia frequently gives good results in spite of difficulty in documenting compartmental pressure increase.[27]

3. *Acute-on-recurrent.* Any athlete with symptoms of recurrent compartment syndrome should be informed that, because of the presence of long-standing symptoms, it is possible to suddenly develop the acute variety, necessitating urgent fascial surgery.

The athlete with recurrent compartment syndrome should be warned that, if the symptoms are more intense than usual and do not subside within a short period of time, urgent medical help should be sought.

Fascial Hernia

ETIOLOGY: Occasionally defects occur in the fascia overlying the compartments, particularly over the anterior and lateral compartments. These defects allow the underlying muscle to bulge through when increased

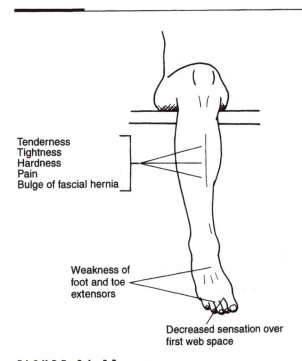

FIGURE 21.33
Symptoms and signs of an anterior compartment compression syndrome

Tenderness
Tightness
Hardness
Pain
Bulge of fascial hernia

Weakness of foot and toe extensors

Decreased sensation over first web space

compartment pressure occurs during exercise. When the muscle herniates through the fascia, it may be caught in this defect and cause pain. This condition is often associated with the compartment compression syndrome.[36]

SYMPTOMS AND SIGNS: Pain and a bulge are the usual symptoms. It is often possible to palpate a hole in the fascia when the limb is in a nonexercised state. A definite bulge can be felt protruding through the defect during or immediately after exercise (Figure 21.34).

TREATMENT: Initial treatment is to tape a felt pad firmly over the defect in an attempt to prevent the muscle from bulging through the fascia. This leads to resolution of the symptoms in some cases. If it does not produce the desired results, a fascial release (incision of the fascia) should be considered, particularly if there are also symptoms of a compartment compression syndrome.

Inflammation of the Anterior Tibial Tendon and Muscle

Inflammation of the anterior tibial tendon and muscle should be differentiated from the anterior compartment compression syndrome.

Inflammation of the muscles and tendons in the anterior compartment appears to be due to microtrauma, which is related to the inability of these muscles to adequately absorb the forces of foot deceleration at or after foot strike. These muscles place the foot in a dorsiflexed position just before impact and then control the speed of pronation during the initial contact and early mid-support phases. Factors frequently precipitating inflammation of these muscles are sudden increase in mileage or hard downhill running.

SYMPTOMS AND SIGNS: Pain, tenderness, and sometimes swelling over the anterior muscle group are present. Occasionally crepitation along the anterior tibial tendon can be felt. There is usually no increase in pressure over the anterior compartment. The tibialis anterior muscle is often weak and/or painful when tested. Other muscles of the lower leg may also be weak, including the tibialis posterior, the extensor hallucis longus, and the extensor digitorum longus muscles.

It is important to feel the tone or firmness of the anterior compartment and to compare this tone with that of the opposite side. This tone should also be felt before, during, and after exercise, particularly when symptoms are present, to rule out the possibility of an

Fascia over anterior compartment

Fascial hernia (with anterior tibialis muscle bulging through)

FIGURE 21.34
A fascial hernia of the anterior compartment of the leg

anterior compartment compression syndrome in which a "woody hardness" is felt.

TREATMENT: Initially, icing and ice massage are performed while gently stretching the anterior muscles in a plantar flexed direction. Good shock-absorbent shoes with beveled heels may take some of the strain off the anterior tibial tendon. If a biomechanical abnormality is present and is considered to be related to the symptoms, an in-shoe orthotic device may be indicated. Training should be done on a softer surface, and the duration and length of training should be decreased until symptoms have subsided. If symptoms are severe, anti-inflammatory medication and physical therapy, such as ultrasound and hydrocortisone, may be useful.

Once symptoms have improved, the anterior and posterior muscle groups should be strengthened and the anterior muscle group should be stretched regularly.

Fibular Stress Reaction and Stress Fracture

ETIOLOGY: The exact etiology is uncertain, but it occurs particularly in the undertrained rather than the more advanced runner. Sometimes it occurs when a well-conditioned athlete suddenly steps up the number of miles run per week. It may be related to the forward movement and torsional forces of the fibula during pronation.

SYMPTOMS AND SIGNS: Pain is commonly localized to the lower end of the fibula, about 7 to 10 cm above (or proximal to) the lateral malleolus, but is sometimes in the mid or upper portion of the fibula (Figure 21.35). Swelling may or may not be present. The

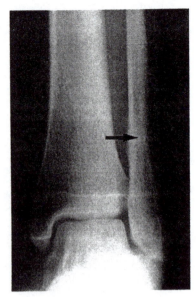

tuning fork vibration test may be positive if a stress fracture is imminent. Others have found that applying ultrasound to the area has been effective at revealing a stress fracture. The vibration of the crystal over the fracture site often causes pain.

TREATMENT: The athlete should be encouraged to decrease mileage and to run on a softer surface. Good shock-absorbent shoes as well as soft orthotic devices may improve the symptoms. Ice and aspirin may also be indicated.

If symptoms persist or increase, or if swelling develops, it may be advisable to stop running for a time. During this time the athlete should run in place in a swimming pool while wearing a life jacket to help maintain cardiovascular endurance (see Chapter 8). Stationary cycling is also useful. If symptoms are severe, it may occasionally be necessary to immobilize the lower leg with a posterior splint.

Popliteal Artery Entrapment Syndrome

The entrapment is an uncommon condition which usually occurs unilaterally in young men who are nonatherosclerotic; it may also occur bilaterally. It can also occur in women.

ETIOLOGY: The cause of this syndrome is intermittent compression or entrapment of the popliteal artery by one of the heads of the gastrocnemius muscle, usually the medial.[37]

SYMPTOMS AND SIGNS: The athlete complains of paresthesia and/or pain in the foot and/or calf after running a specific distance. Walking may relieve the discomfort, after which a return to running may be possible. In some cases, symptoms are produced only while walking, and the athlete is able to run without pain.

There may be a decrease in the dorsalis pedis and posterior tibial artery pulses on active continuous plantar flexion of the foot or after passive dorsiflexion. A Doppler apparatus can be used to define the blood flow more clearly. Angiographic investigation shows entrapment of the popliteal artery.

COMPLICATIONS: Repetitive compression can result in chronic trauma to the popliteal artery, which can lead to an aneurysm or a thrombosis within the artery and subsequent loss of the limb. It is therefore vital to make the diagnosis before complications develop.

TREATMENT: Treatment of the entrapment is surgical. The offending head of the gastrocnemius muscle is completely divided to remove the pressure from the popliteal artery, which may need to be grafted with a saphenous vein graft.

Overuse Injuries to the Achilles Tendon

Though Achilles tendon overuse injuries are common problems, the nomenclature of these injuries is sometimes confusing. As mentioned earlier, the Achilles tendon does not have an actual sheath, but rather a peritendinous tissue (the paratenon), and the classification is based on whether this tissue or the tendon itself is involved:[38]

1. Achilles peritendinitis—inflammation of the peritendinous tissue surrounding the tendon.

2. Achilles peritendinitis with tendinosis—the Achilles tendon itself shows areas of degeneration, in addition to inflammation of the paratenon. Partial tears—either microscopic or macroscopic—may be present. Bone spurs at the attachment of the Achilles to the posterior aspect of the calcaneus can also occur.[39]

3. Partial tears or tendinosis. (See section on lower leg injuries.)

4. Total rupture. (See section on lower leg injuries.)

ETIOLOGY: It is thought that overtraining, biomechanical malalignments, lack of adequate heel height, or unaccustomed use may lead to an inflammatory response to microtrauma of the peritendinous tissue or to microscopic tears within the tendon. If the tendon is involved, areas of necrosis can develop. In some cases, peritendinous inflammation develops as a response to tears within the tendon. Achilles tendinitis is often associated with a cavus foot configuration in conjunction with a tight Achilles, or with compensatory pronation due to a varus position of the lower leg, rearfoot, or forefoot.

SYMPTOMS AND SIGNS: The athlete presents with pain and swelling over the Achilles tendon and inability to perform. There is local tenderness on squeezing the Achilles tendon, and pain is present on forced passive dorsiflexion, resistance to active plantar flexion, or both. Crepitus may occur. A nodular or fusiform swelling of the tendon suggests that microtrauma has led to an area of degeneration within the tendon.

X-RAYS: Soft-tissue lateral views may show changes in the outline of the Achilles tendon or within Kager's triangle (see Chapter 20).

TREATMENT: Initially treatment is with ice and ice massage, heel lifts in the shoes, anti-inflammatory medication, and ultrasound. Running should be limited if symptoms persist.

If symptoms do not improve within a few days, any biomechanical abnormality should be corrected with in-shoe orthotic devices. If symptoms do not improve within a week to ten days with this treatment, it may be necessary to place the foot and ankle into a posterior splint, which rests the tendon but allows physical therapy to continue. If the symptoms are severe, it may be necessary to place the foot and lower leg in a cast, though this measure should be avoided if possible.

On occasion, surgical exploration may need to be undertaken. The paratenon is opened and stripped, the tendon incised to reveal any areas of degeneration, and bone spurs on the calcaneus removed.[40, 41]

Rehabilitation includes gentle Achilles stretching done with the knee bent as well as straight. (See section on stretching.) The whole lower extremity should be thoroughly rehabilitated, isokinetic machines being the most suitable form of resistance. If isokinetic machines are not available, exercises include toe-raises while standing on a 2-inch (5-cm) board or on the edge of a stair, so the heel can drop below the level of the foot.

These exercises should be done carefully, and the number and excursion of dorsiflexion should be progressively increased. Exercises should also be prescribed for the anterior tibial and posterior tibial muscles, the quadriceps, and the hamstrings.

Retrocalcaneal Bursitis

This condition may be divided into two categories:

1. Inflammation of the deep, or retrocalcaneal, bursa lying between the Achilles tendon and the calcaneus

2. Inflammation of the superficial or subcutaneous bursa lying between the skin and the Achilles tendon. (See Chapter 20.)

ETIOLOGY: Excessive compensatory pronation from whatever cause is the usual etiology of irritation of one of the bursa, particularly the deep bursa. However, retrocalcaneal bursitis is frequently found in those with cavus feet, particularly if a bone spur on the posterosuperior aspect of the calcaneus is also present.

SYMPTOMS AND SIGNS: Tenderness, pain, swelling, and redness involving the posterosuperior aspect of the heel and calcaneus, particularly on the lateral side, results in an inability to wear certain types of shoes, and thus performance is often impaired.

TREATMENT: Initially, ice and anti-inflammatory medication should be prescribed. It is important to protect the heel. In the case of the inflamed superficial bursa, the heel counter of the shoe may need to be incised and separated or have a hole cut in it (this will not help the deep retrocalcaneal bursa).

Control of excessive pronation with in-shoe orthotic devices helps control heel eversion and thus reduce inflammation of the deep retrocalcaneal bursa. Cortisone injected into or around the inflamed area may help in resistant cases. Occasionally surgery must be performed to remove irritating soft tissue and bone spurs.

Common Running-Induced Injuries to the Foot

Medial Arch Pain

ETIOLOGY: A number of conditions may present with medial arch pain in the runner. The most common cause of "arch collapse" is associated with stretching of the *spring ligament*, which is caused by inadequate functioning of the supporting tibialis posterior muscle that leads to excessive pronation. This mechanism may also give rise to *entrapment of the medial calcaneal nerve,* with further aggravation of the problem. *Abductor hallucis spasm* may add to medial arch discomfort, and *medial plantar bursitis* is also often present (Figure 21.36).

SYMPTOMS AND SIGNS: Commonly there is pain and tenderness around the medial prominence of the navicular and the talonavicular joints. Swelling is occasionally present. There is often an accessory navicular as well as poor intrinsic foot musculature and insufficient functioning of the tibialis posterior muscle.

TREATMENT: Ice, anti-inflammatory medication, and LowDye taping should be initiated. Excessive pronation should be controlled with in-shoe orthotic devices and with exercises that develop the intrinsic musculature and the tibialis posterior and flexor hallucis longus muscles. Sometimes it is necessary to inject a corticosteroid into the plantar bursa or around an entrapped nerve. Surgery is occasionally necessary to relieve entrapment of the medial calcaneal nerve.

Plantar Fasciitis

Plantar fasciitis can be caused by an acute injury (strain) from sudden excessive loading of the foot. More often it is due to chronic irritation from excessive pronation, resulting in microtears of the plantar fascia. A high-arched, cavus foot is also at risk, as a tight plantar fascia is usually present in this type of foot (Figure 21.9).

SYMPTOMS AND SIGNS: Pain and tenderness are localized to the plantar aspect of the foot, and they usually radiate from the heel forward, particularly when the athlete takes his or her first steps in the morning. Swelling may be observed near the heel. Localized tenderness is present at the plantar fascial attachment into the calcaneus, just distal to this attachment, in the area of the medial arch, over the medial band of the plantar fascia, and in the abductor hallucis muscle. There may be pain on actively and passively dorsiflexing the foot, especially if the big toe is also dorsiflexed. A tight plantar fascial band can be palpated. (See Chapter 20.)

TREATMENT: Ice-massage and anti-inflammatory medication should be initiated. Excessive pronation should be limited by means of LowDye taping, in-shoe orthotic devices, or both. In the case of a high-arched foot, a carefully selected in-shoe orthotic device with

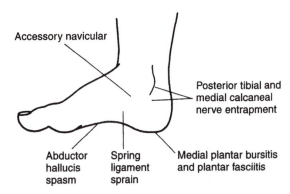

FIGURE 21.36
Various causes of medial arch pain

good shock absorbency can be of help. Local corticosteroid injections should be used judiciously. Surgery is rarely necessary.

Cuboid Dysfunction (Sometimes Called Subluxation)

ETIOLOGY: The etiology is uncertain but may be related in some cases to dysfunction of the calcaneocuboid joint or to passage of the peroneus longus tendon through a groove on the inferior aspect of the cuboid.[39] It occurs particularly in middle- and long-distance runners (Figure 21.37).

SYMPTOMS AND SIGNS: Presentation is fairly acute, with severe pain, tenderness, and sometimes swelling localized to the calcaneoctiboid joint. There is localized tenderness to palpation on the plantar aspect of the foot and laterally over the joint.

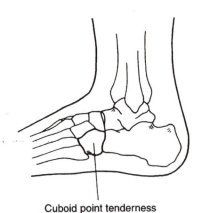

Cuboid point tenderness

FIGURE 21.37
Cuboid "subluxation"

TREATMENT: After X-rays of the foot have excluded bony pathology, the cuboid may be manipulated by one of a number of methods, followed by LowDye taping. If the athlete is seen some time after the onset of the condition, swelling and inflammation may be present, necessitating the use of ice, elevation, and anti-inflammatory medication. In long-standing cases resistant to other forms of therapy, surgical exploration of the cuboid and peroneus longus tendon has been undertaken.

Black Toenails

Black toenails are notorious among runners, but are becoming less frequent with the increased room in the toe box of newer shoes. A shoe that allows the foot to slide forward also predisposes the athlete to this condition,

Black discoloration of a toenail results from pressure that damages the small blood vessels beneath the nail, forming a blood blister. The nail is usually elevated from the nail bed. If this occurs on the big toe, it may be necessary to release the pressure beneath the nail. This is accomplished by heating a straightened paper clip until red hot and melting a number of small holes through the nail with it, thus allowing the fluid to drain. Another effective tool made specifically for this condition is the high-temperature (2200° Fahrenheit) fine-tip catherizer.

Often the injured toenail falls off within two to four weeks. The new nail may be somewhat thicker and deformed compared with the original, however.

Tarsal Tunnel Syndrome

See Chapter 20, Lower Leg, Ankle, and Foot Injuries.

In-Shoe Orthotic Devices for Overuse Running Injuries

In-shoe orthotic devices in athletics, particularly for runners, have gained acceptance and popularity in recent years. In fact, in one study researchers showed that soft orthotics supported the medial longitudinal arch better than traditional taping.

Orthotic devices (or *orthotics* as they are commonly called) are not a panacea for all running-related problems, though they are certainly useful in particular conditions (to be discussed). They may cause new problems if they are not made accurately or are used for conditions for which they are not indicated (Figure 21.38).

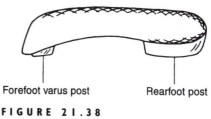

Forefoot varus post   Rearfoot post

FIGURE 21.38
Orthotic posting

In order to judge whether a particular foot type or lower-extremity alignment will respond to orthotics, it is necessary to examine the foot and to note the angular measurements. The athlete should then be observed running; there may be marked pronation when standing but excellent function when running, as the muscles are able to control the position of the feet. Conversion from the flexible adaptor to a rigid lever should take place in the latter half of the mid-support phase. If the foot is still flexible and loose during take-off, it is quite likely that the athlete will benefit from an in-shoe orthotic device.[35, 42]

The purpose of such a device is to place the foot in a position of improved mechanical advantage or efficiency, so the joints and muscles will be more favorably positioned to deal with the repetitive forces applied to them. Some symptom complexes that have been responsive include:

1. Medial longitudinal arch pain and plantar fasciitis

2. Generalized foot pain—the foot is placed in a neutral position and the orthotics are suitably posted

3. Morton's neuroma—a metatarsal bar is added to the orthotic

4. Sesamoid pain—controlled by posting behind the metatarsal head with a cutout made for the sesamoid

5. Heel bruises—cushioned by a donut surrounding the tender area

6. Medial tibial pain from the medial tibial stress syndrome

7. Medial and peripatellar pain due to malalignment, in particular the malalignment syndrome of anteversion, medially squinting patellae, tibia varum, and pronated feet

8. Patellar tendinitis associated with a wide Q angle and excessive pronation

9. Hip pain or backache due to a short leg due to either an anatomical or a functional cause

10. Achilles tendinitis

Be careful with more rigid feet that need precise control. Often additional shock absorbency is needed, especially with the rigid cavus foot, as incorrect posting of the orthotic may produce new symptoms!

With experience in using orthotics, the indications for their use in a particular condition will become clearer and better defined (Figure 21.39).

Types of Orthotics

The numerous types of orthotics can be grouped into three categories:

1. Soft, temporary orthotic devices such as felt placed on podiatry mold or cork, and Spenco, etc.

2. Semirigid devices such as Sporthotics and combinations of Plastazote with Aliplast.

3. Rigid orthotic devices such as one of the many types of Rohadur acrylic (Figure 21.40).

Temporary soft orthotics are often useful initially for evaluating the athlete's response. After that the more permanent semirigid or rigid devices can be prescribed if the response is favorable. Semirigid devices are commonly used for runners and athletes involved in laterally moving sports. A few athletes, mainly long-distance runners, need more precise control of their biomechanical foot function, and they do best with rigid (or acrylic) supports.

The soft devices are usually made by outlining the foot and posting with felt according to the type of foot encountered. Adjustments are made by clinical experience, attempting to balance the foot toward a neutral position (Figure 21.41). Devices such as Plastazote and Aliplast are heat-molded to the foot, with the subtalar joint placed in or near its neutral position because it is

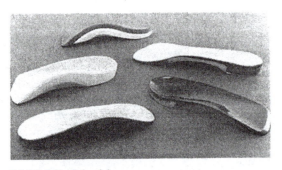

FIGURE 21.40
Various types of orthotics
Starting at the top and moving clockwise: Regalite with Plastazote (very soft); Sporthotic for the long-distance runner (slightly flexible plastic with cushioned undersurface); Rohadur (hard plastic); Sporthotic (slightly flexible plastic); Plastazote with Aliplast (soft but firm).

currently assumed that the foot functions best at, or nearly at, its neutral position (Figure 21.42).

Rigid and some semirigid devices need to be made from a cast of the foot, usually taken when the foot is non-weight-bearing and in the neutral position. Other methods of obtaining casts include: fully-weight-bearing, semi-weight-bearing, non-weight-bearing with the subtalar joint in neutral position but the forefoot brought down perpendicular to the rearfoot. These casts are then sent to a podiatric orthotic laboratory, where a positive mold of the negative cast is made.

Taking the Cast Impression

The technique describes a *non-weight-bearing* cast impression with the subtalar joint in the neutral position.

1. The athlete should have been examined and all necessary measurements recorded. (See examination of a running athlete.)

2. The athlete lies supine with the lower third of the leg unsupported over the end of the examining table. The pelvis should be adjusted so the feet are perpendicular to the ground and neither abducted nor adducted. This is accomplished by placing a pillow under one or both hips to bring the feet to the perpendicular position.

3. Strips of plaster of Paris 4 inches (10 cm) (or sometimes 5 inches [12 cm]) wide are used. The length of each strip is determined by measuring the distance from the head of the fifth metatarsal, around the heel, to the head of the first metatarsal around the toes. Four strips of this length are cut. Two strips are used together to

Soft Plastizote Orthotics	Firm Plastic Orthotics
1. For temporary use during any short term injury recovery	1. Chronic or recurring biomechanical injury
2. Lightweight custom footbed for competition shoegear	2. Training shoegear in which a moderate to high degree of forefoot valgus or forefoot varus is present
3. Sesamoiditis	3. Hallux valgus
4. Plantar fibromatosis	4. Heel spur syndrome (use highly flexible plastic)
	5. Postural problems

FIGURE 21.39
Soft/Firm Orthosis Indications
(*Source:* Ross Leonard, DPM, Corvallis, Oregon. Printed with permission.)

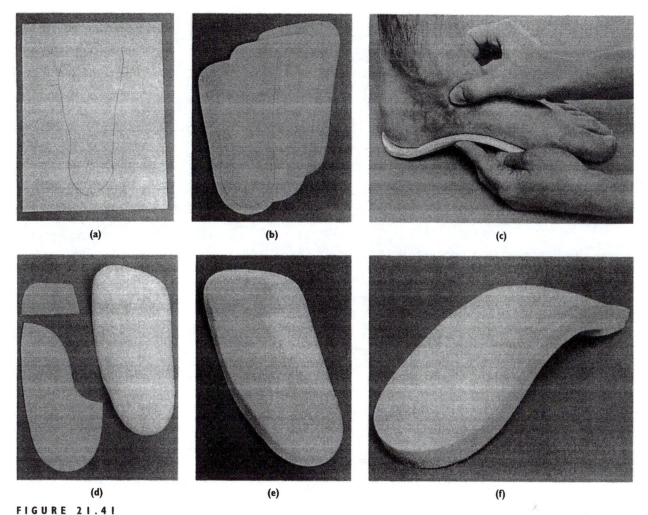

FIGURE 21.41

Manufacturing an orthotic from a heat malleable material such as Plastazote and Aliplast

(a) Draw an outline of the foot, marking the heads of the first and fifth metatarsals. (b) Cut out suitably-sized pieces of Aliplast and Plastazole. (c) Heat these materials in a convection oven at approximately 350°F for about 5 minutes until they are soft. Then place the semi-weight-bearing foot onto the material. Position the foot into neutral, and mold the material to the desired height. (d) When the material has cooled and become firm, cut out the desired posting as illustrated. (e) Glue and grind. (f) The finished product.

provide adequate strength for the cast. The first double layer is dipped into warm water for a few seconds. (A teaspoon [5 ml] of alum is added to facilitate hardening of the cast.) Most of the water is then squeezed out and the plaster is placed along the side of the foot, from the head of the fifth metatarsal around the heel to the head of the first metatarsal, and smoothed down to eliminate creases. The excess plaster is then brought up behind the heel.

4. The second double layer of plaster of Paris is applied from the head of the first metatarsal around the toes to the lateral side of the foot, with the excess folded beneath the toes (Figure 21.42).

5. The foot is then brought into the neutral position by grasping the heads of the fourth and fifth metatarsals just proximal to the metatarsophalangeal joint while palpating the relationship of the head of the talus to the navicular, as previously described. The foot is then dorsiflexed in this position until resistance is felt (which indicates that the midtarsal joint is "locked"). This position is then held until the plaster of Paris has dried.

6. It is important to ensure that the athlete is completely relaxed and does not contract any of the muscles of the lower leg or foot. In particular, the athlete should not be able to palpate the anterior tibial tendon during the casting procedure. If any of the lower leg

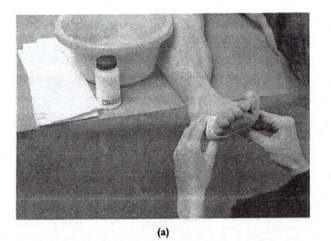

(a)

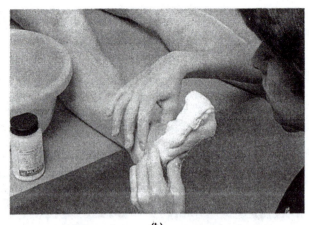

(b)

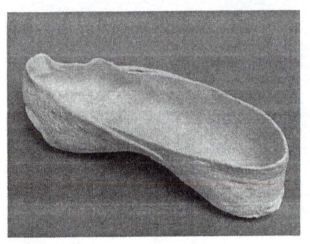

(c)

FIGURE 21.42

Obtaining a neutral cast of the foot, non-weight-bearing, for the manufacture of an orthotic device
(a) Strips of plaster of Paris are applied to the heel and sole. (b) Strips of plaster are then applied to the forefoot and the foot positioned into neutral. The fourth and fifth metatarsal heads are then loaded until resistance is felt. The foot is held in this position until dry. (c) The finished cast.

muscles are tense, a false impression of the rearfoot-to-forefoot relationship will be obtained.

7. The other foot is then put into a cast in the same manner.

8. When the casts are dried they are easily removed from the feet. However care should be taken to ensure that the casts are not distorted as they are removed.

Some painful conditions of the foot are caused by biomechanical malalignment of the foot and ankle complex and may require a custom-made orthotic device. Minor problems often don't require an expensive orthotic and can be corrected or compensated for with a foam or felt pad.

Prevention of Heat Injuries During Long-Distance Running

With more and more recreational athletes participating in an increasing number of distance running events, prevention of heat injuries has assumed an important place in the organization of these races. The body fatigues more easily if a runner loses 3 percent of body weight from sweat and fluid loss during a race. When 5 to 10 percent of body weight is lost the runner is in danger. Dehydration of this magnitude severely limits subsequent sweating, places a dangerous demand on the circulatory system, reduces exercise capacity, and exposes the runner to possible serious heat injury.[43,44] It is thought that middle-aged and aging men and women possess significantly less heat tolerance than their younger counterparts and so are at increased risk. Dehydration is not the only culprit in heat illness. According to Noakes,[45] elevated rectal temperatures (and heat illness) are often the result of the metabolic intensity of the race, not dehydration alone. Obviously athletes who are running in hot, humid conditions need to be monitored, especially if they are running at an aggressive pace.

The American College of Sports Medicine has published a position statement[46] with guidelines for preventing heat injuries in runners. These suggestions include the following:

1. No long-distance race should be run when the wet-bulb globe thermometer (WBGT) is higher than 28°C (82.4°F).

2. Races should be held early in the morning or late in the evening in areas where the daylight dry bulb temperature exceeds 27°C (80°F).[40]

3. Race organizers should provide adequate quantities of fluids at the start of a race and at water stations. Fluids should be available every 3 Km to 4 Km (2 to 2½ miles).

4. There should be adequate medical and paramedical coverage of the race, including medical personnel at each station.

5. Organizational personnel should reserve the right to stop runners who exhibit clear signs of heat stroke or heat exhaustion.

6. Runners should be educated by means of a printed pre-race instruction sheet containing recommendations on training, suggestions on pre-race nutrition and fluid intake, guidelines for consumption of fluids, and suggestions for recognition of heat symptoms during a race.

7. Immediately before the race, the existing as well as the predicted temperature and relative humidity should be announced to the runners, with an interpretation of these values. If the temperature exceeds 24°C (75°F), novice runners should be advised to decrease their planned running pace by about forty-five to sixty seconds per mile.

8. Organizers should remind runners of fluid requirements and the symptoms of heat injury, and should suggest that if a runner notices these symptoms in another runner, he or she should offer or summon aid.

9. Sprinkling the runners down with a garden hose or similar apparatus along the course of the race is a useful way of preventing excessive temperature buildup.

The best protection against development of heat injury is adequate consumption of fluid in the form of water. The athlete should prepare by consuming

1. One liter or more of fluid 2 hours before the race

2. Five hundred milliliters 15 minutes before the race (one tall glass).

3. At least 300 to 500 milliliters of fluid every 15 minutes during the race

Adequate rehydration must be achieved over the 24 hours following the race. Waiting until thirsty is *too late*.

REFERENCES

1. Slocum DB, James SL: Biomechanics of running. *JAMA* 205: 97–104, 1968.

2. James SL, Brubaker CE: Biomechanics of running. *Orthop Clin North Am* 4: 609–615, 1973.

3. Mann RA, Hagy J: Biomechanics of walking, running and sprinting. *Am J Sports Med* 5: 345–350, 1980.

4. Drez Jr, D: Running footwear. Examination of the training shoe, the foot, and functional orthotic devices. Symposium. *Am J Sports Med* 8: 140–141, 1980.

5. Sallade JR, Koch S. Training errors in long distance running. *J Athletic Training* 27:50–53;1992.

6. Scott SH : Internal forces of chronic running injury sites. *Med Sci Sports Exerc* 22: 357–69, 1990.

7. Clement DB, Taunton JE, Smart GW, McNicol KL: A survey of overuse running injuries. *Phys Sports Med* 9(5): 47–58, 1981.

8. Macera CA, Pate RR, Powell KE, Jackson KL: Predicting lower extremity injuries among habitual runners. *Arch Intern Med* 149(11): 2565–2568, 1989.

9. Kalin VX, Denoth J, Stacoff A, Stussi E: Running injuries and running shoe construction: Demonstration of possible correlations. *Sportverletz-Sportschaden* 2: 80–85, 1988.

10. Kurtz TD, Wright J, Poland D: Effect of duration on running injuries among soldiers. *Athletic Training, JNATA* 23:114, 1988.

11. Walter SD, Hart LE, McIntosh JM, Sutton JR: The Ontario cohort study of running related injuries. *Arch Intern Med* 149(11): 2561–2564, 1989.

12. Subotnick SI: The flat foot. *Phys Sports Med* 9:85–91, August 1981.

13. Noble CA: The treatment of iliotibial band friction syndrome. *Br J Sports Med* 13:51–54, 1979.

14. Devas MB: Stress fractures in athletes. *J Sports Med* 1:49–51, 1973.

15. Slocum DB: The shin splint syndrome: Medical aspects and differential diagnosis. Proceedings of 8th National

Conference on the Medical Aspects of Sports, *AMA* November 1966.

16.   Orava S: The iliotibial tract friction syndrome in athletes—an uncommon exertion syndrome on the lateral side of the knee. *Br J Sports Med* 12:69–73, 1978.

17.   Clement DB: Tibial stress syndrome in athletes. *J Sports Med* 2:81–85, 1974.

18.   Mayfield GW: Popliteus tendon tenosynovitis. *Am J Sports Med* 5:31–36, 1977.

19.   Stanitski CL, McMaster JH, Scranton PE: On the nature of stress fractures. *Am J Sports Med* 6:391–396, 1978.

20.   Leach RE, Zohn DA, Stryker WS: Anterior tibial compartment syndrome. Clinical and electromyographic aspects. *Arch Surg* 88:187–192, 1964.

21.   Leach RE, Hammond G, Stryker WS: Anterior tibial compartment syndrome. Acute and chronic. *J Bone Joint Surg* 49A:451–462, 1967.

22.   Leach RE, Corbett M: Anterior tibial compartment syndrome in soccer players. *Am J Sports Med* 7:258–259, 1979.

23.   Lunceford Jr, EM: The peroneal compartment syndrome. *Southern Med J* 58:621–623, 1965.

24.   Lipscomb AB, Ibrahim AA: Acute peroneal compartment syndrome in a well conditioned athlete: A report of a case. *Am J Sports Med* 5:154–157, 1977.

25.   Goodman MJ: Isolated lateral-compartment syndrome. Report of a case. *J Bone Joint Surg* 62A:834, 1980.

26.   Mubarak SJ, Owens CA, Garfin S, et al: Acute exertional superficial posterior compartment syndrome. *Am J Sports Med* 6:287–294, 1978.

27.   Mubarak SJ, Hargens AR, Owen CA, et al: The wick catheter technique for measurement of intramuscular pressure. A new research and clinical tool. *J Bone Joint Surg* 58A:1016–1020, 1976.

28.   Mubarak SJ, Owen CA, Hargens AR et al: Acute compartment syndromes: Diagnosis and treatment with the aid of the wick catheter. *J Bone Joint Surg* 6OA:1091–1095, 1978.

29.   Matsen FA, Winquist RA, Krugmire RB: Diagnosis and management of compartmental syndromes. *J Bone Joint Surg* 62A:286–291, 1980.

30.   Whitesides Jr, TE, Haney TC, Morimoto K, et al: Tissue pressure measurements as a determinant for the need of fasciotomy. *Clin Orthop* 113:43–51, 1975.

31.   Veith RG, Matsen FA III, Newell SG: Recurrent anterior compartmental syndromes. *Phys Sports Med* 8:80–88, November 1980.

32.   Puranen J, Alavaikko A: Intracompartmental pressure increase on exertion in patients with chronic compartment syndrome in the leg. *J Bone Joint Surg* 63A:1304–1309, 1981.

33.   Orava S, Puranen J: Athletes' leg pains. *Br J Sports Med* 13:92–97, 1979.

34.   Puranen J: The medial tibial syndrome. Exercise ischemia in the medial fascial compartment of the leg. *J Bone Joint Surg* 56B:712–715, 1974.

35.   Matsen FA III, Clawson DK: The deep posterior compartmental syndrome of the leg. *J Bone Joint Surg* 57A:34–39, 1975.

36.   Garfin S, Mubarak SJ, Owen CA: Exertional anterolateral-compartment syndrome. Case report with fascial defect, muscle herniation, and superficial peroneal nerve entrapment. *J Bone Joint Surg* 59A:404–405, 1977.

37.   Darling RC, Buckley CJ, Abbott WM, et al: Intermittent claudication in young athletes: Popliteal artery entrapment syndrome. *Trauma* 14:543–552, 1974.

38.   Santilli G: Achilles tendinopathies and paratendinopathies. *J Sports Med* 19:245–259, 1979.

39.   Newell SG, Woodle A: Cuboid syndrome. *Phys Sportmed* 9:71–76, April 1981.

40.   Leach RE, James SL, Wasilewski S: Achilles tendinitis. *Am J Sports Med* 9:93–98, 1981.

41.   Clancy WG, Neidhart D, Brand RL: Achilles tendinitis in runners. A report of five cases. *Am J Sports Med* 4:46–57, 1976.

42.   D'Ambrosia RD, Zelis RF, Chuinard RG: Interstitial pressure measurements in the anterior and posterior compartments in athletes with shin splints. *Am J Sports Med* 5:127–131, 1977.

43.   Wyndham CH, Strydom NB: The danger of an inadequate water intake during marathon running. *S Afr Med J* 43:893–896, 1969.

44.   Wyndham CH: Heat stroke and hyperthermia in marathon runners. *Ann NY Acad Sci* 301:128–138, 1977.

45.   Noakes TD, Myburgh KH, DuPlessis J, et al: Metabolic rate, not percent dehydration, predicts rectal temperature in marathon runners. *Med Sci Sports Exerc* 23: 443–449; 1991.

46.   American College of Sports Medicine Position Statement on prevention of heat injuries during distance running. *Med Sci Sports* 7:VII–IX, 1975.

RECOMMENDED READINGS

Bates BT, Osternig LR, Mason MS, et al: Foot orthotic devices to modify selected aspects of lower extremity mechanics. *Am J Sports Med* 7:338- 342, 1979.

Bates BT, Osternig LR, Mason BR, et al: Functional variability of the lower extremity during the support phase of running. *Med Sci Sports* 11:328–331, 1979.

Blatz DJ: Bilateral femoral and tibial shaft stress fractures in a runner. *Am J Sports Med* 9:322–325, 1981.

Brody DM: Running injuries. *CIBA Clinical Symposia* 32:2–36, 1980.

Brubaker CE, James SL: Injuries to runners. *J Sports Med* 2:189–197, 1974.

Clancy WG: Lower extremity injuries in the jogger and distance runner. *Phys Sports Med* 2:46–50, June 1974.

Clancy WG: Runners' injuries. Part One. Symposium. *Am J Sports Med* 8:137–138, 1980.

Clancy WG: Runners' injuries. Part Two. Evaluation and treatment of specific injuries. Symposium. *Am J Sports Med* 8:287–289, 1980.

Clement DB, Taunton JE: A guide to the prevention of running injuries. *Austr Fam Phys* 10: 156–164, 1981.

Clement DB, Taunton JE, Smart GW, et al: A survey of overuse running injuries. *Phys Sports Med* 9:47–58, May 1981.

Corrigan AD, Fitch KD: Complications of jogging. *Med J Aust* 2:363–368, 1972.

Costill DL, Branam G, Eddy D, et al: Determinants of marathon running success. *Int Z Angew Physiol* 29:249–254, 1971.

Costill DL, Kammer WF, Fisher A: Fluid ingestion during distance running. *Arch Environ Health* 21:520–525, 1970.

Costill DL, Saltin B: Factors limiting gastric empyting during rest and exercise. *J Appl Physiol* 37:679–683, 1974.

Detmer DE: Chronic leg pain. Symposium. *Am J Sports Med* 8:141–144, 1980.

Draper DO: A comparison of shoe inserts to taping for painful arches. *J Pros Orthot* 3:84–89, 1991.

Draper DO. When you're hot, you're hot: Thermal modalities from research to practice. Presented at the 47th Annual Meeting and Clinical Symposium of the National Athletic Trainer's Association, Orlando, FL, June 14, 1996.

Draper DO, Dustman AJ: Avulsion fracture of the anterior superior iliac spine in a collegiate distance runner. *Arch Phys Med Rehabil* 73(9), 1992.

Drez Jr, D, Young JC, Johnston RD, et al: Metatarsal stress fractures. *Am J Sports Med* 8:123–125, 1980.

Goergen TG, Venn-Watson EA, Rossman DJ, et al: Tarsal navicular stress fractures in runners. *Am J Roentg* 136:201–203, 1981.

Gross ML, Davlin LB, Evanski PM: Effectiveness of orthotic shoe inserts in the long distance runner. *Am J Sports Med* 19:409–412, 1991.

Hanson PG: Heat injury in runners. *Phys Sports Med* 7:91–96, June 1979.

Jackson DW: Shin splints: common, painful, and confusing. *Consultant* 16:75–79, February, 1976.

James SL, Bates BT, Osternig LR: Injuries to runners. *Am J Sports Med* 6:40–50, 1978.

James SL, Brubaker CE: Running mechanics. *JAMA* 221:1014–1016, 1972.

Johnson MB, Thiese SM. A review of overtraining syndrome—Recognizing the signs and symptoms. *J Athletic Training* 27:352–354; 1992.

Keskula DR, Tamburello M: Conservative management of piriformis syndrome. *J Athletic Training* 27:102–110, 1992.

Kibler WB, Golberg C, Chandler TJ: Functional biomechanical deficits in running athletes with plantar fasciitis. *Am J Sports Med* 19:66–71, 1991.

Kleiner DM, Glickman SE. Medical considerations and planning for short distance road races. *J Athletic Training* 29:145–151; 1994.

Krissoff WB, Ferris WD: Runners' injuries. *Phys Sports Med* 7:54–64, December 1979.

Lloyd-Smith R, Clement DB, McKenzie DC, Taunton JE: A survey of overuse and traumatic hip and pelvic injuries in athletes. *Phys Sports Med* 13(10):131–41, 1985.

Lohrer H: Design and effect of sports shoe insoles for the runner. *Sportverletz-Sportschaden* 3(3):106–111, 1989.

McNicol K, Tauton JE, Clement DB: Iliotibial tract friction syndrome in athletes. *Can J Appl Sports Sci* 6:77–80, 1981.

Messier SP, Davis SE, Curl WW, Lowert RB, Pack RJ: Etiologic factors associated with patellofemoral pain in runners. *Med Sci Sports Exerc* 23:1008–1015, 1991.

Noakes TD: Why marathon runners collapse. *S Afr Med J* 10:338–45, 1990.

Noble CA: The iliotibial band friction syndrome in runners. *Am J Sports Med* 8:232–234, 1980.

Noble HB, Bachman D: Medical aspects of distance race planning. *Phys Sports Med* 7:78–96, June 1979.

Noble HB, Hajeck MR, Porter M: Diagnosis and treatment of iliotibial band tightness in runners. *Phys Sports Med* 10:67–74, April 1982.

Noble HB, Hajeck MR, Porter M: Diagnosis and treatment of liliotibial band tightness in runners. *Phys Sports Med.* 10:67, 1984

Pudu G, Ippolito E, Postacchini F: A classification of achilles tendon disease. *Am J Sports Med* 4:145–150, 1976.

Raether PM, Lutter LD: Recurrent compartment syndrome in the posterior thigh. Report of a case. *Am J Sports Med* 10:40–43, 1982.

Rasmussen W: Shin splints: Definition and treatment. Sports safety supplement. *J Sports Med* 2:111–117, 1974.

Reneman RS: The anterior and lateral compartmental syndrome of the leg due to intensive use of muscles. *Clin Orthop* 113:69–80, 1975.

Renne J: The iloitibial band friction syndrome. *J Bone Joint Surg* 57A: 1110–1111, 1975.

Root ML, Orien WP, Weed JH, Hughes RJ: *Biomechanical Examination of the Foot.* Los Angeles, Clinical Biomechanics Corporation, 1971.

Root ML, Orien WP, Weed JH: *Normal and Abnormal Function of the Foot.* Los Angeles Clinical Biomechanics Corporation, 1977.

Ryan AJ: Moderator Round Table Discussion on: Leg pains in runners. *Phys Sports Med* 5:42–53, September 1977.

Sallade JR, Koch S. Training errors in long distance running. *J Athletic Training* 27:50–53; 1992.

Scranton Jr, PE, Pedegana LR, Whitesel JP: Gait analysis. Alterations in support phase forces using supportive devices. *Am J Sports Med* 10:6–11, 1982.

Shellock FG, Deutsch AL, Mink JH, Kerr R: Do asymptomatic marathon runners have an increased prevalence of meniscal abnormalities? An MR study of the knee in 23 volunteers. *AJR Am J Roentgenol* 157:1239–41, 1991.

Slocum DB, Bowerman W: Biomechanics of running. *Clin Orthhop* 23:39–45, 1962.

Smart GW, Taunton JE, Clement DB: Achilles tendon disorders in runners—a review. *Med Sci Sports Exerc* 12:231–243, 1980.

Smith WB: Environmental factors in running. Symposium. *Am J Sports Med* 8:138–140, 1980.

Stewart PJ, Posen GA: Case report: Acute renal failure following a marathon. *Phys Sports Med* 8:61–64, 1980.

Sutker AN, Jackson DW, Pagliano JW: Iliotibial band syndrome in distance runners. *Phys Sports Med* 9:69–73, October 1981.

Tippett SR, Voight ML. *Functional Progressions for Sport Rehabilitation*. Champaign: Human Kinetics, 1995.

Tippett SR, Voight ML. Running Activities. Chapter 7. In *Functional Progressions for Sport Rehabilitation*. Champaign: Human Kinetics, 1995.

Torres SM, Draper DO: The effects of a foot strengthening program on the medial longitudinal arch. *Athletic Training, JNATA* 24:124, 1989.

Toy BJ: The incidence of hyponatremia in prolonged exercise activity. *J Athletic Training* 27:116–118, 1992.

Warren BL: Plantar fascitis in runners. Treatment and prevention. *Sports Med* 10:338–45,1990.

Wilcox S, Draper DO: Reusable slip-on padding for painful foot conditions. *Athletic Training, JNATA* 26:265–67, 1991.

Swimming Injuries

Overuse injuries resulting from the long and grueling workouts that competitive (and recreational) swimmers undergo have only recently been explored and documented. Most of these injuries affect the shoulder, the knee, and the anterior aspect of the ankle and are related to a particular swimming stroke. Each stroke is liable to provide its own peculiar injury complex, but freestyle is the most commonly used stroke.

"Swimmer's Shoulder"

A common complaint of competitive swimmers is shoulder pain, with an incidence rate from 40 to 80 percent.[1] Most cases of swimmer's shoulder are due to impingement of the rotator cuff, biceps tendon, bursa, and other soft tissue structures of the subacromial space under the underside of the acromion and coraco-acromial ligament (the coraco-acromial arch).[2,3,4] The mechanism of injury is believed to be excessive humeral head translation, secondary to loss of dynamic stability of the glenohumeral joint. The shoulder of the average competitive swimmer is put through the cycle of abduction/external rotation—forward flexion/internal rotation—many thousands of times each day. This type of activity places a tremendous strain on the dynamic stabilizers of the glenohumeral joint—the rotator cuff. Excessive use leads to fatigue and loss of fine motor (the "steering" function) control. The powerful prime movers of the shoulder (the deltoid and pectoralis major) cause excessive humeral head translation that is not adequately stabilized and counterbalanced by the

rotator cuff.[5] Both stretch and compressive injuries to the capsule, labrum, cuff tendons, and other soft-tissues of the sub-acromial space may result. Pain, secondary to trauma, swelling, and inflammation may also inhibit rotator cuff function serving to further destabilize the shoulder.

PREVENTION: Stretching exercises are sometimes advocated both before and after swim workouts. Discrepancy exists in the literature regarding flexibility and its role in shoulder injury. While some authors have suggested that a lack of flexibility in swimming contributes to shoulder injury, others feel that excessive stretching may compromise capsular integrity, leading to glenohumeral instability.[6,7] Many overhead athletes demonstrate in excess of 10 degrees of external shoulder rotation and abduction as compared with published norms, while at the same time demonstrating limited internal rotation. Stretching activities should be very selective, and any that place excessive stress on capsular restraints should be avoided. In their study on the relationship of flexibility to shoulder pain in competitive swimmers, Beach, et al. stated, "The idea that shoulder mobility may cause shoulder pain may not be important, given that (in their study) the correlation coefficients of shoulder flexibility to shoulder pain in swimmers were extremely low and nonsignificant."[1] The importance of maintaining strength in the dynamic stabilizers of the glenohumeral joint and scapula cannot be overemphasized. Falkel and Murphy reported that swimmers with shoulder pain have significantly lower absolute external rotation endurance than swimmers without shoulder pain.[1] Strength tests of both rotator cuff and scapular stabilizers should be conducted on swimmers at regular intervals in an attempt to elicit weakness before shoulder symptoms and pathological changes occur. An imperfection of technique (both above and below waterline) that could produce an impingement should also be looked for and corrected. A period of easy swimming before any vigorous workout should be routine.

SYMPTOMS: Pain and inability to perform are the usual symptoms. The pain may be anterior or anterolateral but is usually diffuse. Most symptoms are produced during the recovery or pull-through phases of the swimming motion, especially at or just after hand entry, at which the shoulder is fully abducted.

SIGNS:

1. Tenderness over the greater tuberosity and acromial process, the biceps tendon, or both

2. A positive impingement sign (see section on shoulder injuries)

3. Weakness of the posterior deltoid, supraspinatus, external rotators, and other individual shoulder muscles

4. If instability exists, a positive apprehension sign may be noted (see section on shoulder injuries)

TREATMENT: Treatment depends on the phase of the condition.

PHASE I. Symptoms are present only after the workout. Ice is applied to the shoulder before and particularly after workouts. During this time selective stretches can be instituted as long as they do not increase pain in the shoulder. Rotator cuff and scapular stabilizing exercises may be initiated, but only if performed in a pain-free range. Anti-inflammatory medications, starting with aspirin, ibuprofen, or a similar drug, may be initiated. TENS, iontophoresis, and ultrasound may be useful. Changing strokes during the workout is important, as is a change in workout schedule. Examination of the swimmer's technique may bring to light an underlying problem. Swimming with hand paddles should be discontinued.

PHASE II. Symptoms are present during and after workouts. More powerful anti-inflammatory medication may be useful for a short period of time. Icing of the shoulder should continue before and after workouts, and possibly during workouts if the shoulder begins to be uncomfortable. TENS can be used before and after workouts, as can ultrasound. Total yardage swum should be decreased.

PHASE III. Pain is present at all times. At this stage of the condition, the swimmer should cease swimming and continue with the treatment outlined in Phases I and II. Cardiovascular endurance should be maintained by kicking, although a kickboard should not be used because it can put a strain on the arm and possibly produce impingement. Other cardiovascular conditioning exercises include running in place in the swimming pool while wearing a life preserver and dryland exercises such as cycling, running, stairclimbing, and jumping rope.

Corticosteroid injections should not be used except in the most resistant cases, and they should be followed by a layoff of six weeks. The shoulder musculature should be completely rehabilitated before return to the pool. In resistant cases, a decision may need to be made as to whether surgery is indicated.

Anterior Subluxation of the Glenohumeral Joint

Anterior subluxation of the glenohumeral joint can be produced by repeated use of the backstroke. Changes in the rules governing backstroke turns and the techniques now in use have greatly reduced the stress occurring to the anterior shoulder.

SIGNS: The standard apprehension test for anterior subluxation can be used to clinically confirm the diagnosis. X-ray views of the shoulder, particularly the West Point view, may be useful in showing a bony defect of the anterior glenoid (Figure 22.1).

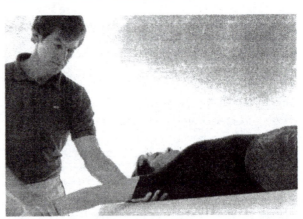

FIGURE 22.1
The apprehension test for anterior subluxation in a swimmer

TREATMENT: Specific muscle testing may expose weakness that can often be strengthened. If a rehabilitation program designed to strengthen the dynamic stabilizers of the shoulder does not succeed, the swimmer will have to decide whether to live with it, stop swimming the backstroke, or undergo surgery for anterior subluxation.

"Breaststroker's Knee"

Breaststroker's knee has long been associated with the whip kick, but the exact pathology and the anatomical area involved appear to be a matter of controversy. Evidence seems to favor an injury of the tibial collateral ligament, but chondromalacia patellae, medial synovitis, or irritation of the medial retinaculum may be involved in certain individuals.[8,9,10] The area involved may depend on the type of technical fault in a particular swimmers whip kick,[11] especially in the less-than-top-level swimmer, while the stress of 15,000 to 20,000 whip kicks per week may play a role in the elite swimmer.

MECHANISM OF INJURY: Studies with underwater photography have shown that during the whip kick a valgus stress is applied to the knee when the hip is in an abducted and internally rotated position and as the knee rapidly moves from flexion to extension in an externally rotated position. This movement may put a considerable strain on the medial aspects of the knee and patella, particularly when external rotation, abduction, or both accompany full extension (Figure 22.2).

PREVENTION:

1. Adjustment of technique, possibly with the aid of an underwater camera, to help prevent an incorrectly performed whip kick from producing symptoms.

2. Isolation and correction of any muscle weakness.

3. General strengthening program for the lower extremity as a part of the training schedule.

4. Slow, static stretching of the muscle groups of the lower extremity. For instance, the swimmer stands with legs apart and feet in external rotation. The knees go slowly into a valgus position, thus placing gentle tension on the medial stabilizing complex. This may allow the tibial collateral ligament and the medial joint structures to adapt to the position that seems to produce the most stress on the knee.

5. Avoidance of the breaststroke for two months each year by the breaststroke swimmer, with frequent variations in the stroke used.

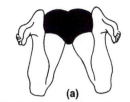
(a)
The knee is moved rapidly from a flexed to an extended position.

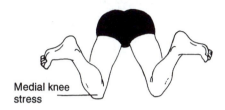
Medial knee stress
(b)
A valgus stress is applied to the knee, especially when there is external rotation as well.

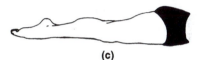
(c)
When extension is reached, the cycle is repeated.

FIGURE 22.2
The whip kick

SYMPTOMS AND SIGNS: Initially, pain is present only when the athlete performs the whip kick, but if participation is continued in spite of pain, symptoms may occur with other strokes and even with walking. Clinically there is usually no swelling, but tenderness may be localized to the course of the tibial collateral ligament, to its attachment to the tibia, or to the medial aspect of the patella. Applying a valgus stress with the tibia in external rotation and the knee in 20° to 30° of flexion may cause pain, as may passively moving the patella laterally.

TREATMENT: As soon as any symptoms arise, the swimmer should be told to ice the affected limb before and after workouts and should be evaluated for any muscle weaknesses. Aspirin or some other anti-inflammatory agent and ultrasound can be started. Consulting the coach about possible technique changes is important because correcting the technical fault can prevent further injury. Should the symptoms persist, the whip kick should not be used for a few weeks.

Irritation of the Extensor Retinaculum of the Ankle

The "flutter kick" is used extensively in freestyle and backstroke swimming. This motion tends to produce a position of excessive plantar flexion of both the foot and the ankle, placing pressure on the structures running under the extensor retinaculum. Tendinitis can develop, with pain, swelling, and crepitation of the anterior tibial, the extensor digitorum longus, and the extensor hallucis longus tendons. The extensor retinaculum itself can become inflamed.

TREATMENT: Changes of technique have been suggested to prevent the problem, that is, using the arms more than the legs and training on a two-beat instead of a six-beat crossover leg kick. Ice, ultrasound, a local corticosteroid injection around the extensor retinaculum, and walking and sleeping in a posterior splint with the ankle at 90° may help reduce symptoms.

REFERENCES

1.   Beach M, Whitney S, Dickhoff-Hoffman S: Relationship of shoulder flexibility, strength, and endurance to shoulder pain in competitive swimmers. *J Orthop Sports Phys Ther* 16 (6):262–268, 1992.

2.   Kennedy JC, Hawkins RJ: Swimmer's shoulder. *Phys Sports Med* 2:34–38, April 1974.

3.   Richardson AB, Jobe FW, Collins HR: The shoulder in competitive swimming. *Am J Sports Med* 8:159–163, 1980.

4.   Dominguez RH: Shoulder pain in swimmers. *Phys Sports Med* 8:37–42, July 1980.

5.   Garrick J, Webb D: *Sports Injuries—Diagnosis and Management.* Philadelphia: WB Saunders, 1990.

6.   Levine M, Lombardo J, McNeeley J, Anderson T: An analysis of individual stretching programs of intercollegiate athletes. *Phys Sports Med* 15:130–136.

7.   Pink M, Jobe F: Shoulder injuries in athletes. *Clin Manag* 11 (6):39–47, 1991.

8.   Stulberg SD, Shulman K, Stuart S, et al: Breaststroker's knee: pathology, etiology, and treatment. *Am J Sports Med* 8:164–171, 1980.

9.   Keskinen K, Eriksson E, Komi P: Breaststroke swimmer's knee: A biomechanical and arthroscopic study. *Am J Sports Med* 8:228–231, 1980.

10.   Kennedy JC, Hawkins RJ: Breaststroker's knee. *Phys Sports Med* 2:33–38, January 1974.

11.   Counsilman JE: *The Science of Swimming.* Upper Saddle River, NJ: Prentice Hall, pp. 117–123, 1968.

RECOMMENDED READINGS

1. Penny JN, Smith C: Prevention and treatment of swimmer's shoulder. *Can J Appl Sport Sci* 5:195–202, 1980.

2. Pink M, Perry J, Brown A, Scovazzo MS, Kerrigan J: The normal shoulder during freestyle swimming. *Am J Sports Med* 6:569–576, 1991.

3. Scovazzo ML, Brown A, Pink M, Jobe FW, Kerrigan J: The painful shoulder during freestyle swimming. *Am J Sports Med* 6:577–582, 1991.

Other Areas for Consideration

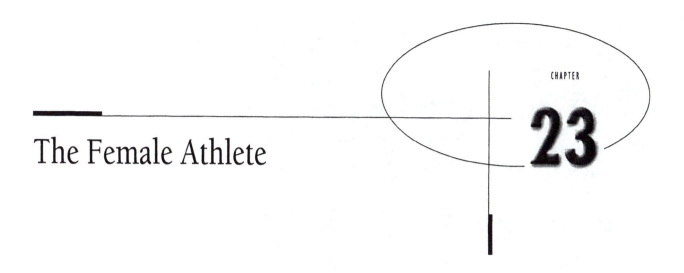

The Female Athlete

Since the 1970s when Title IX became law, there has been a dramatic increase in participation by women in both organized and unorganized athletic activities. This rapid increase in participation among female athletes of all ages has created a need for better understanding of injuries and training-related problems unique to this population.

The Adolescent Female Athlete

Preparation

In all physically active individuals, the ability to sustain a training regime is dependent both on the type and intensity of training, and on the physical maturity of the individual. What must be remembered is that, in addition to the stresses of physical training, adolescents and children are also experiencing rapid and dramatic physical changes due to normal growth and maturation. Fortunately, their systems are extremely adept at managing a variety of stresses placed on them. Because they are so adaptable, we sometimes forget that they still need to be grounded in the concepts of training consistently and gradually, and in the values of proper warm-up and cool-down.

Participation

Programs for young athletes must be individualized as much as possible. The varying rates of physical growth and development should be considered in placing an individual on an athletic "team." The ideal placement would be with peers of similar maturation, ability, and skill level. These determinations are crucial to the athlete's continued development and enjoyment of an activity, and to injury prevention (Figure 23.1).

Pre-Participation Screening

Arguably one of the most important tools for prevention of injuries, the pre-participation screen allows the physician, trainer, or coach to become aware of the individual needs of each athlete. In addition, it provides the opportunity to identify health concerns, and to educate and counsel the athlete on how to manage the demands of the sport on the body. With the information gleaned from the screening process, the health care provider can guide the athlete in making positive progress toward goals for athletic achievement. The particular concerns for female athletes must be included in this screening process. This screening must include a health history questionnaire dealing with menstrual status and history, as well as assessment of nutrition, diet, and eating behaviors (Figure 23.2).[1]

Common Injuries and Health Concerns

A number of injuries are peculiar to the young athlete, and these are discussed in some detail in Chapter 10 (epiphyseal injuries). It has not been demonstrated that female athletes are predisposed to an increased frequency or severity of these types of conditions. It does seem that female athletes may demonstrate patterns of lower extremity malalignment, which causes increased frequency of patellofemoral pain and dysfunction. In some sports, a generalized lack of muscle strength relative to the demands of a particular activity may put the female at some increased risk of injury. For example, it has been noted that female athletes may have an

FIGURE 23.1
Female gymnast
(Photo by Mike Shields)

increased frequency of isolated anterior crutiate ligament disruption. No definitive mechanism for this has as yet been determined.

Body Image and Disordered Eating Behaviors

Adolescent female athletes are particularly susceptible to the development of a poor image of their body shape, size, or physical condition. Due in part to an intense desire to maximize athletic performance, and to conform to socially acceptable standards for appearance, many young females resort to unhealthy behaviors to attain and sustain exceptionally low body weight. These behaviors may include caloric deprivation, induced vomiting, or the use of diuretics, or other types of over-the-counter medications to reduce appetite. Often the desire for success in sports motivates the athlete to set unrealistic weight goals. Underlying this can be a misguided attempt to gain the support and encouragement of a coach or parent. There is a high incidence of denial of these behaviors, and it is often difficult to identify young athletes who engage in these practices. An extensive discussion of the long- and short-term consequences of these behaviors follows in this chapter. It is critical to recognize that these behaviors often begin during adolescence, and may be well entrenched by the time the athletes reach the college level. It is essential to recognize that prevention of these disordered behaviors must include education and communication about how to achieve healthful nutrition and maximize performance. The athlete should recognize that the long-term detrimental effects on health from these behaviors can be devastating, and may be irreversible.

The Female Athlete Triad

The vast majority of women and girls find that participation in sports benefits them both physically and psychologically. However, there is a small subset of exercising females who may be at risk for developing a triad of conditions detrimental to both physical and mental health. Health care providers are beginning to recognize a connection among disordered eating habits, menstrual changes, and premature bone loss (osteoporosis) in the athletically active female (Figure 23.3).[6,7] These interrelated conditions appear to occur more frequently in women who participate in sports that emphasize being lean, such as distance running, and those activities that emphasize appearance and low body fat (gymnastics, ballet). The prevalence of this problem is difficult to estimate, not only in organized sports participants, but also in adults and adolescents who work out on their own. Individuals who work directly with athletes may have observed this "triad" association for years, but it has been directly addressed by sports medicine experts only recently. Our society, in general, pressures women to achieve and maintain often unattainable thinness, and women athletes may have

The purpose of this information is to assess the known factors that may influence your bone health. This information can be vital to decisions regarding injuries you may incur. All of the information is confidential, and will be accessible only to the team physician and medical staff.

Name _____

Date _____

Age _____

Sport _____

Please answer the following questions:

1. At what age did you have your first menstrual period?
2. How often do you have periods now?
3. How many days do your periods last?
4. How many periods have you had in the last 12 months?
5. What date did your last period start?
6. Do you ever have heavy bleeding during your periods?
7. Do you ever experience cramps during your periods?

   ___mild   ___moderate   ___severe

   If so, how do you treat them?
8. Do you take birth control pills or hormones? If so, what type?
9. Do you have any pain or unusual discharge during or between periods?
10. When was your last pelvic exam?
11. Have you ever had an abnormal PAP smear?
    If so, when?
12. Have you ever had a bladder or urinary tract infection? If so, when?
13. Have you ever been diagnosed with anemia? If so, when?
14. How many meals do you eat daily?
15. What have you eaten in the last 24 hours?

16. Are there certain foods you don't eat?
17. What is your current weight?
18. Are you currently on a diet?
19. Are you happy with your weight? If not, how much would you like to weigh?
20. Have you ever tried to control your weight by:
    using laxatives
    vomiting
    taking diet pills
    using diuretics
21. Have you ever had an eating disorder?
22. Do you have questions about healthy ways to control your weight or about diet?

FIGURE 23.2
Health History Questionnaire for Female Athletes

___

even more such pressures placed upon them. Recognizing the potential association among leanness and the triad of menstrual disorders, disordered eating, and premature bone loss is essential for those who work with active women.[2,3,4,5]

Menstrual Changes

Three main types of menstrual dysfunction occur in female athletes: luteal phase deficiency, anovulation (lack of ovulation), and exercise-associated amenorrhea (lack of regular menstruation).[8] Some experts believe that these changes represent a continuum of menstrual dysfunction.

Luteal phase deficiency is postulated to be the first stage in the development of amenorrhea, and may be associated with infertility. The luteal phase of the menstrual cycle occurs after ovulation has occurred. It represents the time in which progesterone normally helps convert the lining of the uterus so that it is capable of supporting a fertilized egg. In luteal phase deficiency this phase is shortened because insufficient progesterone is

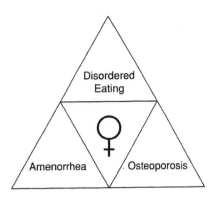

FIGURE 23.3

The Female Athlete Triad

(Developed as a part of a slide series on the female athlete triad by Connie Lebrun for the American College of Sports Medicine—Ad Hoc Task Force on Women's Issues in Sports Medicine, P.O. Box 1440, Indianapolis, IN 46206-1440.)

produced. Because the menstrual cycle may be irregular, women may not notice a problem unless pregnancy is desired but difficult to achieve. The other consequences of luteal deficiency are unclear, and except for treatment of infertility, no therapy is currently recommended.[9,10,11]

Women who do not ovulate (*anovulation*) may have one of many patterns of menstrual cycles. These can include very short cycles of less than 21 days, with frequent spotting, or lapses of several months between periods. These women usually produce adequate estrogen, but inadequate progesterone. Unpredictable bleeding can at the very least be an annoyance, and heavy or frequent bleeding can cause iron deficiency anemia. Because anovulation can have many causes, a complete medical evaluation is recommended.[9] Depending on test results, therapy can include taking progesterone every month to induce a period, or using other hormones to regulate bleeding.

Menarcheal delay (*"primary amenorrhea"*) occurs when menstrual periods have not begun by age 16. It has been linked to slender athletes who begin training regimens before onset of puberty. Some believe that significant exercise itself causes delayed onset of periods. Others feel that girls with primary amenorrhea who are thin are more apt to succeed in their sports while other, more quickly maturing, girls are socialized away from athletics.[11,18] There are multiple causes of delayed periods, and medical examination is mandatory. Concerns have been raised that the relatively low estrogen state associated with amenorrhea increases the risk of osteoporosis, stress fractures, scoliosis, and failure to achieve peak bone mass.[11]

Secondary amenorrhea can be defined as the absence of three to six consecutive cycles, or having less than three periods a year after the established onset of menstruation. Although it occurs in two to five percent of the general population, its prevalence in athletes is thought to be higher, with estimates ranging from 3.4 to 66 percent. The specific mechanism that causes this menstrual irregularity is unknown. For years a widespread popular belief was that a critical percentage of body fat was necessary for menstruation to occur. Research has shown that, while body composition may affect menstrual cycles, its influence on exercise-induced amenorrhea is somewhat less clear. Other factors that have been implicated include both the intensity and volume of training, nutrition, reproductive immaturity, and stress.[11] Another theory implicates a possible "energy drain," in which some women athletes have been found to maintain stable body weights on fewer calories than expected, possibly due to a decreased basal metabolic rate.[13] One or more of these influences may cause the brain's hypothalamus to malfunction by not producing the normal pulsations of gonadatropin-releasing hormone.[8,11] The possibility of lower bone density and osteoporosis, stress fractures, and other injuries necessitate taking this problem seriously.[14,15] Because exercise-associated amenorrhea is a diagnosis of exclusion, medical evaluation to assess the cause is mandatory. One must always consider pregnancy as a possible cause of amenorrhea.

THERAPEUTIC OPTIONS: Options in the treatment of secondary amenorrhea include changing habits (decreasing training regimens, increasing calories), with careful follow-up to ensure that periods resume. Adequate dietary calcium should be stressed during nutritional counseling. Hormonal options include cycling with estrogen and progesterone, similar to a regimen used in post-menopausal women. This option may be protective against amenorrhea, but it is not a form of contraception. Oral contraceptives are often advised when both treatment and contraception are needed. Women athletes may decline the above options, so it becomes especially important to develop a good relationship with a given athlete to continue to advise and monitor her.

Bone Health

Weight-bearing and other skeletal-loading types of exercise are generally promoted as beneficial to the maintenance of bone mass. Unfortunately for some, participating in impact-loading activities when bone mass is not adequate, secondary to low estrogen states (such as secondary amenorrhea), increases the risk of stress fractures.[16] Most young women accumulate their maximum bone mass by their twenties or thirties. It is theorized that if they do not develop a bony "base" while young they may be apt to develop osteoporosis earlier as they age. Several studies have documented bone loss in younger athletes, especially in trabecular type bone, such as that found in the hip and vertebral bodies. More recent studies suggest that even weight-bearing cortical bone may be affected, especially when correlated with longer duration amenorrhea.[17] In other words, these young women have "old" bones. Of great concern is that, if such bone loss is long-standing, some of the loss may be irreversible despite treatment.

A topic currently under intense scrutiny is the determination of factors associated with the development of stress fractures.[19] Some studies suggest that in comparing athletes with similar training schedules, those who develop stress fractures are more likely to have lower dietary calcium intakes, a current menstrual irregularity, and lower bone density.

Disordered Eating

No one knows how prevalent disordered eating is in athletes. Athletes involved in sports and activities that emphasize appearance (ballet, figure skating, gymnastics, diving) may be at higher risk. In addition, participants in sports (such as distance running and swimming) where participants and coaches believe that performance is enhanced by thinness are also at higher risk (Table 23.1).

Eating disorders occur much more commonly in adolescent young women, but they can also occur in males, especially those involved in weight-category sports such as wrestling.[20] Any sport can include athletes with disordered eating patterns,[21] and because these athletes are often reluctant to volunteer information about their problem, diagnosis can often be very difficult. The term "disordered eating" encompasses the spectrum of abnormal eating behavior, with poor nutritional habits on one end and anorexia and bulimia at the other. Many athletes fall somewhere along the spectrum. Although they may not fit the DSM IV criteria for anorexia or bulimia, these athletes are still at risk for developing serious psychiatric and health problems (Table 23.2).[7]

Medical complications of eating disorders can be serious and even fatal. They may include electrolyte disturbances, leading to cardiac rhythm disorders. Potassium depletion can be particularly troublesome because it is often asymptomatic prior to a life-threatening arrhythmia. Other cardiac problems may also involve the heart muscle itself. Endocrine abnormalities can include thyroid dysfunction, as well as changes in cortisol levels. Menstrual disturbances are among the most common medical consequences of disordered eating patterns. Bone loss, especially in anorexia, is very com-

TABLE 23.1 *Warning signs for anorexia nervosa and bulimia distributed to coaches, athletes, and athletic officials by the National Collegiate Athletic Association*

Warning Signs for Anorexia Nervosa
Dramatic loss in weight
Preoccupation with food, calories and weight
Wearing baggy or layered clothing
Relentless, excessive exercise
Mood swings
Avoiding food-related social activities

Warning Signs for Bulimia Nervosa
Noticeable weight loss or gain
Excessive concern about weight
Bathroom visits after meals
Depressive moods
Strict dieting followed by eating binges
Increasing criticism of one's body

Source: Brownell K, Rodin J, Wilmore J. *Eating, Body Weight, and Performance in Athletes: Disorders of Modern Society.* Philadelphia: Lea & Febiger, 1992.

mon and of special concern. Many other symptoms and signs may be evident (Table 23.3).

The emotional and psychiatric aspects of disordered eating are complex, involving depression, anxiety, and compulsive behaviors that are often outside of an athlete's conscious control.

Treatment is a challenge to all concerned and requires a team approach. Prompt referral for diagnosis, and medical and psychological treatment is essential. Coaches, trainers, parents, and others working with athletes can help prevent disturbed eating patterns by encouraging proper nutritional habits and the avoidance of unhealthy and unrealistic weight goals.

Athletic Performance and Hormonal Contraceptives

Although there has been recent research interest in women and sports, much remains to be studied relating to the effect of menstrual cycle or oral contraceptives on athletic performance. Women have set world records during all phases of the menstrual cycle, but a given

TABLE 23.2 *DSM-IV Diagnostic criteria for anorexia nervosa and bulimia nervosa*

Diagnostic criteria for 307.1 Anorexia Nervosa
1. Refusal to maintain body weight at or above a minimally normal weight for age and height (e.g., weight loss leading to maintenance of body weight less than 85% of that expected; or failure to make expected weight gain during period of growth, leading to body weight less than 85% of that expected). 2. Intense fear of gaining weight or becoming fat, even though underweight. 3. Disturbance in the way in which one's body weight or shape is experienced, undue influence of body weight or shape on self-evaluation, or denial of the seriousness of the current low body weight. 4. In postmenarcheal females, amenorrhea, i.e., the absence of at least three consecutive menstrual cycles. (A woman is considered to have amenorrhea if her periods occur only following hormone, e.g., estrogen, administration.)
Specify type:
Restricting Type: During the current episode of Anorexia Nervosa, the person has not regularly engaged in binge-eating or purging behavior (i.e., self-induced vomiting or the misuse of laxatives, diuretics, or enemas) **Binge-Eating/Purging Type:** During the current episode of Anorexia Nervosa, the person has regularly engaged in binge-eating or purging behavior (i.e., self-induced vomiting or the misuse of laxatives, diuretics, or enemas)
Diagnostic criteria for 307.51 Bulimia Nervosa

1. Recurrent episodes of binge eating. An episode of binge eating is characterized by both of the following:
  a. Eating, in a discrete period of time (e.g., within any 2-hour period), an amount of food that is definitely larger than most people would eat during a similar period of time and under similar circumstances.
  b. A sense of lack of control over eating during the episode (e.g., a feeling that one cannot stop eating or control what or how much one is eating).
2. Recurrent inappropriate compensatory behavior in order to prevent weight gain, such as self-induced vomiting; misuse of laxatives, diuretics, enemas, or other medications; fasting; or excessive exercise.
3. The binge eating and inappropriate compensatory behaviors both occur, on average, at least twice a week for 3 months.
4. Self-evaluation is unduly influenced by body shape and weight.
5. The disturbance does not occur exclusively during episodes of Anorexia Nervosa.

Specify type:
Purging Type: During the current episode of Bulimia Nervosa, the person has regularly engaged in self-induced vomiting or the misuse of laxatives, diuretics, or enemas. **Nonpurging Type:** During the current episode of Bulimia Nervosa, the person has used other inappropriate compensatory behaviors, such as fasting or excessive exercise, but has not regularly engaged in self-induced vomiting or the misuse of laxatives, diuretics, or enemas.
From the American Psychiatric Association, *Diagnostic and Statistical Manual of Mental Disorders,* Fourth Edition. Washington, D.C., American Psychiatric Association, 1994.

individual may do better or worse during a particular part of her cycle.[22,23]

Hormones such as estrogen and progesterone may be used by female athletes for a number of reasons. Because of concerns about bone health, hormone therapies, including oral contraceptives, are often offered as one form of treatment for menstrual disorders such as amenorrhea. Of equal importance, women who require

TABLE 23.3 *Common symptoms and signs of eating disorders*

Anorexia Nervosa	Bulimia Nervosa
Symptoms	*Symptoms*
Amenorrhea	Irregular menses
Constipation	Abdominal pain
Abdominal pain	Lethargy
Cold intolerance	Fatigue, headaches
Lethargy	Depression
Anxious energy	Swelling of hands/feet
Fatigue, headaches	Bloating
Signs	*Signs*
Hypotension	Russell's sign
Hypothermia	Parotid gland enlargement
Dry skin	Dental: enamel erosion
Lanugo-like hair	Often appear healthy
Bradycardia	
Edema	
Inanition	

Source: Brownell K, Rodin J, Wilmore J. Eating, Body Weight, and Performance in Athletes: Disorders of Modern Society. Philadelphia: Lea & Febiger, 1992.

a reliable form of contraception may wish to utilize oral contraceptives, progesterone implants, or injectable progesterone. Earlier research was carried out when oral contraceptives contained much higher hormonal dosages than are commonly used now, and conclusions based on those studies may no longer be relevant. Much remains to be learned about contraceptives and their effect on athletic performance.[24,25]

In some individuals, oral contraceptives may increase water retention, cause weight gain or loss, or produce other side effects, some of them serious. Beneficial effects may include elimination of menstruation-related cramping, reduction in menstrually-induced iron deficiency anemia, a reduced risk of endometrial and ovarian cancers, and a reduced risk of osteoporosis in amenorrheic athletes. Injected medroxyprogesterone has potential benefits and risks, and it's effect on bone density is still being debated.[26,27,28] Hormonal contraception may be a preferred option for some athletes, but these decisions need to be individualized.

Athletics and Pregnancy

Increasing numbers of women are continuing their athletic pursuits into pregnancy and the postpartum period.

Because gestation involves not simply the woman's health, but also that of the fetus, recommendations are often requested about exercise during this special time. The basic question revolves around how exercise might affect the course of pregnancy and fetal growth and, conversely, how pregnancy might affect the ability to exercise.[29]

Current official recommendations[30] are based on the theoretical risk to both mother and fetus. Rigorous research is needed to discern real risk in an already-fit pregnant woman with a normal pregnancy. Many available studies are technically flawed, making valid interpretation difficult.

MATERNAL CONSIDERATIONS:

THEORETICAL RISKS. Musculoskeletal trauma, perhaps due to

- Softening of ligaments
- Falls, either due to change in center of gravity, or higher risk sports
- Physiological adaptations (cardiopulmonary, thermoregulatory, metabolic, endocrine[33]
- Nerve compression syndromes

THEORETICAL BENEFITS.[34]

- Avoiding excessive weight gain
- Control of blood pressure
- Decreased backaches, headaches, fatigue
- Shorter labor, easier delivery
- Higher or maintained self-esteem
- Maintenance of fitness level

Pregnancy does influence the ability to exercise. In fact, some of the adaptations to the pregnant state, such as the increase in plasma volume in comparison to red cells, are similar to those found in certain long-term conditioning regimens.[29] Other changes, such as the weight gain associated with pregnancy, eventually do temporarily hamper athletic abilities. Changes in center of gravity and increase in regulatory needs also influence the ability to train and perform.

Much of recent research confirms that mild or moderate exercise during normal pregnancy is not injurious to the gravid (pregnant) woman or to the developing fetus. Each pregnant woman should be counseled individually by her physician or midwife to develop an exercise plan to meet the needs of both mother and fetus. Information should be gathered about the woman's current fitness level, including whether she is just beginning to exercise or is a recreational or top athlete. An exercise prescription should include recommendations about type, frequency, duration, and intensity of exercise. Safety issues should be discussed, including when to avoid such activities as riding, surfing, skiing, team contact, or high-altitude sports and how to avoid body temperatures over 40 degrees centigrade. While adequate research is lacking, common sense and clinical judgment can help to form a successful activity plan for each pregnancy.[31,32]

Urinary Stress Incontinence

Both younger and older women athletes may experience involuntary loss of urine, but many are reluctant to seek help because of embarrassment or because they are unaware of treatment options. This medical problem may negatively influence an athlete's ability to work out, and may also impact her both psychologically and socially. Because denial is so common, athletic trainers, physical therapists, physicians, and other care providers should actively ask about stress incontinence.

Various factors may influence the development of urinary stress incontinence, including family history, previous surgeries (especially urinary or gynecologic), vaginal births, and various medical problems. Stress incontinence is only one of several types or combinations of types of urinary incontinence.[35]

Pelvic floor muscle support plays a key role in maintaining urine control in women, and functional muscular or neurologic damage can contribute to loss of urine or pelvic organ prolapse (a protruding of the pelvic organs into the vaginal canal). High-impact sports involving running or jumping, including basketball, volleyball, certain martial arts, gymnastics, and high-impact aerobic dance, are especially correlated with urinary stress incontinence because the increased intra-abdominal pressures subject the pelvic floor to heavy loads.[36] Even laughing, coughing, or sneezing may bring on symptoms in some women.

Low circulating estrogen levels, common during menopause, can also contribute to urinary stress incontinence because of associated atrophy of the muscles, connective, and vascular tissues of urethral and peri-urethral structures. Certain medications may also cause stress incontinence because of effects on urinary muscle tone or function. Medical evaluation includes detailed history, including voiding diaries, and examination with attention to the pelvic floor muscles, neurologic function, and any evidence of atrophic changes. Special testing may be required depending on initial findings.[35]

Treatment options may include medications, such as estrogen for low-estrogen states, or possibly drugs that affect bladder outlet function. Pelvic floor rehabilitation exercises such as Kegel exercises may be very effective, but proper training is essential for success. Other aids to train or retrain the pelvic floor muscles include biofeed-back, electrical stimulation, and vaginal weights or cones.[36,37,38] Mechanical devices such as vaginal pessaries, bladder neck supports, or even tampons may support the urethral and bladder neck region. Surgery may be the treatment option chosen for selected patients.

Sports medical professionals can play an important role in keeping women physically active by encouraging athletes with urinary stress incontinence to actively seek help.

Nutrition and Anemia

Athletes often have a keen interest in ensuring that their nutritional state is optimum for enhancing their performance. Diet can assume an important role because women athletes often consume fewer calories than their male counterparts and have a higher incidence of disordered eating. In addition to concerns about adequate calories, iron and calcium intakes may need special consideration.

There are three types of low hemoglobin related to athletics:

1. *Dilution pseudoanemia.* This "sports anemia" is not a true loss of red blood cells, but is found in endurance athletes who have a relative increase in their plasma volume. Therefore, the hematocrit may be lower than in general population, but it is a beneficial result of training.[39,40]

2. *Footstrike hemolysis.* Although most commonly seen in runners, this can also occur in "non-impact" activities. Caused by the breaking of red blood cells, it is usually mild and requires no treatment other than attention to body weight, gait, running shoes, and running surface.[39,40] In this anemia, the appearance of the red cells is larger than normal, rather than smaller, as seen in iron deficiency anemia.

3. *Iron Deficiency.* In the past decade, many concerns have been raised about the iron status of athletes, especially women who participate in endurance sports. Some runners, for example, may have extra blood losses from small amounts of gastrointestinal bleeding related to their training. Women, athletes or not, who restrict calories or consume semi-vegetarian diets low in red meat may be at greater risk for this type of anemia due to inadequate iron intake. Women do have higher blood loss because of menstruation, lower iron stores, and higher iron needs during their reproductive years[39,40,41,42]

Much has been made about the possible effect on performance of iron deficiency without anemia, defined as low serum ferritin levels and normal hemoglobin. Some experts now are skeptical of the belief that low iron stores alone decrease athletic achievement.[39]

True iron deficiency anemia may be treated by iron supplementation only after an investigation of its cause. Occasionally significant medical conditions are diagnosed and need to be addressed. If difficulty is experienced distinguishing between "sports anemia" and iron deficiency, a trial of iron for two months may be warranted. If the hemoglobin increases more than 1 g/dl, then iron deficiency may be assumed to have played a role in the condition.

Prevention of iron deficiency includes increasing dietary sources of iron by consuming lean red meat or dark meat poultry, leafy green vegetables, grain and nuts, iron-fortified cereals, and cooking sometimes with cast iron cookware. Drinking a source of vitamin C with meals instead of absorption inhibitors such as tea and coffee also enhances iron absorption.[43]

Some athletes with conditions such as hereditary hemochromatosis are at risk of iron overload, indiscriminate iron supplementation should therefore be avoided.

Exercise and Older Women

By focusing on prevention and fitness, many seniors may enhance the quality of their lives. The majority of older Americans are women, and a healthy woman of 52 today can expect to live to 91 years of age. By the year 2000, the number of women age 65 and older may be twice what it is today.

In order to positively influence function and possibly delay or prevent some aspects of aging, exercise has been advocated.[44] Physical activity can help reduce the risk of several chronic ailments, including high blood pressure, coronary heart disease, non-insulin-dependent diabetes mellitus, and even colon cancer. Exercise may add to a sense of well-being and enjoyment and may decrease anxiety and depression. In fact, physical activity can mean the difference between living independently and needing dependent care. The public health implications of prevention in this age group are tremendous.

With aging, aerobic fitness, strength, and lean muscle mass decline. Without intervention, bone mass declines rapidly in the years around menopause, especially in women who lead a sedentary lifestyle. Osteoporosis disproportionately affects women in the U.S., contributing to 1.3 million fractures per year and costing over $7 to $8 billion per year, with mortalities numbering more than 40,000 per year.[45] Risk factors for osteoporosis in older women include post-menopausal state, family history, cigarette smoking, low calcium intake, certain medications, and lack of weight-bearing exercise. Although prevention is a preferable strategy,

technologies such as dual energy X-ray absorptiometry (DEXA) can be helpful in maintaining bone density.

Treatment and prevention of osteoporosis may include exercise, proper nutrition, smoking cessation, alcohol reduction, and prevention of falls. Hormone replacement, calcium, and medications such as the bisphosphonates or calcitonin may be indicated.[46] Considerations in the design of an exercise program or prescription for an older woman include current functional level, medical conditions, and physician recommendation.[47] Parameters might include increasing duration of exercise before intensity, as well as emphasis on strength, endurance, flexibility, and coordination. To minimize injury, "start low and go slow" is important, and to motivate it helps to work with a mature exercise leader.

REFERENCES

1. Johnson M: Tailoring the preparticipation exam to female athletes. *Phys Sports Med* 20 (7):61–72, 1992.

2. Putukian M: The female triad: Eating Disorders, amenorrhea, and osteoporosis *Med Clin North Am* 78 (2):345–56, 1994.

3. Yurth E: Female athlete triad. *West J Med* 162(2):149–150, 1995.

4. Nattiv, A, Agostini R, Drinkwater B, Yeager, K: The female athletic triad: The inter-relatedness of disordered eating, amenorrhea, and osteoporosis. *Clin Sports Med* 13 (2): 405–18, 1994.

5. American College of Sports Medicine: Position stand—The female athlete triad. *Med Sci Sports Exer* 29(5):i–ix, 1997.

6. Yeager K, Agostini R, Drinkwater B: Commentary—The female athlete triad: Disordered eating, amenorrhea, osteoporosis. *Med Sci Sports Exer* 25 (7):775–777, 1993.

7. Nattiv A, Lynch L: The female athlete triad: Managing an acute risk to long-term health. *Phys Sportsmed* 22 (1):60-68, 1994.

8. Otis C: Exercise-associated amenorrhea, chapter on medical problems. *Clin Sports Med* 24(6), Suppl. 1992.

9. Shangold M, Rebar R, Wentz A, Schiff I: Evaluation and management of menstrual dysfunction in athletes. *JAMA* 263(12):1165–69, 1990.

10. White C, Hergenroeder A: Amenorrhea, osteopenia, and the female athlete. *Pediatr Clin N Am* 37(5):1125–1141, 1990.

11. Loucks A, Vaitukaitis J, Cameron J, Rogol A, Skrinar G, Warren M, Kendrick J, Limacher M: The reproductive system and exercise in women. *Med Sci Sports Exer* 24(6):288–293, Suppl. 1992.

12. Lindholm C, Hagenfeldt K, Ringertz B: Pubertal development in elite juvenile gymnasts: Effects of physical training. *Acta Obstet Gynecol Scand* 73(3):269–73, 1994.

13. Myerson M, Gutin B, Warren M, May M, Contento I, Lee M, Pi-Sunyer F, Pierson R, Brooks-Gunn J: Resting metabolic rate and energy balance in amenorrheic and eumenorrheic runners. *Med Sci Sports Exer* 23(1): 15–22, 1991.

14. Hetland M, Haarbo J, Christiansen C, Larsen T: Running induces menstrual disturbance but bone mass is unaffected, except in amenorrheic women. *Am J Med* 95(1):53–60, 1990.

15. Drinkwater B, Bruemner B, Chesnut C: Menstrual history as a determinant of current bone density in young athletes. *JAMA* 263(4): 545–548, 1990.

16. Marcus R, Drinkwater B, Dalsky G, Raab D, Slemenda C, Snow-Harter C: Osteoporosis and exercise in women. *Med Sci Sports Exer* 24(6):301–307, suppl. 1992.

17. Rencken M, Chesnut C, Drinkwater B: Bone density at multiple skeletal sites in amenorrheic athletes. *JAMA* 276(3):238–240, July 17, 1996.

18. Drinkwater B: Exercise and bones: Lessons learned from female athletes. *Am J Sports Med* 24(6):33–35, 1996.

19. Myburgh K, Hutchins K, Fataar A, Hough S, Noakes T: Low bone density is an etiologic factor for stress fractures in athletes. *Ann Intern Med* 113(10): 754–759, 1990.

20. Brownell K, Rodin J, Wilmore J: *Eating, body weight and performance in athletes: Disorders of modern society.* Philadelphia, Lea and Febiger, 1992.

21. Walberg J, Johnston C: Menstrual function and eating behavior in female recreational weight lifters and competitive body builders. *Med Sci Sports Exer* 23(1):30–36, 1991.

22. Quadagno D, Faquin G, Lim G, Kuminka W, Moffat R: The menstrual cycle: Does it affect athletic performance? *Phys Sportsmed* 19(3): 121–124, 1991.

23. Lebrun C: The effect of the phase of the menstrual cycle and the birth control pill on athletic performance. *Clin Sports Med* 13(2): 419–441, 1994.

24. Shelkun P: Exercise and "the pill": Putting a rumor to rest. *Phys Sportsmed* 19(3): 143–152, 1991.

25. Lebrun, C in Agostini, R: *Medical and orthopedic issues of active and athletic women* Philadelphia, Hanley and Belfus, 1994.

26. Cromer B, Blair J, Mahan J, Zibners L, Naumovski Z: A prospective comparison of bone density in adolescent girls receiving medroxyprogesterone acetate (depo Provera), ievonorgestrel (Norplant), or oral contraceptives. *J Pediatr* 129(5):671–676, 1996.

27. Naessen T, Olsson S, Gudmundson J: Differential effects on bone density of progesterone-only methods for contraception in premenopausal women. *Contraception* 52(1):35–39, 1995.

28. Westhoff C: Depot medroxyprogesterone acetate contraception: Metabolic parameters and mood changes. *J Reproductive Med* 41(5 suppl):401–6, 1996.

29. Huch R, Erkkola R: Pregnancy and exercise—exercise and pregnancy: A short review. *Br J Obstet Gynecol* 97(3): 208–214, March 1990.

30. American College of Obstetrics and Gynecology Technical Bulletin #189, Feb. 1994.

31. Clapp J, Rokey R, Treadway J, Carpenter M, Artal R, Warrnes C: Exercise in pregnancy. *Med Sci Sports Exer* 24(6)(Supplement): 294–300, 1992.

32. Clapp J: A clinical approach to exercise during pregnancy. *Clin Sports Med* 13(2):443–458, 1994.

33. Clapp J: Exercise in pregnancy: A brief clinical review. *Fetal Med Rev* 1990(2):89–101.

34. Jarski R, Trippett D: The risks and benefits of exercise during pregnancy. *J Fam Pract* 30(2):185–189, 1990.

35. American College of Obstetrics and Gynecology technical Bulletin #213, October 1995.

36. Kulpa P: Conservative treatment of urinary stress incontinence. *Phys Sports Med* 24(7): 51–62, July 1996.

37. Miklos J, Karram M: Nonsurgical management of urinary stress incontinence. *The Female Patient* 20(1), 1995.

38. Agostini R: *The medical and orthopedic issues of active and athletic women.* Philadelphia, Hanley and Belfus, 200–212, 1994.

39. Balaban E: Sports anemia. *Clin Sports Med* 11(2): 315–325, April 1992.

40. Eichner E: Sports anemia, iron supplements, and blood doping. *Med Sci Sports Exer* 24(9):(Supplement): S315–318, 1992.

41. Rowland T: Iron deficiency in the young athlete. *Pediatr Clini N Am* 37(5):1153–1163, October 1990.

42. Haymes EM, Lamanca JJ: Iron loss in runners during exercise: Implications and recommendations. *Sports Med* 7(5): 277–285, 1989.

43. Probart C, Bird P, Parker K: Diet and athletic performance. *Med Clin N Am* 77(4): 757–772, July 1993.

44. Public Health Service: *Healthy people 2000: National health promotion and disease prevention objectives.* Washington, D.C., United States Department of Health and Human Services, Public Health Service, 1990.

45. Sazy J, Horstmann H: Exercise participation after menopause. *Clin Sports Med* 10(2):359–369, April 1991.

46. Bellantoni M: Osteoporosis prevention and treatment. *Am Fam Phys* 54(3):986–996, 1996.

47. Pate R, Pratt M, Blair S, Haskell W, Marcera C, Bouchard C, Buchner D, Ettinger W, Heath G, King A: Physical activity and public health: A recommendation from the Centers for Disease Control and Prevention and the American College of Sports Medicine. *JAMA* 273(5):402–407, 1995.

Athletes with Disabilities

It is important that persons interested in the treatment of athletic injuries develop an appreciation for and understanding of issues related to athletes with disabilities. This chapter will provide an overview of such issues, including a brief introduction to various disabled sport organizations, classification systems used for competition, review of research regarding incidence of injuries in disabled sport, considerations for certain disability groups, and recommendations for injury prevention. All athletes have varying physiological and psychological characteristics that must be considered by the athletic trainer in the prevention and treatment of injuries. The only difference for athletes with disabilities is that there may be a greater degree of variation among athletes. Whether a person has mental retardation or a spinal cord injury, he or she deserves the same attention as any athlete—beginning with sound training practices, quality coaching, and injury prevention strategies that enable the athlete to participate at the highest possible level.

History of Disabled Sport

Though the history of competitive sport for persons with disabilities extends from the late 1800s with the Sports Club of the Deaf founded in 1888 in Berlin, Germany, the greatest growth occurred in Europe and the United States following World War II. Sir Ludwig Guttman, a physician at the Stoke Mandeville Hospital in England, was the principal leader in recognizing the need for recreational and sport pursuits for British sol-

diers as an integral part of the rehabilitation process. Similar programs were later established in the United States, with particular interest in wheelchair sports such as basketball. Throughout the 1950s and 1960s wheelchair track and field and basketball prospered with the formulation of leagues and competitive schedules. At that time, wheelchair races were limited to 60, 100, and 200 yards, based on the perception that athletes with disabilities did not have the physical capacity to attempt longer distances. Currently wheelchair athletes compete alongside non-handicapped peers in roadraces including marathons and triathalons. The current wheelchair marathon record easily surpasses that of runners, with times under 1:30 minutes. As discussed later in the chapter, many changes in athletic performances are based on improved training techniques, practice, and competitive opportunities; and on technological advancements.

In the 1970s, President Ford formed a commission on Olympic Sports to review current practices in the United States. An outcome of this commission was the enactment of PL 95-606, the Amateur Sports Act of 1978, which sought the reorganization of the U.S. Olympic Committee (USOC).[1] The USOC constitution included specific language to assist in amateur and competitive programs for handicapped individuals, including the need for expansion of competitive opportunities.[2] A subcommittee was established (Committee on Sports for the Disabled, COSD) to coordinate sports, promote research, and disseminate information regarding sport for persons with disabilities. This legislative act and subsequent action has had a major impact on the continued growth of disabled sport. The following organizations are now Group E members of COSD: American Athletic Association for the Deaf,

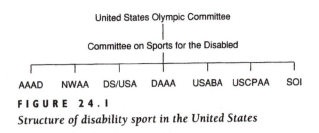

FIGURE 24.1
Structure of disability sport in the United States

United States Association for Blind Athletes, United States Cerebral Palsy Athletic Association, Wheelchair Sports USA, Disabled Sports USA, and Special Olympics International. These organizations are also under the supervision of the International Coordinating Council of the International Olympic Committee, extending the magnitude of the disabled sport movement to local, national, and international perspectives on sport for athletes with disabilities and thousands of participants. As these organizations advocate and promote sport for persons with specific disabilities (e.g., blind, deaf), collectively they advocate for large groups of athletes. Each organization has active programs developing junior level sport opportunities for youth with disabilities in the hope of numerous positive outcomes of a healthy, active lifestyle begun early. It should be noted that the number of participants continues to grow and the development of youth programs will continue to influence many children to become athletes in years to come (Figure 24.1).

Organizational Problems in Disabled Sport

As with any political or highly organized system, problems are often encountered that limit the access to or availability of sport opportunities. The numerous disabled sport organizations often compete against each other for funds, media attention and visibility. Misunderstanding on the part of the general public leads to frustration and tension between the organizations. For example, many persons have the perception that all disabled sport is Special Olympics; in fact, Special Olympics is intended for athletes with mental retardation. Athletes with physical disabilities do not want to be perceived as Special Olympians. Since fundraising and sponsorships play a large role in making sport opportunities available, there is pressure to reduce the numbers of different types of disabled sport organizations and develop a strategy to allow athletes with different disabilities to compete against one another.

Attainment of this goal is particularly complicated by the fact that each organization currently has a classification system intended to equalize competition based on factors such as age, gender, level of injury, previous competitive performance, sensory abilities, neurological function, or a combination of these factors. Because each organization prefers its own classification system, development of an integrated type of classification system that is fair to all athletes has become problematic.

There is currently a major push from international organizations to develop a system to increase the likelihood of inclusion within elite international competitions. Athletes with disabilities have participated in demonstration events during the regular Olympic Games since the 1984 Los Angeles Olympics. It is the goal of many leaders in disabled sport to eventually gain full inclusion into such level of competition. Considering that such inclusion would be improbable if heats were necessary for blind athletes, amputee athletes, wheelchair athletes, and others, integration of athletes into one system may enable inclusion to become a reality. The current move is toward a functional classification system versus a medical classification system,[2,3] though some decisions due to changes in classification have met with much controversy. The medical classification system is based upon documented evidence of dysfunction as evaluated by sensory and muscular innervation. This type of system is used primarily by persons with spinal cord injuries and continues to exist in U.S. wheelchair basketball and track competition. However international competition is moving toward the functional classification system based upon observation and analysis of competitors in a particular sport setting. Classification would thereby be made based upon the characteristics of the sport and the participant, rather than on the athlete independent of the sport. The goal is to create a system of classification in which significant differences are evident between classes.[4]

Problems in classification continue to plague competitive sport for athletes with disabilities. Such problems include athletes cheating during classification or during competition in an attempt to gain an unfair advantage. Competition for media attention, payoffs for athletic performance, sponsorship for only the top athlete, and suspected ergogenic aides to enhance performance are now issues in disabled sport. Unfortunately these are familiar issues in the "regular" sporting world.

Disabled sport is a large yet developing sport arena, with problems and concerns similar to those in any organized structure promoting sport. Yet the number of athletes with disabilities participating in sport and the opportunities for continued growth are significant.

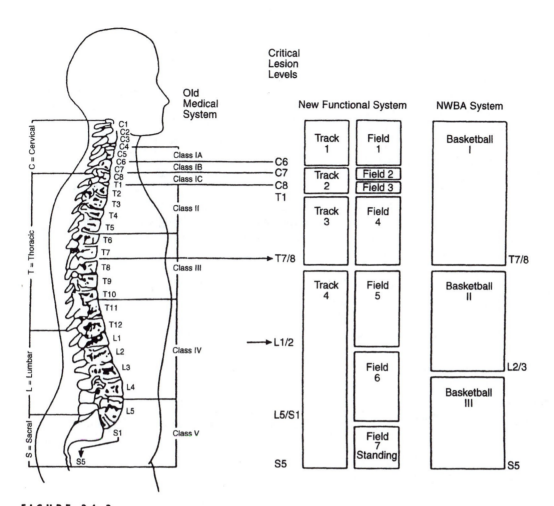

FIGURE 24.2

Medical and functional classifications for wheelchair sports (NWBA refers to National Wheelchair Basketball Association) (From C Sherrill, *Adapted Physical Activity, Recreation, and Sport*, 4th ed. Copyright © Wm. C. Brown Communications, Inc., Dubuque, Iowa. All Rights Reserved. Reprinted by permission.)

Review of Current Research

In contrast to the study of able-bodied counterparts, the study of injuries to athletes with disabilities has attracted relatively little attention of researchers in the sports medicine field. Several studies have documented the necessity of providing medical coverage at competitions for the disabled. Jackson[5] reported that 184 athletes were treated for a variety of injuries at the 1976 Toronto Olympiad for the Physically Disabled. Corcoran[6] described potential risks of participation observed in wheelchair marathon racers, such as chronic musculoskeletal problems and disability/environment-related problems such as hypothermia. Hoeberigs and colleagues[7] reported that 13 of the 40 athletes participating in a one-week international road race required treatment for musculoskeletal problems. An additional six athletes required treatment for conditions resulting from environmental (heat) stress, often disability related.

Burnham and colleagues,[8] studied a multi-disability team of 151 elite athletes and reported that musculoskeletal problems comprised 51 percent of the conditions treated by Canadian medical staff members at the 1988 Paralympic Games. It was found that wheelchair athletes experienced the most upper-extremity injuries. Blind athletes tended to sustain a disproportionate number of leg injuries, and athletes with cerebral palsy seemed to be predisposed to back injury. The remaining 49 percent of medical conditions were primarily acute upper respiratory or gastrointestinal problems and disability-related problems such as urinary tract infections and pressure sores.

Other research in this field has focused on survey design reporting of injuries in relation to training practices. In 1985, Curtis and Dillon[9] first reported the frequency and types of problems sustained by 128 wheelchair athletes who completed a questionnaire survey. The most common injuries reported were upper-extremity soft tissue injuries, blisters, and lacerations. Track, basketball, and road racing were identified as the highest risk sports, accounting for a majority of the injuries reported. Relatively few of these athletes sought medical attention for their injuries. McCormack[10] found similar results with another group of 90 wheelchair athletes.

Exposure and overuse appear to be factors in the prevalence of injuries in wheelchair athletes, and athletes who report more participation hours also report significantly more injuries.[9] It has been reported that athletes who compete in road racing train in excess of 100 miles per week, with a specific repetitive motion that increases the risk of overuse injury.[11] Considerable evidence supports these observations that long-term or intensive upper-extremity use results in chronic shoulder dysfunction.[12,13]

Patterns of muscle imbalance and inflexibility seem to be related to chronic shoulder dysfunction. Burnham and colleagues,[14] reported that wheelchair athletes with shoulder impingement syndromes may exhibit shoulder muscle imbalances, resulting in higher abductor/adductor and abduction/internal rotation strength ratios. Curtis[3] determined that wheelchair athletes who reported a history of a previous injury tended to consistently demonstrate decreased range of motion in shoulder extension. These findings point to the need for preventive strengthening and flexibility programs. Of additional concern was the apparent carpel tunnel syndrome in 23 percent of all athletes using wheelchairs.[15] More recently, a study verified the high prevalence of nerve conduction abnormalities in elite wheelchair athletes. Fifty percent of the 12 athletes tested demonstrated mononeuropathies in either the elbow or wrist. Five of the six athletes who had problems exhibited abnormalities bilaterally.[16]

The types of injuries experienced by athletes with disabilities seem to be similar to those experienced by able-bodied athletes. The impact of those injuries in limiting sport participation and the incidence of injuries over time was studied by Ferrara and colleagues.[17,18,19] The results of several of their studies of athletes with disabilities differed from those in previously described survey research, in that they defined an injury as an event that caused a loss of participation due to an injury or illness, they measured the incidence and impact of reported injuries over a specific period of time, and they recorded the circumstances under which the injury

occurred (training, competition, non-sports-related). These studies demonstrated that athletes with disabilities have approximately the same incidence of injuries as athletes without disabilities in similar sport activities,[17,18] but the injuries may be more severe. Ferrara and Davis[17] determined that major injuries, accounting for over 22 days lost from participation, account for 32 percent of the reported injuries of elite wheelchair athletes.

Athletes who competed in wheelchairs sustained primarily upper-extremity injuries, while athletes with cerebral palsy and visual deficits reported more lower-extremity injuries.[19] Among skiers with disabilities, 51 percent of the injuries involved the upper extremities, compared to 36 percent involving the lower extremities, with chronic injuries reported 50 percent more often than acute injuries.[18]

Injury Prevention

Preventing Common Injuries and Disability-Specific Medical Problems of Athletes with Disabilities

Preventive techniques for athletes with disabilities are essential training for coaches, athletes, event organizers, and medical staff members. Several areas should be addressed on the topic of injury prevention. (Table 24.1)

Musculoskeletal Injuries

The most common injuries to athletes with disabilities are musculoskeletal problems, blisters, and abrasions. Athletes who compete in wheelchairs tend to experience frequent upper-extremity soft tissue injuries. This has been demonstrated in both adult and junior competitors.[17,20]

SOFT TISSUE INJURIES OF UPPER EXTREMITIES: Shoulder impingement syndromes, epicondylitis (tennis elbow), rotator cuff injuries, bicipital tendinitis, and carpal tunnel syndrome are frequent problems for wheelchair and crutch users.[3,8,9,13,21] These injuries are related to the stresses of repetitive wheelchair propulsion, upper extremity weight bearing, and overhead positioning of the arm for both sport and everyday activities.

Flexibility and strengthening programs can play a part in preventing muscle imbalance and the development of poor posture and faulty sport technique that may encourage injuries. Pre- and post-participation stretching and flexibility exercises should be done consistently, emphasizing flexibility into shoulder flexion,

TABLE 24.1 *Means for prevention of injuries and disability-specific medical problems of athletes with disabilities*

Training/Self-Care Procedures
1. Education in proper warm-up techniques including stretching, evaluating core body temperature and sport specific drills
2. Prevention of overuse phenomena by avoiding over-training and incorporating appropriate rest intervals in training schedule.
3. Attention to nutrition, hydration, and hygienic needs, including self-catheterization, adherence to medication schedules, skin inspection and pressure relief.

Safety Considerations
1. Use of recommended safety gear and procedures for each sport. (e.g., helmets for wheelchair athletes)
2. Use of skilled spotters, sighted guides, or assistive personnel to ensure every athlete's safety during training and competition.
3. Removal of architectural barriers, installation of accessible bathrooms and showers
4. Use of equipment (wheelchairs, cushions, crutches, prosthetics, protective gloves and eyewear, orthotics) which is well-maintained, fits properly, and provides adequate support for athletic competition

Environmental Considerations
1. Protection from environmental conditions during competition including proper clothing, hydration, shade and shelter
2. Provision of plentiful clean water, food, appropriate sleeping quarters, and safe transportation to and from competitive venues

Medical Intervention
1. Prompt, appropriate treatment of previous injuries and disability-specific medical problems
2. Inclusion of individualized sport-specific flexibility and strengthening programs
3. Education of athletes and coaches on prevention of injuries and disability-specific medical problems.

extension, horizontal abduction, and external rotation. Strengthening programs should focus on strengthening of the posterior shoulder, including the external and internal rotators of the shoulder as well as the scapular adductor groups.

Some athletes with chronic soft tissue problems may find using ice posttraining to be very helpful. Taping and splinting may also be of value for recurrent hand, wrist, and elbow problems. Anti-inflammatory medications are often prescribed with success for these athletes.

LOW BACK PAIN: In athletes who stand for competition, the dynamics of altered posture, muscle imbalance, and the demands of athletic participation often create the potential for injuries. Due to chronic hip-flexor muscle tightness, some athletes with cerebral palsy and many amputees develop scoliosis, hypermobility, or hyperlordosis of the lumbar spine and experience low-back pain during or following athletic competition. Many of these athletes respond to simple stretching exercises and experience symptomatic relief (Figure 24.3).

Specific muscle stretching exercises to stretch tight hip flexors and ensure flexibility in lumbar flexion, extension, and rotation can be incorporated into their warm-up and cool-down routines. Moist heat or ice, rest, and massage may be useful in relieving symptoms. Normal hip flexibility, together with balanced strengthening of abdominal and hip and back extensor muscle groups, can improve lumbar stability to prevent hypermobility and pain in this area.

SOFT TISSUE INJURIES OF LOWER EXTREMITIES: Ambulatory athletes experience primarily lower-extremity injuries. Athletes with cerebral palsy often show genu valgus; mechanical instability of the knee; and spastic, tight quadriceps muscles; yet these factors do not seem to lead to a higher risk of knee problems. Instead, our experience has been that these athletes experience frequent muscle strain in the quadriceps or hamstrings during competition. Pre- and post-participation stretching and balanced strengthening programs are essential to prevent problems, as is prompt, appropriate medical treatment of muscle pulls.

FIGURE 24.3

Flexibility of amputee athlete prior to competition

Musculoskeletal conditions will often be exacerbated with increased stresses of compensating for a weaker or prosthetic limb. Therefore, bilateral strengthening, stretching and attention to symmetrical technique is very important.

(Photo by Kathleen A. Curtis, Ph.D., RPT)

Below-knee amputees who use prostheses for competition also are not particularly prone to knee injuries, as most socket designs protect the knee by extending above the femoral condyles. Additionally, the prosthetic limb frequently pulls away from the socket during impact, limiting the effect of the rigid prosthetic lever arm on the residual limb. Occasional knee hyperextension injuries do occur and are best managed with appropriate evaluation for serious knee injury; then rest, ice, compression, and elevation encourage a rapid return to participation as soon as feasible.

Blind athletes, ambulatory amputee athletes, and cerebral-palsy athletes are all prone to trips, slips, and falls during competitive activity. Another source of injury is the increased load on a stronger limb or the residual limb of a unilateral amputee. Back, knee, foot, and ankle problems are exacerbated with increased stresses of compensating for a weaker or prosthetic limb. Bilateral strengthening and attention to symmetrical technique are therefore very important in evaluating and preventing these problems.

ABRASIONS AND CONTUSIONS: Abrasions and contusions occur frequently in competitive situations. Falls and contact with equipment account for a large proportion of these injuries. Wheelchair athletes who use racing wheelchairs often experience friction burns on the inner surface of the upper arm from contact with the wheelchair tire during the push stroke. These abrasions can be prevented by wearing protective gear, such as the elasticized end of an athletic sock over the upper arm. Additionally, preventive measures such as examining chair for sharp surfaces and evaluating wheelchair width can help to reduce the likelihood of some injuries.

Falls from wheelchairs most frequently result in abrasions and contusions and infrequently lead to serious problems such as fracture or head or spinal trauma. Nevertheless, head and spinal trauma should be suspected with any contusion to the head sustained as a result of a fall from a wheelchair. In addition, limbs without sensation should be examined closely for edema, bruising, or abnormal alignment that might indicate a potential fracture, as the athlete will frequently have no pain or other symptoms (Figure 24.4).

BLISTERS: Wheelchair athletes frequently have blisters on the fingers and thumbs from contact with the wheelchair push rim. As blisters heal, thick calluses may form and eventually crack with continued trauma, leaving an open wound. Athletes should be encouraged to develop calluses, yet keep them from becoming too thick by filing them with a pumice stone. Open wounds, blisters, and other abrasions should be treated with antibiotic creams and covered with dressings as appropriate. Gloves are a must for both training and competition. Additionally, any athlete who has symptoms of hand weakness, pain, tingling, or numbness should be referred for evaluation of carpal tunnel syndrome, a frequent problem for these athletes.

Lower-extremity amputees frequently experience skin breakdown, blisters, rashes, and edema on the

FIGURE 24.4

Top U.S. track athlete in wheelchair designed for track
Wheelchair athletes who use racing wheelchairs often experience friction burns on the inner surface of the upper arm from contact with the wheelchair tire during the push stroke. Note protective gloves and positioning of lower body to maximize performance.(Photo by Kathleen A. Curtis, Ph.D., RPT)

residual limb in contact with the prosthesis. Sometimes prosthetic adjustment and realignment can prevent these skin lesions. They occur most often over bony prominences. Athletes can wear additional stump socks or use blister protection pads over areas at risk. If skin trauma is severe, it may be appropriate to rest, apply ice or compression, discontinue prosthetic use temporarily, or use a cane or crutches to relieve friction stress.

Disability-Specific Medical Problems

PRESSURE AREAS: Many athletes with disabilities lack sensation over the trunk and/or lower extremities. Without the normal stimulus of discomfort to shift position, the skin and underlying soft tissue may develop ischemic changes. Athletes are subject to the development of these pressure areas primarily over bony prominences. The most common areas are the sacrum, ischium, and greater trochanters, depending on sitting position and competitive activity.

If persistent redness or open sores are noted on skin inspection, the area should be relieved of all pressure from sitting, clothes, or equipment until the problem resolves. Without prompt attention and relief of pressure, the skin will ulcerate and become easily infected. Training and all competitive activity should cease until the area is healed. Athletes with chronic pressure sore problems may benefit from customized seating systems that accommodate their individual needs. A physical or occupational therapist can recommend possible wheelchair and cushion adaptations.

TEMPERATURE REGULATION DISORDERS: Many athletes who have high-level spinal cord injuries (above T6) or multiple sclerosis lack normal sympathetic nervous system function. These athletes are often unable to adapt well to environmental conditions due to their inability to cool themselves in hot weather or to generate heat in colder conditions by normal mechanisms such as sweating or shivering. They are therefore more susceptible to developing both hypothermia and hyperthermia. Additionally, these athletes may be especially at risk for thermal injuries from contact with equipment, ground surfaces, or sun exposure. Even therapeutic heat modalities may inadvertently cause serious burns.

It is important to take several measures to prevent hypothermia in athletes with disabilities. Protective clothing, using multiple layers including head covering, should be emphasized. Adequate fluid intake is essential in cold climates, as well as in hot conditions, as dehydration may accelerate the process of hypothermia. Wet clothing should be removed as soon as possible.[22]

Hyperthermia is also a concern for this population, especially in conditions of high heat and high humidity. Training and competitions should be planned for early morning or evening hours to prevent exposure to peak heat conditions. Since thirst is not always an accurate indicator of hydration, athletes should be encouraged to drink continuously regardless of thirst. Hydration guidelines commonly used include one liter of water one to two hours prior to training or competition and half a liter 30 minutes before the event. Intake of fluids should continue with at least a quarter liter every 10 to 15 minutes during training or competition (Figure 24.5).

Athletes should wear light clothing, including hats, in light colors to provide both shade and skin protection as well as to assist with heat loss. Athletes who are unable to sweat find it helpful to spray the face, neck, upper torso, and arms with water from a spray bottle to assist with dissipation of heat. Sunscreen should be used on exposed areas of skin only, as it can inhibit sweating and cooling as well. Shade should be provided and utilized as much as possible before and between competitive events.

Any athlete showing signs of heat or cold intolerance should be removed to a protected treatment area and immediate measures should be initiated to rewarm or cool the athlete. Hospitalization may be necessary, as hypothermia and hyperthermia may be life-threatening disorders.

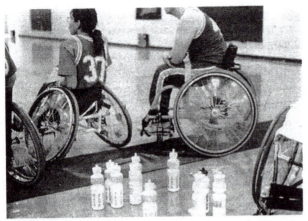

FIGURE 24.5
Basketball athletes need hydration
Adequate hydration is important to maximize performance and as prevention for bladder infection. Note spoke covers as protection of equipment as well as fingers.
(Photo by Kathleen A. Curtis, Ph.D., RPT)

BLADDER DYSFUNCTION: Many athletes with neurological disorders often have a neurogenic bladder, which leaves them susceptible to developing bladder infections, bladder stones, and obstructions. Some athletes have indwelling catheters to drain the bladder; others insert catheters intermittently. Infection in the bladder can spread to the kidneys and system-wide, causing severe illness and possible death. Thus a bladder infection requires prompt treatment with antibiotics. Athletes should not train or compete for at least eight hours after antibiotic treatment has been started and should be without a fever for at least 24 hours before resuming sports participation.

To prevent bladder infections, athletes should be encouraged to frequently flush the bladder by drinking adequate fluids and to maintain a regular catheterization schedule. Access to water and restrooms are therefore essential elements in their training environment. Bladder obstruction may result in a medical emergency, as it may precipitate the onset of symptoms of autonomic dysreflexia, which results in extreme hypertension. This is often treated simply by relieving the bladder obstruction.

HYPERTENSION: Autonomic dysreflexia occurs in individuals with cervical and higher thoracic spinal cord lesions. The onset of symptoms, including facial flushing and sweating, vasodilation, a rapid, pounding heartbeat, and a precipitous rise in blood pressure signal a medical emergency. If untreated, hypertension may reach dangerously high levels, causing cerebral hemorrhage and death.

The symptoms are most often caused by bladder or bowel obstruction, although they may be related to skin trauma. The athlete should assume a sitting position to lower blood pressure. The bladder and bowel should be emptied. If symptoms do not resolve, emergency medical treatment is required to lower blood pressure.

Some wheelchair athletes with quadriplegia attempt to induce autonomic dysreflexia to improve performance during competition. "Boosting" via clamping a catheter or inducing a painful stimulus is a dangerous and foolhardy practice and should be discouraged among all athletes. Unfortunately this dangerous technique has been demonstrated to increase physiological response to exercise.[15] It should be discouraged especially in athletes with high-level spinal cord lesions; if unchecked, the athlete can experience extremely high blood pressure and may be at severe risk for stroke.

HYPOTENSION: Some athletes with poor autonomic nervous system function also experience fluctuations in blood pressure in the upright position, often in combination with heat exposure. Orthostatic hypotension is a risk in athletes with disabilities and should be treated by lowering the athlete's head and raising the lower extremities. Wearing elastic stockings and abdominal corsets may be helpful in promoting venous return in athletes prone to hypotensive episodes.

DYSPHAGIA: Some athletes with cerebral palsy or traumatic brain injury experience difficulty swallowing. Choking on liquids is often a problem, as are drooling and poor control of saliva. Awareness of this problem is essential to prevent dehydration from inadequate fluid intake or excess fluid loss via drooling. Problems with swallowing may be alleviated somewhat by drinking thicker liquids such as fruit juices.

COMMUNICATION DISORDERS: Communication disorders are an occasional problem in the athlete with cerebral palsy; brain injury; or stroke, due to either *dysarthria,* a problem of neuromuscular control and coordination of the vocal musculature or *aphasia,* a problem with either expressive or receptive processing of verbal information in the brain. In providing care to an athlete with either problem, it is important to be patient, speak slowly and clearly, and listen carefully to the athlete's concerns.

BEHAVIORAL PROBLEMS: Occasionally the athlete with a brain injury may become overstimulated in the competitive environment. Agitation and abusive and violent behavior may result. This is not a time to try to reason with the athlete. Instead the athlete should be removed to a quiet environment and his or her attention should be redirected to a more positive focus.

SEIZURE DISORDERS: A small percentage of athletes with cerebral palsy have seizure disorders, and many take medication to control this disorder. Seizures are often brought on under conditions of fatigue, stress, dehydration, and extremes in temperature. Thus, avoiding these conditions is paramount to prevention.

Should a seizure occur, routine safety measures should be carried out during seizure activity. Following the seizure, the athlete should be examined for evidence of traumatic injury and checked frequently for 24 hours for signs of responsiveness. Medications should be reviewed with every athlete, as athletes frequently change their medication schedule during travel and time changes, and this may also precipitate seizure activity.

ATLANTOAXIAL INSTABILITY: This condition is often present in athletes with Down syndrome, a genetic disorder of the 21st chromosome, often causing mental retardation, joint laxity, and other related medical problems. One specific medical concern for these athletes is atlantoaxial instability, which may increase the potential risk of spinal cord injury. As a large percentage of persons with Down syndrome (17%) have this concern, Special Olympics requires all participants with Down syndrome have a medical screening for atlantoaxial instability prior to participation.[23] If the condition is present, activities with hyperflexion or extension of the head and neck are contraindicated. Examples are gymnastics, diving, wrestling, high jumping, or other events where hyperflexion or extension of the head and neck can occur.

Summary

With awareness of potential medical problems of a specific athlete population, sports-medicine professionals will be prepared to minimize risks and to provide appropriate services. Attention to sound training practices, protective gear, equipment, and environmental hazards will prevent many accidental injuries. Athlete and coach education regarding hydration, proper clothing, hygiene, and other preventive practices may serve to discourage the onset of many disability-specific medical problems.

Technological Contributions in Disabled Sport

An interesting outcome of the growth of disabled sport has been the technological revolution in sports equipment. Not only has the evolution of sport-specificity for wheelchairs, prostheses, and other sport-related equipment transformed athletic performance, but it has carried over into the design and development of improved daily-use equipment. The utilization of high-tech metals and alloys has enabled wheelchair designers, prosthetists, and engineers to fabricate lighter and more stable chairs better able to handle the stresses induced via sport competition. In addition, experts in sport biomechanics have assisted in developing various technological modifications that improve sport performance. These new chair designs have no doubt improved the quality and efficiency of athletic performance and may have assisted in the reduction of some types of injuries in wheelchair racing, although with the high speeds now attained in road races, severe injury may be of concern for athletes and sports medicine personnel.

Equipment Modifications for Sport

Following are a variety of examples of modifications utilized in wheelchair sport to assist in performance and reduce injuries. Camber, or angling the wheels, has enabled chairs to be more stable with improved efficiency of the power stroke and recovery phase of propulsion, as well as reduced abrasions caused by upper-arm contact on a moving wheel. Camber usually varies with athlete size and sport-related needs, yet must be determined in order to maximize performance and reduce injury. Handrim sizes are modified to increase the power generated via the rims, thereby increasing the speed of the chair. Modifications include decreasing size according to event and increasing friction by adding rubberized materials to the rim that match gloves so contact time on the rim is maximized. Wheel-spoke covers are used in basketball to reduce finger injuries and spoke damage due to collisions and contact on the court. In racing wheelchairs, steering devices aid in reducing stress on hands and shock absorbers assist in accommodating to terrain-related impact. Chairs usually have interchangable back wheels, front casters, seat cushions, and seat back heights, all of which can improve performance and reduce risk of injury if used correctly.

Aerodynamics play an important role in improving performance, and also reduce physiological stresses imposed by training and racing conditions. Carbon fiber wheels and lightweight metals assist in keeping the overall weight of a chair to approximately 15 pounds, versus 30 pounds of frequently used everyday chairs. With the advent of fast-moving chairs with speeds reaching 40 mph, athletes are using helmets and body suits to protect and aid in aerodynamics. It must be noted that the improved technology in sport and racing wheelchairs has not improved comfort for daily use. Since most chairs are made as narrow as possible (to reduce drag) and are very lightweight, additional materials such as arm rests, high back rests and padding are often not part of the racing chair. This is the case particularly in racing wheelchairs. With comfort and padding at a minimum, athletic-training personnel must be concerned about the increased risk of pressure sores resulting from athletes' increased time in racing chairs.

Technique in propulsion has also changed in recent years, with an emphasis on improved speed, perhaps without consideration for injury prevention. Examples of technique changes that may significantly increase hand- and wrist-related injury include the back hand technique in which athletes with high cervical spinal cord injuries, and thus limited hand function, use the dorsal side of the hand to exert increased pressure on the handrim and tire to increase force exerted on the wheel.

Athletes who have normal hand function yet utilize a wheelchair often use a hard downward striking of the handrim, rather than a grasp, push, and release sequence. This downward striking motion followed by a very fast, explosive pronation of the wrist likely will lead to increased hand- and wrist-related injuries. Though highly padded gloves with high friction tape

(on both glove and handrim) are used to help protect the hands, excessive forces are still generated with this newer technique. As other modifications are developed in wheelchair sport, athletic trainers must be concerned with increased risk of injury due to technique changes.

Prosthesis Modifications for Sport

Current technology for prostheses for lower-extremity amputee athletes has likely superseded that of wheelchair technology in allowing for individuals to perform at levels once inconceivable. Current technologies of lightweight alloys, vacuum suction, hydraulic mechanisms, and air cell design with individualized modifications allow for athletes to modify the stiffness and energy-storing capacity of the prosthesis as necessary relative to sport or movement requirements. An example of the athletic potential was recently demonstrated by Tony Volpentest, a bilateral below-knee amputee from the United States. He won the male 100 and 200 meter races during the 1996 Paralympics in Atlanta with times of 11.36 and 23.28 seconds, respectively. Numerous sport-related prosthetic devices are now available to encourage and assist athletes to participate to the fullest extent possible.

Technology has played a very important role in the improvement of athletic performance in recent years. However, the athletes' training and improvements in technique have also played major roles. Without question, sport pushed prosthetic and wheelchair development forward to enable others to benefit from the technology that was generated to improve athletic performance (Figure 24.6).

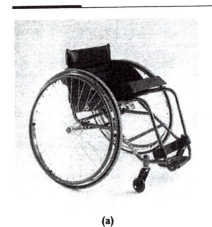
(a)

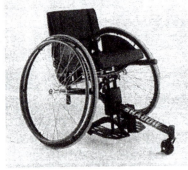
(b)

(c)

FIGURE 24.6
Various designs showing current technology in wheelchair sport
(Photos courtesy of Quickie Designs, a division of Sunrise Medical)

FIGURE 24.7

Amputee athletes waiting prior to start of race
Advanced prosthetic foot components used by top
amputee runners at 1992 Barcelona Paralympic Games.
Note prostheses designed for high performance sport.
(Photo by Kathleen A. Curtis, Ph.D., RPT)

SUMMARY: Familiarity with current issues regarding disabled sport will assist in stimulating interest
among professionals and provide higher quality sports
medicine services to athletes with disabilities. It is imperative that athletes with disabilities receive the same type
of care and prevention of injuries as do other athletes.
Recognition of the athlete with a disability as a person
first will assist the sports-medicine specialist in evaluating and prescribing appropriate treatment. Remember,
athletes with disabilities are much more similar to other
athletes than they are different (Figure 24.7).

REFERENCES

1. Sherrill, C: *Adapted Physical Activity, Recreation and
Sport: Crossdisciplinary and Lifespan.* Dubuque: Brown
Benchmark, fourth edition, 1993.

2. Labanowich S: A case for the integration of the disabled
into the Olympic Games. *Adap Phys Act Quar* 5(4):264–272,
1988.

3. Curtis KA, Brown K, Geisen A, Lee A, Motel S: Shoulder
flexibility and strength in wheelchair athletes: Implications
for preventing shoulder injuries. Presented at *8th International Symposium-International Federation for Adapted Physical Activity,* Miami, FL, November 18, 1991.

4. Higgs C, Babstack P, Buck J, Parsons C, Brewer, J: Wheelchair classification for track and field events: A performance
approach. *Adap Phys Act Quart* 7(1):22–41, 1990.

5. Jackson RW, Fredrickson A: Sports for the physically disabled—The 1976 Olympiad—(Toronto). *Am J Sports Med*
7:293–296, 1979.

6. Corcoran PJ: Sportsmedicine and the physiology of
wheelchair marathon racing. *Orthop Clin N Am* 11:697–716,
1980.

7. Hoeberigs JH, Debets-Eggen HBL, Debets PM: Sports
medical experiences from the international flower marathon
for disabled wheelers. *Am J Sports Med* 18(4):418–421, 1990.

8. Burnham R, Newell E, Steadward R: Sports medicine for
the physically disabled: the Canadian team experience at the
1988 Seoul Paralympic Games. *Clin J Sport Med* 1:193–196,
1991.

9. Curtis KA, Dillon DA: Survey of wheelchair athletic
injuries: common patterns and prevention. *Paraplegia*
23:170–175, 1985.

10. McCormack DAR, Reid DC, Steadward RD, Syrotuik
DG: Injury profiles in wheelchair athletes: results of a retrospective survey. *Clin J Sport Med* 1:35–40, 1991.

11. Curtis, KA: Prevention and treatment of wheelchair
athletic injuries. *Athletic Ther,* in press.

12. Pentland WE, Twomey LT: The weight-bearing upper
extremity in women with long term paraplegia. *Paraplegia*
29:521–530, 1991.

13. Gellman H, Sie I, Waters RL: Late complications of the
weight-bearing upper extremity in the paraplegic patient.
Clin Orthop Rel Res 233:132–135, 1988.

14. Burnham RS, May L, Nelson E, Steadward R: Shoulder
pain in wheelchair athletes—The role of muscle imbalance.
Am J Sports Med 21(2):238–242, 1993.

15. Burnham RS, Wheeler G, Bhambhani Y, Belanger M,
Eriksson P, Steadward R: Intentional induction of autonomic
dysreflexia among quadriplegic athletes for performance
enhancement: Efficacy, safety and mechanism of action. *Clin
J Sport Med* 4(1):1–10, 1994.

16. Bonminger ML, Robertson RN, Wolff M, Cooper RA:
Upper limb nerve entrapments in elite wheelchair racers. *Am
J Phys Med Rehab* 75(3):170–176, 1996.

17. Ferrara MS, Davis RW: Injuries to elite wheelchair athletes. *Paraplegia* 28(5):335–341, 1990.

18. Ferrara MS, Buckley WE, Messner DG, Benedict J: The
injury experience and training history of the competitive
skier with a disability. *Am J Sports Med* 20(1):55–60, 1992a.

19. Ferrara MS, Buckley WE, McCann BC, Limbird TJ,
Powell JW, Robl R: The injury experience of the competitive

athlete with a disability: prevention implications. *Med Sci Sports Exer* 24(2): 184–188, 1992b.

20.   Wilson PE, Washington RL: Pediatric wheelchair athletics: Sports injuries and prevention. *Paraplegia* 31, 330–337, 1993.

21.   Sie I, Waters RL, Adkins RH, Gellman H: Upper extremity pain in the post rehabilitation spinal cord injured patient. *Arch Phys Med Rehab* 73:44–48, 1992.

22.   Stopka C: An overview of common injuries to individuals with disabilities. *Palaestra* Winter: 44–51, 1996.

23.   Cooke RE: Atlantoaxial instability in children with Down's syndrome. *Adap Phys Act Quart* 1:194–195, 1984.

RECOMMENDED READINGS

Bloomquist LE: Injuries to athletes with physical disabilities: Prevention implications. *Phys Sports Med* 14:97–105, 1986.

Curtis KA: Health smarts, part 2, Strategies and solutions for wheelchair athletes—Common injuries prevention and treatment. *Sports n/ Spokes* 22(3):13–19, 1996.

Curtis KA: Health smarts, part 3, Strategies and solutions for wheelchair athletes—Common medical problems prevention and treatment. *Sports n/ Spokes* 22(3):21–28, 1996.

Curtis KA: Health smarts, part 4, Providing sports-medicine services for athletes with disabilities. *Sports n/ Spokes* 22(4):67–73, 1996.

Ferrara MS, Davis RW: Injuries to elite wheelchair athletes. *Paraplegia* 28, 335–341, 1996.

Monahan T: Wheelchair athletes need special treatment but only for injuries. *Phys Sports Med* 14:121–129, 1986.

Gayle GW: Roles of sportsmedicine and the wheelchair athlete: A multidisciplinary relationship. *Palaestra* 1993.

Mangus BC: Medical care for wheelchair athletes. *Adap Phys Act Quart* 5:90–95, 1988.

Mangus BC: Sports injuries, the disabled athletes and the athletic trainer. *Athletic Training* 22:305–310, 1987.

Nilseen R, Nygaard P, Bjorholt PG: Complications that may occur in those with spinal cord injuries who participate in sport. *Paraplegia* 23:152–158, 1985.

Steadward R, Walsh C: Training and fitness programs for disabled athletes: Past, present and future. In *The 1984 Olympics Scientific Congress Proceedings (Vol 9). Sport and disabled athletes* edited by Sherrill C. Champaign, IL: Human Kinetics, 1986 pp. 3–17.

ATHLETIC ORGANIZATIONS FOR ATHLETES WITH DISABILITIES

Disabled Sports USA (DS/USA)
Kirk Bauer, Executive Director
451 Hungerford Dr. Suite 100
Rockville, MD 20850

U.S. Association of Blind Athletes
33 N. Institute St.
Brown Hall, Suite 015
Colorado Springs, CO 80903

U.S. Cerebral Palsy Athletic Association
34518 Warren Rd. Suite 264
Westland, MI 48185

American Athletic Association for the Deaf
3607 Washington Blvd. No. 4
Ogden, Utah 84403-1737

Dwarf Athletic Association
418 Willow Way
Lewisville, TX 75067

United States Les Autres Sports Association
1101 Post Oak Blvd. Suite 9-486
Houston, TX 77056

Special Olympics International
1350 New York Avenue NW
Suite 500
Washington, DC 20005

National Wheelchair Athletic Association
3595 East Fountain Blvd., Suite L-100
Colorado Springs, CO 80910

Canadian Wheelchair Sports Association
1600 James Naismith Dr.
Gloucester, Ontario K1B 5N4, Canada

International Sports Organization for the Disabled
Ferrez 16
28008 Madrid, Spain

International Paralympic Committee
Dr. Robert Steadward
Rick Hansen Centre
W1-67 Van Vliet Centre
University of Alberta
Alberta, Canada T6G 2H9

SPORTS ASSOCIATIONS

Amputee Sports

Eastern Amputee Athletic Association
Jack Graff, President
2080 Ennabrock Road
North Bellmore, NY 11710
(516) 826-8340

National Amputee Summer Sports Association, Ltd.
Susan F. Ehrenfeld, Secretary
215 West 92nd Street, Suite 15A
New York, NY 10025
(212) 874-4138

Archery

American Wheelchair Archers*
Chuck Focht
2065 West Sunbury Road
West Sunbury, PA 16061
(412) 735-4359

Basketball

National Wheelchair Basketball Association
Stan Labanowich
110 Seaton Building
University of Kentucky
Lexington, KY 40506
(606) 257-1623

Bowling

American Wheelchair Bowling Association
Walter A. Roy
Executive Secretary-Treasurer
3620 Tamarack Drive
Redding, CA 96003
(916) 243-2695/244-6651 (fax)

Flying

Freedom's Wings International
1832 Lake Avenue
Scotch Plains, NJ 07076
(908) 232-6354

International Wheelchair Aviators
Bill Blackwood, Secretary
1117 Rising Hill
Escondido, CA 92029
(619) 746-5018

Multisport

Canadian Wheelchair Sports Association
1600 James Naismith Drive
Gloucester, Ontario K1B 5N4
Canada
(619) 748-5685/748-5722 (fax)

National Handicapped Sports
Kirk Bauer, Executive Director
451 Hungerford Drive, Suite 100
Rockville, MD 20850
(301) 217-0960

National Wheelchair Athletic Association
Patricia Long
3595 East Fountain Boulevard, Suite L-1
Colorado Springs, CO 80910
(719) 574-1150

United States Cerebral Palsy Athletic Association, Inc.
Grant Peacock, President
34518 Warren Road, Suite 264

---

*National Governing Body (NGB) of the National Wheelchair Athletic Association (NWAA)

Westland, MI 48185
(313) 425-8961

Quad Sports

Power Soccer
Tim Orr
Bay Area Outreach & Recreation Program (BORP)
605 Eshleman Hall
Berkeley, CA 94720
(510) 849-4663

United States Quad Rugby Association
Brad Mikkelsen
1605 Mathews Street
Fort Collins, CO 80525
(303) 484-7395

Racquet Sports

International Foundation for Wheelchair Tennis
Peter Burwash
2203 Timberloch Place, Suite 126
The Woodlands, TX 77380
(713) 363-4707

International Wheelchair Tennis Federation
Ellen de Lange
Palliser Road, Barons Court
London W14 9EN, England
(011) 44-71-610-1264 (fax)

National Foundation of Wheelchair Tennis
Brad Parks, Director
940 Calle Amanecer, Suite B
San Clemente, CA 92672
(714) 361-6811

National Wheelchair Racquetball Association
Joe Hager
535 Kensington Road, Apt. 4
Lancaster, PA 17603
(717) 394-2111

Recreation

National Association of Handicapped Outdoor Sportsmen, Inc.
R.R. 6, Box 25
Centralia, IL 62801
(618) 532-4565

National Handicap Motorcyclist Association
Bob Nevola, President
35-34 84th Street, #F8
Jackson Heights, NY 11372
(718) 565-1243

North American Riding for the Handicapped Association
Bill Scebbi
P.O. Box 33150
Denver, CO 80233
(800) 369-RIDE

POINT (Paraplegics On Independent Nature Trips)
Shorty Powers, Director
403 Pacific Avenue

Terrell, TX 75160
(214) 524-4231

Wheelchair Motorcycle Association
Dr. Eli Factor
101 Torrey Street
Brockton, MA 02401
(508) 583-8614

Road Racing

International Wheelchair Road Racers Club, Inc.
Joseph M. Dowling, President
30 Myano Lane
Stamford, CT 06902
(203) 967-2231

MUSCLES (Michigan United Sports Chair League Endurance Series)
Scott McDonough
18964 Whitby
Livonia, MI 48152
(313) 478-9325

Shooting

National Wheelchair Shooting Federation*
Sharon R. Scheppke, Chairperson
Dave Baskin, Information
102 Park Avenue
Rockledge, PA 19046
(215) 379-2359/663-9662 (fax)

Skiing

National Handicapped Sports
Kirk Bauer, Executive Director
451 Hungerford Drive, Suite 100
Rockville, MD 20850
(301) 217-0960

Ski for Light, Inc.
Jeff Pagels
Mobility-impaired Coordinator
1400 Carole Lane
Green Bay, WI 54313
(414) 494-5572

US Disabled Ski Team
Jack Benedick
P.O. Box 100
Park City, UT 84060
(801) 649-9090

Softball

National Wheelchair Softball Association
Jon Speake, Commissioner
1616 Todd Court
Hastings, MN 55033
(612) 437-1792

Table Tennis

American Wheelchair Table Tennis Association*
Jennifer Johnson

23 Parker Street
Port Chester, NY 10573
(914) 937-3932

Track & Field

Wheelchair Athletics of the USA*
Judy Einbinder
1475 West Gray
Houston, TX 77019
(713) 526-3000

Water Sports/Recreation

Access to Sailing
Duncan Milne, Director
19744 Beach Boulevard, Suite 340
Huntington Beach, CA 92648
(714) 722-5371

American Canoe Association
7432 Alban Station Boulevard, Suite B-226
Springfield, VA 22150
(703) 451-0141/451-2245 (fax)

American Water Ski Association
Phil Martin, Aquatics Director
Disabled Ski Committee
Adaptive Aquatics, Inc.
P.O. Box 7
Morven, GA 31638
(912) 775-2590

Handicapped Scuba Association
Jim Gatacre
1104 El Prado
San Clemente, CA 92672
(714) 498-6128

National Ocean Access Project
Ed Harrison
P.O. Box 33141, Farragut Station
Washington, DC 20033-0141
(301) 217-9843

US Rowing Association
Richard Tobin
Adaptive Coordinator
201 South Capitol Avenue, Suite 400
Indianapolis, IN 46225
(317) 237-5656/237-5646 (fax)

US Wheelchair Swimming*
Larry Quintiliana
229 Miller Street
Middleboro, MA 02346
(508) 946-1964

Weightlifting

United States Wheelchair Weightlifting Federation*
Bill Hens
39 Michael Place
Levittown, PA 19057
(215) 945-1964

Nutrition and the Athlete

Athletes recognize the importance of healthful nutritional habits as part of a successful program for training and competition. There is great interest not only in developing a competitive edge, but also in maintaining long-term health. It is important for athletes to have access to practical and accurate information that is based on an assessment of individual needs. The temptation to seek a "winning edge" through the use of faddism or questionable nutritional supplementation must be countered with sound principles of the science of nutrition. Individuals demonstrating potential health problems must be referred to appropriate medical personnel for assessment and supervision.

Nutritional Requirements for Athletes

The nutritional concerns of many athletes include "How much should I be eating?" and "What foods are best to allow me to achieve maximal endurance and strength benefits?" The need to maintain adequate calories to allow for energy balance as well as to recover from intense bouts of activity must be recognized. The requirements of the muscles to refuel and provide nutrients for tissue healing and repair are important in the prevention of fatigue and injury. The sources of energy must be reviewed, as well as the desired daily intake of each, and the specific foods containing these nutrients. Recent changes in nutritional guidelines have resulted in the development of the Food Guide Pyramid (Figure 25.1). The pyramid is based on the USDA's (United States Department of Agriculture) research on what

foods Americans eat, what nutrients are in these foods, and how to make the best food choices. There is increasing evidence that our diet plays a significant role both in the development of and the prevention of disease. Because the typical American's diet is excessively high in fat, the food pyramid is designed to illustrate the relative proportion of fat in various food groups, helping consumers to make healthy choices. The consumption of complex carbohydrates forms the large base of the food pyramid diet, with a recommended 6 to 11 servings a day. Also emphasized is the fruit group (2 to 4 servings) and the vegetable group (3 to 5 servings). Meat and milk groups follow with 2 to 3 servings each. Consumption of fats, oils, and sweets are minimized in this ideal diet (Figure 25.1). The minimum number of servings from the food pyramid provides approximately 1,600 Kcal/day, while the maximum number of servings provides approximately 2,800 Kcal/day (Table 25.2).

Carbohydrates

Carbohydrates are the principal source of energy in endurance events and are the only source of energy in explosive or anaerobic activities. High-carbohydrate diets (approximately 70 percent of total calories, or about 8–10 grams of carbohydrate per kilogram of body weight/day) are beneficial for athletes involved in moderate to intense levels of activity. Carbohydrates are converted to glycogen and stored in the liver and muscles as readily-available energy. During sustained exercise, the body consumes carbohydrate at the rate of approximately one gram per minute. Many athletes on intense training schedules don't consume adequate levels of carbohydrate to replenish their glycogen (and blood glucose) stores. A 30 percent reduction in muscle glycogen levels can neg-

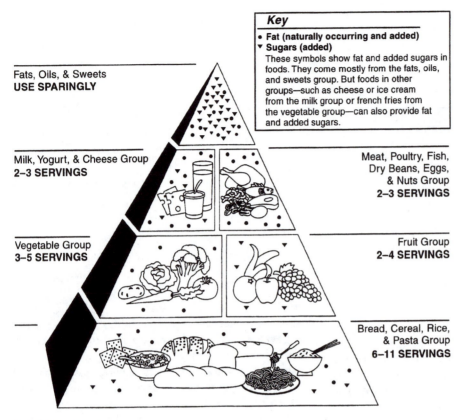

Fats, Oils, & Sweets
USE SPARINGLY

Milk, Yogurt, & Cheese Group
2–3 SERVINGS

Vegetable Group
3–5 SERVINGS

Key
- **Fat (naturally occurring and added)**
- ▼ **Sugars (added)**
These symbols show fat and added sugars in foods. They come mostly from the fats, oils, and sweets group. But foods in other groups—such as cheese or ice cream from the milk group or french fries from the vegetable group—can also provide fat and added sugars.

Meat, Poultry, Fish, Dry Beans, Eggs, & Nuts Group
2–3 SERVINGS

Fruit Group
2–4 SERVINGS

Bread, Cereal, Rice, & Pasta Group
6–11 SERVINGS

FIGURE 25.1
(Source: *The Food Guide Pyramid.* U.S. Department of Agriculture, August 1992, HG 252.)

atively impact training and performance. While it generally takes 90 to 180 minutes of continuous exercise (performed at 60 to 80 percent of VO_2 max.) to deplete muscle glycogen, significant reductions can occur after only 15 to 30 minutes of very intense activity.[1] It takes about 20 hours to resynthesize muscle glycogen stores after a hard exercise bout. The initial two hours following activity seem to represent a particularly critical period. Ivy and colleagues[2] found that delaying the ingestion of carbohydrate by two hours resulted in a 47 percent slower rate of glycogen synthesis when compared with ingesting carbohydrate immediately. The athlete should attempt to eat 50 to 100 grams of carbohydrate every two hours until approximately 500–600 grams have been consumed to ensure rapid replenishment of muscle glycogen and blood glucose levels. A high-fat diet can compromise carbohydrate intake and can slow the refueling of glycogen stores significantly.

Carbohydrate ingestion during endurance activities (in excess of 90 minutes) helps to supplement the glycogen stores found in the liver, muscles, and blood. Coyle and colleagues,[3] studied a group of elite cyclists to determine if carbohydrate feeding during prolonged strenuous exercise would influence muscle glycogen depletion. Athletes consuming a carbohydrate solution were able to exercise an additional hour before fatiguing (4 hours versus 3 hours for the placebo group). About the only time the ingestion of carbohydrate may not be appropriate is during the 30 to 60 minutes prior to exercise. Some athletes may have an exaggerated blood sugar response (hypoglycemia) if they ingest carbohydrates too close to the time they perform.

The cost of converting excess carbohydrate calories to body fat is relatively high (approximately 25% of ingested calories) compared to the cost of converting excess ingested fat calories to body fat (3 to 5%). Calorie for calorie, it is probably more difficult to become overweight if you eat a high-carbohydrate diet compared to an equivalent-calorie diet that contains excess fat.[4] An added benefit: essential vitamins and minerals are plentiful in complex carbohydrate foods. Sources of carbohydrate include breads, cereals, pastas, rice, dried beans and peas, corn, potatoes, fruits, and fruit juices.

CARBOHYDRATE LOADING: The carbohydrate-loading diet has received considerable publicity since it was first described in 1967, and has been used by

TABLE 25.1 *What counts as a serving?*

Bread, Cereal, Rice, and Pasta		
1 slice of bread	1 ounce of ready-to-eat cereal	½ cup cooked cereal, rice, or pasta
Vegetable		
1 cup of raw leafy vegetables	½ cup of other vegetables, cooked or chopped raw	¾ cup of vegetable juice
Fruit		
1 medium apple, banana, orange	½ cup of chopped, cooked, or canned fruit	¾ cup of fruit juice
Milk, Yogurt, and Cheese		
1 cup of milk or yogurt	1-½ ounces of natural cheese	2 ounces of process cheese
Meat, Poultry, Fish, Dry Beans, Eggs, and Nuts		
2–3 ounces of cooked lean meat, poultry, or fish	½ cup of cooked dry beans, 1 egg, or 2 tablespoons of peanut butter count as 1 ounce of lean meat	

Source: The Food Guide Pyramid. U.S. Department of Agriculture, August 1992, HG252.

TABLE 25.2 *Sample diets for a day at 3 calorie levels*

	Lower (about 1,600)	Moderate (about 2,200)	Higher (about 2,800)
Bread Group Servings	6	9	11
Vegetable Group Servings	3	4	5
Fruit Group Servings	2	3	4
Milk Group Servings	2–3[1]	2–3[1]	2-3[1]
Meat Group[2] (ounces)	5	6	7
Total Fat (grams)	53	73	93
Total Added Sugars (teaspoons)	6	12	18

[1]Women who are pregnant or breastfeeding, teenagers, and young adults to age 24 need 3 servings.

[2]Meat group amounts are in total ounces.

Source: The Food Guide Pyramid. U.S. Department of Agriculture, August 1992, HG252.

endurance athletes with varying degrees of success since then.[5] The purpose of the diet is to enhance the glycogen-storing capabilities of the muscles, enabling the athlete to continue to compete at a particular level of activity for an increased period of time. The event must exceed 90 minutes in length in order for the technique to make a difference. It should be realized that the carbohydrate-loading diet does not allow an athlete to participate more intensely. If a marathon runner usually runs a six-minutes-per-mile pace, but becomes exhausted after 20 miles, a carbohydrate-loading diet *may* allow him or her to continue through 26 miles at a six-minute-per-mile pace; however, it will probably not allow a five-minute-per-mile pace for 26 miles.

Originally it was thought that, in order to supercompensate the muscles with glycogen, they first needed to be depleted of their glycogen stores. Depletion was accomplished by an exhaustive workout, after which very little training was done over the next six days. A high-protein, high-fat, low-carbohydrate diet was consumed for the first three days of that six-day period (the depletion phase). This phase was followed by a high-carbohydrate, low-fat, low-protein diet for the remaining three days.

In its unmodified form, a carbohydrate-loading diet can be very taxing to the system and difficult to tolerate; it certainly does not suit everyone. Fortunately, further research has shown the depletion phase to be unnecessary in trained athletes.[6] A modified regimen in which three days of mixed diet together with training, followed by three days of exercise taper and a high-carbohydrate diet, have been found to produce muscle glycogen levels similar to those achieved by the classical regimen. For each gram of glycogen stored, additional water will also be stored. Some athletes note a feeling of stiffness and heaviness associated with increased glycogen storage. These sensations dissipate with exercise. The exercise used to deplete the glycogen stores must be specific to the muscles groups being used for the upcoming activity. For example, a runner needs to deplete his or her glycogen stores by running rather than by cycling.[7]

Fat

There has been much discussion of the need to reduce fat in our diets. In the diet of the average American, about 37 percent of the calories come from fat. The National

Research Council recommends a diet low in total fat (less than 30% of total calories) and saturated fat (less than 10% of total calories) to ensure optimal health. Besides weight gain and the problems associated with obesity (high blood pressure and diabetes), excess fat can contribute to several chronic diseases, including heart disease and cancer of the breast, colon, and prostate.[8] Excessive fat in the diet of an endurance athlete can interfere with the timely reloading of glycogen stores in exercising muscle, and may adversely affect performance.

Fat is calorically dense (9 calories per gram) compared with carbohydrate or protein (4 calories per gram), and converts most easily of any of the energy substrates to body fat. (It takes only 3–5% of ingested calories to convert dietary fat to body fat.) Even a lean athlete has more than 60,000 calories of stored fat.[9] Fat is a significant source of energy during exercise of moderate intensity. Chronic exercise stimulates adaptive changes in our metabolism that increase the ability of the body to mobilize and utilize fat as an energy source. Regular, sustained aerobic activity should be included in any weight loss program. Food sources of fat include oils, cheeses, nuts, butter, sour cream, sausage and most other ground meats, potato chips, some salad dressings, and all fried foods.

Protein

Athletes seem to have many misconceptions about their dietary protein needs, possibly as a result of the conflicting information available. Daily caloric intake should consist of 10 to 15 percent protein, or 1 to 1.5 grams of protein per kilogram of body weight. There is some experimental evidence that athletes in heavy training (e.g., endurance, weightlifters) may have a modest increased need for protein in their diet. It must be noted, however, that the average western diet provides more than enough protein to meet this need.[10] For most athletes there is no need to increase protein intake, particularly for athletes who mistakenly believe that high-protein diets provide additional energy. Protein is an inefficient energy source and cannot be stored and used later, so excess calories from protein will be converted and stored as fat. Excess intake of protein requires increased water consumption as the kidneys attempt to process the nitrogen wastes generated by protein metabolism.[11] Not only does excess protein place a heavy load on the kidneys, but it may also lead to increased urinary calcium excretion, which could be detrimental to the female athlete trying to maintain bone mass.

Amenorrheic athletes tend to consume not only fewer total calories than their regularly menstruating counterparts, but also less protein. Nelson and colleagues[12] found that 82 percent of the amenorrheic athletes ate less than the recommended dietary allowance (RDA) for protein. Low protein consumption may affect the ability to maintain or enhance lean body mass (muscle). In addition, the association among amenorrhea, disordered eating, and bone health puts this group at risk for developing early-onset osteoporosis. A safe intake for female athletes is about 1.1 g to 1.65 g of protein per kilogram of body weight, which is higher than the current RDA for sedentary people. For a 120-pound woman, this comes to 60 to 90 g of protein (13 to 20 percent of an 1,800-calorie diet) and is the equivalent of three or four 8-ounce servings of low-fat milk or yogurt and one 4-to-6-ounce serving of meat. Food sources of protein include red meats, poultry, fish, dry beans, nuts, eggs, milk, and milk products.

Pre-Event Nutrition

The timing and function of the pre-event meal depends to some extent on the type of activity to be performed, the contents of the meal, and personal preference. During exercise, athletes rely primarily on their pre-existing glycogen and fat stores. Although the pre-event meal does not contribute immediate energy, it can provide a significant source of energy (elevated blood glucose) for athletes competing in events lasting more than an hour.

Most authorities favor the intake of a light carbohydrate meal two to four hours prior to activity, and extra fluid in the half hour prior to the event. Good examples of solid high-carbohydrate foods for pre-event meals include fruit, bread products (honey, jam, or jelly may increase caloric content), and low-fat or nonfat yogurt. Fruit juices and nonfat milk provide a fluid source, and are a good high-carbohydrate beverage. Liquid-carbohydrate drinks are suitable for pre-event consumption if it is difficult to ingest adequate calories. High protein or fat content in meals will delay digestion and absorption, and should be avoided or at least limited prior to competitive activities. Spicy foods, beans, raw vegetables, and fried foods are usually difficult to digest. Eating large amounts of food can also delay digestion. As was mentioned previously, about the only time ingestion of carbohydrates may not be appropriate is during the 30 to 60 minutes just prior to activity. The concern is that ingestion of carbohydrate too near the beginning of an event may cause an elevation in blood-insulin levels, resulting in hypoglycemia and fatigue during exercise. To optimize glycogen reloading of muscle, it is necessary to eat a high-carbohydrate meal within two to three hours following activity (Table 25.3).

TABLE 25.3 *Important nutrient sources*

Nutrient	Major Food Source	
Protein	Meat, poultry, fish Eggs Milk	Dried beans, peas Cheeses
Carbohydrate	Cereal Dried beans Bread	Potatoes Corn Sugar
Fat	Shortening, oil Butter, margarine	Salad dressing Sauces
Vitamin A (Retinol)	Liver Sweet potatoes Butter, margarine	Carrots Greens
Vitamin C (Ascorbic Acid)	Broccoli Grapefruit Mango	Orange Papaya Strawberries
Thiamin (B1)	Lean pork Fortified cereals	Nuts
Riboflavin (B2)	Liver Yogurt	Milk Cottage cheese
Niacin	Liver Meat, poultry, fish	Peanuts Fortified cereals
Calcium	Milk, yogurt Sardines, salmon w/ bones	Cheese Collard, kale, mustard and turnip greens
Iron	Enriched farina Liver Dried beans, peas	Prune juice Red meat

Adapted from the National Dairy Council *Guide to Good Eating*. Reprinted with permission.

Vitamins and Minerals

VITAMINS: Vitamins are organic molecules that regulate biochemical reactions within the body. The body cannot manufacture them, which is why we must obtain them through our diet. They help to regulate various processes of growth and to maintain and repair tissues. Currently 13 vitamins have been identified, each with specific functions. Contrary to what many athletes believe, vitamins do not provide a direct source of energy.[13] In general, the vitamin requirements of an athlete are not much greater than those of a sedentary person.

MINERALS: Minerals serve a variety of functions. Some, such as calcium, are used to build tissue. Phosphorus helps build bones and teeth. Others, such as iodine and thyroid hormone, are important components of hormones. Iron is critical in the formation of blood hemoglobin. Minerals are also vital for many of the body's regulatory functions. They regulate contraction of muscle, conduction of nerve impulses, and heart rhythm.[13]

Calcium is necessary to maintain the contractibility of muscles, healthy bones and teeth, to aid in blood clotting and nerve transmission; and possibly to facilitate glycogen breakdown.[7] The typical American diet supplies 450 to 550 milligrams of calcium per day.[13] The National Institute of Health (NIH) and many nutrition experts recommend that women should have at least 1,200 to 1,500 milligrams of calcium per day to reduce the risk of osteoporosis later in life. Female athletes who are amenorrheic may be at even greater risk for developing osteoporosis (see Chapter 23). Calcium supplementation of up to 1,600 milligrams per day may be recommended for this population. Food sources of calcium include dairy products (an 8 oz. glass of milk or carton of yogurt each contain about 330 milligrams of calcium), dark green leafy vegetables, and dried legumes.

Iron assists with the transportation of oxygen and aids in the utilization of oxygen by the muscles. Iron deficiency (characterized by low hemoglobin levels) can lead to anemia. Iron-deficiency anemia can substantially diminish an athlete's performance.[7] The average American diet supplies only 5 to 6 milligrams of iron per 1,000 calories. Athletes who may be at an increased risk for developing anemia include female athletes, teenage athletes, endurance athletes, low-body-weight athletes, and those who do not consume red meat.[7] Women athletes typically consume 10 milligrams per day—far less than the Recommended Dietary Allowance (RDA) of 15 milligrams (for women). In this population an iron supplement may be beneficial. Lean red meat is an excellent source of iron, containing about 1 milligram of iron per ounce. Peas, beans, iron-enriched or fortified cereals and breads, as well as green leafy vegetables are a good source of iron. Consumption of food rich in Vitamin C (fresh fruits, orange juice), along with iron sources, aids in the absorption of iron. Conversely, consumption of caffeine with iron-rich foods can interfere with iron absorption.

SUPPLEMENTS: The Food and Drug Administration estimates that about 40 percent of all Americans take nutritional supplements. In the athletic population, supplementation may be as high as 80 percent.[7] Most athletes tend to abuse vitamin and mineral supplements under the misguided belief that, if some is good, more will be better. Athletes cite three primary reasons for use of supplements:[7]

1. Improve performance
2. Compensate for less-than-optimal diet
3. Meet nutrient demands of heavy exercise

Scientific research has shown that all these reasons for supplementation are invalid. In general, the increased needs for vitamins and minerals associated with a vigorous training schedule are easily met when the athlete increases food consumption. Athletes need to be made aware that there are potential dangers in supplementing the diet with megadoses (at least 10 times the RDA) of vitamins and minerals. At these doses, some vitamins and minerals begin to function more like drugs, producing toxicities and serious side effects.[7] Niacin, one of the B-complex vitamins, is essential in the maintenance of normal energy metabolism and regulation of the nervous and digestive systems. Taken in excess, it may inhibit the release of free fatty acids, and thus force muscle tissue to deplete its stores of glycogen, leading to diminished performance.[14] Excess amounts of zinc in the diet may adversely affect copper and iron levels. Excess amounts of vitamin C can cause decreases in copper levels. High levels of manganese may drive down iron levels. Although athletes on reduced-calorie diets (long-distance runners, gymnasts, dancers, wrestlers) which result in vitamin and mineral intakes below the RDA might benefit from a supplement containing 100 percent of the RDA, they should be made aware that more is not necessarily better. Taking supplements as an alternative to making responsible food choices can have a negative effect on performance by not addressing adequate energy concerns.[7] It is important that coaches, trainers, teachers, and parents understand the principles of nutrition and instill in their athletes a proper, well-balanced eating plan to provide the best diet for both performance and health.[7]

Fluid and Electrolyte Requirements

Often people think of vitamins, minerals, protein, and carbohydrates a being critical to good nutrition; but in reality the most important—yet often overlooked—nutrient is water. An adequate supply of water is necessary for all energy production in the body, for temperature control (particularly during exercise), and for elimination of metabolic waste products. Thirst is not a reliable indicator of fluid needs, so it is important that athletes monitor their fluid intake carefully to avoid dehydration. The loss of as little as 2 percent of body weight (as water) can impair an athlete's performance. Other effects of dehydration include reduced muscular strength, higher resting heart rate, impairment of thermal regulatory processes, and an increase in the loss of electrolytes from the body. It is important to start each exercise session well hydrated. The best pre-event fluid is cold water, and up to one quart can be consumed in the two hours preceding workouts. It is also important to replenish fluids during workouts, ideally 4 to 6 ounces every 10 to 15 minutes. One immediate effect of exercise can be a blunted thirst sensation. Fluid intake should be regulated by a schedule of drinking fluids, rather than by a response to thirst. Monitoring weight loss after activity is an excellent means of assessing fluid loss. A pint (16 ounces) of fluid should be consumed for every pound of weight lost. Another way to monitor sweat loss is to have the athlete check the color and quantity of their urine. Dark and scanty urine indicates it is concentrated with metabolic wastes, and the athlete needs to ingest greater amounts of fluids. Clear urine indicates the body has returned to a more normal water balance.

Plain water is inexpensive and effectively replaces the most crucial nutrient lost during exercise. It is easily absorbed and is palatable for most individuals. Athletes involved in endurance events (longer than one hour) may benefit from one of the numerous sports drinks. Athletes in the early stages of their conditioning programs—who clearly demonstrate increased potential for the loss of electrolytes during strenuous exercise due to excess perspiration and/or lack of acclimatization—may also benefit from an electrolyte replacement drink.

Replacement of fluids after exercise needs to be a deliberate effort because thirst is quenched before body water is replaced fully and because intense exercise blunts the sensation of thirst.[7] Athletes should consume fluid upon completion of activity, even before showering. It is also important to avoid alcohol and beverages containing caffeine, which act as diuretics and can lead to further dehydration. Foods high in salt should be avoided; they may cause fluid retention in the blood plasma and thus increase the amount of water needed for adequate hydration of other body tissues.

Special Considerations

While assisting athletes with their nutritional questions and concerns, it is critical to remember the importance of objective assessment of the individual. This assessment should include a discussion of the athlete's concerns, accurate diet records, perceptions of their optimal weight, goals for weight loss or gain, their current weight, and a weight they have recently attained. An objective measure of body fat must be made and discussed with the athlete to assure their understanding of the concept of body weight versus body fat, and the desired reduction in body fat while maintaining lean body mass. Goals should reflect a reasonable time frame for achieving safe and productive weight changes that will not adversely affect the athlete's performance or health status. There are several excellent software packages which allow for detailed diet analysis based on an accurate reporting of the types and amounts of foods consumed. This process can be very important in increasing awareness of nutritional habits and decisions, and enhancing consciousness of making positive changes. The process is dependent on the accuracy and accountability of the athlete in the reporting process. The most significant part of this process is the education of the athlete as to the significance of diet and proper nutrition in helping to achieve athletic goals and good health. Several patterns seem to be common to many athletes, and can easily be modified:

1. Intake of calories is inadequate for energy expenditure.

2. Percentage of daily total calories from fat is too high.

3. Intake of carbohydrate is too low to maintain energy expenditure.

4. Fluid intake is insufficient.

5. Intake of snacks and meals, which are often high in fat, late in the evening.

6. Excessive intake of caffeine.

Weight Gain

Weight gain requires careful planning in order to be successful. The athlete must understand the need to increase lean body mass and not to consume large amounts of fat, which will be used inefficiently and may have deleterious effects on performance. Therefore, the athlete must be given options for the types of high-carbohydrate foods which will provide energy, and must increase slightly the intake of protein. Regular assessment of body fat can assist in monitoring this process to assure success, and reasonable goals related to length of time must be set to avoid frustration. The importance of the specific training program must be emphasized; this is critical for achieving the goal. Supplemental protein, anabolic steroids, and other magical potions must be discouraged; they are potentially dangerous and can have long-term detrimental effects on health.

Weight Loss

There is frequently interest among athletes in reducing weight in order to enhance conditioning or performance, or to achieve a particular weight standard. A significant number of athletes may be at risk for developing patterns of disordered eating when they attempt to achieve low body weights. It is the responsibility of the coach, athletic trainer, parents, physician, and other support personnel to monitor these behaviors and educate individuals about possible adverse effects on health and performance. (See Chapter 23.) Athletes must realize that rapid weight loss via fasting or severe caloric restriction leads to loss of lean body mass (muscle), liver and muscle glycogen depletion, and dehydration. Health and performance suffer. Consistency is of the utmost importance in proper weight loss. For the majority of athletes desiring to reduce body fat, a long-term program of moderate caloric restriction, appropriate aerobic conditioning, and careful dietary planning to maximize the nutrient composition of food intake should promote maximum loss of body fat, minimum loss of lean tissue and water, and maintenance of adequate nutritional status.[6] Methods of losing weight such as rubber suits, saunas, and dehydration should be avoided (Table 25.4).

Disordered Eating Habits

The pre-participation examination can be helpful in gathering information that may identify at-risk athletes, and it is important to be aware of warning signs. (See Chapter 1.) The side effects of disordered eating behaviors in athletes may include: fatigue, sleep disturbances, decreased immune response, anemia, cardiovascular changes, depression, endocrine abnormalities, decreased hypothalamus and pituitary function, amenorrhea, osteoporosis and stress fractures, metabolic abnormalities, electrolyte imbalances, dehydration, and gastrointestinal problems.

In managing athletes exhibiting these behaviors, a referred plan and prior identification of professional resources is very important. These conditions cannot be managed by forcing an athlete to increase food intake, because there is usually a psychological component to the behavior, which must be addressed. There are many signs for concerns in athletes who are attempting to reduce their weight. The NCAA has produced a videotape addressing some of the important concerns in sports that require maintenance of a low body weight. This video is available free by contacting Karol Video, P. O. Box 7600, Wilkes-Barre, Pennsylvania 18773.

TABLE 25.4 *Weight-loss formula*

A useful formula for determining the amount of weight that can be safely lost is:

(1) $\dfrac{\text{percentage of body fat}}{100} \times \dfrac{\text{weight in kg}}{1}$

= total kg fat

(2) $\dfrac{\text{percentage body fat to lose}}{\text{actual percentage body fat}} \times$ kg fat

= kg to lose

(3) actual weight − kilograms to lose
= goal weight

Example: A 70 kg male wrestler with 15% body fat wishes to achieve an optimum of 5% body fat.

$\dfrac{15}{100} \times 70 = 10.5$ kg of body fat (total)

$\dfrac{10}{15} \times 10.5 = 7$ kg to lose to achieve 5% body fat

70 − 7 = 63 kg—the lowest weight that this wrestler should drop to in order to achieve 5% body fat without becoming dehydrated

Not more than 1 to 1.5 kg (2 to 3 lb) should be lost per week. As 1 kg equals 7,700 Kcal, 1.5 kg per week equals 11,500 Kcal, which equals 1,650 Kcal per day. If this wrestler decreases his caloric intake by 1,000 Kcal per day, and increases the amount of training so that another 700 Kcal per day are lost, the goal weight will be met in 4½ weeks.

While at the present time the nutritional needs of athletes are no different than those of nonathletes, it seems clear there is a great need for practical suggestions that allow athletes to reach their potential and still maintain long-term health. It must be emphasized that it is not possible to compensate for an inadequate, inconsistent nutritional plan with physical conditioning, nor can superior nutrition compensate for inadequate training. Physicians, athletic trainers, coaches, and athletes must work as a team to create a positive environment while providing accurate information and advice in this area. Professional nutritional advice and support should be obtained whenever possible.

REFERENCES

1. Wheeler KB: Sports nutrition for the primary care physician: The importance of carbohydrate. *Phys Sports Med* 17(5):106–117, 1989.

2. Ivy J, Katz A, Cutler C, Sherman W, Coyle E: Muscle glycogen synthesis after exercise: Effect of time of carbohydrate ingestion. *J Appl Physiol* 64(4):1480–1485, 1988.

3. Coyl E, Coggan A, Hemmert M, Ivy J: Muscle glycogen utilization during prolonged strenuous exercise when fed carbohydrate. *J Appl Physiol* 61(1):165–172, 1986.

4. Hill J, Snook J, Mc Ardle W, Wilmore J: Commonly asked questions regarding nutrition and exercise: What does the scientific literature say. *Sports Science Exchange Roundtable*, Chicago: Gatorade Sports Science Institute, Fall 1992.

5. Bergstrom J, Hermansen L, Hultman E, Saltin B: Diet, muscle glycogen and physical performance. *Acta Physiol Scan* 71:140–150, 1967.

6. Burke L, Read R: Sports nutrition—Approaching the nineties. *Sports Med* 8(2):80–100, 1989.

7. Berning J, Steen S: *Sports Nutrition for the Nineties—The Health Professionals Handbook.* Gaithersburg, MD: Ashland Publishers, 1991.

8. Butterfield G, Lemon P, Evans W, Yarasheski K: Protein needs of the active person. *Sports Science Exchange Roundtable*, Chicago: Gatorade Sports Science Institute, Summer 1992.

9. Clark N: *Nancy Clark's Sports Nutrition Guidebook.* Champaign, Ill: Leisure Press, 1990.

10. Lemon P: Effect of exercise on protein requirements. *J Sports Sci* Summer:53–70, 1991.

11. McCarthy P: How much protein do athletes really need. *Phys Sports Med* 17(5):170–175, 1989.

12. Nelson M, Fisher E, Catsos P, Meredith C, Turksoy R, Evans W: Diet and bone status in amenorrheic runners. *Am J Clin Nutr* 43(6):910–916, 1986.

13. Coleman N: *Nutrition to Maximize your Performance* Van Nuys, CA: PM, 1990.

14. Bergstrom J, Hultman E, Jorfeldt L, Pernow B, Wahren J: Effect of nicotinic acid on physical working capacity and on metabolism of muscle glycogen in man. *J Appl Physiol* 26(2):170–176, 1969.

Thermal Injuries

While the focus in this chapter is on heat- and cold-related injuries, it is recognized that other environmental injuries/illness (i.e., topics related to altitude and air quality) are important. The reader should make an effort to research all other environmental topics as they relate to the athlete.

Heat Injuries

Heat injury is preventable, yet cases of heat exhaustion and death from heat stroke continue to occur and in sport, heat injury is as significant a factor in death as are head injuries. Between 1965 and 1981, football in the United States produced 81 heat-related deaths.[1] Another study reports 77 heat-stroke fatalities between 1959 and 1985 among amateur football players and 400 fatalities for football at all levels.[2] Education and constant vigilance have subsequently greatly reduced this figure, but cases still occur.

Football is particularly likely to be associated with heat problems, for a number of reasons. The protective gear effectively reduces the ability of a large portion of the body to dissipate heat, while the added weight actually increases the amount of heat produced, the helmet being a significant factor. In addition, football is often played during the spring and late summer when both temperature and humidity may be dangerously high. Football players are usually highly motivated and tend to overextend themselves, particularly if encouraged to do so by their coaches. Not to be forgotten is a myth that dies hard: "water deprivation makes the players tough!" Obviously anyone who attends to this myth has not read

any sports medicine or physiology text since 1970.[3] Rather, water deprivation causes the players to fatigue more easily and, thus, to be less effective. In actuality the "water deprivation myth" creates more injuries, increases attention loss, and causes significant loss of mental capacity of the sport participant. In fact what restricting fluids causes, which the charts usually do not show, is: a reduction in morale, a lack of vigor, glassy eyes, an apathetic attitude, a "don't-give-a-damn-for-anything" attitude, uncoordinated stumbling, and a shuffling gait.[4] Thus nothing is gained by withholding fluid, and athletes are better prepared if their mental-attentive levels are enhanced, fatigue is reduced, and injury predisposition is reduced by adequate fluid replacement.

Other sports are by no means exempt from the dangers of heat injury, particularly long-distance running, which has become increasingly popular with thousands of recreational athletes. (See Chapter 21.)

Physiology

In order to understand dehydration and heat illness, the function of water in the body and the shell-core concept must be understood. The core must maintain a narrow range of 36° to 40° C, whereas the shell can be exposed to 16° to 60° C in a dry environment and still maintain the internal body temperature. The body's temperature-regulation system is located in the hypothalamus. The regulatory functions of the hypothalamus include constancy of internal body temperature; management of autonomic control; interpretation of stimulus into emotion; control of feeding behaviors, sleeping patterns, and water balance; maintenance of feelings of sanity; and secretion of hormones.[5] Body temperature is almost entirely maintained through a system of stimulus receptors that work in conjunction with the hypothalamus. These sensory receptors are found in the skin, the preoptic area of the hypothalamus, and possibly in some internal organs of the body. The neurons of this area essentially receive and respond to the information yielded from the other receptor sites. Skin receptors and internal receptors found in some organs transmit their impulses to the central nervous system, where they are then relayed to the preoptic area of the hypothalamus, which in turn transmits to the posterior hypothalamus. It is this location that integrates the information to provide the heat-producing or heat-losing reactions of the body. There are both heat-sensitive and cold-sensitive neurons located in the hypothalamus that correlate specifically with the hot and cold receptors of the periphery and internal receptors. When a stimulus is received by the receptors of the hypothalamus from those of the periphery or from the viscera, the neurons increase their rate of firing, sometimes as much as tenfold with an increase of body temperature of 10° C. The messages relayed to the hypothalamus are in anticipation that their signals will induce the appropriate measures for maintaining the body's core temperature.[6]

According to Guyton, the thermostatic system employs three important mechanisms to reduce body heat when the temperature becomes too great:

1. In almost all areas of the body *the skin blood vessels are intensely dilated.* This is caused by inhibition of the sympathetic centers in the posterior hypothalamus that cause vasoconstriction. Full vasodilatation can increase the rate of heat transfer to the skin as much as eightfold.

2. *Sweating is strongly stimulated.* This effect is illustrated by a sharp increase in the rate of evaporative heat loss resulting from sweating when the body core rises above the critical temperature of 37° C. The increase in body temperature causes enough sweating to remove ten times the basal rate of body temperature.

3. Heat production by such mechanisms as shivering and chemical thermogenesis is strongly inhibited.

In contrast, in the cold state, the thermostatic mechanism institutes exactly opposite procedures:

1. *Skin vasoconstriction throughout the body* is caused by stimulation of the posterior hypothalamus sympathetic centers.

2. *Pilo-erection,* that is, hairs "standing on end." The upright projection of the hairs entraps a thick layer of insulator air next to the skin so that the transfer of heat to the surroundings is greatly depressed.

3. *Increase in heat production* by causing shivering, sympathetic excitation, and thyroxine.

When an athlete exercises, the body temperature rises and internal temperatures can reach 40° C. The harder the athlete exercises, the bigger the athlete, and the more subcutaneous fat present, the more heat is produced.[7]

Approximately 60 percent of the body is water. Water is stored in various sections of the body, with continual migration of water dependent upon priority criteria. Water is the universal solvent of the body and plays many essential roles in the body: controlling acid-base balance, sweating, dissolving electrolytes and maintaining the living cell. Water is also the transporter of nutrients, hormones, wastes, and antibodies.

The body is designed to work within a very narrow temperature range. It is constantly striving to keep the core temperature as close to 37° C (98.6° F) as possible. It does this by producing sweat, which, when it evaporates, causes the skin to cool. The important factor is that the sweat must change its form from water to vapor in order to dispose of body heat. Subcutaneous blood vessels dilate and blood is channeled to the skin, where it is cooled. Problems can develop if:

1. Sweat cannot easily *evaporate,* for example, if the humidity is high or if clothing inhibits air exchange.

2. The body is actually being heated by the environment, for example, with temperatures above 37.2° C (99° F). As the ambient temperature approaches the core temperature, it becomes more difficult to cool the body in an exercise state. This is especially true if the humidity level is also high.

3. Water loss from sweat and respiration is not replaced and dehydration occurs.

A combination of these three conditions in an exercising athlete can rapidly prove fatal.

Marathoners have been observed to lose more than 5 liters of fluid during a single race (or 1.5 to 2.5 liters of fluid each hour), and football players who do not replace their fluid may lose 7 to 10 kg (15 to 20 lb.) during the course of a double-day practice session. Unfortunately, the thirst stimulus producing the desire to replace lost fluid is totally inadequate for the body's needs. Athletes may get thirsty only when they are already in danger, and then they usually drink far less than is required. Heat production ranges from 1,000 to 1,500 Kcal per hour or more, and radiant heat can add another 150 Kcal per hour.

The distribution of the body's water changes during exercise, causing a transfer of water from extracellular spaces to intracellular, and the extracellular water is replaced by the water from blood plasma. This reduces the blood volume and urine production. This reduction of water can be cumulative over days, and a progressive dehydration occurs. Fluid loss is also the reason that heat exhaustions signs and symptoms resemble shock.

Certain drugs that facilitate heat-related injuries. Antihistamine drugs increase urine production and interfere with the sweating mechanism. Stimulants increase the metabolic rate and thus increase heat production. Nicotine causes peripheral vasoconstriction and thus reduces the body's ability to dispense the core's heat production.

Prevention

ACCLIMATIZATION: Several physiological changes occur during the process of heat acclimatization. These include the earlier onset of sweating and increased skin blood flow, which allows the temperature-regulating mechanism to come into play at a lower body temperature. Those unacclimatized will, therefore, reach a higher temperature before beginning to sweat adequately (Figure 26.1). The electrolyte content of sweat seems to vary, but is usually hypo-osmolar. With prolonged sweating there may be losses of 5 to 10 percent of the extracellular fluid sodium and chloride, and 1 to 2 percent of body potassium. (Sodium chloride loss is reduced in the athlete who is acclimatized.)

Heat acclimatization takes at least seven days, but can take many weeks. It occurs only if the athlete works out in the heat (Figure 26.2). Workouts should be carefully planned and supervised. They should be short, perhaps repeated twice a day, and then gradually increased in length and intensity, all the time ensuring adequate periods of rest and a copious supply of fluid. Clothing should be light in weight and color.

ENVIRONMENTAL CONDITIONS: Monitoring of atmospheric conditions is vital, so the coach can

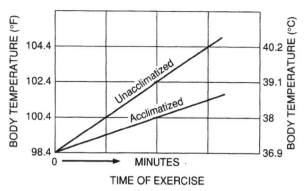

FIGURE 26.2

The effects of acclimatization on body temperature during exercise

judge the amount of work that can safely be handled during a particular workout session. Guesswork should be eliminated. It is necessary to know not only the temperature, but also the humidity and the relative humidity. Cases of severe heat injury have occurred at moderate temperatures but high humidity. It is therefore vitally important that the relative humidity be established so that a true picture of the situation can be obtained. A sophisticated apparatus for obtaining these readings is the wet bulb globe temperature (WBGT) (Table 26.1), but perhaps a more easily obtained and practical apparatus is the sling psychrometer, which measures the dry and the wet bulb temperatures and uses a scale to obtain the relative humidity (Figures 26.3 and 26.4).

CLOTHING: Football uniforms cover much of the available sweat-producing skin of the body. Those involved with the organization of practice sessions and workouts should see to it that modifications are made when the weather is hot and humid. Shorts and white t-shirts should be worn, frequent water breaks allowed, and practices scheduled for early morning and late evening and canceled when necessary. Net jerseys are very useful, as are workouts without helmets, as they allow an increased amount of skin surface to be ventilated and so aid in sweat evaporation and cooling. Any kind of sweatsuit used for the purpose of losing weight by sweating should by banned. These are highly dangerous and the weight lost, being water only, is temporary.

IDENTIFYING SUSCEPTIBLE ATHLETES: The physiology of each athlete varies, and so does each athlete's ability to adapt to and handle heat stress. Big athletes with large muscle mass seem particularly at risk, as

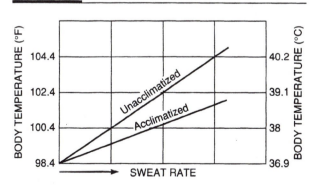

FIGURE 26.1

Representation of sweat rates in acclimatized and unacclimatized athletes

TABLE 26.1 *Planning and conducting practice sessions using a wet bulb temperature guide*

Wet Bulb Temperature	Precautions
Over 24°C (76°F +)	Postpone practice until cooler, or conduct limited practice in light clothing
21.6°C to 23.9°C (71° to 75°F)	Rest periods every 30 minutes—cold water as needed
18.9°C to 21.1°C (66° to 70°F)	Cold water every 20 to 30 minutes, observe carefully
16.1°C to 18.4°C (61° to 65°F)	Observe carefully, water break, no other restrictions
15.6°C (60°F) or below	Normal practice, no restrictions, fluids

Whenever relative humidity is above 95%, irrespective of the temperatures, precautions should be taken and the practice routine modified.

*Assumption = 80% Humidity

Adapted from E. R. Buskirk, *Sports Medicine*, ed. A. Ryan and F. Allman (New York: Academic Press, 1974), p. 211.

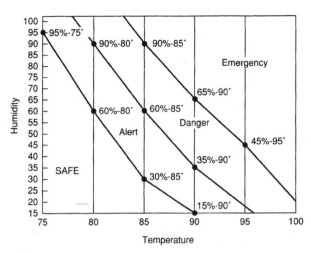

FIGURE 26.4

Temperature–humidity relationship
"Safe" temperature–humidity readings generally allow for normal activity.
(Adapted from the Weather Service Operations Manual.)

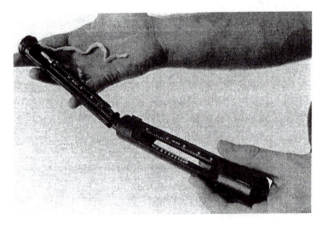

FIGURE 26.3

A sling psychrometer
The trainer should use an apparatus such as this regularly before and during any practice where there is concern that the temperature and/or humidity may be above the minimally acceptable limits.

are those with a thick layer of subcutaneous fat. Any athlete with a previous history of heat injury should take special precautions and should be carefully observed for early signs of a heat problem.

Athletes should be weighed before and after each practice session in order to pick out those who might be inadequately replacing their fluid loss. A loss of up to 3 percent of body weight (3 kg [6 lb] in a 100 kg [200 lb] athlete) is easily corrected with normal fluid replacement. Those who have lost 3 to 5 percent of body weight (3 kg to 5 kg [6 lb to 10 lb] in a 100 kg [200 lb] athlete) are in danger of inadequately replacing their water losses unless fluids are forced. They should have almost regained their normal weight before the next practice session. Those who have lost over 5 percent of body weight (more than 5 kg [10 lb] in a 100 kg [200 lb] athlete) are in danger of developing major heat problems and need to be educated; they have probably not been consuming adequate volumes of fluid. These athletes should be carefully observed on a daily basis to ensure that

1. No practice is undertaken until they have regained and maintained their weight

2. Gradual underhydration over several days and eventual predisposition to severe heat problems do not occur

It should be noted that older athletes, as well as some women, have a low tolerance to heat stress; they begin sweating at a higher temperature and it may take longer for their body temperatures to return to normal. Men do maintain a lower absolute threshold for the onset of sweating.[4] Children and adolescents are more susceptible to heat thermal injury because they have a greater ratio of surface area to body mass, which results in a greater affinity for heat gain or loss. Their metabolic rates are higher, sweating capacity is not as well adapted, and capacity to convey heat by blood from the core to the skin is reduced. Thus, children and young adolescents are at a greater risk than adults.

Numerous studies have suggested a gender difference in thermoregulation. More recent studies appear to indicate that there is little gender difference when aerobic capacities and intensity level are equal and surface area is considered. There may be a thermoregulatory difference during the menstrual cycle.[8]

FLUID REPLACEMENT: The single most important item in preventing heat injury is water. Small amounts of electrolytes may be added (sugar in any form will delay absorption and is not necessary in athletes exercising less than two or three hours), but it is the consumption of adequate quantities of water that has helped to radically reduce the incidence of serious heat-related injuries over the past few years.[9,10]

Athletes are easily educated in this area. They should be given a definite regimen to follow, with the understanding that bigger and heavier athletes need more water, as do athletes who are physiologically more susceptible to heat-induced problems. A suggested fluid intake scheme for preventing heat injuries follows:

1. Two hours before practice—1 liter (34 oz.)
2. Fifteen minutes before practice—400 to 500 milliliters (13–17 oz.)
3. Every 15 to 30 minutes during practice—400 to 500 milliliters (13–17 oz.)
4. After practice—5 to 6 large glasses of fluid

The fluid should be cold water (which has been proven to be more rapidly absorbed than warm water), the exception being during early acclimatization in very hot weather, when part of the replacement fluid may contain up to ten milli-equivalents of sodium and five milli-equivalents of potassium.

As mentioned, sugar should not be included in the fluids because it

1. Delays gastric emptying and water absorption
2. Causes a sense of fullness and sometimes nausea, which decreases the athlete's ability or desire to consume more fluids and so may actually precipitate dehydration.

3. Causes an outpouring of insulin, which results in a secondary hypoglycemic condition a while later (this may not apply to the continuously exercising athlete)

DIET: The diet should contain quantites of fresh salad and a variety of fruit. This helps replace many of the electrolytes that have been lost. During the acclimatization period, it may be useful to lightly salt the food, but this practice should not be continued once the adaptation period is over.

PREDISPOSING FACTORS: Numerous factors predispose an athlete to heat injury. Examples are low fitness level, antihistamine use, and infectious disease, diarrhea, nicotine use, reduced skin-area-to-body-mass ratio, and previous heat stroke.

It is the responsibility of those concerned with the health of the athlete to educate the coaches and the athletes in the prevention and dangers of heat injury, and to ensure that adequate steps are taken to minimize the possibility of such injury.

Heat-Injury Syndromes

Heat-injury syndromes include:

1. Heat cramps
2. Heat fatigue
3. Heat exhaustion
4. Heat stroke
5. Mixed heat-injury syndromes

Heat Cramps

The exact etiology and pathomechanics of heat cramps remain obscure. Numerous electrolytes have been indicted, including sodium, potassium, and magnesium. Empirically it has been observed that the incidence of cramps is reduced when fluid intake is adequate and the diet is adjusted to include bananas, oranges, fresh salads, and a sprinkling of table salt over the food. Always ensure that the athlete does not get behind in fluid replacement. Very few athletes have ever drunk too much water! The calf muscles usually cramp first, then the hamstring group.

Heat Fatigue (Heat Vasomotor Asthenia)

Heat fatigue applies to the unacclimatized athlete who rapidly becomes fatigued and weak when exposed to unusually high temperature or humidity. Recovery after exertion is also slower than normal, and allowance should be made for this. Heat fatigue is a common condition that usually stops short of the more serious problems, often because the athlete is aware of what is happening and tapers off in intensity and/or length of exercise. Treatment is adequate fluid replacement, keeping ahead of predicted fluid losses, adjustment of the diet to include many fresh salads and fruit, and adequate rest.

Heat Exhaustion

Heat exhaustion is caused by excessive water loss that has been inadequately replaced.

SYMPTOMS: A throbbing headache, nausea, hair erection on chest and upper arms, chills, unsteadiness, and fatigue. The athlete may become dizzy and lightheaded when he or she stops exercising or may suddenly collapse. (Collapse is due to the hypovolemia causing a sudden drop in blood pressure, which is usually maintained during exercise in spite of the lack of circulating volume.)

Rectal temperatures should be below 41° C (105.8° F); anything above this should be diagnosed as heat stroke. Usually temperatures range from 39° to 40.5° C (102.2° to 104.9° F). The pulse may be rapid, but more importantly, there is a limited pulse pressure (the range between the systolic and the diastolic pressure is small) and the blood pressure may fall rapidly when the athlete stands (orthostatis hypertension). The skin is usually cool and pale from vasoconstriction. The loss of fluid due to the body's attempt to cool itself through evaporation results in the *shock-like signs and symptoms*. Thus, even though these injuries usually occur in higher temperatures, there is often a cool and clammy feel to the skin. Sweating *usually* remains active. (If it is not active, consider the athlete to have heat stroke.) Sweating does *not* assure an athlete is not a heat stroke victim, especially if the athlete has *collapsed!*

TREATMENT: Intravenous fluids, electrolytes, and glucose because hypoglycemia is often present. Though cooling is not a primary requirement, the athletes should be kept in a cool place and iced towels may be applied.

Urine output and its appearance should be noted for at least twenty-four hours, as complications include delayed rhabdomyolysis with myoglobinuria and renal damage. An athlete who does not pass urine within six to twelve hours has acute renal failure and needs to be referred immediately.

Heat Stroke

Heat stroke implies failure of the body's heat-controlling mechanism and constitutes a dire emergency. The hypothalamus has essentially reset itself to a higher temperature; the situation is analogous to your adjusting the thermostat in your home because you believe the setting is improper.

SYMPTOMS: Heat stroke in athletes is usually the result of heat production from exercise plus the failure of heat-loss mechanisms. Dehydration is an important factor, but heat stroke can occur in the absence of dehydration. The first symptoms may be unusual behavior in the form of incoherent speech, disorientation, and acute confusion or aggressiveness, followed rapidly by unconsciousness. Onset can be rapid! The rectal temperature must be taken to help eliminate other causes of unusual behavior or sudden unconsciousness, such as heat exhaustion or hypoglycemia. Oral (cooled by rapid respiration) and axillary (cooled by wetting) temperatures are usually unreliable, and the classical temperature of 40.5° to 41° C or above probably did occur at the moment of collapse but is rarely measured at the site. It seems obvious that the evaluation of heat stroke may be safely proposed if the athlete has lost consciousness during exertion and demonstrates other signs and symptoms of heat stroke without the measured temperature.[11] Signs include the absence of sweating (though *sweating often persists until the latter phases of this injury*); peripheral vasodilatation with flushed warm skin; and a rapid (> 140), bounding pulse. The blood pressure shows a low diastolic reading and a wide pulse pressure.

TREATMENT: The reduction of the athlete's core temperature as rapidly as possible to 39° C or less (100° to 102° F) is vital, and ice-water immersion is the safest and most effective method to lower the core temperature. This procedure takes 10 to 40 minutes to achieve the required reduction. Ice-water immersion has been practiced for over fifteen years on 252 patients without one fatality at a facility in North Carolina.[2] The alternate method is to take the athlete out of the sun; remove most of his or her clothes; and apply wet cold towels to the trunk, abdomen, and extremities. Ice is then placed in liberal quantities onto the towels. Fanning to stimulate air flow is also useful. Care should be taken to protect and maintain the airway.

As soon as is practical, the athlete should be transferred to an emergency room that is adequately prepared to deal with this problem. Sufficient ice should be loaded onto the ambulance to last through the journey. The emergency room should be warned in advance of what to expect. If possible, an intravenous fluid solution should be started, but this is secondary to reducing the temperature.

If the athlete survives, there are a number of potential problems that manifest only after twenty-four hours, including acute renal failure, acute hepatic failure, rhabdomyolysis that causes blood coagulation defects, cerebral edema, and myocardial infarction.[12]

Mixed Heat-Injury Syndromes

An athlete may present with symptoms and signs associated with both heat exhaustion and heat stroke. He or she needs to be cooled rapidly and requires fluid replacement (Table 26.2).

The athletic trainer needs to appreciate any heat stress signs or symptoms and respond immediately. In addition, in humid climates the skin is usually moist and clammy. The athlete could be in a *heat stroke* situation because the high humidity has disallowed evaporation to occur. **Act immediately if any signs of heat stress occur!**

Cold Injuries

Cold injuries, or hypothermia, is defined simply as the lowering of the core-body temperature. The core temperature must remain within a relatively narrow range to assure body efficiency. With cold exposure, this range becomes even narrower (one to two degrees below normal) than with hyperthermia, and the body will readily sacrifice blood flow to the peripheral structures to maintain this narrow core temperature range. Thus, cold injuries may present with peripheral problems such as frostbite, where a finger or toe is affected, or a central problem, where a few degrees reduction in the body's core temperature creates a serious or even fatal condition. Shivering is the initial response to cold and usually occurs around 35° C (96° F), but if the body's core temperature falls below 34° C (93° F), shivering (involuntary muscular contractions) may cease and death from hypothermia may rapidly occur. At 32° C temperature regulation is seriously disturbed and there is an accelerated fall in the core temperature. Below 30° C a dangerous threshold is passed and the heart develops fibrillation (Figure 26.5).

Cold injuries are most likely to occur when there is a combination of cold plus wind; cold by itself is not

TABLE 26.2 *Symptoms and signs of heat injury*

	Heat Fatigue	Heat Exhaustion	Heat Stroke
Symptoms	Hot, fatigue	Fatigue, nausea	Disorientation, headache, incoherent speech
Mental status	Clear	Usually conscious, may faint (perhaps from orthostatic hypotension)	Confused or unconscious
Rectal temperature	38–39.5°C (100.4–103°F)	40°C + (104°F)	41°C + (105.8°F)
Skin	Flushed	Pale	Flushed
Sweat	+ +	+ +	May not be sweating (but may sweat with heat stroke)
Blood pressure		Narrow pulse pressure; may drop suddenly on standing	Low diastolic pressure with wide pulse pressure
Treatment	Oral fluids, allow to cool down	Give intravenous fluids, electrolytes and glucose, cool with ice	Cool with ice, give intravenous fluids, transfer to emergency room

Adapted from Peter G. Hanson, "Heat Injury in Runners," *Physician and Sportsmedicine* 7:6:93, June 1979.

Effect of cold temperatures on the human body

96.8°F (36°C) to 98.6°F (37°C)	Normal range
Below 96.8°F (36°C) to 93.2°F (34°C)	Slightly hypothermic
Below 93.2°F (34°C) to 89.6°F (32°C)	Temperature regulation system disturbed
Below 89.6°F (32°C) to 82.4°F (28°C)	Dangerously low (possible cardiac fibrillation)
Below 82.4°F (28°C) to 78°F (26°C)	Death upon prolonged exposure

FIGURE 26.5

Effect of cold temperatures on the human body
(Adapted from: E. F. Dubois, *Fever and Regulation of Body Temperatures.* Springfield, Ill: Charles C. Thomas, 1948.)

nearly as dangerous. For instance, –1° C (30° F) is not particularly cold, but if the wind is blowing at 35 miles per hour, the chill factor will reduce the actual temperature to –20.5° C (–50° F) (See Table 26.3). The effects of both cold and wind are intensified if the athlete is also wet and exhausted. In addition, an athlete who has previously suffered from a cold injury is more susceptible.

The insidious aspects of hypothermia may be the most dangerous because, as body temperature gradually falls, the athlete starts to lose coordination. More importantly, the loss of heat to the brain creates impaired judgement. This may be the only noticeable factor and one of which the hypothermic athlete will be unaware. In many situations, any other participants who could observe that an athlete is mentally impaired are also cold. Thus the others exposed to hypothermic effects cannot make rational judgments and treat the hypothermic athlete. Those exposed to cold effects and lowering of core temperature are in a situation analogous to intoxicated individuals treating themselves.

Hypothermia

Heat loss mechanisms are convection, evaporation, radiation, and conduction. Athletes may be more susceptible to hypothermia than others for the following reasons:

1. Convection is the loss of heat from air movement over the surface, and athletes participating in many sports wear a minimal amount of clothing, especially during competition, allowing bare skin to accelerate the heat loss via convection.

2. Wet clothing increases heat loss twenty-fold. Wet clothing, especially absorbent materials like cotton, loses 90 percent of its insulation properties once it

becomes wet. Wool is a better choice, as are many of the newer nonabsorbent materials, to reduce wetting and loss of insulation.

3. Many athletes rarely wear any insulation for the head, and up to 40 percent loss of heat occurs through radiation from the head.

4. The exercising athlete is shunting a significant amount of blood to the extremities during his or her participation. This vasodilatation to the periphery (shell) results in great heat loss.

5. Athletes are generally lean, and the lack of subcutaneous fat—the body's natural insulation—is reduced.

6. Fluid loss through evaporation reduces the blood volume, reducing central circulation of the blood's heating benefits.

7. Exercising may replace or mask the initial sign of hypothermia, shivering. Thus, the athlete may progress into a lower body temperature insidiously.

8. Most athletes prepare for extreme cold, but most hypothermic conditions occur around 10° C (50° F) and many athletes tend to not modify their training and clothing sufficiently for this temperature range. Also certain sport regulations do not take into account environmental factors and require accompanying clothing adjustments for competing athletes.

9. Unfortunately, in certain sports a significant number of players use spit tobacco. Nicotine creates vasoconstriction to the peripheral structures, especially the distal components, thus exposing the user to peripheral cold injury (i.e., frostbite).

SYMPTOMS: The victim is considered to be suffering from severe hypothermia if any of the following signs or symptoms is present:

1. Depressed vital signs

2. Altered level of consciousness

3. Body temperature of 90° F (32° C) or less

4. Lack of shivering (even though the victim is cold)

5. Presence of associated significant illness or injury

PREVENTION: The athlete should be educated in the dangers of the wind chill factor in the causation of hypothermia and other cold injuries. He or she should be taught how to dress for cooler weather and should realize that multiple layers of clothing help trap air and are more effective in insulating the body than is one thick layer. Because a significant percentage of the body's heat is lost from the surface area of the head, special attention should be paid to its insulation. Frostbite

TABLE 26.3 *Wind chill chart*

Wind (mph)	Temperature (Fahrenheit)																				
Calm	40°	35°	30°	25°	20°	15°	10°	5°	0°	-5°	-10°	-15°	-20°	-25°	-30°	-35°	-40°	-45°	-50°	-55°	-60°
	Equivalent Chill Temperature																				
5	35°	30°	25°	20°	15°	10°	5°	0°	-5°	-10°	-15°	-20°	-25°	-30°	-35°	-40°	-45°	-50°	-55°	-65°	-70°
10	30°	20°	15°	10°	5°	0°	-10°	-15°	-20°	-25°	-35°	-40°	-45°	-50°	-60°	-65°	-70°	-75°	-80°	-90°	-95°
15	25°	15°	10°	5°	-5°	-10°	-20°	-25°	-30°	-40°	-45°	-50°	-60°	-65°	-70°	-80°	-85°	-90°	-100°	-105°	-110°
20	20°	10°	5°	0°	-10°	-15°	-25°	-30°	-35°	-45°	-50°	-60°	-65°	-75°	-80°	-85°	-95°	-100°	-105°	-115°	-120°
25	15°	10°	0°	-5°	-15°	-20°	-30°	-35°	-45°	-50°	-60°	-65°	-75°	-80°	-90°	-95°	-105°	-110°	-120°	-125°	-135°
30	10°	5°	0°	-10°	-20°	-25°	-30°	-40°	-50°	-55°	-65°	-70°	-80°	-85°	-95°	-100°	-105°	-115°	-120°	-130°	-140°
35	10°	0°	-5°	-10°	-20°	-25°	-35°	-40°	-50°	-60°	-65°	-75°	-80°	-90°	-100°	-105°	-115°	-120°	-130°	-135°	-145°
40*	10°	0°	-5°	-15°	-20°	-30°	-35°	-45°	-55°	-60°	-70°	-75°	-85°	-95°	-100°	-110°	-110°	-125°	-130°	-140°	-150°

Little danger

Increasing danger
(Flesh may freeze within one minute)

Great danger
(Flesh may freeze within 30 seconds)

*Winds above 40 mph have little additional effect.

prevention is essential for areas that are farthest from the deep organs and large muscle groups, especially the nose, ears, cheeks, fingers, and toes. Fingers and toes are at particular risk of developing frostbite if shoes or gloves are too tight, especially if they are wet. Therefore, a spare pair of dry socks and mittens should be available if the possibility of cold or rain is present. The greatest concern in athletics is the wetting of clothing. When clothes are wet, there is a twenty-fold increase in heat transfer (loss). Sweating saturates the clothes from the inside and participation in wet conditions soaks the clothes from the outside, making the athlete more susceptible to hypothermia. The athlete should wear an outer garment in wet and windy weather to reduce the convection loss by the wind and to reduce or eliminate the saturation of the clothing.

Organizers of long-distance races should be aware of the slow runner (or the cross-country skier) at the back of the pack who may still be on the course after some of the aid stations have closed. This athlete will probably be exhausted and, thus, highly susceptible to cold injury.

TREATMENT: Treatment of the hypothermic patient requires special facilities and is best performed in an intensive care unit. Immediate transfer to the nearest hospital should therefore be undertaken.

Frostbite

In the typical competitive athletic situation, frostbite injuries are quite rare. In some outdoor activities in northern and/or high-altitude locations it is a possibility. In recreational adventure activities the athletic trainer can contribute his/her expertise by counseling these athletes on the hazards of this type of injury.

Frostbite is an injury to a part of the body (mainly the feet, hands, ear, and nose) that is exposed to intensely cold air or liquids. The tissue is actually injured by formation of ice crystals and obstructions of the blood supply.

In most cases, the athletic trainer should be able to recognize the danger of impending frostbite and prevent any serious problems. However on some occasions, the recreational athlete may not have been aware of the predisposing conditions and will present with an already-established case of frostbite.

The five stages of frostbite, in order of increasing severity, are:

Stage 1—initial biting cold, numbness, and some redness and puffiness

Stage 2—more puffiness (edema), violet coloration, and then color progressing to a yellowish-white

Stage 3—rose-violet coloration, blisters; skin may become puffed and shiny

Stage 4—blisters break, tissue scars and peels to second layer of skin

Stage 5—blisters dry, blacken, and slough off

TREATMENT: If an athlete has early signs of frostbite (mild blanching of the skin), the part may be warmed by simply blowing through cupped hands onto the skin or by placing the extremity in the armpit and using body heat for warming. Rubbing the part with hands or with snow may cause permanent injury.

If frostbite is deep, the part requires rewarming and should not be further exposed to the cold.[13] The warming consists of placing the part in a water bath controlled to between 40° to 42° C (104° to 108° F), and the rewarming should be continued until normal color has returned to the entire area. The container should be large enough to allow movement of the part without contact with the sides. Dry heat is not advisable, and even brief exposure to high temperatures can result in serious damage.

REFERENCES

1. Francis K, Feinstein R, Brasher J: Optimal practice times for the reduction of risk of heat illness during fall football practice in the southeastern united states. *J Athletic Training* 26(1):76–80, 1991.

2. Costrini A: Emergency treatment of exertional heat stroke and comparison of whole body cooling techniques. *Med Sci Sports Exerci* 22(1):15–18, 1990.

3. Noakes TD: Fluid replacement during exercise. In *Exercise and Science reviews*, edited by Holloszy JO. Baltimore: Williams & Wilkins, 21:297–330, 1993.

4. Noble BJ: *Physiology of Exercise and Sport.* St. Louis: Times Mirror/Mosby College, 1986.

5. Marieb EN: *Human Anatomy and Physiology.* Redwood City, CA: Benjamin/Cummings Publishing Co., 1992.

6. Guyton AC: *Textbook of Medical Physiology.* Philadelphia: WB Saunders, pp. 886–906, 1986.

7. Wyndham CH, Strydom NB: The danger of an inadequate water intake during marathon running. *S Afr Med J* 43:893–896, 1969.

8. Stehenson LA, Kolka MA: Thermoregulation in women. In *Exercise and Science Reviews*, edited by Holloszy JO. Baltimore: Williams & Wilkins, 21:231–262, 1993.

9. Foster C, Costill DL, Fink WJ: Gastric emptying characteristics of glucose and glucose polymer solutions. *Res Q Exerc Sport* 51:299–305, 1980.

10. Murphy RJ, Matthews DK: Water is the key to heat problems. *Medical Opinion,* July 1976, p 39.

11. Shapiro Y, Seidman DS: Field and clinical observations of exertional heat stroke patients. *Med Sci Sports Exerci* 22(1):6–14, 1990.

12. Costrini AM, Pitt HA, Gustafson AB, et al: Cardiovascular and metabolic manifestations of heat stroke and severe heat exhaustion. *Am J Med* 66:296–302, 1979.

13. Mills Jr, WJ: Out in the cold. *Emergency Med* 8:134–147, 1976.

RECOMMENDED READINGS

American College of Sports Medicine position statement on prevention of heat injuries during distance running. *Med Sci Sports* 7:VII–IX, 1975.

Christensen, CL, Ruhling RO: Thermoregulatory responses during a marathon—a case of a woman runner. *Br J Sports Med* 14:131–132, 1980.

Costill DL: *A Scientific Approach to Distance Running.* Los Altos, Tafnews, 1979.

Costill DL, Coté R, Miller E, et al: Water and electrolyte replacement during repeated days of work in the heat. *Aviat Space Environ Med* 46:795–800, 1975.

Costill DL, Sparks KE: Rapid fluid replacement following thermal dehydration. *J Appl Physiol* 34:299–303, 1973.

Hanson PG: Heat injury in runners. *Phys Sports Med* 7:91–96, June 1979.

Hubbard RW: An introduction: The role of exercise in the etiology of exertional heatstroke. *Med Sci Sports Exerci* 22(1):2–5, 1990.

Maron MB, Wagner JA, Horvath SM: Thermoregulatory responses during competitive marathon running, *J Apply Physiol* 42:909–914, 1977.

Murphy RJ: Heat illness. *J Sports Med* 1:26–29, 1973.

Pugh LG, Corbett JL, Johnson RH: Rectal temperatures, weight losses and sweat rates in marathon running. *J Appl Physiol* 23:347–352, 1967.

Wyndham CH: Heatstroke and hyperthermia in marathon runners. *Ann NY Acad Sci* 301:128–138, 1977.

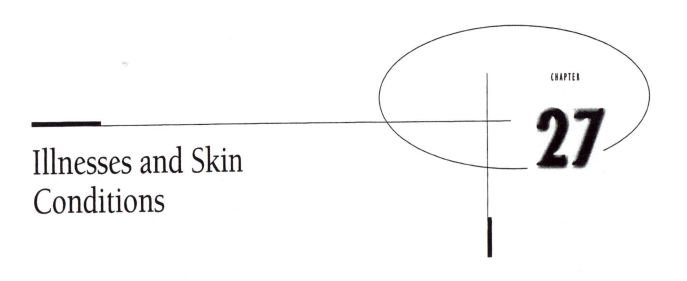

27

Illnesses and Skin Conditions

The Medical Examination and the Trainer

The trainer is often faced with a barrage of complaints, ranging in seriousness from pre-event hypochondriasis to acute emergency, and finds himself or herself in a position similar to that of a triage physician. However, the trainer is not a physician and must not be tempted to practice medicine.

The trainer's responsibility is clear: to evaluate the athlete's problem and refer as appropriate. To adequately assess a complaint, the trainer needs to:

1. Evaluate the history the athlete presents. In order to do this the trainer needs to be informed of the common medical possibilities.
2. Undertake a screening examination to rule out serious conditions and be able to decide on the correct timing of the referral.
3. Have the necessary academic background to communicate with the physician on each referral.

By constantly striving to adequately evaluate each problem, the trainer will advance and expand professionally and become increasingly satisfied with his or her role in the health care of the athlete.

Following is an outline of the medical screening examination of the upper respiratory tract, the chest, and the abdomen.

Examination of an Athlete with Symptoms Related to the Upper Respiratory Tract

The examination of symptoms related to the upper respiratory tract includes taking the temperature and the resting pulse. The throat should be examined for redness, the tonsils for possible exudate, and the neck for tender cervical lymph nodes. Examination of the ears should include the canal and the tympanic membrane. The trainer should become familiar with the appearance of a normal tympanic membrane, so that he or she can recognize when it is inflamed, bulging, or opaque (Figure 27.1).

Examination of the Chest

The trainer should always consult a physician if the athlete presents with severe chest pain. In evaluating a chest complaint, two important conditions need to be kept in mind:

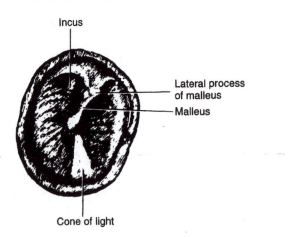

Incus

Lateral process of malleus

Malleus

Cone of light

FIGURE 27.1
The tympanic membrane, as seen through an otoscope

1. *Pneumothorax.* Pneumothorax presents with sudden pain in the chest and shortness of breath. It may occur spontaneously or it may follow closed chest trauma such as a fracture of the ribs. A penetrating injury (such as a stab from a sharp object) can puncture the lung and cause bleeding in addition to the pneumothorax (*hemopneumothorax*).

Signs include poor air entry to one part of the lung. This is detected by asking the athlete to breathe in deeply and comparing the quality and intensity of the breath sounds in corresponding areas on both the left and the right sides of the chest. If one lung is collapsed, the breath sounds may be decreased or absent on the affected side. Percussion of the chest may reveal increased resonance in the case of a pneumothorax or decreased resonance in the case of a hemothorax.

2. *Asthma.* Characteristics of asthma are wheezing and difficulty in breathing. These occur when the bronchi become narrowed by swelling, spasm, or by mucus secretions. Clinical detection is by the presence of wheezing heard throughout the chest on both inspiration and expiration. Mild asthma may present as a dry nonproductive cough without audible wheezing.

Examination of an Athlete with Abdominal Pain

The examiner should be very gentle when evaluating an abdominal complaint. The examination should start with palpating away from the area of discomfort. General palpation reveals if the abdomen is soft and where the tenderness is located. The examiner should carefully feel for possible tenderness or enlargement of the liver or spleen, and for any abnormal masses. This is best done with the abdomen relaxed and the athlete inhaling deeply and rhythmically.

SIGNS:

1. Localized tenderness.

2. Guarding—contraction of the abdominal musculature when a tender area is palpated.

3. Rigidity—involuntary contraction of the abdominal muscles which precludes the examiner from palpating through the muscles. Rigidity is usually due to a serious underlying pathological condition.

4. Rebound tenderness—this test for abdominal peritoneal irritation should be performed very gently. The tender area should be palpated and the hand withdrawn; if positive for rebound tenderness, withdrawal of the hand causes more pain than did the downward pressure. To be certain this maneuver does not cause excessive discomfort, the abdomen should first be gently percussed. The percussion will produce a very mild form of rebound, and, if positive, the regular rebound test need not be performed. If rebound tenderness is present, the patient should immediately be referred for surgical consultation (Figure 27.2).

5. The athlete should also be asked to "blow out" or protrude the abdomen. If unable to do so because of pain, it may again signify a serious problem.

There are many causes of abdominal pain, but the trainer should be familiar with the presenting symptoms and signs of the more common serious conditions. With *appendicitis,* the athlete usually presents with nausea, vomiting, and abdominal pain. There is tenderness either in the central abdominal area or, classically, over

FIGURE 27.2
The rebound test for peritoneal irritation
(a) Downward pressure is applied to the tender area (b) If releasing the pressure causes an increase in the pain, peritoneal irritation should be suspected.

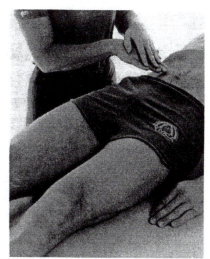

(a)   (b)

the area midway between the umbilicus and the anterior superior iliac spine on the right side (McBurney's point). A *pelvic infection* in the female athlete may present with tenderness in both iliac fossae. An athlete with *gastric discomfort* or a *gastric ulcer* will complain of epigastric pain and discomfort, particularly related to certain foods, and the epigastrium may be tender (Figure 27.3).

Evaluation of the tender abdomen is far from easy, even for experienced physicians. Always refer the athlete if there is any doubt about the significance of the symptoms or signs.

Illnesses as they Affect the Competing Athlete

Respiratory Infections

THE COMMON COLD: The common cold is due to one of the viruses that affect the upper respiratory tract and is a self-limiting condition.

Prevention. There is no indication at this time that any medication or vitamin prevents the common cold. It has been said that large quantities of vitamin C may do so, but the evidence is considered doubtful.

There is no doubt, however, that one of the precipitating factors in the onset of a cold in the competing athlete is overfatigue. The development of an upper respiratory infection may indicate that the athlete is being overtrained and should be given a few days to recover before resuming workouts.

Colds seem to occur more frequently in families or athletes living together. It would therefore be reasonable to partially isolate an affected athlete from the rest of the team.

Screening Examination. Screening should include taking the temperature, counting the resting pulse, examining the pharynx, and inspecting the tympanic membranes. The cervical area should be palpated for enlarged lymph nodes. If the athlete is engaged in contact sports, the abdomen should be examined to exclude the presence of an enlarged spleen or liver.

Laboratory Investigations. Ordinarily no laboratory tests are required. Should a sore throat be present, however, a throat evaluation by rapid streptococcal test, culture, or DNA probe should be performed. A complete blood count (CNC) and a monospot test should be ordered if one suspects that the condition is due to infectious mononucleosis.

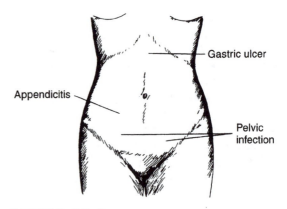

FIGURE 27.3
Differential diagnosis of abdominal pain—areas of tenderness palpation

Treatment. Oral decongestants that do not cause drowsiness may be used. Many antihistamines cause some degree of drowsiness and are therefore not indicated for the competing athlete. Nonsedating prescription antihistamines are preferable. Nasal sprays and nose drops are effective and nonsystemic, but have the disadvantage of causing rebound swelling of the nasal mucous membrane if used for more than a few days. This may lead to more serious nasal stuffiness than before treatment was started. Throat lozenges and gargles, as well as acetominophen or ibuprofin, are useful for sore throat and fever. Antibiotics do not affect the virus; however, bacteria frequently invade areas infected by viruses, especially after 72 hours. If this occurs, antibiotics are indicated to deal with that particular bacterium.

Guidelines For Participation with a Viral Infection. Probably the most important criterion is whether the athlete feels motivated to compete. If the athlete feels too ill, he or she should not be coerced into participation. Many simple viral infections can be worsened by competition, and the athlete should therefore be advised to consider withdrawing if he or she feels ill. On the other hand, if the athlete wants to participate in spite of the infection, the following guidelines as to whether or not he or she should compete may be used:

1. Fever below approximately 102°F (39°C)
2. Resting pulse below 100 beats per minute
3. No complicating features such as infectious mononucleosis

If these guidelines are met, then it is probably permissible for the athlete to participate. It should be remembered, however, that these are rough guidelines only. No definite figures can be given, and each case should be judged individually.

SORE THROAT: A sore throat is commonly due to

1. Viral infection which is part of an upper respiratory infection
2. Streptococcal infection
3. Infectious mononucleosis

Sometimes two of these three may coexist. For instance, it is common to find a streptococcal infection in a patient with infectious mononucleosis. It should be emphasized that the symptoms of a sore throat, whether due to a streptococcal infection or to a virus, are the same. As mentioned before, antibiotics do not influence the course of a viral infection, and a viral sore throat can indeed be very painful and distressing to the athlete.

Investigations. It is advisable to obtain a rapid streptococcal test, throat culture, or DNA probe. A complete blood count and monospot test may be useful as well.

Treatment. Treatment is with the appropriate antibiotic if a streptococcal infection is present. This is usually penicillin unless the athlete is sensitive to it (drug allergy histories should always be obtained), in which case erythromycin should be used. Gargles and throat lozenges may be used as needed, as well as acetominophen or ibuprofin for fever and pain.

CANKER SORES: Canker sores are little ulcers that appear along the gum margins and on the mucous membrane of the mouth. They can be painful and cause considerable distress. Some athletes are susceptible to them and have recurrent attacks. There are two common types of canker sores, namely herpetic ulcers and aphthous ulcers. These may be identical in appearance, although in general aphthous ulcers are deeper and more irregular in shape.

There is no specific therapy for aphthous ulcers. Herpetic ulcers can be treated with oral acyclouir, which may speed healing somewhat. Symptomatic measures include use of a local anaesthetic topical agent and avoidance of acidic foods such as tomatoes, which tend to increase the discomfort.

OTITIS MEDIA: Otitis media is often secondary to an upper respiratory infection in which there is swelling of the mucous membranes. This causes a partial or a complete block of the eustachian tube (the connection between the middle ear and the pharynx). Blockage of this tube allows fluid to accumulate in the middle ear, predisposing it to infection, and also prevents equalization of pressure between the middle ear and the atmosphere.

Symptoms. Pain in the middle ear, a blocked feeling in the ear, and sometimes a decrease in hearing.

Signs. The pharynx may be inflamed and there is usually redness and perhaps a bulging of the tympanic membrane (though it might be opaque in cases where there is an accumulation of fluid without actual infection in the middle ear).

Treatment. An antibiotic is required if there is an infection. In addition, decongestants and nasal spray (for a very limited time only) are used to try to shrink the mucous membranes and open the eustachian tubes.

The athlete should be shown how to perform the *Valsalva maneuver* if there is fluid in the middle ear after the acute infection is over. This maneuver is designed to open the eustachian tubes, equalize pressure, and allow drainage. The nose is held shut and the athlete attempts to blow out against a closed mouth and nose, thereby increasing the pressure in the pharynx and middle ear. At the same time the pressure is being increased, the athlete should swallow. The increase in pressure should not cause pain or discomfort. This maneuver may be performed a number of times a day.

SINUSITIS: One of the commonest reasons for a cold's continuing over a protracted period of time is sinusitis secondary to an upper respiratory infection.

During an upper respiratory infection, the mucous membranes that line the sinuses swell. There is an outpouring of fluid which is normally cleared by the tiny hairs lining the sinuses that sweep the excess fluid toward the sinus opening. If these hairs are immobilized by a secondary bacterial infection, or if so much fluid is produced that it cannot be removed, sinusitis develops.

Symptoms. The main symptoms are facial pain, headache, blocked nose, and at times fever.

Treatment. Treatment includes an antibiotic. Oral decongestants can be helpful, as can a limited course (three to four days only) of a decongestant nasal spray. Antihistamines may help underlying allergy symptoms, but may adversely thicken secretions and inhibit necessary drainage. Corticosteroid nasal sprays can decrease inflammation and improve management of underlying allergies.

BRONCHITIS: Bronchitis is commonly part of a viral upper respiratory infection which becomes secondarily infected by bacteria, or on occasion it may be due to the mycoplasmal organism.

Symptoms and Signs. Fever, a hacking cough, and the production of phlegm (which may be purulent) are the main symptoms. The infection may precipitate the onset of asthma in those susceptible to the development of this condition.

Treatment. An antibiotic is indicated if a bacterial secondary infection exists, or if mycoplasma is a suspected organism. A cough mixture and a decongestant-expectorant may also be indicated.

PNEUMONIA: In the athlete, pneumonia is most commonly due to mycoplasma or a virus. On occasion, the classical pneumococcal pneumonia may occur. Investigations should include a chest X-ray, a sputum culture, and a white blood count (WBC). When mycoplasma is the responsible agent, X-ray changes may be more extensive than the clinical examination would lead one to suspect.

Treatment. The appropriate antibiotic is usually erythromycin for mycoplasma, penicillin for pneumococcal pneumonia, or sometimes amoxicillin. (In less clear-cut cases newer marcrolide or cephalosporin antibiotics may provide an extended spectrum of antimicrobial coverage.)

Systemic Viral Infections

VIRAL HEPATITIS: Viral hepatitis does not occur frequently in athletes. However, an outbreak in a team that is living together can have devastating results, as occurred with members of the Holy Cross football team. Ninety-three percent of the team were found to be infected.[1,2]

Etiology. At this time it is thought that there are three groups of etiologic agents:

1. Hepatitis A virus
2. Hepatitis B virus
3. Hepatitis due to a group of non-A and non-B agents (Hepatitis C, enteric non-A/non-B, hepatitis delta virus).

It is known that the hepatitis A virus is usually transferred via the intestinal-oral route, while the hepatitis B virus is transmitted in a number of ways (via blood and blood products, saliva, sexual intercourse, and needle puncture) but not via the intestinal-oral route.

Approximately 80 percent of non-A, non-B hepatitis is due to hepatitis C, which is spread via blood products, sexual contact, and possibly via unknown types of person-to-person contact. Hepatitis delta virus causes hepatitis only in conjunction with concurrent hepatitis B infection. Enteric non-A/non-B is spread by the fecal-oral route and is similar to hepatitis A.

Symptoms and Signs. Initially the athlete complains of some fatigue, lethargy, and abdominal discomfort. Nausea and an aversion to food, particularly meat, may then be noted. The urine becomes progressively darker in color, approaching dark brown. Stools may become very light or clay colored. A yellow tinge is seen in the conjunctiva in daylight. (Note that this yellow tinge may not be seen if the athlete is examined under an ordinary light bulb.)

Prevention. If the athlete is a member of a team, particularly if the team is living together, blood should be drawn from every team member for a full laboratory examination. If the virus is not found to be type B, it is suggested that standard immune serum globulin (ISG) be given to all the team members. This has been found to prevent the illness from developing in 80 to 90 percent of exposed persons as long as it is given within one to two weeks of exposure. Close contacts of those with the B virus (e.g., spouses) may choose to have hepatitis B immune globulin (HBIG). Hepatitis B vaccine may be indicated in ongoing close contacts.

Treatment. Treatment for most types of hepatitis is largely supportive, with fluids, rest, and good nutrition. Good sanitation and personal hygiene are particularly important in preventing spread. In parenteral types of infection (hepatitis B and hepatitis C) follow-up lab work is necessary to monitor development of immunity. Infectious hepatitis A does not lead to chronic infection.

A team member who is suffering from infectious hepatitis should not share a room with another team member and should not actively participate until the symptoms and signs have returned to normal.

INFECTIOUS MONONUCLEOSIS: Infectious mononucleosis is one of the commonest, and possibly one of the most overtreated, illnesses occurring in young adults. Having said that, it is necessary to point out that serious complications can occur in the occasional case.

Etiology. Most cases of infectious mononucleosis are due to infection from the Epstein-Barr virus. The remainder of the cases are probably due to the cytomegalovirus or other viruses.

Symptoms and Signs. Sore throat and fatigue are the commonest symptoms. Any young athlete presenting with these symptoms should be suspected of having infectious mononucleosis, though of course these symptoms are completely nonspecific and might represent numerous viral or other diseases. Headache and mild generalized aching are also common symptoms. Fever is present in most but not all cases.

Lymph node enlargement is often prominent. The pharynx is usually red and the tonsils are often enlarged, frequently developing characteristic patches of white exudate. Swelling around the eyes and pinpoint red patches on the palate are also characteristic signs.

The abdomen should be carefully palpated to assess if there is splenic or hepatic enlargement. Jaundice develops in about 10 percent of cases.

One of the special features of infectious mononucleosis is a maculopapular rash which may develop if amoxicillin is taken. This antibiotic is therefore avoided in an athlete with suspected infectious mononucleosis unless there are specific indications for its use.

Laboratory Investigations. A throat swab should always be taken initially, as at least 10 to 20 percent of cases are secondarily infected with streptococcus. The white blood cell count is the most commonly performed test, but the results vary depending on the stage of the disease. In the beginning, the count can be quite normal in 50 percent of the cases (5,000 to 10,000 cells per cubic millimeter); in 25 percent of the cases this figure may be less and in 25 percent it may be more. Atypical lymphocytes are also an important finding, as is a large increase in the total number of lymphocytes found on the differential count. An elevated sedimentation rate may also be present.

A positive heterophile antibody test (the mono spot test) is another important test and is fairly conclusive evidence of the diagnosis, but it should always be considered in conjunction with the blood count and with the clinical findings, as it may not become positive for up to three weeks in some cases. Liver function tests are often abnormal.

Treatment. Throat lozenges, acetominophen or ibuprofin for fever, and penicillin in cases of a positive throat culture for streptococcus are the only forms of treatment usually necessary. The use of corticosteroids is controversial. Some physicians use them when tonsillar swelling and throat pain are severe; others feel that they are never appropriate.

Complications. The most well-known complication is *splenic rupture,* and for this reason athletes are kept out of contact participation for four weeks or longer.[3] There are also other complications. Death from infectious mononucleosis occurs every now and then, particularly from agranulocytosis and pneumonitis (Table 27.1).

Hypertension

Hypertension implies blood pressure above "normal" limits as defined by age. Blood pressure is expressed as the systolic over the diastolic pressure (e.g., 120/70).

PREDISPOSING FACTORS: A history of high blood pressure in the family, particularly in the father or mother, increases the chances of an athlete's developing hypertension. This is even more significant if the athlete is black, as blacks have a higher rate of hypertension than the rest of the population. The reason for this is obscure at the present time.

Excessive salt intake (sodium chloride) is thought to be associated with the development of hypertension. Congenital abnormalities of the aorta (e.g., coarctation of the aorta) can produce hypertension that is subject to surgical correction, as is partial blockage of one of the renal arteries.

Raised blood pressure in an athlete is often detected during the physical examination. It is frequently difficult to decide if a particular reading is significant, and sometimes readings need to be repeated on a number of separate occasions while the athlete is resting in order to establish the base-line figures.

TABLE 27.1 *Criteria for return to activity after infectious mononucleosis*

1. Temperature should be normal.
2. Sore throat should be considerably improved.
3. There should be a general feeling of well-being.
4. There should be a decrease in the size of the spleen.
5. At least three to four weeks should have elapsed from the onset to return to activity.

Though these guidelines are clinical, they are very useful and should be used in conjunction with the WBC and differential count, the sedimentation rate, and the liver function tests.

The following are guidelines evaluating blood pressure when the athlete is at rest.

Age	Mild Hypertension	Significant Hypertension
under 15	130/80	140/90
15–18	135/85	145/90
over 18	140/90	150/95

The athlete with mild or borderline hypertension should be given advice such as that in Table 27.2. He or she should also have the blood pressure checked in both arms and femoral pulses palpated (if the femoral pulses are absent, coarctation of the aorta should be suspected). Those with significantly increased blood pressure need to be investigated and possibly treated.

INVESTIGATIONS: Besides specific laboratory tests for individual cases, two important investigations that help clarify the significance of hypertension in a particular athlete are:

1. Follow-up tests of blood pressure at least three to four times a year.

2. Monitoring the rise in blood pressure during a treadmill-exercise stress test. If the blood pressure rises much above 200/95 in an athlete with borderline resting

---

TABLE 27.2 *Advice to athletes with borderline resting hypertension*

1. Decrease salt intake to a minimum.
2. Avoid gaining weight during the off-season.
3. Maintain a year-round aerobic cardiovascular program in addition to any other specialized training.
4. Have blood pressure examinations at regular intervals, e.g., every three to six months.
5. Avoid anabolic steroids and other medications (such as decongestants) that elevate blood pressure.
6. Have a stress test to evaluate the exercise blood pressure response.
7. Maintain adequate dietary potassium, calcium, and magnesium intake.
8. Limit alcohol intake to 1 oz./day.

If this advice is followed, there should be no need to restrict the participation of an athlete with mild high blood pressure.

---

hypertension, it indicates an abnormal response to exercise. This may be more significant than the resting blood pressure.

Urine Abnormalities

The Chemstrip or similar type of urinalysis dipstick is frequently used during the physical examination to pick up the presence of abnormal quantities of protein, glucose, or blood in the urine. If any of these are present in abnormal quantities, the athlete should be referred for further investigation.

PROTEINURIA: The presence of small amounts of protein in the urine on a single urinalysis or dipstick test is relatively common. Benign causes include exercise, orthostatic proteinuria, and fever. More serious causes include renal disease, hypertension, or underlying systemic illnesses.[4,5,6,7] If proteinuria persists after two or more repetitive urinalyses, then further evaluation, including 24-hour urine collection or determination of a ratio of total protein to creatinine from a random urine, may be useful. Microscopic examination of urine sediment and blood chemistry to evaluate renal function are often helpful. Since hypertension can be both a cause and an effect of renal disease, careful blood pressure evaluation is important.

GLUCOSURIA: If glucose is found in the urine, a random (or fasting) blood-sugar level should be obtained to exclude possible diabetes.

HEMATURIA: Athletes frequently have episodes of hematuria, especially after endurance activities.[8] The exact cause of this manifestation of severe exertion is not completely understood but the condition is thought to be harmless. Some reports suggest that bladder contusions are responsible for the bleeding.[9,10] If the athlete complains of hematuria after a workout, the urine should be checked to confirm that the discoloration is actually due to blood and not myoglobinuria (discussed next). The blood pressure should also be taken.

The urine should then be checked daily before workouts. If the hematuria persists more than a day or two, further investigations may be indicated. The urine should also be examined to ensure that no casts, especially red blood cell casts (an indication of renal disease), are present.

Hematuria following exertion needs to be differentiated from acute trauma to the flank or bladder area. Hematuria resulting from such an injury needs to be immediately referred for a specialist's opinion.

A condition that can be mistaken for blood in the urine is *myoglobinuria*, which is the presence of myoglobin in large quantities in the urine. It presents with an appearance similar to blood, but the dipstick is negative. Myoglobinuria results from severe exercise by a poorly conditioned, dehydrated athlete, and as large quantities of myoglobin can lead to renal failure, its appearance in the urine indicates a potentially serious problem requiring prompt referral.[11,12]

Another condition that can cause confusion because of a macroscopic appearance suggesting hematuria is *exertional hemoglobinuria*, which is thought to be due to damaged red blood cells in the soles of the feet. The condition may contribute to anemia, and is prevented by use of good, shock-absorbent running shoes.

Sickle-Cell Trait

Sickle-cell trait has aroused much concern in recent years, particularly since a member of a college football team collapsed during practice and subsequently died, apparently as a result of an acute sickle-cell crisis. There is still controversy as to whether the sickling was the primary cause of this athlete's death or whether it was secondary to some underlying metabolic abnormality.

The sickle-cell trait is an inherited abnormality that affects the hemoglobin content of the red blood cells (RBC). The trait is found mainly in blacks of West African descent, and in a small percentage of descendents of Mediterranean families. The abnormal hemoglobin is hemoglobin S (HbS), which makes up 30 to 40 percent of the hemoglobin, while the normal adult hemoglobin (HbA) makes up the other 60 to 70 percent. If conditions are right, such as very low oxygen tension, the abnormal hemoglobin may induce sickling of the RBC.

In a study done on professional footballers, it was noted that approximately 8 percent of the black athletes investigated had the trait, which is the same percentage as the natural occurrence of the trait in the general black American population. This suggests that the trait does not interfere with an athlete's ability to participate to the limits of his or her potential.

While generally benign, sickle cell trait can rarely be associated with a syndrome of acute sickling, acidosis, rhambdomyolysis, renal failure, hyperkalemia, and death. Contributing factors include high altitude, hot weather, dehydration, and maximal exertion. It is therefore recommended that any such athlete be educated about the need to adequately hydrate at all times, particularly when playing at high altitudes and in hot weather. No restriction from athletic participation is recommended.[13]

Sexually Transmitted Diseases

There is no doubt that sexually transmitted diseases (STDs) are common among athletes. Those concerned with the athlete's health should be aware of what steps to take should an athlete complain of symptoms indicative of an STD. Absolute confidentiality should always be maintained, and the athlete should be aware of this confidentiality so that he or she has the confidence to discuss the matter. The most common sexually transmitted diseases are:

1. Chlamydia
2. Nonspecific urethritis
3. Gonorrhea
4. Condyloma
5. Trichomonas vaginitis
6. Herpes genitalis
7. HIV
8. Syphilis

CHLAMYDIA: Chlamydia is currently the most commonly reported STD. The male often presents with a urethral discharge and dysuria (painful urination), but may be asymptomatic. Females often have no symptoms but may show a friable cervix and mild purulent discharge. Typical pelvic inflammatory disease (PID) with pelvic pain, fever, and elevated white blood count may also occur. Asymptomatic chlamydial infection is believed to be a major contributor to female infertility from low-grade pelvic inflammatory disease with subsequent tubal and ovarian scarring. A urethral or cervical swab for either enzyme immune assay (EIA) or the more recent DNA probe may help confirm the diagnosis. Treatment is usually with tetracyclines, erythromycins, or certain quinolone antibiotics. In confirmed cases, a follow-up test-of-cure swab should be obtained after treatment is completed. Exposed partners should be contacted and treated, and the local health department should be notified. Condoms can help prevent spread of infection.

NONSPECIFIC URETHRITIS (NSU): Nonspecific urethritis is similar to chlamydia in presentation. Responsible organisms include mycoplasma hominus and ureaplasma urealyticum. No specific swabs or cultures for these organisms are currently available, but studies for chlamydia and gonorrhea should be done. Treatment is essentially the same as for chlamydia. Condoms can help prevent spread of infection.

GONORRHEA: Gonorrhea was for years the most common cause of urethritis. In both males and females symptoms tend to be more prominent than with chlamydia or nonspecific urethritis organisms, but asymptomatic cases are relatively common. A yellow-green purulent discharge may suggest gonorrhea rather than the more clear, thin discharge of chlamydia.

Diagnosis includes urethral or cervical swabs for labratory testing. Treatment is usually with appropriate cephalosporin or quinolone antibiotics. Exposed partners should be contacted and treated, and the health department should be notified. Condoms can help prevent transmission.

CONDYLOMA (VENEREAL WARTS) Venereal warts are painless genital lesions ranging from small plaques or papules of thickened skin to larger frondlike lesions. They are often unnoticed by affected individuals and may escape detection on routine genito-urinary physical exam. They are caused by a myriad of subtypes of human papilloma virus (HPV). While they are relatively harmless in males, certain subtypes can lead to a significantly increased rate of cervical cancer in women. Detection is by careful physical exam, often using a weak acetic acid solution to induce a characteristic "aceto-white" color change. More subtle changes in women may be detected only with papanicolou smears (PAP Smear) or microscopic cervical exam (colposcopy). Treatment is problematic. Serial treatments with liquid nitrogen, podophyllin in benzoin, biochloroacetic acid (BCA), or podofilox may eradicate lesions, but the virus often persists after treatment. Careful PAP smear monitoring in women is essential to detect potentially serious cervical changes. Condoms may possibly be helpful in preventing or delaying transmission.

TRICHOMONAS VAGINITIS: A common "minor" sexually transmitted disease of the female genital tract, this seldom produces symptoms in the male. Sexual activity promotes repeated infections unless both partners are treated.

HERPES GENITALIS: The herpes virus is divided into two types: type I occurs above the waist and type II occurs mainly below the waist, though there is some crossover between the two.

Herpes progenitalis is caused by the type II virus and is a sexually transmitted disease that presents with painful blisters on the genitalia. The patient is most infectious during the time the lesions are present, but asymptomatic. No specific treatment is curative, but oral and topical acyclouir can decrease severity and frequency of outbreaks.

HUMAN IMMUNODEFICIENCY VIRUS (HIV-1): has emerged into the limelight in sports medicine. Fueled by the medical attention on sports celebrities with HIV infection, awareness has focused on the risk of infection of active athletes. Compared with other sexually transmitted diseases, risk of infection is small, but the consequences much more significant.

HIV infection is caused by a small retrovirus, with either no initial symptoms or symptoms similar to a flu-like viral infection. These initial symptoms resolve as the body develops initial immunity. The immunity is incomplete, however, and the illness enters a long (2- to 10-year) latent period. During this time immunity gradually wanes (especially T-Cell function) and symptoms emerge. The presence of active disease is then labeled acquired immune deficiency syndrome (AIDS) and includes a pattern of weight loss, chronic diarrhea, fevers, fatigue, and swollen lymph nodes. Opportunistic infections, including pneumonia and eye and central nervous system involvement, occur. Skin and blood system malignancies can also occur. Outcome of AIDS is considered universally fatal, although current treatments have extended survival. A few individuals have survived long-term infection without developing the full-blown active disease.

Transmission occurs through exchange of infected body fluids to an uninfected individual. Infectious fluids include blood and blood products, semen, vaginal secretions, amniotic fluid, and breast milk. The virus has also been found in tears and saliva, although these fluids carry less risk. Sweat carries no risk. The major routes of infection are through unsafe sexual contact and illicit use of drugs, including anabolic steroids. Risk from transfusions is currently minimal, and risk from donating blood is nonexistent. Sports contact is felt to carry very little risk of exposure, although the potential of spread through blood and saliva exposure does exist. The major risk to athletes occurs off the field in unsafe lifestyle activities.[14]

Current prevention includes attempts at education of individuals at risk and the use of latex gloves when treating injuries. The prompt removal of actively bleeding individuals is mandatory. Bleeding should be stopped and wounds covered before the athlete returns to play. Other protective measures may include face shields and gowns.[15,16] Diagnostic testing employs an enzyme linked immunosorbant assay (Elisa), which is usually positive within three to six months after exposure. Treatment includes zidovudine to support immune function, and antibiotics or chemotherapy to treat active disease symptoms as they emerge. Current research is intense, and potential treatments include immune system modulators (such as interleukins) and antiviral drugs. No effective vaccine has yet been developed. Aggressive education and control of transmission continue to be the most effective preventive interventions.

SYPHILIS: Though syphilis had been decreasing in frequency, it now seems to be making a comeback. There are a number of stages in the natural history of syphilis.

1. Primary syphilis presents with a lesion soon after the initial infection called a chancre. This chancre is usually found on the genitals, and is painless. Lymph node swelling of the involved region appears within one week of chancre; these nodes are painless. The chancre heals within about four weeks.

2. Secondary syphilis appears about six weeks after the chancre has healed and often presents with a rash or generalized lymph node enlargement. The secondary rash may subside within two to six weeks.

3. The patient then enters the latent phase, during which there are no clinical manifestations of syphilis on examination, but the diagnosis can be made by a positive blood test.

4. Late syphilis my present many years later with such complications as aortic aneurysm or neurological lesions.

Diagnosis is with a rapid plasma reagin test (RPR). Treatment is varied depending on the clinical stage, but generally includes penicillin.

Whenever an athlete presents with symptoms suggestive of this disease, immediate referral to the appropriate specialist is mandatory.

Allergic Rhinitis ("Hay Fever")

Nasal allergies to grass seed, pollens, ragweed, molds, etc., are very frequent. Where concentrations of these are high during certain times of the year, an athlete's ability to train and participate can be greatly impaired unless the condition is adequately handled. A basic rule, however, is not to make the treatment more unacceptable than the problem. It should also be remembered that asthma can develop in susceptible individuals and may require treatment.

TREATMENT:

1. *Antihistamines*—These are effective for most athletes, but may have the disadvantage of producing drowsiness and slowing reflexes, which may be incompatible with certain sports. Numerous nonsedating prescription versions are currently available.

2. *Eyedrops*—Vasoconstricting eyedrops, with or without antihistamine, are often useful. Corticosteroid eyedrops may occasionally be used for a short period, but they have serious side effects, including the possible development of glaucoma (raised intra-ocular pressure).

3. *Cromolyn sodium*—This has been used successfully, in preventing asthma of allergic origin and exercise-induced asthma. It is also useful in nasal allergies when inserted into the nose. The dosage should be adjusted to the periods of greatest exposure (see exercise-induced asthma in next section).

4. *Immunotherapy*—An increasingly popular and effective treatment, this has the disadvantage of requiring desensitization injections over a long period of time.

5. *Corticosteroids*—Nasal corticosteroid sprays are currently a mainstay of therapy. While they are not useful in treating acute episodes, they work well if used consistently to maintain control of symptoms and prevent flare-ups. Oral corticosteroids may sometimes be used on a short-term basis to achieve control in severe cases. Intramuscular steroids have traditionally been used, but are not currently recommended. Once ingested, there is no control of the blood level and no knowledge of the degree of adrenocortical suppression being produced at any given time. The length of time the corticosteroid is released from the depot in the muscle varies from individual to individual, and it is uncertain if adrenal suppression occurs or for how long it continues.

The National Collegiate Athletic Association (NCAA) and the United States Olympic Committee (USOC) have different policies regarding use of corticosteroids. The NCAA places no restrictions on their use, while the USOC bans intramuscular, intravenous, and oral use. All topical and inhaled forms are allowed by the USOC, and local or intra-articular injections may be allowed by prior written notification.[17]

Exercise-Induced Asthma (EIA)

This condition occurs to varying degrees in 12 to 15 percent of the general population and is found in 70 to 90 percent of asthmatics. It is also found in 40 percent of those with allergic rhinitis. Athletes develop EIA at about the same rate as the general population. Its onset and severity varies with the individual and type of exercise.

Exercise-induced asthma is defined as an acute reversible episode of airway bronchospasm that occurs within six to eight minutes of strenuous exercise. The hyperirritability of the airways is usually due to the inhalation of cold air and leads to bronchospasm during or after activity.[18] Wheezing is one of the main symptoms. If untreated, the bronchospasm peaks within six to eight minutes and then gradually resolves over the next 30 to 60 minutes. Some athletes are able to continue exercise through the initial acute bronchospastic phase into the refractory or "second-wind" phase and are then resistant to further bronchospasm. Approximately 30 percent of affected athletes may encounter a "late phase" of bronchospasm three to six hours after the initial onset of symptoms.

The physiologic mechanism of EIA is uncertain, and the relationship to perennial asthma is unclear. It is felt that hyperventilation during exercise leads to dehydration and cooling of airways, resulting in increased mast cell activity. Primary mediators are released that induce bronchospasm. Sports performed at high intensity (e.g., running, basketball, football, hockey) in cool, dry air are the worst. Lower-risk activities include swimming's warm, moist environment[19] and nonsustained activities like gymnastics and weightlifting. Environmental air pollution and pollens can exacerbate EIA, and some individuals may become susceptible only during periods of upper-respiratory infection.

Diagnosis is usually suggested by a history of previous occurrence or by family history of asthma or allergic rhinitis. Symptoms may be marked, with chest tightness, shortness of breath, and wheezing, or the athlete may simply present with a mild dry cough. Some individuals will have no obvious symptoms at all, with the diagnosis discovered only with spirometry testing of pulmonary function.

Spirometry testing will show a reduction in forced expiratory volume in one second (FEV-1), forced expiratory flow between .25 and .75 seconds (FEF 25–75), and peak expiratory flow rate (PEFR). Once correlated with more sophisticated spirometric testing equipment, an inexpensive peak flow meter can be helpful in the training room or field of play to measure current lung function.[20]

TREATMENT: Management of EIA includes physical conditioning to improve aerobic capacity and medications to prevent or treat acute bronchospasm. Adequate warm-up is also important to allow adaptation and to reach the refractory or "second-wing" phase. If the athlete is exercising in cold weather, a cloth can be worn over the mouth to attempt to decrease the temperature difference of the inspired air.[21]

MEDICATIONS: The National Collegiate Athletic Association (NCAA) currently allows virtually all anti-asthma medications, but the United States Olympic Committee (USOC) is much more restrictive.[17,22]

Beta Agonists. The USOC allows only certain Beta agonists (albuterol and terbutaline), and only in their inhaled forms and with prior notification. Others (metaproterenol, pirbuterol, bitolterol and clenbuterol) are banned outright. The NCAA currently places no restrictions on Beta agonists, and all forms (inhaled or oral) are allowed. Beta agonists effectively prevent the initial bronchospasm response to exercise, but late-phase bronchospasm refractory to Beta agonists may still occur.

Inhaled cromolyn sodium has also been effective in preventing EIA, and is approved by both the NCAA and USOC. It appears to prevent mast-cell release of inflammatory mediators, and can prevent both acute EIA and the late-phase bronchospasm. Once the exercised-induced asthma has occurred, cromolyn sodium is no longer effective. Cromlyn sodium is effective in about 80 percent of the athletes suffering from EIA.[23] Nedocromil is a similar compound that may also be effective.

One recommended approach to management of EIA includes pre-medication with an appropriate Beta agonist and/or cromolyn followed by a brief warm-up period of 5 to 10 minutes of aerobic activity, followed by 5 to 10 minutes of intense aerobic activity. This is followed by a 15 to 30 minute cool-down period to reach the beneficial refractory phase. The Beta agonist and/or cromolyn can then be repeated 15 to 20 minutes before the event.

Other Medications.

1. Corticosteroids can help in managing underlying asthma, but are of limited use in EIA. They have no effect on the acute-phase bronchospasm, but may help prevent the late-phase constriction. The NCAA currently has no restrictions on their use, but the USOC allows only inhaled forms and with prior notification. The USOC bans oral intramuscular and intravenous corticosteroids, but allows (with notification) local or intra-articular injections for musculoskeletal problems.

2. Theophylline compounds are used in chronic asthma, and are approved by both the NCAA and USOC. Their clinical effectiveness in preventing EIA, however, is limited and they are not recommended as primary choices.

3. Anticholinergic agents such as atropine or ipratropium bromide can be helpful in treating bronchospasm once it occurs, but are not considered effective in preventing EIA. They are approved for use in asthma by both the NCAA and USOC. Current NCAA and USOC regulations concerning asthma are changing rapidly and should be reviewed regularly. Current addresses and telephone numbers are listed in the References section of this chapter.

Seizure Disorders

Seizures (epilepsy) occur as a result of abnormal brain electrical activity. Their cause is often unknown, but they may result from infections (meningitis) or acute head trauma. While many seizure disorders are well known from the athlete's history (and are well controlled), new seizures can present in virtually any individual at any age. Generalized seizures (convulsions) usually involve loss of consciousness, widespread repetitive muscular contractions (tonic-clonic activity), and loss of bowel or bladder control. The seizure itself usually lasts only a few minutes and is followed by a "post-ictal" period of up to an hour, during which the individual may remain unconscious, gradually returning to the waking state. Loss of memory of the seizure is common. Partial seizures are more limited and may include staring episodes, repetitive speech or behaviors, confusion or disorientation, or repetitive muscular activity in part of the body. A mild post-ictal period may follow.

Treatment of acute generalized seizures is largely supportive. The airway should be maintained and the head and neck stabilized if any possibility of head trauma exists. Secretions should be cleared as completely as possible, but fingers should never be placed into the mouth. The affected individual should be turned onto one side to alleviate pharyngeal obstruction and to minimize the risk of aspiration of stomach contents. Airway management should be continued through the post-ictal period, with removal of secretions as necessary. An oral airway (or other protective airway) may be useful at this stage. Vital signs (blood pressure, pulse, and respiratory rate) should be monitored periodically.

Partial seizures are usually less pronounced. The individual should be maintained in a calm, supportive atmosphere until the episode passes (Table 27.3).

In the case of an individual with a known seizure disorder, it is seldom necessary to go beyond the procedures described above. In the case of head trauma, however, emergency medical systems should be activated and the individual should be evaluated by appropriate medical personnel. More detailed evaluation by a physi-

TABLE 27.3 *Guidelines for management of acute generalized seizures*

> 1. Maintain airway. Remove secretions but do not force open clenched teeth. Do not place fingers in mouth.
> 2. Stabilize head and neck if any risk of trauma
> 3. Turn athlete onto side. This helps prevent aspiration and keeps pharynx open.
> 4. Monitor vital signs and general status.
> 5. Continue to reassess, especially airway management. Use of oral airway (or other airway) may be appropriate after initial muscle spasms have subsided.
> 6. Refer for further medical care as appropriate.

cian may involve CT or MRI scanning, lumbar puncture, electroencephalograph (EEG), and blood studies.

Long-term management of seizures is primarily by means of medication, of which there are many types. It is beyond the scope of this section to discuss them fully, but most are currently allowed by both the NCAA and USOC. Current guidelines should be consulted. Since many commonly used medications interact with seizure medications, possible drug interactions should be considered.

There is some controversy as to the degree of athletic participation appropriate in individuals with seizure disorders. Some authorities maintain that virtually all activities are allowable if seizure control is adequate. Others feel that all potentially dangerous sports are absolutely contraindicated (e.g., skiing, scuba diving, rock climbing). Adequate control of seizures can at times be problematic, and assessment of risk may be difficult. One reasonable approach is to consider the type of seizure and degree of control, and to assess the likelihood of serious injury if a seizure were to occur. The desires of the individual and parents must also be considered, as must, increasingly, medico-legal risks by the organizing group. It should be emphasized that many individuals with seizure disorders are capable of participating fully and excelling in sports and recreational activities without restriction, and they should be encouraged in their involvement.[24,25]

Syncope

Syncope is a sudden, transient loss of consciousness. It is relatively common in the general population and accounts for approximately 3 percent of emergency room visits. Virtually everyone involved in the care of athletes has witnessed someone with syncope and, while most episodes are benign, underlying serious causes should be considered.

Vasovagal reactions (common faints) are the most common cause of syncope in otherwise healthy individuals. The episode usually is associated with a change in position (sitting or standing) or with an unpleasant or anxiety-provoking situation. There may be preceding nausea, sweating, and lightheadedness. The mechanism of syncope involves venous dilation and increased vagal tone with subsequent bradycardia. The episode usually passes within minutes, especially if the individual lies down when symptoms first occur. While usually easily recognizable in young persons, syncope from orthostasis should be considered only after cardiac causes in individuals with coronary risk factors for heart disease. Syncope associated with dehydration and hypovolemia (low intravascular volume) may result from inadequate fluid and electrolyte intake or excess losses such as from gastroenteritis. Treatment is with appropriate oral or intravenous fluid replacement, with further evaluation as indicated. Occult bleeding can cause orthostatic hypotension (low blood pressure) and can also lead to syncope.

Metabolic disorders such as diabetes can cause syncope. Hypoglycemia is a much more common acute cause than hyperglycemia, and can occur when caloric intake is too low for the level of expended energy, or when relative insulin dosage is too high. Initial treatment of acute hypoglycemia syncope or near syncope is with oral or intravenous glucose solutions as appropriate. Longer-term prevention includes monitoring of glucose levels, intake of adequate calories, and appropriate insulin dosing. Adrenocortical insufficiency (Addison's disease) is an uncommon but serious metabolic cause of syncope.

Cardiac causes of syncope include left ventricular outflow obstruction from various causes (see the section on sudden death.) and electrical dysrhythmias such as supraventricular tachycardias or ventricular dysrhythmias. While many cardiac dysrhythmias causing syncope are not life threatening, any syncopal episode suggesting cardiac involvement should be thoroughly evaluated to eliminate serious underlying problems. Some medications, including antihypertensives, tricyclic antidepressants, and stimulants can at times contribute to syncope.

Intracranial or neurologic conditions causing syncope include seizures or other loss of consciousness due to tumors, trauma, stroke, or intracranial bleeding.[26] Evaluation of the athlete with syncope is important to allow both prompt treatment of benign causes and to identify more serious underlying problems. The athlete

who becomes lightheaded with vigorous prolonged exertion in high temperatures may respond quickly to fluids and rest alone and require no further workup. The athlete with suspicious or unexplained syncope requires further evaluation by a physician. Further evaluation should include a careful history and physical exam, especially cardiac and neurologic, and may utilize other testing. Blood and urine studies may be helpful, and more specific tools such as resting electrocardiogram (ECG), echocardiogram, exercise electrocardiograms (stress ECG), 24-hour Holter monitor, signal-averaged electrocardiogram (SAE), electroencephalogram (EEG), or head-up tilt testing may be indicated.[27] All cases of syncope should be adequately explained and treated before further participation is allowed.

Sudden Death

The dramatic collapse and death of seemingly healthy young athletes has helped force attention on causes of sudden death during exertion. Although highly visible, such episodes are rare, accounting for 10 to 25 deaths per year among the millions of young competitive athletes in the United States.

The causes of sudden death can be grouped with surprising accuracy according to age. Under age 35 most sudden death is related to structural abnormalities of the heart, including hypertrophic cardiomyopathy (HCM), idiopathic left ventricular hypertrophy (LVH), and congenital coronary artery anomalies. Premature atherosclerotic coronary artery disease (CAD), aortic dissection, and mitral valve prolapse are infrequent causes. Other conditions that can lead to sudden death include myocarditis and sarcoidosis. Cardiac dysrhythmias such as Wolff-Parkinson-White (W-P-W) syndrome seldom result in death.

Above the age of 35 atherosclerotic coronary artery disease (CAD) is the predominant cause of death during exercise, often involving previously asymptomatic individuals.[28]

PREVENTION: Prevention in the younger athlete (under 35 years) should focus on information gleaned from the preparticipation history and physical exam. A careful history should be taken, with attention to any symptoms of previous syncope, dyspnea (shortness of breath), chest pains, or palpitations during exercise. A family history for sudden death, cardiomyopathy, Marfan's syndrome, or premature coronary artery disease should stimulate further screening. While large-scale screening exams tend to have a very low yield of positive findings, a careful cardiac exam may disclose abnormalities such as the systolic murmur of hypertrophic cardiomyopathy. A thorough musculoskeletal exam may suggest the possibility of Marfan's syndrome. If suspicions exist, an echocardiogram can be used for further evaluation. Its cost and limited availability make it inappropriate for screening purposes, however.[29]

In the older athlete (over 35 years), screen for a history of previous smoking, hypertension, and known heart disease, as well as a history of any early familial heart disease. Lipid levels will disclose hyperlipidemia. An exercise electrocardiogram (stress ECG) can be helpful in screening men over 40 years and women over 50 years.

Continued participation in strenuous athletics by individuals at risk for sudden death must be assessed on a case-by-case basis. Not all conditions have the same risk or degree of severity, and not all sporting activities are alike in their physiologic demands. Any athlete considered to be at risk should not participate until a full medical evaluation has been performed, and then only with strict medical supervision, if at all.[30]

The trainer or care provider should be familiar with cardiopulmonary resuscitation (CPR), and forethought should be given to the best means to activate the local emergency medical system should the need arise. Thought should be given to potential routes of emergency access and transportation to local emergency facilities. Specialized equipment such as a defibrillator may be useful under rare circumstances, but is generally not necessary. Any observations or concerns regarding any athlete's health should be referred to a physician for evaluation.

Skin Conditions

The trainer will be presented with numerous skin conditions and it is recommended that a color atlas be consulted. (See the Recommended Readings list at end of chapter.)

Fungal Infections

The dermatophytoses are the most common fungal diseases of the skin, and they are commonly seen in athletes.

FUNGAL INFECTIONS OF THE FEET ("ATHLETE'S FOOT"):
The early signs of athlete's foot (tinea pedis) are maceration, scaling, and fissuring of the toe webs, especially the fourth. This leads to desquamation of the flexor aspect of the toes and clear loculated vesicles on the instep. An important clinical feature is that the infection is asymmetrical, though both feet may be infected. A secondary bacterial infection may also be present.

Diagnosis. There are other disorders of the feet that can simulate athlete's foot. It is therefore frequently necessary to obtain a microscopic examination of the skin scrapings (branching threads of mycelia crossing epithelial cells are seen in athlete's foot), and even a culture. Other conditions that should be considered include dermatitis from footwear and psoriasis, both conditions being symmetrical. A primary bacterial infection can also occur (Figure 27.4).

Treatment. The athlete should be instructed to carefully dry the skin between the toes and on the bottoms of the feet. Tinea pedis should be treated vigorously with an antifungal preparation such as miconazole (Monistat) or clotrimazole (Lotrimin). Occasionally oral treatment with griseofulvin or other oral antifungal medication is necessary.

TINEA VERSICOLOR:
Tinea versicolor is due to a mycelia, *Malassezia furfur.* It presents with brownish vesicles on white skins and as partly depigmented patches on pigmented skins. It is an innocent infection that does no harm, aside from causing skin pigment changes.

FIGURE 27.4
Tinea infection of the foot ("athlete's foot")

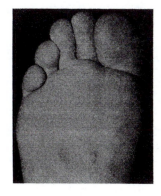 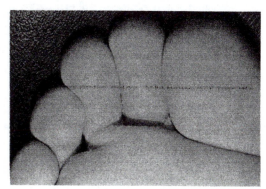

Treatment. Selenium sulfide, 2 ½ percent (Selsun), is available by prescription. It is applied at night and washed off in the morning, and can be used three times. This usually effects a cure. Clotrimazole and other topical antifungals can also be used.

"JOCK ITCH:" Jock itch may be due to a fungal infection. Other causes include:

1. Accumulation of moisture in the groin area

2. Friction of athletic activity

3. Dermatitis caused by sensitivity to a material contained in the underwear

4. Dermatitis from sensitivity to a soap used to wash the underwear

Depending on the etiology, the problem can be treated with an antifungal, or, if the cause is not fungal, with a corticosteroid preparation.

Herpes Simplex Infection

The herpes simplex virus is divided into two types, type I occurring above the waist and type II occurring below the waist. The condition described here is usually due to the type I virus.

ETIOLOGY: Most people have been infected with herpes simplex virus before late adolescence. The virus enters nerve endings in the skin and travels through the peripheral nerves to the dorsal root ganglia, where it remains in its latent form. When the virus is re-activated, it travels down the peripheral nerve to the skin, producing the recurrent lesions which appear in about 25 percent of those who have been infected (but only about 7 percent have significant problems two or more times a year). Primary inoculation (or infection) by the herpes virus can keep occurring at different sites, from autotransmission or by contact, such as in wrestling.

In recurrent herpes, the virus travels from the dorsal root ganglia through the peripheral nerve, using an intracellular pathway that is protected from the body's immunological defense mechanisms. Recurrent herpes may be brought on by an elevation of body temperature, sunlight (ultraviolet light), or occasionally psychological conditions and tension.

INCIDENCE IN ATHLETES: Herpes simplex is a very common problem in wrestlers, occurring mainly from body-to-body contact rather than contact with the mat. For the same reasons, it is also found in rugby players, particularly in forwards. Skiers and mountain climbers, track athletes, and baseball players are likely to suffer repeated recurrent episodes when exposed to ultraviolet light.

CLINICAL COURSE:

1. *Prodromal* herpes consists of a group of symptoms such as itching, burning, or tingling in a given area before the eruption actually becomes visible. On rare occasions there may be symptoms but no lesions.

2. The *primary* infection most frequently occurs in young children, who present with ulcerated lesions in the mouth and on the tongue, as well as with cervical adenopathy, fever, and malaise. There have been reports of herpes pharyngitis in the college-age group; there are no skin signs, only a severely sore throat.

3. The *recurrent* disease first manifests with prodromal symptoms followed by a red spot (papule) which forms a blister (vesicle). After the hard vesicle breaks down, it is covered by a soft crust which later becomes hard. This process takes from five to fourteen days, depending on the size of the lesion. It is probably infectious for five days.

4. *Primary inoculation herpes* is the common type found in wrestlers. The vesicles are small and umbilicated and become pustular and crusted. They tend to form clusters of vesicles (as opposed to the recurrent disease where only one or two lesions occur), and are often mistaken for pyodermia, contact dermatitis, or herpes zoster. The diagnosis can be confirmed by isolation of the virus in tissue culture. Bacterial cultures should also be made, as there is often a secondary infection present.

The commonest areas involved in wrestlers are the cheek and the forehead, due to the lockup position which rubs the right side against the opponent's right side, but the inside of the arm may also be affected. In rugby players it is mainly the forehead and the scalp that are affected. Ultraviolet-induced recurrences in noncontact athletes occur on the face and the lips (Figure 27.5).

PREVENTION: The most important part of treating herpes simplex is prevention. Wrestlers must be removed from all contact activity as soon as they have become symptomatic (some authorities feel they should be removed as soon as the prodromal symptoms appear), and they should be kept out of contact until lesions have healed. Other members on the squad who were wrestling with the infected athlete should be observed daily for any signs of a herpes lesion and, if this occurs, they too should be taken off all contact activities for five days.

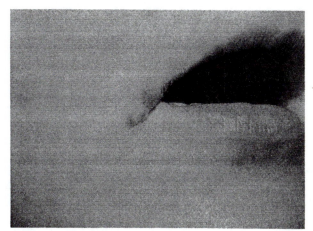

FIGURE 27.5
Herpes simplex involving the corner of the mouth

Ultraviolet-induced herpes is prevented by application of a sunscreen to the lips, face, and other cutaneous areas that might be exposed. This sunscreen should contain para-aminobenzoic acid (PABA) and probably red veterinary petrolatum as well.

TREATMENT: No current treatment is curative. Oral and topical acyclovir (Zovirax) can limit the extent of the outbreak and may promote faster healing and decrease viral shedding. Oral acyclovir can be used to prevent outbreaks. Once present, lesions can be allowed to dry and crust over, and a number of over-the-counter cold sore remedies can be used for comfort. Lesions are infectious until healed.

Herpes Zoster

The virus that causes herpes zoster is the same as the chicken-pox virus. It is thought that the condition is actually a reactivation of the chicken-pox virus which has lain dormant in a sensory ganglion since the time of the primary infection.

SYMPTOMS AND SIGNS: Pain may be felt over the affected nerve root distribution, particularly the intercostal nerves, up to three days before the eruption occurs. Following the eruption, the regional lymph nodes become enlarged and tender. The rash follows a nerve root distribution—this is one of the characteristic features. The rash is initially a raised patch of erythema which becomes a cluster of umbilicated vesicles, and then may become purulent or hemorrhagic and eventually necrotic. In some cases the pain persists for a time after the rash has cleared. If the nasociliary branch or the ophthalmic branch of the temporal nerve is involved, a dangerous irritative conjunctivitis can occur in addition to scalp tenderness, headache, and enlarged lymph nodes.

TREATMENT: Treatment includes possible use of oral acyclovir (Zovirax) and prevention of secondary infections. In the case of nasociliary nerve branch involvement (tip of the nose), the athlete should be referred to an ophthalmologist. Athletes involved in direct contact, such as wrestlers, should avoid participation because they could infect athletes who have not had chicken pox.

Impetigo

Impetigo is usually due to a staphylococcal infection. Some athletes are carriers of the bacteria, particularly in the nose, anus, and under the nails. It commonly infects blisters or damaged skin and is therefore prevalent in wrestlers. It may secondarily infect a herpes simplex or zoster area. The characteristic lesion, once seen, is easy to recognize. The skin beyond the lesion is typically normal. There may be an increase in the size of the regional lymph nodes.

PREVENTION: Carriers of staphylococci should be adequately treated with a topical antibiotic which is applied to the lesion and the nose. Oral antibiotics may be used if necessary. Wrestlers should shower before practice or participation with an antiseptic solution (Betadine or pHisoHex). Nails should be cut short and kept well cleaned. Wrestling mats should be washed daily with an antiseptic solution. All abrasions should be cleaned and treated with a topical antibiotic such as polymixin.

TREATMENT: A culture should be taken to identify the infecting organism and to determine to which antibiotic the organism is sensitive. Many staphylococci are resistant to various antibiotics, penicillins in particular.

Cellulitis

Cellulitis is generally due to a streptococcus. The initial lesion, often on the distal aspect of the limb, becomes painful and red. This may soon be followed by a red streak running up the limb. The regional lymph nodes then become swollen and painful.

TREATMENT: Antibiotics, often a cephalosporin or erythromycin, and a topical antibiotic are combined with rest and elevation of the limb until the infection is under control.

Urticaria

Urticaria is usually due to hypersensitivity, mainly from an allergy. It presents with itchy wheals and can develop into angioneurotic edema with respiratory and laryngeal distress.

TREATMENT: Initial treatment is with an antihistamine. If severe, adrenalin may have to be given subcutaneously or intravenously, and a corticosteroid given orally.

Nonspecific Dermatitis

Nonspecific dermatitis is one of the most common causes of itchy skin in an athlete. The skin is dry and inflamed, particularly on the flexor aspects of the limbs. The usual cause is standing under hot showers for a long period of time or taking two or more showers a day, thus removing the natural oils from the skin and causing the itching and scaling.

TREATMENT: The treatment is to decrease the amount of soap and hot water used and to shower the minimal number of times a day possible. A moisturizing cream should be used after each shower or bath. If this does not work sufficiently, a hydrocortisone or corticosteroid preparation should be applied to the skin.

Infestations

SCABIES: Scabies usually occurs as a result of close physical contact and is a very infectious condition. The scabies mite, *Sarcoptes scabiei*, burrows into the skin, usually between the fingers (60 percent of cases) or on the flexor aspect of the wrists, soles of the feet, or scrotum.

In a person with no previous infestation of scabies, the mite lies dormant for about one month. Dormancy is followed by development of an erythematous reaction around the burrow, and an itchy, papular, urticarial-like eruption appears, commonly on the forearms, axillae, inner thighs and buttocks, and around the ankles. Itching occurs when the athlete gets warm. The eruption is not found on the face or scalp in adults. Vesicles may appear on the hands and feet, and a secondary bacterial infection can develop.

Diagnosis. Diagnosis should be made by finding the burrow on the hands, wrists, or feet (this is most easily achieved by using a magnifying glass).

Treatment. Five percent permethrin (Elimite) or gamma benzene hexachloride (Kwell) is the treatment of choice. The athlete should have a warm bath, then allow the skin to dry and cool, and apply the lotion over all body areas from the neck down. It should be left on for twelve hours, then removed by thorough washing. One application is usually all that is required. All clothing and bedding should also be thoroughly washed.

PEDICULOSIS: Pubic lice are the most frequent form of pediculosis in the athlete, usually contracted by close sexual contact. The athlete presents with itching in the pubic area, nits are seen on the hair shafts, and secondary lymph node swelling is found. There may sometimes be a papular urticarial eruption on the trunk.

Treatment. The treatment for pediculosis pubis is either with 1 percent permethrin (Nix) cream rinse available without prescription or, with prescription, gamma benzene hexachloride (Kwell) in lotion or shampoo form. To use 1 percent permethrin cream rinse, first shampoo and towel dry the area; then saturate hair with the cream rinse, leave on 10 minutes, and rinse out. Repeat applications are seldom necessary.

Gamma benzene hexachloride shampoo can be applied to wet or dry hair and worked in well. After about four minutes water is added, the area is scrubbed to a good lather, and then rinsed. Repeat treatment is recommended in one week. The lotion form can also be used. It is applied to the affected area and washed off after twelve hours. Retreatment is usually not necessary.

All sexual partners should be treated as well. All clothing or linen in contact with the affected person should be washed in hot water or else not worn or used for at least two weeks.

REFERENCES

1. Morse LJ, Bryan JA, Hurley JP, et al: The Holy Cross College football team hepatitis outbreak. *JAMA* 219:706–708, 1972.

2. Bowman JF: Infectious hepatitis in a college football player. *Am J Sports Med* 4:101–106, 1976.

3. de Shazo WF: Returning to athletic activity after infectious mononucleosis. *Phys Sports Med* 8:71–72, December 1980.

4. Ryan AJ: Moderator Round Table on Proteinuria in the athlete. *Phys Sports Med* 6:45–55, July 1978.

5. Bailey RR, Dann E, Gillies AH, et al: What the urine contains following athletic competition. *NZ Med J* 83:309–313, 1976.

6. Castenfors J: Renal clearance and urinary sodium and potassium excretion during supine exercise in normal subjects. *Acta Physio Scand* 70:207–214, 1967.

7. Anderson RE: The significance of proteinuria in athletes. *J Sports Med* 3:133–135, 1975.

8. Siegel AJ, Hennekens CH, Solomon HS, et al: Exercise-related hematuria: Findings in a group of marathon runners. *JAMA* 241:391–392, 1979.

9. Blacklock NJ: Bladder trauma in the long distance runner. *Am J Sports Med* 7:239–241, 1979.

10. Hoover DL, Cromie WJ: Theory and management of exercise-related hematuria. *Phys Sports Med* 9:90–95, November 1981.

11. Schiff HB, MacSearraigh ET, Kallmeyer JC: Myoglobinuria, rhabdomyolysis and marathon running. *Quart J Med* 47:463–472. 1978.

12. Demos MA, Gitin EL: Acute Exertional Rhabdomyolysis. *Arch Intern Med* 133:233–239, 1974.

13. McCurdy PR: Moderator Round Table: Should sickle cell trait ban sports participation? *Phys Sport Med* 4:58–65, January 1976.

14. Calabresse LH, Haupt HA, Hartman L: HIV and sports: What is the risk. *Phys Sports Med* 21(3):172–180. March 1993.

15. Seltzer DG: Educating athletes on HIV disease and aids—The team physician's role. *Phys Sports Med* 21(1):109–115, Jan 1993.

16. Federal Register: Rules and Regulations, 56(235), 1991.

17. United States Olympic Drug Education Handbook. 1750 East Boulder St. Colorado Springs, Colorado 80909, 1989–1992.

18. Burton RM: Case report: Exercise induced asthma in cold weather. *Phys Sports Med* 9:131–132, September 1981.

19. Fitch KD: Exercise-induced asthma and competitive athletics. *Pediatrics* 56:942–943, 1975.

20. Katz RM, Pierson WE: Exercise-induced asthma: Current perspective. *Adv Sports Med Fitness* 1:83–96, 1988.

21. Brenner AM, Weiser PC, Drogh LA, Loren ML: Effectiveness of a portable face mask in attenuating exercise-induced asthma. *JAMA* 244:2196–2198, 1980.

22. NCAA 1992/93 Drug Testing/Education Programs Pamphlet. 6201 College Boulevard, Overland Park, Kansas 66211-2422.

23. Godfrey S, Konig P: Suppression of exercise-induced asthma by salbutamol, theophylline, atropine, cromolyn, and placebo in a group of asthmatic children. *Pediatrics* 56:930–934, 1975.

24. American Academy of Orthopaedic Surgeons: Epilepsy, Chapter 55. In *Athletic Training and Sports Medicine*. Rosemont, IL 60018, second edition, 1991.

25. Preparticipation Physical Exam (PPE). The American Academy of Family Physicians, The American Academy of Pediatrics, The American Society of Sports Medicine, The American Orthopaedic Society for Sports Medicine, The American Osteopathic Academy of Sports Medicine, 1992.

26. Hargarten KM: Syncope: Finding the cause in active people. *Phys Sports Med* 20:123–141, 1992.

27. Cantwell JD, Varughese A, Petlus CW: Cardiovascular syncope: Which patients can resume exercise. *Phys Sports Med* 30:81–92, January 1992.

28. Van Camp S: Sudden death in athletics. *Adv Sports Med Fitness* 1:121–142, 1988.

29. Braden DS, Strong WB: Preparticipation screening for sudden cardiac death in high school and college athletes. *Phys Sports Med* 16(10):128–144, 1988.

30. Bethesda Conference 16: Cardiovascular abnormalities in the athlete: Recommendations regarding eligibility for competition. *J Am Coll Cardiol* 6(6):1185–1232, 1985.

RECOMMENDED READINGS

American Academy of Orthopaedic Surgeons. *Athletic Training and Sports Medicine*. second edition, 1991.

Color Atlas and Synopsis of Clinical Dermatology, New York: McGraw-Hill. second edition, 1992.

Puffer JC: *Medical Problems*. *Clin Sports Med* 11(2) W. B. Saunders, 1992.

Sauer, G: *Manual of Skin Diseases*. Philadelphia: J. P. Lippincott, sixth edition, 1991.

Sexually Transmitted Diseases. Centers for Disease Control and Prevention. MMWR, 42 (No. RR-14), Atlanta Georgia 30333, 1993.

Other Resources

1. National Collegiate Athletic Association (NCAA)
   6201 College Boulevard
   Overland Park, Kansas 66211-2422
   (913)339-1906

2. United States Olympic Committee (USOC)
   1750 East Boulder St.
   Colorado Springs, Colorado 80909
   1-800-233-0393

Medications Commonly Used in Athletics

Medications are used to treat pathological conditions.[1] In athletics, medications are used for two types of therapy:

1. Treatment of athletic injuries
2. Treatment of medical problems

Some of the obvious reasons to use medications in the treatment of athletic injuries are the relief of pain and inflammation, and improvement of mobility. These conditions can be the result of typical athletic injuries (i.e., contusions, sprains, dislocations).[2]

A wide variety of medical problems may be encountered by the athlete. Some of these problems may be related to conditions involving athletic activity (i.e., swimmer's ear, sunburn, athletes foot). Other medical problems may be caused by a functional disorder, such as asthma, diabetes, or epilepsy. Drug therapy for individuals with such disorders is directed at enabling the participant to engage in competitive athletic events more efficiently and safely.

The athletic trainer must be aware of the medications that are commonly encountered in an athletic environment. The trainer and coach are not in a position to dispense prescription drugs or, in some instances, even over-the-counter medication. A trainer may do so only in some instances with a clearly written order from the physician (standing orders) that expressly permits him/her to do so, but there may be some legal definitions even within this situation. Each practicing athletic trainer is responsible for knowing the legal restrictions of advising athletes and/or dispensing medications within his or her own area of employment.

Obviously a trainer in a high-school setting may not be able to give an aspirin to an athlete who is a minor, but the college or professional trainer may be able to administer that same aspirin to his athletes who are adults and can give their own consent. Athletic trainers are in a unique position with regard to informing their athletes about over-the-counter (OTC) medications, the actions of prescription drugs (Rx), and the actions and safety of other drugs.

Drug interactions can be a serious problem.[3,4,5] An example that might occur in an athletic situation is theophylline, a drug taken for asthma, taken simultaneously with erythromycin can result in toxic levels of theophylline in the blood.

Other drug interactions are presented throughout this chapter. In addition, some drug and food interactions need to be considered.

Antibiotics

Antibiotics are used in athletics where infection or the threat of infection occurs, for example in some ankle sprains, bruises, and so on, when blood may accumulate (blood poisoning), or in open wounds.

PENICILLIN (Rx): Penicillin works to destroy susceptible infecting bacteria by interfering with their ability to produce new protective cell walls as they multiply and grow. Certain infections require that this drug be taken for 10 days to prevent the development of rheumatic fever.[6]

To ensure effectiveness, take them at least one hour before or two hours after eating. Do not take them with antacids, erythromycin, or tetracycline.

ERYTHROMYCIN (Rx): Erythromycin works to prevent the growth and multiplication of susceptible bacteria by interfering with their formation of essential proteins. These drugs should not be taken if there is a history of liver disease or impaired liver function. When used to treat infections that predispose to rheumatic fever and kidney disease, take them continuously in full dosage for no fewer than 10 days. Avoid drinking alcohol. Do not take them with penicillin.[6]

Side Effects. Superinfections.

TETRACYCLINE (Rx): Tetracycline prevents the growth and multiplication of susceptible bacteria by interfering with their formation of essential proteins.[6]

Side Effects.

1. Superinfections, often due to yeast organisms. These infections can occur in the mouth, intestinal tract, rectum, and/or vagina, resulting in rectal and vaginal itching.
2. Photosensitivity: Exaggerated sunburn or skin irritation occurs commonly with some tetracyclines.

Drug and Food Interactions. Dairy products can interfere with absorption. Avoid milk for one hour before and after each dose. Avoid alcohol. Antacid, iron, and mineral preparations may decrease absorption. May increase oral anticoagulants.[6]

SULFONAMIDE (Rx): Sulfonamide (sulfa drugs) prevents the growth and multiplication of susceptible bacteria by interfering with their formation of folic acids, an essential nutrient. They may be taken immediately after eating to minimize irritation of stomach. They may increase the effects of alcohol.

ANTIBIOTIC OINTMENTS: Antibiotic ointments are used over open wounds to combat infections. Neosporin (polymyxin B sulfate, bacitracin zinc, neomycin sulfate) (OTC) is a topical first-aid antibiotic ointment used to prevent infections in minor cuts, scrapes, and bruises. It is active against gram-positive and some gram-negative bacteria. Bacitracin (Baciquent) (OTC) is an antibiotic ointment that fights gram-positive bacteria. Polysporin (OTC) is also an antibiotic ointment used in first aid of open wounds.[7]

Side Effects. Hypersensitivity, especially with neomycin, though other topical antibiotics are not immune.

Nonsteroidal Anti-Inflammatory Medications

Nonsteroidal Anti-Inflammatory Agents

Nonsteroidal anti-inflammatory medication (NSAIDS) all cause some gastrointestinal irritation and bleeding, and therefore should be taken with meals. If one type of medication causes gastrointestinal upsets, switching to another that doesn't cause gastrointestinal upset may help. An anti-inflammatory drug should not be taken in combination with another type of anti-inflammatory medication.

IBUPROFEN (MOTRIN, ADVIL) (OTC): Ibuprofen is a nonsteroidal anti-inflammatory agent that also possesses analgesic and antipyretic properties. Its mode of action, like that of other nonsteroidal anti-inflammatories agents, is not completely understood, but may be related to prostaglandin synthetase inhibition. The usual dosage in athletes is 800 mg three times a day. It is thought to be as effective (or perhaps slightly more effective) than aspirin and is better tolerated by some people.

Side Effects. Gastrointestinal side effects do occur, particularly nausea, and occasionally epigastric pain or diarrhea. These are relieved to some extent by combining the drug with meals, milk, or antacids. Dizziness and headache occasionally occur, as does tinnitus. On the whole, however, side effects are relatively infrequent.

Drug and Food Interactions. Do not take with aspirin.

There are many prescription (Rx) anti-inflammatories on the market and new ones are being developed yearly (Figure 28.1).

NABUMETONE (RELAFEN) (Rx): Nabumetone is a nonsteroidal anti-inflammatory drug (NSAID) that exhibits anti-inflammatory, analgesic, and antipyretic properties. It is believed, but not proven, that the ability to inhibit prostaglandin synthesis may be involved in the anti-inflammatory effect.[7]

INDOMETHACIN (INDOCIN) (Rx): Indocin is an NSAID with anti-inflammatory, antipyretic, and analgesic properties. Indocin is a potent inhibitor of prostaglandin synthesis.[6]

DICLOFENAC (VOLTAREN) (Rx): Diclofenac is an NSAID that has shown anti-inflammatory, analgesic, and antipyretic activity. Its mode of action is not known; however its ability to inhibit prostaglandin synthesis may be involved in the anti-inflammatory effect.[7]

FLURBIPROFEN (ANSAID) (Rx): Ansaid is an NSAID with anti-inflammatory, analgesic, and antipyretic properties. Ansaid is a potent prostaglandin synthesis inhibitor, and this property may be involved in this anti-inflammatory effect.[7]

Drug Interactions. May interact with antacids, aspirin, oral hypoglycemic agents, diuretics, and beta blockers.

Side Effects. Gastrointestinal upset.

Aspirin

In spite of many new anti-inflammatory preparations on the market, aspirin (OTC) still has a definite place in sports medicine because of its predictable effectiveness and relatively mild side effects. It is still the basic standby because of its action as:

1. An analgesic (pain killer)
2. A mild anti-inflammatory agent
3. An antipyretic (aid in controlling a fever)

Aspirin, by indirect action on the hypothalamus, reduces fever by dilating blood vessels in the skin, which hastens the loss of body heat. It also reduces the tissue concentration of prostaglandin, chemicals involved in the production of inflammation and pain, and interferes with the blood clotting mechanism by its action on blood platelets.

As an analgesic it is used in a dosage of two tablets (325 mg per tablet) every four to six hours. As an anti-inflammatory agent it has a mild but definite action if taken in a dose of two or three tablets four times a day over a period of a week or more. Aspirin can be taken before participation by athletes with overuse inflammatory lesions such as patellar tendonitis or tennis elbow. These athletes should take two or three aspirin one-half to one hour before participation.

SIDE EFFECTS: The primary side effects of aspirin are related to:

1. The gastrointestinal tract, where gastric irritation and bleeding can be precipitated. This hazard is reduced by taking the aspirin with milk or food, in a buffered form (e.g., with an antacid) or in the "enteric coated" form so that it passes through the stomach into the small intestine before being released. Aspirin should not be taken with alcohol or other stomach irritants.

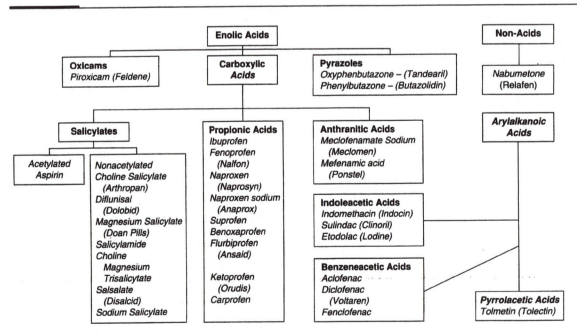

FIGURE 28.1
Anti-inflammatory medications
(Adapted from Upjohn Pharmaceutical Co. Kalamazoo, Michigan)

2. Vestibular effect—tinnitus (buzzing in the ears) is a sign of aspirin intoxication and means the dosage should be reduced.

3. Hypersensitivity reactions, such as the development of bronchospasm, following ingestion.

DRUG AND FOOD INTERACTIONS: Vitamin C in large doses may cause aspirin accumulations and toxicity.

There are a number of prescription nonsteroidal anti-inflammatory agents that are essentially similar in efficacy. However, a particular athlete may find one drug more effective than another, so that some of these can be used in turn on a trial basis.

Dimethyl Sulfoxide (DMSO)

Dimethyl sulfoxide (DMSO) is a drug that still finds its way into sports, even though it has been approved by the FDA only for the treatment of interstitial cystitis.

DMSO is a naturally occurring substance obtained as a byproduct of manufacturing paper. DMSO is sold in various forms: a 50% solution (DMSO-50: Research Laboratories, Inc.) (Rx) approved by the FDA for use in interstitial cystitis, a 50% and 90% veterinary solution, and a 90% industrial solution. Only the solutions approved for human and veterinary usages are purified. Because the bottling process of the industrial grades of DMSO may not take place under sterile conditions, the DMSO itself may contain impurities such as cadmium and lead absorbed through the industrial process.[8]

DMSO was first discovered by a Russian scientist in 1866, but was not used in medicine until 1963, when Stanley Jacob, a physician from the Oregon Health Sciences University, employed it to reduce the swelling and pain of arthritis. Oregon mill workers at Crown Zellerbach (which holds the process patent) reported a decrease of their arthritis symptoms when they were around this by-product of paper manufacturing.[9]

The American Academy of Pediatrics Policy Statement reports that the compound has a number of interesting pharmacological properties that may be beneficial to patients. Its ability to penetrate intact skin, carrying with it a variety of chemicals, offers hope for eliminating painful injections; its inhibition of certain prostaglandins offers hope that various inflammatory diseases may be suppressed; its local analgesics properties may reduce cutaneous pain from burns and injuries; its ability to dissolve compounds such as amyloid and collagen might be harnessed; and DMSO's ability to

reduce intracranial pressure in head injuries could reduce morbidity, if not mortality.[10]

By increasing circulation to the injured area, decreasing swelling, and minimizing pain and inflammation, DMSO seems to hasten the healing process of an acute injury. This may be its most important benefit in sports medicine. The problem is that the DMSO products currently available (veterinary and industrial) cannot be considered safe for human use, and that effectiveness for this purpose has not be established.

SIDE EFFECTS: Musty, garlicky breath odor in 80 percent of patients within minutes of application; local skin sensitivity with erytheria and ulceration; possible injury to the lens of the eyes.

DRUG INTERACTIONS AND PRECAUTIONS: DMSO should not be used by:

1. A person with a history of allergies or hypersensitivity reactions, especially a known sensitivity to sulphur

2. Anyone who has been drinking alcohol

3. Anyone who is also taking a sulphur drug

4. Anyone with unclean skin or skin that has been treated with irritants such as Iodine, tape prep, etc.

5. Anyone whose skin is excessively dry, sunburned, or lacking normal oiliness

6. A pregnant woman or a woman who may be pregnant.[8]

This is not to imply that DMSO should be used in athletics, but serves as a guide to athletes who may be using it on their own. Because the medication may be absorbed into skin, the athletic trainer or coach of an athlete using DMSO may want to use rubber gloves to avoid contact with skin.

Counter-Irritants

Counter-irritants are agents that produce a mild inflammation and act as an analgesic when applied locally to the skin. Counter-irritants are based on the theory that pain in the right thumb can be eliminated by hitting the left thumb with a hammer. Counter-irritants cause a local increase in blood circulation, redness, and a rise in skin temperature. They produce a stimulus to the skin of such intensity as to mask the pain of the original injury. They do not promote healing and may be contraindicated where the feeling of pain is needed to prevent further injury. The more common counter-irritants are analgesic balms (methyl salicylate [menthol] and capsicum oleoresin [red pepper]), which are found in such products as Ben-Gay, Cramergesic, and Mineral Ice.

Corticosteroids

Corticosteroids (Rx) are frequently used in sports medicine, but their role must be understood. The most commonly used form is the intralesional injection. Occasionally oral intramuscular cortisone is used, but this is exceptional. Corticosteroids are very powerful anti-inflammatory agents. However, they also have a number of serious side effects which limit their use, including:

1. Suppression of the adrenal glands
2. Precipitation of diabetes
3. Thinning of bones (osteoporosis)
4. Mental and psychological changes

A number of other side effects can occur if the drug is used for a longer period of time.

INTRALESIONAL CORTICOSTEROIDS: The injection of corticosteroids into a particular area of inflammation is very helpful in many of the injuries sustained by athletes. However, this type of administration still has potential *side effects* that are relevant to the athlete:

1. If cortisone is injected into a tendon or ligament, the structure will be weakened for at least two to six weeks. If athletic activity is continued, the weakened tendon or ligament can undergo complete rupture, particularly if the symptoms are masked by the cortisone.

2. If cortisone is injected into a joint on a number of occasions (particularly into the knee joint), intra-articular degeneration and arthritis can develop.

Corticosteroid injections should thus be used with great discretion. There are a number of anatomical sites where their use is very advantageous and side effects are minimal, including:

1. Shoulder pointer (e.g., contusion of the distal clavicle and acromion process)
2. Hip pointer (e.g., contusion of the iliac crest)
3. Morton's neuroma of the foot

4. Plantar fasciitis and bursitis
5. Iliotibial tract friction syndrome
6. Tenosynovitis of the thumb extensor tendons

A number of other areas are frequently injected, but the use of cortisone in these areas is controversial.

ORAL CORTICOSTEROIDS: These drugs are seldom used in athletic medicine. If they are used, dosage should be limited to about five days, after which adrenal suppression may occur.

INTRAMUSCULAR CORTICOSTEROIDS: Experiments are being conducted using intramuscular corticosteroids away from the site of injury to try to effect a more rapid decrease in inflammation following an injury. Results are uncertain at this time, though the preliminary reports are favorable. The possibility of side effects still needs to be considered.

Analgesics

ACETAMINOPHEN (TYLENOL): Acetaminophen is similar to aspirin in terms of analgesia but has *no* anti-inflammatory effects. It is therefore used purely as a mild painkiller. The usual dosage is two tablets every four to six hours.

Side Effects. With a dosage of two tablets every four to six hours there are relatively few side effects, though occasional liver and other problems have been reported.

ASPIRIN OR ACETAMINOPHEN (TYLENOL) WITH CODEINE: Codeine is a narcotic analgesic that is used in combination with aspirin or acetaminophen for severe pain, for instance, after a fracture.

Side effects. Mainly drowsiness, nausea, and vomiting. Codeine has addictive properties.

Cold Medications

PSEUDOEPHEDRINE HYDROCHLORIDE (e.g., SUDAFED): This vasoconstrictor is useful for dealing with the symptoms of an upper respiratory infection and rhinitis. The advantage for athletes is that pseudoephedrine does not cause drowsiness, which is the main problem with most "cold medications" containing an antihistamine.

Side Effects. Pseudoephedrine does have some side effects, however, including stimulation, which might produce hyperactivity and insomnia in sensitive athletes or if too high a dosage is taken. It should be used with caution if there is a tendency toward hypertension.

Antidiarrheal Medications

DIPHENOXYLATE HYDROCHLORIDE WITH ATROPINE SULFATE (LOMOTIL): Diphenoxylate hydrochloride is an antidiarrheal agent that contains a morphine-like derivative as its main constituent, together with atropine, and is usually effective in treating the nonspecific gastrointestinal upset that plagues many traveling athletes. However, because of the atropine content, some athletes may have difficulty with visual focusing and mouth dryness. The usual dosage is two tablets four times a day for the adult; it should be used cautiously in children, as serious side effects can occur.

ANTINAUSEA AGENTS: Severe nausea and even vomiting are frequent pre-event occurrences. Most antiemetic drugs such as Phenegran have side effects such as drowsiness and are therefore contraindicated before participation. A preparation that has been found useful in such situations is Emetrol, which is an oral solution containing fructose, glucose, and orthophosphoric acid. This has a local action on the wall of the hyperactive gastrointestinal tract and reduces smooth muscle contraction. It should be taken undiluted and with no other fluid for at least 15 minutes afterwards. It helps settle the anxious athlete's stomach without side effects.

Antifungal Agents

These agents are used to treat tinea pedis (athletes foot), tinea versicolor ("jock itch"), and are *tolnaftate* (Tinactin) (OTC) or *Clotrimazole* (Lotrimin), the latter being effective against yeasts as well. Occasionally oral treatment with griseofulvin (Fulvicin, Grisactin) (Rx) is necessary.

GRISEOFULVIN (Rx): An antibiotic derived from a species of penicillin and indicated for the treatment of ringworm infections of the skin, hair, and nails, namely,

tinea corporis, tinea pedis, tinea cruris, tinea barbae, tinea capitis, tinea unguiom.[7]

Asthma and Allergy Medications

CROMOLYN SODIUM (INTAL) (Rx): This inhibits sensitized mast cell degranulation, which occurs after exposure to specific antigens. Cromolyn sodium acts by inhibiting the release of mediators from mast cells. Cromolyn sodium indirectly blocks calcium ions from entering the mast cell, thereby preventing mediator releases (histamine). It is used for the management of patients with bronchial asthma. Intal has no role in the treatment of an acute attack of asthma, especially *status asthmaticus.*

Side Effects. Throat irritation or dryness, bad taste, cough, wheeze, nausea, bronchospasm.

Drug and Food Interactions. Avoid foods or drugs that cause an allergic reaction.

ANTICHOLINERGIC (ATROVENT INHALER) (Rx): Atrovent is an anticholinergic (parasympatholytic) agent that appears to inhibit vagally medicated reflexes by antagonizing the action of acetylcholine, the transmission agent released from the vagus nerve. Anticholinergics prevent the increases in intracellular concentration of cyclic guanosine monophosphate (cycle GMP) caused by interaction of acetylcholine with the muscular receptor on bronchial smooth muscle.[7]

BETA ADRENERGIC STIMULATOR (PROVENTIL, VENTOLIN, METAPREL) (Rx): Proventil inhaler is indicated for the prevention and relief of bronchospasm in patients with reversible obstructive airway disease, and for the prevention of exercise-induced bronchospasm. Proventil causes an increase in C-AMP levels associated with relaxation of bronchial smooth muscle and inhibition of release of mediation of immediate hypersensitivity from cells, especially from mast cells.[7] Ventolin and Proventil are permitted under IOC guidelines in the aerosol or inhalant form only. Written notification required by the USOC.

PREDNISONE (DELTASONE, PARACONE) (Rx): Prednisone is a glucocorticoid (an adrenocortical steroid). It is used for the symptomatic relief of inflammation (i.e., swelling, redness, heat, and pain) in any tissue. The principal actions of therapeutic doses occur at sites of inflammation and/or allergic reactions, regardless of the nature of the causation injury or illness; action may take 24 to 48 hours.[7]

Side Effects.   Retention of salt and water, gain in weight, increased sweating, increased appetite, increased susceptibility to infection.

Drug Interactions.   Aspirin, indocin, barbiturates, and insulin.

Muscle Relaxers

Muscle relaxers are prescribed after an injury that causes muscle spasms in the injured muscle. They are usually prescribed for short periods of time (up to two to three weeks) and in combination with other drugs such as anti-inflammatories and pain relievers.

CYCLOBENZAPRINE HCL (FLEXERIL) (Rx): This drug relieves skeletal muscle spasm of local origin without interfering with muscle function. Cyclobenzaprine acts primarily within the central nervous system at the brain stem as opposed to spinal cord levels, although its action on the latter may contribute to its overall skeletal muscle relaxant activity. Evidence suggests that the net effect of cyclobenzaprine is a reduction of tonic somatic motor activity, influencing both gamma (y) and alpha (x) motor system.[7]

Flexeril is indicated as an adjunct to rest and physical therapy for relief of muscle spasm associated with acute, painful musculoskeletal conditions.

Drug Testing

Drug testing is one strategy to meet the abuse of drugs.[11,12] Present testing using sophisticated technology appears to be very accurate when properly applied to published standards. However, it is expensive and time consuming, and has and will face legal challenges. In order to renew acceptance for testing, the following areas need to be considered: proper administration of the test, protection of the rights of the individual, and proper use of the results (as applied to sanctions and penalties).

A wide variety of testing protocols are being conducted within the athletic community. Examples of testing by various organizations include:

1.   NCAA conducts year-round testing programs for football and track and field, as well as post-NCAA championships and postseason football games.

2.   The Athletic congress (TAC) has a random testing policy that allows for testing of any athlete participating in a TAC-sanctioned meet and for the top 15 athletes in each track and field event.

3.   The National Football League (NFL) tests during the preseason physical examination period.

4.   Individual colleges and universities or entire athletic conferences have testing plans for member schools. These programs supplement those of the NCAA. As an example: Athletes might be randomly and regularly tested during the academic year for substances that may include, but are not necessarily limited to, the following: amphetamines, morphine, barbiturates, codeine, cocaine, PCP (Angel Dust) and analogues, methaqualude, tetrahydrocannabinol (THC or Marijuana), opiates, and anabolic steroids.

Each institution needs to have a drug policy in place and fully presented to the athlete. This detailed policy should include the purpose of the program as well as what drugs will be examined, and should explain how athletes will be selected for testing (Figure 28.2). In addition, if the testing results are positive, the athlete needs to be aware of possible action.

It appears that athletes might continue to use substances until:

1.   More effective educational programs are presented

2.   Research produces more compelling definite clinical evidence of health hazards

3.   Adoption of intervention with sanctions based on the unfair "cheating" concept (Anabolic steroids usage gives the user of steroids an unfair advantage.)

4.   Rehabilitation opportunities for dependent abusers who have physical and/or psychological health problems related to drug use

The athletic trainer may well be a very valuable member of the "team" that can educate the athlete and encourage an honest application effort without chemical enhancements. Some obvious drugs are banned in athletic competition (i.e., heroin, cocaine), but even some over-the-counter drugs are banned (i.e., Sudafed). An athletic trainer needs to be aware of these so that he may inform the coach and athlete what OTC medications he may or may not take during athletic competition. It is very disheartening for an athlete to spend so much time practicing and then win, only to possibly have that championship taken away because he or she used an over-the-counter medication without realizing it was a banned substance. The International Olympic Committee bans drugs listed in Table 28.1.

EXAMPLE
ATHLETIC DEPARTMENT DRUG POLICY

Upon the recommendation of _____ Conference Drug Education Committee, a policy for drug education and testing of intercollegiate athletes at _____ has been drawn up.

Only by being fully appraised of the dangers and consequences of taking drugs can anyone make a fully informed and rational decision on this subject. Therefore, a drug education program has been instituted for all intercollegiate athletes at _____. Educational programs and literature will be made available to each intercollegiate athlete on campus at the beginning of each school term and/or athletic season. This will be a cooperative effort between the Sports Medicine Department and the coaches of each individual sport.

University Student Health Service's Mental Health Unit will assist in this educational program and will also offer individual and/or group counseling for those student-athletes who have, or have had, a problem with drug usage.

To protect student-athletes against the abuse of dangerous drugs and to guard against their athletic standing and eligibility, a random drug testing program has been instituted. The purpose of this drug testing and education program is to help the student-athlete and not to punish him/her.

All drug testing will be analyzed through the University Student Health Center Laboratory and strict confidentiality will be adhered to. Only the Team Physician and the Head Coach of the individual sport will be apprised of the results of the tests.

Student-athletes will be selected on a random basis. (By uniform number—for instance anyone with a 5 on their uniform; by position on the team—for instance all defensive personnel; by alphabet—for instance all players whose last name begins with G through R.)

The drug to be tested are in the categories of:

1. Cannabis—marijuana, hashish, etc.
2. Stimulants—amphetamines, "speed"
3. Cocaine and its derivatives
4. Barbiturates—"downers," quaalude
5. Diazopams—valium, etc.
6. Phencyclidine—"angel dust," PCP

Any one of these, or any combination of them, will be tested. Sometimes only one substance will be examined; on other occasions others will be tested.

The results of the drug tests which are positive will be reported to the Team Physician who will inform the individual athlete of the results of those tests and inform the Head Coach of his/her team. At that time the student-athlete will be given an opportunity to explain and to avail himself/herself of the services of the Student Health Mental Health Unit.

Retesting on those who have previously tested positive will be conducted again at an appropriate time. If repeat testing again is positive, the student-athlete will be required to meet with a committee consisting of the Athletic Director or his representative, the Head Coach, and the Team Physician. At that meeting the athlete should show cause as to why he or she should not be suspended from the team until such time as drug abuse is ended. If the decision is made to remove the athlete from the team, appropriate procedures for retesting and a treatment program will be specified to the athlete so that he/she will know how to be reinstated on the team.

All student-athletes and prospective student-athletes must read and review the _____ Athletic Department drug policy and sign that they agree to submit urine specimens for testing at any time during their athletic career. Results of positive drug tests will be made known only as described above, or as may become legally necessary in the event of any proceedings which develop subsequent to those procedures described above.

I have read the drug policy of _____ and agree to abide by them in all respects.

_____   _____
Signature   Date

FIGURE 28.2
An example of an institution's drug policy

TABLE 28.1   *Drugs banned by the IOC*

Doping Classes	Generic Name	Common Name
1. Stimulants: (partial list)	Dexoxyephedrine	Vicks Inhaler
	Caffeine 12 mcg/mm	4 Vivarin
		8 No Doz
		8 cups coffee in 3 hrs
	Dimentamfetamine	Amphetamine
	Methamphetamine	Desoxyn
	Isoprotenol	Metihaler—ISO
	Pseudoephedrine	Actifed
		Afrin tablets
		Co-Tylenol
		Sudafed
		Chlortrimedine—DC
		Novafed
	Phenylephrine	Coricidin
		Dristan
		Neosynephrine
		Sinex
	Phenylpropanolamine	A.R.M.
		Alka-Seltzer Plus
		Contac
		Sinutab
		Triaminic
	Propylhexedrine	Benzedrex inhaler
	Ephedrine	Bronkaid
		NyQuil Nighttime Medicine
		Herbal tea and medicine containing MA Huang (herbal ephadan)
	Ma Huang	Bishop's tea
	(herbal ephadan)	Mormon Tea
		Brigham Tea
2. Narcotic analgesics (partial list)	Dextroproposyphen	Darvon
	Diamorphine	Heroin
	Pentazocine	Talwin
	Pethidine	Demerol
	Trimeperidine	Demerol
	Oxycodone	Percodan
		Vicodin
3. Anabolic agents (partial list)	Metandienone	Dianabol
	Nandrolone	Deca-Durabolin
	Testosterones	Malogen
Related compound:	Growth Hormone	
	Human chorionic gonadotrophin	
4. Diuretics (partial list)	Acetazolamide	Dazamide
	Chlortalidone	Thalitone
	Furosemide	Lasix
	Spironolactone	Alatone
5. Peptide hormone	Chorionic Gonadotrophin	
	Corticotrophin (ACTH)	
	Growth Hormone (HGH, Somatotrophin)	
	Erythropoietin (EPO)	

Updates on IOC-banned drugs may be obtained by writing to:

U.S. Olympic Committee
Attn: Drug Control
Olympic House
1750 E. Boulder Street
Colorado Springs, CO 80909-5760
or by calling 1-800-233-0393.

Update on NCAA banned drugs may be obtained by writing to:

Clean Data Inc.
P.O. Box 14183
Research Triangle Park, NC 27790-4183

(Products carrying the name "decongestant" generally contain banned substances.)

REFERENCES

1. Arnheim DD: *Principles of Athletic Training.* St. Louis: Mosby-Year Book, eighth edition, 1993.

2. American Academy of Orthopaedic Surgeons: *Athletic Training and Sports Medicine.* Rosemont, Ill: author., second edition, 1991.

3. *PDR Guide to Drug Interactions, Side Effects, Indications.* Montual NJ: Medical Economics Data, forty-seventh edition, 1993.

4. Peck DM, McKeag, DB: Athletes with disabilities: Removing barriers. *Phys Sports Med* 2(4):59–62, 1994.

5. Stopka C: An overview of common injuries to individuals with disabilities. *Palaestra* 44–51, Winter 1996.

6. Long JW: *The Essential Guide to Prescription Drugs.* New York: Harper & Row, 1977.

7. *Physicians Desk Reference.* 47th ed. Montuale, NJ: Medical Economics Data, forty-seventh edition, 1993.

8. Holmer J: *DMSO, the 70% solution. Sports Med* I(1):15–19, 1984.

9. Jacobs S, M.D.: DMSO—Personal communication. 1976.

10. American Academy of Pediatrics Policy Statement: DMSO. *Phys Sports Med* 12(l):192, 1984.

11. Buckley WE, Yesalis C, Friedl KE, Anderson W, Streit A, and Wright J: Estimated incidence of anabolic androgenic steroid use among male high school seniors. *J Am Med Ass* 260:3441–3445, 1988.

12. Wilson JD: Androgen abuse by athletes. *Endocrine Reviews* 9:181–199, 1988.

RECOMMENDED READINGS

American College of Sports Medicine Position Stand on the Use of Anabolic-Androgenic Steroids in Sports. *Amer J Sports Med* 12:13–18, 1984.

Benjamin M, et al: Short children, anxious parents: Is growth hormone the answer? *Hastings Center Rep* 14:5–9, 1984.

Burkett LM, Falduto MT: Steroid use by athletes in a metropolitan area. *Physician Sports Med* 12:69–74, 1984.

Catlin DH, Kammerer RC, Hatton CK, Sekera MH, Merdink JL: Analytical chemistry at the games of the XXIIIrd Olympiad in Los Angeles, 1984. *Clin Chem* 33:319–327, 1987.

Cowart VS: Human growth hormone: the latest ergogenic aid? *Phys Sports Med* 16:175–185, 1988

Dyment PG: Drugs and the adolescent athlete. *Pediatric Annals* 13:602–604, 1984.

Frankle MA, et al: Use of androgenic anabolic steroids by athletes. (letter), *JAMA* 252:482, 1984.

Haupt HA: Anabolic steroids: A review of the literature. *Amer J Sports Med* 12:469–484, 1984.

Johnson WD: Steroids: A problem of huge dimensions, (special report) *Sports Illustrated* 62:38(12), 1985.

Limbird TJ: Anabolic steroids in the training and treatment of athletes. *Comp Ther* 11:25–30, 1985.

Lucking MT: Steroid hormones in sports, Paper presented at the International Conference on Sports Medicine, Utrecht, The Netherlands, 23–26 March 1981.

Macintyre JG: Growth hormone and athletes. *Sports Med* 4:129–142, 1987.

Mellion MB: Anabolic steroids in athletes. *AFP* 30:113–119, 1984.

Overly WL, et al: Androgens and hepatocellular carcinoma in an athlete (letter), *Annals Intern Med* 100:158–159, 1984.

Prokop L: Drug abuse in international athletics. *J Sports Med* 3:85–87, 1975.

Rogol AD: Growth hormone: physiology, therapeutic use, and potential for abuse. *Exer Sports Sci Rev* 17:353–377, 1989.

Ryan AJ: Anabolic steroids are fool's gold. *Federation Proceedings* 40:2682–2688, 1981.

Strauss RH, Wright JE, Finerman GAM, Catlin DH: Side effects of anabolic steroids in weight-trained men. *Phys Sports Med* 11:87–96, 1983.

Strauss RH, et al: Anabolic steroid use and perceived effects in ten weight-trained women athletes. *JAMA* 253:2871–2873, 1985.

Tatro DS: Use of steroids by athletes. *Drug Newsletter* 4:33–34, 1985.

Taylor WN: Growth hormone: Preventing its abuse in sports. *Tech Rev* 88:14(3), 1985.

Taylor WN: *Hormonal Manipulation.* Jefferson, NC: McFarland and Company, 1985.

Underwood LE: Report of Conference on Uses and Possible Abuses of Biosynthetic Human Growth Hormone. *N Engl J Med* 311:606–608, 1984.

Wadler GI, Hainline B: *Drugs and the Athlete.* Philadelphia: F. A. Davis Company, p. 353, 1989.

Webb OL, et al: Severe depression of high-density lipoprotein cholesterol levels in weight lifters and body builders by self-administered exogenous testosterone and anabolic-androgenic steroids. *Metabolism* 33:971–975, 1984.

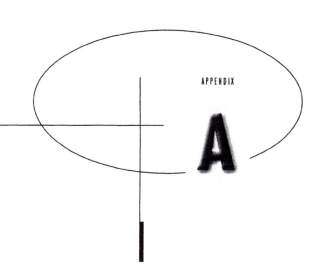

Medical Abbreviations and Symbols

ā   Before

A.A.R.O.M.   Active-assistive range of motion

Abd.   Abduction

a.c.   Before meals

Add   Adduction

ADL   Activities of daily living

Adm   Admit

AJ   Ankle jerk

A/K   Above-knee amputation

Amb   Ambulate

Amp   Amputate

Ant. tib.   Anterior tibialis

@   at

A.R.O.M.   Active range of motion

ASAP   As soon as possible

A.S.I.S.   Anterior superior iliac spine

Asst.   Assist

As Tol   As tolerated

Ⓑ   Bilateral

B.C.   Burn care

B.I.D.   Twice a day

bilat.   Bilateral

BJ   Biceps jerk

B/K   Below-knee amputation

BM   Bowel movement

B/P or B.P.   Blood pressure

bs   Bedside

c̄   with

CC or c/c   Chief complaint

CA   Carcinoma

cerv.; c   cervical

CITx   Intermittent cervical traction

cm.   centimeters

CNS   Central nervous system

c/o   Complains/ed of

cont'd   Continued

contra   Contraindicated

CP   Cerebral palsy

Cryo   Cryotherapy

CSTx   Static cervical traction

CVA   Cerebral vascular accident

CTx/cer. trac   Cervical traction

d   day

D. Dor   Dorsal

DC   Discontinue

DIA   Diathermy

D.I.P.   Distal phalangeal joint

DJD   Degenerative joint disease

DOI   Date of injury

Dx   Diagnosis

fl   Decrease

ed   edema

EMS   Electrical muscle stimulation

E.S.   Electrical stimulation

ER   External rotation

Eval   Evaluation

EXC   Except

EX   Exercise

Ext   Extension

e.g.   Example

Ext. Rot.   External rotation

F   Fair

Flex., fl., or ✓   Flexion

' /ft.   feet

FWB   Full weight bearing

fx   Fracture

G   Good

G.T.   Gait training

gastroc.   Gastronemius

glut   Gluteal

>   Greater than

hams   Hamstring

HP   Hot packs

HPI   History of present injury

HT   Height

hx   History

>   Increase

in vitro   Within a test tube

in vivo   Within a living body

int. rot.   Internal rotation

i.e.   That is

IP jt.   Interphalangeal joint

I.R.   Infrared

IR   Internal rotation

IV   Intravenous

jt.   Joint

KJ   Knee jerk

K.G. or kg.   Kilogram

lat.   lateral

LE.   Lower extremity

lig.   Ligament

LLB   Long leg brace

LB   Low Back

lb   Pound

Ⓛ   Left

LLE   Left lower extremity

LOF   Level of function

LOM   Level of motion

LUE   Left upper extremity

l/s; ls   Lumbo-sacral

L. Lumb.   Lumbar

<   Less than

mass or msg   Massage

max.   Maximal

med.   Medial

MED   Minimal effective dose

min   Minutes, minimal

MD   Muscular dystrophy

ML   Midline

mod   Moderate

mods   Modalities

M.H.   Moist heat

M-P jt   Metacarpalphalangeal joint

mm   Millimeter

Mm   Muscles

ms   Millisecond

MS   Multiple sclerosis

N   Normal

NAD   No acute distress

NBM   Nothing by mouth

neg   Negative

Nn   Nerves

NP   Not palpable

NWB   Nonweight bearing

o/a   On or about

OOB   Out of bed

O.P.   Outpatient

ORIF   Open reduction internal fixation

OTC   Over the counter

O.T.   Occupational therapy

O.T.R.   Registered occupational therapist

p   After

palp   Palpable

PC   After meals

P   Poor

para   parafin

p bars   Parallel bars

PED   Pediatrics

PHx   Past history

P.I.P.   Proximal interphalangeal joint

PITx   Intermittent pelvic traction

pm   Afternoon

PMR   Physical Medicine and Rehabilitation

PNF   Proprioceptive neuromuscular facilitation

post op, p/o   Postoperative

POMR   Problem oriented medical record

Pool add.   Pool additive

Post.   Posterior

PRE-op   Pre-operative

P.R.O.M.   Passive range of motion

P.R.N.   As needed

PSIS   Posterior superior iliac spine

PSTx   Static pelvic traction

pt   Patient

P.T.   Physical therapy

PTA   Prior to admission

P.Tx   Pelvic traction

PVD   Peripheral vascular disease

PWB   Partial weight bearing

|| or //   Parallel bars

/   Per

Pound or number

1'   Primary, first degree

fi   Progressing toward

   Result(ing) in

q   Every

qd/QD   Everyday

qod/QOD   Every other day

q am   Every morning

q h   Every hour

q.d   Four times daily

qn   Every night

Ⓡ   Right

R/A   Rheumatoid arthritis

Rehab.   Rehabilitation

RE   Resistive exercises

Reps.   Repetitions

REUE   Reconditioning (resistive) exercises to uninvolved extremities

RP   Rehabilitation pool

RPT   Registered physical therapist

R/R   Respiratory rate

Rt   Right

RX   Any medication or treatment ordered

2'   Secondary

S   Subjective

s̄   Without

sac   Sacral

SAQ   Short arc quadricep exercises

SCU   Special care unit

SLB   Short leg brace

"   Second or inches

shldr.   Shoulder

SLR   Straight leg raises

S-I   Sacroiliac

sig.   Significant

SOB   Shortness of breath

SOAP   Subjective, objective, assessment & plan

s/p   Status post

SQ   Status quo

s&s   Signs & symptoms

st   Straight

STAT   At once, immediately

Staph   Staphlococcus

STREP   Streptococcus

SWD   Shortwave diathermy

Sup.   Superior

Sx   Signs, symptoms

3°   Tertiary, third degree

TDWB   Touch down weight bearing

TE   Therapeutic exercises

Thor.   Thoracic

TID   Three times a day

TKR   Total knee replacement

THR   Total hip replacement

TLC   Tender loving care

Tol.   Tolerated

T.O.   Telephone order

TP&P   Time, place & person

TR   Trace

Tx   Traction

UE   Upper extremity

US   Ultrasound

UV   Ultraviolet

v.o.   Verbal order

WBT   Weight bearing as tolerated

w/c   Wheel chair

WK   Week

WFL   Within functional limits

WNL   Within normal limits

w/in   Within

Wm's Ex   William's exercises

W.O.   Written order

W.P.   Whirlpool

WTB   Weightbearing

y/o. or y.o.   Year old

Symbols

@   at

fl   decrease

>   increase

=   equivalent to

/   extension

↺↺↺   External rotation

✓   Flexion

>   Greater than

↻↻↻   Internal rotation

<   Less than

−   Minus

+   Plus

#'s   Pounds

fi   Produce, results in

<   The result of

⇄   To and From

1°   Primary, first degree

2°   Secondary, second degree

3°   Tertiary, third degree

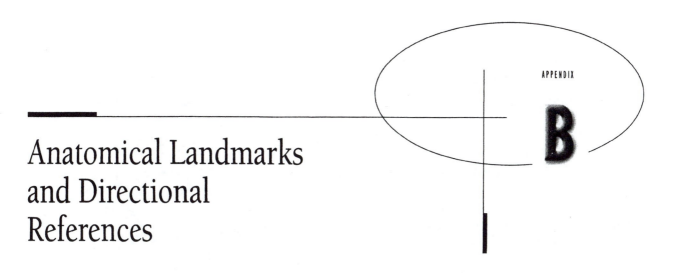

Anatomical Landmarks and Directional References

An understanding of anatomical landmarks and directional references provides for a better understanding of the injury involvement (i.e., type of injury and anatomical structure), the healing process, and the rehabilitation process.

Anatomical Landmarks

Important anatomical landmarks are presented in Figure B.1. The anatomical terms are given in italics, the common names in plain type, and the anatomical adjectives in parentheses.

Understanding the terms and their origins will help you to remember the location of a particular structure, as well as its name.

Standard anatomical illustrations show the human form in the *anatomical position*. In this position the hands are at the sides with the palms facing forward. Figure B.1 shows an individual in the anatomical position as seen from the front and back.

A person lying down in the anatomical position is said to be *supine* (SŪ-pīne) when lying face up and *prone* when lying face down.

Anatomical Regions

In addition to specific landmarks, anatomists and clinicians often need to use regional terms to describe a gen-

eral area of interest or injury. Two approaches have developed, both concerned with mapping the surface of the abdominopelvic region. Clinicians refer to the *abdominopelvic quadrants*. The region is divided into four segments using a pair of imaginary lines that intersect at the *umbilicus* (navel). This simple method, shown in Figure B.2(a), provides useful references for the description of aches, pains, and injuries. The location can assist the doctor in deciding the possible cause; for example, tenderness in the right lower quadrant (RLQ) is a symptom of appendicitis, whereas tenderness in the right upper quadrant (RUQ) may indicate gallbladder or liver problems.

Anatomists like to use more precise regional distinctions to describe the location and orientation of internal organs. They recognize nine *abdominopelvic regions* (Figure B.2[b]). Figure B.2(c) shows the relationship among quadrants, regions, and internal organs.

Anatomical Directions

Table B.1 and Figure B.3 show the principal directional terms and examples of their use. There are many different terms, and some can be used interchangeably. When following anatomical descriptions, you may also find it useful to remember that the terms "left" and "right" always refer to the left and right sides of the *subject*, not of the observer.

Sectional Anatomy

A presentation in sectional view is sometimes the only way to illustrate the relationships between the parts of a three-dimensional object. An understanding of sectional

This chapter is adapted from Frederic Martini, *Fundamentals of Anatomy and Physiology*, 3/e, © 1995, pp. 19–24. Reprinted by permission of Prentice-Hall, Inc., Upper Saddle River, NJ.

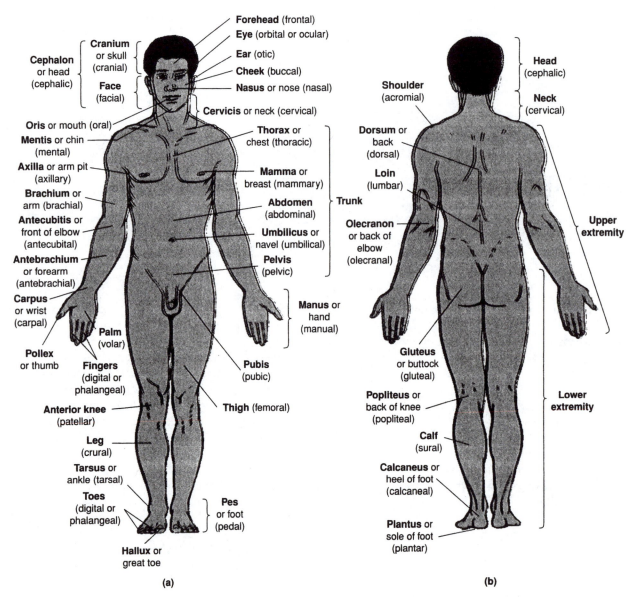

FIGURE B.1

Anatomical landmarks

The anatomical terms are shown in boldface type, the common names are in plain type, and the anatomical adjectives are in parentheses.

views has become increasingly important since the development of procedures that enable us to see inside the living body without resorting to surgery.

Planes and Sections

Any slice through a three-dimensional object can be described with reference to three *sectional planes*, indicated in Table B.2 and Figure B.4. The *transverse plane* lies at right angles to the long axis of the body, dividing it into *superior* and *inferior* sections. A cut in this plane is called a *transverse section*, or *cross section*. The *frontal*, or *coronal*, *plane* and the *sagittal plane* parallel the long axis of the body. The frontal plane extends from side to side, dividing the body into *anterior* and *posterior* sections. The sagittal plane extends from front to back, dividing the body into *left* and *right* sections. A cut that passes along the midline and divides the body into left and right halves is a *midsagittal section*; a cut parallel to the midsagittal line is a *parasagittal section*.

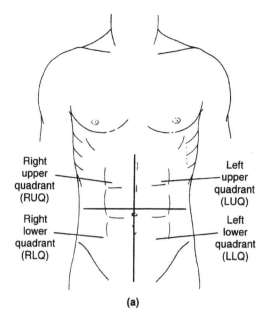

(a)

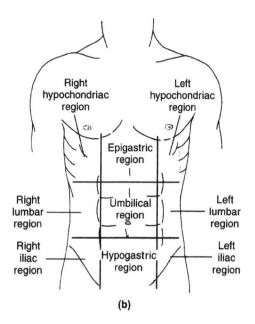

Right hypochondriac region

Left hypochondriac region

Epigastric region

Right lumbar region

Umbilical region

Left lumbar region

Right iliac region

Hypogastric region

Left iliac region

(b)

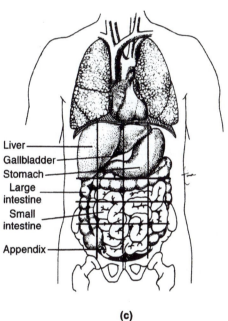

Liver
Gallbladder
Stomach
Large intestine
Small intestine
Appendix

(c)

FIGURE B.2

Abdominopelvic quadrants and regions

(a) Abdominopelvic quadrants divide the area into four sections. These terms, or their abbreviations, are most often used in clinical discussions. (b) More precise regional descriptions are provided by reference to the appropriate abdominopelvic region. (c) Quadrants or regions are useful because there is a known relationship between superficial anatomical landmarks and underlying organs.

Body Cavities

Viewed in sections, the human body is not a solid object, like a rock, in which all of the parts are fused together. Many vital organs are suspended in internal chambers called *body cavities*. These cavities have two essential functions: (1) they protect delicate organs, such as the brain and spinal cord, from accidental shocks, and cushion them from the thumps and bumps that occur during walking, jumping, and running; and (2) they permit significant changes in the size and shape

of visceral organs. For example, because they are situated within body cavities, the lungs, heart, stomach, intestines, urinary bladder, and many other organs can expand and contract without distorting surrounding tissues and disrupting the activities of nearby organs.

Two body cavities form during embryonic development. A *dorsal body cavity* surrounds the brain and spinal cord, and a much larger *ventral body cavity*, or *coelom* (SĒ-lom: *koila*, cavity), surrounds developing organs of the respiratory, cardiovascular, digestive, urinary, and reproductive systems. Relationships between

TABLE B.I *Regional and directional references*

Region of Body	Adjective	Directional Reference	Examples of Descriptive Use
Front	Ventral or anterior	Ventrally	The navel is on the *ventral* (*anterior*) surface of the trunk.
Back	Dorsal or posterior	Dorsally	The *dorsal* body cavity encloses the brain and spinal cord; moving *dorsally* from the navel you find the muscles of the abdominal wall.
Head	Cranial	Cranially	The *cranial* border of the pelvis; moving *cranially* from the pelvis brings you to the umbilicus.
	Cephalic		(Same usage as cranial)
	Superior		(Same as cranial but you refer to the *superior* surface of the skull.)
	Rostral	Rostrally	(Same as cranial but refers to nose); the eyes are on the *rostral* surface of the head; moving *rostrally* from the back of the skull brings you to the face.
Tail (coccyx)	Caudal	Caudally	The hips are *caudal* to the waist; moving *caudally* from the shoulder brings you to the hips.
	Inferior	Inferiorly	(Same as caudal but the soles are on the *inferior* surfaces of the feet.)
Close to long axis of the body	Medial	Medially	The *medial* surfaces of the thighs may be in contact, moving *medially* across the surface of the chest, you arrive at the sternum.
Away from long axis	Lateral	Laterally	The leg articulates with the *lateral* surface of the pelvis; moving *laterally* from the nose brings you to the eyes.
Toward an attached base	Proximal	Proximally	The wrist is *proximal* to the fingers; moving *proximally* from the wrist brings you to the elbow.
Away from an attached base	Distal	Distally	The fingers are *distal* to the wrist; moving *distally* from the elbow brings you to the wrist.

the dorsal and ventral body cavities and their various subdivisions can be seen in Figure B.5.

DORSAL BODY CAVITIES: The dorsal body cavity (Figure B.6[a]) is a fluid-filled space whose limits are established by the *cranium*, the bones of the skull that surround the brain, and the spinal vertebrae. The dorsal body cavity is subdivided into the *cranial cavity*, which encloses the brain, and the *spinal cavity*, which surrounds the spinal cord.

VENTRAL BODY CAVITIES: As development proceeds, internal organs grow and change their relative positions. These changes lead to the subdivision of the ventral body cavity. The formation of the *diaphragm* (DĪ-a-fram), a flat muscular sheet, divides the ventral body cavity into a superior *thoracic cavity*, enclosed by the chest wall, and an inferior *abdominopelvic cavity*, enclosed by the abdomen and pelvic girdle.

By the time of birth, the thoracic cavity has been further subdivided into two *pleural cavities*, each containing a lung, and a *pericardial cavity* that surrounds the heart. Figure B.6 shows the anatomical relationships of these compartments.

A large central mass of connective tissue, the *mediastinum* (mē-dē-as-TĪ-num or mē-dē-AS-ti-num), surrounds the pericardial cavity and separates the two pleural cavities. In addition to the heart and pericardial

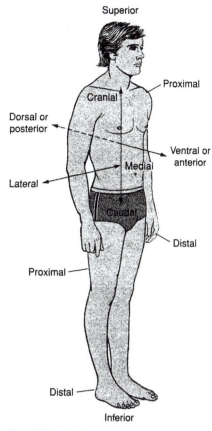

Superior

Cranial

Proximal

Dorsal or
posterior

Ventral or
anterior

Medial

Lateral

Caudal

Distal

Proximal

Distal

Inferior

FIGURE B.3

Directional references

Important directional terms used in this text are indicated by arrows; definitions and descriptions are included in Table B.1.

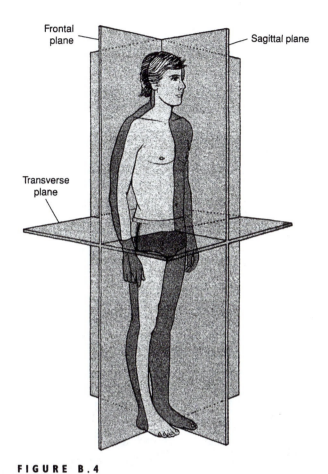

Frontal
plane

Sagittal plane

Transverse
plane

FIGURE B.4

Planes of section

The three primary planes of section are indicated here. Table B.2 defines and describes them.

TABLE B.2   *Terms that indicate planes of section*

Orientation of Plane	Adjective	Directional Reference	Description
Parallel to long axis	Sagittal	Sagittally	A *sagittal* section separates right and left portions. You examine a sagittal section, but you section sagitally.
	Midsagittal		In a *midsagittal* section the plane passes through the midline, dividing the body in half and separating right and left sides.
	Parasagittal		A *parasagittal* section misses the midline, separating right and left portions of unequal size.
	Frontal or coronal	Frontally or coronally	A *frontal*, or *coronal*, section separates anterior and posterior portions of the body; coronal usually refers to sections passing through the skull.
Perpendicular to long axis	Transverse or horizontal	Transversely or horizontally	A *transverse*, or *horizontal*, section separates superior and inferior portions of the body.

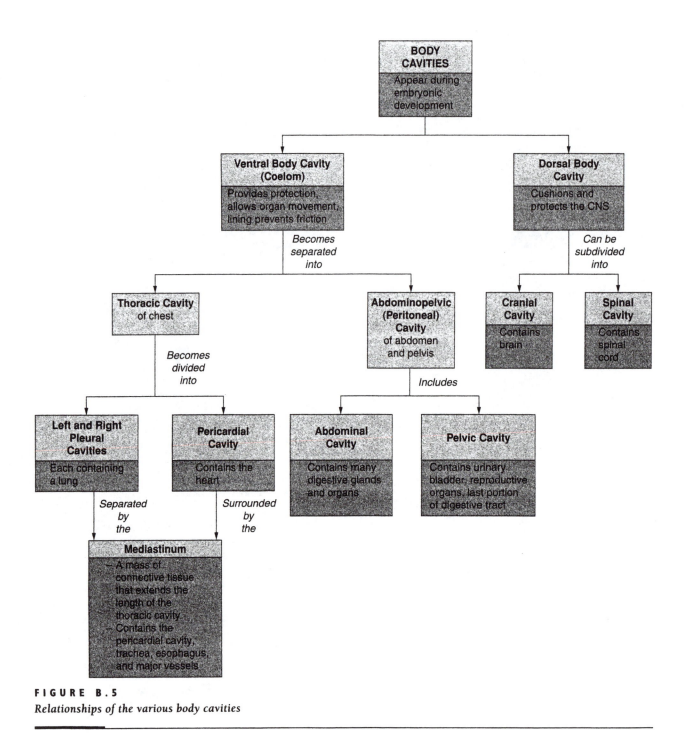

FIGURE B.5
Relationships of the various body cavities

cavity, the mediastinum surrounds the trachea, esophagus, and the large arteries and veins attached to the heart.

The heart projects into the pericardial cavity like a fist pushing into a balloon. The base of the heart, corresponding to the wrist, is embedded in the mediastinum, as is the outer wall of the balloon, or *pericardial sac.*

The abdominopelvic cavity, also known as the *peritoneal* (per-i-tō-NĒ-al) *cavity,* has two subdivisions. The *abdominal cavity* extends from the inferior surface of the diaphragm to an imaginary line drawn from the inferior surface of the lowest spinal vertebra to the anterior and superior margin of the pelvic girdle. The portion of the peritoneal cavity inferior to this imaginary line is the *pelvic cavity.*

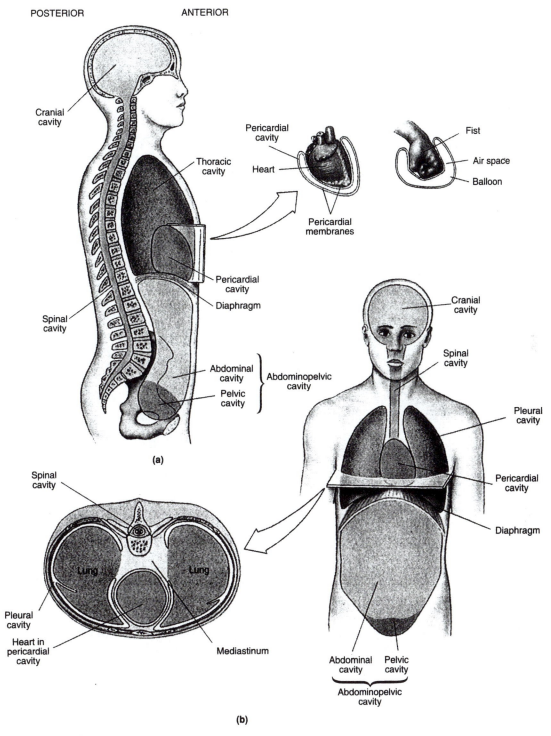

POSTERIOR　　　ANTERIOR

Cranial cavity

Pericardial cavity

Heart

Fist

Air space

Balloon

Pericardial membranes

Thoracic cavity

Pericardial cavity

Diaphragm

Spinal cavity

Abdominal cavity

Pelvic cavity

Abdominopelvic cavity

(a)

Cranial cavity

Spinal cavity

Pleural cavity

Pericardial cavity

Diaphragm

Spinal cavity

Lung

Lung

Pleural cavity

Heart in pericardial cavity

Mediastinum

Abdominal cavity

Pelvic cavity

Abdominopelvic cavity

(b)

FIGURE B.6

Body cavities

(a) The dorsal body cavity is bounded by the bones of the skull and vertebral column. The muscular diaphragm divides the ventral body cavity into a superior thoracic cavity and an inferior abdominopelvic cavity. The pericardial cavity is located inside the chest cavity. The heart is suspended within the pericardial cavity like a fist pushed into a balloon. The attachment site, corresponding to the wrist of the hand in the model, lies at the connection between the heart and major blood vessels. (b) An anterior view of the ventral body cavity, showing the central location of the pericardial cavity within the chest cavity. The relationships are seen more clearly in the sectional plane, which shows how the mediastinum divides the thoracic cavity into two pleural cavities.

Glossary

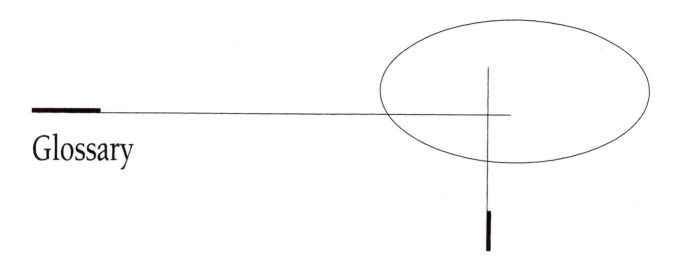

abcess Localized collection of pus (white blood cells) into a cavity formed by the disintegration of tissues

abduction Movement of the limb away from the midline of the body

abrasion Rubbing off or scraping off of the skin or a mucous membrane

acetabulum The socket of the hip joint into which the femoral head fits

actin Protein of the myofibril of the muscle; together with myosin, is responsible for muscle contraction and relaxation

acute Having a short and relatively severe course

addiction Physical or emotional dependence on a specific drug

adduction Movement of the limb toward the midline of the body

adhesion Union of two surfaces that are normally separated; also, any fibrous band that connects two surfaces

amnesia Loss of memory

anabolic steroid Testosterone, or a steroid hormone resembling testosterone, that stimulates anabolism in the body as a whole

analgesic Pain-relieving oral medication

anemia A reduction in the number of circulating red blood cells, hemoglobin, or volume of red cells

aneurysm Weakened, bulging area of a blood vessel

ankylosis Immobility and fixation of a joint due to disease, injury, or surgical procedure

anoxia Lack of oxygen

aortic stenosis Narrowing of the aortic orifice of the heart

apnea Temporary cessation of breathing

aponeurosis Tendinous expansion that helps to connect a number of muscles to the bone

apophyseal injury Injury involving the non-weight-bearing area of the growth plate (epiphyseal plate), to which a tendon is usually attached

arrhythmia Any disturbance in the rhythm of the heartbeat

arthrogram X-ray study in which radio-opaque material is injected into a joint

arthroscopy An alternative to surgical incision and creation of an open wound

aspirate To remove by suction

asystole Lack of a heartbeat

ataxia Muscular incoordination manifested when voluntary movements are attempted

atelectasis Areas of lung collapse

atrophy Wasting away or deterioration of a tissue, organ, or part

auscultation Listening to sounds within the organs during diagnosis and treatment

avascular Without blood vessels

avulsion Injury in which a whole piece of skin, with varying portions of subcutaneous tissue or muscle, is completely or partially torn loose

axilla Armpit

Bennett's fracture Fracture dislocation of the base of the first metacarpal

bilateral On both sides

bronchitis Inflammation of the mucous membrane of the bronchi

bunion   Inflammation and thickening of the bursa of the joint of the great toe, usually associated with marked joint enlargement and toe displacement laterally

bursa   Sac-like cavity that allows a muscle or tendon to slide over bone

calorific value   The availability of calories to an individual according to his or her specific metabolic capability. This value which produces calories in an individual's metabolic conversion cycle

capsule   Fibrous tissues enclosing a joint

carotid pulse (carotid artery pulse)   Pulse felt in the upper portion of the neck

carpal bones   Bones of the wrist

carpal tunnel syndrome   Pressure on the median nerve where it passes through the carpal tunnel of the wrist causing soreness, tenderness, numbness, and weakness of the thumb muscle

chondromalacia   Softening and destruction of articular cartilage

chronic   Of long duration

clinical   Pertaining to or founded on actual observation and treatment of patients

collagen   Fibrous structural protein that constitutes the protein of the white fibers of connective tissues

Colles' fracture   Fracture of the distal radius, with dorsal displacement of the fragments, producing the "silver fork deformity" in which the injured wrist assumes a curvature similar to the side view of a dinner fork

coma   State of unconsciousness from which the patient cannot be aroused

concussion   Jarring injury of the brain resulting in disturbance of brain function

consciousness   State of general wakefulness and responsiveness to one's environment; impairment of consciousness, short of consciousness, is commonly described with no unanimity of precise meaning as lethargy, stupor, coma, and semi-consciousness

contracture   Abnormal shortening of muscle tissue, rendering the muscle highly resistant to stretching

contraindicated   A treatment or medication that should not be given

contralateral   Pertaining to the opposite side

contusion   Injury to tissues without breakage of skin; a bruise

crepitus   Crackling sound or feeling sometimes experienced with fractures or tenosynovitis

cricothyroid cartilage   Tissue connecting the cricoid and thyroid cartilage

cryokinetics   Therapeutic use of cold with exercise movements

cryotherapy   Therapeutic use of cold

cyanosis   Blue color around the lips, fingernails or fingertips, resulting from poor oxygenation of the circulating blood; the blood is very dark

dehydration   Loss of body water

delirium   Mental disturbance marked by hallucinations, cerebral excitement, and physical restlessness, usually lasting only a short time

dermatome   A sensory root field on the skin; the area of skin supplied with various nerve fibers by a single posterior/spinal root

dermis   Inner layer of the skin, containing hair follicles, sweat glands, sebaceous glands, nerve endings, and blood vessels

diabetic coma   State of unconsciousness caused by loss of fluid and increased acidity in diabetes mellitus

diaphysis   Shaft or middle part of a long cylindrical bone

differential diagnosis   The result of distinguishing among various diseases to determine the one from which the patient suffers

dislocation   Displacement of a bone from a joint

distal   Nearer the free end of an extremity; on the trunk farther from the midline or from the point of reference

dorsal   Posterior

dysmenorrhea   Painful menstruation

dyspnea   Difficult or labored breathing

ecchymosis   Bruise; a discoloration of the skin due to subcutaneous and intracutaneous bleeding. Bluish at first, it changes later to greenish-yellow because of chemical changes in the pooled blood

edema   Condition in which fluid escapes into the tissues from vascular or lymphatic spaces and causes local or generalized swelling

effusion   Escape of fluid into a joint

enteritis   Inflammation of the intestine, especially the small intestine

epidermis   The outermost layer of the skin, varying in thickness from 1/200 to 1/20 inch, and containing keratinized, or horny, external protecting cells constantly being rubbed away

epiphyseal injury   Injury involving the growth plate (epiphyseal plate)

epiphyseal plate   Transverse cartilage plate near the end of a child's bone; responsible for growth in length of the bone

epiphysis   End of a long bone

epistaxis   Hemorrhage from the nose

erythema   Reddening

etiology   The study or theory of the causation of any disease

eversion   Turning outward

exostosis   Bony growth projecting outward from the surface of bone or tooth

extracellular   Outside the cell

fascia   Sheet or band of fibrous tissue that covers the body under the skin

fibrillation   Uncontrolled and ineffective beating of the heart, occuring when individual muscle fibers act independently or irregularly; it causes loss of cardiac function

flexion   Bending of a joint, in contrast to *extension*

fracture   Break on a part, especially a bone

Frohlich-type body   Frohlich syndrome is a condition in which a large amount of body fat is combined with lack of sexual development

ganglion   Cluster of nerve cell bodies outside the central nervous system

genu recurvatum   Hyperextension of the knees

genu valgus (knock knees)   Angulation of lower leg away from the midline of the body

genu varum (bowlegs)   Angulation of lower leg toward the midline of body

goniometer   An instrument for measuring angles

heat exhaustion   Disorder resulting from exposure to heat or to the sun causing excessive sweating that removes large quantities of sweat and fluid from the body

heat stroke   Severe life-threatening condition resulting from prolonged exposure to heat

hemarthrosis   Blood within a joint

hematemesis   Vomiting of blood

hematocrit   Volume (%) of erythrocytes (red blood cells) in whole blood

hematoma   A pool of blood collecting within the damaged tissue

hematuria   Blood in the urine

hemiplegia   Paralysis of one side of the body

hemoglobin   The oxygen-carrying component of the red blood cells

hernia   Protrusion of a loop of an organ or tissue through an abnormal opening

hyphema   Bleeding into the anterior chamber of the eye, obscuring the iris

hypothermia   Systemic lowering of the body temperature below 33.3° C (95°F)

hypoxia   Deficiency of oxygen reaching the tissues of the body

inferior   Situated below or directly below

inflammation   Basic response of vascularized tissues to an injurious agent, whether the source is physical, bacterial, thermal, or chemical

inversion   Turning inward toward the body

ipsilateral   Pertaining to the same side

ischemia   Lacking blood; local or temporary anemia due to obstruction of circulation to a body part

isokinetic resistance   Resistance varies but the speed of movement is constant

isometric resistance   Fixed resistance; no movement takes place

isotonic resistance   Resistance is constant but the speed of movement varies

Kager's triangle   A triangular space anterior to the Achilles tendon that is normally visible on x-ray as a radiolucent area

Kehr's sign   Severe pain in the left shoulder in some cases of rupture of the spleen

kinesiology   Study of the motion of the human body

kyphosis   Increased convexity in the curvature of the thoracic spine

laceration   Cut that may leave a smooth or jagged wound through the skin, subcutaneous tissues, muscles, and associated nerves and blood vessels

Lachman test   Test for stability of anterior cruciate ligament of the knee. Originally described by Lanbrinudi; an anterior drawer test performed with the knee flexed 20 degrees

lethargic   Feeling drowsy

leukocytes   White blood cells

ligament   Band of fibrous tissue that connects bone to bone or bone to cartilage and supports and strengthens joints

luxation   Complete dislocation

lymphocyte   Type of leukocyte; responsible primarily for the specific defenses of the body against foreign invaders

meninges Three membranes that envelop the brain and spinal cord: the dura mater, pia mater, and arachnoid

menisci Crescent-shaped discs of fibrocartilage

metaphysis Portion of long bone in the wide part of the extremity containing the growth zone in children

myopia Nearsightedness

myosin Protein of the myofibril of the muscle; together with actin, is responsible for muscle contraction and relaxation

necrosis Destruction and death of tissues

negligence Failure of the actions or behavior of an individual who had a duty to act to conform to the required standard of care, resulting in injury

neuroma Tumor or new growth made up primarily of nerve cells

nociceptors Pain receptors

osteoblast Cell associated with production of osteoid

osteoclast Large multinuclear bone associated with absorption and removal of bone

osteocyte Osteoblast imbedded within bone

otorrhea Discharge from the ear

pain Feeling of distress, suffering, or agony caused by stimulation of specialized nerve endings

palpate To examine by touch

paresis Slight or incomplete paralysis

paresthesia An abnormal sensation, whether spontaneous or evoked

patella Kneecap

patella alta Patella positioned high

patella baja Patella positioned low

pathology Branch of medicine dealing with the essential nature of disease, especially changes in body tissues and organs that cause or are caused by disease

periosteum Specialized connective tissue covering all bones of the body

pinna The external portion of the ear

pleura Membrane lining the thoracic cavity and surrounding the lungs

plexus A network of nerves, blood, or lymphatic vessels

podiatrist Specialist in podiatry which deals with the study and care of the foot

prognosis Prediction of the course and termination of a disease or eventual outcome of injury

pronation Assumption of a prone position; turning the palm of the hand backward

prophylactic Any agent or regimen that contributes to the prevention of injury or disease

proprioception Awareness of posture, movement, and changes in equilibrium and knowledge of posture, weight, and resistance of subjects in relation to the body

pyelogram An X-ray study in which radio-opaque dye is injected in order to outline the kidney, ureter, and bladder

Q angle The angle formed by a line drawn from the anterior superior iliac spine, to the midpoint of the patella and then to the tibial tubercle

recurvatum Deformity in which a joint is bent backwards, i.e., beyond normal extension

referred pain Pain in a part other than that in which the cause is produced or situated

resuscitation Restoring to life or consciousness through the use of assisted breathing to restore ventilation and cardiac massage to restore circulation

retrograde amnesia Inability to recall events that occurred before a head injury

sclera White portion of the eye; the tough outer coating of the eye that protects the delicate, light-sensitive inner layer

sebaceous glands Glands that produce an oily substance called *sebum*, discharged along the shafts of the hairs on the head and body

sepsis Presence in the blood or other tissues of harmful microorganisms or their poisons

shock A critical clinical condition characterized by variable signs and symptoms that arise when the cardiac output is insufficient to fill the arterial tree with blood under sufficient pressure

signs Readily apparent manifestations of changes in body functions

splinting Immobilizing an injured part by means of a device applying a pulling force; or applying a rigid support to an injured part

sprain An injury to a ligament. The severity of the injury is graded by degree: first degree—minimal damage; second degree—partial tearing of the ligament; third degree—complete ligamentous disruption

strain Injury involving the muscle, tendon, or musculotendinous unit, classified into degrees of severity. (*See* sprain)

subluxation   Incomplete or partial dislocation of a joint

superficial   Pertaining to a condition near the surface

superior   Situated directly above

supination   Assumption of a supine position; turning the palm of the hand forward

symptoms   Evidence of changes in body functions apparent to the patient and expressed to the examiner upon questioning

tachycardia   Abnormally fast heart rate; high pulse rate

tendinitis   Inflammation of a tendon

tenosynovitis   Inflammation of a tendon sheath

testosterone   Hormone responsible for the appearance and development of male secondary sex organs

thrombosis   Formation or presence of a blood clot within a blood vessel

trigger point   A small hypersensitive region in muscle, ligament, fascia, or joint capsule from which impulses bombard the CNS, causing referred pain

tubercle   A small rounded elevation or eminence on a bone

tuberosity   A tubercle or nodule

uremia   Toxic condition caused by waste products of metabolism accumulating in the blood as a result of a failure of kidney function

valgus stress   A force applied to a joint in which the distal aspect of the limb is moved away from the midline

varus stress   A force applied to a joint in which the distal aspect of the limb is moved towards the midline

vascularization   The development of blood vessels within the tissue

Volkmann's contracture   Irreversible contracture of muscles produced by fibrosis of dead muscle cells killed by ischemia

Index

Anterior subluxation of the glenohumeral joint, 478–479
Anterior talofibular ligament, 403
Anterior tibial artery, 401, 406
Anterior tibial muscle, 401
Anterior tibial tendon, 465
Antibiotics, 544–545
Anticholinergic (Atrovent inhaler), 549
Aphasia, 500
Apley's mensical test, 359
Apophyses, 169
Appendicitis, 527
Apprehension sign test, 86, 205
Aquatic exercise, 33–34, 144–145
Arachnoid, 178
Arch collapse, 467–468
Arndt-Schultz principle, 112, 128
Arteries:
    and the brain, 178
    of the foot, 406
    in the lower leg, 401
    popliteal, 466
Arthography, 372
Arthroscopy, 372
Articular facet joints, 314
Aspirin, 548
Assessment. *See* Evaluation
Asthma. *See also* Exercise-induced asthma (EIA)
    and the medical examination, 527
    medications for, 549–550
AstroTurf, 352
Athlete's foot, 539, 549
Athletic conditioning. *See* Conditioning
Athletic trainers:
    and assessing medical complaints, 526–528
    and assisting with physical exams, 3
    and EMTs, 94
Atlantoaxial instability, and disabled athletes, 501
Atrovent inhaler, 549
Avascular necrosis, 266
Avulsion injuries, 175, 265, 430
Axillary nerve, 307

Babinski's sign, 319
Back. *See* Spine
Baker's cyst, 386
Ballistic stretching, 27
Bandaging:
    ankles, 420
    continuous finger, 79
    recurrent finger, 80
Bankart lesion, 220, 222
Beam nonuniformity ratio (BNR), 124
Bedside manner, 84
Behavioral problems, and disabled athletes, 501
Bennett's fracture, 285
Beta adrenergic stimulator, 549
Biceps femoris muscle, 346, 460
Biceps femoris tendinitis, 460

Biceps tendon, 31
    description of, 202
    impingement syndrome and, 229–230
    subluxation of the, 230–231, 258
    tendinitis, and wheelchair and crutch users, 496–497
    and tenosynovitis/tendinitis, 258
Bicycle ergometer testing, for cardiopulmonary fitness, 37
Bifurcated ligament, 405
Big toe support, and adhesive taping, 56
Bipartite patella, 384
Bipolar technique, NMES, 129
Black toenails, 469
Bladder dysfunction, and disabled athletes, 500
Bleeding, superficial, 98
Blisters, 436, 498–499
Blood pressure, and testing for head injury, 182
Body fat, estimation of, 15–16
Body image, and eating disorders, 484
Body weight *vs.* gravity, 35
Bone growth, in adolescents, 169–171, 262
Bone scans, 166
Boutonniére deformity, 282–283
Bowler's thumb, 288
Brachial artery, 202
Brachial plexus, 202
Bracing, *vs.* taping, 410–411
Breaststroker's knee, 479–480
Breathing, and stretching, 27
Bridging, 308
Bronchitis, 530
Bucket handle tear, 371
Bulimia, 487
Buoyancy cuffs, 144
Burners/stingers, as a disqualifying condition, 21
Bursitis:
    olecranon, 254
    retrocalcaneal, 467
    subdeltoid, 261–262

Cable tensiometer, 32
Calcaneocuboid joint, 404
Calcaneofibular ligament, 403
Calcaneus, stress fracture of, 165
Calcification, 265, 348, 431
Calipers:
    for head measurements, 42–43
    to measure skinfold thickness, 15
Calluses, 436
Canker sores, 529
Capitellum, 242
Carbohydrate loading, 508–509
Carbohydrates, 507–509
Cardiac conditions:
    congenital aortic stenosis (AS), 21
    contusions, 339
    as a disqualifier for participation, 21
    eating disorders and, 487

Liver, rupture of the, 339
Lomotil, 549
Longissimus capitis muscle, 293
Longissimus cervicis muscle, 293
Longissimus thoracis muscle, 295, 314
Longitudinal arch support, taping, 58
Longitudinal fracture, 164
Long thoracic nerve, 308
Lotrimin, 549
LowDye taping, 57, 432
Lucid interval, 181, 184
Lumbarization, 326
Lumbar spine:
    anatomy of, 313–316
    ankylosing spondylitis, 324
    cauda equina syndrome, 323–324
    contusion to, 324
    examination of, 317–323
    fracture of, 103
    instabilities of, 324–326
    lower back pain, 316–323
    piriformis syndrome, 324
    rehabilitation and, 326–333
    vertebrae, 165
Luteal phase deficiency, 485
Lymphatic drainage, 405

MacIntosh pivot shift test, 358, 370
Magnetic resonance imaging (MRI), 86, 90, 172, 323, 372
Mallet finger, 286–288
Manipulative therapy, 133–134
Marfan syndrome, 4
Massage, 132–133
Maturation:
    sexual development, 21
    skeletal development, 16
Matveyev model of periodization, 38
Maxilla, fracture of, 187
Maximal voluntary contraction (MVC), 140–141
McMurray's mensical test, 359, 361, 86
Measurement:
    for fitting football helmets, 42
    in physical exams, 6
Medial arch pain, 467–468
Medial capsular ligament, 341–342
Medial collateral ligament, 244
Medial lesions, elbow, 266
Medial meniscus, 344–345
Medial patellar, pain from running, 456–457
Medial tibial stress syndrome, 462–463
Median nerve, 278, 294
Medical abbreviations and symbols, 555–558
Medical emergency plan, 107–109
Medical examination, 526–528
Medical history:
    and fitting footbal helmets, 42
    and injury assessment, 83–84
    as part of the preparticipation physical exam, 3–5

Medical plan, for emergencies, 106–109
Medications:
    analgesics, 548
    antibiotics, 544–545
    antidiarrheal, 549
    asthma and allergy, 549–550
    for colds, 548–549
    corticosteroids, 548
    counter-irritants, 547–548
    Dimethyl sulfoxide (DMSO), 547
    muscle relaxers, 550
    nonsteroidal anti-inflammatory (NSAIDS), 545–547
    that facilitate heat injuries, 517
Menisci, 344–345, 359, 371–373
Menstruation, 4–5, 21, 485–486
Metacarpals, 101, 284–285
Metacarpophalangeal (MP) joint, 276, 281, 282, 283–284
Metaprel, 549
Metatarsal arch support, taping, 59
Metatarsals, fractures of, 102
Metatarsal shaft, 165
Microcurrent electrical nerve stimulation (MENS), 130
Microtrauma, 163–164
Microwave diathermy, 122
Middle meningeal artery, 178
Midtarsal joint, 404
Minerals, 511–512
Mini tramps, 35
Mobilization therapy. See Manipulative therapy
Mononucleosis, 97, 530–531
Monopolar technique, NMES, 129
Morton's neuroma, 433–434
Motor level stimulation, 127
Mouthpieces, 46, 187
Muscle relaxers, 550
Muscles:
    abdominal, 315
    cervical, 293–294
    elbow, 245
    foot, 405
    hand, 274–276
    joint, 31
    knee, 345–347
    leg, 402–403
    lower back, 314–315
    and running injuries, 445
    shoulder, 199–202
Musculocutaneous nerve, 294
Myofibrils, 32
Myoglobinuria, 533
Myositis ossificans, 348
    involving the anterolateral aspect of the arm and the brachialis muscle, 246–247
    seriousness of, 252

Nabumetone (Relafin), 546
National Athletic Trainers' Association, guidelines for onsite removal of helmets, 94

Nausea:
    after a head injury, 182
    medicine for, 549
Navicular (scaphoid), 279–280
Neck:
    assessment flowchart, 88
    and head injuries, 183
    emergency treatment of, 94–95
    injuries to, 296–308
    rehabilitation exercises for, 308
Nerve root infiltration, 323
Nerves:
    axillary, 307
    femoral, 315–316
    foot, 405–406
    long thoracic, 308
    lower leg, 401
    median, 294
    musculocutaneous, 294
    nerve plexuses of the cervical spine, 294
    and pinched nerve syndrome, 305, 307
    radial, 277
    sciatic, 315–316
    suprascapular, 307–308
    ulnar, 294
Neuromuscular electrical stimulation (NMES), 128–129
Neuromuscular memory, 26
NOCSAE (National Operating Committee on Standards
    for Athletic Equipment), and certification of
    helmets, 41
Nonspecific dermatitis, 542
Nonspecific urethritis (NSU), 533
Nonsteroidal anti-inflammatory medication (NSAIDS),
    545–547
Nose:
    bleeding of, 191
    fractures of, 191
    and septal hematoma, 191–192
Noxious level stimulation, 127
Nucleus pulposus, 314
Nutrition:
    carbohydrates, 507–509
    diet and dehydration, 519
    eating disorders, 513
    fat, 509–510
    female athletes and, 490–491
    fluids and electrolytes, 512
    pre-event, 510
    protein, 510
    vitamins and minerals, 511–512
    weight, 523
Nystagmus, 182

Oblique fracture, 164
Obliquus externus abdominus muscle, 315
Obliquus internus abdominus muscle, 315
Observation, in injury assessment, 84
Obturators, 315

Ohm, 113
Olecranon bursitis, 254
100-minus-7 test, 85, 182
Open-chain exercises, 148
Orthopedics, examination in physical exams, 6–7
Orthotic devices, 432
    and metatarsal stress fractures, 432
    for overuse running injuries, 469–472
    for patellofemoral joint pain, 384
Osgood-Schlatter disease, 174–175
OSHA standards, for exposure to and disposal
    of blood, 99, 115
Osteitis pubis, 335
Osteochondral fracture, 373, 384–385
    of the dome of the talus, 429
    of the middle of the troclear notch, 267
Osteochondritis dissecans, 266, 373, 385–386
Osteokinematics, 148
Osteolysis, of distal clavicle, 213
Osteoporosis, 486–487
Os trigonum, injury to the, 429
Otitis media, 529
Overuse injuries:
    running and, 444–449
    shoulder injuries and, 263
    swimming and, 477–480
Oxford technique, 147

Pain, and the inflammatory process, 161
Painful arc syndrome, 227
Palmaris longus muscle, 245
Palpation, in injury assessment, 84
Papilledema, and head injury, 183
Paracone, 549–550
Paraffin bath, 120–121
Pars interarticularis, 313
Passive stretching, 27
Patella, 31
    acute dislocation of, 377–381
    anatomy of, 374–376
    and apprehension test, 361–362
    fracture of, 102, 377
    pain of, 459
    subluxation and spontaneous reduction
        of dislocated, 379–381
    taping, 67
    tendinitis and, 457, 459
Patellar tendon ossicles, 175
Patellofemoral articulation, 341
Patellofemoral compression syndrome, 384
Patellofemoral joint, 341, 381–384, 459
Pectoralis major muscle, 200
Pediculosis, 542
Pelvis, 313, 528
Penicillin, 544
Peroneus brevis muscle, 402
Peroneus longus muscle, 402
Peroneus tertius muscle, 402

Pes anserine bursitis, 457
Pes anserine muscles, 31, 345
Petrissage, 133
Phalanges, fractures of, 285–286
Phalen's test, 289
Phonophoresis, 122, 126–127
Pia mater, 178
Pilo-erection, 516
Pinched nerve syndrome, 305, 307
Piriformis gemelli muscle, 315
Piriformis syndrome, 324
Pitching. *See* Throwing
Pivot-shift tests, 358–359
Plantar fascitis, 405, 436, 468
Plantar flexion sprains, ankle, 412
Plantaris muscle, 403, 406, 408
Playing surface, 352, 411, 449
Plyometrics, 35
Pneumatic splints, 100
Pneumonia, 530
Pneumothorax, 96, 338, 527
Popliteal artery, 406, 466
Popliteal oblique ligament, 344
Popliteus muscle, 31, 346–347
Post concussion syndrome, 184
Posterior capsule, 344
Posterior cruciate ligament, 343
Posterior cuff strain, 262
Posterior lesions, elbow, 266–267
Posterior ligamentous system, lumbar, 314
Posterior longitudinal ligament, 293, 314
Posterior oblique ligament, 342
Posterior talofibular ligament, 403–404
Posterior tibial artery, 406
Posterior tibial muscle, 401, 403, 405
Posture, 16
Power, 32
    conditioning and, 35
    and running, 446
Precollege athletes, medical history and, 5
Prednisone, 549–550
Pregnancy, 489–490
Preparticipation physical exam:
    areas involved in, 3–14
    disqualifying conditions as a result of, 21–22
    and female adolescent athletes, 483
    flexibility, 14–15
    maturation, 15, 21, 22–23
    posture, 14
    primary objectives of, 3
    skinfold thickness, 15–16, 19
    strength, 15
    timing of, 3
Pressure areas, and disabled athletes, 499
Prestress fracture, tibial, 461
Prevention. *See also* Conditioning
    of heat injuries, 517–519
    of overuse injuries from running, 446–449

Progressive resistance exercise (PRE), 146–147
Pronation, 404–405, 443
Pronator teres muscle, 245
Proprioception, and leg muscles, 351–352
Proprioceptive Neuromuscular Facilitation (PNF), 27, 29, 139, 149–154
Prostheses, 498, 502
Protein, 510
Proteinuria, 532
Proventil, 549
Proximal humerus, 262
Proximal interphalangeal (PIP) joint, 276
    and boutonniére deformity, 282–283
    dislocations, 284
    sprain of, 282
Pseudo-boutonniére deformity, 283
Pseudoephedrine hydrochloride (Sudafed), 548–549
Psoas major muscle, 315
Psoas minor muscle, 315
Pubic lice, 542
Pubic symphysis, 335
Pubofemoral ligament, at the hip, 314
Pulse, 83, 182
Pulsed current, 113
Pulsed shortwave magnetic waves, 122

Quadratus femoris muscle, 315
Quadratus lumborum muscle, 314
Quadriceps, 345, 347–349
    exercises, 446
    knee injury and, 31, 384
    stretching, 28
    taping, 67
Quadripolar technique, NMES, 129

Radial nerve, and the hand, 277
Radiation, 112
Radio-ulnar-humeral joint, 245
Radio-ulnar joint, 245
Range of motion (ROM):
    neck, 300
    shoulder joint, 205–206
    for shoulder rehabilitation, 234
    techniques to increase, 153–154
    tests for, 85–86, 87
Raynaud's disease, 117
Reciprocal inhibition, 27
Rectus abdominus muscle, 315
Rectus femoris muscle, 345
Referred pain, 96
Reflection, 112
Refraction, 112
Regeneration, in the inflammatory process, 162–163
Regulations:
    for HIV precautions, 99
    for medical eligibility, 3